Thinking Mathematically

Thinking Mathematically

Robert Blitzer
Miami-Dade Community College

PRENTICE HALL
Upper Saddle River, NJ 07458

Library of Congress Cataloging-in-Publication Data
Blitzer, Robert.
    Thinking mathematically / Robert Blitzer.
       p.   cm.
    Includes index.
    ISBN 0-13-948845-6
    1. Mathematics.   I. Title.
QA39.2.B5875   2000
51.0—dc21   99-088495
                             CIP

Executive Acquisitions Editor: Sally Yagan
Assistant Vice President of Production and Manufacturing: David W. Riccardi
Executive Managing Editor: Kathleen Schiaparelli
Senior Managing Editor: Linda Mihatov Behrens
Production Editor: Barbara Mack
Manufacturing Buyer: Alan Fischer
Manufacturing Manager: Trudy Pisciotti
Marketing Manager: Patrice Jones
Marketing Assistant: Vince Jansen
Director of Marketing: John Tweeddale
Development Editor: Shana Ederer
Editor in Chief, Development: Carol Trueheart
Associate Editor, Mathematics/Statistics Media: Audra J. Walsh
Editorial Assistant/Supplements Editor: Sara Beth Newell
Art Director: Maureen Eide
Assistant to the Art Director: John Christiana
Interior Designer: Judy Matz-Coniglio
Cover Designer: Joseph Sengotta
Art Editor: Grace Hazeldine
Art Manager: Gus Vibal
Director of Creative Services: Paul Belfanti
Photo Researcher: Melinda Alexander
Photo Editor: Beth Boyd
Cover Illustration: Garin Baker/Stock Illustration Source, Inc.
Art Studio: Academy Artworks
Compositor: Prepare Inc./Emilcomp srl

Printed in the United States of America
10 9 8 7 6 5 4 3 2 1

ISBN 0-13-948845-6

Prentice-Hall International (UK) Limited, *London*
Prentice-Hall of Australia Pty. Limited, *Sydney*
Prentice-Hall Canada Inc., *Toronto*
Prentice-Hall Hispanoamericana, S.A., *Mexico*
Prentice-Hall of India Private Limited, *New Delhi*
Prentice-Hall of Japan, Inc., *Tokyo*
Pearson Education Asia Pte. Ltd., *Singapore*
Editora Prentice-Hall do Brasil, Ltda., *Rio de Janeiro*

Contents

Chapter 1

Chapter 2

Chapter 6

Chapter 7

Chapter 8

Chapter 9

Chapter 10

Chapter 11

Chapter 12

Chapter 13

About the Author

Bob Blitzer is a native of Manhattan and received a Bachelor of Arts degree with dual majors in mathematics and psychology (minor: English literature) from the City College of New York. His unusual combination of academic interests led him toward a Master of Arts in mathematics from the University of Miami and a doctorate in behavioral sciences from Nova University. Bob is most energized by teaching mathematics and has taught a variety of mathematics courses at Miami-Dade Community College for nearly 30 years. He has received numerous teaching awards, including Innovator of the Year from the League for Innovations in the Community College, and was among the first group of recipients at Miami-Dade for an endowed chair based on excellence in the classroom. In addition to *Thinking Mathematically*, Bob has written four algebra books, all published by Prentice Hall.

To the Student

I've written this book to give you control over the part of your life that involves numbers and mathematical ideas. Gaining an understanding and appreciaton of mathematics will help you participate fully in the twenty-first century. In some ways, you cannot get along in life without the mathematics in this book. For example, if you do not understand the basic ideas of investment, you may find it impossible to achieve your financial goals. If you do not have at least a rudimentary understanding of set theory, you may not be able to meaningfully interpret the vast amount of survey data we are presented with almost daily.

This book has been written so that you can learn about the power of mathematics directly from its pages. All concepts are carefully explained, important definitions and procedures are set off in boxes, and worked-out examples that present solutions in a step-by-step manner appear in every section. Study tip boxes offer hints and suggestions and often point out common errors to avoid. A great deal of attention has been given to show ways to apply mathematics to your life in order to make your learning experience both interesting and relevant.

As you begin your studies, I would like to offer some specific suggestions for using this book and for being successful in this course:

1. Attend all lectures. No book is intended to be a substitute for valuable insights and interactions that occur in the classroom. In addition to arriving for lecture on time and prepared, you will find it useful to read the section before it is covered in lecture. This will give you a clear idea of the new material that will be discussed.

2. Read the book. Read each section with pen (or pencil) in hand. Move through the illustrative examples with great care. These worked-out examples provide a model for doing the exercises in the exercise sets. As you proceed through the reading, do not give up if you do not understand every single word. Things will become clearer as you read on and see how various procedures are applied to specific worked-out examples.

3. Work problems every day and check your answers. The way to learn mathematics is by doing mathematics, which means working the assigned exercises in the exercise sets. The more exercises you work, the better you will understand the material.

4. Prepare for chapter exams. After completing a chapter, study the summary, work the exercises in the chapter review, and work the exercises in the chapter test. Answers to all these exercises are given in the back of the book.

5. Use the supplements available with this book. A solutions manual containing worked-out solutions to the book's odd-numbered exercises and all review exercises, a dynamic web page, and video tapes created for every section of the book are among the supplements created to help you tap into the power of mathematics. Ask your instructor or bookstore what supplements are available and where you can find them.

It is my hope that you will enjoy the pages of this book, as you empower yourself with the mathematics needed to succeed in college, your career, and in your life.

Regards,

Bob

Robert Blitzer

To the Instructor

Thinking Mathematically provides a general survey of mathematical topics that are useful in our contemporary world. My primary purpose in writing the book was to show students how mathematics can be applied to their lives in interesting, enjoyable, and meaningful ways. The book's variety of topics and flexibility of sequence make it appropriate for a one- or two-term course in liberal arts mathematics, finite mathematics, mathematics for education majors, as well as for courses specifically designed to meet state-mandated requirements in mathematics.

I wrote the book with three major goals: first, to help students acquire knowledge of fundamental mathematics; second, to show students how mathematics can solve authentic problems that apply to their lives; and third, to enable students to develop problem-solving skills, fostering critical thinking, within a varied, interesting, and contemporary setting.

I am avidly interested in psychology, philosophy, and literature, as well as mathematics. I've worked as a musician, psychotherapist, and even attempted book, music, and lyrics to an original musical. (Compared to writing for musical theater, authoring mathematics textbooks is a breeze!) I hope that my love for learning, as well as my respect for the diversity of students I have taught and learned from over the years, is apparent in the hundreds of applications that appear throughout the book. By connecting mathematics to the whole spectrum of learning, it is my intent to show students that their world is profoundly mathematical and, indeed, π is in the sky.

Bob
Robert Blitzer

Acknowledgments

I wish to express my appreciation to all the reviewers for their helpful criticisms and suggestions, frequently transmitted with wit, humor, and intelligence. In particular, I would like to thank:

Gerard Buskes, University of Mississippi
David Cochener, Austin Peay State University
Tristen Denley, University of Mississippi
Suzanne Feldberg, Nassau Community College
Margaret H. Finster, Erie Community College
Lyn Geisler III, Randolf–Macon College
Dale Grussing, Miami–Dade Community College
Virginia Harder, College at Oneonta
Julia Hassett, Oakton Community College
Sonya Hensler, St. Petersburg Junior College
Larry Hoehn, Austin Peay State University
Alec Ingraham, New Hampshire College
Mike Marcozzi, University of Nevada, Las Vegas
Diana Martelly, Miami–Dade Community College
Jim Matovina, Community College of Southern Nevada
Erik Matsuoka, Leeward Community College
Marcel Maupin, Oklahoma State University
Diana McCammon, Delgado Community College
Paul Mosbos, State University of New York–Cortland
Frank Pecchioni, Jefferson Community College.
Anthony Pettofrezzo, University of Central Florida
Evelyn Popplo-Cody, Marshall University
Kim Query, Lindenwood College
Shawn Robinson, Valencia Community College
Gary Russell, Brevard Community College
Mary Lee Seitz, Erie Community College
Laurie A. Stahl, State University of New York–Fredonia
Mike Tomme, Community College of Southern Nevada
Karen Villarreal, University of New Orleans
Shirley Wilson, North Central College
James Wooland, Florida State University
Marilyn Zopp, North Illinois University

Additional acknowledgments are extended to Jim Matovina for contributing to the technology essays and exercises throughout the book; James Wooland for writing the Florida CLAST supplement and additional materials; Jacquelyn White for creating the video tape series for each section of the book; the team at Laurel Technical Services for the Herculean task of solving all the book's exercises, preparing the answer section and solutions manuals, as well as serving as accuracy checker; Melinda Alexander, photo researcher, for obtaining the book's photographs; the team of graphic artists at Academy Artworks, whose superb illustrations and graphs provide visual support to the verbal portions of the text; Prepare Inc./Emilcomp srl, the book's compositor, for inputting hundreds of pages with hardly an error; and Barbara Mack, whose talents as production editor contributed to the book's wonderful look.

Most of all, I wish to thank Sally Yagan and Shana Ederer. Shana, my development editor, contributed invaluable edits and suggestions that resulted in a finished product that is both accessible and up to date. Her influence on this book is extraordinary, guiding and coordinating every detail of this project. Sally, executive editor of mathematics at Prentice Hall, is the key person in making this book a reality, and I am grateful to have had an editor with her experience, insight, and professionalism.

Sally Yagan and Shana Ederer are members of the terrific team at Prentice Hall who made this book possible, including President Tim Bozik and Editor-in-Chief Jerome Grant. Thank you Patrice Lumumba Jones, Senior Marketing Manager, for your innovative marketing efforts, as well as the Prentice Hall sales force for your confidence and enthusiasm over the book.

A Guide to Using This Text

You wanted to organize a blood drive on campus with the local Red Cross. The Red Cross asked you whether the number of potential donors warranted a commitment to provide medical staff for the blood drive. So you took a survey to obtain information. Your survey asked students:

1. Would you be willing to donate blood?
2. Would you volunteer to distribute a free breakfast to student donors?
3. Would you be willing to take part in both activities?

Now the survey results are in. How will you organize and present the results to the Red Cross in an efficient manner?

pages 32-33

2   Set Theory

The need to sort and organize information obtained in a survey is related to our need to find order and meaning by classifying things into collections. Mathematicians call such collections **sets**. Sets are groups of objects that usually share some common characteristic. For example, mathematicians classify numbers into sets based on whether or not their decimal representations have repeating patterns. A special set of numbers is used to provide probabilities of events. Sets are even used to describe nature's patterns, from the symmetry of a snowflake to the intricacies of a flower.

Set theory is the thread for the tapestry of mathematics. The set concept finds its way into many topics covered in this book, such as logic, algebra, and probability. Sets provide a precise way of describing and communicating mathematical ideas. Thus, learning to understand set theory will help you appreciate mathematics as a rich and living part of human culture.

33

Chapter-Opening Scenarios present mathematical concepts as they are likely to appear outside the classroom. These scenarios are revisited later in the chapter.

SECTION 2.3   Venn Diagrams and Set Operations

Objectives
1. Use Venn diagrams to visualize set relationships.
2. Perform operations with sets.

You need to determine whether there is sufficient support on campus to have a blood drive. You take a survey to obtain information, asking students:

Would you be willing to donate blood?
Would you be willing to help serve a free breakfast to blood donors?

Set A represents the set of students willing to donate blood. Set B represents the set of students willing to help serve breakfast to donors. Possible survey results include

No students willing to donate blood are willing to serve breakfast, and vice versa.
All students willing to donate blood are willing to serve breakfast.
The same students who are willing to donate blood are willing to serve breakfast.
Some of the students willing to donate blood are willing to serve breakfast.

We begin by using Venn diagrams to visualize these results.

1 Use Venn diagrams to visualize set relationships.

Visualizing Relationships Between Two Sets

Venn diagrams are useful for illustrating relationships between two sets. We consider four basic relationships and their visualizations.

Relationship 1. Disjoint Sets   Two sets that have no elements in common are called **disjoint** sets. Two disjoint sets A and B are shown in the Venn diagram on the left. Disjoint sets are represented as circles that do not overlap. No elements of set A are elements of set B, and vice versa.

If set A represents the set of students willing to donate blood and set B represents the set of students willing to serve breakfast to donors, the set diagram shown above illustrates

page 53

Learning Objectives at the beginning of each section give students a clear idea of the concepts they will cover.

SECTION 3.2 Compound Statements and Connectives

Objectives

1. Express compound statements in symbolic form.
2. Express symbolic statements with parentheses in English.

Percent who smoke
35.7 29.0 22.9 13.6
Level of education
■ Less than 12 years
■ 12 years
■ 13–15 years
■ 16 or more years

Figure 3.1 Percent of people who smoke, by level of education
Source: Centers for Disease Control and Prevention

1 Express English compound statements in symbolic form.

You are reading an article about the percent of people in the United States who smoke, by level of education. Using the graph shown in Figure 3.1, the article concludes:

> The percent of people who smoke decreases as level of education increases and less than 14% of college graduates smoke.

We can break this conclusion down into two sentences:

> The percent of people who smoke decreases as level of education increases.
> Less than 14% of college graduates smoke.

These statements are called **simple statements** because each one conveys one idea with no connecting words. Statements formed by combining two or more simple statements are called **compound statements**. Words called **connectives** are used to join simple statements to form a compound statement. Connectives include words such as **and, or, if … then,** and **if and only if.**

Compound statements appear throughout written and spoken language. We need to be able to understand the logic of such statements to analyze information objectively. In this section, we analyze four kinds of compound statements.

And Statements

If p and q represent two simple statements, then the compound statement "p and q" is symbolized by $p \wedge q$. The compound statement formed by connecting statements with the word **and** is called a **conjunction**. The symbol for *and* is $\wedge$.

EXAMPLE 1   Translating from English to Symbolic Form

Let p and q represent the following simple statements:

p: Harvard is a college.
q: Disney World is a college.

Write each of the compound statements below in its symbolic form.

a. Harvard is a college and Disney World is a college.
b. Harvard is a college and Disney World is not a college.

page 82

EXAMPLE 9   A Person's Actual Pay and the Feeling of Being Underpaid

Research shows that as income rises, people shift from comparing their income to what they need to "get along" to what they require to "get ahead." The formula

$$U = 0.018S^2 - 0.757S + 9.047$$

describes the amount that people feel they are underpaid (U, in thousands of dollars) in terms of their salary S (also expressed in thousands of dollars). If a person earns $40,000 yearly, by how much does that person feel underpaid?

Solution

$U = 0.018S^2 - 0.757S + 9.047$	This is the given formula.
$U = 0.018(40)^2 - 0.757(40) + 9.047$	We are given that the salary is 40 thousand dollars. Because salary S is expressed in thousands of dollars, replace S by 40.
$U = 0.018(1600) - 0.757(40) + 9.047$	Evaluate the exponential expression: $40^2 = (40)(40) = 1600$.
$U = 28.8 - 30.28 + 9.047$	Multiply from left to right: $(0.018)(1600) = 28.8$ and $(0.757)(40) = 30.28$.
$U = 28.8 + (-30.28) + 9.047$	Express subtraction as addition of an additive inverse.
$U = -1.48 + 9.047$	Add from left to right: $28.8 + (-30.28) = -1.48$.
$U = 7.567$	Remember that U, the amount one feels underpaid, is in thousands of dollars.

Thus, a person earning $40,000 yearly feels underpaid by 7.567 thousand dollars = $7.567 \times 1000 = \$7567$.

Study Tip

For the sum

$$28.8 + (-30.28) + 9.047$$

you can also first add the positive numbers

$$28.8 + 9.047 = 37.847$$

and then add the negative number to that result:

$$37.847 + (-30.28) = 7.567.$$

Well-Constructed Examples are clearly written and provide students with step-by-step solutions containing both numerical and verbal explanations. Well-presented examples are essential to students mastering procedural concepts.

page 250

160 as the numerator of the ratio and 100 as the denominator. Thus, the ratio for 1995 to 1980 is:

$$\frac{160}{100} = \frac{160 \div 20}{100 \div 20} = \frac{8}{5}, \text{ or } 8:5 \text{ (8 to 5)}.$$

Ratios in Baseball

A baseball player's batting average is the ratio of the number of hits to the number of times at bat. For example, a player with 60 hits and 200 times at bat has a batting average of

$$\frac{60}{200} = \frac{60 \div 20}{200 \div 20} = \frac{3}{10}$$

or 0.300. Joe DiMaggio was the American League batting champion in 1939 with a 0.381 batting average. The leading batter of all time was left-handed hitter Ty Cobb. Cobb's batting average over 24 years (4191 hits and 11,429 times at bat) was 0.367.

Joe DiMaggio's (1914–1999) grace rivaled that of the great clipper ships, earning him the nickname the "Yankee Clipper."

page 273

SECTION 7.5   *Systems of Linear Equations*

Objectives

1. Decide whether an ordered pair is a solution of a linear system.
2. Solve linear systems by graphing.
3. Solve linear systems by substitution.
4. Solve linear systems by addition.
5. Identify systems that do not have exactly one ordered-pair solution.
6. Solve problems using systems of linear equations.

Key West residents Brian Goss (left), George Wallace, and Michael Mooney (right) hold on to each other as they battle 90 mph winds along Houseboat Row in Key West, Fla., on Friday, Sept. 25, 1998. The three had sought shelter behind a Key West hotel as Hurricane Georges descended on the Florida Keys but were forced to seek other shelter when the storm conditions became too rough. Hundreds of people were killed by the storm when it swept through the Caribbean.

The text uses **Compelling Images** to help students make the connection between their world and the mathematics that permeates it.

Solving real-world problems often involves thousands of equations, sometimes a million variables. Problems ranging from scheduling airline flights to controlling traffic flow to routing phone calls over the nation's communication network often require solutions in a matter of moments. AT&T's domestic long distance network involves 800,000 variables! Meteorologists describing atmospheric conditions surrounding a hurricane must solve problems involving thousands of equations rapidly and efficiently. The difference between a two-hour warning and a two-day warning is a life-and-death issue for thousands of people in the path of one of nature's most destructive forces.

Although we will not be solving 800,000 equations with 800,000 variables, we will turn our attention to two equations with two variables, such as

$$2x - 3y = -4$$
$$2x + y = 4.$$

The methods that we consider for solving such problems provide the foundation for solving far more complex systems with many variables.

Technology Boxes suggest hints for using both computers and graphing calculators. Technology is integrated into both the chapter material and section exercises. Students using technology will find that the text appropriately supports their mode of study. *Expanded coverage of technology complete with tutorials for various calculators can be found on the Website at www.prenhall.com/blitzer.*

> ### Technology
>
> Is your calculator a scientific calculator? Try this. Enter the simple problem $2 + 3 \times 5$, then push =. If your calculator gives the correct answer, 17, it is a scientific calculator and will prove to be useful in your math courses. If your calculator gives the incorrect answer, 25, it will only be useful in problems that do not require multiple steps. Remember this the next time you balance your checkbook!

page 194

> ### Study Tip
>
> You can think of negative integers as amounts of money that you *owe*. It's better to owe less, so
>
> $$-1 > -4.$$

page 189

Study Tips offer suggestions for problem solving, point out common student errors, and provide informal tips and suggestions throughout the text.

EXAMPLE 3   Pet Population

Americans love their pets. The number of cats in the United States exceeds the number of dogs by 7.5 million. The number of cats and dogs combined is 114.7 million. Determine the number of dogs and cats in the United States.

Solution

Step 1   Let x represent one of the quantities. We know something about the number of cats; the cat population exceeds the dog population by 7.5 million. This means that there are 7.5 million more cats than dogs. We will let

$x =$ the number (in millions) of dogs in the United States.

Step 2   Represent other quantities in terms of x. The other unknown quantity is the number of cats. Because there are 7.5 million more cats than dogs, let

$x + 7.5 =$ the number (in millions) of cats in the United States.

Step 3   Write an equation in x that describes the conditions. The number of cats and dogs combined is 114.7 million.

| The number (in millions) of dogs in the U.S. | plus | the number (in millions) of cats in the U.S. | equals | 114.7 million. |
| x | $+$ | $x + 7.5$ | $=$ | 114.7 |

Step 4   Solve the equation and answer the question.

$x + x + 7.5 = 114.7$	This is the equation specified by the conditions of the problem.
$2x + 7.5 = 114.7$	Combine like terms on the left side.
$2x + 7.5 - 7.5 = 114.7 - 7.5$	Subtract 7.5 from both sides.
$2x = 107.2$	Simplify.
$\dfrac{2x}{2} = \dfrac{107.2}{2}$	Divide both sides by 2.
$x = 53.6$	Simplify.

Because x represents the number (in millions) of dogs, there are 53.6 million dogs in the United States. Because $x + 7.5$ represents the number (in millions) of cats, there are $53.6 + 7.5$, or 61.1 million cats in the United States.

U.S. Pet Population

Millions of Pets: Cats, Dogs, Horses 12

Source: American Veterinary Medical Association

Americans spend more than $21 billion a year on their pets. 31.4% of households have cats and 34.3% have dogs.

Real-World Data bring relevance to examples, discussions, and applications.

Step-by-Step Procedures provide a structured resource for learning.

Voice Balloons allow for more specific annotations in examples, further clarifying procedures and concepts for students.

50. $f(x) = 5x^2 + 2$ 51. $f(x) = \dfrac{x}{x^2 + 1}$ 52. $f(x) = \dfrac{x^2}{x^2 + 1}$

$= \dfrac{x}{x^2 - 1}$ 54. $h(x) = \dfrac{x}{x - 1}$ 55. $F(x) = \dfrac{x - 2}{x^3 + x}$ 56. $G(x) = \dfrac{x + 4}{x^3 - 4x}$

$= \sqrt{3x - 12}$ 58. $G(x) = \sqrt{1 - x}$ 59. $f(x) = \dfrac{4}{\sqrt{x - 9}}$ 60. $f(x) = \dfrac{x}{\sqrt{x - 4}}$

$= \sqrt{\dfrac{2}{x - 1}}$ 62. $q(x) = \sqrt{-x - 2}$

n each of the following functions with the graphs that best describe the situation.
he cost of building a house as a function of its square footage
he height of an egg dropped from a 300-foot building as a function of time
he height of a human as a function of time
he demand for Big Macs as a function of price
he height of a child on a swing as a function of time

page 107

---

37. ⌄⌄⌄ ⌄⌄⌄ ⌄⌄⌄   38. ⌄⌄ ⌄⌄ ⌄⌄⌄⌄
39. ⌄⌄ ⌄⌄ ⌄⌄ ⌄⌄   40. ⌄⌄ ⌄⌄ ⌄⌄⌄ ⌄⌄⌄

In Exercises 41–50, use Table 4.2 on page 152 to write each Mayan numeral as a Hindu-Arabic numeral.

41. ▦   42. ▦   43. ▦   44. ▦
45. ▦   46. ▦   47. ▦   48. ▦
49. ▦   50. ▦

 Application Exercises

Exercise 51 contains a Mayan numeral. Exercise 52 contains a Babylonian numeral. Write each numeral as a Hindu-Arabic numeral. The numeral that results represents a year that was not important to the Mayans or the Babylonians but is important to us. Identify the historical event that took place in that year. If necessary, use an appropriate reference.

51. ▦   52. ⌄⌄⌄⌄⌄ ⌄⌄⌄⌄⌄⌄⌄⌄

 Writing in Mathematics

53. Describe the difference between a number and a numeral.

54. Explain how to evaluate 7^3.

55. What is the base in our Hindu-Arabic numeration system? What are the digits in the system?

56. Why is a symbol for zero needed in a positional system?

57. Explain how to write a Hindu-Arabic numeral in expanded form.

58. Describe one way that the Babylonian system is similar to the Hindu-Arabic system and one way that it is different from the Hindu-Arabic system.

59. Describe one way that the Mayan system is similar to the Hindu-Arabic system and one way that it is different from the Hindu-Arabic system.

 Critical Thinking Exercises

61. Write ⌄ ⌄⌄⌄ ⌄⌄ as a Mayan numeral.

62. Write ▦ as a Babylonian numeral.

63. Use Babylonian numerals to write the numeral that precedes and the numeral that follows ⌄⌄ ⌄⌄⌄⌄⌄⌄ ⌄⌄⌄⌄⌄⌄⌄⌄⌄.

 Technology Exercises

Using a calculator, evaluate the following expressions.

64. 4^5 65. 5^4 66. 2^9 67. 84^3

68. For the value of the expression 85^8, a scientific calculator displays 2.724905 15. What is the significance of the space immediately before the final two digits?

 Group Exercises

69. Your group task is to create an original positional numeration system that is different from the three systems discussed in this section.
    a. Construct a table showing your numerals and the corresponding Hindu-Arabic numerals.
    b. Explain how to represent numbers in your system, and express a three-digit and a four-digit Hindu-Arabic numeral in your system.
    c. Explain how two numbers can be added in your system.

70. For many individuals around the world who are blind or visually impaired, Braille numerals are used to represent numbers. Braille numerals can be detected and interpreted by touch. A group of two or three students should research how Braille numerals are formed. Many public and private organizations and schools provide materials and information for the blind and visually impaired. Using your library, resources on the World Wide Web, or local organizations, investigate the basic elements for Braille numerals, including the two-dot by three-dot cell, as well as the dot symbol used to precede a numeral. Present the results of your research to the entire class and bring examples of Braille numerals for each student to interpret by hand with no visual clues.

Exercises are graded by level within six category types:
• Practice Exercises
• Application Exercises
• Writing in Mathematics
• Critical Thinking Exercises
• Technology Exercises
• Group Exercises
This format makes it easy to create well-rounded homework assignments. *Additional exercises are available on the Website at* **www.prenhall.com/blitzer.**

Chapter Summaries and Review Exercises are organized around each section within the chapter. The review exercises conclude with a group exercise based on the chapter opener. *More review is available on the Website at:* **www.prenhall.com/blitzer.**

CHAPTER SUMMARY, REVIEW, AND TEST

SUMMARY

5.1

Divisibility
a. Natural Numbers: $\mathbf{N} = \{1, 2, 3, 4, 5, \ldots\}$
b. $b \mid a$ (b divides a; a is divisible by b) for natural numbers a and b if the operation of dividing a by b leaves a remainder of 0.
c. Rules of divisibility are given in Table 5.1 on page 179.

Prime and Composite Numbers
a. A prime number is a natural number greater than 1 that has only itself and 1 as factors.
b. A composite number is a natural number greater than 1 that is divisible by a number other than itself and 1.
c. The Fundamental Theorem of Arithmetic. Every composite number can be expressed as a product of prime numbers in one and only one way (if the order of the factors is disregarded).

Greatest Common Divisors and Least Common Multiples
a. The greatest common divisor of two or more natural numbers is the largest number that is a divisor (or factor) of all the numbers.
b. The procedure for finding the greatest common divisor is boxed on page 182.
c. The least common multiple of two or more natural numbers is the smallest natural number that is divisible by all of the numbers.
d. The procedure for finding the least common multiple is boxed on page 184.

Absolute Value
a. $|a|$, the absolute value of a, is the distance of a from 0 on a number line.
b. The absolute value of a positive number is the number itself.
c. The absolute value of 0 is 0: $|0| = 0$.
d. The absolute value of a negative number is positive. For example, $|-8| = 8$.

Order of Operations
a. Perform operations in parentheses. Follow the order in b–d listed below.
b. Evaluate all exponential expressions.
c. Do all multiplications and divisions from left to right.
d. Do all additions and subtractions from left to right.

5.3

Rational Numbers
a. The set of rational numbers is the set of all numbers which can be expressed in the form $\frac{a}{b}$, where a and b are integers and b is not equal to 0.
b. Any rational number can be expressed as a decimal. The resulting decimal will either terminate (stop), or it will have a digit that repeats or a block of digits that repeat.
c. The rational number $\frac{a}{b}$ is expressed as a decimal by dividing b into a.
d. To express a terminating decimal as a quotient of integers, the digits to the right of the decimal point are the numerator. The place-value of the last digit to the right of the decimal point is the denominator. To express a repeating decimal as a quotient of integers, use the boxed procedure on page 200.

page 237

CHAPTER 1 TEST

1. Find a counterexample to show that the following statement is false:

   If a two-digit number is multiplied by a one-digit number, the answer is a two-digit number.

In Exercises 2–3, identify a pattern in each list of numbers. Then use this pattern to find the next number.

2. $0, 5, 10, 15, \underline{\hspace{1cm}}$

3. $\frac{1}{6}, \frac{1}{12}, \frac{1}{24}, \frac{1}{48}, \underline{\hspace{1cm}}$

4. Identify a pattern in the following sequence of figures. Then use the pattern to find the next figure in the sequence.

5. Consider the following procedure:

   Select a number. Multiply the number by 4. Add 8 to the product. Divide the sum by 2. Subtract 4 from the quotient.

   a. Repeat this procedure for three numbers of your choice. Write a conjecture that relates the result of the process to the original number selected.
   b. Represent the original number by ▓ and use deductive reasoning to prove the conjecture in part (a).

Work Exercises 6–9 without a calculator. Different rounding results in different estimates, so there is not a single correct answer to these exercises. Use rounding to make the resulting calculations simple.

6. For a spring break vacation, a student needs to spend $47.00 for gas, $311.00 for food, and $405.00 for a hotel room. If the student takes $681.79 from savings, estimate how much more money is needed for the vacation.

7. The cost for opening a restaurant is $485,000. If 19 people decide to share equally in the business, estimate the amount each must contribute.

8. Find an estimate of 0.48992×120.

9. The circle graph shown is based on a survey of 17.1 million acres of lakes in the United States. Using this survey by the Environmental Protection Agency, estimate the number of acres of impaired lakes.

Water Quality in U.S. Lakes

Good 63%

Impaired 37%

Source: U.S. Environmental Protection Agency

10. The bar graph shows the percent of vacations that included the activity listed on the left. Which activities were included on at least 14% of vacations and at most 30%?

Percent of U.S. Vacations that Included the Activity

Source: Travel Industry Association of America

Chapter Tests enable students to test their understanding of the contents from the chapter.

Resources

For the Instructor

Instructor's Solutions Manual

Laurel Technical Services

Complete solutions to the even end-of-section exercises, all of the Review Exercises, and Chapter Tests, all in one complete volume.
ISBN: 0-13-014936-5

Printed Test Bank

Laurel Technical Services

Offers free-response and multiple-choice questions arranged section-by-section as well as grouped in pre-formatted, ready-for-copying exams. For each chapter there are five pre-formatted tests: two multiple-choice and three free-response. There are four pre-formatted final exams: two multiple-choice and two free-response.
ISBN: 0-13- 014935-7

PH Custom Test

Engineering Software Associates

Available in both Windows and MAC formats. Includes all the questions in the Printed Test Bank.
ISBN: WINDOWS: 0-13-014286-6
MAC: 0-13-014287-5

PowerPoint Presentations

Joby Milo Anthony

Designed to enhance an instructor's classroom presentation or create a framework for on-line materials, these mini-presentations correspond to each chapter in the text. These materials can be edited by the user and, if desired, printed and used as overheads. The PowerPoint Presentations can be found on the Website.

For the Student

Student Solutions Manual

Laurel Technical Services

Complete worked-out solutions to all of the odd-numbered exercises, all of the Review Exercises, and Chapter Tests.
ISBN: 0-13-014938-1

Lecture Video Tapes

Jacquelyn White, St. Leo University

This comprehensive set of videos provides a short leture and worked examples for almost every section in the text. These videos provide excellent support for students who missed class or need to study the material at their own pace. They are also an invaluable resource for distance learning or self-paced programs.
ISBN: 0-13-015492-X

Website

The Website provides additional student resources, including:

- The full Student Solutions Manual
- On-line graphing calculator manual, including steps and keystrokes for the TI 81, 83, 85, 86, and 92 calculators as well as Casio and Sharp models
- Additional exercises
- Extension modules on topics meant to expand the text's coverage
- Chapter tests and quizzes
- Syllabus builder
- PowerPoints
- Chapter Website destinations
- Technology projects
- On-line CLAST manual

CLAST Guide

James Wooland, Florida State University

This study guide helps students to prepare for the Florida College Level Academic Skills Test. Available in print format and in electronic format on the Website.

Applications Index

G

Thinking Mathematically

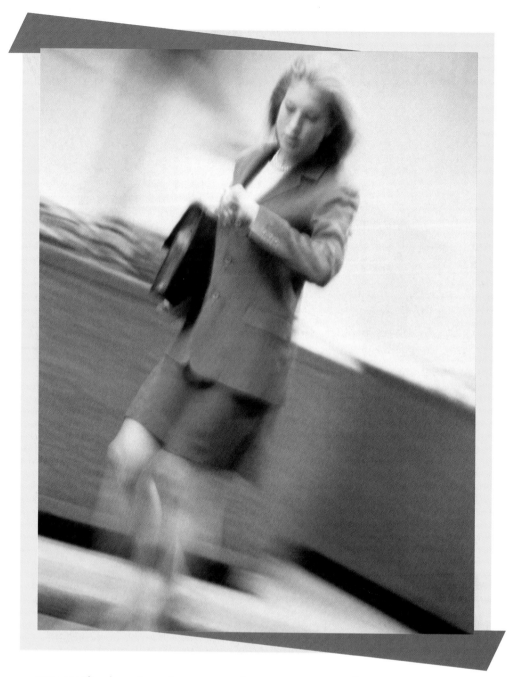

You are the department manager of a company. One of your best employees who is too valuable to fire arrives to work late nearly every morning. What can you do to solve the problem of this employee's tardiness?

1 Problem Solving and Critical Thinking

The ability to solve problems using thought and reasoning is indispensable to every area of our lives. We are all problem solvers. Our work in solving problems in school, on the job, and even in our personal lives involves understanding the problem, devising a plan for solving it, and then carrying out the plan. The aim of this chapter is to help you to better develop your skills of reasoning, estimation, and problem solving. By the time you complete the chapter, you will be a better, more confident problem solver. This will help you as you study the topics throughout the book. You will be able to apply problem-solving techniques used in mathematics to real-life situations such as the one that the department manager is trying to solve. (We will return to this problem in the third section of the chapter.) As you begin your journey through this book, your growing ability to solve problems will result in a BON VOYAGE!

SECTION 1.1   *Inductive and Deductive Reasoning*

Objectives

1. Understand and use inductive reasoning.

2. Understand and use deductive reasoning.

Calvin and Hobbes   by Bill Watterson

Calvin and Hobbes © 1990 Watterson. Reprinted with permission of Universal Press Syndicate. All rights reserved.

Many people associate mathematics with tedious computation, meaningless algebraic procedures, and musty sets of equations. The truth is that mathematics is the most powerful means we have of exploring our world and describing how it works. The word *mathematics* comes from the Greek word *mathematikos*, which means "inclined to learn." To be mathematical literally means to be inquisitive, open-minded, and interested in a lifetime of pursuing knowledge!

Mathematics and Your Life

A major goal of this book is to show you how mathematics can be applied to your life in interesting, enjoyable, and meaningful ways. Here is a brief, although far from complete, preview of what you can expect.

An understanding of logic will help you to determine what is meant and what is not necessarily meant in spoken and written language. It will give you special tools to analyze information objectively, and to avoid arriving at conclusions hastily without considering all the evidence.

Literacy in numbers will provide you with an understanding of what numbers really mean. For example, the national debt of the United States is about $5.5 trillion. What exactly does this huge number mean? How much would each citizen have to pay the government to retire the debt? In Chapter 5, you will be given a technique that will provide a surprising answer to this question.

An understanding of probability theory will enable you to study future courses of events to determine what to expect in the long run. Basic ideas of probability will give you a tool for peering into the future and seeing aspects of the universe that would otherwise be invisible.

Managing your personal finances is not an easy task. Achieving your financial goals depends on understanding basic ideas about savings, loans, and investments. Knowledge of consumer mathematics can pay, literally, by making your financial goals a reality.

You can hardly pick up a newspaper without being bombarded with numbers and graphs that describe how we live, what we want, and even how we are likely to die. These numbers influence which products are sold in stores, which movies are shown in theaters, which treatments are available for disease, and which policies are likely to be supported by politicians. An understanding of statistics will help you comprehend where these numbers come from and how they are used to make decisions.

Mathematics and Your Career

Generally speaking, the income of an occupation is related to the amount of education. This, in turn, is usually related to high skill levels in language and mathematics. With our increasing reliance on technology, the more mathematics you know, the more career choices you will have.

Mathematics and Your World

Mathematics is a science that helps us recognize, classify, and explore the hidden patterns of our universe. Focusing on areas as different as planetary motion, animal markings, shapes of viruses, aerodynamics of figure skaters, and the very origin of the universe, mathematics is the most powerful tool available for revealing the underlying structure of our world. Within the last 30 years, mathematicians have even found order in chaotic events such as the uncontrolled storm of noise in the nerve cells of the brain during an epileptic seizure.

1 Understand and use inductive reasoning.

Inductive Reasoning

Mathematics involves the study of patterns. In everyday life, we frequently rely on patterns and routines that we assume will continue to be helpful in drawing conclusions. Here is an example.

> The last six times I went to the beach, the traffic was light on Wednesdays and heavy on Sundays. My conclusion is that weekdays have lighter traffic than weekends.

This type of reasoning process is referred to as **inductive reasoning**, or **induction**.

Inductive Reasoning

Inductive reasoning is the process of arriving at a general conclusion based on observations of specific examples.

EXAMPLE 1 A Visit to the Florida Keys

A tourist who visited Key West met a number of people from the Keys who were relaxed and laid back. The tourist concluded that all people living in Key West were relaxed and laid back. What reasoning process led to this conclusion?

Solution This conclusion was reached by induction. The tourist reached a general conclusion about people living in Key West based on observing a number of specific people.

Although inductive reasoning is a powerful method of drawing conclusions, we can never be absolutely certain that these conclusions are true. Even if the visitor to Key West met 100 relaxed people who lived on the island, it is possible that Key West resident number 101 is a stressed-out, nervous wreck. Resident number 101 reveals that the conclusion

> All people living in Key West are relaxed and laid back

is false.

As you use inductive reasoning to find patterns, keep in mind that this form of reasoning does not prove that the pattern applies to all cases. For this reason, the conclusion is called a **conjecture**, or an educated guess. If there is just one case for which the conjecture does not work, then the conjecture is false. Such a case is called a **counterexample**. Key West resident number 101, who is a stressed-out wreck, is a counterexample that shows "All people living in Key West are relaxed and laid back" is false.

EXAMPLE 2   Finding a Counterexample

The ten symbols that we use to write numbers, namely 0, 1, 2, 3, 4, 5, 6, 7, 8, and 9, are called **digits**. In each example shown below, the sum of two two-digit numbers is a three-digit number.

$$\begin{array}{r} 47 \\ + 73 \\ \hline 120 \end{array} \quad \text{Two-digit numbers} \quad \begin{array}{r} 56 \\ + 46 \\ \hline 102 \end{array}$$

Three-digit sums

Is the sum of two two-digit numbers always a three-digit number? Find a counterexample to show that the statement

The sum of two two-digit numbers is a three-digit number

is false.

Solution   There are many counterexamples, but we need to find only one. Here is an example that makes the statement false:

Two-digit numbers $\quad \begin{array}{r} 56 \\ + 43 \\ \hline 99 \end{array} \quad$ This is a two-digit sum, not a three-digit sum.

This example is a counterexample that shows

The sum of two two-digit numbers is a three-digit number

is false.

> "When I'm walking in the woods, I find it quite difficult not to look at a fern or the bark of a tree and wonder how it was formed—why is it like that?"
>
> JAMES MURRAY,
> mathematician

You often use inductive reasoning involving number patterns without being aware that you are engaged in this kind of thinking. For example, when a number on the odometer of a car becomes a 9, you use the pattern to conclude that the next number to appear in that column will be a 0. Discovery in mathematics often begins with a search for patterns about numbers.

EXAMPLE 3   Using Inductive Reasoning

Identify a pattern in each list of numbers. Then use this pattern to find the next number.

a. 4, 12, 20, 28, 36, _____   b. 5, 15, 45, 135, _____

Solution

a. Each number in the list

4, 12, 20, 28, 36

is obtained by adding 8 to the previous number. The next number is 36 + 8, or 44.

b. Each number in the list

5, 15, 45, 135

is obtained by multiplying the previous number by 3. The next number is 135 × 3, or 405.

This electron microscope photograph shows the knotty shape of the Ebola virus.

Figure 1.1

2 Understand and use deductive reasoning.

Mathematics is more than recognizing number patterns. It is about the patterns that arise in the world around us. For example, by describing patterns formed by various kinds of knots, mathematicians are helping scientists investigate the knotty shapes and patterns of viruses. One of the weapons used against viruses is based on recognizing visual patterns in the possible ways that knots can be tied.

Our next example deals with recognizing visual patterns.

EXAMPLE 4   Finding the Next Figure in a Visual Sequence

Describe two patterns in this sequence of figures. Use the patterns to draw the next figure in the sequence.

 , , , , _____

Solution   The more obvious pattern is that the figures alternate between circles and squares. We conclude that the next figure will be a circle. We can identify the second pattern in the four regions containing no dots, one dot, two dots, and three dots. The dots are placed in order (no dots, one dot, two dots, three dots) in a clockwise direction. However, the entire pattern of the dots rotates counterclockwise as we follow the figures from left to right.

This means that the next figure should be a circle with a single dot in the right-hand region, two dots in the bottom region, three dots in the left-hand region, and no dots in the top region. This figure is drawn in Figure 1.1.

Deductive Reasoning

We use inductive reasoning in everyday life. Many of the conjectures that come from this kind of thinking seem highly likely, although we can never be absolutely certain that they are true. Another method of reasoning, called **deductive reasoning**, or **deduction**, can be used to prove that some conjectures are true.

> ### Deductive Reasoning
> **Deductive reasoning** is the process of proving a specific conclusion from one or more general statements. A conclusion that is proved true by deductive reasoning is called a **theorem**.

Deductive reasoning allows us to draw specific conclusions based on a general statement. For example, suppose that all college students are required to take mathematics. This general statement applies to every college student. Further suppose that Alberta Einstein is a college student. A specific conclusion is that Alberta Eistein is required to take mathematics. In Chapter 3 you will learn how to prove this conclusion.

Our next example illustrates the difference between inductive and deductive reasoning. The first part of the example involves reasoning that moves from specific examples to a general statement, illustrating inductive reasoning. The second part of the example begins with the general case rather than specific examples, and illustrates deductive reasoning.

Study Tip

In case you have forgotten some basic terms of arithmetic, the following list should be helpful.

Sum: the result of addition

Difference: the result of subtraction

Product: the result of multiplication

Quotient: the result of division

EXAMPLE 5   Using Inductive and Deductive Reasoning

Consider the following procedure:

> Select a number. Multiply the number by 6. Add 8 to the product. Divide this sum by 2. Subtract 4 from the quotient.

a. Repeat this procedure for at least four different numbers. Write a conjecture that relates the result of this process to the original number selected.

b. Represent the original number as ■, and use deductive reasoning to prove the conjecture in part (a).

Solution

a. First, let us pick our starting numbers. We will use 4, 7, 11, and 100, but we could pick any four numbers. Next we will apply the procedure given in this example to 4, 7, 11, and 100, four individual cases, in Table 1.1.

Table 1.1   Applying a Procedure to Four Individual Cases

Select a number.	4	7	11	100
Multiply the number by 6.	$4 \times 6 = 24$	$7 \times 6 = 42$	$11 \times 6 = 66$	$100 \times 6 = 600$
Add 8 to the product.	$24 + 8 = 32$	$42 + 8 = 50$	$66 + 8 = 74$	$600 + 8 = 608$
Divide this sum by 2.	$\frac{32}{2} = 16$	$\frac{50}{2} = 25$	$\frac{74}{2} = 37$	$\frac{608}{2} = 304$
Subtract 4 from the quotient.	$16 - 4 = 12$	$25 - 4 = 21$	$37 - 4 = 33$	$304 - 4 = 300$

Because we are asked to write a conjecture that relates the result of this process to the original number selected, let us focus on the result of each case.

Original number selected	4	7	11	100
Result of the process	12	21	33	300

Do you see a pattern? Our conjecture is that the result of the process is three times the original number selected. We have used inductive reasoning.

b. Now we begin with the general case rather than specific examples. Let us use ■ to stand for any number.

Select a number: ■

Multiply the number by 6: ■ ■ ■ ■ ■ ■

Add 8 to the product: ■ ■ ■ ■ ■ ■ ∷∷

Divide this sum by 2: ■ ■ ■ ° ° ° °

Subtract 4 from the quotient: ■ ■ ■

For any number ■ selected, the result of the process is ■ ■ ■. This proves that the result is three times the original number selected for any number ■. We have used deductive reasoning.

The Patterns of Chaos

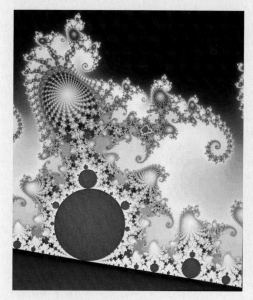

One of the new frontiers of mathematics suggests that there is an underlying order in things that appear to be random, such as the hiss and crackle of background noises as you tune a radio. Irregularities in the heartbeat, some of them severe enough to cause a heart attack, or irregularities in our sleeping patterns, such as insomnia, are examples of chaotic behavior. Chaos in the mathematical sense does not mean a complete lack of form or arrangement. In mathematics, chaos is used to describe something that appears to be random but is not actually random. The patterns of chaos appear in images like the one on the left, called the Mandelbrot set. Magnified portions of this image yield repetitions of the original structure, as well as new and unexpected patterns. The Mandelbrot set transforms the hidden structure of chaotic events into a source of wonder and inspiration.

A magnification of the Mandelbrot set. R. F. Voss
"29-Fold M-set Seahorse" computer-generated
image. © 1990 R. F. Voss/IBM Research.

Exercise Set 1.1

 Practice Exercises

1. Which reasoning process is shown in the following example? Explain your answer.

   We examine the fingerprints of 1000 people. No two individuals in this group of people have identical fingerprints. We conclude that for all people, no two people have identical fingerprints.

2. Which reasoning process is shown in the following example? Explain your answer.

   We observe that the last four mayors in our city have been Democrats. We conclude that the next mayor will be a Democrat.

In Exercises 3–10, find a counterexample to show that each of the statements is false.

3. No U.S. president has been impeached.
4. No singers appear in movies.
5. All books have less than 600 pages.
6. All famous people tell the truth.
7. If a number is multiplied by itself, the result is even.
8. The sum of 2 three-digit numbers is a four-digit number.
9. Adding the same numbers to the top and bottom of a fraction does not change the fraction's value.
10. If the difference between two numbers is odd, then the two numbers are both odd.

In Exercises 11–20, identify a pattern in each list of numbers. Then use this pattern to find the next number. (More than one pattern might exist, so it is possible that there is more than one correct answer.)

11. 8, 12, 16, 20, 24, ____
12. 19, 24, 29, 34, 39, ____
13. 37, 32, 27, 22, 17, ____
14. 33, 29, 25, 21, 17, ____
15. 3, 9, 27, 81, 243, ____
16. 2, 8, 32, 128, 512, ____
17. 1, 2, 4, 8, 16, ____
18. 1, 5, 25, 125, ____
19. 1, 4, 1, 8, 1, 16, 1, ____
20. 1, 4, 1, 7, 1, 10, 1, ____

In Exercises 21–24, identify a pattern in each sequence of figures. Then use the pattern to find the next figure in the sequence.

21.

22.

23.

24.

Exercises 25–28 describe procedures that are to be applied to numbers. In each exercise:

    a. *Repeat the procedure for four numbers of your choice. Write a conjecture that relates the result of the process to the original number selected.*

    b. *Represent the original number as ■ and use deductive reasoning to prove the conjecture in part (a).*

25. Select a number. Multiply the number by 4. Add 8 to the product. Divide this sum by 2. Subtract 4 from the quotient.

26. Select a number. Multiply the number by 3. Add 6 to the product. Divide this sum by 3. Subtract the number you began with from the quotient.

27. Select a number. Add 5. Double the result. Subtract 4. Divide by 2. Subtract the original selected number.

28. Select a number. Add 3. Double the result. Add 4. Divide by 2. Subtract the original selected number.

 Application Exercise

29. The following table relates a man's foot length, in inches, to his shoe size.

Foot length	9	10	11	12	13	14
Shoe size	5	8	11			

    a. Use inductive reasoning to fill in the missing portions of the table.

    b. According to the 1998 *Guinness Book of World Records*, the biggest feet currently known are those of Matthew McGrory (1973–) of Pennsylvania, who wears size 26 shoes. What is the length of his foot?

 Writing in Mathematics

Writing about mathematics will help you to learn mathematics. For all writing exercises in this book, use complete sentences to respond to the questions. Some writing exercises can be answered in a sentence; others require a paragraph or two. You can decide how much you need to write as long as your writing clearly and directly answers the question in the exercise. Standard references such as a dictionary and a thesaurus should be helpful.

30. What is a conjecture?

31. What is a counterexample? Give an example of a conclusion that can be reached using inductive reasoning. Then give a counterexample.

32. Describe what is meant by deductive reasoning. Give an example.

33. Can inductive reasoning be used to prove a theorem? Explain your answer.

34. The word *induce* comes from a Latin term meaning to lead. Explain what leading has to do with inductive reasoning.

35. Give an example of a decision that you made recently in which the reasoning you used to reach the decision was induction. Describe your reasoning process.

36. The March 29, 1999 issue of *Time* magazine is a special issue on the greatest thinkers of the twentieth century. Consult this issue of *Time* and select one of the great thinkers who used inductive or deductive reasoning in his or her work.

    a. Explain how the person you selected used one of these types of reasoning.

    b. Explain why you selected this particular person.

 Critical Thinking Exercises

37. What reasoning process is shown in the following example? Explain your answer.

    I see the same woman leaving the college administration building every day at 5:00 P.M. She must be an administrator at the college.

In Exercises 38–39, identify a pattern and find the next number in the list.

38. 1, 1, 2, 3, 5, 8, 13, 21, 34, ____   39. 15, 23, 33, 45, 59, ____

In Exercises 40–41, use inductive reasoning to predict the next line in the pattern. Then use a calculator or perform the arithmetic by hand to determine whether your conjecture is correct.

40. $37 \times 3 = 111$
    $37 \times 6 = 222$
    $37 \times 9 = 333$
    $37 \times 12 = 444$
    _____

41. $33 \times 3367 = 111,111$
    $66 \times 3367 = 222,222$
    $99 \times 3367 = 333,333$
    $132 \times 3367 = 444,444$
    _____

42. Write a list of numbers that has two patterns so that the next number in the list can be 15 or 20.

 Technology Exercises

43. Using a calculator, find the squares of 75, 175, 275, 375, and 475.

    a. Establish a pattern in the squares.

    b. Use that pattern to predict the squares of 575 and 675.

    c. Is this process an example of inductive or deductive reasoning?

44. Using a calculator, find the squares of 6, 66, 666, and 6666.

    a. Establish a pattern in the squares.

    b. Use that pattern to predict the squares of 66,666 and 666,666.

 Group Exercise

45. Reasoning in real life is often not as clean and simple as the examples of inductive and deductive reasoning presented in this section. Television advertisements often use deceptive reasoning to persuade us to buy products. Each group member should find a television advertisement that uses deceptive logic to get viewers to purchase what they are selling. Upon returning to the group, each member should describe the advertisement and discuss how the advertiser is attempting to fool the viewer into buying something.

SECTION 1.2   *Estimation and Graphs*

Objectives

1. Use estimation techniques to arrive at an approximate answer to a problem.
2. Apply estimation techniques to information given by graphs.

1 Use estimation techniques to arrive at an approximate answer to a problem.

Study Tip

In case you have forgotten, here are the place values for a number.

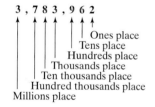

3 , 7 8 3 , 9 6 2

Ones place
Tens place
Hundreds place
Thousands place
Ten thousands place
Hundred thousands place
Millions place

The place that a digit occupies in a number tells us its value in that number.

Estimation

Estimation is the process of arriving at an approximate answer to a question. For example, companies estimate the amount of their products consumers are likely to use, and economists estimate financial trends. If you are about to cross a street, you may estimate the speed of oncoming cars so that you know whether or not to wait before crossing. Rounding numbers is also an estimation method. You might round a number without even being aware that you are doing so. You may say that you are 20 years old, rather than $20\frac{1}{4}$, or that you will be home in about a half-hour rather than 25 minutes.

You will find estimation to be equally valuable in your work for this class. Making mistakes with a calculator or computer is easy. Estimation can tell us whether the answer displayed for a computation makes sense.

In this section, we demonstrate several estimation methods. In the second part of the section, we apply these techniques to information given by graphs.

Performing computations using rounded numbers is one way to check whether an answer displayed by a calculator or a computer is correct.

Rounding numbers

1. Look at the digit to the right of the digit where rounding is to occur.
2. a. If the digit at right is 5 or greater, add 1 to the digit to be rounded. Replace all digits to the right by zeros.
   b. If the digit at right is less than 5, do not change the digit to be rounded. Replace all digits to the right by zeros.

EXAMPLE 1   Rounding a Number

Round 37 to the nearest ten.

Solution

We want to round to the nearest ten. Thus, "3" is the digit where rounding will occur.

Step 1. Look at the digit to the right of where rounding will occur.

37

37

Step 2. "7" is greater than "5".

Add 1 to the digit to be rounded.

37
+1
40

Replace all digits to the right by zeros.

Therefore, 37 rounded to the nearest ten is 40.

The symbol ≈ means *is approximately equal to*. Based on our rounding in Example 1, we can write

$$37 \approx 40.$$

EXAMPLE 2   Estimation by Rounding

You purchased bread for $2.59, detergent for $2.17, a sandwich for $3.65, an apple for $0.47, and coffee for $5.79. The total bill was $18.67. Is this amount reasonable?

Solution   If you are in the habit of carrying a calculator to the store, you can answer the question by finding the exact cost of the purchase. However, estimation can be used to determine if the bill is reasonable even if you do not have a calculator. We will round the cost of each item to the nearest dollar.

| Round to the nearest dollar. | Use digits in this column to do the rounding. |

Bread	$2.59 ≈ $3.00
Detergent	$2.17 ≈ $2.00
Sandwich	$3.65 ≈ $4.00
Apple	$0.47 ≈ $0.00
Coffee	$5.79 ≈ $6.00
	$15.00

The total bill, $18.67, seems a bit high compared to the $15.00 estimate. You should check the bill before paying it.

Estimating Support for a Cause

Police often need to estimate the size of a crowd at a political demonstration. One way to do this is to select a reasonably sized rectangle within the crowd and estimate (or count) the number of people within the rectangle. They then estimate the number of rectangles it would take to completely fill the crowd. The police estimate is obtained by multiplying the number of rectangles by the number of demonstrators in a representative rectangle. The organizers of the demonstration might give a larger estimate than the police to emphasize the strength of their support.

Although different rounding results in different estimates, the whole idea behind the rounding process is to make calculations simple.

EXAMPLE 3   Rounding to Simplify a Calculation

Find a reasonable estimate of

$$\frac{0.47996 \times 88}{0.249}.$$

Solution   Each decimal appears to complicate the calculation. Our goal is to round the decimals to simplify this computation. The decimal 0.47996 is approximately 0.5, which is $\frac{1}{2}$. The decimal 0.249 is approximately 0.25, which is $\frac{1}{4}$. Thus,

$$\frac{0.47996 \times 88}{0.249} \approx \frac{\frac{1}{2} \times 88}{\frac{1}{4}} = \frac{44}{\frac{1}{4}} = 44 \times \frac{4}{1} = 176$$

Using a calculator, the answer displayed for the given computation is 169.624417671. Our estimate, 176, convinces us that the displayed answer makes sense.

EXAMPLE 4   Estimation by Rounding

A carpenter who works full time earns $28 per hour.

a. Estimate the carpenter's weekly salary.
b. Estimate the carpenter's annual salary.

Solution

a. In order to simplify the calculation, we can round the hourly rate of $28 to $30. Be sure to write out the units for each number in the calculation. The work week is 40 hours per week and the rounded salary is $30 per hour. We express this as

$$\frac{40 \text{ hours}}{\text{week}} \quad \text{and} \quad \frac{\$30}{\text{hour}}.$$

The word "per" is represented by the division bar. We multiply these two numbers to estimate the carpenter's weekly salary. We cancel out units that are identical if they are above and below the division bar.

$$\frac{40 \ \text{hours}}{\text{week}} \times \frac{\$30}{\text{hour}} = \frac{\$1200}{\text{week}}$$

Thus, the carpenter earns approximately $1200 per week, written ≈$1200.

b. For the estimate of annual salary, we may round 52 weeks to 50 weeks. The annual salary is approximately the product of $1200 per week and 50 weeks per year:

$$\frac{\$1200}{\text{week}} \times \frac{50 \ \text{weeks}}{\text{year}} = \frac{\$60,000}{\text{year}}$$

Thus, the carpenter earns approximately $60,000 per year, or $60,000 annually, written ≈$60,000.

Study Tip

It does not matter whether a unit is singular, such as *week*, or plural, such as *weeks*. *Week* and *weeks* are identical units and can be canceled out, as shown at the right.

Making estimates is an excellent way to put numbers into perspective. For example, what does the number 1 million really mean? Our next example may help you to comprehend this large number.

EXAMPLE 5 Comprehending Large Numbers

Imagine that you counted 60 numbers per minute and continued to count non-stop until you reached 1 million. What is a reasonable estimate of the number of days it would take you to complete the counting?

Solution We begin by finding how many minutes it will take to count to 1 million. You count 60 numbers per minute. To determine how many minutes it will take to reach 1 million, we divide 1 million numbers by 60 (numbers per minute).

$$\frac{1,000,000 \ \text{numbers}}{\dfrac{60 \ \text{numbers}}{\text{minute}}} = 1,000,000 \ \text{numbers} \times \frac{\text{minute}}{60 \ \text{numbers}}$$

$$= \frac{1,000,000 \ \text{minutes}}{60} = 16,666\tfrac{2}{3} \ \text{minutes}$$

Rounding to the nearest thousand, it will take about 17,000 minutes to count to 1 million.

Now we will convert 17,000 minutes to hours and the hours to days. There are 60 minutes per hour. We divide 17,000 minutes by 60 (minutes per hour) to find how many hours it will take to reach 1 million.

$$\frac{17,000 \ \text{minutes}}{\dfrac{60 \ \text{minutes}}{\text{hour}}} = 17,000 \ \text{minutes} \times \frac{\text{hour}}{60 \ \text{minutes}}$$

$$= \frac{17,000 \ \text{hours}}{60} = 283\tfrac{1}{3} \ \text{hours}$$

Rounding to the nearest ten, it will take about 280 hours to count to 1 million.

There are 24 hours per day. Thus, we can divide 280 hours by 24 (hours per day) to find how many days it will take to reach 1 million.

$$\frac{280 \ \text{hours}}{\dfrac{24 \ \text{hours}}{\text{day}}} = 280 \ \text{hours} \times \frac{\text{day}}{24 \ \text{hours}} = \frac{280}{24} \ \text{days} = 11\tfrac{2}{3} \ \text{days}$$

Study Tip

In case you have forgotten, here is what you need to do in a division situation such as those on the right.

1. Copy the number (and unit) of the number being divided into.
2. Change the division to multiplication.
3. Reverse the positions of the numbers (and units) of the number by which we divide.

Rounding to the nearest day, it will take about 12 days of nonstop counting to reach 1 million.

Were you surprised that 12 days of nonstop counting are required to reach 1 million? If it is difficult to comprehend 1 million, can you imagine trying to comprehend the $90 billion that Bill Gates of Microsoft is worth? It would take Mr. Gates 60 years to exhaust his fortune if he spent close to $4 million per day!

2 Apply estimation techniques to information given by graphs.

Estimation with Graphs

Magazines and newspapers often display information using circle, bar, and line graphs. The following examples illustrate how estimation techniques can be applied to each of these graphs.

Circle graphs, also called **pie charts**, show how a whole quantity is divided into parts. Circle graphs are divided into pieces called **sectors**. Figure 1.2 is an example of a typical circle graph. The graph shows the expected U.S. population by race and Hispanic origin for the year 2050.

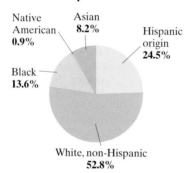

U.S. Population in 2050

Figure 1.2 U.S. population in 2050
Source: Census Bureau

EXAMPLE 6   Applying Estimation Techniques to a Circle Graph

Using Figure 1.2, answer the following:

a. What is the meaning of the sector labeled "White, non-Hispanic"?

b. If the U.S. population for the year 2050 is expected to be 393,931,000, estimate the population for persons of Hispanic origin.

Solution

a. The sector labeled "White, non-Hispanic" shows that 52.8% of the U.S. population for the year 2050 will be white, non-Hispanic. Whites will be the largest racial group in 2050. (To put this number into perspective, in 1999 whites made up 71.8% of the U.S. population.)

b. The circle graph indicates that 24.5% of the population will be Hispanic in 2050. The actual number of Hispanics is 24.5% of the total 393,931,000.

The number of Hispanics	is	24.5%	of	The total population
=		0.245	×	393,931,000

Study Tip

To convert from percent form to decimal form, move the decimal point two places to the left and drop the percent sign. For example,

$$24.5\% = 0.245$$

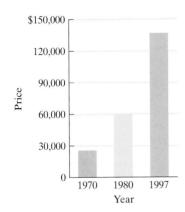

Figure 1.3 Average sales price of existing homes in the Northeast United States
Source: National Association of Realtors

Because 24.5% can be rounded to 25%, which is $\frac{1}{4}$ of the total, we may obtain an estimate as follows:

$$\frac{393,931,000 \;\rightarrow\; 400,000,000}{\times \quad\;\; 0.245 \;\rightarrow\; \times \qquad \frac{1}{4}} \;:\; \frac{400,000,000}{4} = 100,000,000$$

An estimate of the Hispanic population for the year 2050 is 100 million. The actual number can be found by multiplying 0.245 and 393,931,000 with a calculator. The product is 96,513,095, or almost 97 million. Our estimate is close to the actual number.

Bar graphs are convenient for showing comparisons among items. The bars may be either horizontal or vertical, and they are used to show the amounts of different items. Figure 1.3 is an example of a typical bar graph. The graph shows the average sales price of existing homes in the Northeast United States for three years—1970, 1980, and 1997.

EXAMPLE 7 Applying Estimation Techniques to a Bar Graph

Using Figure 1.3, answer the following:
a. Find the average sales price of existing homes in the Northeast United States in 1980.
b. Estimate the average sales price of existing homes in the Northeast United States in 1997.

Solution
a. First, let us find the bar that represents 1980. Based on the labels at the bottom of the graph, we see that this is the bar in the middle of Figure 1.3. We locate the top of the bar representing 1980 and then read across to the corresponding price on the left. The top of the bar extends to 60,000. This means that the average sales price of existing homes in the Northeast United States in 1980 was $60,000.

b. Next, let us find the bar that represents 1997. Based on the labels at the bottom of the graph, we see that this is the bar on the right in Figure 1.3. We locate the top of the bar representing 1997 and then read across to the corresponding price on the left. This bar extends to 120,000 plus approximately half of the distance between the 120,000 and 150,000 lines. Because this distance is 30,000, half the distance is 15,000. Thus, an estimate of the average sales price of existing homes in the Northeast United States in 1997 is 120,000 + 15,000, or $135,000.

Line graphs are often used to illustrate trends over time. Some measure of time, such as months or years, frequently appears on the horizontal axis. Amounts are generally listed on the vertical axis. Figure 1.4 is an example of a typical line

Technology

Spreadsheets, such as Microsoft Excel, are very powerful tools. Spreadsheet programs can generate many different graphs for a particular data set. The type, size, color, labels, and overall look can easily be altered to create a chart or graph that can give a desired visual representation to any set of data. In addition to charts and graphs, spreadsheets allow for rapid and convenient calculations of groups of data, easy sorting and rearrangement of data, and much more. In fact, your instructor may be using a spreadsheet—or a program that utilizes a spreadsheet—to maintain and track the grades for the students in this class.

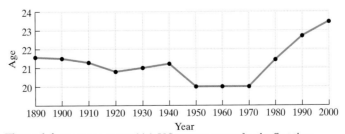

Figure 1.4 Average age at which U.S. women marry for the first time
Source: U.S. Census Bureau

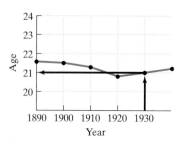

Figure 1.5 In 1930, women were 21 when they married for the first time. *Source:* U.S. Census Bureau

graph. The graph shows the average age at which women in the United States marry for the first time over a 110-year period. The years are listed on the horizontal axis and the ages are listed on the vertical axis.

    Figure 1.5 shows how to find the average age at which women married for the first time in 1930. (Only the part of the graph that reveals what occurred through about 1940 is shown in the margin because we are interested in 1930.)

Step 1 Locate 1930 on the horizontal axis.

Step 2 Locate the point above 1930.

Step 3 Read across to the corresponding age on the vertical axis.

The age is 21. Thus, in 1930 women in the United States married for the first time at an average age of 21.

EXAMPLE 8 Applying Estimation Techniques to a Line Graph

Use Figure 1.4 to estimate the maximum average age at which U.S. women marry for the first time. When does this occur?

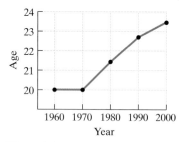

Figure 1.4 Shown again to include 1960–2000

Solution The maximum average age at which U.S. women marry for the first time can be found by locating the highest point on the graph. This point lies above 2000 on the horizontal axis. Read across to the corresponding age on the vertical axis. The age falls approximately midway between 23 and 24, at $23\frac{1}{2}$. Thus, the graph predicts that the average age at which women first marry in the year 2000 will be $23\frac{1}{2}$. This is the oldest average age of first marriage in over 100 years.

Exercise Set 1.2

 Practice Exercises

To help you learn estimation, we suggest that you work this exercise set without a calculator. Different rounding results in different estimates, so there is not a single correct answer to these exercises. Use rounding to make the resulting calculations simple.

1. Estimate the cost of 12 bananas at $0.19 each.

2. Estimate the total distance run by all 297 runners who each complete a 19-mile marathon.

3. Estimate the distance traveled when driving 48 miles per hour for 7 hours, 8 minutes.

4. Estimate the salary of a worker who works for 32.7 hours at $8.95 per hour.

5. Estimate the total cost of six grocery items if their prices are $3.47, $5.89, $19.98, $2.03, $11.85, and $0.23.

6. Estimate the total weight of four people if their individual weights are 137 pounds, 146 pounds, 172 pounds, and 197 pounds.

7. Estimate the tax on a computer that sells for $2037 with a 5% sales tax.

8. If 21% of the population suffers from depression, estimate the number of people who suffer from this disorder in a city with 585,000 residents.

9. If a person earns $19.50 per hour, estimate that person's annual salary.

10. If a person earns $62,400 per year, estimate that person's hourly salary.

11. Find an estimate of $\dfrac{0.57 \times 68}{0.493}$.

12. Find an estimate of $17\frac{7}{8} \div 2\frac{11}{12}$.

13. If the average lifetime expectancy is 78 years, estimate lifetime expectancy in hours.

14. Estimate the number of hours in a decade (ten years).

15. A survey among 347,583 college students indicated that three out of every five owns a computer. Estimate the number of students who do not own a computer.

16. If 5 tablespoons of juice can be obtained by squeezing 2 lemons, estimate the number of tablespoons that can be squeezed from 11 lemons.

17. The area of California is 158,869 square miles and the state's population is 31,878,234. Estimate California's population density, meaning the number of persons per square mile.

18. Alaska's land area is four times as large as California's and its population is 1.9% of California's (see Exercise 17). Estimate Alaska's population density, meaning the number of persons per square mile.

Use this map that shows some of the cities on the main line of a railroad to answer Exercises 19–20.

19. a Estimate the distance from New York to Washington.
    b. If a train travels at an average rate of 40 miles per hour, estimate the traveling time from New York to Washington.

20. a. Estimate the distance from Wilmington to Philadelphia.
    b. If a train travels at an average rate of 40 miles per hour, estimate the travel time from Wilmington to Philadelphia.

 Application Exercises

The circle graph shows the percentage of Americans who belong to various religious groups and who are members of a congregation. The population of the United States in 1998 was 269,816,000. Use the graph to solve Exercises 21–22.

Religious Affiliation

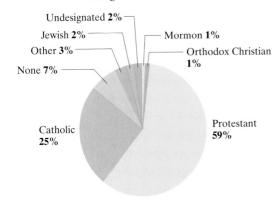

Source: The Gallup Organization

21. Use the circle graph to estimate the number of Protestants.
22. Use the circle graph to estimate the number of Catholics.

The bar graph shows the percentage of teenagers naming the brand as one of three "coolest." Use the graph to solve Exercises 23–26.

"Coolest" Brands for U.S. Teenagers

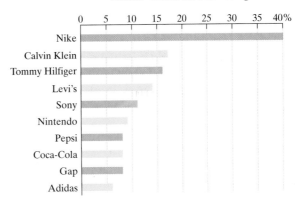

Source: Teenage Research Unlimited Inc.

23. Estimate the percentage of teenagers who named Calvin Klein as one of the three "coolest."
24. Estimate the percentage of teenagers who named Levi's as one of the three "coolest."
25. Which brands were rated "coolest" by at least 10% but not more than 15% of the teenagers surveyed?
26. Which brands were rated "coolest" by at least 15% but not more than 20% of the teenagers surveyed?

The bar graph shows the average price for a ticket on Broadway for plays and musicals. Use the graph to solve Exercises 27–30.

Average Ticket Prices on Broadway

Source: League of American Theatres and Producers

27. Approximately how much money should be set aside so that you and a friend can see a musical at 1997–98 prices?
28. Approximately how much money should be set aside so that you and a friend can see a play at 1997–98 prices?
29. Find an estimate for the increase in the cost of a ticket for a musical from 1984–85 to 1997–98.
30. Find an estimate for the increase in the cost of a ticket for a play from 1984–85 to 1997–98.

The line graph shows the U.S. unemployment rate from 1960 through 1997. Use the graph to solve Exercises 31–34.

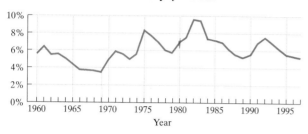

U.S. Unemployment Rate

Year

Source: U.S. Bureau of Labor Statistics

31. Find an estimate for the unemployment rate in 1970.

32. Find an estimate for the unemployment rate in 1980.

33. For the period shown, when did the unemployment rate reach a maximum? What is a reasonable estimate for the rate during that year?

34. For the period shown, when did the unemployment rate reach a minimum? What is a reasonable estimate for the rate during that year?

 Writing in Mathematics

35. Explain how to round 163:
    a. to the nearest ten.
    b. to the nearest hundred.

36. What is estimation? When is it helpful to use estimation?

37. What does the ≈ symbol mean?

38. In this era of calculators and computers, why is there a need to develop estimation skills?

39. Describe a circle graph.

40. What is a sector?

41. Describe a bar graph.

42. Describe a line graph.

43. Describe one way in which you use estimation in a nonacademic area of your life.

44. In Exercises 27–28, if you are indeed planning a trip to New York City and are estimating the cost of theater tickets, is it better to overestimate or underestimate the cost? Explain your answer.

45. A forecaster at the National Hurricane Center needs to estimate the time until a hurricane with high probability of striking South Florida will hit Miami. Is it better to overestimate or underestimate? Explain your answer.

 Critical Thinking Exercises

46. Estimate the height, in miles, of a stack of 1 million dimes.

47. If you spend $1000 each day, estimate how long it will take to spend a billion dollars.

 Technology Exercise

48. Using a spreadsheet, enter the following utility bill data into two columns. The first column should be labeled according to the month. The second column should contain the dollar amount for that month's bill. January's bill was $37.54, February's was $56.98, March's was $45.17, April's was $18.99, May's was $23.13, June's was $31.51, and July's bill was $26.80.

Once the data has been entered, use the computer's mouse to highlight the cells containing the data. Then activate the Chart Option of the spreadsheet by clicking on the Insert pull-down and select Chart (see image). Many types of charts are available. Of these, we will examine the Column, Line, and Pie charts that correspond to the given set of data. Upon selecting a particular type of chart, you can click the "Next" button. Work your way through the options, including the labels and cosmetic effects for each graph. Once you have decided upon all of the options (don't worry, you can go back and change them), click the "Finish" button.

a. Create a Column Chart for the indicated data. Describe any advantages of looking at a utility bill with this type of chart.

b. Create a Line Chart for the indicated data. Describe any advantages of looking at a utility bill with this type of chart.

c. Create a Pie Chart for the indicated data. Describe any advantages of looking at a utility bill with this type of chart.

Additional information on this exercise is available at the Website address http://www.prenhall.com/blitzer.

 Group Exercise

49. Group members should devise an estimation process that can be used to answer each of the following questions. Use input from all group members to describe the best estimation process possible.

a. Is it possible to walk from San Francisco to New York in a year?

b. How much money is spent on ice cream in the United States each year?

SECTION 1.3   *Problem Solving*

Objectives

1. Solve problems using the organization of the four-step problem-solving process.

1 Solve problems using the organization of the four-step problem-solving process.

Study Tip

Problem solving can be thought of in terms of the four steps shown on the right. Think of these steps as *guidelines* that will help you organize the process of problem solving, rather than a list of rigid rules that need to be memorized. You may be able to solve certain problems without thinking about or using every step in the four-step process.

"If you don't know where you're going, you'll probably end up some place else."

YOGI BERRA

Critical thinking and problem solving are essential skills in both school and work. A model for problem solving was established by the charismatic teacher and mathematician George Polya (1887–1985) in *How to Solve It* (Princeton University Press, Princeton, N.J., 1957). This book, first published in 1945, has sold more than 1 million copies and is available in 17 languages. Using a four-step procedure for problem solving, Polya's book demonstrates how to think clearly in any field.

Polya's Four Steps in Problem Solving

Step 1   Understand the problem. Read the problem several times. The first reading can serve as an overview. In the second reading, write down what information is given and determine exactly what it is that the problem requires you to find.

Step 2   Devise a plan. The plan for solving the problem might involve one or more of these suggested problem-solving strategies:

- Use inductive reasoning to look for a pattern.
- Make a systematic list.
- Use estimation to make an educated guess at the solution. Check the guess against the problem's conditions and work backward to eventually determine the solution.
- Try expressing the problem more simply and solve a similar simpler problem.
- Use trial and error.
- List the given information in a chart or table.
- Try making a sketch to illustrate the problem.
- Relate the problem to similar problems that you have seen before. Try applying the procedures used to solve the similar problem to the new one.
- Look for a "catch" if the answer seems too obvious. Perhaps the problem involves some sort of trick question deliberately intended to lead the problem solver in the wrong direction.
- Use the given information to eliminate possibilities.
- Use common sense.

Step 3   Carry out the plan and solve the problem.

Step 4   Look back and check the answer. The answer should satisfy the conditions of the problem. The answer should make sense and be reasonable. If this is not the case, recheck the method and any calculations. Perhaps there is an alternative way to arrive at a correct solution.

The very first step in problem solving involves evaluating the given information in a deliberate manner. Is there enough given to solve the problem? Is the information relevant to the problem's solution, or are some facts not necessary to arrive at a solution?

EXAMPLE 1 Finding What Is Missing

Which necessary piece of information is missing and prevents you from solving the following problem?

A man purchased five shirts, each at the same discount price. How much did he pay for them?

Solution

Step 1 Understand the problem. Here's what is given:

Number of shirts purchased: 5

We must find how much the man paid for the five shirts.

Step 2 Devise a plan. The amount that the man paid for the five shirts is the number of shirts, 5, times the cost of each shirt. The discount price of each shirt is not given. This missing piece of information makes it impossible to solve the problem.

EXAMPLE 2 Finding What Is Unnecessary

In the following problem, one more piece of information is given than is necessary for solving the problem. Identify this unnecessary piece of information. Then solve the problem.

How much change should a customer receive from a $20 bill if she bought three rolls of tape at $1.39 each and five pens for which she paid $2.75?

Solution

Step 1 Understand the problem. Here's what is given:

Purchased: 3 rolls of tape, $1.39 each
          5 pens for $2.75
Amount given to clerk: $20

We must find the change the customer receives.

Step 2 Devise a plan. The amount of change received can be found by subtracting the total amount of the purchase from $20. The total amount of the purchase is found by adding the cost of the tape and the pens. The cost of the three rolls of tape is determined by multiplying $1.39, the cost of each roll, by 3. The cost of the pens is given to be $2.75. Be careful! They do not cost $2.75 each. The customer paid $2.75 for *all five* pens. Only the $2.75 is relevant. The fact that *five* pens were purchased is not needed to solve the problem.

Step 3 Carry out the plan and solve the problem.

$3 \times \$1.39 = \$4.17$ cost of tape $\$20.00$ given to clerk
              $\underline{2.75}$ cost of pens $\underline{-\ 6.92}$ total amount of purchase
              $\$6.92$ total amount of purchase $\$13.08$ change received

The customer should receive $13.08.

Step 4 Look back and check the answer. We can double-check the arithmetic either by hand or with a calculator. We can also see if the answer satisfies the conditions of the problem.

$4.17   cost of tape
2.75   cost of pens
13.08   change received
$20.00   total

The $20.00 total satisfies the condition that the customer paid for the purchase with a $20 bill.

EXAMPLE 3   Applying the Four-Step Procedure

By paying $100 cash up front and the balance at $20 a week, how long would it take to pay for a bicycle costing $680?

Solution

Step 1   Understand the problem. Here's what is given:

Cost of the bicycle: $680
Amount paid in cash: $100
Weekly payments: $20

If necessary, consult a dictionary to look up any unfamiliar words. The word "balance" means the amount still to be paid. We must find the number of weeks required to pay for the bicycle.

Step 2   Devise a plan. Subtract the amount paid in cash from the cost of the bicycle. This results in the amount still to be paid. Because weekly payments are $20, divide the amount still to be paid by 20. This will give the number of weeks required to pay for the bicycle.

Step 3   Carry out the plan and solve the problem. Begin by finding the balance, the amount still to be paid for the bicycle.

$680   cost of the bicycle
− 100   amount paid in cash
$580   amount still to be paid

Now divide the $580 balance by $20, the payment per week. The result of the division is the number of weeks needed to pay off the bicycle.

$$\frac{\$580}{\frac{\$20}{\text{week}}} = \$580 \times \frac{\text{week}}{\$20} = \frac{580 \text{ weeks}}{20} = 29 \text{ weeks}$$

It will take 29 weeks to pay for the bicycle.

Step 4   Look back and check the answer. We can certainly double-check the arithmetic either by hand or with a calculator. We can also see if the answer satisfies the conditions of the ploblem.

$20   weekly payment $580   total of weekly payments
answer → × 29   number of weeks   +$100   amount paid in cash
$580   total of weekly $680   cost of bicycle
payments

The answer of 29 weeks satisfies the condition that the cost of the bicycle is $680.

Making lists is a useful strategy in problem solving.

Study Tip

An effective way to see if you understand a problem is to restate the problem in your own words.

EXAMPLE 4 Solving a Problem by Making a List

Suppose you are an engineer programming the automatic gate for a 50-cent toll. The gate should accept exact change only. It should not accept pennies. How many coin combinations must you program the gate to accept?

Solution

Step 1 Understand the problem. The total change must always be 50 cents. One possible coin combination is two quarters. Another is five dimes. We need to find all such combinations.

Step 2 Devise a plan. Make a list of all possible coin combinations. Begin with the coins of larger value and work toward the coins of smaller value.

Step 3 Carry out the plan and solve the problem. First we must find all of the coins that are not pennies but can combine to form 50 cents. This includes half-dollars, quarters, dimes, and nickels. Now we can set up a table. We will use these coins as table headings.

Half-Dollars	Quarters	Dimes	Nickels

Each row in the table will represent one possible combination for exact change. We start with the largest coin, the half-dollar. Only one half-dollar is needed to make exact change. No other coins are needed. Thus, we put a 1 in the half-dollars column and 0 in the other columns to represent the first possible combination.

Half-Dollars	Quarters	Dimes	Nickels
1	0	0	0

Likewise, two quarters are also exact change for 50 cents. We put a 0 in the half-dollars column, a 2 in the quarters column, and 0s in the columns for dimes and nickels.

Half-Dollars	Quarters	Dimes	Nickels
1	0	0	0
0	2	0	0

In this manner, we can find all possible combinations for exact change for the 50-cent toll. These combinations are shown in Table 1.2.

Table 1.2 Exact Change for 50 Cents; No Pennies

Half-Dollars	Quarters	Dimes	Nickels
1	0	0	0
0	2	0	0
0	1	2	1
0	1	1	3
0	1	0	5
0	0	5	0
0	0	4	2
0	0	3	4
0	0	2	6
0	0	1	8
0	0	0	10

Count the coin combinations shown in Table 1.2. How many coin combinations must the gate accept? You must program the gate to accept 11 coin combinations.

Step 4 Look back and check the answer. Double-check Table 1.2 to make sure that no possible combinations have been omitted and that the total in each row is 50 cents. Double-check your count of the number of combinations.

Sketches and diagrams are sometimes useful in problem solving.

EXAMPLE 5   Solving a Problem by Using a Diagram

Four runners are in a one-mile race: Maria, Aretha, Thelma, and Debbie. Points are awarded only to the women finishing first or second. The first-place winner gets more points than the second-place winner. How many different arrangements of first- and second-place winners are possible?

Solution

Step 1 Understand the problem. Three possibilities for first and second position are

Maria-Aretha
Maria-Thelma
Aretha-Maria

Notice that Maria finishing first and Aretha finishing second is a different outcome than Aretha finishing first and Maria finishing second. Order makes a difference because the first-place winner gets more points than the second-place winner. We must find all possibilities for first and second position.

Step 2 Devise a plan. If Maria finishes first, then each of the other three runners could finish second:

First place	Second place	Possibilities for first and second place
Maria	Aretha	Maria-Aretha
	Thelma	Maria-Thelma
	Debbie	Maria-Debbie

Similarly, we can list each woman as the possible first-place runner. Then we will list the other three women as possible second-place runners. Next we will determine the possibilities for first and second place. This diagram will show how the runners can finish first or second.

Step 3 Carry out the plan and solve the problem. Now we complete the diagram started in step 2. The diagram is shown in Figure 1.6.

First place	Second place	Possibilities for first and second place
Maria	Aretha	Maria-Aretha
	Thelma	Maria-Thelma
	Debbie	Maria-Debbie
Aretha	Maria	Aretha-Maria
	Thelma	Aretha-Thelma
	Debbie	Aretha-Debbie
Thelma	Maria	Thelma-Maria
	Aretha	Thelma-Aretha
	Debbie	Thelma-Debbie
Debbie	Maria	Debbie-Maria
	Aretha	Debbie-Aretha
	Thelma	Debbie-Thelma

*Because of the way Figure 1.6 branches from first to second place, it is called a **tree diagram**. We will be using tree diagrams in Chapter 11 as a problem-solving tool in the study of uncertainty and probability.*

Figure 1.6 Possible ways for four runners to finish first and second

Count the number of possibilities shown under the third column, "Possibilities for first and second place." Can you see that there are 12 possibilities? Therefore, 12 different arrangements of first- and second-place winners are possible.

Step 4 Look back and check the answer. Check the diagram in Figure 1.6 to make sure that no possible first- and second-place outcomes have been left out. Double-check your count for the winning pairs of runners.

George Polya's *How to Solve It* demonstrates how his procedures can be used to methodically approach and solve any problem that involves thought and reasoning. In Examples 6 and 7 we apply his four steps to problems that are not mathematical.

EXAMPLE 6 The Four-Step Procedure and Creative Problem Solving

Look at Figure 1.7. You are the person standing in this room. Two strings are suspended from the ceiling. Your task is to tie the strings together. However, the strings are located so that you cannot reach one string with your outstretched hand while holding the second in your hand. There is nothing in the room, although you do have the resources you normally carry in your pocket. Solve this problem.

Solution

Step 1 Understand the problem. The only way to tie the strings together is to hold both of them. The difficulty is the shortness of reach. There is no way to magically make one of the strings longer. The problem is, "How can I get to the second string?"

Step 2 Devise a plan. I cannot get to the second string. Perhaps there is a way to get the second string to come to me. If I tie a small object that I have in my pocket, such as a key, to the end of the second string and set it swinging like a pendulum, then I can grab it while still holding the end of the first string in my other hand. The plan is illustrated in Figure 1.8.

Step 3 Carry out the plan and solve the problem. Tie the key to the end of the second string and carry out the plan. Notice by defining the problem as "How can the string come to me?" rather than "How can I get to the string?" a solution is possible. Stating the requirements of a problem in the wrong way can prevent you from finding a solution.

Step 4 Look back and check the answer. The solution works, illustrating the need to sometimes consider new directions in problem solving.

Figure 1.7 Your problem is to tie the two strings together.

Figure 1.8

EXAMPLE 7 Taking the First Steps to Solve a Problem That Is Not Mathematical

You are the department manager of a company. One of your employees who is too valuable to fire arrives to work late nearly every morning. Produce ideas that might help correct this employee's tardiness.

Solution When you apply problem-solving techniques to real-life situations, there is often more than one solution.

Trick Questions

Think about the following questions carefully before answering because each contains some sort of trick or catch.

Sample: Do they have a fourth of July in England?

Answer: Of course they do. However, there is no national holiday on that date!

See if you can answer the questions that follow without developing mental whiplash. The answers appear in the answer section.

1. A farmer had 17 sheep. All but 12 died. How many sheep does the farmer have left?

2. If you had only one match and entered a log cabin in which there was a candle, a fireplace, and a woodburning stove, which should you light first?

3. A doctor had a brother, but this brother had no brothers. What was the relationship between doctor and brother?

Step 1 Understand the problem. In spite of frequent lateness, this is one of your best employees. You need to correct the tardiness problem without affecting the excellent work produced by this person.

Step 2 Devise a plan. Write down as many ideas as possible, even if they seem silly or farfetched. Quantity, not quality, is the initial goal. After making an extensive list, select the best suggestions.

Step 3 Carry out the plan and solve the problem. Start by "brainstorming" and write down as many ideas as possible.

- Serve free coffee and donuts to people who are on time.
- Offer a cash bonus to the worker with the best punctuality record over a three-month period.
- Offer to drive the employee to work on your way in.
- Make promotions possible only with consistent on-time arrivals.
- Tell the employee that working hours will begin 30 minutes earlier. In this way, an employee who arrives 30 minutes late will be on time.
- Move the office closer to the employee's home.
- Tell the employee that arriving on time means being able to work on any chosen creative project.
- Reduce the employee's pay for tardiness.
- Hold important 9 A.M. meetings every morning for which the employee would be embarrassed to arrive late.

In the group exercise on page 30, group members will be asked to replace these suggestions with their own ideas for solving the tardiness problem. To be continued…

Becoming more confident as a problem solver will help you as you study the topics throughout this book. Furthermore, you will be able to apply problem-solving techniques to real-life situations. Some people even use these techniques for dealing with personal problems in need of creative solutions. Here's to your continued growth as a problem solver!

Exercise Set 1.3

Everyone can become a better, more confident problem solver. As in learning any other skill, learning problem solving requires hard work and patience. Work as many problems as possible in this exercise set. You may feel confused once in a while, but do not be discouraged. Thinking about a particular problem and trying different methods can eventually lead to new insights. Be sure to check over each answer carefully!

 Practice and Application Exercises

In Exercises 1–4, what necessary piece of information is missing that prevents solving the problem?

1. If a student saves $35 per week, how long will it take to save enough money to buy a computer?

2. If a steak sells for $8.15, what is the cost per pound?

3. If it takes you four minutes to read a page in a book, how many words can you read in one minute?

4. By paying $1500 cash and the balance in equal monthly payments, how many months would it take to pay for a car costing $12,495?

In Exercises 5–8, one more piece of information is given than is necessary for solving the problem. Identify this unnecessary piece of information. Then solve the problem.

5. A salesperson receives a weekly salary of $350. In addition, $15 is paid for every item sold in excess of 200 items. How much extra is received from the sale of 212 items?

6. You have $250 to purchase four new tires. If each tire weighs 21 pounds and costs $42 plus $2.50 tax, how much change will you receive?

7. A parking garage charges $2.50 for the first hour and $0.50 for each additional hour. If a customer gave the parking attendant $20.00 for parking from 10 A.M. to 3 P.M., how much did the garage charge?

8. An architect is designing a house. The scale on the plan is 1 inch = 6 feet. If the house is to have a length of 90 feet and a width of 30 feet, how long will the line representing the house's length be on the blueprint?

Use the four-step method in problem solving to solve Exercises 9–22.

9. One person earns $48,000 per year. Another earns $3750 per month. How much more does the first person earn in a year than the second?

10. At the beginning of a year, the odometer on a car read 25,124 miles. At the end of the year, it read 37,364 miles. If the car averaged 24 miles per gallon, how many gallons of gasoline did it use during the year?

11. A television sells for $750. Instead of paying the total amount at the time of the purchase, the same television can be bought by paying $100 down and $50 a month for 14 months. How much is saved by paying the total amount at the time of the purchase?

12. In a basketball game, the Bulldogs scored 34 field goals, each counting 2 points, and 13 foul goals, each counting 1 point. The Panthers scored 38 field goals and 8 foul goals. Which team won? By how many points did it win?

13. Calculators were purchased at $65 per dozen and sold at $20 for three calculators. Find the profit on six dozen calculators.

14. Pens are bought at 95¢ per dozen and sold in groups of four for $2.25. Find the profit on 15 dozen pens.

15. Each day a small business owner sells 200 pizza slices at $1.50 per slice and 85 sandwiches at $2.50 each. If business expenses come to $60 per day, what is the owner's profit for a ten-day period?

16. A college tutoring center pays math tutors $4.60 per hour. Tutors earn an additional $1.20 per hour for each hour over 40 hours per week. A math tutor worked 42 hours one week and 45 hours the second week. How much did the tutor earn in this two-week period?

17. A car rents for $220 per week plus $0.25 per mile. Find the rental cost for a two-week trip of 500 miles for a group of three people.

18. A college graduate receives a salary of $2750 a month for her first job. During the year she plans to spend $4800 for rent, $8200 for food, $3750 for clothing, $4250 for household expenses, and $3000 for other expenses. With the money that is left, she expects to buy as many shares of stock at $375 per share as possible. How many shares will she be able to buy?

19. Charlene decided to ride her bike from her home to visit her friend Danny. Three miles away from home, her bike got a flat tire, and she had to walk the remaining two miles to Danny's home. She could not repair the tire and had to walk all the way back home. How many more miles did Charlene walk than she rode?

20. A store received 200 containers of juice to be sold by April 1. Each container cost the store $0.75 and sold for $1.25. The store signed a contract with the manufacturer in which the manufacturer agreed to a $0.50 refund for every container not sold by April 1. If 150 containers were sold by April 1, how much profit did the store make?

21. A storeowner ordered 25 calculators that cost $30 each. The storeowner can sell each calculator for $35. The storeowner sold 22 calculators to customers. He had to return 3 calculators and pay a $2 charge for each returned calculator. Find the storeowner's profit.

22. New York City and Washington D.C. are about 240 miles apart. A car leaves New York City at noon traveling directly south toward Washington D.C. at 55 miles per hour. At the same time and along the same route, a second car leaves Washington D.C. bound for New York City traveling directly north at 45 miles per hour. How far has each car traveled when the drivers meet for lunch at 2:24 P.M.?

Solve Exercises 23–24 using the strategy of making a list or using a diagram.

23. A vending machine accepts nickels, dimes, and quarters. Exact change is needed to make a purchase. How many ways can a person with five nickels, three dimes, and two quarters make a 45-cent purchase from the machine?

24. How many ways can you make change for a quarter using only pennies, nickels, and dimes?

Exercises 25–28 involve problems encountered in everyday life. For each of these problematic situations, write seven or more short solutions that might be effective in solving the problem.

25. You started college with your best friend. This semester, you and your friend are taking two classes together. However, your friend frequently misses class and is not doing the necessary homework between classes to succeed. What can you say to your friend, who values your advice and who is in danger of flunking out of college, if things continue on their present course?

26. You started college with your best friend. This semester, you and your friend are taking two classes together. Your friend, who has a job and children, is failing both classes. What suggestions can you offer your friend to help pass the classes and succeed in college?

27. You have just started a job that you love and want to make a great impression with top management. You have been invited to go to an important evening party, and all of your top managers will be there. You have terrific social skills, and you know that your wit and your charm

will help enhance your relationship with the supervisors. However, just before you are to go to the party, a small fire breaks out in your clothes closet. The fire causes almost no damage, although all of your clothes are destroyed. What might you do to be able to attend the party?

28. You have just been hired as the head of the automobile safety department in a large city with an enormous number of car accidents. Your first assignment is to submit a list of creative suggestions for reducing automobile accidents in the city. Your supervisor welcomes all suggestions as long as they do not cost the safety department any money. What are your suggestions?

 Writing in Mathematics

In Exercises 29–31, explain the plan needed to solve the problem.

29. If you know how much was paid for several pounds of steak, find the cost of one pound.

30. If you know a person's age, find the year in which that person was born.

31. If you know how much you earn each hour, find your yearly salary.

32. Write your own problem that can be solved using the four-step procedure. Then use the four steps to solve the problem.

 Critical Thinking Exercises

33. Gym lockers are to be numbered from 1 to 99 using metal numbers to be nailed onto each locker. How many 7's are needed?

34. You are on vacation in an isolated town. Everyone in the town was born there and has never left. You develop a toothache and check out the two dentists in town. One dentist has gorgeous teeth and one has teeth that show the effects of poor dental work. Which dentist should you choose and why?

35. India Jones is standing on a large rock in the middle of a square pool filled with hungry, man-eating piranhas. The edge of the pool is 20 feet away from the rock. India's mom wants to rescue her son, but she is standing on the edge of the pool with only two planks, each $19\frac{1}{2}$ feet long. How can India be rescued using the two planks?

36. The stars in the American flag can be counted in a number of different ways. Counting along the diagonals, we see that there are 50 stars:

$$1 + 3 + 5 + 7 + 9 + 9 + 7 + 5 + 3 + 1 = 50$$

Imagine that a new state (perhaps Washington D.C. or Puerto Rico) joins the United States. You have the task of designing a flag with 51 stars. Arrange the 51 stars to create an attractive pattern.

37. In the figure shown, the large rectangle in the center is a private tennis court. The people living in the triangular houses are allowed to use the court because they paid membership dues. By contrast, the people in the square houses are not allowed to use the court because they have not paid dues. Draw a fence that allows people in the triangular houses to get to the court and keeps people in the square houses from getting to the court.

 Group Exercises

Exercises 38–42 describe problems that have many plans for finding an answer. Group members should describe how the four steps in problem solving can be applied to find a solution. It is not necessary to actually solve each problem. Your professor will let the group know if the four steps should be described verbally by a group spokesperson or in essay form.

38. How much will it cost to install bicycle racks on campus to encourage students to use bikes, rather than cars, to get to campus?

39. How many new counselors are needed on campus to prevent students from waiting in long lines for academic advisement?

40. By how much would taxes in your state have to be increased to cut tuition at community colleges and state universities in half?

41. Is your local electric company overcharging its customers?

42. Should solar heating be required for all new construction in your community?

43. Group members should describe a problem in need of a solution. Then, as in Exercises 38–42, describe how the four steps in problem solving can be applied to find a solution.

 CHAPTER SUMMARY, REVIEW, AND TEST

SUMMARY

1.1 Inductive and Deductive Reasoning

a. Inductive reasoning is the process of arriving at a general conclusion based on observations of specific examples. The conclusion is called a conjecture.

b. A case for which a conjecture is false is called a counterexample.

c. Deductive reasoning is the process of proving a specific conclusion from one or more general statements. The statement that is proved is called a theorem.

1.2 Estimation and Graphs

a. Estimation is the process of arriving at an approximate answer to a question. The symbol $\approx$ means *is approximately equal to*.

b. Estimation is useful when interpreting information given in circle, bar, and line graphs.

1.3 Problem Solving

a. Understand the problem.
b. Devise a plan.
c. Carry out the plan and solve the problem.
d. Look back and check the answer.

REVIEW EXERCISES

1.1

In Exercises 1–2, find a counterexample to show that each of the statements is false.

1. All U.S. states have names whose first letter comes before the letter u in the alphabet.

2. If a number is multiplied by 2 less than itself, the answer is an even number.

In Exercises 3–5, identify a pattern in each list of numbers. Then use this pattern to find the next number.

3. 4, 9, 14, 19, ____   4. 7, 14, 28, 56, ____
5. 1, 3, 6, 10, 15, ____

6. Identify a pattern in the following sequence of figures. Then use the pattern to find the next figure in the sequence.

7. Consider the following procedure:

Select a number. Double the number. Add 4 to the product. Divide the sum by 2. Subtract 2 from the quotient.

a. Repeat the procedure for four numbers of your choice. Write a conjecture that relates the result of the process to the original number selected.

b. Represent the original number as ▧ and use deductive reasoning to prove the conjecture in part (a).

1.2

Work Exercises 8–13 without a calculator. Different rounding results in different estimates, so there is not a single correct answer to these exercises. Use rounding to make the resulting calculations simple.

8. Estimate the total cost of six grocery items if their prices are $8.47, $0.89, $2.79, $0.14, $1.19, and $4.76.

9. Estimate the salary of a worker who works for 78 hours at $6.85 per hour.

10. Estimate the number of seconds in a day.

11. Find an estimate of $27\frac{19}{20} \div 6.823$.

12. At a yard sale, Melissa bought 21 books at $0.85 each, two chairs for $11.95 each, and a ceramic plate for $14.65. Estimate the total amount that Melissa spent.

13. The circle graph shows the regional breakdown for the expected 66.6 million households around the world that will be on-line by 2000. Estimate the number of on-line households for Europe.

World On-line Households by Region Expected by 2000

Europe 25%   Asia/Pacific Rim 15%

Other 3%

North America 57%

Source: Jupiter Communications

14. The circle graphs compare class attendance of successful and unsuccessful students. Write one sentence that summarizes the information conveyed by the graphs.

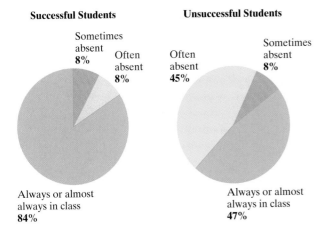

Successful Students

Sometimes absent **8%**

Often absent **8%**

Always or almost always in class **84%**

Unsuccessful Students

Often absent **45%**

Sometimes absent **8%**

Always or almost always in class **47%**

Source: The Psychology of College Success: A Dynamic Approach, by permission of H. C. Lindgren, 1969

The bar graph shows life expectancy in the United States by year of birth. Use the graph to solve Exercises 15–18.

Life Expectancy in the U.S. by Birth Year

Men   Women

0 20 40 60 80 100

1900
1950
1980
1996
2050

Source: National Center for Health Statistics, U.S. Census Bureau

15. Estimate the life expectancy for men born in 1900.

16. Estimate the life expectancy for women born in 2050.

17. By approximately how many more years can women born in 1996 expect to live as compared to men born in 1950?

18. For what genders and for what birth years does life expectancy exceed 40 years but is at most 60 years?

19. The line graph at the top of the next column shows the population of the United States from 1970 to 2000 for people under 16. For the period from 1970 to 2000, in what year was the population for people under 16 at a minimum? Estimate the population for that year.

U.S. Population for People Under 16

Population (millions)

70
60
50
40
30
20
10

1970 1980 1990 2000

Year

Source: U.S. Census Bureau

1.3

20. What necessary piece of information is missing that prevents solving the following problem?

If 3 milligrams of a medicine is given for every 20 pounds of body weight, how many milligrams should be given to a six-year-old child?

21. In the following problem, there is one more piece of information given than is necessary for solving the problem. Identify this unnecessary piece of information. Then solve the problem.

A taxicab charges $3.00 for the first mile and 50 cents for each additional half-mile. After a six-mile trip, a customer handed the taxi driver a $20 bill. Find the cost of the trip.

22. If there are seven frankfurters in one pound, how many pounds would you buy for a picnic to supply 28 people with two frankfurters each?

23. A car rents for $175 per week plus $0.30 per mile. Find the rental cost for a three-week trip of 1200 miles.

24. Membership in Superfit, a fitness club, is $500 per year. The club charges $1.00 for each hour the facility is used. A competing club, Healthy Bodies, charges $400 yearly plus $1.75 per hour used. If you plan to use a fitness club for 80 hours each year, which club offers the better deal? By how much?

25. Miami is on Eastern Standard Time, and San Francisco is on Pacific Standard Time, three hours earlier than Eastern Standard Time. A flight leaves Miami at 10 A.M. Eastern Standard Time, stops for 45 minutes in Houston Texas, and arrives in San Francisco at 1:30 P.M. Pacific time. What is the actual flying time from Miami to San Francisco?

26. An automobile purchased for $37,000 is worth $2600 after eight years. Assuming that the value decreases steadily each year, what was the car worth at the end of the fifth year?

27. Suppose you are an engineer programming the automatic gate for a 35-cent toll. The gate is programmed for exact change only and will not accept pennies. How many coin combinations must you program the gate to accept?

Group Exercise

28. Reread Example 7 on pages 24–25. Group members are now the collective department manager trying to deal with the late employee. Begin by assuming that the nine suggestions for solving the tardiness problem have been tried, and none of them has worked. Group members therefore need to replace the suggestions with their own ideas for solving the problem. The group's final list should contain reasonable solutions. (For example, moving the office closer to the employee's home is not reasonable!)

CHAPTER 1 TEST

1. Find a counterexample to show that the following statement is false:

    If a two-digit number is multiplied by a one-digit number, the answer is a two-digit number.

In Exercises 2–3, identify a pattern in each list of numbers. Then use this pattern to find the next number.

2. 0, 5, 10, 15, _____

3. $\frac{1}{6}, \frac{1}{12}, \frac{1}{24}, \frac{1}{48},$ _____

4. Identify a pattern in the following sequence of figures. Then use the pattern to find the next figure in the sequence.

     _____

5. Consider the following procedure:

    Select a number. Multiply the number by 4. Add 8 to the product. Divide the sum by 2. Subtract 4 from the quotient.

    a. Repeat this procedure for three numbers of your choice. Write a conjecture that relates the result of the process to the original number selected.
    b. Represent the original number by ▢ and use deductive reasoning to prove the conjecture in part (a).

Work Exercises 6–9 without a calculator. Different rounding results in different estimates, so there is not a single correct answer to these exercises. Use rounding to make the resulting calculations simple.

6. For a spring break vacation, a student needs to spend $47.00 for gas, $311.00 for food, and $405.00 for a hotel room. If the student takes $681.79 from savings, estimate how much more money is needed for the vacation.

7. The cost for opening a restaurant is $485,000. If 19 people decide to share equally in the business, estimate the amount each must contribute.

8. Find an estimate of 0.48992 × 120.

9. The circle graph shown is based on a survey of 17.1 million acres of lakes in the United States. Using this survey by the Environmental Protection Agency, estimate the number of acres of impaired lakes.

Water Quality in U.S. Lakes

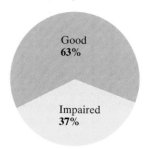

Source: U.S. Environmental Protection Agency

10. The bar graph shows the percent of vacations that included the activity listed on the left. Which activities were included on at least 14% of vacations and at most 30%?

Percent of U.S. Vacations that Included the Activity

Source: Travel Industry Association of America

11. The graph shows the ticket sales from concert tours in North America from 1990 through 1997. For the period shown, in what year did sales reach a maximum? Estimate the sales for that year.

Concert Ticket Sales in North America

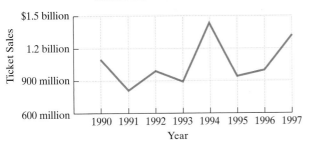

Source: Pollstar

12. The cost of renting a boat from Estes Rental is $9 per 15 minutes. The cost from Ship and Shore Rental is $20 per half-hour. If you plan to rent the boat for three hours, which business offers the better deal and by how much?

13. A bus operates between Miami International Airport and Miami Beach, 10 miles away. It makes 20 round trips per day carrying 32 passengers per trip. If the fare each way is $11.00, how much money is taken in from one day's operation?

14. By paying $50 cash up front and the balance at $35 a week, how long would it take to pay for a computer costing $960?

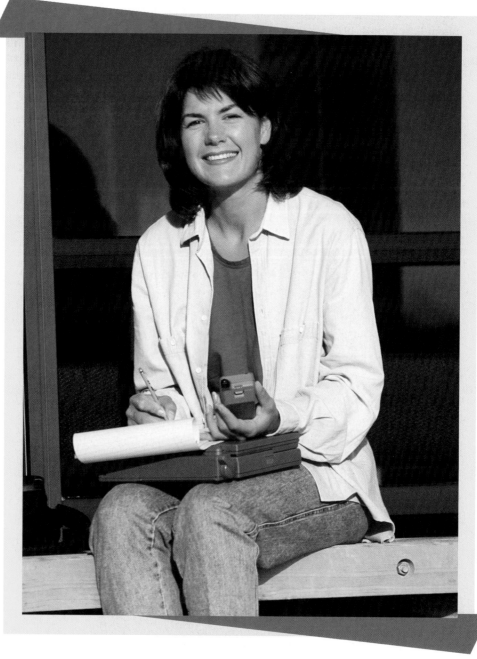

You wanted to organize a blood drive on campus with the local Red Cross. The Red Cross asked you whether the number of potential donors warranted a commitment to provide medical staff for the blood drive. So you took a survey to obtain information. Your survey asked students:

1. Would you be willing to donate blood?
2. Would you volunteer to distribute a free breakfast to student donors?
3. Would you be willing to take part in both activities?

Now the survey results are in. How will you organize and present the results to the Red Cross in an efficient manner?

2 Set Theory

The need to sort and organize information obtained in a survey is related to our need to find order and meaning by classifying things into collections. Mathematicians call such collections **sets**. Sets are groups of objects that usually share some common characteristic. For example, mathematicians classify numbers into sets based on whether or not their decimal representations have repeating patterns. A special set of numbers is used to provide probabilities of events. Sets are even used to describe nature's patterns, from the symmetry of a snowflake to the intricacies of a flower.

Set theory is the thread for the tapestry of mathematics. The set concept finds its way into many topics covered in this book, such as logic, algebra, and probability. Sets provide a precise way of describing and communicating mathematical ideas. Thus, learning to understand set theory will help you appreciate mathematics as a rich and living part of human culture.

SECTION 2.1   *Basic Set Concepts*

Objectives

1. Use three methods to represent sets.
2. Use the symbols $\in$ and $\notin$.
3. Apply set notation to sets of natural numbers.
4. Determine a set's cardinal number.
5. Recognize equal sets.
6. Recognize equivalent sets.

We tend to place things in categories, allowing us to order and structure the world. For example, you can categorize yourself by your age group, your ethnicity, your academic major, or your gender. Our minds cannot find order and meaning without creating collections. Mathematicians call such collections sets. A **set** is a collection of objects whose contents can be clearly determined. The objects in a set are called the **elements**, or **members**, of the set.

An example of a set is the set of the days of the week, whose elements are Monday, Tuesday, Wednesday, Thursday, Friday, Saturday, and Sunday.

Capital letters are generally used to name sets. Let's use W to represent the set of the days of the week.

Three methods are commonly used to designate a set. One method is a word description. We can describe set W as the set of the days of the week. A second method is the **roster method**. This involves listing the elements of a set inside a pair of braces, { }. The braces at the beginning and ending indicate that we are representing a set. The roster form uses commas to separate the elements of the set. Thus, we can designate the set W by listing its elements:

$W = \{$Monday, Tuesday, Wednesday, Thursday, Friday, Saturday, Sunday$\}$.

Grouping symbols such as parentheses, ( ), and square brackets, [ ], are not used to represent sets. Only commas are used to separate the elements of a set. Separators such as colons or semicolons are not used. Finally, the order in which the elements are listed in a set is not important. Thus, another way of expressing the set of the days of the week is

$W = \{$Saturday, Sunday, Monday, Tuesday, Wednesday, Thursday, Friday$\}$.

1 Use three methods to represent sets.

The Loss of Sets

Have you ever considered what would happen if we suddenly lost our ability to recall categories and the names that identify them? This is precisely what happened to Alice, the heroine of Lewis Carroll's *Through the Looking Glass*, as she walked with a fawn in "the woods with no names."

"So they walked on together through the woods, Alice with her arms clasped lovingly round the soft neck of the Fawn, till they came out into another open field, and here the Fawn gave a sudden bound into the air, and shook itself free from Alice's arm. 'I'm a Fawn!' it cried out in a voice of delight. 'And, dear me! you're a human child!' A sudden look of alarm came into its beautiful brown eyes, and in another moment it had darted away at full speed."

By realizing that Alice is a member of the set of human beings, which in turn is part of the set of dangerous things, the fawn is overcome by fear. Thus, the fawn's experience is determined by the way it structures the world into sets with various characteristics.

John Tenniel, colored by Fritz Kredel

EXAMPLE 1 Representing Sets

Write a word description of the set

$$P = \{\text{Washington, Adams, Jefferson, Madison, Monroe}\}.$$

Solution Set P is the set of the first five presidents of the United States.

EXAMPLE 2 Representing Sets

Set C is the set of U.S. coins with a value of less than a dollar. Express this set using the roster method.

Solution

$$C = \{\text{penny, nickel, dime, quarter, half-dollar}\}$$

The third method for representing a set is with **set-builder notation**. Using this method, the set of the days of the week can be expressed as

$$W = \{x \mid x \text{ is a day of the week}\}.$$

We read this notation as "Set W is the set of all elements x such that x is a day of the week." Before the vertical line is the variable x, which represents an element in general. After the vertical line is the condition x must meet in order to be an element of the set.

Table 2.1 contains two examples of sets, each represented with a word description, the roster method, and set-builder notation.

Table 2.1 Sets Using Three Designations

Word Description	Roster Method	Set-Builder Notation
B is the set of members of the rock band the Beatles in 1963.	$B = \{$George Harrison, John Lennon, Paul McCartney, Ringo Starr$\}$	$B = \{x \mid x$ was a member of the Beatles in 1963$\}$
S is the set of states whose names begin with the letter A.	$S = \{$Alabama, Alaska, Arizona, Arkansas$\}$	$S = \{x \mid x$ is a state whose name begins with the letter A$\}$

The Beatles climbed to the top of the British music charts in 1963, conquering the United States a year later.

EXAMPLE 3 Representing Sets

Express set

$$A = \{x \mid x \text{ is a month that begins with the letter M}\}$$

using the roster method.

Solution Set A is the set of all elements x such that x is a month beginning with the letter M. There are two such months, namely March and May. Thus,

$$A = \{\text{March, May}\}.$$

Now let's consider a set similar to the one in Example 3. However, this time set A represents the set of all elements x such that x is a month beginning with the letter R.

$$A = \{x \mid x \text{ is a month that begins with the letter R}\}$$

There are no months that begin with the letter R, and so this set contains no elements. A set such as this that contains no elements is called the **empty set**, or the **null set**.

The Empty Set

The **empty set**, also called the **null set**, is the set that contains no elements. The empty set is represented by { } or ∅.

Notice that { } and ∅ have the same meaning. However, the empty set is not represented by {∅}. This notation represents a set containing the element ∅.

The set of all lowercase letters of the English alphabet is rather long when represented by the roster method. If L is chosen as a name for this set, then we can write

$$L = \{a, b, c, d, e, f, g, h, i, j, k, l, m, n, o, p, q, r, s, t, u, v, w, x, y, z\}.$$

We can shorten the listing in set L by writing

$$L = \{a, b, c, d, \ldots, z\}.$$

The three dots after the d indicate that the elements in the set continue in the same manner up to and including the last element z.

2 Use the symbols ∈ and ∉.

The elements in a set must be clearly determined. The collection of good baseball players is not a set because it would be difficult to determine whether or not a given baseball player belongs to this collection. Not everyone agrees on what makes a "good" baseball player.

Mathematicians have developed a special notation to indicate whether or not a given element belongs to a set.

The Notations ∈ and ∉

The symbol ∈ is used to indicate that an object is an element of a set. The symbol ∈ is used to replace the words "is an element of."

The symbol ∉ is used to indicate that an object is *not* an element of a set. The symbol ∉ is used to replace the words "is not an element of."

EXAMPLE 4 Using the Symbols ∈ and ∉

Determine whether each statement is true or false.

a. $r \in \{a, b, c, \ldots, z\}$
b. $7 \notin \{1, 2, 3, 4, 5\}$

Solution

a. Because r is an element of the set $\{a, b, c, \ldots, z\}$, the statement

$$r \in \{a, b, c, \ldots, z\}$$

is true.

Observe that an element can belong to a set in roster notation when three dots appear even though the element is not listed.

b. Because 7 is not an element of the set $\{1, 2, 3, 4, 5\}$, the statement

$$7 \notin \{1, 2, 3, 4, 5\}$$

is true.

3 Apply set notation to sets of natural numbers.

For the remainder of this section, we will focus on the set of numbers used for counting:

$$\{1, 2, 3, 4, 5, 6, 7, 8, 9, 10, 11, \ldots\}.$$

The set of counting numbers is also called the set of **natural numbers**. We represent this set by the letter **N**.

The Set of Natural Numbers

$$\mathbf{N} = \{1, 2, 3, 4, 5, \ldots\}$$

The three dots after the 5 indicate that there is no final element and that the listing goes on forever.

EXAMPLE 5   Representing Sets With Natural Numbers

Express each of the following sets using the roster method:

a. Set A is the set of natural numbers less than 5.

b. Set B is the set of natural numbers greater than or equal to 25.

c. $E = \{x \mid x \in \mathbf{N} \text{ and } x \text{ is even}\}$.

Solution

a. The natural numbers less than 5 are $1, 2, 3,$ and $4.$ Thus, set A can be expressed using the roster method as

$$A = \{1, 2, 3, 4\}.$$

b. The natural numbers greater than or equal to 25 are $25, 26, 27, 28,$ and so forth. Set B in roster form is

$$B = \{25, 26, 27, 28, \ldots\}.$$

The three dots show that the listing goes on forever.

c. The set-builder notation

$$E = \{x \mid x \in \mathbf{N} \text{ and } x \text{ is even}\}$$

indicates that we want to list all x such that x is an element of the set of natural numbers and x is even. The numbers that meet both conditions are the set of even natural numbers. The set in roster form is

$$E = \{2, 4, 6, 8, \ldots\}.$$

4 Determine a set's cardinal number.

The number of elements in a set is called the **cardinal number** of the set. For example, the set $\{a, e, i, o, u\}$ contains five elements and therefore has a cardinal number 5. We can also say that the set has a cardinality of 5.

Definition of a Set's Cardinal Number

The **cardinal number** of set A, represented by $n(A)$, is the number of elements in set A. The symbol $n(A)$ is read "n of A."

EXAMPLE 6   Determining a Set's Cardinal Number

Find the cardinal number of each of the following sets.

a. $A = \{7, 9, 11, 13\}$
b. $B = \{0\}$
c. $C = \{13, 14, 15, \ldots, 22, 23\}$
d. $\varnothing$

Solution   The cardinal number for each set is found by determining the number of elements in the set.

a. $A = \{7, 9, 11, 13\}$ contains four elements. Thus, the cardinal number of set A is 4. We also say that set A has a cardinality of 4, or $n(A) = 4$.
b. $B = \{0\}$ contains one element, namely 0. The cardinal number of set B is 1. Therefore, $n(B) = 1$.
c. Set $C = \{13, 14, 15, \ldots, 22, 23\}$ lists only five elements. However, the three dots indicate that the natural numbers from 16 through 21 are also in the set. Counting the elements in the set, we find there are 11 natural numbers in set C. The cardinality of set C is 11, and $n(C) = 11$.
d. The empty set, $\varnothing$, contains no elements. Thus, $n(\varnothing) = 0$.

The four sets in Example 6 are all examples of *finite sets*.

Definition of a Finite Set

Set A is a **finite set** if $n(A) = 0$ or $n(A)$ is a natural number. A set that is not finite is called an **infinite set**.

If we have enough time, it is possible to finish counting all the elements in a finite set, thereby obtaining its cardinal number. This is not the case with an infinite set. The counting process never comes to an end. The set

$$\{3, 6, 9, 12, 15, \ldots\}$$

is an example of an infinite set. The three dots indicate that there is no last, or final, element.

5 Recognize equal sets.

Equal and Equivalent Sets

We now turn to another important concept of set theory, equality of sets.

Definition of Equality of Sets

Set A is **equal** to set B means that set A and set B contain exactly the same elements, regardless of order. We symbolize the equality of sets A and B using the statement $A = B$.

For example, if $A = \{w, x, y, z\}$ and $B = \{z, y, w, x\}$, then $A = B$ because the two sets contain exactly the same elements.

Because equal sets contain the same elements, they also have the same cardinal number. For example, the equal sets $A = \{w, x, y, z\}$ and $B = \{z, y, w, x\}$ have four elements each. Thus, both sets have the same cardinal number: 4.

EXAMPLE 7   Determining Whether Sets Are Equal

Determine whether each statement is true or false.

   a. $\{4, 8, 9\} = \{8, 9, 4\}$ b. $\{1, 3, 5\} = \{0, 1, 3, 5\}$

Solution

   a. The sets $\{4, 8, 9\}$ and $\{8, 9, 4\}$ contain exactly the same elements. Therefore, the statement

$$\{4, 8, 9\} = \{8, 9, 4\}$$

      is true.

   b. As we look at the given sets, $\{1, 3, 5\}$ and $\{0, 1, 3, 5\}$, we see that 0 is an element of the second set, but not the first. The sets do not contain exactly the same elements. Therefore, the sets are not equal. This means that the statement

$$\{1, 3, 5\} = \{0, 1, 3, 5\}$$

      is false.

Repeating elements in a set does not add new elements to the set. For example, if $A = \{1, 1, 2, 2, 3\}$ and $B = \{1, 2, 3\}$, then $A = B$ since these sets contain exactly the same elements. Thus, $n(A) = n(B) = 3$.

6 Recognize equivalent sets.

We have seen that because equal sets contain the same elements, they also have the same cardinal number. However, two sets with the same cardinal number are not necessarily equal. For example,

$$A = \{1, 2, 3, \ldots, 49, 50\}$$

and

$$B = \{x \mid x \text{ is a state in the United States}\}$$

both have a cardinal number 50. That is, $n(A) = 50$ and $n(B) = 50$. However, the sets do not contain the same elements.

Sets like these that contain the same number of elements are said to be **equivalent**.

Definition of Equivalent Sets

Set A is **equivalent** to set B means that set A and set B contain the same number of elements. For equivalent sets, $n(A) = n(B)$.

EXAMPLE 8   Recognizing Equivalent Sets

Consider the following sets:

$$A = \{\textit{Midnight Cowboy, The Godfather, Titanic}\}$$

$$B = \{\text{Hoffman, Brando, DiCaprio}\}$$

   a. Are these sets equal? Explain.

   b. Are these sets equivalent? Explain.

Leonardo DiCaprio, star of *Titanic*

Cardinal Numbers of Infinite Sets

P.J. Crook "Time and Time Again" 1981. Courtesy Theo Waddington Fine Art, London & Boca Raton.

The mirrors in the painting "Time and Time Again" have the effect of repeating the image infinitely many times, creating an endless tunnel of mirror images. There is something quite fascinating about the idea of endless infinity. Did you know that for thousands of years religious leaders warned that human beings should not examine the nature of the infinite? Religious teaching often equated infinity with the concept of a Supreme Being. One of the last victims of the Inquisition, Giordano Bruno, was burned at the stake for his explorations into the characteristics of infinity. It was not until the 1870s that the German mathematician Georg Cantor (1845–1918) began a careful analysis of the mathematics of infinity.

Although it is impossible to count the number of elements in the set of natural numbers $\{1,2,3,4,5,6,\ldots\}$, Cantor assigned this set a cardinality. He said that the set of natural numbers has the infinite cardinal number $\aleph_0$ (the first letter of the Hebrew alphabet with a subscript of zero, read "aleph-null"). There are $\aleph_0$ natural numbers, and $\aleph_0$ is called a transfinite cardinal number.

Sets that are equivalent to the set of natural numbers also contain $\aleph_0$ elements. Here are two examples:

Natural Numbers: $\{1, 2, 3, 4, \quad 5, \quad 6,\ldots, \quad n,\ldots\}$
$\updownarrow \updownarrow \updownarrow \updownarrow \quad \updownarrow \quad \updownarrow \qquad \updownarrow$
Even Natural Numbers: $\{2, 4, 6, 8, 10, 12,\ldots, 2n,\ldots\}$

Each natural number n is matched with its double, $2n$, in the set of even natural numbers.

Natural Numbers: $\{1, 2, 3, 4, 5, \quad 6,\ldots, \quad n,\ldots\}$
$\updownarrow \updownarrow \updownarrow \updownarrow \updownarrow \qquad \updownarrow$
Odd Natural Numbers: $\{1, 3, 5, 7, 9, 11,\ldots, 2n - 1,\ldots\}$

Each natural number n is matched with 1 less than its double, $2n - 1$, in the set of odd natural numbers.

These matchings mean that there are $\aleph_0$ even natural numbers and $\aleph_0$ odd natural numbers. Because there are $\aleph_0$ natural numbers, this leads to the strange observations that the "part" (the even or the odd natural numbers) has the same number of elements as the "whole" (all the natural numbers). Cantor's analysis results in unusual statements of transfinite arithmetic, such as

$$\aleph_0 + \aleph_0 = \aleph_0.$$

As Cantor continued studying infinite sets, his observations grew stranger and stranger. He even showed that some infinite sets contain more elements than others. This was too much for Cantor's colleagues, who considered his work ridiculous. His mentor, Leopold Kronecker, told him, "Look at the crazy ideas that are now surfacing with your work with infinite sets. How can one infinity be greater than another? Best to ignore such inconsistencies. By considering these monsters and infinite numbers mathematics, I will make sure that you never gain a faculty position at the University of Berlin." Although Cantor was not burned at the stake, universal condemnation of his work resulted in numerous nervous breakdowns. His final days, sadly, were spent in a psychiatric hospital. However, Cantor's work later regained the respect of mathematicians. Today, he is seen as a great mathematician who de-mystified infinity.

Solution

a. Sets A and B do not contain exactly the same elements. Therefore, the sets are not equal.

b. Sets A and B each contain three elements. Because they contain the same number of elements, the sets are equivalent.

Exercise Set 2.1

 Practice Exercises

Write a description of the sets in Exercises 1–6. There may be more than one correct description.

1. {Mercury, Venus, Earth, Mars, Jupiter, Saturn, Uranus, Neptune, Pluto}
2. {Saturday, Sunday}
3. {Lucy, Ricky, Ethel, Fred}
4. {Jerry, Kramer, Elaine, George, Newman}
5. $\{1, 3, 5, 7, \ldots, 99\}$
6. $\{5, 10, 15, 20, \ldots\}$

In Exercises 7–14, express each set using the roster method.

7. The set of the four seasons in a year
8. The set of months of the year that have exactly 30 days
9. The set of natural numbers less than 4
10. The set of natural numbers less than or equal to 6
11. $\{x \mid x$ is a month that begins with the letter J$\}$
12. $\{x \mid x$ is a college in the county where you live$\}$
13. $\{x \mid x$ is the title of a movie starring Leonardo DiCaprio and Kate Winslet about a tragedy at sea$\}$
14. $\{x \mid x$ is a former football player who was charged with murder$\}$

In Exercises 15–24, determine whether each statement is true or false.

15. $3 \in \{1, 3, 5, 7\}$
16. $6 \in \{2, 4, 6, 8, 10\}$
17. $12 \in \{1, 2, 3, \ldots, 14\}$
18. $10 \in \{1, 2, 3, \ldots, 16\}$
19. $5 \in \{2, 4, 6, \ldots, 20\}$
20. $8 \in \{1, 3, 5, \ldots, 19\}$
21. $11 \notin \{1, 2, 3, \ldots, 9\}$
22. $17 \notin \{1, 2, 3, \ldots, 16\}$
23. $37 \notin \{1, 2, 3, \ldots, 40\}$
24. $26 \notin \{1, 2, 3, \ldots, 50\}$

In Exercises 25–30, fill in the blank with either $\in$ or $\notin$ to make each statement true.

25. Mark McGwire _____ the set of U.S. presidents
26. Sammy Sosa _____ the set of U.S. politicians
27. 13,791 _____ the set of odd natural numbers
28. 26,794 _____ the set of even natural numbers
29. $\varnothing$ _____ $\{\ \}$
30. 0 _____ $\varnothing$

*In Exercises 31–36, express each set using the roster method. Remember that **N** represents the set of natural numbers.*

31. the set of odd natural numbers less than 13
32. the set of even natural numbers less than 10
33. $\{x \mid x \in \mathbf{N}$ and x is greater than 100$\}$
34. $\{x \mid x \in \mathbf{N}$ and x is greater than 50$\}$
35. $\{x \mid x \in \mathbf{N}$ and x lies between 10 and 16$\}$
36. $\{x \mid x \in \mathbf{N}$ and x lies between 23 and 29$\}$

Find the cardinal number for each set in Exercises 37–42.

37. $\{17, 19, 21, 23, 25\}$
38. $\{16, 18, 20, 22, 24, 26\}$
39. $\{2, 4, 6, \ldots, 50\}$
40. $\{1, 3, 5, \ldots, 47\}$
41. $\{x \mid x$ is a day of the week that begins with the letter A$\}$
42. $\{x \mid x$ is a month of the year that begins with the letter W$\}$

In Exercises 43–48, determine whether each statement is true or false.

43. $\{a, b, c, d\} = \{b, d, c, a\}$
44. $\{a, e, i, o, u\} = \{u, a, o, i, e\}$
45. $\{0, 2, 4, 6, 8\} = \{2, 4, 6, 8\}$
46. $\{0, 1, 3, 5\} = \{1, 3, 5\}$
47. $\{1, 1, 8, 8, 13\} = \{1, 8, 13\}$
48. $\{6, 9, 12\} = \{9, 12, 12, 6, 9\}$

In Exercises 49–54:
  a. *Are the sets equal? Explain.*
  b. *Are the sets equivalent? Explain.*

49. A is the set of students at your college.
    B is the set of students majoring in business at your college.
50. A is the set of states in the United States.
    B is the set of people who are now governors of the states in the United States.
51. $A = \{1, 2, 3, 4, 5\}$
    $B = \{0, 1, 2, 3, 4\}$
52. $A = \{1, 3, 5, 7, 9\}$
    $B = \{2, 4, 6, 8, 10\}$
53. $A = \{1, 1, 1, 2, 2, 3, 4\}$
    $B = \{4, 3, 2, 1\}$
54. $A = \{0, 1, 1, 2, 2, 2, 3, 3, 3, 3\}$
    $B = \{3, 2, 1, 0\}$

Application Exercises

The following list shows the ten cities in the United States in which the most crimes per capita are committed. Use the list to represent each of the sets in Exercises 55–58 using the roster method.

City	Crimes per 100,000, 1995
1. Miami	1886.3
2. Pine Bluff, AR	1659.4
3. Los Angeles-Long Beach	1433.6
4. Gainesville, FL	1416.8
5. New York City	1392.8
6. Baton Rouge	1386.0
7. Baltimore	1335.9
8. New Orleans	1334.5
9. Lawton, OK	1330.8
10. Sioux City, IA	1271.4

Source: FBI Uniform Crime Reports, 1996

55. The set of cities where crimes per 100,000 exceeds 1400
56. The set of cities where crimes per 100,000 exceeds 1350 but is less than 1400
57. $\{x \mid x$ is a city in which crimes per 100,000 lies between 1300 and 1350$\}$
58. $\{x \mid x$ is a city in which crimes per 100,000 exceeds 2000$\}$

The following list shows the soggy totals for the ten rainiest cities in the United States. Use the list to represent each of the sets in Exercises 59–62 using the roster method.

Rainiest Cities

City	Avg. Annual Rainfall (inches)
1. Mobile, AL	64.0
2. New Orleans	61.9
3. Miami	55.9
4. Jackson, MS	55.4
5. Juneau, AK	54.3
6. San Juan, PR	52.3
7. Memphis	52.1
8. Jacksonville, FL	51.3
9. Little Rock	50.9
10. Atlanta	50.8

Source: U.S. National Oceanic and Atmospheric Administration, Climatography of the United States

59. The set of cities where average annual rainfall exceeds 55 inches
60. The set of cities where average annual rainfall lies between 55 and 60 inches
61. $\{x \mid x$ is a city in which average annual rainfall exceeds 70 inches$\}$
62. $\{x \mid x$ is a city in which average annual rainfall exceeds 50 inches and is less than 52 inches$\}$

The line graph shows the average monetary awards for discrimination and sexual harassment cases in the United States from 1990 through 1996. Based on the information in the graph, represent each of the sets in Exercises 63–66 using the roster method.

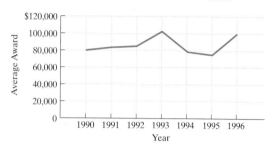

Average Awards for Discrimination and Sexual Harassment Cases in the United States

Source: Jury Verdict Research, Horsham, PA

63. $\{x \mid x$ is a year in which average monetary awards exceeded $90,000$\}$
64. $\{x \mid x$ is a year in which average monetary awards exceeded $81,000, but were less than $90,000$\}$
65. $\{x \mid x$ is a year in which average monetary awards were less than $70,000$\}$
66. $\{x \mid x$ is a year in which average monetary awards were either less than $70,000 or more than $110,000$\}$

 Writing in Mathematics

67. What is a set?
68. Describe the three methods used to represent a set. Give an example of a set represented by each method.
69. What is the empty set?
70. If a set is written in roster notation, describe how to determine if the set is a finite set or an infinite set.
71. Explain what is meant by equal sets.
72. Explain what is meant by equivalent sets.
73. The bar graph shows profits for U.S. corporations from 1980 through 1997. Use the graph to write four problems similar to Exercises 63–66. Each exercise should start with a set in set-builder notation and ask the problem solver to represent the set using the roster method. One of the exercises should have the empty set as the answer.

Corporate Profits

Source: U.S. Commerce Department

74. Write a description of four sets, each of which contains you as an element.

75. Write a description of a set whose cardinality exceeds one million.

 Critical Thinking Exercises

76. Which one of the following is true?
    a. Two sets can be equal but not equivalent.
    b. Any set in roster notation that contains three dots must be an infinite set.
    c. $n(\varnothing) = 1$
    d. Some sets that can be written in set-builder notation cannot be written in roster form.

77. Which one of the following is true?
    a. The set of fractions between 0 and 1 is an infinite set.
    b. The set of multiples of 4 between 0 and 4,000,000,000 is an infinite set.
    c. If the elements in a set cannot be counted in a trillion years, the set is an infinite set.
    d. Because 0 is not a natural number, it can be deleted from any set without changing the set's cardinality.

78. In a certain town, a barber shaves all those men and only those men who do not shave themselves. Consider each of the following sets:
    $A = \{x \mid x \text{ is a man of the town who shaves himself}\}$
    $B = \{x \mid x \text{ is a man of the town who does not shave himself}\}$

The one and only barber in the town is Sweeney Todd. If s represents Sweeney Todd,
a. is $s \in A$?　　　b. is $s \in B$?

 Technology Exercises

Use a calculator to solve Exercises 79 and 81.

79. Is 2684 an element in the set of natural numbers that divide into 968,924 without a remainder?

80. Write the statement that answers Exercise 79 in set-builder notation.

81. Is 244 an element in the set of natural numbers that divide into 140,542 without a remainder?

82. Write the statement that answers Exercise 81 in set-builder notation.

 Group Exercise

83. This activity is a group research project and should result in a presentation made by group members to the entire class. Georg Cantor was certainly not the only genius in history who faced criticism during his lifetime, only to have his work acclaimed as a masterpiece after his death. Describe the life and work of three other people, including at least one mathematician, who faced similar circumstances.

SECTION 2.2　*Venn Diagrams and Subsets*

Objectives

1. Understand the meaning of a universal set.
2. Understand the basic ideas of Venn diagrams.
3. Find a set's complement.
4. Use the symbols $\subseteq, \not\subseteq,$ and $\subset.$
5. Determine the number of subsets of a set.

In discussing sets, it is convenient to refer to a general set that contains all elements under discussion. This general set is called the **universal set**. For example, consider the following sets:

$A = \{\text{Louis Armstrong, Duke Ellington, Charlie Parker, Miles Davis}\}$

$B = \{\text{Quincy Jones, Wynton Marsalis}\}$

Although the people in set A are deceased and those in set B are still alive, they are all jazz musicians of the twentieth century. Thus, a possible universal set that includes all elements under discussion is the set of jazz musicians. Other choices for a universal set are the set of musicians and the set of people in the arts.

1 Understand the meaning of a universal set.

> **Definition of a Universal Set**
>
> A **universal set**, symbolized by U, is a set that contains all the elements being considered in a given discussion or problem.

EXAMPLE 1   Describing a Universal Set

Describe a universal set that includes all elements in sets A and B.

$$A = \{Cats,\ A\ Chorus\ Line,\ Les\ Miserables\}$$
$$B = \{Hello\ Dolly,\ Grease\}$$

Solution   The elements in sets A and B are musicals. A possible universal set is the set of Broadway musicals.

2 Understand the basic ideas of Venn diagrams.

We can obtain a more thorough understanding of sets and their relationship to a universal set by considering diagrams that allow visual analysis. **Venn diagrams**, named for the British logician John Venn (1834–1923), are used to show the visual relationship among sets.

Here are three basic ideas that are used to construct Venn diagrams:

1. In a Venn diagram, the universal set is represented by a region inside a rectangle. The figure at the right represents the universal set U.

2. Sets within the universal set are depicted by circles, or sometimes by ovals or other shapes. In the figure at the right, set A is represented by the region inside the circle. All elements in set A are also elements of the universal set U.

Study Tip

The size of the circle representing set A in a Venn diagram has nothing to do with the number of elements in set A.

3. The region outside the circle, but within the rectangle, represents the set of elements in the universal set U that are not in set A. This region is labeled A' (read "A prime"). This set, called the **complement** of A, contains all elements that are contained in U but not contained in A.

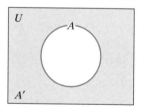

3 Find a set's complement.

Definition of the Complement of a Set

The **complement** of set A, symbolized by A', is the set of all elements in the universal set that are *not* in A. This idea can be expressed in set-builder notation as follows:

$$A' = \{x \mid x \in U \text{ and } x \notin A\}.$$

In order to find A', the universal set U must be given. A fast way to find A' is to cross out the elements in U that are given to be in set A. A' is the set that remains.

EXAMPLE 2   Finding a Set's Complement

Let $U = \{1, 2, 3, 4, 5, 6, 7, 8, 9\}$
and $A = \{1, 3, 4, 7\}$.
Find A'.

Solution   Set A' contains all the elements of set U that are not in set A. Because set A contains the elements $1, 3, 4,$ and 7, these elements cannot be members of set A':

$$\{\cancel{1}, 2, \cancel{3}, \cancel{4}, 5, 6, \cancel{7}, 8, 9\}$$

Thus, set A' contains $2, 5, 6, 8,$ and 9:

$$A' = \{2, 5, 6, 8, 9\}$$

EXAMPLE 3   Illustrating Relationships Among Sets Using a Venn Diagram

Use a Venn diagram to illustrate the relationship among sets U, A, and A' from Example 2.

$$U = \{1, 2, 3, 4, 5, 6, 7, 8, 9\}$$
$$A = \{1, 3, 4, 7\}$$
$$A' = \{2, 5, 6, 8, 9\}$$

Solution

1. Represent the universal set, U, by the region inside a rectangle. Draw a rectangle and label it U in the upper-left-hand corner. This is shown in Figure 2.1.
2. Represent sets A and A'. Depict set A using a circle within the rectangle. Set A is the region inside the circle. A', the complement of set A, is the region outside the circle and inside the rectangle. Label A and A' as shown in Figure 2.2.
3. Because $A = \{1, 3, 4, 7\}$, place these four elements inside circle A, shown in Figure 2.3.
4. Because $A' = \{2, 5, 6, 8, 9\}$, place these five elements outside circle A, in the region labeled A'. This is illustrated in Figure 2.4.

Figure 2.4 represents the required Venn diagram. By joining together the nine elements inside the rectangle, we obtain the universal set

$$U = \{1, 2, 3, 4, 5, 6, 7, 8, 9\}.$$

Technology

Having trouble creating neat and organized Venn diagrams? Many software programs, including options in most popular word processing programs, allow you to draw neat and presentable Venn diagrams. The draw option of Corel WordPerfect allows for the easy manipulation of individual figures within the Venn diagram. Likewise, Microsoft Paint—found in the Accessories folder of any Windows Operating System—can be used to easily create Venn diagrams. You can also add colors to the different regions. The diagram images can be inserted into any document or presentation.

Figure 2.1

Figure 2.2

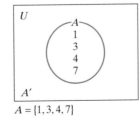

$A = \{1, 3, 4, 7\}$

Figure 2.3

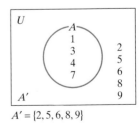

$A' = \{2, 5, 6, 8, 9\}$

Figure 2.4

4 Use the symbols ⊆, ⊄, and ⊂.

Subsets of a Set

In the twentieth century, all U.S. presidents were male. All the elements of the set of twentieth-century U.S. presidents are elements of the set of males. Situations like this, in which all the elements of one set are also elements of another set, are described by the following definition.

> ### Definition of a Subset of a Set
>
> Set A is a **subset** of set B, expressed as
>
> $$A \subseteq B$$
>
> if every element in set A is also in set B.

Because every twentieth-century U.S. president was male, this means that the set of twentieth-century U.S. presidents is a subset of the set of males:

the set of twentieth-century U.S. presidents ⊆ the set of males

The notation $A \not\subseteq B$ means that A **is not a subset** of B. Set A is not a subset of set B if there is at least one element of set A that is not an element of set B. For example, not every drug causes drowsiness. This means that the set of drugs is not a subset of the set of substances that cause drowsiness.

the set of drugs ⊄ the set of substances causing drowsiness

EXAMPLE 4   Using the Symbols ⊆ and ⊄

Write ⊆ or ⊄ in each blank to make a true statement.

a. $A = \{1, 3, 5, 7\}$
   $B = \{1, 3, 5, 7, 9, 11\}$
   A ___ B

b. A = the set of music written in the twentieth century
   B = the set of jazz music
   A ___ B

c. $A = \{x \mid x$ is a planet of Earth's solar system$\}$
   $B = \{$Mercury, Venus, Earth, Mars, Jupiter, Saturn, Uranus, Neptune, Pluto$\}$
   A ___ B

Solution

a. All the elements of $A = \{1, 3, 5, 7\}$ are contained in $B = \{1, 3, 5, 7, 9, 11\}$. Therefore, set A is a subset of set B:

$$A \subseteq B$$

b. Can you think of an example of music written in the twentieth century that is not jazz? One example is the seasonal favorite "White Christmas." This means that not every element of

A = the set of music written in the twentieth century

is an element of

B = the set of jazz music.

Therefore, set A is not a subset of set B:

$$A \not\subseteq B$$

· Pluto

Neptune

Uranus

Saturn

Jupiter

Mars

Earth

Venus

· Mercury

The nine planets in Earth's solar system

c. All the elements of

$$A = \{x \,|\, x \text{ is a planet of the Earth's solar system}\}$$

are contained in

$$B = \{\text{Mercury, Venus, Earth, Mars, Jupiter, Saturn, Uranus, Neptune, Pluto}\}.$$

Furthermore, the sets are equal ($A = B$). Because all elements in set A are also in set B, set A is a subset of set B:

$$A \subseteq B$$

In Example 4(c), the given equal sets suggest that every set is a subset of itself. If we know that set A is a subset of set B and we exclude the possibility of equal sets, then set A is called a **proper subset** of set B, written $A \subset B$.

Definition of a Proper Subset of a Set

Set A is a **proper subset** of set B, expressed as $A \subset B$, if set A is a subset of set B and sets A and B are not equal ($A \neq B$).

Study Tip

For finite sets, the subset symbols are similar to the inequality symbols from algebra.

Sets and Algebra

$A \subseteq B$
A is a subset of B.
$a \leq b$
The number a is less than or equal to the number b.

$A \subset B$
A is a proper subset of B.
$a < b$
The number a is less than the number b.

EXAMPLE 5   Using the Symbols $\subseteq$ and $\subset$

Write $\subseteq$, $\subset$, or both in each blank to make a true statement.

a. $A = \{\text{James Joyce, Virginia Woolf}\}$
   $B = \{\text{James Joyce, Ernest Hemingway, Ralph Ellison, Virginia Woolf}\}$
   $A \underline{\quad} B$

b. $A = \{2, 4, 6, 8\}$
   $B = \{2, 8, 4, 6\}$
   $A \underline{\quad} B$

Solution

a. Every writer in set A is contained in set B, so A is a subset of B:

$$A \subseteq B$$

Because the sets are not equal, set A is a proper subset of set B:

$$A \subset B$$

The symbols $\subseteq$ and $\subset$ can both be placed in the blank to make a true statement.

b. Every number in set A is contained in set B, so A is a subset of B:

$$A \subseteq B$$

Because the sets are equal, set A is *not* a proper subset of set B. The symbol $\subset$ cannot be placed in the blank if we want to form a true statement.

Study Tip

Example 5(b) illustrates that every set is a subset of itself, but no set is a proper subset of itself. Thus, set A is a subset of itself, written

$$A \subseteq A.$$

However, set A is not a proper subset of itself, written

$$A \not\subset A.$$

Subsets and the Empty Set

The meaning of $A \subseteq B$ leads to some interesting properties of the empty set.

EXAMPLE 6   The Empty Set as a Subset

Let $A = \{\ \ \}$ and $B = \{1, 2, 3, 4, 5\}$. Is $A \subseteq B$?

Solution A is not a subset of B ($A \not\subseteq B$) if there is at least one element of set A that is not an element of set B. Because A represents the empty set, there are no elements in set A, period, much less elements in A that do not belong to B. Because we cannot find an element in $A = \{\ \}$ that is not contained in $B = \{1, 2, 3, 4, 5\}$, this means that $A \subseteq B$. Equivalently, $\varnothing \subseteq B$.

Example 6 illustrates the principle that the empty set is a subset of every set. Furthermore, the empty set is a proper subset of every set except itself.

> **The Empty Set as a Subset**
>
> 1. For any set $B, \varnothing \subseteq B$.
> 2. For any set B other than the empty set, $\varnothing \subset B$.

5 Determine the number of subsets of a set.

The Number of Subsets of a Given Set

If a set contains n elements, how many subsets can be formed? Let's observe some special cases, namely sets with $0, 1, 2,$ and 3 elements. We can use inductive reasoning to arrive at a general conclusion. We begin by listing subsets and counting the number of subsets in our list. This is shown in Table 2.2.

Table 2.2   The Number of Subsets: Some Special Cases

Set	Number of Elements	List of All Subsets	Number of Subsets
$\{\ \}$	0	$\{\ \}$	1
$\{a\}$	1	$\{a\},$ $\{\ \}$	2
$\{a, b\}$	2	$\{a, b\},$ $\{a\}, \{b\},$ $\{\ \}$	4
$\{a, b, c\}$	3	$\{a, b, c\},$ $\{a, b\}, \{a, c\}, \{b, c\},$ $\{a\}, \{b\}, \{c\}, \{\ \}$	8

Table 2.2 suggests that when we increase the number of elements in the set by one, the number of subsets doubles. The number of subsets appears to be a power of 2.

Study Tip

Powers of 2 have you in an exponentially increasing state of confusion? No need to panic! Powers and exponents will be reviewed in Chapters 4 and 5.

Number of elements	0	1	2	3
Number of subsets	$1 = 2^0$	$2 = 2^1$	$4 = 2 \times 2 = 2^2$	$8 = 2 \times 2 \times 2 = 2^3$

The power of 2 is the same as the number of elements in the set. Using inductive reasoning, if the set contains n elements, then the number of subsets that can be formed is 2^n.

**Smartest Dogs
Rank/Breed**

1. Border collie

2. Poodle

3. German shepherd

Number of Subsets

The number of subsets of a set with n elements is 2^n.

In Table 2.2, we included the set itself when counting the number of subsets. If we want to find the number of proper subsets, we must exclude counting the given set, thereby decreasing the number by 1.

Number of Proper Subsets

The number of proper subsets of a set with n elements is $2^n - 1$.

EXAMPLE 7 Finding the Number of Subsets and Proper Subsets

According to *The Intelligence of Dogs* by Stanley Coren, the four smartest breeds of dogs are

1. Border collie
2. Poodle
3. German shepherd
4. Golden retriever

A man is trying to decide whether to buy a dog. He can afford up to four dogs, but may buy fewer or none at all. However, if the man makes a purchase, he will buy one or more of the four smartest breeds. The kennel only has one dog from each breed—that is, one border collie, one poodle, one German shepherd, and one golden retriever.

a. Consider the set that represents these breeds:

$$\{border\ collie, poodle, German\ shepherd, golden\ retriever\}$$

Find the number of subsets. What does this number represent in practical terms?

b. List all the subsets and describe what they represent for the prospective dog owner.

c. How many of the subsets are proper subsets?

Solution

a. A set with n elements has 2^n subsets. Because the set of breeds contains four elements, the number of subsets is $2^4 = 2 \times 2 \times 2 \times 2 = 16$. In practical terms, there are 16 different ways to make a selection.

b. Purchase no dogs: $\varnothing$
   Purchase one dog: {border collie}, {poodle}
                        {German shepherd}, {golden retriever}
   Purchase two dogs: {border collie, poodle},
                        {border collie, German shepherd},
                        {border collie, golden retriever},
                        {poodle, German shepherd},
                        {poodle, golden retriever},
                        {German shepherd, golden retriever}

4. Golden retriever

Source: The Intelligence of Dogs

Purchase three dogs: {border collie, poodle, German shepherd},
{border collie, poodle, golden retriever},
{border collie, German shepherd, golden retriever},
{poodle, German shepherd, golden retriever}

Purchase four dogs: {border collie, poodle, German shepherd, golden retriever}

As predicted in part(a), 16 different selections are possible.

c. Every set except

{border collie, poodle, German shepherd, golden retriever}

is a proper subset of the given set. There are $16 - 1$, or 15, proper subsets. Although we obtained this number by counting, we can also use the fact that the number of proper subsets of a set with n elements is $2^n - 1$. Because the set of breeds contains four elements, there are $2^4 - 1$ proper subsets.

$$2^4 - 1 = (2 \times 2 \times 2 \times 2) - 1 = 16 - 1 = 15 \text{ proper subsets}$$

The Smartest and the Dumbest Dogs

In the Venn diagram shown below, the universal set is the set of purebred dogs. Within the universal set, two subsets are shown.

U: Purebred Dogs

Set of Smartest Dogs
{Border collie, Poodle, German shepherd, Golden retriever, Doberman pinscher, Shetland sheepdog, Labrador retriever, Papillon, Rottweiler, Australian cattle dog}

Set of Dumbest Dogs
{Afghan hound, Basenji, Bulldog, Chow Chow, Borzoi, Bloodhound, Pekingese, Beagle, Mastiff, Basset hound}

If Afghans could read, they'd probably disagree with being an element of the set of dumbest dogs.

Source: The Intelligence of Dogs by Stanley Coren, 1994.

Exercise Set 2.2

 Practice Exercises

In Exercises 1–4, describe a universal set U that includes all elements in the given sets. Answers may vary.

1. A = {Bach, Mozart, Beethoven}
   B = {Brahms, Schubert}
2. A = {William Shakespeare, Charles Dickens}
   B = {Mark Twain, Robert Louis Stevenson}
3. A = {Pepsi, Sprite}
   B = {Coca Cola, Seven-Up}
4. A = {Ford Taurus, Honda Accord, Toyota Camry}
   B = {Dodge Intrepid, Buick LeSabre}

In Exercises 5–8, let U = {a, b, c, d, e, f, g}, A = {a, b, f, g}, B = {c, d, e}, C = {a, g}, and D = {a, b, c, d, e, f}. Use the roster method to write each of the following sets.

5. A'   6. B'   7. C'   8. D'

In Exercises 9–12, let U = {1, 2, 3, 4, …, 20}, A = {1, 2, 3, 4, 5}, B = {6, 7, 8, 9}, C = {1, 3, 5, 7, …, 19}, and D = {2, 4, 6, 8, …, 20}. Use the roster method to write each of the following sets.

9. A'   10. B'   11. C'   12. D'

In Exercises 13–16, let U = {1, 2, 3, 4, …}, A = {1, 2, 3, 4, …, 20}, B = {1, 2, 3, 4, …, 50}, C = {2, 4, 6, 8, …}, and D = {1, 3, 5, 7, …}. Use the roster method to write each of the following sets.

13. A'   14. B'   15. C'   16. D'

In Exercises 17–18, place the various elements in the proper regions of the following Venn diagram. Use a separate diagram for each exercise.

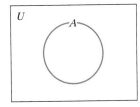

17. Let U = {1, 2, 3, 4, 5, 6, 7} and A = {1, 2, 5}. Find A' and place the elements 1 through 7 in the proper region.
18. Let U = {1, 2, 3, 4, 5, 6, 7, 8} and A = {2, 3, 6, 8}. Find A' and place the elements 1 through 8 in the proper region.
19. Let U = {a, b, c, d, e, f} and A = {a, b, f}. Find A'. Then use a Venn diagram to illustrate the relationship among sets U, A, and A'.
20. Let U = {a, e, i, o, u} and A = {a, u}. Find A'. Then use a Venn diagram to illustrate the relationship among the sets U, A, and A'.
21. If the universal set is the set of the months of the year and set A is the set of months that begin with the letter J, write A' using the roster method. Describe A' in words.

22. If the universal set is the set of the days of the week and set A is the set of days that begin with the letter S, write A' using the roster method. Describe A' in words.

In Exercises 23–34 write ⊆ or ⊄ in each blank so that the resulting statement is true.

23. {1, 2, 5} _____ {1, 2, 3, 4, 5, 6, 7}
24. {2, 3, 7} _____ {1, 2, 3, 4, 5, 6, 7}
25. {−3, 0, 3} _____ {−3, −1, 1, 3}
26. {−4, 0, 4} _____ {−4, −3, −1, 1, 3, 4}
27. {Monday, Friday} _____ {Saturday, Sunday, Monday, Tuesday, Wednesday}
28. {Mercury, Venus, Earth} _____ {Venus, Earth, Mars, Jupiter}
29. {x | x is a key on a piano} _____ {x | x is a black key on a piano}
30. {x | x is a dog} _____ {x | x is a pure-bred dog}
31. {c, o, n, v, e, r, s, a, t, i, o, n} _____ {v, o, i, c, e, s, r, a, n, t, o, n}
32. {r, e, v, o, l, u, t, i, o, n} _____ {t, o, l, o, v, e, r, u, i, n}
33. {4/7, 9/13} _____ {7/4, 13/9}
34. {1/2, 1/3} _____ {2, 3, 5}

In Exercises 35–40, write ⊆, or ⊂, or both to make the statement true. If neither symbol can be placed in the blank so that the resulting statement is true, state this in writing.

35. {V, C, R} _____ {V, C, R, S}
36. {F, I, N} _____ {F, I, N, K}
37. {0, 2, 4, 6, 8} _____ {8, 0, 6, 2, 4}
38. {9, 1, 7, 3, 4} _____ {1, 3, 4, 7, 9}
39. {x | x is a person who is Christian} _____ {x | x is a person who is Catholic}
40. {x | x is a person who is a registered voter} _____ {x | x is a person who is a registered Republican}

Determine whether each statement in Exercises 41–48 is true or false. If the statement is false, explain why.

41. Ralph ∈ {Ralph, Alice, Trixie, Norton}
42. Canada ∈ {Mexico, United States, Canada}
43. Ralph ⊆ {Ralph, Alice, Trixie, Norton}
44. Canada ⊆ {Mexico, United States, Canada}
45. {Ralph} ⊆ {Ralph, Alice, Trixie, Norton}
46. {Canada} ⊆ {Mexico, United States, Canada}
47. ∅ ∈ {Archie, Edith, Mike, Gloria}
48. ∅ ⊆ {Charlie Chaplin, Groucho Marx, Woody Allen}

In Exercises 49–54, list all the subsets of the given set.

49. {border collie, poodle}
50. {Romeo, Juliet}
51. {t, a, b}
52. {Spanish, French, English}
53. {0}
54. ∅

Calculate the number of subsets and the number of proper subsets for each of the sets in Exercises 55–62.

55. $\{2, 4, 6, 8\}$
56. $\{\frac{1}{2}, \frac{1}{3}, \frac{1}{4}, \frac{1}{5}\}$
57. $\{2, 4, 6, 8, 10, 12\}$
58. $\{a, b, c, d, e, f\}$
59. the set of the days of the week
60. the set of U.S. coins containing one kind of each coin worth less than a dollar
61. the set of words describing the colors in the American flag
62. the set containing the Beatles (pictured on page 35) and their original drummer, who was not Ringo Starr

Application Exercises

Use the formula for the number of subsets of a set with n elements to solve Exercises 63–68.

63. Houses in Euclid Estates are all identical. However, a person can purchase a new house with some, all, or none of a set of options. This set includes {pool, screened-in balcony, lake view, alarm system, upgraded landscaping}. How many options are there for purchasing a house in this community?

64. A cheese pizza can be ordered with some, all, or none of the following set of toppings: {beef, ham, mushrooms, sausage, peppers, pepperoni, olives, prosciutto, onion}. How many different variations are available for ordering a pizza?

65. Based on more than 1500 ballots sent to film notables, the American Film Institute rated the top U.S. movies. The Institute selected *Citizen Kane* (1941), *Casablanca* (1942), *The Godfather* (1972), *Gone With the Wind* (1939), *Lawrence of Arabia* (1962), and *The Wizard of Oz* (1939) as the top six films. Suppose that you have all six films on video and decide to view some, all, or none of these films. How many viewing options do you have?

66. A small town has four police cars. If a radio dispatcher receives a call, depending on the nature of the situation, no cars, one car, two cars, three cars, or all four cars can be sent. How many options does the dispatcher have for sending the police cars to the scene of the caller?

67. According to the U.S. Census Bureau, the most ethnically diverse U.S. cities are New York City, Los Angeles, Miami, Chicago, Washington DC, Houston, San Diego, and Seattle. If you decide to visit some, all, or none of these cities, how many travel options do you have?

68. Some of the movies with all-time box office grosses include *Titanic* ($582 million), *Star Wars* ($461 million), *E.T.* ($400 million), *Jurassic Park* ($357 million), *Forrest Gump* ($330 million), *The Lion King* ($313 million), and *Return of the Jedi* ($309 million). Suppose that you have all seven films on video and decide, over the course of a week, to view some, all, or none of these films. How many viewing options do you have?

Writing in Mathematics

69. Describe what is meant by a universal set. Provide an example.
70. What is a Venn diagram and why are they used?
71. Describe what is meant by the complement of a set.
72. Is it possible to find a set's complement if a universal set is not given? Explain your answer.
73. Explain what is meant by a subset.
74. What is the difference between a subset and a proper subset?
75. Explain why the empty set is a subset of every set.
76. Describe the difference between the symbols ∈ and ⊆. Explain how each symbol is used.
77. Describe the formula for finding the number of subsets for a given set. Give an example.
78. Describe how to find the number of proper subsets for a given set. Give an example.
79. In the enrichment essay on page 50, what definitions might be used for the words "smartest" and "dumbest" so that it becomes clear how various breeds were assigned to each of the sets?

Critical Thinking Exercises

80. Which one of the following is true?
    a. The set $\{3\}$ has 2^3 or eight subsets.
    b. The complement of the complement of a set is the set itself.
    c. Every set has a proper subset.
    d. The set $\{3, \{1, 4\}\}$ has eight subsets.

81. Suppose that a nickel, a dime, and a quarter are on a table. You may select some, all, or none of the coins. Specify all of the different amounts of money that can be selected.

82. If a set has 127 proper subsets, how many elements are there in the set?

Technology Exercises

83. Find the draw option in your word processing program. Use it to create a Venn diagram that illustrates the relationships among the sets U, A, and A' described in Example 3 on page 45. Once a figure has been created, you can click on the figure with the right mouse button (right-click) and alter the figure's properties. You can thicken the width of lines in the figure. Set the object to "No Fill" to create a diagram. Create a text box to insert the necessary elements or labels.

84. The symbols ∈, ∉, ⊂, ⊄, ⊆, and ⊈ are all available in any current word processing program. How can you find and use them? Use the option that allows you to insert a symbol or a character. Then, you should be presented with a group of characters to choose from. The symbols are classified in sets and subsets. To find the symbol you desire, you must choose the correct set first.

    Recreate the following statements using the symbols found in your word processor.

a. $2 \in \{2, 4, 6, 8\}$
b. $\{a, b, c\} \subset \{a, b, c, d, e\}$
c. ☺ $\notin \{♦, ♠, ♣, ♥\}$

Group Exercises

85. Take some time to reread Exercises 41–48. In your group, discuss the errors that people make when using set notation, particularly the symbols $\subseteq$ and $\in$. Then present ways of helping students avoid these errors.

86. A state ballot gives citizens the option of voting for or against a particular issue. A political action group is attempting to predict the outcome of the voting. They survey a sample of the state's registered voters. As a group, you should first decide what the issue is. Then propose at least five plans for dividing the voters into subsets so that a sample of people in each subset can be interviewed. Which one of the plans contains the best subsets of the universal set of state voters in terms of predicting the election's outcome?

SECTION 2.3   *Venn Diagrams and Set Operations*

Objectives

1. Use Venn diagrams to visualize set relationships.

2. Perform operations with sets.

You need to determine whether there is sufficient support on campus to have a blood drive. You take a survey to obtain information, asking students:

> Would you be willing to donate blood?
> Would you be willing to help serve a free breakfast to blood donors?

Set A represents the set of students willing to donate blood. Set B represents the set of students willing to help serve breakfast to donors. Possible survey results include

> No students willing to donate blood are willing to serve breakfast, and vice versa.
> All students willing to donate blood are willing to serve breakfast.
> The same students who are willing to donate blood are willing to serve breakfast.
> Some of the students willing to donate blood are willing to serve breakfast.

We begin by using Venn diagrams to visualize these results.

1   Use Venn diagrams to visualize set relationships.

Visualizing Relationships Between Two Sets

Venn diagrams are useful for illustrating relationships between two sets. We consider four basic relationships and their visualizations.

Relationship 1. Disjoint Sets   Two sets that have no elements in common are called **disjoint** sets. Two disjoint sets A and B are shown in the Venn diagram on the left. Disjoint sets are represented as circles that do not overlap. No elements of set A are elements of set B, and vice versa.

     If set A represents the set of students willing to donate blood and set B represents the set of students willing to serve breakfast to donors, the set diagram shown above illustrates

> No students willing to donate blood are willing to serve breakfast, and vice versa.

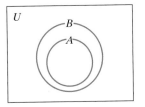

Relationship 2. Proper Subsets   If set A is a proper subset of set B ($A \subset B$), the relationship is shown in the Venn diagram on the left. All elements of set A are elements of set B. If an x representing an element is placed inside circle A, it automatically falls inside circle B.

     If set A represents the set of students willing to donate blood and set B represents the set of students willing to serve breakfast to donors, the set diagram shown above illustrates

> All students willing to donate blood are willing to serve breakfast.

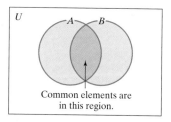

Common elements are
in this region.

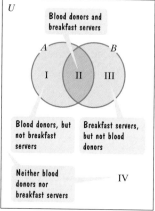

A: Set of blood donors
B: Set of breakfast
    servers

Figure 2.5

2 Perform operations with
    sets.

Relationship 3. Equal Sets   If $A = B$, then set A contains exactly the same elements as set B. This relationship is shown in the Venn diagram on the left. Because all elements in set A are in set B, and vice versa, this diagram illustrates that when $A = B$, then $A \subseteq B$ and $B \subseteq A$.

If set A represents the set of students willing to donate blood and set B represents the set of students willing to serve breakfast to donors, the set diagram shown above illustrates

The same students who are willing to donate blood are willing to serve breakfast.

Relationship 4. Sets with Some Common Elements   In mathematics, the word "some" means *there exists at least one*. If set A and set B have at least one element in common, then the circles representing the sets must overlap. This is illustrated in the Venn diagram on the left.

If set A represents the set of students willing to donate blood and set B represents the set of students willing to serve breakfast to donors, the presence of at least one student in region II in Figure 2.5 illustrates

Some students willing to donate blood are willing to serve breakfast.

Let's make sure that we understand what the other regions in Figure 2.5 represent.

Region I   This region represents the set of students willing to donate blood, but not serve breakfast.

Region III   This region represents the set of students willing to serve breakfast but not donate blood.

Region IV   This region represents the set of students surveyed who are not willing to donate blood and are not willing to serve breakfast.

Operations with Sets

In arithmetic, we use operations such as addition and multiplication to combine numbers. We now turn to two set operations, called **intersection** and **union**, that will enable us to combine sets. We will also revisit the idea of the complement of a set.

Intersection   You are now sorting out the results of the blood-donor, breakfast-server survey. Recall that the Red Cross needs to decide whether the number of potential donors warrants a commitment to provide medical staff for the blood drive. Part of your report to the Red Cross involves reporting the number of students willing to both donate blood *and* serve breakfast. You must focus on the set containing all the students who are common to both set A, the set of donors, *and* set B, the set of breakfast servers. This set is called the **intersection** of sets A and B.

Definition of the Intersection of Sets

The **intersection** of sets A and B, written $A \cap B$, is the set of elements common to both set A and set B. This definition can be expressed in set-builder notation as follows:

$$A \cap B = \{x \mid x \in A \text{ AND } x \in B\}.$$

In Example 1, we are asked to find the intersection of two sets. This is done by listing the common elements of both sets. Because the intersection of two sets is also a set, we enclose these elements with braces.

EXAMPLE 1   Finding the Intersection of Two Sets

Find each of the following intersections.

a. $\{7, 8, 9, 10, 11\} \cap \{6, 8, 10, 12\}$

b. $\{1, 3, 5, 7, 9\} \cap \{2, 4, 6, 8\}$

c. $\{1, 3, 5, 7, 9\} \cap \varnothing$

Solution

a. The elements common to $\{7, 8, 9, 10, 11\}$ and $\{6, 8, 10, 12\}$ are 8 and 10. Thus,

$$\{7, 8, 9, 10, 11\} \cap \{6, 8, 10, 12\} = \{8, 10\}.$$

The Venn diagram in Figure 2.6 illustrates this situation.

b. The sets $\{1, 3, 5, 7, 9\}$ and $\{2, 4, 6, 8\}$ have no elements in common. Thus,

$$\{1, 3, 5, 7, 9\} \cap \{2, 4, 6, 8\} = \varnothing.$$

The Venn diagram in Figure 2.7 illustrates this situation. The sets are disjoint.

c. There are no elements in $\varnothing$, the empty set. This means that there can be no elements belonging to both $\{1, 3, 5, 7, 9\}$ and $\varnothing$. Therefore,

$$\{1, 3, 5, 7, 9\} \cap \varnothing = \varnothing.$$

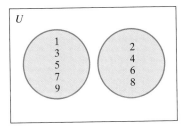

Figure 2.6 The numbers 8 and 10 belong to both sets.

Figure 2.7 These disjoint sets have no common elements.

Study Tip

The word *or* is interpreted to mean *union*.

Union   You continue to sort the results of the survey. The Red Cross also wants a report on the number of students willing to donate blood *or* serve breakfast *or* do both. You must focus on the set containing the students who are in set A, the set of donors, *or* set B, the set of breakfast servers, *or* both of these sets. This set is called the **union** of sets A and B.

Definition of the Union of Sets

The **union** of sets A and B, written $A \cup B$, is the set of elements that are members of set A or of set B or of both sets. This definition can be expressed in set-builder notation as follows:

$$A \cup B = \{x \mid x \in A \text{ OR } x \in B\}.$$

We can find the union of set A and set B by listing the elements of set A. Then, we include any elements of set B that have not already been listed. Enclose all elements that are listed with braces. This shows that the union of two sets is also a set.

EXAMPLE 2   Finding the Union of Sets

Find each of the following unions.

a. $\{7, 8, 9, 10, 11\} \cup \{6, 8, 10, 12\}$

b. $\{1, 3, 5, 7, 9\} \cup \{2, 4, 6, 8\}$

c. $\{1, 3, 5, 7, 9\} \cup \varnothing$

Study Tip

When finding the union of two sets, do not list twice any elements that appear in both sets.

Solution This example uses the same sets as in Example 1. However, this time we are finding the union of the sets, rather than their intersection.

a. To find $\{7, 8, 9, 10, 11\} \cup \{6, 8, 10, 12\}$, start by listing all the elements from the first set, namely 7, 8, 9, 10, and 11. Now list all the elements from the second set that are not in the first set, namely 6 and 12. The union is the set consisting of all these elements. Thus,

$$\{7, 8, 9, 10, 11\} \cup \{6, 8, 10, 12\} = \{6, 7, 8, 9, 10, 11, 12\}.$$

b. To find $\{1, 3, 5, 7, 9\} \cup \{2, 4, 6, 8\}$, list the elements from the first set, namely 1, 3, 5, 7, and 9. Now add to the list the elements in the second set that are not in the first set. This includes every element in the second set, namely 2, 4, 6, and 8. The union is the set consisting of all these elements, so

$$\{1, 3, 5, 7, 9\} \cup \{2, 4, 6, 8\} = \{1, 2, 3, 4, 5, 6, 7, 8, 9\}.$$

c. To find $\{1, 3, 5, 7, 9\} \cup \varnothing$, list the elements from the first set, namely 1, 3, 5, 7, and 9. Because there are no elements in $\varnothing$, the empty set, there are no additional elements to add to the list. Thus,

$$\{1, 3, 5, 7, 9\} \cup \varnothing = \{1, 3, 5, 7, 9\}.$$

EXAMPLE 3   Using Set Operations

Given

$$U = \{1, 2, 3, 4, 5, 6, 7, 8, 9, 10\}$$
$$A = \{1, 3, 7, 9\}$$
$$B = \{3, 7, 8, 10\}$$

find

a. $(A \cup B)'$

b. $A' \cap B'$

Solution

a. To find $(A \cup B)'$, we will first work inside the parentheses and determine $A \cup B$. Then we'll find the complement of $A \cup B$, $(A \cup B)'$.

$$A \cup B = \{1, 3, 7, 9\} \cup \{3, 7, 8, 10\} \qquad \text{These are the given sets.}$$
$$= \{1, 3, 7, 8, 9, 10\} \qquad \text{Join (unite) the elements, listing the common elements (3 and 7) only once.}$$

Now find $(A \cup B)'$, the complement of $A \cup B$.

$$(A \cup B)' = \{1, 3, 7, 8, 9, 10\}'$$
$$= \{2, 4, 5, 6\} \qquad \text{List the elements in the universal set that are not listed in } \{1, 3, 7, 8, 9, 10\}:$$
$$\{1, 2, 3, 4, 5, 6, 7, 8, 9, 10\}$$

b. To find $A' \cap B'$, we must first identify the elements in A' and B'. Set A' is the set of elements of U that are not in set A:

$$A' = \{2, 4, 5, 6, 8, 10\}$$

Set B' is the set of elements of U that are not in set B:

$$B' = \{1, 2, 4, 5, 6, 9\}$$

Now we can find $A' \cap B'$, the set of elements belonging to both A' and to B':

$$A' \cap B' = \{2, 4, 5, 6, 8, 10\} \cap \{1, 2, 4, 5, 6, 9\}$$
$$= \{2, 4, 5, 6\}$$

The numbers 2, 4, 5, and 6 are common to both sets.

It is no coincidence that we obtained the same answer in both parts of Example 3. For any two sets A and B, it is always true that $(A \cup B)' = A' \cap B'$.

We can reverse the union and intersection symbols in the above statement. For any two sets A and B, it is also true that

$$(A \cap B)' = A' \cup B'.$$

These two statements are known as *De Morgan's laws*, named for the British logician Augustus De Morgan (1806–1871).

De Morgan's Laws

$(A \cup B)' = A' \cap B'$: The complement of the union is the intersection of the complements.

$(A \cap B)' = A' \cup B'$: The complement of the intersection is the union of the complements.

Exercise Set 2.3

Practice Exercises

In Exercises 1–24, let

$$U = \{1, 2, 3, 4, 5, 6, 7\}$$
$$A = \{1, 3, 5, 7\}$$
$$B = \{1, 2, 3\}$$
$$C = \{2, 3, 4, 5, 6\}$$

Find each of the following sets.

1. $A \cap B$ 2. $B \cap C$ 3. $A \cup B$ 4. $B \cup C$
5. A' 6. B' 7. $A' \cap B'$ 8. $B' \cap C$
9. $A \cup C'$ 10. $B \cup C'$ 11. $(A \cap C)'$ 12. $(A \cap B)'$
13. $A' \cup C'$ 14. $A' \cup B'$ 15. $(A \cup B)'$ 16. $(A \cup C)'$
17. $A \cup \varnothing$ 18. $C \cup \varnothing$ 19. $A \cap \varnothing$ 20. $C \cap \varnothing$
21. $A \cup U$ 22. $B \cup U$ 23. $A \cap U$ 24. $B \cap U$

In Exercises 25–48, let

$$U = \{a, b, c, d, e, f, g, h\}$$
$$A = \{a, g, h\}$$
$$B = \{b, g, h\}$$
$$C = \{b, c, d, e, f\}$$

Find each of the following sets.

25. $A \cap B$ 26. $B \cap C$ 27. $A \cup B$ 28. $B \cup C$
29. A' 30. B' 31. $A' \cap B'$ 32. $B' \cap C$
33. $A \cup C'$ 34. $B \cup C'$ 35. $(A \cap C)'$ 36. $(A \cap B)'$
37. $A' \cup C'$ 38. $A' \cup B'$ 39. $(A \cup B)'$ 40. $(A \cup C)'$
41. $A \cup \varnothing$ 42. $C \cup \varnothing$ 43. $A \cap \varnothing$ 44. $C \cap \varnothing$
45. $A \cup U$ 46. $B \cup U$ 47. $A \cap U$ 48. $B \cap U$

In Exercises 49–58, use the Venn diagram to list the elements of each set in roster form.

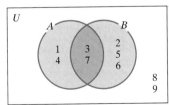

49. A 50. B 51. U 52. $A \cup B$
53. $A \cap B$ 54. A' 55. B' 56. $(A \cap B)'$
57. $(A \cup B)'$ 58. $A' \cap B$

Application Exercises

We have seen that the word and *is interpreted to mean intersection. The word* or *is interpreted to mean union. Based on our work in the previous section, the word* not *is interpreted to mean complement—that is A′ is the set of elements in U that are* not *in A. Use these interpretations and the following sets to write a verbal description of each set in Exercises 59–64.*

> *U is the set of all cities in the United States.*
>
> *A is the set of U.S. cities in which average homes cost more than $200,000.*
>
> *B is the set of U.S. cities with more than one million convention attendees each year.*

Sample: B′ is the set of U.S. cities that do not *have more than 1 million convention attendees each year.*

59. A' 60. $A \cap B$ 61. $A \cup B$
62. $(A \cap B)'$ 63. $A \cup A'$ 64. $A \cap A'$

 Writing in Mathematics

65. Describe the Venn diagram for two disjoint sets. How does this diagram illustrate that the sets have no common elements?

66. Describe the Venn diagram for proper subsets. How does this diagram illustrate that the elements of one set are also in the second set?

67. Describe the Venn diagram for two equal sets. How does this diagram illustrate that the sets are equal?

68. Describe the Venn diagram for two sets with common elements. How does this diagram illustrate this relationship?

69. Describe what is meant by the intersection of sets. Give an example.

70. Describe what is meant by the union of sets. Give an example.

 Critical Thinking Exercises

71. Which one of the following is true?
    a. $n(A \cup B) = n(A) + n(B)$
    b. $A \cap A' = \varnothing$
    c. $(A \cup B) \subseteq A$
    d. If $A \subseteq B$, then $A \cap B = B$

72. Which one of the following is true?
    a. $A \cap U = U$
    b. $A \cup \varnothing = \varnothing$
    c. If $A \subseteq B$, then $A \cap B = \varnothing$
    d. If $B \subseteq A$, then $A \cap B = B$

73. Find a counterexample to show that $(A \cup B)' = A' \cup B'$ is false.

 Technology Exercise

74. Using the Paint Program in Windows, create four Venn diagrams, each with two sets, A and B. The diagrams must include shaded regions corresponding to the following:
    a. $A \cap B$ b. $A \cup B$ c. $A' \cup B'$ d. $(A \cap B)'$

Group Exercise

75. The sentence "All apes are mammals" means that the set of apes is a proper subset of the set of mammals. If set A is the set of apes and set B is the set of mammals, this relationship can be visualized with a Venn diagram in which circle A is drawn inside circle B. Group members should write four true sentences that illustrate each of the four set relationships on pages 53–54. Then, rewrite each sentence using the language of sets. Finally, use a Venn diagram to illustrate each of the group's sentences.

SECTION 2.4 Set Operations and Venn Diagrams with Three Sets

Objectives

1. Perform set operations with three sets.

2. Use Venn diagrams with three sets.

3. Use Venn diagrams to illustrate equality of sets.

Set Operations with Three Sets

We now know how to find the union and intersection of two sets. We also know how to find a set's complement. In Example 1, we apply set operations to situations containing three sets. Always begin by finding the set within parentheses.

1 Perform set operations with three sets.

EXAMPLE 1   Set Operations with Three Sets

Given

$$U = \{1, 2, 3, 4, 5, 6, 7, 8, 9\}$$
$$A = \{1, 2, 3, 4, 5\}$$
$$B = \{1, 2, 3, 6, 8\}$$
$$C = \{2, 3, 4, 6, 7\}$$

find

a. $A \cup (B \cap C)$

b. $(A \cup B) \cap (A \cup C)$

c. $A \cap (B \cup C')$

Solution

a. To find $A \cup (B \cap C)$, first find the set within the parentheses, $B \cap C$. The elements common to B and C are 2, 3, and 6, so

$$B \cap C = \{2, 3, 6\}.$$

Now finish the problem by finding $A \cup (B \cap C)$. List all elements in A and add to this list any elements in $B \cap C$ that have not already been listed. The elements in A are 1, 2, 3, 4, and 5. The only element in $B \cap C$ that has not already been listed is 6. Thus,

$$A \cup (B \cap C) = \{1, 2, 3, 4, 5, 6\}.$$

b. To find $(A \cup B) \cap (A \cup C)$, first find the sets within parentheses. Starting with $A \cup B$, list the elements in set A, namely 1, 2, 3, 4, 5. Add any unlisted numbers that appear in set B, namely 6 and 8. Thus,

$$A \cup B = \{1, 2, 3, 4, 5, 6, 8\}.$$

Now identify the elements in $A \cup C$ by first listing the elements in set A, namely 1, 2, 3, 4, 5. Add any unlisted numbers that appear in set C, namely 6 and 7. Thus,

$$A \cup C = \{1, 2, 3, 4, 5, 6, 7\}.$$

Now finish the problem by finding $(A \cup B) \cap (A \cup C)$, listing the numbers that are common to the $A \cup B$ set and the $A \cup C$ set. Numbers common to both sets are 1, 2, 3, 4, 5, and 6, so

$$(A \cup B) \cap (A \cup C) = \{1, 2, 3, 4, 5, 6\}.$$

c. As in parts (a) and (b), to find $A \cap (B \cup C')$, begin with the set in parentheses. First we must find C', elements in U that are not in C. Looking at sets U and C, we see that 1, 5, 8, and 9 are not in C, so

$$C' = \{1, 5, 8, 9\}.$$

Now we can identify elements of $B \cup C'$ by listing all elements of set B, namely 1, 2, 3, 6, 8, and adding any unlisted elements that appear in C', namely 5 and 9. Listing the numbers from smallest to largest, we see that

$$B \cup C' = \{1, 2, 3, 5, 6, 8, 9\}.$$

Now finish the problem by finding $A \cap (B \cup C')$, identifying numbers that are common to set A and set $B \cup C'$. Set A contains the numbers 1, 2, 3, 4, 5. Looking above for set $B \cup C'$, we see that the common numbers are 1, 2, 3, and 5. Thus,

$$A \cap (B \cup C') = \{1, 2, 3, 5\}.$$

2 Use Venn diagrams with three sets.

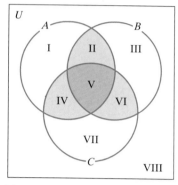

Figure 2.8 Three intersecting sets separate the universal set into eight regions.

Venn Diagrams with Three Sets

Venn diagrams can contain three or more sets, such as the diagram in Figure 2.8. The three sets in the figure separate the universal set U into eight regions. The numbering of these regions is arbitrary—that is, we can number any region as I, any region as II, and so on. Here is a description of each region.

Region I	This region represents elements in set A that are in neither sets B nor C.
Region II	This region represents elements in both sets A and B that are not in set C.
Region III	This region represents elements in set B that are in neither sets A nor C.
Region IV	This region represents elements in both sets A and C that are not in set B.
Region V	This region represents elements that are common to sets A, B, and C.
Region VI	This region represents elements in both sets B and C that are not in set A.
Region VII	This region represents elements in set C that are in neither sets A nor B.
Region VIII	This region represents elements in the universal set U that are not in sets A, B, or C.

EXAMPLE 2   Understanding a Venn Diagram with Three Sets

The Venn diagram with three sets is shown again on the right.

a. Which regions represent set A?
b. Which regions represent $A \cup B$?
c. Which regions represent $B \cap C$?
d. Which regions represent A'?
e. Which region represents $A \cap B \cap C$?

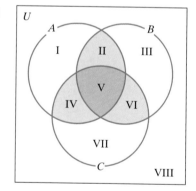

Solution

a. Set A is represented by the regions inside circle A. Therefore, set A is represented by regions I, II, IV, and V.
b. Set $A \cup B$ is found in the Venn diagram by uniting, or joining, all the regions inside circles A and B. Therefore, $A \cup B$ is represented by regions I, II, III, IV, V, and VI.
c. Set $B \cap C$ is found in the Venn diagram by taking the regions common to circles B and C. Therefore, $B \cap C$ is represented by regions V and VI.
d. Set A' is represented by the regions outside circle A. Therefore, A' is represented by regions III, VI, VII, and VIII.
e. Set $A \cap B \cap C$ is found in the Venn diagram by taking the region common to circles A, B, and C. Therefore, $A \cap B \cap C$ is represented by region V.

Venn Diagrams and Color Mixing

Venn diagrams with three intersecting circles can be used to illustrate the blending of the three primary colors—red, green, and blue-violet. The intersection of the three regions, white light, is the blending of all three primary colors.

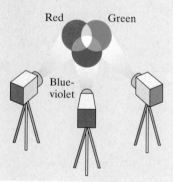

3 Use Venn diagrams to illustrate equality of sets.

Illustrating the Equality of Sets

In Section 2.3, we presented a De Morgan Law that stated

$$(A \cap B)' = A' \cup B'.$$

To illustrate that $(A \cap B)'$ and $A' \cup B'$ are equal, we use a Venn diagram. If both sets represent the same regions of the diagram, then they are equal. Example 3 shows how this is done.

EXAMPLE 3   Illustrating a De Morgan Law with a Venn Diagram

Use the Venn diagram in Figure 2.9 to show that

$$(A \cap B)' = A' \cup B'.$$

Solution   Begin with the regions represented by $(A \cap B)'$.

Set	Regions in the Venn Diagram
A	I, II
B	II, III
$A \cap B$	II (This is the region common to A and B.)
$(A \cap B)'$	I, III, IV (These are the regions in U that are not in $A \cap B$.)

Next, find the regions represented by $A' \cup B'$.

Set	Regions in the Venn Diagram
A'	III, IV (These are the regions not in A.)
B'	I, IV (These are the regions not in B.)
$A' \cup B'$	I, III, IV (These are the regions obtained by uniting the regions representing A' and B'.)

Both $(A \cap B)'$ and $A' \cup B'$ are represented by the same regions, I, III, and IV, of the Venn diagram. This illustrates that

$$(A \cap B)' = A' \cup B'$$

for all sets A and B.

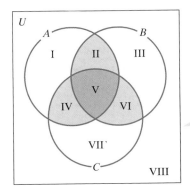

Figure 2.9

Figure 2.10

In Example 1, did you notice that we obtained the same set when finding $A \cup (B \cap C)$ and $(A \cup B) \cap (A \cup C)$? Although one example does not prove that these sets are equal, we can use a Venn diagram to illustrate the equality of these sets. We do this in Example 4.

EXAMPLE 4   Illustrating the Equality of Sets

Use a Venn diagram to show that

$$A \cup (B \cap C) = (A \cup B) \cap (A \cup C).$$

Solution   Use a Venn diagram with three sets A, B, and C, drawn in Figure 2.10. Begin with the regions represented by $A \cup (B \cap C)$.

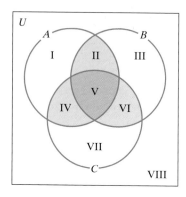

Figure 2.10 Shown again so you do not have to turn back a page

Set	Regions in the Venn Diagram
A	I, II, IV, V
$B \cap C$	V, VI (These are the regions common to B and C.)
$A \cup (B \cap C)$	I, II, IV, V, VI (These are the regions obtained by uniting the regions representing A and $B \cap C$.)

Next, find the regions represented by $(A \cup B) \cap (A \cup C)$.

Set	Regions in the Venn Diagram
A	I, II, IV, V
B	II, III, V, VI
C	IV, V, VI, VII
$A \cup B$	I, II, III, IV, V, VI (Unite the regions representing A and B.)
$A \cup C$	I, II, IV, V, VI, VII (Unite the regions representing A and C.)
$(A \cup B) \cap (A \cup C)$	I, II, IV, V, VI (These are the regions common to $A \cup B$ and $A \cup C$.)

Both $A \cup (B \cap C)$ and $(A \cup B) \cap (A \cup C)$ are represented by the same regions, I, II, IV, V, and VI, of the Venn diagram. This illustrates that

$$A \cup (B \cap C) = (A \cup B) \cap (A \cup C)$$

for all sets A, B, and C.

Blood Types and Venn Diagrams

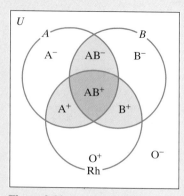

Figure 2.11 Human blood types

In 1900, the Austrian immunologist Karl Landsteiner discovered that all blood is not the same. Blood serum drawn from one person often clumped when mixed with the blood cells of another. The clumping was caused by different antigens, proteins and carbohydrates that trigger antibodies and fight infection. Landsteiner classified blood types based on the presence or absence of the antigens A, B, and Rh in red blood cells. The Venn diagram in Figure 2.11 contains eight regions representing the eight common blood groups.

In the Venn diagram, blood with the Rh antigen is labeled positive and blood lacking the Rh antigen is labeled negative. The region where the three circles intersect represents type AB⁺, indicating that a person with this blood type has the antigens A, B and Rh. Observe that type O blood (both positive and negative) lacks A and B antigens. Type O⁻ lacks all three antigens, A, B, and Rh.

In blood transfusions, the recipient must have all or more of the antigens present in the donor's blood. This discovery rescued surgery patients from random, often lethal, transfusions. This knowledge made the massive blood drives during World War I possible. Eventually, it made the modern blood bank possible as well.

Exercise Set 2.4

 Practice Exercises

In Exercises 1–12, let

$$U = \{1, 2, 3, 4, 5, 6, 7\}$$
$$A = \{1, 3, 5, 7\}$$
$$B = \{1, 2, 3\}$$
$$C = \{2, 3, 4, 5, 6\}$$

Find each of the following sets.

1. $A \cup (B \cap C)$
2. $A \cap (B \cup C)$
3. $(A \cup B) \cap (A \cup C)$
4. $(A \cap B) \cup (A \cap C)$
5. $A' \cap (B \cup C')$
6. $C' \cap (A \cup B')$
7. $(A' \cap B) \cup (A' \cap C')$
8. $(C' \cap A) \cup (C' \cap B')$
9. $(A \cup B \cup C)'$
10. $(A \cap B \cap C)'$
11. $(A \cup B)' \cap C$
12. $(B \cup C)' \cap A$

In Exercises 13–24, let

$$U = \{a, b, c, d, e, f, g, h\}$$
$$A = \{a, g, h\}$$
$$B = \{b, g, h\}$$
$$C = \{b, c, d, e, f\}$$

Find each of the following sets.

13. $A \cup (B \cap C)$
14. $A \cap (B \cup C)$
15. $(A \cup B) \cap (A \cup C)$
16. $(A \cap B) \cup (A \cap C)$
17. $A' \cap (B \cup C')$
18. $C' \cap (A \cup B')$
19. $(A' \cap B) \cup (A' \cap C')$
20. $(C' \cap A) \cup (C' \cap B')$
21. $(A \cup B \cup C)'$
22. $(A \cap B \cap C)'$
23. $(A \cup B)' \cap C$
24. $(B \cup C)' \cap A$

In Exercises 25–32, use the Venn diagram shown to answer each question.

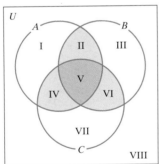

25. What regions represent set B?
26. What regions represent set C?
27. What regions represent $A \cup C$?
28. What regions represent $B \cup C$?
29. What regions represent $A \cap B$?
30. What regions represent $A \cap C$?
31. What regions represent B'?
32. What regions represent C'?

Use the Venn diagram shown to solve Exercises 33–40.

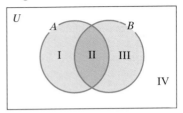

33. a. Which region is represented by $(A \cup B)'$?
    b. Which region is represented by $A' \cap B'$?
    c. Based on parts (a) and (b), what can you conclude?
34. a. Which regions are represented by $A \cup B$?
    b. Which regions are represented by $B \cup A$?
    c. Based on parts (a) and (b), what can you conclude?
35. a. Which region(s) is/are represented by $(A \cap B)'$?
    b. Which region(s) is/are represented by $A' \cap B'$?
    c. Based on parts (a) and (b), are $(A \cap B)'$ and $A' \cap B'$ equal for all sets A and B? Explain your answer.
36. a. Which region(s) is/are represented by $(A \cup B)'$?
    b. Which region(s) is/are represented by $A' \cup B'$?
    c. Based on parts (a) and (b), are $(A \cup B)'$ and $A' \cup B'$ equal for all sets A and B? Explain your answer.
37. a. Which region(s) is/are represented by $A' \cup B$?
    b. Which region(s) is/are represented by $A \cap B'$?
    c. Based on parts (a) and (b), are $A' \cup B$ and $A \cap B'$ equal for all sets A and B? Explain your answer.
38. a. Which region(s) is/are represented by $A' \cap B$?
    b. Which region(s) is/are represented by $A \cup B'$?
    c. Based on parts (a) and (b), are $A' \cap B$ and $A \cup B'$ equal for all sets A and B? Explain your answer.
39. Show that $(A' \cap B)' = A \cup B'$.
40. Show that $(A \cup B')' = A' \cap B$.

Use the Venn diagram shown to solve Exercises 41–46.

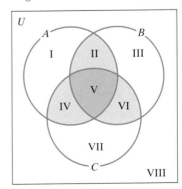

41. a. Which regions are represented by $A \cap (B \cup C)$?
    b. Which regions are represented by $(A \cap B) \cup (A \cap C)$?
    c. Based on parts (a) and (b), what can you conclude?

42. a. Which regions are represented by $(A \cup B) \cap C$?
    b. Which regions are represented by $(A \cap C) \cup (B \cap C)$?
    c. Based on parts (a) and (b), what can you conclude?
43. a. Which regions are represented by $A \cap (B \cup C)$?
    b. Which regions are represented by $A \cup (B \cap C)$?
    c. Based on parts (a) and (b), are $A \cap (B \cup C)$ and $A \cup (B \cap C)$ equal for all sets A, B, and C? Explain your answer.
44. a. Which regions are represented by $C \cup (B \cap A)$?
    b. Which regions are represented by $C \cap (B \cup A)$?
    c. Based on parts (a) and (b), are $C \cup (B \cap A)$ and $C \cap (B \cup A)$ equal for all sets A, B, and C? Explain your answer.
45. Show that $B \cup (A \cap C) = (A \cup B) \cap (B \cup C)$.
46. Show that $B \cap (A \cup C) = (A \cap B) \cup (B \cap C)$.

 Application Exercises

In Exercises 47–50, use the Venn diagram shown to indicate the region in which each company should be placed.

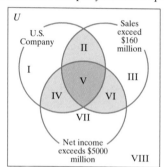

The Four Largest World Companies in the Dow Jones Index

Name	Country	Sales in millions	Net Income in millions
47. General Motors	United States	$178,174	$6698
48. Shell Group	United Kingdom	171,657	7753
49. Ford	United States	153,627	6920
50. Mitsui	Japan	134,157	253

Source: Dow Jones Global Indexes

 Writing in Mathematics

51. If you are given four sets, A, B, C, and U, describe what is involved in determining $(A \cup B)' \cap C$. Be as specific as possible in your description.
52. Describe how a Venn diagram can be used to visualize that $(A \cup B)'$ and $A' \cap B'$ are equal sets.

 Critical Thinking Exercises

The eight blood types discussed in the essay on page 62 are shown once again in the accompanying Venn diagram. In blood transfusions, the set of antigens in a donor's blood must be a subset of the set of antigens in a recipient's blood. Thus, the recipient must have all or more of the antigens present in the donor's blood. Use this information to solve Exercises 53–56.

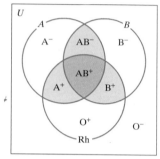

Human blood types

53. What is the blood type of a universal recipient?
54. What is the blood type of a universal donor?
55. Can an A^+ person donate blood to an A^- person?
56. Can an A^- person donate blood to an A^+ person?

 Technology Exercise

57. Using the Paint Program in Windows, create a single Venn diagram in three sets, A, B, and C, which has the following properties:
    a. The region corresponding to $A \cap B \cap C$ is colored black.
    b. The region corresponding to $A \cap B \cap C'$ is colored orange.
    c. The region corresponding to $A' \cap B \cap C$ is colored green.
    d. The region corresponding to $A \cap B' \cap C$ is colored purple.
    e. The region corresponding to $A \cap (B \cup C)'$ is colored red.
    f. The region corresponding to $B \cap (A \cup C)'$ is colored yellow.
    g. The region corresponding to $C \cap (A \cup B)'$ is colored blue.
    h. The region corresponding to $(A \cup B \cup C)'$ is colored gray.

 Group Exercise

58. Each group member should find out his or her blood type. (If you cannot obtain this information, select a blood type that you find appealing!) Read the introduction to Exercises 53–56. Referring to the Venn diagram for these exercises, each group member should determine all other group members to whom blood can be donated and from whom it can be received.

SECTION 2.5 *Surveys and Cardinal Numbers*

Objectives

1. Use Venn diagrams to visualize a survey's results.
2. Use the formula for $n(A \cup B)$.
3. Use survey results to complete Venn diagrams and answer questions about the survey.

In this section, we focus on using sets and Venn diagrams to tabulate information collected in surveys. In survey problems, it is helpful to remember that **and** means **intersection, or** means **union,** and **not** means **complement**.

In Section 2.1 we defined the cardinal number of set A, denoted by $n(A)$, as the number of elements in set A. Venn diagrams are helpful in determining a set's cardinality.

1	Use Venn diagrams to visualize a survey's results.

EXAMPLE 1   Using a Venn Diagram to Visualize the Results of a Survey

We return to the campus survey in which students were asked:

> Would you be willing to donate blood?
>
> Would you be willing to help serve a free breakfast to blood donors?

Set A represents the set of students willing to donate blood. Set B represents the set of students willing to help serve breakfast to donors. The survey results are summarized in Figure 2.12. Use the diagram to answer the following questions.

A: Set of students
    willing to donate
    blood
B: Set of students
    willing to serve
    breakfast to
    donors

Figure 2.12 Results of a survey

a. How many students are willing to donate blood?
b. How many students are willing to help serve a free breakfast to blood donors?
c. How many students are willing to both donate blood and serve breakfast?
d. How many students are willing to donate blood or serve breakfast?
e. How many students are willing to donate blood but not serve breakfast?
f. How many students are willing to serve breakfast but not donate blood?
g. How many students are neither willing to donate blood nor serve breakfast?
h. How many students were surveyed?

Solution

a. The number of students willing to donate blood can be determined by adding the numbers in regions I and II. Thus, $n(A) = 370 + 120 = 490$. There are 490 students willing to donate blood.

b. The number of students willing to help serve a free breakfast to blood donors can be determined by adding the numbers in regions II and III. Thus, $n(B) = 120 + 220 = 340$. There are 340 students willing to help serve breakfast.

c. The number of students willing to both donate blood and serve breakfast appears in region II, the region representing the intersection of the two sets. Thus, $n(A \cap B) = 120$. Therefore, 120 students are willing to both donate blood and serve breakfast.

d. The number of students willing to donate blood or serve breakfast is found by adding the numbers in regions I, II, and III, representing the union of the two sets. We see that $n(A \cup B) = 370 + 120 + 220 = 710$. Therefore, 710 students in the survey are willing to donate blood or serve breakfast.

e. The region representing students who are willing to donate blood but not serve breakfast is region I. We see that 370 of the students surveyed are willing to donate blood but not serve breakfast.

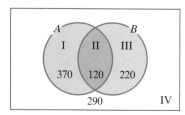

Figure 2.12 Survey results shown again so you do not have to turn back a page

f. Region III represents students willing to serve breakfast but not donate blood. We see that 220 students surveyed are willing to help serve breakfast but not donate blood.

g. Students who are neither willing to donate blood nor serve breakfast fall within the universal set, but outside circles A and B. These students fall in region IV, where the Venn diagram indicates that there are 290 elements. There are 290 students in the survey who are neither willing to donate blood nor serve breakfast.

h. We can find the number of students surveyed by adding the numbers in regions I, II, III, and IV. Thus, $n(U) = 370 + 120 + 220 + 290 = 1000$. Therefore, 1000 students were surveyed.

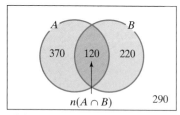

$n(A) = 370 + 120 = 490$
$n(B) = 220 + 120 = 340$
$n(A \cup B) = 370 + 120 + 220 = 710$

Figure 2.13

The Venn diagram for the survey in Example 1 is shown again in Figure 2.13. The diagram indicates that

$$n(A) = 490$$
$$n(B) = 340$$
$$n(A \cap B) = 120$$
$$\text{and } n(A \cup B) = 710.$$

Notice that

$$n(A \cup B) = n(A) + n(B) - n(A \cap B)$$

because

$$710 = 490 + 340 - 120.$$

This relationship is true for any two finite sets A and B.

2 Use the formula for $n(A \cup B)$.

Formula for the Cardinal Number of the Union of Two Sets

$$n(A \cup B) = n(A) + n(B) - n(A \cap B)$$

To find the cardinal number in the union of sets A and B, add the number of elements in sets A and B and then subtract the number of elements common to both sets.

We subtract $n(A \cap B)$ in the formula for $n(A \cup B)$ so that we do not count the number in the intersection twice, once for $n(A)$, and again for $n(B)$.

EXAMPLE 2 Using the Formula for the Cardinality of the Union of Two Sets

Set A contains 30 elements, set B contains 18 elements, and 6 elements are common to sets A and B. How many elements are in $A \cup B$?

Solution

$$n(A \cup B) = n(A) + n(B) - n(A \cap B)$$
$$= 30 + 18 - 6$$
$$= 42$$

There are 42 elements in $A \cup B$.

3 Use survey results to complete Venn diagrams and answer questions about the survey.

Venn diagrams are used to solve problems involving surveys. Here are the steps needed to solve survey problems.

Solving Survey Problems

1. Use the survey's description to define sets and draw a Venn diagram.
2. Use the survey's results to determine the cardinality for each region in the Venn diagram. Start with the intersection of the sets, the innermost region, and work outward.
3. Use the completed Venn diagram to answer the problem's questions.

EXAMPLE 3   Surveying People's Attitudes

In a Gallup poll, 2000 U.S. adults were selected at random and asked to agree or disagree with the following statement:

Job opportunities for women are not equal to those for men.

The results of the survey showed that

1190 people agreed with the statement.

700 women agreed with the statement.

Source: The People's Almanac

If half the people surveyed were women,

a. How many men agreed with the statement?

b. How many men disagreed with the statement?

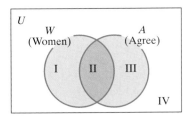

Given: $n(U) = 2000$
$n(W) = 1000$
$n(A) = 1190$
$n(W \cap A) = 700$

Figure 2.14 Our goal is to put numbers in regions I, II, III, and IV.

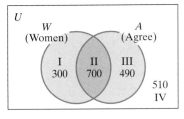

Figure 2.15

Solution   The Venn diagram in Figure 2.14 shows two sets. Set W (labeled "Women") is the set of women surveyed. Set A (labeled "Agree") is the set of people surveyed who agreed with the statement. The problem provides the following cardinalities:

There were 2000 people surveyed: $n(U) = 2000$.
Half the people surveyed were women: $n(W) = 1000$.
The number of people who agreed with the statement was 1190: $n(A) = 1190$.
There were 700 women who agreed with the statement: $n(W \cap A) = 700$.

We can tabulate this information on the Venn diagram in Figure 2.15. Begin with the region of intersection, region II. This region is the set of women who agreed with the statement, given to be 700. Because $n(W \cap A) = 700$, we write 700 in region II, shown in Figure 2.15. Set W contains 1000 women and consists of regions I and II. Therefore region I contains $1000 - 700$, or 300, women. We write the number 300 in region I. Set A consists of regions II and III, representing the set of people who agreed with the statement. We know that $n(A) = 1190$. With 700 people already in region II, this leaves $1190 - 700$, or 490, for region III.

The Venn diagram now shows that $n(W \cup A) = 300 + 700 + 490 = 1490$. The number of people in region IV is the difference between $n(U)$, the number of people surveyed, and $n(W \cup A)$. There are $2000 - 1490$, or 510, people in region IV.

a. The men who agreed with the statement are those members of the set of people who agreed who are not women, shown in region III. This means that 490 men surveyed agreed that job opportunities are unequal.

b. The men who disagreed with the statement can be found outside the circles of people who agreed and people who are women. This corresponds to region IV, whose cardinality is 510. Thus, 510 men surveyed disagreed that job opportunities are unequal.

Did you observe how we drew the Venn diagram in Example 3? By representing the women surveyed with circle W, we did not need a separate circle for the men. The group of people outside circle W must be the set of men. Similarly, by visualizing the set of people who agreed with the statement as circle A, we did not need a separate circle for those who disagreed. The group of people outside the A (agree) circle must be the set of people disagreeing with the statement.

EXAMPLE 4   Constructing a Venn Diagram

A Time/CNN poll sought to determine how Americans felt about reserving a certain number of college scholarships exclusively for minorities and women. Respondents were asked the following question:

> Do you agree or disagree with the following statement: Colleges should reserve a certain number of scholarships exclusively for minorities and women?

Source: Time 1999 Almanac

Construct a Venn diagram that allows the respondents to the poll to be identified by gender (man or woman), ethnicity (black or other), and whether or not they agreed with the statement. Then identify the following regions in the diagram:

a. Black men who agreed with the statement.

b. Women who agreed with the statement.

c. Women who are not black who disagreed with the statement.

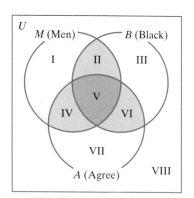

Figure 2.16

Solution   Based on our work in Example 3, we only need one circle to indicate the gender of the respondent. If we use the set M for men, the set of women respondents is M'. M' is represented by the region outside circle M. Similarly, if we use circle B for black respondents, the region outside this circle accounts for all other respondents. Finally, we'll use A for the circle of those who agreed with the statement. Those who disagreed lie outside this circle. A Venn diagram into which the results of the survey can be tabulated is shown in Figure 2.16.

a. The set of black men who agreed with the statement ($M \cap B \cap A$) is represented by region V.

b. The group of women who agreed with the statement is the set of people not found in set M (men) who are in set A (agree). Women who agreed with the statement, $M' \cap A$, are represented by regions VI and VII. Notice that region VI describes black women who agreed with the statement and region VII corresponds to the set of nonblack women who agreed with the statement.

c. Women who are not black are represented by regions VII and VIII. Region VIII corresponds to nonblack women who disagreed with the statement.

Exercise Set 2.5

 Practice Exercises

Use the accompanying Venn diagram that shows the number of elements in regions I through IV to answer the questions in Exercises 1–8.

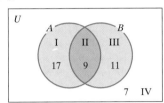

1. How many elements belong to set *A*?
2. How many elements belong to set *B*?
3. How many elements belong to set *A* but not set *B*?
4. How many elements belong to set *B* but not set *A*?
5. How many elements belong to set *A* or set *B*?
6. How many elements belong to set *A* and set *B*?
7. How many elements belong to neither set *A* nor set *B*?
8. How many elements are there in the universal set?

Use the formula for the cardinal number of the union of two sets to solve Exercises 9–12.

9. Set *A* contains 17 elements, set *B* contains 20 elements, and 6 elements are common to sets *A* and *B*. How many elements are in $A \cup B$?
10. Set *A* contains 30 elements, set *B* contains 18 elements, and 5 elements are common to sets *A* and *B*. How many elements are in $A \cup B$?
11. Set *A* contains 8 letters and 9 numbers. Set *B* contains 7 letters and 10 numbers. Four letters and 3 numbers are common to both sets *A* and *B*. Find the number of elements in set *A* or set *B*.
12. Set *A* contains 12 numbers and 18 letters. Set *B* contains 14 numbers and 10 letters. One number and 6 letters are common to both sets *A* and *B*. Find the number of elements in set *A* or set *B*.

 Application Exercises

13. A pollster conducting a telephone poll asked two questions:
    1. Do you currently smoke cigarettes?
    2. Regardless of your answer to question 1, would you support a total ban on smoking in restaurants?
    a. Construct a Venn diagram that allows the respondents to the poll to be identified by whether or not they smoke cigarettes and whether or not they support the total ban.
    b. Write the letter b in the region of the diagram that identifies smokers polled who support the total ban.

c. Write the letter c in the region of the diagram that identifies nonsmokers polled who support the ban.
d. Write the letter d in the region of the diagram that identifies nonsmokers polled who do not support the ban.

14. A pollster conducting a telephone poll at a college campus asked students two questions:
    1. Do you binge drink three or more times per month?
    2. Regardless of your answer to question 1, are you frequently behind in your school work?
    a. Construct a Venn diagram that allows the respondents to the poll to be identified by whether or not they binge drink and whether or not they frequently fall behind in school work.
    b. Write the letter b in the region of the diagram that identifies binge drinkers who are frequently behind in school work.
    c. Write the letter c in the region of the diagram that identifies students polled who do not binge drink but who are frequently behind in school work.
    d. Write the letter d in the region of the diagram that identifies students polled who do not binge drink and who do not frequently fall behind in their school work.

15. A pollster conducting a telephone poll asked three questions:
    1. Are you religious?
    2. Have you spent time with a person during his or her last days of a terminal illness?
    3. Should assisted suicide be an option for terminally ill people?
    a. Construct a Venn diagram with three circles that can assist the pollster in tabulating the responses to the three questions.
    b. Write the letter b in the region of the diagram that identifies all religious persons polled who are not in favor of assisted suicide for the terminally ill.
    c. Write the letter c in the region of the diagram that identifies the people polled who do not consider themselves religious, who have not spent time with a terminally ill person during his or her last days, and who are in favor of assisted suicide for the terminally ill.
    d. Write the letter d in the region of the diagram that corresponds to the people polled who consider themselves religious, have not spent time with a terminally ill person during his or her last days, and who are not in favor of assisted suicide for the terminally ill.
    e. Write the letter e in a region of the Venn diagram other than those in parts (b)–(d) and then describe who in the poll is represented by this region.

16. The following figures are from the American Medical Association.

> There are 720,325 physicians in the United States.
> 149,404 are women.
> 59,345 physicians have family practice as their specialty.
> 13,971 women physicians specialize in family practice.

a. Construct a Venn diagram in which U is the set of all U.S. physicians, W is the set of all women physicians in the United States, and F is the set of all U.S. physicians specializing in family practice. Fill in each of the four regions of the Venn diagram with the number of physicians who belong to that region.

Use your Venn diagram to answer each of the following questions.

b. How many physicians are there in the United States who are men specializing in family practice?

c. How many male physicians in the United States do not specialize in family practice?

17. The following figures, from January 1993 to December 1995, are from the U.S. Bureau of Labor Statistics.

> A total of 9,367,000 U.S. workers lost jobs in this period.
> 5,315,000 were men.
> 1,117,000 of the U.S. workers who lost jobs were under 25.
> 638,000 men under 25 lost jobs.

a. Construct a Venn diagram in which U is the set of U.S. workers who lost jobs in this period, M is the set of men who lost jobs, and T is the set of workers under 25 who lost jobs. Fill in each of the four regions of the Venn diagram with the number of U.S. workers who lost jobs who belong to that region.

Use your Venn diagram to answer each of the following questions.

b. How many female U.S. workers under 25 lost jobs in this period?

c. How many female U.S. workers 25 or older lost jobs in this period?

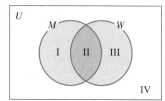

Writing in Mathematics

18. Suppose that you are drawing a Venn diagram to sort and tabulate the results of a survey. If results are being tabulated along gender lines, explain why only a circle representing women is needed, rather than two separate circles representing the women surveyed and the men surveyed.

19. Suppose that you decide to use two sets, M and W, to sort and tabulate the responses for men and women in a survey. Describe the set of people represented by regions II and IV in the Venn diagram shown. What conclusion can you draw?

Critical Thinking Exercises

20. Which one of the following is true?

a. In a survey, 110 students were taking mathematics, 90 were taking psychology, and 20 were taking neither. Thus, 220 students were surveyed.

b. If $A \cap B = \varnothing$, then $n(A \cup B) = n(A) + n(B)$.

c. When filling in cardinalities for regions in a two-set Venn diagram, the innermost region, the intersection of the two sets, should be the last region to be filled in.

d. $n(A')$ cannot be obtained by subtracting $n(A)$ from $n(U)$.

21. In a survey of 150 students, 90 were taking mathematics and 30 were taking psychology.

a. What is the least number of students who could have been taking both courses?

b. What is the greatest number of students who could have been taking both courses?

c. What is the greatest number of students who could have been taking neither course?

22. A person applying for the position of college registrar submitted the following report to the college president on 90 students: 31 take math; 28 take chemistry; 42 take psychology; 9 take math and chemistry; 10 take chemistry and psychology; 6 take math and psychology; 4 take all three subjects; and 20 take none of these courses. The applicant was not hired. Explain why.

Technology Exercises

23. Using the Paint Program in Windows, create a Venn diagram that represents the data given in Example 3 on page 67.

24. Using the Paint Program in Windows, create a Venn diagram that represents the situation given in Example 4 on page 68.

Group Exercise

25. This group activity is intended to provide practice in the use of Venn diagrams to sort responses to a survey. The group will determine the topic of the survey. Although you will not actually conduct the survey, it might be helpful to imagine carrying out the survey using the students on your campus.

a. In your group, decide on a topic for the survey.

b. Devise three questions that the pollster will ask to the people who are interviewed.

c. Construct a Venn diagram that will assist the pollster in sorting the answers to the three questions. The Venn diagram should contain three intersecting circles within a universal set and eight regions.

d. Describe what each of the regions in the Venn diagram represents in terms of the questions in your poll.

CHAPTER SUMMARY, REVIEW, AND TEST

SUMMARY

2.1 Sets and Their Designations

a. A set is a collection of objects. The objects in a set are called the elements, or members, of the set.

b. Sets can be designated by word descriptions, the roster method (a listing within braces, separating elements with commas), or set-builder notation:

Basic Concepts and Notations

a. The empty set, or the null set, represented by { } or $\varnothing$, is a set that contains no elements.

b. The symbol $\in$ means that an object is an element of a set. The symbol $\notin$ means that an object is not an element of a set.

c. The set of natural numbers is $\mathbf{N} = \{1, 2, 3, 4, 5, \ldots\}$.

d. The cardinal number of a set A, $n(A)$, is the number of elements in set A.

e. Set A is a finite set if $n(A) = 0$ or if $n(A)$ is a natural number. A set that is not finite is an infinite set.

f. Equal sets have exactly the same elements. Equivalent sets have the same number of elements.

2.2 The Universal Set and a Set's Complement

a. A universal set, symbolized by U, is a set that contains all the elements being considered in a given discussion or problem.

b. The complement of set A, symbolized by A', is the set of all elements in the universal set that are not in A.

Subsets

a. Set A is a subset of set B, expressed as $A \subseteq B$, if every element in set A is also in set B. The notation $A \nsubseteq B$ means that set A is not a subset of set B, so there is at least one element of set A that is not an element of set B.

b. Set A is a proper subset of set B, expressed as $A \subset B$, if A is a subset of B and $A \neq B$.

c. The empty set is a subset of every set.

d. A set with n elements has 2^n subsets and $2^n - 1$ proper subsets.

2.3 Venn Diagrams

No A are B.
A and B are disjoint.

All A are B.
$A \subset B$.

A and B are equal sets.

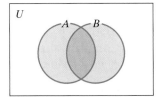

Some (at least one) A are B.

Set Operations

a. $A \cap B$ (A intersection B), read set A **and** set B, is the set of elements common to both set A and set B.

b. $A \cup B$ (A union B), read set A **or** set B, is the set of elements that are members of set A or of set B or of both sets.

c. A' (the complement of set A), read **not** A, is the set of all elements in the universal set that are not in A.

De Morgan's Laws

$$(A \cap B)' = A' \cup B' \quad \text{and} \quad (A \cup B)' = A' \cap B'$$

2.4 Set Operations and Venn Diagrams with Three Sets

a. When using set operations involving three sets, begin by finding the set within parentheses.

b. A Venn diagram with three sets is given in Figure 2.8 on page 60.

c. If two sets represent the same regions of a Venn diagram, then they are equal.

2.5 Surveys and Cardinal Numbers

a. Cardinal Number of the Union of Two Sets

$$n(A \cup B) = n(A) + n(B) - n(A \cap B)$$

b. Survey problems can be solved using the three steps in the box on page 67.

REVIEW EXERCISES

2.1

1. Write a description of the set $\{1, 2, 3, \ldots, 10\}$.
2. Express the set of the days of the week that begin with the letter T using the roster method.

In Exercises 3–4, fill in the blank with either $\in$ or $\notin$ to make each statement true.

3. 93 ____ $\{1, 2, 3, 4, \ldots, 99, 100\}$
4. $\{d\}$ ____ $\{a, b, c, d, e\}$

Find the cardinal number for each set in Exercises 5–6.

5. $\{x \mid x$ is a month of the year$\}$
6. $\{18, 19, 20, \ldots, 31, 32\}$

In Exercises 7–8, fill in the blank with either $=$ or $\neq$ to make each statement true.

7. $\{0, 2, 4, 6, 8\}$ ____ $\{8, 2, 6, 4\}$
8. $\{x \mid x$ is a natural number greater than 7$\}$ ____ $\{8, 9, 10, \ldots, 100\}$

In Exercises 9–10, determine if the pairs of sets are equal, equivalent, both, or neither.

9. $A = \{x \mid x$ is a lowercase letter that comes before f in the English alphabet$\}$
   $B = \{2, 4, 6, 8, 10\}$
10. $A = \{x \mid x$ is a natural number between 3 and 7$\}$
    $B = \{4, 5, 6\}$

2.2

11. Let $U = \{1, 2, 3, 4, 5, 6, 7, 8, 9\}$ and $A = \{3, 4, 5, 6, 7\}$. Find A' and place the elements 1 through 9 in the proper region of the Venn diagram shown.

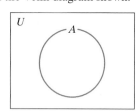

12. If U is the set of the months of the year and A is the set of months that contain exactly 30 days, use the roster method to represent A'.

In Exercises 13–15, write $\subseteq$ or $\nsubseteq$ in each blank so that the resulting statement is true.

13. $\{$penny, nickel, dime$\}$ ____ $\{$half-dollar, quarter, dime, nickel, penny$\}$
14. $\{-1, 0, 1\}$ ____ $\{-3, -2, -1, 1, 2, 3\}$
15. $\varnothing$ ____ $\{x \mid x$ is an odd natural number$\}$

In Exercises 16–17, write $\subseteq$, $\subset$, or both to make the statement true.

16. $\{1, 2\}$ ____ $\{1, 1, 2, 2\}$
17. $\{x \mid x$ is a person who is Baptist$\}$ ____ $\{x \mid x$ is a person who belongs to an organized religion$\}$

Determine whether each statement in Exercises 18–21 is true or false. If the statement is false, explain why.

18. Texas $\in \{$Oklahoma, Louisiana, Georgia, South Carolina$\}$
19. $4 \subseteq \{2, 4, 6, 8, 10, 12\}$
20. $\{e, f, g\} \subset \{d, e, f, g, h, i\}$
21. $\{\ominus, \varnothing\} \subset \{\varnothing, \ominus\}$
22. List all subsets for the set $\{1, 5\}$. Which one of these subsets is not a proper subset?

Find the number of subsets and the number of proper subsets for each of the sets in Exercises 23–24.

23. $\{2, 4, 6, 8, 10\}$
24. $\{x \mid x$ is a month that begins with the letter J$\}$

2.3

In Exercises 25–29, let $U = \{1, 2, 3, 4, 5, 6, 7, 8\}$, $A = \{1, 2, 3, 4\}$, and $B = \{1, 2, 4, 5\}$. Find each of the following sets.

25. $A \cap B$ 26. $A \cup B'$ 27. $A' \cap B$
28. $(A \cup B)'$ 29. $A' \cap B'$

In Exercises 30–37, use the Venn diagram to list the elements of each set in roster form.

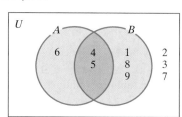

30. A 31. B' 32. $A \cup B$ 33. $A \cap B$
34. $(A \cap B)'$ 35. $(A \cup B)'$ 36. $A \cap B'$ 37. U

2.4

In Exercises 38–39, let

$$U = \{1, 2, 3, 4, 5, 6, 7, 8\}$$
$$A = \{1, 2, 3, 4\}$$
$$B = \{1, 2, 4, 5\}$$
$$C = \{1, 5\}$$

Find each of the following sets.

38. $A \cup (B \cap C)$ 39. $(A \cap C)' \cup B$
40. Use a Venn diagram with two intersecting circles to show that $(A \cup B)' = A' \cap B'$.
41. Use a Venn diagram with thee intersecting circles to determine whether the following statement is true.

$$A \cap (B \cup C) = A \cup (B \cap C)$$

2.5

42. Set A contains 25 elements, set B contains 17 elements, and 9 elements are common to sets A and B. How many elements are in $A \cup B$?

43. The results of a survey of 1000 college students were as follows:

   650 received the news through television.
   550 received the news through newspapers.
   400 received the news through both television and newspapers.

   a. Construct a Venn diagram with two circles, one for each way of receiving the news. Fill in the number for each of the four regions in the diagram.
   b. How many students received the news through television or newspapers?
   c. How many students received the news through television only?
   d. How many students did not receive the news from either source mentioned in the survey?

44. A pollster conducting a telephone survey of college students asked two questions:

   1. Are you a registered Republican?
   2. Are you in favor of the death penalty?

   a. Construct a Venn diagram with two circles that can assist the pollster in tabulating the responses to the two questions.
   b. Write the letter b in the region of the diagram that corresponds to students polled who are registered Republicans who are not in favor of the death penalty.

CHAPTER 2 TEST

1. Express the following set using the roster method:
   $\{x \mid x$ is a natural number that lies between 17 and 26$\}$.
2. Find the cardinal number for the following set:
   $$\{23, 25, 27, 29, \ldots, 45\}.$$

Determine whether each statement in Exercises 3–10 is true or false. If the statement is false, explain why.

3. $\{6\} \in \{1, 2, 3, 4, 5, 6, 7\}$
4. If $A = \{x \mid x$ is a day of the week$\}$ and $B = \{2, 4, 6, \ldots, 14\}$, then sets A and B are equivalent.
5. $\{2, 4, 6, 8\} = \{8, 8, 6, 6, 4, 4, 2\}$
6. $\{d, e, f, g\} \subseteq \{a, b, c, d, e, f\}$
7. $\{3, 4, 5\} \subset \{x \mid x$ is a natural number less than 6$\}$
8. $14 \notin \{1, 2, 3, 4, \ldots, 39, 40\}$
9. $\{a, b, c, d, e\}$ has 25 subsets.
10. The empty set is a proper subset of any set, including itself.
11. List all subsets for the set $\{6, 9\}$. Which of these subsets is not a proper subset?

In Exercises 12–15, let
$$U = \{a, b, c, d, e, f, g\}$$
$$A = \{a, b, c, d\}$$
$$B = \{c, d, e, f\}$$
$$C = \{a, e, g\}$$

Find each of the following sets.

12. $A \cup B$ 13. $(B \cap C)'$ 14. $A \cap C'$ 15. $(A \cup B) \cap C$

c. Write the letter c in the region of the diagram that corresponds to students polled who are not registered Republicans who are in favor of the death penalty.

Group Exercise

45. We now return to the campus blood drive problem and the survey questions:

   Would you be willing to donate blood?
   Would you volunteer to distribute a free breakfast to student donors?
   Would you be willing to take part in both activities?

   You have learned how to sort the information obtained by these questions using a Venn diagram. However, there are still unresolved issues. Where will the free breakfast be served? Could this site be used for the blood drive itself?

   a. Group members should devise three questions that can be asked to to help settle unresolved issues related to the blood drive.
   b. Group members should construct a Venn diagram that will assist the pollster in sorting the answers to these questions.

16. Which region or regions in the Venn diagram shown represent(s) $(A \cup B) \cap (A \cup C)$?

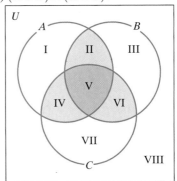

17. In a survey, 150 college students were asked if they owned a car, a computer, or both. The results showed that

   63 owned a car.
   84 owned a computer.
   27 owned both.

   a. Construct a Venn diagram with two circles, one for students owning a car, and one for students owning a computer. Fill in the number for each of the four regions in the diagram.
   b. How many students owned none of the items mentioned in the survey?
   c. How many students owned a computer only?
   d. How many students owned a car only?
   e. How many students owned a car or a computer?

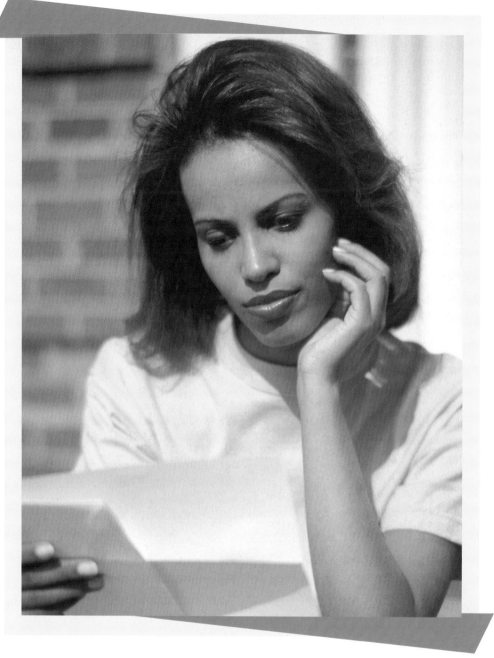

You are sorting through your mail and notice an envelope with this claim: If you follow the instructions inside and you return the winning number, then you win $7 million! Are you about to become a very wealthy person or should you tear up the envelope?

3 Logic

L
ogic, the science of correct reasoning, enables us to analyze given information, like that in the claim about winning $7 million, and arrive at truly inescapable conclusions. In all disciplines, the ability to reason abstractly in solving problems is an important tool. We need to be able to understand the writing and speech of reasonable people to analyze information objectively and to avoid arriving at conclusions that are untrue.

In this chapter, you will analyze information through the study of symbolic logic. In symbolic logic, letters and symbols represent English sentences and their relationships to one another. This new language will enable you to think more clearly, providing you with an important tool for living a more thoughtful life.

SECTION 3.1   *Statements, Negations, and Quantified Statements*

Objectives

1. Identify English sentences that are statements.
2. Express statements using symbols.
3. Form the negation of a statement.
4. Express negations using symbols.
5. Translate a negation represented by symbols into English.
6. Express quantified statements in two ways.
7. Write negations of quantified statements.

1   Identify English sentences that are statements.

2   Express statements using symbols.

3   Form the negation of a statement.

Statements and Using Symbols to Represent Statements

In everyday English, we use many different kinds of sentences. Some of these sentences are clearly true or false. Others are opinions, questions, and exclamations such as *Help!* or *Fire!* However, in logic we are concerned solely with statements, and not all English sentences are statements.

> **Definition of a Statement**
>
> A **statement** is a sentence that is either true or false, but not both simultaneously.

Here are two examples of statements.

1. London is the capital of England.
2. William Shakespeare wrote the last episode of "Seinfeld."

Statement 1 is true and statement 2 is false. Shakespeare had nothing to do with "Seinfeld" (perhaps writer's block after *Macbeth*).

We do not need to know whether a given sentence is true or false to determine whether it is a statement. For example, the sentence

> 123,456,787,654,321 is 11,111,111 multiplied by itself

is a statement. Actually, the statement is true. The sentence

> 123,456,787,654,321 is 22,222,222 multiplied by itself

is also a statement, but this statement is false.

Some sentences, such as commands, questions, and certain opinions are not statements because they cannot be labeled as true or false. The following sentences are not statements.

1. Read pages 23–57.
2. Is there order within chaos?
3. *Titanic* is the greatest movie of all time.

In symbolic logic, we use lowercase letters such as p, q, r, and s to represent statements. Here are two examples.

> p: London is the capital of England.
> q: William Shakespeare wrote the last episode of "Seinfeld."

The letter p represents the first statement.
The letter q represents the second statement.

Negating Statements

The sentence "London is the capital of England" is a true statement. The **negation** of this statement, "London is not the capital of England," is a false statement. The negation of a statement has a meaning that is opposite that of the original meaning. Thus, the negation of a true statement is a false statement, and the negation of a false statement is a true statement.

Technology

This chapter introduces many symbols that may be unfamiliar to you. They can be found in the character map of any of the recent word processors. Usually, you can find this character map by first selecting the "Insert" option, and then either "Symbol" or "Character." You will find literally thousands of symbols to choose from. The symbols are categorized in sets; look for a set labeled "Mathematical Operators." However, it may take a bit of searching to find the symbols you want. You may even have to change fonts.

4 Express negations using symbols.

Not written by Shakespeare!

5 Translate a negation represented by symbols into English.

EXAMPLE 1   Forming Negations

Form the negation of each statement.

a. Shakespeare wrote the last episode of "Seinfeld."
b. Today is not Monday.

Solution

a. The most common way to negate this statement is to introduce *not* into the sentence. The negation is:

Shakespeare did not write the last episode of "Seinfeld."

The English language provides many ways of expressing a statement's meaning. Here is another way to express the negation:

It is not true that Shakespeare wrote the last episode of "Seinfeld."

b. The negation of "Today is not Monday" is:

It is not true that today is not Monday.

This sentence is more naturally expressed in English as:

Today is Monday.

The negation of statement p is expressed by writing $\sim p$. We read this as "not p" or "It is not true that p."

EXAMPLE 2   Expressing Negations Symbolically

Let p and q represent the following statements:

p: Shakespeare wrote the last episode of "Seinfeld."
q: Today is not Monday.

Express each of the following statements symbolically.

a. Shakespeare did not write the last episode of "Seinfeld."
b. Today is Monday.

Solution

a. This statement is the negation of statement p.
Therefore, it is expressed symbolically as $\sim p$.
b. This statement is the negation of statement q.
Therefore, it is expressed symbolically as $\sim q$.

In Example 2, we translated English statements into symbolic statements. In Example 3, we reverse the direction of our translation.

EXAMPLE 3   Translating a Symbolic Statement into Words

Let p represent the following statement:

p: Harvard is a college.

Express the symbolic statement $\sim p$ in words.

Solution The symbol ~ is translated as "not." Therefore ~ *p* represents

Harvard is not a college.

This can also be expressed as:

It is not true that Harvard is a college.

6 Express quantified statements in two ways.

Quantified Statements

In English, we frequently encounter statements containing the words **all**, **some**, and **no** (or **none**). These words are called **quantifiers**. A statement that contains one of these words is a **quantified statement**. Here are some examples:

All poets are writers.
Some people are bigots.
No math books have pictures.
Some students do not work hard.

Using our knowledge of the English language, we can express each of the quantified statements above in two equivalent ways, that is, in two ways that both have exactly the same meaning. These equivalent statements are shown in Table 3.1.

Table 3.1 Equivalent Ways of Expressing Quantified Statements

Statement	An Equivalent Way to Express the Statement	Example (Two Equivalent Quantified Statements)
All *A* are *B*.	There are no *A* that are not *B*.	All poets are writers. There are no poets that are not writers.
Some *A* are *B*.	There exists at least one *A* that is a *B*.	Some people are bigots. At least one person is a bigot.
No *A* are *B*.	All *A* are not *B*.	No math books have pictures. All math books do not have pictures.
Some *A* are not *B*.	Not all *A* are *B*.	Some students do not work hard. Not all students work hard.

7 Write negations of quantified statements.

Forming the negation of a quantified statement can be a bit tricky. Keep in mind that if a statement is false, its negation must be true, and vice versa. This means that the negation of

All writers are poets

cannot be

No writers are poets,

because both statements are false. However, the negation of

All writers are poets

is

Not all writers are poets.

The last entry in Table 3.1 indicates that we can express this negation as:

Some writers are not poets.

In short, the negation of

All writers are poets

is

Some writers are not poets.

This observation works in both directions. Thus, the negation of "some writers are not poets" is "all writers are poets."

In general, the negation of "all are" is "some are not." Likewise, the negation of "some are not" is "all are."

Now let's try negating a "some" statement such as:

Some canaries weigh 50 pounds.

Equivalently,

There is at least one canary that weighs 50 pounds.

The negation is:

It is not true that there is at least one canary that weighs 50 pounds.

Because it is not true that there is even one such critter, we can conclude that

No canary weighs 50 pounds.

In short, the negation of

Some canaries weigh 50 pounds

Not quite 50 pounds!

is

No canary weighs 50 pounds.

In general, the negation of "some A are B" is "no A are B." Likewise, the negation of "no A are B" is "some A are B."

Negations of quantified statements are summarized in Table 3.2.

Table 3.2   Negations of Quantified Statements

Statement	Negation	Example (A Quantified Statement and Its Negation)
All A are B.	Some A are not B.	All people take exams honestly. The negation is: Some people do not take exams honestly.
Some A are B.	No A are B.	Some roads are open. The negation is: No roads are open.

(The negations of the statements in the second column are the statements in the first column.)

Study Tip

This diagram should help you remember the negations for quantified statements. The statements diagonally opposite each other are negations.

All *A* are *B.*   No *A* are *B.*

Some *A* are *B.*   Some *A* are not *B.*

EXAMPLE 4   Negating a Quantified Statement

The mechanic told me, "All piston rings were replaced." I later learned that the mechanic never tells the truth. What can I conclude?

Solution   Let's begin with the mechanic's statement:

All piston rings were replaced.

Because the mechanic never tells the truth, I can conclude that the truth is the negation of what I was told. The negation of "All *A* are *B*" is "Some *A* are not *B.*" Thus, I can conclude that:

Some piston rings were not replaced.

Because "some" means "at least one," I can also correctly conclude that:

At least one piston ring was not replaced.

Logic and "Star Trek"

Four *Enterprise* officers (clockwise from lower left); Kirk, McCoy, Uhura, Spock.

In the television series "Star Trek," the crew of the *Enterprise* is held captive by an evil computer. The crew escapes after one of them tells the computer, "I am lying to you." If he says that he is lying and he *is* lying, then he isn't lying. But consider this: If he says that he is lying and he *isn't* lying, then he is lying. The sentence "I am lying to you" is not a statement because it is true and false simultaneously. Thinking about this sentence destroys the computer.

Exercise Set 3.1

 Practice Exercises

In Exercises 1–12, determine whether or not each sentence is a statement.

1. Manhattan Island from end to end is less than 1 million inches long.
2. There are 2,500,000 rivets in the Eiffel Tower.
3. $9 + 6 = 16$
4. $9 \times 6 = 64$
5. What's a nice person like you doing in a place like this?
6. Was Andrew Johnson impeached?
7. Give me a break.
8. Take a long walk on a short pier.
9. Bill Clinton won the 1996 presidential election.
10. Richard Nixon won the 1992 presidential election.
11. No U.S. presidents were assassinated.
12. Some women have served as U.S. presidents.

In Exercises 13–16, form the negation of each statement.

13. It is raining.
14. It is snowing.
15. *Macbeth* is not a comedy show on television.
16. Albert Einstein was not offered the presidency of Israel.

In Exercises 17–20, let p, q, r, and s represent the following statements:

    p: One works hard.
    q: One succeeds.
    r: The temperature outside is not freezing.
    s: It is not true that the heater is working.

Express each of the following statements symbolically.

17. One does not work hard.
18. One does not succeed.
19. The temperature outside is freezing.
20. The heater is working.

In Exercises 21–24, let p, q, r, and s represent the following statements:

> *p: "I Love Lucy" is a Broadway musical.*
> *q: Mark McGwire is a U.S. president.*
> *r: Benjamin Franklin did not invent the rocking chair.*
> *s: Bill Clinton was not impeached.*

Express each of the following symbolic statements in words.
21. ~p   22. ~q   23. ~r   24. ~s

In Exercises 25–28, let p, q, r, and s represent the following statements:

> *p: The United States is the country with the most Internet users.*
> *q: New Jersey is a planet.*
> *r: It is not true that Michael is the most common of boys' names.*
> *s: The final exam was not easy.*

Express each of the following symbolic statements in words.
25. ~p   26. ~q   27. ~r   28. ~s

Exercises 29–36 contain quantified statements. For each exercise:

   a. *Express the quantified statement in an equivalent way, that is, in a way that has exactly the same meaning.*
   b. *Write the negation of the quantified statement. (The negation should begin with "all," "some," or "no.")*

29. All whales are mammals.
30. All journalists are writers.
31. Some students are business majors.
32. Some movies are comedies.
33. Some thieves are not criminals.
34. Some pianists are not keyboard players.
35. No Democratic presidents have been impeached.
36. No women have served as Supreme Court justices.

 Application Exercises

37. The City Council of a large northern metropolis promised its citizens that in the event of snow, all major roads connecting the city to its airport would remain open. The City Council did not keep its promise during the first blizzard of the season. Therefore, during the first blizzard:
   a. No major roads connecting the city to the airport were open.
   b. At least one major road connecting the city to the airport was not open.
   c. At least one major road connecting the city to the airport was open.
   d. The airport was forced to close.

38. During the Watergate scandal in 1974, President Richard Nixon assured the American people that "In all my years of public service, I have never obstructed justice." Later, events indicated that the president was not telling the truth. Therefore, in his years of public service:
   a. Nixon always obstructed justice.
   b. Nixon sometimes did not obstruct justice.
   c. Nixon sometimes obstructed justice.
   d. Nixon never obstructed justice.

 Writing in Mathematics

39. What is a statement? Explain why commands, questions, and opinions are not statements.
40. Explain how to form the negation of a given English statement. Give an example.
41. Describe how the negation of statement p is expressed using symbols.
42. List the words identified as quantifiers. Give an example of a statement that uses each of these quantifiers.
43. Explain how to write the negation of a quantified statement in the form "All A are B." Give an example.
44. Explain how to write the negation of a quantified statement in the form "Some A are B." Give an example.
45. If the ancient Greek god Zeus could do anything, could he create a rock so huge that he could not move it? Explain your answer.

 Technology Exercise

46. The symbol ~ can usually be found on your computer's keyboard. You can also find it in your word processor's character map. Let p represent a given statement. Using the symbol in the character map, indicate the notation for the negation of p. (There will be more activities like this one as more symbols are introduced.)

 Critical Thinking Exercises

47. Make up an example of a sentence that is not a statement because it is true and false simultaneously.
48. Give an example in which the statement "Some A are not B" is true, but the statement "Some B are not A" is false.
49. The statement
    > She isn't dating him because he is muscular
    is confusing because it can mean two different things. Describe the two different meanings that make this statement ambiguous.

SECTION 3.2 Compound Statements and Connectives

Objectives

1. Express compound statements in symbolic form.

2. Express symbolic statements with parentheses in English.

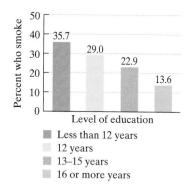

Percent who smoke
50
40 — 35.7
30 | 29.0
20 | | 22.9
10 | | | 13.6
0

Level of education

■ Less than 12 years
☐ 12 years
■ 13–15 years
■ 16 or more years

Figure 3.1 Percent of people who smoke, by level of education
Source: Centers for Disease Control and Prevention

You are reading an article about the percent of people in the United States who smoke, by level of education. Using the graph shown in Figure 3.1, the article concludes:

> The percent of people who smoke decreases as level of education increases and less than 14% of college graduates smoke.

We can break this conclusion down into two sentences:

> The percent of people who smoke decreases as level of education increases.
> Less than 14% of college graduates smoke.

These statements are called **simple statements** because each one conveys one idea with no connecting words. Statements formed by combining two or more simple statements are called **compound statements**. Words called **connectives** are used to join simple statements to form a compound statement. Connectives include words such as **and, or, if … then**, and **if and only if**.

Compound statements appear throughout written and spoken language. We need to be able to understand the logic of such statements to analyze information objectively. In this section, we analyze four kinds of compound statements.

And Statements

If p and q represent two simple statements, then the compound statement "p and q" is symbolized by $p \wedge q$. The compound statement formed by connecting statements with the word **and** is called a **conjunction**. The symbol for *and* is $\wedge$.

EXAMPLE 1 Translating from English to Symbolic Form

1 Express English compound statements in symbolic form.

Let p and q represent the following simple statements:

p: Harvard is a college.
q: Disney World is a college.

Write each of the compound statements below in its symbolic form.

a. Harvard is a college and Disney World is a college.
b. Harvard is a college and Disney World is not a college.

Solution

a.

The symbolic form is $p \wedge q$.

b.

The symbolic form is $p \wedge {\sim}q$.

In English, the connective *and* can also be expressed using *but* or *although*. Here are some examples:

Harvard is a college and Disney World is not.
Harvard is a college, but Disney World is not.
Harvard is a college, although Disney World is not.

Each of these statements is symbolized as $p \wedge \sim q$.

Or Statements

The connective *or* can mean two different things. For example, consider this statement:

I visited London or Paris.

The statement can mean

I visited London or Paris, but not both.

This is an example of the **exclusive or**, which means "one or the other, but not both." By contrast, the statement can mean

I visited London or Paris or both.

This is an example of the **inclusive or**, which means "either or both."

In this chapter and in mathematics in general, when the connective *or* appears, it means the *inclusive or*. If p and q represent two simple statements, then the compound statement "p or q" means p or q or both. The compound statement formed by connecting statements with the word *or* is called a **disjunction**. The symbol for *or* is $\vee$. Thus, we can symbolize the compound statement "p or q or both" by $p \vee q$.

EXAMPLE 2   Translating from English to Symbolic Form

Let p and q represent the following simple statements:

p: The bill receives majority approval.
q: The bill becomes a law.

Write each of the compound statements below in its symbolic form.

a. The bill receives majority approval or the bill becomes a law.
b. The bill receives majority approval or the bill does not become a law.

Solution

a.

The bill receives majority approval	or	the bill becomes a law.
p	$\vee$	q

The symbolic form is $p \vee q$.

b.

The bill receives majority approval	or	the bill does not become a law.
p	$\vee$	$\sim q$

The symbolic form is $p \vee \sim q$.

Figure 3.2 All poets are writers.

If–Then Statements

The diagram in Figure 3.2 shows that:

> All poets are writers.

In Section 3.1, we saw that this can be expressed as:

> There are no poets that are not writers.

Another way of expressing this statement is:

> If a person is a poet, then that person is a writer.

The form of this statement is "If p, then q." The compound statement "If p, then q" is symbolized by $p \rightarrow q$. The compound statement formed by connecting statements with "if–then" is called a **conditional statement**. The symbol for "if–then" is $\rightarrow$.

EXAMPLE 3   Translating from English to Symbolic Form

Let p and q represent the following simple statements:

> p: Ed is a poet.
> q: Ed is a writer.

Write each of the compound statements below in its symbolic form.

a. If Ed is a poet, then Ed is a writer.
b. If Ed is a writer, then Ed is a poet.
c. If Ed is not a writer, then Ed is not a poet.

Solution

a.

The symbolic form is $p \rightarrow q$.

b.

The symbolic form is $q \rightarrow p$.

c.

The symbolic form is $\sim q \rightarrow \sim p$.

Conditional statements in English often omit the word "then" and simply use a comma. When "then" is included, the comma can be included or omitted. Here are some examples:

If Ed is a poet, then he is a writer.

If Ed is a poet then he is a writer.

If Ed is a poet, he is a writer.

If And Only If Statements

Consider the conditional statement:

If you're in Tokyo, then you're in Japan.

This statement is true; Tokyo is the capital of Japan. Now think about this statement:

If you're in Japan, then you're in Tokyo.

This statement is not necessarily true. For example, a person visiting another large city in Japan, such as Osaka, is certainly in Japan. However, this person is not in Tokyo. If a conditional statement is true, changing the order of its simple statements may result in a statement that is no longer true.

However, some conditional statements are true regardless of which simple statement comes first. Let's consider an example.

Let p be: A number is greater than zero.

Let q be: A number is positive.

Notice that both of the following conditionals are true.

$p \rightarrow q$: If a number is greater than zero, then it is positive.

$q \rightarrow p$: If a number is positive, then it is greater than zero.

Rather than deal with two separate conditionals, we can combine them into one **biconditional statement**:

A number is greater than zero if and only if a number is positive.

The biconditional is symbolized by $\leftrightarrow$ and is read "if and only if." The phrase "if and only if" can be abbreviated as "iff."

EXAMPLE 4   Translating from English to Symbolic Form

Let p and q represent the following simple statements:

p: The word is *set*.

q: The word has 464 meanings.

Write each of the compound statements below in its symbolic form.

a. The word is *set* if and only if the word has 464 meanings.

b. The word does not have 464 meanings if and only if the word is not *set*.

Solution

a.

The word is set	if and only if	the word has 464 meanings.
p	$\leftrightarrow$	q

The symbolic form is $p \leftrightarrow q$. Observe that each of the following statements is true:

Words with the Most Meanings in the *Oxford English Dictionary*

Word	Meanings
Set	464
Run	396
Go	368
Take	343
Stand	334

Source: *The Top 10 of Everything*, 1999, Russell Ash, DK Publishing, Inc.

If the word is *set*, then it has 464 meanings.
If the word has 464 meanings, then it is *set*.

b.

The word does not have 464 meanings	if and only if	the word is not set.
$\sim q$	$\leftrightarrow$	$\sim p$

The symbolic form is $\sim q \leftrightarrow \sim p$.

Table 3.3 summarizes the statements discussed in the first two sections of this chapter.

Table 3.3   Statements of Symbolic Logic

Name	Symbolic Form	Read
Negation	$\sim p$	Not p.
Conjunction	$p \wedge q$	p and q.
Disjunction	$p \vee q$	p or q.
Conditional	$p \rightarrow q$	If p, then q.
Biconditional	$p \leftrightarrow q$	p if and only if q.

2 Express symbolic statements with parentheses in English.

Symbolic Statements with Parentheses

Consider the following statements:

It is not true that Tony and Maria like each other.

and

Tony does not like Maria, but Maria likes Tony.

These statements do not mean the same thing. We can express each statement in symbolic form by letting p and q represent the following simple statements:

p: Tony likes Maria.
q: Maria likes Tony.

Using these representations, $p \wedge q$ translates as:

Tony likes Maria and Maria likes Tony.

This means that:

Tony and Maria like each other.

Parentheses in symbolic statements indicate which statements are to be grouped together. Thus, $\sim(p \wedge q)$ means the negation of the entire statement $p \wedge q$. Because $p \wedge q$ represents:

Tony and Maria like each other.

then $\sim(p \wedge q)$ means that:

It is not true that Tony and Maria like each other.

Now, consider this statement:

Tony does not like Maria, but Maria likes Tony.

This means that

> Tony does not like Maria   and   Maria likes Tony.
>
> ~p   ∧   q

The symbolic form is $\sim p \wedge q$. Only statement p is negated.

In general, $\sim(p \wedge q)$ means the negation of the entire statement $p \wedge q$. By contrast, $\sim p \wedge q$ means that only statement p is negated. We read $\sim(p \wedge q)$ as "it is not true that p and q." We read $\sim p \wedge q$ as "not p and q." Unless parentheses appear in a symbolic statement, the symbol $\sim$ negates only the statement that immediately follows it.

EXAMPLE 5   Expressing Symbolic Statements with and without Parentheses in English

Let p and q represent the following simple statements:

p: Mark McGwire is a baseball player.
q: Mark McGwire is a basketball player.

Write each of the following symbolic statements in words:

a. $\sim(p \wedge q)$ b. $\sim p \wedge q$ c. $\sim(p \vee q)$

Solution

In 1998, Mark McGwire, first baseman for the St. Louis Cardinals, hit 70 home runs in a single season, breaking Roger Maris's home-run record of 61 from 1961.

a. A translation of $\sim(p \wedge q)$ is:

   It is not true that Mark McGwire is a baseball player and a basketball player.

   We can also express this statement as:

   It is not true that Mark McGwire is both a baseball player and a basketball player.

b. A translation of $\sim p \wedge q$ is:

   Mark McGwire is not a baseball player and he is a basketball player.

c. The symbolic statement $\sim(p \vee q)$ means the negation of the entire statement $p \vee q$.

   A translation of $p \vee q$ is:

   Mark McGwire is a baseball player or a basketball player.

   A translation of $\sim(p \vee q)$ is:

   It is not true that Mark McGwire is a baseball player or a basketball player.

   We can express this statement as:

   Mark McGwire is neither a baseball player nor a basketball player.

Because parentheses in symbolic statements tell us which statements are to be grouped together, the symbolic statements

$$(q \wedge \sim p) \rightarrow \sim r$$

and

$$q \wedge (\sim p \rightarrow \sim r)$$

do not mean the same thing. Here is a table that explains the difference between these statements.

Statement	Statements to Group Together	Translation
$(q \wedge \sim p) \rightarrow \sim r$	$q \wedge \sim p$	If q and not p, then not r.
$q \wedge (\sim p \rightarrow \sim r)$	$\sim p \rightarrow \sim r$	q, and if not p then not r.

The statement in the first row is an "if–then" conditional statement. Notice that the symbol $\rightarrow$ is outside the parentheses. By contrast, the statement in the second row is an "and" conjunction. In this case, the symbol $\wedge$ is outside the parentheses.

EXAMPLE 6   Expressing Symbolic Statements with Parentheses in English

Let $p, q,$ and r represent the following simple statements:

p: A student misses lecture.
q: A student studies.
r: A student fails.

Write each of the symbolic statements below in words:

a. $(q \wedge \sim p) \rightarrow \sim r$ b. $q \wedge (\sim p \rightarrow \sim r)$

Solution

a. $(q \quad \wedge \quad \sim p) \quad \rightarrow \quad \sim r$

If   A student studies   and   A student does not miss lecture , then   A student does not fail.

One possible English translation for the symbolic statement is:

If a student studies and does not miss lecture, then the student does not fail.

b. $q \quad \wedge \quad (\sim p \quad \rightarrow \quad \sim r)$

A student studies , and if   A student does not miss lecture , then   A student does not fail.

One possible English translation for the symbolic statement is:

A student studies, and if a student does not miss lecture then the student does not fail.

Exercise Set 3.2

 Practice Exercises

In Exercises 1–4, let p and q represent the following simple statements:

> *p:* "I Love Lucy" *is a television show.*
> *q: Macbeth is a television show.*

Write each compound statement in its symbolic form.

1. "I Love Lucy" is a television show and *Macbeth* is a television show.

2. *Macbeth* is a television show and "I Love Lucy" is a television show.

3. "I Love Lucy" is a television show and *Macbeth* is not a television show.

4. *Macbeth* is not a television show and "I Love Lucy" is a television show.

In Exercises 5–8, let p and q represent the following simple statements:

> *p: I study.*
> *q: I pass the course.*

Write each compound statement in its symbolic form.

5. I study or I pass the course.

6. I pass the course or I study.

7. I study or I do not pass the course.

8. I do not study or I do not pass the course.

In Exercises 9–12, let p and q represent the following simple statements:

> *p: This is an alligator.*
> *q: This is a reptile.*

Write each compound statement in its symbolic form.

9. If this is an alligator, then this is a reptile.

10. If this is a reptile, then this is an alligator.

11. If this is not an alligator, then this is not a reptile.

12. If this is not a reptile, then this is not an alligator.

In Exercises 13–16, let p and q represent the following simple statements:

> *p: The campus is closed.*
> *q: It is Sunday.*

Write each compound statement in its symbolic form.

13. The campus is closed if and only if it is Sunday.

14. It is Sunday if and only if the campus is closed.

15. It is not Sunday if and only if the campus is not closed.

16. The campus is not closed if and only if it is not Sunday.

In Exercises 17–24, let p and q represent the following simple statements:

> *p: The heater is working.*
> *q: The house is cold.*

Write each symbolic statement in words.

17. $\sim p \wedge q$

18. $p \wedge \sim q$

19. $p \vee \sim q$

20. $\sim p \vee q$

21. $p \rightarrow \sim q$

22. $q \rightarrow \sim p$

23. $p \leftrightarrow \sim q$

24. $\sim p \leftrightarrow q$

In Exercises 25–32, let q and r represent the following simple statements:

> *q: It is July 4th.*
> *r: We are having a barbecue.*

Write each symbolic statement in words.

25. $q \wedge \sim r$

26. $\sim q \wedge r$

27. $\sim q \vee r$

28. $q \vee \sim r$

29. $r \rightarrow \sim q$

30. $q \rightarrow \sim r$

31. $\sim q \leftrightarrow r$

32. $q \leftrightarrow \sim r$

In Exercises 33–42, let p and q represent the following simple statements:

> *p: Romeo loves Juliet.*
> *q: Juliet loves Romeo.*

Write each symbolic statement in words.

33. $\sim(p \wedge q)$

34. $\sim(q \wedge p)$

35. $\sim p \wedge q$

36. $\sim q \wedge p$

37. $\sim(q \vee p)$

38. $\sim(p \vee q)$

39. $\sim q \vee p$

40. $\sim p \vee q$

41. $\sim p \wedge \sim q$

42. $\sim q \wedge \sim p$

In Exercises 43–48, let p, q, and r represent the following simple statements:

> *p: The temperature outside is freezing.*
> *q: The heater is working.*
> *r: The house is cold.*

Write each compound statement in its symbolic form.

43. The temperature outside is freezing and the heater is working, or the house is cold.

44. If the temperature outside is freezing, then the heater is working or the house is not cold.

45. If the temperature outside is freezing or the heater is not working, then the house is cold.

46. It is not the case that if the house is cold, then the heater is not working.

47. The house is cold, if and only if the temperature outside is freezing and the heater isn't working.

48. If the heater is working, then the temperature outside is freezing if and only if the house is cold.

In Exercises 49–62, let p, q, and r represent the following simple statements:

> *p: The temperature is above 85°.*
> *q: We finished studying.*
> *r: We go to the beach.*

Write each symbolic statement in words.

49. $(p \wedge q) \rightarrow r$
50. $(q \wedge r) \rightarrow p$
51. $p \wedge (q \rightarrow r)$
52. $p \wedge (r \rightarrow q)$
53. $\sim r \rightarrow (\sim p \vee \sim q)$
54. $\sim p \rightarrow (q \vee r)$
55. $(\sim r \rightarrow \sim q) \vee p$
56. $(\sim p \rightarrow \sim r) \vee q$
57. $r \leftrightarrow (p \wedge q)$
58. $r \leftrightarrow (q \wedge p)$
59. $(p \leftrightarrow q) \wedge r$
60. $q \rightarrow (r \leftrightarrow p)$
61. $\sim r \rightarrow \sim(p \wedge q)$
62. $\sim(p \wedge q) \rightarrow \sim r$

 Application Exercises

Exercises 63–66 contain statements made by well-known people or were written in newspapers. Use letters to represent each simple statement and rewrite the given compound statement in symbolic form.

63. "If you give other people permission to do so, then you can be made to feel less than you are." (Eleanor Roosevelt)

64. "If a nationwide strike of Bell System workers goes into effect, some 7000 employees of Southern Bell in Dade County would be affected." (*The Miami Herald*)

65. "If Ed Muskie is ahead on the first ballot and Humphrey is close behind, then we'll switch to Ted Kennedy on the second ballot and start a draft." (California politician)

66. "If I were an intellectual, I would be pessimistic, but since I'm not an intellectual, I am optimistic about America." (General Lewis B. Hershey, Director of the Selective Service during the Vietnam war)
(For simplicity, regard "optimistic" as "not pessimistic.")

 Writing in Mathematics

67. Describe what is meant by a compound statement.

68. What is a conjunction? Describe the symbol that forms a conjunction.

69. What is a disjunction? Describe the symbol that forms a disjunction.

70. What is a conditional statement? Describe the symbol that forms a conditional statement.

71. What is a biconditional statement? Describe the symbol that forms a biconditional statement.

72. Discuss the difference between the symbolic statements $\sim(p \wedge q)$ and $\sim p \wedge q$.

73. Suppose that a friend tells you, "This summer I plan to visit Paris or London." Under what condition can you conclude that if your friend visits Paris, London will not be visited? Under what condition can you conclude that if your friend visits Paris, London might be visited? Assuming your friend has told you the truth, what can you conclude if you know that Paris will not be visited? Explain each of your answers.

 Critical Thinking Exercises

74. Write a compound statement that you feel strongly about. The statement should contain at least two different connectives. Then express the statement in symbolic form.

75. Use letters to represent each simple statement in the compound statement that follows. Then express the compound statement in symbolic form.
Shooting unarmed civilians is morally justifiable if and only if bombing them is morally justifiable, and as the former is not morally justifiable, neither is the latter.

 Technology Exercises

Use the symbols $\sim$, $\wedge$, $\vee$, $\rightarrow$, and $\leftrightarrow$ from the character map of your word processor, and let p, q, and r represent the following simple statements:

> *p: I will pass math.*
> *q: I will pass history.*
> *r: I will graduate.*

Write each compound statement in its symbolic form.

76. I will pass math and history.

77. I will pass math but not history.

78. If I pass math and history, I will graduate.

79. If I do not pass math or history, I will not graduate.

80. I will graduate if and only if I pass math and do not pass history.

 Group Exercise

81. Each group member should find a legal document that contains at least six connectives in one paragraph. The connectives should include at least three different kinds of connectives, such as "and," "or," "if–then," and "if and only if." Share your example with other members of the group, and see if the group can explain what some of the more complicated statements actually mean.

SECTION 3.3 Truth Tables for Negation, Conjunction, and Disjunction

Objectives

1. Use the definitions of negation, conjunction, and disjunction.
2. Construct truth tables.
3. Use a De Morgan law.

In Sections 3.1 and 3.2, we studied the symbols for expressing negation, ~ (not), conjunction, ∧ (and), disjunction, ∨ (or), the conditional, → (if–then), and the bi-conditional, ↔ (if and only if). In this section, we focus on negation, conjunction, and disjunction, determining when these statements are true and when they are false. Classifying a statement as true or false is called **assigning a truth value to the statement**.

---

1 Use the definitions of negation, conjunction, and disjunction.

Negation, ~

The negation of a true statement is a false statement. We can express this in a table in which T represents true and F, false.

p	$\sim p$
T	F

The negation of a false statement is a true statement. This, too, can be shown in table form:

p	$\sim p$
F	T

Combining the two tables shown above results in Table 3.4, called the **truth table for negation**. This truth table expresses the idea that $\sim p$ has the opposite truth value from p.

Table 3.4   Negation

p	$\sim p$
T	F
F	T

$\sim p$ has the opposite truth value from p.

Conjunction, ∧

A friend tells you, "I visited London and I visited Paris." In order to understand the truth values for this statement, let's break it down into its two simple statements:

  p: I visited London.
  q: I visited Paris.

There are four possible cases to consider.

I visited London and I visited Paris.

CASE 1 Your friend actually visited both cities, so p is true and q is true. The conjunction "I visited London and I visited Paris" is true because your friend did both things. If both p and q are true, the conjunction $p \wedge q$ is true. We can show this in truth table form:

p	q	$p \wedge q$
T	T	T

p	q	$p \land q$
T	F	F

p	q	$p \land q$
F	T	F

p	q	$p \land q$
F	F	F

CASE 2 Your friend actually visited London, but did not tell the truth about visiting Paris. In this case, p is true and q is false. Your friend didn't do what was stated, namely visit both cities, so $p \land q$ is false. If p is true and q is false, the conjunction $p \land q$ is false.

CASE 3 This time, London was not visited, but Paris was. This makes p false and q true. As in case 2, your friend didn't do what was stated, namely visit both cities, so $p \land q$ is false. If p is false and q is true, the conjunction $p \land q$ is false.

CASE 4 This time your friend visited neither city, so p is false and q is false. The statement that both were visited, $p \land q$, is false.

Let's use a truth table to summarize all four cases. Only in the case that your friend visited London and visited Paris is the conjunction true. Each of the four cases appears in Table 3.5, the truth table for conjunction, $\land$. The definition of conjunction is given in words to the right of the table.

The Definition of Conjunction

Table 3.5 Conjunction A conjunction is true only when both simple statements are true.

p	q	$p \land q$
T	T	T
T	F	F
F	T	F
F	F	F

Table 3.6 contains an example of each of the four cases in the conjunction truth table.

Table 3.6 Statements of Conjunction and Their Truth Values

Statement	Truth Value	Reason
3 + 2 = 5 and London is in England.	T	Both simple statements are true.
3 + 2 = 5 and London is in France.	F	The second simple statement is not true.
3 + 2 = 6 and London is in England.	F	The first simple statement is not true.
3 + 2 = 6 and London is in France.	F	Both simple statements are not true.

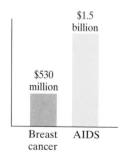

Figure 3.3 Federal research budget, 1998
Source: Centers for Disease Control and Prevention

EXAMPLE 1   Understanding the Definition of Conjunction, $\land$

The bar graph in Figure 3.3 shows the amounts budgeted by the federal government in 1998 for breast cancer and AIDS research. Use the information given by the graph to determine the truth value for the following conjunction:

In 1998, $530 million was allocated for breast cancer research and less than $1 billion was allocated for AIDS research.

Solution A conjunction is true only when both simple statements are true. Consider each of the simple statements that form the conjunction. Begin with:

In 1998, $530 million was allocated for breast cancer research.

Examine the graph in Figure 3.2 to determine the truth value of this statement. The first bar represents the amount allocated for breast cancer research. Because $530 million is printed above the bar, this simple statement is true.

Now consider the second simple statement:

In 1998, less than $1 billion was allocated for AIDS research.

The second bar represents the amount allocated for AIDS research, given to be $1.5 billion. This is more, not less, than $1 billion. Thus, the second simple statement is false.

Because a conjunction, $\wedge$, is true only when both simple statements are true, the given conjunction is false.

The statements that make up a compound statement do not have to be simple statements. Consider, for example, the compound statement

$$(\sim p \vee q) \wedge \sim q.$$

The statements that make up this conjunction are $\sim p \vee q$ and $\sim q$. The conjunction is true only when both $\sim p \vee q$ and $\sim q$ are true. Notice that $\sim p \vee q$ is not a simple statement. We call $\sim p \vee q$ and $\sim q$ the *component statements* of the conjunction. The statements making up a compound statement are called **component statements**.

Disjunction, $\vee$

Now your friend states, "I visited London or I visited Paris." Because we assume that this is the inclusive "or," if your friend visited either or both of these cities, the truth has been told. The disjunction is false only in the event that neither city has been visited. An *or* statement is true in every case, except when both component statements are false.

The truth table for disjunction, $\vee$, is shown in Table 3.7. The definition of disjunction is given in words to the right of the table.

The Definition of Disjunction

Table 3.7 Disjunction   A disjunction is false only when both component statements are false.

p	q	$p \vee q$
T	T	T
T	F	T
F	T	T
F	F	F

Number of Countries Granting Women the Right to Vote

Figure 3.4 Steps Forward: Number of countries in which women were granted the right to vote, by decade *Source:* The United Nations

Table 3.8 contains an example of each of the four cases in the disjunction truth table.

Table 3.8   Statements of Disjunction and Their Truth Values

Statement	Truth Value	Reason
3 + 2 = 5 or London is in England.	T	Both component statements are not false.
3 + 2 = 5 or London is in France.	T	The first component statement is not false.
3 + 2 = 6 or London is in England.	T	The second component statement is not false.
3 + 2 = 6 or London is in France.	F	Both component statements are false.

EXAMPLE 2   Understanding the Definition of Disjunction

In the United States, women were first granted the right to vote in 1920. The graph in Figure 3.4 shows the number of countries that first granted women the right to vote by decade. Use the information given by the graph to determine the truth value for the following disjunction:

> In the 1950s, 32 countries granted women the right to vote or in the 1990s, three countries granted women the right to vote.

Solution   A disjunction is false only when both component statements are false. Thus, we need to determine the truth value of each component statement. We can use Figure 3.4 to do so. Begin with the first component statement:

> In the 1950s, 32 countries granted women the right to vote.

The graph in Figure 3.4 shows that 43 countries granted women the right to vote in the 1950s, not 32. This component statement is false. Now consider the second component statement:

> In the 1990s, three countries granted women the right to vote.

The graph shows that three countries granted women the right to vote in the 1990s. Thus, the second component statement is true. By definition, a disjunction is false only when both component statements are false. In the given disjunction, only one of the two component statements is false. Thus, the given disjunction is true.

2 Construct truth tables.

Constructing Truth Tables

Truth tables can be used to gain a better understanding of English statements. The truth tables in this section are based on the definitions of negation, ~, conjunction, ∧, and disjunction, ∨. It is helpful to remember these definitions in words.

Kurt Gödel (1906–1978)

At the age of 10, Czech mathematician Kurt Gödel was studying mathematics, religion, and several languages. By age 25 he had produced what many mathematicians consider the most important result of twentieth century mathematics: Gödel used deductive reasoning to prove that in logic, as in all other branches of mathematics, there will always be true statements that cannot be proved.

Definitions of Negation, Conjunction, and Disjunction

1. **Negation ~: not**
   The negation of a statement has the opposite truth value from the statement.
2. **Conjunction ∧: and**
   The only case in which a conjunction is true is when both component statements are true.
3. **Disjunction ∨: or**
   The only case in which a disjunction is false is when both component statements are false.

In the examples that follow, we will be constructing truth tables for compound statements that contain the simple statements p and q. In cases like this, there are four possible truth values for p and q. We will always list the four possible combinations of truth values for p and q in the following order. This order is not necessary, but it is a standard and makes for a consistent presentation.

p	q	
T	T	
T	F	
F	T	
F	F	

The final column heading in a truth table should be the given compound statement. Each column heading will tell you exactly how to fill in the four truth values for the statement at the top of the column. If a column heading involves negation, ~ (not), fill in the column by looking back at the column that contains the statement that must be negated. Take the opposite of the truth values in this column.

If a column heading involves the symbol for conjunction, ∧ (and), fill in the truth values in the column by looking back at two columns—the column before the ∧ connective and the column after the ∧ connective. Fill in the column by applying the definition of conjunction, writing T only when both component statements are true.

If a column heading involves the symbol for disjunction, ∨ (or), fill in the truth values in the column by looking back at two columns—the column before the ∨ connective and the column after the ∨ connective. Fill in the column by applying the definition of disjunction, writing F only when both component statements are false.

Let's unravel all this by looking at specific examples.

EXAMPLE 3   Constructing a Truth Table

Construct a truth table for

$$\sim(p \wedge q)$$

to determine when the statement is true and when the statement is false.

Solution   The parentheses indicate that we must first determine the truth values for the conjunction $p \wedge q$. After this, we determine the truth values for the negation $\sim(p \wedge q)$ by taking the opposite of the truth values for $p \wedge q$.

Step 1 As with all truth tables, first list the simple statements on top. Then show all the possible truth values for these statements. In this case there are two simple statements and four possible combinations, or cases.

p	*q*	
T	T	
T	F	
F	T	
F	F	

Step 2 Make a column for $p \land q$, the statement within the parentheses. Use $p \land q$ as the heading for the column, and then fill in the truth values for the conjunction by looking back at the *p* and *q* columns. A conjunction is true only when both component statements are true.

p	*q*	$p \land q$
T	T	T
T	F	F
F	T	F
F	F	F

> *p* and *q* are true, so $p \land q$ is true.

Step 3 Construct one more column for $\sim(p \land q)$. Fill in this column by negating the values in the $p \land q$ column. Use the negation definition, taking the opposite of the truth values in column 3. This completes the truth table for $\sim(p \land q)$.

p	*q*	$p \land q$	$\sim(p \land q)$
T	T	T	F
T	F	F	T
F	T	F	T
F	F	F	T

Bart Simpson

Donald Duck
—Both Cartoon Characters

The final column in the truth table for $\sim(p \land q)$ tells us that the statement is false only when both *p* and *q* are true. For example, using

p: Bart Simpson is a cartoon character. (true)

q: Donald Duck is a cartoon character. (true)

the statement $\sim(p \land q)$ translates as:

It is not true that Bart Simpson and Donald Duck are cartoon characters.

This compound statement is false. It *is* true that Bart Simpson and Donald Duck are cartoon characters.

EXAMPLE 4 Constructing a Truth Table

Construct a truth table for

$$\sim p \lor \sim q$$

to determine when the statement is true and when the statement is false.

Solution   Without parentheses, the negation symbol, ~, negates only the statement that immediately follows it. Therefore, we first determine the truth values for $\sim p$ and for $\sim q$. Then we determine the truth values for the *or* disjunction, $\sim p \vee \sim q$.

Step 1   List the simple statements on top and show the four possible cases for the truth values.

p	q	
T	T	
T	F	
F	T	
F	F	

Step 2   Make columns for $\sim p$ and for $\sim q$. Fill in the $\sim p$ column by looking back at the p column, column 1, and taking the opposite of the truth values in this column. Fill in the $\sim q$ column by taking the opposite of the truth values in column 2, the q column.

p	q	$\sim p$	$\sim q$
T	T	F	F
T	F	F	T
F	T	T	F
F	F	T	T

Step 3   Construct one more column for $\sim p \vee \sim q$. To determine the truth values of $\sim p \vee \sim q$, look back at the $\sim p$ column, column 3, and the $\sim q$ column, column 4. Now use the disjunction definition on columns 3 and 4. Disjunction definition: An *or* statement is false only when both component statements are false. This occurs in the first row.

p	q	$\sim p$	$\sim q$	$\sim p \vee \sim q$
T	T	F	F	F
T	F	F	T	T
F	T	T	F	T
F	F	T	T	T
		column 3	column 4	

$\sim p$ is false and $\sim q$ is false, so $\sim p \vee \sim q$ is false.

3 Use a De Morgan law.

Table 3.9

p	q	$\sim(p \wedge q)$	$\sim p \vee \sim q$
T	T	F	F
T	F	T	T
F	T	T	T
F	F	T	T

$\sim(p \wedge q)$ and $\sim p \vee \sim q$ are equivalent.

Our work in Examples 3 and 4 is summarized in Table 3.9. Notice that $\sim(p \wedge q)$ and $\sim p \vee \sim q$ have the same truth value in each of the four cases. Two statements that have the same truth value in every possible case are said to be **equivalent**. Therefore,

$$\sim(p \wedge q) \text{ is equivalent to } \sim p \vee \sim q.$$

This equivalency is one of the **De Morgan laws** and will be considered in more detail later in this chapter.

EXAMPLE 5   Using a De Morgan Equivalent

$\sim (p \wedge q) = \sim p \vee q$

Write a statement that is equivalent to:

It is not true that James Joyce and Pablo Picasso are both writers.

Table 3.9

p	q	$\sim(p \land q)$	$\sim p \lor \sim q$
T	T	F	F
T	F	T	T
F	T	T	T
F	F	T	T

Solution Let p and q represent the following simple statements:

p: James Joyce is a writer. (true)

q: Pablo Picasso is a writer. (false)

> It is not true that James Joyce and Pablo Picasso are both writers.

The given statement is of the form

$$\sim(p \land q).$$

The truth values of p and q correspond to the second row of Table 3.9. The given statement, $\sim(p \land q)$, is true. An equivalent statement is

$$\sim p \lor \sim q.$$

We can translate this as:

James Joyce is not a writer or Pablo Picasso is not a writer.

The final statement in Example 5 makes sense based on our understanding of the English language. If it's not true that Joyce and Picasso are both writers, then at least one of them is not a writer.

EXAMPLE 6 Constructing a Truth Table

Construct a truth table for

$$(\sim p \lor q) \land \sim q$$

to determine when the statement is true and when the statement is false.

Solution The statement is an *and* conjunction because the conjunction symbol, $\land$, is outside the parentheses. We cannot determine the truth values for the statement until we first determine the truth values for $\sim p \lor q$ and for $\sim q$, the component statements before and after the $\land$ connective:

$$\boxed{(\sim p \ \lor \ q)} \ \land \ \boxed{\sim q}$$

> We'll need a column with truth values for this component statement.

> We'll need a column with truth values for this component statement.

Technology

You can use a word processor to create truth tables. If you desire, you can alter the appearance of the table by merging and splitting cells, removing the table border, and adding background colors. Create one row for each case and one column for each statement whose truth value is to be determined. Then enter "T" for true and "F" for false as needed.

Step 1 The compound statement involves two simple statements and four possible cases.

p	q	
T	T	
T	F	
F	T	
F	F	

Column needed.   Column needed.

Step 2 Because we need a column with truth values for $\sim p \vee q$, begin with $\sim p$. Use $\sim p$ as the heading. Fill in the column by looking back at the p column, column 1, and take the opposite of the truth values in this column.

p	q	$\sim p$
T	T	F
T	F	F
F	T	T
F	F	T
column 1		

Step 3 Now add a $\sim p \vee q$ column. To determine the truth values of $\sim p \vee q$, look back at the $\sim p$ column, column 3, and the q column, column 2. Now use the disjunction definition on columns 3 and 2. Disjunction definition: An *or* statement is false only when both component statements are false. This occurs in the second row.

p	q	$\sim p$	$\sim p \vee q$
T	T	F	T
T	F	F	F
F	T	T	T
F	F	T	T
	column 2	column 3	

$\sim p$ is false and q is false, so $\sim p \vee q$ is false.

Step 4 The statement following the $\wedge$ connective is $\sim q$, so add a $\sim q$ column. Fill in the column by looking back at the q column, column 2, and take the opposite of the truth values in this column.

p	q	$\sim p$	$\sim p \vee q$	$\sim q$
T	T	F	T	F
T	F	F	F	T
F	T	T	T	F
F	F	T	T	T
	column 2			

Step 5 The final column heading is

$$(\sim p \vee q) \wedge \sim q$$

which is our given statement. To determine its truth values, look back at the $\sim p \vee q$ column, column 4, and the $\sim q$ column, column 5. Now use the conjunction definition on columns 4 and 5. Conjunction definition: An *and* statement is true only when both component statements are true. This occurs in the last row.

p	q	$\sim p$	$\sim p \lor q$	$\sim q$	$(\sim p \lor q) \land \sim q$
T	T	F	T	F	F
T	F	F	F	T	F
F	T	T	T	F	F
F	F	T	T	T	T
			column 4	column 5	

$\sim p \lor q$ is true and $\sim q$ is true, so $(\sim p \lor q) \land \sim q$ is true.

The truth table is now complete. By looking at the truth values in the last column, we can see that the compound statement

$$(\sim p \lor q) \land \sim q$$

is true only in case 4, that is, when p is false and q is false.

Exercise Set 3.3

 Practice Exercises

Use the definition of conjunction, ∧, to determine the truth value for each statement in Exercises 1–6.

1. The Beatles were a rock group and Ernest Hemingway was a writer.

2. John Travolta is an actor and Abraham Lincoln was a U.S. president.

3. $3 + 2 = 5$ and 3 is an even number.

4. $7 \times 5 = 35$ and 6 is an odd number.

5. Fir trees produce fur coats and some first basemen are right-handed.

6. Some dogs are not mammals and no number can exceed one million.

Use the definition of disjunction, ∨, to determine the truth value for each statement in Exercises 7–12.

7. $7 \times 3 = 21$ or Martin Luther King fought for racial equality.

8. $11 - 4 = 7$ or George Washington was the first U.S. president.

9. Some athletes are not college professors or Sammy Sosa was a U.S. president.

10. London is the capital of France or some students are not psychology majors.

11. All politicians have law degrees or no students are business majors.

12. All computers cost more than $1000 or no colleges have athletic programs.

In Exercises 13–20, complete the truth table for the given statement by filling in the required columns.

13. $p \lor \sim p$

p	$\sim p$	$p \lor \sim p$
T		
F		

14. $p \land \sim p$

p	$\sim p$	$p \land \sim p$
T		
F		

15. $\sim p \land q$

p	q	$\sim p$	$\sim p \land q$
T	T		
T	F		
F	T		
F	F		

16. $\sim p \lor q$

p	q	$\sim p$	$\sim p \lor q$
T	T		
T	F		
F	T		
F	F		

17. $\sim(p \lor q)$

p	q	$p \lor q$	$\sim(p \lor q)$
T	T		
T	F		
F	T		
F	F		

18. $\sim(p \lor \sim q)$

p	q	$\sim q$	$p \lor \sim q$	$\sim(p \lor \sim q)$
T	T			
T	F			
F	T			
F	F			

19. $\sim p \land \sim q$

p	q	$\sim p$	$\sim q$	$\sim p \land \sim q$
T	T			
T	F			
F	T			
F	F			

20. $p \land \sim q$

p	q	$\sim q$	$p \land \sim q$
T	T		
T	F		
F	T		
F	F		

In Exercises 21–32, construct a truth table for the given statement.

21. $p \land \sim q$ 22. $p \lor \sim q$

23. $\sim(\sim p \lor q)$ 24. $\sim(p \land \sim q)$

25. $(p \lor q) \land \sim p$ 26. $(p \land q) \lor \sim p$

27. $\sim p \lor (p \land \sim q)$ 28. $\sim p \land (p \lor \sim q)$

29. $(p \lor q) \land (\sim p \lor \sim q)$ 30. $(p \land \sim q) \lor (\sim p \land q)$

31. $(p \land \sim q) \lor (p \land q)$ 32. $(p \lor \sim q) \land (p \lor q)$

In Exercises 33–36, use the De Morgan law that states

$$\sim(p \land q) \text{ is equivalent to } \sim p \lor \sim q$$

to write an equivalent English statement for the given statement.

33. It is not true that Texas and Paris are both states.

34. It is not true that Michael Jordan and Garth Brooks are both musicians.

35. It is not the case that *Romeo and Juliet* and *Jurassic Park* were both written by Shakespeare.

36. It is not the case that "Star Wars" and "Frasier" are movies.

 Application Exercises

The accompanying bar graph shows the number of children, in thousands, educated at home in the United States. Use the information given by the graph to determine the truth value for each of the statements in Exercises 37–38.

Source: National Home Education Research Institute

37. The number of children educated at home increased each year from 1993–1997 and in 1997 there were 1,347,000 children educated at home.

38. In 1996 there were 1,220,000 children educated at home and more children were educated at home in 1993 than in 1994.

The accompanying line graphs show the life expectancy at birth for women and men in the United States born between 1900 and 2050. Use the information given by the graphs to determine the truth value for each of the statements in Exercises 39–40.

Life Expectancy at Birth in the U.S.

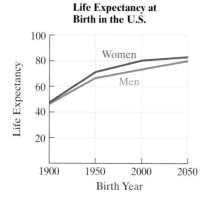

Source: National Center for Health Statistics

39. Men born in 2000 will live longer than women born in 2000 or people in the U.S. are living longer with increasing birth years.

40. Men born in 1950 have a life expectancy of 80 years or women born in any year between 1900 and 2050 live longer than men born in the same year.

The table shows the five countries with the most amount of TV-viewing time. In Exercises 41–48, let p, q, and r represent the following simple statements:

p: *The United States is the top TV-viewing country.*
q: *Italy and Turkey are tied for TV-viewing.*
r: *Spain's TV-viewing time is more than the United Kingdom's.*

Top Five TV-Viewing Countries in the World: 1998

Country	Average Daily Viewing Time (in minutes)
United States	239
Italy	216
Turkey	216
United Kingdom	215
Spain	214

Source: Eurodata TV

Write each symbolic statement in words. Then use the information given by the table to determine the truth value of the statement.

41. $p \wedge \sim q$ 42. $p \wedge \sim r$ 43. $\sim p \wedge r$ 44. $q \wedge \sim p$
45. $p \vee \sim q$ 46. $p \vee \sim r$ 47. $\sim p \vee r$ 48. $q \vee \sim p$

 Writing in Mathematics

49. Under which conditions is a conjunction true?
50. Under which conditions is a conjunction false?

51. Under which conditions is a disjunction true?
52. Under which conditions is a disjunction false?
53. Describe how to construct a truth table for a compound statement.
54. Describe the information given by the truth values in the final column of a truth table.
55. Use the line graphs in Exercises 39–40 to write a true conjunction. Do not use any of the simple statements that appear in Exercises 39–40.
56. Use the line graphs in Exercises 39–40 to write a false disjunction. Do not use any of the simple statements that appear in Exercises 39–40.

 Critical Thinking Exercises

57. Use the bar graph in Exercises 37–38 to write a true compound statement with each of the following characteristics. Do not use any of the simple statements that appear in Exercises 37–38.
    a. The statement contains three different simple statements.
    b. The statement contains two different connectives.
    c. The statement contains one simple statement with the word *not*.
58. The truth table that defines $\vee$, the *inclusive or*, indicates that the compound statement is true if one or both of its component statements are true. The symbol for the *exclusive or* is $\veebar$. The *exclusive or* means *either p or q*, but *not both*. Use this meaning to write the truth table that defines $p \veebar q$.

 Technology Exercises

Use the table function of your word processor and the appropriate symbols from the program's character map to construct a truth table for the statements in Exercises 59–60.

59. $\sim p \wedge q$ 60. $(p \wedge \sim q) \vee q$

 Group Exercise

61. Each member of the group should find a graph that is of particular interest to that person. Share the graphs. The group should select the three graphs that they find most intriguing. For the graphs selected, group members should write four compound statements, two of which are true, and two false. One of the statements should contain three different simple statements and two different connectives.

Objectives

1. Understand the logic behind the definition of the conditional.
2. Construct truth tables for conditional statements.
3. Write a conditional statement's equivalent.
4. Use a truth table to determine if a compound statement is a tautology.
5. Understand the definition of the biconditional.
6. Construct truth tables for biconditional statements.
7. Construct truth tables for statements consisting of three simple statements.

1 Understand the logic behind the definition of the conditional.

Table 3.10
Conditional

	p	q	$p \rightarrow q$
CASE 1	T	T	T
CASE 2	T	F	F
CASE 3	F	T	T
CASE 4	F	F	T

In Section 3.2, we studied the symbols for expressing the conditional, $\rightarrow$ (if–then) and the biconditional, $\leftrightarrow$ (if and only if). In this section, we determine when these statements are true and when they are false.

Conditional Statements, $\rightarrow$

We begin by looking at the truth table for conditional statements. Suppose that your professor promises you:

If you pass the final, then you pass the course.

Break the statement down into its two component statements:

p: You pass the final.
q: You pass the course.

Translated into symbolic form, your professor's statement is $p \rightarrow q$. We now look at the four cases shown in Table 3.10, the truth table for the conditional.

CASE 1 (T, T) You do pass the final and you do pass the course. Your professor did what was promised, and the conditional statement is true.

CASE 2 (T, F) You pass the final, but you do not pass the course. Your professor did not do what was promised, and the conditional statement is false.

CASE 3 (F, T) You do not pass the final, but you do pass the course. Your professor's original statement talks about only what would happen if you passed the final. It says nothing about what would happen if you did not pass the final. Your professor did not break the promise of the original statement, which is consequently true.

CASE 4 (F, F) You do not pass the final and you do not pass the course. As with case 3, your professor's original statement talks about only what would happen if you passed the final. The promise of the original statement has not been broken. Therefore, your professor's statement is true.

The component statement before the $\rightarrow$ connective in any conditional statement is called the **antecedent**. The component statement after the $\rightarrow$ connective is called the **consequent**. Table 3.10 illustrates that a conditional statement is false only when the antecedent is true and the consequent is false. A conditional statement is true in all other cases.

The Definition of the Conditional

p	q	$p \rightarrow q$
T	T	T
T	F	F
F	T	T
F	F	T

A conditional is false only when the antecedent is true and the consequent is false.

Conditional Trickery

We have all received junk mail with this claim. The conditional statement

If you follow the instructions inside and you return the winning number, then you win $7,000,000

consists of three simple statements:

p: You follow the instructions inside. (Might be true.)

q: You return the winning number. (False. There are only losing numbers inside, so you can't return the winning number.)

r: You win $7,000,000 (False.)

The form of the conditional statement is

$$(p \land q) \to r.$$

Because a conjunction is true only when both simple statements are true, $p \land q$ is false. Statement r is also false. Let's substitute these truth values into the conditional statement.

$$(p \land q) \to r$$
$$(T \land F) \to F$$
$$F \to F$$
$$T$$

A conditional is false only when the first part is true and the second part is false. This means the claim that came with the junk mail is true in spite of the fact that you're not going to win one cent!

People who do not think carefully will interpret the conditional claim to read:

If you follow the instructions by returning the winning number that you will find inside this envelope, then you win $7,000,000.

This misreading is wishful thinking. There is no winning number in the envelope. This claim was not made by the conditional statement that entices many people to both open the mail and obediently follow the accompanying instructions. (And to buy magazines, although no purchase is necessary!)

2 Construct truth tables for conditional statements.

Constructing Truth Tables

Our first example shows how truth tables can be used to gain a better understanding of conditional statements.

EXAMPLE 1 Constructing a Truth Table

Construct a truth table for

$$\sim q \rightarrow \sim p$$

to determine when the statement is true and when the statement is false.

Solution Remember that without parentheses, the symbol $\sim$ negates only the statement that immediately follows it. Therefore, we cannot determine the truth values for this conditional statement until we first determine the truth values for $\sim q$ and for $\sim p$, the statements before and after the $\rightarrow$ connective.

Step 1 List the simple statements on top and show the four possible cases for the truth values.

p	q	
T	T	
T	F	
F	T	
F	F	

Steps 2 and 3 Make columns for $\sim q$ and for $\sim p$. Fill in the $\sim q$ column by looking back at the q column, column 2, taking the opposite of the truth values in this column. Fill in the $\sim p$ column by taking the opposite of the truth values in column 1, the p column.

p	q	$\sim q$	$\sim p$
T	T	F	F
T	F	T	F
F	T	F	T
F	F	T	T

Step 4 Construct one more column for $\sim q \rightarrow \sim p$. Look back at the $\sim q$ column, column 3, and the $\sim p$ column, column 4. Now use the conditional definition to determine the truth values for $\sim q \rightarrow \sim p$ based on columns 3 and 4. Conditional definition: An "if–then" statement is false only when the antecedent is true and the consequent is false. This occurs in the second row.

p	q	$\sim q$	$\sim p$	$\sim q \rightarrow \sim p$
T	T	F	F	T
T	F	T	F	F
F	T	F	T	T
F	F	T	T	T
		column 3	column 4	

$\sim q$ is true and $\sim p$ is false, so $\sim q \rightarrow \sim p$ is false.

3 Write a conditional statement's equivalent.

Table 3.11

p	q	$p \rightarrow q$	$\sim q \rightarrow \sim p$
T	T	T	T
T	F	F	F
F	T	T	T
F	F	T	T

$p \rightarrow q$ and $\sim q \rightarrow \sim p$ are equivalent.

The truth values for $p \rightarrow q$, as well as those for $\sim q \rightarrow \sim p$ from Example 1, are shown in Table 3.11. Notice that $p \rightarrow q$ and $\sim q \rightarrow \sim p$ have the same truth value in each of the four cases. Remember that two statements that have the same truth value in every possible case are *equivalent*. Therefore,

$$p \rightarrow q \text{ is equivalent to } \sim q \rightarrow \sim p.$$

This equivalency will be considered in more detail in the next section. The box that follows expresses this equivalency in words.

A Statement That Is Equivalent to the Conditional

The truth value of a conditional statement does not change if the antecedent and consequent are both reversed and negated.

EXAMPLE 2   Writing a Conditional Statement's Equivalent

The following conditional statement is true:

> If I live in Los Angeles, then I live in California.

Write an equivalent conditional statement.

Solution   First, reverse the order of the statements before and after the "if–then" connective. Then negate each statement. The equivalent conditional statement is:

> If I do not live in California, then I do not live in Los Angeles.

Observe that this statement is also true.

4   Use a truth table to determine if a compound statement is a tautology.

Our next example illustrates a statement that is always true. Such a statement is called a **tautology**.

Definition of a Tautology

A **tautology** is a statement that is true in all possible cases.

ALL FINAL ANSWERS ARE TRUE

EXAMPLE 3   Using a Truth Table to Verify a Tautology

Construct a truth table for

$$[(p \vee q) \wedge {\sim}p] \rightarrow q$$

and show that the compound statement is a tautology.

Solution   The statement is a conditional statement because the *if–then* symbol, $\rightarrow$, is outside the grouping symbols. We cannot determine the truth values for this conditional until we first determine the truth values for the statements before and after the $\rightarrow$ connective.

$$\boxed{[(p \vee q) \wedge {\sim}p]} \quad \rightarrow \quad \boxed{q}$$

We'll need a column with truth values for this statement. Prior to this column, we'll need columns for $p \vee q$ and for $\sim p$.

We'll need a column with truth values for this statement. This will be the second column of the truth table.

The disjunction, $\vee$, is false only when both component statements are false.

The truth value of $\sim p$ is opposite that of p.

The conjunction, $\wedge$, is true only when both $p \vee q$ and $\sim p$ are true.

The conditional, $\rightarrow$, is false only when $(p \vee q) \wedge {\sim}p$ is true and q is false.

Show four possible cases.

p	q	$p \vee q$	$\sim p$	$(p \vee q) \wedge {\sim}p$	$[(p \vee q) \wedge {\sim}p] \rightarrow q$
T	T	T	F	F	T
T	F	T	F	F	T
F	T	T	T	T	T
F	F	F	T	F	T

Thus, the conditional statement in the last column, $[(p \lor q) \land \sim p] \to q$, is never false. Equivalently, it is true in all four cases. Because we have shown that $[(p \lor q) \land \sim p] \to q$ is true in all possible cases, we have verified that this compound statement is a tautology.

Conditional statements that are tautologies are called **implications**. For the conditional statement

$$[(p \lor q) \land \sim p] \to q$$

we can say that:

$$(p \lor q) \land \sim p \text{ implies } q.$$

Using p: I visit London and q: I visit Paris, we can say that:

Visiting London or Paris, and not visiting London, implies visiting Paris.

5 Understand the definition of the biconditional.

Biconditional Statements

In Section 3.2, we introduced the biconditional connective, $\leftrightarrow$, translated as "if and only if." The biconditional statement $p \leftrightarrow q$ means that $p \to q$ and $q \to p$. We write this symbolically as

$$(p \to q) \land (q \to p).$$

To create the truth table for $p \leftrightarrow q$, we will first make a truth table for the conjunction of the two conditionals $p \to q$ and $q \to p$.

EXAMPLE 4 Constructing a Truth Table

Construct a truth table for

$$(p \to q) \land (q \to p)$$

to determine when the statement is true and when the statement is false.

Solution The statement is a conjunction because the conjunction symbol, $\land$, is outside the parentheses. We cannot determine the truth values for this conjunction until we determine the truth values for $p \to q$ and $q \to p$, the statements before and after the $\land$ connective.

The conditional is false only when p is true and q is false.

The conditional is false only when q is true and p is false.

The conjunction is true only when both $p \to q$ and $q \to p$ are true.

Show four possible cases.

p	q	$p \to q$	$q \to p$	$(p \to q) \land (q \to p)$
T	T	T	T	T
T	F	F	T	F
F	T	T	F	F
F	F	T	T	T

The truth values in the column for $(p \to q) \land (q \to p)$ show the truth values for the biconditional statement $p \leftrightarrow q$.

The Definition of the Biconditional

p	q	$p \leftrightarrow q$
T	T	T
T	F	F
F	T	F
F	F	T

A biconditional is true only when the component statements have the same truth value.

Before we continue our work with truth tables, let's take a moment to summarize the basic definitions of symbolic logic.

The Definitions of Symbolic Logic

1. Negation ~: not
   The negation of a statement has the opposite truth value from the statement.
2. Conjunction ∧: and
   The only case in which a conjunction is true is when both component statements are true.
3. Disjunction ∨: or
   The only case in which a disjunction is false is when both component statements are false.
4. Conditional →: if–then
   The only case in which a conditional is false is when the first component statement is true and the second component statement is false.
5. Biconditional ↔: if and only if
   The only cases in which a biconditional is true are when the component statements have the same truth value.

6 Construct truth tables for biconditional statements.

EXAMPLE 5   Constructing a Truth Table

Construct a truth table for

$$(p \lor q) \leftrightarrow (\sim q \to p)$$

to determine whether the statement is a tautology.

Solution   The statement is a biconditional because the biconditional symbol, ↔, is outside the parentheses. We cannot determine the truth values for this biconditional until we determine the truth values for the statements in parentheses.

$$\boxed{(p \lor q)} \leftrightarrow \boxed{\sim q \to p}$$

We need a column with truth values for this statement.   We need a column with truth values for this statement.

The completed truth table appears as follows:

p	q	$p \vee q$	$\sim q$	$\sim q \rightarrow p$	$(p \vee q) \leftrightarrow (\sim q \rightarrow p)$
T	T	T	F	T	T
T	F	T	T	T	T
F	T	T	F	T	T
F	F	F	T	F	T

We applied the definition of the biconditional to fill in the last column. In each case, the truth values of $p \vee q$ and $\sim q \rightarrow p$ are the same. Therefore, the biconditional $(p \vee q) \leftrightarrow (\sim q \rightarrow p)$ is true in each case. Because all cases are true, the biconditional is a tautology.

7 Construct truth tables for statements consisting of three simple statements.

Table 3.12

	p	q	r
CASE 1	T	T	T
CASE 2	T	T	F
CASE 3	T	F	T
CASE 4	T	F	F
CASE 5	F	T	T
CASE 6	F	T	F
CASE 7	F	F	T
CASE 8	F	F	F

There are eight different true-false combinations for compound statements consisting of three simple statements.

Compound Statements Consisting of Three Simple Statements

Some compound statements involve three simple statements, usually represented by $p, q,$ and r. In this situation, there are eight different true-false possibilities, shown in Table 3.12. The first column has four Ts followed by four Fs. The second column has two Ts, two Fs, two Ts, and two Fs. Under the third statement, r, T alternates with F. It is not necessary to list the eight cases in this order, but this systematic method ensures that no case is repeated and that all cases are included.

EXAMPLE 6 Constructing a Truth Table With Eight Cases

Construct a truth table for

$$(p \wedge q) \rightarrow r$$

to determine when the statement is true and when the statement is false. Is the statement a tautology?

Solution The statement is a conditional statement because the *if–then* symbol, $\rightarrow$, is outside the parentheses. We cannot determine the truth values for this conditional until we have determined the truth values for $p \wedge q$ and for r, the statements before and after the $\rightarrow$ connective. The completed truth table appears as follows:

The conjunction is true only when p, column 1, is true and q, column 2, is true.

The conditional is false only when $p \wedge q$, column 4, is true and r, column 3, is false.

Show eight possible cases.

p	q	r	$p \wedge q$	$(p \wedge q) \rightarrow r$
T	T	T	T	T
T	T	F	T	F
T	F	T	F	T
T	F	F	F	T
F	T	T	F	T
F	T	F	F	T
F	F	T	F	T
F	F	F	F	T

The truth values in the final column are not all Ts. Therefore, $(p \land q) \to r$ is not true in all possible cases and the statement is not a tautology. We can also say that this conditional statement is not an implication.

The final column in the truth table for $(p \land q) \to r$ tells us that the statement is false only when both p and q are true and r is false. For example, an advertisement claims:

If you use Hair Grow and apply it daily, then your bald spot will disappear.

Use the following representations:

p: You use Hair Grow.

q: You apply it daily.

r: Your bald spot will disappear.

The claim can be expressed in symbolic form as

$$(p \land q) \to r.$$

A client uses Hair Grow (p is true), applies it daily (q is true), but his bald spot does not disappear (r is false). This corresponds to the second row in the truth table for $(p \land q) \to r$. In this case the compound statement $(p \land q) \to r$, like the advertisement's claim, is false.

Exercise Set 3.4

 Practice Exercises

In Exercises 1–8, construct a truth table for the given statement.

1. $p \to {\sim}q$
2. ${\sim}p \to q$
3. ${\sim}(q \to p)$
4. ${\sim}(p \to q)$
5. $(p \land q) \to (p \lor q)$
6. $(p \lor q) \to (p \land q)$
7. $(p \to q) \land {\sim}q$
8. $(p \to q) \land {\sim}p$

In Exercises 9–12, use the result that states

$$p \to q \text{ is equivalent to } {\sim}q \to {\sim}p$$

to write an equivalent English statement for the given statement.

9. If I live in Seattle, then I live in Washington.

10. If I live in Salt Lake City, then I live in Utah.

11. If a plant is not watered, then it wilts.

12. If the exam is tomorrow, then I do not go out tonight.

In Exercises 13–22, construct a truth table for the given statement. Then determine if the statement is a tautology.

13. $[(p \to q) \land q] \to p$
14. $[(p \to q) \land p] \to q$
15. $[(p \to q) \land {\sim}q] \to {\sim}p$
16. $[(p \to q) \land {\sim}p] \to {\sim}q$
17. $[(p \lor q) \land p] \to {\sim}q$
18. $[(p \lor q) \land {\sim}q] \to p$
19. $(p \to q) \to ({\sim}p \lor q)$
20. $(q \to p) \to (p \lor {\sim}q)$
21. $(p \land q) \land ({\sim}p \lor {\sim}q)$
22. $(p \lor q) \land ({\sim}p \land {\sim}q)$

In Exercises 23–32, construct a truth table for the given statement.

23. $p \leftrightarrow {\sim}q$
24. ${\sim}p \leftrightarrow q$
25. ${\sim}(p \leftrightarrow q)$
26. ${\sim}(q \leftrightarrow p)$
27. $(p \leftrightarrow q) \to p$
28. $(p \leftrightarrow q) \to q$
29. $({\sim}p \leftrightarrow q) \to ({\sim}p \to q)$
30. $(p \leftrightarrow {\sim}q) \to (q \to {\sim}p)$
31. $[(p \land q) \land (q \to p)] \leftrightarrow (p \land q)$
32. $[(p \to q) \lor (p \land {\sim}p)] \leftrightarrow ({\sim}q \to {\sim}p)$

In Exercises 33–40, construct a truth table for the given statement. Then determine if the statement is a tautology.

33. $\sim(p \wedge q) \leftrightarrow (\sim p \wedge \sim q)$

34. $\sim(p \vee q) \leftrightarrow (\sim p \wedge \sim q)$

35. $(p \rightarrow q) \leftrightarrow (q \rightarrow p)$

36. $(p \rightarrow q) \leftrightarrow (\sim p \rightarrow \sim q)$

37. $(p \rightarrow q) \leftrightarrow (\sim p \vee q)$

38. $(p \rightarrow q) \leftrightarrow (p \vee \sim q)$

39. $(p \leftrightarrow q) \leftrightarrow \big[(q \rightarrow p) \wedge (p \rightarrow q)\big]$

40. $(q \leftrightarrow p) \leftrightarrow \big[(p \rightarrow q) \wedge (q \rightarrow p)\big]$

In Exercises 41–42, complete the truth table for the given statement by filling in the required columns.

41. $(p \wedge \sim q) \vee r$

p	q	r	$\sim q$	$p \wedge \sim q$	$(p \wedge \sim q) \vee r$
T	T	T			
T	T	F			
T	F	T			
T	F	F			
F	T	T			
F	T	F			
F	F	T			
F	F	F			

42. $(p \vee \sim q) \wedge r$

p	q	r	$\sim q$	$p \vee \sim q$	$(p \vee \sim q) \wedge r$
T	T	T			
T	T	F			
T	F	T			
T	F	F			
F	T	T			
F	T	F			
F	F	T			
F	F	F			

In Exercises 43–50, construct a truth table for the given statement. Then determine if the statement is a tautology.

43. $(p \vee q) \rightarrow r$

44. $p \rightarrow (q \vee r)$

45. $(p \wedge q) \rightarrow (p \vee r)$

46. $(p \vee r) \rightarrow (q \wedge r)$

47. $r \rightarrow (p \wedge q)$

48. $r \rightarrow (p \vee q)$

49. $\big[(p \rightarrow q) \wedge (q \rightarrow r)\big] \rightarrow (p \rightarrow r)$

50. $\big[(p \rightarrow q) \wedge (q \rightarrow r)\big] \rightarrow (\sim r \rightarrow \sim p)$

 Application Exercises

The accompanying bar graph shows the population of the United States, in millions, that is expected for the years 2000, 2010, and 2020. Use the information given by the graph to determine the truth value for each of the statements in Exercises 51–52.

Expected U.S. Population

Source: U.S. Census Bureau

51. If the U.S. population in 2000 is 275 million, then the U.S. population in 2010 is expected to be 350 million.

52. If the U.S. population decreases from the year 2000 to the year 2020, then the U.S. population in 2020 is expected to be less than 300 million.

The table shows the top ten soundtrack albums in the United States. In Exercises 53–58, let p, q, and r represent the following simple statements:

   p: Titanic sold 9 million albums.
   q: Dirty Dancing is the best-selling soundtrack album.
   r: The Lion King sold 3 million more soundtrack albums than Purple Rain.

Write each symbolic statement in words. Then use the information given by the table to determine the truth value of the statement.

Top Selling Soundtrack Albums in the U.S. Through 1998

Album	Sales in Millions
The Bodyguard	16
Purple Rain	13
Saturday Night Fever	11
Dirty Dancing	11
The Lion King	10
Titanic	9

Source: RIAA

53. $r \rightarrow p$ 54. $r \rightarrow q$ 55. $p \rightarrow r$

56. $q \rightarrow r$ 57. $\sim q \rightarrow \sim p$ 58. $\sim p \rightarrow \sim q$

59. The statement *p unless q* means $\sim q \rightarrow p$.
   a. Fill in the truth table that defines *p unless q*.

p	q	~q	p unless q
T	T		
T	F		
F	T		
F	F		

   b. Rewrite the following statement in symbolic form. Indicate the letter that represents each simple statement.

   The curfew will not be lifted unless the violence ends.

   When is this statement false?

Writing in Mathematics

60. Explain when conditional statements are true and when they are false.
61. Explain when biconditional statements are true and when they are false.
62. What is a tautology?
63. Describe how to set up the eight different true-false combinations for a compound statement consisting of three simple statements.
64. Based on the meaning of the inclusive or, explain why it is reasonable that if $p \vee q$ is true, then $\sim p \rightarrow q$ must also be true.
65. Based on the meaning of the inclusive or, explain why if $p \vee q$ is true, then $p \rightarrow \sim q$ is not necessarily true.

Critical Thinking Exercises

66. Which one of the following is true?
   a. A conditional statement is false only when the consequent is true and the antecedent is false.
   b. Some implications are not tautologies.
   c. An equivalent for a conditional statement is obtained by reversing the antecedent and consequent, and then negating the resulting statement.
   d. A compound statement consisting of two simple statements that are both false can be true.
67. Consider the statement "If you get an A in the course, I'll take you out to eat." If you complete the course and I do take you out to eat, can you conclude that you got an A? Explain your answer.

In Exercises 68–69, the headings for the columns in the truth tables are missing. Fill in the statements to replace the missing headings. (More than one correct statement may be possible.)

Do not repeat the column 3 statement.

68.

p	q				
T	T	T	F	T	T
T	F	F	F	F	T
F	T	T	T	T	T
F	F	T	T	T	T

Do not repeat the previous statement.

69.

p	q				
T	T	T	T	F	F
T	F	T	F	T	T
F	T	T	F	T	T
F	F	F	F	T	T

70. A compound statement involving two simple statements has 4 different true-false possibilities. A compound statement involving three simple statements has 8 different true-false possibilites, and one with four simple statements has 16 different true-false possibilities. How many true-false possibilities are there for a compound statement involving n simple statements?

Technology Exercises

Use the table function of your word processor and the appropriate symbols from the program's character map to construct a truth table for the statements in Exercises 71–72.

71. $\sim p \rightarrow q$ 72. $(p \rightarrow \sim q) \vee q$

Group Exercise

73. Each group member should write a compound statement that contains at least three connectives. One of the connectives should be the word unless (see Exercise 59). The group should then select the three statements that members find the most intriguing. For each statement selected, the group should rewrite it in symbolic form, indicating the letters that represent the simple statements.

SECTION 3.5   Equivalent Statements, Conditional Statements, and De Morgan's Laws

Objectives

1. Use a truth table to show that statements are equivalent.

2. Write the equivalent contrapositive for a conditional statement.

3. Write a conditional statement's nonequivalent converse and inverse.

4. Write the negation of a conditional statement.

5. Write equivalent statements using De Morgan's laws.

6. Use De Morgan's laws to negate a conjunction, $\wedge$, and a disjunction, $\vee$.

Equivalent Statements

We have seen that equivalent compound statements are made up of the same simple statements. Equivalent compound statements also have the same corresponding truth values for all true-false interpretations of these simple statements. If a compound statement is true, then its equivalent statement must also be true. Likewise, if a compound statement is false, its equivalent statement must be false.

Truth tables are used to show that two statements are equivalent. When translated into English, equivalencies can be used to gain a better understanding of English statements.

EXAMPLE 1   Showing That Statements Are Equivalent

a. Show that $p \vee q$ and $\sim p \rightarrow q$ are equivalent.

b. Use the result from part (a) to write a statement that is equivalent to:

The bill receives majority approval or the bill does not become law.

Solution

a. Construct a truth table for $p \vee q$ and for $\sim p \rightarrow q$. The truth table for each statement is shown below.

p	q	$p \vee q$	$\sim p$	$\sim p \rightarrow q$
T	T	T	F	T
T	F	T	F	T
F	T	T	T	T
F	F	F	T	F

Corresponding truth values are the same.

The table shows that the truth values for $p \vee q$ and $\sim p \rightarrow q$ are the same. Therefore, the statements are equivalent.

b. The statement

The bill receives majority approval or the bill does not become law

can be expressed in symbolic form using the following representations:

p: The bill receives majority approval.
q: The bill does not become law.

In symbolic form, the statement is $p \vee q$. Based on the truth table in (a), we know that an equivalent statement is $\sim p \rightarrow q$. The equivalent statement can be expressed in words as:

If the bill does not receive majority approval, then the bill does not become law.

Notice that the given statement and its equivalent are both true.

> **1** Use a truth table to show that statements are equivalent.

A special symbol, ≡, is used to show that two statements are equivalent. Because $p \vee q$ and $\sim p \rightarrow q$ are equivalent, we can express this equivalency by writing

$$p \vee q \equiv \sim p \rightarrow q \qquad \text{and} \qquad \sim p \rightarrow q \equiv p \vee q.$$

EXAMPLE 2 Showing That Statements Are Equivalent

Show that $\sim(\sim p) \equiv p$.

Solution Determine the truth values for $\sim(\sim p)$ and p. These are shown in the truth table on the left.

The truth values for $\sim(\sim p)$ were obtained by taking the opposite of each truth value for $\sim p$. The table shows that the truth values for $\sim(\sim p)$ and p are the same. Therefore, the statements are equivalent:

$$\sim(\sim p) \equiv p$$

p	$\sim p$	$\sim(\sim p)$
T	F	T
F	T	F

Corresponding truth values are the same.

The equivalence in Example 2 illustrates that the double negation of a statement is equivalent to the statement. For example, the statement "It is not true that Ernest Hemingway was not a writer" means the same thing as "Ernest Hemingway was a writer."

EXAMPLE 3 Equivalencies and Truth Tables

Select the statement that is not equivalent to:

Miguel is blushing or sunburned.

a. If Miguel is blushing, then he is not sunburned.
b. Miguel is sunburned or blushing.
c. If Miguel is not blushing, then he is sunburned.
d. If Miguel is not sunburned, then he is blushing.

Solution To determine which of the choices is not equivalent to the given statement, begin by writing the given statement and the choices in symbolic form. Then construct a truth table and compare each statement's truth values to those of the given statement. The nonequivalent statement is the one that does not have exactly the same truth values as the given statement.

The simple statements that make up "Miguel is blushing or sunburned" can be represented as follows:

p: Miguel is blushing.

q: Miguel is sunburned.

Here are the symbolic representations for the given statement and the four choices:

Miguel is blushing or sunburned: $p \vee q$

a. If Miguel is blushing, then he is not sunburned: $p \rightarrow \sim q$
b. Miguel is sunburned or blushing: $q \vee p$
c. If Miguel is not blushing, then he is sunburned: $\sim p \rightarrow q$
d. If Miguel is not sunburned, then he is blushing: $\sim q \rightarrow p$

Next, construct a truth table that contains the truth values for the given statement, $p \vee q$, as well as those for the four options. The truth table is shown as follows:

		Given		(a)	(b)		(c)	(d)
p	q	$p \vee q$	$\sim q$	$p \to \sim q$	$q \vee p$	$\sim p$	$\sim p \to q$	$\sim q \to p$
T	T	T	F	F	T	F	T	T
T	F	T	T	T	T	F	T	T
F	T	T	F	T	T	T	T	T
F	F	F	T	T	F	T	F	F

Not equivalent

The statement in option (a) does not have the same corresponding truth values as those for $p \vee q$. Therefore, this statement is not equivalent to the given statement.

We can use our understanding of the inclusive *or* to see why the following statements are not equivalent:

Miguel is blushing or sunburned.

If Miguel is blushing, then he is not sunburned.

Let us assume that the first statement is true. The inclusive *or* tells us that Miguel might be both blushing and sunburned. This means that the second statement might not be true. The fact that Miguel is blushing does not indicate that he is not sunburned; he might be both.

2 Write the equivalent contrapositive for a conditional statement.

The Conditional Statement $p \to q$

In Section 3.4, we learned that $p \to q$ is equivalent to $\sim q \to \sim p$. The truth value of a conditional statement does not change if the antecedent and the consequent are reversed and then both of them are negated. The **contrapositive** is a statement obtained by reversing and negating the antecedent and the consequent.

p	q	$p \to q$	$\sim q \to \sim p$
T	T	T	T
T	F	F	F
F	T	T	T
F	F	T	T

$p \to q$ and $\sim q \to \sim p$ are equivalent.

A Conditional Statement and Its Equivalent Contrapositive

$$p \to q \equiv \sim q \to \sim p$$

The truth value of a conditional statement does not change if the antecedent and consequent are both reversed and negated. The statement $\sim q \to \sim p$ is called the **contrapositive** of the conditional $p \to q$.

EXAMPLE 4 Writing Equivalent Contrapositives

Write the equivalent contrapositive for each of the following statements.

a. If it is a Chevrolet, then it is a vehicle.

b. If the cable is out, then we do not watch TV.

c. If all people obey the law, then no prisons are needed.

Art by Henry L. Small, Ceramic caricature of a classic Chevy

Negations of Quantified Statements

Solution In each part, first reverse the order of the statements before and after the "if–then" connective. Then negate each statement.

a. The equivalent contrapositive of

If it's a Chevrolet, then it's a vehicle.

is:

If it's not a vehicle, then it's not a Chevrolet.

Notice that both of these statements are true.

b. The equivalent contrapositive of

If the cable is out, then we do not watch TV.

is:

If we do watch TV, then the cable is not out.

c. Recall, as shown in the margin, that the negation of "no" is "some," and the negation of "all" is "some … not." We need to reverse and negate the statements before and after "if–then." Our result can be expressed initially using words and symbols:

$\sim$(no prisons are needed) $\rightarrow$ $\sim$(all people obey the law).

Using the correct negations, the contrapositive is:

If some prisons are needed, then some people do not obey the law.

3 Write a conditional statement's nonequivalent converse and inverse.

The truth value of a conditional statement does not change if the antecedent and the consequent are reversed and then both of them are negated. But what happens to the conditional's truth values if just one, but not both, of these changes is made? If the antecedent and the consequent are reversed, the resulting statement is called the **converse** of the conditional statement. By negating both the antecedent and the consequent, we obtain the **inverse** of the conditional statement.

Converses in *Alice's Adventures in Wonderland*

Alice has a problem with logic: She believes that a conditional and its converse mean the same thing. In the passage that follows, she states that

If I say it, I mean it
is the same as
If I mean it, I say it.

She is corrected, told that
If I eat it, I see it
is not the same as
If I see it, I eat it.

(continued)

Variations of the Conditional Statement

Name	Symbolic Form	English Translation
Conditional	$p \rightarrow q$	If p, then q.
Converse	$q \rightarrow p$	If q, then p.
Inverse	$\sim p \rightarrow \sim q$	If not p, then not q.
Contrapositive	$\sim q \rightarrow \sim p$	If not q, then not p.

EXAMPLE 5   Writing the Converse and Inverse

Consider the true conditional statement:

If it's a Chevrolet, then it's a vehicle.

Write the converse and inverse of this true statement.

The group continues its logical humiliation of poor Alice:

"Come, we shall have some fun now" thought Alice. "I'm glad they've begun asking riddles—I believe I can guess that," she added aloud.

"Do you mean that you think you can find out the answer to it?" said the March Hare.

"Exactly so." said Alice.

"Then you should say what you mean," the March Hare went on.

"I do," Alice hastily replied; "at least—at least I mean what I say—that's the same thing, you know."

"Not the same thing a bit!" said the Hatter. "Why, you might just as well say that 'I see what I eat' is the same thing as 'I eat what I see'!"

"You might just as well say," added the March Hare, "that 'I like what I get' is the same thing as 'I get what I like'!"

"You might just as well say," added the Dormouse, which seemed to be talking in its sleep, "that 'I breathe when I sleep' is the same thing as 'I sleep when I breathe'!"

Solution   To form the converse of "If it's a Chevrolet, then it's a vehicle," we reverse the order of the antecedent and consequent:

If it's a vehicle, then it's a Chevrolet.

This statement is not necessarily true. It can be a vehicle, but it might be a make other than a Chevrolet.

To form the inverse of "If it's a Chevrolet, then it's a vehicle," negate the antecedent and consequent:

If it's not a Chevrolet, then it's not a vehicle.

This statement is also not necessarily true. Just because it's not a Chevrolet does not mean that it's not a vehicle. A Ford is not a Chevrolet, yet it certainly is a vehicle.

Example 5 illustrates that if a conditional statement is true, its converse and inverse are not necessarily true. Because the equivalent of a true statement must be true, we see that a conditional statement is not equivalent to its converse or its inverse.

The relationship among the truth values for a conditional statement, its converse, its inverse, and its contrapositive is shown in the truth table that follows.

p	q	Conditional $p \rightarrow q$	Converse $q \rightarrow p$	Inverse $\sim p \rightarrow \sim q$	Contrapositive $\sim q \rightarrow \sim p$
T	T	T	T	T	T
T	F	F	T	T	F
F	T	T	F	F	T
F	F	T	T	T	T

The truth table reveals that a conditional statement is equivalent to its contrapositive. The table also shows that a conditional statement is not equivalent to its converse; in some cases they have the same truth value, but in other cases they have opposite truth values. Also, a conditional statement is not equivalent to its inverse. By contrast, the converse and the inverse are equivalent.

4 Write the negation of a conditional statement.

The Negation of the Conditional Statement $p \rightarrow q$

Suppose that your accountant makes the following statement:

If you itemize deductions, then you pay less in taxes.

When will your accountant have told you a lie? The only case in which you have been lied to is when you itemize deductions and you do *not* pay less in taxes. We can analyze this situation symbolically with the following representations:

p: You itemize deductions.

q: You pay less in taxes.

We represent each compound statement in symbolic form.

$p \rightarrow q$: If you itemize deductions, then you pay less in taxes.

$p \wedge \sim q$: You itemize deductions and you do not pay less in taxes.

The truth table that follows shows that the negation of $p \rightarrow q$ is $p \wedge \sim q$.

p	q	$p \rightarrow q$	$\sim q$	$p \wedge \sim q$
T	T	T	F	F
T	F	F	T	T
F	T	T	F	F
F	F	T	T	F

These columns have opposite truth values, so $p \wedge \sim q$ negates $p \rightarrow q$.

The Negation of a Conditional Statement

The negation of $p \rightarrow q$ is $p \wedge \sim q$. This can be expressed as

$$\sim(p \rightarrow q) \equiv p \wedge \sim q.$$

To form the negation of a conditional statement, leave the antecedent (the first part) unchanged, change the "if–then" connective to "and," and negate the consequent (the second part).

EXAMPLE 6   Writing the Negation of a Conditional Statement

Write the negation of:

If it rains, then I bring my umbrella.

Solution

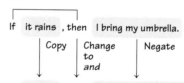

The negation of the given statement is:

It rains and I do not bring my umbrella.

The box that follows summarizes what we have learned about conditional statements.

The Conditional Statement $p \rightarrow q$

Equivalent Contrapositive
   $p \rightarrow q$ is equivalent to $\sim q \rightarrow \sim p$ (the contrapositive).
Nonequivalent Converse and Inverse
   1. $p \rightarrow q$ is not equivalent to $q \rightarrow p$ (the converse).
   2. $p \rightarrow q$ is not equivalent to $\sim p \rightarrow \sim q$ (the inverse).
Negation
   The negation of $p \rightarrow q$ is $p \wedge \sim q$.

5 Write equivalent statements using De Morgan's laws.

p	q	$\sim(p \wedge q)$	$\sim p \vee \sim q$
T	T	F	F
T	F	T	T
F	T	T	T
F	F	T	T

$\sim(p \wedge q)$ and $\sim p \vee \sim q$ are equivalent.

The Rolling Stones

Augustus De Morgan
They don't all rock and roll!

De Morgan's Laws

In Section 3.3, we learned that $\sim(p \wedge q)$ is equivalent to $\sim p \vee \sim q$. Using the symbol for equivalence, $\equiv$, we can write

$$\sim(p \wedge q) \equiv \sim p \vee \sim q.$$

This equivalency is one of two equivalences known as **De Morgan's laws**, named after Augustus De Morgan (1806–1871), an English mathematician.

> **De Morgan's Laws**
>
> 1. $\sim(p \wedge q) \equiv \sim p \vee \sim q$
> 2. $\sim(p \vee q) \equiv \sim p \wedge \sim q$

EXAMPLE 7   Using a De Morgan Law

Write a statement that is equivalent to:

> It is not true that the Rolling Stones and De Morgan's Laws are both rock groups.

Solution   Let p and q represent the following simple statements:

p: The Rolling Stones is a rock group.

q: De Morgan's Laws is a rock group.

The statement is of the form $\sim(p \wedge q)$. An equivalent statement is $\sim p \vee \sim q$. We can translate this as:

The Rolling Stones is not a rock group or De Morgan's Laws is not a rock group.

EXAMPLE 8   Using a De Morgan Law

Write a statement that is equivalent to:

> It is not true that *Jaws* is a musical or a comedy.

Solution   Let p and q represent the following simple statements:

p: *Jaws* is a musical.

q: *Jaws* is a comedy.

The statement is of the form $\sim(p \vee q)$. An equivalent statement is $\sim p \wedge \sim q$. We can translate this as:

Jaws is not a musical and *Jaws* is not a comedy.

This can also be expressed as:

Jaws is neither a musical nor a comedy.

6 Use De Morgan's laws to negate a conjunction, ∧, and a disjunction, ∨.

De Morgan's Laws and Negations

De Morgan's laws can be used to write the negation of a compound statement involving conjunction (∧, and) and disjunction (∨, or).

> ## De Morgan's Laws and Negations
>
> 1. $\sim(p \wedge q) \equiv \sim p \vee \sim q$
>   The negation of $p \wedge q$ is $\sim p \vee \sim q$. To negate a conjunction, negate each component statement and change *and* to *or*.
> 2. $\sim(p \vee q) \equiv \sim p \wedge \sim q$
>   The negation of $p \vee q$ is $\sim p \wedge \sim q$. To negate a disjunction, negate each component statement and change *or* to *and*.

EXAMPLE 9 Negating a Disjunction, ∨

The Ten Greatest Americans of All Time

American	Score
1. Abraham Lincoln	36
2. George Washington	35
3. Franklin D. Roosevelt	31
4. Thomas Edison	27
5. Benjamin Franklin	24
6. Martin Luther King, Jr.	21
7. Henry Ford	19
8. Theodore Roosevelt	18
9. Clara Barton	16
Eleanor Roosevelt	16

Who is the greatest American ever? The editors of *The Definitive Guide to the Best and Worst of Everything* (Prentice Hall, 1997) used a 0 to 40 score to arrive at the list in the margin. Write the negation of this statement that was used to form the list:

An American citizen scores more than 15 or that person is not on the greatest-of-all-time list.

Solution By using De Morgan's law for negating a disjunction, we can write the negation in English without having to first translate into symbolic form. To negate this disjunction, negate each component statement and change *or* to *and*.

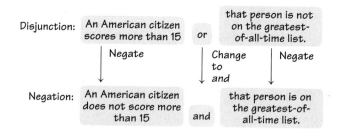

The negation of the given statement is:

An American citizen does not score more than 15 and that person is on the greatest-of-all-time list.

Table 3.13 Negations of Compound Statements

Statement	Negation
$p \wedge q$	$\sim p \vee \sim q$
$p \vee q$	$\sim p \wedge \sim q$
$p \rightarrow q$	$p \wedge \sim q$

Table 3.13 summarizes the negations of the three compound statements discussed in this section.

Exercise Set 3.5

 Practice Exercises

1. a. Use a truth table to show that $p \rightarrow q$ and $\sim p \vee q$ are equivalent.

   b. Use the result from part (a) to write a statement that is equivalent to:

   If a major dam on the upper Nile River is not in place, then the lower Nile overflows its banks each year.

2. a. Use a truth table to show that $p \vee q$ and $\sim q \rightarrow p$ are equivalent.

   b. Use the result from part (a) to write a statement that is equivalent to:

   I study or I fail.

3. Select the statement that is equivalent to:

   I saw *Rent* or *Ragtime*.
   a. If I did not see *Rent*, I saw *Ragtime*.
   b. I saw both *Rent* and *Ragtime*.
   c. If I saw *Rent*, I did not see *Ragtime*.
   d. If I saw *Ragtime*, I did not see *Rent*.

4. Select the statement that is equivalent to:

   Citizen Kane or *Howard the Duck* appear in a list of greatest U.S. movies.
   a. If *Citizen Kane* appears in the list of greatest U.S. movies, *Howard the Duck* does not.
   b. It *Howard the Duck* does not appear in the list of greatest U.S. movies, then *Citizen Kane* does.
   c. Both *Citizen Kane* and *Howard the Duck* appear in a list of greatest U.S. movies.
   d. If *Howard the Duck* appears in the list of greatest U.S. movies, *Citizen Kane* does not.

5. Select the statement that is *not* equivalent to:

   It is not true that Sondheim and Picasso are both musicians.
   a. Sondheim is not a musician or Picasso is not a musician.
   b. If Sondheim is a musician, then Picasso is not a musician.
   c. Sondheim is not a musician and Picasso is not a musician.
   d. If Picasso is a musician, then Sondheim is not a musician.

6. Select the statement that is *not* equivalent to:

   It is not true that England and Africa are both countries.
   a. If England is a country, then Africa is not a country.
   b. England is not a country and Africa is not a country.
   c. England is not a country or Africa is not a country.
   d. If Africa is a country, then England is not a country.

Write the equivalent contrapositive for each statement in Exercises 7–16.

7. If I am in Chicago, then I am in Illinois.

8. If I am in Birmingham, then I am in the South.

9. If the stereo is playing, then I cannot hear you.

10. If it is blue, then it is not an apple.

11. "If you don't laugh, you die." (humorist Alan King)

12. "If Sears does not bring out a riding vacuum cleaner, then the floor stays messy." (Roseanne doing her "domestic goddess" routine)

13. If the president is telling the truth, then all troops were withdrawn.

14. If the review session is successful, then no students fail the test.

15. If all institutions place profit above human need, then some people suffer.

16. If all hard workers are successful, then some people are not hard workers.

Write the nonequivalent converse and inverse for each statement in Exercises 17–26.

17. If you touch poison oak, then you get a skin rash.

18. If I am sick, then I miss class.

19. If the play is *Macbeth*, then Shakespeare is the author.

20. If the movie is *Saving Private Ryan*, then Tom Hanks appears.

21. If you are driving the car, then you are not sleeping.

22. If you are in class, then you are not listening to the radio.

23. If I am in Charleston, then I am not in the West.

24. If I am in London, then I am not in Spain.

25. If it's St. Patrick's Day, then some people wear green.

26. If it's Thanksgiving, then some people eat turkey.

Write the negation of each conditional statement in Exercises 27–34.

27. If I am in Los Angeles, then I am in California.

28. If I am in Houston, then I am in Texas.

29. If it is purple, then it is not a carrot.

30. If the TV is playing, then I cannot concentrate.

31. If he doesn't, I will.

32. If she says yes, he says no.

33. If there is a blizzard, then all schools are closed.

34. If there is a tax cut, then all people have extra spending money.

Use De Morgan's laws to write a statement that is equivalent to each statement in Exercises 35–42.

35. It is not true that Australia and China are both islands.

36. It is not true that Florida and California are both peninsulas.

37. It is not the case that my high school encouraged creativity and diversity.

38. It is not the case that the course covers logic and dream analysis.

39. It is not true that Babe Ruth was a writer or a lawyer.

40. It is not true that Martin Luther King supported violent protest or the Vietnam war.
41. It is not the case that the United States has eradicated poverty or racism.
42. It is not the case that the movie is interesting or entertaining.

Use De Morgan's laws to write the negation of each statement in Exercises 43–50.

43. I'm going to Seattle or San Francisco.
44. This course covers logic or statistics.
45. I study or I do not pass.
46. I give up tobacco or I am not healthy.
47. I am not going and he is going.
48. I do not apply myself and I succeed.
49. A bill becomes law and it does not receive majority approval.
50. They see the show and they do not have tickets.

 Application Exercises

Cosmetic surgery in the United States is a multi-billion dollar industry. Use the information given by the table to solve Exercises 51–53.

Cosmetic Surgery in the U.S.

Procedure	Number of Operations in One Year	Percent of Patients Who Are Women
Chemical Peel	29,072	96%
Nose Reshaping	35,927	71%
Face Lift	32,283	92%
Collagen Injection	27,052	96%
Breast Lift	10,053	100%
Breast Enlargement	39,247	100%
Tummy Tuck	16,829	95%
Buttock Lift	314	93%
Liposuction	51,072	87%

Source: American Society of Plastic and Reconstructive Surgeons

51. Consider the statement:

    If the procedure is a chemical peel, then 96% of the patients are women.
    a. Is this statement true or false?
    Write this statement's: b. contrapositive c. converse d. inverse e. negation. Indicate whether each of these statements is true or false.

For each statement in Exercise 52–53:
   a. *Use the information in the table shown to determine if the statement is true or false.*
   b. *Use a De Morgan's law to write the statement's negation.*
   c. *Use the table to determine if the negation in part (b) is true or false.*

52. There are 51,072 liposuctions each year and 93% of the liposuction patients are women.
53. There are 32,283 face lifts each year or 8% of the face-lift patients are men.

 Writing in Mathematics

54. What are equivalent statements?
55. Describe how to determine if two statements are equivalent.
56. Describe how to obtain the contrapositive of a conditional statement.
57. Describe how to obtain the converse and the inverse of a conditional statement.
58. Make up an example of a conditional statement that is true, but whose converse and inverse are not necessarily true. Try to make the statement somewhat different from the conditional statements that you have encountered throughout this section. Explain why the converse and the inverse that you wrote are not necessarily true.
59. Explain how to write the negation of a conditional statement.
60. Explain how to write the negation of a conjunction.
61. Make up an example of a disjunction that is true, even though one of its component statements is false. Then write the negation of the disjunction and explain why the negation is false.
62. Read the essay on pages 116–117. The Dormouse's last statement is the setup for a joke. The punchline, delivered by the Hatter to the Dormouse, is, "For you, it's the same thing." Explain the joke. What does this punchline have to do with the difference between a conditional and a biconditional statement?

 Critical Thinking Exercises

63. Which one of the following is true?
    a. $\sim q \to (p \wedge r)$ is equivalent to $\sim(p \vee r) \to q$.
    b. The inverse of a statement's converse is the statement's contrapositive.
    c. A conditional statement can sometimes be true if its contrapositive is false.
    d. A conditional statement can never be false if its converse is true.
64. Write the contrapositive for the statement:
    If you are at least 18 and a citizen, then you can vote.
65. Write the contrapositive for the statement:
    I do not get a ticket if I observe the speed limit.

66. Write the negation for the following conjunction:
We will neither replace nor repair the roof, and we will sell the house.

67. Write the converse, the inverse, the contrapositive and the negation of $p \rightarrow (\sim q \vee r)$. If $\sim$ appears outside parentheses, rewrite using one of De Morgan's laws.

Technology Exercises

Use the table function of your word processor and the appropriate symbols from the program's character map to construct a table that verifies the equivalencies in Exercises 68–69.

68. $p \rightarrow q \equiv \sim p \vee q$ 69. $p \rightarrow (q \rightarrow r) \equiv (p \wedge q) \rightarrow r$

Group Exercise

70. Can you think of an advertisement in which the person using a product is extremely attractive or famous? It is true that if you are this attractive or famous person, then you use the product. (Or at least pretend, for monetary gain, that you use the product!) In order to get you to buy the product, here is what the advertisers would *like* you to believe: If I use this product, then I will be just like this attractive or famous person. This, the converse, is not necessarily true and, for most of us, is unfortunately false. Each group member should find an example of this kind of deceptive advertising, sharing the example with other group members.

SECTION 3.6   Arguments and Truth Tables

Objectives

1. Use truth tables to determine validity.
2. Use forms of valid arguments to draw logical conclusions.

In Section 3.5, we used truth tables to determine that statements are equivalent. In this section, we use truth tables to determine whether arguments are valid or invalid.

An **argument** consists of two parts: the given statements, called the **premises**, and a **conclusion**. Here's an example of an argument:

Premise 1: If the toll ticket is lost, then the fare from the farthest point is paid.

Premise 2: I lost the toll ticket.

Conclusion: Therefore, I pay the fare from the farthest point.

It appears that if the premises are true, then I have to pay the fare from the farthest point. The true premises force the conclusion to be true, making this an example of a **valid argument**.

1 Use truth tables to determine validity.

> ### Definition of a Valid Argument
> An argument is **valid** if the conclusion is true whenever the premises are assumed to be true. An argument that is not valid is said to be an **invalid argument**, also called a **fallacy**.

Truth tables can be used to test validity. We begin by writing the argument in symbolic form. Let's do this for the argument involving the lost ticket. Represent each simple statement with a letter. Let p and q be:

p: The toll ticket is lost.

q: The fare from the farthest point is paid.

Now we write the two premises and the conclusion in symbolic form:

Premise 1:	$p \rightarrow q$	If the toll ticket is lost, then the fare from the farthest point is paid.
Premise 2:	p	I lost the toll ticket.
Conclusion:	$\therefore q$	Therefore, I pay the fare from the farthest point.

(The three-dot triangle, $\therefore$, is read "therefore.")

To decide whether this argument is valid, we rewrite it in the following form:

If $\left[premise\ 1\ \textbf{and}\ premise\ 2 \right]$ **then** *conclusion.*

$$\left[(p \rightarrow q) \quad \wedge \quad p \quad \right] \rightarrow \quad q$$

At this point, we must determine whether the conjunction of the premises implies that the conclusion is true for all possible truth values for p and q. We construct a truth table for the statement

$$\left[(p \rightarrow q) \wedge p \right] \rightarrow q.$$

If the final column in the truth table is true in every case, then the statement is a tautology and the argument is valid. If the conditional statement in the last column is false in at least one case, then the statement is not a tautology, and the argument is invalid. The truth table is shown below.

p	q	$p \rightarrow q$	$(p \rightarrow q) \wedge p$	$\left[(p \rightarrow q) \wedge p \right] \rightarrow q$
T	T	T	T	T
T	F	F	F	T
F	T	T	F	T
F	F	T	F	T

The final column in the table is true in every case. The conditional statement is a tautology. This means that the true premises imply the conclusion. The conclusion necessarily follows from the premises. Therefore, the argument is valid.

The form of the argument in the lost-toll-ticket example,

$$p \rightarrow q$$
$$\underline{p}$$
$$\therefore q$$

is called **direct reasoning**. All arguments that have the direct reasoning form are valid regardless of the English statements that p and q represent.

Here's a step-by-step procedure to test the validity of an argument using truth tables.

Testing the Validity of an Argument with a Truth Table

1. Use a letter to represent each simple statement in the argument.
2. Express the premises and the conclusion symbolically.
3. If the argument contains two premises, write a symbolic conditional statement of the form:

$$\left[(\text{premise 1}) \wedge (\text{premise 2}) \right] \rightarrow \text{conclusion.}$$

4. Construct a truth table for the conditional statement in step 3.
5. If the final column of the truth table has all trues, the conditional statement is a tautology, and the argument is valid. If the final column does not have all trues, the conditional statement is not a tautology, and the argument is invalid.

EXAMPLE 1   An Identity Crisis as an Argument

Poor Alice! In Lewis Carroll's *Alice's Adventures in Wonderland*, she falls into a rabbit hole, eats a piece of cake, and suddenly begins to grow. Because she is no longer the same (at least not the same height), she wonders who she is. She thinks of her friend Mabel, who knows very little. After deciding that $4 \times 5 = 12$ and London is the capital of Paris, she realizes that she, too, knows very little. She concludes that she must be Mabel.

Alice's thinking can be expressed in the form of an argument.

> If one is Mabel, then one knows very little.
> I know very little.
> _____
> Therefore, I am Mabel.

Determine whether this argument is valid or invalid.

Solution

Step 1   Use a letter to represent each simple statement in the argument.

We introduce the following representations:

p: One is Mabel.
q: One knows very little.

Step 2   Express the premises and the conclusion symbolically.

$$p \rightarrow q \qquad \text{If one is Mabel, then one knows very little.}$$
$$\underline{q} \qquad\qquad \underline{\text{I know very little.}}$$
$$\therefore p \qquad\quad\ \text{Therefore, I am Mabel.}$$

Step 3   Write a symbolic statement of the form:

$$[(\text{premise 1}) \wedge (\text{premise 2})] \rightarrow \text{conclusion.}$$

The symbolic statement is:

$$[(p \rightarrow q) \wedge q] \rightarrow p.$$

Step 4   Construct a truth table for the conditional statement in step 3.

p	q	$p \rightarrow q$	$(p \rightarrow q) \wedge q$	$[(p \rightarrow q) \wedge q] \rightarrow p$
T	T	T	T	T
T	F	F	F	T
F	T	T	T	F
F	F	T	F	T

Step 5   Use the truth values in the final column to determine if the argument is valid or invalid.

The entries in the final column of the truth table are not all true, so the conditional statement is not a tautology. Alice's argument is invalid or a fallacy.

The form of the argument in Alice's identity crisis,

$$p \rightarrow q$$
$$\underline{q}$$
$$\therefore p$$

is called the **fallacy of the converse**. It should remind you that a conditional is not equivalent to its converse. All arguments that have this form are invalid regardless of the English statements that p and q represent.

Because a conditional statement is not equivalent to its converse or its inverse, there is an invalid form of an argument called the **fallacy of the inverse**:

$$p \rightarrow q$$
$$\underline{\sim p}$$
$$\therefore \sim q$$

An example of such a fallacy is "If I study, I pass. I do not study. Therefore, I do not pass." For most students, the conclusion is true, but it does not have to be. If an argument is invalid, then the conclusion is not necessarily true. This, however, does not mean that the conclusion must be false.

EXAMPLE 2   A Rush Limbaugh Argument

Conservative radio talk show host Rush Limbaugh directed the following argument at Al Gore.

> You would think that if Algore and company believe so passionately in their environmental crusading that [sic] they would first put these ideas to work in their own lives, right? ... Algore thinks the automobile is one of the greatest threats to the planet, but he sure as heck still travels in one of them—a gas guzzler too.

(See, *I Told You So*, p. 168)

Limbaugh's passage can be expressed in the form of an argument.

> If Gore really believed that the automobile were a threat to the planet, he would not travel in a gas-guzzler.
> Gore does travel in a gas-guzzler.
> Therefore, Gore does not really believe that the automobile is a threat to the planet.

Rush Limbaugh, conservative radio talk show host, intrigues some people and infuriates others.

Determine whether this argument is valid or invalid.

Solution

Step 1   Use letters to represent each statement in the argument.

We introduce the following representations:

p: Gore really believes that the automobile is a threat to the planet.
q: He does not travel in a gas-guzzler.

Step 2   Express the premises and the conclusion symbolically.

$p \rightarrow q$	If Gore really believed that the automobile were a threat to the planet, he would not travel in a gas-guzzler.
$\underline{\sim q}$	Gore does travel in a gas-guzzler.
$\therefore \sim p$	Therefore, Gore does not really believe that the automobile is a threat to the planet.

Step 3   Write a symbolic statement of the form:

$$[(\text{premise 1}) \wedge (\text{premise 2})] \rightarrow \text{conclusion}.$$

The symbolic statement is:

$$[(p \rightarrow q) \wedge \sim q] \rightarrow \sim p.$$

Step 4 Construct a truth table for the conditional statement in step 3.

p	q	$p \rightarrow q$	$\sim q$	$(p \rightarrow q) \wedge \sim q$	$\sim p$	$[(p \rightarrow q) \wedge \sim q] \rightarrow \sim p$
T	T	T	F	F	F	T
T	F	F	T	F	F	T
F	T	T	F	F	T	T
F	F	T	T	T	T	T

Step 5 Use the truth values in the final column to determine if the argument is valid or invalid.

The entries in the final column of the truth table are all true, so the conditional statement is a tautology. Limbaugh's argument is valid.

The form of the argument in the Limbaugh example,

$$p \rightarrow q$$
$$\underline{\sim q}$$
$$\therefore \sim p$$

should remind you that a conditional statement is equivalent to its contrapositive:

$$p \rightarrow q \equiv \sim q \rightarrow \sim p.$$

The form is called **contrapositive reasoning**.
   The Limbaugh argument in Example 2 is valid because the conclusion is true *relative to the premises.* If the premises are true, then the conclusion is true. But are the premises indeed true? If they are not, or if they are flawed in some manner, then the relatively true conclusion of the argument might not be true in the real world. For example, the second premise, Gore does travel in a gas-guzzler, is assumed true. But do we know whether Gore really traveled in a gas-guzzler at the time of the argument?

EXAMPLE 3   Sally's Argument in a *Peanuts* Cartoon

Take a moment to read the *Peanuts* cartoon shown below.

Peanuts. Reprinted by permission of United Feature Syndicate, Inc.

We can express Sally's argument as follows:

If you do not know how to read, then you cannot read "War and Peace."
If you cannot read "War and Peace," then Leo Tolstoy will hate you.

Therefore, if you do not know how to read, then Leo Tolstoy will hate you.

Determine whether this argument is valid or invalid.

Solution

Step 1   Use letters to represent each statement in the argument.

We introduce the following representations:
   p: You do not know how to read.
   q: You cannot read "War and Peace."
   r: Leo Tolstoy will hate you.

Step 2   Express the premises and the conclusion symbolically.

$p \rightarrow q$	If you do not know how to read, then you cannot read "War and Peace."
$q \rightarrow r$	If you cannot read "War and Peace," then Leo Tolstoy will hate you.
$\therefore p \rightarrow r$	Therefore, if you do not know how to read, then Leo Tolstoy will hate you.

Step 3   Write a symbolic statement of the form:

$$\big[(\text{premise 1}) \wedge (\text{premise 2})\big] \rightarrow \text{conclusion}.$$

The symbolic statement is:

$$\big[(p \rightarrow q) \wedge (q \rightarrow r)\big] \rightarrow (p \rightarrow r).$$

Step 4   Construct a truth table for the conditional statement in step 3.

p	q	r	$p \rightarrow q$	$q \rightarrow r$	$p \rightarrow r$	$(p \rightarrow q) \wedge (q \rightarrow r)$	$\big[(p \rightarrow q) \wedge (q \rightarrow r)\big] \rightarrow (p \rightarrow r)$
T	T	T	T	T	T	T	T
T	T	F	T	F	F	F	T
T	F	T	F	T	T	F	T
T	F	F	F	T	F	F	T
F	T	T	T	T	T	T	T
F	T	F	T	F	T	F	T
F	F	T	T	T	T	T	T
F	F	F	T	T	T	T	T

Step 5   Use the truth values in the final column to determine if the argument is valid or invalid. The entry in each of the eight rows in the final column of the truth table is true, so the conditional statement is a tautology. Sally's argument is valid.

The form of Sally's argument,

$$p \rightarrow q$$
$$q \rightarrow r$$
$$\therefore p \rightarrow r,$$

is called **transitive reasoning.** If p implies q and q implies r, then p must imply r. Because $p \rightarrow r$ is a valid conclusion, the contrapositive, $\sim r \rightarrow \sim p$, is also a valid conclusion. Not necessarily true are the converse, $r \rightarrow p$, and the inverse, $\sim p \rightarrow \sim r$.

Table 3.14 contains the standard forms of commonly used valid and invalid arguments. If an English argument translates into one of these forms, you can immediately determine whether or not it is valid without using a truth table.

Table 3.14 Standard Forms of Arguments

Valid Arguments

Direct Reasoning	Contrapositive Reasoning	Disjunctive Reasoning	Transitive Reasoning
$p \rightarrow q$ p $\therefore q$	$p \rightarrow q$ $\sim q$ $\therefore \sim p$	$p \vee q \quad p \vee q$ $\sim p \quad\quad \sim q$ $\therefore q \quad\quad \therefore p$	$p \rightarrow q$ $q \rightarrow r$ $\therefore p \rightarrow r$ $\therefore \sim r \rightarrow \sim p$

Invalid Arguments

Fallacy of the Converse	Fallacy of the Inverse	Misuse of Disjunctive Reasoning	Misuse of Transitive Reasoning
$p \rightarrow q$ q $\therefore p$	$p \rightarrow q$ $\sim p$ $\therefore \sim q$	$p \vee q \quad\quad p \vee q$ $p \quad\quad\quad q$ $\therefore \sim q \quad\quad \therefore \sim p$	$p \rightarrow q$ $q \rightarrow r$ $\therefore r \rightarrow p$ $\therefore \sim p \rightarrow \sim r$

2 Use forms of valid arguments to draw logical conclusions.

Drawing Logical Conclusions

A **logical** or **valid conclusion** is one that forms a valid argument when it follows the set of given premises. Suppose that the premises of an English argument translate into any one of the symbolic forms of premises for the valid arguments in Table 3.14. The symbolic conclusion can be used to find a valid English conclusion. Example 4 shows how this is done.

EXAMPLE 4 Drawing a Logical Conclusion

Draw a valid conclusion from the following premises.

If all people have the same idea of what is humorous, then no jokes bomb.

Some jokes bomb.

Solution

Let p be: All people have the same idea of what is humorous.
Let q be: No jokes bomb.

The form of the premises is:

$p \rightarrow q$:   If all people have the same idea of what is humorous, then no jokes bomb.

$\sim q$:   Some jokes bomb. (Recall that the negation of "no" is "some.")

$\therefore\ ?$

The conclusion $\sim p$ is valid because it forms the contrapositive reasoning form of a valid argument when it follows the given premises. The conclusion $\sim p$ translates as:

Not all people have the same idea of what is humorous.

Because the negation of "all" is "some…not," we can equivalently conclude that:

Some people do not have the same idea of what is humorous.

Exercise Set 3.6

 Practice Exercises

In Exercises 1–8, use a truth table to determine whether the symbolic form of the argument is valid or invalid.

1. $p \rightarrow q$
$\dfrac{\sim p}{\therefore \sim q}$

2. $p \rightarrow q$
$\dfrac{\sim p}{\therefore q}$

3. $p \rightarrow \sim q$
$\dfrac{q}{\therefore \sim p}$

4. $\sim p \rightarrow q$
$\dfrac{\sim q}{\therefore p}$

5. $p \wedge \sim q$
$\dfrac{p}{\therefore \sim q}$

6. $\sim p \vee q$
$\dfrac{p}{\therefore q}$

7. $p \rightarrow q$
$q \rightarrow p$
$\therefore p \wedge q$

8. $(p \rightarrow q) \wedge (q \rightarrow p)$
$\dfrac{p}{\therefore p \vee q}$

In Exercises 9–14, translate each argument into symbolic form. Then use a truth table to determine whether each argument is valid or invalid. (You can ignore differences in past, present, and future tense.)

9. If it is cold, my motorcycle will not start.
My motorcycle started.

  ∴ It is not cold.

10. If a metrorail system is not in operation, there are traffic delays.
Over the past year there have been no traffic delays.

  ∴ Over the past year a metrorail system has been in operation.

11. There must be a dam or there is flooding.
This year there is flooding.

  ∴ This year there is no dam.

12. You must eat well or you will not be healthy.
I eat well.

  ∴ I am healthy.

13. If all people obey the law, then no jails are needed.
Some people do not obey the law.

  ∴ Some jails are needed.

14. If all people obey the law, then no jails are needed.
Some jails are needed.

  ∴ Some people do not obey the law.

In Exercises 15–20, use a truth table with eight cases to determine whether the symbolic form of the argument is valid or invalid.

15. $p \rightarrow q$
$q \rightarrow r$
$\therefore r \rightarrow p$

16. $p \rightarrow q$
$q \rightarrow r$
$\therefore \sim p \rightarrow \sim r$

17. $p \rightarrow q$
$q \wedge r$
$\therefore p \vee r$

18. $\sim p \wedge q$
$p \leftrightarrow r$
$\therefore p \wedge r$

19. $p \leftrightarrow q$
$q \rightarrow r$
$\therefore \sim r \rightarrow \sim p$

20. $q \rightarrow \sim p$
$q \wedge r$
$\therefore r \rightarrow p$

In Exercises 21–28, translate each argument into symbolic form. Then use a truth table with eight cases to determine whether each argument is valid or invalid. (Ignore differences in past, present, and future tense.)

21. If Tim and Janet play, then the team wins.
    Tim played and the team lost.

    ∴ Janet did not play.

22. If *The Graduate* and *Midnight Cowboy* are shown, then the performance is sold out.
    Midnight Cowboy was shown and the peformance was not sold out.

    ∴ *The Graduate* was not shown.

23. If it rains or snows, then I read.
    I am not reading.

    ∴ It is neither raining nor snowing.

24. If I am tired or hungry, I cannot concentrate.
    I can concentrate.

    ∴ I am neither tired nor hungry.

25. If it rains or snows, then I read.
    I am reading.

    ∴ It is raining or snowing.

26. If I am tired or hungry, I cannot concentrate.
    I cannot concentrate.

    ∴ I am tired or hungry.

27. If it is hot and humid, I complain.
    It is not hot or it is not humid.

    ∴ I am not complaining.

28. If I watch *Schindler's List* and *Guess Who's Coming to Dinner*, I am aware of the destructive nature of intolerance.
    Today I did not watch *Schindler's List* or I did not watch *Guess Who's Coming to Dinner*.

    ∴ Today I am not aware of the destructive nature of intolerance.

In Exercises 29–36, translate each argument into symbolic form. Then use the forms of valid and invalid arguments in Table 3.14 on page 129 to determine whether each argument is valid or invalid.

29. If we close the door, then there is less noise.
    There is less noise.

    ∴ We closed the door.

30. If the temperature is in the 90s, then at least two county pools are open.
    It is in the 90s today.

    ∴ Two or more county pools are open today.

31. We criminalize drugs or we damage the future of young people.
    We will not damage the future of young people.

    ∴ We criminalize drugs.

32. He is intelligent or an over-achiever.
    He is intelligent.

    ∴ He is not an over-achiever.

33. If I am at the beach, then I swim in the ocean.
    If I swim in the ocean, then I feel refreshed.

    ∴ If I am at the beach, then I feel refreshed.

34. If I'm tired, I'm edgy.
    If I'm edgy, I'm nasty.

    ∴ If I'm not nasty, I'm not tired.

35. If I'm at the beach, then I swim in the ocean.
    If I swim in the ocean, then I feel refreshed.

    ∴ If I'm not at the beach, then I don't feel refreshed.

36. If I'm tired, I'm edgy.
    If I'm edgy, I'm nasty.

    ∴ If I'm nasty, I'm tired.

In Exercises 37–44, draw a valid conclusion from the given premises. (Use the standard forms of valid arguments in Table 3.14 on page 129.)

37. If a person is a chemist, then that person has a college degree.
    My best friend does not have a college degree.
    Therefore,...

38. If the Westway Expressway is not in operation, automobile traffic makes the East Side Highway look like a parking lot.
    On June 2, the Westway Expressway was completely shut down because of an overturned truck.
    Therefore,...

39. The writers of "My Mother the Car" were told by the network to improve their scripts or be dropped from prime time.
    The writers of "My Mother the Car" did not improve their scripts.
    Therefore,...

40. You exercise or you do not feel energized.
    I do not exercise.
    Therefore,...

41. If all electricity is off, then no lights work.
    Some lights work.
    Therefore,...

42. If all houses meet the hurricane code, then none of them are destroyed by a category 4 hurricane.
    Some houses were destroyed by Andrew, a category 4 hurricane.
    Therefore,...

43. If I vacation in Paris, I eat French pastries.
    If I eat French pastries, I gain weight.
    Therefore,...

44. If I am full time student, I cannot work.
    If I cannot work, I cannot afford a rental apartment costing more than $500 per month.
    Therefore,...

Application Exercises

45. Conservative commentator Rush Limbaugh directed the following passage at liberals and the way they think about crime.

> Of course, liberals will argue that these actions [contemporary youth crime] can be laid at the foot of socioeconomic inequities, or poverty. However, the Great Depression caused a level of poverty unknown to exist in America today, and yet I have been unable to find any accounts of crime waves sweeping our large cities. Let the liberals chew on that.
> (*See, I Told You So*, p. 83)

Limbaugh's passage can be expressed in the form of an argument.

> If poverty causes crime, then crime waves would have swept American cities during the Great Depression.
> Crime waves did not sweep American cities during the Great Depression.
> _____
> ∴ Poverty does not cause crime. (Liberals are wrong.)

Translate this argument into symbolic form and determine whether it is valid or invalid.

46. In his *Autobiography*, Bertrand Russell writes:

> I had had from the first a dark suspicion that the invitation [to lecture in China] might be a practical joke, and in order to test its genuineness I had got the Chinese to pay my passage money before I started. I thought that few people would spend £125 on a joke....

Write Russell's passage in the form of an argument using the following simple statements:

p: The invitation is not genuine.
q: People would not spend 125 pounds.

The argument's conclusion should be:

> The invitation is genuine.

Determine if the argument is valid or invalid.

 Writing in Mathematics

47. Describe what is meant by a valid argument.

48. If you are given an argument in words that contains two premises and a conclusion, describe how to determine if the argument is valid or invalid.

49. Write an original argument in words for the direct reasoning form.

50. Write an original argument in words for the contrapositive reasoning form.

51. Write an original argument in words for the transitive reasoning form.

52. What is a valid conclusion?

 Critical Thinking Exercises

53. Write an original argument in words that has a true conclusion, yet is invalid.

54. Draw a valid conclusion from the given premises. Then use a truth table to verify your answer.

> If you only spoke when spoken to and I only spoke when spoken to, then nobody would ever say anything.
> Some people do say things.
> Therefore,...

55. Translate the following argument into symbolic form. Then use a truth table to determine if the argument is valid or invalid.

> It's wrong to smoke in public if secondary cigarette smoke is a health threat.
> If secondary cigarette smoke were not a health threat, the American Lung Association would not say that it is.
> The American Lung Association says that secondary cigarette smoke is a health threat.
> _____
> ∴ It's wrong to smoke in public.

 Technology Exercises

Use the table function of your word processor and the appropriate symbols from the program's character map to construct a table that shows that each statement in Exercises 56–57 is a tautology.

56. $[(p \rightarrow q) \wedge p] \rightarrow q$

57. $[p \rightarrow (q \rightarrow r)] \vee [(p \wedge q) \wedge \sim r]$

 Group Exercise

58. In this section, we used examples from *Alice's Adventures in Wonderland*, Rush Limbaugh's *See, I Told You So*, and the cartoon *Peanuts* to illustrate symbolic arguments.

  a. From any source that is of particular interest to you (these can be the words of someone you truly admire or a person who really gets under your skin), select a paragraph or two in which the writer argues a particular point. Rewrite the reasoning in the form of an argument using words. Then translate the argument into symbolic form and use a truth table to determine if it is valid or invalid.

  b. Each group member should share the selected passage with other people in the group. Explain how it was expressed in argument form. Then tell why the argument is valid or invalid.

SECTION 3.7 *Arguments and Euler Diagrams*

Objective

1. Use Euler diagrams to determine validity.

1 Use Euler diagrams to determine validity.

In this section, our interest is in determining the validity of arguments whose premises contain the words *all*, *some*, and *no*. The technique for doing this involves four basic diagrams known as **Euler diagrams**. These diagrams are attributed to the Swiss mathematician Leonhard Euler (1707–1783), who used the diagrams to study the validity of arguments.

We can represent the four basic quantified statements in Euler diagrams, illustrated in Figure 3.5.

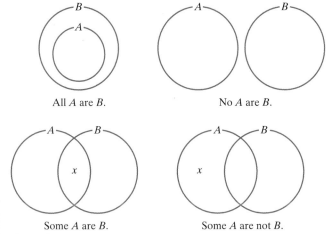

All *A* are *B*.   No *A* are *B*.

Some *A* are *B*.   Some *A* are not *B*.

Figure 3.5 Euler diagrams for quantified statements

The Euler diagrams in Figure 3.5 are just like the Venn diagrams that we used in studying sets. However, there is no need to enclose the circles inside a rectangle representing a universal set. In these diagrams, circles are used to indicate relationships of premises to conclusions.

Here's a step-by-step procedure for using Euler diagrams to determine whether or not an argument is valid.

Euler Diagrams and Arguments

1. Make an Euler diagram for the first premise.
2. Make an Euler diagram for the second premise on top of the one for the first premise.
3. The argument is valid if and only if every possible diagram illustrates the conclusion of the argument. If there is even *one* possible diagram that contradicts the conclusion, this indicates that the conclusion is not true in every case, so the argument is invalid.

The goal of this procedure is to produce, if possible, *a diagram that does* **not** *illustrate the argument's conclusion*. The method of Euler diagrams boils down to determining whether such a diagram is possible. If it is, this serves as a counterexample to the argument's conclusion, and the argument is immediately invalid.

The technique of using Euler diagrams is illustrated in Examples 1–6.

Leonhard Euler

The Swiss mathematician Leonhard Euler (1707–1783) was the most prolific mathematician who ever lived. His collected books and papers fill some 80 volumes, and his introductory algebra text is still available in English translation. Euler was also an astronomer, botanist, chemist, physicist, and linguist. His productivity was not at all slowed down by the total blindness he experienced the last 17 years of his life.

EXAMPLE 1 Arguments and Euler Diagrams

Is the following argument valid?

> All people who arrive late cannot perform.
> All people who cannot perform are ineligible for scholarships.
> ___
> Therefore, all people who arrive late are ineligible for scholarships.

Solution

Step 1 Make an Euler diagram for the first premise. We begin by diagramming the premise:

> All people who arrive late cannot perform.

The region inside the smaller circle represents people who arrive late. The region inside the larger circle represents people who cannot perform.

Step 2 Make an Euler diagram for the second premise on top of the one for the first premise. We add to our previous figure the diagram for the second premise:

> All people who cannot perform are ineligible for scholarships.

A third, larger, circle representing people who are ineligible for scholarships is drawn outside the circle representing people who cannot perform.

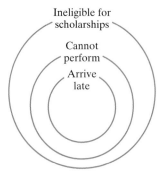

Step 3 The argument is valid if and only if every possible diagram illustrates the argument's conclusion.

There is only one possible diagram. Let's see if this diagram illustrates the argument's conclusion, namely:

> All people who arrive late are ineligible for scholarships.

This is indeed the case because the Euler diagram shows the circle representing the people who arrive late contained within the circle of people who are ineligible for scholarships. The Euler diagram supports the conclusion and the given argument is valid.

EXAMPLE 2 Arguments and Euler Diagrams

Use Euler diagrams to determine whether the following argument is valid or invalid.

> All poets appreciate language.
> All writers appreciate language.
> ___
> Therefore, all poets are writers.

Solution

Step 1 Make an Euler diagram for the first premise. We begin by diagramming the premise:

   All poets appreciate language.

Up to this point, our work is similar to what we did in Example 1.

Step 2 Make an Euler diagram for the second premise on top of the one for the first premise. We add to our previous figure the diagram for the second premise:

   All writers appreciate language.

A third circle representing writers must be drawn inside the circle representing people who appreciate language. There are at least three ways to do this. (In each case, we had to enlarge the "appreciate language" circle to make things fit.)

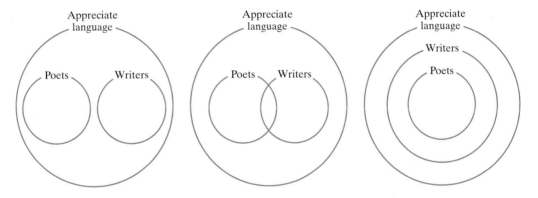

Step 3 The argument is valid if and only if every possible diagram illustrates the argument's conclusion.

The argument's conclusion is:

   All poets are writers.

This conclusion is not illustrated by the figure shown above on the left. This diagram shows "no poets are writers." There is no need to examine the other two diagrams.

The diagram on the left serves as a counterexample to the argument's conclusion. This means that the given argument is invalid.

EXAMPLE 3   Arguments and Euler Diagrams

Use Euler diagrams to determine whether the following argument is valid or invalid.

   All freshmen live on campus.
   No people who live on campus can own cars.

   Therefore, no freshmen can own cars.

Solution

Step 1 Make an Euler diagram for the first premise. The diagram for

All freshmen live on campus

is shown on the right. The region inside the smaller circle represents freshmen. The region inside the larger circle represents people who live on campus.

Step 2 Make an Euler diagram for the second premise on top of the one for the first premise. We add to our previous figure the diagram for the second premise:

No people who live on campus can own cars.

A third circle representing people who own cars is drawn outside the circle representing people who live on campus.

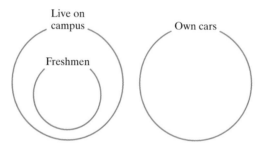

Step 3 The argument is valid if and only if every possible diagram illustrates the argument's conclusion.

There is only one possible diagram. The argument's conclusion is:

No freshmen can own cars.

This is supported by the diagram because it shows the circle representing freshmen drawn outside the circle representing people who own cars. The Euler diagram supports the conclusion, and it is impossible to find a counterexample that does not. The given argument is valid.

Let's see what happens to validity if we reverse the second premise and the conclusion of the argument in Example 3.

EXAMPLE 4   Euler Diagrams and Validity

Use Euler diagrams to determine whether the following argument is valid or invalid.

All freshmen live on campus.
No freshmen can own cars.
_____
Therefore, no people who live on campus can own cars.

Solution

Step 1 Make an Euler diagram for the first premise. We once again begin with the diagram for:

All freshmen live on campus.

So far, our work is exactly the same as in the previous example.

Step 2 Make an Euler diagram for the second premise on top of the one for the first premise. We add to our previous figure the diagram for the second premise:

No freshmen can own cars.

The circle representing people who own cars is drawn outside the freshmen circle. At least two Euler diagrams are possible.

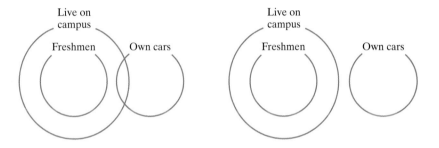

Step 3 The argument is valid if and only if every possible diagram illustrates the argument's conclusion.

The argument's conclusion is:

No people who live on campus can own cars.

This conclusion is not supported by the Euler diagram shown above on the left. The "live on campus" circle and the "own cars" circle intersect. This diagram serves as a counterexample to the argument's conclusion. This means that the argument is invalid.

So far, the arguments that we have looked at have contained "all" or "no" in the premises and conclusions. The quantifier "some" is a bit trickier to work with. Because the statement "Some A are B" means there exists at least one A that is a B, we diagram this existence by showing an element x in the region where A and B intersect, illustrated in Figure 3.6.

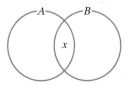

Figure 3.6 Some A are B.

Suppose that it is true that "Some *A* are not *B*," illustrated by element *x* in Figure 3.7. This Euler diagram does not let us conclude that "Some *B* are not *A*" because there is not an *x* in the part of the *B* circle that is not in the *A* circle. Conclusions with the word "some" must be shown by existence of at least one element *x* in an Euler diagram.

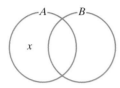

Figure 3.7 Illustrated by the *x* is some *A* are not *B*. We cannot validly conclude that some *B* are not *A*.

Here is an example that shows the premise "Some *A* are not *B*" does not enable us to logically conclude that "Some *B* are not A."

Some U.S. citizens are not U.S. senators. (true)
∴ Some U.S. senators are not U.S. citizens. (false)

EXAMPLE 5 Euler Diagrams and the Quantifier "Some"

Use Euler diagrams to determine whether the following argument is valid or invalid.

All people are mortal.
Some mortals are students.

Therefore, some people are students.

Solution

Step 1 Make an Euler diagram for the first premise. Begin with the premise:

All people are mortal.

The Euler diagram is shown on the right.

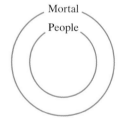

Step 2 Make an Euler diagram for the second premise on top of the one for the first premise. We add to our previous figure the diagram for the second premise:

Some mortals are students.

The circle representing students intersects the circle representing mortals. The *x* in the region of intersection shows that at least one mortal is a student.

Step 3 The argument is valid if and only if every possible diagram illustrates the conclusion of the argument. The argument's conclusion is:

Some people are students.

This conclusion is not supported by the Euler diagram. The diagram does not show the "people" circle and the "students" circle intersecting with an *x* in the re-

Aristotle 384–322 B.C.

The first systematic attempt to describe the logical rules that may be used to arrive at a valid conclusion was made by the ancient Greeks, in particular Aristotle. Aristotelian forms of valid arguments are built into the ways that Westerners think and view the world. In this detail of Raphael's painting *The School of Athens*, Aristotle (on the left) is debating with his teacher and mentor, Plato.

gion of intersection. Although this conclusion is true in the real world, the Euler diagram serves as a counterexample that shows it does not follow from the premises. Therefore, the argument is invalid.

Some arguments show existence without using the word "some." Instead, a particular person or thing is mentioned in one of the premises. This particular person or thing is represented by an *x*. Here is an example.

> All men are mortal.
> Aristotle is a man.
> _____
> Therefore, Aristotle is mortal.

The two premises can be represented by the following Euler diagrams:

 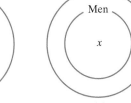

All men are mortal.   Aristotle (*x*) is a man.

The Euler diagram on the right shows Aristotle (*x*) winding up in the "mortal" circle. The diagram supports the conclusion that Aristotle is mortal. This argument is valid.

EXAMPLE 6   An Argument Mentioning One Person

Use Euler diagrams to determine whether the following argument is valid or invalid.

> All children love to swim.
> Jeff Rouse loves to swim.
> _____
> Therefore, Jeff Rouse is a child.

Solution

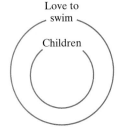

Step 1   Make an Euler diagram for the first premise: Begin with the premise:

> All children love to swim.

The Euler diagram is shown on the right.

Step 2   Make an Euler diagram for the second premise on top of the one for the first premise. We add to our previous figure the diagram for the second premise:

> Jeff Rouse loves to swim.

Jeff Rouse is represented by an *x*. The *x* must be placed in the "love to swim" circle. At least two Euler diagrams are possible.

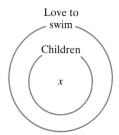

Step 3   The argument is valid if and only every possible diagram illustrates the conclusion of the argument. The argument's conclusion is:

Jeff Rouse is a child.

This conclusion is not supported by the Euler diagram shown above on the left. The *x* representing Jeff Rouse is outside the "children" circle. Jeff Rouse might not be a child. This diagram serves as a counterexample to the argument's conclusion. The argument is invalid.

Exercise Set 3.7

 Practice Exercises

Use Euler diagrams to determine whether each argument in Exercises 1–24 is valid or invalid.

1. All writers appreciate language.
   All poets are writers.

   Therefore, all poets appreciate language.

2. All physicists are scientists.
   All scientists attended college.

   Therefore, all physicists attended college.

3. All clocks keep time accurately.
   All time-measuring devices keep time accurately.

   Therefore, all clocks are time-measuring devices.

4. All cowboys live on ranches.
   All cowherders live on ranches.

   Therefore, all cowboys are cowherders.

5. All insects have six legs.
   No spiders have six legs.

   Therefore, no spiders are insects.

6. All humans are warm-blooded.
   No reptiles are warm-blooded.

   Therefore, no reptiles are human.

7. All insects have six legs.
   No spiders are insects.

   Therefore, no spiders have six legs.

8. All humans are warm-blooded.
   No reptiles are human.

   Therefore, no reptiles are warm-blooded.

9. All professors are wise people.
   Some wise people are actors.

   Therefore, some professors are actors.

10. All comedians are funny people.
    Some funny people are professors.

    Therefore, some comedians are professors.

11. All professors are wise people.
    Some professors are actors.

    Therefore, some wise people are actors.

12. All comedians are funny people.
    Some comedians are professors.

    Therefore, some funny people are professors.

13. All dancers are athletes.
    Savion Glover is a dancer.

    Therefore, Savion Glover is an athlete.

14. All actors are artists.
    Kim Basinger is an actor.

    Therefore, Kim Basinger is an artist.

15. All dancers are athletes.
    Savion Glover is an athlete.

    Therefore, Savion Glover is a dancer.

16. All actors are artists.
    Kim Basinger is an artist.

    Therefore, Kim Basinger is an actor.

17. Some people enjoy reading.
    Some people enjoy TV.

    Therefore, some people who enjoy reading enjoy TV.

18. All thefts are immoral acts.
    Some thefts are justifiable.
    _____
    Therefore, some immoral acts are justifiable.

19. All dogs have fleas.
    Some dogs have rabies.
    _____
    Therefore, all dogs with rabies have fleas.

20. All logic problems make sense.
    Some jokes make sense.
    _____
    Therefore, some logic problems are jokes.

21. No blank disks contain data.
    Some blank disks are formatted.
    _____
    Therefore, some formatted disks do not contain data.

22. Some houses have two stories.
    Some houses have air conditioning.
    _____
    Therefore, some houses with air conditioning have two stories.

23. All multiples of 6 are multiples of 3.
    Eight is not a multiple of 3.
    _____
    Therefore, 8 is not a multiple of 6.

24. All multiples of 6 are multiples of 3.
    Eight is not a multiple of 6.
    _____
    Therefore, 8 is not a multiple of 3.

 Writing in Mathematics

25. Explain how to use Euler diagrams to determine whether or not an argument is valid.

26. Under what circumstances should Euler diagrams rather than truth tables be used to determine whether or not an argument is valid?

 Critical Thinking Exercises

27. Write an example of an argument with two quantified premises that is invalid but that has a true conclusion.

28. No animals that eat meat are vegetarians.
    No cat is a vegetarian.
    Felix is a cat.
    Therefore, . . .
    a. Felix is a vegetarian.
    b. Felix is not a vegetarian.
    c. Felix eats meat.
    d. All animals that do not eat meat are vegetarians.

29. Supply the missing first premise that will make this argument valid.

    _____
    Some opera singers are terrible actors.
    _____
    Therefore, some people who take voice lessons are terrible actors.

30. Supply the missing first premise that will make this argument valid.

    _____
    All amusing people are entertaining.
    _____
    Therefore, some teachers are entertaining.

 Technology Exercises

Using the Windows Paint program, create an Euler diagram to determine whether each argument in Exercises 31–32 is valid or invalid.

31. All math teachers are intelligent people.
    All intelligent people went to college.
    _____
    ∴ Therefore, all intelligent people are math teachers.

32. All dachshunds are small dogs.
    Some dachshunds are red.
    _____
    ∴ Therefore, some small dogs are red.

 CHAPTER SUMMARY, REVIEW, AND TEST

SUMMARY

3.1 and 3.2

Definition of a Statement

A statement is a sentence that is either true or false, but not both simultaneously.

Statements of Symbolic Logic

a. Negation
   $\sim p$: Not p. It is not true that p.

b. Conjunction
   $p \wedge q$: p and q.

c. Disjunction
   $p \vee q$: p or q.

d. Conditional
   $p \rightarrow q$: If p, then q.

e. Biconditional
   $p \leftrightarrow q$: p if and only if q.

Quantified Statements

(In the diagram, each quantified statement's equivalent is written in parentheses below the statement. The statements diagonally opposite each other are negations).

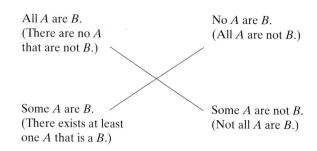

All *A* are *B*.
(There are no *A* that are not *B*.)

No *A* are *B*.
(All *A* are not *B*.)

Some *A* are *B*.
(There exists at least one *A* that is a *B*.)

Some *A* are not *B*.
(Not all *A* are *B*.)

3.3 and 3.4 The Definitions of Symbolic Logic

p q	Negation $\sim p$	Conjunction $p \wedge q$	Disjunction $p \vee q$	Conditional $p \rightarrow q$	Biconditional $p \leftrightarrow q$
T T	F	T	T	T	T
T F	F	F	T	F	F
F T	T	F	T	T	F
F F	T	F	F	T	T

Opposite truth values from p

True only when both component statements are true

False only when both component statements are false

False only when the antecedent is true and the consequent is false

True only when the component statements have the same truth value

3.5

Equivalent Statements

Two statements are equivalent, symbolized ≡, if they have the same truth value in every possible case.

The Conditional Statement: $p \rightarrow q$

a. $p \rightarrow q$ is equivalent to $\sim q \rightarrow \sim p$, the contrapositive.
b. $p \rightarrow q$ is not equivalent to $q \rightarrow p$, the converse.
c. $p \rightarrow q$ is not equivalent to $\sim p \rightarrow \sim q$, the inverse.
d. The negation of $p \rightarrow q$ is $p \wedge \sim q$.

De Morgan's Laws

a. $\sim(p \wedge q) \equiv \sim p \vee \sim q$ The negation of $p \wedge q$ is $\sim p \vee \sim q$.
b. $\sim(p \vee q) \equiv \sim p \wedge \sim q$ The negation of $p \vee q$ is $\sim p \wedge \sim q$.

3.6 Testing the Validity of an Argument with a Truth Table

a. Use a letter to represent each simple statement in the argument.
b. Express the premises and the conclusion symbolically.
c. If the argument contains two premises, write a symbolic conditional statement of the form:

[(premise 1) ∧ (premise 2)] → conclusion.

d. Construct a truth table for the conditional statement in part (c).

e. If the conditional statement is a tautology (true in all cases), the argument is valid. If not, the argument is invalid.

3.7 Euler Diagrams for Quantified Statements

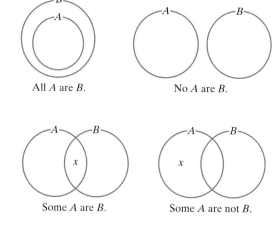

All *A* are *B*.

No *A* are *B*.

Some *A* are *B*.

Some *A* are not *B*.

Testing the Validity of an Argument with an Euler Diagram

a. Make an Euler diagram for the first premise.
b. Make an Euler diagram for the second premise on top of the one for the first premise.
c. The argument is valid if and only if every possible diagram illustrates the conclusion of the argument.

REVIEW EXERCISES

3.1 and 3.2

In Exercises 1–6, let p, q, and r represent the following simple statements:

p: The temperature is below 32°.
q: We finished studying.
r: We go to the movies.

Express each symbolic compound statement in English.

1. $(p \land q) \to r$
2. $\sim r \to (\sim p \lor \sim q)$
3. $p \land (q \to r)$
4. $r \leftrightarrow (p \land q)$
5. $\sim (p \land q)$
6. $\sim r \leftrightarrow (\sim p \lor \sim q)$

In Exercises 7–10, let p, q, and r represent the following simple statements:

p: The outside temperature is at least 80°.
q: The air conditioner is working.
r: The house is hot.

Express each English statement in symbolic form.

7. The outside temperature is at least 80° and the air conditioner is working, or the house is hot.
8. If the outside temperature is at least 80° or the air conditioner is not working, then the house is hot.
9. If the air conditioner is working, then the outside temperature is at least 80° if and only if the house is hot.
10. The house is hot, if and only if the outside temperature is at least 80° and the air conditioner is not working.

In Exercises 11–14, write the negation of each statement.

11. All houses are made with wood.
12. No students major in business.
13. Some crimes are motivated by passion.
14. Some Democrats are not registered voters.
15. The speaker stated that, "All new taxes are for education." We later learned that the speaker was not telling the truth. What can we conclude about new taxes and education?

3.3 and 3.4

The accompanying graph shows the average number of students per computer in America's public schools. Use the information, given by the graph to determine the truth value for each of the statements in Exercises 16–18.

Average Number of Students per Computer

Source: Quality Education Data

16. There are 13.7 students per computer in elementary schools and 10.1 students per computer in senior high schools.
17. There are 13.7 students per computer in elementary schools or 10.1 students per computer in senior high schools.
18. If the number of students per computer decreases as the grade level increases, then there are 10.1 students per computer in senior high schools.

In Exercises 19–25, construct a truth table for the statement.

19. $p \lor (\sim p \land q)$
20. $\sim p \lor \sim q$
21. $p \to (\sim p \lor q)$
22. $p \leftrightarrow \sim q$
23. $\sim (p \lor q) \to (\sim p \land \sim q)$
24. $(p \lor q) \to \sim r$
25. $(p \land q) \leftrightarrow (p \land r)$

3.5

26. a. Use a truth table to show that $p \lor q$ and $\sim q \to p$ are equivalent.
    b. Use the result from part (a) to write a statement that is equivalent to:
       I learn the lines or I do not get the part.
27. Select the statement that is equivalent to:
    Joe grows mangos or oranges.
    a. If Joe grows mangos, he does not grow oranges.
    b. If Joe grows oranges, he does not grow mangos.
    c. If Joe does not grow mangos, he grows oranges.
    d. Joe grows both mangos and oranges.

Write the contrapositive for each statement in Exercises 28–30.

28. If I am in Atlanta, then I am in the South.
29. If I am in class, then today is not a holiday.
30. If I work hard, then I pass all courses.

Write the converse and the inverse for each statement in Exercises 31–32.

31. If there is a storm, then classes are cancelled.
32. If the television is on, then we do not talk.

Write the negation for each conditional statement in Exercises 33–34.

33. If I am in Bogota, then I am in Colombia.
34. If I do not work hard, then I do not succeed.

Use De Morgan's laws to write a statement that is equivalent to each statement in Exercises 35–36.

35. It is not true that both Chicago and Maine are cities.
36. It is not true that Ernest Hemingway was a musician or an actor.

Use De Morgan's laws to write the negation of each statement in Exercises 37–38.

37. I work hard or I do not succeed.
38. She is not using her car and she is taking a bus.

3.6

In Exercises 39–40, use a truth table to determine whether the symbolic form of the argument is valid or invalid.

39. $p \rightarrow q$
$\underline{\sim q}$
$\therefore p$

40. $p \wedge q$
$\underline{q \rightarrow r}$
$\therefore p \rightarrow r$

In Exercises 41–45, translate each argument into symbolic form. Then use a truth table to determine whether each argument is valid or invalid.

41. If one is a good baseball player, one must have good eye-hand coordination.
Todd does not have good eye-hand coordination.
∴ Todd is not a good baseball player.

42. If Tony plays, the team wins.
The team won.
∴ Tony played.

43. My plant is fertilized or it turns yellow.
My plant is turning yellow.
∴ My plant is not fertilized.

44. A majority of legislators vote for a bill or that bill does not become law.
A majority of legislators did not vote for bill *x*.
∴ Bill *x* did not become law.

45. If I purchase season tickets to the football games, then I do not attend all lectures.
If I do not attend all lectures, then I do not do well in school.
∴ If I do not do well in school, then I purchased season tickets to the football games.

3.7

Use Euler diagrams to determine whether each argument in Exercises 46–50 is valid or invalid.

46. All birds have feathers.
All parrots have feathers.
∴ All parrots are birds.

47. All botanists are scientists.
All scientists have college degrees.
∴ All botanists have college degrees.

48. All native desert plants can withstand severe drought.
No tree ferns can withstand severe drought.
∴ No tree ferns are native desert plants.

49. All native desert plants can withstand severe drought.
No tree ferns are native desert plants.
∴ No tree ferns can withstand severe drought.

50. All poets are writers.
Some writers are wealthy.
∴ Some poets are wealthy.

 Group Exercise

51. Read the essay on page 104. Group members are working for the advertising department of a company that sells magazine subscriptions by mail. It is time to replace the claim in the essay with a new compound statement. The statement must be a true claim that will entice people into opening the envelope and ordering magazines. Group members should use their knowledge of logic to write as many such statements as possible.

CHAPTER 3 TEST

Use the following representations in Exercises 1–5:
p: I'm registered.
q: I'm a citizen.
r: I vote.

Express each compound statement in English.

1. $(p \wedge q) \rightarrow r$
2. $\sim r \leftrightarrow (\sim p \vee \sim q)$
3. $\sim (p \vee q)$

Express each English statement in symbolic form.

4. I am registered and a citizen, or I do not vote.
5. If I am not registered or not a citizen, then I do not vote.

In Exercises 6–7, write the negation of the statement.

6. All numbers are divisible by 5.
7. Some people wear glasses.

In Exercises 8–10, construct a truth table for the statement.

8. $p \wedge (\sim p \vee q)$
9. $\sim (p \wedge q) \leftrightarrow (\sim p \vee \sim q)$
10. $p \leftrightarrow (q \vee r)$

11. Select the statement below that is equivalent to:
Gene is an actor or a musician.
a. If Gene is an actor, then he is not a musician.
b. If Gene is not an actor, then he is a musician.
c. It is false that Gene is not an actor or not a musician.
d. If Gene is an actor, then he is a musician.

12. Write the contrapositive of:
If it is August, it does not snow.

13. Write the converse and the inverse of the following statement:
If the radio is playing, then I cannot concentrate.

14. Write the negation of the following statement:

    If it is cold, we do not use the pool.

15. Write a statement that is equivalent to:

    It is not true that the test is today or the party is tonight.

16. Write the negation of the following statement:

    The banana is green and it is not ready to eat.

Determine whether each argument in Exercises 17–20 is valid or invalid.

17. If a parrot talks, it is intelligent.
    This parrot is intelligent.
    ∴ This parrot talks.

18. I am sick or I am tired.
    I am not tired.
    ∴ I am sick.

19. All mammals are warm-blooded.
    All dogs are warm-blooded.
    ∴ All dogs are mammals.

20. All writers love language.
    No insects love language.
    ∴ No writers are insects.

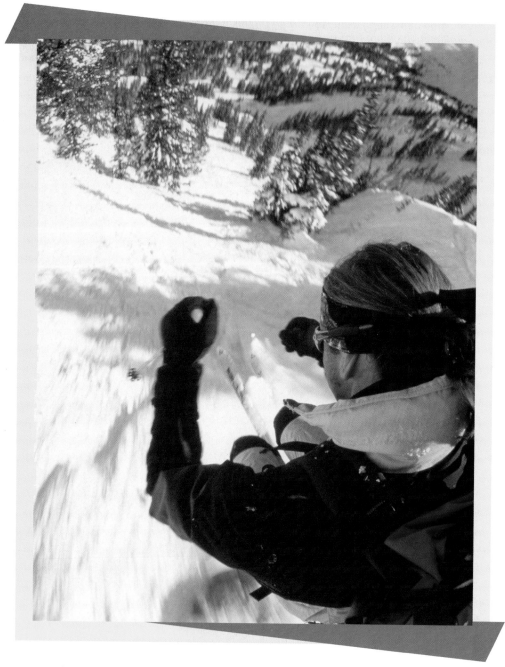

You don't have the money to go on the ski club trip, so you head out to the local arcade where there is a ski simulator game. Instead of the clunky old machine, there is a new virtual reality machine. You slip your money in and put on your headset. Suddenly you are at the top of a mountain, skiing down slopes at 20, 30, 40 miles per hour. Your heart races as you leap off jumps and dodge other skiers. The experience is so realistic! As you walk home you wonder, how do they do that?

4 Number Representation and Calculation

A system for representing numbers, called a **numeration system**, gives the computer its extraordinary powers. The information fed into the computer to create the exhilarating experience of the virtual reality ski game is converted into a binary system, using 0s and 1s. Without an understanding of how we represent numbers, the computer could not exist. In this chapter, our focus is on the system that we use to represent numbers, called the Hindu-Arabic system. The idea behind this system will eventually enable you, a "cybernaut," to see, hear, and interact with three-dimensional, digitally simulated worlds.

SECTION 4.1 Our Hindu-Arabic System and Early Positional Systems

Objectives

1. Evaluate an exponential expression.
2. Write a Hindu-Arabic numeral in expanded form.
3. Express a number's expanded form as a Hindu-Arabic numeral.
4. Understand and use the Babylonian numeration system.
5. Understand and use the Mayan numeration system.

Figure 4.1

All of us have an intuitive understanding of *more* and *less*. As humanity evolved, this sense of more and less was used to develop a system of counting. A tribe needed to know how many sheep it had, and whether the flock was increasing or decreasing in number. The earliest way of keeping count probably involved some tally method, using one vertical mark on a cave wall for each sheep. Later, a variety of vocal sounds developed as a tally for the number of things in a group. Finally, written symbols, or numerals, were used to represent numbers.

A **number** is an abstract idea that addresses the question, "How many?" A **numeral** is a symbol used to represent a number. Different symbols may be used to represent the same number. Numerals used to represent how many buffalo are shown in Figure 4.1 include:

JHT IIII	IX	9
Tally method	Roman numeral	Hindu-Arabic numeral

We take numerals and the numbers that they represent for granted and use them every day. A **system of numeration** consists of a set of basic numerals and rules for combining them to represent numbers. It took humanity thousands of years to invent numeration systems that made computation a reasonable task. Today we use a system of writing numerals that was invented in India and brought to Europe by the Arabs. Our numerals are therefore called **Hindu-Arabic numerals**.

Like literature or music, a numeration system has a profound effect on the culture that created it. Computers, which affect our everyday lives, are based on an understanding of our Hindu-Arabic system of numeration. In this section, we study the characteristics of our numeration system. We also take a brief journey through history to look at two numeration systems that pointed the way toward an amazing cultural creation, our Hindu-Arabic system.

1 Evaluate an exponential expression.

$$Base \rightarrow 10^2 \rightarrow Exponent$$

Exponential Notation

An understanding of exponents is important in understanding the characteristics of our numeration system. Consider each of the following multiplications:

$$10 \times 10 \qquad 10 \times 10 \times 10 \qquad 10 \times 10 \times 10 \times 10$$

These multiplications can be expressed more simply using what is called **exponential notation.** In this notation 10×10 is expressed as 10^2. The 10 that is to be repeated when multiplying is called the **base**. The small 2 above and at the right of 10 is called the **exponent**. The exponent tells the number of times the base is to be used when multiplying. In 10^3, the base is 10 and the exponent is 3.

EXAMPLE 1 Understanding Exponential Notation

Evaluate the following.

a. 10^2 b. 10^3 c. 10^4

Solution

a. $10^2 = 10 \times 10 = 100$

b. $10^3 = 10 \times 10 \times 10 = 1000$

c. $10^4 = 10 \times 10 \times 10 \times 10 = 10,000$

The number represented by an expression like 10^2 is called a **power**. Because $10^2 = 100$, we say that 100 expressed as a **power of 10** is 10^2. Similarly, because $1000 = 10^3$, 10^3 expresses 1000 as a power of 10.

Any number with an exponent of 1 is the number itself. Thus, $10^1 = 10$.

Multiplications that are expressed in exponential notation are read as follows:

10^1 : "ten to the first power"

10^2 : "ten to the second power" or "ten squared"

10^3 : "ten to the third power" or "ten cubed"

10^4 : "ten to the fourth power"

10^5 : "ten to the fifth power"

POWERS OF TEN
$10 = 10^1$
$100 = 10^2$
$1000 = 10^3$
$10,000 = 10^4$
$100,000 = 10^5$
$1,000,000 = 10^6$

Become familiar with the powers of ten shown at the left because they play an important role in our system of numeration. Notice that the number of zeros appearing to the right of the 1 in any numeral that expresses a power of 10 is the same as the exponent in that power of 10. For example, in $10,000 = 10^4$, there are 4 zeros at the right of 1 in 10,000, and the exponent in 10^4 is 4. Therefore, 10^9 can be written as 1 followed by 9 zeros,

$$1,000,000,000,$$

or one billion.

Numbers other than 10 may also be used as the base.

Technology

You can use a calculator to evaluate exponential expressions. For example, to evaluate 5^3, press the following keys:

Scientific Calculator

5 $\boxed{x^y}$ 3 $\boxed{=}$

Graphing Calculator

5 $\boxed{\wedge}$ 3 $\boxed{\text{ENTER}}$

Although calculators have special keys to evaluate powers of ten and squaring bases, you can always use one of the sequences shown above.

Don't have a calculator? You can use the standard calculator in the Accessories folder of your Windows operating system. Just be sure to choose the Scientific option under the View menu, and use the $\boxed{x^\wedge y}$ key for calculations with exponents.

EXAMPLE 2   Using Exponential Notation

Evaluate the following.

a. 7^2 b. 5^3 c. 2^6 d. 9^1

Solution

a. $7^2 = 7 \times 7 = 49$

b. $5^3 = 5 \times 5 \times 5 = 125$

c. $2^6 = 2 \times 2 \times 2 \times 2 \times 2 \times 2 = 64$

d. $9^1 = 9$

Our Hindu-Arabic Numeration System

An important characteristic of our Hindu-Arabic system is that we can write the numeral for any number, large or small, by using only ten symbols. The ten symbols that we use are

$$0, 1, 2, 3, 4, 5, 6, 7, 8, \text{and } 9.$$

These symbols are called **digits**, from the Latin word for fingers.

With the use of exponents, Hindu-Arabic numerals can be written in **expanded form** in which the value of the digit in each position is made clear. In a Hindu-Arabic numeral, the place value of the first digit on the right is 1. The place value of the second digit from the right is 10. The place value of the third digit from the right is 100, or 10^2. For example, we can write 663 in expanded form by thinking of 663 as 6 100s plus 6 10s plus 3 1s. This means that 663 in expanded form is

$$663 = (6 \times 100) + (6 \times 10) + (3 \times 1)$$
$$= (6 \times 10^2) + (6 \times 10^1) + (3 \times 1).$$

2 Write a Hindu-Arabic numeral in expanded form.

Because the value of a digit varies according to the position it occupies in a numeral, the Hindu-Arabic numeration system is called a **positional-value**, or **place-value** system. The positional values in the system are based on powers of ten and are:

$$\ldots, 10^5, 10^4, 10^3, 10^2, 10^1, 1.$$

EXAMPLE 3   Writing Hindu-Arabic Numerals in Expanded Form

Write each of the following in expanded form.

a. 3407   b. 53,525

Solution

a. $3407 = (3 \times 10^3) + (4 \times 10^2) + (0 \times 10^1) + (7 \times 1)$

   or $= (3 \times 1000) + (4 \times 100) + (0 \times 10) + (7 \times 1)$

Because $0 \times 10^1 = 0$, this term could be left out, but the expanded form is clearer when it is included.

b. $53{,}525 = (5 \times 10^4) + (3 \times 10^3) + (5 \times 10^2) + (2 \times 10^1) + (5 \times 1)$

   or $= (5 \times 10{,}000) + (3 \times 1000) + (5 \times 100) + (2 \times 10) + (5 \times 1)$

3   Express a number's expanded form as a Hindu-Arabic numeral.

EXAMPLE 4   Expressing a Number's Expanded Form as a Hindu-Arabic Numeral

Express each expanded form as a Hindu-Arabic numeral.

a. $(7 \times 10^3) + (5 \times 10^1) + (4 \times 1)$
b. $(6 \times 10^5) + (8 \times 10^1)$

Solution   For clarification, we begin by showing all powers of ten, starting with the highest exponent given. Any power of ten that is left out is expressed as 0 times that power of ten.

a. $(7 \times 10^3) + (5 \times 10^1) + (4 \times 1)$

   $= (7 \times 10^3) + (0 \times 10^2) + (5 \times 10^1) + (4 \times 1)$

   $= 7054$

b. $(6 \times 10^5) + (8 \times 10^1)$

   $= (6 \times 10^5) + (0 \times 10^4) + (0 \times 10^3) + (0 \times 10^2) + (8 \times 10^1) + (0 \times 1)$

   $= 600{,}080$

"The ingenious method of expressing all numbers by means of ten symbols appears so simple to us now that we ignore its true merits. But its very simplicity puts our arithmetic in the first rank of useful inventions."

PIERRE-SIMON LAPLACE
(French mathematician, 1749–1827)

Examples 3 and 4 show how there would be no Hindu-Arabic system without an understanding of zero and the invention of a symbol to represent nothingness. The system must have a symbol for zero to serve as a placeholder in case one or more powers of ten are not needed. The concept of zero was a new and radical invention, one that changed our ability to think about the world.

Hindu 300 B.C.

Arabic 10th century

Arabic 15th century

European 15th century

20th century typewriter

1 2 3 4 5 6 7 8 9 0

20th century bank check

1 2 3 4 5 6 7 8 9 0

Bar codes read by computers

0 76950 45026 4

The evolution of digits in the Hindu-Arabic numeration system

4 Understand and use the Babylonian numeration system.

Table 4.1
Babylonian Numerals

Babylonian numerals	∨	<
Hindu-Arabic numerals	1	10

Early Positional Systems

Our Hindu-Arabic system developed over many centuries. Its digits can be found carved on ancient Hindu pillars over 2200 years old. In 1202, the Italian mathematician Leonardo Fibonacci (1170–1250) introduced the system to Europe, writing of its special characteristic: "With the nine Hindu digits and the Arab symbol 0, any number can be written." The Hindu-Arabic system came into widespread use only when printing was invented in the fifteenth century.

The Hindu-Arabic system uses powers of 10. However, positional systems can use powers of any number, not just 10. Think about our system of time, based on powers of 60:

$$1 \text{ minute} = 60 \text{ seconds}$$

$$1 \text{ hour} = 60 \text{ minutes} = 60 \times 60 \text{ seconds} = 60^2 \text{ seconds}$$

What is significant in a positional system is position and the powers that positions convey. The first early positional system that we will look at uses powers of 60, just like those used for units of time.

The Babylonian Numeration System

The city of Babylon, 55 miles south of present-day Baghdad, was the center of Babylonian civilization that lasted for about 1400 years between 2000 B.C. and 600 B.C. The Babylonians used wet clay as a writing surface. Their clay tablets were heated and dried to give a permanent record of their work, which we are able to decipher and read today. Table 4.1 gives the numerals of this civilization's numeration system.

The place values in the Babylonian system use powers of 60. The place values are:

$$\ldots, \qquad 60^3, \qquad 60^2, \qquad 60^1, \qquad 1$$

| | or | or | or | |
| | 216,000 | 3600 | 60 | |

The Babylonians left a space to distinguish the various place values in a numeral from one another. For example,

means

$$\qquad \downarrow \qquad\qquad \downarrow \qquad\qquad \downarrow$$

$$(1 \times 60^2) + (10 \times 60^1) + (1 + 1) \times 1$$

$$= (1 \times 3600) + (10 \times 60) + (2 \times 1)$$

$$= 3600 + 600 + 2 = 4202$$

EXAMPLE 5 Converting from a Babylonian Numeral to a Hindu-Arabic Numeral

Write

∨ ∨   < ∨   < < ∨ ∨

as a Hindu-Arabic numeral.

Table 4.1
Babylonian Numerals

Babylonian numerals	∨	<
Hindu-Arabic numerals	1	10

Solution From left to right, the place values are $60^2, 60^1$, and 1. Represent the numeral in each place as a familiar Hindu-Arabic numeral using Table 4.1. Multiply each Hindu-Arabic numeral by its respective place value. Then find the sum of these products.

$$\underset{\downarrow}{\text{∨ ∨}} \qquad\qquad \underset{\downarrow}{\text{< ∨}} \qquad\qquad \underset{\downarrow}{\text{< < ∨ ∨}}$$

means

$$(1 + 1) \times 60^2 + (10 + 1) \times 60^1 + (10 + 10 + 1 + 1) \times 1$$
$$= (2 \times 60^2) + (11 \times 60^1) + (22 \times 1)$$
$$= (2 \times 3600) + (11 \times 60) + (22 \times 1)$$
$$= 7200 + 660 + 22 = 7882$$

This sum indicates that the given Babylonian numeral is 7882 as a Hindu-Arabic numeral.

A major disadvantage of the Babylonian system is that it did not contain a symbol for zero. Some Babylonian tablets have a larger gap between the numerals or the insertion of the symbol ⟨ to indicate a missing place value, but this led to some ambiguity and confusion.

5 Understand and use the Mayan numeration system.

Numbers and Bird Brains

Birds have large, well-developed brains and are more intelligent than is suggested by the slur "bird brain." Parakeets can learn to *(continued)*

The Mayan Numeration System

The Maya, a tribe of Central American Indians, lived on the Yucatan Peninsula. At its peak, between 300 and 1000 A.D., their civilization covered an area including parts of Mexico, all of Belize and Guatemala, and part of Honduras. They were famous for their magnificent architecture, their astronomical and mathematical knowledge, and their excellence in the arts. Their numeration system was the first to have a symbol for zero. Table 4.2 gives the Mayan numerals.

Table 4.2 Mayan Numerals

0	1	2	3	4	5	6	7	8	9
👁	•	••	•••	••••	—	•̲	••̲	•••̲	••••̲
10	11	12	13	14	15	16	17	18	19
═	•̳	••̳	•••̳	••••̳	≡	•̳	••̳	•••̳	••••̳

The place values in the Mayan system are:

$$\ldots, \quad 18 \times 20^3, \quad 18 \times 20^2, \quad 18 \times 20, \quad 20, \quad 1$$
$$\text{or} \qquad\qquad \text{or} \qquad\qquad \text{or}$$
$$144{,}000 \qquad\quad 7200 \qquad\qquad 360$$

Notice that instead of giving the third position a place value of 20^2, the Mayans used 18×20. This was probably done so that their calendar year of 360 days would be a basic part of the numeration system.

count to seven. They have been taught to identify a box of food by counting the number of small objects in front of the box.

Some species of birds can tell the difference between two and three. If a nest contains four eggs and one is taken, the bird will stay in the nest to protect the remaining three eggs. However, if two of the four eggs are taken, the bird recognizes that only two remain and will desert the nest, leaving the remaining two eggs unprotected.

Birds easily master complex counting problems. The sense of *more* and *less* that led to the development of numeration systems is not limited to the human species.

Numerals in the Mayan system are expressed vertically. The place value at the bottom of the column is 1.

EXAMPLE 6   Using the Mayan Numeration System

Write

$$
\begin{array}{c}
\overset{\bullet\bullet\bullet\bullet}{=} \\
\ominus \\
\overset{\bullet\bullet}{} \\
\overset{\bullet\bullet}{=}
\end{array}
$$

as a Hindu-Arabic numeral.

Solution   The given Mayan numeral has four places. From top to bottom, the place values are 7200, 360, 20, and 1. Represent the numeral in each row as a familiar Hindu-Arabic numeral using Table 4.2. Multiply each Hindu-Arabic numeral by its respective place value. Then find the sum of these products.

Mayan numeral		Hindu-Arabic numeral		Place value		
$\overset{\bullet\bullet\bullet\bullet}{=}$	=	14	×	7200	=	100,800
$\ominus$	=	0	×	360	=	0
$\overset{\bullet\bullet}{}$	=	7	×	20	=	140
$\overset{\bullet\bullet}{=}$	=	12	×	1	=	12
						100,952

The sum on the right indicates that the given Mayan numeral is 100,952 as a Hindu-Arabic numeral.

Exercise Set 4.1

 Practice Exercises

In Exercises 1–8, evaluate the expression.

1. 5^2 2. 6^2 3. 2^3 4. 4^3

5. 3^4 6. 2^4 7. 10^5 8. 10^6

In Exercises 9–22, write each Hindu-Arabic numeral in expanded form.

9. 36   10. 65   11. 249   12. 698

13. 703   14. 902   15. 4856   16. 5749

17. 3070   18. 9007   19. 34,569   20. 67,943

21. 230,007,004   22. 909,006,070

In Exercises 23–32, express each expanded form as a Hindu-Arabic numeral.

23. $(7 \times 10^1) + (3 \times 1)$

24. $(9 \times 10^1) + (4 \times 1)$

25. $(3 \times 10^2) + (8 \times 10^1) + (5 \times 1)$

26. $(7 \times 10^2) + (5 \times 10^1) + (3 \times 1)$

27. $(5 \times 10^5) + (2 \times 10^4) + (8 \times 10^3) + (7 \times 10^2)$
$+ (4 \times 10^1) + (3 \times 1)$

28. $(7 \times 10^6) + (4 \times 10^5) + (2 \times 10^4) + (3 \times 10^3)$
$+ (1 \times 10^2) + (9 \times 10^1) + (6 \times 1)$

29. $(7 \times 10^3) + (0 \times 10^2) + (0 \times 10^1) + (2 \times 1)$

30. $(9 \times 10^4) + (0 \times 10^3) + (0 \times 10^2) + (4 \times 10^1)$
$+ (5 \times 1)$

31. $(6 \times 10^8) + (2 \times 10^3) + (7 \times 1)$

32. $(3 \times 10^8) + (5 \times 10^4) + (4 \times 1)$

In Exercises 33–40, use Table 4.1 on page 151 to write each Babylonian numeral as a Hindu-Arabic numeral.

33. < < ∨ ∨ ∨

34. < < < ∨ ∨

35. < < ∨   ∨ ∨

36. < <   < ∨ ∨

37. ∨ ∨ ∨   < ∨ ∨   ∨ ∨ ∨

38. ∨ ∨   < ∨   < < ∨ ∨

39. < ∨   < ∨   < ∨   < ∨

40. < <   < <   < ∨ ∨   < ∨ ∨

In Exercises 41–50, use Table 4.2 on page 152 to write each Mayan numeral as a Hindu-Arabic numeral.

41. •••• with bar below

42. ••• with two bars below

43. •••• with two bars, then oval below

44. •••• with oval and bar, then dot below

45. ••• / ••• / •••

46. • / • / •

47. •• / oval / oval / two bars

48. ••• / two bars / oval / oval

49. two bars / oval / two bars

50. two bars / oval / three bars

Application Exercises

Exercise 51 contains a Mayan numeral. Exercise 52 contains a Babylonian numeral. Write each numeral as a Hindu-Arabic numeral. The numeral that results represents a year that was not important to the Mayans or the Babylonians but is important to us. Identify the historical event that took place in that year. If necessary, use an appropriate reference.

51. •••• with dot, then two bars, then two bars

52. < < ∨ ∨ ∨ ∨   < < < < < ∨ ∨

Writing in Mathematics

53. Describe the difference between a number and a numeral.

54. Explain how to evaluate 7^3.

55. What is the base in our Hindu-Arabic numeration system? What are the digits in the system?

56. Why is a symbol for zero needed in a positional system?

57. Explain how to write a Hindu-Arabic numeral in expanded form.

58. Describe one way that the Babylonian system is similar to the Hindu-Arabic system and one way that it is different from the Hindu-Arabic system.

59. Describe one way that the Mayan system is similar to the Hindu-Arabic system and one way that it is different from the Hindu-Arabic system.

60. *Research activity* Write a report on the history of the Hindu-Arabic system of numeration. Useful references include history of mathematics books, encyclopedias, and the World Wide Web.

Critical Thinking Exercises

61. Write ∨   < ∨ ∨   < ∨ as a Mayan numeral.

62. Write •• / •• / •• as a Babylonian numeral.

63. Use Babylonian numerals to write the numeral that precedes and the numeral that follows < ∨   < < < < < ∨ ∨ ∨ ∨ ∨ ∨ ∨ ∨ ∨.

Technology Exercises

Using a calculator, evaluate the following expressions.

64. 4^5

65. 5^4

66. 2^9

67. 84^3

68. For the value of the expression 85^8, a scientific calculator displays 2.724905 15. What is the significance of the space immediately before the final two digits?

Group Exercises

69. Your group task is to create an original positional numeration system that is different from the three systems discussed in this section.
    a. Construct a table showing your numerals and the corresponding Hindu-Arabic numerals.
    b. Explain how to represent numbers in your system, and express a three-digit and a four-digit Hindu-Arabic numeral in your system.
    c. Explain how two numbers can be added in your system.

70. For many individuals around the world who are blind or visually impaired, Braille numerals are used to represent numbers. Braille numerals can be detected and interpreted by touch. A group of two or three students should research how Braille numerals are formed. Many public and private organizations and schools provide materials and information for the blind and visually impaired. Using your library, resources on the World Wide Web, or local organizations, investigate the basic elements for Braille numerals, including the two-dot by three-dot cell, as well as the dot symbol used to precede a numeral. Present the results of your research to the entire class and bring examples of Braille numerals for each student to interpret by hand with no visual clues.

SECTION 4.2   *Number Bases in Positional Systems*

Objectives

1. Change numerals in bases other than ten to base ten.
2. Change base ten numerals to numerals in other bases.

In this section, we study numeration systems with bases other than ten. Three such systems are used in computer applications. An understanding of systems with bases other than ten will help you to appreciate the nature of a positional system. You will also attain a better understanding of the computations you have used all of your life. You will even get to see how the world looks from a computer's point of view.

1 Change numerals in bases other than ten to base ten.

Changing Numerals in Bases Other Than Ten to Base Ten

The base of a positional numeration system refers to the number of individual digit symbols that can be used in that system as well as to the powers of the number used in place values. For example, the digit symbols in a base 5 system are 0, 1, 2, 3, and 4. The place values in a base 5 system are powers of 5:

$$\ldots, 5^4, 5^3, 5^2, 5^1, 1$$

$$= \ldots, 5 \times 5 \times 5 \times 5, \; 5 \times 5 \times 5, \; 5 \times 5, \; 5, \; 1$$

$$= \ldots, 625, 125, 25, 5, 1$$

When a numeral appears without a subscript, it is assumed that the base is ten. Bases other than ten are indicated with a spelled-out subscript, as in the numeral

$$122_{\text{five}}.$$

This numeral is read "one two two base five." Do not read it as "one hundred twenty two" because that terminology implies a base ten numeral, naming 122 in base ten.

We can convert 122_{five} to a base ten numeral by following the same procedure used in Section 4.1 to change the Babylonian and Mayan numerals to base ten Hindu-Arabic numerals. In the case of 122_{five}, the numeral has three places. From left to right, the place values are 5^2, 5^1, and 1. Multiply each digit in the numeral by its respective place value. Then add these products.

$$122_{\text{five}} = (1 \times 5^2) + (2 \times 5^1) + (2 \times 1)$$

$$= (1 \times 25) + (2 \times 5) + (2 \times 1)$$

$$= \quad 25 \quad + \quad 10 \quad + \quad 2$$

$$= \quad 37$$

Thus,

$$122_{\text{five}} = \quad 37.$$

In base five, we do not need a digit symbol for 5 because

$$10_{\text{five}} = (1 \times 5^1) + (0 \times 1) = 5.$$

Table 4.3

Base Ten	Base Five
0	0
1	1
2	2
3	3
4	4
5	10
6	11
7	12
8	13
9	14
10	20
11	21
12	22
13	23
14	24
15	30
16	31
17	32
18	33
19	34
20	40

Likewise, the base ten numeral 6 is represented as 11_{five}, the base ten numeral 7 as 12_{five}, and so on. Table 4.3 shows base ten numerals from 0 through 20 and their base five equivalents.

In any base, the digit symbols begin at 0 and go up to one less than the base. In base b, the digit symbols begin at 0 and go up to $b - 1$. The place values in a base b system are powers of b:

$$\ldots b^4, b^3, b^2, b, 1.$$

Table 4.4 shows the digit symbols and place values in various bases.

Table 4.4 Digit Symbols and Place Values in Various Bases

Base	Digit Symbols	Place Values
two	0, 1	$\ldots, 2^4, 2^3, 2^2, 2^1, 1$
three	0, 1, 2	$\ldots, 3^4, 3^3, 3^2, 3^1, 1$
four	0, 1, 2, 3	$\ldots, 4^4, 4^3, 4^2, 4^1, 1$
five	0, 1, 2, 3, 4	$\ldots, 5^4, 5^3, 5^2, 5^1, 1$
six	0, 1, 2, 3, 4, 5	$\ldots, 6^4, 6^3, 6^2, 6^1, 1$
seven	0, 1, 2, 3, 4, 5, 6	$\ldots, 7^4, 7^3, 7^2, 7^1, 1$
eight	0, 1, 2, 3, 4, 5, 6, 7	$\ldots, 8^4, 8^3, 8^2, 8^1, 1$
nine	0, 1, 2, 3, 4, 5, 6, 7, 8	$\ldots, 9^4, 9^3, 9^2, 9^1, 1$
ten	0, 1, 2, 3, 4, 5, 6, 7, 8, 9	$\ldots, 10^4, 10^3, 10^2, 10^1, 1$

We have seen that in base five, 10_{five} represents one group of 5 and no groups of 1. Thus, $10_{\text{five}} = 5$. Similarly, in base six, 10_{six} represents one group of 6 and no groups of 1. Thus, $10_{\text{six}} = 6$. In general $10_{\text{base } b}$ represents one group of b and no groups of 1. This means that $10_{\text{base } b} = b$.

Here is the procedure for changing a numeral in a base other than ten to base ten.

Jasper Johns, *The Number Zero*, oil on canvas, 1959, Private collection.

❝ *It took men about five thousand years, counting from the beginning of number symbols, to think of a symbol for nothing.* **❞**

ISAAC ASIMOV,
Asimov on Numbers

Changing to Base Ten

To change a numeral in a base other than ten to a base ten numeral:
1. Find the place value for each digit in the numeral.
2. Multiply each digit in the numeral by its respective place value.
3. Find the sum of the products in step 2.

EXAMPLE 1   Converting to Base Ten

Convert 4726_{eight} to base ten.

Solution   The given base eight numeral has four places. From left to right, the place values are:

$$\ldots, 8^3, 8^2, 8^1, 1.$$

Talking to Computers

Base two, or binary notation, is the basis for all computer functions. The use of the binary system in the coding of numbers, and in expressing the logic discussed in Chapter 3, gives the computer its extraordinary powers of calculation. From the computer's point of view, sequences of 1s and 0s, the digits in base two, are convenient. The computer uses a code based on electric signals: The passage of electrical current expresses 1, its interruption 0. When a computer receives a command or data, every character is converted into a binary number so that the machine can understand and use it.

Multiply each digit in the numeral by its respective place value. Then find the sum of these products.

Place value: 8^3	Place value: 8^2	Place value: 8^1	Place value: 1
4	7	2	6_{eight}

$$4726_{eight} = (4 \times 8^3) + (7 \times 8^2) + (2 \times 8^1) + (6 \times 1)$$
$$= (4 \times 8 \times 8 \times 8) + (7 \times 8 \times 8) + (2 \times 8) + (6 \times 1)$$
$$= 2048 + 448 + 16 + 6$$
$$= 2518$$

EXAMPLE 2   Converting to Base Ten

Convert 100101_{two} to base ten.

Solution   Multiply each digit in the numeral by its respective place value. Then find the sum of these products.

Place value: 2^5	Place value: 2^4	Place value: 2^3	Place value: 2^2	Place value: 2^1	Place value: 1
1	0	0	1	0	1_{two}

$$100101_{two} = (1 \times 2^5) + (0 \times 2^4) + (0 \times 2^3) + (1 \times 2^2) + (0 \times 2^1) + (1 \times 1)$$
$$= (1 \times 32) + (0 \times 16) + (0 \times 8) + (1 \times 4) + (0 \times 2) + (1 \times 1)$$
$$= 32 + 0 + 0 + 4 + 0 + 1$$
$$= 37$$

Three base systems are used in computer applications. These are base two, called a **binary system**, base eight, called an **octal system**, and base sixteen, called a **hexadecimal system**. Base sixteen presents a problem because digit symbols are needed from 0 up to one less than the base. This means that we need more digit symbols than the ten (0, 1, 2, 3, 4, 5, 6, 7, 8, and 9) used in our base ten system. Computer programmers use the letters A, B, C, D, E, and F as base sixteen digit symbols for the numbers ten through fifteen, respectively.

EXAMPLE 3   Converting to Base Ten

Convert $EC7_{sixteen}$ to decimal form.

Solution   From left to right, the place values are:

$$..., 16^2, 16^1, 1.$$

The digit symbol E represents 14 and the digit symbol C represents 12. Although this numeral looks a bit strange, follow the usual procedure: Multiply

Additional digit symbols in Base 16:
 A = 10,   B = 11,
 C = 12,   D = 13,
 E = 14,   F = 15

2 Change base ten numerals to numerals in other bases.

each digit in the numeral by its respective place value. Then find the sum of these products.

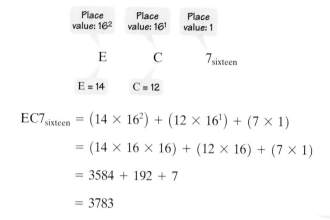

$$EC7_{sixteen} = (14 \times 16^2) + (12 \times 16^1) + (7 \times 1)$$

$$= (14 \times 16 \times 16) + (12 \times 16) + (7 \times 1)$$

$$= 3584 + 192 + 7$$

$$= 3783$$

Changing Base Ten Numerals to Numerals in Other Bases

To convert a base ten numeral to a numeral in a base other than ten, we need to find how many groups of each place value are contained in the base ten numeral. When the base ten numeral consists of one or two digits, we can do this mentally. For example, suppose that we want to convert the base ten numeral, 6, to a base four numeral. The place values in base four are:

$$..., 4^3, 4^2, 4, 1.$$

The place values that are less than 6 are 4 and 1. We can express 6 as one group of four and two ones:

$$6_{ten} = (1 \times 4) + (2 \times 1) = 12_{four}$$

EXAMPLE 4   A Mental Conversion from Base Ten to Base Five

Convert the base ten numeral, 8, to a base five numeral.

Solution   The place values in base five are:

$$..., 5^3, 5^2, 5, 1.$$

The place values that are less than 8 are 5 and 1. We can express 8 as one group of five and three ones:

$$8_{ten} = (1 \times 5) + (3 \times 1) = 13_{five}$$

Tally Sticks

This notched reindeer antler dates from 15,000 B.C. Humans learned how to keep track of numbers by tallying notches on bones with the same intelligence that led them to preserve and use fire, and at around the same time. Using tally sticks, early people grasped the idea that nine buffalo and nine sheep had something in common: the abstract idea of *nine*. As the human mind conceived of numbers separately from the things they represented, systems of numeration developed.

Technology

Some scientific calculators will convert between and perform calculations within different bases. To tell if your scientific calculator will handle other bases, look for buttons labeled with the capital letters A, B, C, D, E, and F. The calculator found in the Accessories folder of Windows allows for such calculations. By default, numbers are displayed as decimals — that is, in base ten. If you enter a number such as 95 and then click the radio button (little black circle) next to Hex (short for hexadecimal, or base 16), you will see the number displayed as 5F:

$5F = (5 \times 16^1) + (15 \times 1)$
$= 80 + 15$
$= 95.$

Similar conversions can be done for base 8 (octal) and base 2 (binary) systems.

If a conversion cannot be performed mentally, you can use divisions to determine how many groups of each place value are contained in a base ten numeral.

EXAMPLE 5 Using Divisions to Convert from Base Ten to Base Eight

Convert the base ten numeral, 299, to a base eight numeral.

Solution The place values in base eight are:

$$\ldots, 8^3, 8^2, 8^1, 1, \quad \text{or} \quad \ldots, 512, 64, 8, 1.$$

The place values that are less than 299 are 64, 8, and 1. We can use divisions to show how many groups of each of these place values are contained in 299. Divide 299 by 64. Divide the remainder by 8:

```
      4  ← 4 groups          5  ← 5 groups
64)299      of 64        8)43      of 8
  256                      40
   43 ───────────→          3  ← 3 ones left over
```

These divisions show that 299 can be expressed as 4 groups of 64, 5 groups of 8, and 3 ones:

$$299 = (4 \times 64) + (5 \times 8) + (3 \times 1)$$
$$= (4 \times 8^2) + (5 \times 8^1) + (3 \times 1)$$
$$= 453_{\text{eight}}$$

EXAMPLE 6 Using Divisions to Convert from Base Ten to Base Six

Convert the base ten numeral, 3444, to a base six numeral.

Solution The place values in base six are:

$$\ldots, 6^5, 6^4, 6^3, 6^2, 6^1, 1, \quad \text{or} \quad \ldots 7776, 1296, 216, 36, 6, 1.$$

We use the powers of 6 that are less than 3444.

```
        2  ← 2 groups         3  ← 3 groups         5  ← 5 groups         4  ← 4 groups
1296)3444     of 1296    216)852      of 216    36)204      of 36      6)24      of 6
    2592                    648                    180                    24
     852 ───────────→       204 ───────────→        24 ───────────→        0  ← 0 ones
                                                                                  left over
```

Using these four quotients and the final remainder on the right, we can immediately write the answer.

$$3444 = 23540_{\text{six}}$$

Exercise Set 4.2

 Practice Exercises

In Exercises 1–18, convert the numeral to a numeral in base ten.

1. 43_{five}
2. 34_{five}
3. 52_{eight}
4. 67_{eight}
5. 132_{four}
6. 321_{four}
7. 1011_{two}
8. 1101_{two}
9. 2035_{six}
10. 2073_{nine}
11. 70355_{eight}
12. 41502_{six}
13. 2096_{sixteen}
14. 3104_{fifteen}
15. 110101_{two}
16. 101101_{two}
17. $\text{ACE5}_{\text{sixteen}}$
18. $\text{EDF7}_{\text{sixteen}}$

In Exercises 19–28, mentally convert each base ten numeral to a numeral in the given base.

19. 7 to base five
20. 9 to base five
21. 11 to base seven
22. 12 to base seven
23. 2 to base two
24. 3 to base two
25. 13 to base four
26. 19 to base four
27. 37 to base six
28. 25 to base six

In Exercises 29–40, use divisions to convert each base ten numeral to a numeral in the given base.

29. 87 to base five
30. 85 to base seven
31. 108 to base four
32. 199 to base four
33. 19 to base two
34. 23 to base two
35. 138 to base three
36. 129 to base three
37. 386 to base six
38. 428 to base nine
39. 1599 to base seven
40. 1346 to base eight

 Application Exercises

Use a procedure similar to the one used in Exercises 29–40 to solve Exercises 41–43.

41. Change 153 days to weeks and days.
42. Change 273 hours to days and hours.
43. Change \$8.79 to quarters, nickels, and pennies.

 Writing in Mathematics

44. Explain how to determine the place values for a four-digit numeral in base six.

45. Describe how to change a numeral in a base other than ten to a base ten numeral.

46. Describe how to change a base ten numeral to a numeral in another base.

 Critical Thinking Exercises

In Exercises 47–48, write in the indicated base the counting numbers that precede and follow the number expressed by the given numeral.

47. 888_{nine}
48. $\text{EC5}_{\text{sixteen}}$
49. Arrange from smallest to largest:
$11111011_{\text{two}}, 3\text{A}6_{\text{twelve}}, 673_{\text{eight}}$.

 Technology Exercises

In Exercises 50–54, use the scientific calculator in Windows (or any scientific calculator that handles different base conversions) to convert each numeral to a numeral in the indicated base. Note: If you are unsure how to convert to a different base on your calculator, consult the owner's manual.

50. 45 to octal
51. 100101_{two} to decimal
52. 100101_{two} to hexadecimal
53. 567 to binary
54. 333_{eight} to hexadecimal

 Group Exercises

The following topics are appropriate for either individual or group research projects. A report should be given to the class on the researched topic. Useful references include history of mathematics books, books whose purpose is to excite the reader about mathematics, encyclopedias, and the World Wide Web.

55. Societies That Use Numeration Systems with Bases Other Than Ten

56. The Use of Fingers to Represent Numbers

57. Applications of Bases Other Than Ten

58. Binary, Octal, Hexadecimal Bases and Computers

59. Negative Bases (See "Numeration Systems with Unusual Bases," by David Ballow in *The Mathematics Teacher*, May 1974, pp. 413–414.)

60. Babylonian and Mayan Civilizations and Their Contributions

SECTION 4.3   *Computation in Positional Systems*

Objectives

1. Add in bases other than ten.
2. Subtract in bases other than ten.
3. Multiply in bases other than ten.
4. Divide in bases other than ten.

The Hindu-Arabic system of numeration made computation simpler and less mysterious. More people were able to perform computation with ease, leading to the widespread use of the system.

All computations in bases other than ten are performed exactly like those in base ten. However, when a computation is equal to or exceeds the given base, use the mental conversions discussed in the previous section to convert from the base ten numeral to a numeral in the desired base.

1   Add in bases other than ten.

The 4^1, or fours' column   The ones' column

$$33_{\text{four}}$$
$$+\ 13_{\text{four}}$$

Letters and Words in Base Two

Wilhelm Leibniz (1646–1716)

Letters are converted into base two numbers for computer processing. A through Z are assigned 65 through 90, with each number expressed in base two. Similarly, a through z are assigned 97 through 122 in base two.

The German mathematician Wilhelm Leibniz was the first modern thinker to promote the base two system. He never imagined that one day the base two system would enable computers to process information and communicate with one another.

Addition

EXAMPLE 1   Addition in Base Four

Add:

$$33_{\text{four}}$$
$$+13_{\text{four}}$$

Solution   We will begin by adding the numbers in the right-hand column. In base four, the digit symbols are 0, 1, 2, and 3. If a sum in this, or any, column exceeds 3, we will have to convert this base ten number to base four. We begin by adding the numbers in the right-hand, or ones', column:

$$3_{\text{four}} + 3_{\text{four}} = 6$$

6 is not a digit symbol in base four. However, we can express 6 as one group of four and two ones left over:

$$3_{\text{four}} + 3_{\text{four}} = 6_{\text{ten}} = (1 \times 4) + (2 \times 1) = 12_{\text{four}}$$

Now we record the sum of the right-hand column, 12_{four}:

We place the digit on the left above the fours' column.

$$\overset{1}{3}3_{\text{four}}$$
$$+\ 13_{\text{four}}$$
$$\overline{2}$$

12_{four}

We place the digit on the right under the ones' column.

Next, we add the three digits in the fours' column:

$$1_{\text{four}} + 3_{\text{four}} + 1_{\text{four}} = 5$$

5 is not a digit symbol in base four. However, we can express 5 as one group of four and one left over:

$$1_{\text{four}} + 3_{\text{four}} + 1_{\text{four}} = 5_{\text{ten}} = (1 \times 4) + (1 \times 1) = 11_{\text{four}}$$

Record the 11_{four}.

$$\overset{1}{3}3_{\text{four}}$$
$$+\ 13_{\text{four}}$$
$$\overline{112_{\text{four}}}$$

The 2^2, or fours' column

The 2^1, or twos' column

The ones' column

$$111_{two}$$
$$+\ 101_{two}$$

EXAMPLE 2 Addition in Base Two

Add:

$$\begin{array}{r} 111_{two} \\ +\ 101_{two} \\ \hline \end{array}$$

Solution   We begin by adding the numbers in the right-hand, or ones', column:

$$1_{two} + 1_{two} = 2$$

2 is not a digit symbol in base two. We can express 2 as one group of 2 and zero ones left over:

$$1_{two} + 1_{two} = 2_{ten} = (1 \times 2) + (0 \times 1) = 10_{two}$$

Now we record the sum of the right-hand column, 10_{two}:

We place the digit on the left above the twos' column.

$$\begin{array}{r} 1\ \ \ \ \\ 111_{two} \\ +\ 101_{two} \\ \hline 0 \end{array}$$

10_{two}

We place the digit on the right under the ones' column.

Next, we add the three digits in the twos' column:

$$1_{two} + 1_{two} + 0_{two} = 2_{ten} = (1 \times 2) + (0 \times 1) = 10_{two}$$

Now we record the sum of the middle column, 10_{two}:

We place the digit on the left above the fours' column.

$$\begin{array}{r} 1\ 1\ \ \ \ \\ 111_{two} \\ +\ 101_{two} \\ \hline 00 \end{array}$$

10_{two}

We place the digit on the right under the twos' column.

Finally, we add the three digits in the fours' column:

$$1_{two} + 1_{two} + 1_{two} = 3$$

3 is not a digit symbol in base two. We can express 3 as one group of 2 and one 1 left over:

$$1_{two} + 1_{two} + 1_{two} = 3_{ten} = (1 \times 2) + (1 \times 1) = 11_{two}$$

Record the 11_{two}.

$$\begin{array}{r} 1\ 1\ \ \ \ \\ 111_{two} \\ +\ 101_{two} \\ \hline 1100_{two} \end{array}$$

2 Subtract in bases other than ten.

Subtraction

To subtract in bases other than ten, we line up the digits with the same place values and subtract column by column, beginning with the column on the right. If borrowing is necessary to perform the subtraction, borrow the amount of the base. For example, when we borrow in base ten subtraction, we borrow 10. Likewise, we borrow 2 in base two, 3 in base three, 4 in base four, and so on.

EXAMPLE 3　Subtraction in Base Four

Subtract:

$$31_{\text{four}}$$
$$-12_{\text{four}}$$

Solution　We start by performing subtraction in the right column, $1_{\text{four}} - 2_{\text{four}}$. Because 2_{four} is greater than 1_{four}, we need to borrow from the preceding column. We are working in base four, so we borrow one group of 4. This gives a sum of $4 + 1$, or 5, in base ten. Now we subtract 2 from 5, obtaining a difference of 3:

We borrow one group of 4. Now there are 2 groups of 4 for this place value, not 3.

$$\overset{2}{\cancel{3}}\,5\;\;1_{\text{four}}$$
$$-\;1\;2_{\text{four}}$$
$$\overline{3_{\text{four}}}$$

We add the borrowed group of 4 to 1 in base ten.
$$1 + 4 = 5$$

Now we perform the subtraction in the second column from the right:

We subtract 1 from 2.

$$\overset{2}{\cancel{3}}\,5\;\;1_{\text{four}}$$
$$-\;1\;2_{\text{four}}$$
$$\overline{1\;3_{\text{four}}}$$

EXAMPLE 4　Subtraction in Base Five

Subtract:

$$3431_{\text{five}} - 1242_{\text{five}}$$

Solution

Step **(1.)** Borrow a group of 5 from the preceding column. This gives a sum of $5+1$, or 6, in base ten.

$$\overset{2\;6}{343\cancel{1}}_{\text{five}}$$
$$-\;1242_{\text{five}}$$
$$\overline{4_{\text{five}}}$$

Step **(2.)** $6 - 2 = 4$

Step **(3.)** Borrow a group of 5 from the preceding column. This gives a sum of $5 + 2$, or 7, in base ten.

$$\overset{7}{\overset{3\,2\,6}{343\cancel{1}}}_{\text{five}}$$
$$-\;1242_{\text{five}}$$
$$\overline{34_{\text{five}}}$$

Step **(4.)** $7 - 4 = 3$

Step **(5.)** No borrowing is needed for these two columns.

$$\overset{7}{\overset{3\,2\,6}{343\cancel{1}}}_{\text{five}}$$
$$-\;1242_{\text{five}}$$
$$\overline{2134_{\text{five}}}$$

Step **(7.)** $3 - 1 = 2$　Step **(6.)** $3 - 2 = 1$

Thus, $3431_{\text{five}} - 1242_{\text{five}} = 2134_{\text{five}}$.

3 Multiply in bases other than ten.

Base Two, Logic, and Computers

Logic in the form of base two is used to simplify the design of the thousands of switches, or gates, used by a computer. Each switch determines whether or not current will flow. The current will flow through a closed switch, represented as 1. It will not flow through an open switch, represented as 0. The switches should remind you of conjunction, disjunction, and negation in logic, except that T is now 1 and F is now 0. Without the merging of base two and logic, computers as we know them would not exist.

And switch   **Or** switch

Not switch

Multiplication

EXAMPLE 5   Multiplication in Base Six

Multiply:

$$34_{six}$$
$$\times\ 2_{six}$$

Solution   We multiply just as we do in base ten. That is, first we will multiply the digit 2 by the digit 4 directly above it. Then we will multiply the digit 2 by the digit 3 in the left column. Keep in mind that only the digit symbols 0, 1, 2, 3, 4, and 5 are permitted in base six. We begin with:

$$2_{six} \times 4_{six} = 8_{ten} = (1 \times 6) + (2 \times 1) = 12_{six}.$$

Record the 2 and carry the 1:

$$\overset{1}{34}_{six}$$
$$\times\ 2_{six}$$
$$2$$

Our next computation involves both multiplication and addition:

$$(2_{six} \times 3_{six}) + 1_{six} = 6 + 1 = 7_{ten} = (1 \times 6) + (1 \times 1) = 11$$

Record the 11_{six}.

$$34_{six}$$
$$\times\ 2_{six}$$
$$112_{six}$$

Division

The answer in a division problem is called a **quotient**. A multiplcation table showing products in the same base as the division problem is helpful.

4 Divide in bases other than ten.

EXAMPLE 6

Use Table 4.5, showing products in base four, to perform the following division:

$$3_{four}\overline{)222_{four}}$$

Solution   We can use the same method to divide in base four that we use in base ten. Begin by dividing 22_{four} by 3_{four}. Use Table 4.5 to find in the vertical column headed by 3 the largest product that is less than or equal to 22_{four}. This product is 21_{four}. Because $3_{four} \times 3_{four} = 21_{four}$, the first number in the quotient is 3_{four}.

$$3 \quad \leftarrow \text{Quotient}$$
$$\text{Divisor} \rightarrow 3_{four}\overline{)222_{four}} \leftarrow \text{Dividend}$$

Table 4.5   Multiplication: Base Four

×	0	1	2	3
0	0	0	0	0
1	0	1	2	3
2	0	2	10	12
3	0	3	12	21

Mechanical Computing

In 1944, scientists at IBM produced Mark I (shown here), the world's biggest calculator. Mark I performed basic arithmetic, multiplying and dividing huge numbers in mere seconds. Its greatest drawback was its size: 50 feet long and 35 tons!

Calculating without thought and skill was the motivating factor in the history of mechanical computing. Today's handheld calculators provide the mathematical power of a computer, allowing the user to perform computations, graph equations, analyze data, write and use original programs, and even perform algebra's symbolic manipulations. Also, the World Wide Web now offers virtual calculators that simulate the format of actual calculators.

Now multiply $3_{four} \times 3_{four}$ and write the product, 21_{four}, under the first two digits of the dividend.

$$3_{four} \overline{)222_{four}}$$
$$\phantom{3_{four})}\,\underline{21}$$
$$\phantom{3_{four})}\,3$$

Subtract: $22_{four} - 21_{four} = 1_{four}$.

$$3_{four} \overline{)222_{four}}$$
$$\phantom{3_{four})}\,\underline{21}$$
$$\phantom{3_{four})}\,1$$

Bring down the next digit in the dividend, 2_{four}:

$$3_{four} \overline{)222_{four}}$$
$$\phantom{3_{four})}\,\underline{21}$$
$$\phantom{3_{four})}\,12$$

We now return to Table 4.5. Find in the vertical column headed by 3 the largest product that is less than or equal to 12_{four}. Because $3_{four} \times 2_{four} = 12_{four}$, the next numeral in the quotient is 2_{four}. We use this information to finish the division:

$$\overset{32_{four}}{3_{four} \overline{)222}}$$
$$\phantom{3_{four})}\,\underline{21}$$
$$\phantom{3_{four})}\,12$$
$$\phantom{3_{four})}\,\underline{12}$$
$$\phantom{3_{four})}\,0$$

Exercise Set 4.3

  Practice Exercises

In Exercises 1–12, add in the indicated base.

1. $\begin{array}{r} 23_{four} \\ +13_{four} \\ \hline \end{array}$

2. $\begin{array}{r} 31_{four} \\ +22_{four} \\ \hline \end{array}$

3. $\begin{array}{r} 11_{two} \\ +11_{two} \\ \hline \end{array}$

7. $\begin{array}{r} 645_{seven} \\ +324_{seven} \\ \hline \end{array}$

8. $\begin{array}{r} 632_{seven} \\ +564_{seven} \\ \hline \end{array}$

9. $\begin{array}{r} 6784_{nine} \\ +7865_{nine} \\ \hline \end{array}$

4. $\begin{array}{r} 101_{two} \\ +11_{two} \\ \hline \end{array}$

5. $\begin{array}{r} 342_{five} \\ +413_{five} \\ \hline \end{array}$

6. $\begin{array}{r} 323_{five} \\ +421_{five} \\ \hline \end{array}$

10. $\begin{array}{r} 1021_{three} \\ +2011_{three} \\ \hline \end{array}$

11. $\begin{array}{r} 14632_{seven} \\ +5604_{seven} \\ \hline \end{array}$

12. $\begin{array}{r} 53B_{sixteen} \\ +694_{sixteen} \\ \hline \end{array}$

In Exercises 13–24, subtract in the indicated base.

13. 32_{four}
-13_{four}

14. 31_{four}
-12_{four}

15. 23_{five}
-14_{five}

16. 32_{seven}
-16_{seven}

17. 475_{eight}
-267_{eight}

18. 712_{nine}
-483_{nine}

19. 563_{seven}
-164_{seven}

20. 462_{eight}
-177_{eight}

21. 1001_{two}
$-\ 111_{\text{two}}$

22. 1000_{two}
$-\ 101_{\text{two}}$

23. 1200_{three}
-1012_{three}

24. $4C6_{\text{sixteen}}$
-198_{sixteen}

In Exercises 25–34, multiply in the indicated base.

25. 25_{six}
$\times\ 4_{\text{six}}$

26. 34_{five}
$\times\ 3_{\text{five}}$

27. 11_{two}
$\times\ 1_{\text{two}}$

28. 21_{four}
$\times\ 3_{\text{four}}$

29. 543_{seven}
$\times\ 5_{\text{seven}}$

30. 243_{nine}
$\times\ 6_{\text{nine}}$

31. 623_{eight}
$\times\ 4_{\text{eight}}$

32. 543_{six}
$\times\ 5_{\text{six}}$

33. 21_{four}
$\times\ 12_{\text{four}}$

34. 32_{four}
$\times\ 23_{\text{four}}$

In Exercises 35–38, use the multiplication tables shown below to divide in the indicated base.

Multiplication: Base Four

×	0	1	2	3
0	0	0	0	0
1	0	1	2	3
2	0	2	10	12
3	0	3	12	21

Multiplication: Base Five

×	0	1	2	3	4
0	0	0	0	0	0
1	0	1	2	3	4
2	0	2	4	11	13
3	0	3	11	14	22
4	0	4	13	22	31

35. $2_{\text{four}}\overline{)100_{\text{four}}}$

36. $2_{\text{four}}\overline{)321_{\text{four}}}$

37. $3_{\text{five}}\overline{)224_{\text{five}}}$

38. $4_{\text{five}}\overline{)134_{\text{five}}}$

Writing in Mathematics

39. Describe how to add two numbers in a base other than ten. How do you express and record the sum of numbers in a column if that sum exceeds the base?

40. Describe how to subtract two numbers in a base other than ten. How do you subtract a larger number from a smaller number in the same column?

41. Describe two difficulties that youngsters encounter when learning to add, subtract, multiply, and divide using Hindu-Arabic numerals. Base your answer on difficulties that are encountered when performing these computations in bases other than ten.

Critical Thinking Exercise

42. Divide: $31_{\text{seven}}\overline{)2426_{\text{seven}}}$.

Technology Exercises

In Exercises 43–46, use the scientific calculator in Windows (or any scientific calculator that handles different base conversions) to perform the calculation in the indicated base. Note: You need to put the calculator in the appropriate mode before you perform these calculations. If you are unsure how to do this, consult your owner's manual.

43. $712_{\text{eight}} + 455_{\text{eight}}$

44. $712_{\text{eight}} - 455_{\text{eight}}$

45. $65_{\text{sixteen}} \times 3_{\text{sixteen}}$

46. $516_{\text{sixteen}} \div 6_{\text{sixteen}}$

Group Exercises

47. Group members should research various methods that societies have used to perform computations. Include finger multiplication, the galley method (sometimes called the Gelosia method), Egyptian duplation, subtraction by complements, Napier's bones, and other methods of interest in your presentation to the entire class.

48. Organize a debate. One side represents people who favor performing computations by hand, using the methods and procedures discussed in this section, but applied to base ten numerals. The other side represents people who favor the use of calculators for performing all computations. Include the merits of each approach in the debate.

SECTION 4.4   *Looking Back at Early Numeration Systems*

Objectives

1. Understand and use the Egyptian system.
2. Understand and use the Roman system.
3. Understand and use the traditional Chinese system.
4. Understand and use the Ionic Greek system.

In this section, we embark on a brief journey through time and numbers. Our Hindu-Arabic numeration system, the focus of this chapter, is successful because it expresses numbers with just ten symbols and makes computation with these numbers relatively easy. By these standards, the early numeration systems discussed in this section are unsuccessful. By looking briefly at these systems, you will see that our system is outstanding when compared with other historical systems.

The Egyptian Numeration System

1 Understand and use the Egyptian system.

Like most great civilizations, ancient Egypt had several numeration systems. The oldest is hieroglyphic notation, which developed around 3400 B.C. Table 4.6 lists the Egyptian hieroglyphic numerals with the equivalent Hindu-Arabic numerals. Notice that the numerals are powers of ten. Their numeral for 1,000,000, or 10^6, looks like someone who just won the lottery!

Study Tip

It is not necessary to memorize the symbols for the four numeration systems discussed in this section. Focus your attention on understanding the idea behind each system and how these ideas have been incorporated into our Hindu-Arabic system.

Table 4.6   Egyptian Hieroglyphic Numerals

Hindu-Arabic Numeral	Egyptian Numeral	Description
1		Staff
10		Heel bone
100		Spiral
1000		Lotus blossom
10,000		Pointing finger
100,000		Tadpole
1,000,000		Astonished person

It takes far more space to represent most numbers in the Egyptian system than in our system. This is because a number is expressed by repeating each numeral the required number of times. However, no numeral, except perhaps the astonished person, should be repeated more than nine times. If we were to use the Egyptian system to represent 764, we would need to write

100 100 100 100 100 100 100 10 10 10 10 10 10 1 1 1 1

and then represent each of these symbols with the appropriate hieroglyphic numeral from Table 4.6. Thus, 764 as an Egyptian numeral is

Hieroglyphic Numerals on Ancient Egyptian Tombs

Egyptian tombs from as early as 2600 B.C. contained hieroglyphic numerals. The funeral rites of ancient Egypt provided the dead with food and drink. The numerals showed how many of each item were included in the offering. Thus, the deceased had nourishment in symbolic form even when the offerings of the rite itself were gone.

The ancient Egyptian system is an example of an **additive system**, one in which the number represented is the sum of the values of the numerals.

EXAMPLE 1 Using the Egyptian Numeration System

Write the following numeral as a Hindu-Arabic numeral:

Solution Using Table 4.6, find the value of each of the Egyptian numerals. Then add them.

$$1,000,000 + 10,000 + 10,000 + 10 + 10 + 10 + 1 + 1 + 1 + 1 = 1,020,034$$

EXAMPLE 2 Using the Egyptian Numeration System

Write 1752 as an Egyptian numeral.

Solution First break down the Hindu-Arabic numeral into quantities that match the Egyptian numerals:

$$1752 = 1000 + 700 + 50 + 2$$
$$= 1000 + 100 + 100 + 100 + 100 + 100 + 100 + 100$$
$$+ 10 + 10 + 10 + 10 + 10 + 1 + 1.$$

Now, use Table 4.6 to find the Egyptian symbol that matches each quantity. For example, the lotus blossom, matches 1000. Write each of these symbols and leave out the addition signs. Thus, the number 1752 can be expressed as:

2 Understand and use the Roman system.

The Roman Numeration System

The Roman numeration system was developed between 500 B.C. and A.D. 100. It evolved as a result of tax collecting and commerce in the vast Roman Empire. The Roman numerals shown in Table 4.7 were used throughout Europe until the eighteenth century. They are still commonly used in outlining, on clocks, for certain copyright dates, and in numbering some pages in books. Roman numerals are selected letters from the Roman alphabet.

Table 4.7 Roman Numerals

Roman numeral	I	V	X	L	C	D	M
Hindu-Arabic numeral	1	5	10	50	100	500	1000

If the symbols in Table 4.7 decrease in value from left to right, then add their values to obtain the value of the Roman numeral as a whole. For example,

CX = 100 + 10 = 110. On the other hand, if symbols increase in value from left to right, then subtract the value of the symbol on the left from the symbol on the right. For example, IV means 5 − 1 = 4 and IX means 10 − 1 = 9.

EXAMPLE 3   Using Roman Numerals

Write CLXVII as a Hindu-Arabic numeral.

Solution   Because the numerals decrease in value from left to right, we add their values to find the value of the Roman numeral as a whole.

$$CLXVII = 100 + 50 + 10 + 5 + 1 + 1 = 167$$

EXAMPLE 4   Using Roman Numerals

Write MCMXCVI as a Hindu-Arabic numeral.

Solution

$$\begin{array}{ccccc} M & CM & XC & V & I \\ \downarrow & \downarrow & \downarrow & \downarrow & \downarrow \end{array}$$
$$= 1000 + (1000 - 100) + (100 - 10) + 5 + 1$$
$$= 1000 + 900 + 90 + 5 + 1 = 1996$$

Study Tip

The Roman numeration system is filled with complicated rules about which numerals are permitted in subtraction and from which numerals they may be subtracted. Without these details, you may find it possible to represent our numerals as Roman numerals in more than one way.

EXAMPLE 5   Using Roman Numerals

Write 249 as a Roman numeral.

Solution

$$\begin{array}{ccccc} 249 = & 200 & + & 40 & + & 9 \\ = & 100 + 100 & + & (50 - 10) & + & (10 - 1) \\ & \downarrow \quad \downarrow & & \downarrow & & \downarrow \\ = & C \quad\; C & & XL & & IX \end{array}$$

Thus, 249 = CCXLIX.

3 Understand and use the traditional Chinese system.

The Traditional Chinese Numeration System

The numerals used in the traditional Chinese numeration system are given in Table 4.8. At least two things are missing—a symbol for zero and a surprised lottery winner!

Table 4.8   Traditional Chinese Numerals

Traditional Chinese numerals	一	二	三	四	五	六	七	八	九	十	百	千
Hindu-Arabic numerals	1	2	3	4	5	6	7	8	9	10	100	1000

7
100
8
10
3

Representing 783 vertically is the first step in expressing it as a Chinese numeral.

$$3000: \begin{cases} 3 & \equiv \\ 1000 & \mathcal{F} \end{cases}$$

$$200: \begin{cases} 2 & = \\ 100 & \text{百} \end{cases}$$

$$60: \begin{cases} 6 & \text{六} \\ 10 & \text{十} \end{cases}$$

$$4: \quad 4 \quad \text{四}$$

Writing 3264 as a Chinese numeral

4 Understand and use the Ionic Greek system.

So, how are numbers represented with this set of symbols? Chinese numerals are written vertically. Using our digits, the number 783 is expressed as shown in the margin.

The next step is to replace each of these five symbols with a traditional Chinese numeral from Table 4.8. Our next example illustrates this procedure using 3264.

EXAMPLE 6   Using the Traditional Chinese Numeration System

Write 3264 as a Chinese numeral.

Solution   First, break down the Hindu-Arabic numeral into quantities that match the Chinese numerals. Represent each quantity vertically. Then, use Table 4.8 to find the Chinese symbol that matches each quantity. This procedure, with the resulting Chinese numeral, is shown in the margin.

The Chinese system does not need a numeral for zero because it is not positional. For example, we write 8006, using zeros as placeholders, to indicate that two powers of ten, namely 10^2, or 100, and 10^1, or 10, are not needed. The Chinese leave this out, writing

8 　　八
1000 　千
6 , or 　六

The Ionic Greek Numeration System

The ancient Greeks, masters of art, architecture, theater, literature, philosophy, geometry, and logic, were not masters when it came to representing numbers. The Ionic Greek numeration system, which can be traced back as far as 450 B.C., used letters of their alphabet for numerals. Table 4.9 shows the many symbols (too many symbols!) used to represent numbers.

To represent a number from 1 to 999, the appropriate symbols are written next to one another. For example, the number $21 = 20 + 1$. When 21 is expressed as a Greek numeral, the plus sign is left out:

$$21 = \kappa\alpha$$

Similarly, the number 823 written as a Greek numeral is $\omega\kappa\gamma$.

Table 4.9   Ionic Greek Numerals

1	α	alpha	10	ι	iota	100	ρ	rho
2	β	beta	20	κ	kappa	200	σ	sigma
3	γ	gamma	30	λ	lambda	300	τ	tau
4	δ	delta	40	μ	mu	400	υ	upsilon
5	ε	epsilon	50	ν	nu	500	ϕ	phi
6	ζ	vau	60	ξ	xi	600	χ	chi
7	ζ	zeta	70	o	omicron	700	ψ	psi
8	η	eta	80	π	pi	800	ω	omega
9	θ	theta	90	Q	koph	900	π	sampi

EXAMPLE 7   Using the Greek Numeration System

Write $\psi\lambda\delta$ as a Hindu-Arabic numeral.

Solution $\psi = 700, \lambda = 30$, and $\delta = 4$. Adding these numbers gives 734.

One of the many unsuccessful features of the Greek numeration system is that new symbols have to be added to represent higher numbers. It is like an alphabet that gets bigger each time a new word is used and has to be written.

Exercise Set 4.4

 Practice Exercises

Use Table 4.6 on page 167 to solve Exercises 1–12.
In Exercises 1–6, write each Egyptian numeral as a Hindu-Arabic numeral.

1. ⑨⑨⑨∩∩| |

2. 👤👤👤 ⫸⫸⫸⫸ ⑨⑨ ∩| | | |

3. ⌐ ⌐ ⌐ ⑨⑨⑨⑨ ∩∩| | |

4. ⌐⌐ ⑨⑨ ∩| | |

5. ⑨∩∩∩| |

6. ⌐ ⫸⫸ 𝍠 ⑨⑨⑨⑨| |

In Exercises 7–12, write each Hindu-Arabic numeral as an Egyptian numeral.

7. 423   8. 825   9. 1846

10. 1425   11. 23,547   12. 2,346,031

Use Table 4.7 on page 168 to solve Exercises 13–34.
In Exercises 13–26, write each Roman numeral as a Hindu-Arabic numeral.

13. XI   14. CL   15. XVI
16. LVII   17. XL   18. CM
19. LIX   20. XLIV   21 CXLVI
22. CLXI   23. MDCXXI   24. MMCDXLV
25. MMDCLXXVII   26. MDXCXXXVI

In Exercises 27–34, write each Hindu-Arabic numeral as a Roman numeral. There may be more than one correct answer.

27. 43   28. 96   29. 129   30. 469
31. 1896   32. 4578   33. 6892   34. 5847

Use Table 4.8 on page 169 to solve Exercises 35–46.
In Exercises 35–40, write each traditional Chinese numeral as a Hindu-Arabic numeral.

35. 八十八
36. 七百五
37. 五百二十七
38. 三千二百八十一
39. 二千七百七十六
40. 八千二百三十六

In Exercises 41–46, write each Hindu-Arabic numeral as a traditional Chinese numeral.

41. 43   42. 269   43. 583
44. 2965   45. 4870   46. 7605

Use Table 4.9 on page 170 to solve Exercises 47–54.
In Exercises 47–50, write each Ionic Greek numeral as a Hindu-Arabic numeral.

47. $\iota\beta$ 48. $\phi\varepsilon$ 49. $\sigma\lambda\delta$ 50. $\psi o \theta$

In Exercises 51–54, write each Hindu-Arabic numeral as an Ionic Greek numeral.

51. 43   52. 257   53. 483   54. 895

 Application Exercises

55. Look at the back of a U.S. one dollar bill. What date is written in Roman numerals along the base of the pyramid with an eye? What is this date's significance?

56. A construction crew demolishing a very old building was surprised to find the numeral MCMLXXXIX inscribed on the cornerstone. Explain why they were surprised.

 Writing in Mathematics

57. Describe how a number is represented in the Egyptian numeration system.

58. If you are interpreting a Roman numeral, when do you add values and when do you subtract them? Give an example to illustrate each case.

59. Describe how a number is represented in the traditional Chinese numeration system.

60. Describe one disadvantage of the Ionic Greek numeration system.

61. If you could use only one system of numeration described in this section, which would you prefer? Discuss the reasons for your choice.

 ## Critical Thinking Exercises

62. Arrange these three numerals from greatest to least.

CCCCXLIX

63. Use Egyptian numerals to write the numeral that precedes and the numeral that follows

64. After reading this section, a student had a numeration nightmare about selling flowers in a time-warped inter-

national market. She started out with 200 flowers, selling XLVI of them to a Roman,

$$\cap\cap\cap\mathsf{II}$$

to an Egyptian,

$$\frac{=}{+}$$

to a traditional Chinese family, and the remainder to a Greek. How many flowers were sold to the Greek? Express the answer in the Ionic Greek numeration system.

 ## Group Exercises

Take a moment to read the introduction to the group exercises on page 160. Exercises 65–67 list some additional topics for individual or group research projects.

65. A Time Line Showing Significant Developments in Numeration Systems

66. Animals and Number Sense

67. The Hebrew Numeration System (or any system not discussed in this chapter)

68. The Rhind Papyrus and What We Learned from It

69. Computation in an Early Numeration System

 # CHAPTER SUMMARY, REVIEW, AND TEST

SUMMARY

4.1 Our Hindu-Arabic System and Early Positional Systems

a. In a positional-value, or place-value, numeration system, the value of each symbol, called a digit, varies according to the position it occupies in the number.

b. The Hindu-Arabic numeration system is a base ten system with the digits 0, 1, 2, 3, 4, 5, 6, 7, 8, and 9. The place values in the system are:

$$\ldots, 10^5, 10^4, 10^3, 10^2, 10^1, 1.$$

c. The Babylonian numeration system is a base 60 system, with place values given by:

$$\ldots, \quad 60^3, \quad 60^2, \quad 60^1, \quad 1.$$
$$\text{or} \qquad \text{or} \qquad \text{or}$$
$$216,000 \quad 3600 \quad 60$$

Babylonian numerals are given in Table 4.1 on page 151.

d. The Mayan numeration system has place values given by:

$$\ldots, \quad 18 \times 20^3, \quad 18 \times 20^2, \quad 18 \times 20, \quad 20, \quad 1.$$
$$\text{or} \qquad \text{or} \qquad \text{or}$$
$$144,000 \quad 7200 \quad 360$$

Mayan numerals are given in Table 4.2 on page 152.

4.2 Number Bases in Positional Systems

a. The base of a positional numeration system refers to the number of individual digit symbols used in the system as well as to the way in which grouping is to occur. In base b, there are b digit symbols (from 0 through $b - 1$ inclusive) with place values given by:

$$\ldots, b^4, b^3, b^2, b^1, 1.$$

b. To change a numeral in a base other than ten to a base ten numeral
   1. Multiply each digit in the numeral by its respective place value.
   2. Find the sum of the products in step 1.
c. To change a base ten numeral to a base b numeral, use mental conversions or repeated divisions by powers of b to find how many groups of each place value are contained in the base ten numeral.

4.3 Computation in Positional Systems

a. Computations in bases other than ten are performed using the same procedures as in ordinary base ten arithmetic. When a computation is equal to or exceeds the given base, use mental conversions to convert from the base ten numeral to a numeral in the desired base.

b. To divide in bases other than ten, it is convenient to use a multiplication table for products in the required base.

4.4 Looking Back at Early Numeration Systems

a. A successful numeration system expresses numbers with relatively few symbols and makes computation with these numbers fairly easy.

b. By the standard in (a), the Egyptian system (Table 4.6 on page 167), the Roman system (Table 4.7 on page 168), the Chinese system (Table 4.8 on page 169), and the Greek system (Table 4.9 on page 170) are all unsuccessful. Unlike our Hindu-Arabic, system, these systems are not positional and contain no symbol for zero.

REVIEW EXERCISES

4.1

In Exercises 1–2, evaluate the expression.

1. 11^2 2. 7^3

In Exercises 3–5, write each Hindu-Arabic numeral in expanded form.

3. 472   4. 8076   5. 70,329

In Exercises 6–7, express each expanded form as a Hindu-Arabic numeral.

6. $(7 \times 10^5) + (0 \times 10^4) + (6 \times 10^3) + (9 \times 10^2) + (5 \times 10^1) + (3 \times 1)$

7. $(7 \times 10^8) + (4 \times 10^7) + (3 \times 10^2) + (6 \times 1)$

Use Table 4.1 on page 151 to write each Babylonian numeral in Exercises 8–9 as a Hindu-Arabic numeral.

8. ᐸ∨ ᐸ∨∨∨   9. ∨∨ ᐸᐸ ᐸᐸᐸ

Use Table 4.2 on page 152 to write each Mayan numeral in Exercises 10–11 as a Hindu-Arabic numeral.

10. ·⋯· ⋯ ·⋯· ═
11. ⋯·· ⋯ ⊜ ≡ ·

12. Describe how a positional system is used to represent a number.

4.2

In Exercises 13–18, convert the numeral to a numeral in base ten.

13. 34_{five} 14. 110_{two} 15. 643_{seven}
16. 1084_{nine} 17. $FD3_{\text{sixteen}}$ 18. 202202_{three}

In Exercises 19–24, convert each base ten numeral to a numeral in the given base.

19. 89 to base five   20. 21 to base two
21. 473 to base three   22. 7093 to base seven
23. 9348 to base six   24. 554 to base twelve

4.3

In Exercises 25–28, add in the indicated base.

25. 46_{seven} 26. 574_{eight} 27. 11011_{two} 28. $43C_{\text{sixteen}}$
$+53_{\text{seven}}$ $+605_{\text{eight}}$ $+10101_{\text{two}}$ $+694_{\text{sixteen}}$

In Exercises 29–32, subtract in the indicated base.

29. 34_{six} 30. 624_{seven} 31. 1001_{two} 32. 4121_{five}
-25_{six} -246_{seven} -110_{two} -1312_{five}

In Exercises 33–35, multiply in the indicated base.

33. 32_{four} 34. 43_{seven} 35. 123_{five}
$\times 3_{\text{four}}$ $\times 6_{\text{seven}}$ $\times 4_{\text{five}}$

In Exercises 36–37, divide in the indicated base. Use the multiplication tables on page 166.

36. $2_{\text{four}}\overline{)332_{\text{four}}}$ 37. $4_{\text{five}}\overline{)103_{\text{five}}}$

Use Table 4.6 on page 167 to solve Exercises 38–41. In Exercises 38–39, write each Egyptian numeral as a Hindu-Arabic numeral.

38. ⚬ 𝒮 ◗◗◗ ∩∩∩∩∩ |||||

39. 𓂝 ⚬⚬ 𝒮 ◗◗◗◗◗ ∩∩ ||

In Exercises 40–41, write each Hindu-Arabic numeral as an Egyptian numeral.

40. 2486   41. 34,573

In Exercises 42–43, assume a system that represents numbers exactly like the Egyptian system, but with different symbols. In particular, A = 1, B = 10, C = 100, and D = 1000.

42. Write DDCCCBAAAA as a Hindu-Arabic numeral.

43. Write 5492 as a numeral in terms of A, B, C and D.

44. Describe how the Egyptian system or the system in Exercises 42–43 is used to represent a number. Discuss one disadvantage of such a system when compared to our Hindu-Arabic system.

Use Table 4.7 on page 168 to solve Exercises 45–49. In Exercises 45–47, write each Roman numeral as a Hindu-Arabic numeral.

45. CLXIII   46. MXXXIV   47. MCMXC

In Exercises 48–49, write each Hindu-Arabic numeral as a Roman numeral.

48. 49   49. 2965

50. Explain when to subtract the value of symbols when interpreting a Roman numeral. Give an example.

Use Table 4.8 on page 169 to solve Exercises 51–54. In Exercises 51–52 write each traditional Chinese numeral as a Hindu-Arabic numeral.

51. 五   52. 八
　　百　　　　千
　　五　　　　二
　　十　　　　百
　　四　　　　五
　　　　　　　十
　　　　　　　三

In Exercises 53–54, write each Hindu-Arabic numeral as a traditional Chinese numeral.

53. 274   54. 3587

In Exercises 55–58, assume a system that represents numbers exactly like the traditional Chinese system, but with different symbols. The symbols are shown as follows:

Numerals in the System	A	B	C	D	E	F	G	H	I	X	Y	Z
Hindu-Arabic Numerals	1	2	3	4	5	6	7	8	9	10	100	1000

Express each numeral in Exercises 55–56 as a Hindu-Arabic numeral.

55. C   56. D
　　Y　　　　Z
　　F　　　　E
　　X　　　　Y
　　E　　　　B
　　　　　　　X

Express each Hindu-Arabic numeral in Exercises 57–58 as a numeral in the system described above.

57. 793   58. 6854

59. Describe how the Chinese system or the system in Exercises 55–58 is used to represent a number. Discuss one disadvantage of such a system when compared to our Hindu-Arabic system.

Use Table 4.9 on page 170 to solve Exercises 60–63. In Exercises 60–61 write each Ionic Greek numeral as a Hindu-Arabic numeral.

60. χνγ   61. χοη

In Exercises 62–63, write each Hindu-Arabic numeral as an Ionic Greek numeral.

62. 453   63. 902

In Exercises 64–68, assume a system that represents numbers exactly like the Greek Ionic system, but with different symbols. The symbols are shown as follows:

Decimal	1	2	3	4	5	6	7	8	9
Ones	A	B	C	D	E	F	G	H	I
Tens	J	K	L	M	N	O	P	Q	R
Hundreds	S	T	U	V	W	X	Y	Z	a
Thousands	b	c	d	e	f	g	h	i	j
Ten thousands	k	l	m	n	o	p	q	r	s

In Exercises 64–66, express each numeral as a Hindu-Arabic numeral.

64. UNG   65. mhZRD   66. rXJH

In Exercises 67–68, express each Hindu-Arabic numeral as a numeral in the system described above.

67. 597   68. 25,483

69. Discuss one disadvantage of the Greek Ionic system or the system described in Exercises 64–68 when compared to our Hindu-Arabic system.

 Group Exercise

70. We opened the chapter with a virtual reality ski simulator in the not-too-distant future. As we enter the twenty-first century, it is difficult to imagine the kind of future that computer technology will bring us. For this activity, group members should research cutting-edge applications of computing devices and calculators that will transform our lives in the twenty-first century. You can visit a computer store to discover what is "hot" in the industry, consult the World Wide Web, or talk with creative people in the arts who are using computers in innovative ways. Include examples in your class presentation that will truly amaze your fellow students, making this a presentation they will never forget.

CHAPTER 4 TEST

1. Evaluate 9^3.
2. Write 567 in expanded form.
3. Write 63,028 in expanded form.
4. Express as a Hindu-Arabic numeral:
   $(7 \times 10^3) + (4 \times 10^2) + (9 \times 10^1) + (3 \times 1)$.
5. Express as a Hindu-Arabic numeral:
   $(4 \times 10^5) + (2 \times 10^2) + (6 \times 1)$.
6. What is the difference between a number and a numeral?
7. Explain why a symbol for zero is needed in a positional system.
8. Place values in the Babylonian system are:

   $\ldots, 60^3, 60^2, 60^1, 1$.

   Use the numerals shown to write the following Babylonian numeral as a Hindu-Arabic numeral:

   $<<\quad <\vee\vee\quad <\vee$.

Babylonian	$\vee$	$<$
Hindu-Arabic	1	10

9. Place values in the Mayan system are:

   $\ldots, 18 \times 20^3, 18 \times 20^2, 18 \times 20, 20, 1$.

   Use the numerals shown to write the following Mayan numeral as a Hindu-Arabic numeral:

Mayan	⊖	•	••	•••	••••	—	$\underline{\cdot}$
Hindu-Arabic	0	1	2	3	4	5	6

In Exercises 10–12, convert the numeral to a numeral in base ten.

10. 423_{five} 11. 267_{nine} 12. 110101_{two}

In Exercises 13–15, convert each base ten numeral to a numeral in the given base.

13. 77 to base three
14. 56 to base two
15. 1844 to base five

In Exercises 16–18, perform the indicated operation.

16. 234_{five}
    $+423_{\text{five}}$

17. 562_{seven}
    -145_{seven}

18. 54_{six}
    $\times 3_{\text{six}}$

19. Use the multiplication table shown to perform this division: $3_{\text{five}} \overline{)1213_{\text{five}}}$.

A Multiplication Table for Base Five

$\times$	0	1	2	3	4
0	0	0	0	0	0
1	0	1	2	3	4
2	0	2	4	11	13
3	0	3	11	14	22
4	0	4	13	22	31

Use the symbols in the tables shown below to solve Exercises 20–23.

Hindu-Arabic Numeral	Egyptian Numeral
1	|
10	∩
100	⑨
1000	⚱
10,000	⌒
100,000	⌒
1,000,000	𓁨

Hindu-Arabic Numeral	Roman Numeral
1	I
5	V
10	X
50	L
100	C
500	D
1000	M

20. Write the following numeral as a Hindu-Arabic numeral: ⫫⑨⑨⑨|||
21. Write 32,634 as an Egyptian numeral.
22. Write the Roman numeral MCMXCIV as a Hindu-Arabic numeral.
23. Express 459 as a Roman numeral.
24. Describe one difference between how a number is represented in the Egyptian system and the Roman system.

Listening to the radio, you hear candidates in the upcoming election discussing the problem of the country's 5.5 trillion dollar deficit. It seems like this is a real problem, but then you realize that you don't really know what that number means. How can you look at this deficit in the proper perspective? If the national debt were evenly divided among all citizens of the country, how much would each citizen have to pay? Does the deficit seem like such a significant problem now?

5 Number Theory and the Real Number System

Throughout the new millenium, literacy with numbers, called **numeracy**, will be a prerequisite for functioning in a meaningful way personally, professionally, and as a citizen. In this chapter, our focus is on understanding numbers, their properties, and their applications. After completing the chapter, you will be in a position to put numbers like 5.5 trillion in perspective, giving you a better understanding of the important policy issues that will shape the twenty-first century.

SECTION 5.1 Number Theory: Prime and Composite Numbers

Objectives

1. Determine divisibility.
2. Write the prime factorization of a composite number.
3. Find the greatest common divisor of two numbers.
4. Solve problems using the greatest common divisor.
5. Find the least common multiple of two numbers.
6. Solve problems using the least common multiple.

Number Theory and Divisibility

You are organizing an intramural league at your school. You need to divide 40 men and 24 women into all-male and all-female teams so that each team has the same number of people. The men's teams should have the same number of players as the women's teams. What is the largest number of people that can be placed on a team?

This problem can be solved using a branch of mathematics called **number theory**. Number theory is primarily concerned with the properties of numbers used for counting, namely 1, 2, 3, 4, 5, and so on. The set of counting numbers is also called the set of **natural numbers**. We represent this set by the letter **N**.

The Set of Natural Numbers

$$\mathbf{N} = \{1, 2, 3, 4, 5, 6, 7, 8, 9, 10, 11, \ldots\}$$

We can solve the intramural league problem. However, to do so we must understand the concept of divisibility. For example, there are a number of different ways to divide the 24 women into teams, including

1 team with all 24 women:	$1 \times 24 = 24$
2 teams with 12 women per team:	$2 \times 12 = 24$
3 teams with 8 women per team:	$3 \times 8 = 24$
4 teams with 6 women per team:	$4 \times 6 = 24$
6 teams with 4 women per team:	$6 \times 4 = 24$
8 teams with 3 women per team:	$8 \times 3 = 24$
12 teams with 2 women per team:	$12 \times 2 = 24$
24 teams with 1 woman per team:	$24 \times 1 = 24$

The natural numbers that are multiplied together resulting in a product of 24 are called the **factors** of 24. Notice that a natural number may have many factors.

$$2 \times 12 = 24 \qquad 3 \times 8 = 24 \qquad 6 \times 4 = 24$$

Factors of 24   Factors of 24   Factors of 24

The numbers 1, 2, 3, 4, 6, 8, 12, and 24 are all factors of 24. Each of these numbers divides 24 without a remainder.

In general, let a and b represent natural numbers. We say that a is **divisible** by b if the operation of dividing a by b leaves a remainder of 0.

A natural number is divisible by all of its factors. Thus, 24 is divisible by 1, 2, 3, 4, 6, 8, 12, and 24. Using the factor 8, we can express this divisibility in a number of ways:

Study Tip

The words *factor* and *divisor* mean the same thing. Thus, 8 is a factor and a divisor of 24.

24 is **divisible** by 8.

8 is a **divisor** of 24.

8 **divides** 24.

Study Tip

Do not confuse the notations $b|a$ and b/a. The symbol $b|a$ means b divides a. The symbol b/a means b divided by a (that is $b \div a$, the quotient of b and a). For example, $5|35$ means 5 divides 35, whereas $5/35$ means 5 divided by 35, which is the fraction $\frac{1}{7}$.

Mathematicians use a special notation to indicate divisibility.

Divisibility

If a and b are natural numbers, a is **divisible** by b if the operation of dividing a by b leaves a remainder of 0. This is the same as saying that b is a **divisor** of a, or b **divides** a. All three statements are symbolized by writing

$$b|a.$$

Using this new notation, we can write

$$12|24.$$

Twelve divides 24 because 24 divided by 12 leaves a remainder of 0. By contrast, 13 does not divide 24 because 24 divided by 13 does not leave a remainder of 0. The notation

$$13 \nmid 24$$

means that 13 does not divide 24.

Table 5.1 shows some common rules for divisibility. Divisibility rules for 7 and 11 are difficult to remember and are not included in the table.

1 Determine divisibility

Table 5.1 Rules of Divisibility

Divisible By	Test	Example
2	The last digit is 0, 2, 4, 6, or 8.	5,892,796 is divisible by 2 because the last digit is 6.
3	The sum of the digits is divisible by 3.	52,341 is divisible by 3 because the sum of the digits is $5 + 2 + 3 + 4 + 1 = 15$, and 15 is divisible by 3.
4	The last two digits form a number divisible by 4.	3,947,136 is divisible by 4 because 36 is divisible by 4.
5	The number ends in 0 or 5.	28,160 and 72,805 end in 0 and 5, respectively. Both are divisible by 5.
6	The number is divisible by both 2 and 3.	954 is divisible by 2 because it ends in 4. 954 is also divisible by 3 because the digit sum is 18, which is divisible by 3. Because 954 is divisible by both 2 and 3, it is divisible by 6.
8	The last three digits form a number that is divisible by 8.	593,777,832 is divisible by 8 because 832 is divisible by 8.
9	The sum of the digits is divisible by 9.	5346 is divisible by 9 because the sum of the digits, 18, is divisible by 9.
10	The last digit is 0.	998,746,250 is divisible by 10 because the number ends in 0.
12	The number is divisible by both 3 and 4.	614,608,176 is divisible by 3 because the digit sum is 39, which is divisible by 3. It is also divisible by 4 because the last two digits form 76, which is divisible by 4. Because 614,608,176 is divisible by both 3 and 4, it is divisible by 12.

Technology

Calculators and Divisibility

You can use a calculator to verify each result in Example 1. Consider part (a):

$$4 \mid 3,754,086$$

Divide 3,754,086 by 4 using the following keystrokes:

$$3754086 \; \boxed{\div} \; 4$$

Press $\boxed{=}$ or $\boxed{\text{ENTER}}$. The number displayed is 938521.5. This is not a natural number. The 0.5 shows that the division leaves a nonzero remainder. Thus, 4 does not divide 3,754,086. The given statement is false.

Now consider part (b):

$$9 \nmid 4,119,706,413$$

Use your calculator to divide the number on the right by 9:

$$4119706413 \; \boxed{\div} \; 9$$

Pressing $\boxed{=}$ or $\boxed{\text{ENTER}}$, the display is 457745157. This is a natural number. The remainder of the division is 0, so 9 does divide 4,119,706,413. The given statement is false.

EXAMPLE 1   Using the Rules of Divisibility

Which one of the following statements is true?

a. $4 \mid 3,754,086$ b. $9 \nmid 4,119,706,413$ c. $8 \mid 677,840$

Solution

a. $4 \mid 3,754,086$ states that 4 divides 3,754,086. Table 5.1 indicates that for 4 to divide a number, the last two digits must form a number that is divisible by 4. Because 86 is not divisible by 4, the given statement is false.

b. $9 \nmid 4,119,706,413$ states that 9 does *not* divide 4,119,706,413. Based on Table 5.1, if the sum of the digits is divisible by 9, then 9 does indeed divide this number. The sum of the digits is $4 + 1 + 1 + 9 + 7 + 0 + 6 + 4 + 1 + 3 = 36$, which is divisible by 9. Because 4,119,706,413 is divisible by 9, the given statement is false.

c. $8 \mid 667,840$ states that 8 divides 677,840. Table 5.1 indicates that for 8 to divide a number, the last three digits must form a number that is divisible by 8. Because 840 is divisible by 8, then 8 divides 677,840, and the given statement is true.

The statement given in part (c) is the only true statement.

Prime Factorization

By developing some other ideas of number theory, we will be able to solve the intramural league problem. We begin with the definition of a prime number.

> **Prime Numbers**
>
> A **prime number** is a natural number greater than 1 that has only itself and 1 as factors.

Study Tip

The number 2 is the only even prime number. Every other even number has at least three factors: 1, 2, and the number itself.

Using this definition, we see that the number 7 is a prime number because it has only 1 and 7 as factors. Said in another way, 7 is prime because it is divisible by only 1 and 7. The first ten prime numbers are 2, 3, 5, 7, 11, 13, 17, 19, 23, and 29. Each number in this list has exactly two divisors, itself and 1. By contrast, 9 is not a prime number; in addition to being divisible by 1 and 9, it is also divisible by 3. The number 9 is an example of a composite number.

> **Composite Numbers**
>
> A **composite number** is a natural number greater than 1 that is divisible by a number other than itself and 1.

Using this definition, the first ten composite numbers are 4, 6, 8, 9, 10, 12, 14, 15, 16, and 18. Each number in this list has at least three divisors.

2 Write the prime factorization of a composite number.

Every composite number can be expressed as the product of prime numbers. For example, the composite number 45 can be expressed as:

$$45 = 3 \times 3 \times 5.$$

Note that 3 and 5 are prime numbers. Expressing a composite number as the product of prime numbers is called **prime factorization.** The prime factorization of 45 is $3 \times 3 \times 5$. The order in which we write these factors does not matter. This means that

$$45 = 3 \times 3 \times 5$$
$$\text{or } 45 = 5 \times 3 \times 3$$
$$\text{or } 45 = 3 \times 5 \times 3$$

In Chapter 1, we defined a **theorem** as a statement that can be proved using deductive reasoning. The ancient Greeks proved that if the order of the factors is disregarded, there is only one prime factorization possible for any given composite number. This statement is called the **Fundamental Theorem of Arithmetic.**

The Fundamental Theorem of Arithmetic

Every composite number can be expressed as a product of prime numbers in one and only one way (if the order of the factors is disregarded).

One method used to find the prime factorization of a composite number is called a **factor tree.** To use this method, begin by selecting any two numbers whose product is the number to be factored. If one or both of the factors are not prime numbers, continue to factor each composite number. Stop when all numbers are prime.

EXAMPLE 2   Prime Factorization Using a Factor Tree

Find the prime factorization of 700.

Solution   Start with any two numbers whose product is 700, such as 7 and 100. This forms the first branch of the tree. Continue factoring the composite number or numbers that result (in this case 100), branching until the end of each branch contains a prime number

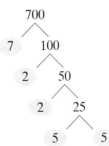

The prime factors are circled. Thus, the prime factorization of 700 is:

$$700 = 7 \times 2 \times 2 \times 5 \times 5.$$

We can use exponents to show the repeated prime factors:

$$700 = 7 \times 2^2 \times 5^2.$$

Using a dot to indicate multiplication, we can write:

$$700 = 7 \cdot 2^2 \cdot 5^2.$$

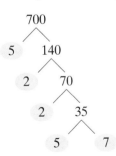

3 Find the greatest common divisor of two numbers.

Greatest Common Divisor

The greatest common divisor of two or more natural numbers is the largest number that is a divisor (or factor) of all the numbers. For example, 8 is the greatest common divisor of 32 and 40 because it is the largest natural number that divides both 32 and 40. Some pairs of numbers have 1 as their greatest common divisor. For example, the greatest common divisor of 5 and 26 is 1.

The greatest common divisor can be found using prime factorizations.

Finding The Greatest Common Divisor of Two or More Numbers Using Prime Factorizations

To find the greatest common divisor of two or more numbers:

1. Write the prime factorization of each number.
2. Select each prime factor with the smallest exponent that is common to each of the prime factorizations.
3. The greatest common divisor is the product of the factors found in step 2.

EXAMPLE 3 Finding the Greatest Common Divisor

Find the greatest common divisor of 216 and 234.

Solution

1. Begin by writing the prime factorizations of 216 and 234.

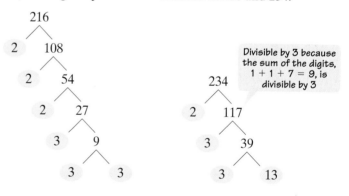

Divisible by 3 because the sum of the digits, $1 + 1 + 7 = 9$, is divisible by 3

The factor tree at left indicates that:

$$216 = 2^3 \times 3^3.$$

The factor tree at right indicates that:

$$234 = 2 \times 3^2 \times 13.$$

2. Select each prime factor with the smallest exponent that is common to each of the prime factorizations.

Look at the factorizations of 216 and 234 from step 1. Can you see that 2 is a prime number common to the factorizations of 216 and 234? Likewise, 3 is also a prime number common to the two factorizations. By contrast, 13 is a prime number that is not common to both factorizations.

$$216 = 2^3 \times 3^3$$
$$234 = 2 \times 3^2 \times 13$$

| 2 is a prime number common to both factorizations. | 3 is a prime number common to both factorizations. |

Now we need to determine which exponent is appropriate for 2 and which exponent is appropriate for 3. The appropriate exponent is the smallest exponent associated with the prime number in the factorizations. The exponents associated with 2 in the factorizations are 1 and 3, so we select 1. Therefore, one factor for the greatest common divisor is 2^1, or 2. The exponents associated with 3 in the factorizations are 2 and 3, so we select 2. Therefore, another factor for the greatest common divisor is 3^2.

3. Form the product of the numbers from step 2.

$$\text{Greatest common divisor} = 2 \times 3^2 = 2 \times 9 = 18$$

The greatest common divisor of 216 and 234 is 18.

4 Solve problems using the greatest common divisor.

EXAMPLE 4 Solving a Problem Using the Greatest Common Divisor

For an intramural league, you need to divide 40 men and 24 women into all-male and all-female teams so that each team has the same number of people. What is the largest number of people that can be placed on a team?

Solution   Because 40 men are to be divided into teams, the number of men on each team must be a divisor of 40. Because 24 women are to be divided into teams, the number of women placed on a team must be a divisor of 24. Although the teams are all-male and all-female, the same number of people must be placed on each team. The largest number of people that can be placed on a team is the largest number that will divide into 40 and 24 without a remainder. This is the greatest common divisor of 40 and 24.

To find the greatest common divisor of 40 and 24, begin with their prime factorizations.

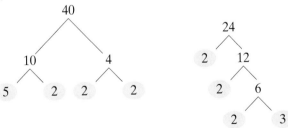

The factor trees indicate that:

$$40 = 2^3 \times 5 \quad \text{and} \quad 24 = 2^3 \times 3.$$

We see that 2 is a prime number common to both factorizations. The exponents associated with 2 in the factorizations are 3 and 3, so we select 3.

$$\text{Greatest common divisor} = 2^3 = 2 \times 2 \times 2 = 8$$

The largest number of people that can be placed on a team is 8. Thus, the 40 men can form five teams with 8 men per team. The 24 women can form three teams with 8 women per team.

5 Find the least common multiple of two numbers.

Least Common Multiple

The **least common multiple** of two or more natural numbers is the smallest natural number that is divisible by all of the numbers. One way to find the least common multiple is to make a list of the numbers that are divisible by each number. This list represents the **multiples** of each number. For example, if we wish to find the least common multiple of 15 and 20, we can list the sets of multiples of 15 and multiples of 20.

$$\begin{cases} \text{Numbers Divisible by 15} : \\ \text{Multiples of 15:} \end{cases} \quad \{15, 30, 45, 60, 75, 90, 105, 120, \dots \}$$

$$\begin{cases} \text{Numbers Divisible by 20} : \\ \text{Multiples of 20:} \end{cases} \quad \{20, 40, 60, 80, 100, 120, 140, 160, \dots \}$$

Some common multiples of 15 and 20 are 60 and 120. The least common multiple is 60. Equivalently, 60 is the smallest number that is divisible by both 15 and 20.

Sometimes a partial list of the multiples for each of two numbers does not reveal the smallest number that is divisible by both given numbers. A more efficient method for finding the least common multiple is to use prime factorizations.

Finding the Least Common Multiple Using Prime Factorizations

To find the least common multiple of two or more numbers:
1. Write the prime factorization of each number.
2. Select every prime factor that occurs, raised to the greatest power to which it occurs, in these factorizations.
3. The least common multiple is the product of the factors found in step 2.

EXAMPLE 5 Finding the Least Common Multiple

Find the least common multiple of 144 and 300.

Solution
1. Write the prime factorizations of 144 and 300.

$$144 = 2^4 \times 3^2$$
$$300 = 2^2 \times 3 \times 5^2$$

2. Select every prime factor that occurs, raised to the greatest power to which it occurs, in these factorizations.
   The prime factors that occur are 2, 3, and 5. The greatest exponent that appears on 2 is 4, so we select 2^4. The greatest exponent that appears on 3 is 2, so we select 3^2. The greatest exponent that occurs on 5 is 2, so we select 5^2. Thus, we have selected 2^4, 3^2, and 5^2.

3. Form the product of the numbers from step 2.

$$\text{Least common multiple} = 2^4 \times 3^2 \times 5^2 = 16 \times 9 \times 25 = 3600$$

The least common multiple of 144 and 300 is 3600. The smallest natural number divisible by 144 and 300 is 3600.

6 Solve problems using the least common multiple.

EXAMPLE 6   Solving a Problem Using the Least Common Multiple

A movie theater runs its films continuously. One movie runs for 80 minutes and a second runs for 120 minutes. Both movies begin at 4:00 P.M. When will the movies begin again at the same time?

Solution   The shorter movie lasts 80 minutes, or 1 hour, 20 minutes. It begins at 4:00, so it will be shown again at 5:20. The longer movie lasts 120 minutes, or 2 hours. It begins at 4:00, so it will be shown again at 6:00. We are asked to find when the movies will begin again at the same time. Therefore, we are looking for the least common multiple of 80 and 120. Find the least common multiple and then add this number of minutes to 4:00 P.M.

Begin with the prime factorizations of 80 and 120:

$$80 = 2^4 \times 5$$
$$120 = 2^3 \times 3 \times 5$$

Now select each prime factor, with the greatest exponent from each factorization.

$$\text{Least common multiple} = 2^4 \times 3 \times 5 = 16 \times 3 \times 5 = 240$$

Therefore, it will take 240 minutes, or 4 hours, for the movies to begin again at the same time. By adding 4 hours to 4:00 P.M., they will start together again at 8:00 P.M.

Study Tip

Example 6 can also be solved by making a partial list of starting times for each movie.
Shorter Movie (Runs 1 hour, 20 minutes):
    4:00,   5:20,   6:40,   8:00,   …
Longer Movie (Runs 2 hours):
    4:00,   6:00,   8:00,   …
The list reveals that both movies start together again at 8:00 P.M.

Exercise Set 5.1

 Practice Exercises

Use rules of divisibility to determine if each number given in Exercises 1–10 is divisible by:

a. 2   b. 3   c. 4   d. 5   e. 6
f. 8   g. 9   h. 10   i. 12

1. 6944   2. 7245   3. 21,408   4. 25,025
5. 26,428   6. 89,001   7. 374,832   8. 347,712
9. 6,126,120   10. 5,941,221

In Exercises 11–24, use a calculator to determine if each statement is true or false. If the statement is true, explain why this is so using one of the rules of divisibility in Table 5.1.

11. 3|5958   12. 3|8142   13. 4|10,612
14. 4|15,984   15. 5|38,814   16. 5|48,659
17. 6|104,538   18. 6|163,944   19. 8|20,104
20. 8|28,096   21. 9|11,378   22. 9|23,772
23. 12|517,872   24. 12|785,172

In Exercises 25–44, find the prime factorization of each composite number.

25. 75   26. 45   27. 56   28. 48   29. 105
30. 180   31. 500   32. 360   33. 663   34. 510
35. 885   36. 999   37. 1440   38. 1280   39. 1996
40. 1575   41. 3675   42. 8316   43. 85,800   44. 30,600

In Exercises 45–56, find the greatest common divisor of the numbers.

45. 42 and 56   46. 25 and 70   47. 16 and 42
48. 66 and 90   49. 60 and 108   50. 96 and 212
51. 72 and 120   52. 220 and 400   53. 342 and 380
54. 224 and 430   55. 240 and 285   56. 150 and 480

In Exercises 57–68, find the least common multiple of the numbers.

57. 42 and 56   58. 25 and 70   59. 16 and 42
60. 66 and 90   61. 60 and 108   62. 96 and 212
63. 72 and 120   64. 220 and 400   65. 342 and 380
66. 224 and 430   67. 240 and 285   68. 150 and 480

Application Exercises

69. A relief worker needs to divide 300 bottles of water and 144 cans of food into groups that each contain the same number of items. Also, each group must have the same type of item (bottled water or canned food). What is the largest number of relief supplies that can be put in each group?

70. A choral director needs to divide 180 men and 144 women into all-male and all-female singing groups so that each group has the same number of people. What is the largest number of people that can be placed in each singing group?

71. You have in front of you 310 five-dollar bills and 460 ten-dollar bills. Your problem: Place the five-dollar bills and the ten-dollar bills in stacks so that each stack has the same number of bills, and each stack contains only one kind of bill (five-dollar or ten-dollar). What is the largest number of bills that you can place in each stack?

72. Harley collects sports cards. He has 360 football cards and 432 baseball cards. Harley plans to arrange his cards in stacks so that each stack has the same number of cards. Also, each stack must have the same type of card (football or baseball). Every card in Harley's collection is to be placed in one of the stacks. What is the largest number of cards that can be placed in each stack?

73. You and your brother both work the 4:00 P.M. to midnight shift. You have every sixth night off. Your brother has every tenth night off. Both of you were off on June 1. Your brother would like to see a movie with you. When will the two of you have the same night off again?

74. A movie theater runs its films continuously. One movie is a short documentary that runs for 40 minutes. The other movie is a full-length feature that runs for 100 minutes. Each film is shown in a separate theater. Both movies begin at noon. When will the movies begin again at the same time?

75. Two people are jogging around a circular track in the same direction. One person can run completely around the track in 15 minutes. The second person takes 18 minutes. If they both start running in the same place at noon, how long will it take them to be at this place together if they continue to run?

76. Two people are in a bicycle race around a circular track. One rider can race completely around the track in 40 seconds. The other rider takes 45 seconds. If they both begin the race at a designated starting point, how long will it take them to be together at this starting point again if they continue to race around the track?

 Writing in Mathematics

77. If a and b are factors of c, what does this mean?

78. Why is 45 divisible by 5?

79. What does "a is divisible by b" mean?

80. Describe the difference between a prime number and a composite number.

81. What does the Fundamental Theorem of Arithmetic state?

82. What is the greatest common divisor of two or more natural numbers?

83. Describe how to find the greatest common divisor of two numbers.

84. What is the least common multiple of two or more natural numbers?

85. Describe how to find the least common multiple of two natural numbers.

86. The process of finding the greatest common divisor of two natural numbers is similar to finding the least common multiple of the numbers. Describe how the two processes differ.

87. What does the essay on page 182 have to do with Gödel's discovery about mathematics and logic, described on page 95?

 Critical Thinking Exercises

88. Write a four-digit natural number that is divisible by 4 and not by 8.

89. Find the greatest common divisor and the least common multiple of $2^{17} \cdot 3^{25} \cdot 5^{31}$ and $2^{14} \cdot 3^{37} \cdot 5^{30}$. Express answers in the same form as the numbers given.

90. A middle-age man observed that his present age was a prime number. He also noticed that the number of years in which his age would again be prime was equal to the number of years ago in which his age was prime. How old is the man?

91. A movie theater runs its films continuously. One movie runs for 85 minutes and a second runs for 100 minutes. The theater has a 15-minute intermission after each movie, at which point the movie is shown again. If both movies start at noon, when will the two movies start again at the same time?

 Technology Exercises

Using the divisibility rules listed in Table 5.1, determine if the following are divisible by the indicated numbers. Then, using a calculator, perform the actual division to determine if you are correct.

92. Is 67,234,096 divisible by 4?

93. Is 12,541,750 divisible by 3?

94. Is 48,201,651 divisible by 9?

Group Exercises

The following topics from number theory are appropriate for either individual or group research projects. A report should be given to the class on the researched topic. Useful references include liberal arts mathematics textbooks, books about numbers and number theory, books whose purpose is to excite the reader about mathematics, history of mathematics books, encyclopedias, and the World Wide Web.

95. Euclid and Number Theory

96. An Unsolved Problem from Number Theory

97. Perfect Numbers

98. Mersenne Primes

99. Deficient and Abundant Numbers

100. Formulas that Yield Primes

101. The Sieve of Eratosthenes

SECTION 5.2   The Integers; Order of Operations

Objectives

1. Define the integers.
2. Graph integers on a number line.
3. Use the symbols < and >.
4. Find the absolute value of an integer.
5. Perform operations with integers.
6. Use the order of operations agreement.

1   Define the integers.

Defining the Integers

In Section 5.1 we applied some ideas of number theory to the set of natural, or counting, numbers:

$$\text{Natural numbers} = \{1, 2, 3, 4, 5, \ldots\}.$$

When we combine the number 0 with the natural numbers, we obtain the set of **whole numbers**:

$$\text{Whole numbers} = \{0, 1, 2, 3, 4, 5, \ldots\}.$$

The whole numbers do not allow us to describe certain everyday situations. For example, if the balance in your checking account is $30 and you write a check for $35, your checking account is overdrawn by $5. We can write this as −5, read *negative* 5. The set consisting of the natural numbers, 0, and the negatives of the natural numbers is called the set of **integers**.

$$\text{Integers} = \{\ldots, -4, -3, -2, -1, 0, 1, 2, 3, 4, \ldots\}$$

$$\underbrace{\qquad\qquad\qquad}_{\text{Negative integers}} \quad \underbrace{\qquad\qquad}_{\text{Positive integers}}$$

Notice that the term *positive integers* is another name for the natural numbers. The positive integers can be written in two ways:

1. Use a "+" sign. For example, +4 is "positive four."
2. Do not write any sign. For example, 4 is assumed to be "positive four."

The idea of every negative integer as the opposite of a positive integer is found in M. C. Escher's print *Day and Night*. White geese, representing positive integers, fly over a night view of the town. By contrast, black geese, representing negative integers, fly over a sunlit mirror image of the same scene. © 1997 Cordon Art–Baarn–Holland. All rights reserved.

The Number Line; The Symbols $<$ and $>$

The **number line** is a graph we use to visualize the set of integers, as well as sets of other numbers. The number line is shown in Figure 5.1.

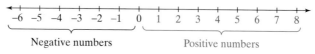

Negative numbers   Positive numbers

Figure 5.1 The number line

The number line extends indefinitely in both directions, shown by the arrows on the left and the right. Zero separates the positive numbers from the negative numbers on the number line. The positive integers are located to the right of 0, and the negative integers are located to the left of 0. 0 is neither positive nor negative. For every positive integer on a number line, there is a corresponding negative integer on the opposite side of 0.

2 Graph integers on a number line.

Integers are graphed on a number line by placing a dot at the correct location for each number.

EXAMPLE 1   Graphing Integers on a Number Line

Graph: a. −3   b. 4   c. 0.

Solution   Place a dot at the correct location for each integer.

3 Use the symbols $<$ and $>$.

We will use the following symbols for comparing two integers:

$<$ means "is less than."

$>$ means "is greater than."

Figure 5.2

On the number line, the integers increase from left to right. The *lesser* of two integers is the one farther to the *left* on a number line. The *greater* of two integers is the one farther to the *right* on a number line.

Look at the number line in Figure 5.2. The integers 2 and 5 are graphed. Observe that 2 is to the left of 5 on the number line. This means that 2 is less than 5:

$2 < 5$:   2 is less than 5 because 2 is to the *left* of 5 on the number line.

In Figure 5.2, we can also observe that 5 is to the right of 2 on the number line. This means that 5 is greater than 2.

$5 > 2$:   5 is greater than 2 because 5 is to the right of 2 on the number line.

Study Tip

The symbols $<$ and $>$ always point to the lesser of the two integers when the inequality is true.

$2 < 5$ The symbol points to 2, the lesser number.

$5 > 2$ The symbol points to 2, the lesser number.

EXAMPLE 2   Using the Symbols $<$ and $>$

Insert either $<$ or $>$ in the shaded area between the integers to make the statement true.

a. −4 ▉ 3   b. −1 ▉ −4   c. −5 ▉ −2   d. 0 ▉ −3

Solution   The solution is illustrated by the number line in Figure 5.3.

Figure 5.3 The integers in Example 2 are graphed on this number line.

a. $-4 < 3$ (negative 4 is less than 3) because −4 is to the left of 3 on the number line.

b. $-1 > -4$ (negative 1 is greater than negative 4) because -1 is to the right of -4 on the number line.

c. $-5 < -2$ (negative 5 is less than negative 2) because -5 is to the left of -2 on the number line.

d. $0 > -3$ (zero is greater than negative 3) because 0 is to the right of -3 on the number line.

The symbols $<$ and $>$ are called **inequality symbols**. They may be combined with an equal sign, as shown in the following table.

Symbols	Meaning	Example	Explanation
$a \leq b$	a is less than or equal to b.	$3 \leq 7$	Because $3 < 7$
		$7 \leq 7$	Because $7 = 7$
$b \geq a$	b is greater than or equal to a.	$7 \geq 3$	Because $7 > 3$
		$-5 \geq -5$	Because $-5 = -5$

4 Find the absolute value of an integer.

Absolute Value

Suppose you are feeling a bit lazy. Instead of your usual jog, you decide to use your finger to stroll along the number line. You start at 0 and end the finger-walk at -5. You have covered a distance of 5 units.

 Absolute value describes distance from 0 on a number line. If a represents an integer, the symbol $|a|$ represents its absolute value, read "the absolute value of a." In terms of your walk, we can write

$$|-5| = 5.$$

The absolute value of -5 is 5 because -5 is 5 units from 0 on the number line. The absolute value of a positive integer or 0 is the number itself. The absolute value of a negative integer, such as -5, is positive.

EXAMPLE 3   Finding Absolute Value

Find the absolute value.

a. $|-3|$ b. $|2|$ c. $|0|$

Solution

a. $|-3| = 3$ The absolute value of -3 is 3 because -3 is 3 units from 0.

b. $|2| = 2$ 2 is 2 units from 0.

c. $|0| = 0$ 0 is 0 units from itself.

Absolute value describes distance from 0 on a number line.

5 Perform operations with integers.

Addition of Integers

It has not been a good day! First, you lost your wallet with $30 in it. Then, you borrowed $10 to get through the day, which you somehow misplaced. Your loss of $30 followed by a loss of $10 is an overall loss of $40. This can be written:

$$-30 + (-10) = -40.$$

Technology

Calculators and Adding Integers

You can use a calculator to add integers. Here are the keystrokes for finding −30 + (−10):

Scientific Calculator

30 + 10 =

Graphing Calculator

(−) 30 + (−) 10 ENTER

Here are the keystrokes for finding −17 + 13:

Scientific Calculator

17 + 13 =

Graphing Calculator

(−) 17 + 13 ENTER

Debts and Negative Numbers

Wall Street in New York City is the financial capital of the United States. In 1929, the financial crash on Wall Street saw stock values fall, leaving many people who had invested in stocks in debt. In accounting, a debt is usually written in parentheses. For example, ($2500) shows a debt of $2500, indicating that $2500 is owed. In mathematics, we write −2500.

The result of adding two or more numbers is called the **sum** of the numbers. The sum of −30 and −10 is −40. You can think of gains and losses of money to find sums. For example, to find 17 + (−13), think of a gain of $17 followed by a loss of $13. There is an overall gain of $4. Thus, 17 + (−13) = 4. In the same way, to find −17 + 13, think of a loss of $17 followed by a gain of $13. There is an overall loss of $4, so −17 + 13 = −4.

Using gains and losses, we can develop the following rules for adding integers.

Rules for Addition of Integers

Rule	Examples
If the integers have the same sign:	
1. Add their absolute values.	$7 + 4 = |7| + |4| = 11$
2. The sign of the sum is the same as the sign of the two numbers.	$-7 + (-4) = -(|-7| + |-4|)$ $= -(7 + 4)$ $= -11$
If the integers have different signs:	
1. Subtract the smaller absolute value from the larger absolute value.	$7 + (-4) = +(|7| - |-4|)$ $= +(7 - 4)$ $= +3 = 3$
2. The sign of the sum is the same as the sign of the number with the larger absolute value.	$-7 + 4 = -(|-7| - |4|)$ $= -(7 - 4)$ $= -3$

Can you guess what number is displayed if you use a calculator to find a sum such as 18 + (−18)? If you gain 18 and then lose 18, there is neither an overall gain or loss. Thus,

$$18 + (-18) = 0.$$

We call 18 and −18 **additive inverses**. Additive inverses have the same absolute value, but lie on opposite sides of zero on the number line. Thus, −7 is the additive inverse of 7, and 5 is the additive inverse of −5. In general, the sum of any integer and its additive inverse is 0:

$$a + (-a) = 0.$$

Subtraction of Integers

Time for a new computer! Your favorite model, which normally sells for $1500, has an incredible price reduction of $600. The computer's reduced price, $900, can be expressed in two ways:

$$1500 - 600 = 900 \quad \text{or} \quad 1500 + (-600) = 900.$$

This means that:

$$1500 - 600 = 1500 + (-600).$$

To subtract 600 from 1500, we add 1500 and the additive inverse of 600. Generalizing from this situation, we define subtraction as follows.

Technology

Calculators and Subtracting Integers

You can use a calculator to subtract integers. Here are the keystrokes for finding $17 - (-11)$:

Scientific Calculator

Graphing Calculator

Here are the keystrokes for finding $-18 - (-5)$:

Scientific Calculator

Graphing Calculator

Don't confuse the subtraction key on a graphing calculator, $\boxed{-}$, with the sign change or additive inverse key, $\boxed{(-)}$.

What happens if you do?

Definition of Subtraction

For all integers a and b,

$$a - b = a + (-b).$$

In words: To subtract b from a, add the additive inverse of b to a. The result of subtraction is called the **difference**.

EXAMPLE 4 Subtracting Integers

Subtract: a. $17 - (-11)$ b. $-18 - (-5)$ c. $-18 - 5$.

Solution

a. $17 - (-11) = 17 + 11 = 28$

> Change the subtraction to addition. Replace −11 with its additive inverse.

b. $-18 - (-5) = -18 + 5 = -13$

> Change the subtraction to addition. Replace −5 with its additive inverse.

c. $-18 - 5 = -18 + (-5) = -23$

Subtraction is used to solve problems in which the word "difference" appears. The difference between integers a and b is expressed as $a - b$.

EXAMPLE 5 An Application of Subtraction Using the Word *Difference*

The bar graph in Figure 5.4 shows that in 1995, Social Security had an annual cash surplus of $233 billion. By 2020, this amount is expected to be a negative number—a deficit of $244 billion. What is the difference between the 1995 surplus and the 2020 deficit?

Solution

$= \$233 + \$244 = \$477$

The difference between the 1995 surplus and the 2020 deficit is $477 billion.

Figure 5.4 Social Security annual operating budget
Source: U.S. Office of Management and Budget

Multiplication of Integers

Suppose that things go from bad to worse for Social Security, and the $244 deficit in 2020 doubles by the middle of the twenty-first century. The new deficit is $2(-\$244)$ or $-\$488$. Notice that multiplying a positive integer and a negative integer gives a negative integer. The result of the multiplication, -488, called the **product**, has the opposite sign of the first number in the multiplication. Using this observation, we would expect $-2(-244)$ to have the opposite sign as -2. Thus, the product is positive:

$$-2(-244) = 488.$$

These observations give us the following rules for multiplying integers.

Rules for Multiplying Integers

Rule	Examples
1. The product of two integers with the same sign is found by multiplying their absolute values. The product is positive.	$3(11) = 33$ $-5(-9) = 45$
2. The product of two integers with different signs is found by multiplying their absolute values. The product is negative.	$7(-10) = -70$ $(-7)(11) = -77$
3. The product of 0 and any integer is 0.	$6(0) = 0$ $0(-23) = 0$

Visualizing Powers of 3

The triangles contain $3, 3^2, 3^3$, and 3^4 circles.

Exponential Notation

The product $10 \cdot 10$ can be written as 10^2, read "ten to the second power" or "ten squared." The small raised number 2 is called an **exponent**. The number 10 is called the **base**. Writing 10^2 as 100 is called **evaluating the exponential expression**. Exponents are used to write repeated products. For example,

$$3^2 = \underbrace{3 \cdot 3}_{\text{Two factors of 3}} = 9 \quad \text{and} \quad 5^3 = \underbrace{5 \cdot 5 \cdot 5}_{\text{Three factors of 5}} = 125.$$

where the braces are labeled "Exponent" and "Exponent."

EXAMPLE 6   Evaluating Exponential Expressions

Evaluate the following:

a. 4^2 b. $(-4)^2$ c. 6^3 d. $(-6)^3$ e. $(-2)^4$

Solution

a. $4^2 = 4 \cdot 4 = 16$

b. $(-4)^2 = (-4)(-4) = 16$

c. $6^3 = 6 \cdot 6 \cdot 6 = 36 \cdot 6 = 216$

d. $(-6)^3 = (-6)(-6)(-6) = 36(-6) = -216$

e. $(-2)^4 = (-2)(-2)(-2)(-2) = 4(-2)(-2) = (-8)(-2) = 16$

Study Tip

Do not confuse -2^4 and $(-2)^4$:

$-2^4 = -2 \cdot 2 \cdot 2 \cdot 2 = -16$

$(-2)^4 = (-2)(-2)(-2)(-2) = 16$

In Example 6, notice the difference between the signs of the answers in parts (d) and (e). In general, if a negative number is raised to an odd power, the sign of the answer is negative. If a negative number is raised to an even power, the sign of the answer is positive.

Division of Integers

The result of dividing the integer a by the nonzero integer b is called the **quotient** of the numbers. We can write this quotient as $a \div b$ or $\frac{a}{b}$.

A relationship exists between multiplication and division. For example,

$$\frac{-12}{4} = -3 \text{ means that } 4(-3) = -12.$$

$$\frac{-12}{-4} = 3 \text{ means that } -4(3) = -12.$$

Because of the relationship between multiplication and division, the rules for obtaining the sign of a quotient are the same as those for obtaining the sign of a product.

Technology

Multiplying and Dividing on a Calculator

Example: $(-173)(-256)$

Scientific Calculator

173 $\boxed{^+/_-}$ $\boxed{\times}$ 256 $\boxed{^+/_-}$ $\boxed{=}$

Graphing Calculator

$\boxed{(-)}$ 173 $\boxed{\times}$ $\boxed{(-)}$ 256 $\boxed{\text{ENTER}}$

The number 44288 should be displayed.

Division is performed in the same manner, using $\boxed{\div}$ instead of $\boxed{\times}$. What happens when you divide by 0? Try entering

8 $\boxed{\div}$ 0

pressing $\boxed{=}$ or $\boxed{\text{ENTER}}$.

Rules for Dividing Integers

Rule	Examples
1. The quotient of two integers with the same sign is found by dividing their absolute values. The quotient is positive.	$\dfrac{27}{9} = 3$ $\dfrac{-45}{-3} = 15$
2. The quotient of two integers with different signs is found by dividing their absolute values. The quotient is negative.	$\dfrac{80}{-4} = -20$ $\dfrac{-15}{5} = -3$
3. Zero divided by any nonzero integer is zero.	$\dfrac{0}{-5} = 0$ (because $-5(0) = 0$)
4. Division by 0 is undefined.	$\dfrac{-8}{0}$ is undefined (because 0 cannot be multiplied by an integer to obtain -8)

6 Use the order of operations agreement.

Order of Operations

Suppose that you want to find the value of $3 + 7 \cdot 5$. Which procedure shown below is correct?

$$3 + 7 \cdot 5 = 3 + 35 = 38 \quad \text{or} \quad 3 + 7 \cdot 5 = 10 \cdot 5 = 50$$

If you know the answer, you probably know certain rules, called the **order of operations**, to make sure that there is only one correct answer. One of these rules states that if a problem contains no parentheses, perform multiplication before addition. Thus, the procedure on the left is correct because the multiplication of 7 and 5 is done first. Then the addition is performed. The correct answer is 38.

Order of Operations

1. Perform operations within parentheses or other grouping symbols following steps 2 to 4.
2. Evaluate all exponential expressions.
3. Do all multiplications and divisions from left to right.
4. Do all additions and subtractions from left to right.

In the third step, be sure to do all multiplications and divisions *as they occur* from left to right. For example,

$$8 \div 4 \times 2 = 2 \times 2 = 4$$

Do the division first because it occurs first.

$$8 \times 4 \div 2 = 32 \div 2 = 16$$

Do the multiplication first because it occurs first.

EXAMPLE 7   Using the Order of Operations

Simplify: $6^2 - 24 \div 2^2 \cdot 3 - 1$.

Solution

$$6^2 - 24 \div 2^2 \cdot 3 - 1$$

Evaluate exponential expressions: $6^2 = 36$ and $2^2 = 4$.

$$= 36 - 24 \div 4 \cdot 3 - 1$$

Perform the multiplications and divisions from left to right. Start with $24 \div 4 = 6$.

$$= 36 - 6 \cdot 3 - 1$$

Now do the multiplication: $6 \cdot 3 = 18$.

$$= 36 - 18 - 1$$

Finally, perform the subtraction from left to right.

$$= 18 - 1$$
$$= 17$$

EXAMPLE 8   Using the Order of Operations

Simplify: $(-6)^2 - (5 - 7)^2(-3)$.

Solution

$$(-6)^2 - (5 - 7)^2(-3)$$

Work inside parentheses first: $5 - 7 = 5 + (-7) = -2$.

$$= (-6)^2 - (-2)^2(-3)$$

Evaluate exponential expressions: $(-6)^2 = (-6)(-6) = 36$ and $(-2)^2 = (-2)(-2) = 4$.

$$= 36 - 4(-3)$$

Multiply: $4(-3) = -12$.

$$= 36 - (-12)$$

Subtract.

$$= 36 + 12$$

Add the additive inverse of -12 to 36.

$$= 48$$

Exercise Set 5.2

✓ Practice Exercises

In Exercises 1–4, start by drawing a number line that shows integers from −5 to 5. Then graph each of the following integers on your number line.

1. 3   2. 5   3. −4   4. −2

In Exercises 5–12, insert either < or > in the shaded area between the integers to make the statement true.

5. −2 ▩ 7   6. −1 ▩ 13   7. −13 ▩ −2

8. −1 ▩ −13   9. 8 ▩ −50   10. 7 ▩ −9

11. −100 ▩ 0   12. 0 ▩ −300

In Exercises 13–18, find the absolute value.

13. $|-14|$ 14. $|-16|$ 15. $|14|$

16. $|16|$ 17. $|-300{,}000|$ 18. $|-1{,}000{,}000|$

In Exercises 19–30, find each sum.

19. $-7 + (-5)$ 20. $-3 + (-4)$ 21. $12 + (-8)$

22. $13 + (-5)$ 23. $6 + (-9)$ 24. $3 + (-11)$

25. $-9 + (+4)$ 26. $-7 + (+3)$ 27. $-9 + (-9)$

28. $-13 + (-13)$ 29. $9 + (-9)$ 30. $13 + (-13)$

In Exercises 31–42, perform the indicated subtraction.

31. $13 - 8$ 32. $14 - 3$ 33. $8 - 15$

34. $9 - 20$ 35. $4 - (-10)$ 36. $3 - (-17)$

37. $-6 - (-17)$ 38. $-4 - (-19)$ 39. $-12 - (-3)$

40. $-19 - (-2)$ 41. $-11 - 17$ 42. $-19 - 21$

In Exercises 43–52, find each product.

43. $6(-9)$ 44. $5(-7)$ 45. $(-7)(-3)$

46. $(-8)(-5)$ 47. $(-2)(6)$ 48. $(-3)(10)$

49. $(-13)(-1)$ 50. $(-17)(-1)$ 51. $0(-5)$

52. $0(-8)$

In Exercises 53–66, evaluate each exponential expression.

53. 5^2 54. 6^2 55. $(-5)^2$ 56. $(-6)^2$

57. 4^3 58. 2^3 59. $(-5)^3$ 60. $(-4)^3$

61. $(-5)^4$ 62. $(-4)^4$ 63. -3^4 64. -1^4

65. $(-3)^4$ 66. $(-1)^4$

In Exercises 67–80, find each quotient, or, if applicable, state that the expression is undefined.

67. $\frac{-12}{4}$ 68. $\frac{-40}{5}$ 69. $\frac{21}{-3}$ 70. $\frac{60}{-6}$

71. $\frac{-90}{-3}$ 72. $\frac{-66}{-6}$

73. $\frac{0}{-7}$ 74. $\frac{0}{-8}$

75. $\frac{-7}{0}$ 76. $\frac{0}{0}$

77. $(-480) \div 24$ 78. $(-300) \div 12$

79. $(465) \div (-15)$ 80. $(-594) \div (-18)$

Use the order of operations to find the value of each expression in Exercises 81–98.

81. $7 + 6 \cdot 3$ 82. $-5 + (-3) \cdot 8$

83. $(-5) - 6(-3)$ 84. $-8(-3) - 5(-6)$

85. $6 - 4(-3) - 5$ 86. $3 - 7(-1) - 6$

87. $3 - 5(-4 - 2)$ 88. $3 - 9(-1 - 6)$

89. $(2 - 6)(-3 - 5)$ 90. $9 - 5(6 - 4) - 10$

91. $3(-2)^2 - 4(-3)^2$ 92. $5(-3)^2 - 2(-2)^3$

93. $(2 - 6)^2 - (3 - 7)^2$

94. $(4 - 6)^2 - (5 - 9)^3$

95. $6(3 - 5)^3 - 2(1 - 3)^3$

96. $-3(-6 + 8)^3 - 5(-3 + 5)^3$

97. $8^2 - 16 \div 2^2 \cdot 4 - 3$

98. $10^2 - 100 \div 5^2 \cdot 2 - (-3)$

⭐ Application Exercises

99. The greatest temperature variation recorded in a day is 100 degrees in Browning, Montana on January 23, 1916. The low temperature was −56°F. What was the high temperature?

100. A football team started with the football on the 27-yard line, advancing toward the center of the field (the 50-yard line). Four successive plays resulted in a 4-yard gain, a 2-yard loss, an 8-yard gain, and a 12-yard loss. What was the location of the football at the end of the fourth play?

101. The peak of Mount Kilimanjaro, the highest point in Africa, is 19,321 feet above sea level. Qattara Depression, Egypt, the lowest point in Africa, is 436 feet below sea level. What is the difference in elevation between these geographic locations?

102. The greatest recorded temperature ranges are around the Siberian "cold pole" in the east of Russia. Temperatures in Verkhoyansk have ranged from −90°F to 98°F. What is the difference between the high and low temperature?

The table below shows the amount of money, in millions of dollars, collected and spent by the U.S. government from 1998–2002. The information for 2000-2002 is what is expected to occur.

Year	Money Collected	Money Spent
1998	1,631,600	1,689,900
1999	1,694,300	1,751,800
2000	1,753,900	1,795,300
2001	1,824,800	1,831,800
2002	1,921,900	1,858,800

Money is expressed in millions of dollars.
Source: Office of Management and Budget

Use this information to solve Exercises 103–106.

103. In 1998, what was the difference between the amount of money collected and the amount spent? Was there a budget surplus or deficit in 1998?

104. Repeat Exercise 103 for 1999.
105. Repeat Exercise 103 for 2001.
106. Repeat Exercise 103 for 2002.

 Writing in Mathematics

107. How does the set of integers differ from the set of whole numbers?
108. Explain how to graph an integer on a number line.
109. If you are given two integers, explain how to determine which one is the lesser.
110. Explain how to add integers.
111. Explain how to subtract integers.
112. Explain how to multiply integers.
113. Explain how to divide integers.
114. Describe what it means to raise a number to a power. In your description, include a discussion of the difference between -5^2 and $(-5)^2$.
115. Why is $\frac{0}{4}$ equal to 0, but $\frac{4}{0}$ is undefined?

 Critical Thinking Exercises

116. We have used a code to describe an activity that is important to your success in school and at work. Here is the coded message:

$$(20, 18) \quad (-8, -12) \quad (0, 9) \quad (-14, -17)$$
$$(0, 11) \quad (-17, 9) \quad (-16, 14) \quad (-22, 7)$$

Read across the two rows. Each number pair represents one letter of the coded message. The first number pair represents the first letter, the second pair, the second letter, and so on. Use the table below to decode the message.

First Decoding	Second Decoding				
Use the greater of the two numbers in each pair. If the greater number is negative, then use its absolute value.	0 = blank space	1 = A	2 = B	3 = C	4 = D
	5 = E	6 = F	7 = G	8 = H	9 = I	10 = J
	11 = K	12 = L	13 = M	14 = N	15 = O	16 = P
	17 = Q	18 = R	19 = S	20 = T	21 = U	22 = V
	23 = W	24 = X	25 = Y	26 = Z		

In Exercises 117–118, insert one pair of parentheses to make each calculation correct.

117. $8 - 2 \cdot 3 - 4 = 10$

118. $8 - 2 \cdot 3 - 4 = 14$

 Technology Exercises

Scientific calculators that have parentheses keys allow for the entry and computation of relatively complicated expressions in a single step. For example, the expression $15 + (10 - 7)^2$ can be evaluated by entering the following keystrokes:

$15 \boxed{+} \boxed{(} 10 \boxed{-} 7 \boxed{)} \boxed{x^y} 2 \boxed{=}$.

Find the value of each expression in Exercises 119–121 using the parentheses keys on your scientific calculator.

119. $8 - 2 \cdot 3 - 9$
120. $(8 - 2) \cdot (3 - 9)$
121. $5^3 + 4 \cdot 9 - (8 + 9 \div 3)$

 Group Exercise

122. How do we first learn about numbers? At what age do we begin to understand what they mean? For this activity, group members should research the work of the innovative Swiss psychologist Jean Piaget (1896–1980) and present a group report on numbers and psychology.

SECTION 5.3   *The Rational Numbers*

Objectives

1. Define the rational numbers.
2. Reduce rational numbers.
3. Express rational numbers as decimals.
4. Express decimals in the form $\frac{a}{b}$.
5. Perform operations with rational numbers.
6. Apply the density property of rational numbers.
7. Solve problems involving rational numbers.

1 Define the rational numbers.

Study Tip

We know that the quotient of two numbers with different signs is a negative number. Thus,

$$\frac{-3}{4} = -\frac{3}{4} \text{ and } \frac{3}{-4} = -\frac{3}{4}.$$

Defining the Rational Numbers

People frequently invest their money by buying stock in a company. Stock prices use fractions to show parts of a dollar. For example, a share of a particular stock might be $43\frac{1}{4}$, which means that the value of a share is $43.25.

If the change in the price of a share is $-\frac{3}{4}$, this means that the price went down by $0.75. If the change is $+\frac{1}{2}$, the price went up by $0.50. The numbers $-\frac{3}{4}$ and $\frac{1}{2}$ are quotients of two integers. For $-\frac{3}{4}$, which can be expressed as $\frac{-3}{4}$, the integers are -3 and 4. For $\frac{1}{2}$, the integers are 1 and 2. A number that can be written as the quotient of two integers is a **rational number**.

The Rational Numbers

The set of **rational numbers** is the set of all numbers which can be expressed in the form $\frac{a}{b}$, where a and b are integers and b is not equal to 0. The integer a is called the **numerator** and the integer b is called the **denominator**.

The following numbers are examples of rational numbers:

$$\frac{1}{2}, \frac{-3}{4}, 5, 0.$$

The integer 5 is a rational number because it can be expressed as the quotient of integers: $5 = \frac{5}{1}$. Similarly, 0 can be written as $\frac{0}{1}$.

In general, every integer a is a rational number because it can be expressed in the form $\frac{a}{1}$.

2 Reduce rational numbers.

Reducing Rational Numbers

The graph in Figure 5.5 shows the profile of stock owners in the United States by age. For example, the 12% for the 45–49 age group means that for every 100 people who own stock, 12 are in the 45–49 age group. The rational number describing stock owners in this age group is $\frac{12}{100}$.

The numerator and denominator in $\frac{12}{100}$ have the common divisor 4. In a case like this, we can *reduce* the rational number *to lowest terms*.

A rational number is **reduced to its lowest terms** when the numerator and denominator have no common divisors other than 1. A rational number is reduced to its lowest terms by dividing both the numerator and the denominator by the greatest common divisor.

For the rational number $\frac{12}{100}$, the greatest common divisor of 12 and 100 is 4. We reduce to lowest terms as follows:

$$\frac{12}{100} = \frac{12 \div 4}{100 \div 4} = \frac{3}{25}$$

Thus, for every 25 people who own stock, 3 are in the 45–49 age group.

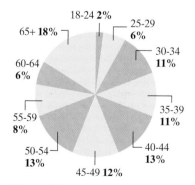

Figure 5.5 Age of U.S. stock owners
Source: Peter D. Hart Research Associates

(pie chart labels) 18-24 **2%**, 25-29 **6%**, 30-34 **11%**, 35-39 **11%**, 40-44 **13%**, 45-49 **12%**, 50-54 **13%**, 55-59 **8%**, 60-64 **6%**, 65+ **18%**

EXAMPLE 1 Reducing a Rational Number

Reduce $\frac{130}{455}$ to lowest terms.

Solution Begin by finding the greatest common divisor of 130 and 455.

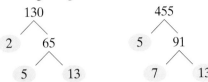

Thus, $130 = 2 \cdot 5 \cdot 13$, and $455 = 5 \cdot 7 \cdot 13$. The greatest common divisor is $5 \cdot 13$, or 65. Divide the numerator and the denominator of the given rational number by 65.

$$\frac{130}{455} = \frac{130 \div 65}{455 \div 65} = \frac{2}{7}$$

There are no common divisors of 2 and 7 other than 1. Thus, this rational number is in its lowest terms.

Rational Numbers and Decimals

We have seen that a rational number is the quotient of integers. Rational numbers can also be expressed as decimals. As shown in the place-value chart in the margin, it is convenient to represent rational numbers with denominators of 10, 100, 1000, and so on as decimals. For example,

$$\frac{7}{10} = 0.7, \quad \frac{3}{100} = 0.03, \quad \text{and} \quad \frac{8}{1000} = 0.008.$$

Any rational number $\frac{a}{b}$ can be expressed as a decimal by dividing the denominator, b, into the numerator, a.

Place-Value Chart

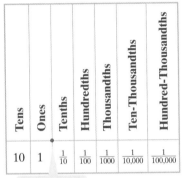

decimal point

3 Express rational numbers as decimals.

Technology

Calculators and Decimals

Given a rational number $\frac{a}{b}$, you can express it as a decimal by entering

$$a \boxed{\div} b$$

into a calculator. In the case of a repeating decimal, the calculator rounds off in the final decimal place displayed. The display for $\frac{7}{11}$ shows

.636363636364

rather than

.636363636363…

When you enter $a \boxed{\div} b$, the display should be greater than 1 if $a > b$. The display should be less than 1 if $a < b$.

EXAMPLE 2 Expressing Rational Numbers as Decimals

Express each rational number as a decimal.

a. $\frac{5}{8}$ b. $\frac{7}{11}$

Solution In each case, divide the denominator into the numerator.

a.
```
      0.625
  8)5.000
    4 8
      20
      16
      40
      40
       0
```

b.
```
       0.6363 …
  11)7.0000 …
     6 6
       40
       33
       70
       66
       40
       33
       70
        ⋮
```

In Example 2, the decimal for $\frac{5}{8}$, namely 0.625, stops and is called a **terminating decimal**. Other examples of terminating decimals are:

$$\frac{1}{4} = 0.25, \quad \frac{2}{5} = 0.4, \quad \frac{7}{8} = 0.875.$$

By contrast, the division process for $\frac{7}{11}$ results in $0.6363\ldots$, with the digits 63 repeating over and over indefinitely. To indicate this, write a bar over the digits that repeat. Thus,

$$\frac{7}{11} = 0.\overline{63}.$$

The decimal for $\frac{7}{11}, 0.\overline{63}$, is called a **repeating decimal**. Other examples of repeating decimals are:

$$\frac{1}{3} = 0.333\ldots = 0.\overline{3} \qquad \frac{2}{3} = 0.666\ldots = 0.\overline{6}.$$

Rational Numbers and Decimals

Any rational number can be expressed as a decimal. The resulting decimal will either terminate (stop), or it will have a digit that repeats or a block of digits that repeat.

4 Express decimals in the form $\frac{a}{b}$.

Place-Value Chart

Tens	Ones	Tenths	Hundredths	Thousandths	Ten-Thousandths	Hundred-Thousandths
10	1	$\frac{1}{10}$	$\frac{1}{100}$	$\frac{1}{1000}$	$\frac{1}{10,000}$	$\frac{1}{100,000}$

decimal point

Reversing Directions: Expressing Decimals as a Quotient of Two Integers

Terminating decimals can be expressed with denominators of 10, 100, 1000, 10,000, and so on. Use the place-value chart shown in the margin. The digits to the right of the decimal point are the numerator of the rational number. To find the denominator, observe the last digit to the right of the decimal point. The place-value of this digit will indicate the denominator.

EXAMPLE 3   Expressing Terminating Decimals in $\frac{a}{b}$ Form

Express each terminating decimal as a quotient of integers.
   a. 0.7   b. 0.49   c. 0.048

Solution
   a. $0.7 = \frac{7}{10}$ because the 7 is in the tenths position.
   b. $0.49 = \frac{49}{100}$ because the digit on the right, 9, is in the hundredths position.
   c. $0.048 = \frac{48}{1000}$ because the digit on the right, 8, is in the thousandths position. Reducing to lowest terms, $\frac{48}{1000} = \frac{48 \div 8}{1000 \div 8} = \frac{6}{125}$.

If you are given a rational number as a repeating decimal, there is a technique for expressing the number as a quotient of integers. Although we will not be discussing algebra until Chapter 6, the basic algebra used in this technique may be familiar to you. We begin by illustrating the technique with an example. Then we will summarize the steps in the procedure and apply them to another example.

EXAMPLE 4   Expressing a Repeating Decimal in $\frac{a}{b}$ Form

Express $0.\overline{6}$ as a quotient of integers.

Solution

Step 1   Let $n = 0.\overline{6}$, so that $n = 0.66666\ldots$.

Step 2 Because there is only one repeating digit, multiply both sides of $n = 0.66666\ldots$ by 10.

$$n = 0.66666\ldots$$
$$10n = 10(0.66666\ldots)$$
$$10n = 6.66666\ldots$$

Step 3 Subtract the expression for n from the expression for $10n$.

$$10n = 6.66666\ldots$$
$$-\quad n = 0.66666\ldots$$
$$9n = 6$$

Remember from algebra that n means $1n$. Thus, $10n - 1n = 9n$.

Step 4 Solve for n by dividing both sides by 9.

$$9n = 6$$
$$\frac{9n}{9} = \frac{6}{9}$$
$$n = \frac{6}{9} = \frac{2}{3}$$

We began the solution process with $n = 0.\overline{6}$, and now we have $n = \frac{2}{3}$. Therefore,

$$0.\overline{6} = \frac{2}{3}.$$

Here are the steps for expressing a repeating decimal as a quotient of integers. Assume that the repeating digit or digits begin directly to the right of the decimal point.

Expressing a Repeating Decimal as a Quotient of Integers

Step 1 Let n equal the repeating decimal.

Step 2 Multiply both sides of the equation in step 1 by 10 if one digit repeats, by 100 if two digits repeat, by 1000 if three digits repeat, and so on.

Step 3 Subtract the equation in step 1 from the equation in step 2.

Step 4 Divide both sides of the equation in step 3 by an appropriate number and solve for n.

EXAMPLE 5 Expressing a Repeating Decimal in $\frac{a}{b}$ Form

Express $0.\overline{53}$ as a quotient of integers.

Solution

Step 1 Let $n = 0.\overline{53}$, so that $n = 0.535353\ldots$.

Step 2 With two repeating digits, multiply both sides of $n = 0.535353\ldots$ by 100.

$$100n = 100(0.535353\ldots)$$
$$100n = 53.535353\ldots$$

Step 3 Subtract the expression for n from the expression for $100n$.

$$100n = 53.535353\ldots$$
$$- \quad n = \underline{0.535353\ldots}$$
$$99n = 53$$

Step 4 Solve for n by dividing both sides by 99.

$$99n = 53$$
$$\frac{99n}{99} = \frac{53}{99}$$
$$n = \frac{53}{99}$$

Because n equals $0.\overline{53}$,

$$0.\overline{53} = \frac{53}{99}.$$

---

5 Perform operations with rational numbers.

Operations with Rational Numbers

There is no integer between two consecutive integers, such as 6 and 7. However, you can always find a rational number between any two given rational numbers. This can be done by adding the rational numbers and dividing the sum by 2. In order to carry out this process, we begin by reviewing how to multiply, divide, add, and subtract rational numbers. A partial review appears in Table 5.2. Always reduce answers to lowest terms when possible.

Table 5.2 Operations with Rational Numbers

Operation	Procedure	Examples
Multiplication	The product of two rational numbers is the product of their numerators divided by the product of their denominators.	$\frac{3}{8} \cdot \frac{5}{11} = \frac{3 \cdot 5}{8 \cdot 11} = \frac{15}{88}$ $\left(-\frac{2}{3}\right)\left(-\frac{7}{15}\right) = \frac{(-2)(-7)}{3 \cdot 15} = \frac{14}{45}$
Division	The quotient of two rational numbers is the product of the first rational number and the second rational number with numerator and denominator reversed.	$\frac{4}{5} \div \frac{1}{10} = \frac{4}{5} \cdot \frac{10}{1} = \frac{4 \cdot 10}{5 \cdot 1} = \frac{40}{5} = 8$ $-\frac{3}{5} \div \frac{7}{11} = -\frac{3}{5} \cdot \frac{11}{7} = \frac{-3(11)}{5 \cdot 7} = -\frac{33}{35}$
Addition and Subtraction with Identical Denominators	The sum or difference of two rational numbers with identical denominators is the sum or difference of their numerators over the common denominator.	$\frac{3}{7} + \frac{2}{7} = \frac{3 + 2}{7} = \frac{5}{7}$ $\frac{11}{12} - \frac{5}{12} = \frac{11 - 5}{12} = \frac{6}{12} = \frac{1}{2}$ $-\frac{21}{4} - \left(-\frac{11}{4}\right) = \frac{-21}{4} + \frac{11}{4} = \frac{-21 + 11}{4}$ $= -\frac{10}{4} = -\frac{5}{2} \left(\text{or} -2\frac{1}{2}\right)$

Technology

Does your calculator have an $\boxed{a^b/_c}$, key? If so, it will perform calculations involving rational numbers. Because the typical display of a scientific calculator cannot display a /, the symbol $\sqsubset$ is often used to separate the numerator and denominator. For example, the fraction 5/7 is often displayed as 5 $\sqsubset$ 7. Also, if you use this feature to make a calculation involving rational numbers, be aware that the result will be displayed as a decimal. The calculator can show only a limited number of digits for each decimal, and will automatically round a long decimal to fit its display. Graphing calculators have a fraction feature that can display a /. For example, to find $\frac{3}{4} + \frac{1}{6}$, a possible keystroke sequence is:

3 $\boxed{\div}$ 4 $\boxed{+}$ 1 $\boxed{\div}$ 6 $\boxed{\blacktriangleright\text{Frac}}$

$\boxed{\text{ENTER}}$.

The calculator display should read 11/12. Check your owner's manual under *fractions* for details on how to use this feature.

If the rational numbers to be added or subtracted have different denominators, we use the least common multiple of their denominators to rewrite the rational numbers. The least common multiple of the denominators is called the **least common denominator**.

EXAMPLE 6   Adding Rational Numbers with Unlike Denominators

Find the sum of $\frac{3}{4} + \frac{1}{6}$.

Solution   The smallest number divisible by both 4 and 6 is 12. Therefore, 12 is the least common multiple of 4 and 6, and will serve as the least common denominator. To obtain a denominator of 12, multiply the denominator and the numerator of the first rational number, $\frac{3}{4}$, by 3. To obtain a denominator of 12, multiply the denominator and the numerator of the second rational number, $\frac{1}{6}$, by 2.

$$\frac{3}{4} + \frac{1}{6} = \frac{3}{4} \cdot \frac{3}{3} + \frac{1}{6} \cdot \frac{2}{2}$$

Rewrite each rational number with a denominator of 12. $\frac{3}{3} = 1$ and $\frac{2}{2} = 1$, and multiplying by 1 does not change a number's value.

$$= \frac{9}{12} + \frac{2}{12}$$

Multiply.

$$= \frac{11}{12}$$

Add numerators and put this sum over the least common denominator.

If the least common denominator cannot be found by inspection, use prime factorizations of the denominators and the method for finding their least common multiple, discussed in Section 5.1.

EXAMPLE 7   Subtracting Rational Numbers with Unlike Denominators

Perform the indicated operation: $\frac{1}{15} - \frac{7}{24}$.

Solution   We need to first find the least common denominator, which is the least common multiple of 15 and 24. What is the smallest number divisible by both 15 and 24? The answer is not obvious, so we begin with the prime factorization of each number.

$$15 = 5 \cdot 3$$

$$24 = 8 \cdot 3 = 2^3 \cdot 3$$

The different factors are 5, 3, and 2. Using the greatest number of times each factor appears in any factorization, the least common multiple $= 5 \cdot 3 \cdot 2^3$ $= 5 \cdot 3 \cdot 8 = 120$.

We will now express each rational number with a denominator of 120, which is the least common denominator. For the first rational number, $\frac{1}{15}$, 120 divided by 15 is 8. Thus, we will multiply the numerator and denominator by 8. For the second rational number, $\frac{7}{24}$, 120 divided by 24 is 5. Thus, we will multiply the numerator and denominator by 5.

Technology

Here is a possible keystroke sequence on a graphing calculator for the subtraction problem on the right:

$1 \boxed{\div} 15 \boxed{-} 7 \boxed{\div} 24$

$\boxed{\blacktriangleright \text{Frac}} \boxed{\text{ENTER}}.$

The calculator display should read $-9/40$.

$$\frac{1}{15} - \frac{7}{24} = \frac{1}{15} \cdot \frac{8}{8} - \frac{7}{24} \cdot \frac{5}{5} \qquad \textit{The least common denominator is 120.}$$

$$= \frac{8}{120} - \frac{35}{120} \qquad \textit{Multiply.}$$

$$= \frac{8 - 35}{120} \qquad \textit{Subtract the numerators and put this difference over the least common denominator.}$$

$$= \frac{-27}{120}$$

$$= \frac{-27 \div 3}{120 \div 3} \qquad \textit{Reduce to lowest terms.}$$

$$= -\frac{9}{40}$$

6 Apply the density property of rational numbers.

Density of Rational Numbers

As we mentioned earlier, you can always find a rational number between any two given rational numbers. Mathematicians express this idea by saying that the set of rational numbers is **dense**.

> **Density of the Rational Numbers**
>
> If r and t represent rational numbers, with $r < t$, then there is a rational number s such that
>
> $$r < s < t.$$

One way to find a rational number between two given rational numbers is to find the rational number halfway between them. Add the given rational numbers and divide their sum by 2, thereby finding the average of the numbers.

EXAMPLE 8   Illustrating the Density Property

Find a rational number halfway between $\frac{1}{2}$ and $\frac{3}{4}$.

Solution   First, add $\frac{1}{2}$ and $\frac{3}{4}$.

$$\frac{1}{2} + \frac{3}{4} = \frac{2}{4} + \frac{3}{4} = \frac{5}{4}$$

Next, divide this sum by 2.

$$\frac{5}{4} \div \frac{2}{1} = \frac{5}{4} \cdot \frac{1}{2} = \frac{5}{8}$$

The number $\frac{5}{8}$ is halfway between $\frac{1}{2}$ and $\frac{3}{4}$. Thus,

$$\frac{1}{2} < \frac{5}{8} < \frac{3}{4}.$$

Study Tip

The inequality $\frac{1}{2} < \frac{5}{8} < \frac{3}{4}$ is more obvious if all denominators are changed to 8:

$$\frac{4}{8} < \frac{5}{8} < \frac{6}{8}$$

We can repeat the procedure of Example 8 and find a rational number halfway between $\frac{1}{2}$ and $\frac{5}{8}$. Repeated application of this procedure implies the following surprising result:

Between any two given rational numbers are *infinitely many* rational numbers.

7 Solve problems involving rational numbers.

Problem Solving

In everyday use, we generally call a quotient of integers a **fraction** rather than a rational number. For example, consider one of the questions in a 1999 Time/CNN poll, shown in the margin. The 23% means $\frac{23}{100}$. We can say that the *fraction* of black teens who have experienced discrimination is $\frac{23}{100}$. Many problems use the term *fraction* instead of *rational number*.

Have you ever been a victim of discrimination because you are black?

Black Teens	Black Adults
Yes: 23%	Yes: 55%
No: 77%	No: 45%

Source: Time/CNN

EXAMPLE 9 Problem Solving with Rational Numbers

At a workshop on enhancing creativity, $\frac{1}{4}$ of the participants are musicians, $\frac{2}{5}$ are artists, $\frac{1}{10}$ are actors, and the remaining participants are writers. What fraction of the people attending the workshop are writers?

Solution We begin by finding the fraction of participants for the group that are musicians, artists, and actors. Add the three given fractions:

$$\frac{1}{4} + \frac{2}{5} + \frac{1}{10}$$ The least common denominator is 20.

$$= \frac{1}{4} \cdot \frac{5}{5} + \frac{2}{5} \cdot \frac{4}{4} + \frac{1}{10} \cdot \frac{2}{2}$$ Rewrite each fraction with a denominator of 20.

$$= \frac{5}{20} + \frac{8}{20} + \frac{2}{20}$$ Multiply.

$$= \frac{5 + 8 + 2}{20}$$ Add the numerators and put this sum over the least common denominator.

$$= \frac{15}{20}$$ Simplify.

$$= \frac{15 \div 5}{20 \div 5}$$ Reduce the fraction to lowest terms by dividing the numerator and denominator by the greatest common divisor.

$$= \frac{3}{4}$$

Thus, $\frac{3}{4}$ of the participants are musicians, artists, and actors. This does not include the writers, the only other group at the workshop. The fractions representing all four groups at the workshop must add up to 1. Therefore, the fraction of writers at the workshop can be found by subtracting $\frac{3}{4}$ from 1. The fraction of the people at the workshop who are writers is:

$$1 - \frac{3}{4} = \frac{4}{4} - \frac{3}{4} = \frac{1}{4}.$$

We see that $\frac{1}{4}$ of the participants are writers.

Exercise Set 5.3

 Practice Exercises

In Exercises 1–12, reduce each rational number to its lowest terms.

1. $\frac{10}{15}$ 2. $\frac{18}{45}$ 3. $\frac{15}{18}$ 4. $\frac{16}{64}$

5. $\frac{24}{42}$ 6. $\frac{32}{80}$ 7. $\frac{60}{108}$ 8. $\frac{112}{128}$

9. $\frac{342}{380}$ 10. $\frac{210}{252}$ 11. $\frac{308}{418}$ 12. $\frac{144}{300}$

In Exercises 13–24, express each rational number as a decimal.

13. $\frac{3}{4}$ 14. $\frac{3}{5}$ 15. $\frac{7}{20}$ 16. $\frac{3}{20}$

17. $\frac{7}{8}$ 18. $\frac{5}{16}$ 19. $\frac{9}{11}$ 20. $\frac{3}{11}$

21. $\frac{22}{7}$ 22. $\frac{20}{3}$ 23. $\frac{2}{7}$ 24. $\frac{5}{7}$

In Exercises 25–36, express each terminating decimal as a quotient of integers. If possible, reduce to lowest terms.

25. 0.3   26. 0.9   27. 0.4   28. 0.6

29. 0.39   30. 0.59   31. 0.82   32. 0.64

33. 0.725   34. 0.625   35. 0.5399   36. 0.7006

In Exercises 37–44, express each repeating decimal as a quotient of integers. If possible, reduce to lowest terms.

37. $0.\overline{7}$ 38. $0.\overline{1}$ 39. $0.\overline{9}$ 40. $0.\overline{3}$

41. $0.\overline{36}$ 42. $0.\overline{81}$ 43. $0.\overline{257}$ 44. $0.\overline{529}$

In Exercises 45–74, perform the indicated operations. Where possible, reduce the answer to its lowest terms.

45. $\frac{3}{8} \cdot \frac{7}{11}$ 46. $\frac{5}{8} \cdot \frac{3}{11}$ 47. $\left(-\frac{1}{10}\right)\left(\frac{7}{12}\right)$

48. $\left(-\frac{1}{8}\right)\left(\frac{5}{9}\right)$ 49. $\left(-\frac{2}{3}\right)\left(-\frac{9}{4}\right)$ 50. $\left(-\frac{5}{4}\right)\left(-\frac{6}{7}\right)$

51. $\frac{5}{4} \div \frac{3}{8}$ 52. $\frac{5}{8} \div \frac{4}{3}$ 53. $-\frac{7}{8} \div \frac{15}{16}$

54. $-\frac{13}{20} \div \frac{4}{5}$ 55. $\frac{2}{11} + \frac{3}{11}$ 56. $\frac{5}{13} + \frac{2}{13}$

57. $\frac{5}{6} - \frac{1}{6}$ 58. $\frac{7}{12} - \frac{5}{12}$ 59. $\frac{7}{12} - \left(-\frac{1}{12}\right)$

60. $\frac{5}{16} - \left(-\frac{5}{16}\right)$ 61. $\frac{1}{2} + \frac{1}{5}$ 62. $\frac{1}{3} + \frac{1}{5}$

63. $\frac{3}{4} + \frac{3}{20}$ 64. $\frac{2}{5} + \frac{2}{15}$ 65. $\frac{5}{24} + \frac{7}{30}$

66. $\frac{7}{108} + \frac{55}{144}$ 67. $\frac{13}{18} - \frac{2}{9}$ 68. $\frac{13}{15} - \frac{2}{45}$

69. $\frac{4}{3} - \frac{3}{4}$ 70. $\frac{3}{2} - \frac{2}{3}$ 71. $\frac{1}{15} - \frac{27}{50}$

72. $\frac{4}{15} - \frac{1}{6}$ 73. $\left(\frac{1}{2} - \frac{1}{3}\right) \div \frac{5}{8}$ 74. $\left(\frac{1}{2} + \frac{1}{4}\right) \div \left(\frac{1}{2} + \frac{1}{3}\right)$

In Exercises 75–80, find a rational number halfway between the two numbers in each pair.

75. $\frac{1}{4}$ and $\frac{1}{3}$ 76. $\frac{2}{3}$ and $\frac{5}{6}$ 77. $\frac{1}{2}$ and $\frac{2}{3}$

78. $\frac{3}{5}$ and $\frac{2}{3}$ 79. $-\frac{2}{3}$ and $-\frac{5}{6}$ 80. -4 and $-\frac{7}{2}$

Different operations with the same rational numbers usually result in different answers. Exercises 81–82 illustrate some curious exceptions.

81. Show that $\frac{13}{4} + \frac{13}{9}$ and $\frac{13}{4} \times \frac{13}{9}$ give the same answer.

82. Show that $\frac{169}{30} + \frac{13}{15}$ and $\frac{169}{30} \div \frac{13}{15}$ give the same answer.

 Application Exercises

83. You purchase 40 shares of stock at \$12 per share. When you sell the stock, the change is $-\frac{3}{4}$ per share. How much do you lose on this investment?

84. You purchase 60 shares of stock at \$16 per share. When you sell the stock, the change is $-\frac{1}{2}$ per share. How much do you lose on this investment?

Exercises 85–90 are based on a 1999 Time/CNN poll focusing on teenagers and adults and their opinions on racial issues.

85. Of the 800 white adults surveyed, 512 replied that racism is a big problem. What fractional part of the white adults, expressed in lowest terms, felt that racism is a big problem?

86. Of the 400 black adults surveyed, 312 replied that racism is a big problem. What fractional part of the black adults, expressed in lowest terms, felt that racism is a big problem?

87. Of the 300 black teenagers surveyed, 186 replied that racism is a big problem. What fractional part of the black teenagers, expressed in lowest terms, felt that racism is *not* a big problem?

88. Of the 300 white teenagers surveyed, 174 replied that racism is a big problem. What fractional part of the white teenagers, expressed in lowest terms, felt that racism is *not* a big problem?

89. $\frac{19}{20}$ of the 300 black teenagers surveyed said that they were planning to go to college. How many planned on college?

90. $\frac{23}{25}$ of the 300 white teenagers surveyed said that they were planning to go to college. How many planned on college?

91. A recipe calls for $\frac{3}{4}$ cup of sugar. How much is needed to make half of the recipe?

92. A recipe calls for $\frac{3}{4}$ cup of shortening. How much is needed to triple the recipe?

93. Some companies pay people extra when they work more than a regular 40-hour work week. The overtime pay is often $1\frac{1}{2}$, or $\frac{3}{2}$, times the regular hourly rate. This is called time and a half. A summer job for students pays \$12 an hour and offers time and a half for the hours worked over 40. If a student works 46 hours during one week, what is the student's total pay before taxes?

94. A will states that $\frac{3}{5}$ of the estate is to be divided among relatives. Of the remaining estate, $\frac{1}{4}$ goes to the National Foundation for AIDS Research. What fraction of the estate goes to the National Foundation for AIDS Research?

95. The graph shows how a particular student spends her weekdays. What fraction of the day is spent in class?

The Weekdays of a Student

 Writing in Mathematics

96. What is a rational number?

97. Explain how to reduce a rational number to its lowest terms.

98. Explain how to write a rational number as a decimal.

99. Explain how to write 0.083 as a quotient of integers.

100. Explain how to write $0.\overline{9}$ as a quotient of integers.

101. Explain how to multiply rational numbers. Use $\frac{5}{6} \cdot \frac{1}{2}$ as an example.

102. Explain how to divide rational numbers. Use $\frac{5}{6} \div \frac{1}{2}$ as an example.

103. Explain how to add rational numbers with different denominators. Use $\frac{5}{6} + \frac{1}{2}$ as an example.

104. What does it mean when we say that the set of rational numbers is dense?

105. Explain what is wrong with this statement. "If you'd like to save some money, I'll be happy to sell you my computer system for only $\frac{3}{2}$ of the price I originally paid for it."

 Technology Exercises

106. Use a calculator to express the following rational numbers as decimals.
a. $\frac{197}{800}$ b. $\frac{4539}{3125}$ c. $\frac{7}{6250}$

107. If you have access to a calculator that performs operations with fractions, use it to verify your answers to Exercises 45–74.

 Critical Thinking Exercises

108. If 2 servings of rice call for $\frac{1}{4}$ teaspoon of salt, and 4 servings require $\frac{1}{2}$ teaspoon of salt, how much salt is needed for 3 servings?

109. Shown below is a short excerpt from "The Star-Spangled Banner." The time is $\frac{3}{4}$, which means that each measure must contain notes that add up to $\frac{3}{4}$. The values of the different notes tell musicians how long to hold each note.

$$\mathbf{o} = 1 \qquad \mathbf{\downarrow} = \frac{1}{2} \qquad \mathbf{\downarrow} = \frac{1}{4} \qquad \mathbf{\downarrow} = \frac{1}{8}$$

Use vertical lines to divide this line of "The Star-Spangled Banner" into measures.

 Group Exercise

110. Each member of the group should present an application of rational numbers. The application can be based on research or on how the group member uses rational numbers in his or her life. If you are not sure where to begin, ask yourself how your life would be different if fractions and decimals were concepts unknown to our civilization.

SECTION 5.4 *The Irrational Numbers*

Objectives

1. Define the irrational numbers.

2. Simplify square roots.

3. Perform operations with square roots.

4. Rationalize the denominator.

For the followers of the Greek mathematician Pythagoras in the sixth century B.C., numbers took on a life-and-death importance. The "Pythagorean Brotherhood" was a secret group whose members were convinced that properties of whole numbers were the key to understanding the universe. Members of the Brotherhood (which admitted women) thought that all numbers that were not whole numbers could be represented as the ratio of whole numbers. A crisis occurred for the Pythagoreans when they discovered the existence of a number that was not rational. Because the Pythagoreans viewed numbers with reverence and awe, the punishment for speaking about this nonrational number was death. However, a member of the Brotherhood revealed the secret of the nonrational

Pythagoras, ca. 530–600 B.C.

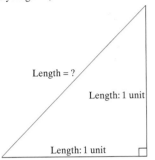

Length = ?

Length: 1 unit

Length: 1 unit

Figure 5.6

1 Define the irrational numbers.

Technology

Calculators and Square Roots

A calculator with a square root key gives a decimal approximation for $\sqrt{2}$, not the exact value.

Scientific calculator

2 $\sqrt{\ }$ or 2 $\boxed{\substack{\text{2ND} \\ \text{INV}}}$ $\boxed{x^2}$

Graphing calculator

$\sqrt{\ }$ 2 $\boxed{\text{ENTER}}$

The number displayed,

1.41421356237

can be rounded:
to the nearest tenth
1.41 ≈ 1.4

less than 5

to the nearest hundredth
1.414 ≈ 1.41

less than 5

to the nearest thousandth
1.4142 ≈ 1.414

less than 5

and so on.

number's existence. When he later died in a shipwreck, his death was viewed as punishment from the gods.

The triangle in Figure 5.6 led the Pythagoreans to the discovery of a number that could not be expressed as the quotient of integers. Based on their understanding of the relationship among the sides of this triangle, they knew that the length of the side shown in red had to be a number that, when squared, is equal to 2. The Pythagoreans discovered that this number seemed to be close to the rational numbers

$$\frac{14}{10}, \frac{141}{100}, \frac{1414}{1000}, \frac{14{,}141}{10{,}000}, \text{ and so on.}$$

However, they were shocked to find that there is no quotient of integers whose square is equal to 2.

The positive number whose square is equal to 2 is written $\sqrt{2}$. We read this "the square root of 2," or "radical 2." The symbol $\sqrt{\ }$ is called the **radical sign**. The number under the radical sign, in this case 2, is called the **radicand**. The entire symbol $\sqrt{2}$ is called a **radical**.

Using deductive reasoning, mathematicians have proved that $\sqrt{2}$ cannot be represented as a quotient of integers. This means that there is no terminating or repeating decimal that can be multiplied by itself to give 2. We can, however, give a decimal approximation for $\sqrt{2}$. We use the symbol ≈, which means "is approximately equal to." Thus,

$$\sqrt{2} \approx 1.414214.$$

We can verify that this is only an approximation by multiplying 1.414214 by itself. The product is not exactly 2:

$$1.414214 \times 1.414214 = 2.0000012378.$$

A number like $\sqrt{2}$, whose decimal representation does not come to an end and does not have a block of repeating digits, is an example of an **irrational number**.

The Irrational Numbers

The set of **irrational numbers** is the set of numbers whose decimal representations are neither terminating nor repeating.

Perhaps the best known of all the irrational numbers is π (pi). This irrational number represents the distance around a circle (its circumference) divided by the diameter of the circle. In the *Star Trek* episode "Wolf in the Fold," Spock foils an evil computer by telling it to "compute the last digit in the value of π." Because π is an irrational number, there is no last digit in its decimal representation:

$$\pi = 3.1415926535897932384626433832795\ldots.$$

The nature of the irrational number π has fascinated mathematicians for centuries. Amateur and professional mathematicians have taken up the challenge of calculating π to more and more decimal places.

Computing π is the ultimate stress test for a computer. Brothers Gregory and David Chudnovsky put their homemade computer to the test, calculating π to over 8 billion digits. If printed on ordinary type, the number would stretch over 9600 miles!

The U.N. building is designed with three golden rectangles.

"The senses delight in things duly proportional."

THOMAS AQUINAS (1225–1274)

2 Simplify square roots.

Study Tip

In general, $\sqrt{a + b}$ is *not* equal to $\sqrt{a} + \sqrt{b}$. If $a = 9$ and $b = 16$, $\sqrt{9 + 16} = \sqrt{25} = 5$. However,

$\sqrt{9} + \sqrt{16} = 3 + 4$, or 7, *not* 5. In general,

$$\sqrt{a + b} \neq \sqrt{a} + \sqrt{b}$$
$$\sqrt{a - b} \neq \sqrt{a} - \sqrt{b}$$

Square Roots

The United Nations Building in New York was designed to represent its mission of promoting world harmony. Viewed from the front, the building looks like three rectangles stacked upon each other. In each rectangle, the ratio of width to height is $\sqrt{5} + 1$ to 2, approximately 1.618 to 1. The ancient Greeks believed that such a rectangle, called a **golden rectangle**, was the most pleasing of all rectangles.

The ratio 1.618 to 1 is approximate because $\sqrt{5}$ is an irrational number. The **principal square root** of a nonnegative number n, written $\sqrt{n}$, is the positive number that when multiplied by itself gives n. Thus,

$$\sqrt{36} = 6 \text{ because } 6 \cdot 6 = 36$$

and

$$\sqrt{81} = 9 \text{ because } 9 \cdot 9 = 81.$$

Notice that both $\sqrt{36}$ and $\sqrt{81}$ are rational numbers because 6 and 9 are terminating decimals. Thus, not all square roots are irrational.

Numbers such as 36 and 81 are called **perfect squares**. A **perfect square** is a number that is the square of a whole number. The first few perfect squares are listed below.

0 $= 0^2$	**16** $= 4^2$	**64** $= 8^2$	**144** $= 12^2$
1 $= 1^2$	**25** $= 5^2$	**81** $= 9^2$	**169** $= 13^2$
4 $= 2^2$	**36** $= 6^2$	**100** $= 10^2$	**196** $= 14^2$
9 $= 3^2$	**49** $= 7^2$	**121** $= 11^2$	**225** $= 15^2$

The square root of a perfect square is a rational number. For example,

$$\sqrt{0} = 0, \sqrt{1} = 1, \sqrt{4} = 2, \sqrt{9} = 3, \sqrt{16} = 4, \sqrt{25} = 5, \sqrt{36} = 6,$$ and so on.

Simplifying Square Roots

A rule for simplifying square roots can be generalized by comparing $\sqrt{25 \cdot 4}$ and $\sqrt{25} \cdot \sqrt{4}$. Notice that:

$$\sqrt{25 \cdot 4} = \sqrt{100} = 10 \text{ and } \sqrt{25} \cdot \sqrt{4} = 5 \cdot 2 = 10.$$

Because we obtain 10 in both situations, the original radicals must be equal. That is,

$$\sqrt{25 \cdot 4} = \sqrt{25} \cdot \sqrt{4}.$$

In general, if a and b are nonnegative, then

$$\sqrt{a \cdot b} = \sqrt{a} \cdot \sqrt{b}.$$

We can use this result to *simplify* some irrational square roots. Write the square root as a product of two square roots. One of the square roots should contain the greatest perfect square that is a factor of the number under the square root symbol in the given expression. Then simplify the square root that contains the perfect square factor.

EXAMPLE 1 Simplifying Square Roots

Simplify: a. $\sqrt{75}$ b. $\sqrt{500}$ c. $\sqrt{17}$

Solution

a. $\sqrt{75} = \sqrt{25 \cdot 3}$ 25 is the largest perfect square that is a factor of 75.

$\phantom{\sqrt{75}} = \sqrt{25} \cdot \sqrt{3}$ $\sqrt{ab} = \sqrt{a}\sqrt{b}$

$\phantom{\sqrt{75}} = 5\sqrt{3}$ $\sqrt{25} = 5$

b. $\sqrt{500} = \sqrt{100 \cdot 5}$ 100 is the largest perfect square factor of 500.

$\phantom{\sqrt{500}} = \sqrt{100} \cdot \sqrt{5}$ $\sqrt{ab} = \sqrt{a}\sqrt{b}$

$\phantom{\sqrt{500}} = 10\sqrt{5}$ $\sqrt{100} = 10$

c. Because 17 has no perfect square factors (other than 1), $\sqrt{17}$ cannot be simplified.

Multiplying Square Roots

3 Perform operations with square roots.

If a and b are nonnegative, then we can use

$$\sqrt{a} \cdot \sqrt{b} = \sqrt{a \cdot b}$$

to multiply square roots. The product of the square roots is the square root of the product. Once the square roots are multiplied, simplify the square root of the product when possible.

EXAMPLE 2 Multiplying Square Roots

Multiply: a. $\sqrt{2} \cdot \sqrt{5}$ b. $\sqrt{7} \cdot \sqrt{7}$ c. $\sqrt{6} \cdot \sqrt{12}$

Solution

a. $\sqrt{2} \cdot \sqrt{5} = \sqrt{2 \cdot 5} = \sqrt{10}$

b. $\sqrt{7} \cdot \sqrt{7} = \sqrt{7 \cdot 7} = \sqrt{49} = 7$

c. $\sqrt{6} \cdot \sqrt{12} = \sqrt{6 \cdot 12} = \sqrt{72} = \sqrt{36} \cdot \sqrt{2} = 6\sqrt{2}$

Study Tip

Because

$$\sqrt{7} \cdot \sqrt{7} = \sqrt{49} = 7,$$

it is possible to multiply irrational numbers and get a rational number for an answer.

Dividing Square Roots

The quotient of two square roots is the square root of the quotient:

$$\frac{\sqrt{a}}{\sqrt{b}} = \sqrt{\frac{a}{b}}, a \geq 0, b > 0.$$

Once the square roots are divided, simplify the square root of the quotient when possible.

EXAMPLE 3 Dividing Square Roots

Find the quotient: a. $\dfrac{\sqrt{75}}{\sqrt{3}}$ b. $\dfrac{\sqrt{90}}{\sqrt{2}}$

Elephants and π

The height of a fully grown elephant, measured from its foot to its shoulder, is approximately

$$2\pi \cdot \text{the diameter of its foot.}$$

Source: The Joy of π

Solution

a. $\dfrac{\sqrt{75}}{\sqrt{3}} = \sqrt{\dfrac{75}{3}} = \sqrt{25} = 5$

b. $\dfrac{\sqrt{90}}{\sqrt{2}} = \sqrt{\dfrac{90}{2}} = \sqrt{45} = \sqrt{9 \cdot 5} = \sqrt{9} \cdot \sqrt{5} = 3\sqrt{5}$

Adding and Subtracting Square Roots

The number that multiplies a square root is called the square root's **coefficient**. For example, in $3\sqrt{5}$, 3 is the coefficient of the square root.

Square roots with the same radicand can be added or subtracted by adding or subtracting their coefficients:

$$a\sqrt{c} + b\sqrt{c} = (a + b)\sqrt{c} \qquad\qquad a\sqrt{c} - b\sqrt{c} = (a - b)\sqrt{c}$$

Sum of coefficients times the common square root

Difference of coefficients times the common square root

EXAMPLE 4   Adding and Subtracting Square Roots

Add or subtract as indicated.

a. $7\sqrt{2} + 5\sqrt{2}$ b. $2\sqrt{5} - 6\sqrt{5}$ c. $3\sqrt{7} + 9\sqrt{7} - \sqrt{7}$

Solution

a. $7\sqrt{2} + 5\sqrt{2} = (7 + 5)\sqrt{2}$
$$= 12\sqrt{2}$$

b. $2\sqrt{5} - 6\sqrt{5} = (2 - 6)\sqrt{5}$
$$= -4\sqrt{5}$$

c. $3\sqrt{7} + 9\sqrt{7} - \sqrt{7} = 3\sqrt{7} + 9\sqrt{7} - 1\sqrt{7}$ Write $\sqrt{7}$ as $1\sqrt{7}$.
$$= (3 + 9 - 1)\sqrt{7}$$
$$= 11\sqrt{7}$$

In some situations, it is possible to add and subtract square roots that do not contain a common square root by first simplifying.

Study Tip

Sums or differences of square roots that cannot be simplified and that do not contain a common square root cannot be combined into one term by adding or subtracting coefficients. Some examples:

- $5\sqrt{3} + 3\sqrt{5}$ cannot be combined by adding coefficients. The square roots, $\sqrt{3}$ and $\sqrt{5}$, are different.
- $28 + 7\sqrt{3}$, or $28\sqrt{1} + 7\sqrt{3}$, cannot be combined by adding coefficients. The square roots, $\sqrt{1}$ and $\sqrt{3}$, are different.

EXAMPLE 5   Adding and Subtracting Square Roots by First Simplifying

Add or subtract as indicated.

a. $\sqrt{2} + \sqrt{8}$ b. $4\sqrt{50} - 6\sqrt{32}$

Solution

a. $\sqrt{2} + \sqrt{8}$
$$= \sqrt{2} + \sqrt{4 \cdot 2}$$ Split 8 into two factors such that one is a perfect square.
$$= 1\sqrt{2} + 2\sqrt{2}$$ $\sqrt{4 \cdot 2} = \sqrt{4} \cdot \sqrt{2} = 2\sqrt{2}$
$$= (1 + 2)\sqrt{2}$$ Add coefficients.
$$= 3\sqrt{2}$$

b. $4\sqrt{50} - 6\sqrt{32}$

$= 4\sqrt{25 \cdot 2} - 6\sqrt{16 \cdot 2}$ 25 is the largest perfect square factor of 50 and 16 is the largest perfect square factor of 32.

$= 4 \cdot 5\sqrt{2} - 6 \cdot 4\sqrt{2}$ $\sqrt{25 \cdot 2} = \sqrt{25}\sqrt{2} = 5\sqrt{2}$ and $\sqrt{16 \cdot 2} = \sqrt{16}\sqrt{2} = 4\sqrt{2}$

$= 20\sqrt{2} - 24\sqrt{2}$ Multiply.

$= (20 - 24)\sqrt{2}$ Subtract coefficients.

$= -4\sqrt{2}$

4 Rationalize the denominator.

Rationalizing the Denominator

You can use a calculator to compare the approximate values for $\frac{1}{\sqrt{3}}$ and $\frac{\sqrt{3}}{3}$. The two approximations are the same. This is not a coincidence:

$$\frac{1}{\sqrt{3}} = \frac{1}{\sqrt{3}} \cdot \boxed{\frac{\sqrt{3}}{\sqrt{3}}} = \frac{\sqrt{3}}{\sqrt{9}} = \frac{\sqrt{3}}{3}$$

Any number divided by itself is 1. Multiplication by 1 does not change the value of $\frac{1}{\sqrt{3}}$.

This process involves rewriting a radical to remove the square root from the denominator without changing the value of the radical. The process is called **rationalizing the denominator**. If the denominator contains the square root of a natural number that is not a perfect square, multiply the numerator and denominator by the smallest number that produces the square root of a perfect square in the denominator.

EXAMPLE 6   Rationalizing Denominators

Rationalize the denominator: a. $\dfrac{15}{\sqrt{6}}$ b. $\sqrt{\dfrac{3}{5}}$ c. $\dfrac{12}{\sqrt{8}}$

Solution

a. If we multiply numerator and denominator by $\sqrt{6}$, the denominator becomes $\sqrt{6} \cdot \sqrt{6} = \sqrt{36} = 6$. Therefore, we multiply by 1, choosing $\dfrac{\sqrt{6}}{\sqrt{6}}$ for 1:

$$\frac{15}{\sqrt{6}} = \frac{15}{\sqrt{6}} \cdot \frac{\sqrt{6}}{\sqrt{6}} = \frac{15\sqrt{6}}{\sqrt{36}} = \frac{15\sqrt{6}}{6} = \frac{5\sqrt{6}}{2}$$

Multiply by 1.   Simplify $\frac{15}{6} = \frac{15 \div 3}{6 \div 3} = \frac{5}{2}$.

b. $\sqrt{\dfrac{3}{5}} = \dfrac{\sqrt{3}}{\sqrt{5}} = \dfrac{\sqrt{3}}{\sqrt{5}} \cdot \dfrac{\sqrt{5}}{\sqrt{5}} = \dfrac{\sqrt{15}}{\sqrt{25}} = \dfrac{\sqrt{15}}{5}$

Multiply by 1.

c. The *smallest* number that will produce a perfect square in the denominator of $\dfrac{12}{\sqrt{8}}$ is $\sqrt{2}$, because $\sqrt{8} \cdot \sqrt{2} = \sqrt{16} = 4$. We multiply by 1, choosing $\dfrac{\sqrt{2}}{\sqrt{2}}$ for 1.

$$\frac{12}{\sqrt{8}} = \frac{12}{\sqrt{8}} \cdot \frac{\sqrt{2}}{\sqrt{2}} = \frac{12\sqrt{2}}{\sqrt{16}} = \frac{12\sqrt{2}}{4} = 3\sqrt{2}$$

Irrational Numbers and Other Kinds of Roots

Irrational numbers appear in roots other than square roots. The symbol $\sqrt[3]{\ }$ represents the **cube root** of a number. For example,

$$\sqrt[3]{8} = 2 \text{ because } 2 \cdot 2 \cdot 2 = 8 \text{ and } \sqrt[3]{64} = 4 \text{ because } 4 \cdot 4 \cdot 4 = 64.$$

Although these cube roots are rational numbers, most cube roots are not. For example,

$$\sqrt[3]{217} \approx 6.0092 \text{ because } (6.0092)^3 \approx 216.995, \text{ not exactly 217.}$$

There is no end to the kinds of roots for numbers. For example $\sqrt[4]{\ }$ represents the **fourth root** of a number. Thus, $\sqrt[4]{81} = 3$ because $3 \cdot 3 \cdot 3 \cdot 3 = 81$. Although the fourth root of 81 is rational, most fourth roots, fifth roots, and so on tend to be irrational.

Exercise Set 5.4

 Practice Exercises

Evaluate each expression in Exercises 1–10.

1. $\sqrt{9}$ 2. $\sqrt{16}$ 3. $\sqrt{25}$ 4. $\sqrt{49}$

5. $\sqrt{64}$ 6. $\sqrt{100}$ 7. $\sqrt{121}$ 8. $\sqrt{144}$

9. $\sqrt{169}$ 10. $\sqrt{225}$

In Exercises 11–16, use a calculator with a square root key to find a decimal approximation for each square root. Round the number displayed to the nearest a. tenth, b. hundredth, c. thousandth.

11. $\sqrt{173}$ 12. $\sqrt{3176}$ 13. $\sqrt{17{,}761}$
14. $\sqrt{779{,}264}$ 15. $\sqrt{\pi}$ 16. $\sqrt{2\pi}$

In Exercises 17–24, simplify the square root.

17. $\sqrt{20}$ 18. $\sqrt{50}$ 19. $\sqrt{80}$ 20. $\sqrt{12}$

21. $\sqrt{250}$ 22. $\sqrt{192}$ 23. $7\sqrt{28}$ 24. $3\sqrt{52}$

In Exercises 25–56, perform the indicated operation. Simplify the answer when possible.

25. $\sqrt{7} \cdot \sqrt{6}$ 26. $\sqrt{19} \cdot \sqrt{3}$ 27. $\sqrt{6} \cdot \sqrt{6}$

28. $\sqrt{5} \cdot \sqrt{5}$ 29. $\sqrt{3} \cdot \sqrt{6}$ 30. $\sqrt{12} \cdot \sqrt{2}$

31. $\sqrt{2} \cdot \sqrt{26}$ 32. $\sqrt{5} \cdot \sqrt{50}$ 33. $\dfrac{\sqrt{54}}{\sqrt{6}}$

34. $\dfrac{\sqrt{75}}{\sqrt{3}}$ 35. $\dfrac{\sqrt{90}}{\sqrt{2}}$ 36. $\dfrac{\sqrt{60}}{\sqrt{3}}$

37. $\dfrac{-\sqrt{96}}{\sqrt{2}}$ 38. $\dfrac{-\sqrt{150}}{\sqrt{3}}$ 39. $7\sqrt{3} + 6\sqrt{3}$

40. $8\sqrt{5} + 11\sqrt{5}$ 41. $4\sqrt{13} - 6\sqrt{13}$

42. $6\sqrt{17} - 8\sqrt{17}$ 43. $\sqrt{5} + \sqrt{5}$

44. $\sqrt{3} + \sqrt{3}$ 45. $4\sqrt{2} - 5\sqrt{2} + 8\sqrt{2}$

46. $6\sqrt{3} + 8\sqrt{3} - 16\sqrt{3}$ 47. $\sqrt{5} + \sqrt{20}$

48. $\sqrt{3} + \sqrt{27}$ 49. $\sqrt{50} - \sqrt{18}$

50. $\sqrt{63} - \sqrt{28}$ 51. $3\sqrt{18} + 5\sqrt{50}$

52. $4\sqrt{12} + 2\sqrt{75}$ 53. $\dfrac{1}{4}\sqrt{12} - \dfrac{1}{2}\sqrt{48}$

54. $\dfrac{1}{5}\sqrt{300} - \dfrac{2}{3}\sqrt{27}$ 55. $3\sqrt{75} + 2\sqrt{12} - 2\sqrt{48}$

56. $2\sqrt{72} + 3\sqrt{50} - \sqrt{128}$

In Exercises 57–66, rationalize the denominator.

57. $\dfrac{5}{\sqrt{3}}$

58. $\dfrac{12}{\sqrt{5}}$

59. $\dfrac{21}{\sqrt{7}}$

60. $\dfrac{30}{\sqrt{5}}$

61. $\dfrac{12}{\sqrt{30}}$

62. $\dfrac{15}{\sqrt{50}}$

63. $\dfrac{15}{\sqrt{12}}$

64. $\dfrac{13}{\sqrt{40}}$

65. $\sqrt{\dfrac{2}{5}}$

66. $\sqrt{\dfrac{5}{7}}$

67. In the Peanuts cartoon shown below, Woodstock appears to be working steps mentally. Fill in the missing steps that show how to go from $\dfrac{7\sqrt{2\cdot2\cdot3}}{6}$ to $\dfrac{7}{3}\sqrt{3}$.

PEANUTS reprinted by permission of United Feature Syndicate, Inc.

 Application Exercises

68. The greatest speed s (in miles per hour) at which a bicyclist can safely turn a corner of radius r feet is $s = 4\sqrt{r}$. Find the greatest speed at which a bicyclist can safely turn a corner with a 25-foot radius.

69. The time t (in seconds) it takes an object dropped from a certain height (in feet) to hit the ground is

$$t = \sqrt{\dfrac{\text{height in feet}}{16}}.$$

Find how long it will take a rock dropped from the top of a 320-foot tall cliff to hit the ground. Write the answer as a simplified square root.

 Writing in Mathematics

70. Describe the difference between a rational number and an irrational number.

71. Describe what is wrong with this statement: $\pi = \frac{22}{7}$.

72. Using $\sqrt{50}$, explain how to simplify a square root.

73. Describe how to multiply square roots.

74. Explain how to add square roots with the same radicand.

75. Explain how to add $\sqrt{3} + \sqrt{12}$.

76. Describe what it means to rationalize a denominator. Use $\dfrac{2}{\sqrt{5}}$ in your explanation.

 Critical Thinking Exercises

77. Which one of the following is true?
    a. The product of any two irrational numbers is always an irrational number.
    b. $\sqrt{9} + \sqrt{16} = \sqrt{25}$
    c. $\sqrt{\sqrt{16}} = 2$
    d. $\dfrac{\sqrt{64}}{2} = \sqrt{32}$

In Exercises 78–80, insert either $<$ or $>$ in the shaded area between the numbers to make the statement true.

78. $\sqrt{2}$ ▦ 1.5

79. $-\pi$ ▦ -3.5

80. $-\dfrac{3.14}{2}$ ▦ $-\dfrac{\pi}{2}$

81. How does doubling a number affect its square root?

82. Between which two consecutive integers is $-\sqrt{47}$?

83. Simplify: $\sqrt{2} + \sqrt{\dfrac{1}{2}}$.

84. Decribe the kinds of numbers that have rational cube roots.

 Group Exercises

The following topics related to irrational numbers are appropriate for either individual or group research projects. A report should be given to the class on the researched topic.

85. A History of How Irrational Numbers Developed

86. Pi: Its History, Applications, and Curiosities

87. Proving That $\sqrt{2}$ Is Irrational

88. Imaginary Numbers: Their History, Applications, and Curiosities

89. The Golden Rectangle in Art and Architecture

SECTION 5.5 *Real Numbers and Their Properties*

Objectives

1. Recognize subsets of the real numbers.
2. Recognize properties of real numbers.

1 Recognize subsets of the real numbers.

The Set of Real Numbers

Those people are *weird*! These people are *friendly*! All of us use categories like *weird* and *friendly* to order and make sense of our world. In the same way, mathematicians place numbers into categories, or sets, helping them to order and structure a universe of numbers in which each one has its very special characteristics. They even use the labels *weird* and *friendly* to describe sets of numbers. However, the label that appears most frequently is *real*. The union of the rational numbers and the irrational numbers is the set of **real numbers**.

The sets that make up the real numbers are summarized in Table 5.3. We refer to these sets as **subsets** of the real numbers, meaning that all elements in each subset are also elements in the set of real numbers.

This diagram shows that every real number is rational or irrational.

Table 5.3 Important Subsets of the Real Numbers

Name	Description	Examples
Natural numbers $\mathbb{N}$	$\{1, 2, 3, 4, 5, \ldots\}$ These numbers are used for counting and are also called the *counting numbers*.	$87, 104, 2001$
Whole numbers $\mathbb{W}$	$\{0, 1, 2, 3, 4, 5, \ldots\}$ The whole numbers add 0 to the set of natural numbers.	$0, 87, 104, 2001$
Integers $\mathbb{Z}$	$\{\ldots, -5, -4, -3, -2, -1, 0, 1, 2, 3, 4, 5, \ldots\}$ The integers add the negatives of the natural numbers to the set of whole numbers.	$-2001, -104, -87, 0, 87,$ $104, 2001$
Rational numbers $\mathbb{Q}$	These numbers can be expressed as an integer divided by a nonzero integer: $\frac{a}{b}$: a and b are integers: $b \neq 0$. Rational numbers can be expressed as terminating or repeating decimals.	$-2000 = \frac{-2000}{1}$, $-104 = \frac{-104}{1}, -87, 0, 87,$ $104, 2001, \frac{87}{104}, \frac{-87}{2001}, \frac{-2000}{87}$
Irrational numbers $\mathbb{I}$	This is the set of numbers whose decimal representations are neither terminating nor repeating. Irrational numbers cannot be expressed as a quotient of integers.	$\pi, \sqrt{2}, \sqrt{3}, \sqrt{8}$

EXAMPLE 1 Classifying Real Numbers

List the numbers in the given set that belong to each of the subsets of the real numbers.

$$\left\{-7, -\frac{3}{4}, 0, 0.\overline{6}, \sqrt{5}, \pi, 7.3, \sqrt{81}\right\}$$

a. Natural numbers
b. Whole numbers
c. Integers

Weird Numbers

Mathematicians use the label **weird** to describe a number if:
1. The sum of its factors, excluding the number itself, is greater than the number.
2. No partial collection of the factors adds up to the number.

The number 70 is weird. Its factors are 1, 2, 5, 7, 10, 14, and 35. The sum of these factors is 74, which is greater than 70. Two or more numbers in the list of factors cannot be added to obtain 70.

Weird numbers are rare. Below 10,000, the weird numbers are 70, 836, 4030, 5830, 7192, 7912, and 9272. It is not known whether an odd weird number exists.

2 Recognize properties of real numbers.

d. Rational numbers
e. Irrational numbers

Solution

a. Natural numbers: The only natural number in the set is $\sqrt{81}$ because $\sqrt{81} = 9$. (9 multiplied by itself is 81.)

b. Whole numbers: The whole numbers consist of the natural numbers and 0. The elements of the set that are whole numbers are 0 and $\sqrt{81}$.

c. Integers: The integers consist of the natural numbers, 0, and the negatives of the natural numbers. The elements of the set that are integers are $\sqrt{81}$, 0, and -7.

d. Rational numbers: All numbers in the set that can be expressed as the quotient of integers are rational numbers. These include $-7 \left(-7 = -\frac{7}{1}\right), -\frac{3}{4}$, $0 \left(0 = \frac{0}{1}\right)$, and $\sqrt{81} \left(\sqrt{81} = \frac{9}{1}\right)$. Furthermore, all numbers in the set that are terminating or repeating decimals are also rational numbers. These include $0.\overline{6}$ and 7.3.

e. Irrational numbers: The irrational numbers in the set are $\sqrt{5} (\sqrt{5} \approx 2.236)$ and $\pi (\pi \approx 3.14)$. Both $\sqrt{5}$ and π are only approximately equal to 2.236 and 3.14, respectively. In decimal form, $\sqrt{5}$ and π neither terminate nor have blocks of repeating digits.

Properties of the Real Numbers

When you use your calculator to add two real numbers, you can enter them in any order. The fact that two real numbers can be added in any order is called the **commutative property of addition**. You probably use this property, as well as other properties of real numbers listed in Table 5.4, without giving it much thought. The properties of the real numbers are especially useful in algebra, as we shall see in Chapter 6.

Table 5.4   Properties of the Real Numbers

Name	Meaning	Examples
Closure Property of Addition	The sum of any two real numbers is a real number.	$4\sqrt{2}$ is a real number and $5\sqrt{2}$ is a real number, so $4\sqrt{2} + 5\sqrt{2}$, or $9\sqrt{2}$, is a real number.
Closure Property of Multiplication	The product of any two real numbers is a real number.	10 is a real number and $\frac{1}{2}$ is a real number, so $10 \cdot \frac{1}{2}$, or 5, is a real number.
Commutative Property of Addition	Two real numbers can be added in any order. $a + b = b + a$	$13 + 7 = 7 + 13$
Commutative Property of Multiplication	Two real numbers can be multiplied in any order. $ab = ba$	$13 \cdot 7 = 7 \cdot 13$ $\sqrt{2} \cdot \sqrt{5} = \sqrt{5} \cdot \sqrt{2}$

continued

Table 5.4 *continued*   **Properties of the Real Numbers**

Name	Meaning	Examples
Associative Property of Addition	If three real numbers are added, it makes no difference which two are added first. $(a + b) + c = a + (b + c)$	$(7 + 2) + 5 = 7 + (2 + 5)$ $9 + 5 = 7 + 7$ $14 = 14$
Associative Property of Multiplication	If three real numbers are multiplied, it makes no difference which two are multiplied first. $(a \cdot b) \cdot c = a \cdot (b \cdot c)$	$(7 \cdot 2) \cdot 5 = 7 \cdot (2 \cdot 5)$ $14 \cdot 5 = 7 \cdot 10$ $70 = 70$
Distributive Property of Multiplication over Addition	Multiplication distributes over addition. $a \cdot (b + c) = a \cdot b + a \cdot c$	$7(4 + \sqrt{3}) = 7 \cdot 4 + 7 \cdot \sqrt{3}$ $= 28 + 7 \cdot \sqrt{3}$

Commutative Words and Sentences

The commutative property states that a change in order produces no change in the answer. The words and sentences listed here are commutative; they read the same from left to right and from right to left!

dad	Draw, o coward!	Revolting is error. Resign it, lover.
repaper	Dennis sinned.	Naomi, did I moan?
never odd or even	Ma is a nun, as I am.	Al lets Della call Ed Stella.

EXAMPLE 2   Identifying Properties of the Real Numbers

Name the property illustrated:

a. $\sqrt{3} \cdot 7 = 7 \cdot \sqrt{3}$

b. $(4 + 7) + 6 = 4 + (7 + 6)$

c. $2(3 + \sqrt{5}) = 6 + 2\sqrt{5}$

d. $\sqrt{2} + (\sqrt{3} + \sqrt{7}) = \sqrt{2} + (\sqrt{7} + \sqrt{3})$

Study Tip

Commutative: Changes *order.*
Associative: Changes *grouping.*

Solution

a. $\sqrt{3} \cdot 7 = 7 \cdot \sqrt{3}$ *Commutative property of multiplication*

b. $(4 + 7) + 6 = 4 + (7 + 6)$ *Associative property of addition*

c. $2(3 + \sqrt{5}) = 6 + 2\sqrt{5}$ *Distributive property of multiplication over addition*

d. $\sqrt{2} + (\sqrt{3} + \sqrt{7}) = \sqrt{2} + (\sqrt{7} + \sqrt{3})$ *The only change between the left and the right sides is in the order that $\sqrt{3}$ and $\sqrt{7}$ are added. The order is changed from $\sqrt{3} + \sqrt{7}$ to $\sqrt{7} + \sqrt{3}$ using the commutative property of addition.*

Although the entire set of real numbers is closed with respect to addition and multiplication, some of the subsets of the real numbers do not satisfy the closure property for a given operation. If the operation results in just one answer that is not in the set, then the set is not closed for that operation.

EXAMPLE 3   Verifying Closure

   a. Are the integers closed with respect to multiplication?
   b. Are the irrational numbers closed with respect to multiplication?
   c. Are the natural numbers closed with respect to division?

Solution
   a. Consider some examples of the multiplication of integers:

$$3 \cdot 2 = 6 \qquad 3(-2) = -6 \qquad -3(-2) = 6 \qquad -3 \cdot 0 = 0.$$

     The product of any two integers is always a positive integer, a negative integer, or zero, which is an integer. Thus, the integers are closed under the operation of multiplication.

   b. If we multiply two irrational numbers, must the product always be an irrational number? The answer is no. Here is an example:

$$\sqrt{7} \cdot \sqrt{7} = \sqrt{49} = 7$$

           Both irrational   Not an irrational number

     This means that the irrational numbers are not closed under the operation of multiplication.

   c. If we divide any two natural numbers, must the quotient always be a natural number? The answer is no. Here is an example:

$$4 \div 8 = \frac{1}{2}$$

          Both natural numbers   Not a natural number

     Thus, the natural numbers are not closed under the operation of division.

     The commutative property involves a change in order with no change in the final result. However, changing the order in which we subtract and divide real numbers can produce different answers. For example,

$$7 - 4 \neq 4 - 7 \qquad \text{and} \qquad 6 \div 2 \neq 2 \div 6.$$

Because the real numbers are not commutative with respect to subtraction and division, it is important that you enter numbers in the correct order when using a calculator to perform these operations.

     The associative property does not hold for the operations of subtraction and division. The examples below show that if we change groupings when subtracting or dividing three numbers, the answer changes.

$$(6 - 1) - 3 \neq 6 - (1 - 3) \qquad (8 \div 4) \div 2 \neq 8 \div (4 \div 2)$$
$$5 - 3 \neq 6 - (-2) \qquad\qquad 2 \div 2 \neq 8 \div 2$$
$$2 \neq 8 \qquad\qquad\qquad\qquad 1 \neq 4$$

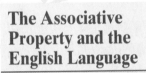

The Associative Property and the English Language

In the English language, phrases can take on different meanings depending on the way the words are associated. For example, (man eating) tiger does not mean the same thing as man (eating tiger).

Beyond the Real Numbers

THE KID WHO LEARNED ABOUT MATH
ON THE STREET

If you divide 6,973 by 0, you die.

Once, this guy tried to find the square root of -9, and his eyeballs turned black.

This girl my brother knows found out exactly what π equals, but she went nuts.

n. Chast

Only real numbers greater than or equal to zero have real number square roots. The square root of −1, $\sqrt{-1}$, is not a real number. This is because there is no real number that can be multiplied by itself that results in −1. Multiplying any real number by itself can never give a negative product. In the sixteenth century, mathematician Girolamo Cardano wrote that square roots of negative numbers would cause "mental tortures." In spite of these "tortures," mathematicians invented a new number, called i, to represent $\sqrt{-1}$. The number i is not a real number; it is called an **imaginary number**. Thus, $\sqrt{9} = 3$, $-\sqrt{9} = -3$, but $\sqrt{-9}$ is not a real number.

Exercise Set 5.5

 Practice Exercises

In Exercises 1–4, list all numbers from the given set that are:
a. natural numbers,   b. whole numbers,   c. integers,
d. rational numbers,   e. irrational numbers.

1. $\left\{-9, -\frac{4}{5}, 0, 0.25, \sqrt{3}, 9.2, \sqrt{100}\right\}$

2. $\left\{-7, -0.\overline{6}, 0, \sqrt{49}, \sqrt{50}\right\}$

3. $\left\{-11, -\frac{5}{6}, 0, 0.75, \sqrt{5}, \pi, \sqrt{64}\right\}$

4. $\left\{-5, -0.\overline{3}, 0, \sqrt{2}, \sqrt{4}\right\}$

5. Give an example of a whole number that is not a natural number.

6. Give an example of an integer that is not a whole number.

7. Give an example of a rational number that is not an integer.

8. Give an example of a rational number that is not a natural number.

9. Give an example of a number that is an integer, a whole number, and a natural number.

10. Give an example of a number that is a rational number, an integer, and a real number.

11. Give an example of a number that is an irrational number and a real number.

12. Give an example of a number that is a real number, but not an irrational number.

Complete each statement in Exercises 13–15 to illustrate the commutative property.

13. $3 + (4 + 5) = 3 + (5 + \underline{\quad})$

14. $\sqrt{5} \cdot 4 = 4 \cdot \underline{\quad}$

15. $9 \cdot (6 + 2) = 9 \cdot (2 + \underline{\quad})$

Complete each statement in Exercises 16–17 to illustrate the associative property.

16. $(3 + 7) + 9 = \underline{\quad} + (7 + \underline{\quad})$

17. $(4 \cdot 5) \cdot 3 = \underline{\quad} \cdot (5 \cdot \underline{\quad})$

Complete each statement in Exercises 18–20 to illustrate the distributive property.

18. $3 \cdot (6 + 4) = 3 \cdot 6 + 3 \cdot \underline{\quad}$

19. $\underline{\quad} \cdot (4 + 5) = 7 \cdot 4 + 7 \cdot 5$

20. $2 \cdot (\underline{\quad} + 3) = 2 \cdot 7 + 2 \cdot 3$

Use the distributive property to simplify the radical expressions in Exercises 21–28.

21. $5(6 + \sqrt{2})$

22. $4(3 + \sqrt{5})$

23. $\sqrt{7}(3 + \sqrt{2})$

24. $\sqrt{6}(7 + \sqrt{5})$

25. $\sqrt{3}(5 + \sqrt{3})$

26. $\sqrt{7}(9 + \sqrt{7})$

27. $\sqrt{6}(\sqrt{2} + \sqrt{6})$

28. $\sqrt{10}(\sqrt{2} + \sqrt{10})$

In Exercises 29–38, state the name of the property illustrated.

29. $6 + (-4) = (-4) + 6$

30. $11 \cdot (7 + 4) = 11 \cdot 7 + 11 \cdot 4$

31. $6 + (2 + 7) = (6 + 2) + 7$

32. $6 \cdot (2 \cdot 3) = 6 \cdot (3 \cdot 2)$

33. $(2 + 3) + (4 + 5) = (4 + 5) + (2 + 3)$

34. $7 \cdot (11 \cdot 8) = (11 \cdot 8) \cdot 7$

35. $2(-8 + 6) = -16 + 12$

36. $-8(3 + 11) = -24 + (-88)$

37. $(2\sqrt{3}) \cdot \sqrt{5} = 2(\sqrt{3} \cdot \sqrt{5})$

38. $\sqrt{2}\pi = \pi\sqrt{2}$

In Exercises 39–43, use two numbers to show that:

39. the natural numbers are not closed with respect to subtraction.

40. the natural numbers are not closed with respect to division.

41. the integers are not closed with respect to division.

42. the irrational numbers are not closed with respect to subtraction.

43. the irrational numbers are not closed with respect to multiplication.

 Application Exercises

44. Are first putting on your left shoe and then putting on your right shoe commutative?

45. Are first getting undressed and then taking a shower commutative?

46. Give an example of two things that you do that are not commutative.

47. Give an example of two things that you do that are commutative.

48. Closure illustrates that a characteristic of a set is not necessarily a characteristic of all of its subsets. The real numbers are closed with respect to multiplication, but the irrational numbers, a subset of the real numbers, are not. Give an example of a set that is not mathematical that has a particular characteristic, but which has a subset without this characteristic.

 Writing in Mathematics

49. What does it mean when we way that the rational numbers are a subset of the real numbers?

50. What does it mean if we say that a set is closed under a given operation?

51. State the commutative property of addition and give an example.

52. State the commutative property of multiplication and give an example.

53. State the associative property of addition and give an example.

54. State the associative property of multiplication and give an example.

55. State the distributive property of multiplication over addition and give an example.

56. Does $7 \cdot (4 \cdot 3) = 7 \cdot (3 \cdot 4)$ illustrate the commutative property or the associative property? Explain your answer.

 Critical Thinking Exercises

57. Which one of the following statements is true?
    a. Every rational number is an integer.
    b. Some whole numbers are not integers.
    c. Some rational numbers are not positive.
    d. Irrational numbers cannot be negative.

58. Which one of the following statements is true?
    a. Subtraction is a commutative operation.
    b. $(24 \div 6) \div 2 = 24 \div (6 \div 2)$
    c. $7 \cdot a + 3 \cdot a = a \cdot (7 + 3)$
    d. $2 \cdot a + 5 = 5 \cdot a + 2$

SECTION 5.6   *Exponents and Scientific Notation*

Objectives

1. Use properties of exponents.

2. Convert from scientific to decimal notation.

3. Convert from decimal to scientific notation.

4. Perform computations using scientific notation.

5. Solve applied problems using scientific notation.

We frequently encounter very large and very small numbers. Governments throughout the world are concerned about the billions of tons of carbon dioxide that the global population of 6 billion people release into the atmosphere each year. The national debt of the United States is about $5.5 trillion. A typical atom has a diameter of about one-ten-billionth of a meter. Exponents provide a way of putting these large and small numbers in perspective.

Properties of Exponents

We have seen that exponents are used to indicate repeated multiplication. For example,

$$2^4 \cdot 2^3$$

1 Use properties of exponents.

means that we are multiplying 4 factors of 2 and 3 factors of 2:

$$\boxed{2 \cdot 2 \cdot 2 \cdot 2} \cdot \boxed{2 \cdot 2 \cdot 2}$$

This is 2^4.   This is 2^3.

We have a total of 7 factors of 2. Thus,

$$2^4 \cdot 2^3 = 2^7.$$

We can quickly find the exponent on the product, 7, by adding 4 and 3, the original exponents. Products of exponential expressions with the same base are found by adding exponents. For example,

$$3^2 \cdot 3^6 = 3^{2+6} = 3^8.$$

Properties of exponents allow us to perform operations with exponential expressions without having to write out long strings of factors. Three such properties are shown in Table 5.5.

Table 5.5   Properties of Exponents

Name	Meaning	Examples
The Product Rule	Add exponents when multiplying with the same base. $b^m \cdot b^n = b^{m+n}$	$9^6 \cdot 9^{12} = 9^{6+12} = 9^{18}$
The Power Rule	Multiply exponents when an exponential expression is raised to a power. $\left(b^m\right)^n = b^{m \cdot n}$	$\left(3^4\right)^5 = 3^{4 \cdot 5} = 3^{20}$ $\left(5^3\right)^8 = 5^{3 \cdot 8} = 5^{24}$
The Quotient Rule	Subtract exponents when dividing with the same base. $\dfrac{b^m}{b^n} = b^{m-n}$	$\dfrac{5^{12}}{5^4} = 5^{12-4} = 5^8$ $\dfrac{9^{40}}{9^5} = 9^{40-5} = 9^{35}$

The third property in Table 5.5, the quotient rule, can lead to a zero exponent when subtracting exponents. Here is an example:

$$\frac{4^3}{4^3} = 4^{3-3} = 4^0.$$

We can see what this zero exponent means by evaluating 4^3 in the numerator and the denominator:

$$\frac{4^3}{4^3} = \frac{4 \cdot 4 \cdot 4}{4 \cdot 4 \cdot 4} = \frac{64}{64} = 1.$$

This means that 4^0 must equal 1. This example illustrates the zero exponent rule.

The Zero Exponent Rule

If b is any real number other than 0,

$$b^0 = 1.$$

EXAMPLE 1   Using the Zero Exponent Rule

Use the zero exponent rule to simplify.

a. 7^0 b. π^0 c. $(-5)^0$

Solution

a. $7^0 = 1$ b. $\pi^0 = 1$ c. $(-5)^0 = 1$

The quotient rule can result in a negative exponent. Consider, for example, $4^3 \div 4^5$.

$$\frac{4^3}{4^5} = 4^{3-5} = 4^{-2}$$

We can see what this negative exponent means by evaluating the numerator and the denominator.

$$\frac{4^3}{4^5} = \frac{4 \cdot 4 \cdot 4}{4 \cdot 4 \cdot 4 \cdot 4 \cdot 4} = \frac{1}{4^2}$$

Notice that $\frac{4^3}{4^5}$ equals both 4^{-2} and $\frac{1}{4^2}$. This means that 4^{-2} must equal $\frac{1}{4^2}$. This example is a special case of the negative exponent rule.

Study Tip

$\frac{4^3}{4^5}$ and $\frac{4^5}{4^3}$ represent different numbers:

$$\frac{4^3}{4^5} = 4^{3-5} = 4^{-2} = \frac{1}{4^2} = \frac{1}{16}$$

$$\frac{4^5}{4^3} = 4^{5-3} = 4^2 = 16$$

The Negative Exponent Rule

If b is any real number other than 0,

$$b^{-m} = \frac{1}{b^m}.$$

EXAMPLE 2   Using the Negative Exponent Rule

Use the negative exponent rule to simplify.

a. 4^{-2} b. 5^{-3} c. 7^{-1}

Solution

a. $4^{-2} = \dfrac{1}{4^2} = \dfrac{1}{4 \cdot 4} = \dfrac{1}{16}$

b. $5^{-3} = \dfrac{1}{5^3} = \dfrac{1}{5 \cdot 5 \cdot 5} = \dfrac{1}{125}$

c. $7^{-1} = \dfrac{1}{7^1} = \dfrac{1}{7}$

Putting Powers of Ten in Perspective

- Although people do a great deal of talking, the total output since the beginning of gabble to the present day, including all baby talk, love songs, and congressional debates, only amounts to about 10^{16} (10 million billion) words.
- A googol is 10^{100}. The number of raindrops falling on New York in a century is much less than a googol.
- A googol times a googol is $10^{100} \cdot 10^{100}$, or 10^{200}, which is much less than a googolplex! A googolplex is 10 to the googol power, or $10^{10^{100}}$, or 1 with a googol of zeros! If you tried to write a googolplex without using exponential notation, there would not be enough room to write it if you went to the farthest star, touring all the nebulae, and putting down zeros every inch of the way.
- The number of grains of sand on the beach at Coney Island, New York, is about 10^{20}.
- The number of snow crystals necessary to form the Ice Age was approximately 10^{30}.
- The number 10^{80} is greater than the total number of atoms in our entire universe.

Powers of Ten

Exponents and their properties allow us to represent and compute with numbers that are large and small. For example, one billion, or 1,000,000,000 can be written as 10^9. In terms of exponents, 10^9 might not look very large, but consider this: If you can count to 200 in one minute and decide to count for 12 hours a day at this rate, it would take you in the region of 19,024 years, 68 days, 10 hours, and 40 minutes to count to 10^9!

Powers of 10 follow two basic rules:

1. A positive exponent tells how many 0s follow the 1. For example, 10^9 (one billion) is a 1 followed by nine zeros: 1,000,000,000.

2. A negative exponent tells how many places there are to the right of the decimal point. For example, 10^{-9} (one billionth) has nine places to the right of the decimal point. The nine places contain eight 0s and the 1.

$$10^{-9} = 0.000000001$$

nine places

Earthquakes and Powers of Ten

The earthquake that ripped through northern California on October 17, 1989, measured 7.1 on the Richter scale, killed more than 60 people, and injured more than 2400. Shown here is San Francisco's Marina district, where shock waves tossed houses off their foundations and into the street.

The Richter scale is misleading because it is not actually a 1 to 8, but rather a 1 to 10 million scale. Each level indicates a tenfold increase in magnitude from the previous level, making a 7.0 earthquake a million times greater than a 1.0 quake.

Below is a translation of the Richter scale.

Richter number (R)	Magnitude (10^{R-1})
1	$10^{1-1} = 10^0 = 1$
2	$10^{2-1} = 10^1 = 10$
3	$10^{3-1} = 10^2 = 100$
4	$10^{4-1} = 10^3 = 1000$
5	$10^{5-1} = 10^4 = 10{,}000$
6	$10^{6-1} = 10^5 = 100{,}000$
7	$10^{7-1} = 10^6 = 1{,}000{,}000$
8	$10^{8-1} = 10^7 = 10{,}000{,}000$

Scientific Notation

The national debt of the United States is about $5.5 trillion. A stack of $1 bills equaling the national debt would rise to twice the distance from the Earth to the moon. Because a trillion is 10^{12}, the national debt can be expressed as

$$5.5 \times 10^{12}.$$

The number 5.5×10^{12} is written in a form called **scientific notation**. A number in scientific notation is expressed as a number greater than or equal to 1 and less than 10 multiplied by some power of 10. It is customary to use the multiplication $\times$ rather than a dot in scientific notation.

Here are two examples of numbers in scientific notation:

Each day, 2.6×10^7 pounds of dust from the atmosphere settle on Earth.
The diameter of a hydrogen atom is 1.016×10^{-8} centimeter.

2 Convert from scientific to decimal notation.

We can use the exponent on the 10 to change a number in scientific notation to decimal notation. If the exponent is *positive*, move the decimal point in the number to the *right* the same number of places as the exponent. If the exponent is *negative*, move the decimal point in the number to the *left* the same number of places as the exponent.

EXAMPLE 3   Converting from Scientific to Decimal Notation

Write each number in decimal notation.

a. 2.6×10^7 b. 1.016×10^{-8}

Solution

a. We express 2.6×10^7 in decimal notation by moving the decimal point in 2.6 seven places to the right. We need to add six zeros.

$$2.6 \times 10^7 = 26{,}000{,}000$$

b. We express 1.016×10^{-8} in decimal notation by moving the decimal point in 1.016 eight places to the left. We need to add seven zeros to the right of the decimal point.

$$1.016 \times 10^{-8} = 0.00000001016$$

3 Convert from decimal to scientific notation.

To convert from decimal notation to scientific notation, we reverse the procedure of Example 3.

- Move the decimal point in the given number to obtain a number greater than or equal to 1 and less than 10.
- The number of places the decimal point moves gives the exponent on 10; the exponent is positive if the given number is greater than 10 and negative if the given number is less than 1.

EXAMPLE 4 Converting from Decimal Notation to Scientific Notation

Write each number in scientific notation.

a. 4,600,000   b. 0.00023

Solution

a. $4{,}600{,}000 = 4.6 \times 10^?$ $\xrightarrow[\text{moves 6 places.}]{\text{Decimal point}}$ 4.6×10^6

b. $0.00023 = 2.3 \times 10^{-?}$ $\xrightarrow[\text{moves 4 places.}]{\text{Decimal point}}$ 2.3×10^{-4}

Fermat's Last Theorem

Pierre de Fermat (1601–1665) was a lawyer who enjoyed studying mathematics. In a margin of one of his books, he claimed that no natural numbers satisfy:

$$a^n + b^n = c^n$$

if n is greater than 2.

If $n = 2$, we can find numbers satisfying the equation:

$$3^2 + 4^2 = 5^2.$$

However, Fermat claimed that no natural numbers satisfy:

$$a^3 + b^3 = c^3, a^4 + b^4 = c^4,$$

and so on.

Fermat claimed to have a proof of his conjecture, but added, "The margin of my book is too narrow to write it down." Some believe that he never had a proof and his intent was to frustrate his colleagues.

In June 1993, 40-year-old Princeton math professor Andrew Wiles claimed that he discovered a proof of the theorem. Subsequent study revealed flaws, but Wiles corrected them. In 1995, his final proof served as a classic example of how great mathematicians accomplish great things: a combination of genius, hard work, frustration, and trial and error.

Andrew Wiles (1953–   )

4 Perform computations using scientific notation.

Computations with Scientific Notation

We use the product rule for exponents to multiply numbers in scientific notation. Add the exponents on 10 and multiply the other parts of the numbers separately.

EXAMPLE 5   Multiplying Numbers in Scientific Notation

Multiply $(3.4 \times 10^9)(2 \times 10^{-5})$. Write the product in decimal notation.

Solution

$$
\begin{aligned}
(3.4 \times 10^9)(2 \times 10^{-5}) &= (3.4 \times 2) \times (10^9 \times 10^{-5}) \\
&= 6.8 \times 10^{9+(-5)} \\
&= 6.8 \times 10^4 \\
&= 68{,}000
\end{aligned}
$$

We use the quotient rule for exponents to divide numbers in scientific notation. Subtract the exponents on 10 and divide the other parts of the numbers separately.

EXAMPLE 6   Dividing Numbers in Scientific Notation

Divide $\dfrac{8.4 \times 10^{-7}}{4 \times 10^{-4}}$. Write the quotient in decimal notation.

Solution

$$
\begin{aligned}
\frac{8.4 \times 10^{-7}}{4 \times 10^{-4}} &= \left(\frac{8.4}{4}\right) \times \left(\frac{10^{-7}}{10^{-4}}\right) \\
&= 2.1 \times 10^{-7-(-4)} \\
&= 2.1 \times 10^{-7+4} \\
&= 2.1 \times 10^{-3} \\
&= 0.0021
\end{aligned}
$$

Multiplication and division involving very large or very small numbers can be performed by first converting each number to scientific notation.

EXAMPLE 7   Using Scientific Notation to Multiply

Multiply $0.00064 \times 9{,}400{,}000{,}000$. Express the product in a. scientific notation and b. decimal notation.

Solution

a. $0.00064 \times 9{,}400{,}000{,}000$

$$
\begin{aligned}
&= 6.4 \times 10^{-4} \times 9.4 \times 10^9 &&\text{Write each number in scientific notation.} \\
&= (6.4 \times 9.4) \times (10^{-4} \times 10^9) &&\text{Rearrange factors.} \\
&= 60.16 \times 10^5 &&\text{Add the exponents.} \\
&= 6.016 \times 10 \times 10^5 &&\text{Express 60.16 in scientific notation.} \\
&= 6.016 \times 10^6 &&\text{Add the exponents when multiplying.}
\end{aligned}
$$

b. The answer in decimal notation is obtained by moving the decimal point in 6.016 six places to the right. The product is 6,016,000.

5 Solve applied problems using scientific notation.

Putting Numbers in Perspective

Due to tax cuts and spending increases, the United States began accumulating large deficits in the 1980s. To finance the deficit, the government had borrowed 5.5 trillion as of the end of 1998. The line graph in Figure 5.7 shows the national debt increasing over time.

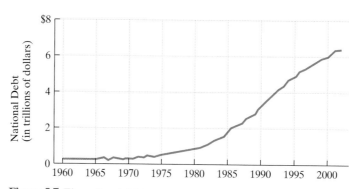

Figure 5.7 The national debt
Source: Office of Management and Budget

Example 8 shows how we can use scientific notation to comprehend the meaning of a number such as 5.5 trillion.

EXAMPLE 8   The National Debt

As of the end of 1998, the national debt was $5.5 trillion, or 5.5×10^{12} dollars. At that time, the U.S. population was approximately 270,000,000 (270 million), or 2.7×10^8. If the national debt were evenly divided among every individual in the United States, how much would each citizen have to pay?

Solution   The amount each citizen must pay is the total debt, 5.5×10^{12} dollars, divided by the number of citizens, 2.7×10^8.

$$\frac{5.5 \times 10^{12}}{2.7 \times 10^8} = \left(\frac{5.5}{2.7}\right) \times \left(\frac{10^{12}}{10^8}\right)$$

$$\approx 2.04 \times 10^{12-8}$$

$$= 2.04 \times 10^4$$

$$= 20,400$$

Every U.S. citizen would have to pay about $20,400 to the federal government to pay off the national debt. A family of three would owe $61,200!

Exercise Set 5.6

 Practice Exercises

In Exercises 1–12, use properties of exponents to simplify each expression. First, express the answer in exponential form. Then, evaluate the expression.

1. $2^2 \cdot 2^3$ 2. $3^3 \cdot 3^2$ 3. $4 \cdot 4^2$ 4. $5 \cdot 5^2$

5. $(2^2)^3$ 6. $(3^3)^2$ 7. $(1^4)^5$ 8. $(1^3)^7$

9. $\dfrac{4^7}{4^5}$ 10. $\dfrac{6^7}{6^5}$ 11. $\dfrac{2^8}{2^4}$ 12. $\dfrac{3^8}{3^4}$

In Exercises 13–24, use the zero and negative exponent rules to simplify each expression.

13. 3^0 14. 9^0 15. $(-3)^0$ 16. $(-9)^0$

17. 2^{-2} 18. 3^{-2} 19. 4^{-3} 20. 2^{-3}

21. 2^{-5} 22. 2^{-6} 23. 4^{-1} 24. 5^{-1}

In Exercises 25–30, use properties of exponents to simplify each expression. First, express the answer in exponential form. Then, evaluate the expression.

25. $3^4 \cdot 3^{-2}$ 26. $2^5 \cdot 2^{-2}$ 27. $3^{-3} \cdot 3$

28. $2^{-3} \cdot 2$ 29. $\dfrac{2^3}{2^7}$ 30. $\dfrac{3^4}{3^7}$

In Exercises 31–46, express the number in decimal notation.

31. 2.7×10^2 32. 4.7×10^3 33. 9.12×10^5

34. 8.14×10^4 35. 8×10^7 36. 7×10^6

37. 1×10^5 38. 1×10^8 39. 7.9×10^{-1}

40. 8.6×10^{-1} 41. 2.15×10^{-2} 42. 3.14×10^{-2}

43. 7.86×10^{-4} 44. 4.63×10^{-5} 45. 3.18×10^{-6}

46. 5.84×10^{-7}

In Exercises 47–60, express the number in scientific notation.

47. 370   48. 530   49. 3600

50. 2700   51. 32,000   52. 64,000

53. 220,000,000   54. 370,000,000,000 55. 0.027

56. 0.014   57. 0.0037   58. 0.00083

59. 0.00000293   60. 0.000000647

In Exercises 61–74, perform the indicated operation and express each answer in decimal notation.

61. $(2 \times 10^3)(3 \times 10^2)$ 62. $(5 \times 10^2)(4 \times 10^4)$

63. $(2 \times 10^9)(3 \times 10^{-5})$ 64. $(4 \times 10^8)(2 \times 10^{-4})$

65. $(4.1 \times 10^2)(3 \times 10^{-4})$ 66. $(1.2 \times 10^3)(2 \times 10^{-5})$

67. $\dfrac{12 \times 10^6}{4 \times 10^2}$ 68. $\dfrac{20 \times 10^{20}}{10 \times 10^{15}}$

69. $\dfrac{15 \times 10^4}{5 \times 10^{-2}}$ 70. $\dfrac{18 \times 10^2}{9 \times 10^{-3}}$

71. $\dfrac{6 \times 10^3}{2 \times 10^5}$ 72. $\dfrac{8 \times 10^4}{2 \times 10^7}$

73. $\dfrac{6.3 \times 10^{-6}}{3 \times 10^{-3}}$ 74. $\dfrac{9.6 \times 10^{-7}}{3 \times 10^{-3}}$

In Exercises 75–84, perform the indicated operation by first expressing each number in scientific notation. Write the answer in scientific notation.

75. $(82,000,000)(3,000,000,000)$

76. $(94,000,000)(6,000,000,000)$

77. $(0.0005)(6,000,000)$

78. $(0.000015)(0.004)$

79. $\dfrac{9,500,000}{500}$ 80. $\dfrac{30,000}{0.0005}$

81. $\dfrac{0.00008}{200}$ 82. $\dfrac{0.0018}{0.0000006}$

83. $\dfrac{480,000,000,000}{0.00012}$ 84. $\dfrac{0.000000096}{16,000}$

 Application Exercises

In Exercises 85–88, rewrite the number in each statement in scientific notation.

85. King Mongut of Siam (the king in the musical *The King and I*) had 9200 wives.

86. The top-selling music album of all time is Michael Jackson's "Thriller," selling 25,000,000 copies.

87. The volume of a bacterium is 0.00000000000000025 cubic meter.

88. Home computers can perform a multiplication in 0.00000000036 second.

In Exercises 89–92, use 10^6 for one million and 10^9 for one billion to rewrite the number in each statement in scientific notation.

89. In 1999, the U.S. government collected $1,694,300 million.

90. In 1999, the U.S. government spent $1,751,800 million.

91. The federal government is expected to provide nearly $60 billion in student aid in 2002.

92. In 1998, U.S. consumers spent $5,493.7 billion.

93. By the year 2000, there will be 66.8 million on-line house-holds around the world.
    a. Express the number of on-line households in scientific notation.
    b. Use the graph shown to write the number of on-line households for Europe in scientific notation.

**World On-line Households
by Region Expected by 2000**

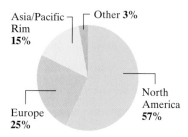

Source: Jupiter Communications

94. If the population of the United States is 2.7×10^8 and each person spends about $120 per year on ice cream, express the total annual spending on ice cream in scientific notation.

95. There are approximately 2×10^4 runners in the New York City Marathon. Each runner runs a distance of 26 miles. Write the total distance covered by all the runners (assuming that each person completes the marathon) in scientific notation.

Writing in Mathematics

96. Explain the product rule for exponents. Use $2^3 \cdot 2^5$ in your explanation.

97. Explain the power rule for exponents. Use $\left(3^2\right)^4$ in your explanation.

98. Explain the quotient rule for exponents. Use $\dfrac{5^8}{5^2}$ in your explanation.

99. Explain the zero exponent rule and give an example.

100. Explain the negative exponent rule and give an example.

101. How do you know if a number is written in scientific notation?

102. Explain how to convert from scientific to decimal notation and give an example.

103. Explain how to convert from decimal to scientific notation and give an example.

104. Suppose you are looking at a number in scientific notation. Describe the size of the number you are looking at if the exponent on ten is a. positive b. negative c. zero.

105. Describe one advantage of expressing a number in scientific notation over decimal notation.

 Critical Thinking Exercises

106. Which one of the following is true?
    a. $4^{-2} < 4^{-3}$
    b. $5^{-2} > 2^{-5}$
    c. $(-2)^4 = 2^{-4}$
    d. $5^2 \cdot 5^{-2} > 2^5 \cdot 2^{-5}$

107. Which one of the following is true?
    a. $534.7 = 5.347 \times 10^3$
    b. $\dfrac{8 \times 10^{30}}{4 \times 10^{-5}} = 2 \times 10^{25}$
    c. $\left(7 \times 10^5\right) + \left(2 \times 10^{-3}\right) = 9 \times 10^2$
    d. $\left(4 \times 10^3\right) + \left(3 \times 10^2\right) = 43 \times 10^2$

108. Give an example of a number where there is no advantage to using scientific notation instead of decimal notation. Explain why this is the case.

109. The mad Dr. Frankenstein has gathered enough bits and pieces (so to speak) for $2^{-1} + 2^{-2}$ of his creature-to-be. Write a fraction that represents the amount of his creature that must still be obtained.

 Technology Exercises

To enter a number in scientific notation into your calculator, you will use the calculator's $\boxed{\text{EXP}}$ *(or* $\boxed{\text{EE}}$ *) key. For example, the expression* $\left(6 \times 10^{23}\right)\left(7 \times 10^8\right)$ *can be entered with the following keystrokes:*

$$6 \boxed{\text{EXP}} 23 \boxed{\times} 7 \boxed{\text{EXP}} 8 \boxed{=}.$$

Use the scientific notation function on your calculator to perform the operations in Exercises 110–112.

110. $\left(4 \times 10^{21}\right)\left(7 \times 10^{18}\right)$ 111. $\left(5.01 \times 10^{33}\right)\left(8.3 \times 10^{24}\right)$

112. $\left(3.024 \times 10^{-9}\right) \div \left(7.1 \times 10^{-51}\right)$

 Group Exercise

113. **The Oddball's Oddball.** In their March 29, 1999 issue on the century's greatest minds, *Time* magazine called Paul Erdös (1913–1996) "the most prolific and arguably the cleverest mathematician of the century." Mathematicians gathered to hear his fascinating ideas about integers, whole numbers, and primes. Erdös solved problems about the nature of numbers, although he could not figure out how to boil an egg or wash his underwear. Speaking of mathematicians in general and Erdös in particular, the writers of *Time* stated, "In a profession with no shortage of oddballs, he was the strangest." Group members should do research on Paul Erdös, presenting a report on his work with numbers and his eccentricities.

SECTION 5.7 *Arithmetic and Geometric Sequences*

Objectives

1. Write terms of an arithmetic sequence.
2. Find a specified term of an arithmetic sequence.
3. Write terms of a geometric sequence.
4. Find a specified term of a geometric sequence.

Fibonacci Numbers on the Piano Keyboard

One Octave

Numbers in the Fibonacci sequence can be found in an octave on the piano keyboard. The octave contains 2 black keys in one cluster, 3 black keys in another cluster, 5 black keys, and a total of 13 keys altogether. The numbers 2, 3, 5, 8, and 13 are the third through seventh terms of the Fibonacci sequence.

Sequences

Many creations in nature involve intricate mathematical designs, including a variety of spirals. For example, the arrangement of the individual florets in the head of a sunflower forms spirals. In some species, there are 21 spirals in the clockwise direction and 34 in the counterclockwise direction. The precise numbers depend on the species of sunflower: 21 and 34, or 34 and 55, or 55 and 89, or even 89 and 144.

This observation becomes even more interesting when we consider a sequence of numbers investigated by Leonardo of Pisa, also known as Fibonacci, an Italian mathematician of the thirteenth century. The *Fibonacci sequence* of numbers is an infinite sequence that begins as follows:

$$1, 1, 2, 3, 5, 8, 13, 21, 34, 55, 89, 144, 233, \ldots.$$

The first two terms are 1. Every term thereafter is the sum of the two preceding terms. For example, the third term (2) is the sum of the first and second terms ($1 + 1 = 2$). The fourth term (3) is the sum of the second and third terms ($1 + 2 = 3$), and so on. Did you know that the number of spirals in a daisy or a sunflower (21 and 34) are two Fibonacci numbers? The number of spirals in a pine cone (8 and 13) and a pineapple (8 and 13) are also Fibonacci numbers.

We can think of a **sequence** as a list of numbers that are related to each other by a rule. The numbers in a sequence are called its **terms**. The letter a with a subscript is used to represent the terms of a sequence. Thus, a_1 represents the first term of the sequence, a_2 represents the second term, a_3 the third term, and so on. This notation is shown for the first six terms of the Fibonacci sequence:

$$1, \qquad 1, \qquad 2, \qquad 3, \qquad 5, \qquad 8$$

$a_1 = 1 \quad a_2 = 1 \quad a_3 = 2 \quad a_4 = 3 \quad a_5 = 5 \quad a_6 = 8$

Arithmetic Sequences

A mathematical formula for the average annual salaries of major league baseball players generates the following data:

Year	1990	1991	1992	1993	1994	1995	1996
Salary	710,000	801,000	892,000	983,000	1,074,000	1,165,000	1,256,000

From 1990 to 1991, salaries increased by $801,000 - $710,000 = $91,000$. From 1991 to 1992, salaries increased by $892,000 - $801,000 = $91,000$. Continuing these computations, there is a yearly salary increase of $91,000. The sequence of annual salaries shows that each term after the first ($710,000) differs from the preceding term by a constant amount, namely $91,000. The sequence of annual salaries

$$710,000, 801,000, 892,000, 983,000, 1,074,000, 1,165,000, 1,256,000$$

is an example of an **arithmetic sequence**.

> **Definition of an Arithmetic Sequence**
>
> An **arithmetic sequence** is a sequence in which each term after the first differs from the preceding term by a constant amount. The difference between consecutive terms is called the **common difference** of the sequence.

The common difference, d, is found by subtracting any term from the term that directly follows it. In the examples shown below, the common difference is found by subtracting the first term from the second term $(a_2 - a_1)$.

Arithmetic sequence	**Common difference**
$710,000, 801,000, 892,000, 983,000, \ldots$	$d = 801,000 - 710,000 = 91,000$
$2, 6, 10, 14, 18, \ldots$	$d = 6 - 2 = 4$
$-9, -6, -3, 0, 3, \ldots$	$d = -6 - (-9) = -6 + 9 = 3$

1 Write terms of an arithmetic sequence.

EXAMPLE 1 Writing the Terms of an Arithmetic Sequence

Write the first six terms of the arithmetic sequence with first term 6 and common difference 4.

Solution The first term is 6. The second term is $6 + 4$, or 10. The third term is $10 + 4$, or 14, and so on. The first six terms are:

$$6, 10, 14, 18, 22, 26.$$

EXAMPLE 2 Writing the Terms of an Arithmetic Sequence

Write the first six terms of the arithmetic sequence with first term 5 and common difference -2.

Solution The first term is 5. To find the second term, we add -2 to 5, giving 3. For the next term, we add -2 to 3, and so on. The first six terms are:

$$5, 3, 1, -1, -3, -5.$$

EXAMPLE 3   Writing the Terms of an Arithmetic Sequence

Write the first six terms of the arithmetic sequence with first term a_1, and common difference d.

Solution   The first term is a_1. The second term is $a_1 + d$. The third term is $a_1 + d + d$ or $a_1 + 2d$. Starting with a_1 and adding d to each successive term, the first six terms are:

$$a_1, a + d, a_1 + 2d, a_1 + 3d, a_1 + 4d, a_1 + 5d.$$

We use the notation a_n to represent the **nth term**, or **general term**, of a sequence. This means that a sequence can be represented as:

$$a_1, a_2, a_3, a_4, \ldots, a_n, \ldots.$$

Using the pattern of the terms in Example 3 results in the following formula for the general or nth term of an arithmetic sequence.

2 Find a specified term of an arithmetic sequence.

General Term of an Arithmetic Sequence

The nth term (the general term) of an arithmetic sequence with first term a_1 and common difference d is:

$$a_n = a_1 + (n - 1)d.$$

EXAMPLE 4   Using the Formula for the General Term of an Arithmetic Sequence

Find the eighth term of the arithmetic sequence whose first term is 4 and whose common difference is -7.

Solution   To find the eighth term, or a_8, we replace n in the formula with 8, a_1 with 4, and d with -7.

$$a_n = a_1 + (n - 1)d$$
$$a_8 = 4 + (8 - 1)(-7)$$
$$= 4 + (7)(-7)$$
$$= 4 + (-49)$$
$$= -45$$

The eighth term is -45. We can check this result by writing the first eight terms of the sequence:

$$4, -3, -10, -17, -24, -31, -38, -45.$$

EXAMPLE 5   Money Spent by U.S. Travelers

According to the U.S. Bureau of Economic Analysis, U.S. travelers spent $12,808 million in other countries in 1984. This amount has increased by approximately $2350 million yearly. How much will U.S. travelers spend in other countries by the year 2000?

Solution We can represent money spent abroad by the following arithmetic sequence:

$$12,808, 15,158, 17,508, \ldots$$

In this sequence a_1, the first term, represents the amount spent in millions of dollars in 1984. Each subsequent year this amount increases by 2350 million dollars, so $d = 2350$. Because $n = 1$ corresponds to 1984, $n = 2$ corresponds to 1985, $n = 3$ corresponds to 1986, and so on. Therefore, $n = 17$ corresponds to the year 2000. We are looking for the 17th term of the arithmetic sequence. Using the formula for the general term of an arithmetic sequence, we obtain:

$$a_n = a_1 + (n - 1)d$$
$$a_{17} = 12,808 + (17 - 1)2350 = 12,808 + 16 \cdot 2350 = 50,408.$$

The 17th term is 50,408. Therefore, U.S. travelers will spend $50,408 million in other countries by the year 2000.

Geometric Sequences

Figure 5.8 shows a sequence in which the number of squares is increasing. From left to right, the number of squares is $1, 5, 25, 125,$ and 625. In this sequence, each term after the first (1) is obtained by multiplying the preceding term by a constant amount, namely 5. This sequence of increasing number of squares is an example of a **geometric sequence**.

Figure 5.8 A geometric sequence of squares

> **Definition of a Geometric Sequence**
>
> A **geometric sequence** is a sequence in which each term after the first is obtained by *multiplying* the preceding term by a fixed nonzero constant. The amount by which we multiply each time is called the **common ratio** of the sequence.

The common ratio, r, is found by dividing any term after the first term by the term that directly precedes it. In the examples below, the common ratio is found by dividing the second term by the first term.

Geometric sequence	Common ratio
$1, 5, 25, 125, 625, \ldots$	$r = \frac{5}{1} = 5$
$4, 8, 16, 32, 64, \ldots$	$r = \frac{8}{4} = 2$
$6, -12, 24, -48, 96, \ldots$	$r = \frac{-12}{6} = -2$
$9, -3, 1, -\frac{1}{3}, \frac{1}{9}, \ldots$	$r = \frac{-3}{9} = -\frac{1}{3}$

3 Write terms of a geometric sequence.

To write out the terms of a geometric sequence when the first term and the common ratio are known, multiply the first term by the common ratio to get the second term, multiply the second term by the common ratio to get the third term, and so on.

EXAMPLE 6 Writing the Terms of a Geometric Sequence

Write the first six terms of the geometric sequence with first term 6 and common ratio $\frac{1}{3}$.

Solution The first term is 6. The second term is $6 \cdot \frac{1}{3}$ or 2. The third term is $2 \cdot \frac{1}{3}$ or $\frac{2}{3}$. The fourth term is $\frac{2}{3} \cdot \frac{1}{3}$ or $\frac{2}{9}$, and so on. The first six terms are:

$$6, 2, \frac{2}{3}, \frac{2}{9}, \frac{2}{27}, \frac{2}{81}.$$

EXAMPLE 7 Writing the Terms of a Geometric Sequence

Write the first six terms of the geometric sequence with first term a_1 and common ratio r.

Solution The first term is a_1. The second term is $a_1 r$. The third term is $a_1 r \cdot r$ or $a_1 r^2$. The fourth term is $a_1 r^2 \cdot r$ or $a_1 r^3$, and so on. The first six terms are:

$$a_1,\ a_1 r,\ a_1 r^2,\ a_1 r^3,\ a_1 r^4,\ a_1 r^5.$$

Using the pattern of the terms in Example 7 results in the following formula for the general or nth term of a geometric sequence.

4 Find a specified term of a geometric sequence.

General Term of a Geometric Sequence

The nth term (the general term) of a geometric sequence with first term a_1 and common ratio r is:

$$a_n = a_1 r^{n-1}.$$

EXAMPLE 8 Using the Formula for the General Term of a Geometric Sequence

Find the eighth term of the geometric sequence whose first term is -4 and whose common ratio is -2.

Solution To find the eighth term, a_8, we replace n in the formula with 8, a_1 with -4, and r with -2.

$$a_n = a_1 r^{n-1}$$
$$a_8 = -4(-2)^{8-1}$$
$$= -4(-2)^7$$
$$= -4(-128)$$
$$= 512$$

Study Tip

Be careful with the order of operations when evaluating $a_1 r^{n-1}$. First find r^{n-1}. Then multiply the result by a_1.

The eighth term is 512. We can check this result by writing the first eight terms of the sequence:

$$-4, 8, -16, 32, -64, 128, -256, 512.$$

EXAMPLE 9 Geometric Population Growth

The population of Florida from 1980 through 1987 is shown below.

Year	1980	1981	1982	1983	1984	1985	1986	1987
Population in millions	9.75	10.03	10.32	10.62	10.93	11.25	11.57	11.91

a. Show that the population is increasing geometrically.
b. Write the general term for the geometric sequence describing population growth for Florida, where $n = 1$ corresponds to 1980.
c. Estimate Florida's population (in millions) for the year 2000.

Geometric Population Growth

Economist Thomas Malthus (1766–1834) predicted that population growth would increase as a geometric sequence and food production would increase as an arithmetic sequence. He concluded that eventually population would exceed food production. If two sequences, one geometric and one arithmetic, are increasing, the geometric sequence will eventually overtake the arithmetic sequence, regardless of any head start that the arithmetic sequence might initially have.

Solution

a. First, we divide the population for each year by the population in the preceding year.

$$\frac{10.03}{9.75} \approx 1.029, \quad \frac{10.32}{10.03} \approx 1.029, \quad \frac{10.62}{10.32} \approx 1.029$$

Continuing in this manner, we will keep getting approximately 1.029. This means that the population is increasing geometrically with $r \approx 1.029$. In this situation, the common ratio is the growth rate, indicating that the population of Florida in any year shown in the table is approximately 1.029 times the population the year before.

b. The sequence of Florida's population growth is:

$$9.75, 10.03, 10.32, 10.62, 10.93, 11.25, 11.57, 11.91, \dots.$$

Because the population is increasing geometrically, we can find the general term of this sequence using

$$a_n = a_1 r^{n-1}.$$

In this sequence, $a_1 = 9.75$ and r [from part (a)] $= 1.029$. We substitute these values into the formula for the general term. This gives the general term for the geometric sequence describing Florida's population.

$$a_n = 9.75(1.029)^{n-1}$$

c. We can use the formula for the general term, a_n, in part (b) to predict Florida's population for the year 2000. Because $n = 1$ corresponds to 1980, $n = 2$ corresponds to 1981, $n = 3$ to 1982, $n = 4$ to 1983, and so on. Therefore, $n = 21$ corresponds to the year 2000. We substitute 21 for n.

$$a_{21} = 9.75(1.029)^{21-1} = 9.75(1.029)^{20} \approx 17.27$$

The formula predicts that Florida will have a population of approximately 17.27 million in the year 2000.

Exercise Set 5.7

 Practice Exercises

In Exercises 1–20, write the first six terms of the arithmetic sequence with the first term, a_1, and common difference, d.

1. $a_1 = 8, d = 2$
2. $a_1 = 5, d = 3$
3. $a_1 = 200, d = 20$
4. $a_1 = 300, d = 50$
5. $a_1 = -7, d = 4$
6. $a_1 = -8, d = 5$
7. $a_1 = -400, d = 300$
8. $a_1 = -500, d = 400$
9. $a_1 = 7, d = -3$
10. $a_1 = 9, d = -5$
11. $a_1 = 200, d = -60$
12. $a_1 = 300, d = -90$
13. $a_1 = \frac{5}{2}, d = \frac{1}{2}$
14. $a_1 = \frac{3}{4}, d = \frac{1}{4}$
15. $a_1 = \frac{3}{2}, d = \frac{1}{4}$
16. $a_1 = \frac{3}{2}, d = -\frac{1}{4}$
17. $a_1 = 4.25, d = 0.3$
18. $a_1 = 6.3, d = 0.25$
19. $a_1 = 4.5, d = -0.75$
20. $a_1 = 3.5, d = -1.75$

In Exercises 21–40, find the indicated term for the arithmetic sequence with first term, a_1, and common difference, d.

21. Find a_6, when $a_1 = 13, d = 4$.
22. Find a_{16}, when $a_1 = 9, d = 2$.
23. Find a_{50}, when $a_1 = 7, d = 5$.
24. Find a_{60}, when $a_1 = 8, d = 6$.
25. Find a_9, when $a_1 = -5, d = 9$.
26. Find a_{10}, when $a_1 = -8, d = 10$.
27. Find a_{200}, when $a_1 = -40, d = 5$.
28. Find a_{150}, when $a_1 = -60, d = 5$.
29. Find a_{10}, when $a_1 = -8, d = 10$.
30. Find a_{11}, when $a_1 = 10, d = -6$.
31. Find a_{60}, when $a_1 = 35, d = -3$.
32. Find a_{70}, when $a_1 = -32, d = 4$.
33. Find a_{12}, when $a_1 = 12, d = -5$.
34. Find a_{20}, when $a_1 = -20, d = -4$.
35. Find a_{90}, when $a_1 = -70, d = -2$.
36. Find a_{80}, when $a_1 = 106, d = -12$.
37. Find a_{12}, when $a_1 = 6, d = \frac{1}{2}$.
38. Find a_{14}, when $a_1 = 8, d = \frac{1}{4}$.
39. Find a_{50}, when $a_1 = 14, d = -0.25$.
40. Find a_{110}, when $a_1 = -12, d = -0.5$.

In Exercises 41–62, write the first six terms of the geometric sequence with the first term, a_1, and common ratio, r.

41. $a_1 = 4, r = 2$
42. $a_1 = 2, r = 3$
43. $a_1 = 1000, r = 1$
44. $a_1 = 5000, r = 1$
45. $a_1 = 3, r = -2$
46. $a_1 = 2, r = -3$
47. $a_1 = 10, r = -4$
48. $a_1 = 20, r = -4$
49. $a_1 = 2000, r = -1$
50. $a_1 = 3000, r = -1$
51. $a_1 = -2, r = -3$
52. $a_1 = -4, r = -2$
53. $a_1 = -6, r = -5$
54. $a_1 = -8, r = -5$
55. $a_1 = \frac{1}{4}, r = 2$
56. $a_1 = \frac{1}{2}, r = 2$
57. $a_1 = \frac{1}{4}, r = \frac{1}{2}$
58. $a_1 = \frac{1}{5}, r = \frac{1}{2}$
59. $a_1 = -\frac{1}{16}, r = -4$
60. $a_1 = -\frac{1}{8}, r = -2$
61. $a_1 = 2, r = 0.1$
62. $a_1 = -1000, r = 0.1$

In Exercises 63–82, find the indicated term for the geometric sequence with first term, a_1, and common ratio, r.

63. Find a_7, when $a_1 = 4, r = 2$.
64. Find a_5, when $a_1 = 4, r = 3$.
65. Find a_{20}, when $a_1 = 2, r = 3$.
66. Find a_{20}, when $a_1 = 2, r = 2$.
67. Find a_{100}, when $a_1 = 50, r = 1$.
68. Find a_{200}, when $a_1 = 60, r = 1$.
69. Find a_7, when $a_1 = 5, r = -2$.
70. Find a_4, when $a_1 = 4, r = -3$.
71. Find a_{30}, when $a_1 = 2, r = -1$.
72. Find a_{40}, when $a_1 = 6, r = -1$.
73. Find a_6, when $a_1 = -2, r = -3$.
74. Find a_5, when $a_1 = -5, r = -2$.
75. Find a_8, when $a_1 = 6, r = \frac{1}{2}$.
76. Find a_8, when $a_1 = 12, r = \frac{1}{2}$.
77. Find a_6, when $a_1 = 18, r = -\frac{1}{3}$.
78. Find a_4, when $a_1 = 9, r = -\frac{1}{3}$.
79. Find a_{40}, when $a_1 = 1000, r = -\frac{1}{2}$.
80. Find a_{30}, when $a_1 = 8000, r = -\frac{1}{2}$.
81. Find a_8, when $a_1 = 1,000,000, r = 0.1$.
82. Find a_8, when $a_1 = 40,000, r = 0.1$.

Determine whether each sequence in Exercises 83–98 is arithmetic or geometric. In each sequence, find the next two terms.

83. $2, 6, 10, 14, \ldots$
84. $3, 8, 13, 18, \ldots$
85. $5, 15, 45, 135, \ldots$
86. $15, 30, 60, 120, \ldots$
87. $-7, -2, 3, 8, \ldots$
88. $-9, -5, -1, 3, \ldots$
89. $3, \frac{3}{2}, \frac{3}{4}, \frac{3}{8}, \ldots$
90. $6, 3, \frac{3}{2}, \frac{3}{4}, \ldots$
91. $\frac{1}{2}, 1, \frac{3}{2}, 2, \ldots$
92. $\frac{2}{3}, 1, \frac{4}{3}, \frac{5}{3}, \ldots$
93. $7, -7, 7, -7, \ldots$
94. $6, -6, 6, -6, \ldots$
95. $7, -7, -21, -35, \ldots$
96. $6, -6, -18, -30, \ldots$
97. $\sqrt{5}, 5, 5\sqrt{5}, 25, \ldots$
98. $\sqrt{3}, 3, 3\sqrt{3}, 9, \ldots$

 Application Exercises

Use the formula for the nth term of an arithmetic sequence to solve Exercises 99–102.

99. According to the U.S. Bureau of Labor Statistics, in 1990 there were 126,424 thousand employees in the United States. This number has increased by approximately 1265 thousand employees each year. How many employees will there be in the United States in the year 2000? (Let $n = 1$ correspond to 1990, so $n = 11$ corresponds to 2000.)

100. According to the National Center for Education Statistics, the total enrollment in U.S. public elementary and secondary schools in 1985 was 39.05 million. Enrollment has increased by approximately 0.45 million each year. Predict total enrollment for the year 2000. (Let $n = 1$ correspond to 1985, so $n = 16$ corresponds to 2000.)

101. According to *Fortune Investor's Guide*, the average annual cost to reside in a nursing home in 1980 was $29,930. Average increases have amounted to $1800 yearly. Predict the average annual cost for the year 2000. (Let $n = 1$ correspond to 1980, so $n = 21$ corresponds to 2000.)

102. Company A pays $12,000 yearly with raises of $800 per year. Company B pays $14,000 yearly with raises of $500 per year. Which company will pay more in year 10? How much more?

Use the formula for the nth term of a geometric sequence to solve Exercises 103–104.

103. Suppose you save $1 the first day of a month, $2 the second day, $4 the third day, and so on. That is, each day you save twice as much as you did the day before.
   a. What will you put aside for savings on the fifteenth day of the month?
   b. What will you put aside for savings on the thirtieth day of the month?

104. *E. coli* is a rod-shaped bacterium approximately 10^{-6} meter long found in the intestinal tracts of humans. The cells of *E. coli* reproduce quite rapidly, as shown in the table.

Initial Population = 100 Bacteria

20-Minute Time Interval	Number of *E. coli* Bacteria
1	200
2	400
3	800
4	1600
5	3200
6	6400

   a. Write the formula for the nth term of the geometric sequence for the number of bacteria:
$$200, 400, 800, 1600, 3200, 6400, \ldots.$$
   b. Use the formula to find the number of bacteria after 8 hours, which is the twenty-fourth time period.

Writing in Mathematics

105. What is a sequence? Give an example with your description.

106. What is an arithmetic sequence? Give an example with your description.

107. What is the common difference in an arithmetic sequence?

108. What is a geometric sequence? Give an example with your description.

109. What is the common ratio in a geometric sequence?

110. If you are given a sequence that is arithmetic or geometric, how can you determine what type of sequence it is?

111. For the first 30 days of a flu outbreak, the number of students on your campus who become ill is increasing. Which is worse: The number of students with the flu is increasing arithmetically or is increasing geometrically? Explain your answer.

Critical Thinking Exercises

112. Which one of the following is true?
   a. The common difference for the arithmetic sequence given by $1, -1, -3, -5, \ldots$ is 2.
   b. The sequence $1, 4, 8, 13, 19, 26, \ldots$ is an arithmetic sequence.
   c. The nth term of an arithmetic sequence whose first term is a_1 and whose common difference is d is $a_n = a_1 + nd$.
   d. If the first term of an arithmetic sequence is 5 and the third term is -3, then the fourth term is -7.

113. Which one of the following is true?
   a. The sequence $2, 6, 24, 120, \ldots$ is an example of a geometric sequence.
   b. Adjacent terms in a geometric sequence have a common difference.
   c. A sequence that is not arithmetic must be geometric.
   d. If a sequence is geometric, we can write as many terms as we want by repeatedly multiplying by the common ratio.

114. A person is investigating two employment opportunities. They both have a beginning salary of $20,000 per year. Company A offers an increase of $1000 per year. Company B offers 5% more than during the preceding year. Which company will pay more in the sixth year?

Technology Exercises

In Exercises 115–116, use your calculator to determine the indicated term for the arithmetic sequence with first term, a_1, and common difference, d.

115. Find a_{327}, when $a_1 = 7721, d = -905$.

116. Find a_{3126}, when $a_1 = -3121, d = 698$.

In Exercises 117–118, use your calculator to determine the indicated term for the geometric sequence with first term, a_1, and common ratio, r.

117. Find a_{32}, when $a_1 = 7721, r = 5$.

118. Find a_{126}, when $a_1 = 196,200, r = 0.925$.

Group Exercise

119. Enough curiosities involving the Fibonacci sequence exist to warrant a flourishing Fibonacci Association. It publishes a quarterly journal. Do some research on the Fibonacci sequence by consulting the research department of your library or the Internet, and find one property that interests you. After doing this research, get together with your group to share these intriguing properties.

CHAPTER SUMMARY, REVIEW, AND TEST

SUMMARY

5.1

Divisibility

a. Natural Numbers: $\mathbf{N} = \{1, 2, 3, 4, 5, \ldots\}$

b. $b\,|\,a$ (b divides a; a is divisible by b) for natural numbers a and b if the operation of dividing a by b leaves a remainder of 0.

c. Rules of divisibility are given in Table 5.1 on page 179.

Prime and Composite Numbers

a. A prime number is a natural number greater than 1 that has only itself and 1 as factors.

b. A composite number is a natural number greater than 1 that is divisible by a number other than itself and 1.

c. The Fundamental Theorem of Arithmetic. Every composite number can be expressed as a product of prime numbers in one and only one way (if the order of the factors is disregarded).

Greatest Common Divisors and Least Common Multiples

a. The greatest common divisor of two or more natural numbers is the largest number that is a divisor (or factor) of all the numbers.

b. The procedure for finding the greatest common divisor is boxed on page 182.

c. The least common multiple of two or more natural numbers is the smallest natural number that is divisible by all of the numbers.

d. The procedure for finding the least common multiple is boxed on page 184.

5.2

Whole Numbers and Integers

a. Whole Numbers $= \{0, 1, 2, 3, 4, 5, \ldots\}$

b. Integers $= \{\ldots, -3, -2, -1, 0, 1, 2, 3, \ldots\}$

The Symbols < and >

a. $a < b$ (a is less than b) means a is to the left of b on a number line.

b. $a > b$ (a is greater than b) means a is to the right of b on a number line.

Absolute Value

a. $|a|$, the absolute value of a, is the distance of a from 0 on a number line.

b. The absolute value of a positive number is the number itself.

c. The absolute value of 0 is 0: $|0| = 0$.

d. The absolute value of a negative number is positive. For example, $|-8| = 8$.

Order of Operations

a. Perform operations in parentheses. Follow the order in b–d listed below.

b. Evaluate all exponential expressions.

c. Do all multiplications and divisions from left to right.

d. Do all additions and subtractions from left to right.

5.3

Rational Numbers

a. The set of rational numbers is the set of all numbers which can be expressed in the form $\frac{a}{b}$, where a and b are integers and b is not equal to 0.

b. Any rational number can be expressed as a decimal. The resulting decimal will either terminate (stop), or it will have a digit that repeats or a block of digits that repeat.

c. The rational number $\frac{a}{b}$ is expressed as a decimal by dividing b into a.

d. To express a terminating decimal as a quotient of integers, the digits to the right of the decimal point are the numerator. The place-value of the last digit to the right of the decimal point is the denominator.

e. To express a repeating decimal as a quotient of integers, use the boxed procedure on page 200.

Operations with Rational Numbers

a. Reduce a rational number to lowest terms by dividing the numerator and denominator by the greatest common divisor.

b. Multiply rational numbers by taking the product of their numerators divided by the product of their denominators.

c. Divide rational numbers by multiplying the first by the second with numerator and denominator reversed.

d. Add or subtract rational numbers with identical denominators by adding or subtracting numerators and putting this result over the common denominator.

e. Add or subtract rational numbers with unlike denominators by first expressing each rational number with the least common denominator and then following part (d) above.

Density of the Rational Numbers

a. Given any two rational numbers, there is always a rational number between them.

b. To find the rational number halfway between two rational numbers, add the rational numbers and divide their sum by 2.

5.4

Irrational Numbers

a. The set of irrational numbers is the set of numbers whose decimal representations are neither terminating nor repeating.

b. Examples of irrational numbers:
$\sqrt{2} \approx 1.414$, $\pi \approx 3.142$

Operations with Square Roots

a. Simplifying square roots: If the radicand contains a perfect square factor, express it as the product of the largest perfect square factor and some other number. Use $\sqrt{ab} = \sqrt{a}\sqrt{b}$. Take the square root of the perfect square factor and leave the other factor under the square root.

b. Multiplying square roots: $\sqrt{a}\sqrt{b} = \sqrt{ab}$. The product of square roots is the square root of the product.

c. Dividing square roots: $\dfrac{\sqrt{a}}{\sqrt{b}} = \sqrt{\dfrac{a}{b}}$. The quotient of the square roots is the square root of the quotient.

d. Adding and subtracting square roots: If the radicals have the same radicand, add or subtract their coefficients. The answer is the sum or difference of the coefficients times the common square root.

e. Rationalizing denominators: Multiply the numerator and denominator by the smallest number that results in a perfect square radicand in the denominator.

5.5

The Real Numbers

a. The set of real numbers is obtained by combining the rational numbers with the irrational numbers.

b. The important subsets of the real numbers are summarized in Table 5.3 on page 214.

c. A diagram representing the relationships among the subsets of the real numbers is given to the left of Table 5.3 on page 214.

Properties of Real Numbers

a. Closure property of addition and multiplication
$a + b$ and $a \cdot b$ are real numbers.

b. Commutative property of addition and multiplication
$a + b = b + a$ $a \cdot b = b \cdot a$

c. Associative property of addition and multiplication
$(a + b) + c = a + (b + c)$ $(a \cdot b) \cdot c = a \cdot (b \cdot c)$

d. Distributive property of multiplication over addition
$a \cdot (b + c) = a \cdot b + a \cdot c$

5.6

Properties of Exponents

a. Product rule: $b^m \cdot b^n = b^{m+n}$

b. Power rule: $(b^m)^n = b^{m \cdot n}$

c. Quotient rule: $\dfrac{b^m}{b^n} = b^{m-n}, b \neq 0$

d. Zero exponent rule: $b^0 = 1, b \neq 0$

e. Negative exponent rule: $b^{-m} = \dfrac{1}{b^m}$

Scientific Notation

a. A number in scientific notation is expressed as a number greater than or equal to 1 and less than 10 multiplied by some power of 10.

b. Changing from Scientific to Decimal Notation
   1. If the exponent is positive, move the decimal point in the number to the right the same number of places as the exponent.
   2. If the exponent is negative, move the decimal point in the number to the left the same number of places as the exponent.

c. Changing from Decimal to Scientific Notation
   1. Move the decimal point in the given number to obtain a number greater than or equal to 1 and less than 10.
   2. The number of places the decimal point moves gives the exponent on 10; the exponent is positive if the given number is greater than 10 and negative if the given number is less than 1.

5.7

Arithmetic Sequence

a. Each term after the first differs from the preceding term by a constant, the common difference. Subtract any term from the term that directly follows to find the common difference.

b. General term or nth term: $a_n = a_1 + (n - 1)d$. The first term is a_1 and the common difference is d.

Geometric Sequence

a. Each term after the first is obtained by multiplying the preceding term by a constant, the common ratio. Divide any term after the first term by the term that directly precedes it to find the common ratio.

b. General term or nth term: $a_n = a_1 r^{n-1}$. The first term is a_1 and the common ratio is r.

REVIEW EXERCISES

5.1

In Exercises 1 and 2, determine if the number is divisible by each of the following numbers: 2, 3, 4, 5, 6, 8, 9, 10, and 12. If you are using a calculator, explain the divisibility shown by your calculator using one of the rules of divisibility.

1. 238,632
2. 421,153,470

In Exercises 3–5, find the prime factorization of each composite number.

3. 705
4. 960
5. 6825

In Exercises 6–8, find the greatest common divisor and the least common multiple of the numbers.

6. 30 and 48
7. 36 and 150
8. 216 and 254

9. For an intramural league, you need to divide 24 men and 60 women into all-male and all-female teams so that each team has the same number of people. What is the largest number of people that can be placed on a team?

10. The media center at a college runs videotapes of two lectures continuously. One videotape runs for 42 minutes and a second runs for 56 minutes. Both videotapes begin at 9:00 A.M. When will the videos of the two lectures begin again at the same time?

5.2

In Exercises 11–12, insert either $<$ or $>$ in the shaded area between the integers to make the statement true.

11. $-93 \quad \blacksquare \quad 17$
12. $-2 \quad \blacksquare \quad -200$

In Exercise 13–15, find the absolute value.

13. $|-860|$
14. $|53|$
15. $|0|$

Perform the indicated operations in Exercises 16–28.

16. $8 + (-11)$
17. $-6 + (-5)$
18. $-7 - 8$
19. $-7 - (-8)$
20. $(-9)(-11)$
21. $5(-3)$
22. $\frac{-36}{-4}$
23. $\frac{20}{-5}$
24. $-40 \div 5 \cdot 2$
25. $-6 + (-2) \cdot 5$
26. $6 - 4(-3 + 2)$
27. $28 \div (2 - 4^2)$
28. $36 - 24 \div 4 \cdot 3 - 1$

5.3

In Exercises 29–31, reduce each rational number to its lowest terms.

29. $\frac{40}{75}$
30. $\frac{36}{150}$
31. $\frac{165}{180}$

In Exercises 32–35, express each rational number as a decimal.

32. $\frac{4}{5}$
33. $\frac{3}{7}$
34. $\frac{5}{8}$
35. $\frac{9}{16}$

In Exercises 36–39, express each terminating decimal as a quotient of integers in its lowest terms.

36. 0.6
37. 0.68
38. 0.588
39. 0.0084

In Exercises 40–42, express each repeating decimal as a quotient of integers in its lowest terms.

40. $0.\overline{5}$
41. $0.\overline{34}$
42. $0.1\overline{13}$

In Exercises 43–49, perform the indicated operations. Where possible, reduce the answer to its lowest terms.

43. $\frac{3}{5} \cdot \frac{7}{10}$
44. $\frac{4}{5} \div \frac{3}{10}$
45. $\frac{2}{9} + \frac{4}{9}$
46. $\frac{7}{9} + \frac{5}{12}$
47. $\frac{3}{4} - \frac{2}{15}$
48. $\frac{1}{3} + \frac{1}{2} \cdot \frac{4}{5}$
49. $\frac{3}{8}\left(\frac{1}{2} + \frac{1}{3}\right)$

In Exercises 50–51, find a rational number halfway between the two numbers in each pair.

50. $\frac{1}{7}$ and $\frac{1}{8}$
51. $\frac{3}{4}$ and $\frac{3}{5}$

52. The gas tank of a car is filled to its capacity. The first day, $\frac{1}{4}$ of the tank's gas is used for travel. The second day, $\frac{1}{3}$ of the tank's original amount of gas is used for travel. What fraction of the tank is filled with gas at the end of the second day?

5.4

In Exercises 53–56, simplify the square root.

53. $\sqrt{28}$
54. $\sqrt{72}$
55. $\sqrt{150}$
56. $\sqrt{300}$

In Exercises 57–65, perform the indicated operation. Simplify the answer when possible.

57. $\sqrt{6} \cdot \sqrt{8}$
58. $\sqrt{10} \cdot \sqrt{5}$
59. $\frac{\sqrt{24}}{\sqrt{2}}$
60. $\frac{\sqrt{27}}{\sqrt{3}}$
61. $\sqrt{5} + 4\sqrt{5}$
62. $7\sqrt{11} - 13\sqrt{11}$
63. $\sqrt{50} + \sqrt{8}$
64. $\sqrt{3} - 6\sqrt{27}$
65. $2\sqrt{18} + 3\sqrt{8}$

In Exercises 66–67, rationalize the denominator.

66. $\frac{30}{\sqrt{5}}$
67. $\sqrt{\frac{2}{3}}$

5.5

68. Consider the set
$$\left\{-17, -\frac{9}{13}, 0, 0.75, \sqrt{2}, \pi, \sqrt{81}\right\}$$
List all numbers from the set that are: a. natural numbers, b. whole numbers, c. integers, d. rational numbers, e. irrational numbers.

69. Give an example of an integer that is not a natural number.

70. Give an example of a rational number that is not an integer.

71. Give an example of a real number that is not a rational number.

In Exercises 72–77, state the name of the property illustrated.

72. $3 + 17 = 17 + 3$

73. $(6 \cdot 3) \cdot 9 = 6 \cdot (3 \cdot 9)$

74. $\sqrt{3}(\sqrt{5} + \sqrt{3}) = \sqrt{15} + 3$

75. $(6 \cdot 9) \cdot 2 = 2 \cdot (6 \cdot 9)$

76. $\sqrt{3}(\sqrt{5} + \sqrt{3}) = (\sqrt{5} + \sqrt{3})\sqrt{3}$

77. $(3 \cdot 7) + (4 \cdot 7) = (4 \cdot 7) + (3 \cdot 7)$

Use two numbers to show that:

78. the natural numbers are not closed with respect to division.

79. the whole numbers are not closed with respect to subtraction.

5.6

In Exercises 80–90, evaluate each expression.

80. $6 \cdot 6^2$

81. $2^3 \cdot 2^3$

82. $(2^2)^2$

83. $(3^3)^2$

84. $\dfrac{5^6}{5^4}$

85. 7^0

86. $(-7)^0$

87. 6^{-3}

88. 2^{-4}

89. $\dfrac{7^4}{7^6}$

90. $3^5 \cdot 3^{-2}$

In Exercises 91–94, express the number in decimal notation.

91. 4.6×10^2

92. 3.74×10^4

93. 2.55×10^{-3}

94. 7.45×10^{-5}

In Exercises 95–98, express the number in scientific notation.

95. 7520   96. 3,590,000   97. 0.00725   98. 0.000000409

In Exercises 99–102, perform the indicated operation and express each answer in decimal notation.

99. $(3 \times 10^7)(1.3 \times 10^{-5})$

100. $(5 \times 10^3)(2.3 \times 10^2)$

101. $\dfrac{6.9 \times 10^3}{3 \times 10^5}$

102. $\dfrac{2.4 \times 10^{-4}}{6 \times 10^{-6}}$

In Exercises 103–106, perform the indicated operation by first expressing each number in scientific notation. Write the answer in scientific notation.

103. $(60,000)(540,000)$

104. $(91,000)(0.0004)$

105. $\dfrac{8,400,000}{4000}$

106. $\dfrac{0.000003}{0.00000006}$

107. If you earned \$1 million per year ($\$10^6$), how long would it take to accumulate \$1 billion dollars ($\$10^9$)?

108. If the population of the United States is 2.7×10^8 and each person spends about \$150 per year going to the movies (or renting movies), express the total annual spending on movies in scientific notation.

5.7

In Exercises 109–111, write the first six terms of the arithmetic sequence with the first term, a_1, and common difference, d.

109. $a_1 = 7, d = 4$

110. $a_1 = -4, d = -5$

111. $a_1 = \frac{3}{2}, d = -\frac{1}{2}$

In Exercises 112–114, find the indicated term for the arithmetic sequence with first term, a_1, and common difference, d.

112. Find a_6, when $a_1 = 5, d = 3$.

113. Find a_{12}, when $a_1 = -8, d = -2$.

114. Find a_{14}, when $a_1 = 14, d = -4$.

In Exercises 115–117, write the first six terms of the geometric sequence with the first term, a_1, and common ratio, r.

115. $a_1 = 3, r = 2$

116. $a_1 = \frac{1}{2}, r = \frac{1}{2}$

117. $a_1 = 16, r = -\frac{1}{2}$

In Exercises 118–120, find the indicated term for the geometric sequence with first term, a_1, and common ratio, r.

118. Find a_4, when $a_1 = 2, r = 3$.

119. Find a_6, when $a_1 = 16, r = \frac{1}{2}$.

120. Find a_5, when $a_1 = -3, r = 2$.

Determine whether each sequence in Exercises 121–124 is arithmetic or geometric. In each sequence, find the next two terms.

121. $4, 9, 14, 19, \ldots$

122. $2, 6, 18, 54, \ldots$

123. $1, \frac{1}{4}, \frac{1}{16}, \frac{1}{64}, \ldots$

124. $0, -7, -14, -21, \ldots$

125. Use the formula for the nth term of an arithmetic sequence to solve this problem. According to the National Center for Education Statistics, in 1985 the average salary for public school teachers in the United States was \$27,966. Average increases have amounted to \$553 yearly. Predict the average salary for public school teachers for the year 2000. (Let $n = 1$ correspond to 1985, so $n = 16$ corresponds to 2000.)

126. A job pays a salary of \$30,000 the first year, with raises of 8% each year. The salaries for the first five years are given by the geometric sequence 30,000, 30,000(1.08), $30,000(1.08)^2$, $30,000(1.08)^3$, $30,000(1.08)^4$, ... Use the formula for the nth term of a geometric sequence to find the salary for year 20.

Group Exercise

127. **Putting Numbers into Perspective**. A large number can be put into perspective by comparing it with another number. For example, we put the $5.5 trillion national debt into perspective by comparing it to the number of U.S. citizens. The total distance covered by all the runners in the New York City Marathon (Exercise 95 in Exercise Set 5.6 on page 228) can be put into perspective by comparing this distance with, say, the distance from New York to San Francisco.

For this project, each group member should consult an almanac, a newspaper, or the World Wide Web to find a number greater than one million. Explain to other members of the group the context in which the large number is used. Express the number in scientific notation. Then put the number into perspective by comparing it with another number.

CHAPTER 5 TEST

1. Which of the numbers 2, 3, 4, 5, 6, 8, 9, 10, and 12 divide 391,248?

2. Find the prime factorization of 252.

3. Find the greatest common divisor and the least common multiple of 48 and 72.

Perform the indicated operations in Exercises 4–6.

4. $-6 - (5 - 12)$ 5. $(-3)(-4) \div (7 - 10)$

6. $(6 - 8)^2(5 - 7)^3$

7. Express $\frac{7}{12}$ as a decimal.

8. Express $0.\overline{64}$ as a quotient of integers in lowest terms.

In Exercises 9–11, perform the indicated operations. Where possible, reduce the answer to its lowest terms.

9. $\left(-\frac{3}{7}\right) \div \left(-\frac{15}{7}\right)$ 10. $\frac{19}{24} - \frac{7}{40}$ 11. $\frac{1}{2} - 8\left(\frac{1}{4} + 1\right)$

12. Find a rational number halfway between $\frac{1}{2}$ and $\frac{2}{3}$.

13. Multiply and simplify: $\sqrt{10} \cdot \sqrt{5}$.

14. Add: $\sqrt{50} + \sqrt{32}$.

15. Rationalize the denominator: $\dfrac{6}{\sqrt{2}}$.

16. List all the rational numbers in this set.

$$\left\{-7, -\tfrac{4}{5}, 0, 0.25, \sqrt{3}, \sqrt{4}, \tfrac{22}{7}, \pi\right\}$$

In Exercises 17–18, state the name of the property illustrated.

17. $3(2 + 5) = 3(5 + 2)$ 18. $6(7 + 4) = 6 \cdot 7 + 6 \cdot 4$

In Exercises 19–21, evaluate each expression.

19. $3^3 \cdot 3^2$ 20. $\dfrac{4^6}{4^3}$ 21. 8^{-2}

22. Multiply and express the answer in decimal notation.
$$\left(3 \times 10^8\right)\left(2.5 \times 10^{-5}\right)$$

23. Divide by first expressing each number in scientific notation. Write the answer in scientific notation.
$$\dfrac{49,000}{0.007}$$

24. Write the first six terms of the arithmetic sequence with first term, a_1, and common difference, d.
$$a_1 = 1, d = -5$$

25. Find a_9, the ninth term of the arithmetic sequence with the first term a_1, and common difference, d.
$$a_1 = -2, d = 3$$

26. Write the first six terms of the geometric sequence with first term, a_1, and common ratio, r.
$$a_1 = 16, r = \tfrac{1}{2}$$

27. Find a_7, the seventh term of the geometric sequence with the first term, a_1, and common ratio, r.
$$a_1 = 5, r = 2$$

Sitting in the biology department office, you overhear two of the professors discussing the possible adult heights of their respective children. Looking at the blackboard that they've been writing on, you see that there are formulas that can estimate the height a child will attain as an adult. If the child is x years old and h inches tall, that child's adult height, H, in inches, is approximated by one of the following formulas.

Girls: $$H = \frac{h}{0.00028x^3 - 0.0071x^2 + 0.0926x + 0.3524}$$

Boys: $$H = \frac{h}{0.00011x^3 - 0.0032x^2 + 0.0604x + 0.3796}$$

6 Algebra: Equations and Inequalities

When you encounter formulas with symbols such as those that appear in the estimation of a child's adult height, don't panic! You are already familiar with many symbols—the smiley face, the peace symbol, the heart symbol, the dollar sign, and even symbols on your calculator or computer. At one point in time, all of these symbols were unfamiliar to you, although it may be hard to remember when that was. In this chapter, you will become familiar with the special symbolic notation of algebra. As you look at the symbols in formulas, we will show you how to take one symbol at a time and ask yourself, "What does this mean?" You will see that the special language of algebra describes your world and holds the power to solve many of its problems.

SECTION 6.1   *Algebraic Expressions and Formulas*

Objectives

1. Evaluate algebraic expressions.
2. Understand the vocabulary of algebraic expressions.
3. Simplify algebraic expressions.
4. Evaluate formulas.

Algebraic Expressions

Feeling attractive with a suntan that gives you a "healthy glow?" Think again. Direct sunlight is known to promote skin cancer. Although sunscreens protect you from burning, skin doctors are concerned with the long-term damage that results from the sun even without sunburn.

Algebra uses letters, such as x and y, to represent numbers. Such letters are called **variables**. For example, we can let x represent the number of minutes that a person can stay in the sun without burning with no sunscreen. With a number 6 sunscreen, exposure time without burning is six times as long, or 6 times x. This can be written $6 \cdot x$, but it is usually expressed as $6x$. Placing a number and a letter next to one another indicates multiplication.

Notice that $6x$ combines the number 6 and the variable x using the operation of multiplication. A combination of variables and numbers using the operations of addition, subtraction, multiplication, or division, as well as powers or roots, is called an **algebraic expression**. Here are some examples of algebraic expressions:

$$x + 6, \ x - 6, \ 6x, \ \frac{x}{6}, \ 3x + 5, \ \sqrt{x} + 7.$$

1 Evaluate algebraic expressions.

Evaluating Algebraic Expressions and Using the Order of Operations

Evaluating an algebraic expression means to find the value of the expression for a given value of the variable. For example, we can evaluate $6x$ (from the sunscreen example) when $x = 15$. We substitute 15 for x. We obtain $6 \cdot 15$, or 90. This means if you can stay in the sun for 15 minutes without burning when you don't put on any lotion, then with a number 6 lotion, you can "cook" for 90 minutes with no visible damage.

Many algebraic expressions contain more than one operation. Evaluating an algebraic expression correctly involves carefully applying the order of operations agreement that we studied in Chapter 5. This agreement is summarized on the top of the next page.

Order of Operations

1. Perform operations within parentheses or other grouping symbols following steps 2 to 4.
2. Evaluate all exponential expressions.
3. Do all multiplications and divisions from left to right.
4. Do all additions and subtractions from left to right.

EXAMPLE 1   Evaluating an Algebraic Expression

Evaluate $7x + 5$ for $x = 10$.

Solution   We substitute 10 for x and carry out the multiplication and addition.

$$7x + 5 \qquad \text{This is the given algebraic expression.}$$
$$= 7 \cdot 10 + 5 \quad \text{Substitute 10 for x.}$$
$$= 70 + 5 \quad \text{Multiply: } 7 \cdot 10 = 70.$$
$$= 75 \quad \text{Add.}$$

EXAMPLE 2   Evaluating an Algebraic Expression

Evaluate $x^2 + 5x - 3$ for $x = 6$.

Solution   We substitute 6 for each of the two occurrences of x. Then we use the order of operations to evaluate the algebraic expression.

$$x^2 + 5x - 3 \qquad \text{This is the given algebraic expression.}$$
$$= 6^2 + 5 \cdot 6 - 3 \quad \text{Substitute 6 for each x.}$$
$$= 36 + 5 \cdot 6 - 3 \quad \text{Evaluate the exponential expression:}$$
$$ 6^2 = 6 \cdot 6 = 36.$$
$$= 36 + 30 - 3 \quad \text{Multiply: } 5 \cdot 6 = 30.$$
$$= 66 - 3 \quad \text{Add and subtract from left to right.}$$
$$ \text{First add: } 36 + 30 = 66.$$
$$= 63 \quad \text{Subtract.}$$

EXAMPLE 3   Evaluating an Algebraic Expression

Evaluate $-2x^2 + 5xy - y^2$ for $x = 4$ and $y = 2$.

Solution   We substitute 4 for each x and 2 for each y. Then we use the order of operations to evaluate the algebraic expression.

$$-2x^2 + 5xy - y^2$$ This is the given algebraic expression.

$$= -2 \cdot 4^2 + 5 \cdot 4 \cdot 2 - 2^2$$ Substitute 4 for x and 2 for y.

$$= -2 \cdot 16 + 5 \cdot 4 \cdot 2 - 4$$ Evaluate the exponential expressions: $4^2 = 4 \cdot 4 = 16$ and $2^2 = 2 \cdot 2 = 4$.

$$= -32 + 40 - 4$$ Multiply: $-2 \cdot 16 = -32$ and $5 \cdot 4 \cdot 2 = 20 \cdot 2 = 40$.

$$= 8 - 4$$ Add and subtract from left to right. First add: $-32 + 40 = 8$.

$$= 4$$ Subtract.

EXAMPLE 4   Evaluating an Algebraic Expression

The algebraic expression $962x + 18{,}667$ describes average yearly earnings in the United States x years after 1990. Evaluate the algebraic expression when $x = 7$. Describe what the answer means in practical terms.

Solution   We begin by substituting 7 for x. Because $x = 7$, we will be finding average weekly earnings 7 years after 1990, or in 1997.

$$962x + 18{,}667$$ This is the given algebraic expression.

$$= 962 \cdot 7 + 18{,}667$$ Substitute 7 for x.

$$= 6734 + 18{,}667$$ Multiply: $962 \cdot 7 = 6734$.

$$= 25{,}401$$ Add.

This means that 7 years after 1990, or in 1997, American workers earned an average of $25,401.

2 Understand the vocabulary of algebraic expressions.

The Vocabulary of Algebraic Expressions

We have seen that an algebraic expression combines numbers and variables. Here is another example of an algebraic expression:

$$7x - 9y - 3.$$

The **terms** of an algebraic expression are those parts that are separated by addition. For example, we can rewrite $7x - 9y - 3$ as:

$$7x + (-9y) + (-3).$$

This expression contains three terms, namely $7x$, $-9y$, and -3.

The numerical part of a term is called its **numerical coefficient**. In the term $7x$, the 7 is the numerical coefficient. In the term $-9y$, the -9 is the numerical coefficient.

A term that consists of just a number is called a **constant term**. The constant term of $7x - 9y - 3$ is -3.

Like terms are terms that have the same variables with the same exponents on the variables. Here are some examples of like terms.

$7x$ and $3x$ These terms have the same variable, x.

$4y$ and $9y$ These terms have the same variable, y.

$5x^2$ and $-3x^2$ These terms have the same variable with the same exponent, x^2.

Constant terms are like terms. Thus, the constant terms 7 and -12 are like terms.

3 Simplify algebraic expressions.

Simplifying Algebraic Expressions

The properties of real numbers that we discussed in Chapter 5 can be applied to algebraic expressions.

Properties of Real Numbers

Property	Example
Commutative Property of addition $a + b = b + a$	$4192 + 30.5x^2 = 30.5x^2 + 4192$
Commutative Property of multiplication $ab = ba$	$x \cdot 6 = 6x$
Associative Property of addition $(a + b) + c = a + (b + c)$	$3 + (8 + x) = (3 + 8) + x = 11 + x$
Associative Property of multiplication $(ab)c = a(bc)$	$-2(3x) = (-2 \cdot 3)x = -6x$
Distributive Property $a(b + c) = ab + ac$	$5(3x + 7) = 5 \cdot 3x + 5 \cdot 7 = 15x + 35$
$a(b - c) = ab - ac$	$4(2x - 5) = 4 \cdot 2x - 4 \cdot 5 = 8x - 20$

The distributive property can be used to rewrite some algebraic expressions without parentheses.

EXAMPLE 5 Applying the Distributive Property

The optimum heart rate is the rate that a person should achieve during exercise for the exercise to be most beneficial. The algebraic expression

$$0.6(220 - a)$$

describes a person's optimum heart rate in beats per minute, where a represents the age of the person in years.

 a. Use the distributive property to rewrite the algebraic expression without parentheses.
 b. Use each form of the algebraic expression to determine the optimum heart rate for a 20-year-old runner.

Solution

a. $0.6(220 - a) = 0.6(220) - 0.6a$ Use the distributive property to remove parentheses.

$= 132 - 0.6a$ Multiply: $0.6(220) = 132$.

 b. To determine the optimum heart rate for a 20-year-old runner, substitute 20 for a in each form of the algebraic expression.

Using 0.6(220 − a):

$0.6(220 − 20)$

$= 0.6(200)$

$= 120$

Using 132 − 0.6a:

$132 − 0.6(20)$

$= 132 − 12$

$= 120$

Both forms of the algebraic expression indicate that the optimum heart rate for a 20-year-old runner is 120 beats per minute.

The distributive property (in reverse) can also be used to combine like terms such as $7x$ and $3x$:

$$7x + 3x = (7 + 3)x = 10x.$$

When combining like terms, you may find yourself leaving out the details of the distributive property and simply writing:

$$7x + 3x = 10x.$$

It might be useful to think along these lines: Seven things plus three of the (same) things give ten of those things. To add like terms, add the numerical coefficients and copy the common variable.

EXAMPLE 6   Combining Like Terms

Combine like terms in each expression.

a. $12y + 9y$ 　　　　b. $8x − 10x$ 　　　　c. $x + 7x$ 　　　　d. $3x^2 − 7x^2$

Solution

a. $12y + 9y = (12 + 9)y = 21y$

b. $8x − 10x = (8 − 10)x = −2x$

c. $x + 7x = 1x + 7x = (1 + 7)x = 8x$

d. $3x^2 − 7x^2 = (3 − 7)x^2 = −4x^2$

> **Study Tip**
>
> You can work each part of Example 6 without writing the middle step. Add or subtract the numerical coefficients of the terms. Use this result as the numerical coefficient of the terms' common variable.

When an expression contains three or more terms, use the commutative and associative properties to group like terms. Then combine the like terms.

EXAMPLE 7   Grouping and Combining Like Terms

Group and combine like terms in each expression.

a. $7x + 5 + 3x + 8$ 　　　　　　　　b. $4x + 7y + 11 − 2x − 9y − 3$

Solution

a. The like terms are $7x$ and $3x$, as well as 5 and 8. Group the like terms and then combine them.

$$7x + 5 + 3x + 8$$

$$= \underbrace{7x + 3x} + \underbrace{5 + 8}$$

$$= \quad 10x \quad + \quad 13$$

b. The pairs of like terms are $4x$ and $-2x$, $7y$ and $-9y$, and 11 and -3. Group the like terms and then combine them.

$$4x + 7y + 11 - 2x - 9y - 3$$
$$= \underbrace{4x - 2x}_{2x} + \underbrace{7y - 9y}_{-2y} + \underbrace{11 - 3}_{+8}$$

An algebraic expression is **simplified** when parentheses have been removed and like terms have been combined.

EXAMPLE 8   Simplifying an Algebraic Expression

Simplify: $5(3x - 7) - 6x$.

Solution

$$\overbrace{5(3x - 7)} - 6x$$

$= 5 \cdot 3x - 5 \cdot 7 - 6x$ Use the distributive property to remove the parentheses.

$= 15x - 35 - 6x$ Multiply.

$= (15x - 6x) - 35$ Group like terms.

$= 9x - 35$ Combine like terms.

4 Evaluate formulas.

Formulas

One aim of algebra is to provide a compact, symbolic description of the world. These descriptions involve the use of **formulas**, statements of equality expressing a relationship among two or more variables. For example, crickets chirp faster as the temperature rises. You can calculate the temperature by counting the number of times a cricket chirps per minute and applying the following formula:

$$T = 0.3n + 40$$

Einstein's Famous Formula: $E = mc^2$

One of the most famous formulas in the world is $E = mc^2$, formulated by Albert Einstein. Einstein showed that any form of energy has mass and that mass itself is a form of energy. In this formula, E represents energy in ergs, m represents mass in grams, and c represents the speed of light. Because light travels at 30 billion centimeters per second, the formula indicates that 1 gram of mass will produce 900 billion ergs of energy.

Einstein's formula implies that the mass of a golf ball could provide the daily energy needs of the metropolitan Boston area. Mass and energy are equivalent, and the transformation of even a tiny amount of mass releases an enormous amount of energy. If this energy is released suddenly, a destructive force is unleashed, as in an atom bomb. When the release is gradual and controlled, the energy can be used to generate power.

The theoretical results implied by Einstein's formula $E = mc^2$ have not been realized because scientists have not yet developed a way of converting a mass completely to energy.

In the formula, T is the temperature in degrees Fahrenheit and n is the number of cricket chirps per minute. We can use this formula to determine the temperature if you are sitting on your porch and count 80 chirps per minute. Here is how to do so.

$$T = 0.3n + 40 \qquad \text{This is the given formula.}$$
$$T = 0.3(80) + 40 \qquad \text{Substitute 80 for } n.$$
$$T = 24 + 40 \qquad \text{Multiply: } 0.3(80) = 24.$$
$$T = 64 \qquad \text{Add.}$$

When there are 80 cricket chirps per minute, the temperature is 64 degrees.

Formulas express relationships between quantities. People use formulas in almost all academic disciplines, as well as in everyday life. For example, there are formulas that estimate what height H a child who is x years old and is h inches tall will attain as an adult. The formulas for girls and boys are:

Girls: $\qquad H = \dfrac{h}{0.00028x^3 - 0.0071x^2 + 0.0926x + 0.3524}$

Boys: $\qquad H = \dfrac{h}{0.00011x^3 - 0.0032x^2 + 0.0604x + 0.3796}.$

In both formulas, H represents adult height in inches.

EXAMPLE 9   A Person's Actual Pay and the Feeling of Being Underpaid

Research shows that as income rises, people shift from comparing their income to what they need to "get along" to what they require to "get ahead." The formula

$$U = 0.018S^2 - 0.757S + 9.047$$

describes the amount that people feel they are underpaid (U, in thousands of dollars) in terms of their salary S (also expressed in thousands of dollars). If a person earns \$40,000 yearly, by how much does that person feel underpaid?

Solution

$U = 0.018S^2 - 0.757S + 9.047$ — This is the given formula.

$U = 0.018(40)^2 - 0.757(40) + 9.047$ — We are given that the salary is 40 thousand dollars. Because salary S is expressed in thousands of dollars, replace S by 40.

$U = 0.018(1600) - 0.757(40) + 9.047$ — Evaluate the exponential expression: $40^2 = (40)(40) = 1600.$

$U = 28.8 - 30.28 + 9.047$ — Multiply from left to right: $(0.018)(1600) = 28.8$ and $(0.757)(40) = 30.28.$

$U = 28.8 + (-30.28) + 9.047$ — Express subtraction as addition of an additive inverse.

$U = -1.48 + 9.047$ — Add from left to right: $28.8 + (-30.28) = -1.48.$

$U = 7.567$ — Remember that U, the amount one feels underpaid, is in thousands of dollars.

Thus, a person earning \$40,000 yearly feels underpaid by 7.567 thousand dollars = \$7.567 $\times$ 1000 = \$7567.

Study Tip

For the sum

$$28.8 + (-30.28) + 9.047$$

you can also first add the positive numbers

$$28.8 + 9.047 = 37.847$$

and then add the negative number to that result:

$$37.847 + (-30.28) = 7.567.$$

Exercise Set 6.1

✓ Practice Exercises

In Exercises 1–30, evaluate the algebraic expression for the given value or values of the variables.

1. $5x + 7$; $x = 4$
2. $9x + 6$; $x = 5$
3. $-7x - 5$; $x = -4$
4. $-6x - 13$; $x = -3$
5. $x^2 + 4$; $x = 5$
6. $x^2 + 9$; $x = 3$
7. $x^2 - 6$; $x = -2$
8. $x^2 - 11$; $x = -3$
9. $x^2 + 4x$; $x = 10$
10. $x^2 + 6x$; $x = 9$
11. $8x^2 + 17$; $x = 5$
12. $7x^2 + 25$; $x = 3$
13. $x^2 - 5x$; $x = -11$
14. $x^2 - 8x$; $x = -5$
15. $x^2 + 5x - 6$; $x = 4$
16. $x^2 + 7x - 4$; $x = 6$
17. $2x^2 - 5x - 6$; $x = -3$
18. $3x^2 - 4x - 9$; $x = -5$
19. $-5x^2 - 4x - 11$; $x = -1$
20. $-6x^2 - 11x - 17$; $x = -2$
21. $4xy$; $x = -3, y = -1$
22. $6xy$; $x = -4, y = -1$
23. $x^2 - 4xy + y^2$; $x = -1, y = -3$
24. $x^2 - 6xy + y^2$; $x = -2, y = -1$
25. $3x^2 + 2xy + 5y^2$; $x = 2, y = 3$
26. $4x^2 + 3xy + 2y^2$; $x = 3, y = 2$
27. $-x^2 - 4xy + 3y^2$; $x = -1, y = -2$
28. $-x^2 - 3xy + 4y^2$; $x = -3, y = -1$
29. $x^3 - 5x^2 + 2$; $x = -4$
30. $x^3 - 4x^2 + 3$; $x = -5$

In Exercises 31–46, use the distributive property to rewrite each expression without parentheses.

31. $3(x + 5)$
32. $4(x + 6)$
33. $8(2x + 3)$
34. $9(2x + 5)$
35. $\frac{1}{3}(12 + 6r)$
36. $\frac{1}{4}(12 + 8r)$
37. $5(x + y)$
38. $7(x + y)$
39. $3(x - 2)$
40. $4(x - 5)$
41. $2(4x - 5)$
42. $6(3x - 2)$
43. $-4(2x - 3)$
44. $-3(4x - 5)$
45. $-3(-2x + 4)$
46. $-4(-3x + 2)$

In Exercises 47–72, simplify each algebraic expression.

47. $7x + 10x$
48. $5x + 13x$
49. $11x - 3x$
50. $14x - 5x$
51. $x + 9x$
52. $x + 12x$
53. $5y - 7y$
54. $8y - 11y$
55. $-5y + y$
56. $-6y + y$
57. $2x^2 + 5x^2$
58. $4x^2 + 6x^2$
59. $5x^2 - 8x^2$
60. $7x^2 - 10x^2$
61. $5x - 3 + 6x$
62. $8x - 7 + 10x$
63. $11y + 12 - 3y - 2$
64. $13y + 15 - 2y - 11$
65. $3x + 10y + 12 + 7x - 2y - 14$
66. $5x + 7y + 13 - 2x - 3y - 15$

67. $5(3x + 4) - 4$
68. $2(5x + 4) - 3$
69. $5(3x - 2) + 12x$
70. $2(5x - 1) + 14x$
71. $7(3y - 5) + 2(4y + 3)$
72. $4(2y - 6) + 3(5y + 10)$

⭐ Application Exercises

73. Suppose you can stay in the sun for x minutes without burning when you don't put on any lotion. The algebraic expression $15x$ describes how long you can tan without burning with a number 15 lotion. Evaluate the algebraic expression when $x = 20$. Describe what the answer means in practical terms.

74. Suppose that the cost of an item, excluding tax, is x dollars. The algebraic expression $0.06x$ describes the sales tax on that item. Evaluate the algebraic expression when $x = 400$. Describe what the answer means in practical terms.

75. The algebraic expression $1527x + 31,290$ describes average yearly earnings for elementary and secondary teachers in the United States x years after 1990. Evaluate the algebraic expression when $x = 10$. Describe what the answer means in practical terms.

76. The algebraic expression $3,184,000x + 48,264,000$ describes the number of cable television subscribers in the United States x years after 1990. Evaluate the algebraic expression when $x = 10$. Describe what the answer means in practical terms.

77. The fuel efficiency of a car can be described in terms of the number of cylinders in its engine. The formula $m = -2.5c + 44$ describes the number of miles per gallon, m, that a car with c cylinders gets in highway driving.
    a. Use the formula to find the number of miles per gallon in highway driving for a car engine with 4 cylinders, a car engine with 6 cylinders, and a car engine with 8 cylinders.
    b. Describe what happens to the number of miles per gallon as the number of cylinders increases by 2.

78. Comedian David Letterman has been known to drop watermelons out of windows and watch them fall. Letterman drops a melon from a window that is 200 feet high. The formula $h = -16t^2 + 200$ describes the height of the watermelon in feet above the ground, h, after t seconds. How far above the ground is the watermelon when it has been falling for 3 seconds?

79. In Silicon Valley, California, a government agency ordered computer-related companies to contribute to a monetary pool to clean up underground water supplies. (The companies had stored toxic chemicals in leaking underground containers.) The required monetary pool M (in millions of dollars) depends on the percent of the contaminant removed, given by the formula

$$M = \frac{2x}{1 - x},$$

where x is the percentage of the total contaminant removed, expressed as a decimal. Complete the following table.

Percentage of Contaminant Removed	Required Amount of Money in Monetary Pool
50% (Let $x = 0.5$.)	$2 million
60% (Let $x = 0.6$.)	$3 million
70% (Let $x = 0.7$.)	
80%	
90%	
95%	
99%	

What happens to the cost of the cleanup as the desired percentage of contaminant removed gets closer and closer to 100%?

Writing in Mathematics

80. What is an algebraic expression? Provide an example with your description.

81. What does it mean to evaluate an algebraic expression? Provide an example with your description.

82. What is a term? Provide an example with your description.

83. What are like terms? Provide an example with your description.

84. Explain how to add like terms. Give an example.

85. What does it mean to simplify an algebraic expression?

86. An algebra student incorrectly used the distributive property and wrote $3(5x + 7) = 15x + 7$. If you were that student's teacher, what would you say to help the student avoid this kind of error?

Critical Thinking Exercises

87. Which of the following is true?
   a. The term x has no numerical coefficient.
   b. $5 + 3(x - 4) = 8(x - 4) = 8x - 32$
   c. $-x - x = -x + (-x) = 0$
   d. $x - 0.02(x + 200) = 0.98x - 4$

88. Which one of the following is true?
   a. $3 + 7x = 10x$
   b. $b \cdot b = 2b$
   c. $(3y - 4) - (8y - 1) = -5y - 3$
   d. $-4y + 4 = -4(y + 4)$

89. A business that manufactures small alarm clocks has weekly fixed costs of $5000. The average cost per clock for the business to manufacture x clocks is described by

$$\frac{0.5x + 5000}{x}.$$

   a. Find the average cost when $x = 100, 1000$, and $10,000$.
   b. Like all other businesses, the alarm clock manufacturer must make a profit. To do this, each clock must be sold for at least 50¢ more than what it costs to manufacture. Due to competition from a larger company, the clocks can be sold for $1.50 each and no more. Our small manufacturer can only produce 2000 clocks weekly. Does this business have much of a future? Explain.

90. Write and solve a problem similar to Example 9 on page 250. However, do not use the "feeling-underpaid" formula. Instead, use one of the formulas that estimates the adult height of a child given in the chapter introduction. Make your problem realistic by using the actual height of a child whose age, x, and height in inches, h, you know. A calculator will be helpful.

Technology Exercise

91. Using the table feature in MS Word, create a table with two columns and five rows. This can be done by choosing the "Insert Table…" option in the Table pull-down menu. In the top row, label the columns x and y. In the column with the x in the top row, enter the values 3, 4, 5, and 6 (see figure). Click into the table cell to the right of the 3 and under the y. Enter the formula for 1 plus the product of 2 multiplied by the number in the cell to the left (in this case, 3). To do this, select the "Formula…" option in the table pull-down menu. In the corresponding formula box, type: =SUM (PRODUCT (2, left), 1). Repeat the procedure for the remaining cells in the column under the y. If you change a number in the x column, the corresponding value in the y column can be updated by clicking in the corresponding y-cell with the right mouse button. Then choose the "Update Field" option in the menu that appears.

x	y
3	
4	
5	
6	

Group Exercise

92. By consulting algebra books or liberal arts mathematics books, each group member should find an algebraic formula that he or she finds particularly intriguing. Group members should present these formulas to the entire class and illustrate their use.

SECTION 6.2   *Solving Linear Equations*

Objectives

1. Solve linear equations.
2. Solve linear equations containing fractions.
3. Solve for a variable in an equation or formula.
4. Identify equations with no solution or infinitely many solutions.

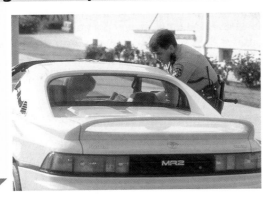

Unfortunately, many of us have been fined for driving over the speed limit. The amount of the fine depends on how fast we are speeding. Suppose that a highway has a speed limit of 60 miles per hour. The amount that speeders are fined, F, is described by the formula

$$F = 10x - 600,$$

where x is the speed in miles per hour. A friend, whom we shall call Leadfoot, borrows your car and returns a few hours later with a $400 speeding fine. Leadfoot is furious, protesting that the car was barely driven over the speed limit. Should you believe Leadfoot?

In order to decide if Leadfoot is telling the truth, use the formula

$$F = 10x - 600.$$

Leadfoot was fined $400, so substitute 400 for F:

$$400 = 10x - 600.$$

Now you need to find the value for x. This variable represents Leadfoot's speed, which resulted in the $400 fine.

The use of algebra in a variety of everyday applications often leads to *equations*. An **equation** consists of two algebraic expressions joined by an equal sign. Thus, $400 = 10x - 600$ is an example of an equation. The equal sign divides the equation into two parts, the left side and the right side:

$$\boxed{400} = \boxed{10x - 600}$$

Left side   Right side

The two sides of an equation can be reversed, so we can express this equation as

$$10x - 600 = 400.$$

The form of this equation is $ax + b = c$, with $a = 10$, $b = -600$, and $c = 400$. Any equation in this form is called a **linear equation in one variable**. The exponent on the variable in such an equation is 1.

In this section, we will study how to solve linear equations. **Solving an equation** is the process of finding the set of numbers that will make the equation a true statement. These numbers are called the **solutions** of the equation, and we say that they **satisfy** the equation. The set of all solutions is called the **solution set** of the equation.

1 Solve linear equations.

Solving Linear Equations

The idea in solving a linear equation is to get the variable (the letter) by itself on one side of the equal sign and a number by itself on the other side. For example, consider the equation $x - 3 = 8$. To get x by itself on the left side, add 3 to the left side, because $x - 3 + 3$ gives $x + 0$, or just x. You must then add 3 to the right side also. By doing this, we are using the **addition property of equality**.

The Addition Property of Equality

The same real number (or algebraic expression) may be added to both sides of an equation without changing the solution set. This can be expressed symbolically as follows:

If $a = b$, then $a + c = b + c$.

EXAMPLE 1   Solving an Equation Using the Addition Property

Solve the equation: $x - 3 = 8$.

Solution

We can isolate the variable x by adding 3 to both sides of the equation.

$$x - 3 = 8 \qquad \text{This is the given equation.}$$
$$x - 3 + 3 = 8 + 3 \qquad \text{Add 3 to both sides.}$$
$$x + 0 = 11 \qquad \text{This step is often done mentally and not listed.}$$
$$x = 11$$

Check.

$$x - 3 = 8 \qquad \text{This is the original equation.}$$
$$11 - 3 \overset{?}{=} 8 \qquad \text{Substitute 11 for x. The question mark over the equal sign indicates that we do not know yet if the statement is true.}$$
$$8 = 8 \qquad \text{This true statement indicates that 11 is the solution.}$$

This verifies that the solution set is $\{11\}$.

A second property used to isolate the variable is the subtraction property.

The Subtraction Property of Equality

The same real number (or algebraic expression) may be subtracted from both sides of an equation without changing the solution set.

If $a = b$, then $a - c = b - c$.

EXAMPLE 2   Solving an Equation Using the Subtraction Property

Solve the equation: $x + 7 = -15$.

Solution   We can isolate the variable x by subtracting 7 from both sides of the equation.

$$x + 7 = -15 \qquad \text{This is the given equation.}$$

$$x + 7 - 7 = -15 - 7 \qquad \text{Subtract 7 from both sides.}$$

$$x = -22$$

By substituting -22 for x in the given equation, we obtain the true statement $-15 = -15$. This verifies that the solution set is $\{-22\}$.

A third property used to isolate the variable is the multiplication property.

The Multiplication Property of Equality

The same nonzero real number (or algebraic expression) may multiply both sides of an equation without changing the solution set.

If $a = b$ and $c \neq 0$, then $ac = bc$.

EXAMPLE 3   Solving an Equation Using the Multiplication Property

Solve the equation: $\dfrac{x}{5} = 9$.

Solution   We can isolate the variable x by multiplying both sides of the equation by 5.

$$\frac{x}{5} = 9 \qquad \text{This is the given equation.}$$

$$5 \cdot \frac{x}{5} = 5 \cdot 9 \qquad \text{Multiply both sides by 5.}$$

$$\frac{5x}{5} = 45 \qquad 5 \cdot \frac{x}{5} = \frac{5}{1} \cdot \frac{x}{5} = \frac{5x}{5}$$

$$1x = 45 \qquad \text{Like the step above, this step is often done mentally and not listed.}$$

$$x = 45$$

By substituting 45 for x in the given equation, we obtain the true statement $9 = 9$. This verifies that the solution set is $\{45\}$.

A fourth property used to isolate the variable is the division property.

The Division Property of Equality

Both sides of an equation may be divided by the same nonzero real number (or algebraic expression) without changing the solution set.

If $a = b$ and $c \neq 0$, then $\dfrac{a}{c} = \dfrac{b}{c}$.

EXAMPLE 4   Solving an Equation Using the Division Property

Solve the equation: $6x = 30$.

Solution We can isolate the variable x by dividing both sides of the equation by 6.

$$6x = 30 \quad \text{This is the given equation.}$$

$$\frac{6x}{6} = \frac{30}{6} \quad \text{Divide both sides by 6.}$$

$$x = 5$$

By substituting 5 for x in the given equation, we obtain the true statement $30 = 30$. This verifies that the solution set is $\{5\}$.

Example 5 illustrates that it is often necessary to use more than one property of equality to solve an equation.

EXAMPLE 5   Solving a Linear Equation (Is Leadfoot Telling the Truth?)

Solve the equation: $10x - 600 = 400$.

Solution Remember that x represents Leadfoot's speed that resulted in the $400 fine. Our goal is to get x by itself on the left side. We do this by getting $10x$ by itself, adding 600 to both sides. Then we isolate x from $10x$ by dividing both sides of the equation by 10.

$$10x - 600 = 400 \quad \text{This is the given equation.}$$

$$10x - 600 + 600 = 400 + 600 \quad \text{Add 600 to both sides.}$$

$$10x = 1000 \quad \text{Combine like terms.}$$

$$\frac{10x}{10} = \frac{1000}{10} \quad \text{Divide both sides by 10.}$$

$$x = 100$$

Can this possibly be correct? Was Leadfoot doing 100 miles per hour in your borrowed car? To find out, check the proposed solution, 100, in the original equation. Check

$$10x - 600 = 400 \quad \text{This is the original equation.}$$

$$10(100) - 600 \stackrel{?}{=} 400 \quad \text{Substitute 100 for x.}$$

$$1000 - 600 \stackrel{?}{=} 400 \quad \text{Multiply: } 10(100) = 1000.$$

$$400 = 400 \quad \text{Subtract: } 1000 - 600 = 400.$$

The true statement $400 = 400$ indicates that 100 is the solution. This verifies that the solution set is $\{100\}$. Leadfoot was doing an outrageous 100 miles per hour, and lied with the claim that your car was barely driven over the speed limit.

Study Tip

If your proposed solution is incorrect, you will get a false statement when you check your answer. For example, 65 is not a solution of $10x - 600 = 400$. Look what happens when we substitute 65 for x:

$$10x - 600 = 400$$
$$10(65) - 600 \stackrel{?}{=} 400$$
$$650 - 600 \stackrel{?}{=} 400$$
$$50 = 400 \text{ False}$$

Study Tip

With increased practice in solving linear equations, try working some steps mentally. For example, consider

$$7x - 8 = -22,$$

the simplified equation, on the right. Add 8 to both sides without listing all the steps:

$$7x = -14.$$

Now, divide both sides by 7:

$$x = -2.$$

EXAMPLE 6   Solving a Linear Equation by First Simplifying

Solve the equation: $2(x - 4) + 5x = -22$.

Solution

$2(x - 4) + 5x = -22$	This is the given equation.
$2x - 8 + 5x = -22$	Apply the distributive property on the left.
$7x - 8 = -22$	Combine like terms on the left.
$7x - 8 + 8 = -22 + 8$	Add 8 to both sides.
$7x = -14$	Combine like terms.
$\dfrac{7x}{7} = \dfrac{-14}{7}$	Divide both sides by 7.
$x = -2$	Simplify.

Check

Check by substituting the proposed solution, -2, into the original equation.

$2(x - 4) + 5x = -22$	This is the original equation.
$2(-2 - 4) + 5(-2) \overset{?}{=} -22$	Substitute -2 for x.
$2(-6) + 5(-2) \overset{?}{=} -22$	Simplify inside parentheses.
$-12 + (-10) \overset{?}{=} -22$	Multiply.
$-22 = -22$	This true statement indicates that -2 is the solution.

The solution set is $\{-2\}$.

Study Tip

You can solve

$$5x - 12 = 8x + 24$$

by collecting x-terms on the right and numbers on the left. To collect x-terms on the right, subtract $5x$ from both sides:

$$5x - 12 - 5x = 8x + 24 - 5x$$
$$-12 = 3x + 24.$$

To collect numbers on the left, subtract 24 from both sides:

$$-12 - 24 = 3x + 24 - 24$$
$$-36 = 3x.$$

Now isolate x by dividing both sides by 3:

$$\dfrac{-36}{3} = \dfrac{3x}{3}$$
$$-12 = x.$$

This is the same solution that we obtained in Example 7.

In Example 7, we solve a linear equation by subtracting the same algebraic expression from both sides.

EXAMPLE 7   Solving a Linear Equation

Solve the equation: $5x - 12 = 8x + 24$.

Solution   As always, our goal is to isolate the variable x. One way to do this is to collect all x-terms on the left and all numbers on the right. This is accomplished by subtracting $8x$ from both sides and adding 12 to both sides. Once this is done, we will have the term $-3x$ on the left. We isolate x by dividing both sides by -3. Here are the details.

$5x - 12 = 8x + 24$	This is the given equation.
$5x - 12 - 8x = 8x + 24 - 8x$	Subtract $8x$ from both sides.
$-3x - 12 = 24$	Simplify.
$-3x - 12 + 12 = 24 + 12$	Collect numbers on the right, adding 12 to both sides.
$-3x = 36$	Simplify.
$\dfrac{-3x}{-3} = \dfrac{36}{-3}$	Isolate x by dividing both sides by -3.
$x = -12$	Simplify.

Now do a check to verify that the solution set is $\{-12\}$.

Let us summarize the major steps involved in solving a linear equation. Not all of these steps are necessary in every equation.

Solving a Linear Equation

1. Simplify the algebraic expression on each side.
2. Collect all the variable terms on one side and all the constant terms on the other side.
3. Isolate the variable and solve.
4. Check the proposed solution in the original equation.

EXAMPLE 8 Solving a Linear Equation

Solve the equation: $2(x - 3) - 17 = 13 - 3(x + 2)$.

Solution

Step 1 Simplify the algebraic expression on each side.

$$2(x - 3) - 17 = 13 - 3(x + 2) \quad \text{This is the given equation.}$$

$$2x - 6 - 17 = 13 - 3x - 6 \quad \text{Use the distributive property.}$$

$$2x - 23 = -3x + 7 \quad \text{Combine numbers.}$$

Step 2 Collect variable terms on one side and constant terms on the other side. We will collect variable terms on the left by adding $3x$ to both sides. We will collect the numbers on the right by adding 23 to both sides.

$$2x - 23 + 3x = -3x + 7 + 3x \quad \text{Add 3x to both sides.}$$

$$5x - 23 = 7 \quad \text{Simplify.}$$

$$5x - 23 + 23 = 7 + 23 \quad \text{Add 23 to both sides.}$$

$$5x = 30 \quad \text{Simplify.}$$

Step 3 Isolate the variable and solve. We isolate the variable x by dividing both sides by 5.

$$\frac{5x}{5} = \frac{30}{5} \quad \text{Divide both sides by 5.}$$

$$x = 6 \quad \text{Simplify.}$$

Step 4 Check the proposed solution in the original equation. Substitute 6 for x in the original equation. You should obtain $-11 = -11$. This true statement verifies that the solution set is $\{6\}$.

2 Solve linear equations containing fractions.

Linear Equations with Fractions

Equations are easier to solve when they do not contain fractions. How do we solve equations involving fractions? We begin by multiplying each term of the equation by the least common denominator, the smallest number that all the denominators will divide into. Example 9 shows how this is done.

The compact, symbolic notation of algebra enables us to use a clear step-by-step method for solving equations, designed to avoid the confusion shown in Carnwath's painting.
Squeak Carnwath, *Equations*, 1981, oil on cotton canvas 96 in. h × 72 in. w.

EXAMPLE 9 Solving a Linear Equation Involving Fractions

Solve the equation: $\dfrac{3x}{2} = \dfrac{x}{5} - \dfrac{39}{5}$.

Solution The denominators are 2, 5, and 5. The smallest number that is divisible by 2, 5, and 5 is 10. We begin by multiplying both sides of the equation by 10, the least common denominator.

$$\dfrac{3x}{2} = \dfrac{x}{5} - \dfrac{39}{5}$$ This is the given equation.

$$10 \cdot \dfrac{3x}{2} = 10\left(\dfrac{x}{5} - \dfrac{39}{5}\right)$$ Multiply both sides by 10.

$$10 \cdot \dfrac{3x}{2} = 10 \cdot \dfrac{x}{5} - 10 \cdot \dfrac{39}{5}$$ Use the distributive property. Be sure to multiply all terms by 10.

$$\left(\dfrac{5 \cdot 2}{1} \cdot \dfrac{3}{2}\right)x = \left(\dfrac{2 \cdot 5}{1} \cdot \dfrac{1}{5}\right)x - \left(\dfrac{2 \cdot 5}{1} \cdot \dfrac{39}{5}\right)$$ Divide out common factors in the multiplication.

$$15x = 2x - 78$$ Complete the multiplication. The fractions are now cleared.

Isolate the variable terms on one side and the constant terms on the other side.

$$15x - 2x = 2x - 2x - 78$$ Subtract 2x to get the x-terms on the left.

$$13x = -78$$ Simplify.

Use the division property to isolate x.

$$\dfrac{13x}{13} = \dfrac{-78}{13}$$ Divide both sides by 13.

$$x = -6$$ Simplify.

Check the proposed solution in the original equation. Substitute -6 for x in the original equation. You should obtain $-9 = -9$. This true statement verifies the solution set is $\{-6\}$.

EXAMPLE 10 An Application: Weight and Height

The formula

$$\dfrac{W}{2} - 3H = 53$$

describes the recommended weight W, in pounds, for a male, where H represents the man's height in inches over 5 feet. What is the recommended weight for a man who is 6 feet, 3 inches tall?

Solution Keep in mind that H represents height in inches *above 5 feet*. A man who is 6 feet, 3 inches tall is 1 foot, 3 inches above 5 feet. Because 12 inches = 1 foot, he is $12 + 3$, or 15 inches, above 5 feet tall. To find his recommended weight, we substitute 15 for H in the formula and solve for W:

$$\frac{W}{2} - 3H = 53 \qquad \text{This is the given formula.}$$

$$\frac{W}{2} - 3 \cdot 15 = 53 \qquad \text{Substitute 15 for } H.$$

$$\frac{W}{2} - 45 = 53 \qquad \text{Multiply: } 3 \cdot 15 = 45.$$

Multiply both sides of the equation by 2, the least common denominator:

$$2\left(\frac{W}{2} - 45\right) = 2 \cdot 53$$

$$2 \cdot \frac{W}{2} - 2 \cdot 45 = 2 \cdot 53 \qquad \text{Use the distributive property.}$$

$$W - 90 = 106 \qquad \text{Multiply: } 2 \cdot \frac{W}{2} = \frac{2}{1} \cdot \frac{W}{2} = \frac{W}{1} = W.$$

$$W - 90 + 90 = 106 + 90 \qquad \text{Add 90 to both sides.}$$

$$W = 196$$

The recommended weight for a man whose height is 6 feet, 3 inches is 196 pounds.

3 Solve for a variable in an equation or formula.

Solving for a Variable in an Equation or Formula

If an equation or formula contains two or more variables, it is often convenient to express one variable in terms of the others. For example, in the next chapter we will be studying graphing and we will need to solve an equation such as $3x + 7y = 14$ for y. This is done by isolating y on one side of the equation. We solve for y using the same properties that we used to solve linear equations in one variable. This procedure is illustrated in Example 11.

EXAMPLE 11   Solving for a Variable in an Equation

Solve the equation $3x + 7y = 14$ for y.

Solution   First, isolate $7y$ on the left by subtracting $3x$ from both sides. Then, isolate y from $7y$ by dividing both sides of the equation by 7.

$$3x + 7y = 14 \qquad \text{This is the given equation.}$$

$$3x - 3x + 7y = -3x + 14 \qquad \text{Subtract } 3x \text{ from both sides.}$$

$$7y = -3x + 14 \qquad \text{Simplify.}$$

$$\frac{7y}{7} = \frac{-3x + 14}{7} \qquad \text{Divide both sides by 7.}$$

$$y = \frac{-3x + 14}{7} \qquad \text{Simplify.}$$

We have now solved for y. We can express the answer by dividing each term in the numerator by 7.

$$y = \frac{-3x}{7} + \frac{14}{7}$$

$$y = -\frac{3}{7}x + 2$$

EXAMPLE 12   Deferred Payment Buying

The total price of an article purchased on a monthly deferred payment plan is described by the following formula:

$$T = D + pm.$$

In this formula, T is the total price, D is the down payment, p is the monthly payment, and m is the number of months one pays. Solve the formula for p.

Solution   First, isolate pm on the right by subtracting D from both sides. Then, isolate p from pm by dividing both sides of the formula by m.

We need to isolate p.

$T = D + pm$	This is the given formula. We want p alone.
$T - D = D - D + pm$	Isolate pm by subtracting D from both sides.
$T - D = pm$	Simplify.
$\dfrac{T - D}{m} = \dfrac{pm}{m}$	Now isolate p by dividing both sides by m.
$\dfrac{T - D}{m} = p$	Simplify: $\dfrac{pm}{m} = \dfrac{p\cancel{m}}{\cancel{m}} = \dfrac{p}{1} = p.$

The formula solved for p is $p = \dfrac{T - D}{m}$.

What does this all-black canvas by artist Ad Reinhardt, entitled *Abstract Painting*, have to do with Example 13? Read the essay on page 262 to discover the connection.
Ad Reinhardt, *Abstract Painting*, 1960–61. Oil on canvas, 60 × 60 in. (152.4 × 152.4 cm). Courtesy of The Museum of Modern Art, New York. Purchase (by exchange). Photograph © 2000 The Museum of Modern Art, New York.

Linear Equations with No Solution and Infinitely Many Solutions

Up to this point we have considered linear equations having exactly one solution. Example 13 illustrates a linear equation that has no solution.

EXAMPLE 13   An Equation with No Solution

4 Identify equations with no solution or infinitely many solutions.

Solve the equation: $-4x - 3(2 - 2x) = 7 + 2x$.

Solution

$-4x - 3(2 - 2x) = 7 + 2x$	This is the given equation.
$-4x - 6 + 6x = 7 + 2x$	Use the distributive property.
$2x - 6 = 7 + 2x$	Combine like terms.
$2x - 6 - 2x = 7 + 2x - 2x$	Subtract 2x from both sides.
$-6 = 7$	This statement is false.

The Empty Set in the Arts

In Example 13, we saw that

$$-4x - 3(2 - 2x) = 7 + 2x$$

has $\varnothing$, the empty set, as its solution. The empty set denotes the notion of nothingness, such as the set of people in an empty room.

Nothingness appears not only in solution sets of equations but also in the arts. John Cage's *4'33"* is musical work written for the piano that requires 4 minutes and 33 seconds of total silence as a musician sits frozen at a piano stool. (Some critics, not impressed with Cage's philosophy that the ultimate order is chaos, rate *4'33"* as his best composition!) In the Gershwin folk opera *Porgy and Bess*, Ira Gershwin wrote, "I've got plenty of nothing." And the painting shown on page 261, a 60" by 60" all-black canvas by the American abstract painter Ad Reinhardt, is a visual depiction of nothingness on permanent display at New York's Museum of Modern Art.

If you obtain a false statement such as $-6 = 7$ in solving an equation, this means that the equation has no solution. The solution set for such an equation contains no elements and is called the empty set, written $\varnothing$.

Our final example illustrates a linear equation that has infinitely many solutions.

EXAMPLE 14 An Equation That Is Satisfied by All Real Numbers

Solve the equation: $3x - 3(2 - x) = 6(x - 1)$.

Solution

$3x - 3(2 - x) = 6(x - 1)$	This is the given equation.
$3x - 6 + 3x = 6x - 6$	Distribute -3 on the left and 6 on the right.
$6x - 6 = 6x - 6$	Combine like terms. Notice that this equation is true for all real numbers.
$6x - 6 - 6x = 6x - 6 - 6x$	Let's see what happens if we continue and subtract 6x from both sides.
$-6 = -6$ ~~Identity~~	

We have a trivial statement of equality in the final step, namely, $-6 = -6$. The left and right sides are equal regardless of what number is substituted for the variable. The solution set consists of the set of all real numbers. Try substituting any number of your choice for x in the original equation. You will obtain a true statement.

Exercise Set 6.2

 Practice Exercises

In Exercises 1–42, solve each equation. Be sure to check your proposed solution by substituting it for the variable in the given equation.

1. $x - 7 = 3$
2. $x - 3 = -17$
3. $x + 5 = -12$
4. $x + 12 = -14$
5. $\dfrac{x}{3} = 4$
6. $\dfrac{x}{5} = 3$
7. $5x = 45$
8. $6x = 18$
9. $8x = -24$
10. $5x = -25$
11. $-8x = 2$
12. $-6x = 3$
13. $5x + 3 = 18$
14. $3x + 8 = 50$
15. $6x - 3 = 63$
16. $5x - 8 = 72$
17. $4x - 14 = -82$
18. $9x - 14 = -77$
19. $14 - 5x = -41$
20. $25 - 6x = -83$
21. $9(5x - 2) = 45$
22. $10(3x + 2) = 70$

23. $5x - (2x - 10) = 35$
24. $11x - (6x - 5) = 40$
25. $3x + 5 = 2x + 13$
26. $2x - 7 = 6 + x$
27. $8x - 2 = 7x - 5$
28. $13x + 14 = -5 + 12x$
29. $7x + 4 = x + 16$
30. $8x + 1 = x + 43$
31. $8y - 3 = 11y + 9$
32. $5y - 2 = 9y + 2$
33. $2(4 - 3x) = 2(2x + 5)$
34. $3(5 - x) = 4(2x + 1)$
35. $8(y + 2) = 2(3y + 4)$
36. $3(3y - 1) = 4(3 + 3y)$
37. $3(x + 1) = 7(x - 2) - 3$
38. $5x - 4(x + 9) = 2x - 3$
39. $5(2x - 8) - 2 = 5(x - 3) + 3$
40. $7(3x - 2) + 5 = 6(2x - 1) + 24$
41. $5(x - 2) - 2(2x + 1) = 2 + 5x$
42. $2(5x + 4) + 3(2x + 11) = 4x - 19$

Solve and check each equation in Exercises 43–50. Begin your work by rewriting each equation without fractions.

43. $\dfrac{x}{3} + \dfrac{x}{2} = \dfrac{5}{6}$

44. $\dfrac{x}{4} - 1 = \dfrac{x}{5}$

45. $\dfrac{x}{2} = 20 - \dfrac{x}{3}$

46. $\dfrac{x}{5} - \dfrac{1}{2} = \dfrac{x}{6}$

47. $\dfrac{3y}{4} - 3 = \dfrac{y}{2} + 2$

48. $y + \dfrac{1}{2} = 1 - \dfrac{y}{3}$

49. $\dfrac{3x}{5} - x = \dfrac{x}{10} - \dfrac{5}{2}$

50. $2x - \dfrac{2x}{7} = \dfrac{x}{2} + \dfrac{17}{2}$

In Exercises 51–60, solve each equation for y.

51. $3x + y = 6$

52. $5x + y = 7$

53. $x + 2y = 6$

54. $x + 4y = 8$

55. $2x + 6y = 12$

56. $3x + 9y = 18$

57. $-2x + 4y = 0$

58. $-3x + 9y = 0$

59. $2x - 3y = 5$

60. $9x - 4y = 7$

In Exercises 61–74, solve each formula for the specified variable. Do you recognize the formula? If so, what does it describe?

61. $A = LW$ for L

62. $D = RT$ for R

63. $A = \frac{1}{2}bh$ for b

64. $V = \frac{1}{3}Bh$ for B

65. $I = Prt$ for P

66. $C = 2\pi r$ for r

67. $E = mc^2$ for m

68. $V = \pi r^2 h$ for h

69. $y = mx + b$ for m

70. $P = C + MC$ for M

71. $A = \frac{1}{2}(a + b)$ for a

72. $A = \frac{1}{2}(a + b)$ for b

73. $S = P + Prt$ for r

74. $S = P + Prt$ for t

For Exercises 75–80, indicate whether each equation has no solution or is true for all real numbers. If neither is the case, solve for the variable.

75. $10x - 2(4 + 5x) = -8$

76. $9x - 3(-5 + 3x) = 15$

77. $10x - 2(4 + 5x) = 8$

78. $9x - 3(-5 + 3x) = -15$

79. $2(3x + 4) - 4 = 9x + 4 - 3x$

80. $3(x - 4) - 5 = -2x + 5x - 9$

 Application Exercises

81. The formula $d = 5000c - 525{,}000$ describes the relationship between the annual number of deaths (d) in the United States from heart disease and the average cholesterol level (c) of blood. (Cholesterol level, c, is expressed in milligrams per deciliter of blood.)

   a. In 1990, 500,000 Americans died from heart disease. Substitute 500,000 for d in the given formula and then solve for c to determine the average cholesterol level in 1990.

   b. Suppose that the average cholesterol level for people in the United States could be reduced to 180. Substi-

tute 180 for c in the given formula and then compute the value for d to determine the number of annual deaths from heart disease with this reduced cholesterol level. Compared to the number of deaths in 1990, how many lives would be saved by this cholesterol reduction?

82. There is a relationship between the vocabulary of a child and its age. The formula $60A - V = 900$ describes this relationship, where A is the age of the child in months and V is the number of words that the child uses. Suppose that a child uses 1500 words. Substitute 1500 for V in the formula to determine the child's age in months.

83. The formula $E = 0.215t + 71.05$ describes the life expectancy, E, for women born in the United States t years after 1950. If a woman has a life expectancy of 77.5 years, how many years after 1950 was she born? What is her birth year with this life expectancy?

84. The formula

$$p = 15 + \frac{15d}{33}$$

describes the pressure of sea water (p, in pounds per square foot) at a depth of d feet below the surface. The record depth for breath-held diving, by Francisco Ferreras (Cuba) off Grand-Bahama Island, on November 14, 1993, involved pressure of 201 pounds per square foot. To what depth did Ferraras descend on this ill-advised venture? (He was underwater for 2 minutes and 9 seconds!)

 Writing in Mathematics

85. What is the solution set of an equation?

86. State the addition property of equality and give an example.

87. State the subtraction property of equality and give an example.

88. State the multiplication property of equality and give an example.

89. State the division property of equality and give an example.

90. How do you know if a linear equation has one solution, no solution, or infinitely many solutions?

91. What is the difference between solving an equation such as $2(y - 4) + 5y = 34$ and simplifying an algebraic expression such as $2(y - 4) + 5y$? It there is a difference, which topic should be taught first? Why?

92. We discussed formulas in this section after we considered procedures for solving linear equations. Does working with formulas simply mean substituting given numbers into a formula and using the order of operations? Is it really necessary to know how to solve equations to work with formulas? Explain.

93. Suppose you were an algebra teacher grading the following solution on an examination:

$$-3(x - 6) = 2 - x$$
$$-3x - 18 = 2 - x$$
$$-2x - 18 = 2$$
$$-2x = -16$$
$$x = 8$$

Try substituting 8 for x in the given equation. Checking shows the solution set is $\{8\}$. The student who worked the problem therefore wants full credit. Can you find any errors in the solution? If full credit is 10 points, how many points should you give the student? Justify your position.

Critical Thinking Exercises

94. Which one of the following is true?
    a. If $3x + 7 = 0$, then $x = \frac{7}{3}$.
    b. Solving $A = LW$ for W gives $W = \dfrac{L}{A}$.
    c. The equation $6x = 0$ has exactly one solution.
    d. The final step in solving $x - b = 6x - c$ for x is $x = 6x - c + b$.

95. Write three equations whose solution set is $\{5\}$.

96. The formula $P = -0.5d + 100$ describes the percentage (P) of lost hikers found in search and rescue missions when members of the search team walk parallel to one another separated by a distance of d yards.

    a. The formula indicates that the chance of lost hikers being found increases as searchers in any area get closer to one another. If this is the case, why not simply have almost no distance separating members of the search team to obtain near certainty of finding the lost hikers?

    b. The formula was determined from actual data collected by search and rescue teams in the desert of the American Southwest. How does this limit the usefulness of the formula?

97. A woman's height (h) is related to the length of the femur (f) (the bone from the knee to the hip socket) by the formula $f = 0.432h - 10.44$. Both h and f are measured in inches. A partial skeleton is found of a woman in which the femur is 16 inches long. Police find the skeleton in an area where a woman slightly over 5 feet tall has been missing for over a year. Can the partial skeleton be that of the missing woman? Explain.

Femur

f in.

h in.

Group Exercise

98. In your group, describe the best procedure for solving an equation like

$$0.47x + \frac{19}{4} = -0.2 + \frac{2}{5}x.$$

Use this procedure to actually solve the equation. Then compare procedures with other groups working on this problem. Which group devised the most streamlined method?

SECTION 6.3   *Applications of Linear Equations*

Objective

1. Solve problems using linear equations.

Problem solving is an important part of algebra. The problems in this book are presented in English. We must *translate* from the ordinary language of English into the language of algebraic equations. To translate, however, we must understand the English prose and be familiar with the forms of algebraic language. Here are some general steps we will follow in solving word problems.

1 Solve problems using linear equations.

Strategy for Solving Word Problems

Step 1   Read the problem and determine the quantities that are involved. Let x (or any variable) represent one of the quantities in the problem.

continued

Step 2   If necessary, write expressions for any other unknown quantities in the problem in terms of x.

Step 3   Write an equation in x that describes the verbal conditions of the problem.

Step 4   Solve the equation written in step 3 and answer the problem's question.

Step 4   Check the solution *in the original wording* of the problem, not in the equation obtained from the words.

Take great care with step 1. Reading a word problem is not the same as reading a newspaper. Reading the problem involves slowly working your way through its parts, making notes on what is given, and perhaps rereading the problem a few times. Only at this point should you let x represent one of the quantities.

The most difficult step in this process is step 3 because it involves translating verbal conditions into an algebraic equation. Translations of some commonly used English phrases are listed in Table 6.1. We choose to use x to represent the variable, but we can use any letter.

Table 6.1   Algebraic Translations of English Phrases

Study Tip

Cover the right column in Table 6.1 with a sheet of paper and attempt to formulate the algebraic expression in the column on your own. Then slide the paper down and check your answer. Work through the entire table in this manner.

English Phrase	Algebraic Expression
Addition	
The sum of a number and 7	$x + 7$
Five more than a number; A number plus 5	$x + 5$
A number increased by 6; 6 added to a number	$x + 6$
Subtraction	
A number minus 4	$x - 4$
A number decreased by 5	$x - 5$
A number subtracted from 8	$8 - x$
The difference between a number and 6	$x - 6$
The difference between 6 and a number	$6 - x$
Seven less than a number	$x - 7$
Seven minus a number	$7 - x$
Nine fewer than a number	$x - 9$
Multiplication	
Five times a number	$5x$
The product of 3 and a number	$3x$
Two-thirds of a number (used with fractions)	$\frac{2}{3}x$
Seventy-five percent of a number (used with decimals)	$0.75x$
Thirteen multiplied by a number	$13x$
A number multiplied by 13	$13x$
Twice a number	$2x$

continued

Table 6.1 *continued* **Algebraic Translations of English Phrases**

English Phrase	Algebraic Expression
Division	
A number divided by 3	$\frac{x}{3}$
The quotient of 7 and a number	$\frac{7}{x}$
The quotient of a number and 7	$\frac{x}{7}$
The reciprocal of a number	$\frac{1}{x}$
More than one operation	
The sum of twice a number and 7	$2x + 7$
Twice the sum of a number and 7	$2(x + 7)$
Three times the sum of 1 and twice a number	$3(1 + 2x)$
Nine subtracted from 8 times a number	$8x - 9$
Twenty-five percent of the sum of 3 times a number and 14	$0.25(3x + 14)$
Seven times a number, increased by 24	$7x + 24$
Seven times the sum of a number and 24	$7(x + 24)$

EXAMPLE 1   Solving a Word Problem

Nine subtracted from eight times a number is 39. Find the number.

Solution

Step 1   Let x represent one of the quantities. Because we are asked to find a number, let

$$x = \text{the number.}$$

Step 2   Represent other quantities in terms of x. There are no other unknown quantities to find, so we can skip this step.

Step 3   Write an equation in x that describes the conditions.

Step 4   Solve the equation and answer the question.

$$8x - 9 = 39 \qquad \text{This is the equation for the problem's conditions.}$$

$$8x - 9 + 9 = 39 + 9 \qquad \text{Add 9 to both sides.}$$

$$8x = 48 \qquad \text{Simplify.}$$

$$\frac{8x}{8} = \frac{48}{8} \qquad \text{Divide both sides by 8.}$$

$$x = 6 \qquad \text{Simplify.}$$

The number is 6.

Step 5 Check the proposed solution in the original wording of the problem.

"Nine subtracted from eight times a number is 39." The proposed number is 6. Eight times 6 is 8 · 6, or 48. Nine subtracted from 48 is 48 − 9, or 39. The proposed solution checks in the problem's wording, verifying that the number is 6.

EXAMPLE 2 Renting a Car

Rent-a-Heap Agency charges $125 per week plus $0.20 per mile to rent a small car. How many miles can you travel for $335?

Solution

Step 1 Let x represent one of the quantities. Because we are asked to find the number of miles we can travel for $335, let

$$x = \text{the number of miles.}$$

Step 2 Represent other quantities in terms of x. There are no other unknown quantities to find, so we can skip this step.

Step 3 Write an equation in x that describes the conditions.
Before writing the equation, let us consider a few specific values for the number of miles traveled. The rental charge is $125 plus $0.20 for each mile.

3 miles: The rental charge is $125 + $0.20(3).

30 miles: The rental charge is $125 + $0.20(30).

100 miles: The rental charge is $125 + $0.20(100).

x miles: The rental charge is $125 + 0.20x$.

The weekly charge of $125	plus	the charge of $0.20 per mile for x miles	equals	the total $335 rental charge.
125	+	0.20x	=	335

Step 4 Solve the equation and answer the question.

$125 + 0.20x = 335$	This is the equation specified by the conditions of the problem.
$125 + 0.20x - 125 = 335 - 125$	Subtract 125 from both sides.
$0.20x = 210$	Simplify.
$\dfrac{0.20x}{0.20} = \dfrac{210}{0.20}$	Divide both sides by 0.20.
$x = 1050$	Simplify.

You can travel 1050 miles for $335.

Step 5 Check the proposed solution in the original wording of the problem. Traveling 1050 miles should result in a total rental charge of $335. The mileage charge of $0.20 per mile is

$$\$0.20(1050) = \$210.$$

Adding this to the $125 weekly charge gives a total rental charge of

$$\$125 + \$210 = \$335.$$

Because this results in the given rental charge of $335, this verifies that you can travel 1050 miles.

EXAMPLE 3   Pet Population

Americans love their pets. The number of cats in the United States exceeds the number of dogs by 7.5 million. The number of cats and dogs combined is 114.7 million. Determine the number of dogs and cats in the United States.

Solution

Step 1 Let x represent one of the quantities. We know something about the number of cats; the cat population exceeds the dog population by 7.5 million. This means that there are 7.5 million more cats than dogs. We will let

$$x = \text{the number (in millions) of dogs in the United States.}$$

Step 2 Represent other quantities in terms of x. The other unknown quantity is the number of cats. Because there are 7.5 million more cats than dogs, let

$$x + 7.5 = \text{the number (in millions) of cats in the United States.}$$

Step 3 Write an equation in x that describes the conditions. The number of cats and dogs combined is 114.7 million.

The number (in millions) of dogs in the U.S.	plus	the number (in millions) of cats in the U.S.	equals	114.7 million.
x	$+$	$x + 7.5$	$=$	114.7

Step 4 Solve the equation and answer the question.

$x + x + 7.5 = 114.7$	This is the equation specified by the conditions of the problem.
$2x + 7.5 = 114.7$	Combine like terms on the left side.
$2x + 7.5 - 7.5 = 114.7 - 7.5$	Subtract 7.5 from both sides.
$2x = 107.2$	Simplify.
$\dfrac{2x}{2} = \dfrac{107.2}{2}$	Divide both sides by 2.
$x = 53.6$	Simplify.

Because x represents the number (in millions) of dogs, there are 53.6 million dogs in the United States. Because $x + 7.5$ represents the number (in millions) of cats, there are 53.6 + 7.5, or 61.1 million cats in the United States.

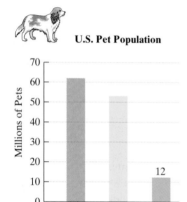

U.S. Pet Population

Millions of Pets

Source: American Veterinary Medical Association

Americans spend more than $21 billion a year on their pets. 31.4% of households have cats and 34.3% have dogs.

Step 5   Check the proposed solution in the original wording of the problem.
The problem states that the number of cats and dogs combined is 114.7 million.
By adding 53.6 million, the dog population, and 61.1 million, the cat population,
we do, indeed, obtain a sum of 114.7 million.

EXAMPLE 4   Solar and Electric Heating Systems

The costs for two different kinds of heating systems for a three-bedroom home
are given below.

System	Cost to Install	Operating Cost/Year
Solar	$29,700	$150
Electric	$5000	$1100

After how many years will total costs for solar heating and electric heating
be the same? What will be the cost at that time?

Solution

Steps 1 and 2   Represent unknown quantities in terms of x. Let x = the number of years where total costs for the two systems will be the same.

Step 3   Write an equation in x that describes the conditions. We begin by writing algebraic expressions for the total costs for the two systems.

Total costs for the solar system	equals	installation cost	plus	yearly operating cost	times	the number of years the system is used.
=		29,700	+	150	·	x

Total costs for the electric system	equals	installation cost	plus	yearly operating cost	times	the number of years the system is used.
=		5000	+	1100	·	x

Because we are interested in the number of years in which total costs for the two
systems will be the same, we set the algebraic expressions for the costs for the two
systems equal to each other.

$$29,700 + 150x \quad = \quad 5000 + 1100x$$

Step 4   Solve the equation and answer the question.

$$29{,}700 + 150x = 5000 + 1100x$$
This is the equation for the problem's conditions.

$$29{,}700 + 150x - 150x = 5000 + 1100x - 150x$$
Subtract 150x from both sides.

$$29{,}700 = 5000 + 950x$$
Simplify.

$$29{,}700 - 5000 = 5000 + 950x - 5000$$
Subtract 5000 from both sides.

$$24{,}700 = 950x$$
Simplify.

$$\frac{24{,}700}{950} = \frac{950x}{950}$$
Divide both sides by 950.

$$26 = x$$
Simplify.

After 26 years the total costs for the two systems will be the same.

Step 5   Check the proposed solution in the original wording of the problem.
The installation cost for the solar system is $29,700 and the yearly operating cost is $150. Thus, the total costs after 26 years are:

$$\$29{,}700 + \$150(26) = \$29{,}700 + \$3900 = \$33{,}600.$$

The installation cost for the electric system is $5000 and the yearly operating cost is $1100. Thus, the total costs after 26 years are:

$$\$5000 + \$1100(26) = \$5000 + \$28{,}600 = \$33{,}600.$$

This verifies that after 26 years the two systems will cost the same amount. The cost for each system at that time will be $33,600.

Exercise Set 6.3

 Practice Exercises

In Exercises 1–14, let x represent the number. Write each English phrase as an algebraic expression.

1. The sum of a number and 9
2. A number increased by 13
3. A number subtracted from 20
4. 13 less than a number
5. 8 decreased by 5 times a number
6. 14 less than the product of 6 and a number
7. The quotient of 15 and a number
8. The quotient of a number and 15
9. The sum of twice a number and 20
10. Twice the sum of a number and 20
11. 30 subtracted from 7 times a number
12. The quotient of 12 and a number, decreased by 3 times the number
13. Four times the sum of a number and 12
14. Five times the difference of a number and 6

In Exercises 15–34, let x represent the number. Use the given conditions to write an equation. Solve the equation and find the number.

15. A number increased by 40 is equal to 450. Find the number.
16. The sum of a number and 29 is 54. Find the number.
17. A number decreased by 13 is equal to 123. Find the number.
18. The difference between a number and 14 is 28. Find the number.
19. The product of 7 and a number is 91. Find the number.
20. The product of 8 and a number is 184. Find the number.
21. The quotient of a number and 18 is 6. Find the number.
22. The quotient of a number and 13 is 9. Find the number.
23. The sum of four and twice a number is 36. Find the number.
24. The sum of five and three times a number is 29. Find the number.
25. Seven subtracted from five times a number is 123. Find the number.
26. Eight subtracted from six times a number is 184. Find the number.

27. A number increased by 5 is two times the number. Find the number.

28. A number increased by 12 is four times the number. Find the number.

29. Twice the sum of four and a number is 36. Find the number.

30. Three times the sum of five and a number is 48. Find the number.

31. Nine times a number is 30 more than three times that number. Find the number.

32. Five more than four times a number is that number increased by 35. Find the number.

33. If the quotient of three times a number and five is increased by four, the result is 34. Find the number.

34. If the quotient of three times a number and 4 is decreased by three, the result is 9. Find the number.

Application Exercises

In Exercises 35–50, use the five-step strategy to solve each problem.

35. A car rental agency charges $200 per week plus $0.15 per mile to rent a car. How many miles can you travel in one week for $320?

36. A car rental agency charges $180 per week plus $0.25 per mile to rent a car. How many miles can you travel in one week for $395?

37. The average weight for female infants at birth is 7 pounds, with a monthly weight gain of 1.5 pounds. After how many months does a baby girl weigh 16 pounds?

38. In 1980, the average yearly salary for teachers in the United States was $16,116. If the salary increases by $1496 per year, in which year will the salary reach $44,540?

39. During the 1998 baseball season, Mark McGwire hit four more home runs than Sammy Sosa. Combined, the two athletes hit 136 home runs. Determine the number of home runs hit by McGwire and Sosa.

40. Two of the top-selling music albums of all time are *Jagged Little Pill* (Alanis Morissette) and *Saturday Night Fever* (Bee Gees). The Morissette album sold 5 million more copies than that of the Bee Gees. Combined, the two albums sold 27 million copies. Determine the number of sales for each of the albums.

41. The annual salary of a surgeon is $18,600 more than six times that of a teacher. If teachers and surgeons have a combined annual salary of $258,000, find the salary for each of the two professions.

42. In the United States, the two leading causes of death are heart disease and cancer. The number of annual deaths from heart disease is 345,705 less than twice that from cancer. Both diseases combined kill 1,272,894 Americans each year. Find the number of annual deaths from each disease.

43. An automobile repair shop charged a customer $448, listing $63 for parts and the remainder for labor. If the cost

of labor is $35 per hour, how many hours of labor did it take to repair the car?

44. A repair bill on a yacht came to $1603, including $532 for parts and the remainder for labor. If the cost of labor is $63 per hour, how many hours of labor did it take to repair the yacht?

45. The sum of the page numbers on the facing pages of a book is 629. What are the page numbers?

46. The sum of the page numbers on the facing pages of a book is 525. What are the page numbers?

47. The bus fare in a city is $1.25. People who use the bus have the option of purchasing a monthly coupon book for $21.00. With the coupon book, the fare is reduced to $0.50.
    a. Write algebraic expressions for the total monthly costs of using the bus x times in a month both without and with the coupon book. Be sure to include the $21.00 in the expression with the coupon book.
    b. Use the algebraic expressions to determine the number of times in a month the bus must be used so that the total monthly cost without the coupon book is the same as the total monthly cost with the coupon book.

48. A coupon book for a bridge costs $21 per month. The toll for the bridge is normally $2.50, but is reduced to $1 for people who have purchased the coupon book.
    a. Write algebraic expressions for the total monthly costs of using the bridge x times in a month both with and without the coupon book. Be sure to include the $21.00 in the expression with the coupon book.
    b. Use the algebraic expressions to determine the number of times in a month the bridge must be crossed so that the total monthly cost without the coupon book is the same as the total monthly cost with the coupon book.

49. Among male college graduates, whites on average earn $9350 more than blacks. The average annual income for the two groups is $39,015. Find the average annual income for white and black male college graduates.

50. Among female college graduates, whites on average earn $2390 more than blacks. The average annual income for the two groups is $29,325. Find the average annual income for white and black female college graduates.

Writing in Mathematics

51. In your own words, describe a step-by-step approach for solving algebraic word problems.

52. Many students find solving linear equations much easier than solving algebraic word problems. Discuss some of the reasons why this is the case.

53. Did you have some difficulties solving some of the problems that were assigned in this exercise set? Discuss what you did if this happened to you. Did your course of action enhance your ability to solve algebraic word problems?

Critical Thinking Exercises

54. An HMO pamphlet contains the following recommended weight for women: "Give yourself 100 pounds for the first 5 feet plus 5 pounds for every inch over 5 feet tall." Using this description, which height corresponds to an ideal weight of 135 pounds?

55. The rate for a particular long distance telephone call is $0.55 for the first minute and $0.40 for each additional minute. Determine the length of a call that cost $6.95.

56. Every year, approximately 1760 Americans suffer spinal cord injuries due to falls. This represents 22% of the total number of Americans who suffer spinal cord injuries yearly. Determine the number of Americans who suffer spinal cord injuries each year. Then use the circle graph to find the number of Americans in each of the remaining four categories.

Causes of U.S. Spinal Cord Injuries

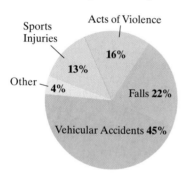

Source: U.S. News and World Report

57. In a film, the actor Charles Coburn plays an elderly "uncle" character criticized for marrying a woman when he is 3 times her age. He wittily replies, "Ah, but in 20 years time I shall only be twice her age." How old is the "uncle" and the woman?

58. Suppose that we agree to pay you 8¢ for every problem in this chapter that you solve correctly and fine you 5¢ for every problem done incorrectly. If at the end of 26 problems we do not owe each other any money, how many problems did you solve correctly?

 Group Exercise

59. One of the best ways to learn how to *solve* a word problem in algebra is to *design* word problems of your own. Creating a word problem makes you very aware of precisely how much information is needed to solve the problem. You must also focus on the best way to present information to a reader and on how much information to give. As you write your problem, you gain skills that will help you solve problems created by others.

   The group should design five different word problems that can be solved using an algebraic equation. All of the problems should be on different topics. For example, the group should not have more than one problem on finding a number. The group should turn in both the problems and their algebraic solutions.

SECTION 6.4   *Ratio, Proportion, and Variation*

Objectives

1. Find ratios.
2. Solve proportions.
3. Solve problems using proportions.
4. Solve direct variation problems.
5. Solve inverse variation problems.

The possibility of seeing a blue whale, the largest mammal ever to grace the earth, increases the excitement of gazing out over the ocean's swell of waves. Blue whales were hunted to near extinction in the last half of the nineteenth and the first half of the twentieth centuries. Using a method for estimating wildlife populations that we discuss in this section, by the mid-1960s it was determined that the world population of blue whales was less than 1000. This led the International Whaling Commission to ban the killing of blue whales to prevent their extinction. A dramatic increase in blue whale sightings indicates an ongoing increase in their population and the success of the killing ban.

1 Find ratios.

Ratios

A **ratio** compares quantities by division. For example, a group contains 60 women and 30 men. The ratio of women to men is $\frac{60}{30}$. We can express this ratio as a fraction reduced to lowest terms:

$$\frac{60}{30} = \frac{60 \div 30}{30 \div 30} = \frac{2}{1}.$$

This ratio can be expressed as 2:1, or 2 to 1.

EXAMPLE 1   Finding Ratios

The bar graph in Figure 6.1 shows the number of divorced people for every thousand married persons. The figure for the year 2000 is a projection. Find the ratio of the number of divorced people for every thousand married persons in 1995 to the number in 1980.

Solution   The ratio we must find shows the following information:

$$\frac{\text{The number of divorced persons per thousand married persons in 1995}}{\text{The number of divorced persons per thousand married persons in 1980}}.$$

First, we must use Figure 6.1 to find the number of divorced persons per thousand married persons in 1995. In 1995, the graph indicates that there were 160 divorced persons for every thousand married persons. Likewise, the graph shows that there were 100 divorced persons for every thousand married persons in 1980. We use 160 as the numerator of the ratio and 100 as the denominator. Thus, the ratio for 1995 to 1980 is:

$$\frac{160}{100} = \frac{160 \div 20}{100 \div 20} = \frac{8}{5}, \text{ or } 8:5 \ (8 \text{ to } 5).$$

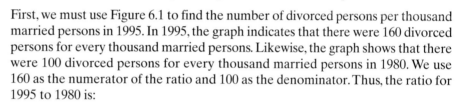

Figure 6.1
Source: U.S. Bureau of the Census

Ratios in Baseball

A baseball player's batting average is the ratio of the number of hits to the number of times at bat. For example, a player with 60 hits and 200 times at bat has a batting average of

$$\frac{60}{200} = \frac{60 \div 20}{200 \div 20} = \frac{3}{10}$$

or 0.300. Joe DiMaggio was the American League batting champion in 1939 with a 0.381 batting average. The leading batter of all time was left-handed hitter Ty Cobb. Cobb's batting average over 24 years (4191 hits and 11,429 times at bat) was 0.367.

Joe DiMaggio's (1914–1999) grace rivaled that of the great clipper ships, earning him the nickname the "Yankee Clipper."

2 Solve proportions.

Proportions

A **proportion** is a statement that says that two ratios are equal. If the ratios are $\frac{a}{b}$ and $\frac{c}{d}$, then the proportion is:

$$\frac{a}{b} = \frac{c}{d}.$$

We can clear this equation of fractions by multiplying both sides by bd, the least common denominator:

$$\frac{a}{b} = \frac{c}{d} \qquad \text{This is the given proportion.}$$

$$bd \cdot \frac{a}{b} = bd \cdot \frac{c}{d} \qquad \text{Multiply both sides by } bd(b \neq 0 \text{ and } d \neq 0). \text{ Then simplify. On}$$

$$\text{the left: } \frac{\cancel{b}d}{1} \cdot \frac{a}{\cancel{b}} = da = ad. \text{ On the right: } \frac{b\cancel{d}}{1} \cdot \frac{c}{\cancel{d}} = bc.$$

$$ad = bc$$

We see that the following principle is true for any proportion.

The cross products principle: $ad = bc$

The Cross Products Principle for Proportions

If $\dfrac{a}{b} = \dfrac{c}{d}$, then $ad = bc$. ($b \neq 0$ and $d \neq 0$.)

The cross products ad and bc are equal.

For example, if $\frac{2}{3} = \frac{6}{9}$, we see that $2 \cdot 9 = 3 \cdot 6$, or $18 = 18$.

If three of the numbers in a proportion are known, the value of the missing quantity can be found by using the cross products principle. This idea is illustrated in Example 2.

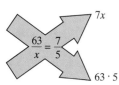

Cross products

EXAMPLE 2   Solving Proportions

Solve each proportion for x.

a. $\dfrac{63}{x} = \dfrac{7}{5}$ b. $\dfrac{20}{x - 10} = \dfrac{30}{x}$

Solution

a. $\qquad \dfrac{63}{x} = \dfrac{7}{5} \qquad$ This is the given proportion.

$\qquad 63 \cdot 5 = 7x \qquad$ Apply the cross products principle.

$\qquad 315 = 7x \qquad$ Simplify.

$\qquad \dfrac{315}{7} = \dfrac{7x}{7} \qquad$ Divide both sides by 7.

$\qquad 45 = x \qquad$ Simplify.

The solution set is $\{45\}$.

Check

$$\frac{63}{45} \stackrel{?}{=} \frac{7}{5}$$ Substitute 45 for x.

$$\frac{63 \div 9}{45 \div 9} \stackrel{?}{=} \frac{7}{5}$$ Reduce $\frac{63}{45}$ to lowest terms.

$$\frac{7}{5} = \frac{7}{5}$$ This verifies that the solution set is {45}.

b. $\dfrac{20}{x - 10} = \dfrac{30}{x}$

$$20x = 30(x - 10)$$ Apply the cross products principle.

$$20x = 30x - 30 \cdot 10$$ Use the distributive property.

$$20x = 30x - 300$$ Simplify.

$$20x - 30x = 30x - 300 - 30x$$ Subtract 30x from both sides.

$$-10x = -300$$ Simplify.

$$\frac{-10x}{-10} = \frac{-300}{-10}$$ Divide both sides by −10.

$$x = 30$$ Simplify.

The solution set is {30}.

Check

$$\frac{20}{30 - 10} \stackrel{?}{=} \frac{30}{30}$$ Substitute 30 for x.

$$\frac{20}{20} \stackrel{?}{=} \frac{30}{30}$$

$$1 = 1$$ This verifies that the solution set is {30}.

3 Solve problems using proportions.

Applications of Proportions

We now turn to practical application problems that can be solved using proportions. Here is a procedure for solving these problems.

Solving Applied Problems Using Proportions

1. Read the problem and represent the unknown quantity by x (or any letter).
2. Set up a proportion by listing the given ratio on one side and the ratio with the unknown quantity on the other side.
3. Drop units and apply the cross products principle.
4. Solve for x and answer the question.

When setting up a proportion, each quantity should occupy the same corresponding position on each side. For example, two acceptable proportions are:

$$\frac{\text{Taxes}}{\text{Assessed value}} = \frac{\text{Taxes}}{\text{Assessed value}} \quad \text{and} \quad \frac{\text{Assessed value}}{\text{Taxes}} = \frac{\text{Assessed value}}{\text{Taxes}}.$$

An incorrect proportion is:

$$\frac{\text{Taxes}}{\text{Assessed value}} = \frac{\text{Assessed value}}{\text{Taxes}}.$$

In the incorrect proportion, the like units do not occupy the same corresponding positions on the left and right side.

EXAMPLE 3 Applying Proportions: Calculating Taxes

The tax on a house whose assessed value is $65,000 is $825. Determine the tax on a house with an assessed value of $180,000, assuming the same tax rate.

Solution

Step 1 Represent the unknown by x. Let x = the tax on a $180,000 house.

Step 2 Set up a proportion. We will set up a proportion comparing taxes to assessed value.

$$\underbrace{\frac{\text{Tax on \$65,000 house}}{\text{Assessed value (\$65,000)}}}_{} \quad \text{equals} \quad \underbrace{\frac{\text{Tax on \$180,000 house}}{\text{Assessed value (\$180,000)}}}_{}$$

$$\left.\begin{array}{c} \text{Given} \\ \text{ratio} \end{array}\right\{ \frac{\$825}{\$65,000} \qquad = \qquad \frac{\$x}{\$180,000} \begin{array}{l} \longleftarrow \text{Unknown} \\ \longleftarrow \text{Given quantity} \end{array}$$

Step 3 Drop the units and apply the cross products principle. We drop the dollar signs and begin to solve for x.

$$\frac{825}{65,000} = \frac{x}{180,000}$$

$$65,000x = (825)(180,000) \qquad \text{Apply the cross products principle.}$$

$$65,000x = 148,500,000 \qquad \text{Multiply.}$$

Step 4 Solve for x and answer the question.

$$\frac{65,000x}{65,000} = \frac{148,500,000}{65,000} \qquad \text{Divide both sides by 65,000.}$$

$$x \approx 2284.62 \qquad \text{Round the value of } x \text{ to the nearest cent.}$$

The tax on the $180,000 house is approximately $2284.62.

Sampling in Nature

The method that was used to estimate the blue whale population is called the **capture-recapture method**. Because it is impossible to count each individual animal within a population, wildlife biologists randomly catch and tag a given number of animals. Sometime later they recapture a second sample of animals and count the number of recaptured tagged animals. The total size of the wildlife population is then estimated using the following proportion.

$$\begin{array}{c} \text{Initially} \\ \text{unknown} \\ (x) \longrightarrow \end{array} \frac{\text{Original number of}}{\underset{\text{population}}{\underset{\text{of animals in the}}{\text{Total number}}}} = \left.\frac{\underset{\text{tagged animals}}{\text{Number of recaptured}}}{\underset{\text{in second sample}}{\text{Number of animals}}}\right\} \begin{array}{c} \text{Known} \\ \text{ratio} \end{array}$$

Although this is called the capture-recapture method, it is not necessary to recapture animals in order to observe whether or not they are tagged. This could be done from a distance, with binoculars for instance.

EXAMPLE 4 Applying Proportions: Estimating Wildlife Population

Wildlife biologists catch, tag, and then release 135 deer back into a wildlife refuge. Two weeks later they observe a sample of 140 deer, 30 of which are tagged. Assuming the ratio of tagged deer in the sample holds for all deer in the refuge, approximately how many deer are in the refuge?

Solution

Step 1 **Represent the unknown by x.** Let x = the total number of deer in the refuge.

Step 2 **Set up a proportion.**

$$\frac{135}{x} = \frac{30}{140}$$

Steps 3 and 4 **Apply the cross products principle, solve, and answer the question.**

$$\frac{135}{x} = \frac{30}{140}$$

$(135)(140) = 30x$ Apply the cross products principle.

$18{,}900 = 30x$ Multiply.

$\dfrac{18{,}900}{30} = \dfrac{30x}{30}$ Divide both sides by 30.

$630 = x$ Simplify.

There are approximately 630 deer in the refuge.

---

4 Solve direct variation problems.

Direct Variation

In Example 3, we saw that as the assessed value on a house goes up, so do the taxes. When the assessed value is doubled, the taxes are doubled; when the assessed value is tripled, the taxes are tripled. Because of this, the tax on a house is said to **vary directly** as its assessed value. Direct variation situations can be solved using a proportion.

EXAMPLE 5 Solving a Direct Variation Problem

The amount of garbage, G, varies directly as the population, P. Allegheny County, Pennsylvania, has a population of 1.3 million and creates 26 million pounds of garbage each week. Find the weekly garbage produced by New York City with a population of 7.3 million.

Solution

Step 1 Represent the unknown by *x*. Let x = the weekly garbage produced by New York City (in millions of pounds).

Step 2 Set up a proportion. We will set up a proportion comparing amount of garbage to population.

$$\frac{\text{Garbage produced by Allegheny County}}{\text{Population of Allegheny County}} \quad \text{equals} \quad \frac{\text{Garbage produced by N.Y.C.}}{\text{Population of N.Y.C.}}$$

Given ratio $\left\{\dfrac{26 \text{ million pounds}}{1.3 \text{ million}}\right.$ $=$ $\dfrac{x \quad \longleftarrow \text{Unknown}}{7.3 \text{ million} \quad \longleftarrow \text{Given quantity}}$

Steps 3 and 4 Apply the cross products principle, solve, and answer the question.

$$\frac{26}{1.3} = \frac{x}{7.3}$$

$$1.3x = (26)(7.3) \qquad \text{Apply the cross products principle.}$$

$$1.3x = 189.8 \qquad \text{Multiply.}$$

$$\frac{1.3x}{1.3} = \frac{189.8}{1.3} \qquad \text{Divide both sides by 1.3.}$$

$$x = 146 \qquad \text{Divide.}$$

The weekly garbage produced by New York City is 146 million pounds.

EXAMPLE 6 Solving a Direct Variation Problem

The distance that the sky divers shown in the photograph fall varies directly as the square of the time in which they fall. The sky divers fall 64 feet in 2 seconds. How far will they fall in 5 seconds?

Solution

Step 1 Represent the unknown by *x*. Let x = the distance the sky divers fall in 5 seconds.

Step 2 Set up a proportion. We will set up a proportion comparing the distance that the sky divers fall to the square of the time in which they fall.

$$\frac{\text{Distance they fall in 2 seconds}}{\text{Square of the time they fall}} \quad \text{equals} \quad \frac{\text{Distance they fall in 5 seconds}}{\text{Square of the time they fall}}$$

Given ratio $\left\{\dfrac{64 \text{ feet}}{2^2 \text{ seconds}}\right.$ $=$ $\dfrac{x \quad \longleftarrow \text{Unknown}}{5^2 \text{ seconds} \quad \longleftarrow \text{Given quantity}}$

Steps 3 and 4 Apply the cross products principle, solve, and answer the question.

$$\frac{64}{2^2} = \frac{x}{5^2}$$

$$\frac{64}{4} = \frac{x}{25} \qquad \text{Square 2 and 5:} 2^2 = 2 \cdot 2 = 4 \text{ and } 5^2 = 5 \cdot 5 = 25.$$

$$4x = 64 \cdot 25 \qquad \text{Apply the cross products principle.}$$

$$4x = 1600 \qquad \text{Multiply.}$$

$$\frac{4x}{4} = \frac{1600}{4} \qquad \text{Divide both sides by 4.}$$

$$x = 400 \qquad \text{Divide.}$$

The sky divers fall 400 feet in 5 seconds.

5 Solve inverse variation problems.

Inverse Variation

So far, we have looked at problems in which as one variable (or quantity) increases, so does the second one. However, in other problems one quantity increases as the other decreases, or vice versa. For example, if you drive to campus, consider the rate at which you drive and the time it takes you to get there. As your driving rate increases, the time it takes you to get to campus decreases. This is an example of *inverse variation*. When two quantities **vary inversely**, as one quantity increases the other decreases and vice versa.

The distance from Atlanta, Georgia, to Orlando, Florida, is 450 miles. If you average 45 miles per hour, the time for the drive is 10 hours. If you average 75 miles per hour, the time for the drive is 6 hours. The following proportion represents this situation in which time varies inversely as driving rate:

$$\frac{\text{time at the slower rate}}{\text{the faster rate}} = \frac{\text{time at the faster rate}}{\text{the slower rate}}$$

$$\frac{10 \text{ hours}}{75 \text{ miles per hour}} = \frac{6 \text{ hours}}{45 \text{ miles per hour}}$$

The cross products are equal:

$$\frac{10 \text{ hours}}{1} \cdot \frac{45 \text{ miles}}{\text{hour}} = 10 \cdot 45 \text{ miles} = 450 \text{ miles}$$

$$\frac{75 \text{ miles}}{\text{hour}} \cdot \frac{6 \text{ hours}}{1} = 75 \cdot 6 \text{ miles} = 450 \text{ miles}$$

Because the product of rate and time is distance, each cross product gives the distance from Atlanta to Orlando.

There is something unusual about the placement of quantities in a proportion in an inverse variation situation:

These quantities correspond to each other. 6 hours is the travel time at 75 miles per hour.

$$\frac{\boxed{10 \text{ hours}}}{\boxed{75 \text{ miles per hours}}} = \frac{\boxed{6 \text{ hours}}}{\boxed{45 \text{ miles per hours}}}$$

These quantities correspond to each other. 10 hours is the travel time at 45 miles per hour.

In an inverse variation situation, corresponding values are not placed in the same ratio. *Placing corresponding values in opposite ratios* allows one variable to increase while the other decreases, or vice versa.

Setting Up a Proportion When *y* Varies Inversely as *x*

$$\frac{\text{The first value for } y}{\substack{\text{The value for } x \text{ corresponding} \\ \text{to the second value for } y}} = \frac{\text{The second value for } y}{\substack{\text{The value for } x \text{ corresponding} \\ \text{to the first value for } y}}$$

EXAMPLE 7 Solving an Inverse Variation Problem

To continue making money, the number of new songs a rock band needs to record each year varies inversely as the number of years the band has been recording. If, after 4 years of recording, a band needs 60 new songs, how many new songs will it need to record after 6 years?

Solution

This is not a real rock band, but rather actors in the mock rock "documentary" film *This Is Spinal Tap.*

Step 1 **Represent the unknown by *x*.** Let *x* = the number of new songs the band needs to record after 6 years.

Step 2 **Set up a proportion.** We will set up a proportion comparing the number of new songs the band needs to record each year to the number of years the band has been recording. Because this is an inverse variation situation, we place corresponding values in opposite ratios.

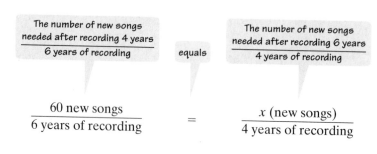

The number of new songs needed after recording 4 years / 6 years of recording   equals   The number of new songs needed after recording 6 years / 4 years of recording

$$\frac{60 \text{ new songs}}{6 \text{ years of recording}} = \frac{x \text{ (new songs)}}{4 \text{ years of recording}}$$

Steps 3 and 4 **Apply the cross products principle, solve, and answer the question.**

$$\frac{60}{6} = \frac{x}{4}$$

$6x = 60 \cdot 4$ Apply the cross products principle.

$6x = 240$ Multiply.

$$\frac{6x}{6} = \frac{240}{6}$$ Divide both sides by 6.

$x = 40$ Divide.

The band will need to record 40 new songs after 6 years.

Exercise Set 6.4

 Practice Exercises

In Exercises 1–6, express each ratio as a fraction reduced to lowest terms.

1. 24 to 48
2. 14 to 49
3. 48 to 20
4. 24 to 15
5. 27:36
6. 25:40

In a class, there are 20 men and 10 women. Find each ratio in Exercises 7–10. First express the ratio as a fraction reduced to lowest terms. Then rewrite the ratio using the reduced fraction and a colon.

7. Find the ratio of the number of men to the number of women.
8. Find the ratio of the number of women to the number of men.
9. Find the ratio of the number of women to the number of students in the class.
10. Find the ratio of the number of men to the number of students in the class.

Solve each proportion in Exercises 11–22.

11. $\dfrac{24}{x} = \dfrac{12}{7}$

12. $\dfrac{56}{x} = \dfrac{8}{7}$

13. $\dfrac{x}{6} = \dfrac{18}{4}$

14. $\dfrac{x}{32} = \dfrac{3}{24}$

15. $\dfrac{x}{3} = -\dfrac{3}{4}$

16. $\dfrac{x}{2} = -\dfrac{1}{5}$

17. $\dfrac{-3}{8} = \dfrac{x}{40}$

18. $\dfrac{-3}{8} = \dfrac{6}{x}$

19. $\dfrac{x-2}{5} = \dfrac{3}{10}$

20. $\dfrac{x+4}{8} = \dfrac{3}{16}$

21. $\dfrac{y+10}{10} = \dfrac{y-2}{4}$

22. $\dfrac{2}{y-5} = \dfrac{3}{y+6}$

 Application Exercises

Use a proportion to solve Exercises 23–28.

23. The tax on a property with an assessed value of $65,000 is $725. Find the tax on a property with an assessed value of $100,000.

24. The maintenance bill for a shopping center containing 180,000 square feet is $45,000. What is the bill for a store in the center that is 4800 square feet?

25. St. Paul Island in Alaska has 12 fur seal rookeries (breeding places). In 1961, to estimate the fur seal pup population in the Gorbath rookery, 4963 fur seal pups were tagged in early August. In late August, a sample of 900 pups was observed and 218 of these were found to have been previously tagged. Estimate the total number of fur seal pups in this rookery.

26. To estimate the number of bass in a lake, wildlife biologists tagged 50 bass and released them in the lake. Later they netted 108 bass and found that 27 of them were tagged. Approximately how many bass are in the lake?

27. The ratio of monthly child support to a father's yearly income is 1:40. How much should a father earning $38,000 annually pay in monthly child support?

28. A person who weighs 55 kilograms on earth weighs 8.8 kilograms on the moon. Find the moon weight of a person who weighs 90 kilograms on earth.

Exercises 29–36 involve direct and inverse variation. Use a proportion to solve each exercise.

29. Height varies directly as foot length. A person whose foot length is 10 inches is 67 inches tall. In 1951, photos of large footprints were published. Some believed that these footprints were made by the "Abominable Snowman." Each footprint was 23 inches long. If indeed they belonged to the Abominable Snowman, how tall is the critter?

30. A person's hair length varies directly as the number of years it has been growing. After 2 years, a person's hair length is 8 inches. The longest moustache on record was grown by Kalyan Sain of India. Sain grew his moustache for 17 years. How long was it?

31. The Mach number is a measurement of speed named after the man who suggested it, Ernst Mach (1838–1916). The speed of an aircraft varies directly as its Mach number. Shown here are two aircraft. Use the figures for the Concord to determine the Blackbird's speed.

Concord
Mach 2.03
Speed = 1502.2 miles per hour

SR-71 Blackbird
Mach 3.3
Speed = ?

32. Do you still own records, or are you strictly a CD person? Record (vinyl) owners claim that the quality of sound on good vinyl surpasses that of a CD, although this is up for debate. This, however, is not debatable: The number of revolutions a record makes as it is being played varies directly as the time that it is on the turntable. A record that lasted 3 minutes made 135 revolutions. If a record takes 2.4 minutes to play, how many revolutions does it make?

33. If all men had identical body types, their weight would vary directly as the cube of their height. Shown above is Robert Wadlow, who reached a record height of 8 feet 11 inches (107 inches) before his death at age 22. If a man who is 5 feet 10 inches tall (70 inches) with the same body type as Mr. Wadlow weighs 170 pounds, what was Robert Wadlow's weight shortly before his death?

34. The distance required to stop a car varies directly as the square of its speed. If 200 feet are required to stop a car traveling 60 miles per hour, how many feet are required to stop a car traveling 100 miles per hour?

35. The volume of a gas in a container at a constant temperature varies inversely as the pressure. If the volume is 32 cubic centimeters at a pressure of 8 pounds, find the pressure when the volume is 40 cubic centimeters.

36. The current in a circuit varies inversely as the resistance. The current is 20 amperes when the resistance is 5 ohms. Find the current for a resistance of 16 ohms.

 Writing in Mathematics

37. What is a ratio? Give an example with your description.

38. What is a proportion? Give an example with your description.

39. Explain the difference between a ratio and a proportion.

40. Explain how to solve a proportion. Illustrate your explanation with an example.

41. Explain the meaning of this statement: A company's monthly sales vary directly as its advertising budget.

42. Explain the meaning of this statement: A company's monthly sales vary inversely as the price of its product.

43. Explain the difference between setting up proportions for direct and inverse variation problems.

 Critical Thinking Exercises

44. The front sprocket on a bicycle has 60 teeth, and the rear sprocket has 20 teeth. For mountain biking, an owner needs a 5 : 1 front : rear ratio. If only one of the sprockets is to be replaced, describe the two ways in which this can be done.

45. The graph shows the yearly income in the United States for women and men in six different categories, each based on years of education. For each category, write a fraction expressing the ratio of a woman's income to a man's income. Then express each of these fractions as a decimal. (A calculator will be helpful.) Describe the trend indicating what happens to the ratio of a woman's income to that of a man's income with increasing years of education.

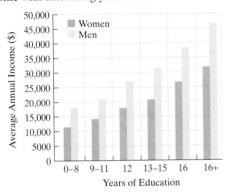

Source: The American Woman: A Status Report,
New York: Norton

46. My friend is 44 years old. My dog Phideaux is 7 years old. If Phideaux were human, he would be 56. Phideaux thinks my friend is another dog, which makes me wonder. If my friend were a dog, how old would my friend be?

47. A person's body-mass index is used to assess levels of fatness, with an index from 20 to 26 considered in the desirable range. The index varies directly as one's weight in pounds and inversely as one's height in inches. A person who weighs 150 pounds and is 70 inches tall has an index of 21. What is the body-mass index of a person who weighs 240 pounds and is 74 inches tall? Since the index is rounded to the nearest whole number, do so and then determine if this person's level of fatness is in the desirable range.

Group Exercise

48. When shopping at the supermarket, a useful ratio to keep in mind is the **unit price** of an item. The unit price is the ratio of the total price to the total units. The word *per* is used to state unit prices. For example, if a 12-ounce box of cereal sells for $3.00, its unit price is:

$$\text{Unit price} = \frac{\text{Total price}}{\text{Total units}} = \frac{\$3.00}{12 \text{ ounces}} = \$0.25 \text{ per ounce.}$$

Each person in your group is to go to the supermarket and find one brand item that is packaged in more than one size. Determine and record the unit price of each size package. Share your results with other people in the group. Describe the pattern that emerges from the group's results.

SECTION 6.5   *Solving Linear Inequalities*

Objectives

1. Graph the solutions of an inequality on a number line.

2. Solve linear inequalities.

3. Solve applied problems using linear inequalities.

Do you remember Rent-a-Heap, the car rental company that charged $125 per week plus $0.20 per mile to rent a small car? In Example 2 on page 267 we asked the question: How many miles can you travel for $335? We let x represent the number of miles and set up a linear equation as follows:

The weekly charge of $125	plus	the charge of $0.20 per mile for x miles	equals	the total $335 rental charge.
125	+	0.20x	=	335

Because we are limited by how much money we can spend on everything from buying clothing to renting a car, it is also possible to ask: How many miles can you travel if you can spend *at most* $335? We again let x represent the number of miles. Spending *at most* $335 means that the amount spent on the weekly rental must be *less than or equal to* $335:

The weekly charge of $125	plus	the charge of $0.20 per mile for x miles	must be less than or equal to	$335.
125	+	0.20x	≤	335

Using the commutative property of addition, we can express this inequality as $0.20x + 125 \leq 335$. The form of this inequality is $ax + b \leq c$, with $a = 0.20$, $b = 125$, and $c = 335$. Any inequality in this form is called a **linear inequality in one variable**. The symbol between $ax + b$ and c can be $\leq$ (is less than or equal to), $<$ (is less than), $\geq$ (is greater than or equal to), or $>$ (is greater than). The greatest exponent on the variable in such an inequality is 1.

In this section, we will study how to solve linear inequalities such as $0.20x + 125 \leq 335$. **Solving an inequality** is the process of finding the set of numbers that will make the inequality a true statement. These numbers are called the **solutions** of the inequality, and we say that they **satisfy** the inequality. The set of all solutions is called the **solution set** of the inequality.

1 Graph the solutions of an inequality on a number line.

Graphs of Inequalities

There are infinitely many solutions to the inequality $x < 3$, namely, all real numbers that are less than 3. Although we cannot list all the solutions, we can make a drawing on a number line that represents these solutions. Such a drawing is called the **graph of the inequality**.

Graphs of linear inequalities are shown on a number line by shading all points representing numbers that are solutions. *Open dots* ($\circ$) indicate endpoints that are *not solutions* and *closed dots* ($\bullet$) indicate endpoints that *are solutions*.

EXAMPLE 1   Graphing Inequalities

Graph the solutions of:

   a. $x < 3$ b. $x \geq -1$ c. $-1 < x \leq 3$.

Solution

a. The solutions of $x < 3$ are all real numbers that are less than 3. They are graphed on a number line by shading all points to the left of 3. The open dot at 3 indicates that 3 is not a solution, but numbers such as 2.9999 and 2.6 are.

b. The solutions of $x \geq -1$ are all real numbers that are greater than or equal to -1. We shade all points to the right of -1 and the point for -1 itself. The closed dot at -1 shows that -1 is a solution for the given inequality.

c. The inequality $-1 < x \leq 3$ is read "-1 is less than x *and* x is less than or equal to 3," or "x is greater than -1 *and* less than or equal to 3." The solutions of $-1 < x \leq 3$ are all real numbers between -1 and 3, not including -1 but including 3. In the graph for all real numbers between -1, exclusive, and 3, inclusive, the open dot at -1 indicates that -1 is not a solution. The closed dot at 3 shows that 3 is a solution. Shading indicates the other solutions.

Study Tip

Because an inequality symbol points to the smaller number, $x < 3$ (x is less than 3) may be expressed as $3 > x$ (3 is greater than x).

Solution Sets

The solutions of $x < 3$ are all real numbers that are less than 3. We can use the set concept introduced in Chapter 2 and state that the solution is the *set of all real numbers less than 3*. Using set-builder notation, the solution set of $x < 3$ is:

$$\{x \mid x < 3\}.$$

We read this as "the set of all x such that x is less than 3." Solutions of inequalities should be expressed in set-builder notation.

2 Solve linear inequalities.

Solving Linear Inequalities

We return, once again, to Rent-a-Heap and our question: How many miles can you travel if you can spend at most $335? We answer the question by solving

$$0.20x + 125 \leq 335$$

for x. The solution procedure is nearly identical to that for solving $0.20x + 125 = 335$. Our goal is to get x by itself on the left side. We do this by getting $0.20x$ by itself, subtracting 125 from both sides:

$$0.20x + 125 \leq 335$$
$$0.20x + 125 - 125 \leq 335 - 125$$
$$0.20x \leq 210$$

Finally, we isolate x from $0.20x$ by dividing both sides of the inequality by 0.20:

$$\frac{0.20x}{0.20} \leq \frac{210}{0.20}$$
$$x \leq 1050$$

Now that x is isolated, we can express the inequality $x \leq 1050$ in at least three ways. With at most $335 to spend:

- you can travel at most 1050 miles.
- you can travel no more than 1050 miles.
- your travel cannot exceed 1050 miles.

We isolated x from $0.20x$ by dividing both sides of $0.20x \leq 210$ by 0.20, a positive number. Let's see what happens if we divide both sides of an inequality by a negative number. Consider the inequality $10 < 14$. Divide 10 and 14 by -2:

$$\frac{10}{-2} = -5 \quad \text{and} \quad \frac{14}{-2} = -7.$$

Because -5 lies to the right of -7 on the number line, -5 is greater than -7:

$$-5 > -7.$$

Notice that the direction of the inequality symbol is reversed:

$$10 < 14$$
$$-5 > -7$$

In general, **when we multiply or divide both sides of an inequality by a negative number, the direction of the inequality symbol is reversed**. When we reverse the direction of the inequality symbol, we say that we change the *sense* of the inequality. We can summarize this discussion with the following statement.

Solving Linear Inequalities

The procedure for solving linear inequalities is the same as the procedure for solving linear equations, with one important exception: When multiplying or dividing by a negative number, reverse the direction of the inequality symbol, changing the sense of the inequality.

EXAMPLE 2   Solving a Linear Inequality

Solve and graph the solution set: $4x - 7 \geq 5$.

Solution   Our goal is to get x by itself on the left side. We do this by getting $4x$ by itself, adding 7 to both sides.

$$4x - 7 \geq 5$$
$$4x - 7 + 7 \geq 5 + 7$$
$$4x \geq 12$$

Next, we isolate x from $4x$ by dividing both sides by 4. The inequality symbol stays the same because we are dividing by a positive number.

$$\frac{4x}{4} \geq \frac{12}{4}$$
$$x \geq 3$$

The solution set is $\{x \mid x \geq 3\}$. We read this as "the set of all x such that x is greater than or equal to 3." The graph of the solution set is shown in Figure 6.2.

Figure 6.2 Real numbers greater than or equal to 3

EXAMPLE 3   Solving Linear Inequalities

Solve and graph the solution set.

a. $\frac{1}{3}x < 5$ b. $-3x < 21$

Solution   In each case, our goal is to isolate x. In the first inequality, this is accomplished by multiplying both sides by 3. In the second inequality, we can do this by dividing both sides by -3.

a. $\frac{1}{3}x < 5$ This is the given inequality

$3 \cdot \frac{1}{3}x < 3 \cdot 5$ Isolate x by multiplying by 3 on both sides.
                         The symbol $<$ stays the same because we are multiplying by a positive number.

$x < 15$ Simplify.

The solution set is $\{x \mid x < 15\}$. The graph of the solution set is shown in Figure 6.3.

Figure 6.3 Real numbers less than 15

b. $-3x < 21$ This is the given inequality.

$\frac{-3x}{-3} > \frac{21}{-3}$ Isolate x by dividing by -3 on both sides.
                          The symbol $<$ must be reversed because we are dividing by a negative number.

$x > -7$ Simplify.

Figure 6.4 Real numbers greater than -7

The solution set is $\{x \mid x > -7\}$. The graph of the solution set is shown in Figure 6.4.

EXAMPLE 4 Solving a Linear Inequality

Solve and graph the solution set: $6x - 12 > 8x + 2$.

Solution We will get x by itself on the left side. We begin by subtracting $8x$ from both sides so that the x-term appears on the left.

$$6x - 12 > 8x + 2 \qquad \text{This is the given inequality.}$$

$$6x - 8x - 12 > 8x - 8x + 2 \qquad \text{Subtract } 8x \text{ on both sides with the goal of isolating } x \text{ on the left.}$$

$$-2x - 12 > 2 \qquad \text{Simplify.}$$

Next, we get $-2x$ by itself, adding 12 to both sides.

$$-2x - 12 + 12 > 2 + 12 \qquad \text{Add 12 to both sides.}$$

$$-2x > 14 \qquad \text{Simplify.}$$

In the last step, we isolate x from $-2x$ by dividing both sides by -2. The direction of the inequality symbol must be reversed because we are dividing by a negative number.

$$\frac{-2x}{-2} < \frac{14}{-2} \qquad \text{Divide both sides by } -2 \text{ and reverse the sense of the inequality.}$$

$$x < -7 \qquad \text{Simplify.}$$

The solution set is $\{x \mid x < -7\}$. The graph of the solution set is shown in Figure 6.5.

Figure 6.5 Real numbers less than -7

EXAMPLE 5 Solving a Linear Inequality

Solve and graph the solution set:

$$2(x - 3) + 5x \leq 8(x - 1).$$

Solution Begin by simplifying the algebraic expression on each side.

$$2(x - 3) + 5x \leq 8(x - 1) \qquad \text{This is the given inequality.}$$

$$2x - 6 + 5x \leq 8x - 8 \qquad \text{Use the distributive property.}$$

$$7x - 6 \leq 8x - 8 \qquad \text{Add like terms on the left.}$$

We will get x by itself on the left side. Subtract $8x$ from both sides.

$$7x - 8x - 6 \leq 8x - 8x - 8$$

$$-x - 6 \leq -8$$

Next, we get $-x$ by itself, adding 6 to both sides.

$$-x - 6 + 6 \leq -8 + 6$$

$$-x \leq -2$$

To isolate x, we must eliminate the negative sign in front of the x. Because $-x$ means $-1x$, we can do this by dividing both sides of the inequality by -1. This reverses the direction of the inequality symbol.

$$\frac{-x}{-1} \geq \frac{-2}{-1} \qquad \text{Divide both sides by } -1 \text{ and reverse the sense of the inequality.}$$

$$x \geq 2 \qquad \text{Simplify.}$$

The solution set is $\{x \mid x \geq 2\}$. The graph of the solution set is shown in Figure 6.6.

Study Tip

You can solve

$$7x - 6 \leq 8x - 8$$

by isolating x on the right side. Subtract $7x$ from both sides and add 8 to both sides:

$$7x - 6 - 7x \leq 8x - 8 - 7x$$

$$-6 \leq x - 8$$

$$-6 + 8 \leq x - 8 + 8$$

$$2 \leq x$$

This last inequality means the same thing as

$$x \geq 2$$

Figure 6.6 Real numbers greater than or equal to 2

As you know, different professors may use different grading systems to determine your final course grade. Some professors require a final examination; others do not. In our next example, not only is a final exam required, but it also counts as two grades.

3 Solve applied problems using linear inequalities.

EXAMPLE 6 An Application: Final Course Grade

To earn an A in a course, you must have a final average of at least 90%. On the first four examinations, you have grades of 86%, 88%, 92%, and 84%. If the final examination counts as two grades, what must you get on the final to earn an A in the course?

Solution   We will use our five-step strategy for solving algebraic word problems.

Steps 1 and 2   Represent unknown quantities in terms of x. Let $x =$ your grade on the final examination.

Step 3   Write an inequality in x that describes the conditions. The average of the six grades is found by adding the grades and dividing the sum by 6.

$$\text{Average} = \frac{86 + 88 + 92 + 84 + x + x}{6}$$

Because the final counts as two grades, the x (your grade on the final examination) is added twice. This is also why the sum is divided by 6.

In order to get an A, your average must be at least 90. This means that your average must be greater than or equal to 90.

| Your average | must be greater than or equal to | 90. |

$$\frac{86 + 88 + 92 + 84 + x + x}{6} \qquad \geq \qquad 90$$

Step 4   Solve the inequality and answer the problem's question.

$$\frac{86 + 88 + 92 + 84 + x + x}{6} \geq 90 \qquad \text{This is the inequality for the given conditions.}$$

$$\frac{350 + 2x}{6} \geq 90 \qquad \text{Combine like terms in the numerator.}$$

$$6\left(\frac{350 + 2x}{6}\right) \geq 6(90) \qquad \text{Multiply both sides by 6, clearing fractions.}$$

$$350 + 2x \geq 540 \qquad \text{Multiply.}$$

$$350 + 2x - 350 \geq 540 - 350 \qquad \text{Subtract 350 from both sides.}$$

$$2x \geq 190 \qquad \text{Simplify.}$$

$$\frac{2x}{2} \geq \frac{190}{2} \qquad \text{Divide both sides by 2.}$$

$$x \geq 95 \qquad \text{Simplify.}$$

You must get at least 95% on the final examination to earn an A in the course.

Step 5 Check. We can check by computing the average with any grade that is at least 95. We will use 96. If you get 96% on the final examination, your average is:

$$\frac{86 + 88 + 92 + 84 + 96 + 96}{6} = \frac{542}{6} = 90\frac{1}{3}.$$

Because $90\frac{1}{3} > 90$, you earn an A in the course.

Exercise Set 6.5

Practice Exercises

In Exercises 1–12, graph the solutions of each inequality on a number line.

1. $x > 6$ 2. $x > -2$ 3. $x < -4$
4. $x < 0$ 5. $x \geq -3$ 6. $x \geq -5$
7. $x \leq 4$ 8. $x \leq 7$ 9. $-2 < x \leq 5$
10. $-3 \leq x < 7$ 11. $-1 < x < 4$ 12. $-7 \leq x \leq 0$

Solve the inequalities in Exercises 13–54 and graph the solution sets.

13. $x - 3 > 2$ 14. $x + 1 < 5$
15. $x + 4 \leq 9$ 16. $x - 5 \geq 1$
17. $x - 3 < 0$ 18. $x + 4 \geq 0$
19. $4x < 20$ 20. $6x \geq 18$
21. $3x \geq -15$ 22. $7x < -21$
23. $2x - 3 > 7$ 24. $3x + 2 \leq 14$
25. $3x + 3 < 18$ 26. $8x - 4 > 12$
27. $\frac{1}{2}x < 4$ 28. $\frac{1}{2}x > 3$
29. $\frac{x}{3} > -2$ 30. $\frac{x}{4} < -1$
31. $-3x < 15$ 32. $-7x > 21$
33. $-3x \geq -15$ 34. $-7x \leq -21$
35. $3x + 4 \leq 2x + 7$ 36. $2x + 9 \leq x + 2$
37. $5x - 9 < 4x + 7$ 38. $3x - 8 < 2x + 11$
39. $-2x - 3 < 3$ 40. $14 - 3x > 5$
41. $3 - 7x \leq 17$ 42. $5 - 3x \geq 20$
43. $-x < 4$ 44. $-x > -3$
45. $5 - x \leq 1$ 46. $3 - x \geq -3$
47. $2x - 5 > -x + 6$ 48. $6x - 2 \geq 4x + 6$
49. $2x - 5 < 5x - 11$ 50. $4x - 7 > 9x - 2$
51. $3(x + 1) - 5 < 2x + 1$
52. $4(x + 1) + 2 \geq 3x + 6$
53. $8x + 3 > 3(2x + 1) - x + 5$
54. $7 - 2(x - 4) < 5(1 - 2x)$

⭐ Application Exercises

The list shown ranks the ten best-educated cities in the United States measured by the percent of the population with 16 or more years of education. Let x represent the percent of the population with 16 or more years of education. In Exercises 55–60 write the name or names of the city or cities described by the given inequality.

Most Educated

City	% with 16+ Years of Education
1. Raleigh, NC	40.6%
2. Seattle	37.9
3. San Francisco	35.0
4. Austin, TX	34.4
5. Washington, DC	33.3
6. Lexington-Fayette, KY	30.6
7. Minneapolis	30.3
8. Boston	30.0
Arlington, TX	30.0
10. San Diego	29.8

Source: U.S. Census Bureau

55. $x \geq 34.4\%$ 56. $x > 35.0\%$
57. $x < 30.0\%$ 58. $x \leq 30.3\%$
59. $30.0\% \leq x < 34.4\%$ 60. $30.6\% < x \leq 35.0\%$

In Exercises 61–64, let x represent the percent of the population with 16 or more years of education. Translate each sentence into an inequality.

61. The percentage is at most 40.6%.
62. The percentage is no more than 40.6%.
63. The percentage exceeds 29%.
64. The percentage is no less than 29.8%.

65. On three examinations, you have grades of 88, 78, and 86. There is still a final examination, which counts as one grade.
   a. In order to get an A, your average must be at least 90. If you get 100 on the final, compute your average and determine if an A in the course is possible.
   b. To earn a B in the course, you must have a final average of at least 80. What must you get on the final to earn a B in the course?

66. On two examinations, you have grades of 86 and 88. There is an optional final examination, which counts as one grade. You decide to take the final in order to get a course grade of A, meaning a final average of at least 90.
   a. What must you get on the final to earn an A in the course?
   b. By taking the final, if you do poorly, you might risk the B that you have in the course based on the first two exam grades. If your final average is less than 80, you will lose your B in the course. Describe the grades on the final that will cause this to happen.

67. A car can be rented from Continental Rental for $80 per week plus 25 cents for each mile driven. How many miles can you travel if you can spend at most $400 for the week?

68. A fitness club charges $440 yearly plus $1.75 per hour for use of their equipment. How many hours can you work out yearly if you can spend at most $790 for the year?

Writing in Mathematics

69. When graphing the solutions of an inequality, what is the difference between an open dot and a closed dot?
70. When solving an inequality, when is it necessary to change the direction of the inequality symbol? Give an example.
71. Describe ways in which solving a linear inequality is similar to solving a linear equation.
72. Describe ways in which solving a linear inequality is different than solving a linear equation.

Critical Thinking Exercises

73. A car can be rented from Basic Rental for $260 per week with no extra charge for mileage. Continental charges $80 per week plus 25 cents for each mile driven to rent the same car. How many miles should be driven in a week to make the rental cost for Basic Rental a better deal than Continental's?
74. Membership in a fitness club costs $500 yearly plus $1 per hour spent working out. A competing club charges $440 yearly plus $1.75 per hour for use of their equipment. How many hours must a person work out yearly to make membership in the first club cheaper than membership in the second club?

SECTION 6.6   *Solving Quadratic Equations*

Objectives

1. Multiply binomials using the FOIL method.
2. Factor trinomials.
3. Solve quadratic equations by factoring.
4. Solve quadratic equations using the quadratic formula.

The crocodile, an endangered species, was the subject of a protection program at Florida's Everglades National Park. Park rangers used the formula

$$P = -10x^2 + 475x + 3500$$

to estimate the crocodile population, P, after x years of the protection program. Their goal was to bring the population up to 7250. To find out how long the program had to be continued for this to occur, it is necessary to substitute 7250 for P in the formula and solve for x:

$$7250 = -10x^2 + 475x + 3500.$$

Do you see how this equation differs from a linear equation? The exponent on x is 2. Solving such an equation involves finding the set of numbers that will make the equation a true statement. In this section, we focus on two methods for solving equations in the form $ax^2 + bx + c = 0$: (1) factoring and (2) using a formula. Equations in this form are called **quadratic equations**. The greatest exponent on the variable in such an equation is 2.

1 Multiply binomials using the FOIL method.

Multiplying Two Binomials Using the FOIL Method

Before we learn about the first method, factoring, we need to consider the FOIL method for multiplying two binomials. A **binomial** is an algebraic expression that contains two terms in which each exponent that appears on a variable is a whole number.

Examples of Binomials

$$x + 3, \quad x + 4, \quad 3x + 4, \quad 5x - 3$$

Two binomials can be multiplied using the FOIL method. In FOIL, F represents the product of the *first* two terms in each binomial, O represents the product of the two *outside* or *outermost* terms, I represents the product of the two *inside* or *innermost* terms, and L represents the product of the *last* two terms in each binomial.

$$\text{First} \quad \text{Outside} \quad \text{Inside} \quad \text{Last}$$
$$(a + b)(c + d) = a \cdot c + a \cdot d + b \cdot c + b \cdot d$$

Once you have multiplied first, outside, inside, and last terms, combine all like terms.

EXAMPLE 1   Using the FOIL Method

Multiply: $(x + 3)(x + 4)$.

Solution

$$F : \text{First terms} = (x + 3)(x + 4) = x \cdot x = x^2$$
$$O: \text{Outside terms} = (x + 3)(x + 4) = x \cdot 4 = 4x$$
$$I : \text{Inside terms} = (x + 3)(x + 4) = 3 \cdot x = 3x$$
$$L : \text{Last terms} = (x + 3)(x + 4) = 3 \cdot 4 = 12$$

$$\begin{array}{ccccc} & F & O & I & L \\ (x + 3)(x + 4) &= x \cdot x &+ x \cdot 4 &+ 3 \cdot x &+ 3 \cdot 4 \end{array}$$
$$= x^2 + 4x + 3x + 12$$
$$= x^2 + 7x + 12 \qquad \textit{Combine like terms.}$$

EXAMPLE 2   Using the FOIL Method

Multiply: $(3x + 4)(5x - 3)$.

Solution

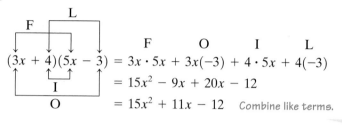

$$(3x + 4)(5x - 3) = \overset{F}{3x \cdot 5x} + \overset{O}{3x(-3)} + \overset{I}{4 \cdot 5x} + \overset{L}{4(-3)}$$
$$= 15x^2 - 9x + 20x - 12$$
$$= 15x^2 + 11x - 12 \quad \text{Combine like terms.}$$

2   Factor trinomials.

Factoring Trinomials Whose Leading Coefficient Is 1

The algebraic expression $x^2 + 7x + 12$ is called a trinomial. A **trinomial** contains three terms in which all variables have whole number exponents.

We can use the FOIL method to multiply two binomials to obtain the trinomial $x^2 + 7x + 12$:

Factored Form   **F   O   I   L**   **Trinomial Form**
$$(x + 3)(x + 4) = x^2 + 4x + 3x + 12 = x^2 + 7x + 12$$

Because the product of $x + 3$ and $x + 4$ is $x^2 + 7x + 12$, we call $x + 3$ and $x + 4$ the **factors** of $x^2 + 7x + 12$. **Factoring** an algebraic expression is the process of writing the expression as the product of two or more expressions. Thus, to factor $x^2 + 7x + 12$, we write:

$$x^2 + 7x + 12 = (x + 3)(x + 4).$$

Now, we can make several important observations.

$$x^2 + 7x + 12 = (x + 3)(x + 4) \qquad x^2 + 7x + 12 = (x + 3)(x + 4) \qquad x^2 + 7x + 12 = (x + 3)(x + 4)$$

The product of the
First terms is $x \cdot x = x^2$.

The product of the
Last terms is $3 \cdot 4 = 12$.

I: $3x$
O: $4x$

The sum of the Outside
and Inside products
is $4x + 3x = 7x$.

These observations provide us with a procedure for factoring $x^2 + bx + c$.

A Strategy for Factoring $x^2 + bx + c$

1. Enter x as the first term of each factor.
$$(x \qquad)(x \qquad) = x^2 + bx + c$$

2. List all pairs of factors of the constant c.

3. Try various combinations of these factors. Select the combination in which the sum of the *Outside* and *Inside* products is equal to bx.
$$(x + \square)(x + \square) = x^2 + bx + c$$

I

O

Sum of O + I

continued

4. Check your work by multiplying the factors using the FOIL method. You should obtain the original trinomial.

If none of the possible combinations yield an *Outside* product and an *Inside* product whose sum is equal to bx, the trinomial cannot be factored using integers and is called **prime**.

EXAMPLE 3   Factoring a Trinomial in $x^2 + bx + c$ Form

Factor: $x^2 + 6x + 8$.

Solution

Step 1   Enter x as the first term of each factor.

$$x^2 + 6x + 8 = (x \qquad)(x \qquad)$$

Step 2   List all pairs of factors of the constant, 8. The possible factors of 8 are $8(1), 4(2), -8(-1),$ and $-4(-2)$.

Step 3   Try various combinations of these factors. The correct factorization of $x^2 + 6x + 8$ is the one in which the sum of the *Outside* and *Inside* products is equal to $6x$. Here is a list of the possible factors.

Possible Factors of $x^2 + 6x + 8$	Sum of Outside and Inside Products (Should Equal $6x$)	
$(x + 8)(x + 1)$	$x + 8x = 9x$	
$(x + 4)(x + 2)$	$2x + 4x = 6x$	This is the required middle term.
$(x - 8)(x - 1)$	$-x - 8x = -9x$	
$(x - 4)(x - 2)$	$-2x - 4x = -6x$	

Thus, $x^2 + 6x + 8 = (x + 4)(x + 2)$.
　　Check this result by multiplying the right side using the FOIL method. You should obtain the original trinomial. Because of the commutative property, we can also say that:

$$x^2 + 6x + 8 = (x + 2)(x + 4).$$

EXAMPLE 4   Factoring a Trinomial in $x^2 + bx + c$ Form

Factor: $x^2 + 2x - 35$.

Solution

Step 1   Enter x as the first term of each factor.

$$x^2 + 2x - 35 = (x \qquad)(x \qquad)$$

Step 2   List all pairs of factors of the constant, −35. The possible factors of −35 are $-1(35), 1(-35), -7(5),$ and $7(-5)$.

Step 3   Try various combinations of these factors. The correct factorization of $x^2 + 2x - 35$ is the one in which the sum of the *O*utside and *I*nside products is equal to $2x$. Here is a list of the possible factors.

Possible Factors of $x^2 + 2x - 35$	Sum of Outside and Inside Products (Should Equal $2x$)
$(x - 1)(x + 35)$	$35x - x = 34x$
$(x + 1)(x - 35)$	$-35x + x = -34x$
$(x - 7)(x + 5)$	$5x - 7x = -2x$
$(x + 7)(x - 5)$	$-5x + 7x = 2x$

This is the required middle term.

Thus, $x^2 + 2x - 35 = (x + 7)(x - 5)$ or $(x - 5)(x + 7)$.
   Check this result using the FOIL method.

Factoring Trinomials Whose Leading Coefficient Is Not 1

How do we factor a trinomial such as $3x^2 - 20x + 28$? Notice that the leading coefficient is 3. We must find two binomials whose product is $3x^2 - 20x + 28$. The product of the *F*irst terms must be $3x^2$:

$$(3x \quad)(x \quad)$$

From this point on, the factoring strategy is exactly the same as the one we use to factor trinomials whose leading coefficient is 1.

EXAMPLE 5   Factoring a Trinomial

Factor: $3x^2 - 20x + 28$.

Solution

Step 1   Find two *First* terms whose product is $3x^2$.
$$3x^2 - 20x + 28 = (3x \quad)(x \quad)$$

Step 2   List all pairs of factors of the constant, 28. The number 28 has pairs of factors that are either both positive or both negative. Because the middle term, $-20x$, is negative, both factors must be negative. The negative factors of 28 are $-1(-28)$, $-2(-14)$, and $-4(-7)$.

Step 3   Try various combinations of these factors. The correct factorization of $3x^2 - 20x + 28$ is the one in which the sum of the *O*utside and *I*nside products is equal to $-20x$. Here is a list of the possible factors.

> **Study Tip**
>
> With practice, you will find that it is not necessary to list every possible factor of the trinomial. As you practice factoring, you will be able to narrow down the list of possible factors to just a few. When it comes to factoring, practice makes perfect. (Sorry about the cliché!)

Possible Factors of $3x^2 - 20x + 28$	Sum of Outside and Inside Products (Should Equal $-20x$)
$(3x - 1)(x - 28)$	$-84x - x = -85x$
$(3x - 28)(x - 1)$	$-3x - 28x = -31x$
$(3x - 2)(x - 14)$	$-42x - 2x = -44x$
$(3x - 14)(x - 2)$	$-6x - 14x = -20x$
$(3x - 4)(x - 7)$	$-21x - 4x = -25x$
$(3x - 7)(x - 4)$	$-12x - 7x = -19x$

This is the required middle term.

The correct factorization is:

$$3x^2 - 20x + 28 = (3x - 14)(x - 2) \quad \text{or} \quad (x - 2)(3x - 14).$$

Step 4   Check by multiplying the factors using the FOIL method.

$$\begin{array}{cccc} \text{F} & \text{O} & \text{I} & \text{L} \end{array}$$
$$(3x - 14)(x - 2) = 3x \cdot x + 3x(-2) + (-14) \cdot x + (-14)(-2)$$
$$= 3x^2 - 6x - 14x + 28$$
$$= 3x^2 - 20x + 28$$

Because this is the trinomial we started with, the factoring is correct.

EXAMPLE 6   Factoring a Trinomial

Factor: $8y^2 - 10y - 3$.

Solution

Step 1   Find two *First* terms whose product is $8y^2$.

$$8y^2 - 10y - 3 \stackrel{?}{=} (8y \quad)(y \quad)$$
$$8y^2 - 10y - 3 \stackrel{?}{=} (4y \quad)(2y \quad)$$

Step 2   List all pairs of factors of the constant, -3. The possible factors are $1(-3)$ and $-1(3)$.

Step 3   Try various combinations of these factors. The correct factorization of $8y^2 - 10y - 3$ is the one in which the sum of the *O*utside and *I*nside products is equal to $-10y$. Here is a list of the possible factors.

Possible Factors of $8y^2 - 10y - 3$	Sum of Outside and Inside Products (Should Equal $-10y$)	
$(8y + 1)(y - 3)$	$-24y + y = -23y$	
$(8y - 3)(y + 1)$	$8y - 3y = 5y$	
$(8y - 1)(y + 3)$	$24y - y = 23y$	
$(8y + 3)(y - 1)$	$-8y + 3y = -5y$	
$(4y + 1)(2y - 3)$	$-12y + 2y = -10y$	This is the required middle term.
$(4y - 3)(2y + 1)$	$4y - 6y = -2y$	
$(4y - 1)(2y + 3)$	$12y - 2y = 10y$	
$(4y + 3)(2y - 1)$	$-4y + 6y = 2y$	

Thus,

$$8y^2 - 10y - 3 = (4y + 1)(2y - 3) \quad \text{or} \quad (2y - 3)(4y + 1).$$

Show that this factorization is correct by multiplying the factors using the FOIL method. You should obtain the original trinomial.

3 Solve quadratic equations by factoring.

Solving Quadratic Equations by Factoring

To solve a quadratic equation by factoring, begin by setting one side of the equation equal to 0, writing the equation in **standard form**. The standard form of a quadratic equation is shown in the box.

> ## Standard Form of a Quadratic Equation
>
> $$ax^2 + bx + c = 0, \quad a \neq 0$$

An example of a quadratic equation in standard form is $x^2 - 7x + 10 = 0$. The coefficient of x^2 is $1(a = 1)$, the coefficient of x is $-7(b = -7)$, and the constant term is $10(c = 10)$. Notice that we can factor the left side of this equation.

$$x^2 - 7x + 10 = 0$$

$$(x - 5)(x - 2) = 0$$

If a quadratic equation has 0 on one side and a factored trinomial on the other side, it can be solved using the **zero-product principle.**

> ## The Zero-Product Principle
>
> If the product of two factors is 0, then one (or both) of the factors must have a value of 0.
>
> If $A \cdot B = 0$, then $A = 0$ or $B = 0$.

EXAMPLE 7   Solving a Quadratic Equation Using the Zero-Product Principle

Solve: $(x - 5)(x - 2) = 0$.

Solution   The product $(x - 5)(x - 2)$ is equal to 0. By the zero-product principle, the only way that this product can be 0 is if at least one of the factors is 0. We set each individual factor equal to 0 and solve each resulting equation for x.

$$(x - 5)(x - 2) = 0$$

$$x - 5 = 0 \quad \text{or} \quad x - 2 = 0$$

$$x = 5 \qquad\qquad x = 2$$

Check each proposed solution by substituting it for x in the original equation.

Check 5:	Check 2:
$(x - 5)(x - 2) = 0$	$(x - 5)(x - 2) = 0$
$(5 - 5)(5 - 2) \stackrel{?}{=} 0$	$(2 - 5)(2 - 2) \stackrel{?}{=} 0$
$0(3) \stackrel{?}{=} 0$	$-3(0) \stackrel{?}{=} 0$
$0 = 0$	$0 = 0$

The resulting true statements indicate that the solutions are 5 and 2. The solution set is $\{5, 2\}$.

Solving a Quadratic Equation by Factoring

1. If necessary, rewrite the equation in the form $ax^2 + bx + c = 0$, setting one side equal to 0.
2. Factor.
3. Apply the zero-product principle, setting each factor equal to 0.
4. Solve the equations in step 3.
5. Check the solutions in the original equation.

EXAMPLE 8   Using Factoring to Solve a Quadratic Equation

Solve: $x^2 - 2x = 35$.

Solution

Step 1   Set one side of the equation equal to 0. Subtract 35 from both sides and write the equation in standard form.

$$x^2 - 2x = 35$$
$$x^2 - 2x - 35 = 35 - 35$$
$$x^2 - 2x - 35 = 0$$

Step 2   Factor.

$$x^2 - 2x - 35 = 0$$
$$(x - 7)(x + 5) = 0$$

Steps 3 and 4   Set each factor equal to 0 and solve each resulting equation.

$$x - 7 = 0 \quad \text{or} \quad x + 5 = 0$$
$$x = 7 \qquad\qquad x = -5$$

Step 5   Check the solutions in the original equation.

Check 7:	Check −5:
$x^2 - 2x = 35$	$x^2 - 2x = 35$
$7^2 - 2 \cdot 7 \overset{?}{=} 35$	$(-5)^2 - 2(-5) \overset{?}{=} 35$
$49 - 14 \overset{?}{=} 35$	$25 + 10 \overset{?}{=} 35$
$35 = 35$	$35 = 35$

The resulting true statements indicate that the solutions are 7 and −5. The solution set is $\{7, -5\}$.

EXAMPLE 9   Solving a Quadratic Equation by Factoring

Solve: $5x^2 - 33x + 40 = 0$.

Solution   One side of the equation is equal to 0, so we can factor the trinomial on the left side. $5x^2 - 33x + 40$ factors as $(5x - 8)(x - 5)$.

$$5x^2 - 33x + 40 = 0$$

$$(5x - 8)(x - 5) = 0 \qquad \text{Factor.}$$

$$5x - 8 = 0 \quad \text{or} \quad x - 5 = 0 \qquad \text{Set each factor equal to 0.}$$

$$5x = 8 \qquad\qquad x = 5 \qquad \text{Solve the resulting equations.}$$

$$x = \frac{8}{5}$$

Checking these values in the original equation confirms that the solution set is $\{\frac{8}{5}, 5\}$.

---

4 Solve quadratic equations using the quadratic formula.

Solving Quadratic Equations Using the Quadratic Formula

The solutions of a quadratic equation cannot always be found by factoring. Some trinomials are difficult to factor, and others cannot be factored (that is, they are prime). However, there is a formula that can be used to solve all quadratic equations, whether or not they contain factorable trinomials. The formula is called the **quadratic formula**.

Study Tip

The entire numerator of the quadratic formula must be divided by $2a$. Always write the fraction bar all the way across the numerator.

$$x = \frac{-b \pm \sqrt{b^2 - 4ac}}{2a}$$

The Quadratic Formula

The solutions of a quadratic equation in standard form $ax^2 + bx + c = 0$, with $a \neq 0$, are given by the *quadratic formula*

$$x = \frac{-b \pm \sqrt{b^2 - 4ac}}{2a}.$$

To use the quadratic formula, if necessary begin by writing the quadratic equation in standard form. Then determine the numerical values for a (the coefficient of the squared term), b (the coefficient of the x term), and c (the constant term). Substitute the values of a, b, and c in the quadratic formula and evaluate the expression. The $\pm$ sign indicates that there are two solutions of the equation. Example 10 illustrates that to find each of the solutions, we first use $+$ and then use $-$.

EXAMPLE 10 Using the Quadratic Formula

Using the quadratic formula, solve $2x^2 + 9x - 5 = 0$.

Solution

$$2x^2 + 9x - 5 = 0$$
$$\updownarrow \quad\; \updownarrow \quad\;\; \updownarrow$$
$$ax^2 + bx + c = 0$$

In this equation, $a = 2$, $b = 9$, and $c = -5$. Substituting these values into the quadratic formula and simplifying gives the equation's solutions.

To Die at Twenty

Can the equations
$$7x^5 + 12x^3 - 9x + 4 = 0$$
and
$$8x^6 - 7x^5 + 4x^3 - 19 = 0$$
be solved using a formula similar to the quadratic formula? The first equation has five solutions and the second has six solutions, but they cannot be found using a formula. How do we know? In 1832, a 20-year-old Frenchman, Evariste Galois, wrote down a proof showing that there is no general formula to solve equations when the exponent on the variable is 5 or greater. Galois was jailed as a political activist several times while still a teenager. The day after his brilliant proof he fought a duel over a woman. The duel was a political setup. As he lay dying, Galois told his brother, Alfred, of the manuscript that contained his proof: "Mathematical manuscripts are in my room. On the table. Take care of my work. Make it known. Important. Don't cry, Alfred. I need all my courage—to die at twenty." (Our source is Leopold Infeld's biography of Galois, *Whom the Gods Love*. Some historians, however, dispute the story of Galois' ironic death the very day after his algebraic proof. Mathematical truths seem more reliable than historical ones!)

$$x = \frac{-b \pm \sqrt{b^2 - 4ac}}{2a}$$ Use the quadratic formula.

$$= \frac{-9 \pm \sqrt{9^2 - 4(2)(-5)}}{2(2)}$$ Substitute the values for a, b, and c. $a = 2$, $b = 9$, and $c = -5$

$$= \frac{-9 \pm \sqrt{81 + 40}}{4}$$ $9^2 - 4(2)(-5) = 81 - (-40) = 81 + 40$

$$= \frac{-9 \pm \sqrt{121}}{4}$$ Add under the radical sign.

$$= \frac{-9 \pm 11}{4}$$ $\sqrt{121} = 11$

Now we will evaluate this expression in two different ways to obtain the two solutions. At left, we will *add* 11 to −9. At right, we will *subtract* 11 from −9.

$$x = \frac{-9 + 11}{4} \quad \text{or} \quad x = \frac{-9 - 11}{4}$$
$$= \frac{2}{4} = \frac{1}{2} \qquad\qquad = \frac{-20}{4} = -5$$

The solution set is $\{-5, \frac{1}{2}\}$.

The quadratic equation in Example 10 has rational solutions, namely −5 and $\frac{1}{2}$. The equation can also be solved by factoring. Take a few minutes to do this now.

Any quadratic equation that has rational solutions can be solved by factoring or using the quadratic formula. However, quadratic equations with irrational solutions cannot be solved by factoring. These equations can be readily solved using the quadratic formula.

EXAMPLE 11   Using the Quadratic Formula

Using the quadratic formula, solve $2x^2 - 4x = 1$.

Solution We must first write the quadratic equation in standard form to determine the values of a, b, and c. Set the right side of the equation equal to 0 by subtracting 1 from both sides.

$$2x^2 - 4x = 1$$
$$2x^2 - 4x - 1 = 1 - 1$$
$$2x^2 - 4x - 1 = 0$$
$$\updownarrow \qquad \updownarrow \qquad \updownarrow$$
$$ax^2 + bx + c = 0$$

Can you see that $a = 2$, $b = -4$, and $c = -1$? Substitute these values into the quadratic formula.

Technology

Most inexpensive scientific calculators are sufficient for performing calculations and evaluating expressions. However, some more advanced, and, hence, expensive, calculators can determine the solutions to linear and quadratic equations. If your calculator handles this type of function (most graphing calculators do), you will probably need to be familiar with imaginary numbers in order to gain a complete understanding of the results.

$$x = \frac{-b \pm \sqrt{b^2 - 4ac}}{2a}$$ Use the quadratic formula.

$$= \frac{-(-4) \pm \sqrt{(-4)^2 - 4(2)(-1)}}{2(2)}$$ $a = 2$, $b = -4$, and $c = -1$.

$$= \frac{4 \pm \sqrt{16 - (-8)}}{4}$$ $(-4)^2 = (-4)(-4) = 16$ and $4(2)(-1) = 8(-1) = -8$.

$$= \frac{4 \pm \sqrt{24}}{4}$$ Subtract under the radical sign.

The solutions are $\dfrac{4 + \sqrt{24}}{4}$ and $\dfrac{4 - \sqrt{24}}{4}$. These solutions are irrational numbers. You can use a calculator to obtain a decimal approximation for each solution. Because $\sqrt{24} \approx 4.9$,

$$x = \frac{4 + \sqrt{24}}{4} \qquad\qquad x = \frac{4 - \sqrt{24}}{4}$$

$$\approx \frac{4 + 4.9}{4} \qquad\qquad \approx \frac{4 - 4.9}{4}$$

$$x \approx 2.2 \qquad\qquad\qquad x \approx -0.2$$

For applied problems, such as solving the quadratic equation for the crocodile population that opened this section, it is usually preferable to express irrational answers as rounded decimals. In a nonapplied situation such as this, it is best to express the irrational solutions as exact numbers in radical form. In some cases, we can simplify this radical form. Using methods for simplifying square roots discussed in Section 5.4, we can simplify $\sqrt{24}$:

$$\sqrt{24} = \sqrt{4 \cdot 6} = \sqrt{4}\,\sqrt{6} = 2\sqrt{6}$$

Study Tip

Avoid these common errors by factoring the numerator *before* you divide.

Incorrect:

$$\frac{\overset{1}{\cancel{4}} \pm \sqrt{24}}{\underset{1}{\cancel{4}}} = 1 \pm \sqrt{24}$$

Incorrect:

$$\frac{4 \pm \overset{1}{\cancel{2}}\sqrt{6}}{\underset{2}{\cancel{4}}} = \frac{4 \pm \sqrt{6}}{2}$$

Now we can use this result to simplify the two solutions. First, use the distributive property to factor out 2 from both terms in the numerator. Then, divide the numerator and the denominator by 2.

$$x = \frac{4 \pm \sqrt{24}}{4} = \frac{4 \pm 2\sqrt{6}}{4} = \frac{\overset{1}{\cancel{2}}(2 \pm \sqrt{6})}{\underset{2}{\cancel{4}}} = \frac{2 \pm \sqrt{6}}{2}$$

In simplified radical form, the equation's solution set is:

$$\left\{ \frac{2 + \sqrt{6}}{2},\ \frac{2 - \sqrt{6}}{2} \right\}.$$

Examples 10 and 11 illustrate that the solutions of quadratic equations can be rational or irrational numbers. In Example 10, the expression under the square root was 121, a perfect square $\left(\sqrt{121} = 11\right)$, and we obtained rational solutions. In Example 11, this expression was 24, which is not a perfect square $\left(\text{although we simplified } \sqrt{24} \text{ to } 2\sqrt{6}\right)$, and we obtained irrational solutions. If the expression under the square root simplifies to a negative number, then the quadratic equation has **no real solution**.

Exercise Set 6.6

 Practice Exercises

Use FOIL to find the products in Exercises 1–8.

1. $(x + 3)(x + 5)$
2. $(x + 7)(x + 2)$
3. $(x - 5)(x + 3)$
4. $(x - 1)(x + 2)$
5. $(2x - 1)(x + 2)$
6. $(2x - 5)(x + 3)$
7. $(3x - 7)(4x - 5)$
8. $(2x - 9)(7x - 4)$

Factor the trinomials in Exercises 9–20, or state that the trinomial is prime. Check your factorization using FOIL multiplication.

9. $x^2 + 5x + 6$
10. $x^2 + 8x + 15$
11. $x^2 - 2x - 15$
12. $x^2 - 4x - 5$
13. $x^2 - 8x + 15$
14. $x^2 - 14x + 45$
15. $x^2 - 9x - 36$
16. $x^2 - x - 90$
17. $x^2 - 8x + 32$
18. $x^2 - 9x + 81$
19. $x^2 + 17x + 16$
20. $x^2 - 7x - 44$

Factor the trinomials in Exercises 21–32, or state that the trinomial is prime. Check your factorization using FOIL multiplication. Unlike the trinomials you factored in Exercises 9–20, the trinomials that follow have coefficients of squared terms that are not equal to 1.

21. $2x^2 + 7x + 3$
22. $3x^2 + 7x + 2$
23. $2x^2 - 17x + 30$
24. $5x^2 - 13x + 6$
25. $3x^2 - x - 2$
26. $2x^2 + 5x - 3$
27. $3x^2 - 25x - 28$
28. $3x^2 - 2x - 5$
29. $6x^2 - 11x + 4$
30. $6x^2 - 17x + 12$
31. $4x^2 + 16x + 15$
32. $8x^2 + 33x + 4$

In Exercises 33–36, solve each equation using the zero-product principle.

33. $(x - 8)(x + 3) = 0$
34. $(x + 11)(x - 5) = 0$
35. $(4x + 5)(x - 2) = 0$
36. $(x + 9)(3x - 1) = 0$

Solve the quadratic equations in Exercises 37–52 by factoring.

37. $x^2 + 8x + 15 = 0$
38. $x^2 + 5x + 6 = 0$
39. $x^2 - 2x - 15 = 0$
40. $x^2 + x - 42 = 0$
41. $x^2 - 4x = 21$
42. $x^2 + 7x = 18$
43. $x^2 + 9x = -8$
44. $x^2 - 11x = -10$
45. $x^2 - 12x = -36$
46. $x^2 - 14x = -49$
47. $2x^2 = 7x + 4$
48. $3x^2 = x + 4$
49. $5x^2 + x = 18$
50. $3x^2 - 4x = 15$
51. $x(6x + 23) + 7 = 0$
52. $x(6x + 13) + 6 = 0$

Solve the equations in Exercises 53–72 by using the quadratic formula.

53. $x^2 + 8x + 15 = 0$
54. $x^2 + 8x + 12 = 0$
55. $x^2 + 5x + 3 = 0$
56. $x^2 + 5x + 2 = 0$
57. $x^2 + 4x - 6 = 0$
58. $x^2 + 2x - 4 = 0$
59. $x^2 + 4x - 7 = 0$
60. $x^2 + 4x + 1 = 0$
61. $x^2 - 3x - 18 = 0$
62. $x^2 - 3x - 10 = 0$
63. $6x^2 - 5x - 6 = 0$
64. $9x^2 - 12x - 5 = 0$
65. $x^2 - 2x - 10 = 0$
66. $x^2 + 6x - 10 = 0$
67. $x^2 - x = 14$
68. $x^2 - 5x = 10$
69. $6x^2 + 6x + 1 = 0$
70. $3x^2 - 5x + 1 = 0$
71. $4x^2 - 12x + 9 = 0$
72. $9x^2 + 6x + 1 = 0$

⭐ **Application Exercises**

73. As we mentioned in the introduction, rangers at Everglades National Park used the formula
$$P = -10x^2 + 475x + 3500$$
to estimate the crocodile population, P, after x years of a protection program.
   a. The goal of the rangers was to bring the population up to 7250. Substitute 7250 for P in the formula and write the resulting quadratic equation so that one side is equal to 0.
   b. Use the quadratic formula (and perhaps a calculator, because the numbers are relatively large) to solve the equation in part (a).
   c. Based on your solution in part (b), how many years will it take to bring the population up to 7250?

74. The formula $N = 2x^2 + 22x + 320$ describes the number of inmates in thousands, N, in federal and state prisons x years after 1980.
   a. Substitute 480 for N in the formula and write the resulting quadratic equation so that one side is equal to 0.
   b. Use the quadratic formula (and perhaps a calculator, because the numbers are relatively large) to solve the equation in part (a).
   c. Based on your solution in part (b), fill in the blanks: The U.S. federal and state prison population was 480 thousand _____ years after 1980, in the year _____ .

 Writing in Mathematics

75. Explain how to multiply two binomials using the FOIL method. Give an example with your explanation.
76. Explain how to factor $x^2 - 5x + 6$.
77. Explain how to solve a quadratic equation by factoring. Use the equation $x^2 + 6x + 8 = 0$ in your explanation.
78. Explain how to solve a quadratic equation using the quadratic formula. Use the equation $x^2 + 6x + 8 = 0$ in your explanation.

Critical Thinking Exercises

79. The radicand of the quadratic formula, $b^2 - 4ac$, can be used to determine whether $ax^2 + bx + c = 0$ has solutions that are rational, irrational, or not real numbers. Explain how this works. Is it possible to determine the kinds of answers that one will obtain to a quadratic equation without actually solving the equation? Explain.

In Exercises 80–81, find all integers b so that the trinomial can be factored.

80. $x^2 + bx + 15$

81. $x^2 + 4x + b$

82. Factor: $x^{2n} + 20x^n + 99$.

83. A person throws a rock upward from the edge of an 80-foot cliff. The height, h, in feet, of the rock above the water at the bottom of the cliff after t seconds is described by the formula

$$h = -16t^2 + 64t + 80.$$

How long will it take for the rock to reach the water?

Technology Exercise

84. If you have access to a calculator that solves quadratic equations, consult the owner's manual to determine how to use this feature. Then use your calculator to solve any five of the equations in Exercises 37–72.

CHAPTER SUMMARY, REVIEW, AND TEST

SUMMARY

6.1 Algebraic Expressions and Formulas

a. An algebraic expression combines variables and numbers using addition, subtraction, multiplication, division, powers, or roots.

b. Evaluating an algebraic expression means finding its value for a given value of the variable.

c. Terms of an algebraic expression are separated by addition. Like terms have the same variables with the same exponents on the variables. To add or subtract like terms, add or subtract the numerical coefficients and copy the common variable.

d. An algebraic expression is simplified when parentheses have been removed (using the distributive property) and like terms have been combined.

e. Formulas are statements of equality expressing a relationship among two or more variables.

6.2 Solving Linear Equations

a. A linear equation in one variable can be written in the form $ax + b = c$. The greatest exponent on the variable is 1.

b. Solving a linear equation is the process of finding the set of numbers that will make the equation a true statement. These numbers are the solutions.

c. A step-by-step procedure for solving a linear equation is given in the box on page 258.

d. If an equation contains fractions, begin by multiplying each term by the least common denominator, thereby clearing the fractions.

e. If a false statement (such as $-6 = 7$) is obtained in solving an equation, the equation has no solution. The solution set is $\varnothing$, the empty set.

f. If a true statement (such as $-6 = -6$) is obtained, the equation has infinitely many solutions. The solution set is the set of all real numbers.

6.3 Applications of Linear Equations

a. A step-by-step strategy for solving word problems using linear equations is given in the box on pages 264–265.

b. Algebraic translations of English phrases are given in Table 6.1 on pages 265–266.

6.4 Ratio, Proportion, and Variation

a. The ratio of a to b is written $\dfrac{a}{b}$, or $a:b$.

b. A proportion is a statement in the form $\dfrac{a}{b} = \dfrac{c}{d}$.

c. The cross products principle states that if $\dfrac{a}{b} = \dfrac{c}{d}$, then $ad = bc$.

d. A step-by-step procedure for solving applied problems using proportions is given in the box on page 275.

e. If two quantities vary directly, as one increases, so does the other. As one decreases, so does the other. Proportions can be used to solve direct variation problems.

f. If two quantities vary inversely, as one increases, the other decreases. As one decreases, the other increases. Proportions, as explained in the box on page 280, can be used to solve inverse variation problems.

6.5 Solving Linear Inequalities

A procedure for solving a linear inequality is given in the box on page 286. Remember to reverse the direction of the inequality symbol when multiplying or dividing by a negative number.

6.6 Solving Quadratic Equations

a. The standard form of a quadratic equation is $ax^2 + bx + c = 0, a \neq 0$.

b. Some quadratic equations can be solved using factoring and the zero-product principle. A step-by-step procedure is given in the box on page 297.

c. All quadratic equations can be solved using the quadratic formula $x = \dfrac{-b \pm \sqrt{b^2 - 4ac}}{2a}$.

REVIEW EXERCISES

6.1

In Exercises 1–3, evaluate the algebraic expression for the given value of the variable.

1. $6x + 9, x = 4$
2. $4x^2 - 3x + 2, x = 5$
3. $7x^2 + 4x - 5, x = -2$

In Exercises 4–6, simplify each algebraic expression.

4. $7x + 9 - 12 - x$
5. $6(5x + 3) - 20$
6. $4(7x - 1) + 11x$

7. Suppose you can stay in the sun for x minutes without burning when you don't put on any lotion. The algebraic expression $9x$ describes how long you can tan without burning with a number 9 lotion. Evaluate the expression when $x = 15$. Describe what the answer means in practical terms.

8. Suppose that a store is selling all computers at 25% off the regular price. If x is the regular price, the algebraic expression $x - 0.25x$ describes the sale price. Evaluate the expression when $x = 2400$. Describe what the answer means in practical terms.

9. The formula
$$T = 3(A - 20)^2 \div 50 + 10$$
describes the average running time, T, in seconds, for a person who is A years old to run the 100-yard dash. How long does it take a 30-year-old runner to run the 100-yard dash?

6.2

Solve each equation in Exercises 10–14.

10. $4x + 9 = 33$
11. $5x - 3 = x + 5$
12. $3(x + 4) = 5x - 12$
13. $2(x - 2) + 3(x + 5) = 2x - 2$
14. $\dfrac{2x}{3} = \dfrac{x}{6} + 1$

In Exercises 15–16, solve each equation for y.

15. $3x + y = 9$
16. $4x + 2y = 16$

In Exercises 17–20, solve each formula for the specified variable.

17. $D = RT$, for T
18. $P = 2l + 2w$, for w
19. $A = \dfrac{1}{2} bh$, for h
20. $A = \dfrac{B + C}{2}$, for B

21. The formula $y = 420x + 720$ describes the amount of money, y, in millions of dollars, lost to credit card fraud worldwide x years after 1989. In how many years after 1989 did losses amount to 4080 million dollars? In what year was that?

6.3

In Exercises 22–25, let x represent the number. Write each English phrase as an algebraic expression.

22. 17 decreased by 9 times a number
23. 3 times a number, decreased by 7
24. 8 more than 5 times a number
25. The quotient of 6 and a number, increased by triple the number

In Exercises 26–29, let x represent the number. Use the given conditions to write an equation. Solve the equation and find the number.

26. Seventeen decreased by 4 times a number is 5. Find the number.

27. The product of 5 and a number, increased by 2, is 22 more than the number. Find the number.

28. When 7 times a number is decreased by 1, the result is 9 more than 5 times the number. Find the number.

29. Eight times the difference of a number and 5 is 56. Find the number.

In Exercises 30–32, use an equation to solve each problem.

30. In 1993, the average weekly salary for workers in the United States was $462. If this amount is increasing by $15 yearly, in how many years after 1993 will the average weekly salary reach $807? In what year will that be?

31. In the 1998 Super Bowl, Denver scored 7 points more than Green Bay. If the sum of their scores was 55, what were the scores?

32. Costs for two different kinds of heating systems for a three-bedroom house are given below.

System	Cost to Install	Operating Cost/Year
Electric	$5000	$1100
Gas	$12,000	$700

After how long will total costs for electric heating and gas heating be the same? What will be the cost at that time?

6.4

33. The bar graph indicates countries where ten or more languages have become extinct. Use the graph to find each of the following ratios. First express the ratio as a fraction reduced to lowest terms. Then rewrite the ratio using the reduced fraction and a colon.

 a. The number of extinct languages in Brazil to that of the United States
 b. The number of extinct languages in Australia and India combined to that of Colombia

Countries Where Ten or More Languages Have Become Extinct (Number of Languages)

Source: Grimes

Solve each proportion in Exercises 34–37.

34. $\dfrac{3}{x} = \dfrac{15}{25}$

35. $\dfrac{-7}{5} = \dfrac{91}{x}$

36. $\dfrac{x + 2}{3} = \dfrac{4}{5}$

37. $\dfrac{5}{x + 7} = \dfrac{3}{x + 3}$

Use a proportion to solve Exercises 38–39.

38. If a school board determines that there should be 3 teachers for every 50 students, how many teachers are needed for an enrollment of 5400 students?

39. To determine the number of trout in a lake, a conservationist catches 112 trout, tags them, and returns them to the lake. Later, 82 trout are caught, and 32 of them are found to be tagged. How many trout are in the lake?

Exercises 40–42 involve direct and inverse variation. Use a proportion to solve each exercise.

40. The owners of Rollerblades Now determine that the monthly sales of its skates varies directly as their advertising budget. When $60,000 is spent on advertising, the company sells 12,000 rollerblades in a month. What will be the monthly sales if they spend $96,000 on advertising?

41. The distance that an object falls varies directly as the square of the time it has been falling. An object falls 144 feet in 3 seconds. Find how far it will fall after 7 seconds.

42. The weight that can be supported by a 2-inch by 4-inch piece of pine (called a 2-by-4) varies inversely as its length. A 10-foot 2-by-4 pine can support 500 pounds. What weight can be supported by a 125-foot 2-by-4 pine?

6.5

Solve the inequalities in Exercises 43–48 and graph the solution sets.

43. $2x - 5 < 3$

44. $\dfrac{x}{2} > -4$

45. $3 - 5x \le 18$

46. $4x + 6 < 5x$

47. $6x - 10 \ge 2(x + 3)$

48. $4x + 3(2x - 7) \le x - 3$

49. To pass a course, a student must have an average on three examinations of at least 60. If a student stores 42 and 74 on the first two tests, what must be earned on the third test to pass the course?

6.6

Use FOIL to find the products in Exercises 50–51.

50. $(x + 9)(x - 5)$

51. $(4x - 7)(3x + 2)$

Factor the trinomials in Exercises 52–57, or state that the trinomial is prime.

52. $x^2 - x - 12$

53. $x^2 - 8x + 15$

54. $x^2 + 2x + 3$

55. $3x^2 - 17x + 10$

56. $6x^2 - 11x - 10$

57. $3x^2 - 6x - 5$

Solve the quadratic equations in Exercises 58–61 by factoring.

58. $x^2 + 5x - 14 = 0$

59. $x^2 - 4x = 32$

60. $2x^2 + 15x - 8 = 0$

61. $3x^2 = -21x - 30$

Solve the quadratic equations in Exercises 62–65 by using the quadratic formula.

62. $x^2 - 4x + 3 = 0$

63. $x^2 - 5x = 4$

64. $2x^2 + 5x - 3 = 0$

65. $3x^2 - 6x = 5$

Group Exercise

66. We have seen examples throughout the chapter of algebraic expressions and formulas that predict future values for things that are changing. These changing quantities included teachers' salaries (Exercise 75, page 251), number of cable TV subscribers (Exercise 76, page 251), life expectancy for women (Exercise 83, page 263), crocodile population (Exercise 73 on page 301), and the number of inmates in federal and state prisons (Exercise 74 on page 301). Group members should select one of these algebraic expressions or formulas and:

a. Use the expression or formula to predict a future value for the changing quantity.

b. Use the expression or formula to write and solve a word problem. The solution should require a linear equation, a linear inequality, or a quadratic equation.

c. Describe changes that might take place in the future that will affect the accuracy of the prediction made by the expression or formula.

CHAPTER 6 TEST

1. Evaluate $5x^2 - 7x - 2$ when $x = -3$.

2. Simplify: $5(3x - 2) + 7x$.

3. The formula $S = 91t + 164$ describes the average annual salary, S, of major league baseball players, in thousands of dollars, t years after 1984. What was the average annual salary in 1994?

In Exercises 4 and 5, solve each equation.

4. $8x - 5(x - 2) = x + 26$

5. $3(2x - 4) = 9 - 3(x + 1)$

6. The formula $S = 1472t + 21,700$ describes the average annual salary, S, for teachers in the United States t years after 1984. How many years after 1984 will teachers be earning $48,196 annually? What year will that be?

7. Solve for y: $2x + 4y = 8$.

8. Solve for P: $L = \dfrac{P - 2W}{2}$.

In Exercises 9–11, use an equation to solve each problem.

9. The product of 5 and a number, decreased by 9, is 310. What is the number?

10. A person with no education can expect to earn $7200 yearly with annual income increases of $2600 for each year of education. How many years of education are needed to earn $35,800 per year?

11. In a class, there are 15 men and 10 women. Find the ratio of the number of women to the number of students in the class. First express the ratio as a fraction reduced to lowest terms. Then rewrite the ratio using a second method.

In Exercises 12 and 13, solve each proportion.

12. $\dfrac{5}{8} = \dfrac{x}{12}$

13. $\dfrac{x + 5}{8} = \dfrac{x + 2}{5}$

14. Park rangers catch, tag, and release 200 tule elk back into a wildlife refuge. Two weeks later they observe a sample of 150 elk, of which 5 are tagged. Assuming that the ratio of tagged elk in the sample holds for all elk in the refuge, how many elk are there in the park?

15. The pressure of water on an object below the surface varies directly as its distance below the surface. If a submarine experiences a pressure of 25 pounds per square inch 60 feet below the surface, how much pressure will it experience 330 feet below the surface?

16. The time that it takes you to get to campus varies inversely as your driving rate. Averaging 20 miles per hour in terrible traffic, it takes you 1.5 hours to get to campus. How long would the trip take averaging 60 miles per hour?

Solve the inequalities in Exercises 17–18 and graph the solution sets.

17. $6 - 9x \geq 33$

18. $4x - 2 > 2(x + 6)$

19. A student has grades on three examinations of 76, 80, and 72. What must the student earn on a fourth examination in order to have an average of at least 80?

20. Use FOIL to find this product: $(2x - 5)(3x + 4)$.

21. Factor: $2x^2 - 9x + 10$.

22. Solve by factoring: $x^2 + 5x = 36$.

23. Solve by using the quadratic formula: $2x^2 + 4x = -1$.

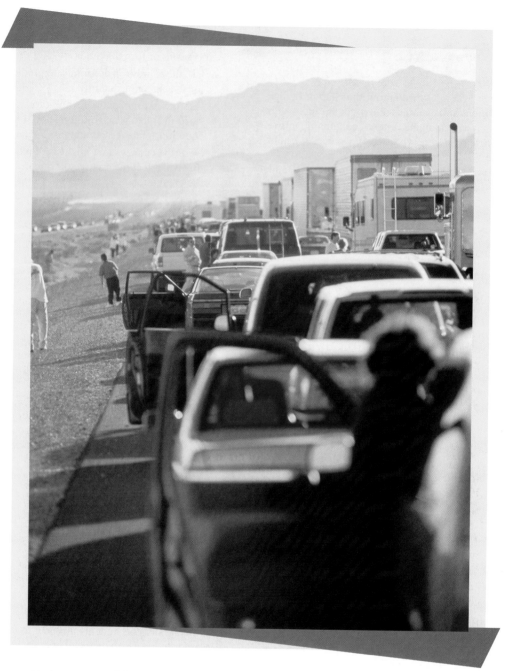

It's been one of those days! Traffic is really backed up on the highway. Finally, you see the source of the traffic jam—a minor fender-bender. Still stuck in traffic, you notice that the driver appears to be quite young. This might seem like a strange observation. After all, what does a driver's age have to do with his or her chances of getting into an accident?

7 Algebra: Graphs, Functions, and Linear Systems

We have seen that the language of algebra provides a compact symbolic description of your world. There is even a formula that describes the number of car accidents as a function of a driver's age. (We'll have lots to say about functions in this chapter.) Do you have any idea about the age at which drivers get into the least number of car accidents? The answer to this question will unfold as we study a technique for making pictures of formulas.

Understanding formulas as functions and representing them with pictures provide powerful tools for describing your world and solving some of its problems.

SECTION 7.1 *Graphing and Functions*

Objectives

1. Plot ordered pairs in the rectangular coordinate system.
2. Graph equations.
3. Use $f(x)$ notation.
4. Graph functions.
5. Use the vertical line test.

Figure 7.1 A picture of a formula

A picture, as they say, is worth a thousand words. Have you seen pictures of gas-guzzling cars from the 1950s, with their huge fins and overstated designs? The worst year for automobile fuel efficiency was 1958, when U.S. cars averaged a dismal 12.4 miles per gallon.

There is a formula that describes fuel efficiency of U.S. cars over time. The formula is:

$$y = 0.0075x^2 - 0.2672x + 14.8.$$

The variable x represents the number of years after 1940. The variable y represents the average number of miles per gallon for U.S. automobiles. Looking at the formula does not make it obvious that 1958, 18 years after 1940, was the worst year for fuel efficiency. However, if we could somehow make a picture of the formula, such as the one shown in Figure 7.1, the lowest point on the picture would reveal approximately 1958 as the year in which gas-guzzling cars averaged less than 13 miles per gallon. The shape of the graph also shows decreasing fuel efficiency from 1940 through 1958 and increasing fuel efficiency after 1958. In this section, we will be making pictures of formulas. We can use these pictures to visualize the behavior of the variables in the formula.

1 Plot ordered pairs in the rectangular coordinate system.

Points and Ordered Pairs

Making a picture of an equation with two variables, such as the formula for automobile fuel efficiency over time, is accomplished using the **rectangular coordinate system**. The rectangular coordinate system is based on the work of the French mathematician René Descartes (1596–1650). It is also called the **Cartesian coordinate system.**

Figure 7.2 The rectangular coordinate system

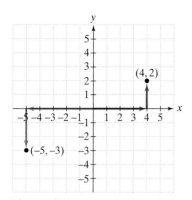

Figure 7.3 Plotting $(4, 2)$ and $(-5, -3)$

Descartes used two number lines that intersect at right angles at their zero points, as shown in Figure 7.2. The horizontal line is the *x*-axis and the vertical line is the *y*-axis. The point of intersection of these axes is the **origin**. Positive numbers are shown to the right and above the origin. Negative numbers are shown to the left and below the origin. The axes divide the plane into four quarters, called **quadrants**. The points located on the axes are not in any quadrant.

Each point in the plane corresponds to an **ordered pair** of real numbers, (x, y). Examples of such pairs are $(4, 2)$ and $(-5, -3)$. The first number in each pair, called the **x-coordinate**, denotes the distance and direction from the origin along the *x*-axis. The second number, called the **y-coordinate**, denotes vertical distance and direction along a line parallel to the *y*-axis or along the *y*-axis itself.

Figure 7.3 shows how we **plot**, or locate, the points corresponding to the ordered pairs $(4, 2)$ and $(-5, -3)$. We plot $(4, 2)$ by going 4 units from 0 to the right along the *x*-axis. Then we go 2 units up parallel to the *y*-axis. We plot $(-5, -3)$ by going 5 units from 0 to the left along the *x*-axis and 3 units down parallel to the *y*-axis. The phrase "the point corresponding to the ordered pair $(-5, -3)$" is often abbreviated as "the point $(-5, -3)$."

EXAMPLE 1 Plotting Points in the Rectangular Coordinate System

Plot the points $A(-3, 5)$, $B(2, -4)$, $C(5, 0)$, $D(5, 3)$, $E(0, 4)$, and $F(0, 0)$.

Solution   See Figure 7.4. We plot the points in the following way:

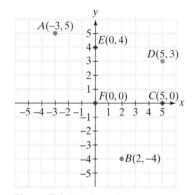

Figure 7.4 Plotting points

$$
\begin{array}{ll}
A(-3, 5)\colon & \text{3 units left, 5 units up} \\
B(2, -4)\colon & \text{2 units right, 4 units down} \\
C(5, 0)\colon & \text{5 units right, 0 units up or down} \\
D(5, 3)\colon & \text{5 units right, 3 units up} \\
E(0, 4)\colon & \text{0 units right or left, 4 units up} \\
F(0, 0)\colon & \text{0 units right or left, 0 units up or down}
\end{array}
$$

The origin is represented by $(0, 0)$.

2 Graph equations.

Graphing Equations

The rectangular coordinate system allows us to visualize relationships between two variables by connecting any equation in two variables with a geometric figure. Consider, for example, the following equation in two variables: $y = x^2 - 4$. A **solution** to this equation is an ordered pair of real numbers with the following property: When the *x*-coordinate is substituted for *x* and the *y*-coordinate is substituted for *y* in the equation, we obtain a true statement. For example, if we let $x = 3$, then $y = 3^2 - 4 = 9 - 4 = 5$. The ordered pair $(3, 5)$ is a solution to the equation $y = x^2 - 4$. We also say that $(3, 5)$ **satisfies** the equation.

We can generate as many ordered-pair solutions as desired to $y = x^2 - 4$ by substituting numbers for *x* and then finding the values for *y*. The **graph of the equation** is the set of all points whose coordinates satisfy the equation.

One method for graphing an equation such as $y = x^2 - 4$ is the **point-plotting method**. First, we find several ordered pairs that are solutions to the equation. Next, we plot these ordered pairs as points in the rectangular coordinate system. Finally, we connect the points with a smooth curve or line. This often gives us a picture of all ordered pairs that satisfy the equation.

EXAMPLE 2 Graphing an Equation Using the Point-Plotting Method

Graph $y = x^2 - 4$. Select integers for x, starting with -3 and ending with 3.

Solution For each value of x we find the corresponding value for y.

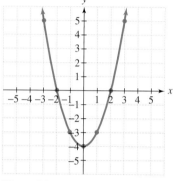

Figure 7.5 The graph of $y = x^2 - 4$

x	$y = x^2 - 4$	Ordered Pair (x, y)
-3	$y = (-3)^2 - 4 = 9 - 4 = 5$	$(-3, 5)$
-2	$y = (-2)^2 - 4 = 4 - 4 = 0$	$(-2, 0)$
-1	$y = (-1)^2 - 4 = 1 - 4 = -3$	$(-1, -3)$
0	$y = 0^2 - 4 = 0 - 4 = -4$	$(0, -4)$
1	$y = 1^2 - 4 = 1 - 4 = -3$	$(1, -3)$
2	$y = 2^2 - 4 = 4 - 4 = 0$	$(2, 0)$
3	$y = 3^2 - 4 = 9 - 4 = 5$	$(3, 5)$

Now we plot the seven points and join them with a smooth curve, as shown in Figure 7.5. The graph of $y = x^2 - 4$ is a curve where the part of the graph to the right of the y-axis is a reflection of the part to the left of it and vice versa.

Part of the beauty of the rectangular coordinate system is that it allows us to "see" mathematical formulas and visualize the solution to a problem. This idea is demonstrated in Example 3.

EXAMPLE 3 An Application Using the Rectangular Coordinate System

The toll to a bridge costs $2.50. Commuters who use the bridge frequently have the option of purchasing a monthly coupon book for $21.00. With the coupon book, the toll is reduced to $1.00. The monthly cost, y, of using the bridge x times can be described by the following formulas.

Without the coupon book:

$$y = 2.50x$$

The monthly cost, y, is $2.50 times the number of times, x, that the bridge is used.

With the coupon book:

$$y = 21 + 1 \cdot x$$
$$y = 21 + x$$

The monthly cost, y, is $21 for the book plus $1 times the number of times, x, that the bridge is used.

a. Let $x = 0, 2, 4, 10, 12, 14$, and 16. Make a table of the x- and y-coordinates for each of the formulas.
b. Graph the formulas in the same rectangular coordinate system.
c. What are the coordinates of the intersection point for the two graphs? Interpret the coordinates in practical terms.

Solution

a. A table of x- and y-coordinates for each formula follows.

Without the Coupon Book

x	$y = 2.5x$	(x, y)
0	$y = 2.5(0) = 0$	$(0, 0)$
2	$y = 2.5(2) = 5$	$(2, 5)$
4	$y = 2.5(4) = 10$	$(4, 10)$
10	$y = 2.5(10) = 25$	$(10, 25)$
12	$y = 2.5(12) = 30$	$(12, 30)$
14	$y = 2.5(14) = 35$	$(14, 35)$
16	$y = 2.5(16) = 40$	$(16, 40)$

With the Coupon Book

x	$y = 21 + x$	(x, y)
0	$y = 21 + 0 = 21$	$(0, 21)$
2	$y = 21 + 2 = 23$	$(2, 23)$
4	$y = 21 + 4 = 25$	$(4, 25)$
10	$y = 21 + 10 = 31$	$(10, 31)$
12	$y = 21 + 12 = 33$	$(12, 33)$
14	$y = 21 + 14 = 35$	$(14, 35)$
16	$y = 21 + 16 = 37$	$(16, 37)$

b. Now we are ready to graph the two formulas. Because the x- and y-coordinates are nonnegative, it is only necessary to use the origin, the positive portions of the x- and y-axes, and the first quadrant of the rectangular coordinate system. The x-coordinates begin at 0 and end at 16. We will let each tick-mark on the x-axis represent one unit. However, the y-coordinates begin at 0 and get as large as 40 in the formula without the coupon book. So that our y-axis does not get too long, we will let each tick-mark on the y-axis represent two units. Using this setup and the two tables of coordinates, we construct the graphs of $y = 2.5x$ and $y = 21 + x$, shown in Figure 7.6.

c. The graphs intersect at $(14, 35)$. This means that if the bridge is used 14 times in a month, the total monthly cost without the coupon book is the same as the total monthly cost with the coupon book, namely $35.

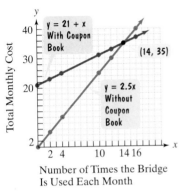

Figure 7.6 Options for a toll

In Figure 7.6, look at the two graphs to the right of the intersection point $(14, 35)$. The red graph of $y = 21 + x$ lies below the blue graph of $y = 2.5x$. This means that if the bridge is used more than 14 times in a month $(x > 14)$, the monthly cost, y, with the coupon book is cheaper than the monthly cost, y, without the coupon book.

3   Use $f(x)$ notation.

Functions

Reconsider the equation from Example 4, $y = 2.5x$. Recall that this equation describes the monthly cost, y, of using the bridge x times, with a toll cost of $2.50 each time the bridge is used. The monthly cost, y, depends on the number of times the bridge is used, x. For each value of x, there is one and only one value of y. If an equation in two variables (x and y) yields precisely one value of y for each value of x, we say that y is a **function** of x.

The notation $y = f(x)$ indicates that the variable y is a function of x. The notation $f(x)$ is read "f of x."

For example, the formula for the cost of the bridge

$$y = 2.5x$$

can be expressed in function notation as

$$f(x) = 2.5x.$$

We read this as "f of x is equal to $2.5x$." If, say, x equals 10 (meaning that the bridge is used 10 times), we can find the corresponding value of y (monthly cost) using the equation $f(x) = 2.5x$.

Study Tip

The notation $f(x)$ does not mean "f times x." The notation describes the "output" for the function f when the "input" is x.

$$f(x) = 2.5x$$

$$f(10) = 2.5(10) \qquad \text{To find f(10), read "f of 10," replace x by 10.}$$

$$= 25$$

Because $f(10) = 25$, this means that if the bridge is used 10 times in a month, the total monthly cost is $25.

Table 7.1 compares our previous notation with the new notation of functions.

Table 7.1 Function Notation

"y Equals" Notation	"f(x) Equals" Notation
$y = 2.5x$	$f(x) = 2.5x$
If $x = 10$, $\quad y = 2.5(10) = 25$	$f(10) = 2.5(10) = 25$ f of 10 equals 25.

We now return to our formula for fuel efficiency of U.S. cars over time.

EXAMPLE 4   Using Function Notation

The formula $y = 0.0075x^2 - 0.2672x + 14.8$ describes the average number of miles per gallon of U.S. automobiles, y, as a function of time, x, in which x is the number of years after 1940.

a. Express the equation in function notation.

b. Find and interpret $f(18)$.

The Road to Nowhere

Fortunately, the miles-per-gallon for American cars has increased since the 1950s. However, with increasingly efficient automobile engines, Americans are driving more and purchasing more automobiles. In spite of appeals to save gasoline, the falling cost of driving a mile has encouraged more driving. The plan for increased gas savings due to the increased fuel efficiency predicted by the function in Example 4 backfired; increased consumption is instead the result.

Solution

a. We can express $y = 0.0075x^2 - 0.2672x + 14.8$ in function notation by replacing y by $f(x)$. The formula in function notation is:

$$f(x) = 0.0075x^2 - 0.2672x + 14.8.$$

b. We can find $f(18)$, f of 18, by replacing each occurrence of x by 18. The arithmetic gets somewhat "messy," so it is probably a good idea to use a calculator.

$$f(x) = 0.0075x^2 - 0.2672x + 14.8 \qquad \text{This is the given formula in function notation.}$$

$$f(18) = 0.0075(18)^2 - 0.2672(18) + 14.8 \qquad \text{Replace each x by 18.}$$

$$= 0.0075(324) - 0.2672(18) + 14.8 \qquad \text{Use the order of operations, evaluating the exponential expression.}$$

$$= 2.43 - 4.8096 + 14.8 \qquad \text{Perform the multiplications.}$$

$$= 12.4204 \qquad \text{Subtract and add as indicated.}$$

Figure 7.7 Eighteen years after 1940, in 1958, fuel efficiency was at its worst—12.4 miles per gallon.

We see that $f(18) = 12.4204$—that is, f of 18 is 12.4204. Because 18 represents the number of years after 1940, this means that in 1958, U.S. automobiles averaged about 12.4 miles per gallon of gasoline. Figure 7.7 shows that $(18, 12.4)$ is the lowest point on the graph of the function. Thus, automobile fuel efficiency was at its very worst in 1958.

Graphing Functions

The **graph of a function** is the graph of its ordered pairs. In our next example, we will graph two functions. It would be awkward to call both of them f. We will call one function f and the other g. These letters are the most frequently used to name functions.

EXAMPLE 5   Graphing Functions

4 Graph functions.

Graph the functions $f(x) = 2x$ and $g(x) = 2x + 4$ in the same rectangular coordinate system. Let $x = -4, -2, 0,$ and 2.

Solution   For each function we use the suggested values for x, and then *evaluate* $f(x)$ and $g(x)$. Then we can create a table of some of the coordinates for the functions.

x	$f(x) = 2x$	$(x, f(x))$
-4	$f(-4) = 2(-4) = -8$	$(-4, -8)$
-2	$f(-2) = 2(-2) = -4$	$(-2, -4)$
0	$f(0) = 2(0) = 0$	$(0, 0)$
2	$f(2) = 2(2) = 4$	$(2, 4)$

x	$g(x) = 2x + 4$	$(x, g(x))$
-4	$g(-4) = 2(-4) + 4 = -4$	$(-4, -4)$
-2	$g(-2) = 2(-2) + 4 = 0$	$(-2, 0)$
0	$g(0) = 2(0) + 4 = 4$	$(0, 4)$
2	$g(2) = 2(2) + 4 = 8$	$(2, 8)$

Before we graph the functions, keep in mind that $f(x)$ and $g(x)$ can both be replaced by y. The ordered pairs in the last column of each table, $(x, f(x))$ and $(x, g(x))$, are the same as (x, y). We plot the points and connect them, resulting in the graphs in Figure 7.8. Notice that the graph of function g can be obtained from the graph of function f by moving the graph of f up four units.

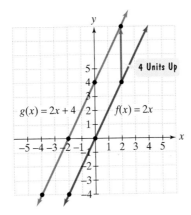

Figure 7.8 Shifting the graph of f four units up gives the graph of g.

EXAMPLE 6   Graphing a Formula

The function $f(x) = 2x^2 + 22x + 320$ describes the number of inmates in federal and state prisons, in thousands, x years after 1980, where $0 \le x \le 20$. Graph the function and use the graph to estimate the number of prisoners for the year 1997.

Solution   We begin by creating a table of some of the coordinates for the function. The graph is the curve passing through these ordered pairs.

x	$f(x) = 2x^2 + 22x + 320$	$(x, f(x))$
0	$f(0) = 2(0)^2 + 22(0) + 320$ $= 320$	$(0, 320)$
5	$f(5) = 2(5)^2 + 22(5) + 320$ $= 480$	$(5, 480)$
10	$f(10) = 2(10)^2 + 22(10) + 320$ $= 740$	$(10, 740)$
15	$f(15) = 2(15)^2 + 22(15) + 320$ $= 1100$	$(15, 1100)$
20	$f(20) = 2(20)^2 + 22(20) + 320$ $= 1560$	$(20, 1560)$

Figure 7.9 The graph of $f(x) = 2x^2 + 22x + 320$

The values of x start at 0 and end at 20. Many scales on the x-axis are possible; we will use one in which each tick mark represents 5 units. Values of y are rather large, starting at 320 thousand and ending at 1560 thousand. We will use a scale on the y-axis in which each tick-mark represents 500 thousand. Plotting the five ordered pairs and connecting them with a smooth curve gives the graph shown in Figure 7.9.

1997 is 17 years after 1980. To estimate from the graph the number of prisoners in 1997, locate the point on the graph that is directly above 17. Estimate the second coordinate by moving horizontally from the point to the vertical axis. As shown by the dashed blue line in Figure 7.9, the second coordinate is about three-fifths of the distance between 1000 and 1500.

$$y \approx 1000 + \tfrac{3}{5} \cdot 500 = 1000 + 300 = 1300$$

Thus, in the year 1997, there were approximately 1300 thousand, or 1,300,000, prisoners.

5 Use the vertical line test.

The Vertical Line Test

Not every graph in the rectangular coordinate system is the graph of a function. The definition of a function specifies that no value of x can be paired with two or more different values of y. Consequently, if a graph contains two or more different points with the same first coordinate, the graph cannot represent a function. This is illustrated in Figure 7.10. Observe that points sharing a common first coordinate are vertically above or below each other.

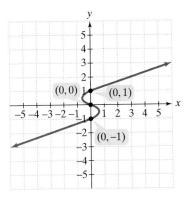

Figure 7.10 y is not a function of x because 0 is paired with three values of y, namely, 1, 0, and -1.

This observation is the basis of a useful test for determining whether a graph defines y as a function of x. The test is called the *vertical line test*.

Technology

Graphing calculators are powerful tools that allow you to view a function and its values at the same time. By using a graphing calculator to quickly generate the graph of a particular function, you can focus on the properties of the graph rather than worrying about how to create the graph by hand. These calculators also allow for the graphing of several functions on the same rectangular coordinate system, thus allowing you to quickly determine the solutions to systems of equations. http://oscar.ctc.edu/precalc/ReferenceCenter/Tech.html provides online tutorials for several different graphing calculator models.

Note: Technology Exercises throughout this chapter reference the TI-82 Graphics Calculator. Other calculators may be used, but the exact key sequences will be different. Consult your calculator's owner's manual for instructions.

The Vertical Line Test for Functions

If any vertical line intersects a graph in more than one point, the graph does not define y as a function of x.

EXAMPLE 7   Using the Vertical Line Test

Use the vertical line test to identify graphs in which y is a function of x.

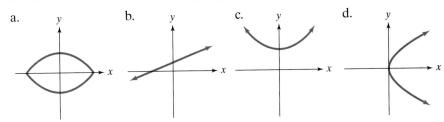

Solution y is a function of x for the graphs in (b) and (c).

Exercise Set 7.1

 Practice Exercises

In Exercises 1–20, plot the given point in a rectangular coordinate system.

1. $(1, 4)$ 2. $(2, 5)$ 3. $(-2, 3)$ 4. $(-1, 4)$
5. $(-3, -5)$ 6. $(-4, -2)$ 7. $(4, -1)$ 8. $(3, -2)$
9. $(-4, 0)$ 10. $(-5, 0)$ 11. $(0, -3)$ 12. $(0, -4)$
13. $(0, 0)$ 14. $(-3, -1\frac{1}{2})$ 15. $(-2, -3\frac{1}{2})$ 16. $(-5, -2.5)$
17. $(3.5, 4.5)$ 18. $(2.5, 3.5)$
19. $(1.25, -3.25)$ 20. $(2.25, -4.25)$

Graph each equation in Exercises 21–30. Let $x = -3, -2, -1,$ 0, 1, 2, and 3.

21. $y = x^2 - 2$ 22. $y = x^2 + 2$
23. $y = x - 2$ 24. $y = x + 2$
25. $y = 2x + 1$ 26. $y = 2x - 4$
27. $y = -\frac{1}{2}x$ 28. $y = -\frac{1}{2}x + 2$
29. $y = x^3$ 30. $y = x^3 - 1$

In Exercises 31–40, find f of each given value of x.

31. $f(x) = x - 4$ a. $f(8)$ b. $f(1)$
32. $f(x) = x - 6$ a. $f(9)$ b. $f(2)$
33. $f(x) = 3x - 2$ a. $f(7)$ b. $f(0)$
34. $f(x) = 4x - 3$ a. $f(7)$ b. $f(0)$
35. $f(x) = x^2 + 1$ a. $f(2)$ b. $f(-2)$
36. $f(x) = x^2 + 4$ a. $f(3)$ b. $f(-3)$
37. $f(x) = 3x^2 + 5$ a. $f(4)$ b. $f(-1)$
38. $f(x) = 2x^2 - 4$ a. $f(5)$ b. $f(-1)$
39. $f(x) = 2x^2 + 3x - 1$ a. $f(3)$ b. $f(-4)$
40. $f(x) = 3x^2 + 4x - 2$ a. $f(2)$ b. $f(-1)$

In Exercises 41–48, evaluate $f(x)$ for the given values for x. Then use the ordered pairs $(x, f(x))$ from your table to graph the function.

41. $f(x) = x^2 - 1$ 42. $f(x) = x^2 + 1$

x	$f(x) = x^2 - 1$
-2	
-1	
0	
1	
2	

x	$f(x) = x^2 + 1$
-2	
-1	
0	
1	
2	

43. $f(x) = x - 1$ 44. $f(x) = x + 1$

x	$f(x) = x - 1$
-2	
-1	
0	
1	
2	

x	$f(x) = x + 1$
-2	
-1	
0	
1	
2	

45. $f(x) = (x - 2)^2$ 46. $f(x) = (x + 1)^2$

x	$f(x) = (x - 2)^2$
0	
1	
2	
3	
4	

x	$f(x) = (x + 1)^2$
-3	
-2	
-1	
0	
1	

47. $f(x) = x^3 + 1$ 48. $f(x) = (x + 1)^3$

x	$f(x) = x^3 + 1$
-2	
-1	
0	
1	
2	

x	$f(x) = (x + 1)^3$
-3	
-2	
-1	
0	
1	

For Exercises 49–56, use the vertical line test to identify graphs in which y is a function of x.

49.

50.

51.

52.

53.

54.

55.

56.

Application Exercises

57. The graph shows defense spending in the United States from 1988 through 1998.
    a. Estimate the ordered pairs that correspond to points A, B, and C in the graph. The x-coordinate should be a year. The y-coordinate should be defense spending, expressed in billions of dollars.
    b. Describe the meaning of each of the three ordered pairs.

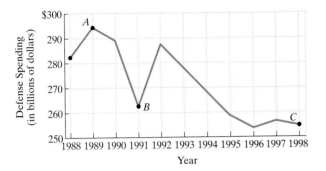

Source: Office of Management and Budget

58. The graph shows the gasoline mileage for compact and medium-sized cars traveling at various constant speeds.
    a. Determine the coordinates for points A and B. Interpret the coordinates in practical terms.
    b. Find the difference in the y-coordinates for points A and B. What does this mean?

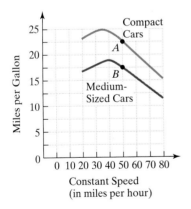

59. A rental company charges $40.00 a day plus $0.35 per mile to rent a moving truck. The total cost (y) for a day's rental if x miles are driven is described by $y = 40 + 0.35x$. A second company charges $36.00 a day plus $0.45 per mile, so the daily cost (y) if x miles are driven is described by $y = 36 + 0.45x$. The graphs of the two equations are shown at the top of the next column.
    a. What is the x-coordinate of the intersection point of the graphs? Describe what this x-coordinate means in practical terms.

b. What is a reasonable estimate for the y-coordinate of the intersection point?
c. Substitute the x-coordinate of the intersection point into each of the equations and find the corresponding value for y. Describe what this value represents in practical terms. How close is this value to your estimate from part (b)?

60. The graphs in the figure indicate the percent of unemployed blacks and whites in the United States. The graph for blacks is designated by f and the graph for whites by g.
    a. How do we know that f and g each represent graphs of functions?
    b. Estimate the coordinates of the highest point on the graph of f. What exactly does this mean?
    c. Find a reasonable estimate of

$$f(1998) - g(1998).$$

Describe what this means in practical terms.

Percent of U.S. Unemployed Blacks and Whites

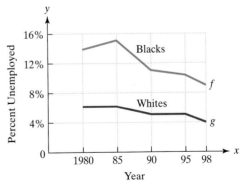

Source: U.S. Bureau of the Census

61. Although the level of air pollution varies from day to day and from hour to hour, during the summer the level of air pollution is a function of the time of day. The function

$$f(x) = 0.1x^2 - 0.4x + 0.6$$

describes the level of air pollution (in parts per million [ppm]), where x corresponds to the number of hours after 9 A.M.

a. Construct a table of values using integers from 0 to 5 for x, and graph the function from 0 to 5.

b. Researchers have determined that a level of 0.3 ppm of pollutants in the air can be hazardous to your health. Based on the graph, at what time of day should runners exercise to avoid unsafe air?

Writing in Mathematics

62. What is the rectangular coordinate system?

63. Explain how to plot a point in the rectangular coordinate system. Give an example with your explanation.

64. Explain why $(5, -2)$ and $(-2, 5)$ do not represent the same ordered pair.

65. Explain how to graph an equation in the rectangular coordinate system.

66. What is a function?

67. Explain how the vertical line test is used to determine whether a graph is a function.

Critical Thinking Exercises

68. Researchers at Yale University have suggested that levels of passion and commitment are functions of time. Based on the shapes of the graphs shown at the top of the next column, which do you think depicts passion and which represents commitment? Explain how you arrived at your answer.

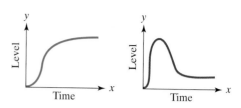

69. Consider a function defined by

$f(1) = 1$
$f(2) = 1 - 2 = -1$
$f(3) = 1 - 2 + 3 = 2$
$f(4) = 1 - 2 + 3 - 4 = -2$
$f(5) = 1 - 2 + 3 - 4 + 5 = 3$
$f(6) = 1 - 2 + 3 - 4 + 5 - 6 = -3$

a. What is the formula for $f(x)$ if x is even?
b. What is the formula for $f(x)$ if x is odd?
c. Find $f(20) + f(40) + f(65)$.

70. Re-examine Figure 7.6 on page 311. Explain why it is more realistic to graph each formula using only the points shown rather than connecting them with lines.

 ## Technology Exercise

71. Using the TI-82 Graphics Calculator, you can practice plotting points. First, push the GRAPH button. To display the DRAW POINTS menu, press 2nd [DRAW] > . Select option 1 to turn on a point. Then, to plot a point, position the cursor at the location on the display where you want to draw the point, and press ENTER. When you hit ENTER, the point will be plotted on the graph. The coordinates of the point are displayed at the bottom of the screen. Use this feature to plot any five of the points in Exercises 1–20.

 ## Group Exercise

72. In Exercise 68, passion and commitment are graphed over time. For this activity, you will be creating a graph of a particular experience that involved your feelings of love, anger, sadness, or any other emotion you choose. The horizontal axis should be labeled time and the vertical axis the emotion you are graphing. You will not be using your algebra skills to create your graph; however, you should try to make the graph as precise as possible. You may use negative numbers on the vertical axis, if appropriate. After each group member has created a graph, pool together all of the graphs and study them to see if there are any similarities in the graphs for a particular emotion or for all emotions.

SECTION 7.2   *Linear Functions and Their Graphs*

Objectives

1. Use intercepts to graph a linear equation.
2. Calculate slope.
3. Use the slope and *y*-intercept to graph a line.
4. Graph horizontal or vertical lines.
5. Interpret slope and *y*-intercept in applied situations.

We hope that you are not watching the horror film *Anaconda* as you glance at the image above. If you are, think of smaller snakes whose body lengths range from 160 millimeters (about 6.25 inches) to 1800 millimeters (about 5.8 feet, which is large enough if you are phobic about snakes). The graph in Figure 7.11 indicates that a snake's body length is a function of its tail length. The point $(30, 231.8)$ shows that a snake with a 30-millimeter tail length has a body length of 231.8 millimeters.

The graph in Figure 7.11 is a straight line. The equation for this line is:

$$y = 7.44x + 8.6.$$

The variable *x* represents the snake's tail length in millimeters. The variable *y* represents the snake's body length in millimeters. Using function notation, we can rewrite the equation as:

$$f(x) = 7.44x + 8.6.$$

A function such as this, whose graph is a straight line, is called a **linear function**. In this section we will study linear functions and their graphs.

Figure 7.11 The graph of $y = 7.44x + 8.6$, a linear function

1 Use intercepts to graph a linear equation.

Graphing Using Intercepts

There is another way that we can write the equation

$$y = 7.44x + 8.6.$$

We will collect the *x*- and *y*-terms on the left side. This is done by subtracting $7.44x$ from both sides:

$$-7.44x + y = 8.6.$$

All equations of the form $Ax + By = C$ are straight lines when graphed as long as *A* and *B* are not both zero. Such equations are called **linear equations in two variables**. We can quickly obtain the graph for equations in this form by finding the points where the graph crosses the *x*-axis and the *y*-axis. The *x*-coordinate of the point where the graph crosses the *x*-axis is called the **x-intercept**. The *y*-coordinate of the point where the graph crosses the *y*-axis is called the **y-intercept**.

Locating Intercepts

To locate the *x*-intercept, set $y = 0$ and solve the equation for *x*.
To locate the *y*-intercept, set $x = 0$ and solve the equation for *y*.

An equation of the form $Ax + By = C$ can be graphed by finding the x- and y-intercepts, plotting the intercepts, and drawing a straight line through these points. When graphing using intercepts, it is a good idea to use a third point, a checkpoint, before drawing the line. A checkpoint can be obtained by selecting a value for x, other than 0, and finding the corresponding value for y. The checkpoint should lie on the same line as the x- and y-intercepts. If it does not, recheck your work and find the error.

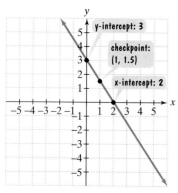

Figure 7.12 The graph of $3x + 2y = 6$

EXAMPLE 1   Using Intercepts to Graph a Linear Equation

Graph: $3x + 2y = 6$.

Solution

Find the x-intercept by letting	**Find the y-intercept by letting**
$y = 0$ and solving for x.	**$x = 0$ and solving for y.**
$3x + 2 \cdot 0 = 6$	$3 \cdot 0 + 2y = 6$
$3x = 6$	$2y = 6$
$x = 2$	$y = 3$

The x-intercept is 2, so the line passes through $(2, 0)$. The y-intercept is 3, so the line passes through $(0, 3)$.

For our checkpoint, we will let $x = 1$ and find the corresponding value for y.

$$3x + 2y = 6 \qquad \text{This is the given equation.}$$
$$3(1) + 2y = 6 \qquad \text{Substitute 1 for x.}$$
$$3 + 2y = 6$$
$$2y = 3 \qquad \text{Subtract 3 from both sides.}$$
$$y = \tfrac{3}{2} \qquad \text{Divide by 2.}$$

The checkpoint is the ordered pair $\left(1, \tfrac{3}{2}\right)$ or $(1, 1.5)$.

The three points in Figure 7.12 lie along the same line. Drawing a line through the three points results in the graph of $3x + 2y = 6$.

2 Calculate slope.

These lines have various steepnesses, or slopes.

Slope

Mathematicians have developed a useful measure of the steepness of a line, called the **slope** of the line. Slope compares the vertical change (the **rise**) to the horizontal change (the **run**) when moving from one fixed point to another along the line. To calculate the slope of a line, mathematicians use a ratio comparing the change in y (the rise) to the change in x (the run).

Definition of Slope

The *slope* of the line through the distinct points (x_1, y_1) and (x_2, y_2) is:

$$\frac{\text{Change in } y}{\text{Change in } x} = \frac{\text{Rise}}{\text{Run}}$$

$$= \frac{y_2 - y_1}{x_2 - x_1} = \frac{y_1 - y_2}{x_1 - x_2}$$

where $x_2 - x_1 \neq 0$.

It is common notation to let the letter m represent the slope of a line. The letter m is used because it is the first letter of the French verb *monter*, meaning to rise or to ascend.

EXAMPLE 2   Using the Definition of Slope

Calculate the slope of the line passing through the points $(-3, -1)$ and $(-2, 4)$.

Solution   Figure 7.13(a) shows the two points and the line. We will let $(x_1, y_1) = (-3, -1)$ and $(x_2, y_2) = (-2, 4)$.

$$m = \frac{\text{Change in } y}{\text{Change in } x} = \frac{y_2 - y_1}{x_2 - x_1} = \frac{4 - (-1)}{-2 - (-3)} = \frac{5}{1} = 5$$

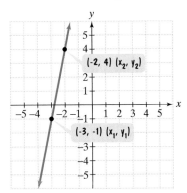

Figure 7.13(a)

The slope of 5 indicates that there is a vertical change, a rise, of 5 units for each horizontal change, a run, of 1 unit. This is shown in Figure. 7.13(b). The slope is positive, and the line rises from left to right.

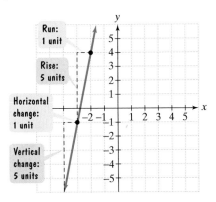

Figure 7.13(b)

The line in Example 2 has a positive slope, rising from left to right. A line may also have a negative slope. Such a line falls from left to right. A horizontal line neither rises nor falls and has a slope of 0. A vertical line has no horizontal change, so $x_2 - x_1 = 0$. Because we cannot divide by 0, the slope of a vertical line is undefined.

3 Use the slope and y-intercept to graph a line.

The Slope-Intercept Form of a Line

We opened this section with the linear function

$$y = 7.44x + 8.6.$$

Recall that x represents the snake's tail length and y represents its body length. A linear equation such as this, in the form $y = mx + b$, is said to be in **slope-intercept form**.

> ## Slope-Intercept Form of the Equation of a Line
> The equation $y = mx + b$ is called the **slope-intercept form of a line**. The coefficient of x is the slope of the line, and the constant term is its y-intercept.

EXAMPLE 3   Graphing by Using the Slope and y-Intercept

Graph the linear function $y = \dfrac{2}{3}x + 2$ by using the slope and y-intercept.

Solution   The equation of the linear function is in the form $y = mx + b$. We can find the slope, m, by identifying the coefficient of x. We can find the y-intercept by identifying the constant term, b.

$$y = \frac{2}{3}x + 2$$

The slope is $\dfrac{2}{3}$.

The y-intercept is 2.

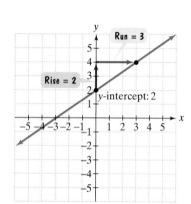

Figure 7.14 The graph of $y = \frac{2}{3}x + 2$

We need two points in order to graph the linear function. We can use the y-intercept, 2, to obtain the first point $(0, 2)$. Plot this point on the y-axis, shown in Figure 7.14.

We know the slope and one point on the line. We can use the slope, $\frac{2}{3}$, to determine a second point on the line. By definition,

$$m = \frac{2}{3} = \frac{\text{Rise}}{\text{Run}}.$$

We plot the second point on the line by starting at $(0, 2)$, the first point. Based on the slope, we move 2 units *up* (the rise) and 3 units to the *right* (the run). This puts us at a second point on the line, shown in Figure 7.14.

We use a straightedge to draw a line through the two points. The graph of $y = \frac{2}{3}x + 2$ is shown in Figure 7.14. Using function notation, this is also the graph of $f(x) = \frac{2}{3}x + 2$.

Using y-intercept -3 and slope 4 to graph a line

> ## Graphing $y = mx + b$ by Using the Slope and y-Intercept
> 1. Plot the y-intercept on the y-axis. This is the point $(0, b)$.
> 2. Obtain a second point using the slope, m. Write m as a fraction, and use rise over run starting at the y-intercept to plot this point.
> 3. Use a straightedge to draw a line through the two points. Draw arrowheads at the ends of the line to show that the line continues infinitely in both directions.

Earlier in this section, we considered linear functions whose equations are of the form $Ax + By = C$. We used x- and y-intercepts to graph these functions.

It is also possible to obtain the graph by using the slope and y-intercept. To do this, begin by solving $Ax + By = C$ for y. This will put the equation in slope-intercept form. Then use the three steps in the box to graph the equation. This procedure is illustrated in Example 4.

EXAMPLE 4   Graphing by Using the Slope and y-Intercept

Graph the linear function $2x + 5y = 0$ by using the slope and y-intercept.

Solution   We put the equation in slope-intercept form by solving for y.

$$2x + 5y = 0 \qquad \text{This is the given equation.}$$

$$2x - 2x + 5y = -2x + 0 \qquad \text{Subtract 2x from both sides.}$$

$$5y = -2x + 0 \qquad \text{Simplify.}$$

$$\frac{5y}{5} = \frac{-2x + 0}{5} \qquad \text{Divide both sides by 5.}$$

$$y = \frac{-2x}{5} + \frac{0}{5} \qquad \text{Divide each term in the numerator by 5.}$$

$$y = -\frac{2}{5}x + 0 \qquad \text{Simplify.}$$

Now that the equation is in slope-intercept form, we can use the slope and y-intercept to obtain its graph. Examine the slope-intercept form:

$$y = -\frac{2}{5}x + 0$$

slope: $-\dfrac{2}{5}$ y-intercept: 0

Note that the slope is $-\frac{2}{5}$ and the y-intercept is 0. Use the y-intercept to plot $(0, 0)$ on the y-axis. Then locate a second point by using the slope.

$$m = \frac{-2}{5} = \frac{\text{Rise}}{\text{Run}}$$

Because the rise is -2 and the run is 5, move *down* 2 units and to the *right* 5 units, starting at the y-intercept. The graph is the line drawn through these points, shown in Figure 7.15.

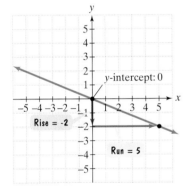

Figure 7.15 The graph of $2x + 5y = 0$, or $y = -\frac{2}{5}x + 0$

If you try graphing $2x + 5y = 0$ using intercepts, you will find that the x-intercept is 0 and the y-intercept is 0. This means that the graph passes through the origin. A second point must be found to graph the line. In Example 4, the line's slope gave us the second point.

4 Graph horizontal or vertical lines.

Horizontal and Vertical Lines

EXAMPLE 5   Graphing a Horizontal Line

Graph $y = -4$ in the rectangular coordinate system.

Solution   All ordered pairs that are solutions to $y = -4$ have a value of y that is always -4. Any value can be used for x. Let us select three of the possible values for x: -2, 0, and 3. So, the ordered pairs that are solutions to $y = -4$ are $(-2, -4)$, $(0, -4)$, and $(3, -4)$. Plot each of these points. Drawing a line that passes through the three points gives the horizontal line shown in Figure 7.16.

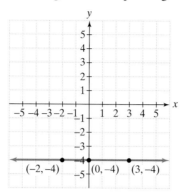

Figure 7.16 The graph of $y = -4$

Horizontal Lines

The graph of $y = b$ is a horizontal line that intersects the y-axis at b. In particular, the graph of $y = 0$ is the x-axis.

EXAMPLE 6   Graphing a Vertical Line

Graph $x = 5$ in the rectangular coordinate system.

Solution   All ordered pairs that are solutions to $x = 5$ have a value of x that is always 5. Any value can be used for y. Let us select three of the possible values for y: -2, 0, and 3. So, the ordered pairs that are solutions to $x = 5$ are $(5, -2)$, $(5, 0)$, and $(5, 3)$. Plot each of these points. Drawing a line that passes through the three points gives the vertical line shown in Figure 7.17.

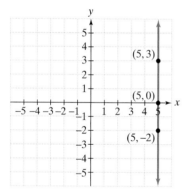

Figure 7.17 The graph $x = 5$

By generalizing from Example 6, we obtain the following result.

Vertical Lines

The graph of $x = a$ is a vertical line that intersects the x-axis at a. In particular, the graph of $x = 0$ is the y-axis.

The graph of a vertical line does not pass the vertical line test. One of the vertical lines that can be drawn will coincide with the given vertical line. This line will certainly intersect the graph more than once; it will intersect it in infinitely many points! Thus, a vertical line does not define y as a function of x. All other lines are graphs of functions.

5 Interpret slope and y-intercept in applied situations.

Applications of Linear Functions

You probably do not need to be told this: The cost of a college education continues to skyrocket. The linear function $y = 166x + 1781$ describes the approximate cost (tuition and fees per year) of a four-year public college. The variable x represents the number of years after 1990. The variable y represents the cost per year. We can use the function to find the tuition and fees back in the "good old days."

Year	x	Tuition and fees: $y = 166x + 1781$
1990, 0 years after 1990	0	$y = 166 \cdot 0 + 1781 = \$1781$
1991, 1 year after 1990	1	$y = 166 \cdot 1 + 1781 = \$1947$
1992, 2 years after 1990	2	$y = 166 \cdot 2 + 1781 = \$2113$
1993, 3 years after 1990	3	$y = 166 \cdot 3 + 1781 = \$2279$

Tuition and fees are increasing by \$166 per year. Observe that 166 is the slope of $y = 166x + 1781$. In situations like this, in which an equation in slope-intercept form describes some real-world situation, the slope and the y-intercept can be interpreted in terms of that situation. This is illustrated in Table 7.2.

Table 7.2   Interpreting Slope and y-Intercept

Linear Function	What the Function Describes	Interpretation
$y = 166x + 1781$ Slope y-intercept	The approximate cost (tuition and fees per year) of a four-year public college x years after 1990	1781 is the y-intercept. At the beginning (in 1990), the cost of college was \$1781 per year. 166 is the slope. The cost of college is increasing \$166 per year.
$y = -6.9x + 40.3$ Slope y-intercept	The percentage of men injured in the Boston Marathon by age group x: 0: under 20 3: 40–49 1: 20–29 4: 50–59 2: 30–39 *Source: The Boston Globe,* April 20, 1992.	40.3 is the y-intercept. For group 0 (men under 20), 40.3% were injured. -6.9 is the slope. The percentage injured decreases by 6.9% for each subsequent age group.

Railroads and Highways

The steepest part of Mt. Washington Cog Railway in New Hampshire has a 37% grade. This is equivalent to a slope of $\frac{37}{100}$. For every horizontal change of 100 feet, the railroad ascends 37 feet vertically. Engineers denote slope by grade, expressing slope as a percentage.

4 feet ⌐5 feet

100 feet
4% Grade

100 feet
−5% Grade

Railroad grades are usually less than 2%, although in the mountains they may go as high as 4%. The grade of the Mt. Washington Cog Railway is phenomenal, making it necessary for locomotives to *push* single cars up its steepest part.

A Mount Washington Cog Railway locomotive pushing a single car up the steepest part of the railroad. The locomotive is about 120 years old.

Exercise Set 7.2

✓ Practice Exercises

In Exercises 1–8, use the x- and y-intercepts to graph each linear equation.

1. $x - y = 3$
2. $x + y = 4$
3. $3x - 4y = 12$
4. $2x - 5y = 10$
5. $2x + y = 6$
6. $x + 3y = 6$
7. $5x = 3y - 15$
8. $3x = 2y + 6$

In Exercises 9–20, calculate the slope of the line passing through the given points. If the slope is undefined, so state. Then indicate whether the line rises, falls, is horizontal, or is vertical.

9. $(2, 6)$ and $(3, 5)$
10. $(4, 2)$ and $(3, 4)$
11. $(-2, 1)$ and $(2, 2)$
12. $(-1, 3)$ and $(2, 4)$
13. $(-2, 4)$ and $(-1, -1)$
14. $(6, -4)$ and $(4, -2)$
15. $(5, 3)$ and $(5, -2)$
16. $(3, -4)$ and $(3, 5)$
17. $(2, 0)$ and $(0, 8)$
18. $(3, 0)$ and $(0, -9)$
19. $(5, 1)$ and $(-2, 1)$
20. $(-2, 3)$ and $(1, 3)$

In Exercises 21–32, graph each linear function using the slope and y-intercept.

21. $y = 2x + 3$
22. $y = 2x + 1$
23. $y = -2x + 4$
24. $y = -2x + 3$
25. $y = \frac{1}{2}x + 3$
26. $y = \frac{1}{2}x + 2$
27. $y = \frac{2}{3}x - 4$
28. $y = \frac{3}{4}x - 5$
29. $y = -\frac{3}{4}x + 4$
30. $y = -\frac{2}{3}x + 5$
31. $y = -\frac{5}{3}x$
32. $y = -\frac{4}{3}x$

In Exercises 33–40:

   a. *Put the equation in slope-intercept form by solving for y.*
   b. *Identify the slope and the y-intercept.*
   c. *Use the slope and y-intercept to graph the line.*

33. $3x + y = 0$
34. $2x + y = 0$
35. $3y = 4x$
36. $4y = 5x$
37. $2x + y = 3$
38. $3x + y = 4$
39. $7x + 2y = 14$
40. $5x + 3y = 15$

In Exercises 41–48, graph each horizontal or vertical line.

41. $y = 4$
42. $y = 2$
43. $y = -2$
44. $y = -3$
45. $x = 2$
46. $x = 4$
47. $x + 1 = 0$
48. $x + 5 = 0$

⭐ Application Exercises

49. The linear function $y = 2.35x + 179.5$ describes the population of the United States, y, in millions, x years after 1960.

   a. Use the formula to find the U.S. population in 1960, 1961, 1962, 1963, and 1964.
   b. What is the slope of this function? What does it represent in this situation?
   c. What is the y-intercept of this function? What does it represent in this situation?
   d. The function can also be expressed as $f(x) = 2.35x + 179.5$. Find $f(40)$. What does your answer represent?

50. A salesperson receives a fixed salary plus a percentage of all sales. The linear function $y = 0.05x + 400$ describes the weekly salary, y, in dollars, as a function of weekly sales, x, also in dollars.

   a. Use the formula to find the weekly salary for sales of $0, $1, $2, $3, $4, and $5.
   b. What is the slope of this function? What does it represent in this situation?
   c. What is the y-intercept of this function? What does it represent in this situation?
   d. The function can be written as $f(x) = 0.05x + 400$. Find $f(6000)$. What does your answer represent?

✍ Writing in Mathematics

51. Describe how to find the x-intercept of a linear equation.
52. Describe how to find the y-intercept of a linear equation.
53. What is the slope of a line?
54. Describe how to calculate the slope of a line passing through two points.
55. Describe how to graph a line using the slope and y-intercept. Provide an original example with your description.
56. What does it mean if the slope of a line is 0?
57. What does it mean if the slope of a line is undefined?
58. How many points are needed to graph a line? How many should actually be used? Explain.
59. Explain why the y-values can be any number for the equation $x = 5$. How is this shown in the graph of the equation?

💻 Technology Exercise

60. To graph a linear function using the TI-82 Graphics Calculator, push the Y=button. Enter a linear function, such as $y = 2x + 3$, and press ENTER (the X is obtained from the X, T, Θ key). The function will be plotted when you push the GRAPH button. Use this feature to graph any five of the linear functions in Exercises 21–32.

Critical Thinking Exercises

61. The graph shows the life expectancy in years for U.S. women whose year of birth is indicated on the *x*-axis. Find the slope of the line passing through the points whose coordinates are shown on the graph. Describe what the slope represents.

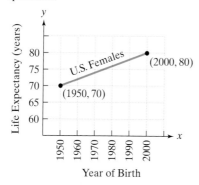

Year of Birth

62. The graph shown at the right indicates that lower fertility rates (the number of births per woman) are related to the percent of the population using contraceptives. A line that best fits the data is shown. Estimate the *y*-intercept and the slope of this line. Then write the line's slope-intercept equation. Use the equation to find the number of births per woman if 90% of married women of child-bearing age used contraceptives.

Contraceptive Prevalence and Births per Woman, Selected Countries

*Percent of married women of child-bearing age.

Source: Peter J. Donaldson and Amy Ong Tsui. "International Family Planning Movement," *Population Bulletin 45,* November 1990, Population Reference Bureau. Inc.

SECTION 7.3   *Quadratic Functions and Their Graphs*

Objectives

1. Graph a parabola.
2. Solve applied problems based on knowing a parabola's vertex.

In the opening to this chapter, we mentioned that a driver's age has something to do with his or her chances of getting into a car accident. The equation

$$y = 0.4x^2 - 36x + 1000$$

describes the number of accidents, *y*, per 50 million miles driven, as a function of a driver's age, *x*, in years, where *x* is an age between 16 and 74 inclusive ($16 \le x \le 74$). Can you see how this function differs from the linear functions studied in the previous section? The exponent on *x* is 2. In a linear function, the greatest exponent on the variable is 1. The equation

$$y = 0.4x^2 - 36x + 1000$$

is of the form $y = ax^2 + bx + c$. An equation of this form, in which the greatest exponent on the variable is 2, is called a **quadratic function**. Using function notation, we can also express this equation as:

$$f(x) = 0.4x^2 - 36x + 1000.$$

EXAMPLE 1   Using a Quadratic Function

Use the quadratic function described on page 327 to find and interpret $f(20)$.

Solution

We can find $f(20)$, f of 20, by replacing each x by 20.

$$f(x) = 0.4x^2 - 36x + 1000 \qquad \text{This is the given quadratic function.}$$

$$f(20) = 0.4(20)^2 - 36(20) + 1000 \qquad \text{Replace each x by 20.}$$

$$= 0.4(400) - 36(20) + 1000 \qquad \text{Use the order of operations, evaluating the exponential expression.}$$

$$= 160 - 720 + 1000 \qquad \text{Perform the multiplications.}$$

$$= 440 \qquad \text{Subtract and add as indicated.}$$

We see that $f(20) = 440$—that is, f of 20 is 440. In practical terms, this indicates that 20-year-olds have 440 accidents per 50 million miles driven.

1 Graph a parabola.

Graphs of Quadratic Functions

The graph of the quadratic function $y = ax^2 + bx + c$ is called a **parabola**. Parabolas are shaped like cups, as shown in Figure 7.18. If the coefficient of x^2 (a in $ax^2 + bx + c$) is positive, the parabola opens upward. When the coefficient of x^2 is negative, the graph opens downward. The **vertex** (or turning point) of the parabola is the lowest point on the graph when it opens upward and the highest point on the graph when it opens downward.

Parabola opens upward.

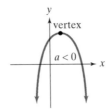

Parabola opens downward.

Figure 7.18 The graph of $y = ax^2 + bx + c$ for $a > 0$ and $a < 0$

EXAMPLE 2   Using Point-Plotting to Graph a Parabola

Consider the equation $y = x^2 + 4x + 3$.

a. Is the graph a parabola that opens upward or downward?

b. Use point-plotting to graph the parabola.

Solution

a. To determine whether a parabola opens upward or downward, we begin by identifying a, the coefficient of x^2. Shown below are the values for $a, b,$ and c in $y = x^2 + 4x + 3$. Notice that we wrote x^2 as $1x^2$.

$$y = 1x^2 + 4x + 3$$

| a, the coefficient of x^2, is 1. | b, the coefficient of x, is 4. | c, the constant term, is 3. |

When a is greater than 0, the parabola opens upward. When a is less than 0, the parabola opens downward. Because $a = 1$, which is greater than 0, the parabola opens upward.

b. To use point-plotting to graph the parabola, we first make a table of x- and y-coordinates.

x	$y = x^2 + 4x + 3$	(x, y)
-5	$y = (-5)^2 + 4(-5) + 3 = 8$	$(-5, 8)$
-4	$y = (-4)^2 + 4(-4) + 3 = 3$	$(-4, 3)$
-3	$y = (-3)^2 + 4(-3) + 3 = 0$	$(-3, 0)$
-2	$y = (-2)^2 + 4(-2) + 3 = -1$	$(-2, -1)$
-1	$y = (-1)^2 + 4(-1) + 3 = 0$	$(-1, 0)$
0	$y = 0^2 + 4(0) + 3 = 3$	$(0, 3)$
1	$y = 1^2 + 4(1) + 3 = 8$	$(1, 8)$

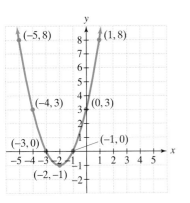

Figure 7.19 The graph of $y = x^2 + 4x + 3$

Then we plot the points and connect them with a smooth curve. The graph of $y = x^2 + 4x + 3$ is shown in Figure 7.19.

A number of points are important when graphing a quadratic function. These points, labeled in Figure 7.20, are the x-intercepts (although not every parabola has two x-intercepts), the y-intercept, and the vertex. Let us see how we can locate these points.

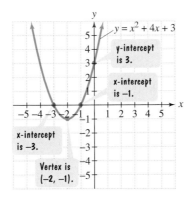

Figure 7.20 Useful points in graphing a parabola

Finding a Parabola's x-Intercepts

At each point where a parabola crosses the x-axis, the value of y equals 0. Thus, the x-intercepts can be found by replacing y with 0 in the quadratic function. Use factoring or the quadratic formula to solve the resulting quadratic equation for x.

EXAMPLE 3   Finding a Parabola's x-Intercepts

Find the x-intercepts for the parabola whose equation is $y = x^2 + 4x + 3$.

Solution   Replace y with 0 in $y = x^2 + 4x + 3$. We obtain $0 = x^2 + 4x + 3$, or $x^2 + 4x + 3 = 0$. We can solve this equation by factoring.

$$x^2 + 4x + 3 = 0$$
$$(x + 3)(x + 1) = 0$$
$$x + 3 = 0 \qquad \text{or} \qquad x + 1 = 0$$
$$x = -3 \qquad\qquad\qquad x = -1$$

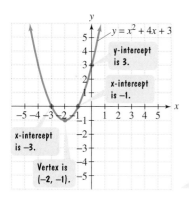

Figure 7.20 repeated so you do not have to turn back a page

Thus, the x-intercepts are -3 and -1. The parabola passes through $(-3, 0)$ and $(-1, 0)$, shown in Figure 7.20.

Finding a Parabola's y-Intercept

At the point where a parabola crosses the y-axis, the value of x equals 0. Thus, the y-intercept can be found by replacing x with 0 in the quadratic function. Simple arithmetic will produce a value for y, which is the y-intercept.

EXAMPLE 4   Finding a Parabola's y-Intercept

Find the y-intercept for the parabola whose equation is $y = x^2 + 4x + 3$.

Solution   Replace x with 0 in $y = x^2 + 4x + 3$.

$$y = 0^2 + 4 \cdot 0 + 3 = 0 + 0 + 3 = 3$$

The y-intercept is 3. The parabola passes through $(0, 3)$, shown in Figure 7.20.

Finding a Parabola's Vertex

Keep in mind that a parabola's vertex is its turning point. The x-coordinate of the vertex for the parabola in Figure 7.20, -2, is midway between the x-intercepts, -3 and -1. However, not every parabola has two x-intercepts. There is a formula that can be used to determine the vertex of a parabola regardless of how many x-intercepts it has. The x-coordinate of the vertex is found by using the following equation:

$$x = \frac{-b}{2a}.$$

Once the x-coordinate of the vertex is determined, you can find the y-coordinate by substituting the x-coordinate into $y = ax^2 + bx + c$. Evaluating this equation gives the y-coordinate of the vertex. This procedure is illustrated in Example 5.

EXAMPLE 5   Finding a Parabola's Vertex

Find the vertex for the parabola whose equation is $y = x^2 + 4x + 3$.

Solution   To find the x-coordinate of the vertex, we use the equation $x = \frac{-b}{2a}$. In the equation $y = x^2 + 4x + 3$, $a = 1$, $b = 4$, and $c = 3$. The x-coordinate of the vertex is found as follows:

$$x = \frac{-b}{2a} = \frac{-4}{2 \cdot 1} = \frac{-4}{2} = -2$$

To find the y-coordinate of the vertex, we substitute -2 for x in $y = x^2 + 4x + 3$ and then evaluate.

$$y = x^2 + 4x + 3 \qquad \text{This is the given quadratic function.}$$

$$y = (-2)^2 + 4(-2) + 3 \qquad \text{Replace each occurrence of x by } -2.$$

$$= 4 + (-8) + 3$$

$$= -4 + 3 = -1$$

The y-coordinate of the vertex is -1. On page 330, we found that the x-coordinate is -2. Therefore, the vertex of the parabola is located at the point $(-2, -1)$. This is shown in Figure 7.20.

Here is a general procedure to sketch the graph of a quadratic function.

Graphing the Quadratic Function

$$y = ax^2 + bx + c,$$

whose graph is called a parabola

1. Determine whether the parabola opens upward or downward. If $a > 0$, it opens upward. If $a < 0$, it opens downward.

2. Determine the vertex of the parabola. The x-coordinate is $x = \dfrac{-b}{2a}$.
   The y-coordinate is found by substituting the x-coordinate in the parabola's equation.

3. Find any x-intercepts by replacing y with 0. Solve the resulting quadratic equation for x.

4. Find the y-intercept by replacing x with 0.

5. Plot the intercepts and the vertex.

6. Connect these points with a smooth curve that is shaped like a cup.

Look at the unusual image of the word "mirror" shown below. The artist, Scott Kim, has created the image so that the two halves of the whole are mirror images of each other. A parabola shares this kind of symmetry, in which the vertex divides the figure in half. The movements of gymnasts, divers, and swimmers can approximate this symmetry.

From INVERSIONS © 1989 by Scott Kim. Used with permission of W.H. Freeman and Company.

EXAMPLE 6 Graphing a Parabola

Graph the quadratic function: $y = x^2 - 2x - 3$.

Solution We can graph this equation by following the steps in the box.

Step 1 Determine how the parabola opens. Note that a, the coefficient of x^2 is 1. Thus, $a > 0$; this positive value tells us that the parabola opens upward.

Step 2 Find the vertex. We know that the x-coordinate of the vertex is $x = \dfrac{-b}{2a}$.

Let us identify the numbers a, b, and c in the given equation, which is in the form $y = ax^2 + bx + c$.

$$y = x^2 - 2x - 3$$

| $a = 1$ | $b = -2$ | $c = -3$ |

Now we substitute the values of a and b into the equation for the x-coordinate:

$$x = \frac{-b}{2a} = \frac{-(-2)}{2(1)} = \frac{2}{2} = 1$$

The x-coordinate of the vertex is equal to 1. We can substitute 1 for x in the equation of the function to find the y-coordinate:

$$y = x^2 - 2x - 3 = 1^2 - 2 \cdot 1 - 3 = 1 - 2 - 3 = -4$$

The vertex is at $(1, -4)$.

Step 3 Find the x-intercepts. Replace y with 0 in $y = x^2 - 2x - 3$. We obtain $0 = x^2 - 2x - 3$ or $x^2 - 2x - 3 = 0$. We can solve this equation by factoring.

$$x^2 - 2x - 3 = 0$$
$$(x - 3)(x + 1) = 0$$
$$x - 3 = 0 \quad \text{or} \quad x + 1 = 0$$
$$x = 3 \qquad\qquad x = -1$$

The x-intercepts are 3 and -1. The parabola passes through $(3, 0)$ and $(-1, 0)$.

Step 4 Find the y-intercept. Replace x with 0 in $y = x^2 - 2x - 3$:

$$y = 0^2 - 2 \cdot 0 - 3 = 0 - 0 - 3 = -3$$

The y-intercept is -3. The parabola passes through $(0, -3)$.

Steps 5 and 6 Plot the intercepts and the vertex. Connect these points with a smooth curve. The intercepts and the vertex are shown as the four labeled points in Figure 7.21. Also shown is the graph of the parabola, obtained by connecting the points with a smooth curve.

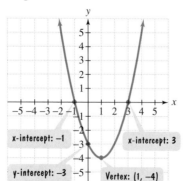

Figure 7.21 The graph of $y = x^2 - 2x - 3$

Parabola

Suspension Bridge

Parabola

Arch Bridge

Cables hung between structures to form suspension bridges form parabolas. Arches whose main purpose is strength are usually parabolic in shape.

EXAMPLE 7   Graphing a Parabola

Graph the quadratic function: $f(x) = -x^2 + 4x - 1$.

Solution   In order to follow the steps in the box on graphing parabolas, we begin by replacing $f(x)$ with y. Thus, we express the quadratic function as:

$$y = -x^2 + 4x - 1.$$

Step 1   Determine how the parabola opens. Note that a, the coefficient of x^2, is -1. Thus, $a < 0$; this negative value tells us that the parabola opens downward.

Step 2   Find the vertex. We know that the x-coordinate of the vertex is $x = \dfrac{-b}{2a}$. Once again, we identify a, b, and c in $y = ax^2 + bx + c$.

$$y = -x^2 + 4x - 1$$

$a = -1$ $b = 4$ $c = -1$

Substitute the values of a and b into the equation for the x-coordinate:

$$x = \frac{-b}{2a} = \frac{-4}{2(-1)} = \frac{-4}{-2} = 2$$

The x-coordinate of the vertex is 2. We substitute 2 for x in the equation of the function to find the y-coordinate:

$$y = -x^2 + 4x - 1 = -2^2 + 4 \cdot 2 - 1 = -4 + 8 - 1 = 3$$

The vertex is at $(2, 3)$.

Step 3   Find the x-intercepts. Replace y with 0 in $y = -x^2 + 4x - 1$. We obtain $0 = -x^2 + 4x - 1$ or $-x^2 + 4x - 1 = 0$. This equation cannot be solved by factoring. We will use the quadratic formula to solve it.

$$a = -1, \quad b = 4, \quad c = -1$$

$$x = \frac{-b \pm \sqrt{b^2 - 4ac}}{2a}$$

$$= \frac{-4 \pm \sqrt{4^2 - 4(-1)(-1)}}{2(-1)}$$

$$= \frac{-4 \pm \sqrt{16 - 4}}{-2}$$

$$= \frac{-4 \pm \sqrt{12}}{-2}$$

If you evaluate this expression with your calculator, rather than first rounding $\sqrt{12}$, the rounded x-intercept will be 3.7

Because $\sqrt{12} \approx 3.5$,

$$x \approx \frac{-4 + 3.5}{-2} \approx \frac{-0.5}{-2} \approx 0.3 \quad \text{or} \quad x \approx \frac{-4 - 3.5}{-2} \approx \frac{-7.5}{-2} \approx 3.8.$$

The x-intercepts are approximately 0.3 and 3.8 The parabola passes through $(0.3, 0)$ and $(3.8, 0)$.

Technology

A Revolution in Hand-Held Computers

A graphing calculator easily provides the graphs of the functions that we have been drawing by hand. You need only enter the function's equation, determine the number of tick-marks and their value along each axis, press **GRAPH**, and there you have it! A graph is instantly displayed in the rectangular coordinate system.

Shown below are the graphs of $y = 2x - 4$ and $y = x^2 - 4$, each obtained using a graphing calculator. Typically, the calculator shows tick-marks more widely spaced along the x-axis than along the y-axis. However the user can change the spacing of the tick-marks.

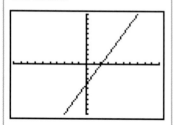

The graph of $y = 2x - 4$

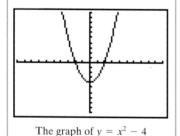

The graph of $y = x^2 - 4$

2 Solve applied problems based on knowing a parabola's vertex.

Step 4 **Find the y-intercept.** Replace x with 0 in $y = -x^2 + 4x - 1$:

$$y = -0^2 + 4 \cdot 0 - 1 = 0 + 0 - 1 = -1$$

The y-intercept is -1. The parabola passes through $(0, -1)$.

Steps 5 and 6 **Plot the intercepts and the vertex. Connect these points with a smooth curve.** The intercepts and the vertex are shown as the four labeled points in Figure 7.22. Also shown is the graph of the parabola, obtained by connecting the points with a smooth curve.

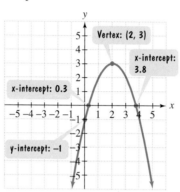

Figure 7.22 The graph of $f(x) = -x^2 + 4x - 1$

If you use the quadratic formula to find the x-intercepts for a parabola, the expression under the radical, $b^2 - 4ac$, indicates whether or not there are x-intercepts. If $b^2 - 4ac$ is a negative number, the graph has no x-intercepts. The parabola lies totally above or below the x-axis.

Applications of Quadratic Functions

We opened this section with a formula that described accidents as a function of age. We saw that 20-year-olds have 440 car accidents per 50 million miles driven. Do you have a guess about the age of a driver who has the least number of accidents per 50 million miles driven? We answer this question in Example 7.

EXAMPLE 8   Car Accidents as a Function of Age

We have seen that the equation

$$y = 0.4x^2 - 36x + 1000$$

describes the number of accidents, y, per 50 million miles driven, as a function of a driver's age, x, in years, where $16 \leq x \leq 74$. The graph of the resulting parabola is shown in Figure 7.23. Find the coordinates of the vertex and describe what this represents in practical terms.

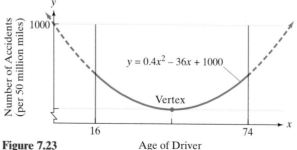

Figure 7.23

Solution Because $y = 0.4x^2 - 36x + 1000$, a (the coefficient of x^2) is 0.4 and b (the coefficient of x) is -36. The x-coordinate of the vertex is:

$$x = \frac{-b}{2a} = \frac{-(-36)}{2(0.4)} = \frac{36}{0.8} = 45.$$

We now substitute 45 for x in the equation of the function to find the y-coordinate of the vertex.

$$y = 0.4x^2 - 36x + 1000$$
$$= 0.4(45)^2 - 36(45) + 1000$$
$$= 0.4(2025) - 36(45) + 1000 = 810 - 1620 + 1000 = 190$$

The y-coordinate of the vertex is 190. The vertex is at $(45, 190)$. In practical terms, this indicates that 45-year-olds have the least number of car accidents, 190 per 50 million miles driven. Drivers both younger and older than 45 have more accidents per 50 million miles driven.

Exercise Set 7.3

 Practice Exercises

1. The quadratic function $f(x) = -43x^2 + 3806x - 38{,}526$ describes the average income in the United States, y, for a person who is x years old. Find and interpret $f(30)$.
2. The quadratic function $f(x) = -0.018x^2 + 1.93x - 25.34$ describes the miles per gallon of a Ford Taurus diven at x miles per hour. Find and interpret $f(50)$. Round to the nearest whole number.

In Exercises 3–6, determine if the parabola whose equation is given opens upward or downward.

3. $y = x^2 - 4x + 3$
4. $y = x^2 - 6x + 5$
5. $y = -2x^2 + x + 6$
6. $y = -2x^2 - 4x + 6$

In Exercises 7–12, find the x-intercepts for the parabola whose equation is given. If the x-intercepts are irrational numbers, round your answers to the nearest tenth.

7. $y = x^2 - 4x + 3$
8. $y = x^2 - 6x + 5$
9. $y = -x^2 + 8x - 12$
10. $y = -x^2 - 2x + 3$
11. $y = x^2 + 2x - 4$
12. $y = x^2 + 8x + 14$

In Exercises 13–20, find the y-intercept for the parabola whose equation is given.

13. $y = x^2 - 4x + 3$
14. $y = x^2 - 6x + 5$
15. $y = -x^2 + 8x - 12$
16. $y = -x^2 - 2x + 3$
17. $y = x^2 + 2x - 4$
18. $y = x^2 + 8x + 14$
19. $y = x^2 + 6x$
20. $y = x^2 + 8x$

In Exercises 21–26, find the vertex for the parabola whose equation is given.

21. $y = x^2 - 4x + 3$
22. $y = x^2 - 6x + 5$
23. $y = 2x^2 + 4x - 6$
24. $y = -2x^2 - 4x - 2$
25. $y = x^2 + 6x$
26. $y = x^2 + 8x$

In Exercises 27–38, graph the parabola whose equation is given.

27. $y = x^2 + 6x + 5$
28. $y = x^2 + 4x + 3$
29. $y = x^2 - 2x - 8$
30. $y = x^2 + 4x - 5$
31. $y = -x^2 + 4x - 3$
32. $y = -x^2 + 2x + 1$
33. $y = x^2 - 1$
34. $y = x^2 - 4$
35. $y = x^2 + 2x + 1$
36. $y = x^2 - 2x + 1$
37. $y = -2x^2 + 4x + 5$
38. $y = -3x^2 + 6x - 2$

 Application Exercises

39. The equation $y = -0.02x^2 + x + 1$ describes the number of inches, y, that a young redwood tree grows per year as a function of annual rainfall, x, in inches. The graph of the resulting parabola was obtained using a graphing calculator and is shown here. Find the coordinates of the vertex. Then describe what the vertex represents in practical terms.

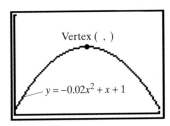

Vertex (,)

$y = -0.02x^2 + x + 1$

40. One would think that the more avocado trees planted per acre, the higher the yield of avocados. However, this is not the case. When more than a certain number of trees are present per acre, they tend to crowd one another and the yield per tree drops. The equation $y = -0.01x^2 + 0.8x$ describes the yield, y, in bushels of avocados per tree as a function of the number of trees per acre, x. The graph of the resulting parabola was obtained with a graphing calculator and is shown here. Find the coordinates of the vertex. Then describe what the vertex represents in practical terms.

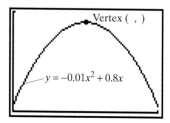

Vertex (,)

$y = -0.01x^2 + 0.8x$

Use the coordinates of the vertex to solve Exercises 41–42.

41. A person standing close to the edge of an 80-foot cliff throws a rock upward with an initial speed of 64 feet per second. The height of the rock above the water at the bottom of the cliff is a function of time, described by the equation

$$y = -16x^2 + 64x + 80.$$

The variable x describes the number of seconds that the rock is in motion. The variable y describes the height of the rock in feet above the water at the bottom of the cliff. After how many seconds will the rock reach its maximum height above the water? How many feet above the water is the rock at that time?

42. Use the quadratic function in Exercise 1 in this Exercise Set to find the age (to the nearest whole year) at which an individual can expect to earn the most income. What income can a person of that age expect to earn?

 Writing in Mathematics

43. What is a quadratic function?

44. What is a parabola? Describe its shape.

45. Explain how to decide whether a parabola opens upward or downward.

46. Describe how to find a parabola's x-intercepts. Use $y = x^2 + x - 6$ as an example.

47. Describe how to find a parabola's y-intercept. Use $y = x^2 + x - 6$ as an example.

48. Describe how to find a parabola's vertex. Use $y = x^2 - 6x + 8$ as an example.

49. A parabola that opens downward has its vertex at $(1, 5)$. Describe as much as you can about this parabola based on this information. Include in your discussion the number of x-intercepts (if any) for the parabola.

50. Suppose that you own a Ford Taurus. Describe how you can use the quadratic function in Exercise 2 in this Exercise Set to save money.

 Critical Thinking Exercises

51. A quadratic function presented in this section indicated that 45-year-olds have the least number of car accidents. Discuss one reason why this is so.

In Exercises 52–54, the value of a in $y = ax^2 + bx + c$ and the vertex of the parabola are given. How many x-intercepts does the parabola have? Explain how you arrived at this number.

52. $a = -2$; vertex at $(4, 8)$

53. $a = 1$; vertex at $(2, 0)$

54. $a = 3$; vertex at $(3, 1)$

 Technology Exercise

55. Use a graphing calculator to graph the parabolas that you graphed by hand in Exercises 27–38. Describe similarities and differences between the graphs obtained by hand and those that appear in the calculator's viewing window.

 Group Exercise

56. Group members should be people who are familiar with graphing calculators. The group should prepare a presentation to the entire class that will amaze people with what graphing calculators can do. Show how functions are graphed. Take some of the topics studied in our two algebra chapters and show how the calculator does the things that we have been doing by hand. Make the presentation as entertaining as possible. *Note*: Your professor will need to have the graphing calculator equipped with an attachment so that the calculator display can be shown on a large screen using an overhead projector.

SECTION 7.4 Exponential Functions

Objectives

1. Graph exponential functions.
2. Solve applied problems using exponential functions.

In 1980, U.S. doctors diagnosed 41 cases of a rare form of cancer, Kaposi's sarcoma, that involved skin spots, pneumonia, and severe immunological deficiencies. All cases involved gay men ranging in age from 26 to 51. By the end of 1997, 633,000 Americans, straight and gay, male and female, old and young, were infected with the AIDS virus.

The function

$$y = 9420.9(1.492)^x$$

describes the number of AIDS cases in the United States x years after 1983. Can you see how this function is different from linear and quadratic functions? The variable, x, is in the exponent. Functions whose equations contain a variable in the exponent are called **exponential functions**. Many real-life situations, including population growth, growth of epidemics, radioactive decay, and other changes that involve rapid increase or decrease, can be described using exponential functions.

1 Graph exponential functions.

Graphing Exponential Functions

We begin by looking at the graph of an exponential function of the form

$$y = b^x \quad \text{or} \quad f(x) = b^x$$

where b is greater than 1.

EXAMPLE 1 Graphing an Exponential Function

Graph: $y = 2^x$.

Solution We start by selecting numbers for x and finding the corresponding values for y.

Let $x = -3$: $\quad y = 2^{-3} = \dfrac{1}{2^3} = \dfrac{1}{8}$

Let $x = -2$: $\quad y = 2^{-2} = \dfrac{1}{2^2} = \dfrac{1}{4}$

Let $x = -1$: $\quad y = 2^{-1} = \dfrac{1}{2^1} = \dfrac{1}{2}$

Let $x = 0$: $\quad y = 2^0 = 1$

Let $x = 1$: $\quad y = 2^1 = 2$

Let $x = 2$: $\quad y = 2^2 = 4$

Let $x = 3$: $\quad y = 2^3 = 8$

x	y
-3	$\frac{1}{8}$
-2	$\frac{1}{4}$
-1	$\frac{1}{2}$
0	1
1	2
2	4
3	8

We plot these points, connecting them with a smooth curve. Figure 7.24 shows the graph of $y = 2^x$.

Figure 7.24 The graph of $y = 2^x$

All exponential functions of the form $y = b^x$, where b is a number greater than 1, have the shape of the graph shown in Figure 7.24. The graph approaches, but never touches, the negative portion of the x-axis.

Technology

Visualizing the Spread of an Epidemic Using a Graphing Calculator

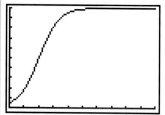

The graph shown here was generated by a graphing calculator using a function describing the number of people, y, who became ill with influenza, x weeks after its initial outbreak. Look at how fast the graph increases at the beginning. This shows the rapid spread of the epidemic during the first few weeks. The curve finally tapers off, indicating that there is a limit to the number of people who become ill.

EXAMPLE 2   Graphing an Exponential Function

Graph: $y = \left(\frac{1}{2}\right)^x$.

Solution   We begin by selecting numbers for x and finding the corresponding values for y.

Let $x = -3$: $y = \left(\frac{1}{2}\right)^{-3} = \dfrac{1}{\left(\frac{1}{2}\right)^3} = \dfrac{1}{\frac{1}{8}} = 8$

Let $x = -2$: $y = \left(\frac{1}{2}\right)^{-2} = \dfrac{1}{\left(\frac{1}{2}\right)^2} = \dfrac{1}{\frac{1}{4}} = 4$

Let $x = -1$: $y = \left(\frac{1}{2}\right)^{-1} = \dfrac{1}{\left(\frac{1}{2}\right)^1} = \dfrac{1}{\frac{1}{2}} = 2$

Let $x = 0$: $y = \left(\frac{1}{2}\right)^{0} = 1$

Let $x = 1$: $y = \left(\frac{1}{2}\right)^{1} = \frac{1}{2}$

Let $x = 2$: $y = \left(\frac{1}{2}\right)^{2} = \frac{1}{4}$

Let $x = 3$: $y = \left(\frac{1}{2}\right)^{3} = \frac{1}{8}$

x	y
-3	8
-2	4
-1	2
0	1
1	$\frac{1}{2}$
2	$\frac{1}{4}$
3	$\frac{1}{8}$

We plot these points, connecting them with a smooth curve. Figure 7.25 shows the graph of $y = \left(\frac{1}{2}\right)^x$.

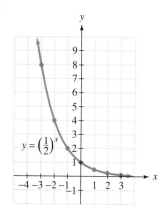

Figure 7.25 The graph of $y = \left(\frac{1}{2}\right)^x$

All exponential functions of the form $y = b^x$, where b is a number between 0 and 1 exclusive $(0 < b < 1)$, have the shape of the graph shown in Figure 7.25. The graph approaches, but never touches, the positive portion of the x-axis.

2 Solve applied problems using exponential functions.

Applications of Exponential Functions

Mathematicians used the number of AIDS cases in the United States from 1983 through 1992 to obtain the exponential function

$$y = 9420.9(1.492)^x.$$

The variable x represents the number of years after 1983 and the variable y represents the number of U.S. AIDS cases. Suppose we are interested in using the function to find the number of cases for the year 1992. Because 1992 is 9 years after 1983, we substitute 9 for x:

$$y = 9420.9(1.492)^9.$$

Use a scientific or graphing calculator to evaluate $(1.492)^9$. Press the following keys on your calculator to do this:

Scientific calculator: 1.492 $\boxed{x^y}$ 9 $\boxed{=}$

Graphing calculator: 1.492 $\boxed{\wedge}$ 9 $\boxed{\text{ENTER}}$

The display should be approximately 36.6369581353. Multiplying this number by 9420.9, we obtain:

$$y = 9420.9(1.492)^9 \approx 345,153.$$

The exponential function indicates that 9 years after 1983, that is, in 1992, there were 345,153 AIDS cases in the United States. The actual number in 1992 was 326,648. Notice that the function gives an approximate, but not exact, description of the number of cases for 1992.

EXAMPLE 3   The Chernobyl Disaster

The 1986 explosion at the Chernobyl nuclear power plant in the former Soviet Union sent about 1000 kilograms of radioactive cesium-137 into the atmosphere. The formula

$$A = 1000(0.5)^{t/30}$$

Chernobyl

The spread of radioactive fallout from the Chernobyl accident is expected to result in at least 100,000 deaths from cancer in the Northern Hemisphere.

describes the amount, A, in kilograms, of cesium-137 remaining in Chernobyl after t years. If even 100 kilograms of cesium-137 remain in Chernobyl's atmosphere, the area is considered unsafe for human habitation. Will people be able to live in the area 80 years after the accident?

Solution   We substitute 80 for t in the given formula. If the resulting value of A is 100 or greater, the area will still be unsafe for human habitation.

$$A = 1000(0.5)^{t/30} \qquad \text{This is the given formula.}$$
$$= 1000(0.5)^{80/30} \qquad \text{Substitute 80 for } t.$$
$$\approx 157 \qquad\qquad\quad \text{Use a calculator.}$$

After 80 years, 157 kilograms of cesium-137 will be in the atmosphere. Because this exceeds 100, even by the year 2066 the Chernobyl area will be unsafe for human habitation.

The Role of e in Applied Exponential Functions

An irrational number, symbolized by the letter e, appears in many applied exponential functions. This irrational number is approximately equal to 2.72:

$$e \approx 2.72.$$

The function

$$y = e^x \quad \text{or} \quad f(x) = e^x$$

is called the **natural exponential function**.

Use a scientitic or graphing calculator with an e^x key to evaluate e to various powers. For example, to find e^2, press the following keys on most calculators:

Scientific calculator: $2\;\boxed{e^x}$

Graphing calculator: $\boxed{e^x}\;2\;\boxed{\text{ENTER}}$

The display is approximately 7.389.

$$e^2 \approx 7.389$$

The number e lies between 2 and 3. Because $2^2 = 4$ and $3^2 = 9$, it makes sense that e^2, approximately 7.389, lies between 4 and 9.

EXAMPLE 4   World Population

In a report entitled *Resources and Man*, the U.S. National Academy of Sciences concluded that a world population of 10 billion "is close to (if not above) the maximum that an intensely managed world might hope to support with some degree of comfort and individual choice." At the time the report was issued, in 1969, the world population was approximately 3.6 billion, with a growth rate of 2% per year. The function

$$y = 3.6e^{0.02x}$$

describes world population, y, in billions, x years after 1969. Use the function to find world population in the year 2020. Is there cause for alarm?

Solution   Because 2020 is 51 years after 1969, we substitute 51 for x:

$$y = 3.6e^{0.02(51)}.$$

Although this computation can be done on your calculator in one step, we will break it down into smaller steps so that you can clearly see how we use the $\boxed{e^x}$ key. First find 0.02(51):

$$0.02(51) = 1.02.$$

Now find $e^{1.02}$:

Scientific calculator: $1.02\;\boxed{e^x}$

Graphing calculator: $\boxed{e^x}\;1.02\;\boxed{\text{ENTER}}$

The display is approximately 2.7731948. Multiplying this number by 3.6, we obtain:

$$y = 3.6e^{0.02(51)} = 3.6e^{1.02} \approx 9.98.$$

This indicates that world population in the year 2020 will be approximately 9.98 billion. Because this number is quite close to 10 billion, the given function suggests that there may be cause for alarm.

World population in 1998 was 5.93 billion, but the growth rate was no longer 2%. It had slowed down to 1.5%. Using this current growth rate, exponential functions now predict a world population of 7.58 billion in the year 2020.

Exercise Set 7.4

 Practice Exercises

In Exercises 1–10, graph the exponential function whose equation is given. Start by using −2, −1, 0, 1, and 2 for x and find the corresponding values for y.

1. $y = 3^x$
2. $y = 4^x$
3. $y = 2^{x+1}$
4. $y = 2^{x-1}$
5. $y = 3^{x-1}$
6. $y = 3^{x+1}$
7. $y = \left(\frac{1}{3}\right)^x$
8. $y = \left(\frac{1}{4}\right)^x$
9. $y = \left(\frac{1}{2}\right)^{x-1}$
10. $y = \left(\frac{1}{2}\right)^x$

 Application Exercises

Use a calculator with an $\boxed{x^y}$ key or a $\boxed{\wedge}$ key to solve Exercises 11–12.

11. The exponential function $y = 67.38(1.026)^x$ describes the population of Mexico, y, in millions, x years after 1980.
    a. Substitute 0 for x and, without using a calculator, find Mexico's population in 1980.
    b. Substitute 27 for x and use your calculator to find Mexico's population in the year 2007 as predicted by this function.
    c. Find Mexico's population in the year 2034 as predicted by this function.
    d. Find Mexico's population in the year 2061 as predicted by this function.
    e. What appears to be happening to Mexico's population every 27 years?

12. The space shuttle Challenger exploded approximately 73 seconds into flight on January 28, 1986. The tragedy involved O-rings used to seal the connections between different sections of the shuttle engines. The number of O-rings damaged increases dramatically with falling temperature. The exponential function
    $$y = 13.49(0.967)^x - 1$$
    describes the number of O-rings expected to fail, y, at a temperature of x degrees. On the morning the Challenger was launched, the temperature was 31 degrees, colder than any previous launching. Find the number of O-rings expected to fail at this temperature.

Use a calculator with an $\boxed{e^x}$ key to solve Exercises 13–14.

13. The exponential function $y = 24{,}000e^{0.21x}$ describes the number of AIDS cases in the United States among intravenous drug users, y, x years after 1989. How many cases of AIDS will be expected for this population by the end of: a. 2000? b. 2020?

14. In college, we study large volumes of information—information that, unfortunately, we do not often retain for very long. The function
    $$y = 80e^{-0.5x} + 20$$
    describes the percentage of information, y, that a particular person remembers x weeks after learning the information.
    a. Substitute 0 for x and, without using a calculator, find the percentage of information remembered at the moment it is first learned.
    b. Substitute 1 for x and find the percentage of information that is remembered after 1 week.
    c. Find the percentage of information that is remembered after 4 weeks.
    d. Find the percentage of information that is remembered after one year (52 weeks).

 Writing in Mathematics

15. What is an exponential function?
16. Look at the graph of $y = 2^x$ (Figure 7.24 on page 337) and explain why the graph defines y as a function of x.
17. What is the natural exponential function?

 Critical Thinking Exercises

18. Explain why the graph of $y = 2^x$ does not cross the x-axis.
19. The graphs labeled a–d in the accompanying figure represent $y = 3^x$, $y = 5^x$, $y = \left(\frac{1}{3}\right)^x$, and $y = \left(\frac{1}{5}\right)^x$, but not necessarily in that order. Which is which? Describe the process that enables you to make your decision.

 Technology Exercise

20. Use a graphing calculator to graph the exponential functions that you graphed by hand in Exercises 1–10. Describe similarities and differences between the graphs obtained by hand and those that appear in the calculator's viewing window.

Group Exercise

21. Group members should consult the current edition of *The World Almanac* or an equivalent reference, including the Internet. Select data that is of interest to the group that can be described with an exponential function. Then consult a person who is familiar with graphing calculators who can use the exponential regression feature of the calculator to show you how to obtain a function that describes your data. Once you have this function, each group member should make one prediction based on the exponential function, and then discuss a consequence of this prediction. What factors might change the accuracy of each prediction?

SECTION 7.5 *Systems of Linear Equations*

Objectives

1. Decide whether an ordered pair is a solution of a linear system.
2. Solve linear systems by graphing.
3. Solve linear systems by substitution.
4. Solve linear systems by addition.
5. Identify systems that do not have exactly one ordered-pair solution.
6. Solve problems using systems of linear equations.

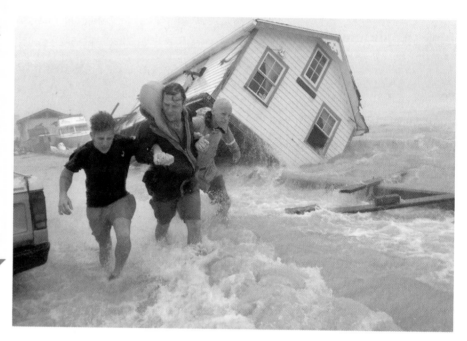

Key West residents Brian Goss (left), George Wallace, and Michael Mooney (right) hold on to each other as they battle 90 mph winds along Houseboat Row in Key West, Fla., on Friday, Sept. 25, 1998. The three had sought shelter behind a Key West hotel as Hurricane Georges descended on the Florida Keys but were forced to seek other shelter when the storm conditions became too rough. Hundreds of people were killed by the storm when it swept through the Caribbean.

Solving real-world problems often involves thousands of equations, sometimes a million variables. Problems ranging from scheduling airline flights to controlling traffic flow to routing phone calls over the nation's communication network often require solutions in a matter of moments. AT&T's domestic long distance network involves 800,000 variables! Meteorologists describing atmospheric conditions surrounding a hurricane must solve problems involving thousands of equations rapidly and efficiently. The difference between a two-hour warning and a two-day warning is a life-and-death issue for thousands of people in the path of one of nature's most destructive forces.

Although we will not be solving 800,000 equations with 800,000 variables, we will turn our attention to two equations with two variables, such as

$$2x - 3y = -4$$

$$2x + y = 4.$$

The methods that we consider for solving such problems provide the foundation for solving far more complex systems with many variables.

1 Decide whether an ordered pair is a solution of a linear system.

Systems of Linear Equations and Their Solutions

We have seen that all equations in the form $Ax + By = C$ are straight lines when graphed. Two such equations, such as those listed on page 342, are called a **system of linear equations**. A **solution to a system of linear equations** is the ordered pair that satisfies all equations in the system. For example, $(3, 4)$ satisfies the system

$$x + y = 7 \quad \text{(3 + 4 is, indeed, 7.)}$$
$$x - y = -1 \quad \text{(3 - 4 is, indeed, -1.)}$$

Thus, $(3, 4)$ satisfies both equations and is a solution of the system. The solution can be described by saying that $x = 3$ and $y = 4$. The solution can also be described using set notation. The solution set to the system is $\{(3, 4)\}$—that is, the set consisting of the ordered pair $(3, 4)$.

A system of linear equations can have exactly one solution, no solution, or infinitely many solutions. We will focus on systems with exactly one solution.

EXAMPLE 1   Determining Whether an Ordered Pair Is a Solution of a System

Determine whether $(1, 2)$ is a solution of the system

$$2x - 3y = -4$$
$$2x + y = 4.$$

Solution   Because 1 is the x-coordinate and 2 is the y-coordinate of $(1, 2)$, we replace x by 1 and y by 2.

$2x - 3y = -4$	$2x + y = 4$
$2(1) - 3(2) \overset{?}{=} -4$	$2(1) + 2 \overset{?}{=} 4$
$2 - 6 \overset{?}{=} -4$	$2 + 2 \overset{?}{=} 4$
$-4 = -4$ true	$4 = 4$ true

The pair $(1, 2)$ satisfies both equations—that is, it makes each equation true—so it is a solution of the system. The solution set to the system is $\{(1, 2)\}$.

2 Solve linear systems by graphing.

Solving Linear Systems by Graphing

The solution to a system of linear equations can be found by graphing both of the equations in the same rectangular coordinate system. For a system with one solution, the coordinates of the point of intersection of the lines is the system's solution.

EXAMPLE 2   Solving a Linear System by Graphing

Solve by graphing:

$$x + 2y = 2$$
$$x - 2y = 6.$$

Solution   We find the solution by graphing both $x + 2y = 2$ and $x - 2y = 6$ in the same rectangular coordinate system. We will use intercepts to graph each equation.

All points are solutions of x + 2y = 2.

All points are solutions of x - 2y = 6.

Point of intersection (4, -1) gives the common solution.

Figure 7.26 Visualizing a system's solution

$$x + 2y = 2$$

x-intercept: Set y = 0.

$$x + 2 \cdot 0 = 2$$

$$x = 2$$

y-intercept: Set x = 0.

$$0 + 2y = 2$$

$$2y = 2$$

$$y = 1$$

$$x - 2y = 6$$

x-intercept: Set y = 0.

$$x - 2 \cdot 0 = 6$$

$$x = 6$$

y-intercept: Set x = 0.

$$0 - 2y = 6$$

$$-2y = 6$$

$$y = -3$$

The system is graphed in Figure 7.26. To ensure that the graph is accurate, check the coordinates of the intersection point, $(4, -1)$, in both equations. We replace x by 4 and y by -1.

$$x + 2y = 2$$

$$4 + 2(-1) \overset{?}{=} 2$$

$$4 + (-2) \overset{?}{=} 2$$

$$2 = 2 \quad \text{true}$$

$$x - 2y = 6$$

$$4 - 2(-1) \overset{?}{=} 6$$

$$4 - (-2) \overset{?}{=} 6$$

$$4 + 2 \overset{?}{=} 6$$

$$6 = 6 \quad \text{true}$$

The pair $(4, -1)$ satisfies both equations—that is, it makes each equation true. This verifies that the system's solution set is $\{(4, -1)\}$.

3 Solve linear systems by substitution.

Solving Linear Systems by the Substitution Method

Finding a system's solution using the graphing method can be awkward. For instance, a solution of $\left(-\frac{2}{3}, \frac{157}{29}\right)$ would be difficult to "see" as an intersection point.

We will now consider the substitution method. This method does not depend on finding a system's solution visually using a graph. Instead, it involves eliminating a variable, leading to a linear equation in one variable, such as $7x + 3 = 24$. We already know how to solve such an equation—that is, subtract 3 from both sides and then divide both sides by 7.

Example 3 illustrates the substitution method. We will give you the steps of the method as we show you how it works with a specific example. Then we will summarize the steps used in the substitution method.

EXAMPLE 3   Solving a System by Substitution

Solve by the substitution method:

$$y = -x - 1$$

$$4x - 3y = 24.$$

Solution

Intersecting lines and the repetition of simple forms play a role in modern architecture.

Step 1   Solve one of the equations for one variable in terms of the other. This step has already been done for us. The first equation, $y = -x - 1$, has y solved in terms of x.

Step 2   Substitute the expression from step 1 into the other equation.
We substitute the expression $-x - 1$ for y in the other equation:

$$y = \boxed{-x - 1} \qquad 4x - 3 \boxed{y} = 24 \qquad \text{Substitute } -x - 1 \text{ for } y.$$

This gives us an equation in one variable, namely

$$4x - 3(-x - 1) = 24.$$

The variable y has been eliminated.

Step 3   Solve the resulting equation containing one variable.

$4x - 3(-x - 1) = 24$	This is the equation containing one variable.
$4x + 3x + 3 = 24$	Apply the distributive property.
$7x + 3 = 24$	Combine like terms.
$7x = 21$	Subtract 3 from both sides.
$x = 3$	Divide both sides by 7.

Step 4   Back-substitute the obtained value into the equation from step 1.
We now know that the x-coordinate of the solution is 3. To find the y-coordinate, we back-substitute the x-value into the equation from step 1,

$$y = -x - 1.$$

Substitute 3 for x.

$$y = -3 - 1 = -4$$

With $x = 3$ and $y = -4$, the proposed solution is $(3, -4)$.

Step 5   Check the proposed solution in both of the system's given equations.
Replace x with 3 and y with -4.

$$y = -x - 1 \qquad\qquad 4x - 3y = 24$$
$$-4 \stackrel{?}{=} -3 - 1 \qquad\qquad 4(3) - 3(-4) \stackrel{?}{=} 24$$
$$-4 = -4 \quad \text{true} \qquad\qquad 12 + 12 \stackrel{?}{=} 24$$
$$24 = 24 \quad \text{true}$$

The pair $(3, -4)$ satisfies both equations. The system's solution set is $\{(3, -4)\}$.

Before considering additional examples, let's summarize the steps used in the substitution method.

ISECT
X = 3   Y = −4

A graphing calculator can be used to solve the system in Example 3. By graphing each equation and using the calculator's intersection (ISECT) feature, the calculator displays the solution $(3, -4)$ as $x = 3, y = -4$.

Study Tip

In step 1, if possible, solve for a variable whose coefficient is 1 or −1 to avoid working with fractions.

Solving Linear Systems by Substitution

1. Solve one of the equations for one variable in terms of the other. (If one of the equations is already in this form, you can skip this step.)
2. Substitute the expression found in step 1 into the other equation. This will result in an equation in one variable.
3. Solve the equation obtained in step 2.
4. Back-substitute the value found from step 3 into the equation from step 1. Simplify and find the value of the remaining variable.
5. Check the proposed solution in both of the system's given equations.

EXAMPLE 4   Solving a System by Substitution

Solve by the substitution method:

$$5x - 4y = 9$$

$$x - 2y = -3.$$

Solution

Step 1   Solve one of the equations for one variable in terms of the other.
We begin by isolating one of the variables in either of the equations. By solving
for x in the second equation, which has a coefficient of 1, we can avoid fractions.

$$x - 2y = -3 \qquad \text{This is the second equation in the given system.}$$

$$x = 2y - 3 \qquad \text{Solve for x by adding 2y to both sides.}$$

Step 2   Substitute the expression from step 1 into the other equation.
We substitute $2y - 3$ for x in the first equation.

$$x = \boxed{2y - 3} \qquad 5\,\boxed{x} - 4y = 9$$

This gives us an equation in one variable, namely

$$5(2y - 3) - 4y = 9.$$

The variable x has been eliminated.

Step 3   Solve the resulting equation containing one variable.

$$5(2y - 3) - 4y = 9 \qquad \text{This is the equation containing one variable.}$$

$$10y - 15 - 4y = 9 \qquad \text{Apply the distributive property.}$$

$$6y - 15 = 9 \qquad \text{Combine like terms.}$$

$$6y = 24 \qquad \text{Add 15 to both sides.}$$

$$y = 4 \qquad \text{Divide both sides by 6.}$$

Step 4   Back-substitute the obtained value into the equation from step 1.
Now that we have the y-coordinate of the solution, we back-substitute 4 for y in
the equation $x = 2y - 3$.

$$x = 2y - 3 \qquad \text{Use the equation obtained in step 1.}$$

$$x = 2(4) - 3 \qquad \text{Substitute 4 for y.}$$

$$x = 8 - 3 \qquad \text{Multiply.}$$

$$x = 5 \qquad \text{Subtract.}$$

Study Tip

Get into the habit of checking
ordered-pair solutions in *both*
equations of the system.

With $x = 5$ and $y = 4$, the proposed solution is $(5, 4)$.

Step 5   Check. Take a moment to show that $(5, 4)$ satisfies both given equations. The solution set is $\{(5, 4)\}$.

4 Solve linear systems by addition.

Solving Linear Systems by the Addition Method

The substitution method is most useful if one of the given equations has an isolated variable. A third, and frequently the easiest, method for solving a linear system is the addition method. Like the substitution method, the addition method involves eliminating a variable and ultimately solving an equation containing only one variable. However, this time we eliminate a variable by adding the equations. In Example 5, the *x*-terms are eliminated when the two equations are added.

EXAMPLE 5   Solving a System by the Addition Method

Solve by the addition method:

$$3x - 4y = 11$$
$$-3x + 2y = -7.$$

Solution   Because the coefficients of *x* in the two equations differ only in sign, we can add the two left sides and add the two right sides, thereby eliminating the *x*-terms.

$$3x - 4y = 11$$
$$\underline{-3x + 2y = -7}$$

Add: $-2y = 4$

$$y = -2 \qquad \text{Solve for } y, \text{ dividing both sides by } -2.$$

Now we can back-substitute -2 for *y* into one of the original equations to find *x*. We will use both equations to show that we obtain the same value for *x* in either case.

Using the First Equation   **Using the Second Equation**

$$3x - 4y = 11 \qquad\qquad -3x + 2y = -7$$
$$3x - 4(-2) = 11 \qquad\qquad -3x + 2(-2) = -7 \qquad \text{Replace } y \text{ with } -2.$$
$$3x + 8 = 11 \qquad\qquad -3x - 4 = -7 \qquad \text{Solve for } x.$$
$$3x = 3 \qquad\qquad -3x = -3$$
$$x = 1 \qquad\qquad x = 1$$

The solution $(1, -2)$ can be shown to satisfy both equations in the system. Consequently, the solution set is $\{(1, -2)\}$.

The object of the addition method is to obtain two equations whose sum is an equation containing only one variable. The key step is to obtain, for one of the variables, coefficients that differ only in sign. Then when the two equations are added, this variable is eliminated.

For example, consider the following equations:

$$3x - 4y = 11$$
$$-3x + 2y = -7.$$

When we add these two equations, the *x*-terms are eliminated. This occurs because the coefficients of the *x*-terms, 3 and -3, are opposites of each other. When this is not the case, we must multiply one or both equations by some nonzero

Mathematical Blossom

Graph of an equation in a three-dimensional cartesian plane

This picture is a graph in a three-dimensional rectangular coordinate system. For many, the picture is more interesting than its equation:

$$z = \left(|x| - |y|\right)^2 + \frac{2|xy|}{\sqrt{x^2 + y^2}}.$$

Sometimes it's pleasant to simply get the "feel" of an equation by seeing its picture. Turning equations into visual images hints at the beauty that can be derived from mathematics.

number so that the coefficients of one of the variables, x or y, become opposites. Let's see exactly how this works by considering Example 6.

EXAMPLE 6   Solving a System by the Addition Method

Solve by the addition method:

$$3x + 2y = 48$$
$$9x - 8y = -24.$$

Solution   We must rewrite one or both equations in equivalent forms so that the coefficients of the same variable (either x or y) will be opposites of each other. Consider the terms in x in each equation, that is, $3x$ and $9x$. To eliminate x, we can multiply each term of the first equation by -3 and then add the equations.

$$3x + 2y = 48 \qquad \text{Multiply by } -3. \qquad -9x - 6y = -144$$
$$9x - 8y = -24 \qquad \underline{\text{No change}} \qquad \underline{9x - 8y = -24}$$
$$\text{Add:} \qquad -14y = -168$$
$$y = 12 \qquad \text{Solve for } y, \text{ dividing both sides by } -14.$$

Thus, $y = 12$. We back-substitute this value into either one of the given equations. We'll use the first one.

$$3x + 2y = 48 \qquad \text{This is the first equation in the given system.}$$
$$3x + 2(12) = 48 \qquad \text{Substitute 12 for } y.$$
$$3x + 24 = 48 \qquad \text{Multiply.}$$
$$3x = 24 \qquad \text{Subtract 24 from both sides.}$$
$$x = 8 \qquad \text{Divide both sides by 3.}$$

Finally, we verify that the ordered pair $(8, 12)$ satisfies both equations in the system.

$$3x + 2y = 48 \qquad\qquad 9x - 8y = -24 \qquad \text{These are the given equations.}$$
$$3(8) + 2(12) \overset{?}{=} 48 \qquad 9(8) - 8(12) \overset{?}{=} -24 \qquad \text{Replace } x \text{ with 8 and } y \text{ with 12.}$$
$$24 + 24 \overset{?}{=} 48 \qquad\qquad 72 - 96 \overset{?}{=} -24$$
$$48 = 48 \quad \text{true} \qquad\qquad -24 = -24 \quad \text{true}$$

Since $(8, 12)$ satisfies both equations, the system's solution set is $\{(8, 12)\}$.

Solving Linear Systems by Addition

1. If necessary, rewrite both equations in the form $Ax + By = C$.
2. If necessary, multiply either equation or both equations by appropriate nonzero numbers so that the sum of the x-coefficients or the sum of the y-coefficients will be 0.
3. Add the equations in step 2. The sum is an equation in one variable.
4. Solve the equation from step 3.
5. Back-substitute the value obtained in step 4 into either of the given equations and solve for the other variable.
6. Check the solution in both of the original equations.

EXAMPLE 7   Solving a System by the Addition Method

Solve by the addition method:

$$7x = 5 - 2y$$
$$3y = 16 - 2x.$$

Solution

Step 1   Rewrite both equations in the form $Ax + By = C$. We first arrange the system so that variable terms appear on the left and constants appear on the right. We obtain:

$$7x + 2y = 5 \qquad \text{Add 2y to both sides in the first equation.}$$
$$2x + 3y = 16 \qquad \text{Add 2x to both sides in the second equation.}$$

Step 2   If necessary, multiply either equation or both equations by appropriate numbers so that the sum of the x-coefficients or the sum of the y-coefficients will be 0.

We can eliminate x or y. Let's eliminate y by multiplying the first equation by 3 and the second equation by -2.

$$7x + 2y = 5 \quad \underrightarrow{\text{Multiply by 3.}} \quad 3 \cdot 7x + 3 \cdot 2y = 3 \cdot 5 \quad \rightarrow \quad 21x + 6y = 15$$
$$2x + 3y = 16 \quad \underrightarrow{\text{Multiply by } -2.} \quad -2 \cdot 2x + (-2) \cdot 3y = -2 \cdot 16 \quad \rightarrow \quad -4x - 6y = -32$$

Steps 3 and 4   Add the equations and solve for the remaining variable.

$$21x + 6y = 15$$
$$\underline{-4x - 6y = -32}$$
$$\text{Add:} \quad 17x = -17$$
$$x = -1 \qquad \text{Divide both sides by 17.}$$

Step 5   Back-substitute and find the value for the other variable.

$$3y = 16 - 2x \qquad \text{This is the second equation in the given system.}$$
$$3y = 16 - 2(-1) \qquad \text{Replace x by } -1.$$
$$3y = 16 + 2 \qquad \text{Multiply.}$$
$$3y = 18 \qquad \text{Add.}$$
$$y = 6 \qquad \text{Divide both sides by 3.}$$

Step 6   Check. The solution $(-1, 6)$ can be shown to satisfy both equations in the system. Consequently, the solution set is $\{(-1, 6)\}$.

5 Identify systems that do not have exactly one ordered-pair solution.

Linear Systems Having No Solution or Infinitely Many Solutions

Because the graph of a linear equation is a straight line, there are three possibilities for the number of solutions to a system of two linear equations.

The Number of Solutions to a System of Two Linear Equations

The number of solutions to a system of two linear equations in two variables is given by one of the following. (See Figure 7.27.)

Number of Solutions	What This Means Graphically
Exactly one ordered-pair solution	The two lines intersect at one point.
No solution	The two lines are parallel.
Infinitely many solutions	The two lines are identical.

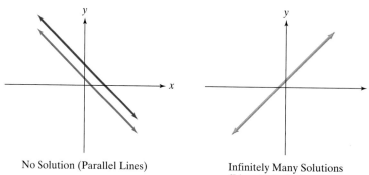

Exactly One Solution   No Solution (Parallel Lines)   Infinitely Many Solutions (Lines Coincide)

Figure 7.27 Possible graphs for a system of two linear equations in two variables

EXAMPLE 8   A System with No Solution

Solve the system:

$$4x + 6y = 12$$
$$6x + 9y = 12.$$

Solution   Because no variable is isolated, we will use the addition method. To obtain coefficients of x that differ only in sign, we multiply the first equation by 3 and multiply the second equation by -2.

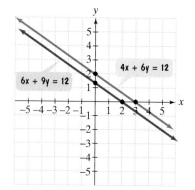

$$\begin{array}{ll} 4x + 6y = 12 & \underrightarrow{\text{Multiply by 3.}} \quad 12x + 18y = 36 \\ 6x + 9y = 12 & \underrightarrow{\text{Multiply by }-2.} \quad -12x - 18y = -24 \\ & \text{Add:} \quad \; 0 = 12 \end{array}$$

There are no values of x and y for which $0 = 12$.

The false statement $0 = 12$ indicates that the system has no solution. The solution set is the empty set, $\varnothing$.

Figure 7.28 The graph of a system with no solution

The lines corresponding to the two equations in Example 8 are shown in Figure 7.28. The lines are parallel and have no point of intersection.

EXAMPLE 9   A System with Infinitely Many Solutions

Solve the system:

$$y = 3 - 2x$$
$$4x + 2y = 6.$$

Solution Because the variable y is isolated in the first equation, we can use the substitution method. We substitute the expression for y in the other equation.

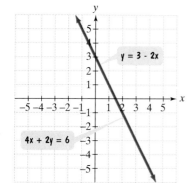

$$y = \boxed{3 - 2x} \quad 4x + 2\boxed{y} = 6 \qquad \text{Substitute } 3 - 2x \text{ for } y.$$

$$4x + 2y \qquad = 6 \qquad\qquad \text{This is the second equation in the given system.}$$

$$\downarrow$$

$$4x + 2(3 - 2x) = 6 \qquad\qquad \text{Substitute } 3 - 2x \text{ for } y.$$

$$4x + 6 - 4x = 6 \qquad\qquad \text{Apply the distributive property.}$$

$$6 = 6 \qquad\qquad \text{Simplify. This statement is true for all values of x and y.}$$

Figure 7.29 The graph of a system with infinitely many solutions

In our final step, both variables have been eliminated, and the resulting statement $6 = 6$ is true. This true statement indicates that the system has infinitely many solutions. The solution set consists of all points (x, y) lying on the line $y = 3 - 2x$, as shown in Figure 7.29.

We express the solution set for the system in one of two equivalent ways:

$$\{(x, y) \mid y = 3 - 2x\} \qquad \text{The set of all ordered pairs (x, y) such that y = 3 - 2x.}$$

$$\text{or} \quad \{(x, y) \mid 4x + 2y = 6\} \qquad \text{The set of all ordered pairs (x, y) such that 4x + 2y = 6.}$$

Linear Systems Having No Solution or Infinitely Many Solutions

If both variables are eliminated when a system of linear equations is solved by substitution or addition, one of the following is true.

1. There is no solution if the resulting statement is false.
2. There are infinitely many solutions if the resulting statement is true.

---

6 Solve problems using systems of linear equations.

Problem Solving

When we solved word problems in Section 6.3, we let x represent a quantity that was unknown. Problems in this section involve *two* unknown quantities. We will let x and y represent these quantities. We then translate from the verbal conditions of the problem to a *system* of linear equations.

EXAMPLE 10 Cholesterol and Heart Disease

The verdict is in. After years of research, the nation's health experts agree that high cholesterol in the blood is a major contributor to heart disease. Thus, cholesterol intake should be limited to 300 mg or less each day. Fast foods provide a cholesterol carnival. All together, two McDonald's Quarter Pounders and three Burger King Whoppers with cheese contain 520 mg of cholesterol. Three Quarter Pounders and one Whopper with cheese exceed the suggested daily cholesterol intake by 53 mg. Determine the cholesterol content in each item.

Solution

Step 1 Use variables to represent the unknown quantities. Let x represent the cholesterol content of a Quarter Pounder and y the cholesterol content of a Whopper with cheese.

About 15 million hamburgers are eaten every day in the United States.

Step 2   Write a system of equations describing the problem's conditions.

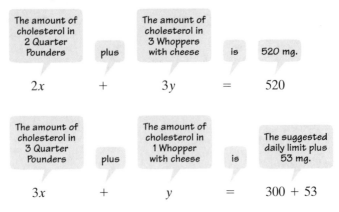

$$2x + 3y = 520$$

$$3x + y = 300 + 53$$

Top Meat Eaters

Country	Pounds Consumed per Person per Year
United States	257
Australia	229
New Zealand	222

Source: International Food Policy Research Institute

Step 3   Solve the system and answer the problem's question. The system

$$2x + 3y = 520$$
$$3x + y = 353$$

can be solved by substitution or addition. Substitution works well because y in the second equation has a coefficient of 1. We can solve for y by subtracting $3x$ from both sides, thereby avoiding fractions. Addition also works well; if we multiply the second equation by -3, adding equations will eliminate y. We will use addition.

$$2x + 3y = 520 \quad \text{No change} \qquad 2x + 3y = 520$$
$$3x + y = 353 \quad \text{Multiply by } -3. \qquad -9x - 3y = -1059$$
$$\text{Add:} \qquad -7x = -539$$

$$x = \frac{-539}{-7} = 77$$

Because x represents the cholesterol content of a Quarter Pounder, we see that a Quarter Pounder contains 77 mg of cholesterol. Now we can find y, the cholesterol content of a Whopper with cheese. We do so by back-substituting 77 for x in either of the system's equations.

$$3x + y = 353 \qquad \text{We'll use the second equation.}$$
$$3(77) + y = 353 \qquad \text{Back-substitute 77 for } x.$$
$$231 + y = 353 \qquad \text{Multiply.}$$
$$y = 122 \qquad \text{Subtract 231 from both sides.}$$

Because $x = 77$ and $y = 122$, a Quarter Pounder contains 77 mg of cholesterol and a Whopper with cheese contains 122 mg of cholesterol.

Step 4   Check the proposed answers in the original wording of the problem. Two Quarter Pounders and three Whoppers with cheese contain

$$2(77 \text{ mg}) + 3(122 \text{ mg}) = 520 \text{ mg},$$

which checks with the given conditions. Furthermore, three Quarter Pounders and one Whopper with cheese contain

$$3(77 \text{ mg}) + 1(122 \text{ mg}) = 353 \text{ mg},$$

which does exceed the daily limit of 300 mg by 53 mg.

Exercise Set 7.5

 Practice Exercises

In Exercises 1–4, determine whether the given ordered pair is a solution of the system.

1. $(2, 3)$
   $x + 3y = 11$
   $x - 5y = -13$

2. $(-3, 5)$
   $9x + 7y = 8$
   $8x - 9y = -69$

3. $(2, 5)$
   $2x + 3y = 17$
   $x + 4y = 16$

4. $(8, 5)$
   $5x - 4y = 20$
   $3y = 2x + 1$

In Exercises 5–12, solve each system by graphing. Check the coordinates of the intersection point in both equations.

5. $x + y = 6$
   $x - y = 2$

6. $x + y = 2$
   $x - y = 4$

7. $2x - 3y = 6$
   $4x + 3y = 12$

8. $4x + y = 4$
   $3x - y = 3$

9. $y = x + 5$
   $y = -x + 3$

10. $y = x + 1$
    $y = 3x - 1$

11. $y = -x - 1$
    $4x - 3y = 24$

12. $y = 3x - 4$
    $2x + y = 1$

In Exercises 13–24, solve each system by the substitution method.

13. $x + y = 4$
    $y = 3x$

14. $x + y = 6$
    $y = 2x$

15. $x + 3y = 8$
    $y = 2x - 9$

16. $2x - 3y = -13$
    $y = 2x + 7$

17. $x + 3y = 5$
    $4x + 5y = 13$

18. $x + 2y = 5$
    $2x - y = -15$

19. $2x - y = -5$
    $x + 5y = 14$

20. $2x + 3y = 11$
    $x - 4y = 0$

21. $2x - y = 3$
    $5x - 2y = 10$

22. $-x + 3y = 10$
    $2x + 8y = -6$

23. $x + 8y = 6$
    $2x + 4y = -3$

24. $-4x + y = -11$
    $2x - 3y = 5$

In Exercises 25–36, solve each system by the addition method.

25. $x + y = 1$
    $x - y = 3$

26. $x + y = 6$
    $x - y = -2$

27. $2x + 3y = 6$
    $2x - 3y = 6$

28. $3x + 2y = 14$
    $3x - 2y = 10$

29. $x + 2y = 2$
    $-4x + 3y = 25$

30. $2x - 7y = 2$
    $3x + y = -20$

31. $4x + 3y = 15$
    $2x - 5y = 1$

32. $3x - 7y = 13$
    $6x + 5y = 7$

33. $3x - 4y = 11$
    $2x + 3y = -4$

34. $2x + 3y = -16$
    $5x - 10y = 30$

35. $2x = 3y - 4$
    $-6x + 12y = 6$

36. $5x = 4y - 8$
    $3x + 7y = 14$

In Exercises 37–44, solve by the method of your choice. Identify systems with no solution and systems with infinitely many solutions, using set notation to express their solution sets.

37. $x = 9 - 2y$
    $x + 2y = 13$

38. $6x + 2y = 7$
    $y = 2 - 3x$

39. $y = 3x - 5$
    $21x - 35 = 7y$

40. $9x - 3y = 12$
    $y = 3x - 4$

41. $3x - 2y = -5$
    $4x + y = 8$

42. $2x + 5y = -4$
    $3x - y = 11$

43. $x + 3y = 2$
    $3x + 9y = 6$

44. $4x - 2y = 2$
    $2x - y = 1$

 Application Exercises

In Exercises 45–48, let x represent one number and let y represent the other number. Use the given conditions to write a system of equations. Solve the system and find the numbers.

45. The sum of two numbers is 7. If one number is subtracted from the other, their difference is -1. Find the numbers.

46. The sum of two numbers is 2. If one number is subtracted from the other, their difference is 8. Find the numbers.

47. Three times a first number decreased by a second number is 1. The first number increased by twice the second number is 12. Find the numbers.

48. The sum of three times a first number and twice a second number is 8. If the second number is subtracted from twice the first number, the result is 3. Find the numbers.

In Exercises 49–52, let x represent one quantity and let y represent the other quantity. Use the given conditions to write a system of equations. Solve the system and answer the problem's question.

49. The royal python and the anaconda are the world's longest snakes. The maximum length for each of these snakes is implied by the following description:

    Three royal pythons and two anacondas measure 161 feet. The royal python's length increased by triple the anaconda's length is 119 feet. What is the maximum length for each of these snakes?

50. Cholesterol intake should be limited to 300 mg or less each day. One serving of scrambled eggs from McDonalds and one Double Beef Whopper from Burger King exceed this intake by 241 mg. Two servings of scrambled eggs and three Double Beef Whoppers provide 1257 mg of cholesterol. What is the cholesterol content in each item?

51. If x represents a year, such as 1990, the formula $x + 10y = 2120$ describes the relationship between deaths from gunfire in the United States, y, in deaths per hundred thousand Americans, in year x. The formula $7x + 8y = 14{,}065$ describes deaths from car accidents in the United States, y, in deaths per hundred thousand Americans, in year x. Solve the linear system formed by the two formulas. Then describe what the solution means in terms of the variables in the given formulas.

52. The calorie-nutrient information for an apple and an avocado is given in the table. How many of each should be eaten to get exactly 1000 calories and 100 grams of carbohydrates?

	One Apple	One Avocado
Calories	100	350
Carbohydrates (grams)	24	14

Writing in Mathematics

53. What is a system of linear equations? Provide an example with your description.

54. What is the solution to a system of linear equations?

55. Explain how to solve a system of equations by using graphing.

56. Explain how to solve a system of equations by using the substitution method. Use $y = 3 - 3x$ and $3x + 4y = 6$ to illustrate your explanation.

57. Explain how to solve a system of equations by using the addition method. Use $3x + 5y = -2$ and $2x + 3y = 0$ to illustrate your explanation.

58. What is the disadvantage to solving a system of equations using the graphing method?

59. When is it easier to use the addition method rather than the substitution method when solving a system of equations?

60. When using the addition or substitution method, how can you tell if a system of linear equations has infinitely many solutions? What is the relationship between the graphs of the two equations?

61. When using the addition or substitution method, how can you tell if a system of linear equations has no solution? What is the relationship between the graphs of the two equations?

Critical Thinking Exercises

62. Write a word problem that can be solved by translating to a system of linear equations. Then solve the problem.

63. Write a system of equations having $\{(-2, 7)\}$ as a solution set. (More than one system is possible.)

64. One apartment is directly above a second apartment. The resident living downstairs calls his neighbor living above him and states, "If one of you is willing to come downstairs, we'll have the same number of people in both apartments." The upstairs' resident responds, "We're all too tired to move. Why don't one of you come up here? Then we will have twice as many people up here as you've got down there." How many people are in each apartment?

Technology Exercise

65. Use a graphing calculator to solve the systems in Exercises 5–12 by graphing. To see the point of intersection, you may need to adjust the viewing window, or use the ZOOM OUT feature. Read the section of your manual that describes how to use the INTERSECTION feature and have the calculator display the coordinates of the intersection point in each exercise.

Group Exercise

66. a. In solving

$$3x + 5y = 26$$
$$y = 2x$$

by substitution, a student found that $x = 2$. At that point the student asserted that the system's solution is $x = 2$. What is the error?

b. In solving

$$y = 4 - x$$
$$2x + 2y = 8$$

by substitution, a student obtained $0 = 0$, giving the solution as $(0, 0)$. What is the error?

c. In your group, discuss other common errors that can occur in solving linear systems by any of the three methods discussed in this section. Give specific examples of these kinds of errors, What suggestions can group members offer for avoiding these errors?

SECTION 7.6 *Linear Inequalities in Two Variables*

Objectives

1. Graph a linear inequality.
2. Graph a system of linear inequalities.

Had a good workout lately? If so, could you tell if you were overdoing it or not pushing yourself hard enough? In this section, we will use inequalities in two variables to help you to establish a target zone for your workouts.

Graphing a Linear Inequality in Two Variables

1 Graph a linear inequality.

We have seen that equations in the form $Ax + By = C$ are straight lines when graphed. If we change the $=$ sign to $>, <, \geq,$ or $\leq,$ we obtain a **linear inequality in two variables**. Some examples of linear inequalities in two variables are $x + y > 4, 3x - 5y \leq 15,$ and $2x - y < 4.$

Figure 7.30 shows the graph of the linear equation $x + y = 2.$ The line divides the points in the rectangular coordinate system into three sets. First, there is the set of points along the line, satisfying $x + y = 2.$ Next, there is the set of points in the green region above the line. Points in the green region satisfy the linear inequality $x + y > 2.$ Finally, there is the set of points in the pink region below the line. Points in the pink region satisfy the linear inequality $x + y < 2.$

A **half-plane** is the set of all the points on one side of a line. In Figure 7.30, the green region is a half-plane. The pink region is also a half-plane. A half-plane is the solution set of an inequality that involves $>$ or $<.$ The solution set of an inequality that involves $\geq$ or $\leq$ is a half-plane and a line. A solid line is used to show that the line is part of the solution set. A dashed line is used to show that a line is not part of a solution set.

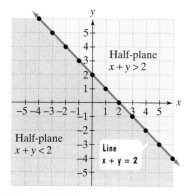

Figure 7.30 All points on the line satisfy $x + y = 2.$ All points in the green half-plane above the line satisfy $x + y > 2.$ All points in the pink half-plane below the line satisfy $x + y < 2.$

Graphing a Linear Inequality in Two Variables

1. Replace the inequality symbol with an equal sign and graph the corresponding linear equation. Draw a solid line if the original inequality contains a $\leq$ or $\geq$ symbol. Draw a dashed line if the original inequality contains a $<$ or $>$ symbol.
2. Choose a test point in one of the half-planes that is not on the line. Substitute the coordinates of the test point into the inequality.
3. If a true statement results, shade the half-plane containing this test point. If a false statement results, shade the half-plane not containing this test point.

EXAMPLE 1 Graphing a Linear Inequality in Two Variables

Graph: $x + y > 4.$

Solution

Step 1 Replace the inequality symbol by $=$ and graph the linear equation. We need to graph $x + y = 4.$ We can use intercepts to graph this line.

We set $y = 0$ to find the x-intercept:	We set $x = 0$ to find the y-intercept:
$x + y = 4$	$x + y = 4$
$x + 0 = 4$	$0 + y = 4$
$x = 4$	$y = 4$

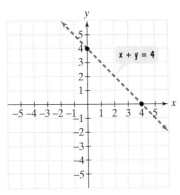

Figure 7.31 Preparing to graph $x + y > 4$

Study Tip

If a line passes through the origin, then $(0, 0)$ is on the line and cannot be chosen as a test point.

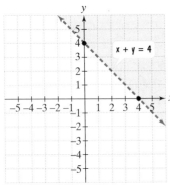

Figure 7.32 The graph of $x + y > 4$

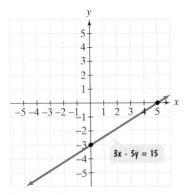

Figure 7.33 Preparing to graph $3x - 5y \leq 15$

The x-intercept is 4, so the line passes through $(4, 0)$. The y-intercept is 4, so the line passes through $(0, 4)$. The graph is indicated by a dashed line because the inequality $x + y > 4$ contains a $>$ symbol, rather than $\geq$. The dashed line, shown in Figure 7.31, indicates that points on the line are not part of the solution set.

Step 2   Choose a test point in one of the half-planes that is not on the line. Substitute its coordinates into the inequality.

The line $x + y = 4$ divides the plane into three parts—the line itself and two-half planes. The points in one half-plane satisfy $x + y > 4$. The points in the other half-plane satisfy $x + y < 4$. We need to find which half-plane is the solution. To do so, we test a point from either half-plane. The origin, $(0, 0)$, is easiest.

$$x + y > 4 \qquad \text{This is the given inequality.}$$

$$\text{Is} \quad 0 + 0 > 4? \qquad \text{Test (0, 0) by substituting 0 for x and 0 for y.}$$

$$0 > 4, \text{ false}$$

Step 3   If a false statement results, shade the half-plane not containing the test point.

Because 0 is not greater than 4, the test point $(0, 0)$ is not part of the solution set. Thus, the half-plane above the dashed line $x + y = 4$ is the solution set. We shade the half-plane that does not contain $(0, 0)$. The graph is shown using green shading in Figure 7.32.

EXAMPLE 2   Graphing a Linear Inequality in Two Variables

Graph: $3x - 5y \leq 15$.

Solution

Step 1   Replace the inequality symbol by = and graph the linear equation.
We need to graph $3x - 5y = 15$. We can use intercepts to graph this line.

We set $y = 0$ to find the x-intercept:	We set $x = 0$ to find the y-intercept:
$3x - 5y = 15$	$3x - 5y = 15$
$3x - 5 \cdot 0 = 15$	$3 \cdot 0 - 5y = 15$
$3x = 15$	$-5y = 15$
$x = 5$	$y = -3$

The x-intercept is 5, so the line passes through $(5, 0)$. The y-intercept is -3, so the line passes through $(0, -3)$. The graph is indicated by a solid line because the inequality $3x - 5y \leq 15$ contains a $\leq$ symbol, in which equality is included. The graph of the line is shown in Figure 7.33.

Step 2   Choose a test point in one of the half-planes that is not on the line. Substitute its coordinates into the inequality.

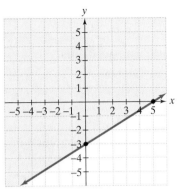

Figure 7.34 The graph of
$3x - 5y \leq 15$

Take $(0, 0)$ as the test point.

$$3x - 5y \leq 5$$ This is the given inequality.

Is $\quad 3 \cdot 0 - 5 \cdot 0 \leq 15?$ Test $(0, 0)$ by substituting 0 for x and 0 for y.

$$0 - 0 \leq 15$$

$$0 \leq 15, \text{true}$$

Step 3 **If a true statement results, shade the half-plane containing the test point.**
Because 0 is less than or equal to 15, the test point $(0, 0)$ is part of the solution set. All the points on the same side of the line $3x - 5y = 15$ as the point $(0, 0)$ are members of the solution set. The solution set is the line and the half-plane that contains the point $(0, 0)$, indicated by shading this half-plane. The graph is shown using green shading and a blue line in Figure 7.34.

Systems of Linear Inequalities

2 Graph a system of linear inequalities.

We have seen that a system of linear equations can be solved by graphing the individual equations in the system and then finding the intersection of the lines. To solve a system of inequalities, we graph each inequality and then find the intersection of the graphs.

EXAMPLE 3 Graphing a System of Linear Inequalities

Graph the solution of the system:

$$2x - y < 4$$
$$x + y \geq -1.$$

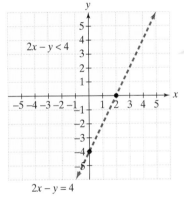

Figure 7.35 The graph of
$2x - y < 4$

Solution We begin by graphing $2x - y < 4$. Because the inequality contains a $<$ symbol, rather than $\leq$, we graph $2x - y = 4$ as a dashed line. (If $x = 0$, then $y = -4$, and if $y = 0$, then $x = 2$. The x-intercept is 2 and the y-intercept is -4.) Because $(0, 0)$ makes the inequality $2x - y < 4$ true, we shade the half-plane containing $(0, 0)$, shown in yellow in Figure 7.35.

Now we graph $x + y \geq -1$ on the same coordinate axes. Because the inequality contains a $\geq$ symbol, in which equality is included, we graph $x + y = -1$ as a solid line. (If $x = 0$, then $y = -1$, and if $y = 0$, then $x = -1$. The x-intercept and y-intercept are both -1.) Because $(0, 0)$ makes the inequality true, we shade the half-plane containing $(0, 0)$. This is shown in Figure 7.36 using green vertical shading. The solution of the system is shown graphically by the intersection (the overlap) of the two half-planes. This is shown in Figure 7.36 as the region in which the yellow shading and the green vertical shading overlap. The solution of the system is shown again in Figure 7.37.

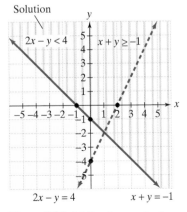

Figure 7.36 Adding the graph of
$x + y \geq -1$

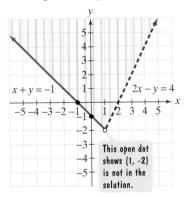

Figure 7.37 The graph of
$2x - y < 4$ and $x + y \geq -1$

Example 4 illustrates that it is not necessary to use test points when graphing inequalities involving vertical and horizontal lines.

EXAMPLE 4 Graphing a System of Linear Inequalities

Graph the solution of the system:

$$x \leq 4$$
$$y > -2.$$

Solution   We begin by graphing $x \leq 4$. Because the inequality contains a $\leq$ symbol, in which equality is included, we graph $x = 4$ as a solid vertical line. The points in the half-plane to the left of the line satisfy $x < 4$. The graph of $x \leq 4$ is shown using a blue vertical line and yellow shading in Figure 7.38.

Now we graph $y > -2$ on the same coordinate axes. Because the inequality contains a $>$ symbol, rather than $\geq$, we graph $y = -2$ as a dashed horizontal line. The points in the half-plane above the line satisfy $y > -2$. This is shown in Figure 7.39 using green vertical shading. The solution set, shown in Figure 7.39, is the region in which the yellow shading and the green vertical shading overlap and includes the part of the blue vertical line that lies above the dashed red horizontal line.

The solution of the system is shown again in Figure 7.40. The point of intersection of the two lines, $(4, -2)$, is not part of the solution set because it does not satisfy the inequality $y > -2$.

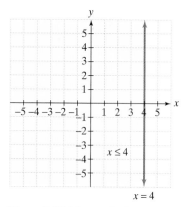

Figure 7.38 The graph of $x \leq 4$

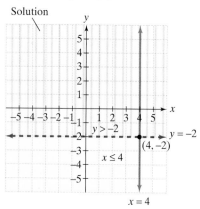

Figure 7.39 Adding the graph of $y > -2$

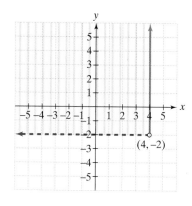

Figure 7.40 The graph of $x \leq 4$ and $y > -2$

EXAMPLE 5 Inequalities and Aerobic Exercise

For people between ages 10 and 70, inclusive, the target zone for aerobic exercise is given by the following system of inequalities in which a represents one's age and p is one's pulse rate.

$$2a + 3p \geq 450$$
$$a + p \leq 190$$

The graph of this target zone is shown in Figure 7.41. As you find your age, the shaded region indicates upper and lower limits for your pulse rate, in beats per minute, when engaging in aerobic exercise.

a. What are the coordinates of point A and what does this mean in terms of age and pulse rate?

Figure 7.41

b. Show that the coordinates of point *A* satisfy each inequality in the system.

Solution

a. Point *A* has coordinates (20, 160). This means that a pulse rate of 160 beats per minute is within the target zone for a 20-year-old person engaged in aerobic exercise.

b. We can show that (20, 160) satisfies each inequality by substituting 20 for *a* and 160 for *p*.

$$2a + 3p \geq 450 \qquad\qquad\qquad a + p \leq 190$$

$$\text{Is}\quad 2(20) + 3(160) \geq 450? \qquad\qquad \text{Is}\quad 20 + 160 \leq 190?$$

$$40 + 480 \geq 450 \qquad\qquad\qquad 180 \leq 190, \text{true}$$

$$520 \geq 450, \text{true}$$

The pair (20, 160) makes each inequality true, so it satisfies each inequality in the system.

Exercise Set 7.6

 Practice Exercises

Graph each linear inequality in Exercises 1–12.

1. $x + y \geq 2$
2. $x - y \leq 1$
3. $3x - y \geq 6$
4. $3x + y \leq 3$
5. $2x + 3y > 12$
6. $2x - 5y < 10$
7. $5x + 3y \leq -15$
8. $3x + 4y \leq -12$
9. $2y - 3x > 6$
10. $2y - x > 4$
11. $x > 4$
12. $y \leq 3$

Graph each system of linear inequalities in Exercises 13–24.

13. $3x + 6y \leq 6$
    $2x + y \leq 8$
14. $x - y \geq 4$
    $x + y \leq 6$
15. $2x + y < 3$
    $x - y > 2$
16. $x + y < 4$
    $4x - 2y < 6$
17. $2x + y < 4$
    $x - y > 4$
18. $2x - y < 3$
    $x + y < 6$
19. $x \geq 2$
    $y \leq 3$
20. $x \geq 4$
    $y \leq 2$
21. $x \leq 5$
    $y > -3$
22. $x \leq 3$
    $y > -1$
23. $x - y \leq 1$
    $x \geq 2$
24. $4x - 5y \geq -20$
    $x \geq -3$

 Application Exercises

25. Use Figure 7.41 on page 358 to solve this exercise.
    a. Find a pulse rate that lies within the target zone for a person your age engaged in aerobic exercise.

b. Express your answer in part (a) as an ordered pair. Show that the coordinates of this ordered pair satisfy each inequality in the system.

26. Suppose a patient is not allowed to have more than 330 milligrams of cholesterol from a diet of eggs and meat. Each egg provides 165 milligrams of cholesterol and each ounce of meat provides 110 milligrams of cholesterol. Thus, $165x + 110y \leq 330$, where *x* is the number of eggs and *y* the number of ounces of meat. Graph the inequality in the first quadrant. Give the coordinates of any two points in the solution set. Describe what each set of coordinates means in terms of the variables in the problem.

27. Many elevators have a capacity of 2000 pounds. If a child averages 50 pounds and an adult 150 pounds, write an inequality that describes when *x* children and *y* adults will cause the elevator to be overloaded. Graph the inequality. Select an ordered pair satisfying the inequality. Describe what this means in practical terms.

 Writing in Mathematics

28. What is a half-plane?
29. What does a dashed line mean in the graph of an inequality?
30. Write a paragraph explaining how to graph $2x - 3y < 6$.
31. Compare the graphs of $3x - 2y > 6$ and $3x - 2y \leq 6$. Discuss similarities and differences between the graphs.
32. Describe how to solve a system of linear inequalities.

Technology Exercise

33. The TI-82 can shade the area between two graphs quite easily. For example, try shading the area between the functions $y = x + 1$ and $y = -2x + 5$. Press 2nd [DRAW] and select the **Shade(** option. Then, press X, T, Θ + **1**, to define the function above which you want to shade, and $(-)$ **2** X, T, Θ + **5**, to define the function below which you want to shade. Then press **2)** to define the resolution for shading the graph (resolution can be set from 1 to 9). Finally, press ENTER to execute the instruction.

 Critical Thinking Exercises

34. Which one of the following is true?
    a. The graph of $4x - y > 2$ is the half-plane above the line whose equation is $4x - y = 2$.
    b. The graph of $x < -2$ is the region to the left of the vertical line whose equation is $x = 2$.
    c. The graph of $-\frac{5}{12}x + \frac{1}{4}y \geq \frac{3}{4}$ includes a boundary line whose y-intercept is 3.
    d. The graph of a half-plane in rectangular coordinates is the graph of a function.

35. Graph the system of inequalities:
$$x + 2y \geq 8$$
$$x - y \leq 2$$
$$y \leq 4.$$

SECTION 7.7   *Linear Programming*

Objectives

1. Write an objective function describing a quantity that must be maximized or minimized.
2. Use inequalities to describe limitations in a situation.
3. Use linear programming to solve problems.

In this section, we will look at an important application of systems of linear inequalities. Such systems arise in **linear programming**, a method for solving problems in which a particular quantity that must be maximized or minimized is limited. Linear programming is one of the most widely used tools in management science. Linear programming helps businesses allocate resources to manufacture products in a way that will maximize profit.

Objective Functions in Linear Programming

Many problems involve quantities that must be maximized or minimized. Businesses are interested in maximizing profit. An operation in which bottled water and medical kits are shipped to earthquake victims needs to maximize the number of victims helped by this shipment. An **objective function** is an algebraic expression in two or more variables describing a quantity that must be maximized or minimized.

1 Write an objective function describing a quantity that must be maximized or minimized.

EXAMPLE 1   Writing an Objective Function

Bottled water and medical supplies are to be shipped to victims of an earthquake by plane. Each container of bottled water will serve 10 people and each medical kit will aid 6 people. If x represents the number of bottles of water to be shipped and y represents the number of medical kits, write the objective function that describes the number of people that can be helped.

Solution   Because each bottle of water serves 10 people and each medical kit aids 6 people, we have:

Using z to represent the objective function, we have:

$$z = 10x + 6y.$$

Unlike the functions that we have seen so far, the objective function is an equation in three variables. For a value of x and a value of y, there is one and only one value of z.

2 Use inequalities to describe limitations in a situation.

Constraints in Linear Programming

Ideally, the number of earthquake victims helped in Example 1 should increase without restriction so that every victim receives water and medical kits. However, the planes that ship these supplies are subject to weight and volume restrictions. In linear programming problems, such restrictions are called **constraints**. Each constraint is expressed as a linear inequality. The list of constraints forms a system of linear inequalities.

EXAMPLE 2   Writing a Constraint

Each plane can carry no more than 80,000 pounds. The bottled water weighs 20 pounds per container and each medical kit weighs 10 pounds. If x represents the number of bottles of water to be shipped and y represents the number of medical kits, write an inequality that describes this constraint.

Solution   Because each plane can carry no more than 80,000 pounds, we have:

The total weight of the water bottles	plus	The total weight of the medical kits	must be less than or equal to	80.000 pounds.
$20x$	$+$	$10y$	$\leq$	80,000
Each bottle weighs 20 pounds.		Each kit weighs 10 pounds.		

The plane's weight constraint is described by the inequality

$$20x + 10y \leq 80,000.$$

In addition to a weight constraint on its cargo, each plane has a limited amount of space in which to carry supplies. Example 3 demonstrates how to express this constraint.

EXAMPLE 3   Writing a Constraint

Planes can carry a total volume for supplies that does not exceed 6000 cubic feet. Each water bottle is 1 cubic foot and each medical kit also has a volume of 1 cubic foot. With x still representing the number of water bottles and y the number of medical kits, write an inequality that describes this second constraint.

Solution   Because each plane can carry a volume for supplies that does not exceed 6000 cubic feet, we have:

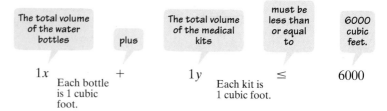

The plane's volume constraint is described by the inequality $x + y \leq 6000$.

In summary, here's what we have described in this aid-to-earthquake-victims situation:

$$z = 10x + 6y$$

This is the objective function describing the number of people helped with x bottles of water and y medical kits.

$$20x + 10y \leq 80,000$$
$$x + y \leq 6000$$

These are the constraints based on each plane's weight and volume limitations.

3 Use linear programming to solve problems.

Solving Problems with Linear Programming

The Berlin Airlift (1948–1949) was an operation by the United States and Great Britain. It was a response to military action by the former Soviet Union: The Soviet troops closed all roads and rail lines between West Germany and Berlin, cutting off supply routes to the city. The Allies used linear programming to maximize the amount of supplies that could be transported. The 11-month airlift, in 272,264 flights, provided basic necessities to blockaded Berlin, saving one of the world's great cities.

Linear programming is an example of new mathematics that developed during and shortly after World War II. We can use linear programming to solve problems involving a quantity that must be maximized or minimized subject to a number of constraints.

West Berlin children at Tempelhof airport watch fleets of U.S. airplanes bringing in supplies to circumvent the Russian blockade. The airlift began June 25, 1948 and continued for 11 months.

Solving a Linear Programming Problem

Let $z = ax + by$ be an objective function that depends on x and y. Furthermore, z is subject to a number of constraints on x and y. If a maximum or minimum value of z exists, it can be determined as follows:

1. Graph the system of inequalities representing the constraints.
2. Find the value of the objective function at each corner of the graphed region. The maximum and minimum of the objective function will occur at one or more of the corner points.

EXAMPLE 4   Solving the Linear Programming Problem

Solve the problem of determining how many bottles of water and how many medical kits should be sent on each plane to maximize the number of earthquake victims who can be helped.

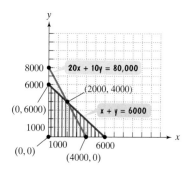

Figure 7.42 The region in quadrant 1 representing the constraints

$$20x + 10y \le 80,000$$
$$x + y \le 6000$$

Solution We must maximize $z = 10x + 6y$ subject to the constraints

$$20x + 10y \le 80,000$$

$$x + \quad y \le 6000.$$

Step 1   Graph the system of inequalities representing the constraints. Because x (the number of bottles of water per plane) and y (the number of medical kits per plane) must be nonnegative, we need to graph the system of inequalities in quadrant 1 and its boundary only. To graph the inequality $20x + 10y \le 80,000$, we graph the equation $20x + 10y = 80,000$ as a solid line. Setting $y = 0$, the x-intercept is 4000 and setting $x = 0$, the y-intercept is 8000. Using $(0, 0)$ as a test point, the inequality is satisfied, so we shade below the line, as shown in yellow in Figure 7.42.

Now we graph $x + y \le 6000$ by first graphing $x + y = 6000$ as a solid line. Setting $y = 0$, the x-intercept is 6000. Setting $x = 0$, the y-intercept is 6000. Using $(0, 0)$ as a test point, the inequality is satisfied, so we shade below the line, as shown using green vertical shading in Figure 7.42.

We use the addition method to find where the lines $20x + 10y = 80,000$ and $x + y = 6000$ intersect.

$$
\begin{array}{lll}
20x + 10y = 80,000 & \text{No change} & 20x + 10y = 80,000 \\
x + y = 6000 & \text{Multiply by} -10. & -10x - 10y = -60,000 \\
\cline{2-3}
& \text{Add:} & 10x = 20,000 \\
& & x = 2000
\end{array}
$$

Back-substituting 2000 for x in $x + y = 6000$, we find $y = 4000$, so the intersection point is $(2000, 4000)$.

The system of inequalities representing the constraints is shown by the region in which the yellow shading and the green vertical shading overlap in Figure 7.42. The graph of the system of inequalities is shown again in Figure 7.43. The red and blue line segments are included in the graph.

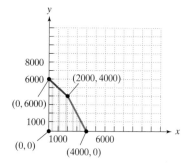

Figure 7.43

Step 2   Find the value of the objective function at each corner of the graphed region. The maximum and minimum of the objective function will occur at one or more of the corner points.

We must evaluate the objective function, $z = 10x + 6y$, at the four corners of the region in Figure 7.43.

Corner (x, y)	Objective Function $z = 10x + 6y$
$(0,0)$	$z = 10(0) + 6(0) = 0$
$(4000,0)$	$z = 10(4000) + 6(0) = 40,000$
$(2000, 4000)$	$z = 10(2000) + 6(4000) = 44,000$ ← maximum
$(0, 6000)$	$z = 10(0) + 6(6000) = 36,000$

Thus, the maximum value of z is 44,000 and this occurs when $x = 2000$ and $y = 4000$. In practical terms, this means that the maximum number of earthquake victims who can be helped with each plane shipment is 44,000. This can be accomplished by sending 2000 water bottles and 4000 medical kits per plane.

Exercise Set 7.7

 Practice Exercises

In Exercises 1–4, find the value of the objective function at each corner of the graphed region. What is the maximum value of the objective function? What is the minimum value of the objective function?

1. Objective Function
   $z = 5x + 6y$

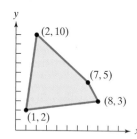

2. Objective Function
   $z = 3x + 2y$

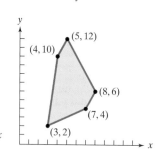

3. Objective Function
   $z = 40x + 50y$

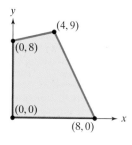

4. Objective Function
   $z = 30x + 45y$

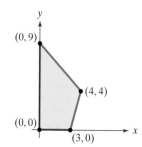

In Exercises 5–8, an objective function and a system of linear inequalities representing constraints are given.

a. *Graph the system of inequalities representing the constraints.*

b. *Find the value of the objective function at each corner of the graphed region.*

c. *Use the values in part (b) to determine the maximum and minimum values of the objective function and the values of x and y for which they occur.*

5. Objective Function
   $z = x + y$
   Constraints
   $x \leq 6$
   $y \geq 1$
   $2x - y \geq -1$

6. Objective Function
   $z = 3x - 2y$
   Constraints
   $x \geq 1$
   $x \leq 5$
   $y \geq 2$
   $x - y \geq -3$

7. Objective Function
   $z = 6x + 10y$
   Constraints
   $x + y \leq 12$
   $x + 2y \leq 20$

   $\left. \begin{array}{l} x \geq 0 \\ y \geq 0 \end{array} \right\}$ Quadrant 1 and its boundary

8. Objective Function
   $z = x + 3y$
   Constraints
   $x + y \geq 2$
   $x \leq 6$
   $y \leq 5$

   $\left. \begin{array}{l} x \geq 0 \\ y \geq 0 \end{array} \right\}$ Quadrant 1 and its boundary

 Application Exercises

9. a. A student earns $10 per hour for tutoring and $7 per hour as a teacher's aid. Let x = the number of hours each week spent tutoring, and y = the number of hours each week spent as a teacher's aid. Write the objective function that describes total weekly earnings.

   b. The student is bound by the following constraints:
      To have enough time for studies, the student can work no more 20 hours a week.
      The tutoring center requires that each tutor spend at least three hours a week tutoring.
      The tutoring center requires that each tutor spend no more than eight hours a week tutoring.
      Write a system of three inequalities that describes these constraints.

   c. Graph the system of inequalities in part (b). Use only the first quadrant and its boundary, because x and y are nonnegative.

   d. Evaluate the objective function for total weekly earnings at each of the four vertices of the graphed region. (The vertices should occur at $(3, 0)$, $(8, 0)$, $(3, 17)$, and $(8, 12)$.)

   e. Complete the missing portions of this statement: The student can earn the maximum amount per week by tutoring for ____ hours per week and working as a teacher's aid for ____ hours per week. The maximum amount that the student can earn each week is $____.

10. A television manufacturer makes console and wide-screen televisions The profit per unit is $125 for the console televisions and $200 for the wide-screen televisions.
    a. Let

       x = the number of consoles manufactured in a month and

       y = the number of wide-screens manufactured in a month.

       Write the objective function that describes the total monthly profit.

    b. The manufacturer is bound by the following constraints:
       1. Equipment in the factory allows for making at most 450 console televisions in one month.

2. Equipment in the factory allows for making at most 200 wide-screen televisions in one month.

3. The cost to the manufacturer per unit is $600 for the console televisions and $900 for the wide-screen televisions. Total monthly costs cannot exceed $360,000.

Write a system of three inequalities that describes these constraints.

c. Graph the system of inequalities in part (b). Use only the first quadrant and its boundary, because x and y must both be nonnegative.

d. Evaluate the objective function for total monthly profit at each of the five vertices of the graphed region. (The vertices should occur at $(0, 0)$, $(0, 200)$, $(300, 200)$, $(450, 100)$, and $(450, 0)$.)

e. Complete the missing portions of this statement: The television manufacturer will make the greatest profit by manufacturing ____ console televisions each month and ____ wide-screen televisions each month. The maximum monthly profit is $____.

Use the two steps for solving a linear programming problem, given in the box on page 362 to solve the problems in Exercises 11–12.

11. A manufacturer produces two models of mountain bicycles. The times (in hours) required for assembling and painting each model are given in the following table.

	Model A	Model B
Assembling	5	4
Painting	2	3

The maximum total weekly hours available in the assembly department and the paint department are 200 hours and 108 hours, respectively. The profits per unit are $25 for model A and $15 for model B. How many of each type should be produced to maximize profit?

12. A theater is presenting a program on drinking and driving for students and their parents. The proceeds will be donated to a local alcohol information center. Admission is $2.00 for parents and $1.00 for students. However, the situation has two constraints: The theater can hold no more than 150 people and every two parents must bring at least one student. How many parents and students should attend to raise the maximum amount of money?

Writing in Mathematics

13. What kinds of problems are solved using the linear programming method?

14. What is an objective function in a linear programming problem?

15. What is a constraint in a linear programming problem? How is a constraint represented?

16. In your own words, describe how to solve a linear programming problem.

17. Describe a situation in your life in which you would really like to maximize something, but you are limited by at least two constraints. Can linear programming be used in this situation? Explain your answer.

Critical Thinking Exercise

18. Suppose that you inherit $10,000. The will states how you must invest the money. Some (or all) of the money must be invested in stocks and bonds. The requirements are that at least $3000 be invested in bonds, with expected returns of $0.08 per dollar, and at least $2000 be invested in stocks, with expected returns of $0.12 per dollar. Because the stocks are medium risk, the final stipulation requires that the investment in bonds should never be less than the investment in stocks. How should the money be invested so as to maximize your expected returns?

Technology Exercise

19. Similar to the shading exercise in Section 7.6, the TI-82 can shade the area between two graphs with a lower limit for the x value. For example, to shade the area between the functions $y = x + 1$ and $y = -2x + 5$ with the constraint of $x > 1$, press 2nd [DRAW] and select the **Shade(** option. Then, press X, T, ↑ + **1**, to define the function above which you want to shade, and $(-)$ **2** X, T, ↑ + **5**, to define the function below which you want to shade. Then press **2**, to define the resolution for shading the graph (resolution can be set from 1 to 9. Include the lower limit for the x value by pressing **1**). Finally, press ENTER to execute the instruction.

Group Exercises

20. Group members should choose a particular field of interest. Research how linear programming is used to solve problems in that field. If possible, investigate the solution of a specific practical problem. Present a report on your findings, including the contributions of George Dantzig, Narendra Karmarkar, and L.G. Khachion to linear programming.

21. Members of the group should interview a business executive who is in charge of deciding the product mix for a business. How are production policy decisions made? Are other methods used in conjunction with linear programming? What are these methods? What sort of academic background, particularly in mathematics, does this executive have? Write a group report addressing these questions, emphasizing the role of linear programming for the business.

CHAPTER SUMMARY, REVIEW, AND TEST

SUMMARY

7.1 Graphing and Functions

a. The rectangular coordinate system is formed using two number lines that intersect at right angles at their zero points. See Figure 7.2 on page 308. The horizontal line is the x-axis and the vertical line is the y-axis. Their point of intersection, $(0, 0)$, is the origin.

b. If an equation in x and y yields one value of y for each value of x, then y is a function of x, indicated by writing $f(x)$ for y.

c. The Vertical Line Test: If any vertical line intersects a graph in more than one point, the graph does not define y as a function of x.

7.2 Linear Functions and Their Graphs

a. A function whose graph is a straight line is a linear function.

b. The graph of $Ax + By = C$, a linear equation in two variables, is a straight line. The line can be graphed using intercepts and a checkpoint. To locate the x-intercept, set $y = 0$ and solve for x. To locate the y-intercept, set $x = 0$ and solve for y.

c. The slope of the line through (x_1, y_1) and (x_2, y_2) is:
$$m = \frac{\text{Rise}}{\text{Run}} = \frac{y_2 - y_1}{x_2 - x_1} = \frac{y_1 - y_2}{x_1 - x_2}.$$

d. The equation $y = mx + b$ is the slope-intercept form of a line, in which m is the slope and b is the y-intercept.

e. Horizontal and Vertical Lines
  1. The graph of $y = b$ is a horizontal line that intersects the y-axis at b.
  2. The graph of $x = a$ is a vertical line that intersects the x-axis at a.

7.3 Quadratic Functions and Their Graphs

a. An equation of the form $y = ax^2 + bx + c$ is called a quadratic function.

b. The graph of the quadratic function is called a parabola.

c. The x-coordinate of a parabola's vertex is $x = \frac{-b}{2a}$. The y-coordinate is found by substituting the x-coordinate in the parabola's equation. The vertex, or turning point, is the low point when the graph opens upward and the high point when the graph opens downward.

d. The six steps for graphing a parabola are given in the box on page 331.

7.4 Exponential Functions

a. Functions whose equations contain a variable in the exponent are called exponential functions.

b. All exponential functions of the form $y = b^x$, where $b > 1$, have the shape of the graph in Figure 7.24 on page 337.

c. All exponential functions of the form $y = b^x$, where $0 < b < 1$, have the shape of the graph in Figure 7.25 on page 338.

d. The irrational number e, $e \approx 2.72$, appears in many applied exponential functions.

7.5 Systems of Linear Equations

a. Two equations in the form $Ax + By = C$ are called a system of linear equations. A solution to the system is an ordered pair that satisfies both equations in the system.

b. Linear systems can be solved by graphing, substitution (see the box on page 345) and addition (see the box on page 348).

c. Some linear systems have no solution; others have infinitely many solutions. For details, see the box on page 351.

7.6 Linear Inequalities in Two Variables

a. A linear inequality in two variables can be written in the form $Ax + By > C$, $Ax + By \geq C$, $Ax + By < C$, or $Ax + By \leq C$.

b. The procedure for graphing a linear inequality in two variables is given in the box on page 355.

c. Graphing Systems of Linear Inequalities
  1. Graph each inequality in the system in the same rectangular coordinate system.
  2. Find the intersection of the individual graphs.

7.7 Linear Programming

a. An objective function is an algebraic expression in three variables describing a quantity that must be maximized or minimized.

b. Constraints are restrictions, expressed as linear inequalities.

c. Steps for solving a linear programming problem are given in the box on page 362.

REVIEW EXERCISES

7.1

In Exercises 1–4, plot the given point in a rectangular coordinate system.

1. $(2, 5)$ 2. $(-4, 3)$

3. $(-5, -3)$ 4. $(2, -5)$

Graph each equation in Exercises 5–7. Let $x = -3, -2, -1, 0, 1, 2,$ and 3.

5. $y = 2x - 2$ 6. $y = x^2 - 3$ 7. $y = x$

8. If $f(x) = 4x + 11,$ find $f(-2)$.

9. If $f(x) = -7x + 5,$ find $f(-3)$.

10. If $f(x) = 3x^2 - 5x + 2,$ find $f(4)$.

11. If $f(x) = -3x^2 + 6x + 8,$ find $f(-4)$.

In Exercises 12–13, evaluate $f(x)$ for the given values for x. Then use the ordered pairs $(x, f(x))$ from your table to graph the function.

12. $f(x) = \frac{1}{2}x$

x	$f(x) = \frac{1}{2}x$
-6	
-4	
-2	
0	
2	
4	
6	

13. $f(x) = x^2 - 2$

x	$f(x) = x^2 - 2$
-2	
-1	
0	
1	
2	

In Exercises 14–16, use the vertical line test to identify graphs in which y is a function of x.

14.

15.

16.

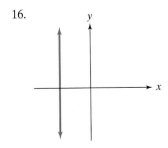

7.2

In Exercises 17–19, use the x- and y-intercepts to graph each linear equation.

17. $2x + y = 4$ 18. $2x - 3y = 6$

19. $5x - 3y = 15$

In Exercises 20–23, calculate the slope of the line passing through the given points. If the slope is undefined, so state. Then indicate whether the line rises, falls, is horizontal, or is vertical.

20. $(3, 2)$ and $(5, 1)$ 21. $(-1, 2)$ and $(-3, -4)$

22. $(-3, 4)$ and $(6, 4)$ 23. $(5, 3)$ and $(5, -3)$

In Exercises 24–27, graph each linear function using the slope and y-intercept.

24. $y = 2x - 4$ 25. $y = -\frac{2}{3}x + 5$

26. $y = \frac{3}{4}x - 2$ 27. $y = \frac{1}{2}x + 0$

In Exercises 28–30, a. Put the equation in slope-intercept form by solving for y; b. Identify the slope and the y-intercept; and c. Use the slope and y-intercept to graph the line.

28. $2x + y = 0$ 29. $3y = 5x$ 30. $3x + 2y = 4$

In Exercises 31–33, graph each horizontal or vertical line.

31. $x = 3$ 32. $y = -4$ 33. $x + 2 = 0$

7.3

In Exercises 34–36, for each quadratic function: a. Determine whether the parabola opens upward or downward; Find the b. vertex, c. x-intercepts, and d. y-intercept; e. Graph the parabola.

34. $y = x^2 - 6x + 7$ 35. $y = -x^2 - 2x + 3$

36. $y = -3x^2 + 6x + 1$

37. The equation $y = -0.02x^2 + 0.16x + 3.95$ describes the number of secretaries, y, in millions, in the United States x years after 1983. The graph of the resulting parabola is shown. Find the coordinates of the vertex. Then describe what the vertex represents in practical terms.

7.4

In Exercises 38–40, graph the exponential function whose equation is given. Start by using −2, −1, 0, 1, and 2 for x and find the corresponding values for y.

38. $y = 2^x$ 39. $y = 4^{x-1}$ 40. $y = \left(\frac{1}{2}\right)^{2x}$

41. Use a calculator with an $\boxed{x^y}$ key or a $\boxed{\wedge}$ key to solve this exercise. The exponential function $y = 126.4(2)^{0.04x}$ describes the population of Pakistan, y, in millions, x years after 1994. Find Pakistan's population in the year 2020 as predicted by this function.

42. Use a calculator with an $\boxed{e^x}$ key to solve this exercise. The exponential function $y = 14.6e^{0.041x}$ describes the number of residents of Hispanic origin living in the United States, y, in millions, x years after 1980. Find the Hispanic resident population of the United States in the year 2025 as predicted by this function.

7.5

In Exercises 43–45, solve each system by graphing. Check the coordinates of the intersection point in both equations.

43. $x + y = 5$
$3x - y = 3$

44. $2x - y = -1$
$x + y = -5$

45. $y = -x + 5$
$2x - y = 4$

In Exercises 46–48, solve each system by the substitution method.

46. $2x + 3y = 2$
$x = 3y + 10$

47. $y = 4x + 1$
$3x + 2y = 13$

48. $x + 4y = 14$
$2x - y = 1$

In Exercises 49–51, solve each system by the addition method.

49. $x + 2y = -3$
$x - y = -12$

50. $2x - y = 2$
$x + 2y = 11$

51. $5x + 3y = 1$
$3x + 4y = -6$

In Exercises 52–54, solve by the method of your choice. Identify systems with no solution and systems with infinitely many solutions, using set notation to express their solution sets.

52. $y = -x + 4$
$3x + 3y = -6$

53. $3x + y = 8$
$2x - 5y = 11$

54. $3x - 2y = 6$
$6x - 4y = 12$

Use a system of equations to solve Exercises 55–56.

55. The sum of three times a first number and eight times a second number is −1. When twice the second number is subtracted from the first number, the result is −5. What are the numbers?

56. Health experts agree that cholesterol intake should be limited to 300 mg or less each day. Three ounces of shrimp and 2 ounces of scallops contain 156 mg of cholesterol. Five ounces of shrimp and 3 ounces of scallops contain 45 mg of cholesterol less than the suggested maximum daily intake. Determine the cholesterol content in an ounce of each item.

7.6

Graph each inequality in Exercises 57–60.

57. $x - 3y \leq 6$ 58. $2x + 3y \geq 12$

59. $2x - 7y > 14$ 60. $x \leq 2$

Graph each system of linear inequalities in Exercises 61–64.

61. $3x - y \leq 6$
$x + y \geq 2$

62. $x + y < 4$
$x - y < 4$

63. $x \leq 3$
$y > -2$

64. $4x + 6y \leq 24$
$y > 2$

65. Find the value of the objective function $z = 2x + 3y$ at each corner of the graphed region shown. What is the maximum value of the objective function? What is the minimum value of the objective function?

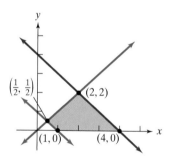

66. Consider the objective function $z = 2x + 3y$ and the following constraints:

$$x \leq 6, \, y \leq 5, \, \underbrace{x + y \geq 2, \, x \geq 0, \, y \geq 0}_{\substack{\text{Quadrant 1 and} \\ \text{its boundary}}}$$

a. Graph the system of inequalities representing the constraints.

b. Find the value of the objective function at each corner of the graphed region.

c. Use the values in part (b) to determine the maximum and minimum values of the objective function and the values of x and y for which they occur.

Group Exercise

67. Figure 7.23 on page 334 and the accompanying quadratic function show that the number of car accidents is a function of a driver's age. In Exercise 1 on page 335, we saw that income is also a function of age. For this activity, group members should list as many characteristics as possible that are functions of a person's age. For each characteristic, group members should create a graph. The horizontal axis should be labeled age and the vertical axis the characteristic you are graphing. Is the shape of the graph linear, quadratic, exponential, or something quite different? Group members should consider what happens to the characteristic from childhood to old age as they create each graph. Are there similarities in some of the graphs even though they describe different characteristics?

CHAPTER 7 TEST

1. Graph $y = (x - 1)^2$. Let $x = -1, 0, 1, 2,$ and 3.
2. If $f(x) = 3x^2 - 7x - 5$, find $f(-2)$.
3. Use the x- and y-intercepts to graph $4x - 2y = -8$.
4. Find the slope of the line passing through $(-3, 4)$ and $(-5, -2)$.

In Exercises 5–6, graph each linear function using the slope and y-intercept.

5. $y = \frac{2}{3}x - 1$ 6. $y = -2x + 3$
7. For the equation $y = x^2 - 2x - 8$:
   a. Determine whether the parabola opens upward or downward;
   b. Find the vertex;
   c. Find the x-intercepts;
   d. Find the y-intercept;
   e. Graph the parabola.
8. Graph $y = 3^x$. Start by using $-2, -1, 0, 1,$ and 2 for x and find the corresponding values for y.
9. Use a calculator with an $\boxed{x^y}$ or $\boxed{\wedge}$ key to solve this problem. The exponential function

$$y = 74{,}741(1.17)^x$$

   describes the average annual salary of baseball players, y, in dollars, x years after 1976. What will a baseball player's average annual salary be in the year 2005 as predicted by this function?

10. Solve by graphing.
    $x + y = 6$
    $4x - y = 4$

11. Solve by substitution.
    $x = y + 4$
    $3x + 7y = -18$

12. Solve by addition.
    $5x + 4y = 10$
    $3x + 5y = -7$

13. Graph the linear inequality: $3x - 2y < 6$.

14. Graph the system of linear inequalities.
    $$2x - y \le 4$$
    $$2x - y > -1$$

15. Find the value of the objective function $z = 3x + 2y$ at each corner of the graphed region shown. What is the maximum value of the objective function? What is the minimum value of the objective function?

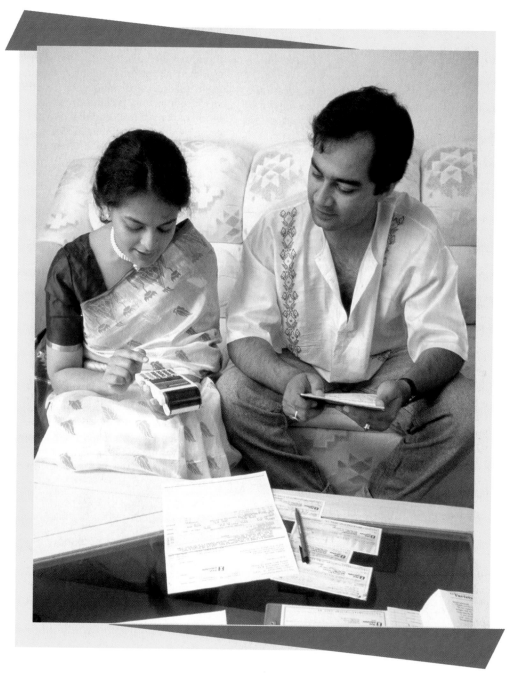

Writing out the checks to cover your monthly bills gets you thinking about the future. Last night you heard an infomercial selling the idea that if you invest a small amount of money while you are young, you will be a millionaire by the time you are 50 and can retire early. How can this be true?

8

Consumer Mathematics and Financial Management

anaging your personal finances is not an easy task. At one time, it did not involve much thought and planning: Everything was purchased using cash, and banks were the only reliable place for savings. Now we face numerous choices. Money invested may increase in value over time. If $1000 is not invested, the amount of goods it can buy diminishes over time. If it's spent, it's gone, although what it's spent on may be life-affirming in ways that cannot be measured in dollars and cents. However, we also know that if the $1000 is invested wisely, its value may increase considerably in a few years.

We all want a wonderful life with fulfilling work, good health, and loving relationships. And let's be honest: Financial security wouldn't hurt! Achieving this goal depends on understanding basic ideas about savings, loans, and investments. A solid understanding of the topics in this chapter can pay, literally, by making your financial goals a reality. And how can that small investment now be worth a million dollars in the future? The chapter concludes with an essay that answers this question.

SECTION 8.1   Percent

Objectives

1. Express a fraction as a percent.

2. Express a decimal as a percent.

3. Express a percent as a decimal.

4. Solve applied problems involving percent.

5. Investigate some of the ways percent can be abused.

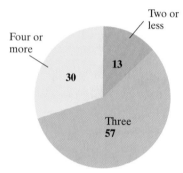

Figure 8.1 Number of bedrooms in privately owned one-family U.S. houses per 100 houses
Source: U.S. Census Bureau and HUD

1 Express a fraction as a percent.

2 Express a decimal as a percent.

> **❝**And if elected, it is my solemn pledge to cut your taxes by 10% for each of my first three years in office, for a total cut of 30%. **❞**

Did you know that one of the most common ways that you are given numerical information is with percents? This section will provide you with the tools to make sense of the politician's promise, as we present the uses, and abuses, of percent.

Basics of Percent

Percents are the result of expressing numbers as a part of 100. The word *percent* means *per hundred*. For example, the circle graph in Figure 8.1 shows that 57 out of every 100 one-family houses have three bedrooms. Thus, $\frac{57}{100} = 57\%$, indicating that 57% of the houses have three bedrooms. The percent sign, %, is used to indicate the number of parts out of one hundred parts.

A fraction can be expressed as a percent using the following procedure.

Expressing a Fraction as a Percent

1. Divide the numerator by the denominator.
2. Multiply the quotient by 100. Equivalently, move the decimal point in the quotient two places to the right.
3. Add a percent sign.

EXAMPLE 1   Expressing a Fraction as a Percent

Express $\frac{5}{8}$ as a percent.

Solution

Step 1   Divide the numerator by the denominator.

$$5 \div 8 = 0.625$$

Step 2   Multiply the quotient by 100.

$$0.625 \times 100 = 62.5$$

Step 3   Add a percent sign.

$$62.5\%$$

Thus, $\frac{5}{8} = 62.5\%$.

Our work in Example 1 shows that $0.625 = 62.5\%$. This illustrates the procedure for expressing a decimal number as a percent.

Expressing a Decimal Number as a Percent

1. Move the decimal point two places to the right.
2. Add a percent sign.

EXAMPLE 2   Expressing a Decimal as a Percent

Express 0.47 as a percent.

Solution

> Move decimal point
> two places right.

$$0.47 \, \% \quad \text{Add a percent sign.}$$

Thus, $0.47 = 47\%$.

3 Express a percent as a decimal.

We reverse the procedure of Example 2 to express a percent as a decimal number.

Expressing a Percent as a Decimal Number

1. Move the decimal point two places to the left.
2. Remove the percent sign.

EXAMPLE 3   Expressing Percents as Decimals

Express each percent as a decimal.

    a. 19%   b. 180%

Solution   Use the two steps in the box.

    a. $19\% = 19.\% = 0.19 \, \%$
> The percent sign
> is removed.

> The decimal
> point starts at
> the far right.

> The decimal point
> is moved two places
> to the left.

    Thus, $19\% = 0.19$.

    b. $180\% = 1.80 \, \% = 1.80$ or 1.8.

If a fraction is part of a percent, as in $\frac{1}{4}\%$, begin by expressing the fraction as a decimal, retaining the percent sign. Then, use the two steps in the box to express the percent as a decimal number. For example:

$$\tfrac{1}{4}\% = 0.25\% = 00.25 \, \% = 0.0025.$$

4 Solve applied problems involving percent.

Applications of Percent

Many applications of percent involve expressing a problem's conditions as a fraction and then writing the fraction as a percent.

EXAMPLE 4   Expressing a Fraction as a Percent

A charity has raised $16,400, with a goal of raising $80,000. What percent of the goal has been raised?

Solution   Of the $80,000 goal, $16,400 has been raised. The fraction of the goal that has been raised is the amount raised, $16,400, divided by the total, $80,000.

$$\frac{\$16,400}{\$80,000} \quad \text{or} \quad \frac{16,400}{80,000}$$

To find the percent of the goal that has been raised, express this fraction as a percent.

$$\text{Percent of the goal raised} = \frac{16,400}{80,000} = 0.205 = 20.5\%$$

Thus, 20.5% of the charity's goal has been raised.

EXAMPLE 5   Expressing a Fraction as a Percent

The leading causes of death in the United States are given in the margin. What percent of deaths are caused by heart disease?

Solution

$$\text{Percent caused by heart disease} = \frac{\text{the number of deaths caused by heart disease}}{\text{the total number of deaths}}$$

$$= \frac{733,361}{2,314,690} \approx 0.32 = 32\%$$

Approximately 32% of all deaths in the United States are caused by heart disease.

Suppose that 60 of 200 students decide to consult an academic advisor before enrolling for next semester's classes. The percent of students who consult an academic advisor is:

$$\frac{60}{200} = 0.3 = 30\%.$$

The number of students who decide to consult an advisor is 30% of the total, or 0.3 times 200.

$$30\% \text{ of } 200 = 30\% \times 200 = 0.3 \times 200 = 60$$

In general, to find a percent of a number, change the percent to a decimal and multiply the decimal and the number.

EXAMPLE 6   Finding the Percent of a Number

The circle graph in Figure 8.2 shows that 59% of hate crimes in the United States in 1997 were motivated by racial bias. If there were approximately 8000 hate-crime incidents in 1997, how many were motivated by racial bias?

Leading Causes of Death

		No. of Deaths
1	Heart disease	733,361
2	Cancer	539,533
3	Stroke	159,942
4	Respiratory diseases	106,027
5	Accidents	94,948
6	Pneumonia and Flu	83,727
7	Diabetes	61,767
8	HIV	31,130
9	Suicide	30,903
10	Chronic liver disease	25,047
	All causes	**2,314,690**

Source: Centers for Disease Control and Prevention

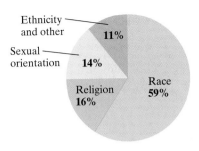

Figure 8.2 Motivation for U.S. hate-crime incidents, 1997
Source: FBI

Solution

$$\text{The number motivated by racial bias} = 59\% \text{ of } 8000$$
$$= 0.59 \times 8000 = 4720$$

Thus, 4720 hate crimes in 1997 were motivated by racial bias.

A common application of percent involves **sales tax** collected by states, counties, and cities on sales of items to customers. The sales tax is a percent of the cost of an item, implying the following formula:

Sales tax amount = tax rate × item's cost

EXAMPLE 7   Percents and Sales Tax

Suppose that the local sales tax rate is 5% and you purchase a bicycle for $394.

a. How much tax is paid?
b. What is the bicycle's total cost?

Solution
a. Sales tax amount = tax rate × item's cost
$$= 5\% \times \$394 = 0.05 \times \$394 = \$19.70$$

The tax paid is $19.70.
b. The bicycle's total cost is the purchase price, $394, plus the sales tax, $19.70.
$$\text{Total cost} = \$394.00 + \$19.70 = \$413.70$$

The bicycle's total cost is $413.70.

None of us is thrilled about sales tax, but we do like buying things that are *on sale*. Businesses reduce prices, or **discount**, to attract customers. The discount rate is a percent of the original price, implying the following formula:

Discount amount = discount rate × original price

EXAMPLE 8   Percents and Sale Price

A computer with an original price of $1460 is on sale at 15% off.

a. What is the discount amount?
b. What is the computer's sale price?

Solution

a. Discount amount = discount rate × original price

$$= 15\% \times \$1460 = 0.15 \times \$1460 = \$219$$

The discount amount is $219.

b. The computer's sale price is the original price, $1460, minus the discount amount, $219.

$$\text{Sale price} = \$1460 - \$219 = \$1241$$

The computer's sale price is $1241.

Percents are used for comparing changes, such as increases or decreases in sales, population, prices, and production. If a quantity changes by increasing, the **percent increase** can be found as follows.

Finding Percent Increase

1. Use subtraction to find the amount of increase.
2. Find the fraction for the percent increase, using

$$\frac{\text{amount of increase}}{\text{original amount}}.$$

3. Find the percent increase by expressing the fraction in step 2 as a percent.

Figure 8.3 Total world on-line households (in millions), 1999–2000
Source: Jupiter Communications

EXAMPLE 9   Finding Percent Increase

Use the bar graph in Figure 8.3 to find the percent increase of on-line households from 1999 to 2000.

Solution

Step 1   Use subtraction to find the amount of increase.

$$\text{Amount of increase} = 66.6 - 56.7 = 9.9 \text{ (million)}$$

Step 2   Find the fraction for the percent increase.

$$\frac{\text{amount of increase}}{\text{original amount}} = \frac{9.9}{56.7}$$

Step 3 **Express the fraction in step 2 as a percent.**

$$\text{Percent increase} = \frac{9.9}{56.7} \approx 0.17 = 17\%$$

From 1999 to 2000, the percent increase in on-line households is approximately 17%.

If a quantity changes by decreasing, the **percent decrease** is found using a procedure nearly identical to the one used to find percent increase.

Finding Percent Decrease

1. Use subtraction to find the amount of decrease.
2. Find the fraction for the percent decrease, using

$$\frac{\text{amount of decrease}}{\text{original amount}}.$$

3. Find the percent decrease by expressing the fraction in step 2 as a percent.

EXAMPLE 10 Finding Percent Decrease

A jacket regularly sells for $135.00. The sale price is $60.75. Find the percent decrease of the sale price from the regular price.

Solution

Step 1 **Use subtraction to find the amount of decrease.**

$$\text{Amount of decrease} = \$135.00 - \$60.75 = \$74.25$$

Step 2 **Find the fraction for the percent decrease.**

$$\frac{\text{amount of decrease}}{\text{original amount}} = \frac{\$74.25}{\$135.00} = \frac{74.25}{135}$$

Step 3 **Express the fraction in step 2 as a percent.**

$$\text{Percent decrease} = \frac{74.25}{135} = 0.55 = 55\%$$

The percent decrease of the sale price from the regular price is 55%. This means that the sale price of the jacket is 55% lower than the regular price.

Go West (or Someplace Warm)

Americans are migrating West and South. This map shows the percent increase in population by region from 1900 to 2000.

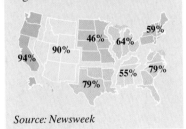

94%   90%   46%   64%   59%

55%   79%

79%

Source: Newsweek

5 Investigate some of the ways percent can be abused.

Abuses of Percent

In our next examples, we look at a few of the many ways that percent can be used incorrectly. Confusion often arises when percent increase (or decrease) refers to a changing quantity that is itself a percent.

EXAMPLE 11   Percents of Percents

John Tesh, when he was still co-anchoring "Entertainment Tonight," reported that the PBS series "The Civil War" had an audience of 13% versus the usual 4% PBS audience, "an increase of more than 300%." Did Tesh report the percent increase correctly?

Solution   We begin by finding the percent increase.

$$\text{percent increase} = \frac{\text{amount of increase}}{\text{original amount}}$$

$$= \frac{13\% - 4\%}{4\%} = \frac{9\%}{4\%} = \frac{9}{4} = 2.25 = 225\%$$

The percent increase for PBS is 225%. This is not more than 300%, so Tesh did not report the percent increase correctly.

EXAMPLE 12   Promises of a Politician

A politician states, "If you elect me to office, I promise to cut your taxes for each of my first three years in office by 10% each year, for a total reduction of 30%." Evaluate the accuracy of the politician's statement.

Solution   To make things simple, let's assume that a taxpayer paid $100 in taxes in the year previous to the politician's election. A 10% reduction during year 1 is 10% of $100.

$$10\% \text{ of previous year tax} = 10\% \text{ of } \$100 = 0.10 \times \$100 = \$10$$

With a 10% reduction the first year, the taxpayer will pay only $100 − $10, or $90, in taxes during the politician's first year in office.
   The following table shows how we calculate the new, reduced tax for each of the first three years in office.

Year	Tax paid the year before	10% reduction	Taxes paid this year
1	$100	0.10 × $100 = $10	$100 − $10 = $90
2	$ 90	0.10 × $90 = $9	$90 − $9 = $81
3	$ 81	0.10 × $81 = $8.10	$81 − $8.10 = $72.90

Technology

When you use a calculator to compute percents, are you ever confused about what you need to do with the decimal point? If you use the $\boxed{\%}$ key on your calculator, the calculator will take care of the decimal point for you. For example, to compute the total cost (purchase price + 8% sales tax) of a $14 shirt, you can enter:

$14 \boxed{+} 8 \boxed{\%} \boxed{\times} 14 \boxed{=}$.

The calculator gives you the total amount of the shirt, $15.12. Be careful! If you do not use the $\boxed{\%}$ key, make sure you can account for the correct placement of the decimal point in your calculations.

Percents and College Students' Dreams

Sixty-one percent of college students think they will retire between 40 and 50.
   Seventy-seven percent of college students think they will be millionaires.
Source: Newsweek, July 5, 1999

Now, we determine the percent decrease in taxes over the three years.

$$\text{percent decrease} = \frac{\text{amount of decrease}}{\text{original amount}}$$

$$= \frac{\$100 - \$72.90}{\$100} = \frac{\$27.10}{\$100} = \frac{27.1}{100} = 0.271 = 27.1\%$$

The taxes decline by 27.1%, not by 30%. The politician is ill-informed in saying that three consecutive 10% cuts add up to a total tax cut of 30%. In our calculation, which serves as a counterexample to the promise, the total tax cut is only 27.1%.

Exercise Set 8.1

 Practice Exercises

In Exercises 1–10, express each fraction as a percent.

1. $\frac{2}{5}$ 2. $\frac{3}{5}$ 3. $\frac{1}{4}$ 4. $\frac{3}{4}$

5. $\frac{3}{8}$ 6. $\frac{7}{8}$ 7. $\frac{1}{40}$ 8. $\frac{3}{40}$

9. $\frac{9}{80}$ 10. $\frac{13}{80}$

In Exercises 11–20, express each decimal as a percent.

11. 0.59   12. 0.96   13. 0.3844   14. 0.003

15. 2.87   16. 9.83   17. 14.87   18. 19.63

19. 100   20. 95

In Exercises 21–34, express each percent as a decimal.

21. 72%   22. 38%   23. 43.6%   24. 6.25%

25. 130%   26. 260%   27. 2%   28. 6%

29. $\frac{1}{2}$%   30. $\frac{3}{4}$%   31. $\frac{5}{8}$%   32. $\frac{1}{8}$%

33. $62\frac{1}{2}$%   34. $87\frac{1}{2}$%

 Application Exercises

35. A charity has raised $7500, with a goal of raising $60,000. What percent of the goal has been raised?

36. A charity has raised $225,000, with a goal of raising $500,000. What percent of the goal has been raised?

The circle graph in the next column shows the market share of different means of intercity transportation for 1230 million passengers in 1997. Use the graph to solve Exercises 37–38.

37. Find the percent of passengers traveling by bus.

38. Find the percent of passengers traveling by air.

Number of Passengers on Intercity Transportation in the United States in 1997

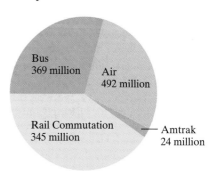

Source: Eno Transportation Foundation Inc.

39. The U.S. population in 2000 is projected to be approximately 275,000,000. If 12% of this population is African-American, find the U.S. African-American population in 2000.

40. The U.S. population in 2050 is projected to be approximately 394,000,000. If 20% of this population will be people ages 65 and older, how many people ages 65 and older will there be in the U.S. in 2050?

41. A restaurant bill came to $60. If 15% of this bill was left as a tip, how much was the tip?

42. If income tax is $3502 plus 28% of taxable income over $23,000, how much is the income tax on a taxable income of $35,000?

43. Suppose that the local sales tax rate is 6% and you purchase a car for $16,800.
    a. How much tax is paid?
    b. What is the car's total cost?

44. Suppose that the local sales tax rate is 7% and you purchase a graphing calculator for $96.
    a. How much tax is paid?
    b. What is the calculator's total cost?

45. An exercise machine with an original price of $860 is on sale at 12% off.
    a. What is the discount amount?
    b. What is the exercise machine's sale price?

46. A dictionary that normally sells for $16.50 is on sale at 40% off.
    a. What is the discount amount?
    b. What is the dictionary's sale price?

47. According to the National Basketball Association, the average salary of a professional basketball player in the 1995–1996 season was $2,000,000. For the 1996–1997 season, this amount increased to $2,200,000. Find the percent increase.

48. With more women using fertility drugs, the number of babies born as quintuplets and larger multiples has increased rapidly. In 1995, there were 57 births in the United States involving quintuplets and larger multiples. By 1996, this number had increased to 81. Find the percent increase, rounded to the nearest tenth of a percent. (*Source: National Center for Health Statistics*)

49. A sofa regularly sells for $840. The sale price is $714. Find the percent decrease of the sale price from the regular price.

50. A FAX machine regularly sells for $380. The sale price is $266. Find the percent decrease of the sale price from the regular price.

51. According to the Centers for Disease Control and Prevention, in 1955, 56.9% of the men in the United States age 18 and older smoked cigarettes. By 1995, this percent had decreased to 28.2%. Find the percent decrease from 1955 to 1995, rounded to the nearest tenth of a percent.

52. According to the Centers for Disease Control and Prevention, in 1955, 28.4% of the women in the United States age 18 and older smoked cigarettes. By 1995, this percent had decreased to 23.1%. Find the percent decrease from 1955 to 1995, rounded to the nearest tenth of a percent.

53. Suppose that you have $10,000 in a rather risky investment recommended by your financial advisor. During the first year, your investment decreases by 30% of its original value. During the second year, your investment increases by 40% of its first-year value. Your advisor tells you that there must have been a 10% overall increase of your original $10,000 investment. Is your financial advisor using percentages properly? If not, what is your actual percent gain or loss of your original $10,000 investment?

54. The price of a color printer is reduced by 30% of its original price. When it still does not sell, its price is reduced by 20% of the reduced price. The salesperson informs you that there has been a total reduction of 50%. Is the salesperson using percentages properly? If not, what is the actual percent reduction from the original price?

Writing in Mathematics

55. What is a percent?

56. Describe how to express a decimal number as a percent and give an example.

57. Describe how to express a percent as a decimal number and give an example.

58. Describe how to find percent increase and give an example.

59. Describe two ways in which you use percents in your daily life.

60. Give an example of a situation in which you might use percent increase or percent decrease in your daily life. Then write a problem using this example and explain how to solve it.

Critical Thinking Exercises

61. Which one of the following is true?
    a. If your weight increases by 5% this year and 5% next year, the increase in weight over two years is 10%.
    b. A grade point average that increases by 10% this semester and decreases by 10% next semester will be unchanged after two semesters.
    c. If $\frac{1}{10}$ of a person's salary is spent for clothing, $\frac{1}{3}$ for food, and $\frac{1}{5}$ for rent, the percent of the salary that is left is $36\frac{2}{3}\%$.
    d. If the amount that a person spends on rent increases from 20% to 30% of that person's income, the percent increase is 10%.

62. A condominium is taxed based on its $78,500 value. The tax rate is $3.40 for every $100 of value. If the tax is paid before March 1, 3% of the normal tax is given as a discount. How much tax is paid if the condominium owner takes advantage of the discount?

63. In January, each of 60 people purchased a $200 washing machine. In February, 10% fewer customers purchased the same washing machine that had increased in price by 20%. What was the change in sales from January to February?

Technology Exercises

Use the %̲ *key on your calculator to solve Exercises 64–66.*

64. Find the total cost of a $758 refrigerator if the sales tax rate is 7.5%

65. Find the sale price of a $24.95 tennis racket if it is on sale at 25% off.

66. With Tricia's promotion, she receives a 15% pay raise. If her old salary was $45,365 a year, what is her new salary?

67. The circle graphs you have seen throughout this section are a convenient way to display percents. They are easily generated within a spreadsheet program, such as

Microsoft Excel. Using Excel, enter the following sales information. Last week, UBS Distributing sold 5249 magazines, 3243 newspapers, 891 paperback books, and 351 hardcover books.

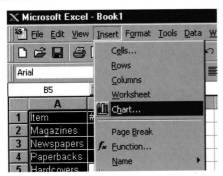

First, enter the given data. Then, use the computer's mouse to highlight the cells containing the data. Activate the Chart Option of the spreadsheet by clicking on the Insert pulldown and selecting Chart (see image). Choose the pie chart type with a 3D visual effect. Click the "Next" button and work your way through the options, including the labels and cosmetic effects. In the third of four option pages, click on the "Data Labels" tab and select the option to "Show label and percent." Once you have decided on all of the options (don't worry, you can go back and change them), click the "Finish" button. According to the displayed chart, what percent of the company's sales were:

a. magazines?
b. newspapers?
c. paperback books?
d. hardcover books?

Group Exercise

68. Each person should find two examples in which percents are used in news reports. Share these examples with other members of the group. If possible, try to find an example in which percent is used incorrectly.

SECTION 8.2 Interest

Objectives

1. Calculate simple interest and maturity value.
2. Use compound interest formulas.
3. Calculate present value.
4. Understand the meaning of effective annual yield.

In 1626, Peter Minuit convinced the Wappinger Indians to sell him Manhattan Island for $24. If the native Americans had put the $24 into a bank account at a 5% interest rate compounded monthly, by the year 2000 there would be well over $5 billion in the account!

Although you may not yet understand terms such as *interest rate* and *compounded monthly*, one thing seems clear: Money in certain savings accounts grows in remarkable ways. You, too, can take advantage of such accounts with astonishing results. In this section we will show you how.

1 Calculate simple interest and maturity value.

Simple Interest

Interest is the price that we get paid for lending money or pay for borrowing money. When we deposit money in a savings institution, the institution pays us interest for its use. When we borrow money, interest is the price we pay for the privilege of using the money until we repay it.

The amount of money that we deposit or borrow is called the **principal**. For example, if you deposit $2000 in a savings account, then $2000 is the principal. The charge for interest is given as a percent, and is called the **rate**. The rate is assumed to be per year.

Simple interest involves interest calculated only on the principal. The following formula is used to find simple interest.

> ### Calculating Simple Interest
>
> $$\text{Interest} = \text{principal} \times \text{rate} \times \text{time}$$
> $$I = prt$$
>
> The rate, r, is expressed as a decimal when calculating simple interest.

EXAMPLE 1   Calculating Simple Interest for a Year

You deposit $2000 in a savings account at Hometown Bank, which has a rate of 6%. Find the interest at the end of the first year.

Solution   The amount deposited, or principal (p), is $2000. The rate (r) is 6%, or 0.06. The time of the deposit (t) is one year. The interest is:

$$I = prt = \$2000 \times 0.06 \times 1 = \$120.$$

At the end of the first year, the interest is $120. You can withdraw the $120 in interest, and you still have $2000 in the savings account.

EXAMPLE 2   Calculating Simple Interest for More Than a Year

A student took out a simple interest loan for $1800 for two years at a rate of 8% to purchase a used car. What is the interest on the loan?

Solution   The amount borrowed, or principal (p), is $1800. The rate (r) is 8%, or 0.08. The time of the loan (t) is two years. The interest is:

$$I = prt = \$1800 \times 0.08 \times 2 = \$288.$$

The interest on the loan is $288.

When a loan is repaid, the interest is added to the original principal to find the total amount due. In Example 2, at the end of two years the student will have to repay

$$\text{principal} + \text{interest} = \$1800 + \$288 = \$2088.$$

The amount due, principal + interest, is called the **maturity value** of the loan.

EXAMPLE 3   Calculating Interest and Maturity Value for Less Than a Year

A loan of $1060 has been made at 6.5% for three months.
  a. Find the interest.
  b. Find the maturity value of the loan.

Solution

  a. The amount borrowed, or principal (p), is $1060. The rate (r) is 6.5%, or 0.065. The time, t, is given as 3 months. We need to express the time in years because the rate is understood to be 6.5% per year. Because 3 months is $\frac{3}{12}$ of a year, $t = \frac{3}{12} = \frac{1}{4}$. The interest is:

$$I = prt = \$1060 \times 0.065 \times \tfrac{1}{4} \approx \$17.23.$$

Rounded to the nearest cent, the interest on the loan is $17.23.
  b. The maturity value of the loan is the amount due when the loan is repaid.

$$\text{maturity value} = \text{principal} + \text{interest}$$
$$= \$1060 + \$17.23 = \$1077.23$$

The maturity value, the total amount due, is $1077.23.

Simple interest is used for many short-term loans, including automobile and consumer loans. Imagine that a short-term loan is taken for 125 days. The time of the loan is $\frac{125}{365}$ because there are 365 days in a year. However, the **Banker's rule** allows financial institutions to use 360 in the denominator of such a fraction, claiming that this simplifies the interest calculation. The time (t) for a 125-day short-term loan is:

$$\frac{125 \text{ days}}{360 \text{ days}} = \frac{125}{360}.$$

Consumer groups question whether a year should be simplified to 360 days. Why? Compare the values for time, t, for a 125-day short-term loan using denominators of 360 and 365.

$$\frac{125}{360} \approx 0.347 \qquad \frac{125}{365} \approx 0.342$$

The denominator of 360 benefits the bank by resulting in a greater period of time for the loan, and consequently more interest.

Borrowers have the option of paying off part or all of a debt before the day the principal and interest are due. For example, in order to complete construction on a house, a borrower takes out a 90-day loan for $80,000 at an interest rate of 12%. On day 50, a partial loan repayment of $30,000 is made. The interest on the principal from the date of the loan to day 50 is:

$$I = prt = \$80{,}000 \times 0.12 \times \frac{50}{360} \approx \$1333.33.$$

This interest is deducted from the payment of $30,000: $30,000 − $1333.33 = $28,666.67. The $28,666.67 is then deducted from the original $80,000 principal. This leaves $80,000 − $28,666.67, or $51,333.33, as the unpaid amount of the loan. If no other payments are made until the due date, day 90, the interest is:

$$I = prt = \$51{,}333.33 \times 0.12 \times \tfrac{40}{360} \approx \$684.44.$$

> The number of days from the payment on day 50 to the due date on day 90 is 40.

The maturity value of the loan, the amount due on day 90, is $51,333.33 + $684.44, or $52,017.77.

When paying off part of a loan before the due date, the interest due is subtracted from this partial payment. The rest of the payment is used to reduce the original principal. This method of crediting payments made before a loan's due date is called the **United States rule**.

Compound Interest

2 Use compound interest formulas.

Compound interest is interest computed on the original principal as well as on any accumulated interest. Many savings accounts pay compound interest. For example, let's return to Example 1. You deposited $2000 in a savings account at Hometown Bank at a rate of 6%. The interest at the end of the first year is $120 ($I = prt = \$2000 \times 0.06 \times 1 = \$120$). Unlike the situation in Example 1, you do not withdraw the $120 interest. Thus, the amount in the account during year 2 is $2000 + $120, or $2120. The interest paid at the end of the second year is computed using $2120:

$$I = prt = \$2120 \times 0.06 \times 1 = \$127.20$$

Hometown Bank now adds $127.20 to the $2120 in your account. Thus, during year 3 the account contains $2120 + $127.20, or $2247.20. The interest paid at the end of the third year is computed using $2247.20:

$$I = prt = \$2247.20 \times 0.06 \times 1 \approx \$134.83.$$

The amount in the savings account at the end of year three is $2247.20 + $134.83, or $2382.03.

A faster way to determine the amount, A, in an account subject to compound interest is to use the following formula and a calculator.

continued next page

Technology

Here are the calculator keystroke sequences to compute $2000(1.06)^3$:

Scientific Calculator:

2000 $\boxed{x}$ 1.06 $\boxed{x^y}$ 3 $\boxed{=}$

Graphing Calculator:

2000 $\boxed{\times}$ 1.06 $\boxed{\wedge}$ 3 $\boxed{\text{ENTER}}$

Technology

Some calculators, such as the Texas Instruments BA-35, are explicitly created for financial calculations. With it, you can determine the future value in an account or the present value needed to accumulate to a specified future value with just a few keystrokes. You may have to first put the calculator in Financial mode. The keys for the financial calculations are $\boxed{\text{N}}$ for the total number of compounding periods, $\boxed{\%i}$ for the percent interest per compounding period, $\boxed{\text{PMT}}$ for the amount of regular payment, $\boxed{\text{PV}}$ for present value, $\boxed{\text{FV}}$ for future value, and $\boxed{\text{CPT}}$ for compute. For example, you deposit $100 in a savings account that has a rate of 6% compounded monthly. The following sequence gives the amount of money in the account after three years, called the future value.

Calculating the Amount in an Account for Compound Interest Paid Once a Year

If p dollars are deposited at rate r, in decimal form, subject to compound interest, then the amount, A, of money in the account after t years is given by:

$$A = p(1 + r)^t.$$

EXAMPLE 4 Using the Compound Interest Formula

You deposit $2000 in a savings account at Hometown Bank, which has a rate of 6%.

a. Find the amount, A, of money in the account after 3 years subject to compound interest.

b. Find the interest.

Solution

a. The amount deposited, or principal (p), is $2000. The rate ($r$) is 6%, or 0.06. The time of the deposit (t) is three years. The amount in the account after three years is:

$$A = p(1 + r)^t = \$2000(1 + 0.06)^3 = \$2000(1.06)^3 \approx \$2382.03.$$

Rounded to the nearest cent, the amount in the savings account after three years is $2382.03.

b. Because the amount in the account is $2382.03 and the original principal is $2000, the interest is $2382.03 − $2000, or $383.03.

Compound Interest Paid More Than Once a Year

The period of time between two interest payments is called the **compounding period**. When compound interest is paid once a year, the compounding period is one year. We say that the interest is **compounded annually**.

Most savings institutions have plans in which interest is paid more than once a year. If compound interest is paid twice a year, the compounding period is six months. We say that the interest is **compounded semiannually**. When compound interest is paid four times a year, the compounding period is three months and the interest is said to be **compounded quarterly**. Some plans allow for monthly compounding or daily compounding.

In general, when compound interest is paid n times a year, we say that there are n **compounding periods per year**. The following formula is used to calculate

36 $\boxed{\text{N}}$ 100 $\boxed{\text{PV}}$ 0.5 $\boxed{\%i}$
$\boxed{\text{CPT}}$ $\boxed{\text{FV}}$.

$\boxed{\text{N}}$, the total number of compounding periods, is 36 because with monthly compounding, there are 36 compounding periods over three years. $\boxed{\text{PV}}$, the present value, is 100 because you deposited $100 in the present. $\boxed{\%i}$, the percent interest per compounding period, is the interest rate, 6%, divided by the number of compounding periods per year, $12 : \frac{6\%}{12} = 0.5\%$. The calculator gives $119.67 as the future value.

the amount in an account subject to compound interest with n compounding periods per year.

Calculating the Amount in an Account for Compound Interest Paid n Times a Year

If p dollars are deposited at rate r, in decimal form, subject to compound interest paid n times a year, then the amount, A, of money in the account after t years is given by:

$$A = p\left(1 + \frac{r}{n}\right)^{nt}.$$

EXAMPLE 5   Using the Compound Interest Formula

You deposit $7500 in a savings account that has a rate of 6%. The interest is compounded monthly.

a. How much money will you have after five years?
b. Find the interest after five years.

Solution

a. The amount deposited, or principal (p), is $7500. The rate ($r$) is 6%, or 0.06. Because interest is compounded monthly, there are 12 compounding periods per year, so $n = 12$. The time of the deposit (t) is five years. The amount in the account after five years is:

$$A = p\left(1 + \frac{r}{n}\right)^{nt} = \$7500\left(1 + \frac{0.06}{12}\right)^{12 \cdot 5} = \$7500(1.005)^{60} \approx \$10{,}116.38.$$

Rounded to the nearest cent, you will have $10,116.38 after five years.

b. Because the amount in the account is $10,116.38 and the original principal is $7500, the interest after five years is $10,116.38 − $7500, or $2616.38.

EXAMPLE 6   Choosing Between Savings Accounts

Which is the better choice: an 8.25% rate compounded quarterly, or an 8.3% rate compounded semiannually?

Solution   One way to decide is to assume that $1000 is put into each account for one year. The better choice is the one that results in the greater amount of money in the account at the end of the year.

Begin with the 8.25% rate compounded quarterly. We have $r = 0.0825$. Quarterly compounding means that the bank pays interest four times a year (that is, once every three months), so $n = 4$. The amount of money in the account after one year is:

$$A = p\left(1 + \frac{r}{n}\right)^{nt} = \$1000\left(1 + \frac{0.0825}{4}\right)^{4 \cdot 1} \approx \$1085.09.$$

Next, consider the 8.3% rate compounded semiannually. We have $r = 0.083$. Semiannual compounding means that the bank pays interest two times a year (that is, once every six months), so $n = 2$. The amount of money in the account after one year is:

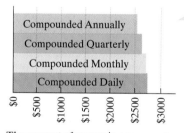

The amount of money in an account when $1000 is invested at a 10% rate after 10 years; the increasing bar lengths show greater amounts as the number of compounding periods in a year increases.

$$A = p\left(1 + \frac{r}{n}\right)^{nt} = \$1000\left(1 + \frac{0.083}{2}\right)^{2 \cdot 1} \approx \$1084.72.$$

The option of 8.25% compounded quarterly results in a slightly greater amount of money, ($1085.09, as opposed to $1084.72), so this is the better choice.

3 Calculate present value.

Planning for the Future with Compound Interest

Consumers often need to consider how much money needs to be deposited now in order to have a certain amount in the future. For example, how much should be deposited in an account today at a given rate so that it will accumulate to $20,000 in four years to pay for a car? The principal, p, that needs to be invested now is called the **present value**.

Calculating Present Value

If A dollars are to be accumulated in t years in an account that pays rate r compounded n times a year, then the amount, p, that needs to be invested now is given by:

$$p = \frac{A}{\left(1 + \dfrac{r}{n}\right)^{nt}}.$$

The principal p that must be invested now is called the **present value**.

EXAMPLE 7   Calculating Present Value

How much money should be deposited in an account today that earns 8% compounded monthly so that it will accumulate to $20,000 in five years to pay for a car?

Solution   The amount we need today is determined by the present value formula. Because the interest is compounded monthly, $n = 12$. Furthermore, A (the accumulated amount) = $20,000, r (the rate) = 8% = 0.08, and t (time in years) = 5.

$$p = \frac{A}{\left(1 + \dfrac{r}{n}\right)^{nt}} = \frac{\$20,000}{\left(1 + \dfrac{0.08}{12}\right)^{12 \cdot 5}} \approx \frac{\$20,000}{1.4898457} \approx \$13,424.21$$

4 Understand the meaning of effective annual yield.

Approximately $13,424.21 should be invested today in order to accumulate to $20,000 in five years.

Hometown Bank
8% Rate
Quarterly Compounding
8.24%
Effective Annual Yield

Effective Annual Yield

The advertisement for Hometown Bank shown in the margin is, at first, a bit confusing. Does Hometown Bank offer two different rates for savings accounts? The answer is no. The first rate, 8%, is the rate paid for compound interest calculated at the end of every three-month period. The second rate, 8.24%, means that if a sum of money is deposited at a *simple interest* rate of 8.24% and the same sum is deposited at 8% compounded quarterly, the interest from both investments at the end of the year is the same. The second rate, 8.24%, is called the **effective annual yield**.

Technology

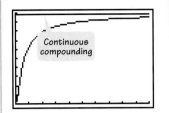

This graph, obtained using a graphing calculator, shows the effects of increasing the number of compounding periods per year on the amount of money in an account. The amount of money gets closer and closer to the amount obtained using continuous compounding, graphed as a horizontal line.

Effective Annual Yield

The **effective annual yield** is the simple interest rate that produces the same amount of money in an account at the end of one year as there is when the account is subjected to compound interest at a stated rate.

In a previous example, we used two different compound rates with different compounding periods to show you how to choose between savings accounts. If the effective annual yield is known for two different accounts, the choice is easy: **The better choice is the account with the greater effective annual yield.** However, there are differences in the types of accounts that you need to take into consideration. Some pay interest from the day of deposit to the day of withdrawal. Other accounts start paying interest the first day of the month that follows the day of deposit. Some savings institutions stop paying interest if the balance in the account falls below a certain amount.

Some banks use **continuous compounding**, where the compounding periods increase infinitely (compounding interest every trillionth of a second, every quadrillionth of a second, etc.). Although continuous compounding sounds terrific, it yields only a fraction of a percent more interest over a year than daily compounding.

Saving to Reach a Goal

Table 8.1 shows how $100 invested monthly at various rates compounded annually will grow with the passing years. The future values in the table illustrate how much you need to save now to reach a specific goal.

Table 8.1 is also helpful if you have a current savings plan. For example, if you're putting aside $200 a month in a tax-deferred account that pays an annual return of 10%, you can determine the amount that you'll have in 15 years by finding the intersection of 10% and 15 years ($41,790) and multiplying that figure by two to reflect a $200-a-month contribution. In 15 years, you will have saved $41,790 × 2, or $83,580.

Table 8.1   How $100 a Month Will Grow

YEAR	3%	4%	5%	6%	7%	8%	9%	10%	11%	12%	13%
						Rate					
1	$ 1220	$ 1230	$ 1230	$ 1240	$ 1250	$ 1250	$ 1260	$ 1270	$ 1270	$ 1280	$ 1290
2	2480	2500	2530	2560	2580	2610	2640	2670	2700	2720	2750
3	3770	3830	3890	3950	4020	4080	4150	4210	4280	4350	4420
4	5110	5210	5320	5440	5550	5670	5800	5920	6050	6180	6320
5	6480	6650	6830	7010	7200	7400	7600	7810	8020	8250	8480
6	7900	8150	8410	8680	8970	9260	9570	9890	10,230	10,580	10,940
7	9360	9710	10,080	10,460	10,860	11,290	11,730	12,200	12,680	13,200	13,740
8	10,860	11,330	11,820	12,340	12,890	13,480	14,090	14,740	15,430	16,150	16,920
9	12,410	13,020	13,660	14,350	15,070	15,850	16,670	17,550	18,490	19,480	20,540
10	14,010	14,770	15,590	16,470	17,410	18,420	19,500	20,660	21,900	23,230	24,670
15	22,750	24,690	26,840	29,230	31,880	34,830	38,120	41,790	45,890	50,460	55,570
20	32,910	36,800	41,280	46,440	52,400	59,290	67,290	76,570	87,360	99,910	114,550
25	44,710	51,580	59,800	69,650	81,480	95,740	112,950	133,790	159,060	189,760	227,140
30	58,420	69,640	83,570	100,950	122,710	150,030	184,450	227,930	283,020	352,990	442,060

Exercise Set 8.2

 Practice Exercises

In Exercises 1–12, the principal represents an amount of money borrowed at the given rate for the specified time.

    a. *Find the simple interest. (Assume 360 days in a year.)*
    b. *Find the maturity value of the loan.*

	Principal	Rate	Time
1.	$4000	6%	1 year
2.	$7000	5%	1 year
3.	$180	3%	2 years
4.	$260	4%	3 years
5.	$900	4%	9 months
6.	$1100	6%	8 months
7.	$9200	6.5%	18 months
8.	$18,000	7.5%	18 months
9.	$20,000	5.25%	3 months
10.	$30,000	5.75%	2 months
11.	$15,500	11%	90 days
12.	$12,600	9%	60 days

In Exercises 13–24, the principal represents an amount of money deposited in a savings account subject to compound interest at the given rate.

    a. *Use the formula $A = p(1 + r)^t$ for one compounding period per year or $A = p\left(1 + \frac{r}{n}\right)^{nt}$ for n compounding periods per year to find how much money there will be in the account after the given number of years.*
    b. *Find the interest earned.*

	Principal	Rate	Compounding Periods per Year	Time
13.	$10,000	4%	1	2 years
14.	$8000	6%	1	3 years
15.	$3000	5%	2	4 years
16.	$4000	4%	2	5 years
17.	$9500	6%	4	5 years
18.	$2500	8%	4	6 years
19.	$4500	4.5%	12	3 years
20.	$2500	6.5%	12	4 years
21.	$1500	8.5%	360	2.5 years
22.	$1200	8.5%	360	3.5 years
23.	$20,000	4.5%	360	20 years
24.	$25,000	5.5%	360	20 years

In Exercises 25–26, assume that $1000 is put into each account for one year.

25. Which is the better choice: a 5.5% rate compounded semi-annually or a 5.4% rate compounded monthly?

26. Which is the better choice: a 6.5% rate compounded semi-annually or a 6.3% rate compounded 360 times per year?

27. Suppose that you have $16,000 to invest. Which investment yields the greater return over three years: 7% compounded monthly or 6.85% compounded 360 times per year?

28. Suppose that you have $14,000 to invest. Which investment yields the greater return over four years: 5% with one compounding period per year or 4.85% with 360 compounding periods per year?

Solve Exercises 29–32 using the present value formula:

$$p = \frac{A}{\left(1 + \dfrac{r}{n}\right)^{nt}}$$

29. How much money should be deposited today in an account that earns 6% compounded semiannually so that it will accumulate to $10,000 in three years?

30. How much money should be deposited today in an account that earns 7% compounded semiannually so that it will accumulate to $12,000 in four years?

31. How much money should be deposited today in an account that earns 9.5% compounded monthly so that it will accumulate to $10,000 in three years?

32. How much money should be deposited today in an account that earns 10.5% compounded monthly so that it will accumulate to $22,000 in four years?

 Application Exercises

33. In order to start a small business, a student takes out a simple interest loan for $4000 for 9 months at a rate of 8.25%.
    a. How much interest must the student pay?
    b. Find the maturity value of the loan.

34. In order to pay for baseball uniforms, a school takes out a simple interest loan for $20,000 for 7 months at a rate of 12%.
    a. How much interest must the school pay?
    b. Find the maturity value of the loan.

35. In 1626, Peter Minuit convinced the Wappinger Indians to sell him Manhattan Island for $24. If the Native Americans had put the $24 into a bank account paying compound interest at a 5% rate, how much would the investment be worth in the year 2000 ($t = 374$ years) if interest were compounded: a. Monthly? b. 360 times per year?

36. In 1777, Jacob DeHaven loaned George Washington's army $450,000 in gold and supplies. Due to a disagreement over the method of repayment (gold versus Continental money), DeHaven was never repaid, dying penniless. In 1989, his descendants sued the U.S. Government over the 212-year-old debt. If the DeHavens used an interest rate of 6% and daily compounding (the rate offered by the Continental Congress in 1777), how much money did the DeHaven family demand in their suit? (*Hint*: Use the compound interest formula with $n = 360$ and $t = 212$ years.)

37. At the time of her grandson's birth, a grandmother deposits $10,000 in an account that pays 9% compounded monthly. What will be the value of the account at the child's twenty-first birthday, assuming that no other deposits or withdrawals are made during this period?

38. Parents wish to have $80,000 available for a child's education. If the child is now 5 years old, how much money must be set aside at 6% compounded semiannually to meet their financial goal when the child is 18?

39. A 30-year-old worker plans to retire at age 65. He believes that $500,000 is needed to retire comfortably. How much should be deposited now at 9% compounded monthly to meet the $500,000 retirement goal?

Writing in Mathematics

40. Describe how a loan's maturity value is determined.

41. What is the Banker's rule?

42. Describe the difference between simple and compound interest.

43. What is meant by present value? Give an example of a practical situation in which present value is used.

44. What is effective annual yield?

45. Shown are figures in an actual advertisement for Great Western Bank. Explain the meaning of the given percents, as well as the statement below these percents.

9.21%	8.85%
Yield	*Rate*

Interest compounded monthly.

Critical Thinking Exercises

46. A depositor opens a new savings account with $6000 at 5% compounded semiannually. At the beginning of year 3, an additional $4000 is deposited. At the end of six years, what is the balance in the account?

47. A depositor opens a money market account with $5000 at 8% compounded monthly. After two years, $1500 is withdrawn from the account to buy a new computer. A year later, $2000 is put in the account. What will be the ending balance if the money is kept in the account for another three years?

48. Explain how to use the compound interest formula, $A = p\left(1 + \frac{r}{n}\right)^{nt}$, to obtain the formula for calculating present value.

Technology Exercises

Use a financial calculator such as the Texas Instruments BA-35 to solve Exercises 49–51.

49. Find the future value of $5000 invested at 10% compounded monthly after six years.

50. How much money should be deposited today in an account that earns 6% compounded quarterly so that it will accumulate to $12,000 in three years?

51. What rate is needed so that $5000 will accumulate to $10,000 in five years subject to monthly compounding?

Group Exercises

52. This activity is a group research project intended for four or five people. Present your research in a seminar on the history of interest and banking. The seminar should last about 30 minutes. Address the following questions:
    When was interest first charged on loans? How was lending money for a fee opposed historically? What is usury? What connection did banking and interest rates play in the historic European rivalries between Christians and Jews? When and where were some of the highest interest rates charged? What were the rates? Where does the word "interest" come from? What is the origin of the word "shylock"? What is the difference between usury and interest in modern times? What is the history of a national bank in the United States?

53. Group members should conduct a survey of banks, savings and loan companies, and credit unions in the area. Report to the class on the different kinds of savings accounts available and the interest rates they pay. What are the methods of payment?

SECTION 8.3 *Installment Buying*

Objectives

1. Determine the amount financed, the installment price, and the finance charge for a fixed loan.
2. Determine the APR.
3. Compute unearned interest and the payoff amount for a loan paid off early.
4. Find the interest, the balance due, and the minimum monthly payment for credit card loans.
5. Calculate interest on credit cards using three methods.

Do you buy products with a credit card? Your card lets you use a product while paying for it. However, the costs associated with such cards contributed to nearly 1.5 million U.S. consumers filing for bankruptcy in 1998. If you use a credit card, you are engaging in **installment buying**, in which you repay a loan for the cost of a product on a monthly basis. A loan that you pay off with weekly or monthly payments, or payments in some other time period, is called an **installment loan**. The advantage of an installment loan is that the consumer gets to use a product immediately. In this section, we will see that the disadvantage is that it can add a substantial amount to the cost of a purchase. When it comes to installment buying, consumer beware!

Fixed Installment Loans

You decide to purchase a pick-up truck that cost $9345. You can finance the truck by paying $300 at the time of purchase, called the **down payment**, and $194.38 per month for 60 months. A loan like this that has a schedule for paying a fixed amount each period is called a **fixed installment loan**. We begin with three terms associated with such loans.

1 Determine the amount financed, the installment price, and the finance charge for a fixed loan.

The Vocabulary of Fixed Installment Loans

The **amount financed** is what the consumer borrows:

Amount financed = Cash price − Down payment

The **total installment price** is the sum of all monthly payments plus the down payment:

Total installment price = Total of all monthly payments + Down payment

The **finance charge** is the interest on the installment loan:

Finance charge = Total installment price − Cash price

EXAMPLE 1 Buying a Pick-up Truck Using a Fixed Installment Loan

The cost of a pick-up truck is $9345. We can finance the truck by paying $300 down and $194.38 per month for 60 months.

  a. Determine the amount financed.
  b. Determine the total installment price.
  c. Determine the finance charge.

Solution

  a. Amount financed = Cash price − Down payment

$$= \$9345 - \$300$$

$$= \$9045$$

The amount financed is $9045.

b. The total installment price is obtained by adding the the total of all monthly payments and the down payment. Because we are paying $194.38 per month for 60 months, the total of all monthly payments is:

$$\frac{\$194.38}{\text{month}} \times 60 \text{ months} = \$194.38 \times 60.$$

Total installment price = Total of all monthly payments + Down payment

$$= \$194.38 \times 60 + \$300$$

$$= \$11,662.80 + \$300$$

$$= \$11,962.80$$

The total installment price is $11,962.80.

c. Finance charge = Total installment price − Cash price

$$= \$11,962.80 - \$9345$$

$$= \$2617.80$$

The finance charge for the loan is $2617.80.

2 Determine the APR.

In Example 1, the finance charge for the loan, $2617.80, is the **interest** paid to finance the truck. What interest rate are we paying when we pay $2617.80 interest over 60 months? The interest rate per year is called the **annual percentage rate**, abbreviated **APR**. In 1969, the Federal Reserve Board established the **Truth-in-Lending Act**. It requires lending institutions to inform borrowers in writing of a loan's APR. When comparing two or more loans with different terms, the loan with the lowest APR is the one that charges the least interest. For many people, an important factor in deciding on a fixed installment loan is the cash down payment that is required. If you do not have a lot of cash at the time of purchase, you might select a loan with a smaller down payment even though it has a not-so-desirable APR.

The APR for a fixed installment loan can be determined using a table similar to the abbreviated version shown in Table 8.2 on page 392. Here are the steps involved in using an APR table. These steps are illustrated in Example 2.

Study Tip

As you read steps 2 and 3 on the right, be sure to turn the page and examine Table 8.2. Make sure you understand how to use Table 8.2 to carry out each step.

Steps in Using an APR Table

1. Compute the finance charge per $100 financed

$$= \frac{\text{Finance charge}}{\text{Amount financed}} \times \$100.$$

2. Look in the row corresponding to the number of payments to be made, and find the entry closest to the value in step 1.
3. Find the APR at the top of the column in which the entry from step 2 is found. (This is the APR rounded to the nearest $\frac{1}{2}\%$.)

Table 8.2 Annual Percentage Rate (APR) for Monthly Payment Loans

Number of Monthly Payments	Annual Percentage Rate (APR)												
	10.0%	10.5%	11.0%	11.5%	12.0%	12.5%	13.0%	13.5%	14.0%	14.5%	15.0%	15.5%	16.0%
	(Finance charge per $100 of amount financed)												
6	$2.94	$3.08	$3.23	$3.38	$3.53	$3.68	$3.83	$3.97	$4.12	$4.27	$4.42	$4.57	$4.72
12	5.50	5.78	6.06	6.34	6.62	6.90	7.18	7.46	7.74	8.03	8.31	8.59	8.88
18	8.10	8.52	8.93	9.35	9.77	10.19	10.61	11.03	11.45	11.87	12.29	12.72	13.14
24	10.75	11.30	11.86	12.42	12.98	13.54	14.10	14.66	15.23	15.80	16.37	16.94	17.51
30	13.43	14.13	14.83	15.54	16.24	16.95	17.66	18.38	19.10	19.81	20.54	21.26	21.99
36	16.16	17.01	17.86	18.71	19.57	20.43	21.30	22.17	23.04	23.92	24.80	25.68	26.57
48	21.74	22.90	24.06	25.23	26.40	27.58	28.77	29.97	31.17	32.37	33.59	34.81	36.03
60	27.48	(28.96)	30.45	31.96	33.47	34.99	36.52	38.06	39.61	41.17	42.74	44.32	45.91

EXAMPLE 2 Determining the APR

In Example 1, we found that the amount financed for the truck was $9045 and the finance charge was $2617.80. The borrower financed the truck with 60 monthly payments. Use Table 8.2 to determine the APR.

Solution

Step 1 Find the finance charge per $100 of the amount financed.

$$\text{Finance charge per \$100 financed} = \frac{\text{Finance charge}}{\text{Amount financed}} \times \$100$$

$$= \frac{\$2617.80}{\$9045.00} \times \$100$$

$$\approx \$28.94$$

This means that the borrower pays $28.94 interest for each $100 being financed.

Step 2 Look in the row corresponding to the number of payments to be made (60) and find the entry closest to the value in step 1 ($28.94). Table 8.2 presents three types of information: the number of monthly payments, the APR, and the finance charge per $100 financed. There are 60 monthly payments, so look for 60 in the left column. Then move across to the right until you find the amount closest to the finance charge per $100 financed, namely $28.94. This amount, $28.96, is circled in the table.

Step 3 Find the APR at the top of the column in which the entry from step 2 is found. Take a second look at the circled entry, $28.96. At the top of this column is 10.5%. Thus, the APR for the fixed installment truck loan is approximately 10.5%.

Study Tip

Use Table 8.2 for this example as follows.

$$\begin{array}{cc} & 10.5\% \\ \downarrow & \uparrow \\ 60 & \rightarrow 28.96 \end{array}$$

3 Compute unearned interest and the payoff amount for a loan paid early.

A fixed installment loan can be paid off early so that a borrower need not pay the entire finance charge. The amount by which the finance charge is reduced is called the **unearned interest**. The interest saved by paying off the loan early can be calculated by one of two methods, the **actuarial method** or the **rule of 78**. The

Study Tip

Keep in mind that a loan's finance charge is the same thing as the loan's interest.

actuarial method uses the APR table, and the rule of 78 does not. The Truth-in-Lending Act requires that the method for calculating the reduction of finance charge be disclosed at the time the loan is signed.

Here are two formulas for computing unearned interest.

Methods for Computing Unearned Interest

Unearned interest is the amount by which a loan's finance charge is reduced when the loan is paid off early

Actuarial Method	Rule of 78
$$u = \dfrac{kRV}{100 + V}$$	$$u = \dfrac{k(k+1)}{n(n+1)} \times F$$
u = unearned interest	u = unearned interest
k = remaining number of scheduled payments (excluding current payment)	k = remaining number of scheduled payments (excluding current payment)
R = regular monthly payment	n = original number of payments
V = finance charge per $100 (from the APR table) for a loan with the same APR and k monthly payments	F = original finance charge

Pick-up truck
cost: $9345
Financing: $300 + $194.38 per month for 60 months
Amount financed: $9045
Total installment price: $11,962.80
Finance charge (interest): $2617.80
Finance charge per $100 financed: $28.94
APR: 10.5%.

The total amount due on the day that a loan is paid off early is called the **payoff amount**. Unearned interest is subtracted from the payoff amount. Examples 3 and 4 illustrate how this is done using the actuarial method in Example 3 and the rule of 78 in Example 4. Both examples refer back to the pick-up truck in Example 1. Shown in the margin is a summary of given and computed amounts for the truck.

EXAMPLE 3 Early Payoff: The Actuarial Method

You got a big bonus at work—and a raise. Instead of making the thirty-sixth payment on your truck, you decide to pay the remaining balance and terminate the loan.

a. Use the actuarial method to determine how much interest will be saved (the unearned interest, u) by repaying the loan early.

b. Find the payoff amount.

Solution

a. We will use the formula $u = \dfrac{kRV}{100 + V}$ to find u, the unearned interest. We need values for k, R, and V. The current payment is payment number 36. There are 60 payments total. We subtract the number of the current payment from the total number of payments to find the number of remaining payments, k: $k = 60 - 36 = 24$. The value of R, the regular monthly payment, is given: $R = \$194.38$. To find the value for the finance charge per $100,

V, use the APR table (Table 8.2 on page 392). In the Number of Monthly Payments Column, find the number of remaining payments, 24, and then look to the right until you reach the column headed by 10.5%, the APR. This row and column intersect at 11.30. Thus, $V = 11.30$. This is the finance charge per $100 for a loan with the same APR and $k(k = 24)$ monthly payments. We substitute these values into the actuarial method formula.

$$u = \frac{kRV}{100 + V} = \frac{24 \times 194.38 \times 11.30}{100 + 11.30} \approx 473.64$$

Approximately $473.64 will be saved in interest by terminating the loan early using the actuarial method.

b. The payoff amount, the amount due on the day of the loan's termination, is determined as follows:

Payoff amount	=	Payment number 36	plus	Total of remaining payments after payment 36	minus	Interest saved (unearned interest)
	=	$194.38	+	24 × $194.38	−	$473.64
	=	$4385.86				

The payment needed to terminate the loan at the end of 36 months is $4385.86.

EXAMPLE 4   Early Payoff: The Rule of 78

The loan in Example 3 is paid off at the time of the thirty-sixth monthly payment. Use the rule of 78 to find:

a. the unearned interest.

b. the payoff amount.

Pick-up truck
cost: $9345
Financing: $300 + $194.38 per month for 60 months
Amount financed: $9045
Total installment price: $11,962.80
Finance charge (interest): $2617.80
Finance charge per $100 financed: $28.94
APR: 10.5%.

Solution

a. We will use the formula

$$u = \frac{k(k + 1)}{n(n + 1)} \times F$$

to find u, the unearned interest. We need values for k, n, and F. From Example 3, k, the number of remaining payments, is 24: $k = 24$. The original number of payments, n, is 60: $n = 60$. The summary of figures for the pick-up truck shown in the margin lists the finance charge: $F = \$2617.80$ We substitute these values into the rule of 78 formula.

$$u = \frac{k(k + 1)}{n(n + 1)} \times F = \frac{24(24 + 1)}{60(60 + 1)} \times \$2617.80 \approx \$429.15$$

By the rule of 78, the borrower will save $429.15 in interest.

b. Next, we determine the payoff amount.

$$\begin{array}{ccccc}\text{Payoff} \\ \text{amount} \end{array} = \boxed{\begin{array}{c}\text{Payment} \\ \text{number 36}\end{array}} \; \text{plus} \; \boxed{\begin{array}{c}\text{Total of remaining} \\ \text{payments after} \\ \text{payment 36}\end{array}} \; \text{minus} \; \boxed{\begin{array}{c}\text{Interest saved} \\ \text{(unearned interest)}\end{array}}$$

$$= \$194.38 \quad + \quad 24 \times \$194.38 \quad - \quad \$429.15$$

$$= \$4430.35$$

The payoff amount is $4430.35.

In Example 3, we found that $473.64 is saved in interest using the actuarial method, while in Example 4, we found that $429.15 is saved in interest using the rule of 78. These examples illustrate that the actuarial method is more beneficial to the borrower than the rule of 78 because it results in greater savings in interest at the loan's termination. For loans of 61 months or longer, only the actuarial method is allowed. Also, some states have shorter loan periods that do not allow the rule of 78.

4 Find the interest, the balance due, and the minimum monthly payment for credit card loans.

Open-End Installment Loans

Using a credit card is an example of an open-end installment loan, commonly called **revolving credit**. Open-end loans differ from fixed installment loans in that there is no schedule for paying a fixed amount each period. Credit card loans require users to make only a minimum monthly payment that depends on the unpaid balance and the interest rate. Credit cards have high interest rates compared to other kinds of loans. The interest on credit cards is computed using the simple interest formula $I = prt$. However, r represents the *monthly* interest rate and t is time in months rather than years. A typical interest rate is 1.57% monthly. This is equivalent to a yearly rate of $12 \times 1.57\%$, or 18.84%. With such a high APR, credit card balances should be paid off as quickly as possible.

Most credit card customers are billed every month. A typical billing period is May 1 through May 31, but it can also run from, say, May 5 through June 4. Customers receive a statement, called an **itemized billing**, that contains the unpaid balance on the first day of the billing period, the total balance owed on the last day of the billing period, a list of purchases and cash advances made during the billing period, the date of the last day of the billing period, the payment due date, and the minimum payment required.

Customers who make a purchase during the billing period and pay the entire amount of the purchase by the payment due date are not charged interest. By contrast, customers who make cash advances using their credit cards must pay interest from the day the money is advanced until the day it is repaid.

One method for calculating interest on credit cards is the **unpaid balance method**. Interest is calculated on the unpaid balance on the first day of the billing period less payments and credits.

EXAMPLE 5   Balance Due on a Credit Card

A particular VISA card calculates interest using the unpaid balance method. The monthly interest rate is 1.3% on the unpaid balance on the first day of the billing period less payments and credits. Here are some of the details in the May 1–May 31 itemized billing:

Study Tip

You can search the Internet for the most current information regarding annual fees and interest rates for credit cards.

Charge It

With features such as miles toward air travel, insurance on rental cars, and special introductory rates, consumers are using credit cards more and more. The big winner in the spendfest has been VISA, with nearly a 50 percent market share and a charge volume of $431.8 billion. The big losers are the 55 to 60 million U.S. households that each owe more than $7000 on their credit cards. This means that they pay at least $1000 a year in interest.

May 1 Unpaid Balance: $1350

Payment Received May 8: $250

Purchases Charged to the VISA Account: Airline tickets: $375 Books: $57 Meals: $65

Last Day of the Billing Period: May 31

Payment Due Date: June 9

a. Find the interest due on the payment due date.

b. Find the total balance owed on the last day of the billing period.

c. This credit card requires a $10 minimum monthly payment if the total balance owed on the last day of the billing period is less than $360. Otherwise, the minimum monthly payment is $\frac{1}{36}$ of the balance owed on the last day of the billing period, rounded to the nearest whole dollar. What is the minimum monthly payment due by June 9?

Solution

a. The monthly interest rate is 1.3% on the unpaid balance on the first day of the billing period, $1350, less payments and credits, $250:

$$I = prt = (\$1350 - \$250) \times 0.013 \times 1 = \$1100 \times 0.013 \times 1 = \$14.30$$

> Time, t, is measured in months, and $t = 1$ month.

The interest due on the payment due date is $14.30.

b. The total balance owed on the last day of the billing period is determined as follows:

$$\text{Balance owed} = \underset{\substack{\text{Unpaid balance} \\ \text{on the first day} \\ \text{of the billing period} \\ \text{minus payments}}}{} \text{plus} \quad \text{interest} \quad \text{plus} \quad \underset{\substack{\text{charges for three items} \\ \text{during billing period}}}{}$$

$$= \$1100 \quad + \quad \$14.30 \quad + \quad \$375 + \$57 + \$65$$

$$= \$1611.30$$

The total balance owed on the last day of the billing period is $1611.30.

c. Because the balance owed on the last day of the billing period exceeds $360, the customer must pay a minimum of $\frac{1}{36}$ of the balance owed.

$$\text{Minimum monthly payment} = \frac{\text{balance owed}}{36} = \frac{\$1611.30}{36} \approx \$45$$

Rounded to the nearest whole dollar, the minimum monthly payment due by June 9 is $45.

5 Calculate interest on credit cards using three methods.

Methods for calculating interest on credit cards vary, and the interest can differ on credit cards that show the same APR. The three methods for calculating interest are summarized in the box.

The Dark Side of Credit Cards

- The average APR is a steep 18.84% and increasing each year.
- Half the credit card companies charge a late fee of more than $18.
- Some credit card companies charge their cardholders a fee for not charging during a six-month period.
- Some credit card companies charge a fee if you cancel your account.
- In addition to high interest rates, many credit card companies charge annual fees.

Methods for Calculating Interest on Credit Cards

For all three methods, $I = prt$, where r is the monthly rate and t is one month.

Unpaid balance method: The principal, p, is the balance on the first day of the billing period less payments and credits.

Previous balance method: The principal, p, is the unpaid balance on the first day of the billing period.

Average daily balance method: The principal, p, is the **average daily balance**. This is determined by adding the unpaid balances for each day in the billing period and dividing by the number of days in the billing period.

EXAMPLE 6   Comparing Methods for Calculating Interest

A credit card has a monthly rate of 1.75%. (The APR is 21%.) In the January 1–January 31 itemized billing, the January 1 unpaid balance is $2500. A payment of $1000 was received on January 8. There are no purchases or cash advances in this billing period. The payment due date is February 9. Find the interest due on this date using each of the three methods for calculating credit card interest.

Solution   Because the monthly rate is 1.75%, for all three methods $I = prt = p \times 0.0175 \times 1$ month. The principal, p, is different for each method.

a. The Unpaid Balance Method
    The principal, p, is the unpaid balance on the first day of the billing period, $2500, less payments and credits, $1000. The interest is:

$$I = prt = (\$2500 - \$1000) \times 0.0175 \times 1 = \$1500 \times 0.0175 \times 1 = \$26.25.$$

The interest due on the payment due date is $26.25.

b. The Previous Balance Method
    The principal, p, is the unpaid balance on the first day of the billing period, $2500. The interest is:

$$I = prt = \$2500 \times 0.0175 \times 1 = \$43.75.$$

The interest due on the payment due date is $43.75.

c. The Average Daily Balance Method
    The principal, p, is the average daily balance. Add the unpaid balances for each day in the billing period and divide by the number of days in the billing period, 31. The unpaid balance on the first day of the billing period is $2500, and a $1000 payment is recorded on January 8. The sum of the balances owed for each day of the billing period is $2500 added for each of the first 7 days, expressed as $2500 × 7, plus $1500 added for each of the remaining 24 days, expressed as $1500 × 24.

$$\text{Average daily balance} = \frac{\text{Sum of the unpaid balances for each day in the billing period}}{\text{Number of days in the billing period}}$$

$$= \frac{\$2500(7) + \$1500(24)}{31} \approx \$1725.81$$

The average daily balance serves as the principal. The interest is:

$$I = prt = \$1725.81 \times 0.0175 \times 1 \approx \$30.20.$$

The interest due on the payment due date is $30.20.

Most credit cards use the average daily balance method to determine interest due. Calculating the average daily balance by hand can be quite tedious when there are numerous transactions during a billing period. Credit card customers who are charged interest by the average daily balance method will find the average daily balance provided on monthly statements.

Collecting Credit Cards

The largest collection of credit cards is 1397 different cards by Walter Cavanagh of Santa Clara, California. His cards offer over $1.65 million in credit and are kept in a 250-foot long wallet that weighs 38 pounds 8 ounces.

Source: The Guinness Book of World Records

Exercise Set 8.3

  Practice and Application Exercises

1. The cost of a sports utility vehicle is $27,000. We can finance this by paying $5000 down and $410 per month for 60 months. Determine: a. the amount financed; b. the total installment price; c. the finance charge.

2. The cost of a computer is $2450. We can finance this by paying $550 down and $94.50 a month for 24 months. Determine: a. the amount financed; b. the total installment price; c. the finance charge.

3. The cost of a washer-dryer is $1100. We can finance this by paying $100 down and $110 per month for 12 months. Determine: a. the amount financed; b. the total installment price; c. the finance charge.

4. The cost of a used car is $5675. We can finance this by paying $1223 down and $125 per month for 48 months. Determine: a. the amount financed; b. the total installment price; c. the finance charge.

5. You plan to pay for a computer in 12 equal monthly payments. The finance charge per $100 financed is $6.90. Use Table 8.2 on page 392 to find the APR for this loan.

6. You plan to pay for a refrigerator in 18 equal monthly payments. The finance charge per $100 financed is $12.72. Use Table 8.2 on page 392 to find the APR for this loan.

7. The finance charge per $100 financed for a computer that is paid off in 24 equal monthly payments is $15.80. Use Table 8.2 to find the Annual Percentage Rate (the APR) for this loan.

8. The finance charge per $100 financed for a refrigerator that is paid off in 12 monthly payments is $8.59. Use Table 8.2 to find the Annual Percentage Rate (the APR) for this loan.

9. A used car is financed for $4450 over 48 months. If the total finance charge is $1279, find the APR for this loan.

10. A desk is financed for $1200 over 30 months. If the total finance charge is $264, find the APR for this loan.

11. The cash price for furniture for all rooms of a three-bedroom house is $17,500. The furniture can be financed by paying $500 down and $360.55 per month for 60 months.
   a. Determine the amount financed.
   b. Determine the total installment price.
   c. Determine the finance charge.
   d. What is the APR for this loan?

12. The cost of a Blazer is $18,000, which can be financed by paying $600 down and $385 per month for 60 months.
   a. Determine the amount financed.
   b. Determine the total installment price.
   c. Determine the finance charge.
   d. What is the APR for this loan?

13. In Exercise 11, instead of making the twenty-fourth payment, the borrower decides to pay the remaining balance and terminate the loan for the furniture.
   a. Use the actuarial method to determine how much interest will be saved by repaying the loan early.
   b. By the actuarial method, what is the total amount due on the day of the loan's termination?
   c. Use the rule of 78 to determine how much interest will be saved by repaying the loan early.
   d. By the rule of 78, what is the total amount due on the day of the loan's termination?

14. In Exercise 12, instead of making the twenty-fourth payment, the borrower decides to pay the remaining balance and terminate the loan for the Blazer.
   a. Use the actuarial method to determine how much interest will be saved by repaying the loan early.
   b. By the actuarial method, what is the total amount due on the day of the loan's termination?
   c. Use the rule of 78 to determine how much interest will be saved by repaying the loan early.
   d. By the rule of 78, what is the total amount due on the day of the loan's termination?

15. A particular VISA card calculates interest using the unpaid balance method. The monthly interest rate is 1.3% on the unpaid balance on the first day of the billing period less payments and credits. Here are some of the details in the May 1–May 31 itemized billing:
   May 1 Unpaid Balance: $950
   Payment Received May 8: $100
   Purchases Charged to the VISA Account: clothing, $85 and car repair, $67
   Last Day of the Billing Period: May 31
   Payment Due Date: June 9
   a. Find the interest due on the payment due date.
   b. Find the total balance owed on the last day of the billing period.
   c. This credit card requires a $10 minimum monthly payment if the total balance owed on the last day of the billing period is less than $360. Otherwise, the minimum monthly payment is $\frac{1}{36}$ of the balance owed on the last day of the billing period, rounded to the nearest whole dollar. What is the minimum monthly payment due by June 9?

16. A particular credit card calculates interest using the unpaid balance method. The monthly interest rate is 1.75% on the unpaid balance on the first day of the billing period less payments and credits. Here are some of the details in the September 1–September 30 itemized billing:
   September 1 Unpaid Balance: $425
   Payment Received September 6: $75
   Purchases Charged to the Account: groceries, $45 and clothing, $77
   Last Day of the Billing Period: September 30
   Payment Due Date: October 9
   a. Find the interest due on the payment due date.
   b. Find the total balance owed on the last day of the billing period.
   c. Terms for this credit card are shown below. What is the minimum monthly payment due by October 9?

New Balance	Minimum Payment
$ 0.01 to $ 10.00	No payment due
10.01 to 200.00	$10.00
200.01 to 250.00	15.00
250.01 to 300.00	20.00
300.01 to 350.00	25.00
350.01 to 400.00	30.00
400.01 to 450.00	35.00
450.01 to 500.00	40.00
Over $500.00	1/10 of New Bal.

17. A credit card has a monthly rate of 1.5% and uses the average daily balance method for calculating interest. Here are some of the details in the April 1–April 30 itemized billing:
   April 1 Unpaid Balance: $445.59
   Payment Received April 5: $110
   Purchases Charged to the Account: $278.06
   Average Daily Balance: $330.90
   Last Day of the Billing Period: April 30
   Payment Due Date: May 9
   a. Find the interest due on the payment due date.
   b. Find the total balance owed on the last day of the billing period.
   c. Terms for this credit card are given in Exercise 16. What is the minimum monthly payment due by May 9?

18. A credit card has a monthly rate of 1.8% and uses the average daily balance method for calculating interest. Here are some of the details in the December 1–December 31 itemized billing:
   December 1 Unpaid Balance: $220
   Payment Received December 7: $60
   Purchases Charged to the Account: $90

Average Daily Balance: $205.60
Last Day of the Billing Period: December 31
Payment Due Date: January 9

a. Find the interest due on the payment due date.
b. Find the total balance owed on the last day of the billing period.
c. Terms for this credit card are given in Exercise 16 on page 399. What is the minimum monthly payment due on January 9?

19. A credit card has a monthly rate of 1.5%. In the September 1–September 30 itemized billing, the September 1 unpaid balance is $3000. A payment of $2500 was received on September 6. There are no purchases or cash advances in this billing period. The payment due date is October 9. Find the interest due on this date using:
a. the unpaid balance method.
b. the previous balance method.
c. the average daily balance method.

20. A credit card has a monthly rate of 2.2%. In the October 1–October 31 itemized billing, the October 1 unpaid balance is $2000. A payment of $400 was received on October 6. There are no purchases or cash advances in this billing period. The payment due date is November 9. Find the interest due on this date using:
a. the unpaid balance method.
b. the previous balance method.
c. the average daily balance method.

Writing in Mathematics

21. Describe the difference between a fixed installment loan and an open-end installment loan.

22. For a fixed installment loan, what is the total installment price?

23. For a fixed installment loan, how is the total finance charge determined?

24. What is the APR?

25. What are the two methods for computing unearned interest when a loan is paid off early? Describe how the payoff amount is determined regardless of which method is used in the computation.

26. Name and describe each of the three methods for calculating interest on credit cards.

27. For a credit card billing period, describe how the average daily balance is determined. Why is this computation somewhat tedious when done by hand?

28. Which method for calculating interest on credit cards is most beneficial to the borrower and which is least beneficial? Explain why this is so.

29. A Sears Revolving Charge Card has a monthly rate of 1.75%. The interest is a minimum of 50¢ if the average daily balance is $28.50 or less. Explain how this policy is beneficial to Sears.

Critical Thinking Exercises

30. Which one of the following is true?
a. The finance charge on a fixed installment loan is the cash price minus the total installment price.
b. It is to a borrower's advantage to have unearned interest computed by the rule of 78 rather than by the actuarial method.
c. It is not necessary to know the number of days in a credit card billing period to determine the average daily balance.
d. If a credit card has a 2.2% monthly interest rate, the annual rate exceeds 25%.

Use estimation and not calculation to select the most reasonable value in Exercises 31–32.

31. If you purchase a $1400 item, put $200 down, and pay the balance in 30 monthly installments, what is a reasonable estimate of the monthly payment?
a. $35   b. $47   c. $70   d. $100

32. A reasonable estimate of the monthly interest on an average daily balance of $359.58 at a 1.3% monthly rate is:
a. $50   b. $10   c. $5   d. $2

33. A bank bills its credit card holders on the first of each month for each itemized billing. The card provides a 20-day period in which to pay the bill before charging interest. If the card holder wants to buy an expensive gift for a September 30 wedding but can't pay for it until November 5, explain how this can be done without adding an interest charge.

34. A $1500 computer can be purchased using a credit card that charges a monthly rate of 1.5% using the unpaid balance method. The borrower is considering one of the following options:

Option A: Make a credit card payment of $300 at the end of each month for five months and pay off the balance at the end of the sixth month.

Option B: Make a credit card payment of $300 plus the month's interest at the end of each months for five months.

How much is saved in interest using option B?

Technology Exercises

35. Set up a spreadsheet with one column each for the balance, number of days at that balance, payments, charges, and the product of each balance and the number of days at that balance. The balance on John and Jane Doe's credit card on July 5, their billing date, was $375.80. For the period ending August 4, they had the following transactions.
July 13, Payment: $150.00
July 15, Charge: Computer Store, $74.35
July 23, Charge: Clothing, $123.50
July 29, Charge: Restaurant, $42.50

a. Use the summation capabilities of the spreadsheet to determine the number of days in the billing period and the average daily balance.

b. Find the finance charge (the interest) that is owed on August 4. Assume the monthly rate is 1.3%.

c. Find the balance that is owed on August 4.

36. Set up a spreadsheet with one column each for the balance, number of days at that balance, payments, charges, and the product of each balance and the number of days at that balance. The balance on the Does' credit card on May 12, their billing date, was $378.50. For the period ending June 11, they had the following transactions.

May 13, Charge: Toys, $129.79
May 15, Payment: $50.00
May 18, Charge: Clothing, $135.85
May 29, Charge: Housewares, $37.63

a. Use the summation capabilities of the spreadsheet to determine the number of days in the billing period and the average daily balance.

b. Find the finance charge (the interest) that is owed on June 11. Assume the monthly rate is 0.75%.

c. Find the balance that is owed on June 11.

Group Exercise

37. Credit card trouble can compound quickly, and many people get into financial trouble as a result. As a group, present ten guidelines for avoiding credit card trouble. Assume that these guidelines are to be distributed to all students at your college by the Student Government Association.

SECTION 8.4   *The Cost of Home Ownership*

Objectives

1. Understand mortgage options.
2. Compute interest costs for a mortgage.
3. Prepare a partial loan amortization schedule.
4. Determine how much to spend when buying a home.

Percentage of People in the United States Who Are Homeowners, by Race or Hispanic Origin

White   Black   Hispanic

Figure 8.4
Source: U.S. Census Bureau

Figure 8.4 shows the percentage of Americans who are homeowners. For most people, buying a home is a major lifetime decision and their largest purchase ever.

Many factors must be considered before deciding to purchase a home. Two major questions are "Does this house have what I require?" and, if it does, "Can I afford it?" In this section, we focus on the cost of home ownership, a centerpiece of the American dream.

Mortgages

A **mortgage** is a long-term loan (perhaps up to 30 or even 40 years) for the purpose of buying a home, and for which the property is pledged as security for payment. If payments are not made on the loan, the lender gets to take possession of the property. The **down payment** is the portion of the sale price of the home that the buyer initially pays to the seller. The minimum required down payment is computed as a percentage of the sale price. For example, suppose you decide to buy a $120,000 home that requires you to pay the seller 10% of the sale price. You must pay 10% of $120,000, which is $0.10 \times \$120,000$, or $12,000 to the seller. Thus, $12,000 is the down payment. The **amount of the mortgage** is the difference between the sale price and the down payment. For your $120,000 home, the amount of the mortgage is $120,000 − $12,000, or $108,000.

There are many types of lenders and types of mortgages to choose from. Many banks, savings associations, mortgage companies, and credit unions provide mortgage loans. Some companies, called **mortgage brokers**, offer to find you a mortgage lender willing to make you a loan. Computer loan origination systems, or CLOs, are computer terminals sometimes available in real estate offices to help buyers sort through the various types of loans offered by different lenders.

Monthly payments for a mortgage depend on the amount of the mortgage, or the principal, and the interest rate. Mortgages can have a fixed interest rate or a variable interest rate. **Fixed-rate mortgages** have the same monthly payment during the entire time of the loan. **Variable-rate mortgages**, also known as **adjustable-rate mortgages** (ARMs), have payment amounts that change from

1 Understand mortgage options.

time to time depending on changes in the interest rate. ARMS are less predictable than fixed-rate mortgages. They start out at lower rates than fixed-rate mortgages. Caps limit how high rates can go over the term of the loan.

There are many other mortgage options. One option involves a short-term loan in which only the interest is paid, followed by a final payment (called a "balloon payment") for the entire loan amount. This kind of mortgage might appeal to a buyer who plans to sell the house in a short period of time. Some buyers are eligible for a mortgage insured through the Federal Housing Administration (FHA) or guaranteed by the Department of Veteran Affairs or similar programs operated by cities or states. These programs require a smaller down payment than standard loans.

Computation Involved with Buying a Home

Although monthly payments for a mortgage depend on the amount of the mortgage and the interest rate, the rate is not the only cost of a mortgage. Most lending institutions require the buyer to pay one or more **points** at the time of closing—that is, the time at which the mortgage begins. A point is a one-time charge that equals 1 percent of the loan amount. For example, two points means that the buyer must pay 2 percent of the loan amount at closing. Often, a buyer can pay fewer points in exchange for a higher interest rate or more points for a lower rate. A document, called the **Truth-in-Lending Disclosure Statement**, shows the buyer the APR for the mortgage. The APR takes into account the interest rate and points.

A monthly mortgage payment is used to repay the principal plus interest. In addition, lending institutions can require that part of the monthly payment be deposited into an **escrow account**, an account used by the lender to pay real estate taxes and insurance. Interest is paid to the buyer on the amount in an escrow account.

Table 8.3 gives the monthly mortgage payment for each $1000 of mortgage at various interest rates for mortgage loans of 15, 20, 25, 30, 35, and 40 years. The entries in the table do not include amounts deposited monthly into an escrow account.

Dream homes in the United State are growing larger each year.
Source: U.S. Department of Housing and Urban Development

Study Tip

Do not use Table 8.3 to conclude that rates lower than 6.5% or higher than 12.5% are not possible. Interest rates on 30-year-fixed mortgages peaked at 16.63% in 1981. The essay on page 407 will help you to put the rates in Table 8.3 in perspective.

Table 8.3 Monthly Payment per $1000 of Mortgage, Including Principal and Interest

Rate %	Number of Years					
	15	20	25	30	35	40
6.5	$8.71	$7.46	$6.75	$6.32	$6.04	$5.85
7	8.99	7.75	7.70	6.65	6.39	6.21
7.5	9.28	8.06	7.39	6.99	6.74	6.58
8	9.56	8.36	7.72	7.34	7.10	6.95
8.5	9.85	8.68	8.05	7.69	7.47	7.33
9	10.15	9.00	8.40	8.05	7.84	7.72
9.5	10.45	9.33	8.74	8.41	8.22	8.11
10	10.75	9.66	9.09	8.70	8.60	8.50
10.5	11.06	9.98	9.44	9.15	8.98	8.89
11	11.37	10.32	9.80	9.52	9.37	9.28
11.5	11.69	10.66	10.16	9.90	9.76	9.68
12	12.01	11.01	10.53	10.29	10.16	10.08
12.5	12.33	11.36	10.90	10.67	10.55	10.49

2 Compute interest costs for a mortgage.

EXAMPLE 1 Computing the Total Cost of Interest over the Life of a Fixed-Rate Mortgage

The price of a home is $195,000. The bank requires a 10% down payment and two points at the time of closing. The cost of the home is financed with a 30-year fixed-rate mortgage at 7.5%.

a. Find the required down payment.
b. Find the amount of the mortgage.
c. How much must be paid for the two points at closing?
d. Find the monthly payment (excluding escrowed taxes and insurance).
e. Find the total cost of interest over 30 years.

Solution

a. The required down payment is 10% of $195,00 or

$$0.10 \times \$195,000 = \$19,500.$$

b. The amount of the mortgage is the difference between the price of the home and the down payment.

$$\begin{array}{ccc} \text{Amount of} & = & \text{Sale} & - & \text{Down} \\ \text{the mortgage} & & \text{price} & & \text{payment} \end{array}$$

$$= \$195,000 - \$19,500$$

$$= \$175,500$$

c. To find the cost of two points on a mortgage of $175,500, find 2% of $175,500.

$$0.02 \times \$175,500 = \$3510$$

The down payment ($19,500) is paid to the seller and the cost of two points ($3510) is paid to the lending institution.

d. We need to find the monthly mortgage payment. To do so, we will use Table 8.3, which shows the monthly payment *per $1000 of the mortgage amount*. For a mortgage of 30 years at 7.5%, the monthly payment *per $1000* (including the interest payment and the principal payment) is $6.99. This amount is circled in Table 8.3.

We can multiply this amount, $6.99, by the number of thousands of dollars in the mortgage amount to find the monthly payment for the entire mortgage amount. We divide the mortgage amount, $175,500, by $1000 to find the number of thousands of dollars in the mortgage amount.

$$\frac{\$175,500}{\$1000} = 175.5$$

The monthly mortgage payment is found by multiplying the number of thousands of dollars in the mortgage, 175.5, by the amount shown in Table 8.3.

$$\$6.99 \times 175.5 \approx \$1226.75$$

The monthly mortgage payment for principal and interest is $1226.75. (Keep in mind that this payment does not include escrowed taxes and insurance.)

e. The total cost of interest over 30 years is equal to the difference between the total of all monthly payments and the amount of the mortgage. The total of all monthly payments is equal to the amount of the monthly payment multiplied by the number of payments. We found the amount of the monthly payment in

404 • Consumer Mathematics and Financial Management • Chapter 8

(d): $1226.75. The number of payments is equal to the number of months in a year, 12, multiplied by the number of years in the mortgage, 30: $12 \times 30 = 360$. Thus, the total of all monthly payments = 1226.75×360. Now we can calculate the interest over 30 years.

$$\begin{array}{c} \text{Total cost} \\ \text{of interest} \end{array} = \begin{array}{c} \text{Total of all} \\ \text{monthly payments} \end{array} \text{ minus } \begin{array}{c} \text{Amount of} \\ \text{the mortgage} \end{array}$$

$$= \$1226.75 \times 360 - \$175,500$$

$$= \$441,630 - \$175,500 = \$266,130$$

The total cost of interest over 30 years is $266,130.

Buying the American Dream

Characteristics of home buyers in major metropolitan areas have varied in each decade of the twentieth century.

	1976	1997
Average home price	$43,340	$159,700
Average monthly payment	$329	$1114
Average age of first-time buyer	28.1	32.1
Average household income of buyer	$20,840	$66,100

Source: Chicago Title and Trust Co.

3 Prepare a partial loan amortization schedule.

In Example 1, were you surprised that over the 30 years of a $195,000 mortgage loan, the amount paid in interest is $266,130? What adds to the cost of the loan is the long time period over which it is financed. Although each payment is the same, with each successive payment the interest portion decreases and the principal portion increases. The interest is computed using the simple interest formula $I = prt$. The principal, p, is equal to the balance of the loan, which changes each month. The rate, r, is the annual interest rate of the mortgage loan (the APR). Because a payment is made each month, the time, t, is

$$\frac{1 \text{ month}}{12 \text{ months}} = \frac{1 \text{ month}}{12 \text{ months}}$$

or $\frac{1}{12}$ of a year.

The process of making regular payments on the principal and interest until the loan is paid off is called **amortizing the loan**. A document showing important information about the status of the mortgage is called a **loan amortization schedule**. Typically, the document includes the number of the most recent payment and those of any previous monthly payments, the interest for each monthly payment, the principal payment for each monthly payment, and the balance of the loan.

EXAMPLE 2   Preparing a Loan Amortization Schedule

Prepare a loan amortization schedule for the first two months of the mortgage loan shown on page 405.

Loan Amortization Schedule

Annual % rate: 9.5% Amount of Mortgage: $130,000 Number of Monthly Payments: 180		Monthly payment: $1357.50 Term: Years 15, Months 0	
Payment Number	**Interest Payment**	**Principal Payment**	**Balance of Loan**
1			
2			

Solution We begin with payment number 1.

$$\text{Interest for the month} = prt = \$130{,}000 \times 0.095 \times \tfrac{1}{12} \approx \$1029.17$$

$$\text{Principal payment} = \text{Monthly payment} - \text{Interest payment}$$
$$= \$1357.50 - \$1029.17 = \$328.33$$

$$\text{Balance of loan} = \text{Principal balance} - \text{Principal payment}$$
$$= \$130{,}000 - \$328.33 = \$129{,}671.67$$

Now, starting with a loan balance of $129,671.67, we repeat these computations for the second month.

$$\text{Interest for the month} = prt = \$129{,}671.67 \times 0.095 \times \tfrac{1}{12} = \$1026.57$$

$$\text{Principal payment} = \text{Monthly payment} - \text{Interest payment}$$
$$= \$1357.50 - \$1026.57 = \$330.93$$

$$\text{Balance of loan} = \text{Principal balance} - \text{Principal payment}$$
$$= \$129{,}671.67 - \$330.93 = \$129{,}340.74$$

The results of these computations are included in Table 8.4, a partial loan amortization schedule. By using the simple interest formula month-to-month on the loan's balance, a complete loan amortization schedule for all 180 payments can be calculated. Many lenders supply such a schedule. The loan amortization schedule shows how the buyer pays slightly less in interest and more in principal for each payment over the entire life of the loan.

Table 8.4   Loan Amortization Schedule

Annual % rate: 9.5% Amount of Mortgage: $130,000 Number of Monthly Payments: 180		Monthly payment: $1357.50 Term: Years 15, Months 0	
Payment Number	**Interest Payment**	**Principal Payment**	**Balance of Loan**
1	$1029.17	$328.33	$129,671.67
2	1026.57	330.93	129,340.74
3	1023.96	333.54	129,007.22
4	1021.32	336.18	128,671.04
30	944.82	412.68	118,931.35
31	941.55	415.95	118,515.52
125	484.62	872.88	60,340.84
126	477.71	879.79	59,461.05
179	21.26	1336.24	1347.74
180	9.76	1347.74	

4 Determine how much to spend when buying a home.

Qualifying for a Mortgage Loan

How much can you afford to pay for a home? The following two commonly accepted guidelines are used by most lenders:

1. Your monthly housing costs, including principal, interest, and payments deposited into an escrow account, should total no more than 28% of your monthly gross (before taxes) income.

2. Your monthly housing costs plus other long-term debts should total no more than 36% of your monthly gross income. Long-term debts may include payments on car loans, student loans, or other installment loans with more than ten months left to repay.

Table 8.5 can help you determine how large a mortgage you might qualify for based on your yearly gross (before taxes) income and the interest rate for a 30-year fixed-rate mortgage. Rather than using 28% of your gross income, this table uses 25% and assumes that the amount needed to set aside to pay for taxes and insurance is approximately the 3% difference. Table 8.5 should give you a fairly accurate answer to the question: How large a mortgage do I qualify for?

Table 8.5   How Large Is the Mortgage for Which You Qualify?

Interest rates	Annual income					
	$15,000	**$20,000**	**$25,000**	**$30,000**	**$35,000**	**$40,000**
6.5%	$49,400	$65,900	$82,400	$98,800	$115,300	$131,800
7.0	47,000	62,600	78,300	93,900	109,600	125,300
7.5	44,600	59,600	74,500	89,400	104,300	119,200
8.0	45,000	56,700	70,900	85,100	99,300	113,500
8.5	40,600	54,100	67,700	81,200	94,800	108,300
9.0	38,800	51,700	64,700	77,700	90,600	103,500
9.5	37,200	49,500	61,900	74,300	86,700	99,100
10.0	35,600	47,400	59,300	71,200	83,000	94,900
10.5	34,200	45,500	56,900	68,300	79,700	91,100
	$45,000	**$50,000**	**$55,000**	**$60,000**	**$65,000**	**$70,000**
6.5%	$148,300	$164,800	$181,300	$197,700	$214,200	$230,000
7.0	140,900	156,600	172,300	187,900	203,600	219,200
7.5	134,100	149,000	163,900	178,800	193,700	208,600
8.0	127,700	141,900	156,100	170,300	184,500	198,700
8.5	121,900	135,400	149,000	162.500	176,100	189,600
9.0	116,500	129,400	142,400	155,300	168,200	181,200
9.5	111,400	123,800	136,200	148,600	161,000	173,400
10.0	106,800	118,600	130,500	142,400	154,300	166,100
10.5	102,400	113,800	125.200	136,600	148,000	159,400

Source: Fannie Mae

EXAMPLE 3   Qualifying for a Mortgage

Use Table 8.5 to answer this question. How large is the fixed-rate mortgage at 7.5% interest for which a person with a yearly gross income of $35,000 qualifies?

Solution Locate 7.5% in the left column of Table 8.5 and $35,000 in the first row. The entry in the table where this column and row meet is $104,300. Thus, a person with a yearly income of $35,000 qualifies for a $104,300 mortgage at 7.5%.

Suppose that the buyer in Example 3 has fallen in love with a home that requires a $120,000 mortgage. Just because the buyer qualifies for only $104,300 at a fixed-rate 7.5% does not necessarily mean that a $120,000 mortgage is not possible. A loan such as an adjustable-rate mortgage starts out at a lower interest rate than a fixed-rate mortgage. The lower monthly payments enable the buyer to qualify for a greater mortgage loan. A good loan officer will work with a buyer and explore mortgage options before determining that he or she does not qualify for the purchase of a much-loved dream home.

The Rise and Fall of Mortgage Rates

Average annual interest rates on a 30-year fixed-rate mortgage peaked at 16.63% in 1981.

Average Annual Interest Rates on 30-Year Fixed-Rate Mortgages

Source: Federal Home Loan Mortgage Corp.

Exercise Set 8.4

Practice and Application Exercises

1. The price of a home is $125,000. The bank requires a 20% down payment and three points at the time of closing. The cost of the home is financed with a 30-year fixed-rate mortgage at 7%.
   a. Find the required down payment.
   b. Find the amount of the mortgage.
   c. How much must be paid for the three points at closing?
   d. Find the monthly payment (excluding escrowed taxes and insurance).
   e. Find the total cost of interest over 30 years.

2. The price of a condominium is $85,000. The bank requires a 5% down payment and one point at the time of closing. The cost of the condominium is financed with a 30-year fixed-rate mortgage at 8%.
   a. Find the required down payment.
   b. Find the amount of the mortgage.
   c. How much must be paid for the one point at closing?

d. Find the monthly payment (excluding escrowed taxes and insurance).
   e. Find the total cost of interest over 30 years.

3. The price of a small cabin is $40,000. The bank requires a 5% down payment. The buyer is offered two mortgage options: 20-year fixed at 8% or 30-year fixed at 8%. Calculate the amount of interest paid for each option. How much does the buyer save in interest with the 20-year option?

4. The price of a home is $160,000. The bank requires a 15% down payment. The buyer is offered two mortgage options: 15-year fixed at 8% or 30-year fixed at 8%. Calculate the amount of interest paid for each option. How much does the buyer save in interest with the 15-year option?

5. In terms of paying less in interest, which is more economical for a $100,000 mortgage: a 30-year fixed-rate at 8% or a 20-year fixed-rate at 7.5%?

6. In terms of paying less in interest, which is more economical for a $90,000 mortgage: a 30-year fixed-rate at 8% or a 15-year fixed-rate at 7.5%?

7. Prepare a loan amortization schedule for the first three months of the following mortgage loan.

Amortization Schedule

Annual % rate: 8%

Amount of Mortgage: $100,000

Monthly payment: $734

Number of Monthly Payments: 360

Term: Years 30, Months 0

Payment Number	Interest Payment	Principal Payment	Balance of Loan
1			
2			
3			

8. Prepare a loan amortization schedule for the first three months of the following mortgage loan.

Amortization Schedule

Annual % rate: 9%

Amount of Mortgage: $300,000

Monthly payment: $2415

Number of Monthly Payments: 360

Term: Years 30, Months 0

Payment Number	Interest Payment	Principal Payment	Balance of Loan
1			
2			
3			

Use Table 8.5 on page 406 to solve Exercises 9–12. Assume a fixed-rate 30-year mortgage.

9. How much of a mortgage at 7.0% interest does a person with a yearly gross income of $55,000 qualify for?

10. How much of a mortgage at 8.5% interest does a person with a yearly gross income of $65,000 qualify for?

11. At an interest rate of 6.5%, if a buyer wants to qualify for a $98,800 mortgage, what should be that buyer's annual income?

12. At an interest rate of 10.5%, if a buyer wants to qualify for a $79,700 mortgage, what should be that buyer's annual income?

13. According to the *Guinness Book of World Records*, the most expensive private house ever built is the Hearst Ranch in San Simeon, California. It was built 1922–1939 for William Randolph Hearst (1863–1951), at a cost of over $30 million. Suppose that you do very well in your career and decide to treat yourself to this 100-room home, complete with a 104-foot-long heated pool, an 83-foot-long assembly hall, and a garage for 25 limousines. The house is yours for a "steal"—namely $80 million, with 30% down and a 30-year fixed-rate mortgage at 12%. Find the total cost of interest over 30 years. (By the way, if you do get the roof of the Hearst Ranch over your head, you may need some help to keep things in tip-top shape. Hearst originally maintained the house with 60 servants.)

 ## Writing in Mathematics

14. What is a mortgage?

15. What is a down payment?

16. How is the amount of a mortgage determined?

17. Describe why a buyer would select a 30-year fixed-rate mortgage instead of a 15-year fixed-rate mortgage if interest rates are $\frac{1}{4}\%$ to $\frac{1}{2}\%$ lower on a 15-year mortgage.

18. Describe one advantage and one disadvantage of an adjustable-rate mortgage over a fixed-rate mortgage.

19. What is the worst thing that can happen with a balloon-payment mortgage?

20. In terms of current interest rates for mortgage loans, describe the type of mortgage that best suits your needs at this time. What features of the mortgage are compatible with your vocational goals and your projected future earnings?

21. What is a loan amortization schedule?

22. Describe one advantage and one disadvantage of home ownership over renting.

 ## Critical Thinking Exercise

23. Suppose that upon graduation from college, you find a job that pays a starting salary of $30,000 per year. Assuming that you could get a mortgage at 8% interest,
   a. How large of a mortgage do you qualify for?
   b. What is the monthly payment?
   c. Do you think you can actually afford this monthly payment? Remember that the $30,000 is your gross income, not your take-home pay. Explain your answer.

 ## Technology Exercises

A spreadsheet offers a convenient way to compute an amortization schedule. Using Microsoft Excel, assign columns to the payment number, total monthly payment, interest payment, principal payment, and balance of loan. When telling Excel to perform a calculation, click into the appropriate cell and type = and then the corresponding expression. The expression can be composed of numbers or other cell references. For more specific directions on how to use Microsoft Excel to create an amortization schedule, visit http://www.prenhall.com/blitzer.

24. Use a spreadsheet such as Microsoft Excel to create an amortization schedule for a mortgage of $125,000 for 30 years at 7.5% APR. The monthly payment will be $873.75.

25. Use a spreadsheet such as Microsoft Excel to create an amortization schedule for a mortgage of $100,000 for 30 years at 7% APR. The monthly payment will be $665.00.

Group Exercises

26. Group members work for a company that works with local banks. A client with a monthly income of $4000 needs a loan to purchase a $125,000 home. This client has $16,000 in savings that can be used as a down payment. Find the current rates available from two local banks for both fixed- and adjustable-rate mortgages. Analyze the offerings and then write a report for this client summarizing the best mortgage options, along with the advantages and disadvantages of each option.

27. Should I rent or buy? Perhaps before having to weigh the pros and cons of renting versus buying, you might have to deal with this difficult question: Should I lease or buy my next car? The December 1997 issue of *Consumer Reports* contains an article addressing this question. Group members should consult the article and present a report on the pros and cons of leasing versus buying. Be sure to present some of the costly traps of leasing, as well as how to use good negotiating to save thousands of dollars over a three-year lease. Discuss the finance charges and the interest rates on car leases in the report.

SECTION 8.5   *Investing in Stocks, Bonds, and Mutual Funds*

Objectives

1. Understand stocks, bonds, and mutual funds as investments.
2. Read stock tables.
3. Calculate costs involved in trading stock.

Projected Number of U.S. Households, in Millions, Investing On-line

Source: Tradeline/IDD Information Services

1 Understand stocks, bonds, and mutual funds as investments.

Wade Brown is a 31-year-old financial manager. "Every time I've lost on a stock it's because of impatience," he says. "As I look back, the stock has always gone back up." He's planning to get his portfolio to $1 million in four years. "Age 35 is what I've been thinking," he says matter-of-factly.

With a computer and access to the Internet, the world of on-line investing in stocks, bonds, and mutual funds is creating a new generation of millionaires. These investments are not without risk. In this section we provide you with information about these kinds of investments so that you can make informed choices in managing your finances and achieving your financial goals.

Investments

When you deposit money into a bank account, you are making a **cash investment**. Bank accounts up to $100,000 are insured by the federal government, so there is no risk of losing the principal you've invested. The account's interest rate guarantees a certain percent increase in your investment, called its **return**. For example, if you deposit $7500 in a savings account that has a rate of 4% compounded annually, the annual return is 4%. There are other kinds of investments that are riskier, meaning that it is possible to lose all or part of your principal. These investments include **stocks** and **bonds**. We begin by discussing these investment categories.

Stocks

Investors purchase **stock**, shares of ownership in a company. The shares indicate the percent of ownership. For example, if a company has issued a total of one million shares, and an investor owns 20,000 of these shares, that investor owns

$$\frac{20,000 \text{ shares}}{1,000,000 \text{ shares}} = 0.02$$

or 2% of the company. Any investor who owns some percentage of the company is called a **shareholder**.

Occupation of Shareholders

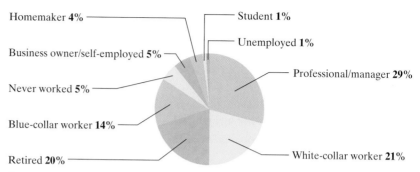

Source: Study by Peter D. Hart Research Associates for the Nasdaq Stock Market

Technology

It's wise to be cautious about making investments using the Internet. The rapidly changing prices of stocks can cause an on-line trader to see a huge profit and an even bigger loss in a very short amount of time. Just like any investment, on-line trading should be thoroughly investigated before you commit your hard-earned money. Many of the largest on-line brokers offer extensive Web sites. You may be able to access many features of these sites without even investing. For more information, visit http://www.prenhall.com/blitzer.

Buying or selling stock is referred to as **trading**. Shares of stock need both a seller and a buyer to be traded. Stocks are traded on a **stock exchange**. The price of a share of stock is determined by the law of supply and demand. If a company is prospering, investors will be willing to pay a good price for its stock, and so the stock price goes up. If the company does not do well, investors may decide to sell, and the stock price goes down. Stock prices indicate the performance of the companies they represent, as well as the state of the national and global economies.

Stock exchanges provide an orderly place for determining the price of a share of stock. The New York Stock Exchange on Wall Street in Manhattan is the largest stock exchange. Only **stockbrokers** are allowed on the floor of the exchange. Investors buy and sell stock through stockbrokers, who charge a commission for their services.

Americans now have more money invested in stocks than in their homes. Stock ownership grew dramatically in the last decade of the twentieth century. Today, over 43% of adult Americans are stock owners. Many people with computers and access to the Internet use the world of on-line investing to buy and sell stocks. With the click of a mouse, industry research suggesting companies to invest in is now available to on-line investors. A note of caution: Some of the information on the Web may be inaccurate or posted for fraudulent reasons.

Gender of U.S. Shareholders

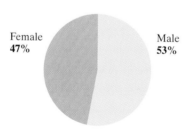

Source: Study by Peter D. Hart Research Associates for the Nasdaq Stock Market

Percentage of All Stock Trades Handled by On-line Brokers

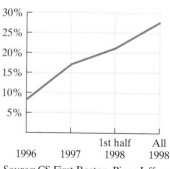

Source: CS First Boston, Piper Jaffray

Investors make money with stock by selling a stock for more money than they paid for it. Since 1926, the return on stocks has been 10.9% a year on average, and from 1994 through the end of the century, stock prices have had an average annual percent increase of 33%. Although the stock market has been a proven wealth builder for millions of Americans, all stocks have some risk. Even with an average 33% annual return, some stocks go down and stay down. Outsized returns year in and year out may not last forever and investors should not exclude the possibility of huge losses.

If you make money by selling stock for more than you paid for it, you have a **capital gain** on the sale of stock. With more and more average Americans investing and making money, the federal government cut the capital-gains tax rate in 1997.

Investors can make money while they own stock if a company distributes all or part of its profits to shareholders as **dividends**. Each share of stock is paid the same dividend, so the amount of money received by an investor depends on the number of shares owned. Some companies do not pay dividends, reinvesting all profits within the company.

The Dow Jones Industrial Average: Bull Markets and Bear Markets

The Dow Jones Industrial Average (DJIA) is an index of 30 U.S. stocks. It is computed by adding up stock prices and dividing by the number of stocks. The DJIA is the best-known market indicator in the world. A **bull market** requires a 30% rise in the DJIA over 50 calendar days or a 13% rise over 155 calendar days. A **bear market** requires a 30% drop in the DJIA over 50 calendar days or a 13% decline over 145 calendar days. The Great Bull Market of the 1990s, which began just after a modest recession, is the longest in history.

The 30 Stocks in the Dow Jones Industrial Average

AT&T Corp.	Home Depot Inc.
AlliedSignal Inc.	Intel Corp.
Aluminum Co. of America	International Business Machines Corp.
American Express Co.	International Paper Co.
Boeing Co.	Johnson & Johnson
Caterpillar Inc.	McDonald's Corp.
Citigroup Inc.	Merck & Co.
Coca-Cola Co.	Microsoft Corp.
Walt Disney Co.	Minnesota Mining & Manufacturing Co.
DuPont Co.	J.P. Morgan & Co.
Eastman Kodak Co.	Philip Morris Cos.
Exxon Corp.	Procter & Gamble Co.
General Electric Co.	SBC Communications Inc.
General Motors Corp.	United Technologies Corp.
Hewlett-Packard Co.	Wal-Mart Stores Inc.

Best Years for the Dow Jones Industrial Average

Rank	Date	Close	% Change
1	1915	99.15	81.66
2	1933	99.90	66.69
3	1928	300.00	48.22
4	1908	86.15	46.64
5	1954	404.39	43.96
6	1904	69.61	41.74
7	1935	144.13	38.53
8	1975	852.41	38.32
9	1905	96.20	38.20
10	1958	583.65	33.96

Worst Years for the Dow Jones Industrial Average

Rank	Date	Close	% Change
1	1931	77.90	−52.67
2	1907	58.75	−37.73
3	1930	164.58	−33.77
4	1920	71.95	−32.90
5	1937	120.85	−32.82
6	1914	54.58	−30.72
7	1974	616.24	−27.57
8	1903	49.11	−23.61
9	1932	59.93	−23.07
10	1917	74.38	−21.71

Source: Dow Jones & Co.

Bonds

People who buy stock become part owners in a company. In order to raise money and not dilute the ownership of current stockholders, companies sell **bonds**. People who buy a bond are **lending money** to the company from which they buy the bond. Bonds are a commitment from a company to pay the price an investor pays for the bond at the time it was purchased, called the **face value**, along with interest payments at a given rate.

There are many reasons for issuing bonds. A company might need to raise money for research on a drug that has the potential for curing AIDS, so it issues bonds. The U.S. Treasury Department issues 30-year bonds at a fixed 7% annual rate to borrow money to cover possible federal deficits. Local governments often issue bonds to borrow money to build schools, parks, and libraries.

Bonds are traded like stock, and their price is a function of supply and demand. If a company goes bankrupt, bondholders are the first to claim the company's assets. They make their claims before the stockholders, even though (unlike stockholders) they do not own a share of the company. Buying and selling bonds is frequently done through on-line investing.

Generally speaking, investing in bonds is less risky than investing in stocks, although the return is lower. A listing of all the investments that a person holds is called a **financial portfolio**. Most financial advisors recommend a portfolio with a mixture of low-risk and high-risk investments, called a **diversified portfolio**.

Mutual Funds

Growth of Mutual Funds

Year	Number of Funds
1956	1967
1960	5608
1965	7642
1970	13,678
1975	7137
1980	3642
1985	6300
1990	7085
1991	7360
1992	8267
1993	10,033
1994	12,429
1995	16,054
1996	25,409
1997	34,618

Source: National Association of Investment Clubs

It is not an easy job to determine which stocks and bonds to buy or sell, or when to do so. Many small investors have decided that they do not have the time to stay informed about the progress of corporations, even with the help of on-line industry research. Instead, they invest in a **mutual fund**. A mutual fund is a group of stocks and/or bonds managed by a professional investor. When you purchase shares in a mutual fund, you give your money to the **fund manager**. Your money is combined with the money of other investors in the mutual fund. The fund manager invests this pool of money, buying and selling shares of stocks and bonds to obtain the maximum possible returns.

Investors in mutual funds own a small portion of many different companies, protecting them against the poor performance of a single company. In the United States, there are more mutual funds that invest in stocks than there are stocks listed on the New York Stock Exchange. A total of $2.2 trillion reside in stock mutual funds, and this is increasing by $20 billion a month. New funds, some specializing in high-risk investments, others in low-risk investments, some investing in U.S. markets only, others investing in foreign markets, are forming at the rate of three per day.

Newspapers publish ratings from 1 (worst) to 5 (best) of mutual fund performance based on whether the fund manager is doing a good job with its investors' money. Two numbers are given. The first number compares the performance of the mutual fund to a large group of similar funds. The second number compares the performance to funds that are nearly identical. The best rating a fund manager can receive is 5/5; the worst is 1/1.

Profile of Mutual Fund Investors

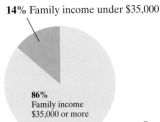

14% Family income under $35,000

34.7% Male

65.3% Female

86% Family income $35,000 or more

Source: National Association of Investment Clubs

Reading Stock Tables

Daily newspapers and on-line services give current stock prices and other information about stocks. We will use Citigroup stock to learn how to read these daily stock tables. Look at the following newspaper listing of Citigroup stock.

52-week High	Low	Stock	SYM	Div	Yld %	PE	Vol 100s	Hi	Lo	Close	Net Chg
77	$28\frac{1}{2}$	Citigroup	C	.84	1.1	29	64981	76	$74\frac{7}{16}$	$74\frac{9}{16}$	$-\frac{15}{16}$

The headings indicate the meanings of the numbers across the row.

The heading **52-Week High** refers to the *highest price* at which Citigroup stock traded during the past 52 weeks. The highest price was $77.00 per share. This means that during the past 52 weeks an investor was willing to pay $77.00 for a share of stock. Notice that 77 represents a quantity in dollars, although the stock table does not show the dollar sign.

The heading **52-Week Low** refers to the *lowest price* that Citigroup stock reached during the past 52 weeks. This price is $28\frac{1}{2}$. The fraction, $\frac{1}{2}$, represents a fractional part of a dollar. The number of cents can be obtained by dividing the numerator by the denominator:

$$1 \div 2 = 0.5, \text{ or } 0.50.$$

Thus, $28\frac{1}{2}$ means that the lowest price per share was $28.50.

The heading **Stock** is the *company name*, Citigroup. The heading **SYM** is the *symbol* the company uses for trading. Citigroup uses the symbol C.

The heading **Div** refers to *dividends* paid per share to stockholders last year. Citigroup paid a dividend of $0.84 per share. Once again, the dollar symbol does not appear in the table. Thus, if you owned 100 shares, you received a dividend of $0.84 × 100, or $84.00.

The heading **Yld %** stands for *percent yield*. In this case, the percent yield is 1.1%. (The stock table does not show the percent sign.) This means that the dividends alone give investors an annual return of 1.1%. This is much lower than interest rates offered by most banks. However, this percent does not take into account the fact that Citigroup stock prices might rise. If an investor sells shares for more than what they were paid for, the gain will probably make Citigroup stock a much better investment than a bank account.

In order to understand the meaning of the heading PE, we need to understand some of the other numbers in the table. We will return to this column.

The heading **Vol 100s** stands for *sales volume in hundreds*. This is the number of shares traded yesterday, in hundreds. The number in the table is 64,981. This means that yesterday, a total of 64,981 × 100, or 6,498,100 shares of Citigroup were traded.

2 Read stock tables.

52-week High
77

52-week Low
$28\frac{1}{2}$

Stock	SYM
Citigroup	C

Div
.84

Yld %
1.1

Vol 100s
64981

Hi
76

The heading **Hi** stands for the *highest price* at which Citigroup stock traded *yesterday*. This number is 76. Yesterday, Citigroup's highest trading price was $76 a share.

Lo
$74\frac{7}{16}$

The heading **Lo** stands for the *lowest price* at which Citigroup stock traded *yesterday*. This number is $74\frac{7}{16}$. The fraction, $\frac{7}{16}$, represents a fractional part of a dollar.

$$7 \div 16 = 0.4375$$

Thus, Citigroup's lowest trading price yesterday was $74\frac{7}{16}$, approximately $74.44 per share.

Close
$74\frac{9}{16}$

The heading **Close** stands for the *price* at which shares traded *when the stock exchange closed yesterday*. This number is $74\frac{9}{16}$. Because

$$9 \div 16 = 0.5625$$

the price at which shares of Citigroup traded when the stock exchange closed yesterday was $74\frac{9}{16}$, approximately $74.56 per share. This is called yesterday's **closing price**.

Net Chg
$-\frac{15}{16}$

The heading **Net Chg** stands for *net change*. This is the change in price from the market close two days ago to yesterday's market close. This number is $-\frac{15}{16}$. Because

$$15 \div 16 = 0.9375$$

the price of a share of Citigroup stock went down by approximately $0.94. For some stock listings, the notation … appears under Net Chg. This means that there was *no change in price* for a share of stock from the market close two days ago to yesterday's market close.

PE
29

Now, we are ready to return to the heading **PE**, standing for the *price-to-earnings ratio*.

$$\text{PE ratio} = \frac{\text{Yesterday's closing price per share}}{\text{Annual earnings per share}}$$

This can be expressed as:

$$\text{Annual earnings per share} = \frac{\text{Yesterday's closing price per share}}{\text{PE ratio}}.$$

The PE ratio for Citigroup is given to be 29. Yesterday's closing price per share was $74\frac{9}{16}$. We can substitute these numbers into the formula to find annual earnings per share:

$$\text{Annual earnings per share} = \frac{74\frac{9}{16}}{29} = \frac{74.5625}{29} \approx 2.57.$$

The annual earnings per share for Citigroup are $2.57. The PE ratio, 29, tells us that yesterday's closing price per share, approximately $74.56, is 29 times greater than the earnings per share, $2.57.

EXAMPLE 1   Reading Stock Tables

52-week					Yld		Vol				Net
High	Low	Stock	SYM	Div	%	PE	100s	Hi	Lo	Close	Chg
$42\frac{3}{8}$	$22\frac{1}{2}$	Disney	DIS	.21	.6	43	115900	$32\frac{1}{2}$	$31\frac{1}{4}$	$32\frac{1}{2}$	…

Study Tip

An excellent reference on financial management is *The Wall Street Journal Guide to Personal Finance* (New York: Lightbulb Press). This guide explains how to read bond tables and mutual fund tables.

Percent of U.S. Households with Net Worth Over $1 Million

Source: Forrester Research Inc.

Use the stock table for Disney to answer the following questions.

a. What were the high and low prices for the past 52 weeks?

b. If you owned 3000 shares of Disney stock last year, what dividend did you receive?

c. What is the annual return for dividends alone? How does this compare to a bank account offering a 3.5% interest rate?

d. How many shares of Disney were traded yesterday?

e. What were the high and low prices for Disney shares yesterday?

f. What was the price at which Disney shares traded when the stock exchange closed yesterday?

g. What does … in the net change column mean?

h. Compute Disney's annual earnings per share using

$$\text{Annual earnings per share} = \frac{\text{Yesterday's closing price per share}}{\text{PE ratio}}.$$

Solution

a. We find the high price for the past 52 weeks by looking under the heading *High.* The price is listed in dollars, given as $42\frac{3}{8}$. Because $3 \div 8 = 0.375$, the high price for a share of stock for the past 52 weeks was $42.375, or approximately $42.38. We find the low price for the past 52 weeks by looking under the heading *Low.* This price is also listed in dollars, given as $22\frac{1}{2}$. Because $1 \div 2 = 0.50$, the low price for a share of Disney stock for the past 52 weeks was $22.50.

b. We find the dividend paid for a share of Disney stock last year by looking under the heading *Div.* The price is listed in dollars, given as .21. Thus, Disney paid a dividend of $0.21 per share to stockholders last year. If you owned 3000 shares, you received a dividend of $0.21 × 3000, or $630.

c. We find the annual return for dividends alone by looking under the heading *Yld %,* standing for percent yield. The number in the table, .6, is a percent. This means that the dividends alone give Disney investors an annual return of 0.6%. This is much lower than the 3.5% interest rate for the bank account. However, if Disney shares increase in value, the gain might make Disney stock a better investment than the bank account.

d. We find the number of shares of Disney traded yesterday by looking under the heading *Vol 100s,* standing for sales volume in hundreds. The number in the table is 115900. This means that yesterday, a total of 115,900 × 100, or 11,590,000 shares, were traded.

e. We find the high and low prices for Disney shares yesterday by looking under the headings *Hi* and *Lo.* Both prices are listed in dollars, given as $32\frac{1}{2}$ and $31\frac{1}{4}$. Because $\frac{1}{2} = 1 \div 2 = 0.50$ and $\frac{1}{4} = 1 \div 4 = 0.25$, the high and low prices for Disney shares yesterday were $32.50 and $31.25, respectively.

f. We find the price at which Disney shares traded when the stock exchange closed yesterday by looking under the heading *Close.* The price is listed in dollars, given as $32\frac{1}{2}$. Thus, when the stock exchange closed yesterday, the price of a share of Disney stock was $32.50.

g. The … under *Net Chg* means that there was no change in price in Disney stock from the market close two days ago to yesterday's market close. In part (f), we found that the price of a share of Disney stock at yesterday's close was $32.50, so the price at the market close two days ago was also $32.50.

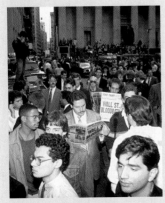
h. We are now ready to use

$$\text{Annual earnings per share} = \frac{\text{Yesterday's closing price per share}}{\text{PE ratio}}$$

to compute Disney's annual earnings per share. We have found that yesterday's closing price per share was $32.50. We find the PE ratio under the heading *PE*. The given number is 43. Thus,

$$\text{Annual earnings per share} = \frac{\$32.50}{43} \approx \$0.76.$$

The annual earnings per share for Disney are $0.76. The PE ratio, 43, tells us that yesterday's closing price per share, $32.50, is 43 times greater than the earnings per share, approximately $0.76.

Costs Involved in Trading Stock

Frank and Ernest reprinted by permission of Newspaper Enterprise Association, Inc.

A broker must be used to buy or sell stock. The broker has representatives at the stock exchange who carry out an investor's order. Brokers charge commissions for their service. They make most of their money by persuading customers to trade into and out of individual stocks. Commissions are competitive and vary among brokers.

Brokers also charge commissions for buying and selling bonds. On-line investing also involves paying commissions, although these are usually at a discount. Investors must also pay fees for subscribing to on-line research offering advice about which stocks and bonds to buy and sell and when to do so. There are management fees for mutual funds, although many funds trade shares with no commission charge.

3 Calculate costs involved in trading stock.

EXAMPLE 2 Selling Stock

Suppose that you bought 400 shares of Citigroup stock at the 52-week low, $28.50 per share, and sold at the 52-week high, $77.00 per share.

a. Ignoring dividends, how much money did you make on this transaction?

b. If the broker charges 2.5% of the total sale price, find the broker's commission.

Solution

a. The difference between the high price per share, $77.00, and the low price per share, $28.50, is $77.00 − $28.50, or $48.50. Because you bought at the low price and sold at the high price, you made $48.50 per share. For 400 shares, you made $48.50 × 400, or $19,400.

b. You are selling the stock at $77.00 per share. The total sale price for 400 shares is $77.00 × 400, or $30,800. The broker charges 2.5% of this price:

$$2.5\% \text{ of } \$30,800 = 0.025 \times \$30,800 = \$770.00$$

The broker's commission is $770.00.

The vast amount of money flowing into stocks, bonds, and mutual funds in the 1990s has generated record profits on Wall Street. Realtors watch with joy as young stockbrokers engage in bidding wars for Manhattan's million-dollar apartments. What will bring this all to a screeching stop? As of this writing, the thing that will spoil the love affair between investors and the stock market is probably going to be totally unexpected and unpredictable.

How to Make Your Child a Millionaire

People in charge of pension funds and retirement accounts invest the money collected by members in stocks. Based on an average annual return of 10%, *The Wall Street Journal* article on the right explains how to make your child a millionaire at age 65.

> ### Make a Child a Millionaire
> #### By JONATHAN CLEMENTS
> *Staff Reporter of* THE WALL STREET JOURNAL
>
> Thanks a million.
> Even if you haven't got a lot of money, you can easily give $1 million or more to your children, grandchildren or favorite charity. All it takes is a small initial investment and a lot of time.
> Suppose your 16-year-old daughter plans to take a summer job that will pay her at least $2000. Because she has earned income, she can open an individual retirement account. If you would like to help fund her retirement, Kenneth Klegon, a financial planner in Lansing, Mich., suggests giving her $2000 to set up the IRA. He then advises doing the same in each of the next five years, so that your daughter stashes away a total of $12,000.
> Result? If the money is invested in stocks, and stocks deliver their historical average annual return of 10%, your daughter will have more than $1 million by the time she turns 65.
>
> (c) 1994 Dow Jones & Company, Inc.

Exercise Set 8.5

Practice and Application Exercises

Exercises 1 and 2 refer to the stock tables for Goodyear (the tire company) and JC Penney (the store) given on page 418. In each exercise, use the stock table to answer the following questions. Where necessary, round dollar amounts to the nearest cent.

a. *What were the high and low prices for a share for the past 52 weeks?*

b. *If you owned 700 shares of this stock last year, what dividend did you receive?*

c. *What is the annual return for the dividends alone? How does this compare to a bank offering a 3% interest rate?*

d. *How many shares of this company's stock were traded yesterday?*

e. *What were the high and low prices for a share yesterday?*

f. *What was the price at which a share traded when the stock exchange closed yesterday?*

g. *What was the change in price for a share of stock from the market close two days ago to yesterday's market close?*

h. *Compute the company's annual earnings per share using:*

Annual earnings per share =

$$\frac{\textit{Yesterday's closing price per share}}{\textit{PE ratio}}.$$

1.

52-week					Yld		Vol				Net
High	Low	Stock	SYM	Div	%	PE	100s	Hi	Lo	Close	Chg
$73\frac{1}{4}$	$45\frac{7}{16}$	Goodyear	GT	1.20	2.2	17	5915	$56\frac{3}{8}$	$54\frac{3}{8}$	$55\frac{1}{2}$	$+1\frac{1}{4}$

2.

52-week					Yld		Vol				Net
High	Low	Stock	SYM	Div	%	PE	100s	Hi	Lo	Close	Chg
$78\frac{3}{4}$	$35\frac{3}{8}$	Penney JC	JCP	2.18	4.7	22	7473	$48\frac{3}{16}$	$46\frac{5}{8}$	$46\frac{7}{8}$	$-1\frac{5}{16}$

3. Suppose that you bought 250 shares of Sears stock at its 52-week low, $39.06 per share, and sold at the 52-week high, $65.00 per share.
   a. Ignoring dividends, how much did you make on this transaction?
   b. If the broker charges 2.5% of the total sale price, find the broker's commission.

4. Suppose that you bought 350 shares of Walmart stock at its 52-week low, $36.75 per share, and sold at the 52-week high, $72.44 per share.
   a. Ignoring dividends, how much did you make on this transaction?
   b. If the broker charges 2.5% of the total sale price, find the broker's commission.

5. An investor purchased 400 shares of stock for $37\frac{1}{2}$ per share.
   a. Find the cost of the stock.
   b. If the broker charges 2% of the cost of the stock, find the broker's commission.

6. An investor purchased 600 shares of stock for $56\frac{1}{4}$ per share.
   a. Find the cost of the stock.
   b. If the broker charges 2% of the cost of the stock, find the broker's commission.

7. An investor purchased 240 shares of stock for $17\frac{3}{4}$ per share.
   a. Find the cost of the stock.
   b. The broker charges 2.5% of the cost of the stock plus 12.5¢ per share for 40 of the shares purchased. Find the broker's commission.

8. An investor purchased 370 shares of stock for $22\frac{3}{4}$ per share.
   a. Find the cost of the stock.
   b. The broker charges 2.5% of the cost of the stock plus 12.5¢ per share for 70 of the shares purchased. Find the broker's commission.

Writing in Mathematics

9. What is stock?

10. Describe how to find the percent ownership that a stockholder has in a company.

11. Describe the two ways that investors make money with stock.

12. What is a bond? Describe the difference between a stock and a bond.

13. What is a mutual fund? Describe two advantages to investing in mutual funds.

14. Using a recent newspaper, copy the stock table for a company of your choice. Then explain the meaning of the numbers in the columns.

15. If an investor sees that the dividends for a stock have a lower annual rate than those for a no-risk bank account, should the stock be sold and the money placed in the bank account? Explain your answer.

Use the following investments to answer Exercises 16–19.

   Investment 1. 1000 shares of IBM stock
   Investment 2. A 5-year bond with a 22% interest rate issued by a small company that is testing and planning to sell delicious, nearly zero-calorie desserts
   Investment 3. A 30-year U.S. treasury bond at a fixed 7% annual rate

16. Which of these investments has the greatest risk? Explain why.

17. Which of these investments has the least risk? Explain why.

18. Which of these investments is likely to have the greatest return? Explain why.

19. If you could be given one of these investments as a gift, which one would you choose? Explain why.

Critical Thinking Exercise

20. Use mathematics to show that the *Wall Street Journal* article on page 417 is correct. In particular, use one or more formulas to show that the $12,000 will be worth more than $1 million by the time the teenager turns 65.

Group Exercises

21. Each group should have a newspaper with current stock quotations. Choose nine stocks that group members think would make good investments. Imagine that you invest $1000 in each of these nine investments. Check the value of your stock each day over the next five weeks and then sell the nine stocks after five weeks. What is the group's profit or loss over the five-week period? Compare this figure with the profit or loss of other groups in your class for this activity.

22. This activity is a group research project intended for four or five people. Use the research to present a seminar on investments. The seminar is intended to last about 30 minutes and should result in an interesting and informative presentation to the entire class. The seminar should include investment considerations, how to read the bond section of the newspaper, how to read the mutual fund section, and higher risk investments.

23. Group members have inherited $1 million. However, the group cannot spend any of the money for ten years. As a group, determine how to invest this money in order to maximize the money you will make over ten years. The money can be invested in as many ways as the group decides. Explain each investment decision. What are the risks involved in this investment plan?

CHAPTER SUMMARY, REVIEW, AND TEST

SUMMARY

8.1 Percent

a. Percent means per hundred. Thus, $97\% = \frac{97}{100}$.

b. To express a fraction as a percent, divide the numerator by the denominator, move the decimal point in the quotient two places to the right, and add a percent sign.

c. To express a decimal number as a percent, move the decimal point two places to the right and add a percent sign.

d. To express a percent as a decimal number, move the decimal point two places to the left and remove the percent sign.

e. To find the percent of a number, change the percent to a decimal and multiply the decimal and the number.

f. Sales tax amount = tax rate × item's cost.

g. Discount amount = discount rate × original price.

h. The fraction for percent increase (or decrease) is:

$$\frac{\text{amount of increase (or decrease)}}{\text{original amount}}.$$

Find the percent increase (or decrease) by expressing this fraction as a percent.

8.2 Interest

a. Interest is the price we are paid for lending money or pay for borrowing money. The amount deposited or borrowed is the principal. The charge for interest, given as a percent, is the rate, assumed to be per year.

b. Simple interest involves interest calculated only on the principal and is computed using $I = prt$.

c. The amount due on a loan, called the maturity value, is the principal plus the interest.

d. Compound interest involves interest computed on the original principal as well as on any accumulated interest. The amount in an account for one compounding period per year is $A = p(1 + r)^t$. For n compoundings per year, the amount is $A = p\left(1 + \frac{r}{n}\right)^{nt}$.

e. Calculating Present Value
If A dollars are to be accumulated in t years in an account that pays rate r compounded n times a year, then the amount p (the present value) that needs to be invested now is given by:

$$p = \frac{A}{\left(1 + \dfrac{r}{n}\right)^{nt}}.$$

8.3 Installment Buying

a. A fixed installment loan is paid off with a series of equal periodic payments. An open-end installment loan is paid off with variable monthly payments. Credit card loans are open-end installment loans.

b. The terms of fixed installment loans—the amount financed, the total installment price, and the finance charge—are explained in the box on page 390.

c. The interest rate per year on a loan is called the Annual Percentage Rate (APR). The box on page 391 shows how to find the APR for a fixed installment loan.

d. Unearned interest is the amount by which the original finance charge is reduced when a fixed installment loan is paid off early. The two methods for computing unearned interest—the actuarial method and the rule of 78—are explained in the box on page 393.

e. Open-end installment loans such as credit cards calculate interest using the simple interest formula $I = prt$. The methods for determining the interest, the unpaid balance method, the previous balance method, and the average daily balance method, are described in the box on page 397.

8.4 The Cost of Home Ownership

a. A mortgage is a long-term loan for the purpose of buying a home, and for which the property is pledged as security for payment. The term of the mortgage is the number of years until final payoff. The down payment is the portion of the sale price of the home that the buyer initially pays. The amount of the mortgage is the difference between the sale price and the down payment.

b. Fixed-rate mortgages have the same monthly payment during the entire time of the loan. Variable-rate mortgages, or adjustable-rate mortgages, have payment amounts that change from time to time depending on changes in the interest rate.

c. A point is a one-time charge that equals 1 percent of the amount of a mortgage loan.

d. Amortizing the loan is the process of making regular payments on the principal and interest until the loan is paid off. A document containing the payment number, payment toward the interest, payment toward the principal, and balance of the loan is called a loan amortization schedule. Such a schedule shows how the buyer pays slightly less in interest and more in principal for each payment over the entire life of the loan.

8.5 Investing in Stocks, Bonds, and Mutual Funds

a. The return of an investment is the percent increase in the investment.

b. Investors purchase stock, shares of ownership in a company. The shares indicate the percent of ownership. Trading refers to buying and selling stock. Investors make money by selling a stock for more money than they paid for it. They can also make money while they own stock if a company distributes all or part of its profits as dividends. Each share of stock is paid the same dividend.

c. Investors purchase a bond, lending money to the company from which they purchase the bond. The company commits itself to pay the price an investor pays for the bond at the time it was purchased, called its face value, along with interest payments at a given rate.

d. A portfolio is a listing of all the investments that a person holds.

e. A mutual fund is a group of stocks and/or bonds managed by a professional investor, called the fund manager. Investors in mutual funds own a small portion of many different companies, protecting them against the poor performance of a single company.

f. Reading stock tables is explained on pages 413–414.

g. Costs involved in trading stock include commissions to brokers and management fees to fund managers of mutual funds.

REVIEW EXERCISES

8.1

In Exercises 1–3, express each fraction as a percent.

1. $\frac{4}{5}$
2. $\frac{1}{8}$
3. $\frac{3}{4}$

In Exercises 4–6, express each decimal as a percent.

4. 0.72
5. 0.0035
6. 4.756

In Exercises 7–12, express each percent as a decimal.

7. 65%
8. 99.7%
9. 150%
10. 3%
11. 0.65%
12. $\frac{1}{4}$%

13. If $35,000 is invested in stock and there is a total of $50,000 invested, what percent of the invested money is in stock?

14. A restaurant bill came to $78. If 15% of this bill was left as a tip, how much was the tip?

15. Suppose that the local sales tax rate is 6% and you purchase a backpack for $24. a. How much tax is paid? b. What is the backpack's total cost?

16. A television with an original price of $850 is on sale at 35% off. a. What is the discount amount? b. What is the television's sale price?

17. A college that had 40 students for each lecture course increased the number to 45 students. What is the percent increase in the number of students in a lecture course?

18. A dictionary regularly sells for $56.00. The sale price is $36.40. Find the percent decrease of the sale price from the regular price.

8.2

In Exercises 19–22, find the simple interest. (Assume 360 days in a years.)

Principal	Rate	Time
19. $6000	3%	1 year
20. $8400	5%	6 years
21. $20,000	8%	9 months
22. $36,000	15%	60 days

23. In order to pay for tuition and books, a student borrows $3500 for four months at 10.5% interest.
   a. How much interest must the student pay?
   b. Find the maturity value of the loan.

In Exercises 24–26, the principal represents an amount of money deposited in a savings account that provides the lender compound interest at the given rate.

   a. *Use the formula $A = p(1 + r)^t$ for one compounding period per year or $A = p(1 + \frac{r}{n})^{nt}$ for n compounding periods per year to find how much money there will be in the account after the given number of years.*
   b. *Find the interest earned.*

Principal	Rate	Compounding per Year	Time
24. $7000	3%	1	5 years
25. $30,000	2.5%	4	10 years
26. $2500	4%	12	20 years

27. Suppose that you have $5000 to invest. Which investment is the better choice over five years: a 6.25% rate compounded 12 times a year or a 6.3% rate coupounded once a year?

Solve Exercises 28–29 using the present value formula
$$p = \frac{A}{\left(1 + \frac{r}{n}\right)^{nt}}.$$

28. How much money should parents deposit today in an account that earns 10% compounded monthly so that it will accumulate to $100,000 in 18 years for their child's college education?

29. How much money should be deposited today in an account that earns 5% compounded quarterly so that it will accumulate to $75,000 in 35 years for retirement?

8.3

30. The cost of a new car is $16,500. We can finance the purchase by paying $500 down and $350 per month for 60 months.
   a. Determine the amount financed.
   b. Determine the total installment price.
   c. Determine the finance charge.
   d. Use Table 8.2 on page 392 to find the APR for this loan.

31. Use the actuarial method formula
$$u = \frac{kRV}{100 + V}$$
described in the box on page 393 to solve this problem. In Exercise 30, instead of making the forty-eighth payment, the borrower decides to pay the remaining balance and terminate the loan for the car.
   a. How much interest is saved by repaying the loan early?
   b. What is the total amount due on the day of the loan's termination?

32. Use the rule of 78 formula
$$u = \frac{k(k + 1)}{n(n + 1)} \times F$$
described in the box on page 393 to solve this problem. In Exercise 30, instead of making the forty-eighth payment, the borrower decides to pay the remaining balance and terminate the loan for the car.
   a. How much interest is saved by repaying the loan early?
   b. What is the total amount due on the day of the loan's termination?

33. Describe the difference between the answers in Exercises 31 and 32. Which method saves the borrower more money?

34. The terms of a particular credit card are based on the unpaid balance method. The monthly interest rate is 1.5% on the unpaid balance on the first day of the billing period less payments and credits. Here are some of the details in the June 1–June 30 itemized billing:
   June 1 Unpaid Balance: $1300
   Payment Received June 4: $200
   Purchases Charged to the Account: airline ticket, $380; car repair, $120; groceries, $140
   Last Day of the Billing Period: June 30
   Due Date: July 9
   a. Find the interest due on the payment due date.
   b. Find the total balance owed on the last day of the billing period.
   c. Terms for the credit card require a $10 minimum monthly payment if the balance due is less than $360. Otherwise, the minimum monthly payment is $\frac{1}{36}$ of the balance due, rounded to the nearest whole dollar. What is the minimum monthly payment due by July 9?

35. A credit card has a monthly rate of 1.8%. In the March 1–March 31 itemized billing, the March 1 unpaid balance is $3600. A payment of $2000 was received on March 6. There are no purchases or cash advances in this billing period. The payment due date is April 9. Find the interest due on this date using: a. the unpaid balance method; b. the previous balance method; c. the average daily balance method.

8.4

36. The price of a home is $145,000. The bank requires a 20% down payment and two points at the time of closing. The cost of the home is financed with a 30-year fixed-rate mortgage at 7%.
    a. Find the required down payment.
    b. Find the amount of the mortgage.
    c. How much must be paid for the two points at closing?
    d. Use Table 8.3 on page 402 to find the monthly payment (excluding escrowed taxes and insurance).
    e. Find the total cost of interest over 30 years.

37. Use Table 8.3 on page 402 to solve this problem. In terms of paying less in interest, which is more economical for a $70,000 mortgage: a 30-year fixed-rate at 8.5% or a 20-year fixed-rate at 8%? Discuss one advantage and one disadvantage for each mortgage option.

38. Prepare an amortization schedule for the first two months of the following mortgage loan.

Amortization Schedule

Annual % rate: 7.5%			
Amount of Mortgage: $80,000		**Monthly payment: $559.20**	
Number of Monthly Payments: 360		**Term: Years 30, Months 0**	
Payment Number	**Interest Payment**	**Principal Payment**	**Balance of Loan**
1			
2			

39. You need a loan of $100,000 to buy a home. Here are your options:
    Option A: 30-year fixed-rate at 8.5% with no closing costs and no points.
    Option B: 30-year fixed-rate at 7.5% with closing costs of $1300 and three points.
    Determine your monthly payments for each option, and discuss how you would decide between the two options.

8.5

Exercises 40–47, refer to the stock table for Harley Davidson (the motorcycle company). Where necessary, round dollar amounts to the nearest cent.

40. What were the high and low prices for a share for the past 52 weeks?

41. If you owned 900 shares of this stock last year, what dividend did you receive?

42. What is the annual return for the dividends alone?

43. How many shares of this company's stock were traded yesterday?

44. What were the high and low prices for a share yesterday?

45. What was the price at which a share traded when the stock exchange closed yesterday?

46. What was the change in price for a share of stock from the market close two days ago to yesterday's market close?

47. Compute the company's annual earnings per share using:

$$\text{Annual earnings per share} = \frac{\text{Yesterday's closing price per share}}{\text{PE ratio}}.$$

48. Suppose that you bought 600 shares of Pepsi stock at $27\frac{1}{2}$ per share and sold them for $43\frac{3}{4}$ per share.
    a. Ignoring dividends, how much did you make on this transaction?
    b. If the broker charges 2.5% of the total sale price, find the broker's commission.

49. Explain the difference between investing in a stock and investing in a bond.

50. What is a mutual fund? Why might a person want to invest in one?

Group Exercise

51. Group members have $12,000 to invest. The essay on page 417 suggests one way that the investment can be worth over $1 million, but this will take about 45 years. Your group task is to determine strategies for investing this money in order to make it worth over $1 million in a shorter period of time. The money can be invested in as many ways as the group decides. Explain each investment decision, using formulas to show that the $12,000 will be worth more than $1 million in a shorter period than 45 years. What are the risks involved in each investment plan?

| 52-week | | | | | Yld | | Vol | | | | Net |
High	Low	Stock	SYM	Div	%	PE	100s	Hi	Lo	Close	Chg
$64\frac{1}{16}$	$26\frac{1}{8}$	Harley Dav	HDI	.16	.3	41	5458	$61\frac{1}{4}$	$59\frac{1}{4}$	61	$+1\frac{3}{4}$

CHAPTER 8 TEST

1. A CD player with an original price of $120 is on sale at 15% off. a. What is the amount of the discount? b. What is the sale price of the CD player?
2. A club that had 10 members increased its membership to 12. Find the percent increase in the club's membership.

In Exercises 3 and 4, $2400 is borrowed for three months at 12% interest.

3. Find the simple interest.
4. Find the maturity value of the loan.
5. Use the formula $A = p\left(1 + \frac{r}{n}\right)^{nt}$ to find how much money there will be in an account if $2000 is deposited for five years at 6% compounded monthly.
6. In Exercise 5, find the amount of interest earned.
7. Use the formula

$$p = \frac{A}{\left(1 + \frac{r}{n}\right)^{nt}}$$

to answer the following question: How much money should be deposited today in an account that earns 10% compounded semiannually so that it will accumulate to $100,000 in 20 years?

In Exercises 8–13, the cost of a new car is $16,000, which can be financed by paying $3000 down and $300 per month for 60 months.

8. Determine the amount financed.
9. Determine the total installment price.
10. Determine the finance charge.
11. Use Table 8.2 on page 392 to find the APR for this loan.
12. Use the rule of 78 formula

$$u = \frac{k(k + 1)}{n(n + 1)} \times F$$

to solve this problem. Instead of making the thirty-sixth payment, the borrower decides to pay the remaining balance and terminate the loan for the car. How much interest is saved by repaying the loan early?
13. Use the answer from Exercise 12 to find the total amount due on the day of the loan's termination.

Use this information to solve Exercises 14–16. The terms of a particular credit card are based on the unpaid balance method. The monthly interest rate is 2% on the unpaid balance on the first day of the billing period less payments and credits. Here are some of the details in the November 1 –November 30 itemized billing:

> November 1 Unpaid Balance: $880
> Payment Received November 5: $100

Purchases Charged to the Account: clothing, $350; gasoline, $70; groceries, $120
Last Day of the Billing Period: November 30
Due Date: December 8

14. Find the interest due on the payment due date.
15. Find the total balance owed on the last day of the billing period.
16. Terms for the credit card require a $10 minimum monthly payment if the balance due is less than $360. Otherwise, the minimum monthly payment is $\frac{1}{36}$ of the balance due, rounded to the nearest whole dollar. What is the minimum monthly payment due by December 8?
17. A credit card has a monthly rate of 1.6%. In the September 1–September 30 itemized billing, the September 1 unpaid balance is $2400. A payment of $1500 was received on September 4. There are no purchases or cash advances in this billing period. The payment due date is October 10. Find the interest due on this date using the average daily balance method.

Use this information to solve Exercises 18–22. The price of a home is $120,000. The bank requires a 10% down payment and two points at the time of closing. The cost of the home is financed with a 30-year fixed-rate mortgage at 8.5%.

18. Find the required down payment.
19. Find the amount of the mortgage.
20. How much must be paid for the two points at closing?
21. Use Table 8.3 on page 402 to find the monthly payment (excluding escrowed taxes and insurance).
22. Find the total cost of interest over 30 years.
23. You need a loan of $100,000 to buy a home. Here are your options:

Option A: 30-year fixed-rate at $7\frac{1}{2}$% with closing costs of $1200 and one point.

Option B: 15-year fixed-rate at 7% with closing costs of $1500 and three points.

Use Table 8.3 on page 402 to determine your monthly payments for each option. Then discuss how you would decide between the two options.

Use the stock table for AT&T to solve Exercises 24–26.

24. What were the high and low prices for a share yesterday?
25. If you owned 1000 shares of this stock last year, what dividend did you receive?
26. Suppose that you bought 600 shares of AT&T, paying the price per share at which a share traded when the stock exchange closed yesterday. If the broker charges 2.5% of the price paid for all 600 shares, find the broker's commission.

| 52-week | | Stock | SYM | Div | Yld % | PE | Vol 100s | Hi | Lo | Close | Net Chg |
High	Low										
$26\frac{1}{2}$	$24\frac{1}{4}$	AT&T	PNS	2.03	7.9	18	961	$25\frac{3}{4}$	$25\frac{1}{2}$	$25\frac{3}{4}$	$+\frac{1}{8}$

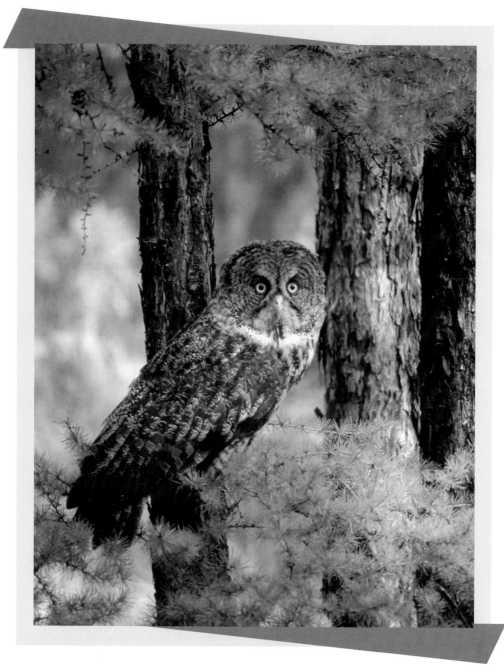

You are feeling crowded in. Perhaps it would be a good time to move to a state with more elbow room. But which state? You can look up the population of each state, but that does not take into account the amount of land the population occupies. How is this land measured and how can you use this measure to select a place where wildlife outnumber humans?

9

Measurement

You use measurements all the time to describe things: the distance you travel to school, the temperature of your room, the size of your house or apartment, and your weight gain after a vacation with lots of great food. Unfortunately, we live in a country that still embraces the units of the English system, whereas most of the world uses metric measurements. This can be extremely disorienting when you travel outside the country.

In this chapter, we explore ways of measuring things in our English system, as well as in the metric system. We will also return to find a state with lots of room to spread out. Knowing how units of measure are used to describe your world will help you to make decisions based on understanding the numbers and units you face every day.

SECTION 9.1   *Measuring Length; The Metric System*

Objectives

1. Use dimensional analysis to change units of measurement.

2. Understand and use metric prefixes.

3. Convert units within the metric system.

4. Use dimensional analysis to change to and from the metric system.

Have you seen the film *Jurassic Park*? The popularity of the movie reflects our fascination with dinosaurs and their incredible size. From end to end, the largest dinosaur from the Jurassic period that lasted from 208 to 146 million years ago was about 88 feet. To **measure** an object such as a dinosaur is to assign a number to its size. The number representing its measure from end to end is called its **length**. Measurements are used to describe properties of length, area, volume, weight, and temperature. Over the centuries, people have developed systems of measurement that are accepted in most of the world.

Length

Every measurement consists of two parts: a number and a unit of measure. For example, if the length of a dinosaur is 88 feet, the number is 88 and the unit of measure is the foot. Many different units are commonly used in measuring length. The foot is from a system of measurement called the **English system**, which is generally used in the United States. In this system of measurement, length is expressed in such units as inches, feet, yards, and miles.

The result obtained from measuring length is called a **linear measurement** and is stated in **linear units**.

Palm
(4 fingers)

Cubit

Span

Linear units of measure were originally based on parts of the body. The Egyptians used the palm (equal to four fingers), the span (a handspan), and the cubit (length of forearm).

Linear Units of Measure: The English System

12 inches (in.) = 1 foot (ft)

3 feet = 1 yard (yd)

36 inches = 1 yard

5280 feet = 1 mile (mi)

1 Use dimensional analysis to change units of measurement.

Because many of us are familiar with the measures in the box, we find it simple to change from one measure to another, say from feet to inches. We know that there are 12 inches in a foot. To convert from 5 feet to a measure in inches, we multiply by 12. Thus, 5 feet = 12 × 5 inches = 60 inches.

Another procedure to convert from one unit of measurement to another is called **dimensional analysis**. Dimensional analysis uses **unit fractions**. A unit fraction has two properties: The numerator and denominator contain different units, and the value of the unit fraction is 1. Here are some examples of unit fractions:

$$\frac{12 \text{ in.}}{1 \text{ ft}} \quad \frac{1 \text{ ft}}{12 \text{ in.}} \quad \frac{3 \text{ ft}}{1 \text{ yd}} \quad \frac{1 \text{ yd}}{3 \text{ ft}} \quad \frac{5280 \text{ ft}}{1 \text{ mi}} \quad \frac{1 \text{ mi}}{5280 \text{ ft}}$$

In each unit fraction, the numerator and denominator are equal, making the value of the fraction 1.

Let's see how to convert 5 feet to inches using a unit fraction.

$$5 \text{ ft} = ? \text{ in.}$$

Measuring Nails

Nail sizes run from 2d to 60d. The "d" is the British symbol for *pence* or *penny*, which is why a 2d nail is called a "2-penny" nail. Listed below are the lengths for the 16 most popular nail sizes. The lengths increase $\frac{1}{4}$ inch for each size under 16d and $\frac{1}{2}$ inch for each size over 16d.

Nail Size	Length	Nail Size	Length
2d	1 in.	10d	3 in.
3d	$1\frac{1}{4}$ in.	12d	$3\frac{1}{4}$ in.
4d	$1\frac{1}{2}$ in.	16d	$3\frac{1}{2}$ in.
5d	$1\frac{3}{4}$ in.	20d	4 in.
6d	2 in.	30d	$4\frac{1}{2}$ in.
7d	$2\frac{1}{4}$ in.	40d	5 in.
8d	$2\frac{1}{2}$ in.	50d	$5\frac{1}{2}$ in.
9d	$2\frac{3}{4}$ in.	60d	6 in.

Study Tip

The abbreviations for units of measurement are written without the period, such as ft for feet, except for the abbreviation for the inch (in.).

We need to eliminate feet and introduce inches. The unit we need to introduce must appear in the numerator of the fraction. The unit we need to eliminate must appear in the denominator. The units will divide out as follows:

$$5 \text{ ft} = \frac{5 \text{ ft}}{1} \cdot \frac{12 \text{ in.}}{1 \text{ ft}} = 5 \cdot 12 \text{ in.} = 60 \text{ in.}$$

unit fraction

Dimensional Analysis

To convert a measurement to a different unit, multiply by a unit fraction (or by unit fractions). The given unit of measurement should appear in the denominator of the unit fraction so that this unit cancels upon multiplication. The unit of measurement that needs to be introduced should appear in the numerator of the fraction so that this unit will be retained upon multiplication.

EXAMPLE 1   Using Dimensional Analysis to Change Units of Measurement

Convert:

a. 40 inches to feet.

b. 13,200 feet to miles.

c. 9 inches to yards.

Solution

a. Because we want to convert 40 inches to feet, feet should appear in the numerator and inches in the denominator. We use the unit fraction

$$\frac{1 \text{ ft}}{12 \text{ in.}}$$

and proceed as follows:

$$40 \text{ in.} = \frac{40 \text{ in.}}{1} \cdot \frac{1 \text{ ft}}{12 \text{ in.}} = \frac{40}{12} \text{ ft} = 3\frac{1}{3} \text{ ft or } 3.\overline{3} \text{ ft}$$

b. To convert 13,200 feet to miles, miles should appear in the numerator and feet in the denominator. We use the unit fraction

$$\frac{1 \text{ mi}}{5280 \text{ ft}}$$

and proceed as follows:

$$13,200 \text{ ft} = \frac{13,200 \text{ ft}}{1} \cdot \frac{1 \text{ mi}}{5280 \text{ ft}} = \frac{13,200}{5280} \text{ mi} = 2.5 \text{ mi}$$

c. To convert 9 inches to yards, yards should appear in the numerator and inches in the denominator. We use the unit fraction

$$\frac{1 \text{ yd}}{36 \text{ in.}}$$

and proceed as follows:

$$9 \text{ in.} = \frac{9 \text{ in.}}{1} \cdot \frac{1 \text{ yd}}{36 \text{ in.}} = \frac{9}{36} \text{ yd} = \frac{1}{4} \text{ yd or } 0.25 \text{ yd}$$

2 Understand and use metric prefixes.

Length and the Metric System

Although the English system of measurement is most commonly used in the United States, most industrialized countries use the metric system of measurement. One of the advantages of the metric system is that units are based on powers of ten, making it much easier than the English system to change from one unit of measure to another.

The basic unit for linear measure in the metric system is the meter (abbreviated as m). A meter is longer than a yard, approximately 39.37 inches. Prefixes are used to denote a multiple or part of a meter. Table 9.1 summarizes the more commonly used metric prefixes and their meanings.

Table 9.1 Commonly Used Metric Prefixes

Prefix	Symbol	Meaning
kilo	k	1000 × base unit
hecto	h	100 × base unit
deka	da	10 × base unit
deci	d	$\frac{1}{10}$ of base unit
centi	c	$\frac{1}{100}$ of base unit
milli	m	$\frac{1}{1000}$ of base unit

Study Tip

Prefixes containing an "i" (deci, centi, milli) are all fractional parts of one unit.

The prefixes kilo, centi, and milli are used more frequently than hecto, deka, and deci. Table 9.2 applies all six prefixes to the meter. The first part of the symbol indicates the prefix and the second part (m) indicates meter.

Table 9.2 Commonly Used Units of Linear Measure in the Metric System

Symbol	Unit	Meaning
km	kilometer	1000 meters
hm	hectometer	100 meters
dam	dekameter	10 meters
m	meter	1 meter
dm	decimeter	0.1 meter
cm	centimeter	0.01 meter
mm	millimeter	0.001 meter

kilodollar

hectodollar

dekadollar

dollar

decidollar

centidollar

In the metric system, the kilometer is used to measure distances comparable to those measured in miles in the English system. One kilometer is about 0.6 mile, and one mile is about 1.6 kilometers.

Metric units of centimeters and millimeters are used to measure what the English system measures in inches. Figure 9.1 shows that a centimeter is less than half an inch; there are approximately 2.54 centimeters in an inch. The smaller markings on the bottom scale are millimeters. A millimeter is approximately the thickness of a dime. The length of a bee or a fly may be measured in millimeters.

Figure 9.1

Those of us born in the United States have a good sense of what a length in the English system tells us about an object. An 88-foot dinosaur is huge, about 15 times the length of a 6-foot man. But what sense can we make of knowing that a whale is 25 meters long? The following lengths and the given approximations can help give you a feel for metric units of linear measure.

$$(1 \text{ meter} \approx 39 \text{ inches} \qquad 1 \text{ kilometer} \approx 0.62 \text{ mile})$$

A screw of length 3 cm or 30 mm

Item	Approximate Length
Width of lead in pencil	2 mm or 0.08 in.
Width of an adult's thumb	2 cm or 0.8 in.
Height of adult male	1.8 m or 6 ft
Typical room height	2.5 m or 8.3 ft
Length of medium-size car	5 m or 16.7 ft
Height of Empire State Building	381 m or 1270 ft
Average depth of ocean	4 km or 2.5 mi
Length of Manhattan Island	18 km or 11.25 mi
Distance from New York City to San Francisco	4800 km or 3000 mi
Radius of Earth	6378 km or 3986 mi
Distance from Earth to the moon	384,401 km or 240,251 mi

3 Convert units within the metric system.

Although dimensional analysis can be used to convert from one unit to another within the metric system, there is an easier, faster way to accomplish this. The procedure is based on the observation that successively smaller units in Table 9.2 involve division by 10 and successively larger units involve multiplication by 10.

km hm dam m dm cm mm

÷ 10

Figure 9.2 From meters to kilometers: 3 places left

× 10

km hm dam m dm cm mm

Figure 9.3 From meters to centimeters: 2 places right

km hm dam m dm cm mm

÷ 10

Figure 9.4 From millimeters to hectometers: 5 places left

Changing Units within the Metric System

Use the following chart to find equivalent measures of length:

1. To change from a larger unit to a smaller unit (moving to the right in the chart), multiply by 10 for each step to the right. Thus, move the decimal point in the given quantity one place to the right for each smaller unit until the desired unit is reached.

2. To change from a smaller unit to a larger unit (moving to the left in the chart), divide by 10 for each step to the left. Thus, move the decimal point in the given quantity one place to the left for each larger unit until the desired unit is reached.

EXAMPLE 2   Changing Units within the Metric System

a. Convert 504.7 meters to kilometers.

b. Convert 27 meters to centimeters.

c. Convert 704 mm to hm.

d. Convert 9.71 dam to dm.

Solution

a. Using Figure 9.2, we start at meters and move three places to the left to obtain kilometers. Hence, we move the decimal point three places to the left.

$$504.7 \text{ m} = 0.5047 \text{ km}$$

Thus, 504.7 meters converts to 0.5047 kilometers. Changing from a smaller unit of measurement (meter) to a larger unit of measurement (kilometer) results in an answer with a smaller number of units.

b. Using Figure 9.3, we once again start at meters and move two places to the right to obtain centimeters. Hence, we move the decimal point two places to the right.

$$27 \text{ m} = 2700 \text{ cm}$$

Thus, 27 meters converts to 2700 centimeters. Changing from a larger unit of measurement (meter) to a small unit of measurement (centimeter) results in an answer with a larger number of units.

c. Figure 9.4 shows that to convert from mm (millimeters) to hm (hectometers), we move the decimal point five places to the left.

$$704 \text{ mm} = 0.00704 \text{ hm}$$

× 10

km hm dam m dm cm mm

Figure 9.5 From dekameters to decimeters: 2 places right

d. Figure 9.5 shows that to convert from dam (dekameters) to dm (decimeters), we move the decimal point two places to the right.

$$9.71 \text{ dam} = 971 \text{ dm}$$

In Example 2(b), we showed that 27 meters converts to 2700 centimeters. This is the average length of the California blue whale, the longest of the great whales. Blue whales can have lengths that exceed 30 meters, making them over 100 feet long.

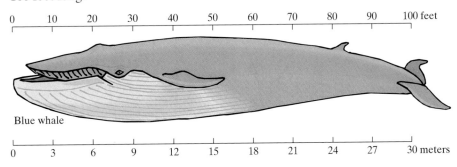

Blue whale

Beyond Commonly Used Metric Prefixes

Have you ever noticed the shimmering patterns of light on a compact disc? These are reflections from billions of pits less than a millionth of a meter wide buried under the CD's surface. One millionth of a meter, or 10^{-6} meter, is called a micrometer, symbolized μm.

There are twenty prefixes to the meter, from the yottameter (10^{24} meters) to the yoctometer (10^{-24} meter). Here is a comprehensive list of all metric prefixes.

Prefix	Symbol	Power of Ten	English Name
yotta-	Y	+24	septillion
zetta-	Z	+21	sextillion
exa-	E	+18	quintillion
peta-	P	+15	quadrillion
tera-	T	+12	trillion
giga-	G	+9	billion
mega-	M	+6	million
kilo-	k	+3	thousand
hecto-	h	+2	hundred
deca-	da	+1	ten

Prefix	Symbol	Power of Ten	English Name
deci-	d	−1	tenth
centi-	c	−2	hundredth
milli-	m	−3	thousandth
micro-	μ	−6	millionth
nano-	n	−9	billionth
pico-	p	−12	trillionth
femto-	f	−15	quadrillionth
atto-	a	−18	quintillionth
zepto-	z	−21	sextillionth
yocto-	y	−24	septillionth

4 Use dimensional analysis to change to and from the metric system.

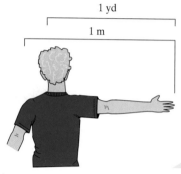

1 yd = 0.9 m

Although dimensional analysis is not necessary when changing units within the metric system, it is a useful tool when converting to and from the metric system. Some approximate linear conversions are given in Table 9.3.

Table 9.3 Approximate English and Metric Equivalents

1 inch (in.) = 2.54 centimeters (cm)
1 foot (ft) = 30 centimeters (cm)
1 yard (yd) = 0.9 meter (m)
1 mile (mi) = 1.6 kilometers (km)

EXAMPLE 3 Using Dimensional Analysis to Change to and from the Metric System

a. Convert 8 inches to centimeters.
b. Convert 125 miles to kilometers.
c. Convert 26,800 millimeters to inches.

Solution

a. To convert 8 inches to centimeters, we use a unit fraction with centimeters in the numerator and inches in the denominator.

$$\frac{2.54 \text{ cm}}{1 \text{ in.}}$$ Table 9.3 shows that 1 in. = 2.54 cm.

We proceed as follows.

$$8 \text{ in.} = \frac{8 \text{ in.}}{1} \cdot \frac{2.54 \text{ cm}}{1 \text{ in.}} = 8(2.54)\text{cm} = 20.32 \text{ cm}$$

b. To convert 125 miles to kilometers, we use a unit fraction with kilometers in the numerator and miles in the denominator.

$$\frac{1.6 \text{ km}}{1 \text{ mi}}$$ Table 9.3 shows that 1 mi = 1.6 km.

Thus,

$$125 \text{ mi} = \frac{125 \text{ mi}}{1} \cdot \frac{1.6 \text{ km}}{1 \text{ mi}} = 125(1.6)\text{km} = 200 \text{ km}$$

c. To convert 26,800 millimeters to inches, we observe that Table 9.3 has only a conversion factor from inches to centimeters. We begin by changing millimeters to centimeters.

$$26{,}800 \text{ mm} = 2680.0 \text{ cm}$$

Now we need to convert 2680 centimeters to inches. We use a unit fraction with inches in the numerator and centimeters in the denominator.

$$\frac{1 \text{ in.}}{2.54 \text{ cm}}$$

Study Tip

Keep in mind that the conversions shown here are *approximate*. More accurately,

1 mi = 1.61 km.

Thus,

125 mi ≈ 1.25(1.61) km

= 201.25 km.

Thus,

$$26{,}800 \text{ mm} = 2680 \text{ cm} = \frac{2680 \text{ cm}}{1} \cdot \frac{1 \text{ in.}}{2.54 \text{ cm}} = \frac{2680}{2.54} \text{ in.} \approx 1055 \text{ in.}$$

This measure is equivalent to about 88 feet, the length of the largest dinosaur from the Jurassic period. The diplodocus, a plant eater, was 26.8 meters, approximately 88 feet, long.

So far, we have used dimensional analysis to change units of length. Dimensional analysis may also be used to convert other kinds of measures, such as speed.

EXAMPLE 4 Using Dimensional Analysis

a. The speed limit on many highways in the United States is 55 miles per hour (mi/hr). How many kilometers per hour (km/hr) is this?
b. If a high-speed train in Japan is capable of traveling at 200 kilometers per hour, how many miles per hour is this?

Solution

a. To change miles per hour to kilometers per hour, we need to concentrate on changing miles to kilometers, so we need a unit fraction with kilometers in the numerator and miles in the denominator.

$$\frac{1.6 \text{ km}}{1 \text{ mi}}$$

Thus,

$$\frac{55 \text{ mi}}{\text{hr}} = \frac{55 \text{ mi}}{\text{hr}} \cdot \frac{1.6 \text{ km}}{1 \text{ mi}} = 55(1.6) \frac{\text{km}}{\text{hr}} = 88 \text{ km/hr}$$

This shows that 55 miles per hour is equivalent to 88 kilometers per hour.

b. To change 200 kilometers per hour to miles per hour, we focus on changing kilometers to miles. We need a unit fraction with miles in the numerator and kilometers in the denominator.

$$\frac{1 \text{ mi}}{1.6 \text{ km}}$$

Thus,

$$\frac{200 \text{ km}}{\text{hr}} = \frac{200 \text{ km}}{\text{hr}} \cdot \frac{1 \text{ mi}}{1.6 \text{ km}} = \frac{200 \text{ mi}}{1.6 \text{ hr}} = 125 \text{ mi/hr}$$

A train capable of traveling at 200 kilometers per hour can therefore travel at 125 miles per hour.

Measuring Eyesight

We know that 20/20 vision is excellent, but what do these 20s measure? The answer is *feet*. We view an eyechart from a distance of 20 feet. If you can read the lines that normal eyes can see at 20 feet, you have 20/20 vision. If you can read only the lines people with normal vision can see at 40 feet, you have 20/40 vision. The first 20 in measuring eyesight never changes.

Some people have eyesight that is better than normal. For example, if you can read the lines in an eyechart at 20 feet that people with normal vision have to get closer to read, say 15 feet, then you have 20/15 vision. Because each eye is tested separately, you can have 20/20 vision in one eye and 20/40 vision in the other.

Exercise Set 9.1

✓ Practice Exercises

In Exercises 1–16, use dimensional analysis to convert the quantity to the indicated units. If necessary, round the answer to two decimal places.

1. 30 in. to ft
2. 100 in. to ft
3. 30 ft to in.
4. 100 ft to in.
5. 6 in. to yd
6. 21 in. to yd
7. 6 yd to in.
8. 21 yd to in.
9. 6 yd to ft
10. 12 yd to ft
11. 6 ft to yd
12. 12 ft to yd
13. 17,160 ft to mi
14. 19,800 ft to mi
15. 0.75 mi to ft
16. 0.25 mi to ft

In Exercises 17–26, use the chart in the box on page 430 to convert the given measurement to the unit indicated.

17. 5 m to cm
18. 8 dam to m
19. 16.3 hm to m
20. 0.37 hm to m
21. 317.8 cm to hm
22. 8.64 hm to cm
23. 0.023 mm to m
24. 0.00037 km to cm
25. 2196 mm to dm
26. 71 dm to km

In Exercises 27–44, use the following English and metric equivalents, along with dimensional analysis, to convert the given measurement to the unit indicated.

Approximate English and Metric Equivalents

1 in. = 2.54 cm
1 ft = 30 cm
1 yd = 0.9 m
1 mi = 1.6 km

27. 14 in. to cm
28. 26 in. to cm
29. 14 cm to in.
30. 26 cm to in.
31. 265 mi to km
32. 776 mi to km
33. 265 km to mi
34. 776 km to mi
35. 12 m to yd
36. 20 m to yd
37. 14 dm to in.
38. 1.2 dam to in.
39. 160 in. to dam
40. 180 in. to hm
41. 5 ft to m
42. 8 ft to mi
43. 5 m to ft
44. 8 m to ft

Use 1 mi = 1.6 km to solve Exercises 45–48.

45. Express 96 kilometers per hour in miles per hour.
46. Express 104 kilometers per hour in miles per hour.
47. Express 45 miles per hour in kilometers per hour.
48. Express 50 miles per hour in kilometers per hour.

☆ Application Exercises

In Exercises 49–58, selecting from millimeter, meter, and kilometer, determine the best unit of measure to express the given length.

49. A person's height
50. The length of a football field
51. The length of a bee
52. The distance from New York City to Washington D.C.
53. The distance around a one-acre lot
54. The length of a car
55. The width of a book
56. The altitude of an airplane
57. The diameter of a screw
58. The width of a human foot

In Exercises 59–66, select the best estimate for the measure of the given item.

59. The length of a pen
    a. 30 cm   b. 19 cm   c. 19 mm
60. The length of this page
    a. 2.5 mm   b. 25 mm   c. 250 mm
61. The height of a skyscraper
    a. 325 m   b. 32.5 km   c. 325 km   d. 3250 km
62. The length of a pair of pants
    a. 700 cm   b. 70 cm   c. 7 cm
63. The height of a room
    a. 4 mm   b. 4 cm   c. 4 m   d. 4 dm
64. The length of a rowboat
    a. 4 cm   b. 4 dm   c. 4 m   d. 4 dam
65. The width of an electric cord
    a. 4 mm   b. 4 cm   c. 4 dm   d. 4 m
66. The dimensions of a piece of typing paper
    a. 22 mm by 28 mm   b. 22 cm by 28 cm
    c. 22 dm by 28 dm   d. 22 m by 28 m
67. A baseball diamond measures 27 meters along each side. If a batter scored two home runs in a game, how many kilometers did the batter run?
68. If you jog six times around a track that is 700 meters long, how many kilometers have you covered?
69. The distance from the Earth to the sun is about 93 million miles. What is this distance in kilometers?
70. The distance from New York City to Los Angeles is 4690 kilometers. What is the distance in miles?

Writing in Mathematics

71. Describe the two parts of a measurement.
72. Describe how to use dimensional analysis to convert 20 inches to feet.
73. Describe advantages of the metric system over the English system.
74. Explain how to change units within the metric system.
75. You jog 500 meters in a given period of time. The next day, you jog 500 yards over the same time period. On which day was your speed faster? Explain your answer.
76. What kind of difficulties might arise if the United States immediately eliminated all units of measure in the English system and replaced the system by the metric system?
77. The United States is the only Westernized country that does not use the metric system as its primary system of measurement. Why are we opposed to switching to the metric system?

Critical Thinking Exercises

In Exercises 78–82, convert to an appropriate unit so that the numerical expression in the given measure does not contain any zeros.

78. 6000 cm   79. 900 m   80. 7000 dm
81. 11,000 mm   82. 0.0002 km
83. Use the unit fractions

$$\frac{36 \text{ in.}}{1 \text{ yd}} \quad \text{and} \quad \frac{2.54 \text{ cm}}{1 \text{ in.}}$$

to convert 5 yards to centimeters.

84. Use the unit fractions

$$\frac{5280 \text{ ft}}{1 \text{ mi}}, \frac{12 \text{ in.}}{1 \text{ ft}}, \text{ and } \frac{2.54 \text{ cm}}{1 \text{ in.}}$$

to convert 30 miles to kilometers.

Group Exercise

85. Jurassic Math: A Matter of Scale

Given only a list of numbers describing the height and length of a dinosaur, would you be able to make realistic judgments about how this historic creature would fit into your world? Could a Tyrannosaurus Rex peer in the window of a three-story building? Could a Stegosaurus fit in your classroom? How many parking spaces would a Brontosaurus fill?

a. In a small group, select a dinosaur to study. Write the approximate dimensions of the dinosaur in terms of height and length in an uncommon unit of measurement, such as inches, centimeters, or a fraction of a mile. Ask several people to make a comparative estimate of the size of the dinosaur from these measurements. For example, you might ask, "Is it bigger than a car?" or "Is it taller than this house?" You may tell the person if the dinosaur walked on two or four legs, but do not reveal the name of the dinosaur. Record the answers from several sources and compare the results with the rest of your group. How accurate were the answers?

b. Conduct another set of interviews, this time giving the information in a more typical form, such as feet or yards. How does the accuracy of the new estimates compare to the ones in part (a)? Share your results with other groups in the class. Does the actual size of the dinosaur seem to affect the estimates? In other words, does the size of larger dinosaurs seem harder to estimate accurately than smaller ones or vice versa?

SECTION 9.2 *Measuring Area and Volume*

Objectives

1. Use square units to measure area.
2. Use dimensional analysis to change units for area.
3. Use cubic units to measure volume.
4. Use English and metric units to measure capacity.

Are you feeling a bit crowded in? Although there are more people on the East coast of the United States than there are bears, there are places in the Northwest where bears outnumber humans. The most densely populated state is New Jersey, with 1042 people per square mile. The least densely populated state is Alaska, with one person per square mile.

A square mile is one way of measuring the **area** of a state. A state's area is the region within its boundaries. Its **population density** is its population divided by its area. In this section, we discuss methods for measuring both area and volume.

1 Use square units to measure area.

Figure 9.6 One square unit

Measuring Area

In order to measure a region that is enclosed by boundaries, we begin by selecting a **square unit**. A square unit is a square, each of whose sides is one unit in length, illustrated in Figure 9.6. The region in Figure 9.6 is said to have an area of **one square unit**. The side of the square can be 1 inch, 1 centimeter, 1 meter, 1 foot, or any linear unit of measure. The corresponding units of area are the square inch (in.^2), the square centimeter (cm^2), the square meter (m^2), the square foot (ft^2), and so on. Figure 9.7 illustrates 1 square inch and 1 square centimeter, drawn to actual size.

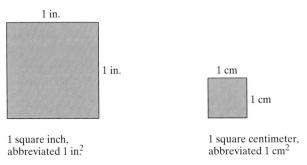

1 square inch, abbreviated 1 in.^{2}

1 square centimeter, abbreviated 1 cm^2

Figure 9.7 Common units of measurement for area, drawn to actual size

Square Unit

Figure 9.8

EXAMPLE 1 Measuring Area

What is the area of the region shown in Figure 9.8?

Solution We can determine the area of the region by counting the number of square units contained within the region. There are 12 such units. Therefore, the area of the region is 12 square units.

Although there are 12 inches in a foot and 3 feet in a yard, these numerical relationships are not the same for square units:

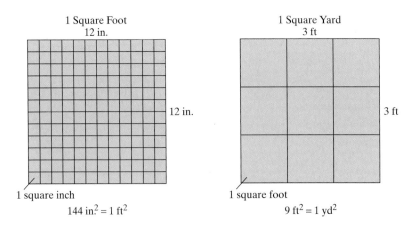

1 square inch
$144 \text{ in.}^2 = 1 \text{ ft}^2$

1 square foot
$9 \text{ ft}^2 = 1 \text{ yd}^2$

Study Tip

A small plot of land is usually measured in square feet, rather than a small fraction of an acre. Curiously, square yards are rarely used.

Square Units of Measure: The English System

$$1 \text{ square foot } (\text{ft}^2) = 144 \text{ square inches } (\text{in.}^2)$$
$$1 \text{ square yard } (\text{yd}^2) = 9 \text{ square feet } (\text{ft}^2)$$
$$1 \text{ acre } (\text{a}) = 43{,}560 \text{ ft}^2 \text{ or } 4840 \text{ yd}^2$$
$$1 \text{ square mile } (\text{mi}^2) = 640 \text{ acres}$$

Most Densely Populated States

State	Population per Square Mile
1. New Jersey	1042.0
2. Rhode Island	960.3
3. Massachusetts	767.6
4. Connecticut	678.4
5. Maryland	489.2
6. New York	381.0
7. Delaware	340.8
8. Pennsylvania	265.1
9. Ohio	264.9
10. Florida	239.6

Source: U.S. Census Bureau

EXAMPLE 2   Using Square Units to Compute Population Density

After Alaska, Wyoming is the least densely populated state. The population of Wyoming is 453,588 and its area is 97,105 square miles. What is Wyoming's population density?

Solution   We compute the population density by dividing Wyoming's population by its area.

$$\text{population density} = \frac{\text{population}}{\text{area}} = \frac{453{,}588 \text{ people}}{97{,}105 \text{ square miles}}$$

Using a calculator and rounding to the nearest tenth, we obtain a population density of 4.7 people per square mile. This means that there is an average of only 4.7 people for each square mile of area.

2   Use dimensional analysis to change units for area.

One theory is that using square units to measure area has its origin in the weaving of fabric.

In Section 9.1, we saw that almost anywhere on our planet, with the exception of the United States, the system of measurement that is used is the metric system. In the metric system, the square centimeter is used instead of the square inch. The square meter replaces the square foot and the square yard.

The English system uses the acre and the square mile to measure large land areas. The metric system uses the hectare (symbolized ha and pronounced "hectair"). A hectare is approximately 2.5 acres. One square mile of land consists of approximately 260 hectares. Just as the hectare replaces the acre, the square kilometer is used instead of the square mile. One square kilometer is approximately 0.38 square mile.

Some basic approximate conversions for square units of area are given in Table 9.4.

Table 9.4   English and Metric Equivalents for Area

1 square inch (in.^2)	= 6.5	square centimeters (cm^2)
1 square foot (ft^2)	= 0.09	square meter (m^2)
1 square yard (yd^2)	= 0.8	square meter (m^2)
1 square mile (mi^2)	= 2.6	square kilometers (km^2)
1 acre	= 0.4	hectare (ha)

EXAMPLE 3   Using Dimensional Analysis on Units of Area

A property in Italy is advertised at $545,000 for 6.8 hectares.

    a. Find the area of the property in acres.

    b. What is the price per acre?

Solution

    a. Using Table 9.4, we see that 1 acre = 0.4 hectare. To convert 6.8 hectares to acres, we use a unit fraction with acres in the numerator and hectares in the denominator.

$$6.8 \text{ ha} = \frac{6.8 \text{ ha}}{1} \cdot \frac{1 \text{ acre}}{0.4 \text{ ha}} = \frac{6.8}{0.4} \text{ acres} = 17 \text{ acres}$$

    The area of the property is 17 acres.

    b. The price per acre is the total price, $545,000, divided by the number of acres.

$$\text{price per acre} = \frac{\$545,000}{17 \text{ acres}} \approx 32,059/\text{acre}$$

    The price is approximately $32,059 per acre.

3   Use cubic units to measure volume.

Measuring Volume

A shoe box and a basketball are examples of three-dimensional figures. **Volume** refers to the amount of space occupied by such a figure. In order to measure this space, we begin by selecting a cubic unit. Two such cubic units are shown in Figure 9.9.

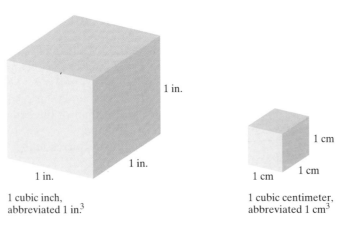

1 in.

1 in.

1 in.

1 cubic inch, abbreviated 1 in.³

1 cm

1 cm

1 cm

1 cubic centimeter, abbreviated 1 cm³

Figure 9.9 Common Units of Measurement for Volume

    The edges of a cube all have the same length. Other cubic units used to measure volume include 1 cubic foot (1 ft^3) and 1 cubic meter (1 m^3). One way to measure the volume of a solid is to calculate the number of cubic units contained in its interior.

Cubic Unit

Volume = ?

Figure 9.10

EXAMPLE 4 Measuring Volume

What is the volume of the solid shown in Figure 9.10?

Solution   We can determine the volume of the solid by counting the number of cubic units contained within the region. Because we have drawn a solid figure on a flat page, some of the small cubic units in the back, left are hidden. The figures below show how the cubic units are used to fill the inside of the solid.

Do these figures help you to see that there are 18 cubic units inside the solid? The volume of the solid is 18 cubic units.

Study Tip

If you have difficulty seeing the detail in Figure 9.11, cubing numbers is helpful:

$$3 \text{ ft} = 1 \text{ yd}$$

$$(3 \text{ ft})^3 = (1 \text{ yd})^3$$

$$3 \cdot 3 \cdot 3 \text{ ft}^3 = 1 \cdot 1 \cdot 1 \text{ yd}^3$$

Conclusion: $27 \text{ ft}^3 = 1 \text{ yd}^3$

$$12 \text{ in.} = 1 \text{ ft}$$

$$(12 \text{ in.})^3 = (1 \text{ ft})^3$$

$$12 \cdot 12 \cdot 12 \text{ in.}^3 = 1 \cdot 1 \cdot 1 \text{ ft}^3$$

Conclusion: $1728 \text{ in.}^3 = 1 \text{ ft}^3$

---

4 Use English and metric units to measure capacity.

We have seen that there are 3 feet in a yard, but 9 square feet in a square yard. Neither of these relationships holds for cubic units. Figure 9.11 illustrates that there are 27 cubic feet in a cubic yard. Furthermore, there are 1728 cubic inches in a cubic foot.

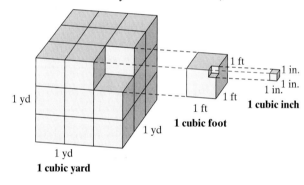

1 yd

1 cubic yard

1 yd

1 yd

1 cubic foot

1 ft 1 ft 1 ft

1 cubic inch

1 in. 1 in. 1 in.

Figure 9.11 $27 \text{ ft}^3 = 1 \text{ yd}^3$ and $1728 \text{ in.}^3 = 1 \text{ ft}^3$

The measure of volume also includes the amount of fluid that a three-dimensional object can hold. This is often called the object's **capacity**. For example, we often refer to the capacity, in gallons, of a gas tank. A cubic yard has a capacity of about 200 gallons and a cubic foot has a capacity of about 7.48 gallons.

Table 9.5 contains information about standard units of capacity in the English system.

Table 9.5   English Units for Capacity

2 pints (pt) = 1 quart (qt)	
4 quarts = 1 gallon (gal)	
1 gallon = 128 ounces (oz)	
1 cup (c) = 8 ounces	
Volume in Cubic Units	**Capacity**
1 cubic yard	about 200 gallons
1 cubic foot	about 7.48 gallons
231 cubic inches	about 1 gallon

EXAMPLE 5   Volume and Capacity in the English System

A swimming pool has a volume of 22,500 cubic feet. How many gallons of water does the pool hold?

Solution   We use the fact that 1 cubic foot has a capacity of about 7.48 gallons to set up our unit fraction.

$$\frac{7.48 \text{ gal}}{1 \text{ ft}^3}$$

We use this unit fraction to find the capacity of the 22,500 cubic feet.

$$22,500 \text{ ft}^3 = \frac{22,500 \text{ ft}^3}{1} \cdot \frac{7.48 \text{ gal}}{1 \text{ ft}^3} = 22,500 \, (7.48) \text{ gal} = 168,300 \text{ gal}$$

The pool holds approximately 168,300 gallons of water.

1 liter   1 quart

As always, things are simpler when the metric system is used to measure capacity. The basic unit is the **liter**, abbreviated L. A liter is slightly larger than a quart.

$$1 \text{ liter} \approx 1.0567 \text{ quarts}$$

The standard metric prefixes are used to denote a multiple or part of a liter. Table 9.6 applies these prefixes to the liter.

Table 9.6   Units of Capacity in the Metric System

Symbol	Unit	Meaning
kL	kiloliter	1000 liters
hL	hectoliter	100 liters
daL	dekaliter	10 liters
L	liter	1 liter ≈ 1.06 quarts
dL	deciliter	0.1 liter
cL	centiliter	0.01 liter
mL	milliliter	0.001 liter

The following list should help give you a feel for capacity in the metric system.

Item	Capacity
Average cup of coffee	250 mL
12-ounce can of soda	355 mL
One quart of fruit juice	0.95 L
One gallon of milk	3.78 L
Average gas capacity of a car (about 18.5 gallons)	70 L

10 cm

10 cm

1 liter

10 cm

1000 cubic centimeters = 1 liter

A solid with a volume of 1000 cubic centimeters has a capacity of 1 liter.

EXAMPLE 6   Volume and Capacity in the Metric System

An aquarium has a volume of 36,000 cubic centimeters. How many liters of water does the aquarium hold?

Solution   We use the fact that 1000 cubic centimeters corresponds to a capacity of 1 liter to set up our unit fraction.

$$\frac{1 \text{ L}}{1000 \text{ cm}^3}$$

We use this unit fraction to find the capacity of the 36,000 cubic centimeters.

$$36,000 \text{ cm}^3 = \frac{36,000 \text{ cm}^3}{1} \cdot \frac{1 \text{ L}}{1000 \text{ cm}^3} = \frac{36,000}{1000} \text{ L} = 36 \text{ L}$$

The aquarium holds 36 liters of water.

Exercise Set 9.2

 Practice Exercises

In Exercises 1–6, use the given figure to find its area in square units.

1.

2.

3.

4.

5.

6.

In Exercises 7–14, use Table 9.4 on page 437, along with dimensional analysis, to convert the given square unit to the square unit indicated. Where necessary, round answers to two decimal places.

7. 14 cm² to in.²

8. 20 m² to ft²

9. 30 m² to yd²

10. 14 mi² to km²

11. 10.2 ha to acres

12. 20.6 ha to acres

13. 14 in.² to cm²

14. 20 in.² to cm²

In Exercises 15–16, use the given figure to find its volume in cubic units.

15.

16.

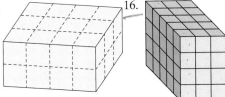

In Exercises 17–24, use Table 9.5 on page 439, along with dimensional analysis, to convert the given unit to the unit indicated. Where necessary, round answers to two decimal places.

17. 10,000 ft³ to gal

18. 25,000 ft³ to gal

19. 8 yd³ to gal

20. 35 yd³ to gal

21. 2079 in.³ to gal

22. 6237 in.³ to gal

23. 2700 gal to yd³

24. 1496 gal to ft³

In Exercises 25–32, use the fact that a solid with a volume of 1000 cubic centimeters has a capacity of 1 liter, along with dimensional analysis, to convert the given unit to the unit indicated.

25. 45,000 cm³ to L

26. 75,000 cm³ to L

27. 17 cm³ to mL

28. 19 cm³ to mL

29. 1.5 L to cm³

30. 4.5 L to cm³

31. 150 mL to cm³

32. 250 mL to cm³

Application Exercises

33. The population of Montana is 799,065 and its area is 145,556 square miles. Find Montana's population density to the nearest tenth.

34. The population of Utah is 1,722,850 and its area is 82,168 square miles. Find Utah's population density to the nearest tenth.

35. A property that measures 8 hectares is for sale.
    a. How large is the property in acres?
    b. If the property is selling for $250,000, what is the price per acre?

36. A property that measures 100 hectares is for sale.
    a. How large is the property in acres?
    b. If the property is selling for $350,000, what is the price per acre?

In Exercises 37–40, selecting from square centimeters, square meters, or square kilometers, determine the best unit of measure to express the area of the object described.

37. The top of a desk
38. A dollar bill
39. A national park
40. The wall of a room

In Exercises 41–44, select the best estimate for the measure of the area of the object described.

41. The area of the floor of a room
    a. 25 cm²   b. 25 m²   c. 25 km²

42. The area of a television screen
    a. 2050 mm²   b. 2050 cm²   c. 2050 dm²

43. The area of the face of a small coin
    a. 6 mm²   b. 6 cm²   c. 6 dm²

44. The area of a parcel of land in a large metropolitan area on which a house can be built
    a. 900 cm²   b. 900 m²   c. 900 ha

45. A swimming pool has a volume of 45,000 cubic feet. How many gallons of water does the pool hold?

46. A swimming pool has a volume of 66,000 cubic feet. How many gallons of water does the pool hold?

47. A container of grapefruit juice has a volume of 4000 cubic centimeters. How many liters of juice does the container hold?

48. An aquarium has a volume of 17,500 cubic centimeters. How many liters of water does the aquarium hold?

 Writing in Mathematics

49. Describe how area is measured. Explain why linear units cannot be used.

50. New Mexico has a population density of 12.5 people per square mile. Describe what this means. Use an almanac or the Internet to compare this population density to that of the state in which you are now living.

51. Describe the difference between the following problems: How much fencing is needed to enclose a garden? How much fertilizer is needed for the garden?

52. Describe how volume is measured. Explain why linear or square units cannot be used.

53. For a swimming pool, what is the difference between the following units of measure: cubic feet and gallons? For each unit, write a sentence about the pool that makes the use of the unit appropriate.

54. If there are 10 decimeters in a meter, explain why there are not 10 cubic decimeters in a cubic meter.

 Critical Thinking Exercises

55. Singapore has the highest population density of any country: 46,690 people per 1000 hectares. How many people are there per square mile?

56. Nebraska has a population density of 20.5 people per square mile and a population of 1,578,417. What is the area of Nebraska?

57. A high population density is a condition common to extremely poor and extremely rich locales. Explain why this is so.

58. Although Alaska is the least densely populated state, over 90 percent of its land is protected Federal property that is off-limits to settlement. A resident of Anchorage, Alaska, might feel hemmed in. In terms of "elbow room," what other important factor must be considered when calculating a state's population density?

59. A solid with a volume of 1000 cubic centimeters has a capacity of 1 liter. Therefore, if a solid has a volume of 1 cubic centimeter, its capacity is 1 ____ (fill in the appropriate unit). A solid with a volume of 1 cubic decimeter has a capacity of 1 ____, and a solid with a volume of 1 cubic meter has a capacity of 1 ____ .

60. A swimming pool has a volume of 540 cubic meters. Find the pool's capacity in liters and kiloliters.

61. Does an adult's body contain approximately 6.5 liters, kiloliters, or milliliters of blood? Explain your answer.

62. Is the volume of a coin approximately 1 cubic centimeter, 1 cubic millimeter, or 1 cubic decimeter? Explain your answer.

 Group Exercise

63. Discovering how a particular measure came into common use requires a look at the history of mathematics and sometimes the history of everyday life. Most of the shorter measures we use for length came from the measure of

different parts of the human body. Ancient Egyptians, Mesopotamians, Greeks, and Romans all had measures based on the width of a finger or the span of a palm. For example, the smallest Roman measure, the width of a finger, was named *uncia*, the Latin word for one-twelfth, which has survived to this day in the form of "inch."

Listed on the right are various units for measuring length and area. For this project, you will select a measure and determine how it came into its current usage. Bring this information to class and share it with other students in the group. Pool the research and prepare a presentation on your findings.

Units for Measuring Length and Area

statute mile	nautical mile
furlong	arc
foot	rod
inch	cubit
yard	span
meter	fathom
acre	hand

SECTION 9.3 *Measuring Weight and Temperature*

Objectives

1. Apply metric prefixes to units of weight.
2. Convert units of weight within the metric system.
3. Use dimensional analysis to change units of weight to and from the metric system.
4. Understand temperature scales.

You are watching CNN International on cable television. The temperature in Honolulu, Hawaii, is reported as 30°C. Are Honolulu's tourists running around in winter jackets? In this section, we will make sense of Celsius temperature readings, as we discuss methods for measuring temperature and weight.

Measuring Weight

You step on the scale at the doctor's office to check your weight, discovering that you are 150 pounds. Compare this to your weight on the moon: 25 pounds. Why the difference? **Weight** is the measure of the gravitational pull on an object. The gravitational pull on the moon is only about one-sixth the gravitational pull on Earth. Although your weight varies depending on the force of gravity, your mass is exactly the same in all locations. **Mass** is a measure of the quantity of matter in an object, determined by its molecular structure. On Earth, as your weight increases, so does your mass. In this section, we will treat weight and mass as equivalent and refer strictly to weight.

About 2.2 lb

1 kilogram   1 pound

Units of Weight: The English System

$$16 \text{ ounces (oz)} = 1 \text{ pound (lb)}$$

$$2000 \text{ pounds (lb)} = 1 \text{ ton (T)}$$

1 Apply metric prefixes to units of weight.

The basic metric unit of weight is the **gram** (g), used for very small objects such as a coin, a candy bar, or a teaspoon of salt. A nickel has a weight of about 5 grams.

As with meters, prefixes are used to denote a multiple or part of a gram. Table 9.7 on page 444 applies the common metric prefixes to the gram. The first part of the symbol indicates the prefix and the second part (g) indicates gram.

Study Tip

The following weights of common objects can help give you a feel for metric units of weight.

Item	Approximate Weight
Grain of sand	1 mg
Paper clip	1 g
Dime	2 g
Quarter	6 g
2-lb can of coffee	1 kg

Table 9.7 Commonly Used Units of Weight in the Metric System

Symbol	Unit	Meaning
kg	kilogram	1000 grams
hg	hectogram	100 grams
dag	dekagram	10 grams
g	gram	1 gram
dg	decigram	0.1 gram
cg	centigram	0.01 gram
mg	milligram	0.001 gram

Weight of paper clip is 1 g.

1 mm thick

1 cm wide

In the metric system, the kilogram is the comparable unit to the pound in the English system. A weight of 1 kilogram is about 2.2 pounds. Thus, an average man has a weight of about 75 kilograms.

A milligram, equivalent to 0.001 gram, is an extremely small unit of weight and is used extensively in the pharmaceutical industry. If you look at the label on a bottle of tablets, you will see that the amounts of different substances in each tablet are expressed in milligrams.

The weight of a very heavy object is expressed in terms of the metric tonne (t), which is equivalent to 1000 kilograms, or about 2200 pounds. This is 10 percent more than the English ton (T) of 2000 pounds.

The chart in Figure 9.12 can be used to change units of weight within the metric system. The chart is used in exactly the same way that we changed units of length. For each step to the right, we multiply by 10 and for each step to the left, we divide by 10.

Figure 9.12 Converting metric units of weight

2 Convert units of weight within the metric system.

EXAMPLE 1 Changing Units within the Metric System

a. Convert 8.7 dg to mg.

b. Convert 950 mg to g.

Solution

a. Figure 9.13 shows that to convert from dg (decigrams) to mg (milligrams), we move the decimal point two places to the right.

$$8.7 \text{ dg} = 870 \text{ mg}$$

Figure 9.13 From decigrams to milligrams: two places right

Thus, 8.7 decigrams is equivalent to 870 milligrams. Changing from a larger unit of weight (decigram) to a small unit (milligram) results in an answer with a larger number of units.

b. Figure 9.14 shows that to convert from mg (milligrams) to g (grams), we move the decimal point three places to the left.

$$950 \text{ mg} = 0.950 \text{ g}$$

Figure 9.14 From milligrams to grams: three places left

Thus, 950 milligrams is equivalent to 0.950 (or 0.95) gram. Changing from a smaller unit of weight (milligrams) to a larger unit (grams) results in an answer with a smaller number of units.

3 Use dimensional analysis to change units of weight to and from the metric system.

We have already seen that although dimensional analysis is not necessary when changing units within the metric system, it is a useful tool when converting to and from the metric system. Some basic conversions are given in Table 9.8.

Table 9.8 Weight: English and Metric Equivalents

1 ounce (oz) = 28 grams (g)
1 pound (lb) = 0.45 kilogram (kg)
1 ton (T) = 0.9 tonne (t)

The SI System

Nothing puts more stress on the average American than the threat of the metric system, officially called the Systemé International d'Unites, abbreviated the SI system. Yemen, Brunei, and the United States are the only countries in the world not using the SI system.

In 1975, the United States prepared to adopt the SI system with the Metric Conversion Act. However, grassroots America rose up and forced Congress to make the conversion voluntary, effectively chasing it off. But it's not as bad as you think; from metric tools to milligram measures of medication, we have been edging, inching, even centimetering toward the metric system.

EXAMPLE 2   Using Dimensional Analysis

a. Convert 160 pounds to kilograms.

b. Convert 300 grams to ounces.

Solution

a. To convert 160 pounds to kilograms, we use a unit fraction with kilograms in the numerator and pounds in the denominator.

$$\frac{0.45 \text{ kg}}{1 \text{ lb}} \qquad \text{Table 9.8 shows that 1 lb} = 0.45 \text{ kg.}$$

Thus,

$$160 \text{ lb} = \frac{160 \text{ lb}}{1} \cdot \frac{0.45 \text{ kg}}{1 \text{ lb}} = 160(0.45) \text{ kg} = 72 \text{ kg}$$

b. To convert 300 grams to ounces, we use a unit fraction with ounces in the numerator and grams in the denominator.

$$\frac{1 \text{ oz}}{28 \text{ g}} \qquad \text{Table 9.8 shows that 1 oz} = 28 \text{ g.}$$

Thus,

$$300 \text{ g} = \frac{300 \text{ g}}{1} \cdot \frac{1 \text{ oz}}{28 \text{ g}} = \frac{300}{28} \text{ oz} \approx 10.7 \text{ oz}$$

Measuring Temperature

You'll be leaving the cold of winter for a Hawaii vacation. CNN International reports a temperature in Hawaii of 30°C. Should you cancel the trip?

The idea of changing from Celsius readings—or is it Centigrade?—to familiar Fahrenheit readings can be disorienting. Reporting a temperature of 30° doesn't have the same impact as the Fahrenheit equivalent of 86 degrees (don't cancel the trip). Why these annoying temperature scales?

The **Fahrenheit temperature scale**, the one we are accustomed to, was established in 1714 by the German physicist Gabriel Daniel Fahrenheit. He took a mixture of salt and ice, then thought to be the coldest possible temperature, and called it 0 degrees. He called the temperature of the human body 96 degrees, dividing the space between 0 and 96 into 96 parts. Fahrenheit was wrong about body temperature. It was later found to be 98.6 degrees. On his scale, water froze (without salt) at 32 degrees and boiled at 212 degrees. The symbol ° was used to replace the word *degree*.

4 Understand temperature scales.

Figure 9.15 The Celsius scale is on the left and the Fahrenheit scale is on the right.

Twenty years later, the Swedish scientist Anders Celsius introduced another temperature scale. He set the freezing point of water at 0° and its boiling point at 100°, dividing the space into 100 parts. Degrees were called centigrade until 1948, when the name was officially changed to honor its inventor. However, "centigrade" is still commonly used in the United States.

Figure 9.15 shows a thermometer that measures temperatures in both degrees Celsius (°C is the scale on the left) and degrees Fahrenheit (°F is the scale on the right). The thermometer should help orient you if you need to know what a temperature in °C means. For example, if it is 40°C, find the horizontal line representing this temperature on the left. Now read across to the °F scale on the right. The reading is above 100°, indicating heat wave conditions.

The following formulas can be used to convert from one temperature scale to the other.

From Celsius to Fahrenheit	**From Fahrenheit to Celsius**
$$F = \frac{9}{5}C + 32$$	$$C = \frac{5}{9}(F - 32)$$

EXAMPLE 3 Converting from Celsius to Fahrenheit

Your European vacation has you feeling a bit feverish, so you decide to take your temperature. The thermometer reads 37°. Should you panic?

Solution
Use the formula

$$F = \frac{9}{5}C + 32$$

and convert 37°C from °C to °F. Substitute 37 for C in the formula and find the value of F.

$$F = \frac{9}{5}(37) + 32$$

$$= 66.6 + 32$$

$$= 98.6$$

No need to panic! Your temperature is 98.6°F, which is perfectly normal.

EXAMPLE 4 Converting from Fahrenheit to Celsius

The temperature on a warm spring day is 77°F. Find the equivalent temperature on the Celsius scale.

Solution   Use the formula

$$C = \frac{5}{9}(F - 32)$$

and convert 77°F from °F to °C. Substitute 77 for F in the formula and find the value of C.

$$C = \frac{5}{9}(77 - 32)$$

$$= \frac{5}{9}(45)$$

$$= 25$$

Thus, 77°F is equivalent to 25°C.

Lake Baikal, Siberia, is one of the coldest places on Earth, reaching −76°F (−60°C) in winter. The lowest temperature possible is absolute zero. Scientists have cooled atoms to a few millionths of a degree above absolute zero.

Because temperature is a measure of heat, scientists do not find negative temperatures meaningful in their work. In 1948, the British physicist Lord Kelvin introduced a third temperature scale. He put 0 degrees at absolute zero, the coldest possible temperature, at which there is no heat and molecules stop moving. Figure 9.16 illustrates the three temperature scales.

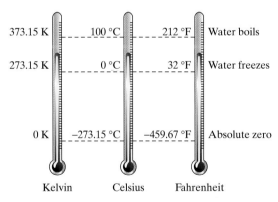

Figure 9.16 The three temperature scales

Figure 9.16 shows that water freezes at 273.15 K (read "K" or "Kelvins," not "degrees Kelvin") and boils at 373.15 K. The Kelvin scale is the same as the Celsius scale, except in its starting (zero) point. This makes it easy to go back and forth from Celsius to Kelvin.

From Celsius to Kelvin	**From Kelvin to Celsius**
$K = C + 273.15$	$C = K - 273.15$

Kelvin's scale was embraced by the scientific community. Today, it is the final authority, as scientists define Celsius and Fahrenheit in terms of Kelvins.

Exercise Set 9.3

 Practice Exercises

In Exercises 1–10, use Figure 9.12 on page 444 to convert the given unit of weight to the unit indicated.

1. 7.4 dg to mg
2. 6.9 dg to mg
3. 870 mg to g
4. 640 mg to g
5. 8 g to cg
6. 7 g to cg
7. 18.6 kg to g
8. 0.37 kg to g
9. 0.018 mg to g
10. 0.029 mg to g

In Exercises 11–22, use the following equivalents, along with dimensional analysis, to convert the given unit to the unit indicated. When necessary, round answers to two decimal places.

$$16 \text{ oz} = 1 \text{ lb}$$
$$2000 \text{ lb} = 1 \text{ T}$$
$$1 \text{ oz} = 28 \text{ g}$$
$$1 \text{ lb} = 0.45 \text{ kg}$$
$$1 \text{ T} = 0.9 \text{ t}$$

11. 36 oz to lb
12. 26 oz to lb
13. 36 oz to g
14. 26 oz to g
15. 540 lb to kg
16. 220 lb to kg
17. 80 lb to g
18. 150 lb to g
19. 540 kg to lb
20. 220 kg to lb
21. 200 t to T
22. 100 t to T

In Exercises 23–30, convert the given Celsius temperature to its equivalent temperature on the Fahrenheit scale. Where appropriate, round to the nearest tenth of a degree.

23. 10°C
24. 20°C
25. 35°C
26. 45°C
27. 57°C
28. 98°C
29. −5°C
30. −10°C

In Exercises 31–42, convert the given Fahrenheit temperature to its equivalent temperature on the Celsius scale. Where appropriate, round to the nearest tenth of a degree.

31. 68°F
32. 86°F
33. 41°F
34. 50°F
35. 72°F
36. 90°F
37. 23°F
38. 14°F
39. 350°F
40. 475°F
41. −22°F
42. −31°F

⭐ **Application Exercises**

In Exercises 43–49, selecting from milligram, gram, kilogram, and tonne, determine the best unit of measure to express the given item's weight.

43. A bee
44. This book
45. A tablespoon of salt
46. A Boeing 747
47. A stacked washer-dryer
48. A pen
49. An adult male

In Exercises 50–56, select the best estimate for the weight of the given item.

50. A newborn infant's weight
   a. 3000 kg   b. 300 kg   c. 30 kg   d. 3 kg
51. The weight of a nickel
   a. 5 kg   b. 5 g   c. 5 mg
52. A person's weight
   a. 60 kg   b. 60 g   c. 60 dag
53. The weight of a box of cereal
   a. 0.5 kg   b. 0.5 g   c. 0.5 t
54. The weight of a glass of water
   a. 400 dg   b. 400 g   c. 400 dag   d. 400 hg
55. The weight of a regular-size car
   a. 1500 dag   b. 1500 hg   c. 1500 kg   d. 15,000 kg
56. The weight of a bicycle
   a. 140 kg   b. 140 hg   c. 140 dag   d. 140 g

57. Six items purchased at a grocery store weigh 14 kilograms. One of the items is detergent weighing 720 grams. What is the total weight, in kilograms, of the other five items?

58. If a nickel weighs 5 grams, how many nickels are there in 4 kilograms of nickels?

59. If the cost to mail a letter is 33 cents for mail weighing up to one ounce and 22 cents for each additional ounce or fraction of an ounce, find the cost of mailing a letter that weighs 85 grams.

60. Using the information given below the pictured finback whale, estimate the weight, in tons and kilograms, of the killer whale.

Finback whale

Weight: 50T, 45,360 kg

Killer whale

61. Which is more economical: purchasing the economy size of a detergent at 3 kilograms for $3.15 or purchasing the regular size at 720 grams for 60¢?

In Exercises 62–65, select the best estimate of the Celsius temperature of:

62. A very hot day.
    a. 85°C   b. 65°C   c. 35°C   d. 20°C
63. A warm winter day in Washington, D.C.
    a. 10°C   b. 30°C   c. 50°C   d. 70°C
64. A setting for a home thermostat.
    a. 20°C   b. 40°C   c. 60°C   d. 80°C
65. The oven temperature for cooking a roast.
    a. 80°C   b. 100°C   c. 175°C   d. 350°C
66. Key West, Florida, has the highest average yearly temperature of any city in the United States: 25.7°C. What is this temperature, in °F, to the nearest tenth of a degree?
67. Plateau Station, Antarctica, has the lowest average yearly temperature of any place on Earth: −7°C. What is this temperature, in °F, to the nearest tenth of a degree?

Writing in Mathematics

68. Describe the difference between weight and mass.
69. Explain how to use dimensional analysis to convert 200 pounds to kilograms.
70. Why do you think that countries using the metric system prefer the Celsius scale rather than the Fahrenheit scale?
71. Describe in words how to convert from Celsius to Fahrenheit.
72. Describe in words how to convert from Fahrenheit to Celsius.
73. If you decide to travel outside the United States, which one of the two temperature conversion formulas should you take? Explain your answer.

Critical Thinking Exercises

74. Which one of the following is true?
    a. A 4-pound object weighs more than a 2000-gram object.
    b. A 100-milligram object weighs more than a 2-ounce object.
    c. A 50-gram object weighs more than a 2-ounce object.
    d. A 10-pound object weighs more than a 4-kilogram object.
75. Which one of the following is true?
    a. Flour selling at 3¢ per gram is a better buy than flour selling at 55¢ per pound.
    b. The measures

       32,600 g,   32.1 kg,   4 lb,   36 oz

       are arranged in order, from greatest to least weight.
    c. If you are taking aspirin to relieve cold symptoms, a reasonable dose is 2 kilograms four times a day.
    d. A large dog weighs about 350 kilograms.
76. Start with the conversion formula from Fahrenheit to Celsius. Use algebra to obtain the conversion formula from Celsius to Fahrenheit.

Group Exercise

77. Present a group report on the current status of the metric system in the United States. At the present, does it appear that the United States will convert to the metric system? Who supports the conversion and who opposes it? Give examples of how our current system of weights and measures is a national embarrassment and an economic liability. What are the current obstacles to metric conversion?

CHAPTER SUMMARY, REVIEW, AND TEST

SUMMARY

9.1 Measuring Length; The Metric System

a. The result obtained from measuring length is called a linear measurement, stated in linear units.

b. Linear Units: The English System
   12 in. = 1 ft, 3 ft = 1 yd, 36 in. = 1 yd, 5280 ft = 1 mi

c. Dimensional Analysis
   Multiply the given expression by a unit fraction with the unit of measurement that needs to be introduced in the numerator and the unit of measurement that needs to be eliminated in the denominator.

d. Linear Units: The Metric System
   The basic unit is the meter (m), approximately 39 inches.
   km = 1000m, hm = 100m, dam = 10m, dm = 0.1m, cm = 0.01m, mm = 0.001m

e. Changing Linear Units Within the Metric System

   $$\times 10$$

   km hm dam m dm cm mm

   $$\div 10$$

f. English and Metric Equivalents
See Table 9.3 on page 432.

9.2 Measuring Area and Volume

a. The area measure of a plane region is the number of square units contained in the given region.

b. The volume measure of a three-dimensional figure is the number of cubic units contained in its interior.

c. Capacity refers to the amount of fluid that a three-dimensional object can hold. English units for capacity include pints, quarts, and gallons: 2 pt = 1 qt; 4 qt = 1 gal; one cubic yard has a capacity of about 200 gallons.

d. The basic unit for capacity in the metric system is the liter (L). One liter is about 1.06 quarts. Prefixes for the liter are the same as throughout the metric system. 1000 cubic centimeters = 1 liter.

9.3 Measuring Weight and Temperature

a. Weight: The English System

$$16 \text{ oz} = 1 \text{ lb}, 2000 \text{ lb} = 1 \text{T}$$

b. Units of Weight: The Metric System
The basic unit is the gram (g).
1000 grams (1 kg) ≈ 2.2 lb,
kg = 1000 g, hg = 100 g, dag = 10 g,
dg = 0.1 g, cg = 0.01 g, mg = 0.001 g

c. Changing Units of Weight within the Metric System

d. English and Metric Equivalents of Weight
See Table 9.8 on page 445.

c. Temperature Scales: Celsius to Fahrenheit

$$F = \frac{9}{5}C + 32$$

f. Temperature Scales: Fahrenheit to Celsius

$$C = \frac{5}{9}(F - 32)$$

REVIEW EXERCISES

9.1

In Exercises 1–4, use dimensional analysis to convert the quantity to the indicated units.

1. 69 in. to ft
2. 9 in. to yd
3. 21 ft to yd
4. 13,200 ft to mi

In Exercises 5–10, convert the given linear measurement to the metric unit indicated.

5. 22.8 m to cm
6. 7 dam to m
7. 19.2 hm to m
8. 144 cm to hm
9. 0.5 mm to m
10. 18 cm to mm

In Exercises 11–16, use the given English and metric equivalents, along with dimensional analysis, to convert the given measurement to the unit indicated. Where necessary, round answers to two decimal places.

11. 23 in. to cm
12. 19 cm to in.
13. 330 mi to km
14. 600 km to mi
15. 14 m to yd
16. 12 m to ft

1 in. = 2.54 cm
1 ft = 30 cm
1 yd = 0.9 m
1 mi = 1.6 km

17. Express 45 kilometers per hour in miles per hour.
18. Express 60 miles per hour in kilometers per hour.
19. Arrange from smallest to largest: 0.024 km, 2400 m, 24,000 cm.
20. If you jog six times around a track that is 800 meters long, how many kilometers have you covered?

9.2

21. Use the given figure to find its area in square units.

22. The population of California is 29,760,000, making it the U.S. state with the largest population. If the area of California is 155,973 square miles, find California's population density to the nearest tenth. Describe what this means.

23. If 1 acre = 0.4 hectare, use dimensional analysis to find the size of a property in acres measured at 7.2 hectares.

24. If 1 ft^2 = 0.09 m^2, convert 30 m^2 to ft^2.

25. If 1 mi^2 = 2.6 km^2, convert 12 mi^2 to km^2.

26. Which one of the following is a reasonable measure for the area of a flower garden in a person's yard?
a. 100 m^2 b. 0.4 ha c. 0.01 km^2

27. Use the given figure to find its volume in cubic units.

28. A swimming pool has a volume of 33,600 cubic feet. If 1 cubic foot has a capacity of about 7.48 gallons, how many gallons of water does the pool hold?

29. An aquarium has a volume of 76,000 cubic centimeters. How many liters of water does the aquarium hold?

30. The capacity of a one-quart container of juice is about:
a. 0.1 kL   b. 0.5 L   c. 1 L   d. 1 mL

31. If there are 3 feet in a yard, explain why there are not 3 square feet in a square yard. If helpful, illustrate your explanation with a diagram.

32. Explain why the area of California could not be measured in cubic miles.

9.3

In Exercises 33–36, use Figure 9.12 on page 444 to convert the given unit of weight to the unit indicated.

33. 12.4 dg to mg   34. 12 g to cg

35. 0.012 mg to g   36. 450 mg to kg

37. If 1 lb = 0.45 kg, convert 210 pounds to kilograms.

38. If 1 oz = 28 g, convert 392 grams to ounces.

39. If you are interested in your weight in the metric system, would it be best to report it in milligrams, grams, or kilograms? Explain why the unit you selected would be most appropriate. Explain why the other two units are not the best choice for reporting your weight.

40. If 16 oz = 1 lb, use dimensional analysis to convert 36 ounces to pounds.

In Exercises 41–42, select the best estimate for the weight of the given item.

41. A dollar bill: a. 1 g   b. 10 g   c. 1 kg   d. 4 kg

42. A hamburger: a. 3 kg   b. 1 kg   c. 200 g   d. 5 g

In Exercises 43–47, convert the given Celsius temperature to its equivalent temperature on the Fahrenheit scale.

43. 15°C   44. 100°C   45. 5°C

46. 0°C   47. −25°C

In Exercises 48–53, convert the given Fahrenheit temperature to its equivalent temperature on the Celsius scale.

48. 59°F   49. 41°F   50. 212°F

51. 98.6°F   52. 0°F   53. 14°F

54. Is a decrease of 15° Celsius more or less than a decrease of 15° Fahrenheit? Explain your answer.

 Group Exercise

55. If you could select any place in the world, where would you like to live? Look up the population and area of your ideal place, and compute its population density. Group members should share both favorite places to live and population densities. What trend, if any, does the group observe?

CHAPTER 9 TEST

1. Change 807 mm to hm.

2. If 1 inch = 2.54 centimeters, use dimensional analysis to change 635 centimeters to inches.

3. If you jog eight times around a track that is 600 meters long, how many kilometers have you covered?

In Exercises 4–6, write the most reasonable metric unit for length in each blank. Select from mm, cm, m, and km.

4. A human thumb is 20 _____ wide.

5. The height of the table is 45 _____ .

6. The towns are 60 _____ apart.

7. If 1 mile = 1.6 kilometers, express 80 miles per hour in kilometers per hour.

8. How many times greater is a square yard than a square foot?

9. Spain has a population of 39,133,966 and an area of 195,365 square miles. Find Spain's population density to the nearest tenth. Describe what this means.

10. If 1 acre = 0.4 hectare, use dimensional analysis to find the area of a property measured at 18 hectares.

11. The area of a dollar bill is:
a. 10 cm^2 b. 100 cm^2 c. 1000 cm^2 d. 1 m^2

12. If there are 10 decimeters in a meter, explain why there are not 10 cubic decimeters in a cubic meter. How many times greater is a cubic meter than a cubic decimeter?

13. A swimming pool has a volume of 10,000 cubic feet. If 1 cubic foot has a capacity of about 7.48 gallons, how many gallons of water does the pool hold?

14. The capacity of a pail used to wash floors is about:
a. 3 L   b. 12 L   c. 80 L   d. 2 kL

15. Change 137 g to kg.

16. If 1 lb = 0.45 kg, convert 90 pounds to kilograms.

In Exercises 17–18, write the most reasonable metric unit for weight in each blank. Select from mg, g, and kg.

17. My suitcase weighs 20 _____ .

18. I took a 350 _____ aspirin.

19. Convert 30°C to Fahrenheit.

20. Convert 176°F to Celsius.

21. Comfortable room temperature is about:
a. 70°C   b. 50°C   c. 30°C   d. 20°C

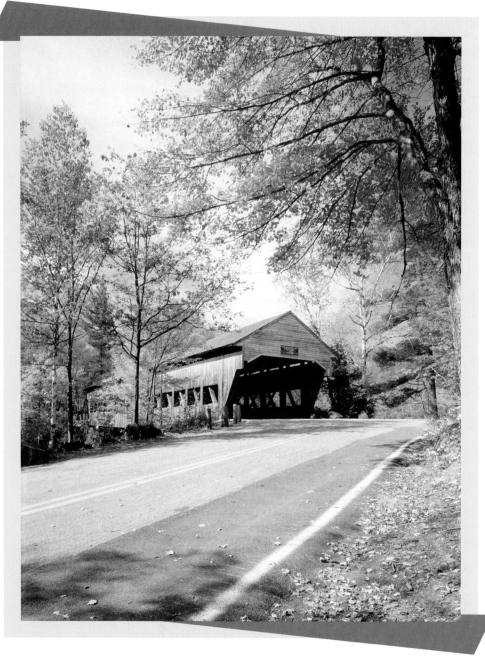

On a summer job, you are delivering three large cylindrical tanks filled with water to a remote country house. Your truck weighs 12 tons and you are worried about the extra weight of the tanks on these poorly paved, winding roads. Up ahead you see a warning sign at the entrance to a wobbly looking small bridge: Weight Not to Exceed 20 Tons. Knowing that making an error would not be a good idea, you pull over to compute the weight of your truck. Your boss told you every cubic inch of water that you are carrying weighs about 0.036 pound. You need to compute the volume of the tanks and then determine the combined weight of the tanks and your truck. What else do you need to know to decide whether to cross the bridge or go home without pay?

10 Geometry

Geometry is about the space you live in and the shapes that surround you. You're even made of it! The human lung consists of nearly 300 spherical air sacs, geometrically designed to provide the greatest surface area within the limited volume of our bodies. Viewed in this way, geometry becomes an intimate experience.

For thousands of years, people have studied geometry in some form in order to obtain a better understanding of the world in which they lived. A study of the shape of your world will provide you with many practical applications and perhaps help to increase your appreciation of its beauty.

SECTION 10.1 Points, Lines, Planes, and Angles

Objectives

1. Understand points, lines, and planes as the basis of geometry.
2. Solve problems involving angle measures.
3. Solve problems involving angles formed by parallel lines and transversals.

1 Understand points, lines, and planes as the basis of geometry.

Point *A*

Line *AB*

P

Plane *P*

Figure 10.1 Representing a point, a line, and a plane

The word *geometry* means *earth measure*. Because it involves the mathematics of shapes, geometry connects mathematics to art and architecture. It also has many practical applications. You can use geometry at home when you buy a carpet, build a fence, tile a floor, or determine whether a piece of furniture will fit through your doorway. In this chapter, we look at the shapes that surround us and their applications.

Points, Lines, and Planes

Points, lines, and planes make up the basis of all geometry. Stars in the night sky look like points of light. Long stretches of overhead power lines that appear to extend endlessly look like lines. The top of a flat table resembles part of a plane. However, stars, power lines, and table tops only approximate points, lines, and planes. Points, lines, and planes do not exist in the physical world. Representations of these forms are shown in Figure 10.1. A **point**, represented as a small dot, has no length, width, or thickness. No object in the real world has zero size. A **line**, connecting two points along the shortest possible path, has no thickness and extends infinitely in both directions. However, no familiar everyday object is infinite in length. A **plane** is a flat surface with no thickness and no boundaries. This page resembles a plane, although it does not extend indefinitely and it does have thickness.

A line may be named using any two of its points. In Figure 10.1, line *AB* is symbolized $\overleftrightarrow{AB}$ or $\overleftrightarrow{BA}$. In practical applications, you often use **line segments**, portions of lines between two points, including the **endpoints**. For example, suppose you are planning a garden in the backyard. You put stakes at each corner of the area you plan to use. Then you tie string between two of the stakes. The string between the two stakes is analogous to a line segment. The stakes are analogous to the endpoints of a line segment. If one stake is named *A* and the other *B*, the line segment approximated by the stakes and the string is line segment *AB*. Line segment *AB* is symbolized $\overline{AB}$ or $\overline{BA}$.

Help! I'm trapped in a plane! Why trapped? As a three-dimensional creature, I can move north or south, east or west, and up or down (or any combination of these three options). My space is *three dimensional* because I can move in *three independent directions*. But if I am trapped in a plane, the up/down option is no longer available. The plane is *two dimensional* because I can now move in only *two independent directions*. The **dimension** of any object is the number of independent directions in which you could move if you "lived" in the object. **Plane geometry** focuses on two-dimensional objects and **solid geometry** on three-dimensional objects. Are there objects that allow even more movement options than the three available to us in our surrounding world? We invite you to read *Flatland* and explore Group Exercise 47 on page 514.

Two Dimensions

Three Dimensions

Four Dimensions ?!

Figure 10.2 Clock with hands forming an angle

Angles

The hour hand of a clock moves from 12 to 2 o'clock. The hour hand suggests a **ray**, a part of a line that has only one endpoint and extends forever in the opposite direction. An *angle* is formed as the ray in Figure 10.2 rotates from 12 to 2.

An **angle**, symbolized ∡, is made up of two rays that have a common endpoint. Figure 10.3 shows an angle. The common endpoint, *B* in the figure, is called the **vertex** of the angle. The two rays that form the angle are called its **sides**. The four ways of naming the angle are shown to the right of Figure 10.3.

Figure 10.3 An angle: two rays with a common endpoint

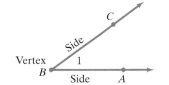

Naming the Angle

∡ 1 ∡ *B* ∡ *ABC* ∡ *CBA*

Vertex alone | Vertex letter in the middle

EXAMPLE 1   Identifying Angle Parts and Naming an Angle

Consider the angle in Figure 10.4.

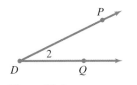

Figure 10.4

a. Name the vertex of the angle.

b. Name the sides of the angle.

c. Name the angle in four different ways.

2 Solve problems involving angle measures.

Solution

a. The vertex, the endpoint common to the two sides, is the point *D*.

b. The sides of the angle are the rays *DQ* and *DP*.

c. The angle can be named ∡ 2, ∡ *D*, ∡ *QDP*, or ∡ *PDQ*.

One way to measure angles is in **degrees**, symbolized by a small, raised circle °. Think of the hour hand of a clock. From 12 noon to 12 midnight, the hour hand moves around in a complete circle. By definition, the ray has rotated through 360 degrees, or 360°. Using 360° as the amount of rotation of a ray back onto itself, a degree, 1°, is $\frac{1}{360}$ of a complete rotation.

A Complete 360° Rotation

EXAMPLE 2   Using Degree Measure

The hour hand of a clock moves from 12 to 2 o'clock (see Figure 10.2). Through how many degrees does it move?

Solution   We know that one complete rotation is 360°. Moving from 12 to 2 o'clock is $\frac{2}{12}$, or $\frac{1}{6}$, of a complete rotation. Thus, the hour hand moves

$$\frac{1}{6} \times 360° = \frac{360°}{6} = 60°$$

in going from 12 to 2 o'clock.

If the hour hand moves from 12 to 3, it has moved through one-quarter of a complete rotation, or $\frac{1}{4} \times 360° = 90°$. An angle that measures 90° is called a **right angle**. If the hour hand moves from 12 to 6, it has moved halfway around a complete rotation, or $\frac{1}{2} \times 360° = 180°$. An angle that measures 180° is called a **straight angle**. The two rays in a straight angle form a straight line.

Figure 10.5 shows angles classified by their degree measurement. An **acute angle** measures less than 90°; a **right angle** measures 90°; an **obtuse angle** measures more than 90°, but less than 180°; a **straight angle** measures 180°. Examine the right angle—do you see a small square at the vertex? This symbol is used to indicate a right angle.

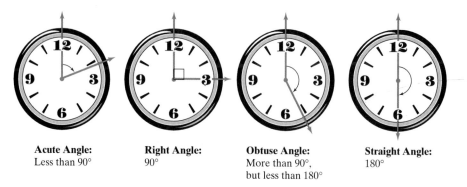

Acute Angle:
Less than 90°

Right Angle:
90°

Obtuse Angle:
More than 90°,
but less than 180°

Straight Angle:
180°

Figure 10.5 Classifying angles by their degree measurement

Figure 10.6 illustrates a **protractor**, used for finding the degree measure of an angle. As shown in the figure, we measure an angle by placing the center point of the protractor on the vertex of the angle and the straight side of the protractor along one side of the angle. The measure of $\angle ABC$ is then read as 50°. Observe that the measure is not 130° because the angle is obviously less than 90°. We indicate the angle's measure by writing

$$m\angle ABC = 50°$$

read "the measure of angle ABC is 50°."

Figure 10.6 Using a protractor to measure an angle: $m\angle ABC = 50°$

Two angles whose measures have a sum of 90° are called **complementary angles**. For example, angles measuring 70° and 20° are complementary angles because $70° + 20° = 90°$. For angles such as those measuring 70° and 20°, each angle is a **complement** of the other: the 70° angle is the complement of the 20° angle and the 20° angle is the complement of the 70° angle. The measure of the complement can be found by subtracting the angle's measure from 90°. For example, we can find the complement of a 25° angle by subtracting 25° from 90°: $90° - 25° = 65°$. Thus, an angle measuring 65° is the complement of one measuring 25°.

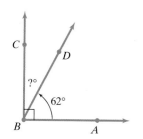

Figure 10.7

EXAMPLE 3   Angle Measures and Complements

Use Figure 10.7 to find $m\sphericalangle DBC$.

Solution   The measure of $\sphericalangle DBC$ is not yet known. It is shown as ?° in Figure 10.7. The acute angles, $\sphericalangle ABD$, which measures 62°, and $\sphericalangle DBC$, form a right angle, indicated by the square at the vertex. This means that the measures of the acute angles add up to 90°. Thus, $\sphericalangle DBC$ is the complement of the angle measuring 62°. The measure of $\sphericalangle DBC$ is found by subtracting 62° from 90°:

$$m\sphericalangle DBC = 90° - 62° = 28°$$

Two angles whose measures have a sum of 180° are called **supplementary angles**. For example, angles measuring 110° and 70° are supplementary angles because 110° + 70° = 180°. For angles such as those measuring 110° and 70°, each angle is a **supplement** of the other: the 110° angle is the supplement of the 70° angle, and the 70° angle is the supplement of the 110° angle. The measure of the supplement can be found by subtracting the angle's measure from 180°. For example, we can find the supplement of a 25° angle by subtracting 25° from 180°: 180° − 25° = 155°. Thus, an angle measuring 155° is the supplement of one measuring 25°.

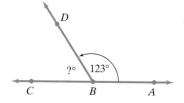

Figure 10.8

EXAMPLE 4   Angle Measures and Supplements

Use Figure 10.8 to find $m\sphericalangle DBC$.

Solution   The measure of $\sphericalangle DBC$ is not yet known. It is shown as ?° in Figure 10.8. The angles $\sphericalangle ABD$ and $\sphericalangle DBC$ form a straight angle. Their measures add up to 180°. Thus, $\sphericalangle DBC$ is the supplement of $\sphericalangle ABD$, whose measure is given as 123°. The measure of $\sphericalangle DBC$ is found by subtracting 123° from 180°:

$$m\sphericalangle DBC = 180° - 123° = 57°$$

Figure 10.9

Figure 10.9 illustrates a highway sign that warns of a railroad crossing. When two lines intersect, the opposite angles formed are called **vertical angles**. In Figure 10.10, there are two pairs of vertical angles. Angles 1 and 3 are vertical angles. Angles 2 and 4 are also vertical angles. **Vertical angles have the same measure**. For example, the measure of angle 1 = the measure of angle 3, and the measure of angle 2 = the measure of angle 4. Re-examine Figure 10.10. Note that angles with equal measure are denoted by the same number of tick marks. For example, angles 1 and 3 have the same measure and both have one tick mark.

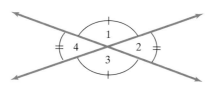

Figure 10.10 Vertical angles:
$m\sphericalangle 1 = m\sphericalangle 3$ and $m\sphericalangle 4 = m\sphericalangle 2$

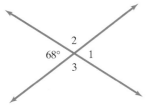

Figure 10.11

EXAMPLE 5   Using Vertical Angles

Figure 10.11 shows that the angle on the left measures 68°. Find the measures of the other three angles.

Solution   Angle 1 and the angle measuring 68° are vertical angles. Because vertical angles have the same measure,

$$m\angle 1 = 68°.$$

Angle 2 and the angle measuring 68° form a straight angle and are supplementary. Because their measures add up to 180°,

$$m\angle 2 = 180° - 68° = 112°.$$

Angle 2 and angle 3 are also vertical angles, so they have the same measure. Because the measure of angle 2 is 112°, then

$$m\angle 3 = 112°.$$

3 Solve problems involving angles formed by parallel lines and transversals.

Parallel Lines

Figure 10.12 shows a diagram of Bush Street, Sutter Street, and Broadway. The diagram indicates that Bush Street and Sutter Street each make an angle of 90° with Broadway. When two lines meet to form a right angle, they are called **perpendicular lines**. Thus, Bush Street and Sutter Street are both perpendicular to Broadway. The edges of this page meet at right angles and are perpendicular to each other.

In Figure 10.12, Bush Street and Sutter Street never cross and are said to be *parallel*. Two lines in the same plane that do not intersect are called **parallel lines**.

In Figure 10.12, we see that Broadway intersects the parallel streets, Bush and Sutter, at two points. A line that crosses two or more other lines is called a **transversal**. If two lines are intersected by a transversal, special names are used for each pair of angles formed. These names are summarized in Table 10.1.

Figure 10.12 Perpendicular lines and parallel lines are shown in this diagram

Table 10.1   Names of Angle Pairs Formed by a Transversal Crossing Two Lines

Name	Description	Sketch	Angle Pairs Described
Alternate interior angles	Interior angles that do not have a common vertex on alternate sides of the transversal		$\angle 3$ and $\angle 6$ $\angle 4$ and $\angle 5$
Alternate exterior angles	Exterior angles that do not have a common vertex on alternate sides of the transversal		$\angle 1$ and $\angle 8$ $\angle 2$ and $\angle 7$
Corresponding angles	One interior and one exterior angle on the same side of the transversal		$\angle 1$ and $\angle 5$ $\angle 2$ and $\angle 6$ $\angle 3$ and $\angle 7$ $\angle 4$ and $\angle 8$

Study Tip

Corresponding angles are the angles that appear to be in the same relative position in each group of four angles.

When two parallel lines are cut by a transversal, the following relationships are true.

Parallel Lines and Angle Pairs

If parallel lines are cut by a transversal,

- alternate interior angles have the same measure,
- alternate exterior angles have the same measure, and
- corresponding angles have the same measure.

Conversely, if an alternate interior angle pair or an alternate exterior angle pair or a pair of corresponding angles has the same measure, then the lines are parallel.

EXAMPLE 6   Finding Angle Measures When Parallel Lines are Intersected by a Transversal

In Figure 10.13, two parallel lines are intersected by a transversal. One of the angles ($\angle 8$) has a measure of 35°. Find the measure of each of the other seven angles.

Solution   Look carefully at Figure 10.13 as you read each line in this solution.

$m\angle 1 = 35°$ $\angle 8$ and $\angle 1$ are vertical angles and vertical angles have the same measure.

$m\angle 6 = 180° - 35° = 145°$ $\angle 8$ and $\angle 6$ are supplementary.

$m\angle 7 = 145°$ $\angle 6$ and $\angle 7$ are vertical angles, so they have the same measure.

$m\angle 2 = 35°$ $\angle 8$ and $\angle 2$ are alternate interior angles, so they have the same measure.

$m\angle 3 = 145°$ $\angle 7$ and $\angle 3$ are alternate interior angles. Thus, they have the same measure.

$m\angle 5 = 35°$ $\angle 8$ and $\angle 5$ are corresponding angles. Thus, they have the same measure.

$m\angle 4 = 180° - 35° = 145°$ $\angle 4$ and $\angle 5$ are supplementary.

Figure 10.13

Study Tip

There is more than one way to solve Example 6. For example, once you know that $m\angle 2 = 35°$, $m\angle 5$ is also 35° because $\angle 2$ and $\angle 5$ are vertical angles.

Exercise Set 10.1

  Practice Exercises

In Exercises 1–2:   a. Name the vertex of the angle.
b. Name the sides of the angle.   c. Name the angle in three
different ways.

1.

2.

3. The hour hand of a clock moves from 12 to 1 o'clock. Through how many degrees does it move?

4. The hour hand of a clock moves from 12 to 4 o'clock. Through how many degrees does it move?

5. The hour hand of a clock moves from 1 to 4 o'clock. Through how many degrees does it move?

6. The hour hand of a clock moves from 1 to 7 o'clock. Through how many degrees does it move?

In Exercises 7–8, use the protractor to find the measure of the angle. Then indicate if the angle is acute, right, obtuse, or straight.

7.

8.

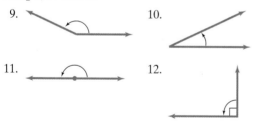

In Exercises 9–12, classify the angle as acute, right, straight, or obtuse.

9.   10.

11.   12.

In Exercises 13–16, find the measure of the angle in which ?° appears.

13.   14.

15.

16.

In Exercises 17–22, find the measure of the complement of each angle.

17. 48°   18. 52°   19. 89°

20. 1°   21. 37.4°   22. $15\frac{1}{3}°$

In Exercises 23–30, find the measure of the supplement of each angle.

23. 111°   24. 95°   25. 16°

26. 9°   27. 90°   28. 179°

29. $93\frac{1}{4}°$ 30. 153.8°

In Exercises 31–34, find the measures of angles 1, 2, and 3.

31.

32.

33.   34.

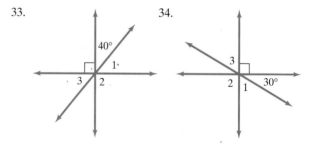

The figures for Exercises 35–36 show two parallel lines intersected by a transversal. One of the angle measures is given. Find the measure of each of the other seven angles.

35.   36.

Application Exercises

For Exercises 37–42, look around the room you are in.

37. Describe a feature of the room that approximates a point.

38. Describe a feature of the room that approximates a line segment.

39. Describe a feature of the room that approximates a plane.

40. Describe a feature of the room that approximates perpendicular lines.

41. Describe a feature of the room that approximates parallel lines.

42. Describe a feature of the room in which an angle can be found. Classify the angle by its size.

 Writing in Mathematics

43. Describe the difference between a line and a line segment.

44. Describe the difference between a line and a ray.

45. What is an angle?

46. What determines the size of an angle?

47. What are complementary angles? Describe how to find the measure of an angle's complement.

48. What are supplementary angles? Describe how to find the measure of an angle's supplement.

49. Describe the difference between perpendicular and parallel lines.

50. If two lines are intersected by a transversal, describe the location of the alternate interior angles, the alternate exterior angles, and the corresponding angles.

51. Describe everyday objects that approximate points, lines, and planes.

52. If a transversal is perpendicular to one of two parallel lines, must it be perpendicular to the other parallel line as well? Explain your answer.

 Critical Thinking Exercises

53. Use the figure shown to find the measure of angle 1.

54. Use the figure shown to select a pair of complementary angles from the following choices.
    a. ∠1 and ∠4
    b. ∠3 and ∠6
    c. ∠2 and ∠5
    d. ∠1 and ∠5

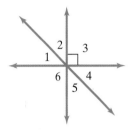

55. If $m\angle AGB = m\angle BGC$, and $m\angle CGD = m\angle DGE$, find $m\angle BGD$.

 Group Exercises

56. Group members should find pictures of interesting shapes in architecture. Bring in a picture of the building that you find interesting so that you can share it with other group members. In each case, the group should discuss what they observe about the angles that are formed in the geometric shape of the building.

57. Have you ever noticed that we use the vocabulary of angles in everyday speech? Here is an example:

    My opinion about the metric system took a 180° turn.

    Group members should explain what this means. Then members should give examples of the vocabulary of angles in everyday use. Describe what the everyday meaning has to do with angles and their measures. Can the group give examples in which the vocabulary of angles takes on a different meaning in everyday speech?

SECTION 10.2   *Triangles*

Objectives

1. Solve problems involving angle relationships in triangles.
2. Solve problems involving similar triangles.
3. Solve problems using the Pythagorean theorem.

Many natural forms can be fit inside geometric figures.

In Chapter 1, we defined deductive reasoning as the process of proving a specific conclusion from one or more general statements. A conclusion that is proved true by deductive reasoning is called a **theorem**. The Greek mathematician Euclid, who lived more than 2000 years ago, used deductive reasoning. In his 13-volume book, the *Elements*, Euclid proved over 465 theorems about geometric figures. Euclid's work established deductive reasoning as a fundamental tool of mathematics.

A **triangle** is a geometric figure that has three sides, all of which lie on a flat surface or plane. If you start at any point along the triangle and trace along the entire figure exactly once, you will end at the same point at which you started. Because the beginning point and ending point are the same, the triangle is called a **closed** geometric figure. Portions of the fly shown in the margin fit inside triangles of various sizes and shapes. Euclid used parallel lines to prove one of the most important properties in the geometry of triangles: The sum of the measures of the three angles of any triangle is 180°. Here is how he did it. He began with the following general statement.

Euclid's Assumption about Parallel Lines

Given a line and a point not on the line, one and only one line can be drawn through the given point parallel to the given line.

In Figure 10.14, triangle *ABC* represents any triangle. Using the general assumption given above, we draw a line through point *B* parallel to line *AC*.

Figure 10.14

Because the lines are parallel, alternate interior angles have the same measure.

$$m\angle 1 = m\angle 2 \quad \text{and} \quad m\angle 3 = m\angle 4$$

Also observe that angles 2, 5, and 4 form a straight angle.

$$m\angle 2 + m\angle 5 + m\angle 4 = 180°$$

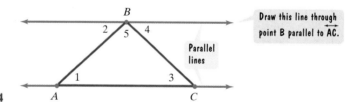

Because $m\angle 1 = m\angle 2$, replace $m\angle 2$ with $m\angle 1$.

Because $m\angle 3 = m\angle 4$, replace $m\angle 4$ with $m\angle 3$.

$$m\angle 1 + m\angle 5 + m\angle 3 = 180°$$

Because $\measuredangle 1$, $\measuredangle 5$, and $\measuredangle 4$ are the three angles of the triangle, this last equation shows that the measures of the triangle's three angles have a 180° sum.

Solve problems involving angle relationships in triangles.

The Angles of a Triangle

The sum of the measures of the three angles of any triangle is 180°.

EXAMPLE 1   Using Angle Relationships in Triangles

Find the measure of angle A for triangle ABC in Figure 10.15.

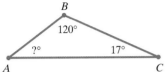

Figure 10.15

Solution   Because $m\measuredangle A + m\measuredangle B + m\measuredangle C = 180°$, we obtain

$$m\measuredangle A + 120° + 17° = 180°$$
$$m\measuredangle A + 137° = 180°$$
$$m\measuredangle A = 180° - 137° = 43°$$

EXAMPLE 2   Using Angle Relationships in Triangles

Find the measures of angles 1 through 5 in Figure 10.16.

Figure 10.16

Solution   Because $\measuredangle 1$ is supplementary to the right angle, $m\measuredangle 1 = 90°$.
$m\measuredangle 2$ can be found using the fact that the sum of the measures of the angles of a triangle is 180°.

$$m\measuredangle 1 + m\measuredangle 2 + 43° = 180°$$
$$90° + m\measuredangle 2 + 43° = 180°$$
$$m\measuredangle 2 + 133° = 180°$$
$$m\measuredangle 2 = 180° - 133° = 47°$$

$m\measuredangle 3$ can be found using the fact that vertical angles have equal measures. $m\measuredangle 3 = m\measuredangle 2$. Thus, $m\measuredangle 3 = 47°$.
$m\measuredangle 4$ can be found using the fact that the sum of the measures of the angles of a triangle is 180°. Refer to the triangle at the top of Figure 10.16.

$$m\measuredangle 3 + m\measuredangle 4 + 60° = 180°$$
$$47° + m\measuredangle 4 + 60° = 180°$$
$$m\measuredangle 4 + 107° = 180°$$
$$m\measuredangle 4 = 180° - 107° = 73°$$

Finally, we can find $m\measuredangle 5$ by observing that angles 4 and 5 form a straight angle.

$$m\measuredangle 4 + m\measuredangle 5 = 180°$$
$$73° + m\measuredangle 5 = 180°$$
$$m\measuredangle 5 = 180° - 73° = 107°$$

2 Solve problems involving similar triangles.

Pedestrian Crossing

Similar Triangles

Shown in the margin is an international road sign. This sign is shaped just like the actual sign, although its size is smaller. Figures that have the same shape, but not the same size, are used in **scale drawings**. A scale drawing always pictures the exact shape of the object that the drawing represents. Architects, engineers, landscape gardeners, and interior decorators use scale drawings in planning their work.

Figures that have the same shape, but not necessarily the same size, are called **similar figures**. In Figure 10.17, triangles *ABC* and *DEF* are similar. Angles *A* and *D* measure the same number of degrees and are called **corresponding angles**. Angles *C* and *F* are corresponding angles, as are angles *B* and *E*. Angles with the same number of tick marks in Figure 10.17 are the corresponding angles.

Figure 10.17

The sides opposite the corresponding angles are called **corresponding sides**. Thus, $\overline{CB}$ and $\overline{FE}$ are corresponding sides. $\overline{AB}$ and $\overline{DE}$ are also corresponding sides, as are $\overline{AC}$ and $\overline{DF}$. Corresponding angles measure the same number of degrees, but corresponding sides may or may not be the same length. For the triangles in Figure 10.17, each side in the smaller triangle is half the length of the corresponding side in the larger triangle.

The triangles in Figure 10.17 illustrate what it means to be similar triangles. Corresponding angles have the same measure and the ratios of the lengths of the corresponding sides are equal.

$$\frac{\text{length of } \overline{AC}}{\text{length of } \overline{DF}} = \frac{6 \text{ in.}}{3 \text{ in.}} = \frac{2}{1}$$

$$\frac{\text{length of } \overline{CB}}{\text{length of } \overline{FE}} = \frac{8 \text{ in.}}{4 \text{ in.}} = \frac{2}{1}$$

$$\frac{\text{length of } \overline{AB}}{\text{length of } \overline{DE}} = \frac{4 \text{ in.}}{2 \text{ in.}} = \frac{2}{1}$$

In similar triangles, the lengths of the corresponding sides are proportional.

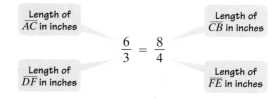

Length of $\overline{AC}$ in inches   Length of $\overline{CB}$ in inches

$$\frac{6}{3} = \frac{8}{4}$$

Length of $\overline{DF}$ in inches   Length of $\overline{FE}$ in inches

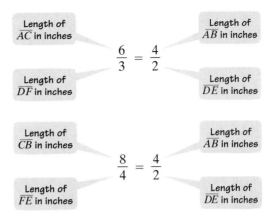

EXAMPLE 3   Using Similar Triangles

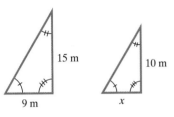

Figure 10.18

The triangles in Figure 10.18 are similar. Find the length of the side marked with an x.

Solution   The sides that measure 15 meters and 10 meters are corresponding sides because they are opposite the equal corresponding angles marked with one tick mark. The ratio of the lengths of these sides can be written as a fraction in lowest terms.

$$\frac{15 \text{ m}}{10 \text{ m}} = \frac{15}{10} = \frac{3}{2}$$

The sides that measure 9 meters and x meters are also corresponding sides because they are opposite the equal corresponding angles marked with two tick marks. The ratio of the lengths of these sides can be written as a fraction.

$$\frac{9 \text{ m}}{x \text{ m}} = \frac{9}{x}$$

The ratios of the lengths of these corresponding sides are equal, so we set the two fractions from above equal to one another.

$$\frac{3}{2} = \frac{9}{x}$$

This proportion states that the ratios $\frac{3}{2}$ and $\frac{9}{x}$ are equal. The lengths of the corresponding sides of similar triangles are proportional. We solve this equation for x by applying the cross products principle for proportions that we discussed in Section 6.4.

$$3x = 2 \cdot 9$$
$$3x = 18$$

Divide both sides by 3.

$$\frac{3x}{3} = \frac{18}{3}$$
$$x = 6$$

The length of the side marked with an x is 6 meters.

How can we quickly determine if two triangles are similar? If the measures of two angles of one triangle are equal to those of two angles of a second triangle, then the two triangles are similar. If the triangles are similar, then their corresponding sides are proportional.

EXAMPLE 4   Problem Solving Using Similar Triangles

A man who is 6 feet tall is standing 10 feet from the base of a lamppost (see Figure 10.19). The man's shadow has a length of 4 feet. How tall is the lamppost?

Solution   The drawing in Figure 10.20 makes the similarity of the triangles easier to see. The large triangle with the lamppost on the left and the small triangle with the man on the left both contain 90° angles. They also share an angle. Thus, two angles of the large triangle are equal in measure to two angles of the small triangle. This means that the triangles are similar and their corresponding sides are proportional. We begin by letting x represent the height of the lamppost, in feet. Because corresponding sides of similar triangles are proportional,

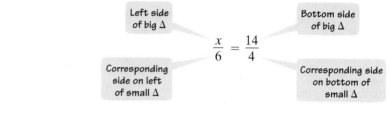

$$\frac{x}{6} = \frac{14}{4}$$

We solve for x by applying the cross products principle.

$$4x = 6 \cdot 14$$

$$4x = 84$$

$$\frac{4x}{4} = \frac{84}{4} \qquad \text{Divide both sides by 4.}$$

$$x = 21$$

The lamppost is 21 feet tall.

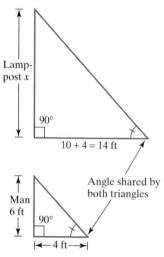

Figure 10.19

Figure 10.20

3 Solve problems using the Pythagorean theorem.

The Pythagorean Theorem

The ancient Greek philosopher and mathematician Pythagoras (approximately 582–500 B.C.) founded a school whose motto was "All is number." Pythagoras is best remembered for his work with the **right triangle**, a triangle with one angle measuring 90°. The side opposite the 90° angle is called the **hypotenuse**. The other sides are called **legs**. Pythagoras found that if he constructed squares on each of the legs, as well as a larger square on the hypotenuse, the sum of the areas of the smaller squares is equal to the area of the larger square. This is illustrated in Figure 10.21.

This relationship is usually stated in terms of the lengths of the three sides of a right triangle and is called the **Pythagorean theorem**.

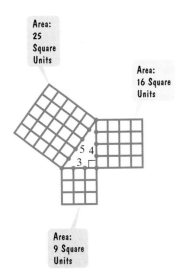

Figure 10.21 The area of the large square equals the sum of the areas of the smaller squares.

The Pythagorean Theorem

The sum of the squares of the lengths of the legs of a right triangle equals the square of the length of the hypotenuse.

If the legs have lengths a and b, and the hypotenuse has length c, then

$$a^2 + b^2 = c^2.$$

EXAMPLE 5   Using the Pythagorean Theorem

Find the length of the hypotenuse c in the right triangle shown in Figure 10.22.

Solution   Let $a = 9$ and $b = 12$. Substituting these values into $c^2 = a^2 + b^2$ enables us to solve for c.

$$c^2 = a^2 + b^2 \qquad \text{Use the symbolic statement of the Pythagorean theorem.}$$
$$c^2 = 9^2 + 12^2 \qquad \text{Let } a = 9 \text{ and } b = 12.$$
$$c^2 = 81 + 144$$
$$c^2 = 225$$
$$c = \sqrt{225} = 15 \qquad \text{Solve for } c \text{ by taking the square root of 225.}$$

The length of the hypotenuse is 15 feet.

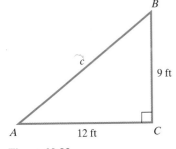

Figure 10.22

EXAMPLE 6   Using the Pythagorean Theorem

In a 25-inch television set, the length of the screen's diagonal is 25 inches. If the screen's height is 15 inches, what is its width?

Solution   Figure 10.23 shows a right triangle that is formed by the height, width, and diagonal. We can find w, the screen's width, using the Pythagorean theorem.

(Leg)^2	plus	(Leg)^2	equals	(Hypotenuse)^2	
w^2	$+$	15^2	$=$	25^2	This is the equation resulting from the Pythagorean theorem.

$$w^2 + 225 = 625 \qquad \text{Square 15 and 25.}$$
$$w^2 = 400 \qquad \text{Subtract 225 from both sides.}$$

$$w = \sqrt{400} \qquad \text{Take the square root of 400.}$$

$$w = 20 \qquad \text{Simplify.}$$

Figure 10.23 A right triangle is formed by the television's height, width, and diagonal.

The screen's width is 20 inches.

Congruent Antiforms

These portraits have the same shape *and the same size* and are called **congruent figures**. However, the colors in the identical corresponding parts would neutralize each other if blended. These images suggest the theory that every form has a congruent antiform; the pair of forms would annihilate each other if they met. So, if you come across a visitor from outer space who looks just like you, be careful before shaking your congruent hands!

Exercise Set 10.2

 Practice Exercises

In Exercises 1–4, find the measure of angle A for the triangle shown.

1.

2.

3.

4.

In Exercises 5–6, find the measures of angles 1 through 5 in the figure shown.

5.

6.
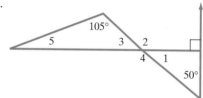

In Exercises 7–10, name the corresponding angles and the corresponding sides in each pair of similar triangles.

7.

8.

9.

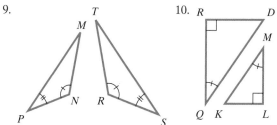

10.

In Exercises 17–24, use the Pythagorean theorem to find the missing length in each right triangle. Use your calculator to find square roots, rounding, if necessary, to the nearest tenth.

17.

18.

In Exercises 11–16, use similar triangles and the fact that corresponding sides are proportional to find the length of the side marked with an x.

11.

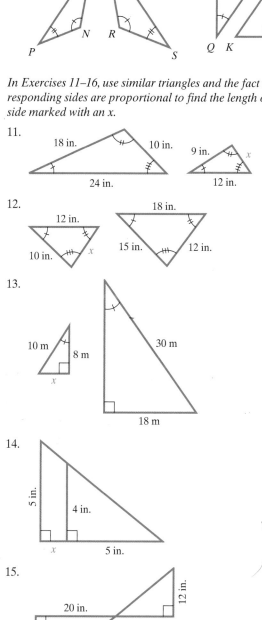

19.

20.

12.

13.

21.

22.

14.

23.

24.

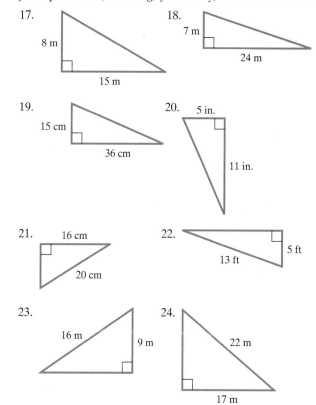

⭐ **Application Exercises**

25. A surveyor measured a triangular plot of ground, measuring the three angles as 46.1°, 58.3°, and 75.9°. Are these measurements correct? If not, how much of an error is there?

Use similar triangles to solve Exercises 26–27.

26. A tree casts a shadow 12 feet long. At the same time, a vertical rod 8 feet high casts a shadow of 6 feet long. How tall is the tree?

15.

16.

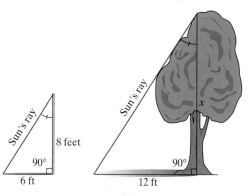

27. Find the height of the lookout tower using the figure that lines up the top of the tower with the top of a stick that is 2 yards long.

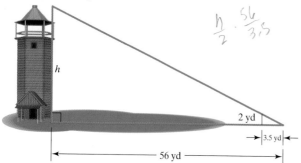

$\dfrac{h}{2} \cdot \dfrac{56}{3.5}$

h

2 yd

3.5 yd

56 yd

Use the Pythagorean theorem to solve Exercises 28–32.

28. Find the length of the ladder.

?

8 ft

10 ft

29. How high is the airplane above the ground?

1000 yd

?

800 yd

30. If you drive 12 miles north, then make a right turn and drive 9 miles east, how far are you, in a straight line, from your starting point?

31. An 8-foot tree is to be supported by two wires that extend from the top of the tree to a point on the ground located 15 feet from the base of the tree. Find the total length of the two support wires.

32. A baseball diamond is actually a square with 90-foot sides. What is the distance from home plate to second base?

 Writing in Mathematics

33. If the measures of two angles of a triangle are known, explain how to find the measure of the third angle.

34. Can a triangle contain two right angles? Explain your answer.

35. What general assumption did Euclid make about a point and a line in order to prove that the sum of the measures of the angles of a triangle is 180°?

36. What are similar triangles?

37. If the ratio of the corresponding sides of two similar triangles is 1 to 1 $\left(\frac{1}{1}\right)$, what must be true about the triangles?

38. What are corresponding angles in similar triangles?

39. Describe how to identify the corresponding sides in similar triangles.

40. In your own words, state the Pythagorean theorem.

41. In the 1939 movie *The Wizard of Oz*, upon being presented with a Th.D (Doctor of Thinkology), the Scarecrow proudly exclaims, "The sum of the square roots of any two sides of an isosceles triangle is equal to the square root of the remaining side." Did the Scarecrow get the Pythagorean theorem right? In particular, describe four errors in the Scarecrow's statement.

Critical Thinking Exercises

42. Find the measure of angle *R*.

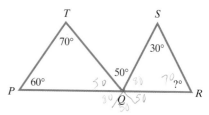

T

S

70°

30°

50°

60°

P

Q

R

43. What is the length of $\overline{AB}$ in the accompanying figure?

13 ft

20 ft

12 ft

A

B

44. A builder is adding a 16-foot by 20-foot rectangular room to a house. Once the floor is constructed, it is found that the length of its diagonal is $24\frac{1}{4}$ feet. Is the floor squared off properly so that once the walls are constructed they will form a right angle?

Group Exercises

45. Group members should write and solve two practical problems that can be solved using similar triangles. The problems should be different from those in this section.

46. Group members should write and solve two practical problems that can be solved using the Pythagorean theorem. As in Exercise 45, be sure that the problems are different from those in this section.

SECTION 10.3   Polygons, Quadrilaterals, and Perimeter

Objectives

1. Name certain polygons according to the number of sides.
2. Recognize the characteristics of certain quadrilaterals.
3. Solve problems involving a polygon's perimeter.
4. Find the sum of the measures of a polygon's angles.

1 Name certain polygons according to the number of sides.

Bees and Regular Hexagons

Bees use honeycombs to store honey and house larvae. They construct honey storage cells from wax. Each cell has the shape of a regular hexagon. The cells fit together perfectly, preventing dirt or predators from entering. Squares or equilateral triangles would fit equally well, but regular hexagons provide the largest storage space for the amount of wax used.

You have just purchased a beautiful plot of land in the country, shown in Figure 10.24. In order to have more privacy, you decide to put fencing along each of its four sides. The cost of this project depends on the distance around the four outside edges of the plot, called its **perimeter**, as well as the cost for each foot of fencing.

Figure 10.24

Your plot of land is a geometric figure: It has four straight sides that are line segments. The plot is on level ground, so that the four sides all lie on a flat surface, or plane. The plot is an example of a *polygon*. Any closed shape in the plane formed by three or more line segments is a **polygon**.

A polygon is named according to the number of sides it has. A three-sided polygon is called a **triangle**. A four-sided polygon is called a **quadrilateral**.

A polygon whose sides are all the same length and whose angles all have the same measure is called a **regular polygon**. Table 10.2 provides the names of six polygons. Also shown are illustrations of regular polygons. A triangle that is a regular polygon is called an **equilateral triangle**. Each angle in an equilateral triangle measures 60°.

Table 10.2   Illustrations of Regular Polygons

Name	Picture	Name	Picture
Triangle 3 sides		Hexagon 6 sides	
Quadrilateral 4 sides		Heptagon 7 sides	
Pentagon 5 sides		Octagon 8 sides	

By contrast to the equilateral triangle shown in Table 10.2, an **isosceles triangle** has two sides with equal length. A **scalene triangle** has no two sides that are equal in length.

2 Recognize the characteristics of certain quadrilaterals.

Decorating with Geometry

When your bathroom wall is tiled, tiles of the same shape are fitted together to cover the wall without leaving any gaps, so that water cannot get through. Tiling the plane means covering the entire plane without leaving any space empty or overlapping any tiles. Shown here is a tiling using regular polygons. If you look at a soccer ball, you will see that the entire surface is filled with regular pentagons and regular hexagons. Designs formed by tiling the plane have been featured in art and architecture for centuries.

3 Solve problems involving a polygon's perimeter.

Quadrilaterals

The plot of land in Figure 10.24 is a four-sided polygon, or a quadrilateral. However, when you first looked at the figure, perhaps you thought of the plot as a rectangular field. A **rectangle** is a special kind of quadrilateral in which both pairs of opposite sides are parallel, have the same measure, and whose angles are right angles. Table 10.3 presents some special quadrilaterals and their characteristics.

Table 10.3 Types of Quadrilaterals

Name	Characteristics	Representation
Parallelogram	Quadrilateral in which both pairs of opposite sides are parallel and have the same measure. Opposite angles have the same measure.	
Rhombus	Parallelogram with all sides having equal length.	
Rectangle	Parallelogram with four right angles. Because a rectangle is a parallelogram, opposite sides are parallel and have the same measure.	
Square	A rectangle with all sides having equal length. Each angle measures 90°, and the square is a regular quadrilateral.	
Trapezoid	A quadrilateral with exactly one pair of parallel sides.	

Perimeter

The **perimeter**, P, of a polygon is the sum of the lengths of its sides. Perimeter is measured in linear units, such as inches, feet, yards, meters, or kilometers.

Example 1 involves the perimeter of a rectangle. Because perimeter is the sum of the lengths of the sides, the perimeter of the rectangle shown in Figure 10.25 is $l + w + l + w$. This can be expressed as

$$P = 2l + 2w.$$

Figure 10.25 A rectangle with length l and width w

EXAMPLE 1 An Application of Perimeter

The rectangular field we discussed at the beginning of this section (see Figure 10.24 on page 471) has a length of 128 feet and a width of 84 feet. If fencing costs $5.25 per foot, find the cost to enclose the rectangle with fencing.

Solution We begin by finding the perimeter of the rectangle. Once we have determined the distance around the four outside edges in feet, we multiply this number by $5.25 because the fencing costs $5.25 per foot.

The length, l, is 128 feet and the width, w, is 84 feet. The perimeter of the rectangle is determined by using the formula $P = 2l + 2w$.

$$P = 2l + 2w$$
$$= 2 \cdot 128 \text{ ft} + 2 \cdot 84 \text{ ft}$$
$$= 256 \text{ ft} + 168 \text{ ft} = 424 \text{ ft}$$

The perimeter of the rectangle is 424 feet. Now we are ready to find the cost of the fencing. We multiply 424 feet by $5.25, the cost per foot.

$$\text{Cost} = \frac{424 \text{ feet}}{1} \cdot \frac{\$5.25}{\text{foot}} = 424(\$5.25) = \$2226$$

The cost to enclose the rectangle with fencing is $2226.

4 Find the sum of the measures of a polygon's angles.

The Sum of the Measures of a Polygon's Angles

We know that the sum of the measures of the three angles of any triangle is 180°. We can use inductive reasoning to find the sum of the measures of the angles of any polygon. Start by drawing line segments from a single point where two sides meet so that nonoverlapping triangles are formed. This is done in Figure 10.26.

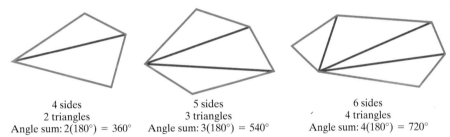

Figure 10.26

4 sides	5 sides	6 sides
2 triangles	3 triangles	4 triangles
Angle sum: $2(180°) = 360°$	Angle sum: $3(180°) = 540°$	Angle sum: $4(180°) = 720°$

In each case, the number of triangles is two less than the number of sides. Thus, for an n-sided polygon, there are $n - 2$ triangles. Because each triangle has an angle-measure sum of 180°, the sum of the measures for the angles in the $n - 2$ triangles is $(n - 2)180°$. Thus, the sum of the measures of the angles of an n-sided polygon is $(n - 2)180°$.

> **The Angles of a Polygon**
>
> The sum of the measures of the angles of a polygon with n sides is $(n - 2)180°$.

EXAMPLE 2   Using the Formula for the Angles of a Polygon

a. Find the sum of the measures of the angles of an octagon.
b. Figure 10.27 shows a regular octagon. Find the measure of angle A.

Solution

a. An octagon has eight sides. Using the formula $(n - 2)180°$ with $n = 8$, we can find the sum of the measures of its eight angles.

The sum of the measures of an octagon's angles

$$= (n - 2)180°$$
$$= (8 - 2)180°$$
$$= 6 \cdot 180°$$
$$= 1080°$$

Figure 10.27 A regular octagon

b. Examine the regular octagon in Figure 10.27. Note that all eight sides have the same length. Likewise, all eight angles have the same degree measure. Angle A is one of these eight angles. We find its measure by taking the sum of the measures of all eight angles, 1080°, and dividing by 8.

$$m \angle A = \frac{1080°}{8} = 135°$$

Exercise Set 10.3

 Practice Exercises

In Exercises 1–4, use the number of sides to name the polygon.

1.

2.

3.

4.

Use these quadrilaterals to solve Exercises 5–10.

a.

b.

c.

d.

e.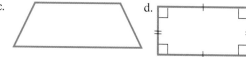

5. Which of these quadrilaterals have opposite sides that are parallel? Name these quadrilaterals.

6. Which of these quadrilaterals have sides of equal length that meet? Name these quadrilaterals.

7. Which of these quadrilaterals have right angles? Name these quadrilaterals.

8. Which of these quadrilaterals do not have four sides of equal length? Name these quadrilaterals.

9. Which of these quadrilaterals is not a parallelogram? Name this quadrilateral.

10. Which of these quadrilaterals is/are a regular polygon? Name this/these quadrilateral(s).

In Exercises 11–20, find the perimeter of the figure named and shown. Express the perimeter using the same unit of measure that appears on the given side or sides.

11. Rectangle

12. Parallelogram

13. Rectangle   14. Rectangle

15. Square   16. Square

17. Triangle

9 ft   7 ft

11 ft

18. Triangle

16 yd

10 yd

8.5 yd

19. Equilateral triangle

6 yd

20. Regular hexagon

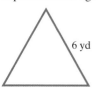

4 mm

In Exercises 21–24, find the perimeter of the figure shown. Express the perimeter using the same unit of measure that appears on the given side or sides.

21.

9 yd

9 yd

12 yd

21 yd

12 yd

21 yd

22.

5 in.

13 in.

17 in.

9 in.

4 in.

14 in.

23.

3 ft

3 ft

6 ft

4 ft

24.

10 m

8 m

3 m

5 m

25. Find the sum of the measures of the angles of a five-sided polygon.

26. Find the sum of the measures of the angles of a six-sided polygon.

27. Find the sum of the measures of the angles of a quadrilateral.

28. Find the sum of the measures of the angles of a heptagon.

In Exercises 29–30, each figure shows a regular polygon. Find the measure of angle 1.

29.

1

30.

1

In Exercises 31–32; a. Find the sum of the measures of the angles for the figure given; b. Find the measure of angle 1.

31.

150°

70°

1

32.

1

42°

⭐ **Application Exercises**

For Exercises 33–40, use the road signs shown.

stop at intersection

one-way traffic

no entry

yield

deer crossing

33. Which sign has a shape that is not a polygon?

34. Describe the shape of the STOP sign as specifically as possible.

35. Which signs have the shape of a regular polygon?

36. Which sign(s) has/have the shape of a polygon that is not regular?

37. Describe the shape of the YIELD sign as specifically as possible.

38. Describe the shape of the DEER CROSSING sign as specifically as possible.

39. Which sign is shaped like a polygon with a 60° angle?

40. Which sign has obtuse angles?

41. A school playground is in the shape of a rectangle 400 feet long and 200 feet wide. If fencing cost $14 a yard, what will it cost to place fencing around the playground?

42. A softball diamond is shaped like a square. A batter who hits a home run must run 240 feet around the bases. What is the distance from third base to home plate?

43. What will it cost to place baseboard around the region shown if the basebord costs $0.25 per foot? No baseboard is needed for the 2-foot doorway.

 Writing in Mathematics

44. What is a polygon?

45. Explain why rectangles and rhombuses are also parallelograms.

46. Explain why every square is a rectangle, a rhombus, a parallelogram, a quadrilateral, and a polygon.

47. Using words only, describe how to find the perimeter of a rectangle.

48. Describe a practical situation in which you needed to apply the concept of a geometric figure's perimeter.

49. Describe how to find the measure of an angle of a regular pentagon.

 Critical Thinking Exercises

In Exercises 50–52, write an algebraic expression that represents the perimeter of the figure shown.

50.

51.

52. Find $m \angle 1$ in the figure shown.

Group Exercise

53. Tiling the plane, in a mathematical sense, is very similar to tiling a floor. Tiling, or tessellating, the plane means covering the entire plane with endless repetitions of a basic design, without leaving any space empty. Present a group report on tiling the plane. Include a discussion of cultures that have used tessellations on fabrics, wall coverings, baskets, rugs, and pottery, with examples. Include the Alhambra, a fourteenth century palace in Granada, Spain, in the presentation, as well as works by the artist M.C. Escher. Finally, be sure to discuss practical applications of tiling the plane.

SECTION 10.4   *Area and Circumference*

Objectives

1. Use area formulas to compute the areas of plane regions and solve applied problems.

2. Use formulas for a circle's circumference and area.

1 Use area formulas to compute the areas of plane regions and solve applied problems.

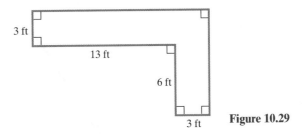

Figure 10.28 The area of the region on the left is 12 square units.

Appraising a House

A house is measured by an appraiser hired by a bank to help establish its value. The appraiser works from the outside, measuring off a rectangle. Then the appraiser adds the living spaces that lie outside the rectangle and subtracts the empty areas inside the rectangle. The final figure, in square feet, includes all the finished floor space in the house. Not included are the garage, outside porches, decks, or an unfinished basement.

A 1000-square-foot house is considered small, one with 1500 square feet average, and one with more than 2000 square feet pleasantly large. If a 1200-square foot house has three bedrooms, the individual rooms might seem snug and cozy. With only one bedroom, the space may feel palatial!

The size of a house is described in square feet. But how do you know from the real estate ad whether the 1200-square-foot home with the backyard pool is large enough to warrant a visit? Faced with hundreds of ads, you need some way to sort out the best bets. What does 1200 square feet mean and how is this area determined? In this section, we discuss how to compute the areas of plane regions.

Formulas for Area

In Section 9.2, we saw that the area of a two-dimensional figure is the number of square units, such as square inches or square miles, it takes to fill the interior of the figure. For example, Figure 10.28 shows that there are 12 square units contained within the rectangular region. The area of the region is 12 square units. Notice that the area can be determined in the following manner:

$$\begin{array}{cc} \textbf{Across} & \textbf{Down} \end{array}$$

$$4 \text{ units} \times 3 \text{ units} = 4 \times 3 \text{ units} \times \text{units}$$

$$= 12 \text{ square units}$$

The area of a rectangular region, usually referred to as the area of a rectangle, is the product of the distance across (length) and the distance down (width).

Area of a Rectangle and a Square

The area A of a rectangle with length l and width w is given by the formula

$$A = lw.$$

The area A of a square with one side measuring s linear units is given by the formula

$$A = s^2.$$

EXAMPLE 1   Solving an Area Problem

You decide to cover the path shown in Figure 10.29 with bricks.

Figure 10.29

a. Find the area of the path.

b. If the path requires four bricks for every square foot, how many bricks are needed for the project?

Solution

a. Because we have a formula for the area of a rectangle, we begin by drawing a dashed line that divides the path into two rectangles. One way of doing this is shown below. We then use the length and width of each rectangle to find its area.

The area of the path is found by adding the areas of the two rectangles.

$$\text{Area of path} = 39 \text{ ft}^2 + 27 \text{ ft}^2 = 66 \text{ ft}^2$$

b. The path requires 4 bricks per square foot. The number of bricks needed for the project is the number of square feet in the path, its area, times 4.

$$\text{Number of bricks needed} = 66 \text{ ft}^2 \cdot \frac{4 \text{ bricks}}{\text{ft}^2} = 66 \cdot 4 \text{ bricks} = 264 \text{ bricks}$$

Thus, 264 bricks are needed for the project.

In Section 9.2, we saw that although there are 3 linear feet in a linear yard, there are 9 square feet in a square yard. If a problem requires measurement of area in square yards and the linear measures are given in feet, to avoid errors first convert feet to yards. Then apply the area formula. This idea is illustrated in Example 2.

EXAMPLE 2   Solving an Area Problem

What will it cost to carpet a rectangular floor measuring 12 feet by 15 feet if the carpet costs $18.50 per square yard?

Solution   We begin by converting the linear measures in feet to linear yards.

$$12 \text{ ft} = \frac{12 \text{ ft}}{1} \cdot \frac{1 \text{ yd}}{3 \text{ ft}} = \frac{12}{3} \text{ yd} = 4 \text{ yd}$$

$$15 \text{ ft} = \frac{15 \text{ ft}}{1} \cdot \frac{1 \text{ yd}}{3 \text{ ft}} = \frac{15}{3} \text{ yd} = 5 \text{ yd}$$

Next, we find the area of the rectangular floor in square yards.

$$A = lw = 5 \text{ yd} \cdot 4 \text{ yd} = 20 \text{ yd}^2$$

Finally, we find the cost of the carpet by multiplying the cost per square yard, $18.50, by the number of square yards in the floor, 20.

$$\text{Cost of carpet} = \frac{\$18.50}{\text{yd}^2} \cdot \frac{20 \text{ yd}^2}{1} = \$18.50(20) = \$370$$

It will cost $370 to carpet the floor.

Figure 10.30

We can use the formula for the area of a rectangle to develop formulas for areas of other polygons. We begin with a parallelogram, a quadrilateral with parallel and equal opposite sides. The **height** of a parallelogram is the perpendicular distance between two of the parallel sides. Height is denoted by h in Figure 10.30. The **base**, denoted by b, is the length of either of these parallel sides.

In Figure 10.31, the red triangular region has been cut off from the right of the parallelogram and attached to the left. The resulting figure is a rectangle with length b and width h. Because bh is the area of the rectangle, it also represents the area of the parallelogram.

Figure 10.31

Study Tip

The height of a parallelogram is the perpendicular distance between two of the parallel sides. It is *not* the length of a side.

Area of a Parallelogram

The area A of a parallelogram with height h and base b is given by the formula

$$A = bh.$$

EXAMPLE 3   Using the Formula for a Parallelogram's Area

Find the area of the parallelogram in Figure 10.32.

Solution   As shown in the figure, the base is 8 centimeters and the height is 4 centimeters. Thus, $b = 8$ and $h = 4$.

$$A = bh$$
$$A = 8 \text{ cm} \cdot 4 \text{ cm} = 32 \text{ cm}^2$$

The area is 32 cm².

Figure 10.32

Figure 10.33 demonstrates how we can use the formula for the area of a parallelogram to obtain a formula for the area of a triangle. The area of the parallelogram in Figure 10.33(a) is given by $A = bh$. The diagonal shown in the parallelogram divides it into two triangles with the same size and shape. This means that the area of each triangle is one-half that of the parallelogram. Thus, the area of the triangle in Figure 10.33(b) is given by $A = \frac{1}{2}bh$.

(a)

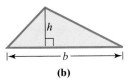

(b)

Figure 10.33

Area of a Triangle

The area A of a triangle with height h and base b is given by the formula

$$A = \frac{1}{2}bh.$$

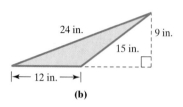

Figure 10.34

EXAMPLE 4   Using the Formula for a Triangle's Area

Find the area of each triangle in Figure 10.34.

Solution   In Figure 10.34(a), the base is 16 meters and the height is 10 meters, so $b = 16$ and $h = 10$. We do not need the 10.5 meters or the 14 meters to find the area. The area of the triangle is

$$A = \frac{1}{2}bh = \frac{1}{2} \cdot 16 \text{ m} \cdot 10 \text{ m} = 80 \text{ m}^2.$$

The area is 80 square meters. In Figure 10.34(b), the base is 12 inches. The base line needs to be extended to draw the height. However, we still use 12 inches for b in the area formula. The height, h, is 9 inches. The area of the triangle is

$$A = \frac{1}{2}bh = \frac{1}{2} \cdot 12 \text{ in.} \cdot 9 \text{ in.} = 54 \text{ in.}^2.$$

The area of the triangle is 54 square inches.

Figure 10.35

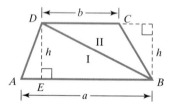

Figure 10.36

The formula for the area of a triangle can be used to obtain a formula for the area of a trapezoid. Consider the trapezoid shown in Figure 10.35. The lengths of the two nonparallel sides, called the **bases**, are represented by a (the lower base) and b (the upper base). The trapezoid's height, denoted by h, is the perpendicular distance between the two parallel sides.

In Figure 10.36, we have drawn line segment BD, dividing the trapezoid into two triangles, I and II. The area of the trapezoid is the sum of the areas of these triangles.

Area of the trapezoid = Area of triangle I + Area of triangle II

$$A = \frac{1}{2}ah \qquad\qquad + \frac{1}{2}bh$$

$$= \frac{1}{2}h(a + b) \qquad \text{Factor out } \frac{1}{2}h.$$

Figure 10.37

Area of a Trapezoid

The area A of a trapezoid with parallel bases a and b and height h is given by the formula

$$A = \frac{1}{2}h(a + b).$$

EXAMPLE 5   Finding the Area of a Trapezoid

Find the area of the trapezoid in Figure 10.37.

Solution   The height, h, is 13 feet. The long base, a, is 46 feet, and the short base, b, is 32 feet. We do not use the 17 foot and 19 foot sides in finding the trapezoid's area.

$$A = \frac{1}{2}h(a + b) = \frac{1}{2} \cdot 13 \text{ ft} \cdot (46 \text{ ft} + 32 \text{ ft})$$

$$= \frac{1}{2} \cdot 13 \text{ ft} \cdot 78 \text{ ft} = 507 \text{ ft}^2$$

The area of the trapezoid is 507 square feet.

2 Use formulas for a circle's circumference and area.

Circles

It's a good idea to know your way around a circle. Clocks, angles, maps, and compasses are based on circles. Circles occur everywhere in nature: in ripples on water, patterns on a butterfly's wings, and cross sections of trees. Some consider the circle to be the most pleasing of all shapes.

A **circle** is actually a set of points in the plane equally distant from a given point, its **center**. Figure 10.38 shows three circles. Each point on the circle on the left is 3 inches away from the center. Each 3-inch line segment is called a **radius** (plural: radii). The radius, r, is a line segment from the center to any point on the circle. For a given circle, all radii have the same length. Each 6-inch line segment is called a **diameter**. The diameter, d, is a line segment through the center whose endpoints both lie on the circle.

The point at which a pebble hits a flat surface of water becomes the center of a number of circular ripples.

  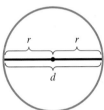

Figure 10.38

The words *radius* and *diameter* refer to both the line segments in Figure 10.38 as well as to their linear measures. The radius of the circle on the left is 3 inches and the diameter is 6 inches. If you double the radius, you obtain the diameter: $2 \cdot 3$ inches $= 6$ inches $=$ diameter. If you half the diameter, you obtain the radius: $\frac{1}{2} \cdot 6$ inches $= 3$ inches $=$ radius. In general,

$$\text{diameter} = 2 \cdot \text{radius } (d = 2r) \quad \text{and} \quad \text{radius} = \frac{\text{diameter}}{2} \left(r = \frac{d}{2} \right).$$

The distance around a circle (its perimeter) is called its **circumference**, C. For all circles, if you divide the circumference by the diameter, or by twice the radius, you will get the same number. This ratio is the irrational number π and is approximately equal to 3.14:

$$\frac{C}{d} = \pi \quad \text{and} \quad \frac{C}{2r} = \pi.$$

Thus,

$$C = \pi d \quad \text{or} \quad C = 2\pi r.$$

Finding the Distance Around a Circle

The circumference, C, of a circle with diameter d and radius r is

$$C = \pi d \quad \text{or} \quad C = 2\pi r.$$

When computing a circle's circumference by hand, round π to 3.14. When using a calculator, use the $\boxed{\pi}$ key, which gives the value of π rounded to approximately 11 decimal places. In either case, calculations involving π give approximate answers. These answers can vary slightly depending on how π is rounded. The symbol $\approx$ (is approximately equal to) will be written in these calculations.

EXAMPLE 6   Finding a Circle's Circumference

Find the circumference of the circle in Figure 10.39.

Solution   The diameter is 40 yards, so we use the formula for circumference with d in it.

$$C = \pi d \approx 3.14(40 \text{ yd}) \approx 126 \text{ yd}$$

The distance around the circle is approximately 126 yards.

Figure 10.39

EXAMPLE 7   Using the Circumference Formula

How much trim is needed to go around the window shown in Figure 10.40?

Solution   The trim covers the 6-foot bottom of the window, the two 8-foot sides, and the half-circle (called a semicircle) on top. The length needed is

$$6 \text{ ft} + 8 \text{ ft} + 8 \text{ ft} + \text{circumference of the semicircle.}$$

The circumference of the semicircle is half the circumference of a circle whose diameter is 6 feet:

$$\text{Circumference of semicircle} = \frac{1}{2}\pi d \approx \frac{1}{2}(3.14)(6 \text{ ft}) \approx 9.42 \text{ ft}$$

Rounding the circumference to the nearest tenth (9.4 feet), the length of trim that is needed is approximately

$$6 \text{ ft} + 8 \text{ ft} + 8 \text{ ft} + 9.4 \text{ ft}$$

or 31.4 feet.

Figure 10.40

We also use π to find the area of a circle in square units.

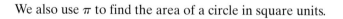

Finding the Area of a Circle
The area A of a circle with radius r is

$$A = \pi r^2.$$

EXAMPLE 8 Problem Solving Using the Formula for a Circle's Area

Which one of the following is the better buy: a large pizza with a 16-inch diameter for $15.00 or a medium pizza with an 8-inch diameter for $7.50?

Solution The better buy is the pizza with the cheaper price per square inch. The radius of the large pizza is $\frac{1}{2} \cdot 16$ inches, or 8 inches, and the radius of the medium pizza is $\frac{1}{2} \cdot 8$ inches, or 4 inches. The area of the surface of each circular pizza is determined using the formula for the area of a circle.

Large pizza: $A = \pi r^2 = \pi(8 \text{ in.})^2 = 64\pi \text{ in.}^2 \approx 201 \text{ in.}^2$

Medium pizza: $A = \pi r^2 = \pi(4 \text{ in.})^2 = 16\pi \text{ in.}^2 \approx 50 \text{ in.}^2$

For each pizza, the price per square inch is found by dividing the price by the area:

$$\text{Price per square inch for large pizza} = \frac{\$15.00}{201 \text{ in.}^2} \approx \frac{\$0.07}{\text{in.}^2}$$

$$\text{Price per square inch for medium pizza} = \frac{\$7.50}{50 \text{ in.}^2} = \frac{\$0.15}{\text{in.}^2}$$

The larger pizza is the better buy.

In Example 8, did you at first think that the price per square inch would be the same for the large and the medium pizzas? After all, the radius of the large pizza is twice that of the medium pizza, and the cost of the large is twice that of the medium. However, the large pizza's area, 64π square inches, is *four times the area* of the medium pizza's, 16π square inches. Doubling the radius of a circle increases its area by four times the original amount. In general, if the radius of a circle is increased by k times its original linear measure, the area is increased by k^2 square units. The same principle is true for any two-dimensional figure: if the shape of the figure is kept the same while linear dimensions are increased k times, the area of the larger, similar, figure is increased by k^2.

Exercise Set 10.4

✓ Practice Exercises

In Exercises 1–12, use the formulas developed in this section to find the area of each figure.

1. 3 m, 6 m

2. 3 ft, 4 ft

3. 4 in., 4 in.

4. 3 cm, 3 cm

5. 50 cm, 44 cm, 42 cm, 44 cm, 50 cm

6. 58 ft, 46 ft, 43 ft, 46 ft, 58 ft

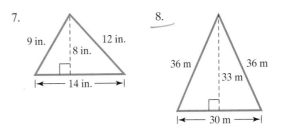

7. 9 in., 12 in., 8 in., 14 in.

8. 36 m, 36 m, 33 m, 30 m

9.

10.

11.

12.

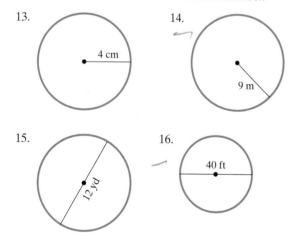

In Exercises 13–16, find the circumference and area of each circle. Round answers to the nearest whole number.

13.

4 cm

14.

9 m

15.

12 yd

16.

40 ft

Find the area of each figure in Exercises 17–20.

17.

4 m

9 m

12 m

8 m

3 m

12 m

18.

7 ft

3 ft

5 ft

12 ft

9 ft

2 ft

19.

13 m   13 m

15 m

10 m   10 m

24 m

20.

6 cm

3 cm

10 cm

7

9 cm   3

⭐ **Application Exercises**

21. What will it cost to carpet a rectangular floor measuring 9 feet by 21 feet if the carpet costs $26.50 per square yard?

22. A plastering contractor charges $18 per square yard. What is the cost of plastering 60 feet of wall in a house with a 9-foot ceiling?

23. A rectangular kitchen floor measures 12 feet by 15 feet. A stove on the floor has a rectangular base measuring 3 feet by 4 feet, and a refrigerator covers a rectangular area of the floor measuring 4 feet by 5 feet. How many square feet of tile will be needed to cover the kitchen floor not counting the area used by the stove and the refrigerator?

24. A rectangular room measures 12 feet by 15 feet. The entire room is to be covered with rectangular tiles that measure 3 inches by 2 inches. If the tiles are sold at ten for 30¢, what will it cost to tile the room?

25. A swimming pool is shaped like a parallelogram. The base is 14 meters and the height is 10 meters. What will it cost to make a cover for the pool at $6.50 per square meter?

26. A yard that is to be covered with mats of grass is shaped like a trapezoid. The bases are 80 feet and 100 feet, and the height is 60 feet. What is the cost of putting the grass mats on the yard if the landscaper charges $0.35 per square foot?

27. The lot in the figure shown, except for the house, shed, and driveway, is lawn. One bag of lawn fertilizer costs $23.95 and covers 4000 square feet.
    a. Determine the minimum number of bags of fertilizer needed for the lawn.
    b. Find the total cost of the fertilizer.

28. Taxpayers with an office in their home may deduct a percentage of their home-related expenses. This percentage is based on the ratio of the office's area to the area of the home. A taxpayer with an office in a 2200 square foot home maintains a 20 foot by 16 foot office. If the yearly electric bills for the home come to $4800, how much of this is deductible?

In Exercises 29–35, round all circumference and area calculations to the nearest whole number.

29. How much fencing is required to enclose a circular garden whose radius is 20 meters?

30. A circular rug is 6 feet in diameter. How many feet of fringe is required to edge this rug?

31. How many plants spaced every 6 inches are needed to surround a circular garden with a 30-foot radius?

32. A stained glass window is to be placed in a house. The window consists of a rectangle, 6 feet high by 3 feet wide, with a semicircle at the top. Approximately how many feet of stripping will be needed to frame the window?

6 ft

3 ft

33. Which one of the following is the best deal: a small pizza (diameter = 12 inches) for $10.25, a medium pizza (diameter = 14 inches) for $13.75, or a large pizza (diameter = 18 inches) for $19.75?

34. If asphalt pavement costs $0.82 per square foot, find the cost to pave the circular road in the figure shown at the top of the next column.

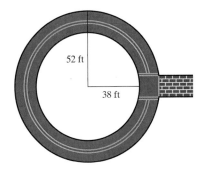

52 ft

38 ft

35. Hardwood flooring costs $9.50 per square foot. How much will it cost (to the nearest cent) to cover the dance floor shown in the figure with hardwood flooring?

20 feet

60 feet

Writing in Mathematics

36. Using the formula for the area of a rectangle, explain how the formula for the area of a parallelogram $(A = bh)$ is obtained.

37. Using the formula for the area of a parallelogram $(A = bh)$, explain how the formula for the area of a triangle $\left(A = \frac{1}{2}bh\right)$ is obtained.

38. Using the formula for the area of a triangle, explain how the formula for the area of a trapezoid is obtained.

39. Explain why a circle is not a polygon.

40. Describe the difference between the following problems: How much fencing is needed to enclose a circular garden? How much fertilizer is needed for a circular garden?

Critical Thinking Exercises

41. Suppose you know the cost for building a rectangular deck measuring 8 feet by 10 feet. If you decide to increase the dimensions to 12 feet by 15 feet, by how much will the cost increase?

42. A rectangular swimming pool measures 14 feet by 30 feet. The pool is surrounded on all four sides by a path that is 3 feet wide. If the cost to resurface the path is $2 per square foot, what is the total cost of resurfacing the path?

43. A proposed oil pipeline will cross 16.8 miles of national forest. The width of the land needed for the pipeline is 200 feet. If the U.S. Forest Service charges the oil company $32 per acre, calculate the total cost. (1 mile = 5280 feet and 1 acre = 43,560 square feet.)

In Exercises 44–45, find the area of the shaded region. If necessary, round to the nearest whole number.

44.

2 cm

2 cm

(Both quadrilaterals are squares.)

45.

6 cm

8 cm

Group Exercise

46. Using a tape measure, group members should determine the area of a floor, a wall, or a roof. Then write and solve a practical problem using the region whose area you determined.

SECTION 10.5 Volume

Objectives

1. Use volume formulas to compute the volumes of three-dimensional figures and solve applied problems.
2. Compute the surface area of a three-dimensional figure.

Your contractor promised to install a water tank that holds 500 gallons of water. Upon delivery, you notice that capacity is not printed anywhere, so you decide to do some measuring. The tank is shaped like a giant tuna can, with a circular top and bottom. You measure the radius of each circle to be 3 feet and you measure the tank's height to be 2 feet 4 inches. You know that 500 gallons is the capacity of a solid figure with a volume of about 67 cubic feet. Now you need some sort of method to compute the volume of the water tank. In this section, we discuss how to compute the volumes of various solid, three-dimensional figures.

Formulas for Volume

1 Use volume formulas to compute the volumes of three-dimensional figures and solve applied problems.

Cubic Unit

In Section 9.2, we saw that **volume** refers to the amount of space occupied by a solid object, determined by the number of cubic units it takes to fill the interior of that object. For example, Figure 10.41 shows that there are 18 cubic units contained within the box. The volume of the box, called a **rectangular solid**, is 18 cubic units. The box has a length of 3 units, a width of 3 units, and a height of 2 units. The volume, 18 cubic units, may be determined by finding the product of the length, the width, and the height:

$$\text{Volume} = 3 \text{ units} \cdot 3 \text{ units} \cdot 2 \text{ units} = 18 \text{ units}^3.$$

In general, the volume, V, of a rectangular solid is the product of its length, l, its width, w, and its height, h:

$$V = lwh.$$

If the length, width, and height are the same, the rectangular solid is called a **cube**. Formulas for these boxlike shapes are given below.

Figure 10.41 Volume = 18 cubic units

$h = 2$

$w = 3$

$l = 3$

Volumes of Boxlike Shapes

Rectangular Solid

h

l

w

$V = lwh$

Cube

s

s

s

$V = sss = s^3$

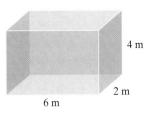

4 m

2 m

6 m

Figure 10.42

EXAMPLE 1 Finding the Volume of a Rectangular Solid

Find the volume of the rectangular solid in Figure 10.42

Solution
As shown in the figure, the length is 6 meters, the width is 2 meters, and the height is 4 meters. Thus, $l = 6$, $w = 2$, and $h = 4$.

$$V = lwh = 6 \text{ m} \cdot 2 \text{ m} \cdot 4 \text{ m} = 48 \text{ m}^3$$

The volume of the rectangular solid is 48 cubic meters.

In Section 9.2, we saw that although there are 3 feet in a yard, there are 27 cubic feet in a cubic yard. If a problem requires measurement of volume in cubic yards and the linear measures are given in feet, to avoid errors first convert feet to yards. Then apply the volume formula. This idea is illustrated in Example 2.

EXAMPLE 2 Solving a Volume Problem

You are about to begin work on a swimming pool in your yard. The first step is to have a hole dug that is 90 feet long, 60 feet wide, and 6 feet deep. You will use a truck that can carry 10 cubic yards of dirt and charges $12 per load. How much will it cost you to have all the dirt hauled away?

Solution   We begin by converting feet to yards:

$$90 \text{ ft} = \frac{90 \text{ ft}}{1} \cdot \frac{1 \text{ yd}}{3 \text{ ft}} = \frac{90}{3} \text{ yd} = 30 \text{ yd}$$

Similarly, 60 ft = 20 yd and 6 ft = 2 yd. Next, we find the volume of dirt that needs to be dug out and hauled off.

$$V = lwh = 30 \text{ yd} \cdot 20 \text{ yd} \cdot 2 \text{ yd} = 1200 \text{ yd}^3$$

Now, we find the number of loads that the truck needs to haul off all the dirt. Because the truck carries 10 cubic yards, divide the number of cubic yards of dirt by 10.

$$\text{Number of truckloads} = \frac{1200 \text{ yd}^3}{\dfrac{10 \text{ yd}^3}{\text{trip}}} = \frac{1200 \text{ yd}^3}{1} \cdot \frac{\text{trip}}{10 \text{ yd}^3} = \frac{1200}{10} \text{ trips} = 120 \text{ trips}$$

Because the truck charges $12 per trip, the cost to have all the dirt hauled away is the number of trips, 120, times the cost per trip, $12.

$$\text{Cost to haul all dirt away} = \frac{120 \text{ trips}}{1} \cdot \frac{\$12}{\text{trip}} = 120(\$12) = \$1440$$

The dirt-hauling phase of the pool project will cost you $1440.

Figure 10.43 The volume of a pyramid is $\frac{1}{3}$ the volume of a rectangular solid having the same base and the same height.

A rectangular solid is an example of a **polyhedron**, a solid figure bounded by polygons. This boxlike shape is bounded by six rectangles. By contrast, a **pyramid** is a polyhedron whose base is a polygon and whose sides are triangles. Figure 10.43 shows a pyramid with a rectangular base drawn inside of a rectangular solid. The contents of three pyramids with rectangular bases exactly fill a rectangular solid of the same base and height. Thus, the formula for the volume of the pyramid is $\frac{1}{3}$ that of the rectangular solid.

Volume of a Pyramid

The volume V of a pyramid is given by the formula

$$V = \frac{1}{3}Bh,$$

where B is the area of the base and h is the height (the perpendicular distance from the top to the base.)

Pyramid

$V = \frac{1}{3}Bh$, where B is the area of the base

EXAMPLE 3   Using the Formula for a Pyramid's Volume

Capped with a pointed spire on top of its 48 stories, the Transamerica Tower in San Francisco is a pyramid with a square base. The pyramid is 256 meters (853 feet) tall. Each side of the square base has a length of 52 meters. Although San Franciscans disliked it when it opened in 1972, they have since accepted it as part of the skyline. Find the volume of the building.

Solution   First find the area of the square base, represented as B in the volume formula. Because each side of the square base is 52 meters, the area of the square base is

$$B = 52\,\text{m} \cdot 52\,\text{m} = 2704\,\text{m}^2.$$

The area of the square base is 2704 square meters. Because the pyramid is 256 meters tall, its height, h, is 256 meters. Now we apply the formula for the volume of a pyramid:

$$V = \frac{1}{3}Bh = \frac{1}{3} \cdot \frac{2704\,\text{m}^2}{1} \cdot \frac{256\,\text{m}}{1} = \frac{2704 \cdot 256}{3}\,\text{m}^3 \approx 230{,}741\,\text{m}^3$$

The volume of the building is about 230,741 cubic meters.

The Transamerica Tower's 3678 windows take cleaners one month to wash. Its foundation is sunk 15.5 m (52 ft) into the ground, and is designed to move with earth tremors.

The San Francisco pyramid is relatively small compared to the Great Pyramid outside Cairo, Egypt. Built about 2550 B.C. by a labor force of 100,000, the Great Pyramid is approximately 11 times the volume of San Francisco's pyramid.

Not every three-dimensional figure is a polyhedron. Take, for example, the right circular cylinder shown in Figure 10.44. Its shape should remind you of a soup can or a piece of pipe. The right circular cylinder is so named because the top and bottom are circles, and the side forms a right angle with the top and bottom. The formula for the volume of a right circular cylinder is given at the top of the next page.

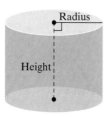

Radius

Height

Figure 10.44

Volume of a Right Circular Cylinder

The volume V of a right circular cylinder is given by the formula

$$V = \pi r^2 h,$$

where r is the radius of the circle at either end and h is the height

Right circular cylinder

EXAMPLE 4 Finding the Volume of a Cylinder

Find the volume of the cylinder in Figure 10.45.

Solution In order to find the cylinder's volume, we need both its radius and its height. Because the diameter is 20 yards, the radius is half this length, or 10 yards. The height of the cylinder is given to be 9 yards. Thus, $r = 10$ and $h = 9$. Now we apply the formula for the volume of a cylinder.

$$V = \pi r^2 h = \pi (10 \text{ yd})^2 \cdot 9 \text{ yd} = 900\pi \text{ yd}^3 \approx 2827 \text{ yd}^3$$

The volume of the cylinder is approximately 2827 cubic yards.

Figure 10.45

Figure 10.46 shows a **right circular cone** inside a cylinder, sharing the same circular base as the cylinder. The height of the cone, the perpendicular distance from the top to the circular base, is the same as that of the cylinder. Three such cones occupy the same amount of space as the cylinder. Therefore, the formula for the volume of the cone is $\frac{1}{3}$ the volume of the cylinder.

Volume of a Cone

The volume V of a right circular cone that has height h and radius r is given by the formula

$$V = \frac{1}{3}\pi r^2 h.$$

Cone

$$V = \frac{1}{3}\pi r^2 h$$

Figure 10.46

EXAMPLE 5 Finding the Volume of a Cone

Find the volume of the cone in Figure 10.47.

Solution The radius of the cone is 7 meters and the height is 10 meters. Thus, $r = 7$ and $h = 10$. Now we apply the formula for the volume of a cone.

$$V = \frac{1}{3}\pi r^2 h = \frac{1}{3}\pi (7 \text{ m})^2 \cdot 10 \text{ m} = \frac{490\pi}{3} \text{ m}^3 \approx 513 \text{ m}^3$$

Figure 10.47

The volume of the cone is approximately 513 cubic meters.

Figure 10.48

Figure 10.48 shows a **sphere**. Its shape may remind you of a basketball. The Earth is not a perfect sphere, but it's close. A *sphere* is the set of points in space equally distant from a given point, its **center**. The **radius** is the line segment from the center to any point on the sphere. The word *radius* is also used to refer to the length of this line segment. A sphere's volume can be found by using π and its radius.

Volume of a Sphere

The volume V of a sphere of radius r is given by the formula

$$V = \frac{4}{3}\pi r^3.$$

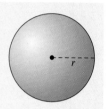

EXAMPLE 6   Applying Volume Formulas

An ice cream cone is 5 inches deep and has a radius of 1 inch. A spherical scoop of ice cream also has a radius of 1 inch. (See Figure 10.49.) If the ice cream melts into the cone, will it overflow?

Solution   The ice cream will overflow if the volume of the ice cream, a sphere, is greater than the volume of the cone. Find the volume of each.

$$V_{\text{cone}} = \frac{1}{3}\pi r^2 h = \frac{1}{3}\pi(1 \text{ in.})^2 \cdot 5 \text{ in.} = \frac{5\pi}{3} \text{ in.}^3 \approx 5 \text{ in.}^3$$

$$V_{\text{sphere}} = \frac{4}{3}\pi r^3 = \frac{4}{3}\pi(1 \text{ in.})^3 = \frac{4\pi}{3} \text{ in.}^3 \approx 4 \text{ in.}^3$$

The volume of the spherical ice cream is less than the volume of the cone, so there will be no overflow.

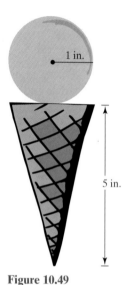

Figure 10.49

2 Compute the surface area of a three-dimensional figure.

Surface Area

Imagine that you fit a piece of cloth to a three-dimensional figure, peel off the cloth, and lay it on a flat surface. The area of the cloth is the three-dimensional figure's **surface area**. Surface area is measured in square units. The surface area of a polyhedron is found by taking the sum of the areas of the polygons that form the outside of the figure.

EXAMPLE 7   Finding the Surface Area of a Solid

Find the surface area of the rectangular solid in Figure 10.50.

Solution   The surface area is the sum of the areas of the six outside rectangles of the solid.

$$\text{Area of front rectangle} = 5 \text{ yd} \cdot 3 \text{ yd} = 15 \text{ yd}^2$$
$$\text{Area of back rectangle: same as front} = 15 \text{ yd}^2$$
$$\text{Area of rectangle on right side} = 8 \text{ yd} \cdot 3 \text{ yd} = 24 \text{ yd}^2$$
$$\text{Area of rectangle on left side: same as right} = 24 \text{ yd}^2$$
$$\text{Area of bottom rectangle} = 8 \text{ yd} \cdot 5 \text{ yd} = 40 \text{ yd}^2$$
$$\text{Area of top rectangle: same as bottom} = 40 \text{ yd}^2$$

$$\text{Sum of these areas: } 158 \text{ yd}^2$$

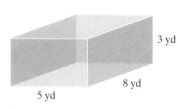

Figure 10.50

The surface area is 158 square yards.

Exercise Set 10.5

 Practice Exercises

In Exercises 1–20, find the volume of each figure. If neces-
sary, round answers to the nearest whole number.

1.

4 in.
3 in.
3 in.

2.

3 cm
3 cm
5 cm

3.
4 cm
4 cm
4 cm

4.
5 in.
5 in.
5 in.

5.
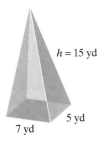
h = 15 yd
5 yd
7 yd

6.

h = 20 yd
15 yd
8 yd

7.

6 in.
7 in.
4 in.

8.

12 m
10 m
10 m

9.

5 cm
6 cm

10.

6 cm
8 cm

11.

24 in.
21 in.

12.

12 cm
14 cm

13.

9 m
4 m

14.

16 m
5 m

15.

6 yd
5 yd

16.

6 yd
7 yd

17.

6 m

18.

15 m

19.

18 cm

20.

24 in.

In Exercises 21–24, find the surface area of each figure.

21.

22.

23.   24.

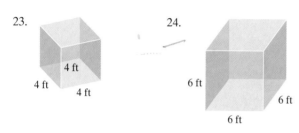

In Exercises 25–26, use two formulas for volume to find the volume of each figure. Round answers to the nearest whole number.

25.

26.

 Application Exercises

27. A building contractor is to dig a foundation 12 feet long, 9 feet wide, and 6 feet deep for a toll booth's foundation. The contractor pays $10 per load for trucks to remove the dirt. Each truck holds 6 cubic yards. What is the cost to the contractor to have all the dirt hauled away?

28. What is the cost of concrete for a walkway that is 15 feet long, 8 feet wide, and 9 inches deep if the concrete is $30 per cubic yard?

29. A furnace is designed to heat 10,000 cubic feet. Will this furnace be adequate for a 1400-square foot house with a 9-foot ceiling?

30. A water reservoir is shaped like a rectangular solid with a base that is 50 yards by 30 yards, and a vertical height of 20 yards. At the start of a three-month period of no rain, the reservoir was completely full. At the end of this period, the height of the water was down to 6 yards. How much water was used in the three-month period?

31. The Great Pyramid outside Cairo, Egypt, has a square base measuring 756 feet on a side and a height of 480 feet.
    a. What is the volume of the Great Pyramid in cubic yards?
    b. The stones used to build the Great Pyramid were limestone blocks with an average volume of 1.5 cubic yards. How many of these blocks were needed to construct the Great Pyramid?

32. Although the Eiffel Tower in Paris is not a solid pyramid, its shape approximates that of a pyramid with a square base measuring 120 feet on a side and a height of 980 feet. If it were a solid pyramid, what would be the Eiffel Tower's volume, in cubic yards?

33. You are about to sue your contractor who promised to install a water tank that holds 500 gallons of water. You know that 500 gallons is the capacity of a tank that holds 67 cubic feet. The cylindrical tank has a radius of 3 feet and a height of 2 feet 4 inches. Does the evidence indicate you can win the case against the contractor if it goes to court?

34. Two cylindrical cans of soup sell for the same price. One can has a diameter of 6 inches and a height of 5 inches. The other has a diameter of 5 inches and a height of 6 inches. Which can contains more soup and, therefore, is the better buy?

35. The shape of Earth is approximately a sphere with a radius of about 3960 miles. Use a calculator with a $\boxed{\pi}$ key to find the volume of Earth.

36. The tunnel under the English Channel that connects England and France is the world's longest tunnel. There are actually three separate tunnels built side by side. Each is a half-cylinder that is 50,000 meters long and 4 meters high. How many cubic meters of dirt had to be removed to build the tunnel?

Writing in Mathematics

37. Explain the following analogy:

    In terms of formulas used to compute volume, a pyramid is to a rectangular solid just as a cone is to a cylinder.

38. Explain why a cylinder is not a polyhedron.

Critical Thinking Exercises

39. What happens to the volume of a sphere if its radius is doubled?

40. A scale model of a car is constructed so that its length, width, and height are each $\frac{1}{10}$ the length, width, and height of the actual car. By how many times does the volume of the car exceed its scale model?

In Exercises 41–42, find the volume of the shaded region. If necessary, round to the nearest whole number.

41.
    7 cm
    6 cm
    6 cm

42.
    2 in.
    10 in.
    6 in.

43. Find the surface area of the figure shown.

6 cm
4 cm
3 cm
5 cm

Group Exercise

44. People who love cars should be members of this group. The group will prepare a presentation to the class on how the power of a car engine is measured. One person, who has worked on car engines, should explain the details of how they work, including cylinders, pistons, fuel, and so on in the discussion. In explaining how the power of the engine is measured, be sure to discuss horsepower, cubic centimeters, and liters. Give examples of the measures of engines for various makes of cars, including more powerful upgrade options that are available.

SECTION 10.6 *Right Triangle Trigonometry*

Objectives

1. Use the lengths of the sides of a right triangle to find trigonometric ratios.

2. Use trigonometric ratios to find missing parts of right triangles.

3. Use trigonometric ratios to solve applied problems.

Ang Rita Sherpa climbed Mount Everest eight times, all without the use of bottled oxygen.

Mountain climbers have forever been fascinated by reaching the top of Mount Everest, sometimes with tragic results. The mountain, on Asia's Tibet-Nepal border, is Earth's highest, peaking at an incredible 29,029 feet. The heights of mountains can be found using **trigonometry**. The word *trigonometry* means *measurement of triangles*. Trigonometry is used in navigation, building, and engineering. For centuries, Muslims have used trigonometry and the stars to navigate across the Arabian desert to Mecca, the birthplace of the prophet Muhammad, the founder of Islam. The ancient Greeks used trigonometry to record the locations of thousands of stars and worked out the motion of the Moon relative to the Earth. Today, trigonometry is used to study the structure of DNA, the master molecule that determines how we grow from a single cell to a complex, fully developed adult.

Ratios in Right Triangles

The right triangle forms the basis of trigonometry. If either acute angle of a right triangle stays the same size, the shape of the triangle does not change even if it is made larger or smaller. Because of properties of similar triangles, this means that the ratios of certain lengths stay the same regardless of the right triangle's size. These ratios have special names and are defined in terms of the **side opposite** an acute angle, the **side adjacent** to the acute angle, and the **hypotenuse**. In Figure 10.51, the length of the hypotenuse, the side opposite the 90° angle, is represented by c. The length of the side opposite angle A is represented by a. The length of the side adjacent to angle A is represented by b.

The three fundamental trigonometric ratios, **sine** (abbreviated sin), **cosine** (abbreviated cos), and **tangent** (abbreviated tan) are defined as ratios of the lengths of the sides of a right triangle. In the box that follows, when a side of a triangle is mentioned, we are referring to the *length* of that side.

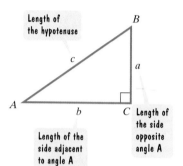

Figure 10.51 Naming a right triangle's sides from the point of view of an acute angle

1 Use the lengths of the sides of a right triangle to find trigonometric ratios.

Trigonometric Ratios

Let A represent an acute angle of a right triangle, with right angle C, shown in Figure 10.51. For A, the trigonometric ratios are defined as follows:

$$\sin A (\text{sine of } A) = \frac{\text{side opposite angle } A}{\text{hypotenuse}} = \frac{a}{c}$$

$$\cos A (\text{cosine of } A) = \frac{\text{side adjacent to angle } A}{\text{hypotenuse}} = \frac{b}{c}$$

$$\tan A (\text{tangent of } A) = \frac{\text{side opposite angle } A}{\text{side adjacent to angle } A} = \frac{a}{b}$$

Study Tip

The word

SOHCAHTOA (pronounced: so-cah-tow-ah)

is a way to remember the definitions of the three trigonometric ratios.

$$\underset{\text{Sine}}{S} \quad \underset{}{\frac{\overset{O}{\text{opp}}\ \overset{H}{}}{\text{hyp}}} \qquad \underset{\text{Cosine}}{C} \quad \underset{}{\frac{\overset{A}{\text{adj}}\ \overset{H}{}}{\text{hyp}}} \qquad \underset{\text{Tangent}}{T} \quad \underset{}{\frac{\overset{O}{\text{opp}}\ \overset{A}{}}{\text{adj}}}$$

"Some Old Hog Came Around Here and Took Our Apples."

EXAMPLE 1 Becoming Familiar with the Trigonometric Ratios

Find the sine, cosine, and tangent of A in Figure 10.52.

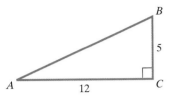

Figure 10.52

Solution We begin by finding the measure of hypotenuse c using the Pythagorean theorem.

$$c^2 = a^2 + b^2 = 5^2 + 12^2 = 25 + 144 = 169$$

$$c = \sqrt{169} = 13$$

Now, we apply the definitions of the trigonometric ratios.

$$\sin A = \frac{\text{side opposite angle } A}{\text{hypotenuse}} = \frac{5}{13}$$

$$\cos A = \frac{\text{side adjacent to angle } A}{\text{hypotenuse}} = \frac{12}{13}$$

$$\tan A = \frac{\text{side opposite angle } A}{\text{side adjacent to angle } A} = \frac{5}{12}$$

2 Use trigonometric ratios to find missing parts of right triangles.

A scientific or graphing calculator in the degree mode will give you decimal approximations for the trigonometric ratios of any angle. For example, to find an approximation for tan 37°, the tangent of 37°, a keystroke sequence similar to one of the following can be used:

Most scientific calculators: 37 $\boxed{\text{Tan}}$
Most graphing calculators: $\boxed{\text{Tan}}$ 37 $\boxed{\text{ENTER}}$

The tangent of 37°, rounded to four decimal places, is 0.7536.

If you do not have your calculator with you, a table of trigonometric ratios appears on page 496. Table 10.4 is quite easy to use. To find tan 37°, simply locate 37° and then select the third decimal to the right under the tangent column.

If we are given the length of one side and the measure of an acute angle of a right triangle, we can use trigonometry to solve for the measures of the other parts. Example 2 illustrates how this is done.

EXAMPLE 2 Finding Missing Parts of a Right Triangle

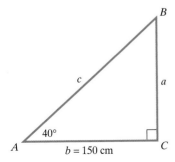

Figure 10.53

Find $m\angle B$ and the lengths a and c for the right triangle in Figure 10.53.

Solution We begin by finding the measure of angle B. We do not need to know trigonometric ratios to do so. Because angle B is the complement of angle A, which measures 40°, its measure is found by subtracting 40° from 90°.

$$m\angle B = 90° - 40° = 50°$$

Now, we need to find a. Let us identify a trigonometric ratio that will make it possible to do so. Our goal is to use a ratio in which two of the quantities are

Table 10.4   Trigonometric Ratios

Angle (degrees)	sine	cosine	tangent	Angle (degrees)	sine	cosine	tangent
0	0.0000	1.0000	0.0000	46	0.7193	0.6947	1.0355
1	0.0175	0.9998	0.0175	47	0.7314	0.6820	1.0724
2	0.0349	0.9994	0.0349	48	0.7431	0.6691	1.1106
3	0.0523	0.9986	0.0524	49	0.7547	0.6561	1.1504
4	0.0698	0.9976	0.0699	50	0.7660	0.6428	1.1918
5	0.0872	0.9962	0.0875	51	0.7771	0.6293	1.2349
6	0.1045	0.9945	0.1051	52	0.7880	0.6157	1.2799
7	0.1219	0.9925	0.1228	53	0.7986	0.6018	1.3270
8	0.1392	0.9903	0.1405	54	0.8090	0.5878	1.3764
9	0.1564	0.9877	0.1584	55	0.8192	0.5736	1.4281
10	0.1736	0.9848	0.1763	56	0.8290	0.5592	1.4826
11	0.1908	0.9816	0.1944	57	0.8387	0.5446	1.5399
12	0.2079	0.9781	0.2126	58	0.8480	0.5299	1.6003
13	0.2250	0.9744	0.2309	59	0.8572	0.5150	1.6643
14	0.2419	0.9703	0.2493	60	0.8660	0.5000	1.7321
15	0.2588	0.9659	0.2679	61	0.8746	0.4848	1.8040
16	0.2756	0.9613	0.2867	62	0.8829	0.4695	1.8807
17	0.2924	0.9563	0.3057	63	0.8910	0.4540	1.9626
18	0.3090	0.9511	0.3249	64	0.8988	0.4384	2.0503
19	0.3256	0.9455	0.3443	65	0.9063	0.4226	2.1445
20	0.3420	0.9397	0.3640	66	0.9135	0.4067	2.2460
21	0.3584	0.9336	0.3839	67	0.9205	0.3907	2.3559
22	0.3746	0.9272	0.4040	68	0.9272	0.3746	2.4751
23	0.3907	0.9205	0.4245	69	0.9336	0.3584	2.6051
24	0.4067	0.9135	0.4452	70	0.9397	0.3420	2.7475
25	0.4226	0.9063	0.4663	71	0.9455	0.3256	2.9042
26	0.4384	0.8988	0.4877	72	0.9511	0.3090	3.0777
27	0.4540	0.8910	0.5095	73	0.9563	0.2924	3.2709
28	0.4695	0.8829	0.5317	74	0.9613	0.2756	3.4874
29	0.4848	0.8746	0.5543	75	0.9659	0.2588	3.7321
30	0.5000	0.8660	0.5774	76	0.9703	0.2419	4.0108
31	0.5150	0.8572	0.6009	77	0.9744	0.2250	4.3315
32	0.5299	0.8480	0.6249	78	0.9781	0.2079	4.7046
33	0.5446	0.8387	0.6494	79	0.9816	0.1908	5.1446
34	0.5592	0.8290	0.6745	80	0.9848	0.1736	5.6713
35	0.5736	0.8192	0.7002	81	0.9877	0.1564	6.3138
36	0.5878	0.8090	0.7265	82	0.9903	0.1392	7.1154
37	0.6018	0.7986	0.7536	83	0.9925	0.1219	8.1443
38	0.6157	0.7880	0.7813	84	0.9945	0.1045	9.5144
39	0.6293	0.7771	0.8098	85	0.9962	0.0872	11.4300
40	0.6428	0.7660	0.8391	86	0.9976	0.0698	14.3007
41	0.6561	0.7547	0.8693	87	0.9986	0.0523	19.0812
42	0.6691	0.7431	0.9004	88	0.9994	0.0349	28.6364
43	0.6820	0.7314	0.9325	89	0.9998	0.0175	57.2900
44	0.6947	0.7193	0.9657	90	1.0000	0.0000	undefined
45	0.7071	0.7071	1.0000				

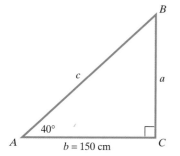

Figure 10.53 Shown again so you do not have to turn back a page.

known and the unknown third quantity is a. This will enable us to solve for a. We know the length of b, namely 150 centimeters. Thus, either the numerator or the denominator of the ratio we select must involve b. Let us consider the three trigonometric ratios.

$$\sin A = \frac{\text{side opposite } A}{\text{hypotenuse}} = \frac{a}{c}$$

$$\cos A = \frac{\text{side adjacent to } A}{\text{hypotenuse}} = \frac{b}{c}$$

$$\tan A = \frac{\text{side opposite } A}{\text{side adjacent to } A} = \frac{a}{b}$$

The third ratio in the list, the tangent of angle A, is the only trigonometric ratio that involves both the given length, b ($b = 150$ cm), and the length we need to find, a. As the measure of angle A is given to be $40°$, we can solve for a as follows:

$$\tan A = \frac{\text{side opposite } A}{\text{side adjacent to } A}$$

$$\tan 40° = \frac{a}{150}$$

Now, use your calculator or Table 10.4 to find $\tan 40°$.

$$0.8391 = \frac{a}{150}$$

We solve for a by multiplying both sides by 150.

$$a = 150(0.8391) \approx 126 \text{ cm}$$

Thus, the measure of one leg is approximately 126 centimeters.

There are a number of different ways to find c. One method is to use the Pythagorean theorem.

$$c^2 = a^2 + b^2 = 126^2 + 150^2 = 38{,}376$$
$$c = \sqrt{38{,}376} \approx 196$$

We can also use a trigonometric ratio to find c. Because c is the hypotenuse and we know the length of the side adjacent to angle A, 150 centimeters, we use the cosine ratio.

$$\cos A = \frac{\text{side adjacent to } A}{\text{hypotenuse}}$$

$$\cos 40° = \frac{150}{c}$$

$$0.766 = \frac{150}{c} \qquad \text{Use a calculator or Table 10.4.}$$

$$0.766c = 150 \qquad \text{Multiply both sides by } c.$$

$$c = \frac{150}{0.766} \approx 196 \qquad \text{Divide both sides by 0.766.}$$

Using either the Pythagorean theorem or a ratio, we see that the hypotenuse measures approximately 196 centimeters.

In summary, $m \angle B = 50°$, $a \approx 126$ centimeters, and $c \approx 196$ centimeters.

3 Use trigonometric ratios to solve applied problems.

Applications of the Trigonometric Ratios

Example 3 illustrates the use of trigonometry in surveying.

EXAMPLE 3 Problem Solving Using a Trigonometric Ratio

The irregular blue shape in Figure 10.54 represents a lake. The distance across the lake, a, is unknown. To find this distance, a surveyor took the measurements shown in the figure. What is the distance across the lake?

Solution We need to identify a trigonometric ratio that will make it possible to find a. In terms of the 24° angle, we are looking for the side opposite the angle. The surveyor measured the side adjacent to the angle as 750 yards. Since we have a known angle, an unknown opposite side, and a known adjacent side, we will select the tangent ratio.

$$\tan A = \frac{\text{side opposite angle } A}{\text{side adjacent to angle } A}$$

$$\tan 24° = \frac{a}{750}$$

$$0.4452 = \frac{a}{750} \qquad \text{Use a calculator or Table 10.4.}$$

$$a = 750(0.4452) \qquad \text{Multiply both sides by 750.}$$

$$a \approx 334$$

The distance across the lake is approximately 334 yards.

Figure 10.54

Many applications of right triangles involve the angle made with an imaginary horizontal line. As shown in Figure 10.55, an angle formed by a horizontal line and the line of sight to an object that is above the horizontal line is called the **angle of elevation**. The angle formed by a horizontal line and the line of sight to

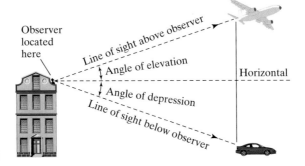

Figure 10.55

an object that is below the horizontal line is called the **angle of depression**. Transits and sextants are instruments used to measure such angles.

EXAMPLE 4   Problem Solving Using an Angle of Elevation

Sighting the top of a building, a surveyor measured the angle of elevation to be 22°. The transit is 5 feet above the ground and 300 feet from the building. Find the building's height.

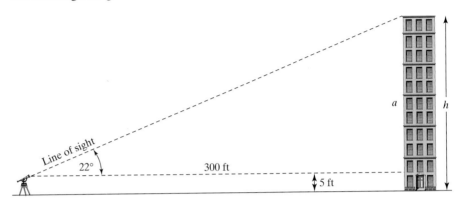

Figure 10.56

Solution   The situation is illustrated in Figure 10.56. If a is the height of the portion of the building that lies above the transit,

$$\tan 22° = \frac{a}{300} \quad \text{and} \quad a = 300 \tan 22° \approx 300(0.404) \approx 121.$$

The height of the part of the building above the transit is 121 feet. Thus, the height of the building is determined by adding the transit's height, 5 feet, to 121 feet.

$$h = 5 + 121 = 126$$

The building's height is 126 feet.

If the measures of two sides of a right triangle are known, the measures of the two acute angles can be found using Table 10.4 or a calculator. For example, Figure 10.57 shows a 50-foot ladder reaching 43.3 feet on a vertical wall. To find the measure of ∡ A, the angle that the ladder makes with the ground, we can use the sine ratio.

Figure 10.57

$$\sin A = \frac{\text{side opposite angle } A}{\text{hypotenuse}} = \frac{43.3}{50}$$

To find the measure of ∡ A using Table 10.4, perform the division on the right, $43.3 \div 50$:

$$\sin A = 0.866$$

Now, look down the sine column in Table 10.4 until you find the displayed decimal that is the closest to 0.866. In this instance, 0.866 occurs in the sine column to the right of 60°, so the measure of angle A is 60°.

Finding the measure of angle A with either a scientific or graphing calculator requires the use of the *inverse sine key*, usually labeled $\boxed{\sin^{-1}}$. Given that

$$\sin A = \frac{43.3}{50},$$

here are the keystroke sequences used on most calculators:

Most scientific calculators:

$$43.3 \boxed{\div} 50 \boxed{=} \boxed{\text{2nd Function}} \boxed{\sin/\sin^{-1}}$$

Most graphing calculators:

$$\boxed{\text{2nd}} \boxed{\sin/\sin^{-1}} \boxed{(} 43.3 \boxed{\div} 50 \boxed{)} \boxed{\text{ENTER}}$$

The display should show approximately 59.99°, which can be rounded to 60°.

EXAMPLE 5 Determining the Angle of Elevation

A building that is 21 meters tall casts a shadow 25 meters long. Find the angle of elevation of the sun.

Solution The situation is illustrated in Figure 10.58. We are asked to find $m\angle A$. We begin with the tangent ratio.

Figure 10.58

$$\tan A = \frac{21}{25} = 0.84$$

Using Table 10.4, the value in the tangent column that comes closest to 0.84 is 0.8391, which appears to the right of 40°. So, the angle of elevation is 40°. Using a calculator, it is necessary to use the inverse tangent key.

Since $\tan A = 0.84$, then $A = \tan^{-1} 0.84$.

Scientific Calculator: .84 $\boxed{\text{2nd Function}}$ $\boxed{\tan/\tan^{-1}}$

Graphing Calculator: $\boxed{\text{2nd}}$ $\boxed{\tan/\tan^{-1}}$ .84 $\boxed{\text{ENTER}}$

The display should show approximately 40°.

Using Table 10.4 or a calculator, the angle of elevation of the sun is approximately 40°.

Exercise Set 10.6

 Practice Exercises

In Exercises 1–8, use the given right triangles to find sin *A*, cos *A*, *and* tan *A*.

1.

2.

3.

4.

5.

6.

7.

8.
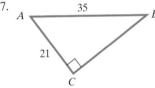

In Exercises 9–18, find the measure of the side of the right triangle whose length is designated by a lowercase letter. Round answers to the nearest whole number.

9.

10.

11.

12.

13.

14.

15.

16.

17.

18.

In Exercises 19–22, find the measures of the parts of the right triangle that are not given. Round all answers to the nearest whole number.

19.

20.

21.

22.

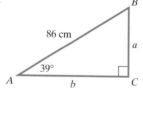

In Exercises 23–26, use Table 10.4 or the inverse trigonometric keys on a calculator to find the measure of angle A, rounded to the nearest whole degree.

23.

24.

25.

26.

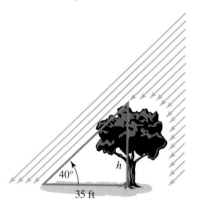

Application Exercises

27. To find the distance across a lake, a surveyor took the measurements in the figure shown. Use these measurements to determine how far it is across the lake. Round to the nearest yard.

28. At a certain time of day, the angle of elevation of the sun is 40°. To the nearest foot, find the height of a tree whose shadow is 35 feet long.

29. A plane rises from a take-off and flies at an angle of 10° with the horizontal runway. When it has gained 500 feet, find the distance, to the nearest foot, the plane has flown.

30. A road is inclined at an angle of 5°. After driving 5000 feet along this road, find the driver's increase in altitude. Round to the nearest foot.

31. Sighting the top of a hill, a surveyor measured the angle of elevation to be 16°. The transit is 5 feet above the ground and 282 feet from the hill. Find the height of the hill, rounded to the nearest foot.

32. If a 40-foot ladder leaning against a vertical wall makes a 75° angle with the horizontal ground, how far up the wall does the ladder reach? Round the answer to the nearest foot.

33. A building that is 65 feet tall casts a shadow 55 feet long. Find the angle of elevation of the sun, rounded to the nearest degree.

34. A person 5.8 feet tall casts a shadow 8.1 feet long. Find the angle of elevation of the sun, rounded to the nearest degree.

35. At a point 70 feet on level ground from the base of a tree, the angle of elevation to the top of the tree is measured to be 65°. Find the height of the tree, rounded to the nearest foot.

36. Radar shows that the distance to an approaching airplane is 7.4 miles. If the angle of elevation to the plane is 24°, find the altitude at which the plane is flying. Round the answer to the nearest mile.

37. From the top of a 200-foot lighthouse, the angle of depression of a ship is 26°. Find the distance of the ship from the foot of the lighthouse, rounded to the nearest foot.

38. At a certain time of the day, the angle of elevation of the sun is 38°. Find the length of the shadow cast by a 90-foot building, rounded to the nearest foot.

 Writing in Mathematics

39. If you are given the lengths of the sides of a right triangle, describe how to find the sine of either acute angle.

40. Describe one similarity and one difference between the sine ratio and the cosine ratio in terms of the sides of a right triangle.

41. If one of the acute angles of a right triangle is 37°, explain why the sine ratio does not increase as the size of the triangle increases.

42. If the measure of one of the acute angles and the hypotenuse of a right triangle are known, describe how to find the measure of the remaining parts of the triangle.

43. Describe what is meant by an angle of elevation and an angle of depression.

44. Give an example of an applied problem that can be solved using one or more trigonometric ratios. Be as specific as possible.

45. Use Table 10.4 or a calculator to find each of the following: sin 32° and cos 58°; sin 17° and cos 73°; sin 50° and cos 40°; sin 88° and cos 2°. Describe what you observe. Based on your observations, what do you think the *co* in *cosine* stands for?

 Critical Thinking Exercises

46. Explain why the sine or cosine of an acute angle cannot be greater than or equal to 1.

47. Describe what happens to the tangent of an angle as the measure of the angle gets close to 90°. What happens at 90°?

48. From the top of a 250-foot lighthouse, a plane is sighted overhead and a ship is observed directly below the plane. The angle of elevation of the plane is 22° and the angle of depression of the ship is 35°. Find a. the distance of the ship from the lighthouse; b. the plane's height above the water. Round to the nearest foot.

SECTION 10.7   *Beyond Euclidean Geometry*

Objectives

1. Gain an understanding of some of the general ideas of other kinds of geometries.

Think of your favorite natural setting. During the last quarter of the twentieth century, mathematicians have developed a new kind of geometry that uses the computer to produce the diverse forms of nature that we see around us. These forms are not polygons, polyhedrons, circles, or cylinders. In this section, we move beyond Euclidean geometry to explore ideas which have extended geometry beyond the boundaries first laid down by the ancient Greek scholars.

1 Gain an understanding of some of the general ideas of other kinds of geometries.

The Geometry of Networks

In the early 1700s, the city of Königsberg, Germany, was connected by seven bridges, shown in Figure 10.59. Many people in the city were interested in finding if it were possible to walk through the city so as to cross each bridge exactly once. After a few trials, you may be convinced that the answer is no. However, it is not easy to prove your answer by trial and error because there are a large number of ways of taking such a walk.

Figure 10.59

Ethane

Network theory is used to show how atoms are linked to form molecules.

The problem was taken to the Swiss mathematician Leonhard Euler (1707–1783). In the year 1736, Euler proved that it is not possible to stroll through the city and cross each bridge exactly once. His solution of the problem opened up a new kind of geometry called network (or graph) theory. Network theory is now used to design city streets, analyze traffic patterns, and find the most efficient routes for public transportation.

Euler solved the problem by introducing the following definitions:

A **vertex** is a point. An **arc** is a line segment or curve that starts and ends at a vertex.

Vertices and arcs form a **network**. A vertex with an odd number of attached arcs is an **odd vertex**. A vertex with an even number of attached arcs is an **even vertex.**

Using these definitions, Figure 10.60 shows that the network in the Königsberg bridge problem has four odd vertices.

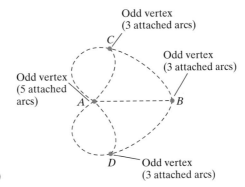

Odd vertex
(3 attached arcs)

Odd vertex
(3 attached arcs)

Odd vertex
(5 attached arcs)

Odd vertex
(3 attached arcs)

Figure 10.60

A network is **traversable** if it can be traced without removing the pencil from the paper and without tracing an arc more than once. Euler proved the following rules of traversability in solving the problem.

1. A network with all even vertices is traversable. One can start at any vertex and end where one began.
2. A network with two odd vertices is traversable. One must start at either of the odd vertices and finish at the other.
3. A network with more than two odd vertices is not traversable.

Because the network in the Königsberg bridge problem has four odd vertices, it cannot be traversed.

EXAMPLE 1   To Traverse or Not to Traverse?

Consider the network in Figure 10.61.
   a. Is this network traversable?
   b. If it is, describe a path that will traverse it.

Solution
   a. Begin by determining if each vertex is even or odd.

Figure 10.61

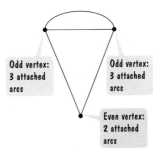

Odd vertex:
3 attached arcs

Odd vertex:
3 attached arcs

Even vertex:
2 attached arcs

Because this network has two odd vertices, by Euler's second rule, it is traversable.
   b. In order to find a path that traverses this network, we again use Euler's second rule. It states that we must start at either of the odd vertices and finish at the other. One of two possible paths is shown in Figure 10.62.

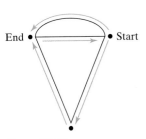

End   Start

Figure 10.62

A floor plan can be represented by a network. Represent rooms as vertices, the outside as a vertex, and doors as arcs. Once this is done, Euler's rules will let you know if it is possible to take a trip through the house in such a way that you would pass through each door exactly once.

EXAMPLE 2   Traversing the Rooms of a House

The floor plan of a four-room house is shown in Figure 10.63. The rooms are labeled $A, B, C,$ and D. The outside of the house is labeled E. The openings represent doors.

Figure 10.63

a. Draw a network that corresponds to the floor plan.
b. Is the network traversable?
c. If it is, determine a path to walk through every room, using each door only once.

Solution

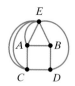

Figure 10.64

a. A network has been created for the floor plan in Figure 10.64. The rooms are vertices $A, B, C,$ and D. The outside of the house is vertex E. Each door is an arc. Two doors connect the outside, E, with room A, so draw two arcs from E to A. One of these arcs is shown as a line segment and the other as a curve. Only one door connects the outside, E, with room B, so draw one arc from E to B, shown as a line segment. Two doors connect the outside, E, to room C; draw two arcs from E to C, both shown as curves. Counting doors from the outside to each room and doors between rooms, the network is completed as shown in Figure 10.64.

b. There are only two odd vertices, B and D. This means that the network is traversable.

Figure 10.65

c. The path must start at either of the odd vertices, B or D. Figure 10.65 shows starting in room B and ending in room D. You can also start in room D and end in room B. Try using the path in the floor plan in Figure 10.65 to trace the same path in the network in Figure 10.64.

Colorful Puzzles

A problem that plagued mathematicians for over 100 years involved the maximum number of colors needed on a plane map so that any two regions that share a common boundary are colored differently. The conjecture that at most four colors are needed, stated in 1850, was proved by Kenneth Appel and Wolfgang Haken of the University of Illinois in 1976. However, many mathematicians question the validity of the Haken-Appel proof. The proof relies heavily on computer computations that are too numerous to check. There are even recent rumors about a flaw in the proof. Network theory played an important role in Appel and Haken's work.

If you take a strip of paper, give it a single half-twist, and paste the ends together, the result is a one-sided surface called a Möbius strip. A map on a Möbius strip requires six colors to make sure that no adjacent areas are the same color.

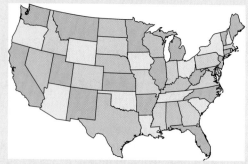

At most four colors are needed on a plane map.

At most six colors are needed on a map drawn on a Möbius strip.

Topology

A branch of modern geometry called **topology** looks at shapes in a completely new way. In Euclidean geometry, shapes are rigid and unchanging. In topology, shapes can be twisted, stretched, bent, and shrunk. Total flexibility is the rule.

A topologist does not know the difference between a doughnut and a coffee cup! This is because, topologically speaking, there is no difference. They both have one hole, and in this strange geometry of transformations, a doughnut can be flattened, pulled, and pushed to form a coffee cup.

In topology, objects are classified according to the number of holes in them, called their **genus**. The genus gives the largest number of complete cuts that can be made in the object without cutting the object into two pieces. Objects with the same genus are **topologically equivalent**.

> ### Study Tip
>
> The genus of an object is the same as the number of holes in the object.

All of these shapes (sphere, cube, irregular blob) have the same genus: 0. No complete cuts can be made without cutting these objects into two pieces.

How can a doughnut be transformed into a coffee cup? It can be stretched and deformed to make a bowl part of the surface. Both the doughnut and the coffee cup have genus 1. One complete cut can be made without cutting these objects into two pieces.

To a topologist, a lump with two holes in it is no different than a sugar bowl with two handles. Both have genus 2. Two complete cuts can be made without cutting these objects into two pieces.

Shown below is a transformation that results in a most unusual topological figure.

Base

Start with a flexible glass tube.

Neck

Pass the neck through a hole.

Join the neck to the base.

The figure that results is called a **Klein bottle**. You couldn't use one to carry water on a long hike. Because the inside surface loops back on itself to merge with the outside, it has neither an outside nor an inside and cannot hold water. A Klein bottle passes through itself without the existence of a hole, which is impossible in three-dimensional space. A true Klein bottle is visible only when generated on a computer.

A Klein bottle generated on a computer

Topology is more than an excursion in geometric fantasy. Topologists study knots and ways in which they are topologically equivalent. Knot theory is used to identify viruses and understand the ways in which they invade our cells. Such an understanding is a first step in finding vaccines for viruses ranging from the common cold to HIV.

Non-Euclidean Geometries

Imagine this: Earth is squeezed and compressed to the size of a golf ball. It becomes a **black hole**, a region in space where everything seems to disappear. Its pull of gravity is now so strong that the space near the golf ball can be thought of as a funnel with the black hole sitting at the bottom. Any object that comes near the funnel will be pulled into it by the immense gravity of the golf-ball-sized Earth. Then the object disappears! Although this sounds like science fiction, some physicists believe that there are billions of black holes in space.

Is there a geometry that describes this bizarre situation? Yes, although it's not the geometry of Euclid. Euclidean geometry is based on the assumption that given a point not on a line, there is one line that can be drawn through the point parallel to the given line, shown as the black line in Figure 10.66. We used this assumption to prove that the sum of the measures of the three angles of any triangle is 180°.

Hyperbolic geometry was developed independently by the Russian mathematician Nikolay Lobachevsky (1792–1856) and the Hungarian mathematician Janos Bolyai (1802–1860). It is based on the assumption that given a point not on a line, there are an infinite number of lines that can be drawn through the point

given point

given line

Figure 10.66

Figure 10.67

Figure 10.68

parallel to the given line. The shapes in this non-Euclidean geometry are not represented on a plane. Instead, they are drawn on a funnel-like surface, called a *pseudosphere*, shown in Figure 10.67. On such a surface, the shortest distance between two points is a curved line. A triangle's sides are composed of arcs, and the sum of the measures of its angles is less than 180°. The shape of the pseudosphere looks like the distorted space near a black hole.

Once the ice had been broken by Lobachevsky and Bolyai, mathematicians were stimulated to set up other non-Euclidean geometries. The best known of these was **elliptic geometry**, proposed by the German mathematician Bernhard Riemann (1826–1866). Riemann began his geometry with the assumption that there are no parallel lines. As shown in Figure 10.68, geometry is on a sphere, and the sum of the measures of the angles of a triangle is greater than 180°.

Riemann's elliptic geometry was used by Albert Einstein in his theory of the universe. The theory claims that if you set off on a journey through space and keep going in the same direction, you will eventually come back to your starting point. The same thing happens on the surface of a sphere. This means that space itself "curved," although the idea is difficult to visualize. It is interesting that Einstein used ideas of non-Euclidean geometry more than 50 years after the system was logically developed. Mathematics often moves ahead of our understanding of the physical world.

The Dutch artist M.C. Escher (1898–1972) is known for combining art and geometry. Many of his images are based on non-Euclidean geometry. In the woodcut shown below, things enlarge as they approach the center and shrink proportionally as they approach the boundary. The shortest distance between two points is a curved line, and the triangles that are formed look like those from hyperbolic geometry.

M.C. Escher, *Circle Limit III* © 1994 M.C. Escher/Cordon Art, Baarn, Holland. All rights reserved.

Table 10.5 compares Euclidean geometry with hyperbolic and elliptic geometry.

Table 10.5   Comparing Three Systems of Geometry

Euclidean Geometry Euclid (300 B.C.)	Hyperbolic Geometry Lobachevsky, Bolyai (1830)	Elliptic Geometry Riemann (1850)
Given a point not on a line, there is one and only one line through the point parallel to the given line.	Given a point not on a line, there are an infinite number of lines through the point that do not intersect the given line.	There are no parallel line.
Geometry is on a plane: *D*　　*C* *A*　　*B*	Geometry is on a pseudosphere: *D*　　*C* *A*　　*B*	Geometry is on a sphere: *D*　　*C* *A*　　*B*
The sum of the measures of the angles of a triangle is 180°. *A* *C*　　*B*	The sum of the measures of the angles of a triangle is less than 180°. *A* *B* *C*	The sum of the measures of the angles of a triangle is greater than 180°. *A* *B*　*C*

Fractal Geometry

magnified portion

How can geometry describe nature's complexity in objects such as ferns, coastlines, or the human circulatory system? Any magnified portion of a fern repeats much of the pattern of the whole fern, as well as new and unexpected patterns. This property is called **self-similarity**.

Through the use of computers, a new geometry of natural shapes, called **fractal geometry**, has arrived. The word *fractal* is from the Latin word *fractus*, meaning *broken up*, or *fragmented*. The fractal shape shown in Figure 10.69 is, indeed, broken up. This shape was obtained by repeatedly subtracting triangles from within triangles. From the midpoints of the sides of triangle *ABC*, remove

Figure 10.69

Figure 10.70 Daryl H. Hepting and Allan N. Snider, "Desktop Tetrahedron" 1990. Computer generated at the University of Regina in Canada

triangle $A'B'C'$. Repeat the process for the three remaining triangles, then with each of the triangles left after that, and so on ad infinitum.

The process of repeating a rule again and again to create a self-similar fractal like the broken-up triangle is called **iteration**. The self-similar fractal shape in Figure 10.70 was generated on a computer by iteration that involved subtracting pyramids within pyramids. Computers can generate fractal shapes by carrying out thousands or millions of iterations.

In 1975, Benoit Mandelbrot (1924–), an American mathematician who developed fractal geometry, published *The Fractal Geometry of Nature*. This book of beautiful computer graphics shows images that look like actual mountains, coastlines, underwater coral gardens, and flowers, all imitating nature's forms. Many of the realistic-looking landscapes that you see in movies are actually computer-generated fractal images.

These images are computer-generated fractals.

Exercise Set 10.7

 Practice Exercises

For each network in Exercises 1–6: a. Is the network traversable? b. If it is, describe a path that will traverse it.

1.

2.

3.

4.

5.

6.
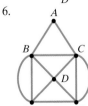

In Exercises 7–10, give the genus of each object.

7.

Pretzel

8.

Pitcher

9.

Wrench

10.

Button

11. In Exercises 7–10, which objects are topologically equivalent?

12. Draw (or find and describe) an object of genus 4 or more.

13. What does the figure shown illustrate about angles in a triangle when the triangle is drawn on a sphere?

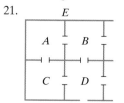

14. The figure shows a quadrilateral that was drawn on the surface of a sphere. Angles *C* and *D* are obtuse angles. What does the figure illustrate about the sum of the measures of the four angles in a quadrilateral in elliptic geometry?

In Exercises 15–17, describe whether each figure shown exhibits self-similarity.

15.

16.

17.

The model shows the way that carbon atoms (black) and hydrogen atoms (white) link together to form a propane molecule. Use the model to answer Exercises 18–20.

Propane

18. Using each of the three black carbon atoms as a vertex and each of the eight white hydrogen atoms as a vertex, draw a network for the propane molecule.

19. Determine if each vertex of the network is even or odd.

20. Is the network traversable?

Each floor plan in Exercises 21–25 represents the floor plan of an art museum.

   a. *Draw a network that corresponds to the floor plan.*
   b. *Is the network traversable?*
   c. *If it is, determine a path to walk through every room, using each door only once.*

21.

22.

23.

24.

25.

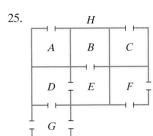

26. The figure shows a map of a portion of New York City with the bridge and tunnel connections.

a. Represent Manhattan, Long Island, Staten Island, and New Jersey as vertices of a network. Represent the bridges and tunnels as arcs. Draw the map as a network.
b. Use the network to determine if it is possible to visit Manhattan, Long Island, Staten Island, and New Jersey using each bridge or tunnel only once.

27. Consult an Internet site devoted to fractals and download two fractal images that imitate nature's forms. How is self-similarity shown in each image?

Writing in Mathematics

28. What is a network?
29. What does it mean if a network is traversable?
30. How do you determine whether or not a network is traversable?
31. Discuss one way in which you can use the geometry of networks in a practical, applied way.
32. Describe one way in which topology is different than Euclidean geometry.
33. What is the genus of an object?
34. Describe how a rectangular solid and a sphere are topologically equivalent.
35. State the assumption that Euclid made about parallel lines that was altered in both hyperbolic and elliptic geometry.
36. How does hyperbolic geometry differ from Euclidean geometry?
37. How does elliptic geometry differ from Euclidean geometry?

38. What is self-similarity? Describe an object in nature that has this characteristic.
39. Some suggest that nature produces its many forms through a combination of both iteration and a touch of randomness. Describe what this means.
40. Find an Internet site devoted to fractals. Use the site to write a paper on a specific use of fractals.
41. Did you know that laid end to end, the veins, arteries, and capillaries of your body would reach over 40,000 miles? However, your vascular system occupies a very small fraction of your body's volume. Describe a self-similar object in nature, such as your vascular system, with enormous length but relatively small volume.
42. Describe a difference between the shapes of man-made objects and objects that occur in nature.
43. Explain what this short poem by Jonathan Swift has to do with fractal images:

> So Nat'ralists observe, A Flea
> Hath Smaller Fleas that on him prey
> and these have smaller Fleas to bite'em
> And so proceed, ad infinitum

44. In Tom Stoppard's play *Arcadia*, the characters talk about mathematics, including ideas from fractal geometry. Rent the movie and write a paper on one of the ideas that the characters discuss that is related to something presented in this section.

Group Exercises

45. This activity is suggested for two or three people. Research some of the practical applications of topology. Present the results of your research in a seminar to the entire class. You may also want to include a discussion of some of topology's more unusal figures, such as the Klein bottle and the Möbius strip.
46. Research non-Euclidean geometry and plan a seminar based on your group's research. Each group member should research one of the five areas described below.
a. Present an overview of the history of the people who developed non-Euclidean geometry. Who first used the term, and why did he never publish his work?
b. Present an overview of the connection between Saccheri quadrilaterals and non-Euclidean geometry. Describe the work of Girolamo Saccheri.
c. Describe how Albert Einstein applied the ideas of Gauss and Riemann. Discuss the notion of curved space and a fourth dimension.
d. Present examples of the work of M.C. Escher that provide ways of visualizing hyperbolic and elliptic geometry.
e. Describe how non-Euclidean geometry changed the direction of subsequent research in mathematics.

After all research has been completed, the group should plan the order in which each group member will speak. Each person should plan on taking about five minutes for his or her portion of the presentation.

47. Albert Einstein's theory of general relativity is concerned with the structure, or the geometry, of the universe. In order to describe the universe, Einstein discovered that he needed four variables: three variables to locate an object in space and a fourth variable describing time. This system is known as space-time.

Because we are three-dimensional beings, how can we imagine four dimensions? One interesting approach to visualizing four dimensions is to consider an analogy of a two-dimensional being struggling to understand three dimensions. This approach first appeared in a book called *Flatland* by Edwin Abbott, written around 1884.

Flatland describes an entire race of beings who are two dimensional, living on a flat plane, unaware of the existence of anything outside their universe. A house in Flatland would look like a blueprint or a line drawing to us. If we were to draw a closed circle around Flatlanders, they would be imprisoned in a cell with no way to see out or escape because there is no way to move up and over the circle. For a two-dimensional being moving only on a plane,

the idea of up would be incomprehensible. We could explain that up means moving in a new direction, perpendicular to the two dimensions they know, but it would be similar to telling us we can move in the fourth dimension by traveling perpendicular to our three dimensions.

An excerpt of *Flatland* can be found on the Web site for this book. Once all group members have read the story, the following questions are offered for group discussion.

a. How does the sphere, the visitor from the third dimension, reflect the same narrow perspective as the Flatlanders?

b. What are some of the sociological problems raised in the story?

c. What happens when we have a certain way of seeing the world that is challenged by coming into contact with something quite different? Be as specific as possible, citing either personal examples or historical examples.

d. How are A. Square's difficulties in visualizing three dimensions similar to those of a three-dimensional dweller trying to visualize four dimensions?

e. How does the author reflect the overt sexism of his time?

f. What "upward not northward" ideas do you hold that, if shared, would result in criticism, rejection, or a fate similar to that of the narrator of *Flatland*?

 CHAPTER SUMMARY, REVIEW, AND TEST

SUMMARY

10.1 Points, Lines, Planes, and Angles

a. Point A, line AB ($\overleftrightarrow{AB}$), and plane P are represented in Figure 10.1 on page 454.

b. Angles are measured in degrees. Acute angles measure less than 90°, right angles 90°, obtuse angles more than 90° but less than 180°, and straight angles 180°.

c. Complementary angles are two angles whose measure have a sum of 90° and supplementary angles a sum of 180°.

d. Vertical angles have the same measure.

e. If parallel lines are cut by a transversal, alternate interior angles, alternate exterior angles, and corresponding angles have the same measure.

10.2 Triangles

a. The sum of the measures of the three angles of any triangle is 180°.

b. Similar triangles have the same shape, but not necessarily the same size. Corresponding angles have

the same measure and corresponding sides are proportional. If the measures of two angles of one triangle are equal to those of two angles of a second triangle, then the two triangles are similar.

c. The Pythagorean theorem: The sum of the squares of the lengths of the legs of a right triangle equals the square of the length of the hypotenuse.

10.3 Polygons, Quadrilaterals, and Perimeter

a. A polygon is a closed geometric figure in a plane formed by three or more line segments. Names of some polygons are given in Table 10.2 on page 471. A regular polygon is one whose sides are all the same length and whose angles all have the same measure. The sum of the measures of the angles of an n-sided polygon is $(n - 2)\,180°$.

b. Quadrilaterals are four-sided polygons. The sum of the measures of the angles is 360°. Types of quadrilaterals and their characteristics are given in Table 10.3 on page 472.

c. The perimeter of a polygon is the sum of the lengths of its sides.

10.4 Area and Circumference

a. Formulas for Area
Rectangle: $A = lw$; Square: $A = s^2$; Parallelogram:
$A = bh$; Triangle: $A = \frac{1}{2}bh$; Trapezoid: $A = \frac{1}{2}h(a + b)$

b. Circles
Circumference: $C = 2\pi r$ or $C = \pi d$; Area: $A = \pi r^2$

10.5 Volume

a. Formulas for Volume
Rectangular Solid: $V = lwh$; Cube: $V = s^3$; Pyramid:
$V = \frac{1}{3}Bh$; Cylinder: $V = \pi r^2 h$; Cone: $V = \frac{1}{3}\pi r^2 h$;
Sphere: $V = \frac{4}{3}\pi r^3$

b. Surface Area
The surface area of a polyhedron is found by taking
the sum of the areas of the polygons that form the outside of the figure.

10.6 Right Triangle Trigonometry

a. Trigonometric Ratios

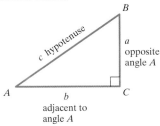

$$\sin A = \frac{\text{side opposite } A}{\text{hypotenuse}} = \frac{a}{c}$$

$$\cos A = \frac{\text{side adjacent to } A}{\text{hypotenuse}} = \frac{b}{c}$$

$$\tan A = \frac{\text{side opposite } A}{\text{side adjacent to } A} = \frac{a}{b}$$

The word SOHCAHTOA is a way to remember these ratios.

b. Given one side and the measure of an acute angle of
a right triangle, the trigonometric ratios can be used
to find the measures of the other parts. Table 10.4 on
page 496 or a calculator is needed.

c. Given the measures of two sides of a right triangle,
the measures of the acute angles can be found using
Table 10.4 on page 496 or the inverse trigonometric
ratio keys, $\sin^{-1}$, $\cos^{-1}$, $\tan^{-1}$, on a calculator.

10.7 Beyond Euclidean Geometry

a. A vertex is a point. An arc is a line segment or curve
that starts and ends at a vertex. Vertices and arcs form
a network. A vertex with an odd number of arcs is
odd; one with an even number of arcs is even. A
traversable network is one that can be traced without
removing the pencil from the paper and without
tracing an arc more than once. A network with all
even vertices or one with two odd vertices is
traversable. With more than two odd vertices, the
network cannot be traversed.

b. In topology, shapes are twisted, stretched, bent, and
shrunk. The genus of an object refers to the number
of holes in the object. Objects with the same genus
are topologically equivalent.

c. Non-Euclidean geometries, including hyperbolic
geometry and elliptic geometry, are outlined in Table
10.5 on page 510.

d. Fractal geometry includes self-similar forms;
magnified portions of such forms repeat much of the
pattern of the whole form. Computer-generated
fractals look like forms produced in nature.

REVIEW EXERCISES

10.1

In Exercises 1–3, classify the angle as acute, right, straight, or obtuse.

1.

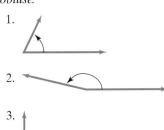

2.

3.

In Exercises 4–5, find the measure of the angle in which $?°$ *appears.*

4.

5.

6. If an angle measures 73°, find the measure of its complement.

7. If an angle measures 46°, find the measure of its supplement.

8. In the figure shown, find the measures of angles 1, 2, and 3.

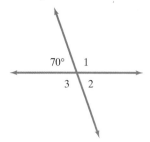

9. In the figure shown, two parallel lines are intersected by a transversal. One of the angle measures is given. Find the measure of each of the other seven angles.

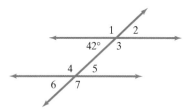

10.2

In Exercises 10–11, find the measure of angle A for the triangle shown.

10.

11.

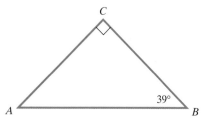

12. Find the measures of angles 1 through 5 in the figure shown.

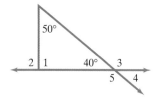

In Exercises 13–14, use similar triangles and the fact that corresponding sides are proportional to find the length of each side marked with an x.

13.

14.

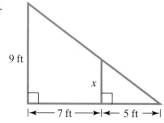

In Exercises 15–17, use the Pythagorean theorem to find the missing length in each right triangle. Round, if necessary, to the nearest tenth.

15.

16.

17.

18. Find the height of the lamppost in the figure.

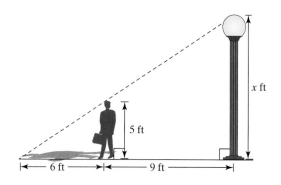

19. How far away from the building in the figure shown is the bottom of the ladder?

20. A vertical pole is to be supported by three wires. Each wire is 13 yards long and is anchored 5 yards from the base of the pole. How far up the pole will the wires be attached?

10.3

21. Write the names of all quadrilaterals that have four right angles.

22. Write the names of all quadrilaterals with four sides having the same measure.

23. Write the names of all quadrilaterals that do not have four angles with the same measure.

In Exercises 24–26, find the perimeter of the figure shown. Express the perimeter using the same unit of measure that appears in the figure.

24.

25.

26.

27. Find the sum of the measures of the angles of a 12-sided polygon.

28. Find the sum of the measures of the angles of an octagon.

29. The figure shown is a regular polygon. Find the measure of angle 1.

30. A carpenter is installing a baseboard around a room that has a length of 35 feet and a width of 15 feet. The room has four doorways, and each doorway is 3 feet wide. If no baseboard is to be put across the doorways and the cost of the baseboard is $1.50 per foot, what is the cost of installing the baseboard around the room?

10.4

In Exercises 31–34, find the area of each figure.

31.

32.

33.

34.

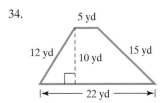

35. Find the circumference and the area of a circle with a diameter of 20 meters. Round answers to the nearest whole number.

In Exercises 36–37, find the area of each figure.

36.

37.

38. What will it cost to carpet a rectangular floor measuring 15 feet by 21 feet if the carpet costs $22.50 per square yard?

39. What will it cost to cover a rectangular floor measuring 40 feet by 50 feet with square tiles that measure 2 feet on each side if a package of 10 tiles costs $13 per package?

40. How much fencing, to the nearest whole yard, is needed to enclose a circular garden that measures 10 yards across?

10.5

In Exercises 41–45, find the volume of each figure. If necessary, round answers to the nearest whole number.

41.

42.

43.

44.

45.

46. Find the surface area of the figure shown.

47. A train is being loaded with shipping boxes. Each box is 8 meters long, 4 meters wide, and 3 meters high. If there are 50 shipping boxes, how much space is needed?

48. An Egyptian pyramid has a square base measuring 145 meters on each side. If the height of the pyramid is 93 meters, find its volume.

49. What is the cost of concrete for a walkway that is 27 feet long, 4 feet wide, and 6 inches deep if the concrete is $40 per cubic yard?

10.6

50. Use the right triangle shown to find $\sin A$, $\cos A$, and $\tan A$.

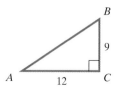

In Exercises 51–53, find the measure of the side of the right triangle whose length is designated by a lowercase letter. Round answers to the nearest whole number.

51.

52.

53.

54. Find the measure of angle *A* in the right triangle shown. Round to the nearest whole degree.

55. A hiker climbs for a half mile up a slope whose inclination is 17°. How many feet of altitude, to the nearest foot, does the hiker gain?

56. To find the distance across a lake, a surveyor took the measurements in the figure shown. What is the distance across the lake? Round to the nearest meter.

57. When a six-foot pole casts a four-foot shadow, what is the angle of elevation of the sun? Round to the nearest whole degree.

10.7

For each network in Exercises 58–59, determine if it is traversable. If it is, describe a path that will traverse it.

58.

59.

In Exercises 60–63, give the genus of each object. Which objects are topologically equivalent?

60.

61.

62.

63.

64. State Euclid's assumption about parallel lines that no longer applies in hyperbolic and elliptic geometry.

65. What is self-similarity? Describe an object in nature that has this characteristic.

Group Exercise

66. a. As a group, write a problem that is based on the situation that opened this chapter. Group members will need to assign realistic values, in inches, to the radius and height of each cylindrical tank. You can decide if each tank is the same size, or if they differ in size. Use these assigned numbers, the formula for the volume of a cylinder, and the information given under the photograph on page 452 to detemine if it is safe to cross the bridge.

   b. We have seen that geometry has many practical applications. Now, group members need to take this one step further. Describe as many situations as possible in which a knowledge of geometry can prevent a disaster (or at least a serious mishap) from happening. Be as creative as possible. It is not necessary to assign specific numbers in each situation or to solve the problem, as you were asked to do in part (a).

CHAPTER 10 TEST

1. If an angle measures 54°, find the measure of its supplement.

In Exercises 2–4, use the figure shown to find the measure of angle 1.

2.

3.

4.

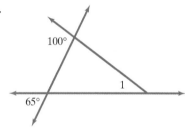

5. The triangles in the figure are similar. Find the length of the side marked with an *x*.

6. A vertical pole is to be supported by three wires. Each wire is 26 feet long and is anchored 24 feet from the base of the pole. How far up the pole should the wires be attached?

7. Find the sum of the measures of the angles of a ten-sided polygon.

8. Find the perimeter of the figure shown.

9. Which one of the following names a quadrilateral in which the sides that meet have the same measure?

   a. rectangle   b. parallelogram
   c. trapezoid   d. rhombus

In Exercises 10–11, find the area of each figure.

10.

11.

12. Find the circumference and area of a circle with a diameter of 40 meters. Round answers to the nearest whole number.

13. A rectangular floor measuring 8 feet by 6 feet is to be completely covered with square tiles measuring 8 inches on each side. How many tiles are needed to completely cover the floor?

In Exercises 14–16, find the volume of each figure. If necessary, round answers to the nearest whole number.

14.

15.

16.

17. Find the measure, to the nearest whole number, of the side of the right triangle whose length is designated by c.

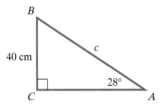

18. At a certain time of day, the angle of elevation of the sun is 34°. If a building casts a shadow measuring 104 feet, find the height of the building to the nearest foot.

19. Determine if the network shown is traversable. If it is, describe a path that will traverse it.

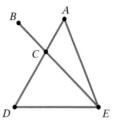

20. Describe a difference between the shapes of fractal geometry and those of Euclidean geometry.

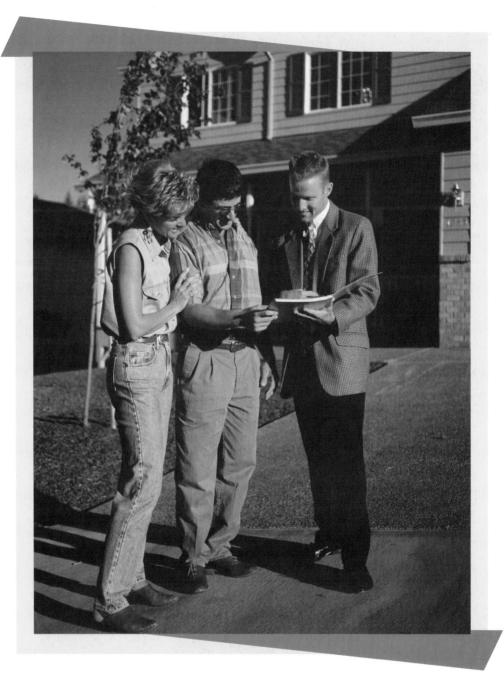

You have a plan to help pay for college. It took a lot of hard work, but you got your real estate license. After a few months of making no money, a great opportunity has come your way. You have the chance to list a relatively expensive house. If it sells during your listing period, you can make enough money to pay for at least a year of college. However, the listing will cost you quite a bit of money for advertising and providing food for other realtors during open showings. If the house does not sell after four months, you lose the listing, along with your out-of-pocket money to cover these expenses. Such a loss will leave you short of money for the fall semester. What should you do?

11 Counting Methods and Probability Theory

L ife is filled with risks and uncertainty. We purchase insurance to compensate ourselves for the possibility of an unpleasant event. Weather forecasters tell us the chances it will rain tomorrow, and on the basis of the information they provide we decide what to wear when we go out. Stock market investments are placed according to the probabilities of future performances of different companies.

The mathematics of uncertainty and risk is called probability theory. In this chapter, you will see how probability theory gives you the tools for making decisions, such as whether or not to list an expensive house. In this sense, the mathematics of uncertainty will give you a way to peer into the future, enabling you to see things that would otherwise be invisible.

SECTION 11.1 *The Fundamental Counting Principle*

Objective

1. Use the Fundamental Counting Principle to determnine the number of possible outcomes in a given situation.

Have you ever imagined what your life would be like if you won the lottery? What changes would you make? Before you fantasize about becoming a person of leisure with a staff of obedient elves, think about this: The probability of winning top prize in the lottery is about the same as the probability of being struck by lightning. There are millions of possible number combinations in lottery games, and only one way of winning the grand prize. Determining the probability of winning involves calculating the chance of getting the winning combination from all possible outcomes. In this section, we begin preparing for the surprising world of probability by looking at methods for counting possible outcomes.

1 Use the Fundamental Counting Principle to determine the number of possible outcomes in a given situation.

The Fundamental Counting Principle with Two Groups of Items

It's early morning, you're groggy, and you have to select something to wear for your 8 A.M. class. (What *were* you thinking of when you signed up for a class at that hour?!) Fortunately, your "lecture wardrobe" is rather limited—just two pairs of jeans to choose from (one blue, one black) and three T-shirts to choose from (one beige, one yellow, and one blue). Your early-morning dilemma is illustrated in Figure 11.1.

Figure 11.1 Selecting a wardrobe

The **tree diagram**, so named because of its branches, shows that you can form six outfits from your two jeans and three T-shirts. Each pair of jeans can be combined with one of three T-shirts. Notice that the total number of outfits can be obtained by multiplying the number of choices for the jeans, 2, by the number of choices for the T-shirts, 3:

$$2 \cdot 3 = 6.$$

We can generalize this idea to any two groups of items—not just jeans and T-shirts—with the **Fundamental Counting Principle.**

The Fundamental Counting Principle

If you can choose one item from a group of M items and a second item from a group of N items, then the total number of two-item choices is $M \cdot N$.

EXAMPLE 1 Applying the Fundamental Counting Principle

The Greasy Spoon Restaurant offers 6 appetizers and 14 main courses. In how many ways can a person order a two-course meal?

Solution Choosing from one of 6 appetizers and one of 14 main courses, the total number of two-course meals is

$$6 \cdot 14 = 84.$$

A person can order a two-course meal in 84 different ways.

EXAMPLE 2 Applying the Fundamental Counting Principle

This is the semester that you decide to take your required psychology and social science courses. Because you decide to register early, there are 15 sections of psychology from which you can choose. Furthermore, there are 9 sections of social science that are available at times that do not conflict with those for psychology. In how many ways can you create two-course schedules that satisfy the psychology-social science requirement?

Solution The number of ways that you can satisfy the requirement is found by multiplying the number of choices for each course. You can choose your psychology course from 15 sections and your social science course from 9 sections. For both courses you have

$$15 \cdot 9, \quad \text{or} \quad 135$$

choices. Thus, you can satisfy the psychology-social science requirement in 135 ways.

The Fundamental Counting Principle with More Than Two Groups of Items

Whoops! You forgot something in choosing your lecture wardrobe—shoes! You have two pairs of sneakers to choose from—one black and one red, for that extra fashion flair! Your possible outfits, including sneakers, are shown in Figure 11.2.

Figure 11.2 Increasing wardrobe selections

The number of possible ways of playing the first four moves on each side in a game of chess is $318, 979, 564, 000.$

The tree diagram shows that you can form 12 outfits from your two jeans, three T-shirts, and two pairs of sneakers. Notice that the number of outfits can be obtained by multiplying the number of choices for jeans, 2, the number of choices for T-shirts, 3, and the number of choices for sneakers, 2:

$$2 \cdot 3 \cdot 2 = 12.$$

Unlike your earlier dilemma, you are now dealing with *three* groups of items. The Fundamental Counting Principle can be extended to determine the number of possible outcomes in situations in which there are three or more groups of items.

The Fundamental Counting Principle

The number of ways in which a series of successive things can occur is found by multiplying the number of ways in which each thing can occur.

For example, if you own 30 pairs of jeans, 20 T-shirts, and 12 pairs of sneakers, you have

$$30 \cdot 20 \cdot 12 = 7200$$

choices for your wardrobe!

EXAMPLE 3   Options in Planning a Course Schedule

Next semester you are planning to take three courses—math, English, and humanities. Based on time blocks and highly recommended professors, there are 8 sections of math, 5 of English, and 4 of humanities that you find suitable. Assuming no scheduling conflicts, how many different three-course schedules are possible?

Solution This situation involves making choices with three groups of items.

Math	English	Humanities
8 choices	5 choices	4 choices

We use the Fundamental Counting Principle to find the number of three-course schedules. Multiply the number of choices for each of the three groups.

$$8 \cdot 5 \cdot 4 = 160$$

Thus, there are 160 different three-course schedules.

EXAMPLE 4 Car of the Future

Car manufacturers are now experimenting with lightweight three-wheel cars, designed for a driver and one passenger, and considered ideal for city driving. Intrigued? Suppose you could order such a car with a choice of 9 possible colors, with or without air-conditioning, with or without a removable roof, and with or without an onboard computer. In how many ways can this car be ordered in terms of these options?

Solution This situation involves making choices with four groups of items.

Color	Air-conditioning	Removable Roof	Computer
9 choices	2 choices: with or without	2 choices: with or without	2 choices: with or without

We use the Fundamental Counting Principle to find the number of ordering options. Multiply the number of choices for each of the four groups.

$$9 \cdot 2 \cdot 2 \cdot 2 = 72$$

Thus, the car can be ordered in 72 different ways.

EXAMPLE 5 A Multiple-Choice Test

You are taking a multiple-choice test that has ten questions. Each of the questions has four choices, with one correct choice per question. If you select one of these options per question and leave nothing blank, in how many ways can you answer the questions?

Technology

4^{10} on many calculators:
Scientific Calculator

4 $\boxed{x^y}$ 10 $\boxed{=}$

Graphing Calculator

4 $\boxed{\wedge}$ 10 $\boxed{\text{ENTER}}$

Solution We use the Fundamental Counting Principle to determine the number of ways you can answer the test. Multiply the number of choices, 4, for each of the ten questions.

$$4 \cdot 4 \cdot 4 \cdot 4 \cdot 4 \cdot 4 \cdot 4 \cdot 4 \cdot 4 \cdot 4 = 4^{10} = 1,048,576$$

Thus, you can answer the questions in 1,048,576 different ways.

Are you surprised that there are over one million ways of answering a ten-question multiple-choice test? Of course, there is only one way to answer the test and receive a perfect score. The probability of guessing your way into a perfect

By the year 2020, portable telephones used for business and pleasure will all be videophones. At that time, U.S. population is expected to be 323 million. Faxes, beepers, cell phones, computer phone lines, and business lines may result in certain areas running out of phone numbers. Solution: Add more digits!

score involves calculating the chance of getting a perfect score, just one way, from all 1,048,576 possible outcomes. In short, prepare for the test and do not rely on guessing!

EXAMPLE 6 Telephone Numbers in the United States

Telephone numbers in the United States begin with three-digit area codes followed by seven-digit local telephone numbers. Area codes and local telephone numbers cannot begin with 0 or 1. How many different telephone numbers are possible?

Solution This situation involves making choices with ten groups of items.

We use the Fundamental Counting Principle to determine the number of different telephone numbers that are possible. The total number of telephone numbers possible is

$$8 \cdot 10 \cdot 10 \cdot 8 \cdot 10 \cdot 10 \cdot 10 \cdot 10 \cdot 10 \cdot 10 = 6{,}400{,}000{,}000.$$

There are six billion four hundred million different telephone numbers that are possible.

Exercise Set 11.1

 Practice and Application Exercises

Solve Exercises 1–6 by applying the Fundamental Counting Principle with two groups of items.

1. A restaurant offers 8 appetizers and 10 main courses. In how many ways can a person order a two-course meal?

2. The model of the car you are thinking of buying is available in nine different colors and three different styles (hatchback, sedan, or station wagon). In how many ways can you order the car?

3. A popular brand of pen is available in three colors (red, green, or blue) and four writing tips (bold, medium, fine, or micro). How many different choices of pens do you have with this brand?

4. In how many ways can a casting director choose a mother character and a father character from five female actors and six male actors?

5. A student is planning a two-part trip. The first leg of the trip is from San Francisco to New York and the second leg of the trip is from New York to Paris. From San Francisco to New York, travel options include airplane, train, or bus. From New York to Paris, the options are limited to airplane or ship. In how many ways can the two-part trip be made?

6. For a temporary job between semesters, you are painting the parking spaces for a new shopping mall with a letter of the alphabet and a single digit from 1 to 9. The first parking space is A1 and the last parking space is Z9. How many parking spaces do you need to paint with these labels?

Solve Exercises 7–22 by applying the Fundamental Counting Principle with three or more groups of items.

7. An ice cream store sells two drinks (sodas or milk shakes), in four sizes (small, medium, large, or jumbo), and five flavors (vanilla, strawberry, chocolate, coffee, or pistachio). In how many ways can a customer order a drink?

8. A pizza can be ordered with three choices of size (small, medium, or large), four choices of crust (thin, thick, crispy, or regular), and six choices of toppings (ground beef, sausage, pepperoni, bacon, mushrooms, or onions). How many one-topping pizzas can be ordered?

9. A restaurant offers the following limited lunch menu.

Main Course	Vegetables	Beverages	Desserts
Ham	Potatoes	Coffee	Cake
Chicken	Peas	Tea	Pie
Fish	Green beans	Milk	Ice cream
Beef		Soda	

If one item is selected from each of the four groups, in how many ways can a meal be ordered? Describe two such orders.

10. An apartment complex offers apartments with four different options, designated by A through D.

A	B	C	D
one bedroom	one bathroom	first floor	lake view
two bedrooms	two bathrooms	second floor	golf course view
three bedrooms			no special view

How many apartment options are available? Describe two such options.

11. Shoppers in a large shopping mall are categorized as male or female, over 30 or 30 and under, and cash or credit card shoppers. In how many ways can the shoppers be categorized?

12. There are three highways from city A to city B, two highways from city B to city C, and four highways from city C to city D. How many different highway routes are there from city A to city D?

13. A person can order a new car with a choice of six possible colors, with or without air conditioning, with or without automatic transmission, with or without power windows, and with or without a CD player. In how many different ways can a new car be ordered in terms of these options?

14. A car model comes in nine colors, with or without air conditioning, with or without a sun roof, with or without automatic transmission, and with or without antilock brakes. In how many ways can the car be ordered in terms of these options?

15. You are taking a multiple-choice test that has six questions. Each of the questions has three choices, with one correct choice per question. If you select one of these options per question and leave nothing blank, in how many ways can you answer the questions?

16. You are taking a multiple-choice test that has eight questions. Each of the questions has three choices, with one correct choice per question. If you select one of these options per question and leave nothing blank, in how many ways can you answer the questions?

17. In the original plan for area codes in 1945, the first digit could be any number from 2 through 9, the second digit was either 0 or 1, and the third digit could be any number except 0. With this plan, how many different area codes were possible?

18. The local seven-digit telephone numbers in Inverness, California, have 669 as the first three digits. How many different telephone numbers are possible?

19. License plates in a particular state display two letters followed by three numbers, such as AT-887 or BB-013. How many different license plates can be manufactured?

20. How many different four-letter radio station call letters can be formed if the first letter must be W or K?

21. A stock can go up, go down, or stay unchanged. How many possibilities are there if you own seven stocks?

22. A social security number contains nine digits, such as 074-66-7795. How many different social security numbers can be formed?

 Writing in Mathematics

23. Explain the Fundamental Counting Principle.

24. Figure 11.2 on page 526 shows that a tree diagram can be used to find the total number of outfits. Describe one advantage of using the Fundamental Counting Principle rather than a tree diagram.

25. Write an original problem that can be solved using the Fundamental Counting Principle. Then solve the problem.

 Critical Thinking Exercises

26. How many four-digit odd numbers are there? Assume that the digit on the left cannot be 0.

27. In order to develop a more appealing hamburger, a franchise used taste tests with 12 different buns, 30 sauces, 4 types of lettuce, and 3 types of tomatoes. If the taste test was done at one restaurant by one tester who took 10 minutes to eat each hamburger, approximately how long would it take the tester to eat all possible hamburgers?

 Group Exercise

28. The group should select real-world situations where the Fundamental Counting Principle can be applied. These can involve the number of possible student ID numbers on your campus, the number of possible phone numbers in your community, the number of meal options at a local restaurant, the number of ways a person in the group can select outfits for class, the number of ways a condominium can be purchased in a nearby community, and so on. Once situations have been selected, group members should determine in how many ways each part of the task can be done. Group members will need to obtain menus, find out about telephone-digit requirements in the community, count shirts, pants, shoes in closets, visit condominium sales offices, and so on. Once the group reassembles, apply the Fundamental Counting Principle to determine the number of available options in each situation. Because these numbers may be quite large, use a calculator.

SECTION 11.2 *Permutations*

Objectives

1. Use the Fundamental Counting Principle to count permutations.
2. Evaluate factorial expressions.
3. Use the permutations formula.

1 Use the Fundamental Counting Principle to count permutations.

Offspring

Ladies and gentlemen: Please give a huge round of applause for

Offspring! Pink Floyd! Sublime! The Rolling Stones!

You are in charge of planning one of the most anticipated concert tours of the new millennium. All four of these groups will appear in concert, which will be seen in a pay-per-view cable special by millions of people throughout the world. One of your jobs is to determine the order in which the groups will perform. Each group will perform once. How many different ways can you put together this four-group concert?

You are familiar with the work of all these musicians *and* you know the Fundamental Counting Principle! (Who could be better qualified for this job?) You can choose any of the four groups as the first performer. Once you've chosen the first group, you'll have three groups left to choose from for the second performer. You'll then have two groups left to choose from for the third performance. After the first three performers are determined, you'll have only one group left for the final appearance in the concert. This situation can be shown as follows:

First Group to Perform	Second Group to Perform	Third Group to Perform	Last Group to Perform
4 choices	3 choices	2 choices	1 choice

We use the Fundamental Counting Principle to find the number of ways you can put together the concert. Multiply the choices:

$$4 \cdot 3 \cdot 2 \cdot 1 = 24.$$

Thus, there are 24 different ways to arrange the concert. One of the 24 possible arrangements is

Sublime-Offspring-Pink Floyd-The Rolling Stones.

Such an ordered arrangement is called a **permutation** of the four rock groups. A permutation of items occurs when:

Pink Floyd

Sublime

The Rolling Stones

- No item is used more than once. (Each rock group performs exactly once.)
- The order of arrangement makes a difference.

  (It will make a difference in terms of how the concert is received if the Rolling Stones are the first group or the last group to perform.)

EXAMPLE 1 Counting Permutations

Based on their long-standing contribution to rock music, you decide that the Rolling Stones should be the last group to perform at the four-group Offspring, Pink Floyd, Sublime, Rolling Stones concert. Given this decision, in how many ways can you put together the concert?

Solution You can now choose any one of the three groups, Offspring, Pink Floyd, or Sublime, as the opening act. Once you've chosen the first group, you'll have two groups left to choose from for the second performance. You'll then have just one group left to choose from for the third performance. There is also just one choice for the closing act—the Rolling Stones. This situation can be shown as follows:

First Group to Perform	Second Group to Perform	Third Group to Perform	Last Group to Perform
3 choices (Offspring, Pink Floyd, or Sublime)	2 choices	1 choice	1 choice: The Rolling Stones will close the concert.

We use the Fundamental Counting Principle to find the number of ways you can put together the concert. Multiply the choices:

$$3 \cdot 2 \cdot 1 \cdot 1 = 6.$$

Thus, there are six different ways to arrange the concert if the Rolling Stones are the final group to perform.

EXAMPLE 2 Counting Permutations

You need to arrange seven of your favorite books along a small shelf. How many different ways can you arrange the books, assuming that the order of the books makes a difference to you?

Solution You may choose any of the seven books for the first position on the shelf. This leaves six choices for second position. After the first two positions are filled, there are five books to choose from for third position, four choices left for the fourth position, three choices left for the fifth position, then two choices for the sixth position, and only one choice for the last position. This situation can be shown as follows:

First Shelf Position	Second Shelf Position	Third Shelf Position	Fourth Shelf Position	Fifth Shelf Position	Sixth Shelf Position	Seventh Shelf Position
7 choices	6 choices	5 choices	4 choices	3 choices	2 choices	1 choice

We use the Fundamental Counting Principle to find the number of ways you can arrange the seven books along the shelf. Multiply the choices:

$$7 \cdot 6 \cdot 5 \cdot 4 \cdot 3 \cdot 2 \cdot 1 = 5040.$$

Thus, you can arrange the books in 5040 ways. There are 5040 different possible permutations.

How to Pass the Time for $2\frac{1}{2}$ Million Years

If you were to arrange 15 different books on a shelf and it took you one minute for each permutation, the entire task would take 2,487,965 years.

Source: Isaac Asimov's Book of Facts

2 Evaluate factorial expressions.

Factorial Notation

The product in Example 2,

$$7 \cdot 6 \cdot 5 \cdot 4 \cdot 3 \cdot 2 \cdot 1$$

is given a special name and symbol. It is called 7 **factorial**, and written 7! Thus,

$$7! = 7 \cdot 6 \cdot 5 \cdot 4 \cdot 3 \cdot 2 \cdot 1.$$

In general, if n is a positive integer, then $n!$ (n *factorial*) is the product of all positive integers from n down through 1. For example,

$$1! = 1$$

$$2! = 2 \cdot 1 = 2$$

$$3! = 3 \cdot 2 \cdot 1 = 6$$

$$4! = 4 \cdot 3 \cdot 2 \cdot 1 = 24$$

$$5! = 5 \cdot 4 \cdot 3 \cdot 2 \cdot 1 = 120$$

$$6! = 6 \cdot 5 \cdot 4 \cdot 3 \cdot 2 \cdot 1 = 720$$

0!	1
1!	1
2!	2
3!	6
4!	24
5!	120
6!	720
7!	5040
8!	40,320
9!	362,880
10!	3,628,800
11!	39,916,800
12!	479,001,600
13!	6,227,020,800
14!	87,178,291,200
15!	1,307,674,368,000
16!	20,922,789,888,000
17!	355,687,428,096,000
18!	6,402,373,705,728,000
19!	121,645,100,408,832,000
20!	2,432,902,008,176,640,000

Factorials from 0 through 20. As n increases, $n!$ grows very rapidly. Factorial growth is more explosive than exponential growth discussed in Chapter 7.

Factorial Notation

If n is a positive integer, the notation $n!$ (read "n factorial") is the product of all positive integers from n down through 1.

$$n! = n(n - 1)(n - 2) \ldots (3)(2)(1)$$

0! (zero factorial), by definition, is 1.

$$0! = 1$$

Technology

Most calculators have a factorial key. Here are the keystrokes on many calculators for finding 9!

Scientific Calculator

9 [n!] [=]

Graphing Calculator

9 [!] [ENTER]

EXAMPLE 3   Using Factorial Notation

Evaluate the following factorial expressions without using the factorial key on your calculator.

a. $\dfrac{8!}{5!}$ b. $\dfrac{26!}{21!}$ c. $\dfrac{500!}{499!}$

Solution

a. We can evaluate the numerator and the denominator. However, it is easier to use the following simplification:

$$\frac{8!}{5!} = \frac{8 \cdot 7 \cdot 6 \cdot \boxed{5 \cdot 4 \cdot 3 \cdot 2 \cdot 1}}{\boxed{5 \cdot 4 \cdot 3 \cdot 2 \cdot 1}} = \frac{8 \cdot 7 \cdot 6 \cdot \boxed{5!}}{\boxed{5!}} = \frac{8 \cdot 7 \cdot 6 \cdot \cancel{5!}}{\cancel{5!}} = 8 \cdot 7 \cdot 6 = 336$$

b. Rather than write out 26! as the product of all integers from 26 down to 1, we can express 26! as

$$26! = 26 \cdot 25 \cdot 24 \cdot 23 \cdot 22 \cdot 21!$$

In this way, we can cancel 21! in the numerator and the denominator of the given expression.

$$\frac{26!}{21!} = \frac{26 \cdot 25 \cdot 24 \cdot 23 \cdot 22 \cdot 21!}{21!} = \frac{26 \cdot 25 \cdot 24 \cdot 23 \cdot 22 \cdot \cancel{21!}}{\cancel{21!}}$$
$$= 26 \cdot 25 \cdot 24 \cdot 23 \cdot 22 = 7{,}893{,}600$$

c. In order to cancel identical factorials in the numerator and the denominator, we can express 500! as $500 \cdot 499!$

$$\frac{500!}{499!} = \frac{500 \cdot 499!}{499!} = \frac{500 \cdot \cancel{499!}}{\cancel{499!}} = 500$$

3 Use the permutations formula.

A Formula for Permutations

You are the coach of a little league baseball team. There are 13 players on the team (and lots of parents hovering in the background, dreaming of stardom for their little "Mark McGwire"). You need to choose a batting order having 9 players. The order makes a difference, because, for instance, if bases are loaded and "Little Mark" is fourth or fifth at bat, his possible home run will drive in three additional runs. How many batting orders can you form?

You can choose any of 13 players for the first person at bat. Then you will have 12 players from which to choose the second batter, then 11 from which to choose the third batter, and so on. The situation can be shown as follows:

Batter 1	Batter 2	Batter 3	Batter 4	Batter 5	Batter 6	Batter 7	Batter 8	Batter 9
13 choices	12 choices	11 choices	10 choices	9 choices	8 choices	7 choices	6 choices	5 choices

The total number of batting orders is

$$13 \cdot 12 \cdot 11 \cdot 10 \cdot 9 \cdot 8 \cdot 7 \cdot 6 \cdot 5 = 259{,}459{,}200.$$

Nearly 260 million batting orders are possible for your 13-player little league team. Each batting order is a permutation because the order of the batters makes a difference. The number of permutations of 13 players taken 9 at a time is 259,459,200.

We can obtain a formula for finding the number of permutations by rewriting our computation:

$$13 \cdot 12 \cdot 11 \cdot 10 \cdot 9 \cdot 8 \cdot 7 \cdot 6 \cdot 5$$
$$= \frac{13 \cdot 12 \cdot 11 \cdot 10 \cdot 9 \cdot 8 \cdot 7 \cdot 6 \cdot 5 \cdot \boxed{4 \cdot 3 \cdot 2 \cdot 1}}{\boxed{4 \cdot 3 \cdot 2 \cdot 1}} = \frac{13!}{4!} = \frac{13!}{(13 - 9)!}$$

Thus, the number of permutations of 13 things taken 9 at a time is $\frac{13!}{(13 - 9)!}$. The special notation $_{13}P_9$ is used to replace the phrase "the number of permutations of 13 things taken 9 at a time." Using this new notation, we can write:

$$_{13}P_9 = \frac{13!}{(13 - 9)!}.$$

The numerator of this expression is the number of items, 13 team members, expressed as a factorial: 13! The denominator is also a factorial. It is the factorial of the difference between the number of items, 13, and the number of items in each permutation, 9 batters: $(13 - 9)!$

The notation $_nP_r$ means the **number of permutations of n things taken r at a time**. We can generalize from the situation in which 9 batters were taken from 13 players. By generalizing, we obtain the following formula for the number of permutations if r items are taken from n items.

Permutations of n Things Taken r at a Time

The number of permutations possible if r items are taken from n items is

$$_nP_r = \frac{n!}{(n-r)!}.$$

EXAMPLE 4   Using the Formula for Permutations

You and 19 of your friends have decided to form an Internet marketing consulting firm. The group needs to choose three officers–a CEO, an operating manager, and a treasurer. In how many ways can those offices be filled?

Solution   Your group is choosing $r = 3$ officers from a group of $n = 20$ people (you and 19 friends). The order in which the officers are chosen matters because the CEO, the operating manager, and the treasurer each have different responsibilities. Thus, we are looking for the number of permutations of 20 things taken 3 at a time. We use the formula

$$_nP_r = \frac{n!}{(n-r)!}$$

with $n = 20$ and $r = 3$.

$$_{20}P_3 = \frac{20!}{(20-3)!} = \frac{20!}{17!} = \frac{20 \cdot 19 \cdot 18 \cdot 17!}{17!} = \frac{20 \cdot 19 \cdot 18 \cdot 17!}{17!} = 20 \cdot 19 \cdot 18 = 6840$$

Thus, there are 6840 different ways of filling the three offices.

EXAMPLE 5   Using the Formula for Permutations

You are working for The Sitcom Television Network. Your assignment is to help set up the television schedule for Monday evenings between 7 and 10 P.M. You need to schedule a show in each of six 30-minute time blocks, beginning with 7 to 7:30 and ending with 9:30 to 10:00. You can select from among the following situation comedies: "Home Improvement," "Seinfeld," "Mad About You," "Cheers," "Friends," "Frasier," "All in the Family," "I Love Lucy," "M*A*S*H," "The Larry Sanders Show," "The Jeffersons," "Married with Children," and "Happy Days." How many different programming schedules can be arranged?

Solution   You are choosing $r = 6$ situation comedies from a collection of $n = 13$ classic sitcoms. The order in which the programs are aired matters. Family-oriented comedies have higher ratings when aired in earlier time blocks, such as 7 to 7:30. By contrast, comedies with adult themes do better in later time blocks.

In short, we are looking for the number of permutations of 13 things taken 6 at a time. We use the formula

$$_nP_r = \frac{n!}{(n-r)!}$$

with $n = 13$ and $r = 6$.

$$_{13}P_6 = \frac{13!}{(13-6)!} = \frac{13!}{7!} = \frac{13 \cdot 12 \cdot 11 \cdot 10 \cdot 9 \cdot 8 \cdot 7!}{7!} = 13 \cdot 12 \cdot 11 \cdot 10 \cdot 9 \cdot 8 = 1{,}235{,}520$$

There are 1,235,520 different programming schedules that can be arranged.

Exercise Set 11.2

Practice and Application Exercises

Use the Fundamental Counting Principle to solve Exercises 1–12.

1. Six performers are to present their comedy acts on a weekend evening at a comedy club. How many different ways are there to schedule their appearances?

2. Five singers are to perform on a weekend evening at a night club. How many different ways are there to schedule their appearances?

3. In the *Cambridge Encyclopedia of Language* (Cambridge University Press, 1987), author David Crystal presents five sentences that make a reasonable paragraph regardless of their order. The sentences are:

   Mark had told him about the foxes.
   John looked out of the window.
   Could it be a fox?
   However, nobody had seen one for months.
   He thought he saw a shape in the bushes.

   In how many different orders can the five sentences be arranged?

4. In how many different ways can a police department arrange eight suspects in a police lineup if each lineup contains all eight people?

5. As in Exercise 1, six performers are to present their comedy acts on a weekend evening at a comedy club. One of the performers insists on being the last stand-up comic of the evening. If this performer's request is granted, how many different ways are there to schedule the appearances?

6. As in Exercise 2, five singers are to perform at a night club. One of the singers insists on being the last performer of the evening. If this singer's request is granted, how many different ways are there to schedule the appearances?

7. You need to arrange nine of your favorite books along a small shelf. How many different ways can you arrange the books, assuming that the order of the books makes a difference to you?

8. You need to arrange ten of your favorite photographs on the mantel above a fireplace. How many ways can you arrange the photographs, assuming that the order of the pictures makes a difference to you?

In Exercises 9–10, use the five sentences that are given in Exercise 3.

9. How many different five-sentence paragraphs can be formed if the paragraph begins with "He thought he saw a shape in the bushes" and ends with "John looked out of the window"?

10. How many different five-sentence paragraphs can be formed if the paragraph begins with "He thought he saw a shape in the bushes" followed by "Mark had told him about the foxes"?

11. A television programmer is arranging the order that five movies will be seen between the hours of 6 P.M. and 4 A.M. Two of the movies have a G rating, and they are to be shown in the first two time blocks. One of the movies is rated NC-17, and it is to be shown in the last of the time blocks, from 2 A.M. until 4 A.M. Given these restrictions, in how many ways can the five movies be arranged during the indicated time blocks?

12. A camp counselor and six campers are to be seated along a picnic bench. In how many ways can this be done if the counselor must be seated in the middle and a camper who has a tendency to engage in food fights must sit to the counselor's immediate left?

In Exercises 13–32, evaluate each factorial expression.

13. $\dfrac{9!}{6!}$

14. $\dfrac{12!}{10!}$

15. $\dfrac{29!}{25!}$

16. $\dfrac{31!}{28!}$

17. $\dfrac{19!}{11!}$

18. $\dfrac{17!}{9!}$

19. $\dfrac{600!}{599!}$

20. $\dfrac{700!}{699!}$

21. $\dfrac{104!}{102!}$

22. $\dfrac{106!}{104!}$

23. $7! - 3!$

24. $6! - 3!$

25. $(7 - 3)!$

26. $(6 - 3)!$

27. $\left(\dfrac{12}{4}\right)!$

28. $\left(\dfrac{45}{9}\right)!$

29. $\dfrac{7!}{(7 - 2)!}$

30. $\dfrac{8!}{(8 - 5)!}$

31. $\dfrac{13!}{(13 - 3)!}$

32. $\dfrac{17!}{(17 - 3)!}$

In Exercises 33–40, use the formula for $_nP_r$ to evaluate each expression.

33. $_9P_4$

34. $_7P_3$

35. $_8P_5$

36. $_{10}P_4$

37. $_6P_6$

38. $_9P_9$

39. $_8P_0$

40. $_6P_0$

Use the formula for $_nP_r$ to solve Exercises 41–48.

41. A club with ten members is to choose three officers—president, vice-president, and secretary-treasurer. If each office is to be held by one person and no person can hold more than one office, in how many ways can those offices be filled?

42. A corporation has seven members on its board of directors. In how many different ways can it elect a president, vice-president, secretary, and treasurer?

43. For a segment of a radio show, a disc jockey can play 7 records. If there are 13 records to select from, in how many ways can the program for this segment be arranged?

44. Suppose you are asked to list, in order of preference, the three best movies you have seen this year. If you saw 20 movies during the year, in how many ways can the three best be chosen and ranked?

45. In a race in which six automobiles are entered and there are no ties, in how many ways can the first three finishers come in?

46. In a production of *West Side Story*, eight actors are considered for the male roles of Tony, Riff, and Bernardo. In how many ways can the director cast the male roles?

47. Nine bands have volunteered to perform at a benefit concert, but there is only enough time for five of the bands to play. How many lineups are possible?

48. How many arrangements can be made using four of the letters of the word COMBINE if no letter is to be used more than once?

 ## Writing in Mathematics

49. What is a permutation?

50. Explain how to find $n!$ if n is a positive integer.

51. Explain the best way to evaluate $\frac{900!}{899!}$ without a calculator.

52. Describe what $_nP_r$ represents.

53. Write a word problem that can be solved by evaluating $5!$.

54. Write a word problem that can be solved by evaluating $_7P_3$.

 ## Critical Thinking Exercises

55. It ten people board an airplane, and there are 12 aisle seats, in how many ways can they be seated if they all select aisle seats?

56. Six horses are entered in a race. If two specific horses are tied for first place, in how many ways can the race end?

57. Performing at a concert are eight rock bands and eight jazz groups. How many ways can the program be arranged if the first, third, and eighth performers are jazz groups?

58. Five men and five women line up at a checkout counter in a store. In how many ways can they line up if the first person in line is a woman, and the people in line alternate woman, man, woman, man, and so on?

59. How many four-digit odd numbers less than 6000 can be formed using the digits 2, 4, 6, 7, 8, and 9?

60. Express $_nP_{n-2}$ without using factorials.

 ## Technology Exercises

Use a calculator with a factorial key to compute the factorials in Exercises 61–64.

61. $8!$

62. $4!$

63. $13!$

64. $31!$

Use a calculator with an $\boxed{_nP_r}$ key to evaluate the expressions in Exercises 65–67.

65. $_{13}P_6$

66. $_{12}P_{11}$

67. $_5P_5$

SECTION 11.3   Combinations

Objectives

1. Distinguish between permutation and combination problems.
2. Solve problems involving combinations using the combinations formula.

1 Distinguish between permutation and combination problems.

As the twentieth century drew to a close, *Time* magazine presented a series of special issues on the most influential people of the century. In their issue on heroes and icons (June 14, 1999), they discussed a number of people whose careers became more profitable after their tragic deaths, including Marilyn Monroe, James Dean, Jim Morrison, Kurt Cobain, and Selena.

Imagine that you ask your friends the following question: "Of these five people, which three would you select to be included in a documentary featuring the best of their work?" You are not asking your friends to rank their three favorite artists in any kind of order—they should merely select the three to be included in the documentary.

One friend answers, "Jim Morrison, Kurt Cobain, and Selena." Another responds, "Selena, Kurt Cobain, and Jim Morrison." These two people have the same artists in their group of selections, even if they are named in a different order. We are interested *in which artists are named, not the order in which they are named* for the documentary. Because the items are taken without regard to order, this is not a permutation problem. No ranking of any sort is involved.

Later on, you ask your roommate which three artists she would select for the documentary. She names Marilyn Monroe, James Dean, and Selena. Her selection is different from those of your two other friends because different entertainers are cited.

Mathematicians describe the group of artists given by your roommate as a *combination*. A **combination** of items occurs when:

- The items are selected from the same group (the five stars who died young and tragically).
- No item is used more than once. (You may adore Selena, but your three selections cannot be Selena, Selena, and Selena).
- The order of items makes no difference. (Morrison, Cobain, Selena is the same group in the documentary as Selena, Cobain, Morrison.)

Marilyn Monroe, Actress (1927–1962)

James Dean, Actor (1931–1955)

Jim Morrison, Musician and Lead Singer of The Doors (1943–1971)

Kurt Cobain, Musician and Front Man for Nirvana (1967–1994)

Selena, Musician of Tejano Music
(1971–1995)

Do you see the difference between a permutation and a combination? A permutation is an ordered arrangement of a given group of items. A combination is a group of items taken without regard to their order. *Permutation* problems involve situations in which *order matters*. *Combination* problems involve situations in which the *order* of items *makes no difference*.

EXAMPLE 1   Distinguishing Between Permutations and Combinations

For each of the following problems, explain if the problem is one involving permutations or combinations. (It is not necessary to solve the problem.)

a. Six students are running for student government president, vice-president, and treasurer. The student with the greatest number of votes becomes the president, the second biggest vote-getter becomes vice-president, and the student who gets the third largest number of votes will be student government treasurer. How many different outcomes are possible for these three positions?

b. Six people are on the volunteer board of supervisors for your neighborhood park. A three-person committee is needed to study the possibility of expanding the park. How many different committees could be formed from the six people on the board of supervisors?

c. Baskin-Robbins offers 31 different flavors of ice cream. One of their items is a bowl consisting of three scoops of ice cream, each a different flavor. How many such bowls are possible?

Solution

a. Students are choosing three student government officers from six candidates. The order in which the officers are chosen makes a difference because each of the offices (president, vice-president, treasurer) is different. Order matters. This is a problem involving permutations. (How many permutations are possible if three candidates are elected from six candidates?)

b. A three-person committee is to be formed from the six-person board of supervisors. The order in which the three people are selected does not matter because they are not filling different roles on the committee. Because order makes no difference, this is a problem involving combinations. (How many different combinations of three people can be chosen from a group of six people?)

c. A three-scoop bowl of three different flavors is to be formed from Baskin-Robbin's 31 flavors. The order in which the three scoops of ice cream are put into the bowl is irrelevant. A bowl with chocolate, vanilla, and strawberry is exactly the same as a bowl with vanilla, strawberry, and chocolate. Different orderings do not change things, and so this is a problem in combinations. (How many ways can three scoops be selected from 31 flavors?)

2 Solve problems involving combinations using the combinations formula.

A Formula for Combinations

You volunteer to pet-sit for your friend, who has quite a collection of animals: a dog, a cat, an iguana, a snake, and a hamster. You offer to take three of the five. How many different pet combinations can you care for?

We cannot find the number of pet-sit possibilities by using the permutation formula, but we could list all possible three-pet combinations and then count the items in our list. The five pets from which you will select three are represented using the letters shown on the next page.

D	C	I	S	H
dog	cat	iguana	snake	hamster

Here is a list of the different pet combinations you can care for:

Combinations that include the dog	DCI, DCS, DCH, DIS, DIH, DSH
Combinations that include the cat but not the dog	CIS, CIH, CSH
Combination that includes neither the dog nor the cat	ISH

Using the combinations shown on the right, we see that there are $6 + 3 + 1 = 10$ combinations. You can care for ten different groups containing three critters each.

You can use sets to describe the pet-sitting scenario. You are selecting subsets with three members from the five-membered set $\{D, C, I, S, H\}$. There are ten such subsets, each of which can be obtained from our list of different pet combinations:

$\{D, C, I\}$ $\{D, C, S\}$ $\{D, C, H\}$ $\{D, I, S\}$ $\{D, I, H\}$

$\{D, S, H\}$ $\{C, I, S\}$ $\{C, I, H\}$ $\{C, S, H\}$ $\{I, S, H\}$

Fortunately, we can find the number of combinations, or subsets, without having to make either list. We begin with the observation that for each three-pet combination, there are $3 \cdot 2 \cdot 1$, or 6, permutations. For example, the single DCI (dog, cat, iguana) combination yields these 6 permutations:

DCI, DIC, CID, CDI, IDC, ICD

There are 6, or 3!, times as many three-pet permutations as there are three-pet combinations. Thus, the number of combinations of five pets taken three at a time is the number of permutations of five pets taken three at a time divided by 3!.

$$\text{Number of combinations of 5 pets taken 3 at a time} = \frac{_5P_3}{3!}$$

The notation $_nC_r$ means the **number of combinations of n things taken r at a time**. We can find this number by generalizing from the situation in which we considered the number of combinations of five things taken three at a time: $_5C_3$. We find the number of combinations of n things taken r at time by dividing the number of permutations of n things taken r at a time by $r!$.

Study Tip

The number of combinations if r items are taken from n items cannot be found using the Fundamental Counting Principle and requires the use of the formula shown on the right.

$$\frac{_nP_r}{r!} = \frac{\dfrac{n!}{(n-r)!}}{r!} = \frac{n!}{(n-r)!r!}$$

Combinations of n Things Taken r at a Time

The number of combinations possible if r items are taken from n items is

$$_nC_r = \frac{n!}{(n-r)!r!}.$$

Technology

Graphing calculators have a key for calculating combinations, usually labeled $_nC_r$. For example, to find $_8C_3$, the keystrokes on most graphing calculators are:

$$8 \;\boxed{_nC_r}\; 3 \;\boxed{\text{ENTER}}.$$

If you are using a scientific calculator, check your manual for the location of the key for calculating combinations and the required keystrokes.

If you use your calculator's factorial key to find $\dfrac{8!}{5!3!}$, be sure to enclose the factorials in the denominator with parentheses,

$$8\;\boxed{!}\;\boxed{\div}\;\boxed{(}\;5\;\boxed{!}\;\boxed{\times}\;3\;\boxed{!}\;\boxed{)},$$

pressing $\boxed{=}$ or $\boxed{\text{ENTER}}$ to obtain the answer.

EXAMPLE 2 Using the Formula for Combinations

A three-person committee is needed to study ways of improving public transportation. How many committees could be formed from the eight people on the board of supervisors?

Solution The order in which the three people are selected does not matter. This is a problem of selecting $r = 3$ people from a group of $n = 8$ people. We are looking for the number of combinations of eight things taken three at a time. We use the formula

$$_nC_r = \frac{n!}{(n-r)!r!}$$

with $n = 8$ and $r = 3$.

$$_8C_3 = \frac{8!}{(8-3)!3!} = \frac{8!}{5!3!} = \frac{8 \cdot 7 \cdot 6 \cdot 5!}{5! \cdot 3 \cdot 2 \cdot 1} = \frac{8 \cdot 7 \cdot 6 \cdot 5!}{5! \cdot 3 \cdot 2 \cdot 1} = 56$$

Thus, 56 committees of three people each can be formed from the eight people on the board of supervisors.

EXAMPLE 3 Using the Formula for Combinations

In poker, a person is dealt 5 cards from a standard 52-card deck. The order in which you are dealt the 5 cards does not matter. How many different 5-card poker hands are possible?

Solution Because the order in which the 5 cards are dealt does not matter, this is a problem involving combinations. We are looking for the number of combinations of $n = 52$ cards drawn $r = 5$ at a time. We use the formula

$$_nC_r = \frac{n!}{(n-r)!r!}$$

with $n = 52$ and $r = 5$.

$$_{52}C_5 = \frac{52!}{(52-5)!5!} = \frac{52!}{47!5!} = \frac{52 \cdot 51 \cdot 50 \cdot 49 \cdot 48 \cdot 47!}{47! \cdot 5 \cdot 4 \cdot 3 \cdot 2 \cdot 1} = 2{,}598{,}960$$

Thus, there are 2,598,960 different 5-card poker hands possible. It surprises many people that more than 2.5 million 5-card hands can be dealt from a mere 52 cards.

If you are a card player, it does not get any better than to be dealt the 5-card poker hand shown in Figure 11.3. This hand is called a *royal flush*. It consists of an ace, king, queen, jack, and 10, all of the same suit: all hearts, all diamonds, all clubs, or all spades. The probability of being dealt a royal flush involves calculating the number of ways of being dealt such a hand: just 4 of all 2,598,960 possible hands. In the next section, we move from counting possibilities to computing probabilities.

Figure 11.3 A royal flush

EXAMPLE 4 Using the Formula for Combinations and the Fundamental Counting Principle

The U.S. Senate of the 104th Congress consisted of 54 Republicans and 46 Democrats. How many committees can be formed if each committee must have 3 Republicans and 2 Democrats?

Solution   The order in which the members are selected does not matter. Thus, this is a problem involving combinations.

We begin with the number of ways of selecting 3 Republicans out of 54 Republicans without regard to order. We are looking for the number of combinations of $n = 54$ people taken $r = 3$ at a time. We use the formula

$$_nC_r = \frac{n!}{(n-r)!r!}$$

with $n = 54$ and $r = 3$.

$$_{54}C_3 = \frac{54!}{(54-3)!3!} = \frac{54!}{51!3!} = \frac{54 \cdot 53 \cdot 52 \cdot 51!}{51! \cdot 3 \cdot 2 \cdot 1} = \frac{54 \cdot 53 \cdot 52}{3 \cdot 2 \cdot 1} = 24{,}804$$

There are 24,804 choices for forming 3-member Republican committees.

Next, we find the number of ways of selecting 2 Democrats out of 46 Democrats without regard to order. We are looking for the number of combinations of $n = 46$ people taken $r = 2$ at a time. Once again, we use the formula

$$_nC_r = \frac{n!}{(n-r)!r!}.$$

This time, $n = 46$ and $r = 2$.

$$_{46}C_2 = \frac{46!}{(46-2)!2!} = \frac{46!}{44!2!} = \frac{46 \cdot 45 \cdot 44!}{44! \cdot 2 \cdot 1} = 1035$$

There are 1035 choices for forming 2-member Democratic committees.

We use the Fundamental Counting Principle to find the number of committees that can be formed:

Committees with Republicans	Committees with Democrats
24,804 choices	1035 choices

Multiply the choices:

$$24{,}804 \cdot 1035 = 25{,}672{,}140.$$

Thus, 25,672,140 committees can be formed.

Exercise Set 11.3

 Practice Exercises

In Exercises 1–10, does the problem involve permutations or combinations? Explain your answer. (It is not necessary to solve the problem.)

1. In a race in which six automobiles are entered and there are no ties, in how many ways can the first three finishers come in?

2. A book club offers a choice of 8 books from a list of 40. In how many ways can a member make a selection?

3. A medical researcher needs 6 people to test the effectiveness of an experimental drug. If 13 people have volunteered for the test, in how many ways can 6 people be selected?

4. Fifty people purchase raffle tickets. Three winning tickets are selected at random. If first prize is $1000, second prize is $500, and third prize is $100, in how many different ways can the prizes be awarded?

5. From a club of 20 people, in how many ways can a group of three members be selected to attend a conference?

6. Fifty people purchase raffle tickets. Three winning tickets are selected at random. If each prize is $500, in how many different ways can the prizes be awarded?

7. How many different four-letter passwords can be formed from the letters A, B, C, D, E, F, and G if no repetition of letters is allowed?

8. Nine comedy acts will perform over two evenings. Five of the acts will perform on the first evening. How many ways can the schedule for the first evening be made?

9. Using 15 flavors of ice cream, how many cones with three different flavors can you create if it is important to you which flavor goes on the top, middle, and bottom?

10. Four of a sample of 50 laser printers will be selected and tested. How many ways are there to make this selection?

In Exercises 11–26, use the formula for $_nC_r$ to evaluate each expression.

11. $_6C_5$ 12. $_8C_7$ 13. $_9C_5$ 14. $_{10}C_6$

15. $_{11}C_4$ 16. $_{12}C_5$ 17. $_8C_1$ 18. $_7C_1$

19. $_7C_7$ 20. $_4C_4$ 21. $_{30}C_3$ 22. $_{25}C_4$

23. $_5C_0$ 24. $_6C_0$ 25. $\dfrac{_7C_3}{_5C_4}$ 26. $\dfrac{_{10}C_3}{_6C_4}$

 Application Exercises

Use the formula for $_nC_r$ to solve Exercises 27–40.

27. An election ballot asks voters to select three city commissioners from a group of six candidates. In how many ways can this be done?

28. A four-person committee is to be elected from an organization's membership of 11 people. How many different committees are possible?

29. Of 12 possible books, you plan to take 4 with you on vacation. How many different collections of 4 books can you take?

30. There are 14 standbys who hope to get seats on a flight, but only 6 seats are available on the plane. How many different ways can the 6 people be selected?

31. You volunteer to help drive children at a charity event to the zoo, but you can fit only 8 of the 17 children present in your van. How many different groups of 8 children can you drive?

32. How many different 4-card hands can be dealt from a deck that has 16 different cards?

33. Baskin-Robbins offers 31 different flavors of ice cream. One of their items is a bowl consisting of three scoops of ice cream, each a different flavor. How many such bowls are possible?

34. Of the 100 people in the U.S. Senate, 18 serve on the Foreign Relations Committee. How many ways are there to select Senate members for this committee (assuming party affiliation is not a factor in selection)?

35. To win at LOTTO in the state of Florida, one must correctly select 6 numbers from a collection of 49 numbers (1 through 49). The order in which the selection is made does not matter. How many different selections are possible?

36. To win in the New York State lottery, one must correctly select 6 numbers from 54 numbers. The order in which the selection is made does not matter. How many different selections are possible?

37. In how many ways can a committee of four men and five women be formed from a group of seven men and seven women?

38. How many different committees can be formed from 5 professors and 15 students if each committee is made up of 2 professors and 10 students?

39. The U.S. Senate of the 106th Congress consisted of 55 Republicans and 45 Democrats. How many committees can be formed if each committee must have 4 Republicans and 3 Democrats?

40. A mathematics exam consists of 10 multiple-choice questions and 5 open-ended problems in which all work must be shown. If an examinee must answer 8 of the multiple-choice questions and 3 of the open-ended problems, in how many ways can the questions and problems be chosen?

 Writing in Mathematics

41. What is a combination?

42. Explain how to distinguish between permutation and combination problems.

43. Write a word problem that can be solved by evaluating $_7C_3$.

Critical Thinking Exercises

44. Write a word problem that can be solved by evaluating $_{10}C_3 \cdot {_7}C_2$.

45. A 6/53 lottery involves choosing 6 of the numbers from 1 through 53 and a 5/36 lottery involves choosing 5 of the numbers from 1 through 36. The order in which the numbers are chosen does not matter. Which lottery is easier to win? Explain your answer.

46. If the number of permutations of n objects taken r at a time is six times the number of combinations of n objects taken r at a time, determine the value of r. Is there enough information to determine the value of n? Why or why not?

47. In a group of 20 people, how long will it take each person to shake hands with each of the other persons in the group, assuming that it takes three seconds for each shake and only 2 people can shake hands at a time? What if the group is increased to 40 people?

48. A sample of 4 telephones is selected from a shipment of 20 phones. There are 5 defective telephones in the shipment. How many of the samples of 4 phones do not include any of the defective ones?

Technology Exercises

Use a calculator with an $\boxed{_nC_r}$ *key to evaluate the expressions in Exercises 49–51.*

49. $_{10}C_6$ 50. $_{12}C_8$ 51. $_{40}C_6$

SECTION 11.4 *Fundamentals of Probability*

Objectives

1. Compute theoretical probability.
2. Compute empirical probability.

Table 11.1 Number of Americans and the Hours of Sleep They Get on a Typical Night

Hours of Sleep	Number of Americans, in millions
4 or less	11
5	24.75
6	68.75
7	82.5
8	74.25
9	8.25
10 or more	5.5
	Total: 275

Source: Discovery Health Media

1 Compute theoretical probability.

How many hours of sleep do you typically get each night? Table 11.1 indicates that 11 million out of 275 million Americans are getting four hours or less sleep on a typical night. The *probability* of an American getting four hours or less sleep on a typical night is $\frac{11}{275}$. This fraction can be reduced to $\frac{1}{25}$, or expressed as 0.04 or 4%. Thus, 4% of Americans get four hours or less sleep each night.

We find a probability by dividing one number by another. Probabilities are assigned to an *event*, such as getting four hours or less sleep on a typical night. Events that are certain to occur are assigned probabilities of 1, or 100%. For example, the probability that a given individual will eventually die is 1. Regrettably, taxes and death are always certain! By contrast, if an event cannot occur, its probability is 0. For example, the probability that Elvis will return from the dead and serenade us with one final reprise of "Heartbreak Hotel" is 0.

Probabilities of events are expressed as numbers ranging from 0 to 1, or 0% to 100%. The closer the probability of a given event is to 1, the more likely it is that the event will occur. The closer the probability of a given event is to 0, the less likely it is that the event will occur.

Theoretical Probability

You toss a coin. If it is equally likely to land on heads or tails, the probability of the coin landing on heads is $\frac{1}{2}$. Before the coin is tossed, we know the set of possible outcomes:

{landing on heads, landing on tails}.

Theoretical probability applies to situations like this, in which the set of all equally likely outcomes is known. Any subset of this known set is called an **event**. For example, the coin landing on heads is an event. We can use the following formula to compute the theoretical probability of an event.

100% or 1 ◀— *Certain*

◀— *Likely*

50% or $\frac{1}{2}$ ◀— *50-50 Chance*

◀— *Unlikely*

0% or 0 ◀— *Impossible*

Possible Values for Probabilities

Figure 11.4 Outcomes when a die is rolled

Computing Theoretical Probability

The **theoretical probability** of event E, denoted by $P(E)$, is:

$$P(E) = \frac{\text{number of ways } E \text{ can occur}}{\text{total number of possible outcomes}}.$$

Theoretical probability applies to many games of chance, including dice rolling, lotteries, card games, and roulette. We begin with rolling a die. Figure 11.4 illustrates that when a die is rolled, there are six equally likely possible outcomes. The set of possible outcomes can be shown as:

$$\{1, 2, 3, 4, 5, 6\}.$$

EXAMPLE 1 Computing Theoretical Probability

A die is rolled once. Find the probability of getting

a. a 3.   b. an even number.   c. a number less than 5.
d. a number less than 10.   e. a number greater than 6.

Solution   The set of equally likely outcomes is

$$\{1, 2, 3, 4, 5, 6\}.$$

The total number of possible outcomes is 6. We use this number in the denominator of each probability fraction.

a. The event of getting a 3 can occur in one way.

$$P(3) = \frac{\text{number of ways a 3 can occur}}{\text{total number of possible outcomes}} = \frac{1}{6}$$

The probability of rolling a 3 is $\frac{1}{6}$.

b. The event of getting an even number can occur in 3 ways: 2, 4, 6.

$$P(\text{even number}) = \frac{\text{number of ways an even number can occur}}{\text{total number of possible outcomes}} = \frac{3}{6} = \frac{1}{2}$$

The probability of rolling an even number is $\frac{1}{2}$.

c. The event of getting a number less than 5 can occur in 4 ways: 1, 2, 3, 4.

$$P(\text{less than 5}) = \frac{\text{number of ways a number less than 5 can occur}}{\text{total number of possible outcomes}} = \frac{4}{6} = \frac{2}{3}$$

The probability of rolling a number less than 5 is $\frac{2}{3}$.

d. The event of getting a number less than 10 can occur in 6 ways: 1, 2, 3, 4, 5, 6. All of the possible outcomes are less than 10. This event is certain to occur.

$$P(\text{less than 10}) = \frac{\text{number of ways a number less than 10 can occur}}{\text{total number of possible outcomes}} = \frac{6}{6} = 1$$

The probability of any certain event is 1.

e. The event of getting a number greater than 6 cannot occur. At most, you can roll a 6. The number of ways a number greater than 6 can occur is 0.

$$P(\text{greater than 6}) = \frac{\text{number of ways a number greater than 6 can occur}}{\text{total number of possible outcomes}} = \frac{0}{6} = 0$$

The probability of an event that cannot occur is 0.

In Example 1, there are six possible outcomes, each with a probability of $\frac{1}{6}$:

$$P(1) = \frac{1}{6} \quad P(2) = \frac{1}{6} \quad P(3) = \frac{1}{6} \quad P(4) = \frac{1}{6} \quad P(5) = \frac{1}{6} \quad P(6) = \frac{1}{6}$$

The sum of these probabilities is 1: $\frac{1}{6} + \frac{1}{6} + \frac{1}{6} + \frac{1}{6} + \frac{1}{6} + \frac{1}{6} = 1$. In general, the sum of the probabilities of all possible outcomes in any situation is 1.

Our next example involves a standard 52-card bridge deck, illustrated in Figure 11.5. The deck has four suits: Hearts and diamonds are red, and clubs and spades are black. Each suit has 13 different face values—A(ace), 2, 3, 4, 5, 6, 7, 8, 9, 10, J(jack), Q(queen), and K(king). Jacks, queens, and kings are called picture cards.

Try a Bench Press with This at the Gym

You have a deck of cards for every permutation of the 52 cards. If each deck weighed only as much as a single hydrogen atom, all the decks together would weigh a billion times as much as the sun.

Source: Isaac Asimov's Book of Facts

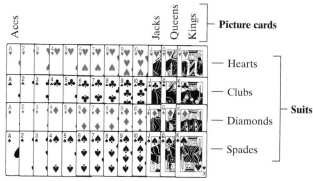

Figure 11.5 A standard 52-card bridge deck

EXAMPLE 2   Probability and a Deck of 52 Cards

You are dealt one card from a standard 52-card deck. Find the probability of being dealt

a. a king.   b. a heart.   c. a king of hearts.

Solution   Because there are 52 cards, the total number of possible ways of being dealt a single card is 52. We use 52, the total number of possible outcomes, as the number in the denominator of each probability fraction.

a. Because there are 4 kings in the deck, the event of being dealt a king can occur in 4 ways.

$$P(\text{king}) = \frac{\text{number of ways a king can occur}}{\text{total number of outcomes}} = \frac{4}{52} = \frac{1}{13}$$

The probability of being dealt a king is $\frac{1}{13}$.

b. Because there are 13 hearts in the deck, the event of being dealt a heart can occur in 13 ways.

$$P(\text{heart}) = \frac{\text{number of ways a heart can occur}}{\text{total number of outcomes}} = \frac{13}{52} = \frac{1}{4}$$

The probability of being dealt a heart is $\frac{1}{4}$.

c. Because there is only one card in the deck that is the king of hearts, the event of being dealt the king of hearts can occur in just one way.

$$P(\text{king of hearts}) = \frac{\text{number of ways a king of hearts can occur}}{\text{total number of outcomes}} = \frac{1}{52}$$

The probability of being dealt the king of hearts is $\frac{1}{52}$.

Probabilities play a valuable role in the science of genetics. Example 3 deals with cystic fibrosis, an inherited lung disease occurring in about 1 out of every 2000 births among Caucasians and in about 1 in 250,000 births among non-Caucasians.

EXAMPLE 3 Probabilities in Genetics

Each person carries two genes that are related to the absence or presence of the disease cystic fibrosis. Most Americans have two normal genes for this trait and are unaffected by cystic fibrosis. However, 1 in 25 Americans carries one normal gene and one defective gene. If we use c to represent a defective gene and C a normal gene, such a carrier can be designated as Cc. Thus, CC is a person who neither carries nor has cystic fibrosis, Cc is a carrier who is not actually sick, and cc is a person sick with the disease. The table below shows the four equally likely outcomes for a child's genetic inheritance from two parents who are both carrying one cystic fibrosis gene. One copy of each gene is passed on to the child from the parents.

Genetic engineering offers some hope for cystic fibrosis patients. Geneticists can now isolate the c gene. It is hoped that it will soon be possible to replace the defective c gene with a normal C gene.

		Second Parent	
		C	c
First	C	CC	Cc
Parent	c	Cc	cc

Shown in the table are the four possibilities for a child whose parents each carry one cystic fibrosis gene.

If each parent carries one cystic fibrosis gene, what is the probability that their child will have cystic fibrosis?

Solution The table shows the four equally likely outcomes. Only the cc child will develop cystic fibrosis. Thus,

$$P(\text{cystic fibrosis}) = \frac{\text{number of ways cystic fibrosis can occur}}{\text{total number of possible outcomes}} = \frac{1}{4}.$$

If each parent carries one cystic fibrosis gene, the probability that their child will have cystic fibrosis is $\frac{1}{4}$.

2 Compute empirical probability.

Empirical Probability

According to Discovery Health Media, the group that runs the Discovery Health Channel, although Americans say they lead active lives, for most of us, walking is as strenuous as it gets. Table 11.2 is based on a survey of 2000 Americans and shows the number of people who regularly participate in various kinds of exercise. For people who do not exercise regularly, the leading obstacle is a perceived lack of time.

Table 11.2   Number of People Surveyed Who Regularly Participate in Various Forms of Exercise

Form of Exercise	Number of People
Walking/hiking	1140
Weight training	320
Running/jogging	280
Biking	240
Aerobics	240
Exercise machines	220
Total people surveyed:	2000

Source: Discovery Health Media

Table 11.2 shows that 1140 of the 2000 people surveyed regularly participate in walking/hiking. We use these numbers, or **observed frequencies**, to find the probability that an American participates in walking/hiking. We take the observed frequency for walking/hiking, 1140, and divide by the total number of people surveyed, 2000:

$$P(\text{participates in walking/hiking}) = \frac{1140}{2000} = \frac{57}{100} \text{ or } 57\%$$

Assuming that this survey is representative of all Americans, about 57 per 100 Americans exercise regularly by walking/hiking.

Theoretical probability is based on a set of equally likely outcomes and the number of elements in the set. By contrast, the probability of participating in walking/hiking uses numbers in the numerator and denominator of the probability fraction that are obtained from observed frequencies. **Empirical probability** applies to situations in which we observe the frequency of occurrence of an event. We use the following formula to compute the empirical probability of an event.

Computing Empirical Probability

The empirical probability of event E is:

$$P(E) = \frac{\text{observed number of times } E \text{ occurs}}{\text{total number of observed occurrences}}.$$

EXAMPLE 4 Computing Empirical Probability

According to a 1997 survey of 6000 college freshmen conducted by the American Council on Education, 2070 freshmen reported that they regularly overslept and missed class. Find the empirical probability of a freshman oversleeping and missing class.

Solution The probability of oversleeping and missing class is the observed number of freshmen who reported doing this, 2070, divided by the total number of freshmen in the survey, 6000.

P(oversleeping and missing class)

$$= \frac{\text{number of freshmen who oversleep and miss class}}{\text{total number of freshmen}} = \frac{2070}{6000} = \frac{69}{200} = 0.345$$

The empirical probability of a freshman oversleeping and missing class is $\frac{2070}{6000}$, or $\frac{69}{200}$. Assuming that this survey is representative of all U.S. college freshmen, about 69 out of every 200 freshmen (34.5%) regularly oversleep and miss class.

In certain situations, we can establish a relationship between the two kinds of probability. Consider, for example, a coin that is equally likely to land heads or tails. Such a coin is called a **fair coin**. Empirical probability can be used to determine if a coin is fair. Suppose we toss a coin 10, 50, 100, 1000, 10,000, and 100,000 times. We record the number of heads observed, shown in Table 11.3. For each of the six cases in the table, the empirical probability of heads is determined by dividing the number of heads observed by the number of tosses.

Table 11.3 Empirical Probabilities of Heads as the Number of Tosses Increases

Number of Tosses	Number of Heads Observed	Empirical Probability of Heads, or $P(H)$
10	4	$P(H) = \frac{4}{10} = 0.4$
50	27	$P(H) = \frac{27}{50} = 0.54$
100	44	$P(H) = \frac{44}{100} = 0.44$
1000	530	$P(H) = \frac{530}{1000} = 0.53$
10,000	4851	$P(H) = \frac{4851}{10,000} = 0.4851$
100,000	49,880	$P(H) = \frac{49,880}{100,000} = 0.4988$

A pattern is exhibited by the empirical probabilities in the right-hand column of Table 11.3. As the number of tosses increases, the empirical probabilities tend to get closer to 0.5, the theoretical probability. These results give us no reason to suspect that the coin is not fair.

Table 11.3 illustrates an important principle when observing uncertain outcomes such as the event of a coin landing on heads. As a process is repeated more and more times, the empirical probability of an event tends to get closer to the theoretical probability of that event. This principle is known as the **law of large numbers**.

Exercise Set 11.4

  Practice and Application Exercises

Exercises 1–54 involve theoretical probability. Use the theoretical probability formula to solve each exercise. Express each probability as a fraction reduced to lowest terms.

In Exercises 1–10, a die is rolled. The set of equally likely outcomes is {1, 2, 3, 4, 5, 6}. Find the probability of getting

1. a 4.
2. a 5.
3. an odd number.
4. a number greater than 3.
5. a number less than 3.
6. a number greater than 4.
7. a number less than 7.
8. a number less than 8.
9. a number greater than 7.
10. a number greater than 8.

In Exercises 11–20, you are dealt one card from a standard 52-card deck. Find the probability of being dealt

11. a queen.
12. a jack.
13. a club.
14. a diamond.
15. a picture card.
16. a card greater than 3 and less than 7.
17. a queen of spades.
18. an ace of clubs.
19. a diamond and a spade.
20. a card with a green heart.

In Exercises 21–26, a fair coin is tossed two times in succession. The set of equally likely outcomes is {HH, HT, TH, TT}. Find the probability of getting

21. two heads.
22. two tails.
23. the same outcome on each toss.
24. different outcomes on each toss.
25. a head on the second toss.
26. at least one head.

In Exercises 27–34, you select a family with three children. If M represents a male child and F a female child, the set of equally likely outcomes is {MMM, MMF, MFM, MFF, FMM, FMF, FFM, FFF}. Find the probability of selecting a family with

27. exactly one female child.
28. exactly one male child.
29. exactly two male children.

30. exactly two female children.
31. at least one male child.
32. at least two female children.
33. four male children.
34. fewer than four female children.

In Exercises 35–40, a single die is rolled twice. The 36 equally likely outcomes are shown as follows:

	Second Roll					
	⚀	⚁	⚂	⚃	⚄	⚅
⚀	(1,1)	(1,2)	(1,3)	(1,4)	(1,5)	(1,6)
⚁	(2,1)	(2,2)	(2,3)	(2,4)	(2,5)	(2,6)
⚂	(3,1)	(3,2)	(3,3)	(3,4)	(3,5)	(3,6)
⚃	(4,1)	(4,2)	(4,3)	(4,4)	(4,5)	(4,6)
⚄	(5,1)	(5,2)	(5,3)	(5,4)	(5,5)	(5,6)
⚅	(6,1)	(6,2)	(6,3)	(6,4)	(6,5)	(6,6)

(First Roll shown vertically at left)

Find the probability of getting

35. two even numbers.
36. two odd numbers.
37. two numbers whose sum is 5.
38. two numbers whose sum is 6.
39. two numbers whose sum exceeds 12.
40. two numbers whose sum is less than 13.

Use the spinner shown to answer Exercises 41–48. Assume that it is equally probable that the pointer will land on any one of the ten colored regions. If the pointer lands on a borderline, spin again.

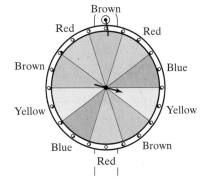

Find the probability that the spinner lands in

41. a red region. ³/₁₀
43. a blue region. ¹/₅
45. a region that is red or blue. ¹/₂
46. a region that is yellow or brown. ¹/₂
47. a region that is red and blue. 0
48. a region that is yellow and brown. 0

42. a yellow region.
44. a brown region.

Exercises 49–54 deal with sickle cell anemia, an inherited disease in which red blood cells become distorted and deprived of oxygen. Approximately 1 in every 500 black infants is born with the disease; only 1 in 160,000 nonblack infants has the disease. A person with two sickle cell genes will have the disease, but a person with only one sickle cell gene will have a mild, nonfatal anemia called sickle cell trait. (Approximately 8%–10% of the black population has this trait.)

		Second Parent	
		S	s
First Parent	S	SS	Ss
	s	Ss	ss

If we use s to represent a sickle cell gene and S a healthy gene, the table shows the four possibilities for the children of two Ss parents. Each parent has only one sickle cell gene, so each has the relatively mild sickle cell trait. Find the probability that these parents give birth to a child who

49. has sickle cell anemia.
50. has sickle cell trait.
51. is healthy.

In Exercises 52–54, use the table that shows the four possibilities for the children of one healthy, SS, parent, and one parent with sickle cell trait, Ss.

		Second Parent (with Sickle Cell Trait)	
		S	s
Healthy First Parent	S	SS	Ss
	S	SS	Ss

Find the probability that these parents give birth to a child who

52. has sickle cell anemia.
53. has sickle cell trait.
54. is healthy.

Exercises 55–66 involve empirical probability. Use the empirical probability formula to solve each exercise. Express answers as fractions. Then use a calculator to express probabilities as decimals, rounded to the nearest thousandth.

Use the table showing U.S. family size to solve Exercises 55–60.

U.S. Families (includes only a householder and his/her relatives) by Size, 1997

Total: 70,241,000 Families	
Size	Number of Families
2 people	29,780,000
3 people	16,239,000
4 people	14,602,000
5 people	6,326,000
6 people	2,108,000
7 people or more	1,186,000

Source: U.S. Bureau of the Census

Find the probability that a U.S. family has

55. 2 people.
56. 3 people.
57. 4 people.
58. 5 people.
59. 6 people.
60. 7 or more people.

Use the table showing world population for selected regions to solve Exercises 61–66.

Populations of Selected Regions of the World

Total World Population: 5926 million	
Region	Population in millions
Africa	761
Near East	165
Asia	3363
Latin America	508
Europe	799
North America	301

Source: U.S. Bureau of the Census

If one person is randomly selected from all people on planet Earth, find the probability of selecting

61. an African.
62. a person from the Near East.
63. an Asian.
64. a Latin American.
65. a European.
66. a North American.

Writing in Mathematics

67. Describe the difference between theoretical probability and empirical probability.

68. Give an example of an event whose probability must be determined empirically rather than theoretically.

69. Use the definition of probability to explain why the probability of an event that cannot occur is 0.

70. Use the definition of probability to explain why the probability of an event that is certain to occur is 1.

71. Write a probability word problem whose answer is one of the following fractions: $\frac{1}{6}$ or $\frac{1}{4}$ or $\frac{1}{3}$.

72. The president of a large company with 10,000 employees is considering mandatory cocaine testing for every employee. The test that would be used is 90% accurate, meaning that it will detect 90% of the cocaine users who are tested, and that 90% of the nonusers will test negative. This also means that the test gives 10% false positive. Suppose that 1% of the employees actually use cocaine. Find the probability that someone who tests positive for cocaine use is, indeed, a user.

Hint: Find the following probability fraction:

$$= \frac{\text{the number of employees who test positive and are cocaine users}}{\text{the number of employees who test positive}}$$

$$= \frac{90\% \text{ of } 1\% \text{ of } 10,000}{\text{the number who test positive who actually use cocaine plus the number who test positive who do not use cocaine}}$$

What does this probability indicate in terms of the percent of employees who test positive who are not actually users? Discuss these numbers in terms of the issue of mandatory drug testing. Write a paper either in favor of or against mandatory drug testing, incorporating the actual percentage accuracy for such tests.

Critical Thinking Exercises

73. The target in the figure shown contains four squares. If a dart thrown at random hits the target, find the probability that it will land in a colored region.

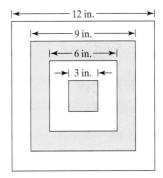

74. Some three-digit numbers, such as 101 and 313, read the same forward and backward. If you select a number from all three-digit numbers, find the probability it will read the same forward and backward.

Group Exercise

75. There is a third type of probability, called **subjective probability**. Subjective probability states a probability value using an estimate or an educated guess, utilizing opinions and inexact information. For example, a sports journalist might say that there is a 60% probability that the Yankees will win the pennant next year. A seismologist might state that there is a 70% probability that a major earthquake will occur on the San Andreas fault within the next ten years.

Each group member should give an example of how subjective probability is used in everyday life, or of how he or she uses this probability.

SECTION 11.5 *Probability with the Fundamental Counting Principle, Permutations, and Combinations*

Objectives

1. Compute probabilities with permutations.

2. Compute probabilities with combinations.

Probability with Permutations

We return to our concert tour with Offspring, Pink Floyd, Sublime, and the Rolling Stones. Now, the surviving members of the Beatles have agreed to join the tour! You really have your work cut out for you. In what order should the five groups in the concert perform? Because order makes a difference, this is a permutation situation. Example 1 is based on this scenario, and uses permutations to solve a probability problem.

1 Compute probabilities with permutations.

Permutations and Rubik's Cube

First.developed in Hungary in the 1970s by Erno Rubik, a Rubik's cube contains $3 \times 3 \times 3 = 27$ small cubes. The square faces of the cubes are colored in six different colors. The cubes can be twisted horizontally or vertically. When first purchased, the cube is arranged so that each face shows a said color. To do the puzzle, you first turn columns and rows in a random way until all of the six faces are multicolored. To solve the puzzle, you must return the cube to its original state—that is, a single color on each of the six faces. With 43,252,003,274,489,856,000 arrangements, this is no easy task! If it takes one-half second for each of these arrangements, it would require over 681,000,000,000 years to move the cube into all possible arrangements.

EXAMPLE 1   Probability and Permutations

The five groups in the tour agree to determine the order of performance based on a random selection. Each band's name is written on one of five cards. The cards are placed in a hat and then five cards are drawn, one at a time. The order in which the cards are drawn determines the order in which the bands perform. What is the probability of the Rolling Stones performing fourth and the Beatles last?

Solution   We begin by applying the definition of probability to this situation.

P(Rolling Stones fourth, Beatles last)

$$= \frac{\text{number of permutations with Rolling Stones fourth, Beatles last}}{\text{total number of possible permutations}}$$

We can use the Fundamental Counting Principle to find the total number of possible permutations. This represents the number of ways you can put together the concert.

First Group to Perform	Second Group to Perform	Third Group to Perform	Fourth Group to Perform	Last Group to Perform
5 choices	4 choices	3 choices	2 choices	1 choice

There are $5 \cdot 4 \cdot 3 \cdot 2 \cdot 1$, or 120, possible permutations. Equivalently, the five groups can perform in 120 different orders.

We can also use the Fundamental Counting Principle to find the number of permutations with the Rolling Stones performing fourth and the Beatles performing last. You can choose any one of the three groups, Offspring, Pink Floyd, or Sublime, as the opening act. This leaves two choices for the second group to perform, and only one choice for the third group to perform. There is only one choice for the fourth group—the Rolling Stones, and one choice for the closing act—the Beatles:

First Group to Perform	Second Group to Perform	Third Group to Perform	Fourth Group to Perform	Last Group to Perform
3 choices (Offspring, Pink Floyd, or Sublime)	2 choices	1 choice	1 choice: The Rolling Stones	1 choice: The Beatles

Thus, there are $3 \cdot 2 \cdot 1 \cdot 1 \cdot 1$, or six possible permutations. Equivalently, there are six lineups with the Rolling Stones perfoming fourth and the Beatles last.

Now we can return to our probability fraction.

P(Rolling Stones fourth, Beatles last)

$$= \frac{\text{number of permutations with Rolling Stones fourth, Beatles last}}{\text{total number of possible permutations}}$$

$$= \frac{6}{120} = \frac{1}{20}$$

The probability of the Rolling Stones performing fourth and the Beatles last is $\frac{1}{20}$.

2 Compute probabilities with combinations.

Probability with Combinations

If your state has a lottery drawing each week, the probability that someone will win the top prize is relatively high. If there is no winner this week, it is virtually certain that eventually someone will be graced with millions of dollars. So, how come you are unlucky compared to this undisclosed someone? In Example 2, we provide an answer to this question.

State lotteries keep 50 cents on the dollar, resulting in $10 billion a year for public funding.

EXAMPLE 2   Probability and Combinations: Winning the Lottery

Florida's lottery game, LOTTO, is set up so that each player chooses six different numbers from 1 to 49. If the six numbers chosen match the six numbers drawn randomly each Saturday evening, the player wins (or shares) the top cash prize. (As of this writing, the top cash prize has ranged from $7 million to $106.5 million.) What is the probability of winning this prize?

Solution   Because the order of the six numbers does not matter, this is a situation involving combinations. We begin with the formula for probability.

$$P(\text{winning}) = \frac{\text{number of ways of winning}}{\text{total number of possible combinations}}$$

We can use the combinations formula

$$_nC_r = \frac{n!}{(n-r)!r!}$$

to find the total number of possible combinations. We are selecting $r = 6$ numbers from a collection of $n = 49$ numbers.

$$_{49}C_6 = \frac{49!}{(49-6)!6!} = \frac{49!}{43!6!} = \frac{49 \cdot 48 \cdot 47 \cdot 46 \cdot 45 \cdot 44 \cdot 43!}{43! \cdot 6 \cdot 5 \cdot 4 \cdot 3 \cdot 2 \cdot 1} = 13,983,816$$

There are nearly 14 million number combinations possible in LOTTO! If a person buys one LOTTO ticket, that person has selected only one combination of the six numbers. With one LOTTO ticket, there is only one way of winning.

Now we can return to our probability fraction.

$$P(\text{winning}) = \frac{\text{number of ways of winning}}{\text{total number of possible combinations}} = \frac{1}{13,983,816} \approx 0.0000000715$$

The probability of winning the top prize with one LOTTO ticket is about 1 in 14 million.

In 1997, Americans spent nearly 17 billion dollars on lotteries set up by revenue-hungry states. If a pigeon, er, person, buys, say 5000 different tickets in Florida's LOTTO, that person has selected 5000 different combinations of the six numbers. The probability of winning is

$$\frac{5000}{13,983,816} \approx 0.000358.$$

The chances of winning top prize are about 358 in a million. At $1 per LOTTO ticket, it is highly probable that Mr. or Ms. Pigeon will be $5000 poorer.

Technology

Although we've shown the computational details for $_{49}C_6$, you can obtain the number of combinations using your calculator by either:

1. Using the $\boxed{_nC_r}$ key.

or

2. Using the factorial key for $\frac{49!}{43!6!}$. Don't forget to enter parentheses around 43! × 6!.

EXAMPLE 3   Probability and Combinations

A club consists of five men and seven women. Three members are selected at random to attend a conference. Find the probability that the selected group consists of

a. three men.

b. one man and two women.

Solution   The order in which the three people are selected does not matter, so this is a problem involving combinations.

a. We begin with the probability of selecting three men.

$$P(3 \text{ men}) = \frac{\text{number of ways of selecting 3 men}}{\text{total number of possible combinations}}$$

First, we consider the denominator of the probability fraction. We are selecting $r = 3$ people from a total group of $n = 12$ people (five men and seven women). The total number of possible combinations is

$$_{12}C_3 = \frac{12!}{(12-3)!3!} = \frac{12!}{9!3!} = \frac{12 \cdot 11 \cdot 10 \cdot 9!}{9! \cdot 3 \cdot 2 \cdot 1} = 220.$$

Thus, there are 220 possible three-person selections.

Next, we consider the numerator of the probability fraction. We are interested in the number of ways of selecting three men. We are selecting $r = 3$ men from a total group of $n = 5$ men. The number of possible combinations of three men is

$$_{5}C_3 = \frac{5!}{(5-3)!3!} = \frac{5!}{2!3!} = \frac{5 \cdot 4 \cdot 3!}{2 \cdot 1 \cdot 3!} = 10.$$

Thus, there are 10 ways of selecting three men. Now we can fill in the numbers in the numerator and the denominator of our probability fraction.

$$P(3 \text{ men}) = \frac{\text{number of ways of selecting 3 men}}{\text{total number of possible combinations}} = \frac{10}{220} = \frac{1}{22}$$

The probability that the group selected to attend the conference consists of three men is $\frac{1}{22}$.

b. We set up the fraction for the probability that the selected group consists of one man and two women.

$$P(1 \text{ man, 2 women}) = \frac{\text{number of ways of selecting 1 man and 2 women}}{\text{total number of possible combinations}}$$

The denominator of this fraction is the same as the denominator in part (a). The total number of possible combinations is found by selecting $r = 3$ people from $n = 12$ people: $_{12}C_3 = 220$.

Next, we move to the numerator of the probability fraction. The number of ways of selecting $r = 1$ man from $n = 5$ men is

$$_{5}C_1 = \frac{5!}{(5-1)!1!} = \frac{5!}{4!1!} = \frac{5 \cdot 4!}{4! \cdot 1} = 5.$$

The number of ways of selecting $r = 2$ women from $n = 7$ women is

$$_7C_2 = \frac{7!}{(7-2)!2!} = \frac{7!}{5!2!} = \frac{7 \cdot 6 \cdot 5!}{5! \cdot 2 \cdot 1} = 21.$$

By the Fundamental Counting Principle, the number of ways of selecting 1 man and 2 women is

$$_5C_1 \cdot {_7C_2} = 5 \cdot 21 = 105.$$

Now we can fill in the numbers in the numerator and the denominator of our probability fraction.

$$P(1 \text{ man, 2 women}) = \frac{\text{number of ways of selecting 1 man and 2 women}}{\text{total number of possible combinations}} = \frac{105}{220} = \frac{21}{44}$$

The probability that the group selected to attend the conference consists of one man and two women is $\frac{21}{44}$.

Exercise Set 11.5

 Practice and Application Exercises

1. Martha, Lee, Nancy, Paul, and Armando have all been invited to a dinner party. They arrive randomly and each person arrives at a different time.
   a. In how many ways can they arrive?
   b. In how many ways can Martha arrive first and Armando last?
   c. Find the probability that Martha will arrive first and Armando will arrive last.

2. Three men and three women line up at a checkout counter in a store.
   a. In how many ways can they line up?
   b. In how many ways can they line up if the first person in line is a woman, and then the line alternates by gender—that is, a woman, a man, a woman, a man, and so on?
   c. Find the probability that the first person in line is a woman and the line alternates by gender.

3. Six stand-up comics, A, B, C, D, E, and F, are to perform on a single evening at a comedy club. The order of performance is determined by random selection. Find the probability that
   a. Comic E will perform first.
   b. Comic C will perform fifth and comic B will perform last.
   c. The comedians will perform in the following order: D, E, C, A, B, F.
   d. Comic A or comic B will perform first.

4. Seven performers, A, B, C, D, E, F, and G, are to appear in a fund raiser. The order of performance is determined by random selection. Find the probability that
   a. D will perform first.
   b. E will perform sixth and B will perform last.

   c. They will perform in the following order: C, D, B, A, G, F, E.
   d. F or G will perform first.

5. A group consists of four men and five women. Three people are selected to attend a conference.
   a. In how many ways can three people be selected from this group of nine?
   b. In how many ways can three women be selected from the five women?
   c. Find the probability that the selected group will consist of all women.

6. A political discussion group consists of five Democrats and six Republicans. Four people are selected to attend a conference.
   a. In how many ways can four people be selected from this group of eleven?
   b. In how many ways can four Republicans be selected from the six Republicans?
   c. Find the probability that the selected group will consist of all Republicans.

7. To play the California lottery, a person has to correctly select 6 out of 51 numbers, paying $1 for each six-number selection. If the six numbers picked are the same as the ones drawn by the lottery, mountains of money are bestowed. What is the probability that a person with one combination of six numbers will win? What is the probability of winning if 100 different lottery tickets are purchased?

8. A state lottery is designed so that a player chooses five numbers from 1 to 30 on one lottery ticket. What is the probability that a player with one lottery ticket will win? What is the probability of winning if 100 different lottery tickets are purchased?

9. A box contains 25 transitors, 6 of which are defective. If 6 are sold at random, find the probability that
   a. all are defective.
   b. none are defective.

10. A committee of five people is to be formed from six lawyers and seven teachers. Find the probability that
    a. all are lawyers.
    b. none are lawyers.

11. A city council consists of six Democrats and four Republicans. If a committee of three people is selected, find the probability of selecting one Democrat and two Republicans.

12. A parent-teacher committee consisting of four people is to be selected from fifteen parents and five teachers. Find the probability of selecting two parents and two teachers.

Exercises 13–18 involve a deck of 52 cards. If necessary, refer to the picture of a deck of cards, Figure 11.5 on page 545.

13. A poker hand consists of five cards.
    a. Find the total number of possible five-card poker hands.
    b. A diamond flush consists of a five-card hand consisting of all diamonds. Find the number of possible five-card diamond flushes.
    c. Find the probability of being dealt a diamond flush.

14. A poker hand consists of five cards.
    a. Find the total number of possible five-card poker hands.
    b. Find the number of ways in which four aces can be selected.
    c. Find the number of ways in which one king can be selected.
    d. Use the Fundamental Counting Principle and your answers from parts (b) and (c) to find the number of ways of getting four aces and one king.
    e. Find the probability of getting a poker hand of four aces and one king.

15. If you are dealt 3 cards from a shuffled deck of 52 cards, find the probability that all 3 cards are picture cards.

16. If you are dealt 4 cards from a shuffled deck of 52 cards, find the probability that all 4 are hearts.

17. If you are dealt 4 cards from a shuffled deck of 52 cards, find the probability of getting two queens and two kings.

18. If you are dealt 4 cards from a shuffled deck of 52 cards, find the probability of getting three jacks and one queen.

Writing in Mathematics

19. If people understood the mathematics involving probabilities and lotteries, as you now do, do you think they would continue to spend hundreds of dollars per year on lottery tickets? Explain your answer.

20. Write and solve an original problem involving probability and permutations.

21. Write and solve an original problem involving probability and combinations whose solution requires $\frac{_{14}C_{10}}{_{20}C_{10}}$.

Critical Thinking Exercises

22. An apartment complex offers apartments with four different options, designated by A through D.

A	B	C	D
one bedroom	one bathroom	first floor	lake view
two bedrooms	two bathrooms	second floor	golf course view
three bedrooms			view
			no special view

If there is only one apartment left, what is the probability that it is precisely what a person is looking for, namely two bedrooms, two bathrooms, first floor, and a lake or golf course view?

23. Reread Exercise 7. How much must a person spend so that the probability of winning the California lottery is $\frac{1}{2}$?

24. Suppose that it is a week in which the cash prize in Florida's LOTTO is promised to exceed $50 million. If a person purchases 13,983,816 tickets in LOTTO at $1 per ticket (all possible combinations), isn't this a guarantee of winning the lottery? Because the probability in this situation is 1, what's wrong with doing this?

25. The digits 1, 2, 3, 4, and 5 are randomly arranged to form a three-digit number. (Digits are not repeated.) Find the probability that the number is even and greater than 500.

26. In a five-card poker hand, what is the probability of being dealt one ace and no picture cards?

Group Exercise

27. Research and present a group report on state lotteries. Include answers to some or all of the following questions. As always, make the report interesting and informative. Which states do not have lotteries? Why not? How much is spent per capita on lotteries? What are some of the lottery games? What is the probability of winning top prize in these games? What income groups spend the greatest amount of money on lotteries? If your state has a lottery, what does it do with the money it makes? Is the way the money is spent what was promised when the lottery first began?

SECTION 11.6   *Events Involving Not and Or; Odds*

Objectives

1. Find the probability an event will not occur.
2. Find the probability of one event or a second event occurring.
3. Understand and use odds.

You take your first trip to London. You are surprised to learn that the British gamble on everything. Shops with bookmakers are available everywhere for placing bets. In such a shop, you overhear a conversation about turning up the king of hearts in a deck of cards. You are expecting to hear something about a probability of $\frac{1}{52}$. Instead, you hear the phrase "51 to 1 against." Are you having difficulty understanding the British accents or did you miss something in your liberal arts math course? Whatever happened to probability?

No, it's not the accent. There are several ways to express the likelihood of an event. For example, we can discuss the probability of an event. We can also discuss *odds against* an event and *odds in favor* of an event. In this section, we expand our knowledge of probability and explain the meaning of odds.

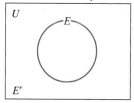

1 Find the probability an event will not occur.

Probability of an Event Not Occurring

A survey (source: Penn, Schoen, and Berland, 1999) asked 500 Americans to rate their health. Of those surveyed, 270 rated their health as good/excellent. This means that $500 - 270$, or 230, people surveyed did not rate their health as good/excellent. Notice that

$$P(\text{good/excellent}) + P(\text{not good/excellent}) = \frac{270}{500} + \frac{230}{500} = \frac{500}{500} = 1.$$

In general, because the sum of the probabilities of all possible outcomes in any situation is 1,

$$P(E) + P(\text{not } E) = 1.$$

We now solve this equation for $P(\text{not } E)$, the probability that event E will not occur, by subtracting $P(E)$ from both sides. The resulting formula is given in the following box.

Sets and Probability

$E \cup E' = U$
$P(E) + P(E') = P(U) = 1$

The Probability of an Event Not Occurring

The probability that an event E will not occur is equal to one minus the probability that it will occur.

$$P(\text{not } E) = 1 - P(E)$$

EXAMPLE 1   The Probability of an Event Not Occurring

If you are dealt one card from a standard 52-card deck, find the probability that you are not dealt a queen.

Solution   Because

$$P(\text{not } E) = 1 - P(E)$$

then

$$P(\text{not a queen}) = 1 - P(\text{queen}).$$

There are four queens in a deck of 52 cards. The probability of being dealt a queen is $\frac{4}{52} = \frac{1}{13}$.

$1 - \frac{1}{13}$

Thus,

$$P(\text{not a queen}) = 1 - P(\text{queen}) = 1 - \frac{1}{13} = \frac{13}{13} - \frac{1}{13} = \frac{12}{13}.$$

The probability that you are not dealt a queen is $\frac{12}{13}$.

EXAMPLE 2 The Probability of Not Winning the Lottery

We have seen that the probability of winning Florida's LOTTO with one ticket is $\frac{1}{13,983,816}$. What is the probability of not winning?

Solution

$$P(\text{not winning}) = 1 - P(\text{winning}) = 1 - \frac{1}{13,983,816} = \frac{13,983,816}{13,983,816} - \frac{1}{13,983,816}$$

$$= \frac{13,983,815}{13,983,816} \approx 0.9999999$$

The probability of not winning is close to 1. It is almost certain that with one LOTTO ticket, a person will not win the top prize.

2 Find the probability of one event or a second event occurring.

Or Probabilities with Mutually Exclusive Events

According to 1998 government data, commuters are not helping to preserve the environment and conserve energy. Table 11.4 shows the primary means of trans-

Table 11.4 How Americans Get to Work

Primary Means of Transportation	Number
Total workers	115,070,274
• Private vehicle	99,592,932
Drove alone	84,215,298
Carpooled	15,377,634
• Public transportation	6,069,589
Bus	3,445,000
Streetcar or trolley car	78,130
Subway or elevated	1,755,476
Railroad	574,052
Ferryboat	37,497
Taxicab	179,434
• Motorcycle	237,404
• Bicycle	466,856
• Walked only	4,488,886
• Worked at home	3,406,025
• All other means	808,582

Source: U.S. Census Bureau

portation for America's 115,070,274 workers. Most people get to work by private vehicle. Only 6,069,589 use public transportation and far fewer, 466,856, use a bicycle. If we randomly select one American worker, we can use these numbers to determine the following probabilities:

$$P(\text{public transportation}) = \frac{6{,}069{,}589}{115{,}070{,}274} \approx 0.053$$

$$P(\text{bicycle}) = \frac{466{,}856}{115{,}070{,}274} \approx 0.004$$

Because Table 11.4 shows the *primary* means of transportation, a worker whose primary means is public transportation excludes the use of a bicycle as the primary way of getting to work, and vice versa. The events of using public transportation and using a bicycle cannot occur simultaneously, and are said to be **mutually exclusive.**

> ### Mutually Exclusive Events
> If it is impossible for events A and B to occur simultaneously, the events are said to be **mutually exclusive.**

We can use the numbers in Table 11.4 to find the probability that a randomly selected worker uses either public transportation or a bicycle as the primary means of getting to work:

$P(\text{public transportation or bicycle})$

$$= \frac{\text{number of workers whose primary way of getting to work is either public transportation or bicycle}}{\text{total number of workers}}$$

$$= \frac{6{,}069{,}589 + 466{,}856}{115{,}070{,}274} = \frac{6{,}536{,}445}{115{,}070{,}274} \approx 0.057$$

We could also find the probability of these mutually exclusive events by adding their individual probabilities:

$$P(\text{public transportation or bicycle}) = P(\text{public transportation}) + P(\text{bicycle}).$$

In general, if A and B are mutually exclusive events, the probability that either A or B will occur is determined by adding their individual probabilities.

Sets and Probability

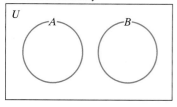

If $A \cap B = \varnothing$, then
$P(A \cup B) = P(A) + P(B)$.
Equivalently,
$P(A \text{ or } B) = P(A) + P(B)$.

> ### *Or* Probabilities with Mutually Exclusive Events
> If A and B are mutually exclusive events, then
> $$P(A \text{ or } B) = P(A) + P(B).$$

EXAMPLE 3   The Probability of Either of Two Mutually Exclusive Events Occurring

If you roll a single, six-sided die, what is the probability of getting either a 4 or a 5?

Solution   Because the outcomes of a 4 and a 5 cannot occur simultaneously, the events are mutually exclusive. We find the probability that either of these events will occur by adding their individual probabilities.

$$P(4 \text{ or } 5) = P(4) + P(5) = \frac{1}{6} + \frac{1}{6} = \frac{2}{6} = \frac{1}{3}$$

The probability of getting a 4 or a 5 is $\frac{1}{3}$.

EXAMPLE 4   The Probability of Either of Two Mutually Exclusive Events Occurring

If one card is randomly selected from a deck of cards, what is the probability of selecting a king or a queen?

Solution   Only one card is selected, so it is impossible to get both a king and a queen. Because the outcomes of selecting a king and a queen cannot both occur simultaneously, the events are mutually exclusive.

We find the probability that either of these events will occur by adding their individual probabilities.

$$P(\text{king or queen}) = P(\text{king}) + P(\text{queen}) = \frac{4}{52} + \frac{4}{52} = \frac{8}{52} = \frac{2}{13}$$

The probability of selecting a king or a queen is $\frac{2}{13}$.

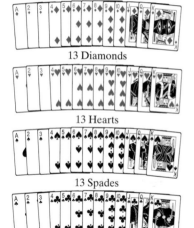

13 Diamonds

13 Hearts

13 Spades

13 Clubs

Figure 11.6 A deck of 52 cards

Or Probabilities with Events That Are Not Mutually Exclusive

Consider the deck of 52 cards shown in Figure 11.6. Suppose that these cards are shuffled and you randomly select one card from the deck. What is the probability of selecting a diamond or a picture card (jack, queen, king)? Begin by adding their individual probabilities:

$$P(\text{diamond}) + P(\text{picture card}) = \frac{13}{52} + \frac{12}{52}$$

> There are 13 diamonds in the deck of 52 cards.

> There are 12 picture cards in the deck of 52 cards.

Figure 11.7 Three diamonds are picture cards.

However, this is not the probability of selecting a diamond or a picture card. The problem is that there are three cards that are simultaneously diamonds and picture cards, shown in Figure 11.7. The events of selecting a diamond and selecting a picture card are not mutually exclusive. It is possible to select a card that is both a diamond and a picture card.

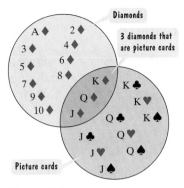

Figure 11.8

Sets and Probability

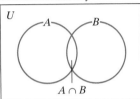

$P(A \cup B) = P(A) + P(B)$
$\quad - P(A \cap B).$
Equivalently,
$P(A \text{ or } B) = P(A) + P(B)$
$\quad - P(A \text{ and } B).$

The situation is illustrated in the Venn diagram in Figure 11.8. Why can't we find the probability of selecting a diamond or a picture card by adding their individual probabilities? The Venn diagram shows that three of the cards, the three diamonds that are picture cards, get counted twice when we add the individual probabilities. First the three cards get counted as diamonds, and then they get counted as picture cards. In order to avoid the error of counting the three cards twice, we need to subtract the probability of getting a diamond and a picture card, $\frac{3}{52}$, as follows:

P(diamond or picture card)

$$= P(\text{diamond}) + P(\text{picture card}) - P(\text{diamond and picture card})$$

$$= \frac{13}{52} + \frac{12}{52} - \frac{3}{52} = \frac{13 + 12 - 3}{52} = \frac{22}{52} = \frac{11}{26}$$

Thus, the probability of selecting a diamond or a picture card is $\frac{11}{26}$.

In general, if A and B are events that are not mutually exclusive, the probability that A or B will occur is determined by adding their individual probabilities and then subtracting the probability that A and B occur simultaneously.

Or Probabilities with Events That Are Not Mutually Exclusive

If A and B are not mutually exclusive events, then

$$P(A \text{ or } B) = P(A) + P(B) - P(A \text{ and } B).$$

EXAMPLE 5 An *Or* Probability with Events That Are Not Mutually Exclusive

In a group of 25 baboons, 18 enjoy picking fleas off of their neighbors, 16 enjoy screeching wildly, while 10 enjoy picking fleas off of their neighbors and screeching wildly. If one baboon is selected at random from the group, find the probability that it enjoys picking fleas off of its neighbors or screeching wildly.

Solution It is possible for a baboon in the group to enjoy picking its neighbors' fleas and screeching wildly. Ten of the brutes are given to engage in both activities. These events are not mutually exclusive.

$$P\left(\begin{array}{c}\text{picking fleas}\\\text{or screeching}\end{array}\right) = P(\text{picking fleas}) + P(\text{screeching}) - P\left(\begin{array}{c}\text{picking fleas}\\\text{and screeching}\end{array}\right)$$

$$= \frac{18}{25} + \frac{16}{25} - \frac{10}{25}$$

> 18 of the 25 baboons enjoy picking fleas.

> 16 of the 25 baboons enjoy screeching.

> 10 of the 25 baboons enjoy both.

$$= \frac{18 + 16 - 10}{25} = \frac{24}{25}$$

The probability that a baboon in the group enjoys picking fleas off of its neighbors or screeching wildly is $\frac{24}{25}$.

Figure 11.9 It is equally probable that the pointer will land on any one of the eight regions.

EXAMPLE 6   An *Or* Probability with Events That Are Not Mutually Exclusive

Figure 11.9 illustrates a spinner. It is equally probable that the pointer will land on any one of the eight regions, numbered 1 through 8. If the pointer lands on a borderline, spin again. Find the probability that the pointer will stop on an even number or a number greater than 5.

Solution   It is possible for the pointer to land on a number that is even and greater than 5. Two of the numbers, 6 and 8, are even and greater than 5. These events are not mutually exclusive. The probability of landing on a number that is even and greater than 5 is:

$$P\left(\begin{array}{c}\text{even or}\\ \text{greater than 5}\end{array}\right) = P(\text{even}) + P(\text{greater than 5}) - P\left(\begin{array}{c}\text{even and}\\ \text{greater than 5}\end{array}\right)$$

$$= \frac{4}{8} + \frac{3}{8} - \frac{2}{8}$$

> Four of the eight numbers, 2, 4, 6, and 8 are even.

> Three of the eight numbers, 6, 7, and 8, are greater than 5.

> Two of the eight numbers, 6 and 8, are even and greater than 5.

$$= \frac{4 + 3 - 2}{8} = \frac{5}{8}.$$

The probability that the pointer will stop on an even number or a number greater than 5 is $\frac{5}{8}$.

EXAMPLE 7   An *Or* Probability with Events That Are Not Mutually Exclusive

A group of people is comprised of 15 U.S. men, 20 U.S. women, 10 Canadian men, and 5 Canadian women. If a person is selected at random from the group, find the probability that the selected person is a man or a Canadian.

Solution   The group is comprised of $15 + 20 + 10 + 5$, or 50 people. It is possible to select a man who is Canadian. We are given that there are 10 Canadian men, so these events are not mutually exclusive.

$$P(\text{man or Canadian}) = P(\text{man}) + P(\text{Canadian}) - P(\text{man and Canadian})$$

$$= \frac{25}{50} + \frac{15}{50} - \frac{10}{50}$$

> Of the 50 people, 25 are men—15 U.S. men and 10 Canadian men.

> Of the 50 people, 15 are Canadian—10 Canadian men and 5 Canadian women.

> Of the 50 people, 10 are Canadian men.

$$= \frac{25 + 15 - 10}{50} = \frac{30}{50} = \frac{3}{5}$$

The probability of selecting a man or a Canadian is $\frac{3}{5}$.

3 Understand and use odds.

Stating the Odds

Time to make a bet: We toss a fair coin. I will give you $10 if it lands on heads. You will give me $10 if it lands on tails. Because there are two outcomes—heads and tails—and they are equally probable, the bet seems fair.

From my point of view, heads is a favorable outcome and tails is unfavorable. The **odds in favor** of heads compares the number of favorable outcomes (just 1, heads) to the number of unfavorable outcomes (just 1, tails). This means that the odds in favor of heads are 1 to 1. Saying that the probability of getting heads on a coin toss is $\frac{1}{2}$ is the same as saying that the odds of a coin landing on heads are 1 to 1.

Odds

If there are a outcomes that are favorable to event E and b outcomes that are unfavorable to event E, then

- The odds in favor of E are a to b, written $a:b$.
- The odds against E are b to a, written $b:a$.

EXAMPLE 8   Stating the Odds

You roll a single, six-sided die.

a. Find the odds in favor of getting 2.

b. Find the odds against getting 2.

Solution   There are six possible outcomes: 1, 2, 3, 4, 5, 6. In terms of the event of getting 2, only one outcome is favorable, namely 2. For rolling a 2, five of the outcomes are unfavorable, namely 1, 3, 4, 5, and 6.

a. The odds in favor of getting 2 are the number of favorable outcomes, 1, to the number of unfavorable outcomes, 5. Thus, the odds in favor of getting 2 are 1 to 5, written 1:5.

b. The odds against getting 2 are the number of unfavorable outcomes, 5, to the number of favorable outcomes, 1. Thus, the odds against getting 2 are 5 to 1, written 5:1.

Odds, like fractions, should be reduced if possible. For example, odds of 44 to 4 should be expressed as 11 to 1.

EXAMPLE 9   Stating the Odds

The winner of a raffle will receive a new sports utility vehicle. If 500 raffle tickets were sold and you purchased ten tickets, what are the odds against your winning the car?

Solution The odds against your winning the car are:

Thus, the odds against your winning the car are 490 to 10, or 49 to 1, written 49:1.

If the odds in favor of event E are a to b and the odds are not reduced, we can assume that there are a favorable outcomes and b unfavorable outcomes. There are $a + b$ total outcomes. Thus, the probability of event E is the number of ways E can occur, a ways, divided by the total number of possible outcomes, $a + b$.

Finding Probabilities from Odds

If the odds in favor of event E are a to b, then the probability of the event is given by

$$P(E) = \frac{a}{a + b}.$$

EXAMPLE 10   From Odds to Probability

The odds in favor of a particular horse winning a race are 2 to 5. What is the probability that this horse will win the race?

Solution Because odds in favor, a to b, means a probability of $\frac{a}{a+b}$, then odds in favor, 2 to 5, means a probability of

$$\frac{2}{2 + 5} = \frac{2}{7}.$$

The probability that this horse will win the race is $\frac{2}{7}$.

The odds given at horse races and at all games of chance are usually *odds against*. The horse in Example 10, with odds of winning at 2 to 5, has odds against winning at 5 to 2. At a horse race, the odds on this particular horse are given simply as 5 to 2. For every \$2 that you bet, you can gain \$5 if you win.

Exercise Set 11.6

 Practice and Application Exercises

In Exercises 1–6, you are dealt one card from a 52-card deck. Find the probability that you are not dealt

1. an ace.   2. a 3.   3. a heart.   4. a club.   5. a picture card.   6. a red picture card.

In 5-card poker, played with a standard 52-card deck, $_{52}C_5$, or 2,598,960, different hands are possible. The probability of being dealt various hands is the number of different ways they can occur divided by 2,598,960. Shown in Exercises 7–10 are various types of poker hands and their probabilities. In each exercise, find the probability of not being dealt this type of hand.

Type of Hand	Illustration	Number of Ways the Hand Can Occur	Probability
7. Straight flush: 5 cards with consecutive numbers, all in the same suit (excluding royal flush)		36	$\dfrac{36}{2,598,960}$
8. Four of a kind: 4 cards with the same number, plus 1 additional card		624	$\dfrac{624}{2,598,960}$
9. Full house: 3 cards of one number and 2 cards of a second number		3744	$\dfrac{3744}{2,598,960}$
10. Flush: 5 cards of the same suit (excluding royal flush and straight flush)		5108	$\dfrac{5108}{2,598,960}$

Use these figures for the U.S. population in 2000 to answer Exercises 11–16.

Total U.S. Population: 274,634 Thousand

Age	under 5	5–13	14–17	18–24	25–34	35–44	45–64	65–84	85 and older
Population (in thousands)	18,987	36,043	15,752	26,258	37,233	44,659	60,992	30,378	4332

Source: U.S. Bureau of the Census

If a U.S. citizen is chosen at random, find the probability that this person is not

11. under 5.

12. in the 18–24 age group.

13. in the 25–34 age group.

14. 85 and older.

Exercises 15–28 involve or probabilities with mutually exclusive events.

15. If a U.S. citizen is chosen at random, find the probability that this person is in the 14–17 or 18–24 age group.

16. If a U.S. citizen is chosen at random, find the probability that this person is in the 25–34 or 35–44 age group.

If one card is randomly selected from a deck of cards, find the probability of selecting

17. a 2 or a 3.

18. a 7 or an 8.

19. a red 2 or a black 3.

20. a red 7 or a black 8.

21. the 2 of hearts or the 3 of spades.

22. the 7 of hearts or the 8 of spades.

In Exercises 23–26, a single die is rolled twice. The 36 equally likely outcomes are shown.

	Second Roll					
	·	··	··	::	:·:	::
·	(1,1)	(1,2)	(1,3)	(1,4)	(1,5)	(1,6)
··	(2,1)	(2,2)	(2,3)	(2,4)	(2,5)	(2,6)
··	(3,1)	(3,2)	(3,3)	(3,4)	(3,5)	(3,6)
::	(4,1)	(4,2)	(4,3)	(4,4)	(4,5)	(4,6)
:·:	(5,1)	(5,2)	(5,3)	(5,4)	(5,5)	(5,6)
::	(6,1)	(6,2)	(6,3)	(6,4)	(6,5)	(6,6)

First Roll

Find the probability of getting

23. a sum of 2 or 3.

24. a sum of 3 or 4.

25. two even numbers or two odd numbers.

26. a sum of 7 or 8.

27. The mathematics faculty at a college consists of 8 professors, 12 associate professors, 14 assistant professors, and 10 instructors. If one faculty member is randomly selected, find the probability of choosing a professor or an instructor.

28. A political discussion group consists of 30 Republicans, 25 Democrats, 8 Independents, and 4 Socialists. If one person is randomly selected from the group, find the probability of choosing an Independent or a Socialist.

Exercises 29–44 involve or probabilities with events that are not mutually exclusive.

In Exercises 29–30, a single die is rolled. Find the probability of getting

29. an even number or a number less than 5.

30. an odd number or a number less than 4.

In Exercises 31–34, you are dealt one card from a 52-card deck. Find the probability that you are dealt

31. a 7 or a red card.

32. a 5 or a black card.

33. a heart or a picture card.

34. a card greater than 2 and less than 7, or a diamond.

In Exercises 35–38, it is equally probable that the pointer on the spinner shown will land on any one of the eight regions, numbered 1 through 8. If the pointer lands on a borderline, spin again.

Find the probability that the pointer will stop on

35. an odd number or a number less than 6.

36. an odd number or a number greater than 3.

37. an even number or a number greater than 5.

38. an even number or a number less than 4.

Use this information to solve Exercises 39–42. The mathematics department of a college has 8 male professors, 11 female professors, 14 male teaching assistants, and 7 female teaching assistants. If a person is selected at random from the group, find the probability that the selected person is

39. a professor or a male.

40. a professor or a female.

41. a teaching assistant or a female.

42. a teaching assistant or a male.

43. In a class of 50 students, 29 are Democrats, 11 are business majors, and 5 of the business majors are Democrats. If one student is randomly selected from the class, find the probability of choosing a Democrat or a business major.

44. A student is selected at random from a group of 200 students in which 135 take math, 85 take English, and 65 take both math and English. Find the probability that the selected student takes math or English.

In Exercises 45–48, a single die is rolled. Find the odds

45. in favor of getting a number greater than 2.

46. in favor of getting a number less than 5.

47. against getting a number greater than 2.

48. against getting a number less than 5.

In Exercises 49–58, one card is randomly selected from a deck of cards. Find the odds

49. in favor of getting a heart.

50. in favor of getting a picture card.

51. in favor of getting a red card.

52. in favor of getting a black card.

53. against getting a 9.

54. against getting a 5.

55. against getting a black king.

56. against getting a red jack.

57. against getting a spade greater than 3 and less than 9.

58. against getting a club greater than 4 and less than 10.

59. The winner of a raffle will receive a 21-foot outboard boat. If 1000 raffle tickets were sold and you purchased 20 tickets, what are the odds against your winning the boat?

60. The winner of a raffle will receive a 30-day all-expense-paid trip throughout Europe. If 5000 raffle tickets were sold and you purchased 30 tickets, what are the odds against your winning the trip?

61. According to the book *What Are the Chances* by Siskin, Staller, and Rorvik, the probability of an American being the victim of a serious crime at some point in his or her lifetime is $\frac{1}{20}$. What are the odds in favor of being the victim of a serious crime?

62. One in four Americans has a high cholesterol level. What are the odds in favor of randomly selecting an American with a high cholesterol level?

63. If you are given odds of 3 to 4 in favor of winning a bet, what is the probability of winning the bet?

64. If you are given odds of 3 to 7 in favor of winning a bet, what is the probability of winning the bet?

65. Based on his skills in basketball, it was computed that when Michael Jordan shot a free throw, the odds in favor of his making it were 4 to 21. Find the probability that when Michael Jordan shot a free throw, he made it. Out of every 100 free throws he attempted, on the average how many did he miss?

66. The odds in favor of a person who is alive at age 20 still being alive at age 70 are 193 to 270. Find the probability that a person who is alive at age 20 will still be alive at age 70.

 Writing in Mathematics

67. Explain how to find the probability of an event not occurring. Give an example.

68. What are mutually exclusive events? Give an example of two events that are mutually exclusive.

69. Explain how to find *or* probabilities with mutually exclusive events. Give an example.

70. Give an example of two events that are not mutually exclusive.

71. Explain how to find *or* probabilities with events that are not mutually exclusive. Give an example.

72. Describe the difference between the probability of an event and the odds in favor of the event.

 Critical Thinking Exercises

73. In Exercise 43, find the probability of choosing: a. a Democrat who is not a business major. b. a student who is neither a Democrat nor a business major.

74. On New Year's Eve, the probability of a person driving while intoxicated or having a driving accident is 0.35. If the probability of driving while intoxicated is 0.32 and the probability of having a driving accident is 0.09, find the probability of a person having a driving accident while intoxicated.

75. Each spinner in the figure shown is spun once and the numbers that the pointers stop at are multiplied. Find the odds in favor of an even product.

 Group Exercise

76. Group members should check the Web for government statistics about transportation safety. Group members should use these numbers to write and solve problems involving *not* and *or*. For example, what is the probability of *not* dying in an airline accident? What is the probability of dying in a car accident *or* an airline accident? Be sure to specify time periods in your problems. If the group writes a probability problem on airline safety, does it seem like a good idea to spend $10 to insure your life on an airplane flight?

SECTION 11.7   Events Involving And; Conditional Probability

Objectives

1. Find the probability of one event and a second event occurring.

2. Compute conditional probabilities.

You are considering a job offer in South Florida. You were thrilled by images of Miami on MTVs "Real World." The job offer is just what you wanted, and you are excited about living in the midst of Miami's tropical diversity. However, there is just one thing: the risk of hurricanes. If you expect to stay in Miami ten years and buy a home, what is the probability that South Florida will be hit by a hurricane at least once in the next ten years?

In this section, we look at the probability that an event occurs at least once by expanding our discussion of probability to events involving *and*.

1 Find the probability of one event and a second event occurring.

And Probabilities with Independent Events

We begin by tossing a fair coin two times in succession. The outcome of the first toss, heads or tails, does not affect what happens when you toss the coin a second time. For example, the occurrence of tails on the first toss does not make tails more likely or less likely to occur on the second toss. The repeated toss of a coin produces **independent events** because the outcome of one toss does not affect the outcome of others. Two events are *independent* if the occurrence of either of them has no effect on the probability of the other.

When a fair coin is tossed two times in succession, the set of equally likely outcomes is

{heads heads, heads tails, tails heads, tails tails}.

We can use this set to find the probability of getting heads on the first toss and heads on the second toss:

$$P(\text{heads and heads}) = \frac{\text{number of ways two heads can occur}}{\text{total number of possible outcomes}} = \frac{1}{4}.$$

We can also determine the probability of two heads, $\frac{1}{4}$, without having to list all the equally likely outcomes. The probability of heads on the first toss is $\frac{1}{2}$. The probability of heads on the second toss is also $\frac{1}{2}$. The product of these probabilities, $\frac{1}{2} \cdot \frac{1}{2}$, results in the probability of two heads, namely $\frac{1}{4}$. Thus,

$$P(\text{heads and heads}) = P(\text{heads}) \cdot P(\text{heads}).$$

In general, if two events are independent, we can calculate the probability of the first occurring and the second occurring by multiplying their probabilities.

> ### *And* Probabilities with Independent Events
> If A and B are independent events, then
> $$P(A \text{ and } B) = P(A) \cdot P(B).$$

EXAMPLE 1   Independent Events on a Roulette Wheel

Figure 11.10 shows a U.S. roulette wheel that has 38 numbered slots (1 through 36, 0, and 00). Of the 38 compartments, 18 are black, 18 are red, and two are green. A play has the dealer spin the wheel and a small ball in opposite directions. As the ball slows to a stop, it can land with equal probability on any one of the 38 numbered slots. Find the probability of red occurring on two consecutive plays.

Figure 11.10 A U.S. roulette wheel

Solution The wheel has 38 equally likely outcomes and 18 are red. Thus, the proballity of red occurring on a play is $\frac{18}{38}$, or $\frac{9}{19}$. The result that occurs on each play is independent of all previous results. Thus,

$$P(\text{red and red}) = P(\text{red}) \cdot P(\text{red}) = \frac{9}{19} \cdot \frac{9}{19} = \frac{81}{361} \approx 0.224.$$

The probability of red occurring on two consecutive plays is $\frac{81}{361}$.

Some roulette players incorrectly believe that if red occurs on two consecutive plays, then another color is "due." Because the events are independent, the outcomes of previous spins have no effect on any other spins.

The *and* rule for independent events can be extended to cover three or more events. Thus, if *A*, *B*, and *C* are independent events, then

$$P(A \text{ and } B \text{ and } C) = P(A) \cdot P(B) \cdot P(C).$$

EXAMPLE 2 Independent Events in a Family

The picture in the margin shows a family that has had nine girls in a row. Find the probability of this occurrence.

Solution If two or more events are independent, we can find the probability of them all occurring by multiplying the probabilities. The probability of a baby girl is $\frac{1}{2}$, so the probability of nine girls in a row is $\frac{1}{2}$ used as a factor nine times.

$$P(\text{nine girls in a row}) = \frac{1}{2} \cdot \frac{1}{2} \cdot \frac{1}{2} \cdot \frac{1}{2} \cdot \frac{1}{2} \cdot \frac{1}{2} \cdot \frac{1}{2} \cdot \frac{1}{2} \cdot \frac{1}{2}$$

$$= \left(\frac{1}{2}\right)^9 = \frac{1}{512}$$

The probability of a run of nine girls in a row is $\frac{1}{512}$. (If another child is born into the family, this event is independent of the other nine, and the probability of a girl is still $\frac{1}{2}$.)

Table 11.5 The Saffir/Simpson Hurricane Scale

The Saffir/Simpson scale assigns numbers 1 through 5 to measure the disaster potential of a hurricane's winds. Table 11.5 describes the scale. According to the National Hurricane Center, the probability that South Florida will be hit by a category 1 hurricane or higher in any single year is $\frac{5}{19}$, or approximately 0.26. In Example 3, we explore the risks of living in "Hurricane Alley."

Category	Winds (Miles per Hour)
1	74–95
2	96–110
3	111–130
4	131–155
5	>155

EXAMPLE 3 Hurricanes and Probabilities

If the probability that South Florida will be hit by a hurricane in any single year is $\frac{5}{19}$,

a. What is the probability that South Florida will be hit by a hurricane in three consecutive years?

b. What is the probability that South Florida will not be hit by a hurricane in the next ten years?

Solution

a. The probability that South Florida will be hit by a hurricane in three consecutive years is:

P(hurricane and hurricane and hurricane)

$$= P(\text{hurricane}) \cdot P(\text{hurricane}) \cdot P(\text{hurricane}) = \frac{5}{19} \cdot \frac{5}{19} \cdot \frac{5}{19} = \frac{125}{6859} \approx 0.018.$$

b. We will first find the probability that South Florida will not be hit by a hurricane in any single year.

$$P(\text{no hurricane}) = 1 - P(\text{hurricane}) = 1 - \frac{5}{19} = \frac{14}{19} \approx 0.737$$

The probability of not being hit by a hurricane in a single year is ≈ 0.737. Therefore, the probability of not being hit by a hurricane ten years in a row is 0.737 used as a factor ten times.

$$P(\text{no hurricanes for ten years}) = (0.737)^{10} \approx 0.047$$

The probability that South Florida will not be hit by a hurricane in the next ten years is approximately 0.047.

Now we are ready to answer your question:

What is the probability that South Florida will be hit by a hurricane at least once in the next ten years?

Because $P(\text{not } E) = 1 - P(E)$,

$P(\text{no hurricane for ten years}) = 1 - P(\text{at least one hurricane in ten years})$.

> In our logic chapter, we saw that the negation of "at least one" is "no."

Equivalently,

$P(\text{at least one hurricane in ten years}) = 1 - P(\text{no hurricane for ten years})$

$$= 1 - 0.047 = 0.953.$$

With a probability of 0.953, it is nearly certain that South Florida will be hit by a hurricane at least once in the next ten years.

And Probabilities with Dependent Events

Chocolate lovers, please help yourself! There are 20 mouth-watering tidbits to select from. What's that? You want 2? And you prefer chocolate-covered cherries? The problem is that there are only 5 chocolate-covered cherries, and it's impossible to tell what is inside each piece. They're all shaped exactly alike. At any rate, reach in, select a piece, enjoy, choose another piece, eat, and be well. There is nothing like savoring a good piece of chocolate in the midst of all this chit-chat about probability and hurricanes.

Another question? You want to know what your chances are of selecting 2 chocolate-covered cherries? Well, let's see. Five of the 20 pieces are chocolate-covered cherries, so the probability of getting one of them on your first selection is $\frac{5}{20}$, or $\frac{1}{4}$. Now, suppose that you did choose a chocolate-covered cherry on your first pick. Eat it slowly; there's no guarantee that you'll select your favorite on the second selection. There are now only 19 pieces of chocolate left. Only 4 are chocolate-covered cherries. The probability of getting a chocolate-covered cherry on your second try is 4 out of 19, or $\frac{4}{19}$. This is a different probability than the $\frac{1}{4}$ probability on your first selection. Selecting a chocolate-covered cherry the first time changes what is in the candy box. The probability of what you select the second time *is* affected by the outcome of the first event. For this reason, we say that these are *dependent events*. The occurrence of one of them has an effect on the probability of the other.

The probability of selecting two chocolate-covered cherries in a row can be found by multiplying the $\frac{1}{4}$ probability on the first selection by the $\frac{4}{19}$ probability on the second selection:

P(chocolate-covered cherry and chocolate-covered cherry)

$$= P(\text{chocolate-covered cherry}) \cdot P\left(\begin{array}{c}\text{chocolate-covered cherry}\\ \text{given that one was selected}\end{array}\right)$$

$$= \frac{1}{4} \cdot \frac{4}{19} = \frac{1}{19}$$

The probability of selecting two chocolate-covered cherries in a row is $\frac{1}{19}$. This is a special case of finding the probability that each of two dependent events occurs.

And Probabilities with Dependent Events

If A and B are dependent events, then

$$P(A \text{ and } B) = P(A) \cdot P(B \text{ given that } A \text{ has occurred}).$$

EXAMPLE 4   Dependent Events with Your Cousins

Good news: You won a free trip to Madrid and can take two people with you, all expenses paid. Bad news: Ten of your cousins have appeared out of nowhere and are begging you to take them. You write each cousin's name on a card, place the cards in a hat, and select one name. Then you select a second name without replacing the first card. If three of your ten cousins speak Spanish, find the probability of selecting two Spanish-speaking cousins.

Solution   Because $P(A \text{ and } B) = P(A) \cdot P(B \text{ given that } A \text{ has occurred})$, then

P(two Spanish-speaking cousins)

$= P(\text{speaks Spanish and speaks Spanish})$

$= P(\text{speaks Spanish}) \cdot P\left(\begin{array}{c}\text{speaks Spanish given that a Spanish-speaking}\\ \text{cousin was selected first}\end{array}\right).$

Because you have ten begging cousins and three speak Spanish, the probability of selecting a cousin who speaks Spanish on the first card selection is $\frac{3}{10}$.

$$P(\text{speaks Spanish}) = \frac{3}{10}$$

Now that this Spanish-speaking cousin has been selected, only nine cards, including the names of two Spanish speakers, remain in the hat. The probability of selecting a cousin who speaks Spanish on the second card pick is $\frac{2}{9}$.

$$P\left(\begin{array}{c}\text{speaks Spanish given that a Spanish-speaking}\\ \text{cousin was selected first}\end{array}\right) = \frac{2}{9}$$

Study Tip

Example 4 can also be solved using the combinations formula.

P(two Spanish speakers)

$= \dfrac{\begin{array}{c}\text{number of ways of}\\ \text{selecting 2 Spanish-}\\ \text{speaking cousins}\end{array}}{\begin{array}{c}\text{number of ways of}\\ \text{selecting 2 cousins}\end{array}}$

$= \dfrac{_3C_2}{_{10}C_2}$

2 Spanish speakers selected from 3 Spanish-speaking cousins

2 cousins selected from 10 cousins

$= \dfrac{3}{45} = \dfrac{1}{15}$

Now, we are ready to substitute the two probabilities into the formula for *and* probabilities with dependent events.

P(speaks Spanish and speaks Spanish)

$$= P(\text{speaks Spanish}) \cdot P\left(\begin{array}{c}\text{speaks Spanish given that a Spanish-speaking} \\ \text{cousin was selected first}\end{array}\right)$$

$$= \frac{3}{10} \cdot \frac{2}{9} = \frac{6}{90} = \frac{1}{15} \approx 0.067$$

The probability of selecting two Spanish-speaking cousins is $\frac{1}{15}$.

The multiplication rule for dependent events can be extended to cover three or more dependent events. For example, in the case of three such events,

$P(A \text{ and } B \text{ and } C)$

$$= P(A) \cdot P(B \text{ given that } A \text{ occurred}) \cdot P(C \text{ given that } A \text{ and } B \text{ occurred})$$

EXAMPLE 5   An *And* Probability with Three Dependent Events

Three people are randomly selected, one person at a time, from five freshmen, two sophomores, and four juniors. Find the probability that the first two people selected are freshmen and the third is a junior.

Solution

P(first two are freshmen and the third is a junior)

$$= P(\text{freshman}) \cdot P\left(\begin{array}{c}\text{freshman given that a} \\ \text{freshman was selected first}\end{array}\right) \cdot P\left(\begin{array}{c}\text{junior given that a freshman was} \\ \text{selected first and a freshman was} \\ \text{selected second}\end{array}\right)$$

$$= \qquad \frac{5}{11} \qquad \cdot \qquad \frac{4}{10} \qquad \cdot \qquad \frac{4}{9}$$

There are 11 people, five of whom are freshmen.   After picking a freshman, there are 10 people left, four of whom are freshmen.   After the first two selections, 9 people are left, four of whom are juniors.

$$= \frac{8}{99}$$

The probability that the first two people selected are freshmen and the third is a junior is $\frac{8}{99}$.

2 Compute conditional probabilities.

Conditional Probability

We have seen that for any two dependent events A and B,

$$P(A \text{ and } B) = P(A) \cdot P(B \text{ given that } A \text{ occurs}).$$

For example, consider the following group of four students:

Ann (freshman) Maria (freshman) Sam (freshman) Mark (sophomore)

Probability and Shared Birthdays

James K. Polk
Born November 2, 1795

Warren G. Harding
Born November 2, 1865

Of the 43 U.S. presidents, two share a birthday (same month and day). The probability of two or more people in a group sharing a birthday rises sharply as the group's size increases. Above 50 people, the probability approaches certainty. You can verify the mathematics of this surprising result by working Exercise 65 in Exercise Set 11.7.

If two people are randomly selected from the group in succession, the probability of first selecting a sophomore and then a woman is:

$$P(\text{sophomore and woman}) = P(\text{sophomore}) \cdot P\left(\begin{array}{c}\text{woman given that a}\\ \text{sophomore was selected}\end{array}\right)$$

$$= \quad \frac{1}{4} \quad \cdot \quad \frac{2}{3} \quad = \quad \frac{1}{6}$$

> There are four people, one of whom, Mark, is a sophomore.

> After picking Mark, there are three freshmen left, two of whom are women.

We can think of the second probability, $\frac{2}{3}$, as the probability of selecting a woman, given that we are selecting from the freshmen. This probability can be expressed as

$$P(\text{woman|selection is from the freshmen})$$

and is called the *conditional probability* of selecting a woman, given that a freshman is selected. The condition that a freshman is selected limits the situation to only three possible outcomes:

$$\{\text{Ann (Freshman), Maria (Freshman), Sam (Freshman)}\}.$$

Because a woman can be selected from these possible outcomes in two ways (Ann or Maria),

$$P(\text{woman|selection is from the freshman}) = \tfrac{2}{3}.$$

Conditional Probability

The **conditional probability** of B, given A, written $P(B|A)$, is the probability that event B occurs computed on the assumption that event A occurs.

EXAMPLE 6 Computing Conditional Probability

A letter is randomly selected from the letters of the English alphabet. Find the probability of selecting a vowel, given that the outcome is a letter that precedes h.

Solution   Because we are given the condition that the outcome is a letter that precedes h, the set of all possible outcomes is

$$\{a, b, c, d, e, f, g\}.$$

There are seven possible outcomes. We can select a vowel from this set in one of two ways: a or e. Therefore, the probability of selecting a vowel, given that the outcome is a letter that precedes h, is $\frac{2}{7}$.

$$P(\text{vowel|outcome precedes h}) = \tfrac{2}{7}$$

Conditional probabilities can sometimes be obtained from numbers in charts and graphs. These conditional probabilities are empirical probabilities. The following formula can be used to find conditional probabilities from observed numbers.

Applying Conditional Probability to Real-World Data

$$P(B|A) = \frac{\text{observed number of times } B \text{ and } A \text{ occur together}}{\text{observed number of times } A \text{ occurs}}$$

EXAMPLE 7   Conditional Probabilities with Real-World Data

Table 11.6 shows the number of active-duty personnel in the U.S. military in 1997. If one person is randomly selected from the U.S. military, find the probability that the person

a. is in the Army if the person is female.
b. is male if the person is in the Marine Corps.

Table 11.6   Active-Duty U.S. Military Personnel, 1997

	Army	Navy	Marine Corps	Air Force
Male	418,880	342,986	164,620	311,550
Female	72,827	52,578	9286	65,835

Source: U.S. Defense Department

Solution

a. We begin with the probability that the selected person is in the Army, given that we are selecting from the females.

$$P(\text{Army}|\text{Female}) = \frac{\text{observed number of personnel who are in the Army and are female}}{\text{observed number of females in the military}}$$

$$= \frac{72{,}827}{72{,}827 + 52{,}578 + 9286 + 65{,}835} = \frac{72{,}827}{200{,}526} \approx 0.363$$

The probability of randomly selecting a person who is in the Army from among female members of the U.S. military is approximately 0.363.

b. Now, we find the probability that the selected person is a male, given that we are selecting from the Marines.

$$P(\text{Male}|\text{Marine Corps}) = \frac{\text{observed number of personnel who are males and Marines}}{\text{observed number of people in the Marines}}$$

$$= \frac{164{,}620}{164{,}620 + 9286} = \frac{164{,}620}{173{,}906} \approx 0.947$$

The probability of selecting a man from among the personnel serving in the Marines is approximately 0.947.

Exercise Set 11.7

  Practice and Application Exercises

Exercises 1–26 involve and probabilities with independent events.

Use the spinner shown to solve Exercises 1–10. It is equally probable that the pointer will land on any one of the six regions. If the pointer lands on a borderline, spin again. If the pointer is spun twice, find the probability it will land on

1. green and then red.   2. yellow and then green.
3. yellow and then yellow.   4. red and then red.
5. a color other than red each time.
6. a color other than green each time.

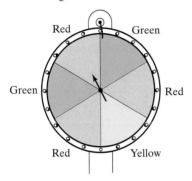

If the pointer is spun three times, find the probability it will land on

7. green and then red and then yellow.
8. red and then red and then green.
9. red every time.   10. green every time.

In Exercises 11–14, a single die is rolled twice. Find the probability of getting

11. a 2 the first time and a 3 the second time.
12. a 5 the first time and a 1 the second time.
13. an even number the first time and a number greater than 2 the second time.
14. an odd number the first time and a number less than 3 the second time.

In Exercises 15–20, you are dealt one card from a 52-card deck. Then the card is replaced in the deck, the deck is shuffled, and you draw again. Find the probability of getting

15. a picture card the first time and a heart the second time.
16. a jack the first time and a club the second time.
17. a king each time.
18. a 3 each time.
19. a red card each time.
20. a black card each time.
21. If you toss a fair coin six times, what is the probability of getting all heads?

22. If you toss a fair coin seven times, what is the probability of getting all tails?

In Exercises 23–24, a coin is tossed and a die is rolled. Find the probability of getting

23. a head and a number greater than 4.
24. a tail and a number less than 5.
25. The probability that South Florida will be hit by a major hurricane (category 4 or 5) in any single year is $\frac{1}{16}$.
    (*Source:* National Hurricane Center)
    a. What is the probability that South Florida will be hit by a major hurricane two years in a row?
    b. What is the probability that South Florida will be hit by a major hurricane in three consecutive years?
    c. What is the probability that South Florida will not be hit by a major hurricane in the next ten years?
    d. What is the probability that South Florida will be hit by a major hurricane at least once in the next ten years?
26. The probability that a region prone to flooding will flood in any single year is $\frac{1}{10}$.
    a. What is the probability of a flood two years in a row?
    b. What is the probability of flooding in three consecutive years?
    c. What is the probability of no flooding for ten consecutive years?
    d. What is the probability of flooding at least once in the next ten years?

Exercises 27–42 involve and probabilities with dependent events.

In Exercises 27–30, we return to our box of chocolates. There are 30 chocolates in the box, all identically shaped. Five are filled with coconut, 10 with caramel, and 15 are solid chocolate. You randomly select one piece, eat it, and then select a second piece. Find the probability of selecting

27. two solid chocolates in a row.
28. two caramel-filled chocolates in a row.
29. a coconut-filled chocolate followed by a caramel-filled chocolate.
30. a coconut-filled chocolate followed by a solid chocolate.

In Exercises 31–36, consider a political discussion group consisting of 5 Democrats, 6 Republicans, and 4 Independents. Suppose that two group members are randomly selected, in succession, to attend a political convention. Find the probability of selecting

31. two Democrats.
32. two Republicans.
33. an Independent and then a Republican.
34. an Independent and then a Democrat.
35. no Independents.
36. no Democrats.

In Exercises 37–42, an ice chest contains six cans of apple juice, eight cans of grape juice, four cans of orange juice, and two cans of mango juice. Suppose that you reach into the container and randomly select three cans in succession. Find the probability of selecting

37. three cans of apple juice.   38. three cans of grape juice.
39. a can of grape juice, then a can of orange juice, then a can of mango juice.
40. a can of apple juice, then a can of grape juice, then a can of orange juice.
41. no grape juice.   42. no apple juice.

In Exercises 43–50, the numbered disks shown are placed in a box and one disk is selected at random.

| 1 | 2 | 3 | 4 |
| red | yellow | red | yellow |

| 5 | 6 | 7 | 8 |
| red | red | yellow | red |

Find the probability of selecting

43. a 3, given that a red disk is selected.
44. a 7, given that a yellow disk is selected.
45. an even number, given that a yellow disk is selected.
46. an odd number, given that a red disk is selected.
47. a red disk, given that an odd number is selected.
48. a yellow disk, given that an odd number is selected.
49. a red disk, given that the number selected is at least 5.
50. a yellow disk, given that the number selected is at most 3.

The table shows the number of people who lost jobs, in thousands, from January 1995–December 1997.

Number of People (in thousands) Who Lost Jobs

	20–24	25–54	55–64	65+
Male	634	4148	401	132
Female	483	3162	306	101

Source: U.S. Bureau of Labor Statistics

In Exercises 51–54, assume that one person will be selected from the group described in the table. Find the probability of selecting

51. a man who lost his job, given that he was in the 20–24 age group.
52. a woman who lost her job, given that she was in the 25–54 age group.
53. a person in the 65+ age group who lost a job, given that the person is female.
54. a person in the 55–64 age group who lost a job, given that the person is male.

Writing in Mathematics

55. Explain how to find *and* probabilities with independent events. Give an example.
56. Explain how to find *and* probabilities with dependent events. Give an example.
57. What does $P(B|A)$ mean? Give an example.

In Exercises 58–62, write a probability problem involving the word <u>and</u> *whose solution results in the probability fractions shown.*

58. $\frac{1}{2} \cdot \frac{1}{2}$ 59. $\frac{1}{6} \cdot \frac{1}{6} \cdot \frac{1}{6}$ 60. $\frac{1}{2} \cdot \frac{1}{6}$

61. $\frac{13}{52} \cdot \frac{12}{51}$ 62. $\frac{1}{4} \cdot \frac{3}{5}$

Critical Thinking Exercises

63. If the probability of being hospitalized during a year is 0.1, find the probability that no one in a family of five will be hospitalized in a year.
64. If a single die is rolled five times, what is the probability it lands on 2 on the first, third, and fourth rolls, but not on any of the other rolls?
65. a. If two people are selected at random, the probability that they do not have the same birthday (day and month) is $\frac{365}{365} \cdot \frac{364}{365}$. Explain why this is so. (Ignore leap years and assume 365 days in a year.)
    b. If three people are selected at random, find the probability that they all have different birthdays.
    c. If three people are selected at random, find the probability that at least two of them have the same birthday.
    d. If 20 people are selected at random, find the probability that at least 2 of them have the same birthday.
    e. How large a group is needed to give a 0.5 chance of at least two people having the same birthday?
66. Nine cards numbered from 1 through 9 are placed into a box, and two cards are selected without replacement. Find the probability that both numbers selected are odd, given that their sum is even.

Group Exercises

67. Do you live in an area prone to catastrophes, such as earthquakes, fires, tornados, hurricanes, and floods? If so, research the probability of this catastrophe occurring in a single year. Group members should then use this probability to write and solve a problem similar to Exercise 25 in this set of exercises.
68. Each group member should bring in one table with data similar to Table 11.6 on page 574 or the table that precedes Exercises 51–54 in this exercise set. Group members should select the three tables they find most interesting. For each table selected, write and solve two problems involving conditional probability similar to Exercises 51–54.

SECTION 11.8   *Expected Value*

Objectives

1. Compute expected value.
2. Use expected value to solve applied problems.
3. Use expected value to determine the average payoff or loss in a game of chance.

1   Compute expected value.

The *Titanic*

It wasn't supposed to happen—especially not to Leonardo and Kate! The British liner *Titanic*, built in 1912, hit an iceberg on its maiden voyage and sank, with the loss of 1513 lives. The probability of this happening was extremely remote because of the ship's safety features. Insurance companies work with probabilities, using past claims as a basis for predicting the probabilities of future ones.

The tragedy of the *Titanic* was captured in the movie's most complex scene. Many watched in amazement as 100 stunt people leapt, fell, and slid 70 feet as the ship broke in half and rose out of the water to a 90° angle.

Would you be willing to spend $50 a year for an insurance policy that pays $200,000 if you become too ill to continue your education? It is unlikely that this will occur. Insurance companies make money by compensating us for events that have a low probability. If one in every 5000 students needs to quit college due to serious illness, the probability of this event is $\frac{1}{5000}$. Multiplying the amount of the claim, $200,000, by its probability, $\frac{1}{5000}$, tells the insurance company what to expect on average for each policy:

$$\$200,000 \times \frac{1}{5000} = \$40$$

Amount of the claim

Probability of paying the claim

Over the long run, the insurance company can expect to pay $40 for each policy it sells. By selling the policy for $50, the expected profit is $10 per policy. If 400,000 students choose to take out this insurance, the company can expect to make 400,000 × $10, or $4,000,000.

Expected value is a mathematical way to use probabilities to determine what to expect in various situations over the long run. Expected value is used to determine premiums on insurance policies, weigh the risks versus the benefits of alternatives in business ventures, and indicate to a player of any game of chance what will happen if the game is played repeatedly.

The standard way to find expected value is to multiply each possible outcome by its probability, and then add these products. We use the letter E to represent expected value.

EXAMPLE 1   Computing Expected Value

Find the expected value for the outcome of the roll of a fair die.

Solution   The outcomes are 1, 2, 3, 4, 5, and 6, each with a probability of $\frac{1}{6}$. The expected value, E, is computed by multiplying each outcome by its probability and then adding these products.

$$E = 1 \cdot \frac{1}{6} + 2 \cdot \frac{1}{6} + 3 \cdot \frac{1}{6} + 4 \cdot \frac{1}{6} + 5 \cdot \frac{1}{6} + 6 \cdot \frac{1}{6}$$

$$= \frac{1 + 2 + 3 + 4 + 5 + 6}{6} = \frac{21}{6} = 3.5$$

The expected value of the roll of a fair die is 3.5. This means that if the die is rolled repeatedly, there are an average of 3.5 dots per roll over the long run. This expected value cannot occur on a single roll of the die. However, it is a long-run average of the various outcomes that can occur when a fair die is rolled.

EXAMPLE 2   Computing Expected Value

Find the expected value for the number of girls for a family with three children.

Solution   A family with three children can have 0, 1, 2, or 3 girls. There are eight ways these outcomes can occur:

Table 11.7 Outcomes and Probabilities for the Number of Girls in a Three-Child Family

Outcome: Number of Girls	Probability
0	$\frac{1}{8}$
1	$\frac{3}{8}$
2	$\frac{3}{8}$
3	$\frac{1}{8}$

No girls : Boy Boy Boy — *One way*

One girl : Girl Boy Boy, Boy Girl Boy, Boy Boy Girl — *Three ways*

Two girls : Girl Girl Boy, Girl Boy Girl, Boy Girl Girl — *Three ways*

Three girls : Girl Girl Girl — *One way*

Table 11.7 shows the probabilities for 0, 1, 2, and 3 girls.

The expected value, E, is computed by multiplying each outcome by its probability and then adding these products.

$$E = 0 \cdot \frac{1}{8} + 1 \cdot \frac{3}{8} + 2 \cdot \frac{3}{8} + 3 \cdot \frac{1}{8} = \frac{0 + 3 + 6 + 3}{8} = \frac{12}{8} = \frac{3}{2} = 1.5$$

The expected value is 1.5. This means that if we record the number of girls in many different three-child families, the average number of girls for all these families will be 1.5. In a three-child family, half the children are expected to be girls, so the expected value of 1.5 is consistent with this observation.

Study Tip

A single family with 1.5 girls *cannot* occur. The expected value, 1.5, is a long-run average of the number of girls that *could* occur. We will discuss averages in more detail in our next chapter on statistics.

2 Use expected value to solve applied problems.

Applications of Expected Value

Empirical probabilities can be determined in many situations by examining what has occurred in the past. For example, an insurance company can tally various claim amounts over many years. If 15% of these amounts are for a $2000 claim, then the probability of this claim amount is 0.15. By studying sales of similar houses in a particular area, a realtor can determine the probability that he or she will sell a listed house, another agent will sell the house, or the listed house will remain unsold. Once probabilities have been assigned to all possible outcomes, expected value can indicate what is expected to happen in the long run. These ideas are illustrated in Examples 3 and 4.

EXAMPLE 3 Determining an Insurance Premium

An automobile insurance company has determined the probabilities for various claim amounts for drivers ages 16 through 21, shown in Table 11.8

a. Calculate the expected value and describe what this means in practical terms.

b. How much should the company charge as an average premium so that it does not lose or gain money on its claim costs?

Table 11.8 Probabilities for Auto Claims

Amount of Claim (to the nearest $2000)	Probability
$0	0.70
$2000	0.15
$4000	0.08
$6000	0.05
$8000	0.01
$10,000	0.01

Solution

a. The expected value, E, is computed by multiplying each outcome by its probability, and then adding these products.

$$E = \$0(0.70) + \$2000(0.15) + \$4000(0.08) + \$6000(0.05)$$
$$+ \$8000(0.01) + \$10,000(0.01)$$
$$= \$0 + \$300 + \$320 + \$300 + \$80 + \$100$$
$$= \$1100$$

The expected value is $1100. This means that in the long run the average cost of a claim is $1100. The insurance company should expect to pay $1100 per car insured to people in the 16–21 age group.

b. At the very least, the amount that the company should charge as an average premium for each person in the 16–21 group is $1100. In this way, it will not lose or gain money on its claims costs. It's quite probable that the company will charge more, moving from break-even to profit.

Business decisions are interpreted in terms of dollars and cents. In these situations, expected value is calculated by multiplying the gain or loss for each possible outcome by its probability. The sum of these products is the expected value.

EXAMPLE 4   Expectation in a Business Decision

You are a realtor considering listing a $500,000 house. The cost of advertising and providing food for other realtors during open showings is anticipated to cost you $5000. The house is quite unusual, and you are given a four-month listing. If the house is unsold after four months, you lose the listing and receive nothing. You anticipate that the probability you sell your own listed house is 0.3, the probability that another agent sells your listing is 0.2, and the probability that the house is unsold after 4 months is 0.5. If you sell your own listed house, the commission is a hefty $30,000. If another realtor sells your listing, the commission is $15,000. The bottom line: You will not take the listing unless you anticipate earning at least $6000. Should you list the house?

Solution   Shown in the margin is a summary of the amounts of money and probabilities that will determine your decision. The expected value in this situation is the sum of each income possibility times its probability. The expected value represents the amount you can anticipate earning if you take the listing. If the expected value is not at least $6000, you should not list the house.

The possible incomes listed in the margin, $30,000, $15,000, and $0, do not take into account your $5000 costs. Because of these costs, each amount needs to be reduced by $5000. Thus, you can gain $30,000 − $5000, or $25,000, or you can gain $15,000 − $5000, or $10,000. Because $0 − $5000 = −$5000, you can also lose $5000. Table 11.9 summarizes possible outcomes if you take the listing, and their respective probabilities.

Table 11.9   Gains, Losses, and Probabilities for Listing a $500,000 House

Outcome	Gain or Loss	Probability
Sells house	$25,000	0.3
Another agent sells house	$10,000	0.2
House doesn't sell	−$5000	0.5

The expected value, E, is computed by multiplying each gain or loss in Table 11.9 by its probability, and then adding these results.

$$E = \$25,000(0.3) + \$10,000(0.2) + (-\$5000)(0.5)$$
$$= \$7500 + \$2000 + (-\$2500) = \$7000$$

You can expect to earn $7000 by listing the house. Because the expected value exceeds $6000, you should list the house.

"Probability theory helps you to put some kind of pattern on randomness. You can't tell what's going to happen from step to step, but you can predict what's going to happen over the long haul."

ED PACKEL
mathematician and gambling expert

The Realtor's Summary Sheet

My Cost:	$5000
My Possible Income:	
I sell house:	$30,000
Another agent sells house:	$15,000
House unsold after 4 months:	$0
The Probabilities:	
I sell house:	0.3
Another agent sells house:	0.2
House unsold after 4 months:	0.5

My Bottom Line: I take the listing only if I anticipate earning at least $6000.

3 Use expected value to determine the average payoff or loss in a game of chance.

Expected Value and Games of Chance

Expected value can be interpreted as the average payoff in a contest or game when either is played a large number of times. To find the expected value of a game, multiply the gain or loss for each possible outcome by its probability. Then add the products.

Gambling It Away

Shown below are amounts of money spent in the United States on various kinds of gambling. Gambling is a $50 billion business that attracts more people than movies or baseball.

U.S. Gambling Revenues in Millions of Dollars, 1997

Horses	$3251.4
Greyhounds	509.4
Jai Alai	50.1
Lotteries	16,566.8
Casinos	20,527.6
Legal Bookmaking	96.3
Card Rooms	700.2
Charitable Bingo	956.9
Charitable Games	1562.2
Indian Reservations	6678.5
Grand Total	**$50,899.4**

Source: International Gaming and Wagering Business

EXAMPLE 5 Expected Value as Average Payoff

A game is played using one die. If the die is rolled and shows 1, 2, or 3, the player wins nothing. If the die shows 4 or 5, the player wins $3. If the die shows 6, the player wins $9. If there is a charge of $1 to play the game, what is the game's expected value? Describe what this means in practical terms.

Solution Because there is a charge of $1 to play the game, a player who wins $9 gains $9 − $1, or $8. A player who wins $3 gains $3 − $1 or $2. If the player gets $0, there is a loss of $1 because $0 − $1 = −$1. The outcomes for the die, with their respective gains, losses, and probabilities, are summarized in Table 11.10

Table 11.10   Gains, Losses, and Probabilities in a Game of Chance

Outcome	Gain or Loss	Probability
1, 2, or 3	−$1	$\frac{3}{6}$
4 or 5	$2	$\frac{2}{6}$
6	$8	$\frac{1}{6}$

Expected value, E, is computed by multiplying each gain or loss in Table 11.10 by its probability and then adding these results.

$$E = (-\$1)\left(\frac{3}{6}\right) + \$2\left(\frac{2}{6}\right) + \$8\left(\frac{1}{6}\right)$$

$$= \frac{-\$3 + \$4 + \$8}{6} = \frac{\$9}{6} = \$1.50$$

The expected value is $1.50. This means that in the long run, a player can expect to win an average of $1.50 for each game played. However, this does not mean that the player will win $1.50 on any single game. It does mean that if the game is played repeatedly, then, in the long run, the player should expect to win about $1.50 per play on the average. If 1000 games are played, one could expect to win $1500. However, if only three games are played, one's net winnings can range between −$3 and $24, even though the expected winnings are $1.50(3), or $4.50.

Figure 11.11 A U.S. roulette wheel

Unlike the game in Example 5, games in gambling casinos are set up so that players will lose in the long run. These games have negative expected values. Such a game is roulette, French for "little wheel." We first saw the roulette wheel in Section 11.7. It is shown again in Figure 11.11. Recall that the wheel has 38 numbered slots (1 through 36, 0, and 00). In each play of the game, the dealer spins the wheel and a small ball in opposite directions. The ball is equally likely to come to rest in any one of the slots, which are colored black, red, or green. Gamblers can place a number of different bets in roulette. Example 6 illustrates one gambling option.

EXAMPLE 6   Expected Value and Roulette

One way to bet in roulette is to place $1 on a single number. If the ball lands on that number, you are awarded $35 and get to keep the $1 that you paid to play the game. If the ball lands on any one of the other 37 slots, you are awarded nothing and the $1 that you bet is collected. Find the expected value for playing roulette if you bet $1 on number 20. Describe what this means.

Solution   Table 11.11 contains the two outcomes of interest: the ball landing on the winning number 20 and the ball landing elsewhere (in any one of the other 37 slots). The outcomes, their respective gains, losses, and probabilities, are summarized in the table.

How to Win at Roulette

A player may win or lose at roulette, but in the long run the casino always wins. Casinos make an average of three cents on every dollar spent by gamblers. There *is* a way to win at roulette in the long run: own the casino.

Table 11.11   Playing One Number with a 35 to 1 Payoff in Roulette

Outcome	Gain or Loss	Probability
Ball lands on 20	$35	$\frac{1}{38}$
Ball does not land on 20	−$1	$\frac{37}{38}$

Expected value, E, is computed by multiplying each gain or loss in Table 11.11 by its probability and then adding these results.

$$E = \$35\left(\frac{1}{38}\right) + (-\$1)\left(\frac{37}{38}\right) = \frac{\$35 - \$37}{38} = \frac{-\$2}{38} \approx -\$0.05$$

The expected value is approximately −$0.05. This means that in the long run, a player can expect to lose about 5¢ for each game played. If 2000 games are played, one could expect to lose $100.

Exercise Set 11.8

  Practice and Application Exercises

In Exercises 1–2, the numbers that each pointer can land on and their respective probabilities are shown. Compute the expected value for the number on which each pointer lands.

1.

Outcome	Probability
1	$\frac{1}{2}$
2	$\frac{1}{4}$
3	$\frac{1}{4}$

2.

Outcome	Probability
1	$\frac{1}{8}$
2	$\frac{1}{8}$
3	$\frac{1}{2}$
4	$\frac{1}{4}$

The tables in Exercises 3–4 show claims and their probabilities for an insurance company.

   a. *Calculate the expected value and describe what this means in practical terms.*

   b. *How much should the company charge as an average premium so that it breaks even on its claim costs?*

   c. *How much should the company charge to make a profit of $50 per policy?*

3. **Probabilities for Homeowners' Insurance Claims**

Amount of claim (to the nearest $50,000)	Probability
$0	0.65
$50,000	0.20
$100,000	0.10
$150,000	0.03
$200,000	0.01
$250,000	0.01

4. **Probabilities for Medical Insurance Claims**

Amount of claim (to the nearest $20,000)	Probability
$0	0.70
$20,000	0.20
$40,000	0.06
$60,000	0.02
$80,000	0.01
$100,000	0.01

5. An architect is considering bidding for the design of a new museum. The cost of drawing plans and submitting a model is $10,000. The probability of being awarded the bid is 0.1, and anticipated profits are $100,000, resulting in a possible gain of this amount minus the $10,000 cost for plans and a model. What is the expected value in this situation? Describe what this value means.

6. A construction company is planning to bid on a building contract. The bid costs the company $1500. The probability that the bid is accepted is $\frac{1}{5}$. If the bid is accepted, the company will make $40,000 minus the cost of the bid. Find the expected value in this situation. Describe what this value means.

7. It is estimated that there are 27 deaths for every 10 million people who use airplanes. A company that sells flight insurance provides $100,000 in case of death in a plane crash. A policy can be purchased for $1. Calculate the expected value and thereby determine how much the insurance company can make over the long run for each policy that it sells.

8. A 25-year old can purchase a one-year life insurance policy for $10,000 at a cost of $100. Past history indicates that the probability of a person dying at age 25 is 0.002. Determine the company's expected gain per policy.

9. A store specializing in mountain bikes is to open in one of two malls. If the first mall is selected, the store anticipates a yearly profit of $300,000 if successful and a yearly loss of $100,000 otherwise. The probability of success is $\frac{1}{2}$. If the second mall is selected, it is estimated that the yearly profit will be $200,000 if successful; otherwise, the annual loss will be $60,000. The probability of success at the second mall is $\frac{3}{4}$. Which mall should be chosen in order to maximize the expected profit?

10. An oil company is considering two sites on which to drill, described as follows:
    Site A: Profit if oil is found: $80 million
    Loss if no oil is found: $10 million
    Probability of finding oil: 0.2
    Site B: Profit if oil is found: $120 million
    Loss if no oil is found: $18 million
    Probability of finding oil: 0.1
    Which site has the larger expected profit? By how much?

11. In a product liability case, a company can settle out of court for a loss of $350,000, or go to trial, losing $700,000 if found guilty and nothing if found not guilty. Lawyers for the company estimate the probability of a not-guilty verdict to be 0.8.
    a. Find the expected value of the amount the company can lose by taking the case to court.
    b. Should the company settle out of court?

12. A service that repairs air conditioners sells maintenance agreements for $80 a year. The average cost for repairing an air conditioner is $350 and 1 in every 100 people who purchase maintenance agreements have air conditioners that require repair. Find the service's expected profit per maintenance agreement.

Exercises 13–17 involve computing expected values in games of chance.

13. A game is played using one die. If the die is rolled and shows a 1, the player wins $5. If the die shows any number other than 1, the player wins nothing. If there is a charge of $1 to play the game, what is the game's expected value? What does this value mean?

14. A game is played using one die. If the die is rolled and shows 1, the player wins $1; if 2, the player wins $2; if 3, the player wins $3. If the die shows 4, 5, or 6, the player wins nothing. If there is a charge of $1.25 to play the game, what is the game's expected value? What does this value mean?

15. Another option in a roulette game (see Example 6 on page 581) is to bet $1 on red. (There are 18 red compartments, 18 black compartments, and two compartments that are neither red nor black.) If the ball lands on red, you get to keep the $1 that you paid to play the game and you are awarded $1. If the ball lands elsewhere, you are awarded nothing and the $1 that you bet is collected. Find the expected value for playing roulette if you bet $1 on red. Describe what this number means.

16. The spinner on a wheel of fortune can land with an equal chance on any one of ten regions. Three regions are red, four are blue, two are yellow, and one is green. A player wins $4 if the spinner stops on red and $2 if it stops on green. The player loses $2 if it stops on blue and $3 if it stops on yellow. What is the expected value? What does this mean if the game is played ten times?

17. For many years, organized crime ran a numbers game that is now run legally by many state governments. The player se-

lects a three-digit number from 000 to 999. There are 1000 such numbers. A bet of $1 is placed on a number, say number 115. If the number is selected, the player wins $500. If any other number is selected, the player wins nothing. Find the expected value for this game and describe what this means

Writing in Mathematics

18. What does the expected value for the outcome of the roll of a fair die represent?

19. Explain how to find the expected value for the number of girls for a family with two children. What is the expected value?

20. How do insurance companies use expected value to determine what to charge for a policy?

21. Describe a situation in which a business can use expected value.

22. If the expected value of a game is negative, what does this mean? Also describe what it means for a positive and a zero expected value.

23. The expected value for purchasing a ticket in a raffle is −$0.75. Describe what this means. Will a person who purchases a ticket lose $0.75?

Critical Thinking Exercises

24. A popular state lottery is the 5/35 lottery, played in Arizona, Connecticut, Illinois, Iowa, Kentucky, Maine, Massachusetts, New Hampshire, South Dakota, and Vermont. In Arizona's version of the game, prizes are set: First prize is $50,000, second prize is $500, and third prize is $5. To win first prize, you must select all five of the winning numbers, numbered from 1 to 35. Second prize is awarded to players who select any four of the five winning numbers, and third prize is awarded to players who select any three of the winning numbers. The cost to purchase a lottery ticket is $1. Find the expected value of Arizona's "Fantasy Five" game, and describe what this means in terms of buying a lottery ticket over the long run.

25. Many multiple-choice exams discourage guessing by subtracting points for wrong answers. Consider such a test in which there are five possible answers for each question. A correct answer is worth 4 points and an incorrect answer is worth −1 point. Points are neither added nor subtracted for questions not answered.
    a. Find the expected value for guessing at an answer. (Only one of the five possible options is the correct choice.)
    b. If a test taker can eliminate one of the possible choices, find the expected value for guessing at an answer among the four remaining options. (Only one of the four possible answers is correct.)
    c. Find the expected value for eliminating two of the possible choices and guessing at an answer among the three remaining options.

d. Find the expected value for eliminating three of the possible choices and guessing at an answer between the two remaining options.

e. Use your answers from parts (a) through (d) to describe a guessing strategy for standardized tests such as the S.A.T that use the grading system described in this exercise.

Group Exercise

26. This activity is a group research project intended for people interested in games of chance at casinos. The research should culminate in a seminar on games of chance and their expected values. The seminar is intended to last about 30 minutes and should result in an interesting and informative presentation made to the entire class.

Each member of the group should research a game available at a typical casino. Describe the game to the class and compute its expected value. After each member has done this, so that class members now have an idea of those games with the greatest and smallest house advantages, a final group member might want to research and present ways for currently treating people whose addiction to these games has caused their lives to swirl out of control.

CHAPTER SUMMARY, REVIEW, AND TEST

SUMMARY

11.1 The Fundamental Counting Principle
The number of ways in which a series of successive things can occur is found by multiplying the number of ways in which each thing can occur.

11.2 Permutations
a. A permutation from a group of items occurs when no item is used more than once and the order of arrangement makes a difference.

b. Factorial Notation
$$n! = n(n - 1)(n - 2)\ldots(3)(2)(1) \quad \text{and} \quad 0! = 1$$

c. Permutations Formula
The number of permutations possible if r items are taken from n items is $_nP_r = \dfrac{n!}{(n - r)!}$.

11.3 Combinations
a. A combination from a group of items occurs when no item is used more than once and the order of items makes no difference.

b. Combinations Formula
The number of combinations possible if r items are taken from n items is $_nC_r = \dfrac{n!}{(n - r)!r!}$.

11.4 Fundamentals of Probability
a. Theoretical probability applies to situations in which the set of all equally likely outcomes is known.

b. The theoretical probability of event E is:
$$P(E) = \frac{\text{number of ways } E \text{ can occur}}{\text{total number of possible outcomes}}.$$

c. Empirical probability applies to situations in which we observe the frequency of occurrence of an event.

d. The empirical probability of event E is:
$$P(E) = \frac{\text{observed number of times } E \text{ occurs}}{\text{total number of observed occurrences}}.$$

11.5 Probability with Permutations and Combinations
a. Probability of a permutation
$$= \frac{\text{the number of ways the permutation can occur}}{\text{total number of possible permutations}}.$$

b. Probability of a combination
$$= \frac{\text{the number of ways the combination can occur}}{\text{total number of possible combinations}}.$$

11.6 Events Involving *Not* and *Or*
a. $P(\text{not } E) = 1 - P(E)$

b. If it is impossible for events A and B to occur simultaneously, the events are mutually exclusive.

c. If A and B are mutually exclusive events, then $P(A \text{ or } B) = P(A) + P(B)$.

d. If A and B are not mutually exclusive events, then $P(A \text{ or } B) = P(A) + P(B) - P(A \text{ and } B)$.

Odds
a. If there are a outcomes that are favorable to event E and b outcomes that are unfavorable to event E, then the odds in favor of E are a to b, written $a:b$, and the odds against E are b to a, written $b:a$.

b. If the odds in favor of event E are a to b, then the probability of the event is $P(E) = \frac{a}{a + b}$.

11.7 Events Involving *And*

a. Two events are independent if the occurrence of either of them has no effect on the probability of the other.
b. If A and B are independent events,
$$P(A \text{ and } B) = P(A) \cdot P(B).$$
c. The probability of a succession of independent events is the product of each of their probabilities.
d. Two events are dependent if the occurrence of one of them has an effect on the probability of the other.
e. If A and B are dependent events,
$$P(A \text{ and } B) = P(A) \cdot P(B \text{ given that } A \text{ has occurred}).$$
f. The multiplication rule can be extended to cover three or more dependent events. In the case of three such events,
$$P(A \text{ and } B \text{ and } C)$$
$$= P(A) \cdot P(B \text{ given } A \text{ occurred}) \cdot P(C \text{ given } A \text{ and } B \text{ occurred}).$$

Conditional Probability

a. The conditional probability of B, given A, written $P(B|A)$, is the probability that event B occurs computed on the assumption that event A occurs.

b. Conditional probability applied to real-world data:
$$P(B|A)$$
$$= \frac{\text{observed number of times } B \text{ and } A \text{ occur together}}{\text{observed number of times } A \text{ occurs}}.$$

11.8 Expected Value

a. Expected value, E, is found by multiplying every possible outcome by its probability and then adding these products.

b. In situations involving business decisions, expected value is calculated by multiplying the gain or loss for each possible outcome by its probability. The sum of these products is the expected value.

c. In a game of chance, expected value is the average payoff when the game is played a large number of times. To find the expected value of a game, multiply the gain or loss for each possible outcome by its probability. Then add the products.

REVIEW EXERCISES

11.1

1. A restaurant offers 20 appetizers and 40 main courses. In how many ways can a person order a two-course meal?

2. A popular brand of pen comes in red, green, blue, or black ink. The writing tip can be chosen from extra bold, bold, regular, fine, or micro. How many different choices of pens do you have with this brand?

3. In how many ways can first and second prize be awarded in a contest with 100 people entered, assuming that each prize is awarded to a different person?

4. You are answering three multiple-choice questions. Each question has five choices, with one correct choice per question. If you select one of these options per question and leave nothing blank, in how many ways can you answer the questions?

5. A stock can go up, go down, or stay unchanged. How many possibilities are there if you own five stocks?

6. A person can purchase a condominium with a choice of five kinds of carpeting, with or without a pool, with or without a porch, and with one, two, or three bedrooms. How many different options are there for the condominium?

11.2

7. Six acts are scheduled to perform in a variety show. How many different ways are there to schedule their appearances?

8. In how many ways can five airplanes line up for departure on a runway?

9. You need to arrange seven of your favorite books along a small shelf. Although you are not arranging the books by height, the tallest of the books is to be placed at the left end and the shortest of the books at the right end. How many different ways can you arrange the books?

In Exercises 10–13, evaluate each factorial expression.

10. $\dfrac{16!}{14!}$

11. $\dfrac{800!}{799!}$

12. $5! - 3!$

13. $\dfrac{11!}{(11-3)!}$

In Exercises 14–15, use the formula for $_nP_r$ to evaluate each expression.

14. $_{10}P_6$

15. $_{100}P_2$

Use the formula for $_nP_r$ to solve Exercises 16–17.

16. A club with 15 members is to choose four officers—president, vice-president, secretary, and treasurer. In how many ways can these offices be filled?

17. Suppose you are asked to list, in order of preference, the five favorite CDs you purchased in the past 12 months. If you bought 20 CDs over this time period, in how many ways can the five favorite be ranked?

11.3

In Exercises 18–20, does the problem involve permutations or combinations? Explain your answer. (It is not necessary to solve the problem.)

18. How many different 4-card hands can be dealt from a 52-card deck?

19. How many different ways can a director select from 20 male actors and cast the roles of Mark, Roger, Angel, and Collins in the musical *Rent*?

20. How many different ways can a director select 4 actors from a group of 20 actors to attend a workshop on performing in rock musicals?

In Exercises 21–22, use the formula for $_nC_r$ to evaluate each expression.

21. $_{11}C_7$ 22. $_{14}C_5$

Use the formula for $_nC_r$ to solve Exercises 23–26.

23. An election ballot asks voters to select four city commissioners from a group of ten candidates. In how many ways can this be done?

24. How many different 5-card hands can be dealt from a deck that has only hearts (13 different cards)?

25. From the 20 CDs that you've bought during the past year, you plan to take 3 with you on vacation. How many different sets of three CDs can you take?

26. A political discussion group consists of 12 Republicans and 8 Democrats. In how many ways can 5 Republicans and 4 Democrats be selected to attend a conference on politics and social issues?

11.4

In Exercises 27–30, a die is rolled. Find the probability of getting

27. a 6.   28. a number less than 5.

29. a number less than 7.   30. a number greater than 6.

In Exercises 31–35, you are dealt one card from a 52-card deck. Find the probability of being dealt

31. a 5.   32. a picture card.

33. a card greater than 4 and less than 8.

34. a 4 of diamonds.   35. a red ace.

In Exercises 36–38, suppose that you reach into a bag and randomly select one piece of candy from 15 chocolates, 10 caramels, and 5 peppermints. Find the probability of selecting

36. a chocolate.   37. a caramel.

38. a peppermint.

39. Tay-Sachs disease occurs in 1 of every 3600 births among Jews from central and eastern Europe, and in 1 in 600,000 births in other populations. The disease causes abnormal accumulation of certain fat compounds in the spinal cord and brain, resulting in paralysis, blindness, and mental impairment. Death generally occurs before the age of five. If we use *t* to represent a Tay-Sachs gene and *T* a healthy gene, the table at the top of the next column shows the four possibilities for the children of one healthy, *TT*, parent, and one parent who carries the disease, *Tt*, but is not sick.

     a. Find the probability that a child of these parents will be a carrier without the disease.

b. Find the probability that a child of these parents will have the disease.

		Second Parent	
		T	*t*
First	*T*	*TT*	*Tt*
Parent	*T*	*TT*	*Tt*

Exercises 40–41 involve empirical probabilities. Express each probability as a fraction. Then use a calculator to express the probability in decimal form, rounded to the nearest thousandth. The table shows the two states with the largest Hispanic populations. Find the probability that

40. a person randomly selected from California is Hispanic.

41. a person randomly selected from Texas is Hispanic.

Largest Hispanic Population, 1997

State	Total Population	Hispanic Population
California	31,878,234	9,630,188
Texas	19,128,261	5,503,372

Source: Bureau of the Census

11.5

42. If cities A, B, C, and D are visited in random order, each city visited once, find the probability that city D will be visited first, city B second, city A third, and city C last.

In Exercises 43–46, suppose that six singers are being lined up to perform at a charity. Call the singers A, B, C, D, E, and F. The order of performance is determined by writing each singer's name on one of six cards, placing the cards in a hat, and then drawing one card at a time. The order in which the cards are drawn determines the order in which the singers perform. Find the probability that

43. singer C will perform last.

44. singer B will perform first and singer A will perform last.

45. the singers will perform in the following order: F, E, A, D, C, B.

46. the performance will begin with singer A or C.

47. A lottery game is set up so that each player chooses five different numbers from 1 to 20. If the five numbers match the five numbers drawn in the lottery, the player wins (or shares) the top cash prize. What is the probability of winning the prize

     a. with one lottery ticket?

     b. with 100 different lottery tickets?

48. A committee of four people is to be selected from six Democrats and four Republicans. Find the probability that

     a. all are Democrats.

     b. two are Democrats and two are Republicans.

49. If you are dealt 3 cards from a shuffled deck of red cards (26 different cards), find the probability of getting 2 picture cards.

11.6

In Exercises 50–54, a die is rolled. Find the probability of

50. not getting a 5.
51. not getting a number less than 4.
52. getting a 3 or a 5.
53. getting a number less than 3 or greater than 4.
54. getting a number less than 5 or greater than 2.

In Exercises 55–60, you are dealt one card from a 52-card deck. Find the probability of

55. not getting a picture card. 56. not getting a diamond.
57. getting an ace or a king. 58. getting a black 6 or a red 7.
59. getting a queen or a red card.
60. getting a club or a picture card.

In Exercises 61–66, it is equally probable that the pointer on the spinner shown will land on any one of the six regions, numbered 1 through 6, and colored as shown. If the pointer lands on a borderline, spin again. Find the probability of

61. not stopping on 4. 62. not stopping on yellow.
63. not stopping on red. 64. stopping on red or yellow.
65. stopping on red or an even number.
66. stopping on red or a number greater than 3.

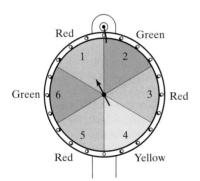

Use the data shown for U.S. population by region to answer Exercises 67–68. Express each probability as a fraction. Then use a calculator to express the probability in decimal form, rounded to the nearest thousandth. Find the probability of randomly selecting a U.S. citizen

67. who does not live in the Northeast.
68. who lives in the South or the West.

U.S. Population by Region: 1997

Total:	267,636,061
Northeast:	51,588,281
Midwest:	62,460,453
South:	94,187,161
West:	59,400,166

Source: U.S. Bureau of the Census

Use this information to solve Exercises 69–70. At a workshop on police work and the black community, there are 50 black male police officers, 20 black female police officers, 90 white male police officers, and 40 white female police officers. If one police officer is selected at random from the people at the workshop, find the probability that the selected person is

69. black or male. 70. female or white.
71. One card is randomly selected from a deck of 52 cards. Find the odds in favor and the odds against getting a queen.
72. The winner of a raffle will receive a two-year scholarship to any college of the winner's choice. If 2000 raffle tickets were sold and you purchased 20 tickets, what are the odds against your winning the scholarship?
73. The odds in favor of a candidate winning an election are given at 3 to 1. What is the probability that this candidate will win the election?

11.7

Use the spinner shown to solve Exercises 74–78. It is equally probable that the pointer will land on any one of the six regions, numbered 1 through 6, and colored as shown. If the pointer lands on a borderline, spin again. If the pointer is spun twice, find the probability it will land on

74. yellow and then red.
75. 1 and then 3
76. yellow both times.

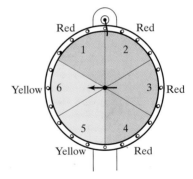

If the pointer is spun three times, find the probability it will land on

77. yellow and then 4 and then an odd number.
78. red every time.
79. What is the probability of a family having five boys born in a row?
80. The probability of a flood in any given year in a region prone to floods is 0.2.
    a. What is the probability of a flood two years in a row?
    b. What is the probability of a flood for three consecutive years?
    c. What is the probability of no flooding for four consecutive years?
    d. What is the probability of a flood at least once in the next four years?

In Exercises 81–82, two students are selected from a group of four psychology majors, three business majors, and two music majors. The two students are to meet with the campus cafeteria manager to voice the group's concerns about food prices and quality. One student is randomly selected and leaves for the cafeteria manager's office. Then, a second student is selected. Find the probability of selecting

81. a music major and then a psychology major.

82. two business majors.

83. A final visit to the box of chocolates: It's now grown to a box of 50, of which 30 are solid chocolate, 15 are filled with jelly, and 5 are filled with cherries. The story is still the same: They all look alike. You select a piece, eat it, select a second piece, eat it, and help yourself to a final sugar rush. Find the probability of selecting a solid chocolate followed by two cherry-filled chocolates.

84. A single die is tossed. Find the probability that the tossed die shows 5, given that the outcome is an odd number.

85. A letter is randomly selected from the letters of the English alphabet. Find the probability of selecting a vowel, given that the outcome is a letter that precedes k.

86. The numbers shown below are each written on a colored chip. The chips are placed into a bag and one chip is selected at random. Find the probability of selecting
    a. an odd number, given that a red chip is selected.
    b. a yellow chip, given that the number selected is at least 3.

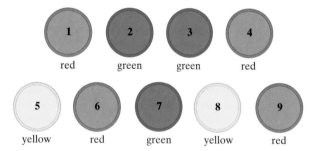

| 1 | 2 | 3 | 4 |
| red | green | green | red |

| 5 | 6 | 7 | 8 | 9 |
| yellow | red | green | yellow | red |

Use the table that shows the number of students at a small liberal arts college to answer Exercises 87–88.

Number of Students at a Small Liberal Arts College

	Freshmen	Sophomores	Juniors	Seniors
Male	342	296	244	192
Female	368	314	262	220

If one student is randomly selected from this college, find the probability of selecting

87. a freshman if the student is female.

88. a woman if the student is a senior.

11.8

89. The numbers that the pointer can land on and their respective probabilities are shown. Compute the expected value for the number on which the pointer lands.

Outcome	Probability
1	$\frac{1}{4}$
2	$\frac{1}{8}$
3	$\frac{1}{8}$
4	$\frac{1}{4}$
5	$\frac{1}{4}$

90. The table shows claims and their probabilities for an insurance company.

Life Insurance for an Airline Flight

Amount of claim	Probability
$0	0.9999995
$1,000,000	0.0000005

a. Calculate the expected value and describe what this value means.

b. How much should the company charge to make a profit of $9.50 per policy?

91. A construction company is planning to bid on a building contract. The bid costs the company $3000. The probability that the bid is accepted is $\frac{1}{4}$. If the bid is accepted, the company will make $30,000 minus the cost of the bid. Find the expected value in this situation. Describe what this value means.

92. A game is played using a fair coin that is tossed twice. The set of possible outcomes is $\{HH, HT, TH, TT\}$. If exactly one head occurs, the player wins $5, and if exactly two tails occur, the player also wins $5. For any other outcome, the player receives nothing. There is a $4 charge to play the game. What is the expected value? What does this value mean?

 Group Exercise

93. We opened the chapter with a decision involving whether or not to accept a real estate listing. In Example 4 on page 579, we saw that it would be worth the risk to accept the listing. In this exercise, each group member should present a situation related to what he or she is doing now or plans to do in the future in which risk and decision making come into play. List all the possible outcomes and assign to each outcome the most realistic probability that you can. The group should select three of these situations. For each, the group should write and solve a problem involving expected value, similar to Example 4 on page 579.

CHAPTER 11 TEST

1. A person can purchase a particular model of a new car with a choice of ten colors, with or without automatic transmission, with or without four-wheel drive, with or without air conditioning, and with two, three, or four radio-CD speakers. How many different options are there for this model of the car?

2. Four acts are scheduled to perform in a variety show. How many different ways are there to schedule their appearances?

3. In how many ways can seven airplanes line up for a departure on a runway if the plane with the greatest number of passengers must depart first?

4. A human resource manager has 11 applicants to fill three different positions. Assuming that all applicants are equally qualified for any of the three positions, in how many ways can this be done?

5. From the ten books that you've recently bought but not read, you plan to take four with you on vacation. How many different sets of four books can you take?

In Exercises 6–8, one student is selected at random from a group of 12 freshmen, 16 sophomores, 20 juniors, and 2 seniors. Find the probability that the person selected is

6. a freshman.   7. not a sophomore.

8. a junior or a senior.

9. If you are dealt one card from a 52-card deck, find the probability of being dealt a card greater than 4 and less than 10.

10. Seven movies (A, B, C, D, E, F, and G) are being scheduled for showing. The order of showing is determined by random selection. Find the probability that film C will be shown first, film A next-to-last, and film E last.

11. A lottery game is set up so that each player chooses six different numbers from 1 to 15. If the six numbers match the six numbers drawn in the lottery, the player wins (or shares) the top cash prize. What is the probability of winning the prize with 50 different lottery tickets?

In Exercises 12–13, it is equally probable that the pointer on the spinner shown will land on any one of the eight colored regions. If the pointer lands on a borderline, spin again.

12. If the spinner is spun once, find the probability that the pointer will land on red or blue.

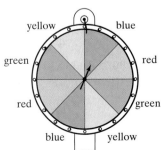

13. If the spinner is spun twice, find the probability that the pointer lands on red on the first spin and blue on the second spin.

14. A region is prone to flooding once every 20 years. What is the probability of flooding for three consecutive years?

15. One card is randomly selected from a deck of 52 cards. Find the probability of selecting a black card or a picture card.

16. A group of students consists of 10 male freshmen, 15 female freshmen, 20 male sophomores, and 5 female sophomores. If one person is randomly selected from the group, find the probability of selecting a freshman or a female.

17. A box contains five red balls, six green balls, and nine yellow balls. Suppose you select one ball at random from the box and do not replace it. Then you randomly select a second ball. Find the probability that both balls selected are red.

18. A quiz consisting of four multiple-choice questions has four available options (a, b, c, or d) for each question. If a person guesses at every question, what is the probability of answering all questions correctly?

19. Describe what is wrong with the following statement: There are 50 states, so the probability of selecting an American who lives in North Dakota is $\frac{1}{50}$.

20. A group is comprised of 20 men and 15 women. If one person is randomly selected from the group, find the odds against the person being a man.

21. The odds against a candidate winning an election are given at 1 to 4.
    a. What are the odds in favor of the candidate winning?
    b. What is the probability that the candidate will win the election?

22. A class is collecting data on eye color and gender. They organize the data they collected into the table shown. Numbers in the table represent the number of students from the class that belong to each of the categories. If one student is selected from the class, find the probability that the student is a man, given that the student has blue eyes.

	Brown	Blue	Green
Male	22	18	10
Female	18	20	12

23. An architect is considering bidding for the design of a new theater. The cost of drawing plans and submitting a model is $15,000. The probability of being awarded the bid is 0.2, and anticipated profits are $80,000, resulting in a possible gain of this amount minus the $15,000 cost for plans and models. What is the expected value if the architect decides to bid for the design? Describe what this value means.

24. A game is played by selecting one bill at random from a bag that contains ten $1 bills, five $2 bills, three $5 bills, one $10 bill, and one $100 bill. The player gets to keep the selected bill. There is a $20 charge to play the game. What is the expected value? What does this value mean?

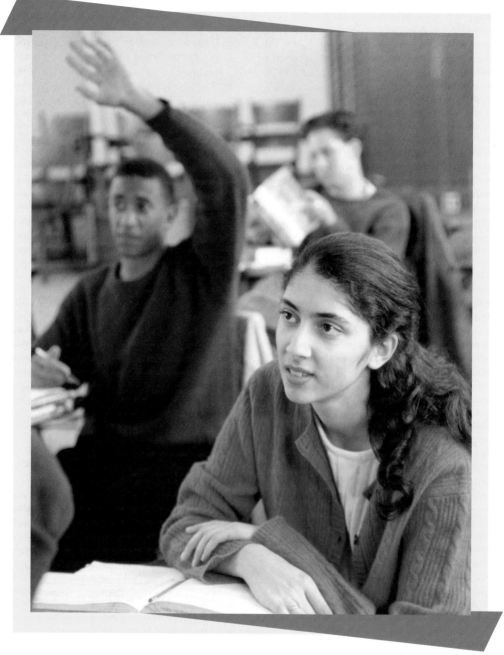

This course is wonderful! You are sitting in a large auditorium classroom, enjoying every second of the lecture. You are energized by your professor's knowledge, delivery, and sense of humor. This is truly what college is all about. Are you the only one so enthused about this course? Well over 100 students are in the room. Is there any way to use the opinions of a small subgroup to find out if a substantial number of all the students share your opinion?

12 statistics

S tatisticians collect numerical data from subgroups of populations to find out everything imaginable about the population, including whom they favor in an election, what they are watching on television, how much money they make, what worries them, and how they feel about the quality of their education. In the twenty-first century, statistics is big business. Because statisticians both record and influence our behavior, it is important to distinguish between good and bad methods for collecting, presenting, and interpreting data. In this chapter, you will gain an understanding of where data come from and how these numbers are used to make decisions.

SECTION 12.1 *Sampling, Frequency Distributions, and Graphs*

Objectives

1. Describe the population whose properties are to be analyzed.
2. Select an appropriate sampling technique.
3. Organize and present data.
4. Identify deceptions in visual displays of data.

"M*A*S*H" took place in the early 1950s, during the Korean War. By the final episode, the show had lasted four times as long as the Korean War.

At the end of the twentieth century, there were 94 million households in the United States with television sets. The television program viewed by the greatest percentage of such households in that century was the final episode of "M*A*S*H." Over 50 million American households watched this program.

Numerical information, such as the information about the top three TV shows of the twentieth century shown in Table 12.1, is called **data**. The word **statistics** is often used when referring to data. However, statistics has a second meaning: Statistics is also a method for collecting, organizing, analyzing, and interpreting data, as well as drawing conclusions based on the data. This methodology divides statistics into two main areas. **Descriptive statistics** is concerned with collecting, organizing, summarizing, and presenting data. **Inferential statistics** has to do with making generalizations about and drawing conclusions from the data collected.

Table 12.1   TV Programs with the Greatest U.S. Audience Viewing Percentage of the Twentieth Century

Program	Households total	Viewing percentage
1. "M*A*S*H" Feb. 28, 1983	50,150,000	60.2%
2. "Dallas" Nov. 21, 1980	41,470,000	53.3%
3. "Roots" Part 8 Jan. 30, 1977	36,380,000	51.1%

Source: Nielsen Media Research

1 Describe the population whose properties are to be analyzed.

Populations and Samples

Consider the set of all American TV households. Such a set is called the *population*. In general, a **population** is the set containing all the people or objects whose properties are to be described and analyzed by the data collector.

The population of American TV households is huge. At the time of the "M*A*S*H" conclusion, there were nearly 84 million such households. Did over 50 million American TV households really watch the final episode of "M*A*S*H"? A friendly phone call to each household ("So, how are you? What's new? Watch any good television last night? If so, what?") is, of course, absurd. A **sample**, which is a subset or subgroup of the population, is needed. In this case, it would be appropriate to have a sample of a few thousand TV households to draw conclusions about the population of all TV housholds.

EXAMPLE 1   Populations and Samples

A group of hotel owners in a large city decide to conduct a survey among citizens of the city to discover their opinions about casino gambling.

a. Describe the population.

b. One of the hotel owners suggests obtaining a sample by surveying all the people at six of the largest nightclubs in the city on a Saturday night. Each person will be asked to express his or her opinion on casino gambling. Does this seem like a good idea?

Solution

a. The population is the set containing all the citizens of the city.

b. Questioning people at six of the city's largest nightclubs is a terrible idea. The nightclub subset is probably more likely to have a more positive attitude toward casino gambling than the population of all the city's citizens.

Random Sampling

There is a way to use a small sample to make generalizations about a large population: Guarantee that every member of the population has an equal chance to be selected for the sample. Surveying people at six of the city's largest nightclubs does not provide this guarantee. Unless it can be established that all citizens of the city frequent these clubs, which seems unlikely, this sampling scheme does not permit each citizen an equal chance of selection.

Random Samples

A **random sample** is a sample obtained in such a way that every element in the population has an equal chance of being selected for the sample.

Suppose you are elated with the quality of one of your courses. Although it's an auditorium section with 120 students, you feel that the professor is lecturing right to you. During a wonderful lecture, you look around the auditorium to see if any of the other students are sharing your enthusiasm. Based on body language, it's hard to tell. You really want to know the opinion of the population of 120 students taking this course. You fantasize about asking students to grade the course on an A to F scale, anticipating a unanimous A. You cannot survey everyone. Eureka! Suddenly you have an idea on how to take a sample. Put cards numbered from 1 to 120, one number per card, in a box. Because the course has assigned seating by number, each numbered card corresponds to a student in the class. Reach in and randomly select six cards. Each card, and therefore each student, has an equal chance of being selected. Then use the opinions of the course from the six randomly selected students to generalize about the course opinion for the entire 120-student population.

Your idea is precisely how random samples are obtained. In random sampling, each element in the population must be identified and assigned a number. The numbers are generally assigned in order. The way to sample from the larger numbered population is to generate random numbers using a computer or calculator. Each numbered element from the population that corresponds to a random number is selected for the sample.

Call-in polls on radio and television are not reliable because those polled do not represent the larger population. A person who calls in is likely to have feelings about an issue that are consistent with the politics of the show's host. For a poll to be accurate, the sample must be chosen randomly from the larger population. The A.C. Nielsen Company uses a random sample of about 5000 TV households to measure the percent of all 94 million households tuned in to every television program.

2 Select an appropriate sampling technique.

LAFF-A-DAY

"We've polled the entire populace, Your Majesty, and we've come up with exactly the results you ordered!"

© 1993 King Features Syndicate Inc. World rights reserved. Reprinted with special permission of King Features Syndicate.

EXAMPLE 2   Selecting an Appropriate Sampling Technique

We return to the hotel owners in the large city who are interested in how the city's citizens feel about casino gambling. Which of the following would be the most appropriate way to select a random sample?

a. Randomly survey people who live in the oceanfront condominiums in the city.
b. Survey the first 200 people whose names appear in the city's telephone directory.
c. Randomly select neighborhoods of the city and then randomly survey people within the selected neighborhoods.

Solution   Keep in mind that the population is the set containing all the city's citizens. A random sample must give each citizen an equal chance of being selected.

a. Randomly selecting people who live in the city's oceanfront condominiums is not a good idea. Many hotels lie along the oceanfront, and the oceanfront property owners might object to the traffic and noise as a result of casino gambling. Furthermore, this sample does not give each citizen of the city an equal chance of being selected.
b. If the hotel owners survey the first 200 names in the city's telephone directory, all citizens do not have an equal chance of selection. For example, individuals whose last name begins with a letter toward the end of the alphabet have no chance of being selected.
c. Randomly selecting neighborhoods of the city and then randomly surveying people within the selected neighborhood is an appropriate technique. Using this method, each citizen has an equal chance of being selected. In summary, given the three options, the sampling technique in part (c) is the most appropriate.

3 Organize and present data.

Frequency Distributions

After data have been collected from a sample of the population, the next task facing the statistician is to present the data in a condensed and manageable form. In this way, the data can be more easily interpreted.

Suppose, for example, that researchers are interested in determining the age at which adolescent males show the greatest rate of physical growth. A random sample of 35 10-year-old boys is measured for height and then remeasured each year until they reach 18. The age of maximum yearly growth for each subject is as follows:

12, 14, 13, 14, 16, 14, 14, 17, 13, 10, 13, 18, 12, 15, 14, 15, 15, 14, 14, 13, 15, 16, 15, 12, 13, 16, 11, 15, 12, 13, 12, 11, 13, 14, 14

A piece of data is called a **data item**. This list of data has 35 data items. Some of the data items are identical. Two of the data items are 11 and 11. Thus, we can say that the **data value** 11 occurs twice. Similarly, because 5 of the data items are 12, 12, 12, 12, and 12, the data value 12 occurs five times.

Collected data can be presented using a **frequency distribution**. Such a distribution consists of two columns. The data values are listed in one column. Numerical data are generally listed from smallest to largest. The adjacent column is labeled **frequency** and indicates the number of times each value occurs.

EXAMPLE 3   Constructing a Frequency Distribution

Construct a frequency distribution for the data of the age of maximum yearly growth for 35 boys:

12, 14, 13, 14, 16, 14, 14, 17, 13, 10, 13, 18, 12, 15, 14, 15, 15, 14, 14, 13, 15, 16, 15, 12, 13, 16, 11, 15, 12, 13, 12, 11, 13, 14, 14

Solution   It is difficult to determine trends in the data above in its current format. Perhaps we can make sense of the data by organizing it into a frequency distribution. Let us create two columns. One lists all possible data values, from smallest (10) to largest (18). The other column indicates the number of times the value occurs in the sample. The frequency distribution is shown in Table 12.2.

The frequency distribution indicates that one subject had maximum growth at age 10, two at age 11, five at age 12, seven at age 13, and so on. The maximum growth for most of the subjects occurred between the ages of 12 and 15. Nine boys experienced maximum growth at age 14, more than at any other age within the sample. The sum of the frequencies, 35, is equal to the original number of data items.

Table 12.2   A Frequency Distribution for a Boy's Age at Maximum Yearly Growth

Age of Maximum Growth	Number of Boys (Frequency)
10	1
11	2
12	5
13	7
14	9
15	6
16	3
17	1
18	1
	35

35 is the sum of the frequencies.

The frequency distribution shows 10 occurs once, 11 twice, 12 five times, 13 seven times, and so on.

A frequency distribution that lists all possible data items can be quite cumbersome when there are many such items. For example, consider the following data items. These are statistics test scores made by a group of 40 students.

82	47	75	64	57	82	63	93
76	68	84	54	88	77	79	80
94	92	94	80	94	66	81	67
75	73	66	87	76	45	43	56
57	74	50	78	71	84	59	76

It's difficult to determine how well the group did when the grades are displayed like this. Because there are so many data items, one way to organize this data so the results are more meaningful is to arrange the grades into groups, or **classes**, based on something that interests us. Many grading systems assign an A to grades in the 90–100 class, B to grades in the 80–89 class, C to grades in the 70–79 class, and so on. These classes provide one way to organize the data.

Looking at the 40 statistics test scores, we see that they range from a low of 43 to a high of 94. We can use classes that run from 40 through 49, 50 through 59, 60 through 69, and so on up to 90 through 99, to organize the scores. In Example 4, we go through the data and tally each item into the appropriate class. This method for organizing data is called a **grouped frequency distribution**.

EXAMPLE 4 Constructing a Grouped Frequency Distribution

Use the classes 40–49, 50–59, 60–69, 70–79, 80–89, and 90–99 to construct a grouped frequency distribution for the 40 test scores listed on page 595.

Solution We use the 40 given scores and tally the number of scores in each interval.

Test Scores (Class)	Tally	Number of Students (Frequency)
40–49	|||	3
50–59	ℍℓ		6
60–69	ℍℓ		6
70–79	ℍℓ ℍℓ		11
80–89	ℍℓ ||||	9
90–99	ℍℓ	5

Table 12.3 A Grouped Frequency Distribution Organizing 40 Test Scores

Class	Frequency
40–49	3
50–59	6
60–69	6
70–79	11
80–89	9
90–99	5
	40

40, the sum of the frequencies, is the number of data items.

Omitting the tally column results in the grouped frequency distribution in Table 12.3. The distribution shows that the greatest frequency of students scored in the 70–79 class. The number of students decreases in classes that contain successively lower and higher scores. The sum of the frequencies, 40, is equal to the original number of data items.

We can use other classes to organize the 40 statistics test scores. Most grading systems assign a grade of F to numerical grades below 60. Thus, the classes 40–59, 60–69, 70–79, 80–89, and 90–99 can be used. The last class can also be selected as 90–100. It is not uncommon to see a grouped frequency distribution in which the first and last class are wider or narrower than the rest.

Histograms and Frequency Polygons

Take a second look at the frequency distribution for the age of a boy's maximum yearly growth, shown in Table 12.2, repeated on page 597. A bar graph with bars that touch can be used to visually display the data. Such a graph is called a **histogram**. Figure 12.1 illustrates a histogram that was constructed using the frequency distribution in Table 12.2. A series of rectangles whose lengths represent the frequencies are placed next to each other. For example, the length of the bar for the data value 10, shown at the far left of Figure 12.1, is 1. This corresponds to

Table 12.2 A Boy's Age at Maximum Yearly Growth

Age of Maximum Growth (Data Value)	Number of Boys (Frequency)
10	1
11	2
12	5
13	7
14	9
15	6
16	3
17	1
18	1
	35

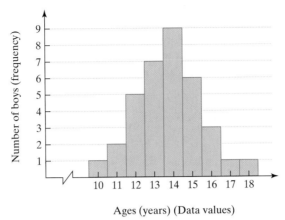

Figure 12.1 A histogram for a boy's age at maximum yearly growth

the frequency for 10 given in Table 12.2. The higher the bar, the more frequent the score. The break along the horizontal axis, symbolized by ⌐/ᴸ, eliminates listing the ages 1 to 9.

A line graph called a **frequency polygon** can also be used to visually convey the information shown in Figure 12.1. The axes are labeled just like those in a histogram. Thus, the horizontal axis shows data values and the vertical axis shows frequencies. Once a histogram has been constructed, it's fairly easy to draw a frequency polygon. Figure 12.2 shows a histogram with a dot at the top of each rectangle at its midpoint. Connect each of these midpoints with a straight line. To complete the frequency polygon at both ends, the lines should be drawn down to touch the horizontal axis. The completed frequency polygon is shown in Figure 12.3.

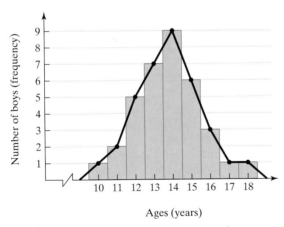

Figure 12.2 A histogram for a boy's age at maximum yearly growth with a superimposed frequency polygon

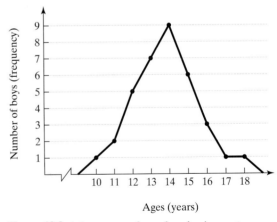

Figure 12.3 A frequency polygon for a boy's age at maximum yearly growth

Stem-and-Leaf Plots

A unique way for displaying data uses a tool called a **stem-and-leaf plot**. Example 5 illustrates how we sort the data, revealing the same visual impression created by a histogram.

EXAMPLE 5   Constructing a Stem-and-Leaf Plot

Use the data showing statistics test scores for 40 students to construct a stem-and-leaf plot.

82	47	75	64	57	82	63	93
76	68	84	54	88	77	79	80
94	92	94	80	94	66	81	67
75	73	66	87	76	45	43	56
57	74	50	78	71	84	59	76

Solution   The plot is constructed by separating each number into two parts. The first part is the *stem*. The **stem** consists of the tens' digit. For example, the stem for the score of 82 is 8. The second part is the *leaf*. The **leaf** consists of the units' digit for a given value. For the score of 82, the leaf is 2. The possible stems for the 40 scores are 4, 5, 6, 7, 8, and 9, entered in the left column of the plot.

Begin by entering each data item in the first row.

**Entering
8 2 :**

Stems	Leaves
4	
5	
6	
7	
8	2
9	

**Adding
4 7 :**

Stems	Leaves
4	7
5	
6	
7	
8	2
9	

**Adding
7 5 :**

Stems	Leaves
4	7
5	
6	
7	5
8	2
9	

**Adding
6 4 :**

Stems	Leaves
4	7
5	
6	4
7	5
8	2
9	

**Adding
5 7 :**

Stems	Leaves
4	7
5	7
6	4
7	5
8	2
9	

**Adding
8 2 :**

Stems	Leaves
4	7
5	7
6	4
7	5
8	2 2
9	

**Adding
6 3 :**

Stems	Leaves
4	7
5	7
6	4 3
7	5
8	2 2
9	

**Adding
9 3 :**

Stems	Leaves
4	7
5	7
6	4 3
7	5
8	2 2
9	3

Figure 12.4 shows the stem-and-leaf plot, constructed by entering the data items from the first row of the given data, from left to right, then the items from the second row, and so on through the fifth row. If you turn the page so that the left margin is on the bottom and facing you, the visual impression created by the enclosed leaves is the same as that created by a histogram. The enclosed leaves extend farthest to the right when the stem is 7. This shows that the greatest frequency of students scored in the 70s.

Stems	Leaves
4	7 5 3
5	7 4 6 7 0 9
6	4 3 8 6 7 6
7	5 6 7 9 5 3 6 4 8 1 6
8	2 2 4 8 0 0 1 7 4
9	3 4 2 4 4

Figure 12.4 A steam-and-leaf plot displaying 40 test scores

4 Identify deceptions in visual displays of data.

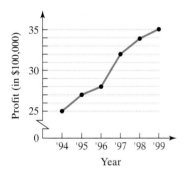

Figure 12.5 The graph on the bottom uses a scale that might exaggerate the increasing profits.

Deceptions in Visual Displays of Data

Benjamin Disraeli, Queen Victoria's prime minister, stated that there are "lies, damned lies, and statistics." The problem is not that statistics lie, but rather that liars use statistics. Graphs can be used to distort the underlying data, making it difficult for the viewer to learn the truth. One potential source of misunderstanding is an exaggerated scale on the vertical axis, illustrated in Figure 12.5. The two graphs convey the same data items, although the scale on the bottom makes the company's profits look as if they are increasing more dramatically over time.

The bottom graph in Figure 12.5 *is* more effective in terms of reading differences between years. The graph does tell the truth, although the deceptive scale can lead to an incorrect interpretation of how quickly profits are increasing over time.

The graph in Figure 12.6 creates the impression that Congress has set forth unreasonable fuel economy standards for automobiles. The line representing 18 miles per gallon for 1978 is 0.6 inch long, so the line representing 27.5 miles per gallon for 1985 should be about 0.92 inch long.

$$\frac{\text{inches}}{\text{miles per gallon}} : \frac{0.6}{18} = \frac{x}{27.5}$$

$$18x = 0.6(27.5)$$

$$x = \frac{0.6(27.5)}{18} \approx 0.92$$

Rather than 0.92 inch, the line is 5.3 inches long. Because this line represents 27.5 miles per gallon, its length compared to that of the short line for 1978 creates the impression that fuel standards for 1985 are unreasonable.

Do you notice anything else that is unusual about the graph in Figure 12.6? The dates on the left are all the same size. The numbers on the right are different sizes. The largest number in the figure is $27\frac{1}{2}$, which also exaggerates the severity of the 1985 mileage standard. Figure 12.7 shows how the data can be presented in a nondeceptive manner.

Figure 12.6 *Source: New York Times*, August 9, 1978, p. D-2. Reprinted by permission.

Required fuel economy standards: new cars built from 1978 to 1985

Figure 12.7 Required fuel economy standards: new cars built from 1978 to 1985

The graph in Figure 12.8 varies both the length and width of each dollar bill as the purchasing power of the bill diminishes. The 1958 dollar was worth $1.00. By contrast, the 1978 dollar is worth 44¢. Thus, the 1978 dollar should be drawn to be slightly less than half the size of the 1958 dollar. If the area of the dollar were drawn to reflect its purchasing power, the 1978 dollar would be approximately twice as large as the one shown in the visual display.

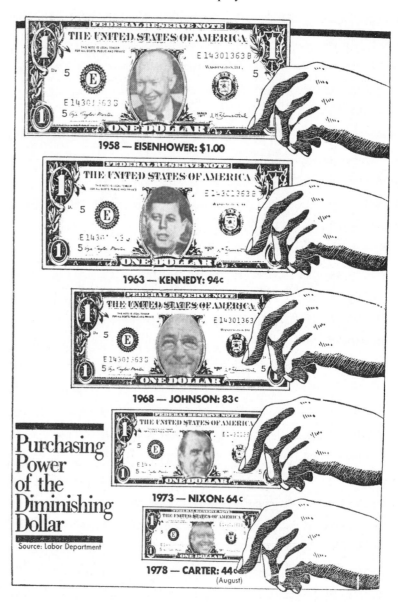

Figure 12.8 *Source: Washington Post,* October 25, 1978, p. 1.

Figure 12.9 Day Mines, Inc., *1974 Annual Report,* p. 1.

Figure 12.9 is another example of a graph that uses deception in its visual display. The company hopes that the viewer will not notice the loss in 1970. This loss is disguised because the graph does not provide a scale on the vertical axis. The bars begin at the bottom at approximately negative $4,200,000.

Examples of graphs that contain visual frauds are endless. We need to become aware of ways that visual displays can be deceptive. With this knowledge, we can avoid interpreting potentially deceptive graphs incorrectly.

Exercise Set 12.1

 Practice and Application Exercises

Exercises 1–6 present numerical information. Describe the population whose properties are analyzed by the data.

1. In 1997, 42.7% of college professors in the United States were women. (*Source:* U.S. Bureau of Labor Statistics)

2. In 1999, using interviews with 1172 U.S. children ages 6 to 14, researchers concluded that 62% of U.S. children would not like to be president of the country. (*Source: Time*, July 5, 1999)

3. In 1997, there were 634 violent crimes in the United States per 100,000 residents. (*Source:* F.B.I.)

4. In 1999, 66% of world on-line households were in North America. (*Source:* Jupiter Comunications)

5. In 1997, 88% of high school students in Connecticut took the SAT. (*Source: New York Times*)

6. Approximately 54% of New York City's workers get to work by public transportation. (*Source:* American Public Transit Association)

7. The government of a large city needs to determine if the city's residents will support the construction of a new jail. The government decides to conduct a survey of a sample of the city's residents. Which one of the following procedures would be most appropriate for obtaining a sample of the city's residents?
   a. Survey a random sample of the employees and inmates at the old jail.
   b. Survey every fifth person who walks into City Hall on a given day.
   c. Survey a random sample of persons within each geographic region of the city.
   d. Survey the first 200 people listed in the city's telephone directory.

8. The city council of a large city needs to know if its residents will support the building of three new schools. The council decides to conduct a survey of a sample of the city's residents. Which procedure would be most appropriate for obtaining a sample of the city's residents?
   a. Survey a random sample of teachers who live in the city.
   b. Survey 100 individuals who are randomly selected from a list of all people living in the state in which the city in question is located.
   c. Survey a random sample of persons within each neighborhood of the city.
   d. Survey every tenth person who enters City Hall on a randomly selected day.

9. A random sample of 30 college students is selected. Each student is asked how much time he or she spent on homework during the previous week. The following times (in hours) are obtained:

16, 24, 18, 21, 18, 16, 18, 17, 15, 21, 19, 17, 17, 16, 19, 18,

15, 15, 20, 17, 15, 17, 24, 19, 16, 20, 16, 19, 18, 17

Construct a frequency distribution for the data.

10. A random sample of 30 male college students is selected. Each student is asked his height (to the nearest inch). The heights are as follows:

72, 70, 68, 72, 71, 71, 71, 69, 73, 71, 73, 75, 66, 67, 75

74, 73, 71, 72, 67, 72, 68, 67, 71, 73, 71, 72, 70, 73, 70

Construct a frequency distribution for the data.

11. The ages of 40 runners who participated in a 10-kilometer run are as follows:

17, 54, 22, 25, 30, 37, 37, 18, 19, 16, 25, 46, 48, 61, 53,

32, 28, 20, 10, 13, 49, 39, 26, 28, 22, 22, 14, 19, 48, 69,

51, 47, 23, 28, 32, 38, 45, 51, 24, 27

Construct a grouped frequency distribution for the data. Use the classes 10–19, 20–29, 30–39, 40–49, 50–59, and 60–69.

12. The IQ scores of 70 students enrolled in a liberal arts course at a college are as follows:

102, 100, 103, 86, 120, 117, 111, 101, 93, 97, 99, 95, 95, 104, 104, 105, 106, 109, 109, 89, 94, 95, 99, 99, 103, 104, 105, 109, 110, 114, 124, 123, 118, 117, 116, 110, 114, 114, 96, 99, 103, 103, 104, 107, 107, 110, 111, 112, 113, 117, 115, 116, 100, 104, 102, 94, 93, 93, 96, 96, 111, 116, 107, 109, 105, 106, 97, 106, 107, 108

Construct a grouped frequency distribution for the data. Use the classes 85–89, 90–94, 95–99, 100–104, 105–109, 110–114, 115–119, and 120–124.

In Exercises 13–14, construct a histogram and a frequency polygon for the given data.

13.

Size of U.S. Family	Number of Families (in millions) (Frequency)
2	30
3	16
4	15
5	6
6	2

Source: U.S. Bureau of the Census

14.

Lifestyle	Number of Americans per 100 Adults
1 Very active	43
2 Somewhat active	44
3 Not very active	10
4 Not at all active	3

Source: Penn, Schoen, and Berland

15. Construct a histogram and a frequency polygon for the data in Exercise 9.

16. Construct a histogram and a frequency polygon for the data in Exercise 10.

17. The histogram shows the distribution of starting salaries (rounded to the nearest thousand) for college graduates based on a random sample of recent graduates.

Starting Salaries of Recent College Graduates

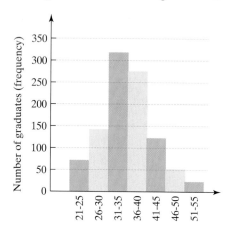

Salary in thousands of dollars

Which one of the following is true according to the graph?
a. The graph is based on a sample of approximately 500 recent college graduates.
b. More college graduates had starting salaries in the $41,000–$45,000 range than in the $26,000–$30,000 range.
c. If the sample is truly representative, then for a group of 400 college graduates, we can expect about 28 of them to have starting salaries in the $21,000–$25,000 range.
d. The percent of starting salaries falling above those shown by any rectangular bar is equal to the percent of starting salaries falling below that bar.

18. The frequency polygon at the top of the next column shows a distribution of IQ scores. Which one of the following is true based upon the graph?
a. The graph is based on a sample of approximately 50 people.
b. More people had an IQ score of 100 than any other IQ score, and as the deviation from 100 increases or decreases, the scores fall off in a symmetrical manner.
c. More people had an IQ score of 110 than a score of 90.

d. The percent of scores above any IQ score is equal to the percent of scores below that score.

IQ score

19. A random sample of 40 college professors is selected from all professors at a university. The following list gives their ages.

63, 48, 42, 42, 38, 59, 41, 44, 45, 28, 54, 62, 51, 44, 63,

66, 59, 46, 51, 28, 37, 66, 42, 40, 30, 31, 48, 32, 29, 42,

63, 37, 36, 47, 25, 34, 49, 30, 35, 50

Construct a stem-and-leaf display for the data. What does the shape of the display reveal about the ages of the professors?

20. Construct a stem-and-leaf display for the data given in Exercise 11.

21. In "Ages of Oscar-Winning Best Actors and Actresses" (*Mathematics Teacher* magazine) by Richard Brown and Gretchen Davis, the stem-and-leaf plots shown compare the ages of actors and actresses for 30 winners of the Oscar at the time they won the award. Use the plot to write the ages of the 30 actors and of the 30 actresses. What differences do you observe between the two sets of data? What explanations can you offer for these differences?

Actors	Stems	Actresses
	2	146667
98753221	3	00113344455778
88767543322100	4	11129
6651	5	
210	6	011
6	7	4
	8	0

22. The stem-and-leaf plot shown on page 603 displays the heights of 218 volcanoes. The unit is 100 feet, so the entry 18|5 represents a volcano whose height is 185(100) = 18,500 feet.
a. What is the height of the tallest volcano?
b. What is the height of the least tall of the volcanoes?

c. What is the greatest height shared by at least two of the volcanoes?

d. Describe a trend shown by the stem-and-leaf display.

0	98766562
1	97719630
2	69987766544422211009850
3	876655412099551426
4	99988443319294333361107
5	9766666655442221009733
6	898665441077761065
7	98855431100652108073
8	653322122937
9	377655421000493
10	0984433165212
11	4963201631
12	45421164
13	47830
14	00
15	676
16	52
17	92
18	5
19	39730

23. The graph shown indicates a decline in commission payments to travel agents in 1978. Or does it? Describe what is misleading about the four "declines" in this visual display.

Source: New York Times, August 8, 1978, p. D-1. Reprinted by permission.

24. Describe the error in the visual display shown. What is misleading about this error? (*Note:* The abbreviation bbl. stands for *barrel*.)

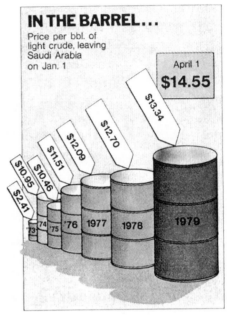

Source: Time, April 9, 1979, p. 57; © 1979 Time Inc. Reprinted by permission.

 Writing in Mathematics

25. What is a population? What is a sample?

26. Describe what is meant by a random sample.

27. Suppose you are interested in whether or not the students at your college would favor a grading system in which students may receive final grades of A+, A, A−, B+, B, B−, C+, C, C−, and so on. Describe how you might obtain a random sample of 100 students from the entire student population.

28. For Exercise 27, would questioning every fifth student as he or she is leaving the campus library until 100 students are interviewed be a good way to obtain a random sample? Explain your answer.

29. What is a frequency distribution?

30. What is a histogram?

31. What is a frequency polygon?

32. Describe how to construct a frequency polygon from a histogram.

33. Describe how to construct a stem-and-leaf plot from a set of data.

34. Describe two ways that graphs can be used to distort data.

35. Did Sir Francis Bacon write some or all of the plays attributed to William Shakespeare? In an attempt to determine whether this is true, scholars sampled words from Shakespeare's plays and Bacon's writings, counting the number of letters per word. The results are presented in the histograms shown on page 604.

Shakespeare's plays

Bacon's writings

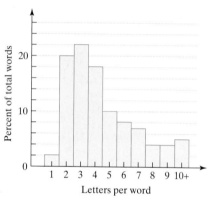

a. Describe what these histograms show about each author's use of words that are less than five letters long.
b. Describe what these histograms show about each author's use of words that are more than five letters long.
c. Do these histograms suggest that Bacon wrote some of Shakespeare's plays? Explain your answer.

 Critical Thinking Exercises

For each frequency polygon shown in Exercises 36–37, describe a situation that might result in a distribution of scores that takes on this shape.

36.

37.

 Technology Exercises

38. Using a spreadsheet, enter the following exam scores into a spreadsheet column: 4 A's, 7 B's, 3 C's, 4 D's, and 1 F.

After entering the data, use the computer's mouse to highlight the cells containing the data. Then activate the Chart Option of the spreadsheet by clicking on the Insert pull-down menu and selecting Chart. (See image.) Select the Column chart option and click the "Next" button. Work your way through the options, including the labels and cosmetic effects. Once you have decided on all of the options (don't worry, you can go back and change them), click the "Finish" button.

39. Use a spreadsheet to create a histogram for the following distribution of grades: 14 A's, 34 B's, 65 C's, 28 D's, and 10 F's.

 Group Exercises

40. The classic book on distortion using statistics is *How to Lie with Statistics* by Darrell Huff. This activity is designed for five people. Each person should select two chapters from Huff's book and then present to the class the common methods of statistical manipulation and distortion that Huff discusses.

41. Each group member should find one example of a graph that presents data with integrity and one example of a graph that is misleading. Use newspapers, magazines, the Internet, books, and so forth. Once graphs have been collected, each member should share his or her graphs with the entire group. Be sure to explain why one graph depicts quantitative data in a forthright manner and how the other graph deliberately misleads the viewer.

SECTION 12.2 *Measures of Central Tendency*

Objectives

1. Determine the mean for a data set.
2. Determine the median for a data set.
3. Determine the mode for a data set.
4. Determine the midrange for a data set.

RELEASE WEEK OF NOVEMBER 29, 1976
Release Monday

© Field Enterprise Inc., 1976. Reprinted with special permission of King Features Syndicate.

Median Age of U.S. Whites, Blacks, and Hispanics

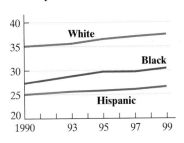

Figure 12.10 *Source*: U.S. Census Bureau

1 Determine the mean for a data set.

Singers Ricky Martin and Jennifer Lopez, television journalist Soledad O'Brien, boxer Oscar De La Hoya, Internet entrepreneur Carlos Cardona, actor John Leguizamo, and political organizer Luigi Crespo are members of a generation of young Hispanics that is changing the way America looks, feels, thinks, eats, dances, and votes. There are 31 million Hispanics in the United States, pumping $300 billion a year into the economy. By 2050, the Hispanic population is expected to reach 96 million—an increase of more than 200 percent. And Hispanics are younger than the rest of the nation: A third are under 18. The graph in Figure 12.10 shows the *median* age of whites, African-Americans, and Americans of Hispanic origin.

The *what* age? Perhaps you have seen the word *median* in the presentation of numerical information. The median age for U.S. Latinos in 1999 was 27: The number of Latinos who are older than 27 is the same as the number who are younger than 27. The single number 27 represents what is "average" or "typical" of the age of Latino-Americans. In statistics, such a value is known as a **measure of central tendency** because it is generally located toward the center of a distribution. Four such measures are discussed in this section: the mean, the median, the mode, and the midrange. Each measure of central tendency is calculated in a different way. Thus, it is better to use a specific term (mean, median, mode, or midrange) than to use the generic descriptive term "average."

Table 12.4 Mean Major League Baseball Salaries

Year	Mean Salary
1990	$597,537
1991	$851,492
1992	$1,028,667
1993	$1,076,089
1994	$1,168,263
1995	$1,110,766
1996	$1,119,981
1997	$1,336,609

Source: Major League Baseball Players Association

The Mean

By far the most commonly used measure of central tendency is the *mean*. The **mean** is obtained by adding all the data items and then dividing the sum by the number of items. For example, Table 12.4 shows the mean U.S. major league baseball salaries. The mean salary for 1997, $1,336,609, was determined by adding up the baseball salaries of all major league players and then dividing the sum by the number of major league players.

EXAMPLE 1 Calculating the Mean

Table 12.5 on page 606 shows the all-time top point scorers in a National Football League season. Find the mean points scored per season for the top 11 scorers.

Paul Hornung of the Green Bay Packers

Table 12.5   Top Point Scorers in an NFL Season (through 1998)

Player	Team	Year	Points
Paul Hornung	Green Bay Packers	1960	176
Mark Moseley	Washington Redskins	1983	161
Gino Cappelletti	Boston Patriots	1964	155
Emitt Smith	Dallas Cowboys	1995	150
Chip Lohmiller	Washington Redskins	1991	149
Gino Cappelletti	Boston Patriots	1961	147
Paul Hornung	Green Bay Packers	1961	146
Jim Turner	New York Jets	1968	145
John Kasay	Carolina Panthers	1996	145
John Riggins	Washington Redskins	1983	144
Kevin Butler	Chicago Bears	1985	144

Source: National Football League

Solution   We find the mean by adding the points scored and dividing this sum by 11, the number of data items.

$$\text{Mean} = \frac{176 + 161 + 155 + 150 + 149 + 147 + 146 + 145 + 145 + 144 + 144}{11}$$

$$= \frac{1662}{11} \approx 151.09$$

The mean points scored per season for the top 11 scorers is approximately 151.

The Mean American Guy According to researchers, "Robert" is 31, 5 feet 10 inches, 172 pounds, watches TV 2567 hours yearly, commutes to work, works 6.1 hours daily, and sleeps 7.7 hours.

One and only one mean can be calculated for any group of numerical data. The mean may or may not be one of the actual data items. In Example 1, the mean was approximately 151. However, none of the 11 players scored 151 points in a season.

The Greek letter sigma, Σ, is called a **symbol of summation**. It is used to indicate the sum of the data items. The notation Σx, read "the sum of x," means to add all the data items. We can use this symbol to give a formula for calculating the mean.

The Mean

The **mean** is the sum of the data items divided by the number of items.

$$\text{Mean} = \frac{\Sigma x}{n},$$

where Σx represents the sum of all the data items and n represents the number of items.

Take another look at the points for the top point scorers in an NFL season (Table 12.5). Some of the data items are identical. Two of the data items are 145 and 145. Thus, the data value 145 occurs twice. Similarly, because two of the data items are 144 and 144, the data value 144 also occurs twice. Table 12.6 shows a frequency distribution for the season points of the top NFL scorers.

Table 12.6   A Frequency Distribution for Points by Top Point Scorers in an NFL Season

Points x	Number of Players with These Points Frequency: f
144	2
145	2
146	1
147	1
149	1
150	1
155	1
161	1
176	1
	11

Total frequency

In Example 1, in computing the mean, we added 145 twice and 144 twice. Another option is to multiply 145 by 2 and 144 by 2. Indeed, if you multiply each value of x in Table 12.6 by its frequency (xf) and then add these products (Σxf), you will get 1662. This is the sum from Example 1 that we obtained by adding all the data items. When many data values occur more than once and a frequency distribution is used to organize the data, we can use the following formula for calculating the mean.

Calculating the Mean for a Frequency Distribution

$$\text{Mean} = \frac{\Sigma xf}{n}$$

in which

x refers to each data value.

f refers to the frequency of that data value.

Σxf refers to the sum of all the products obtained by multiplying each data value by its frequency.

n refers to the *total frequency* of the distribution.

EXAMPLE 2   Calculating the Mean for a Frequency Distribution

Table 12.7 shows the age of maximum growth for a group of 35 boys. Find the mean age of maximum growth.

Solution   We use the formula

$$\text{Mean} = \frac{\Sigma xf}{n}.$$

First, we must find xf, obtained by multiplying each data value, x, by its frequency, f. Then, we need to find the sum of these products: Σxf. We can use the frequency distribution to organize these computations. Add a third column in which each data value is multiplied by its frequency. This column, shown below, is headed xf. Then, find the sum of the values (Σxf) in this column.

Table 12.7   A Boy's Age at Maximum Yearly Growth

Age of Maximum Growth x	Number of Boys Frequency: f
10	1
11	2
12	5
13	7
14	9
15	6
16	3
17	1
18	1
	35

x	f	xf
10	1	$10 \cdot 1 = 10$
11	2	$11 \cdot 2 = 22$
12	5	$12 \cdot 5 = 60$
13	7	$13 \cdot 7 = 91$
14	9	$14 \cdot 9 = 126$
15	6	$15 \cdot 6 = 90$
16	3	$16 \cdot 3 = 48$
17	1	$17 \cdot 1 = 17$
18	1	$18 \cdot 1 = 18$
	35	$\Sigma xf = 482$

Σxf is the sum of the values in the third column:
10 + 22 + 60 + 91 + 126 + 90 + 48 + 17 + 18 = 482

This value is *n*, the total frequency of the distribution.

Mean Weekly Hours and Minutes of Viewing per U.S. TV Household

Year		Time
1971		42:04
1980		46:05
1990		48:29
1994		50:50
1997		50:24

0 10 20 30 40 50 60

Figure 12.11 *Source*: Nielsen Media Research

Colombian-born actor John Leguizamo is a member of a generation of young Hispanics shaping American pop culture.

2 Determine the median for a data set.

Now, substitute these values into the formula for the mean. Remember that *n* is the *total frequency* of the distribution, or 35.

$$\text{Mean} = \frac{\Sigma xf}{n} = \frac{482}{35} \approx 13.77$$

The mean age of maximum growth is approximately 13.77 or, rounded to the nearest whole year, 14 years of age.

We saw that in 1997, the mean salary for major league baseball players was $1,336,609. This is the mean for the *entire population* of 1997 major league baseball players. By contrast, the graph in Figure 12.11 indicates that in 1997, the mean weekly TV viewing time per TV household in the United States was 50 hours, 24 minutes. This mean was obtained *using a random sample* of the population. Unlike the population of major league baseball players, the population of 94 million TV households is too large to obtain a data item from every member. By calculating the mean for a random sample, statisticians can gain a reasonable estimate for the mean in the entire population.

The Median

We have seen that the median age for U.S. Latinos in 1999 was 27. To find this value, researchers begin with a random sample of all U.S. Latinos. The data items—that is, the ages for sampled Latinos—are arranged in order, from youngest to oldest. The **median** age is the data item in the middle of this set of ranked data.

The Median

To find the **median** of a group of data items,
1. Arrange the data items in order, from smallest to largest.
2. If the number of data items is odd, the median is the data item in the middle of the list.
3. If the number of data items is even, the median is the mean of the two middle data items.

EXAMPLE 3   Finding the Median

Find the median for each of the following groups of data.
   a. 84, 90, 98, 95, 88
   b. 68, 74, 7, 13, 15, 25, 28, 59, 34, 47

Solution
   a. Arrange the data items in order, from smallest to largest. The number of data items in the list, five, is odd. Thus, the median is the middle number.

84, 88, 90, 95, 98

Middle data item

The median is 90. Notice that two data items lie above 90 and two data items lie below 90.

b. Arrange the data items in order, from smallest to largest. The number of data items in the list, ten, is even. Thus, the median is the mean of the two middle data items.

$$7, 13, 15, 25, 28, 34, 47, 59, 68, 74$$

Middle data items
are 28 and 34.

$$\text{Median} = \frac{28 + 34}{2} = \frac{62}{2} = 31$$

The median is 31. Five data items lie above 31 and five data items lie below 31.

If a relatively long list of data items is arranged in order, it may be difficult to identify the item or items in the middle. In cases like this, the median can be found by determining its position in the list of items.

Position of the Median

If n data items are arranged in order, from smallest to largest, the median is the value in the

$$\frac{n + 1}{2}$$

position.

EXAMPLE 4   Finding the Median Using the Position Formula

Listed below are the points scored per season by the 11 top point scorers in the NFL. Find the median points scored per season for the top 11 scorers.

$$144, 144, 145, 145, 146, 147, 149, 150, 155, 161, 176$$

Solution   The data items are arranged from smallest to largest.

There are 11 data items, so $n = 11$. The median is the value in the

$$\frac{n + 1}{2} \text{ position} = \frac{11 + 1}{2} \text{ position} = \frac{12}{2} \text{ position} = \text{sixth position.}$$

We find the median by selecting the data item in the sixth position:

Position   Position
3   4

$$144, \; 144, \; 145, \; 145, \; 146, \; 147, \; 149, \; 150, \; 155, \; 161, \; 176$$

Position Position   Position Position
1   2   5   6

The median is 147. Notice that five data items lie above 147 and five data items lie below it. The median points scored per season for the top 11 scorers is 147.

Study Tip

The formula

$$\frac{n + 1}{2}$$

gives the *position* of the median, and not the actual value of the median. When finding the median, be sure to first arrange the data items in order from smallest to largest.

EXAMPLE 5 Finding the Median Using the Position Formula

Find the median for the following group of data items:

$$109, 123, 192, 170, 99, 108, 168, 146, 126, 129.$$

Solution Arrange the data items in order, from smallest to largest:

$$99, 108, 109, 123, 126, 129, 146, 168, 170, 192$$

There are ten data items, so $n = 10$. The median is the value in the

$$\frac{n + 1}{2} \text{ position} = \frac{10 + 1}{2} \text{ position} = \frac{11}{2} \text{ position} = 5.5 \text{ position}.$$

This means that the median is the mean of the data items in positions 5 and 6:

$$99, 108, 109, 123, 126, 129, 146, 168, 170, 192$$

Position 5   Position 6

$$\text{Median} = \frac{126 + 129}{2} = \frac{255}{2} = 127.5$$

The median is 127.5.

When individual data items are listed from smallest to largest, you can find the median by identifying the item or items in the middle or by using the $\frac{n + 1}{2}$ formula for its position. However, the formula for the position of the median is useful when data items are organized in a frequency distribution.

Table 12.2   A Boy's Age at Maximum Yearly Growth

Age of Maximum Growth x	Number of Boys Frequency: f
10	1
11	2
12	5
13	7
14	9
15	6
16	3
17	1
18	1
	35

EXAMPLE 6   Finding the Median for a Frequency Distribution

Table 12.2, showing the age of maximum growth for a group of 35 boys, is repeated in the margin. Find the median age of maximum growth.

Solution There are 35 data items, so $n = 35$. The median is the value in the

$$\frac{n + 1}{2} \text{ position} = \frac{35 + 1}{2} \text{ position} = \frac{36}{2} \text{ position} = 18\text{th position}.$$

We find the median by selecting the data item in eighteenth position. Table 12.2 indicates that the data items begin with

$$10, 11, 11, 12, 12, 12, 12, 12, \ldots$$

and so on. We can write them all out and then select the median, the eighteenth data item. A more efficient way to proceed is to count down the frequency column in the distribution until we reach the eighteenth data item:

x	f	
10	1	We count down the frequency column.
		1
11	2	2, 3
12	5	4, 5, 6, 7, 8
13	7	9, 10, 11, 12, 13, 14, 15
14	9	16, 17, 18
15	6	
16	3	
17	1	
18	1	
	35	

The eighteenth data item is 14. The median age of maximum growth is 14.

Table 12.8 Median Weekly Earnings

For Workers 15 and Older			
Male	**1990**	**1993**	**1997**
Blacks	$303	$311	$348
Whites	$499	$469	$502
Female	**1990**	**1993**	**1997**
Blacks	$196	$203	$250
Whites	$243	$240	$265

Source: Bureau of Labor Statistics

Table 12.8 shows the median weekly earnings for U.S. workers 15 and older. The table indicates that in 1997, the median weekly earning for black men was $348. By definition, in 1997 the number of black men in the United States who earned less than $348 per week is the same as the number who earned more. Notice how these numbers tell a story. For all four groups, the median weekly earnings in 1997 is greater than in 1990. However, there are gaps between blacks and whites, as well as between women and men.

Statisticians generally use the median, rather than the mean, when reporting income. Why? Our next example will help to answer this question.

EXAMPLE 7   Comparing the Median and the Mean

Five employees in the assembly section of a television manufacturing company earn salaries of $19,700, $20,400, $21,500, $22,600, and $23,000 annually. The section manager has an annual salary of $95,000.

a. Find the median annual salary for the six people.
b. Find the mean annual salary for the six people.

Solution

a. To compute the median, first arrange the salaries in order.

$$\$19,700, \$20,400, \$21,500, \$22,600, \$23,000, \$95,000$$

Because the list contains an even number of data items, six, the median is the mean of the two middle items.

$$\text{Median} = \frac{\$21,500 + \$22,600}{2} = \frac{\$44,100}{2} = \$22,050$$

The median annual salary is $22,050.

> *"People generally think of the numbers and less of what is to me the interesting part: using the numbers to make decisions about everything under the sun."*
>
> HAL STERN
> mathematician

3 Determine the mode for a data set.

b. We find the mean annual salary by adding the six annual salaries and dividing by 6.

$$\text{Mean} = \frac{\$19{,}700 + \$20{,}400 + \$21{,}500 + \$22{,}600 + \$23{,}000 + \$95{,}000}{6}$$

$$= \frac{\$202{,}200}{6} = \$33{,}700$$

The mean annual salary is $33,700.

In Example 7, the median annual salary is $22,050 and the mean annual salary is $33,700. Why such a big difference between these two measures of central tendency? The relatively high annual salary of the section manager, $95,000, pulls the mean salary to a value considerably higher than the median salary. When one or more data items are much greater than the other items, these extreme values can greatly influence the mean. In cases like this, the median is often more representative of the data.

This is why the median, rather than the mean, is used to summarize the weekly earnings for black men, white men, black women, and white women in Table 12.8 on page 611. Because no one can earn less than $0 per week, the distribution of weekly income must come to an end at $0 for each of these four groups. By contrast, there is no upper limit on weekly earnings on the high side. In the United States, the wealthiest 5% of the population earn about 21% of the total income. The relatively few people with very high weekly incomes tend to pull the mean income to a value considerably greater than the median income. Reporting mean incomes in Table 12.8 would inflate the numbers shown, making them nonrepresentative of the millions of workers in each of the four groups.

The Mode

Table 12.9 shows the ten longest running national network television series of the twentieth century. Using the number of seasons for the top ten shows, we construct a frequency distribution:

Table 12.9   Ten Longest-Running National Network TV Series of the Twentieth Century

Program	Number of Seasons the Show Ran
"Walt Disney"	33
"60 Minutes"	33
"The Ed Sullivan Show"	24
"Gunsmoke"	20
"The Red Skelton Show"	20
"Meet the Press"	18
"What's My Line?"	18
"I've Got a Secret"	17
"Lassie"	17
"The Lawrence Welk Show"	17

Source: Nielsen Media Research

A Frequency Distribution for the Number of Seasons for the Longest-Running TV Series

Number of Seasons the Show Ran x	Number of Shows Frequency
17	3
18	2
20	2
24	1
33	2

The data value that occurs most often in this distribution is 17. Of the ten longest-running shows, the greatest number ran for 17 seasons; 17 is called the *mode* of this distribution.

The Mode

The **mode** is the data value that occurs most often in a data set.

EXAMPLE 8   Finding the Mode

Find the mode for the following group of data:

$$7, 2, 4, 7, 8, 10.$$

Solution   The number 7 occurs more often than any other. Therefore, 7 is the mode.

If no single data value occurs more frequently than any other data value in a group, the group has no mode. For example, no data value in 2, 1, 4, 5, 3 occurs more than once, and the group has no mode. For the group 3, 3, 4, 5, 6, 6, no single value occurs most frequently, and this group has no mode. (You may find some books that call both 3 and 6 the modes of this group because each of these occurs twice.)

The Midrange

4 Determine the midrange for a data set.

Table 12.10 shows the ten hottest cities in the United States. Because temperature is constantly changing, you might wonder how the mean temperatures shown in the table are obtained.

First, we need to find a representative daily temperature. This is obtained by adding the lowest and highest temperatures for the day and then dividing this sum by 2. Next, we take the representative daily temperatures for all 365 days, add them, and divide the sum by 365. These are the mean temperatures that appear in Table 12.10.

Representative daily temperature,

$$\frac{\text{lowest daily temperature} + \text{highest daily temperature}}{2},$$

is an example of a measure of central tendency called the *midrange*.

The Midrange

The **midrange** is found by adding the lowest and highest data values and dividing the sum by 2.

$$\text{Midrange} = \frac{\text{lowest data value} + \text{highest data value}}{2}$$

Table 12.10   Ten Hottest U.S. Cities

City	Mean Temperature
Key West, FL	77.8°
Miami, FL	75.9°
West Palm Beach, FL	74.7°
Fort Myers, FL	74.4°
Yuma, AZ	74.2°
Brownsville, TX	73.8°
Phoenix, AZ	72.6°
Vero Beach, FL	72.4°
Orlando, FL	72.3°
Tampa, FL	72.3°

Source: National Oceanic and Atmospheric Administration

Technology

Calculators, Software Packages, and Statistics of Central Tendency

Many scientific calculators and all graphing calculators will allow you to enter data items. After you do so, the calculator will automatically display the mean, and perhaps the median and mode. Software packages for statistics automatically give the value for any requested statistic after data items have been entered.

EXAMPLE 9 Finding the Midrange

The best paid state governors are in New York and New Jersey, each earning $130,000 annually. The worst paid is the governor of Montana, earning $59,310 annually. Find the midrange for annual salaries of U.S. governors.

Solution

$$\text{Midrange} = \frac{\text{Lowest annual salary} + \text{highest annual salary}}{2}$$

$$= \frac{\$59,310 + \$130,000}{2} = \frac{\$189,310}{2} = \$94,655$$

The midrange for annual salaries of U.S. governors is $94,655.

We can find the mean annual salary of U.S. governors by adding up the salaries of all 50 governors and then dividing the sum by 50. It is much faster to calculate the midrange, which is often used as an estimate for the mean.

EXAMPLE 10 Finding the Four Measures of Central Tendency

Suppose your six exam grades in a course are

$$52, 69, 75, 86, 86, \text{ and } 92.$$

Compute your final course grade (90–100 = A, 80–89 = B, 70–79 = C, 60–69 = D, below 60 = F) using the

a. mean b. median c. mode d. midrange

Solution

a. The mean is the sum of the data items divided by the number of items, 6.

$$\text{Mean} = \frac{52 + 69 + 75 + 86 + 86 + 92}{6} = \frac{460}{6} \approx 76.67$$

Using the mean, your final course grade is C.

b. The data items are arranged in order. Because the number of data items is even, the median is the mean of the two middle items.

$$\text{Median} = \frac{75 + 86}{2} = \frac{161}{2} = 80.5$$

Using the median, your final course grade is B.

c. The mode is the data value that occurs most frequently. Because 86 occurs most often, the mode is 86. Using the mode, your final course grade is B.

d. The midrange is the mean of the lowest and highest data values.

$$\text{Midrange} = \frac{52 + 92}{2} = \frac{144}{2} = 72$$

Using the midrange, your final course grade is C.

Shrinking Means

The mean number of persons per U.S. household declined from 1850 through 1990. The mean has remained relatively stable since 1990.

Year	Mean Number of Persons per Household
1850	5.55
1860	5.28
1870	5.09
1880	5.04
1890	4.93
1900	4.76
1910	4.54
1920	4.34
1930	4.11
1940	3.67
1950	3.37
1960	3.35
1970	3.14
1975	2.94
1980	2.76
1985	2.69
1990	2.63
1997	2.64

Source: Bureau of the Census

Exercise Set 12.2

 Practice Exercises

In Exercises 1–8, find the mean for each group of data items.

1. 7, 4, 3, 2, 8, 5, 1, 3
2. 11, 6, 4, 0, 2, 1, 12, 0, 0
3. 91, 95, 99, 97, 93, 95
4. 100, 100, 90, 30, 70, 100
5. 100, 40, 70, 40, 60
6. 1, 3, 5, 10, 8, 5, 6, 8
7. 1.6, 3.8, 5.0, 2.7, 4.2, 4.2, 3.2, 4.7, 3.6, 2.5, 2.5
8. 1.4, 2.1, 1.6, 3.0, 1.4, 2.2, 1.4, 9.0, 9.0, 1.8

In Exercises 9–12, find the mean for the data items in the given frequency distribution.

9.

Score x	Frequency f
1	1
2	3
3	4
4	4
5	6
6	5
7	3
8	2

10.

Score x	Frequency f
1	2
2	4
3	5
4	7
5	6
6	4
7	3

128

11.

Score x	Frequency f
1	1
2	1
3	2
4	5
5	7
6	9
7	8
8	6
9	4
10	3

12.

Score x	Frequency f
1	3
2	4
3	6
4	8
5	9
6	7
7	5
8	2
9	1
10	1

2.18

In Exercises 13–20, find the median for each group of data items.

13. 7, 4, 3, 2, 8, 5, 1, 3
14. 11, 6, 4, 0, 2, 1, 12, 0, 0
15. 91, 95, 99, 97, 93, 95
16. 100, 100, 90, 30, 70, 100
17. 100, 40, 70, 40, 60
18. 1, 3, 5, 10, 8, 5, 6, 8
19. 1.6, 3.8, 5.0, 2.7, 4.2, 4.2, 3.2, 4.7, 3.6, 2.5, 2.5
20. 1.4, 2.1, 1.6, 3.0, 1.4, 2.2, 1.4, 9.0, 9.0, 1.8

Find the median for the data items in the frequency distribution in

21. Exercise 9.
22. Exercise 10.
23. Exercise 11.
24. Exercise 12.

In Exercises 25–32, find the mode for each group of data items. If there is no mode, so state.

25. 7, 4, 3, 2, 8, 5, 1, 3
26. 11, 6, 4, 0, 2, 1, 12, 0, 0
27. 91, 95, 99, 97, 93, 95
28. 100, 100, 90, 30, 70, 100
29. 100, 40, 70, 40, 60
30. 1, 3, 5, 10, 8, 5, 6, 8
31. 1.6, 3.8, 5.0, 2.7, 4.2, 4.2, 3.2, 4.7, 3.6, 2.5, 2.5
32. 1.4, 2.1, 1.6, 3.0, 1.4, 2.2, 1.4, 9.0, 9.0, 1.8

Find the mode for the data items in the frequency distribution in

33. Exercise 9.
34. Exercise 10.
35. Exercise 11.
36. Exercise 12.

In Exercises 37–44, find the midrange for each group of data items.

37. 7, 4, 3, 2, 8, 5, 1, 3
38. 11, 6, 4, 0, 2, 1, 12, 0, 0
39. 91, 95, 99, 97, 93, 95
40. 100, 100, 90, 30, 70, 100
41. 100, 40, 70, 40, 60
42. 1, 3, 5, 10, 8, 5, 6, 8
43. 1.6, 3.8, 5.0, 2.7, 4.2, 4.2, 3.2, 4.7, 3.6, 2.5, 2.5
44. 1.4, 2.1, 1.6, 3.0, 1.4, 2.2, 1.4, 9.0, 9.0, 1.8

Find the midrange for the data items in the frequency distribution in

45. Exercise 9.   46. Exercise 10.

47. Exercise 11.   48. Exercise 12.

Application Exercises

49. The mean annual cost for automobile insurance in the United States is $665.52. The cost in each of the five most expensive states is shown. By how much does the mean cost for these five states exceed the national mean?

Rank	State	Cost for Auto Insurance
1	New Jersey	$1013.47
2	Hawaii	963.08
3	District of Columbia	958.58
4	New York	905.90
5	Massachusetts	898.21

Source: National Association of Insurance Commissioners

50. Use the graph to find the mean number of business failures in the United States for the 1990–1997 period.

Number of Business Failures in the U.S.

Source: Dun & Bradstreet

51. The greatest rainfall amount recorded in the United States occurred in Alvin, Texas in a 24-hour period on July 25–26, 1979. It was 43 inches.
    a. What was the mean hourly rainfall during that period?
    b. Does your answer in part (a) mean that this is the number of inches of rain that fell during each hour on July 25–26? Explain your answer.
    c. What was the least amount of rain that could have fallen in Alvin in a single hour on July 25–26?

The weights (to the nearest whole pound) of 40 randomly selected male college students are organized in a histogram with a superimposed frequency polygon, shown at the top of the next column. Use the graph to answer Exercises 52–55.

52. Find the mean weight.
53. Find the median weight.

54. Find the modal weight.
55. Find the midrange weight.

Weights of 40 Male College Students

56. The list shows the total worldwide sales of the top-selling albums of the twentieth century. For these top-selling 11 albums, find
    a. the mean number of sales.
    b. the median number of sales.
    c. the modal number of sales.
    d. the midrange number of sales.

Artist/Album	Worldwide Sales to the Nearest Million
Michael Jackson, *Thriller*	40,000,000
Pink Floyd, *Dark Side of the Moon*	28,000,000
Meat Loaf, *Bat out of Hell*	27,000,000
Soundtrack, *The Bodyguard*	26,000,000
Soundtrack, *Saturday Night Fever*	25,000,000
The Beatles, *Sgt. Pepper's Lonely Hearts Club Band*	24,000,000
Eagles, *Their Greatest Hits 1971–1975*	24,000,000
Mariah Carey, *Music Box*	23,000,000
Carole King, *Tapestry*	22,000,000
Simon and Garfunkel, *Bridge over Troubled Water*	22,000,000
Soundtrack, *Grease*	22,000,000

Source: RIAA

57. An advertisement for a speed-reading course claimed that the "average" reading speed for people completing the course was 1000 words per minute. Shown on page 617 are the actual data for the reading speeds per minute for a sample of 24 people who completed the course.

1000	900	800	1000	900	850
650	1000	1050	800	1000	850
700	750	800	850	900	950
600	1100	950	700	750	650

a. Find the mean, median, mode, and midrange. (If you prefer, first organize the data in a frequency distribution.)

b. Which measure of central tendency was given in the advertisement?

c. Which measure of central tendency is the best indicator of the "average" reading speed in this situation? Explain your answer.

Writing in Mathematics

58. What is the mean and how is it obtained?

59. What is the median and how is it obtained?

60. What is the mode and how is it obtained?

61. What is the midrange and how is it obtained?

Use the median sales prices of existing single-family homes to answer Exercises 62–64.

Median Sales Price of Existing Single-Family Homes

Year	United States	Northeast	Midwest	South	West
1996	118,200	140,900	99,800	102,800	152,900
1997	124,100	145,100	106,100	109,000	160,300

Source: U.S. Department of Housing and Urban Development

62. The median sales price in 1997 for the entire country was $124,100. Explain what this means.

63. Explain why median sales prices, rather than mean sales prices, are reported.

64. Without using specific numbers, write two statements that summarize the trends shown by the median sales prices.

65. The "average" income in the United States can be given by the mean or the median.
a. Which measure would be used in anti-U.S. propaganda? Explain your answer.
b. Which measure would be used in pro-U.S. propaganda? Explain your answer.

66. In a class of 40 students, 21 have examination scores of 77%. Which measure or measures of central tendency can you immediately determine? Explain your answer.

67. A student's parents promise to pay for next semester's tuition if an A average is earned in chemsitry. With examination grades of 97%, 97%, 75%, 70%, and 55%, the student reports that an A average has been earned. Which measure of central tendency is the student reporting as the average? How is this student misrepresenting the course performance with statistics?

68. According to the National Oceanic and Atmospheric Administration, the coldest city in the United States is International Falls, Minnesota, with a mean temperature of 36.8°. Explain how this mean is obtained.

 ## Critical Thinking Exercises

69. Make up a set of six examination grades (from 0 to 100) with each of the following characteristics:
a. The mean and the median have the same value, but the mode has a different value.
b. The mean and the mode have the same value, but the median has a different value.
c. The mean is greater than the median.
d. The mode is greater than the mean.
e. The mean, median, and mode have the same value.
f. The mean and mode have values of 72.

70. On an examination given to 30 students, no student scored below the mean. Describe how this occurred.

 ## Technology Exercises

71. Use the statistical mode of a calculator to determine the mean for the following data items: 3, 9, 6, 10, 5, 6, 9, 9, 3, 6.

72. Use the statistical mode of a calculator to determine the mean for the following data items: 13, 29, 65, 23, 65, 96, 91, 95, 73, 66.

 ## Group Exercise

73. Select a characteristic, such as shoe size or height, for which each member of the group can provide a number. Choose a characteristic of genuine interest to the group. For this characteristic, organize the data collected into a frequency distribution and a graph. Compute the mean, median, mode and midrange. Discuss any differences among these values. What happens if the group is divided (men and women or people under a certain age and people over a certain age) and these measures of central tendency are computed for each of the subgroups? Attempt to use measures of central tendency to discover something interesting about the entire group or the subgroups.

SECTION 12.3   *Measures of Dispersion*

Objectives

1. Determine the range for a data set.
2. Determine the standard deviation for a data set.

When you think of Houston, Texas and Honolulu, Hawaii, do balmy temperatures come to mind? Both cities have a mean temperature of 75°. However, the mean temperature does not tell the whole story. The temperature in Houston differs seasonally from a low of about 40° in January to a high of close to 100° in July and August. By contrast, Honolulu's temperature varies less throughout the year, usually ranging between 60° and 90°.

Measures of dispersion are used to describe the spread of data items in a data set. Two of the most common measures of dispersion, the *range* and the *standard deviation*, are discussed in this section.

1 Determine the range for a data set.

The Range

A quick but rough measure of dispersion is the **range**, the difference between the highest and lowest data values in a data set. For example, if Houston's hottest annual temperature is 103° and its coldest annual temperature is 33°, the range in temperature is

$$103° - 33°, \quad \text{or} \quad 70°.$$

If Honolulu's hottest day is 89° and its coldest day 61°, the range in temperature is

$$89° - 61°, \quad \text{or} \quad 28°.$$

Table 12.11   Highest New Home Costs

City	Mean Home Cost (in thousands of dollars, to the nearest thousand $)
Honolulu	$332
San Francisco	256
San Jose, CA	251
Santa Cruz, CA	235
Stamford, CT	223
Orange County, CA	215
Bergen County, NJ	215
Salinas, CA	213
Long Island, NY	210
Ventura, CA	210

Source: Places Rated Almanac

> **The Range**
>
> The **range**, the difference between the highest and lowest data values in a data set, indicates the total spread of the data.
>
> Range = highest data value − lowest data value

EXAMPLE 1   Computing the Range

Table 12.11 gives the ten most expensive markets for new homes in the United States. The figures are based on the mean cost of a new home and are drawn from a database of approximately 300 cities encompassing the largest metropolitan areas in the country. Find the range of home costs for the ten most expensive cities.

Solution

$$\text{Range} = \text{highest data value} - \text{lowest data value}$$
$$= \$332 - \$210 = \$122$$

Because new home costs are shown in thousands of dollars in Table 12.11, the range of this data is $122,000.

The Standard Deviation

A second measure of dispersion, and one that is dependent on *all* of the data items, is called the **standard deviation**. The standard deviation incorporates how much each data item differs from the mean. To determine how much a data item deviates from the mean, first compute the mean. Then subtract the mean from the data item.

EXAMPLE 2 Finding Deviations from the Mean

Find the deviations from the mean for the ten data items in Table 12.11.

Solution First, calculate the mean.

$$\text{Mean} = \frac{\Sigma x}{n} = \frac{332 + 256 + 251 + 235 + 223 + 215 + 215 + 213 + 210 + 210}{10}$$

$$= \frac{2360}{10} = 236$$

The mean home cost for the ten most expensive markets is $236,000. Now, let's find out by how much the home cost for each city differs from this amount. We do so by subtracting 236, the mean, from the ten data items. For Honolulu, the computation is shown as follows:

$$\text{Deviation from mean} = \text{data item} - \text{mean}$$

$$= 332 - 236 = 96$$

This indicates that home costs in Honolulu exceed the $236,000 mean by $96,000. The computation for Ventura is given by:

$$\text{Deviation from mean} = \text{data item} - \text{mean}$$

$$= 210 - 236 = -26$$

This indicates that home costs in Ventura are $26,000 below the mean.

The deviations from the mean for each of the ten given data items are shown in Table 12.12.

Table 12.12 Deviations from the Mean

Data item	Deviation: Data item − mean
332	$332 - 236 = 96$
256	$256 - 236 = 20$
251	$251 - 236 = 15$
235	$235 - 236 = -1$
223	$223 - 236 = -13$
215	$215 - 236 = -21$
215	$215 - 236 = -21$
213	$213 - 236 = -23$
210	$210 - 236 = -26$
210	$210 - 236 = -26$

The sum of deviations for a set of data is always zero. For the deviations shown in Table 12.12,

$$96 + 20 + 15 + (-1) + (-13) + (-21) + (-21) + (-23) + (-26) + (-26)$$

$$= 131 + (-131) = 0$$

This shows that we cannot find a measure of dispersion by finding the mean of the deviations, because this value is always zero. However, a kind of average of the deviations from the mean, called the **standard deviation**, can be computed. We do so by squaring each deviation and later introducing a square root in the computation. Here are the details on how to find the standard deviation of a set of data.

2 Determine the standard deviation for a data set.

> **Computing the Standard Deviation for a Data Set**
>
> 1. Find the mean of the data items.
> 2. Find the deviation of each data item from the mean:
>
> $$\text{data item} - \text{mean}$$
>
> 3. Square each deviation:
>
> $$(\text{data item} - \text{mean})^2$$
>
> 4. Sum the squared deviations:
>
> $$\Sigma(\text{data item} - \text{mean})^2$$
>
> 5. Divide the sum in step 4 by $n - 1$, where n represents the number of data items:
>
> $$\frac{\Sigma(\text{data item} - \text{mean})^2}{n - 1}$$
>
> 6. Take the square root of the quotient in step 5. This value is the standard deviation for the data set.
>
> $$\text{standard deviation} = \sqrt{\frac{\Sigma(\text{data item} - \text{mean})^2}{n - 1}}$$

Table 12.11 Highest New Home Costs

City	Mean Home Cost (in thousands of dollars, to the nearest thousand $)
Honolulu	$332
San Francisco	256
San Jose, CA	251
Santa Cruz, CA	235
Stamford, CT	223
Orange County, CA	215
Bergen County, NJ	215
Salinas, CA	213
Long Island, NY	210
Ventura, CA	210

Source: Places Rated Almanac.

The computation of the standard deviation can be organized using a table with three columns:

Data item	Deviation: Data item − mean	(Deviation)²: (Data item − mean)²

In Example 2, we worked out the first two columns of such a table. Let's continue working with the data for the most expensive homes in the United States and compute the standard deviation.

EXAMPLE 3 Computing the Standard Deviation

Table 12.11, showing the ten most expensive markets for new homes in the United States, is repeated in the margin. Find the standard deviation of the home costs.

Solution

1. **Find the mean.**

   From our work in Example 2, the mean is 236.

2. **Find the deviation of each data item from the mean: data item − mean.**

This, too, was done in Example 2 for each of the ten data items.

3. **Square each deviation: (data item − mean)^2.** We square each of the numbers in the (data item − mean) column, shown in Table 12.13. Notice that squaring the difference always results in a positive number.

Table 12.13   Computing the Standard Deviation

Data item	Deviation: Data item − mean	(Deviation)^2: (Data item − mean)^2
332	$332 - 236 = 96$	$96^2 = 96 \cdot 96 \qquad = 9216$
256	$256 - 236 = 20$	$20^2 = 20 \cdot 20 \qquad = 400$
251	$251 - 236 = 15$	$15^2 = 15 \cdot 15 \qquad = 225$
235	$235 - 236 = -1$	$(-1)^2 = (-1)(-1) \qquad = 1$
223	$223 - 236 = -13$	$(-13)^2 = (-13)(-13) = 169$
215	$215 - 236 = -21$	$(-21)^2 = (-21)(-21) = 441$
215	$215 - 236 = -21$	$(-21)^2 = (-21)(-21) = 441$
213	$213 - 236 = -23$	$(-23)^2 = (-23)(-23) = 529$
210	$210 - 236 = -26$	$(-26)^2 = (-26)(-26) = 676$
210	$210 - 236 = -26$	$(-26)^2 = (-26)(-26) = 676$
		12,774

> Adding the ten numbers in the third column gives the sum of the squared deviations: $\Sigma(\text{data item}-\text{mean})^2$.

4. **Sum the squared deviations: Σ(data item − mean)^2.** This step is shown in Table 12.13. The squares in the third column were added.

5. **Divide the sum in step 4 by $n - 1$, where n represents the number of data items.** The number of data items is 10, so we divide by 9.

$$\frac{\Sigma(\text{data item} - \text{mean})^2}{n - 1} = \frac{12{,}774}{10 - 1} = \frac{12{,}774}{9} \approx 1419.33$$

6. **The standard deviation is the square root of the quotient in step 5.**

$$\text{Standard deviation} = \sqrt{\frac{\Sigma(\text{data item} - \text{mean})^2}{n - 1}} = \sqrt{\frac{12{,}774}{9}} \approx 37.67$$

The standard deviation of the home costs in Table 12.11 is $37.67 thousand, or $37,670.

Example 4 illustrates that as the spread of data items increases, the standard deviation gets larger.

EXAMPLE 4   Computing the Standard Deviation

Find the standard deviation of the data items in each of the samples on page 622.

Sample A:

$$17, 18, 19, 20, 21, 22, 23$$

Sample B:

$$5, 10, 15, 20, 25, 30, 35$$

Solution Begin by finding the mean for each sample.
Sample A:

$$\text{Mean} = \frac{17 + 18 + 19 + 20 + 21 + 22 + 23}{7} = \frac{140}{7} = 20$$

Sample B:

$$\text{Mean} = \frac{5 + 10 + 15 + 20 + 25 + 30 + 35}{7} = \frac{140}{7} = 20$$

Although both samples have the same mean, the scores in sample B are more spread out. Thus, we would expect sample B to have the greater standard deviation. The computation of the standard deviation requires that we find $\Sigma(\text{data item} - \text{mean})^2$, shown in Table 12.14.

Table 12.14 Computing Standard Deviations for Two Samples

	Sample A			Sample B	
Data item	Deviation: Data item − mean	(Deviation)²: (Data item − mean)²	Data item	Deviation: Data item − mean	(Deviation)²: (Data item − mean)²
17	$17 - 20 = -3$	$(-3)^2 = 9$	5	$5 - 20 = -15$	$(-15)^2 = 225$
18	$18 - 20 = -2$	$(-2)^2 = 4$	10	$10 - 20 = -10$	$(-10)^2 = 100$
19	$19 - 20 = -1$	$(-1)^2 = 1$	15	$15 - 20 = -5$	$(-5)^2 = 25$
20	$20 - 20 = 0$	$0^2 = 0$	20	$20 - 20 = 0$	$0^2 = 0$
21	$21 - 20 = 1$	$1^2 = 1$	25	$25 - 20 = 5$	$5^2 = 25$
22	$22 - 20 = 2$	$2^2 = 4$	30	$30 - 20 = 10$	$10^2 = 100$
23	$23 - 20 = 3$	$3^2 = 9$	35	$35 - 20 = 15$	$15^2 = 225$
	$\Sigma(\text{data item} - \text{mean})^2 = 28$			$\Sigma(\text{data item} - \text{mean})^2 = 700$	

Each sample contains seven pieces of data, so we compute the standard deviation by dividing the sums in Table 12.14 by $7 - 1$, or 6, and taking the square root of each quotient.

$$\text{Standard deviation} = \sqrt{\frac{\Sigma(\text{data item} - \text{mean})^2}{n - 1}}$$

Sample A:

$$\text{Standard deviation} = \sqrt{\frac{28}{6}} \approx 2.16$$

Sample B:

$$\text{Standard deviation} = \sqrt{\frac{700}{6}} \approx 10.80$$

Sample A has a standard deviation of approximately 2.16, and sample B has a standard deviation of approximately 10.80. The scores in sample B are more spread out than those in sample A.

Figure 12.12 The standard deviation gets larger with increased dispersion among scores. In each case, the mean is 4.

Figure 12.12 illustrates four sets of data items organized in histograms. From left to right, the data items are

Figure 12.12 (a): 4, 4, 4, 4, 4, 4, 4

Figure 12.12 (b): 3, 3, 4, 4, 4, 5, 5

Figure 12.12 (c): 3, 3, 3, 4, 5, 5, 5

Figure 12.12 (d): 1, 1, 1, 4, 7, 7, 7

Each data set has a mean of 4. However, as the spread of data items increases, the standard deviation gets larger. Observe that when all the data items are the same, the standard deviation is 0.

EXAMPLE 5 Interpreting Standard Deviation

Two fifth grade classes have nearly identical mean scores on an aptitude test, but one class has a standard deviation three times that of the other. All other factors being equal, which class is easier to teach, and why?

Solution The class with the smaller standard deviation is easier to teach because there is less variation among student aptitudes. Course work can be aimed at the average student without too much concern that the work will be too easy for some or too difficult for others. By contrast, the class with greater dispersion poses a greater challenge. By teaching to the average student, the students whose scores are significantly above the mean will be bored; students whose scores are significantly below the mean will be confused.

In 1997, the mean salary for a U.S. public school teacher was approximately $40,000. Nearly 34 teachers can be hired for the salary of one NFL quarterback.

Technology

Standard Deviation on a Calculator

Many scientific calculators and all graphing calculators will allow you to enter data items, automatically displaying the standard deviation. Graphing calculators require that you specify if data items are from an entire population or a sample of the population. Many calculators use s to represent the sample standard deviation and σ to represent the population standard deviation.

In our discussion of measures of central tendency, we saw that these measures are sometimes given for the entire population. For example, in 1997 the mean salary for National Football League quarterbacks was $1,346,000 (source: NFL Players Association). We can use this mean for the population of NFL quarterbacks to find the standard deviation for their salaries. Subtract the mean salary from each player's salary and use the procedure for computing the standard deviation.

By contrast to the population of NFL quarterbacks, most populations are too large to obtain data items for all members. Means and standard deviations are calculated using data items from a random sample of the population. Over the long run, statisticians expect the mean and the standard deviation for the sample to agree with the mean and the standard deviation for the population. By calculating the standard deviation for a random sample, statisticians can gain a good estimate for the standard deviation of the entire population.

Exercise Set 12.3

 Practice Exercises

In Exercises 1–10, find the range for each group of data items.

1. 1, 2, 3, 4, 5
2. 16, 17, 18, 19, 20
3. 7, 9, 9, 15
4. 11, 13, 14, 15, 17
5. 3, 3, 4, 4, 5, 5
6. 3, 3, 3, 4, 5, 5, 5
7. 1, 1, 1, 4, 7, 7, 7
8. 6, 6, 6, 6, 7, 7, 7, 4, 8, 3
9. 9, 5, 9, 5, 9, 5, 9, 5
10. 6, 10, 6, 10, 6, 10, 6, 10

In Exercises 11–14, a group of data items and their mean are given. Find a. the deviation from the mean for each of the data items and b. the sum of the deviations in part (a).

11. 3, 5, 7, 12, 18, 27; Mean = 12
12. 84, 88, 90, 95, 98; Mean = 91
13. 29, 38, 48, 49, 53, 77; Mean = 49
14. 60, 60, 62, 65, 65, 65, 66, 67, 70, 70; Mean = 65

In Exercises 15–20, find a. the mean; b. the deviation from the mean for each data item; and c. the sum of the deviations in part (b).

15. 85, 95, 90, 85, 100
16. 94, 62, 88, 85, 91
17. 146, 153, 155, 160, 161
18. 150, 132, 144, 122
19. 2.25, 3.50, 2.75, 3.10, 1.90
20. 0.35, 0.37, 0.41, 0.39, 0.43

In Exercises 21–30, find the standard deviation for each group of data items.

21. 1, 2, 3, 4, 5
22. 16, 17, 18, 19, 20
23. 7, 9, 9, 15
24. 11, 13, 14, 15, 17
25. 3, 3, 4, 4, 5, 5
26. 3, 3, 3, 4, 5, 5, 5
27. 1, 1, 1, 4, 7, 7, 7
28. 6, 6, 6, 6, 7, 7, 7, 4, 8, 3
29. 9, 5, 9, 5, 9, 5, 9, 5
30. 6, 10, 6, 10, 6, 10, 6, 10

In Exercises 31–32, compute the mean, range, and standard deviation for the data items in each of the three samples. Then describe one way in which the samples are alike and one way in which they are different.

31. Sample A: 6, 8, 10, 12, 14, 16, 18
    Sample B: 6, 7, 8, 12, 16, 17, 18
    Sample C: 6, 6, 6, 12, 18, 18, 18
32. Sample A: 8, 10, 12, 14, 16, 18, 20
    Sample B: 8, 9, 10, 14, 18, 19, 20
    Sample C: 8, 8, 8, 14, 20, 20, 20

 Application Exercises

33. The table at the top of the next column gives the number of police officers (in thousands, rounded to the nearest thousand) for the ten largest police forces in the United

States. (Miami is included because the city has more police officers than most states.) Find the mean and the standard deviation for this set of data.

State	Police Officers (thousands)
1. New York	68
2. California	66
3. Texas	41
4. Illinois	36
5. Florida	33
6. New Jersey	27
7. Pennsylvania	24
8. Ohio	21
9. Miami	20
10. Georgia	17

Source: U.S. Bureau of Justice Statistics

34. The accompanying table gives the number of U.S. citizens (in thousands) residing in other countries. Find the mean and the standard deviation for this set of data.

Nation	U.S. Citizens (thousands)
1. Mexico	539
2. Germany	354
3. Canada	296
4. United Kingdom	259
5. Israel	112
6. Italy	104
7. Dominican Republic	97
8. Spain	79
9. Australia	62
10. France	59

Source: U.S. Census Bureau

35. From 1918 to 1931, Babe Ruth was the American League home-run champion 12 times. The number of home runs Ruth hit per year for each of the 12 years is shown below. Find the mean and the standard deviation for this set of data.

11, 29, 54, 59, 41, 46, 47, 60, 54, 46, 49, 46

A 1996 study of student achievement in math and science ranked 41 countries. Scoring was on a scale of 200 to 800 points. Results for 15 of the countries in science are shown on the next page. Use these results to solve Exercises 36–38.

**Science Scores
Top Five**

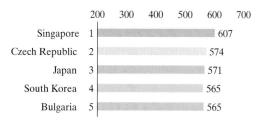

Singapore	1	607
Czech Republic	2	574
Japan	3	571
South Korea	4	565
Bulgaria	5	565

In the Middle

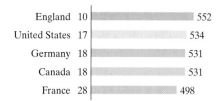

England	10	552
United States	17	534
Germany	18	531
Canada	18	531
France	28	498

Bottom Five

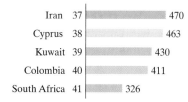

Iran	37	470
Cyprus	38	463
Kuwait	39	430
Colombia	40	411
South Africa	41	326

Source: International Mathematics and Science Study, 1996

36. Find the mean and the standard deviation for the top five countries.

37. Find the mean and the standard deviation for the five countries in the middle.

38. Find the mean and the standard deviation for the bottom five countries.

39. The bar graph shows the number of children home-educated in the United States. Find the mean and the standard deviation for the six data items.

Number of Children Home-Educated in the U.S.

Source: National Home Education Research Institute

40. (Work this exercise with a calculator.) Shown below is the yearly per capita expenditure for the fifty U.S. states and Washington D.C. for police protection. Find the mean per capita expenditure and the standard deviation for the 51 data items.

AL	102.9	AK	532.9	AZ	194.8
AR	76.1	CA	202.6	CO	152.0
CT	135.8	DE	175.9	DC	548.8
FL	160.9	GA	123.9	HI	165.6
ID	102.1	IL	152.7	IN	92.1
IA	108.6	KS	108.9	KY	92.2
LA	144.7	ME	87.5	MD	175.6
MA	139.9	MI	170.8	MN	128.1
MS	74.8	MO	113.6	MT	117.1
NE	111.3	NV	276.4	NH	104.7
NJ	180.5	NM	184.4	NY	216.3
NC	109.0	ND	101.8	OH	121.7
OK	110.8	OR	147.9	PA	124.7
RI	143.2	SC	94.0	SD	103.8
TN	102.1	TX	112.8	UT	133.1
VT	109.9	VA	138.9	WA	169.3
WV	67.2	WI	153.0	WY	202.5

Source: Statistical Abstract of the U.S.

 Writing in Mathematics

41. Describe how to find the range of a data set.

42. Describe why the range might not be the best measure of dispersion.

43. Describe how the standard deviation is computed.

44. Describe what the standard deviation reveals about a data set.

45. If a set of test scores has a standard deviation of zero, what does this mean about the scores?

46. Two classes took a statistics test. Both classes had a mean score of 73. The scores of class A had a standard deviation of 5.6, and those of class B had a standard deviation of 10. Discuss the difference between the two classes' performance on the test.

47. A sample of cereals indicates a mean potassium content per serving of 93 milligrams, and a standard deviation of 2 milligrams. Write a description of what this means for a person who knows nothing about statistics.

Critical Thinking Exercises

48. Which one of the following is true?
    a. If the same number is added to each data item in a set of data, the standard deviation does not change.
    b. If each number in a data set is multiplied by 4, the standard deviation is doubled.
    c. It is possible for a set of scores to have a negative standard deviation.
    d. Data sets with different means cannot have the same standard deviation.

49. Describe a situation in which a relatively large standard deviation is desirable.

50. If a set of test scores has a large range but a small standard deviation, describe what this means about students' performance on the test.

51. Use the data 1, 2, 3, 5, 6, 7. Without actually computing the standard deviation, which of the following best approximates the standard deviation?
    a. 2   b. 6   c. 10   d. 20

Technology Exercises

52. Use the statistical mode of a calculator to determine the standard deviation of the following data items: 3, 9, 6, 10, 5, 6, 9, 9, 3, 6.

53. Use the statistical mode of a calculator to determine the standard deviation of the following data items: 13, 29, 65, 23, 65, 96, 91, 95, 73, 66.

Group Exercises

54. As a follow up to Group Exercise 73 on page 617, the group should reassemble and compute the standard deviation for each data set whose mean you previously determined. Does the standard deviation tell you anything new or interesting about the entire group or subgroups that you did not discover during the previous group activity?

55. Two fascinating sources of data are the *Wall Street Journal Almanac* (filled with terrific graphs) and the *American Almanac: Statistical Abstract of the United States.* Each volume is updated yearly. Group members should consult these sources (or an equivalent Internet source) and select intriguing data. The group's function is to use statistics to tell a story. Once "intriguing" data are identified, as a group:
    a. Summarize the data. Use words, frequency distributions, and graphic displays.
    b. Compute measures of central tendency and variability, using these statistics to discuss the data.

SECTION 12.4   *The Normal Distribution*

Objectives

1. Recognize characteristics of normal distributions.
2. Understand the 68–95–99.7 Rule.
3. Find scores at a specified standard deviation from the mean.
4. Use the 68–95–99.7 Rule.
5. Convert a data item to a *z*-score.
6. Understand and use percentiles.
7. Use and interpret margins of error.
8. Recognize distributions that are not normal.

Mean Adult Heights

5'2" 5'7"   5'5" 5'10"   5'7" 6'0"

1900   2000   2050

Source: National Center for Health Statistics

Our heights are on the rise! In one million B.C., the mean height for men was 4 feet 6 inches. The mean height for women was 4 feet 2 inches. Because of improved diets and medical care, the mean height for men is now 5 feet 10 inches and for women it is 5 feet 5 inches. Mean adult heights are expected to plateau by 2050.

Suppose that a researcher selects a random sample of 100 adult men, measures their heights, and constructs a histogram. The graph is shown in Figure 12.13(a) at the top of the next page. Figure 12.13 illustrates what happens as the sample size increases. In Figure 12.13(c), if you were to fold the graph down the middle, the left side would fit the right side. As we move out from the middle, the heights of the bars are the same to the left and right. Such a histogram is called

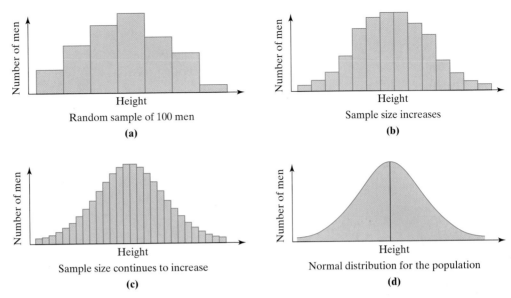

Figure 12.13 Heights of adult males

1 Recognize characteristics of normal distributions.

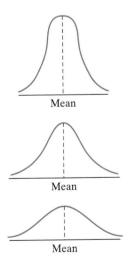

Figure 12.14 As the standard deviation increases from the top distribution to the bottom one, the normal distribution becomes more spread out, but retains its symmetric bell shape.

symmetric. As the sample size increases, so does the graph's symmetry. If it were possible to measure the heights of all adult males, the entire population, the histogram would approach what is called the **normal distribution**, shown in Figure 12.13(d). This distribution is also called the **bell curve** or the **Gaussian distribution**, named for the German mathematician Carl Friedrich Gauss (1777–1855).

Figure 12.13(d) illustrates that the normal distribution is bell-shaped and symmetric about a vertical line through its center. Furthermore, **the mean, median, and mode** of a normal distribution **are all equal** and located at the center of the distribution.

The shape of the normal distribution depends on the mean and the standard deviation. Figure 12.14 illustrates three normal distributions with the same mean, but different standard deviations. As the standard deviation increases, the distribution becomes more dispersed, or spread out.

The normal distribution provides a wonderful model for all kinds of phenomena because many sets of data items closely resemble this population distribution. Examples include heights and weights of adult males, intelligence quotients, SAT scores, prices paid for a new car model, and life spans of light bulbs. In these distributions, the data items tend to cluster around the mean. The more an item differs from the mean, the less likely it is to occur.

The normal distribution is used to make predictions about an entire population using data from a sample. In this section, we focus on the characteristics and applications of the normal distribution.

2 Understand the 68–95–99.7 Rule.

The Standard Deviation and *z*-Scores in Normal Distributions

The standard deviation plays a crucial role in the normal distribution, summarized by the **68–95–99.7 rule**. This rule is illustrated in Figure 12.15 on page 628.

Well-Worn Steps and the Normal Distribution

These ancient steps each take on the shape of a normal distribution when the picture is viewed from upside down. The center of each step is more worn than the outer edges. The greatest number of people have walked in the center, making this the mean, median, and mode for where people have walked.

The 68–95–99.7 Rule for the Normal Distribution

1. Approximately 68% of the data items fall within 1 standard deviation of the mean (in both directions).
2. Approximately 95% of the data items fall within 2 standard deviations of the mean.
3. Approximately 99.7% of the data items fall within 3 standard deviations of the mean.

Figure 12.15

Figure 12.15 illustrates that a very small percentage of the data in a normal distribution lies more than 3 standard deviations above or below the mean. As we move from the mean, the curve falls rapidly, and then more and more gradually, toward the horizontal axis. The tails of the curve approach, but never touch, the horizontal axis, although they are quite close to the axis at 3 standard deviations from the mean. The range of the population normal distribution is infinite. No matter how far out from the mean we move, there is always the probability (although very small) of a data item occurring even farther out.

The SAT is a test that has been taken by many college-bound seniors since 1941. Each part has a mean of 500 and a standard deviation of 100. Although there can be no scores less than 200 or more than 800, the scores can be modeled by the normal distribution.

3 Find scores at a specified standard deviation from the mean.

EXAMPLE 1 Finding Scores at a Specified Standard Deviation from the Mean

With a mean of 500 and a standard deviation of 100, find the SAT score that is

a. 2 standard deviations above the mean.
b. 3 standard deviations below the mean.

Solution

a. First, let us find the SAT score that is 2 standard deviations above the mean.

$$\text{Score} = \text{Mean} + 2 \cdot \text{standard deviation}$$
$$= 500 + 2 \cdot 100 = 500 + 200 = 700$$

An SAT score of 700 is 2 standard deviations above the mean.

b. Next, let us find the SAT score that is 3 standard deviations below the mean.

Score = Mean − 3 · standard deviation

= 500 − 3 · 100 = 500 − 300 = 200

An SAT score of 200 is 3 standard deviations below the mean.

The distribution of SAT scores is illustrated as a population normal distribution in Figure 12.16.

Normal Distribution of SAT Scores

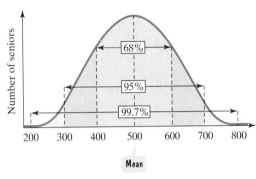

Figure 12.16

4 Use the 68–95–99.7 rule.

EXAMPLE 2   Using the 68–95–99.7 Rule

Use the distribution of SAT scores in Figure 12.16 to find the percentage of seniors who score

a. between 400 and 600.   b. between 500 and 600.   c. above 700.

Solution

a. The 68–95–99.7 rule states that approximately 68% of the data items fall within 1 standard deviation, 100, of the mean, 500.

mean − 1 · standard deviation = 500 − 1 · 100 = 400

mean + 1 · standard deviation = 500 + 1 · 100 = 600

Figure 12.16 shows that 68% of the seniors score between 400 and 600.

b. The percentage of seniors who score between 500 and 600 is not given directly in Figure 12.16 or 12.17. Because of the distribution's symmetry, the percentage who score between 400 and 500 is the same as the percentage who score between 500 and 600. Figure 12.17 indicates that 68% score between 400 and 600. Thus, half of 68%, or 34%, of seniors score between 500 and 600.

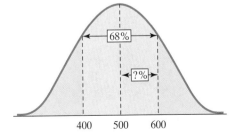

Figure 12.17 What percentage score between 500 and 600?

c. The percentage of seniors who score above 700 is not given directly in Figure 12.16 or 12.18. A score of 700 is 2 standard deviations, $2 \cdot 100$, above the mean, 500. The 68–95–99.7 rule states that approximately 95% of the data items fall within 2 standard deviations of the mean. Thus, approximately $100\% - 95\%$, or 5%, of the data items are farther than 2 standard deviations from the mean. The 5% of the data items are represented by the two shaded green regions in Figure 12.18. Because of the distribution's symmetry, half of 5%, or 2.5%, of the data items are more than 2 standard deviations above the mean. This means that 2.5% of seniors score above 700.

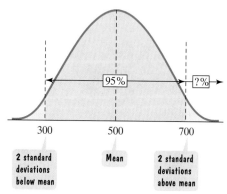

300   500   700

2 standard deviations below mean   Mean   2 standard deviations above mean

Figure 12.18 What percentage score above 700?

Because the SAT has a mean of 500 and a standard deviation of 100, a score of 700 lies 2 standard deviations above the mean. In a normal distribution, a **z-score** describes how many standard deviations a particular data item lies above or below the mean. Thus, the z-score for the data item 700 is 2.

The following formula can be used to express a data item in a normal distribution as a z-score.

5 Convert a data item to a z-score.

> **Computing z-Scores**
>
> A z-score describes how many standard deviations a data item in a normal distribution lies above or below the mean. The z-score can be obtained using
>
> $$z\text{-score} = \frac{\text{data item} - \text{mean}}{\text{standard deviation}}.$$
>
> Data items above the mean have positive z-scores. Data items below the mean have negative z-scores. The z-score for the mean is 0.

EXAMPLE 3 Computing z-Scores

The mean weight of newborn infants is 7 pounds and the standard deviation is 0.8 pound. The characteristic of weight of newborn infants is normally distributed. Find the z-score for a weight of

a. 9 pounds.   b. 7 pounds.   c. 6 pounds.

Solution   We compute the z-score for each weight by using the z-score formula. The mean is 7 and the standard deviation is 0.8.

a. The z-score for a weight of 9 pounds is:

$$z\text{-score for 9} = \frac{\text{data item} - \text{mean}}{\text{standard deviation}} = \frac{9 - 7}{0.8} = \frac{2}{0.8} = 2.5.$$

A 9-pound infant is a chubby little tyke, with a weight that is 2.5 standard deviations above the mean.

b. The z-score for a weight of 7 pounds is:

$$z\text{-score for 7} = \frac{\text{data item} - \text{mean}}{\text{standard deviation}} = \frac{7 - 7}{0.8} = \frac{0}{0.8} = 0.$$

The z-score for the mean is always 0. A 7-pound infant is right at the mean, deviating 0 pounds above or below it.

c. The z-score for a weight of 6 pounds is:

$$z\text{-score for 6} = \frac{\text{data item} - \text{mean}}{\text{standard deviation}} = \frac{6 - 7}{0.8} = \frac{-1}{0.8} = -1.25.$$

A 6-pound infant's weight is 1.25 standard deviations below the mean.

Figure 12.19 shows the normal distribution of weights of newborn infants. The horizontal axis is labeled in terms of weights and z-scores.

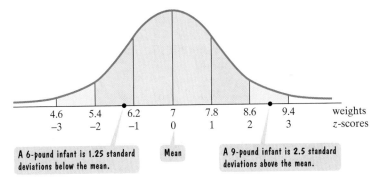

Normal Distribution of Weights of Newborn Infants

Figure 12.19 Infant's weights are normally distributed.

In Example 4, we consider two normally distributed sets of test scores, in which a higher score generally indicates a better result. To compare scores on two different tests in relation to the mean on each test, we can use z-scores. The better score is the item with the greater z-score.

EXAMPLE 4   Using and Interpreting z-Scores

A student scores 70 on an arithmetic test and 66 on a vocabulary test. The scores for both tests are normally distributed. The arithmetic test has a mean of 60 and a standard deviation of 20. The vocabulary test has a mean of 60 and a standard deviation of 2. On which test did the student have the better score?

Solution To answer the question, we need to find the student's z-score on each test, using:

$$z = \frac{\text{data item} - \text{mean}}{\text{standard deviation}}.$$

The arithmetic test has a mean of 60 and a standard deviation of 20.

$$z\text{-score for } 70 = \frac{70 - 60}{20} = \frac{10}{20} = 0.5$$

The vocabulary test has a mean of 60 and a standard deviation of 2.

$$z\text{-score for } 66 = \frac{66 - 60}{2} = \frac{6}{2} = 3$$

The arithmetic score is half a standard deviation above the mean, whereas the vocabulary score is 3 standard deviations above the mean. The student did much better than the mean on the vocabulary test.

The IQ Controversy

Is intelligence something we are born with or is it a quality that can be manipulated through education? Can it be measured accurately and is IQ the way to measure it? There are no clear answers to these questions. Historical misuses of intelligence testing is in evidence from the Nazis to American racists.

In a study by Carolyn Bird (*Pygmalion in the Classroom*), a group of third grade teachers was told that they had classes of students with IQs well above the mean. These classes made incredible progress throughout the year. In reality, these were not gifted kids, but, rather, a random sample of all third-graders. It was the teachers' expectations, and not the IQs of the students, that resulted in increased performance.

EXAMPLE 5   Understanding z-Scores

Intelligence quotients (IQs) are normally distributed with a mean of 100 and a standard deviation of 15. What is the IQ corresponding to a z-score of -1.5?

Solution   The *negative sign* in -1.5 tells us that the score in question is one-and-a-half standard deviations *below* the mean. We need to determine how many units below the mean the score is. We do so by adding one standard deviation, 15, and half of a standard deviation.

$$15 + \tfrac{1}{2} \cdot 15 = 15 + 7.5 = 22.5$$

Thus, the score is 22.5 units below the mean. We find the score by subtracting 22.5 from the mean.

$$100 - 22.5 = 77.5$$

The IQ corresponding to a z-score of -1.5 is 77.5.

6 Understand and use percentiles.

z-Scores and Percentiles

A z-score measures a data item's position in a normal distribution. Another measure of a data item's position is its **percentile**. Percentiles are often associated with scores on standardized tests. If a score is in the 45th percentile, this means that 45% of the scores are less than this score. If a score is in the 95th percentile, this indicates that 95% of the scores are less that this score.

Percentiles

If $n\%$ of the items in a distribution are less than a particular data item, we say that the data item is in the **nth percentile** of the distribution.

EXAMPLE 6   Interpreting Percentile

A student scored in the 93rd percentile on the SAT. What does this mean?

Solution   By scoring in the 93rd percentile, the student did better than about 93% of all those who took the exam.

Table 12.15 gives a percentile interpretation for z-scores. For example, the corresponding percentile for a data item with a z-score of 2 is 97.72. A student with this score on a test whose results are normally distributed outperformed 97.72% of those who took the test.

In a normal distribution, the mean, median, and mode all have a corresponding z-score of 0. Table 12.15 shows that the percentile for a z-score of 0 is 50.00. Thus, 50% of the data items in a normal distribution are less than the mean, median, and mode. Fifty percent of the data items are greater than or equal to the mean, median, and mode.

Table 12.15 z-Scores and Percentiles

z-score	Percentile	z-score	Percentile	z-score	Percentile	z-score	Percentile
−4.0	0.00	−1.0	15.87	0.0	50.00	1.1	86.43
−3.5	0.02	−0.95	17.11	0.05	51.99	1.2	88.49
−3.0	0.13	−0.90	18.41	0.10	53.98	1.3	90.32
−2.9	0.19	−0.85	19.77	0.15	55.96	1.4	91.92
−2.8	0.26	−0.80	21.19	0.20	57.93	1.5	93.32
−2.7	0.35	−0.75	22.66	0.25	59.87	1.6	94.52
−2.6	0.47	−0.70	24.20	0.30	61.79	1.7	95.54
−2.5	0.62	−0.65	25.78	0.35	63.68	1.8	96.41
−2.4	0.82	−0.60	27.43	0.40	65.54	1.9	97.13
−2.3	1.07	−0.55	29.12	0.45	67.36	2.0	97.72
−2.2	1.39	−0.50	30.85	0.50	69.15	2.1	98.21
−2.1	1.79	−0.45	32.64	0.55	70.88	2.2	98.61
−2.0	2.28	−0.40	34.46	0.60	72.57	2.3	98.93
−1.9	2.87	−0.35	36.32	0.65	74.22	2.4	99.18
−1.8	3.59	−0.30	38.21	0.70	75.80	2.5	99.38
−1.7	4.46	−0.25	40.13	0.75	77.34	2.6	99.53
−1.6	5.48	−0.20	42.07	0.80	78.81	2.7	99.65
−1.5	6.68	−0.15	44.04	0.85	80.23	2.8	99.74
−1.4	8.08	−0.10	46.02	0.90	81.59	2.9	99.81
−1.3	9.68	−0.05	48.01	0.95	82.89	3.0	99.87
−1.2	11.51	0.0	50.00	1.0	84.13	3.5	99.98
−1.1	13.57					4.0	99.99

Table 12.15 can be used to find the percentage of data items that are less than any data item in a normal distribution. Begin by converting the data item to a z-score. Then, use the table to find the percentile for this z-score. This percentile is the percentage of data items that are less than the data item in question.

EXAMPLE 7   Finding the Percentage of Data Items Less Than a Given Data Item

According to the Department of Health and Education, cholesterol levels are normally distributed. For men between 18 and 24 years, the mean is 178.1 (measured in milligrams per 100 milliliters) and the standard deviation is 40.7. What percentage of men in this age range have a cholesterol level less than 239.15?

Solution   If you are familiar with your own cholesterol level, you probably recognize that a level of 239.15 is fairly high for a young man. Because of this, we would expect most young men to have a level less than 239.15. Let's see if this is so. Table 12.15 requires that we use z-scores. We compute the z-score for a 239.15 cholesterol level by using the z-score formula.

$$z\text{-score for } 239.15 = \frac{\text{data item } - \text{ mean}}{\text{standard deviation}} = \frac{239.15 - 178.1}{40.7} = \frac{61.05}{40.7} = 1.5$$

A Portion of Table 12.15

z-score	Percentile
1.4	91.92
1.5	93.32
1.6	94.52

A man between 18 and 24 with a 239.15 cholesterol level is 1.5 standard deviations above the mean. Table 12.15 gives the percentile corresponding to $z = 1.5$. Find 1.5 in the z-score column in the right portion of the table. The percentile given to the right of 1.5 is 93.32. This means that 93.32% of men between 18 and 24 have a cholesterol level less than $z = 1.5$, the z-score for a 239.15 cholesterol level.

The normal distribution accounts for all data items, meaning 100% of the scores. This means that Table 12.15 can also be used to find the percentage of data items that are greater than any data item in a normal distribution. Use the percentile in the table to determine the percentage of data items less than the data item in question. Then subtract this percentage from 100% to find the percentage of data items greater than the item in question. In using this technique we will treat the phrase "greater than" and "greater than or equal to" as equivalent.

EXAMPLE 8   Finding the Percentage of Data Items Greater Than a Given Data Item

Lengths of pregnancy of women are normally distributed with a mean of 266 days and a standard deviation of 16 days. What percentage of children are born from pregnancies lasting more than 274 days?

Solution   Table 12.15 requires that we use z-scores. We compute the z-score for a 274-day pregnancy by using the z-score formula.

$$z\text{-score for } 274 = \frac{\text{data item } - \text{ mean}}{\text{standard deviation}} = \frac{274 - 266}{16} = \frac{8}{16} = 0.5$$

A 274-day pregnancy is 0.5 standard deviation above the mean. Table 12.15 gives the percentile corresponding to $z = 0.5$. Turn back to page 633 and find 0.50 in the z-score column in the third part of the table. The percentile given to the right of 0.50 is 69.15. This means that 69.15% of pregnancies last less than 274 days. We find the number of pregnancies lasting more than 274 days by subtracting 69.15% from 100%.

$$100\% - 69.15\% = 30.85\%$$

Thus, 30.85% of children are born from pregnancies lasting more than 274 days.

We have seen how Table 12.15 is used to find the percentage of data items that are less than or greater than any given item. The table can also be used to find the percentage of data items *between* two given items. Because the percentile for each item is the percentage of data items less than the given item, the percentage of data between the two given items is found by subtracting the lesser percent from the greater percent. This is illustrated in Figure 12.20.

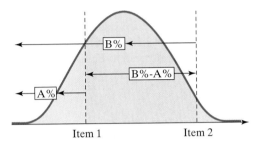

Figure 12.20 The percentile for data item 1 is A. The percentile for data item 2 is B. The percentage of data items between item 1 and item 2 is B% − A%.

Finding the Percentage of Data Items between Two Given Items in a Normal Distribution

1. Convert each given data item to a z-score:

$$z = \frac{\text{data item} - \text{mean}}{\text{standard deviation}}.$$

2. Use Table 12.15 to find the percentile corresponding to each z-score in step 1.
3. Subtract the lesser percentile from the greater percentile and attach a % sign.

EXAMPLE 9 Finding the Percentage of Data Items between Two Given Data Items

According to the National Federation of State High School Associations, the amount of time that high school students work at jobs each week is normally distributed with a mean of 10.7 hours and a standard deviation of 11.2 hours. What percentage of high school students work between 5.1 and 38.7 hours each week?

Solution

Step 1 Convert each given data item to a z-score.

$$z\text{-score for } 5.1 = \frac{\text{data item} - \text{mean}}{\text{standard deviation}} = \frac{5.1 - 10.7}{11.2} = \frac{-5.6}{11.2} = -0.5$$

$$z\text{-score for } 38.7 = \frac{\text{data item} - \text{mean}}{\text{standard deviation}} = \frac{38.7 - 10.7}{11.2} = \frac{28}{11.2} = 2.5$$

A Portion of Table 12.15

z-score	Percentile
−0.55	29.12
−0.50	30.85
−0.45	32.64

Step 2 Use Table 12.15 to find the percentile corresponding to these z-scores. Table 12.15 gives the percentile corresponding to $z = -0.5$. Find −0.50 in the z-score column in the second part of the table. The percentile given to the right of −0.50 is 30.85. This means that 30.85% of high school students work less than 5.1 hours each week.

Table 12.15 also gives the percentile corresponding to $z = 2.5$. Find 2.5 in the z-score column in the far-right portion of the table. The percentile given to the right of 2.5 is 99.38. This means that 99.38% of high school students work less than 38.7 hours per week.

Step 3 Subtract the lesser percentile from the greater percentile and attach a % sign. Subtracting percentiles, we obtain

$$99.38 - 30.85 = 68.53.$$

Thus, 68.53% of high school students work between 5.1 and 38.7 hours each week. The solution is illustrated in Figure 12.21.

A Portion of Table 12.15

z-score	Percentile
2.4	99.18
2.5	99.38
2.6	99.53

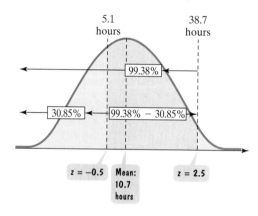

Figure 12.21

---

7 Use and interpret margins of error.

Polls and Margins of Error

When you were between the ages of 6 and 14, how would you have responded to this question:

What Is Bad About Being a Kid?

Kids Say	
Getting bossed around	17%
School, homework	15%
Can't do everything I want	11%
Chores	9%
Being grounded	9%

Source: Penn, Schoen, and Berland using 1172 interviews with children ages 6 to 14 from May 14 to June 1, 1999. Margin of error: ±2.9%

What is bad about being a kid?

In a random sample of 1172 children ages 6 to 14, 17% of the children responded, "Getting bossed around." The problem is that this is a single random sample. Do 17% of kids in the entire population of children ages 6 to 14 think that getting bossed around as a kid is a bad thing?

Statisticians use properties of the normal distribution to estimate the probability that a result obtained from a single sample reflects what is truly happening in the population. If you look at the results of a poll like the one shown in the margin, you will observe that a *margin of error* is reported. Surveys and opinion polls often give a margin of error. Let's use our understanding of the normal distribution to see how to calculate and interpret margins of error.

Suppose that p% of the population of children ages 6 to 14 hold the opinion that getting bossed around is a bad thing about being a kid. Instead of taking only one random sample of 1172 children, we repeat the process of selecting a random sample of 1172 children hundreds of times. Then, we calculate the percentage of children for each sample who think being bossed around is bad. With random sampling, we expect to find the percentage in many of the samples close to p%, with relatively few samples having percent-

Percentage of children who feel
being bossed around is bad

Figure 12.22 Percentage of children
who feel being bossed around is bad

ages far from $p\%$. Figure 12.22 shows that the percentages of children from the hundreds of samples form a normal distribution. The mean of this distribution is the actual population percent, $p\%$, and is the most frequent result from the samples.

Mathematicians have shown that the standard deviation of a normal distribution of samples like the one in Figure 12.22 is approximately $\dfrac{1}{2\sqrt{n}}$, where n is the sample size. Using the 68–95–99.7 rule, approximately 95% of the samples have a percentage within 2 standard deviations of the true population percentage, $p\%$:

$$2 \text{ standard deviations} = 2 \cdot \dfrac{1}{2\sqrt{n}} = \dfrac{1}{\sqrt{n}}$$

If we use a single random sample of size n, there is a 95% probability that the percent obtained will lie within two standard deviations, or $\dfrac{1}{\sqrt{n}}$, of the true population percent. We can be 95% confident that the true population percent lies between

$$\text{the sample percent} - \dfrac{1}{\sqrt{n}}$$

and

$$\text{the sample percent} + \dfrac{1}{\sqrt{n}}.$$

We call $\pm \dfrac{1}{\sqrt{n}}$ the **margin of error**.

Margin of Error in a Survey

If a statistic is obtained from a random sample of size n, there is a 95% probability that it lies within $\dfrac{1}{\sqrt{n}}$ of the true population statistic, where $\pm \dfrac{1}{\sqrt{n}}$ is called the **margin of error**.

What Is Bad About Being a Kid?

Kids Say	
Getting bossed around	17%
School, homework	15%
Can't do everything I want	11%
Chores	9%
Being grounded	9%

Source: Penn, Schoen, and Berland using 1172 interviews with children ages 6 to 14 from May 14 to June 1, 1999. Margin of error: ±2.9%
What Is Bad About Being a Kid? (Reproduced from page 636 so you do not have to turn back a page.)

EXAMPLE 10   Using and Interpreting Margin of Error

In a random sample of 1172 children ages 6 to 14, 17% of the children said getting bossed around is a bad thing about being a kid.

a. Verify the margin of error that was given for this survey.

b. Write a statement about the percentage of children in the population who feel that getting bossed around is a bad thing about being a kid.

Solution

a. The sample size is $n = 1172$. The margin of error is

$$\pm \frac{1}{\sqrt{n}} = \pm \frac{1}{\sqrt{1172}} \approx \pm 0.029 = \pm 2.9\%.$$

b. There is a 95% probability that the true population percentage lies between

$$\text{the sample percent} - \frac{1}{\sqrt{n}} = 17\% - 2.9\% = 14.1\%$$

and

$$\text{the sample percent} + \frac{1}{\sqrt{n}} = 17\% + 2.9\% = 19.9\%.$$

We can be 95% confident that between 14.1% and 19.9% of all children feel that getting bossed around is a bad thing about being a kid.

8 Recognize distributions that are not normal.

Other Kinds of Distributions

The histogram in Figure 12.23 represents the frequencies of the ages of women interviewed by Kinsey and his colleagues in their study of female sexual behavior. This distribution is not symmetric. The greatest frequency of women interviewed was in the 16–20 age range. The bars get shorter and shorter after this. The shorter bars fall on the right, indicating that relatively few older women were included in Kinsey's interviews.

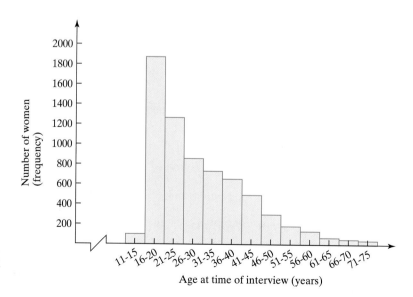

Figure 12.23 Histogram of the ages of females interviewed by Kinsey and his associates.

Although the normal distribution is the most important of all distributions in terms of analyzing data, not all data can be approximated by this symmetric distribution with its mean, median, and mode all having the same value.

In our discussion of measures of central tendency, we mentioned that the median, rather than the mean, is used to summarize weekly earnings. Figure 12.24 illustrates the population distribution of weekly earnings in the United States. There is no upper limit on weekly earnings on the high side. The relatively few people with very high weekly incomes tend to pull the mean income to a value greater than the median. The most frequent income, the mode, occurs toward the low end of the data items. The mean, median, and mode do not have the same value, and a normal distribution is not an appropriate model for describing weekly earnings in the United States.

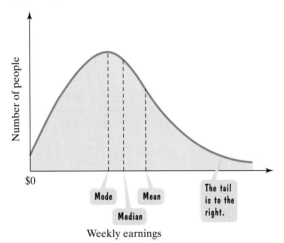

Weekly earnings

Figure 12.24 Skewed to the right

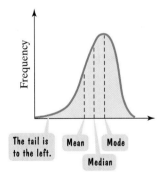

Figure 12.25 Skewed to the left

The distribution in Figure 12.24 is called a *skewed distribution*. A distribution of data is **skewed** if a large number of data items are piled up at one end or the other, with a "tail" at the opposite end. In the distribution of weekly earnings in Figure 12.24, the tail is to the right. Such a distribution is said to be **skewed to the right.**

By contrast to the distribution of weekly earnings, the distribution in Figure 12.25 has more data items at the high end of the scale than at the low end. The tail of this distribution is to the left. The distribution is said to be **skewed to the left.** In many colleges, an example of a distribution skewed to the left is based on the student ratings of faculty teaching performance. Most professors are given rather high ratings, while only a few are rated terrible. These low ratings pull the value of the mean lower than the median.

Exercise Set 12.4

 Practice and Application Exercises

The scores on a test are normally distributed with a mean of 100 and a standard deviation of 20. In Exercises 1–10, find the score that is

1. 1 standard deviation above the mean.
2. 2 standard deviations above the mean.
3. 3 standard deviations above the mean.
4. $1\frac{1}{2}$ standard deviations above the mean.
5. $2\frac{1}{2}$ standard deviations above the mean.
6. 1 standard deviation below the mean.
7. 2 standard deviations below the mean.
8. 3 standard deviations below the mean.

9. one-half a standard deviation below the mean.

10. $2\frac{1}{2}$ standard deviations below the mean.

Not everyone pays the same price for the same model of a car. The figure illustrates a normal distribution for the prices paid for a new car model. The mean is $17,000 and the standard deviation is $500. In Exercises 11–22, use the 68–95–99.7 rule, illustrated in the figure, to find the percentage of buyers who paid

11. between $16,500 and $17,500.

12. between $16,000 and $18,000.

13. between $17,000 and $17,500.

14. between $17,000 and $18,000.

15. between $16,000 and $17,000.

16. between $16,500 and $17,000.

17. between $15,500 and $17,000.

18. between $17,000 and $18,500.

19. more than $17,500. 20. more than $18,000.

21. less than $16,000. 22. less than $16,500.

Scores on the GRE (Graduate Record Examination) are normally distributed with a mean of 530 and a standard deviation of 128. In Exercises 23–32, use the 68–95–99.7 rule to find the percentage of people taking the test who score

23. between 274 and 786. 24. between 402 and 658.

25. between 274 and 530. 26. between 402 and 530.

27. above 658. 28. above 786.

29. below 274. 30. below 402.

31. above 914. 32. below 146.

A set of data items is normally distributed with a mean of 60 and a standard deviation of 8. In Exercises 33–48, convert each data item to a z-score.

33. 68 34. 76 35. 84 36. 92

37. 64 38. 72 39. 74 40. 78

41. 60 42. 100 43. 52 44. 44

45. 48 46. 40 47. 34 48. 30

Lengths of pregnancy of women are normally distributed with a mean of 266 days and a standard deviation of 16 days. In Exercises 49–56, find the z-score for a pregnancy lasting:

49. 290 days. 50. 294 days. 51. 302 days. 52. 318 days.

53. 258 days. 54. 254 days. 55. 242 days. 56. 226 days.

57. A student scores 230 on a math test and 540 on a reading comprehension test. The math test has a mean of 200 and a standard deviation of 10. The reading comprehension test has a mean of 500 and a standard deviation of 15. If the data for both tests are normally distributed, on which test did the student have the better score?

58. A student scores 72 on a grammar test and 255 on a vocabulary test. The grammar test has a mean of 84 and a standard deviation of 10. The vocabulary test has a mean of 300 and a standard deviation of 30. If the data for both tests are normally distributed, on which test did the student have the better score?

A set of data items is normally distributed with a mean of 400 and a standard deviation of 50. In Exercises 59–66, find the data item in this distribution that corresponds to the given z-score.

59. $z = 2$ 60. $z = 3$ 61. $z = 1.5$ 62. $z = 2.5$

63. $z = -3$ 64. $z = -2$ 65. $z = -2.5$ 66. $z = -1.5$

Use Table 12.15 on page 633 to solve Exercises 67–82.

In Exercises 67–74, find the percentage of data items in a normal distribution that lie a. below and b. above the given z-score.

67. $z = 0.6$ 68. $z = 0.8$

69. $z = 1.2$ 70. $z = 1.4$

71. $z = -0.7$ 72. $z = -0.4$

73. $z = -1.2$ 74. $z = -1.8$

In Exercises 75–82, find the percentage of data items in a normal distribution that lie between

75. $z = 0.2$ and $z = 1.4$. 76. $z = 0.3$ and $z = 2.1$.

77. $z = 1$ and $z = 3$. 78. $z = 2$ and $z = 3$

79. $z = -1.5$ and $z = 1.5$. 80. $z = -1.2$ and $z = 1.2$.

81. $z = -2$ and $z = -0.5$. 82. $z = -2.2$ and $z = -0.3$.

We have seen that SAT scores are normally distributed with a mean of 500 and a standard deviation of 100. In Exercises 83–92, begin by converting any given score or scores into z-scores. Then use Table 12.15 on page 633 to find the percentage of seniors who score

83. below 650. 84. below 680.

85. above 560. 86. above 590.

87. above 380. 88. above 360.

89. between 640 and 710. 90. between 660 and 740.

91. between 440 and 560. 92. between 420 and 580.

The weights for 12-month-old baby boys are normally distributed with a mean of 22.5 pounds and a standard deviation of 2.2 pounds. In Exercises 93–96, use Table 12.15 on page 633 to find the percentage of 12-month-old baby boys who weigh

93. more than 25.8 pounds.

94. more than 23.6 pounds.

95. between 19.2 and 21.4 pounds.

96. between 18.1 and 19.2 pounds.

97. Penn, Schoen, and Berland conducted interviews with 397 randomly selected parents. Twenty-six percent of the parents said that crime is a bad thing about being a kid.
    a. Find the margin of error for this survey.
    b. Write a statement about the percentage of parents in the population who feel that crime is a bad thing about being a kid.

98. Penn, Schoen, and Berland conducted interviews with 397 randomly selected parents. Five percent of the parents said that drugs are a bad thing about being a kid.
    a. Find the margin of error for this survey.
    b. Write a statement about the percentage of parents in the population who feel that drugs are a bad thing about being a kid.

99. Using a random sample of 4000 TV households, Nielsen Media Research found that 60.2% watched the final episode of "M*A*S*H."
    a. Find the margin of error in this percent.
    b. Write a statement about the percentage of TV households in the population who tuned into the final episode of "M*A*S*H."

100. Using a random sample of 4000 TV households, Nielsen Media Research found that 51.1% watched "Roots," Part 8.
    a. Find the margin of error in this percent.
    b. Write a statement about the percentage of TV households in the population who tuned into "Roots," Part 8.

101. In 1997, Nielsen Media Research increased their random sample to 5000 TV households. By how much, to the nearest tenth of a percent, did this improve their margin, of error over that in Exercises 99 and 100?

102. If Nielsen Media Research were to increase their random sample from 5000 to 10,000 TV households, by how much, to the nearest tenth of a percent, would this improve their margin of error?

The histograms shown in the next column indicate the frequencies of the number of syllables per word for randomly selected words in English and Japanese. Use the histograms to solve Exercises 103–106.

103. Is either histogram symmetric? Explain your answer.

104. Can the number of syllables in English or Japanese be described using the normal distribution? Explain your answer.

105. Describe one way in which English and Japanese are similar.

106. Describe one way in which English and Japanese are different.

English

Japanese

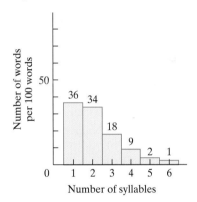

![feather pen icon] **Writing in Mathematics**

107. What is a symmetric histogram?

108. Describe the normal distribution and discuss some of its properties.

109. Describe the 68–95–99.7 rule.

110. Describe how to determine the z-score for a data item in a normal distribution.

111. What does a z-score measure?

112. Give an example of both a common and an unusual z-score. Explain how you arrived at these examples.

113. Describe when a z-score is negative.

114. If you score in the 73rd percentile, what does this mean?

115. Two students have scores with the same percentile, but for different administrations of the SAT. Does this mean that the students have the same score on the SAT? Explain your answer.

116. Give an example of a phenomenon that is normally distributed. Explain why. (Try to be creative and not use one of the distributions discussed in this section.) Estimate what the mean and the standard deviation might be and describe how you determined these estimates.

117. Give an example of a phenomenon that is not normally distributed and explain why.

 Critical Thinking Exercises

118. Find two z-scores so that 40% of the data in the distribution lies between them. (More than one answer is possible.)

119. A woman insists that she will never marry a man as short or shorter than she, knowing that only one man in 400 falls into this category. Assuming a mean height of 69 inches for men with a standard deviation of 2.5 inches (and a normal distribution), approximately how tall is the woman?

120. The placement test for a college has scores that are normally distributed with a mean of 500 and a standard deviation of 100. If the college accepts only the top 10% of examinees, what is the cutoff score on the test for admission?

 Group Exercise

121. For this activity, group members will conduct interviews with a random sample of students on campus. Each student is to be asked, "What is the worst thing about being a student?" One response should be recorded for each student.

a. Each member should interview enough students so that there are at least 50 randomly selected students in the sample.

b. After all responses have been recorded, the group should organize the four most common answers. For each answer, compute the percentage of students in the sample who felt that this is the worst thing about being a student.

c. Find the margin of error for your survey.

d. For each of the four most common answers, write a statement about the percentage of all students on your campus who feel that this is the worst thing about being a student.

SECTION 12.5 *Scatter Plots, Correlation, and Regression Lines*

Objectives

1. Make a scatter plot for a table of data items.

2. Interpret information given in a scatter plot.

3. Compute the correlation coefficient.

4. Write the equation of the regression line.

5. Use a sample's correlation coefficient to determine if there is a correlation in the population.

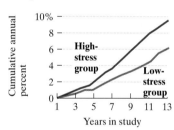

Cumulative Annual Heart-Disease Incidents for High- and Low-Stress Groups

During a 13-year study, men in a high-stress group were more likely to have heart attacks than those in a low-stress group.
Source: "Self-Perceived Psychological Stress and Incidence of Coronary Artery Disease in Middle-Aged Men."

Have you ever noticed that during periods of high stress you tend to get sick? A random sample of 232 subjects each filled in two questionnaires. The first dealt with the amount of stress he or she experienced in the past 12 months. The second questionnaire assessed how often he or she became ill during that period. The researchers found that there is a relationship between stress and illness. An increase in stress tends to be accompanied by increased episodes of ill health. This 1971 study lead to hundreds of followup studies that have enabled medical professionals to better understand how stress is related to physical health.

Up to this point in the chapter, we have studied situations in which data sets involve a single variable, such as SAT scores, weights, cholesterol levels, and lengths of pregnancies. By contrast, the stress-illness study involved data collected on two variables—amount of stress and frequency of illness. In this section, we consider situations in which there are two data items for each randomly selected person or thing. Our interest is in determining whether or not there is a relationship between the two variables and, if so, the strength of that relationship.

1 Make a scatter plot for a table of data items.

Scatter Plots and Correlation

Is there a relationship between education and prejudice? With increased education, does a person's level of prejudice tend to decrease? Notice that we are interested in two quantities—years of education and level of prejudice. For each person in our sample, we will record the number of years of school completed and the score on a test measuring prejudice. Higher scores on this 1 to 10 test indicate greater prejudice. Using x to represent years of education and y to represent scores on a test measuring prejudice, Table 12.16 shows these two quantities for a random sample of ten people.

Table 12.16 Recording Two Quantities in a Sample of Ten People

Respondent	A	B	C	D	E	F	G	H	I	J
Years of education (x)	12	5	14	13	8	10	16	11	12	4
Score on prejudice test (y)	1	7	2	3	5	4	1	2	3	10

When two data items are collected for every person or object in a sample, the data items can be visually displayed using a *scatter plot*. A **scatter plot** is a collection of data points, one data point per person or object. We can make a scatter plot of the data in Table 12.16 by drawing a horizontal axis to represent years of education and a vertical axis to represent scores on a test measuring prejudice. We then represent each of the ten respondents with a single point on the graph. For example, the dot for respondent A is located to represent 12 years of education on the horizontal axis and 1 on the prejudice test on the vertical axis. Plotting each of the ten pieces of data in a rectangular coordinate system results in the scatter plot shown in Figure 12.26.

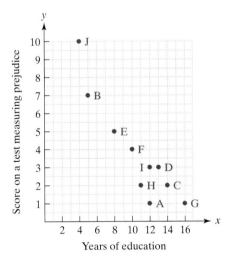

Figure 12.26 A scatter plot for education-prejudice data

A scatter plot like the one in Figure 12.26 can be used to determine if two quantities are related. If there is a clear relationship, the quantities are said to be **correlated**. The scatter plot shows a downward trend among the data points, although there are a few exceptions. People with increased education tend to have a lower score on the test measuring prejudice. **Correlation** is used to determine if there is a relationship between two variables and, if so, the strength and direction of that relationship.

Correlation and Causal Connections

Correlations can often be seen when data items are displayed on a scatter plot. Although the scatter plot in Figure 12.26 indicates a correlation between education and prejudice, we cannot conclude that increased education

Study Tip

The numbered list on the right represents three possibilities. Perhaps you can provide a better explanation about decreasing prejudice with increased education.

causes a person's level of prejudice to decrease. There are at least three possible explanations.

1. The correlation between increased education and decreased prejudice is simply a coincidence.

2. Education usually involves classrooms with a variety of different kinds of people. Increased exposure to diversity in the classroom setting, which accompanies increased levels of education, might be an underlying cause for decreased prejudice.

3. Education, the process of acquiring knowledge, requires people to look at new ideas and see things in different ways. Thus, education causes one to be more tolerant and less prejudiced.

Establishing that one thing causes another is extremely difficult, even if there is a strong correlation between these things. For example, as the air temperature increases, there is an increase in the number of people stung by jellyfish at the beach. This does not mean that an increase in air temperature causes more people to be stung. It might mean that because it is hotter, more people go into the water. With an increased number of swimmers, more people are likely to be stung. In short, correlation is not necessarily causation.

Regression Lines and Correlation Coefficients

Figure 12.27 shows the scatter plot for the education-prejudice data for a second time. Also shown is a straight line that seems to "fit" the data points fairly well. Most of the data points lie either near or on this line. A line that best fits the data points in a scatter plot is called a **regression line**. The regression line is the particular line in which the spread of the data points around it is as small as possible.

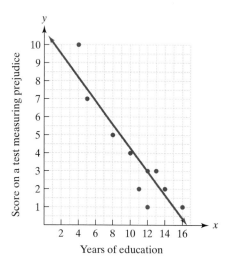

Figure 12.27 A scatter plot with a regression line

The scatter plot in Figure 12.28 on page 645 indicates that as years of education increase, income tends to increase. Each point in the scatter plot depicts two variables, education and income, obtained from one randomly selected person. Also shown is the regression line, the line that best fits the data points. The

Figure 12.28 As years of education increase, income tends to increase

scatter plot indicates a relationship, or correlation, between education and income. However, we cannot conclude that increased education causes annual income to increase.

A measure that is used to describe the strength and direction of a relationship between variables whose data points lie on or near a line is called the **correlation coefficient**, designated by r. Figure 12.29 shows scatter plots and correlation coefficients. Variables are **positively correlated** if they tend to increase or decrease together, as in Figure 12.29 (a), (b), and (c). By contrast, variables are **negatively correlated** if one variable tends to decrease while the other increases, as in Figure 12.29 (e), (f), and (g). Figure 12.29 illustrates that a correlation coefficient, r, is a number between -1 and 1, inclusive. Figure 12.29 (a) shows a value of 1. This indicates a **perfect positive correlation** in which all points in the scatter plot lie precisely on the regression line that rises from left to right. On the far right, Figure 12.29 (g) shows a value of -1. This indicates a **perfect negative correlation** in which all points in the scatter plot lie precisely on the regression line that falls from left to right.

2 Interpret information given in a scatter plot.

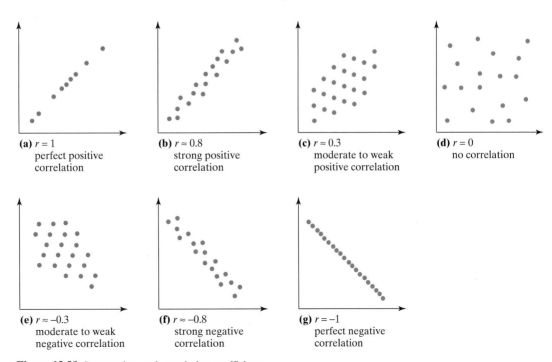

(a) $r = 1$
perfect positive
correlation

(b) $r \approx 0.8$
strong positive
correlation

(c) $r \approx 0.3$
moderate to weak
positive correlation

(d) $r = 0$
no correlation

(e) $r \approx -0.3$
moderate to weak
negative correlation

(f) $r \approx -0.8$
strong negative
correlation

(g) $r = -1$
perfect negative
correlation

Figure 12.29 Scatter plots and correlation coefficients

Beneficial Uses of Correlation Coefficients

- A Florida study showed a high positive correlation between the number of powerboats and the number of manatee deaths. Many of these deaths were seen to be caused by boats' propellers gashing into the manatees' bodies. Based on this study, Florida set up coastal sanctuaries where power boats are prohibited so that these large gentle mammals that float just below the water's surface could thrive.

- In 1986, researchers studied how psychiatric patients readjusted to their community after their release from a mental hospital. A moderate positive correlation ($r = 0.38$) was found between patients' attractiveness and their postdischarge social adjustment. The better-looking patients were better off. The researchers suggested that physical attractiveness plays a role in patients' readjustment to community living because good-looking people tend to be treated better by others than homely people are.

Take another look at Figure 12.29. If r is between 0 and 1, as in (b) and (c), the two variables are positively correlated, but not perfectly. Although all the data points will not lie on the regression line, as in (a), an increase in one variable tends to be accompanied by an increase in the other.

Negative correlations are also illustrated in Figure 12.29. If r is between 0 and -1, as in (e) and (f), the two variables are negatively correlated, but not perfectly. Although all the data points will not lie on the regression line, as in (g), an increase in one variable tends to be accompanied by a decrease in the other.

EXAMPLE 1 Interpreting a Correlation Coefficient

We opened this section with a 1971 study involving 232 subjects. Researchers found a relationship between subjects' level of stress and how often they became ill. The correlation coefficient in this study was 0.32. Does this indicate a strong relationship between stress and illness?

Solution The correlation coefficient $r = 0.32$ means that as stress increases, frequency of illness also tends to increase. However, 0.32 is only a moderate correlation, illustrated in Figure 12.29(c) on page 645. There is not, based on this study, a strong relationship between stress and illness. In this study, the relationship is somewhat weak.

EXAMPLE 2 Interpreting Information Given in a Scatter Plot

The scatter plot in Figure 12.30 shows the relationship between fat intake and deaths per 100,000 women from breast cancer. Use the scatter plot to determine whether each of the statements on page 647 is true or false.

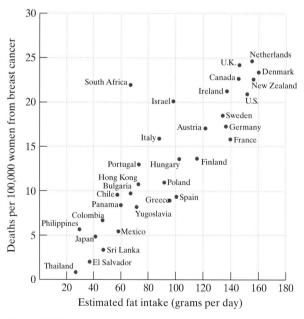

Figure 12.30 *Source:* From "Diet and Cancer" by Leonard A. Cohen, Copyright © 1987 by Scientific American, Inc. All rights reserved

a. Increased fat intake is a cause of breast cancer.

Solution   The variables in the scatter plot, daily fat intake and deaths per 100,000 women, tend to increase together in Figure 12.30. Thus, the values of the first variable (daily fat intake) are positively correlated with those for the second variable (deaths per 100,000 women). However, correlation does not tell us whether there is a cause-and-effect relationship between the first and second variables. Other factors may influence the death rate from breast cancer. (Recent studies from Great Britain show that there is no causal relationship between fat intake and breast cancer.) Based on Figure 12.30, we cannot conclude that increased fat intake is a cause of breast cancer. Correlation is not necessarily causation. The given statement is false.

b. With a fat intake of approximately 150 grams per day in the United States, there are 26 deaths per 100,000 women from breast cancer.

Solution   Find the point in the scatter plot that represents the United States. This point is over about 150 units on the horizontal axis and up about 21 units. This means that with a fat intake of approximately 150 grams per day in the United States, there are 21 deaths per 100,000 women from breast cancer. The given statement is false because of its claim that there are 26 deaths per 100,000 women.

c. There is a strong positive correlation between fat intake and deaths from breast cancer.

Solution   The variables in the scatter plot, daily fat intake and deaths per 100,000 women from breast cancer, tend to increase together. It would not be too difficult to draw a straight line that rises from left to right on or near which most of the data points lie. This indicates that there is a strong positive correlation between fat intake and deaths from breast cancer. The given statement is true.

Cigarettes and Lung Cancer

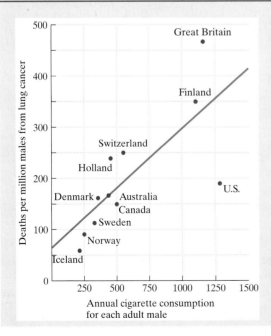

This scatter plot shows a relationship between cigarette consumption among males and deaths due to lung cancer per million males. The data are from 11 countries and date back to a 1964 report by the U.S. Surgeon General. The correlation coefficient for this study was computed to be 0.73, a relatively high positive correlation. At that time, the tobacco industry argued that in spite of this correlation, tobacco use is not the cause of cancer. Although correlation is not causation, recent data do, indeed, show a causal effect between tobacco use and numerous diseases.

Source: Smoking and Health, Washington, D.C., 1964

3 Compute the correlation coefficient.

How to Obtain the Correlation Coefficient and the Equation of the Regression Line

The easiest way to find the correlation coefficient and the equation of the regression line is to use a graphing or statistical calculator. Graphing calculators have statistical menus that enable you to enter the x and y data items for the variables. Based on this information, you can instruct the calculator to display a scatter plot, the equation of the regression line, and the correlation coefficient.

We can also compute the correlation coefficient and the equation of the regression line by hand using formulas. First, we compute the correlation coefficient.

Technology

Gaphing Calculators, Scatter Plots, and Regression Lines

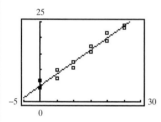

This calculator display was obtained by entering x and y data items and instructing the calculator to display a scatter plot and the regression line.

```
LinReg
  y=ax+b
  a=.7171428571
  b=4.785714286
  r=.9803266536
```

Calculators display equations of regression lines and calculate correlation coefficients. The slope shown above is approximately 0.7. The positive slope reinforces the fact that there is a positive correlation between the variables.

Computing the Correlation Coefficient by Hand

The following formula is used to calculate the correlation coefficient, r.

$$r = \frac{n(\Sigma xy) - (\Sigma x)(\Sigma y)}{\sqrt{n(\Sigma x^2) - (\Sigma x)^2}\sqrt{n(\Sigma y^2) - (\Sigma y)^2}}$$

In the formula

$$n = \text{the number of data points } (x, y)$$
$$\Sigma x = \text{the sum of the } x\text{-values}$$
$$\Sigma y = \text{the sum of the } y\text{-values}$$
$$\Sigma xy = \text{the sum of the product of } x \text{ and } y \text{ in each pair}$$
$$\Sigma x^2 = \text{the sum of the squares of the } x\text{-values}$$
$$\Sigma y^2 = \text{the sum of the squares of the } y\text{-values}$$
$$(\Sigma x)^2 = \text{the square of the sum of the } x\text{-values}$$
$$(\Sigma y)^2 = \text{the square of the sum of the } y\text{-values}$$

When computing the correlation coefficient by hand, organize your work in five columns:

$$x \qquad y \qquad xy \qquad x^2 \qquad y^2$$

Find the sum of the numbers in each column. Then, substitute these values into the formula for r. Example 3 illustrates computing the correlation coefficient for the education-prejudice test data.

EXAMPLE 3   Computing the Correlation Coefficient

Shown again on page 649 are the number of years of school, x, completed by ten randomly selected people and their scores on a test measuring prejudice, y. Recall that higher scores on the measure of prejudice (1 to 10) indicate greater levels of prejudice. Determine the correlation coefficient between years of education and scores on a prejudice test.

Respondent	A	B	C	D	E	F	G	H	I	J
Years of education (x)	12	5	14	13	8	10	16	11	12	4
Score on prejudice test (y)	1	7	2	3	5	4	1	2	3	10

Solution   As suggested, organize the work in five columns.

x	y	xy	x^2	y^2
12	1	12	144	1
5	7	35	25	49
14	2	28	196	4
13	3	39	169	9
8	5	40	64	25
10	4	40	100	16
16	1	16	256	1
11	2	22	121	4
12	3	36	144	9
4	10	40	16	100
$\Sigma x = 105$	$\Sigma y = 38$	$\Sigma xy = 308$	$\Sigma x^2 = 1235$	$\Sigma y^2 = 218$

Add all values in the x-column.	Add all values in the y-column.	Add all values in the xy-column.	Add all values in the x²-column.	Add all values in the y²-column.

"Common wisdom among statisticians is that at least 5% of all data points are corrupted, either when they are initially recorded or when they are entered into the computer. **"**

JESSICA UTTS,
Statistician

We use these five sums in calculating the correlation coefficient.

Another value in the formula for r that we have not yet determined is n, the number of data points (x, y). Because there are ten items in the x-column and ten items in the y-column, the number of data points (x, y) is ten. Thus, $n = 10$.

In order to calculate r, we also need to find the square of the sum of the x-values and the y-values:

$$(\Sigma x)^2 = (105)^2 = 11{,}025 \text{ and } (\Sigma y)^2 = (38)^2 = 1444$$

We are ready to determine the value for r.

$$r = \frac{n(\Sigma xy) - (\Sigma x)(\Sigma y)}{\sqrt{n(\Sigma x^2) - (\Sigma x)^2}\sqrt{n(\Sigma y^2) - (\Sigma y)^2}}$$

$$= \frac{10(308) - 105(38)}{\sqrt{10(1235) - 11{,}025}\sqrt{10(218) - 1444}}$$

$$= \frac{-910}{\sqrt{1325}\sqrt{736}}$$

$$\approx -0.92$$

This value for r is fairly close to -1 and indicates a strong negative correlation. This means that the more education a person has, the less prejudiced that person is (based on scores on the test measuring levels of prejudice).

Once we have determined that two variables are related, we can use the equation of the regression line to determine the exact relationship. Here is the formula for writing the equation of the line that best fits the data.

4 Write the equation of the regression line.

Writing the Equation of the Regression Line by Hand

The equation of the regression line is

$$y = mx + b$$

where

$$m = \frac{n(\Sigma xy) - (\Sigma x)(\Sigma y)}{n(\Sigma x^2) - (\Sigma x)^2}, \text{ and } b = \frac{\Sigma y - m(\Sigma x)}{n}.$$

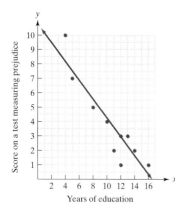

Figure 12.27

EXAMPLE 4   Writing the Equation of the Regression Line

a. Shown, again, in Figure 12.27 is the scatter plot and the regression line for the data in Example 3. Use the data to find the equation of the regression line that relates years of education and scores on a prejudice test.

b. Approximately what score on the test can be anticipated by a person with nine years of education?

Solution

a. We use the sums obtained in Example 3. Thus,

$$m = \frac{n(\Sigma xy) - (\Sigma x)(\Sigma y)}{n(\Sigma x^2) - (\Sigma x)^2} = \frac{10(308) - 105(38)}{10(1235) - (105)^2} = \frac{-910}{1325} \approx -0.69$$

With a negative correlation coefficient, it makes sense that the slope of the regression line is negative. This line falls from left to right, indicating a negative correlation.

Now, we find the y-intercept, b.

$$b = \frac{\Sigma y - m(\Sigma x)}{n} = \frac{38 - (-0.69)(105)}{10} = \frac{110.45}{10} \approx 11.05$$

Therefore, the equation of the regression line is

$$y = mx + b$$

$$y = -0.69x + 11.05$$

where x represents the number of years of education and y represents the score on the prejudice test.

b. To anticipate the score on the prejudice test for a person with nine years of education, substitute 9 for x in the regression line's equation.

$$y = -0.69x + 11.05$$

$$y = -0.69(9) + 11.05 = 4.84$$

5 Use a sample's correlation coefficient to determine if there is a correlation in the population.

A person with nine years of education is anticipated to have a score close to 5 on the prejudice test.

The Level of Significance of r

In Example 3, we found a strong negative correlation between education and prejudice, computing the correlation coefficient, r, to be -0.92. However, the sample size ($n = 10$) was relatively small. With such a small sample, can we truly conclude that a correlation exists in the population? Or could it be that education and prejudice are not related? Perhaps the results we obtained were simply due to sampling error and chance.

Mathematicians have identified values to determine if r, the correlation coefficient for a sample, can be attributed to a relationship between variables in the population. These values are shown in the second and third columns of Table 12.17. They depend on the sample size, n, listed in the left column. If $|r|$, the absolute value of the correlation coefficient computed for the sample, is greater than the value given in the table, a correlation exits between the variables in the population. The column headed $\alpha = 0.05$ denotes a **significance level of 5%**, meaning that there is a 0.05 probability that, when the statistician says the variables are correlated, they are actually not related in the population. The column on the right, headed $\alpha = 0.01$, denotes a **significance level of 1%**, meaning that there is a 0.01 probability that, when the statistician says the variables are correlated, they are actually not related in the population. Values in the $\alpha = 0.01$ column are greater than those in the $\alpha = 0.05$ column. Because of the possibility of sampling error, there is always a probability that when we say the variables are related, there is actually not a correlation in the population from which the sample was randomly selected.

Table 12.17   Values for Determining Correlations in a Population

n	$\alpha = 0.05$	$\alpha = 0.01$
4	0.950	0.990
5	0.878	0.959
6	0.811	0.917
7	0.754	0.875
8	0.707	0.834
9	0.666	0.798
10	0.632	0.765
11	0.602	0.735
12	0.576	0.708
13	0.553	0.684
14	0.532	0.661
15	0.514	0.641
16	0.497	0.623
17	0.482	0.606
18	0.468	0.590
19	0456	0.575
20	0.444	0.561
22	0.423	0.537
27	0.381	0.487
32	0.349	0.449
37	0.325	0.418
42	0.304	0.393
47	0.288	0.372
52	0.273	0.354
62	0.250	0.325
72	0.232	0.302
82	0.217	0.283
92	0.205	0.267
102	0.195	0.254

The larger the sample size n, the smaller is the value of r needed for a correlation in the population.

EXAMPLE 5   Determining a Correlation in the Population

In Example 3, we computed $r = -0.92$ for $n = 10$. Can we conclude that there is a negative correlation between education and prejudice in the population?

Solution   Begin by taking the absolute value of the calculated correlation coefficient.

$$|r| = |-0.92| = 0.92$$

Now, look to the right of $n = 10$ in Table 12.17. Because 0.92 is greater than both of these values (0.632 and 0.765), we may conclude that a correlation does exist between education and prejudice in the population. (There is a probability of 0.01 that the variables are not really correlated in the population and our results could be attributed to chance.)

Exercise Set 12.5

✔ Practice and Application Exercises

In Exercises 1–8, make a scatter plot for the given data. Use the scatter plot to describe whether or not the variables appear to be related.

1.

x	1	6	4	3	7	2
y	2	5	3	3	4	1

2.

x	2	1	6	3	4
y	4	5	10	8	9

3.

x	8	6	1	5	4	10	3
y	2	4	10	5	6	2	9

4.

x	4	5	2	1
y	1	3	5	4

5.

Respondent	A	B	C	D	E	F	G
Years of education of parent (x)	13	9	7	12	12	10	11
Years of education of child (y)	13	11	7	16	17	8	17

6.

Respondent	A	B	C	D	E
IQ (x)	110	115	120	125	135
Annual income (y) (in thousands of dollars)	30	32	36	40	44

7. The data show the number of registered automatic weapons (in thousands) and the murder rate (in murders per 100,000) for eight randomly selected states.

Automatic weapons, x	11.6	8.3	6.9	3.6	2.6	2.5	2.4	0.6
Murder rate, y	13.1	10.6	11.5	10.1	5.3	6.6	3.6	4.4

Source: FBI and Bureau of Alcohol, Tobacco, and Firearms

8. The data show the number of marriages and divorces (in millions) for six selected years in the United States

Year	1970	1975	1980	1985	1990	1994
Marriages, x	2.159	2.153	2.39	2.413	2.443	2.362
Divorces, y	0.708	1.036	1.189	1.19	1.182	1.191

Source: U.S. Center for Health Statistics

The scatter plot in the figure shows the relationship between the percentage of married women of child bearing age and births per woman in selected countries. Use the scatter plot to determine whether each of the statements in Exercises 9–16 is true or false.

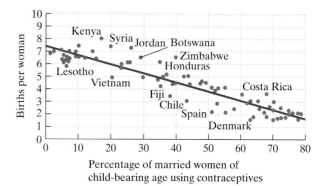

Source: Population Reference Bureau

9. There is a strong positive correlation between contraceptive use and births per woman.

10. There is no correlation between contraceptive use and births per woman.

11. There is a strong negative correlation between contraceptive use and births per woman.

12. There is a causal relationship between contraceptive use and births per woman.

13. With approximately 43% of women of child-bearing age using contraceptives, there are 3 births per woman in Chile.

14. With 20% of women of child-bearing age using contraceptives, there are 6 births per woman in Vietnam.

15. No two countries have a different number of births per woman with the same percentage of married women using contraceptives.

16. The country with the greatest number of births per woman also has the smallest percentage of women using contraceptives.

The scatter plot in the figure shows the relationship between SAT scores and grade point average for the first year in college for a group of randomly selected college students. Use the scatter plot to determine whether each of the statements in Exercises 17–24 is true or false.

17. There is no correlation between SAT scores and grade point averages.
18. There is an almost-perfect positive correlation between SAT scores and grade point averages.
19. There is a positive correlation between SAT scores and grade point averages.
20. As SAT scores decrease, grade point averages also tend to decrease.
21. Most of the data points lie on the regression line.
22. The number of college students in this sample is approximately 200.
23. The student with the lowest SAT score has the worst grade point average.
24. The student with the highest SAT score has the best grade point average.

The scatter plot shows the relationship between the Olympic year and the men's and women's winning times (in seconds) in the Olympic 100-meter freestyle swimming race. Also shown are the regression lines. Use the information given in the figure to determine whether each statement in Exercises 25–28 is true or false.

Men's and women's winning times in the Olympic 100-meter freestyle swimming race

25. There is a strong positive correlation between the Olympic year and winning time in the race for both women and men.
26. Even if present trends continue, women will not swim faster than men in this Olympic event.
27. Many of the data points do not fall exactly on the regression lines for the two sets of data.
28. A reasonable estimate of the correlation coefficient for the data for the women is −0.2.

Use the scatter plots shown, labeled (a)–(f), to solve Exercises 29–32.

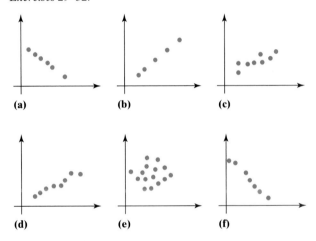

29. Which scatter plot indicates a perfect negative correlation?
30. Which scatter plot indicates a perfect positive correlation?
31. In which scatter plot is $r = 0.9$?
32. In which scatter plot is $r = 0.01$?

Compute r, the correlation coefficient, rounded to the nearest thousandth, for the data in

33. Exercise 1.   34. Exercise 2.

35. Exercise 3.   36. Exercise 4.

37. Use the data in Exercise 5 to solve this exercise.
    a. Determine the correlation coefficient between years of education of parent and child.
    b. Find the equation of the regression line for years of education of parent and child.
    c. Approximately how many years of education can we predict for a child with a parent who has 16 years of education?

38. Use the data in Exercise 6 to solve this exercise.
    a. Determine the correlation coefficient between IQ and income.
    b. Find the equation of the regression line for IQ and income.
    c. Approximately what annual income can be anticipated by a person whose IQ is 123?

39. Use the data in Exercise 7 to solve this exercise.
    a. Determine the correlation coefficient between the number of automatic weapons and the murder rate.
    b. Find the equation of the regression line.
    c. Approximately what murder rate can we anticipate in a state that has 14 thousand registered weapons?

40. Use the data in Exercise 8 to solve this exercise.
    a. Determine the correlation coefficient between the number of marriages and the number of divorces.
    b. Find the equation of the regression line.
    c. Approximately how many divorces can we anticipate for a year in which there are 2.7 million marriages?

In Exercises 41–47, the correlation coefficient, r, is given for a sample of n data points. Use the $\alpha = 0.05$ column in Table 12.17 on page 651 and determine whether or not we may conclude that a correlation does exist in the population. (Using the $\alpha = 0.05$ column there is a probability of 0.05 that the variables are not really correlated in the population and our results could be attributed to chance. Ignore this possibility when concluding whether or not there is a correlation in the population.)

41. $n = 20, r = 0.5$ 42. $n = 27, r = 0.4$

43. $n = 12, r = 0.5$ 44. $n = 22, r = 0.04$

45. $n = 72, r = -0.351$ 46. $n = 37, r = -0.37$

47. $n = 20, r = -0.37$

48. In the 1964 study on cigarette consumption and deaths due to lung cancer (see the essay on page 647), $n = 11$ and $r = 0.73$. What can you conclude using the $\alpha = 0.05$ column in Table 12.17?

 Writing in Mathematics

49. What is a scatter plot?

50. How does a scatter plot indicate that two variables are correlated?

51. Give an example of two variables with a strong positive correlation and explain why this is so.

52. Give an example of two variables with a strong negative correlation and explain why this is so.

53. What is meant by a regression line?

54. When all points in a scatter plot fall on the regression line, what is the value of the correlation coefficient? Describe what this means.

For the pairs of quantities in Exercises 55–58, describe whether a scatter plot will show a positive correlation, a negative correlation, or no correlation. If there is a correlation, is it strong, moderate, or weak? Explain your answers.

55. Height and weight

56. Number of days absent and grade in a course

57. Height and grade in a course

58. Hours of television watched and grade in a course

59. Explain how to use the correlation coefficient for a sample to determine if there is a correlation in the population.

 Critical Thinking Exercises

60. Which one of the following is true?
    a. A scatter plot need not define y as a function of x.
    b. The correlation coefficient and the slope of the regression line for the same set of data can have opposite signs.
    c. When all points in a scatter plot fall on the regression line, the value of the correlation coefficient is 0.
    d. If the same number is subtracted from each x-item, but the y-item stays the same, the correlation coefficient for these new data points decreases.

61. Give an example of two variables with a strong correlation, where each variable is not the cause of the other.

 Technology Exercises

62. Enter the data items from Table 12.16 on page 643 into an Excel spreadsheet.

After you have entered the data, use the computer's mouse to highlight the cells containing the data corresponding to the years of education and test scores. Then, activate the Chart Option of the spreadsheet by clicking on the Insert pull-down menu and selecting Chart. Select the XY(Scatter) option (see picture). Then, click the "Next" button to work your way through the options, including the labels and cosmetic effects. Once you have decided on all of the options (don't worry, you can go back and change them), click the "Finish" button. Excel should generate a scatter plot that looks like Figure 12.26 on page 643.

63. Use MS Excel (or another spreadsheet program) to create a scatter plot for the data in Exercise 6.

Group Exercises

64. The group should select two variables that it believes have a strong positive or negative correlation. Once these variables have been determined,
    a. Collect at least 30 ordered pairs of data (x, y) from a sample of people on your campus.
    b. Draw a scatter plot for the data collected.
    c. Does the scatter plot indicate a positive correlation, a negative correlation, or no relationship between the variables?
    d. Calculate r. Does the value of r reinforce the impression conveyed by the scatter plot?
    e. Find the equation of the regression line.
    f. Use the regression line's equation to make a prediction about a y-value given an x-value.

g. Are the results of this project consistent with the group's original belief about the correlation between the variables, or are there some surprises in the data collected?

65. Group members should consult an almanac, a magazine, or a newspaper in which data about two variables are presented. (See, for example, Exercises 7 and 8 in this exercise set.)
    a. Draw a scatter plot for the data selected by the group.
    b. Does the scatter plot indicate a positive correlation, a negative correlation, or no correlation between the variables?
    c. Calculate r. Does the value of r reinforce the impression conveyed by the scatter plot?
    d. Find the equation of the regression line and use the equation to make a prediction.

CHAPTER SUMMARY, REVIEW, AND TEST

SUMMARY

12.1 Sampling, Frequency Distributions, and Graphs

a. A population is the set containing all objects whose properties are to be described and analyzed. A sample is a subset of the population.

b. Random samples are obtained in such a way that each member of the population has an equal chance of being selected.

c. Data can be organized and presented in frequency distributions, grouped frequency distributions, histograms, frequency polygons, and stem-and-leaf plots.

12.2 Measures of Central Tendency

a. The mean is the sum of the data items divided by the number of items. Mean $= \dfrac{\Sigma x}{n}$.

b. The mean of a frequency distribution is computed using

$$\text{Mean} = \dfrac{\Sigma xf}{n}$$

where x is each data value, f is its frequency, and n is the total frequency of the distribution.

c. The median of data arranged in order is the item in the middle or the mean of the two middlemost items. The median is the value in the $\dfrac{n+1}{2}$ position.

d. The mode of a data set is the value that occurs most often. If there is no such value, there is no mode.

e. The midrange is computed using

$$\dfrac{\text{lowest data value} + \text{highest data value}}{2}.$$

12.3 Measures of Dispersion

a. Range = highest data value − lowest data value

b. Standard deviation $= \sqrt{\dfrac{\Sigma(\text{data item} - \text{mean})^2}{n-1}}$

c. As the spread of data items increases, the standard deviation gets larger.

12.4 The Normal Distribution

a. The normal distribution is a theoretical distribution for the entire population. The distribution is bell-shaped and symmetric about a vertical line through its center, where the mean, median, and mode are located.

b. The 68–95–99.7 Rule

Approximately 68% of the data items fall within 1 standard deviation of the mean, 95% within 2 standard deviations of the mean, and 99.7% within 3 standard deviations of the mean.

c. A z-score describes how many standard deviations a data item in a normal distribution lies above or below the mean.

$$z\text{-score} = \frac{\text{data item} - \text{mean}}{\text{standard deviation}}$$

d. If n% of the items in a distribution are less than a particular data item, that data item is in the nth percentile of the distribution. A table showing z-scores and their percentiles can be used to find the percentage of data items less than or greater than a given data item in a normal distribution, as well as the percentage of data items between two given items.

e. If a statistic is obtained from a random sample of size n, there is a 95% probability that it lies within $\frac{1}{\sqrt{n}}$ of the true population statistic. $\pm \frac{1}{\sqrt{n}}$ is called the margin of error.

12.5 Scatter Plots, Correlation, and Regression Lines

a. A plot of data points is called a scatter plot. If the points lie approximately along a line, the line that best fits the data is called a regression line.

b. A correlation coefficient, r, measures the strength and direction of a possible relationship between variables. If $r = 1$, there is a perfect positive correlation, and if $r = -1$, there is a perfect negative correlation. If $r = 0$, there is no relationship between the variables. Table 12.17 on page 651 indicates whether r denotes a correlation in the population.

c. The formula for computing the correlation coefficient, r, is given in the box on page 648. The equation of the regression line is given in the box on page 650.

REVIEW EXERCISES

12.1

Exercises 1–2 present numerical information. Describe the population whose properties are analyzed by the data.

1. In 1998, 69.4% of American adults earning $100,000 or more each year did volunteer work. (Source: Statistical Abstract of the United States.)

2. In 1998, a random sample of San Francisco's rental apartments revealed one of the most expensive apartment rents in the United States, averaging $1542 per month. (Source: M/PF Research, Inc.)

3. The government of a large city wants to know if its citizens will support a three-year tax increase to provide additional support to the city's community college system. The government decides to conduct a survey of the city's residents before placing a tax increase initiative on the ballot. Which one of the following is most appropriate for obtaining a sample of the city's residents?
   a. Survey a random sample of persons within each geographic region of the city.
   b. Survey a random sample of community college professors living in the city.
   c. Survey every tenth person who walks into the city's government center on two randomly selected days of the week.
   d. Survey a random sample of persons within each geographic region of the state in which the city is located.

A random sample of ten college students is selected and each student is asked how much time he or she spent on homework during the previous weekend. The followinig times (in hours) are obtained:

$$8, 10, 9, 7, 9, 8, 7, 6, 8, 7$$

Use these data items to solve Exercises 4–6.

4. Construct a frequency distribution for the data.
5. Construct a histogram for the data.
6. Construct a frequency polygon for the data.

The 50 grades on a physiology test are shown. Use the data to solve Exercises 7–8.

44	24	54	81	18
34	39	63	67	60
72	36	91	47	75
57	74	87	49	86
59	14	26	41	90
13	29	13	31	68
63	35	29	70	22
95	17	50	42	27
73	11	42	31	69
56	40	31	45	51

7. Construct a grouped frequency distribution for the data. Use the classes 0–39, 40–49, 50–59, 60–69, 70–79, 80–89, and 90–100.
8. Construct a stem-and-leaf display for the data.
9. This 1911 visual display shows the annual cost per patient at five facilities for treating the mentally ill. Describe what is misleading about the display.

South Mountain   Pittsburgh   Harrisburg   Norristown   Warren

Source: Pittsburgh Civic Commission, *Report on Expenditures of the Department of Charities*

12.2

In Exercises 10–11, find the mean for each group of data items.

10. 84, 90, 95, 89, 98
11. 33, 27, 9, 10, 6, 7, 11, 23, 27
12. Find the mean for the data items in the given frequency distribution.

Score x	Frequency f
1	2
2	4
3	3
4	1

In Exercises 13–14, find the median for each group of data items.

13. 33, 27, 9, 10, 6, 7, 11, 23, 27
14. 28, 16, 22, 28, 34
15. Find the median for the data items in the frequency distribution in Exercise 12.

In Exercises 16–17, find the mode for each group of data items. If there is no mode, so state.

16. 33, 27, 9, 10, 6, 7, 11, 23, 27
17. 582, 585, 583, 585, 587, 587, 589
18. Find the mode for the data items in the frequency distribution in Exercise 12.

In Exercises 19–20, find the midrange for each group of data items.

19. 84, 90, 95, 88, 98
20. 33, 27, 9, 10, 6, 7, 11, 23, 27
21. Find the midrange for the data items in the frequency distribution in Exercise 12.

22. In 1997, the mean salary for quarterbacks in the National Football League was $1,346,000 (Source: NFL Players Association). Explain how this figure was obtained.

23. A student took seven tests in a course, scoring between 90% and 95% on three of the tests, between 80% and 89% on three of the tests, and below 40% on one of the tests. In this distribution, is the mean or the median more representative of the student's overall performance in the course? Explain your answer.

24. The data items below are the ages of U.S. presidents at the time of their first inauguration.

57   61   57   57   58   57   61   54   68   51   49   64   50   48
65   52   56   46   54   49   51   47   55   55   54   42   51   56
55   51   54   51   60   62   43   55   56   61   52   69   64   46

a. Organize the data in a frequency distribution.
b. Use the frequency distribution to find the mean age, median age, modal age, and midrange age of the presidents when they were inaugurated.

12.3

In Exercises 25–26, find the range for each group of data items.

25. 28, 34, 16, 22, 28
26. 312, 783, 219, 312, 426, 219
27. The mean for the data items 29, 9, 8, 22, 46, 51, 48, 42, 53, 42 is 35. Find a. the deviation from the mean for each data item and b. the sum of the deviations in part (a).
28. Use the data items 36, 26, 24, 90, and 74 to find a. the mean, b. the deviation from the mean for each data item, and c. the sum of the deviations in part (b).

In Exercises 29–30, find the standard deviation for each group of data items.

29. 3, 3, 5, 8, 10, 13
30. 20, 27, 23, 26, 28, 32, 33, 35
31. A test measuring anxiety levels is administered to a sample of ten college students with the following results. (High scores indicate high anxiety.)

10, 30, 37, 40, 43, 44, 45, 69, 86, 86

Find the mean, range, and standard deviation for the data.

32. Compute the mean and the standard deviation for each of the following data sets. Then, write a brief description of similarities and differences between the two sets based on each of your computations.

  Set A: 80, 80, 80, 80   Set B: 70, 70, 90, 90

33. Describe how you would determine
   a. which of the two groups, men or women, at your college has a higher mean grade point average.
   b. which of the groups is more consistently close to its mean grade point average.

12.4

The scores on a test are normally distributed with a mean of 70 and a standard deviation of 8. In Exercises 34–36, find the score that is

34. 2 standard deviations above the mean.
35. $3\frac{1}{2}$ standard deviations above the mean.
36. $1\frac{1}{4}$ standard deviations below the mean.

The ages of people living in a retirement community are normally distributed with a mean age of 68 years and a standard deviation of 4 years. In Exercises 37–43, use the 68–95–99.7 rule to find the percentage of people in the community whose ages

37. are between 64 and 72.   38. are between 60 and 76.
39. are between 68 and 72.   40. are between 56 and 80.
41. exceed 72.   42. are less than 72.
43. exceed 76.

A set of data items is normally distributed with a mean of 50 and a standard deviation of 5. In Exercises 44–48, convert each data item to a z-score.

44. 50   45. 60   46. 58
47. 35   48. 44

49. A student scores 60 on a vocabulary test and 80 on a grammar test. The data items for both tests are normally distributed. The vocabulary test has a mean of 50 and a standard deviation of 5. The grammar test has a mean of 72 and a standard deviation of 6. On which test did the student have the better score? Explain why this is so.

The number of miles that a particular brand of car tires last is normally distributed with a mean of 32,000 miles and a standard deviation of 4000 miles. In Exercises 50–52, find the data item in this distribution that corresponds to the given z-score.

50. $z = 1.5$ 51. $z = 2.25$ 52. $z = -2.5$

The mean cholesterol level for all men in the United States is 200 and the standard deviation is 15. In Exercises 53–56, use Table 12.15 on page 633 to find the percentage of U.S. men whose cholesterol level

53. is less than 221.
54. is greater than 173.
55. is between 173 and 221.
56. is between 164 and 182.

Use the percentiles for the weights of adult men over 40 to solve Exercises 57–59.

Weight	Percentile
235	86
227	75
180	50
173	25

Find the percentage of men over 40 who weigh

57. less than 227 pounds.
58. more than 235 pounds.
59. between 227 and 235 pounds.
60. Using a random sample of 5000 TV households, Nielsen Media Research found that 9.8% watch "Jeopardy."
   a. Find the margin of error in this percent.
   b. Write a statement about the percentage of TV households in the population who watch "Jeopardy."

12.5

In Exercises 61–62, make a scatter plot for the given data. Use the scatter plot to describe whether or not the variables appear to be related.

61.

x	1	3	4	6	8	9
y	1	2	3	3	5	5

62.

Country	Canada	U.S.	Mexico	Brazil	Costa Rica	Denmark	China	Egypt	Pakistan	Bangla- desh	Australia	Japan	Russia
Life expectancy in years, x	79	76	72	64	76	76	70	62	59	57	80	80	65
Infant deaths per 1000 births, y	5.6	6.4	25.9	40.0	13.1	6.8	45.5	69.3	93.5	97.7	5.3	4.1	23.3

Source: U.S. Bureau of the Census International Database

The scatter plot in the figure shows the relationship between years of education and annual income, in thousands of dollars, for a group of randomly selected U.S. women. Use the scatter plot to determine whether each of the statements in Exercises 63–69 is true or false.

63. There is a perfect positive correlation between years of education and annual income.

64. As years of education increase, annual income tends to increase.

65. The woman with the least amount of education has the lowest annual income.

66. No two women have the same amount of education but different annual incomes.

67. There are more than 10 women in this sample.

68. There is no correlation between years of education and annual income.

69. The woman with 12 years of education earned more than $20,000 annually.

70. Which one of the following scatter plots indicates a correlation coefficient of approximately −0.9?

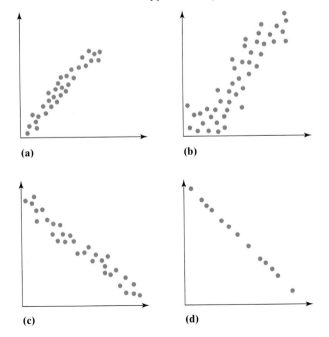

(a)　　　　　(b)

(c)　　　　　(d)

71. Use the data in Exercise 61 to solve this exercise.
    a. Compute r, the correlation coefficient, rounded to the nearest thousandth.
    b. Find the equation of the regression line.

72. The graph shows the number of people in the United States, in millions, receiving care in HMOs from 1986–1996.

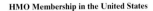

HMO Membership in the United States

Source: American Association of Health Plans

    a. Construct a scatter plot with the year on the horizontal axis.
    b. Let x represent the number of years after 1980 (so $x = 0$ corresponds to 1986, $x = 1$ to 1987, and so on) and y represent the millions of HMO members. Calculate the correlation coefficient.
    c. Using Table 12.17 on page 651 and the $\alpha = 0.05$ column, determine if there is a correlation between time and HMO membership.

Group Exercise

73. What is the opinion of students on your campus about…? Group members should begin by deciding on some aspect of college life around which student opinion can be polled. The poll should consist of the question, "What is your opinion of … ?" Be sure to provide options such as excellent, good, average, poor horrible, or a 1 to 10 scale, or possibly grades of A, B, C, D, F. Use a random sample of students on your campus and conduct the opinion survey. After collecting the data, present and interpret it using as many of the skills and techniques learned in this chapter as possible.

CHAPTER 12 TEST

1. Politicians in the Florida Keys need to know if the residents of Key Largo think the amount of money charged for water is reasonable. The politicians decide to conduct a survey of a sample of Key Largo's residents. Which procedure would be most appropriate for a sample of Key Largo's residents?
   a. Survey all water customers who pay their water bills at Key Largo City Hall on the third day of the month.
   b. Survey a random sample of executives who work for the water company in Key Largo.
   c. Survey 5000 individuals who are randomly selected from a list of all people living in Georgia and Florida.
   d. Survey a random sample of persons within each neighborhood of Key Largo.

Use these scores on a ten-point quiz to solve Exercises 2–4.

   8, 5, 3, 6, 5, 10, 6, 9, 4, 5, 7, 9, 7, 4, 8, 8

2. Construct a frequency distribution for the data.
3. Construct a histogram for the data.
4. Construct a frequency polygon for the data.

Use the 30 test scores listed below to solve Exercises 5–6.

79	51	67	50	78
62	89	83	73	80
88	48	60	71	79
89	63	55	93	71
41	81	46	50	61
59	50	90	75	61

5. Construct a grouped frequency distribution for the data. Use the classes 40–49, 50–59, 60–69, and so on.
6. Construct a stem-and-leaf display for the data.

Use the six data items listed below to solve Exercises 7–10.

   3, 6, 2, 1, 7, 3

7. Find the mean.
8. Find the median.
9. Find the midrange.
10. Find the standard deviation.

Use the frequency distribution shown to solve Exercises 11–13.

Score x	Frequency f
1	3
2	5
3	2
4	2

11. Find the mean.
12. Find the median.
13. Find the mode.
14. The annual salaries of four salespeople and the owner of a bookstore are

$$\$17,500, \$19,000, \$22,000, \$27,500, \$98,500$$

Is the mean or the median more representative of the five annual salaries? Briefly explain your answer.

According to the American Freshman, the number of hours that college freshmen spend studying each week is normally distributed with a mean of 7 hours and a standard deviation of 5.3 hours. In Exercises 15–16, use the 68–95–99.7 Rule to find the percentage of college freshmen who study

15. between 7 and 12.3 hours each week.
16. more than 17.6 hours each week.
17. IQ scores are normally distributed in the population. Who has a higher IQ: a student with a 120 IQ on a scale where 100 is the mean and 10 is the standard deviation, or a professor with a 128 IQ on a scale where 100 is the mean and 15 is the standard deviation? Briefly explain your answer.
18. Use the z-scores and the corresponding percentiles shown below to solve this problem. Test scores are normally distributed with a mean of 74 and a standard deviation of 10. What percentage of the scores are above 88?

z-Score	Percentile
1.1	86.43
1.2	88.49
1.3	90.32
1.4	91.92
1.5	93.32

19. Use the percentiles in the table shown below to find the percentage of scores between 630 and 690.

Score	Percentile
780	99
750	87
720	72
690	49
660	26
630	8
600	1

20. Using a random sample of 100 students from a campus of approximately 12,000 students, 60% of the students in the sample said they were very satisfied with their professors.
    a. Find the margin of error in this percent.
    b. Write a statement about the percentage of the entire population of students from this campus who are very satisfied with their professors.

21. Make a scatter plot for the given data. Use the scatter plot to describe whether or not the variables appear to be related.

x	1	4	3	5	2
y	5	2	2	1	4

The scatter plot at the top of the next column shows the number of minutes each of 16 people exercise per week and the number of headaches per month each person experiences. Use the scatter plot to determine whether each of the statements in Exercises 22–24 is true or false.

22. An increase in the number of minutes devoted to exercise causes a decrease in headaches.

23. There is a perfect negative correlation between time spent exercising and number of headaches.

24. The person who exercised most per week had the least number of headaches per month.

25. Is the relationship between the price of gas and the number of people visiting our national parks a positive correlation, a negative correlation, or is there no correlation? Explain your answer.

It took a while to get your passionflower vine going, but now it's finally taken off. Flowers have appeared and you are overwhelmed by their beauty. What is it about the flower that makes it so visually appealing?

13 Mathematical Systems

Is beauty in the eye of the beholder? Or are there certain objects (or people) that are so well balanced and proportioned that they are universally pleasing to the eye? In this chapter you will learn to use mathematics to describe the characteristics of forms such as the passionflower that many people find alluring.

SECTION 13.1 Mathematical Systems

Objectives

1. Understand what is meant by a mathematical system.
2. Understand properties of certain mathematical systems.

Figure 13.1 A three-way switch on the table lamp

1 Understand what is meant by a mathematical system.

Thanks for the gift. What, exactly, is it? Oh, a lamp. It's—uh—very nice. (What am I ever going to do with this hideous monument to bad taste?) What's that? You want to tell me about some of its special features? I'm all ears. We're going to start with the three-way switch. Looks pretty high-tech: Does it come with a manual? Only kidding. Do go on. So, if I turn the switch once to the right I get low-intensity light. Another turn to the right gives medium-intensity light. Still another turn results in high-intensity light. Finally, one more right turn puts the switch in the off position, resulting in no light. You've even made me a diagram of the switch? (See Figure 13.1.) Nothing like capping off this fascinating tutorial with a visual aid. Life is good.

Despite the sarcasm of the lamp's recipient, there is something mathematical happening. We begin with the obvious: The amount of light that you get depends on the position of the three-way switch when you begin and the number of turns to the right you move the switch. Using $\oplus$ to represent turning the switch to the right (clockwise), here are some examples:

$$0 \qquad \oplus \qquad 2 \qquad = \qquad 2$$

| The switch is in the off position. | Turn the switch clockwise 2 turns. | The final position of the switch is 2, giving medium light. |

$$1 \qquad \oplus \qquad 2 \qquad = \qquad 3$$

| The switch is in the low position. | Turn the switch clockwise 2 turns. | The final position of the switch is 3, giving high-intensity light. |

$$3 \qquad \oplus \qquad 1 \qquad = \qquad 0$$

| The switch is in the high position. | Turn the switch clockwise 1 turn. | The final position of the switch is 0, the off position with no light. |

Table 13.1

Number of clockwise turns

$\oplus$	0	1	2	3
0	0	1	2	3
1	1	2	3	0
2	2	3	0	1
3	3	0	1	2

Starting positions

$\oplus$	0	1	2	3
0	0	1	2	3
1	1	2	3	0
2	2	3	0	①
3	3	0	1	2

Figure 13.2 Using Table 13.1 to find $2 \oplus 3$. The intersecting lines show that $2 \oplus 3 = 1$.

We can use a table to show all possible starting and ending positions for the three-way switch. In Table 13.1, the starting positions are shown in the left column. The number of clockwise turns are shown across the top. The 16 entries in the table represent all possible final positions of the switch. For example, to find $2 \oplus 3$, find 2 in the left column and 3 across the top. Assuming a horizontal line through 2 and a vertical line through 3, as in Figure 13.2, the point of intersection of these lines is 1. Thus, $2 \oplus 3 = 1$. This means that if the switch starts in the 2, medium, position and is turned 3 positions clockwise, its final position is 1, the setting for low-intensity light.

Table 13.1 consists of a set of four elements, namely $\{0, 1, 2, 3\}$. The table provides a rule, designated by $\oplus$, that can be performed on two elements of the set at a time. Such a rule is called a *binary operation*. A **binary operation** is a rule that can be used to combine any two elements of a set, resulting in a single element. A **mathematical system** consists of a set of elements and at least one binary operation. Many mathematical systems are presented in the form of a table, such as Table 13.1.

EXAMPLE 1 An Example of a Mathematical System

If two even or two odd numbers are added, the sum is even. For example, $4 + 4 = 8$ (even + even = even). Likewise, $5 + 5 = 10$ (odd + odd = even). By contrast, if one number is even and the other odd, the sum is odd. For example, $4 + 3 = 7$ (even + odd = odd). Likewise, $7 + 6 = 13$ (odd + even = odd). If we let E represent any even number and O any odd number, these observations are summarized in Table 13.2.

a. What is the set of elements of this mathematical system?
b. What is the binary operation of this mathematical system?
c. Use Table 13.2 to find $E + O$. Explain what this means.

Solution

a. The set of elements of this mathematical system is $\{E, O\}$.
b. The binary operation used to combine any two elements of $\{E, O\}$ is $+$.
c. We find $E + O$ by drawing a horizontal line through E in the left column and a vertical line through O in the top row. These lines intersect at O, shown in Figure 13.3. Thus, $E + O = O$. This means that the sum of an even number and an odd number is an odd number.

Table 13.2

Now add an even or odd number.

+	E	O
E	E	O
O	O	E

Start with an even or odd number.

+	E	O
E	E	Ⓞ
O	O	E

Figure 13.3 Using Table 13.2 to find $E + O$

Properties of Some Mathematical Systems

We now look at five properties that apply to certain mathematical systems. You may recognize some of these properties from our work in Chapter 5, where we studied the set of real numbers with two binary operations: addition and multiplication.

2 Understand properties of certain mathematical systems.

The Closure Property

A mathematical system is **closed** under a binary operation if the answer to any possible combination of two elements of the set is an element that is in the set. For example, take a second look at Table 13.1, which shows all possible starting and ending positions for the three-way switch. The answers in the body of the table are all elements of the set $\{0, 1, 2, 3\}$. Thus, the system is closed under $\oplus$. If an element other than 0, 1, 2, or 3 had appeared in the body of the table, the system would not have been closed under the binary operation.

Table 13.1

$\oplus$	0	1	2	3
0	0	1	2	3
1	1	2	3	0
2	2	3	0	1
3	3	0	1	2

EXAMPLE 2 Understanding the Closure Property

Is the set $\{0, 1, 2, 3\}$ closed under the operation of addition?

Solution Shown on the right is an addition table for $\{0, 1, 2, 3\}$. Is every entry in the table an element in $\{0, 1, 2, 3\}$? The answer is no. The numbers 4, 5, and 6 are not elements of $\{0, 1, 2, 3\}$. The set $\{0, 1, 2, 3\}$ is not closed under addition.

+	0	1	2	3
0	0	1	2	3
1	1	2	3	4
2	2	3	4	5
3	3	4	5	6

EXAMPLE 3   Understanding the Closure Property

Consider the set of integers

$$\{\ldots, -3, -2, -1, 0, 1, 2, 3, \ldots \}.$$

Is this set closed under the operation of multiplication?

Solution   If any two integers are multiplied, the product will be an integer. Thus, the set of integers is closed under multiplication.

EXAMPLE 4   Understanding the Closure Property

Is the set of integers closed under the operation of division?

Solution   If any two integers are divided, the quotient might not be an integer. For example,

$$\underbrace{-3 \text{ and } 9 \text{ are integers.}} \qquad \frac{-3}{9} = -\frac{1}{3} \qquad -\frac{1}{3} \text{ is not an integer.}$$

Thus, the set of integers is not closed under division.

The Commutative Property

Suppose that $\circ$ represents a binary operation for the elements of a set. The set is **commutative** under the operation $\circ$ if for any two elements of the set a and b, $a \circ b = b \circ a$. The order of the two elements being combined in a commutative binary operation can be switched without changing the answer.

In Chapter 5, we saw that the integers are commutative under the operations of addition and multiplication. For example,

$$3 + 7 = 7 + 3 \quad \text{and} \quad 3 \cdot 7 = 7 \cdot 3$$

By contrast, the integers are not commutative under the operations of subtraction and division. For example,

$$8 - 4 \neq 4 - 8 \quad \text{and} \quad 8 \div 4 \neq 4 \div 8$$

In Figure 13.4, we use the table for the three-way lamp switch to show that $2 \oplus 3 = 3 \oplus 2$. Observe that $2 \oplus 3$ is found by first locating 2 on the left and 3 across the top. The green intersecting lines show that $2 \oplus 3 = 1$. We find $3 \oplus 2$ by locating 3 on the left and 2 across the top, again using intersecting lines. These yellow lines show that $3 \oplus 2 = 1$. Thus, $2 \oplus 3 = 3 \oplus 2$ because both binary operations give 1.

To verify that $\{0, 1, 2, 3\}$ is commutative under the operation $\oplus$, we need to verify all possibilities, not just $2 \oplus 3 = 3 \oplus 2$. This might take a while. Fortunately, there is a way to determine if a mathematical system given by a table is commutative under the operation shown in the table. Draw a diagonal line from upper left to lower right, as in Figure 13.5. Observe that for each number in the table, the same number is repeated the same number of times on each side of the green diagonal. For any mathematical system presented in the form of a table, if the part of the table above the diagonal is a mirror image of the part below the diagonal, the system is commutative under the operation given in the table.

$\oplus$	0	1	2	3
0	0	1	2	3
1	1	2	3	0
2	2	3	0	①
3	3	0	①	2

$2 \oplus 3 = 1$

$3 \oplus 2 = 1$

Figure 13.4 Showing that $2 \oplus 3 = 3 \oplus 2$

$\oplus$	0	1	2	3
0	0	1	2	3
1	1	2	3	0
2	2	3	0	1
3	3	0	1	2

Figure 13.5 Showing that $\{0, 1, 2, 3\}$ is commutative under $\oplus$

The Associative Property

A set of elements is **associative** under a given operation ∘ if for any three elements a, b, and c of the set,

$$(a \circ b) \circ c = a \circ (b \circ c).$$

If a binary operation is associative, the answer does not change depending on which two of any three elements are combined first.

In Chapter 5, we saw that the integers are associative under the operations of addition and multiplication. For example,

$$(3 + 4) + 2 = 3 + (4 + 2) \qquad\qquad (3 \cdot 4) \cdot 2 = 3 \cdot (4 \cdot 2)$$
$$7 + 2 = 3 + 6 \qquad\qquad\qquad 12 \cdot 2 = 3 \cdot 8$$
$$9 = 9 \qquad\qquad\qquad\qquad 24 = 24$$

By contrast, the integers are not associative under the operations of subtraction and division. For example,

$$(6 - 3) - 2 \neq 6 - (3 - 2) \qquad\qquad (6 \div 3) \div 2 \neq 6 \div (3 \div 2)$$
$$3 - 2 \neq 6 - 1 \qquad\qquad\qquad 2 \div 2 \neq 6 \div 1.5$$
$$1 \neq 5 \qquad\qquad\qquad\qquad 1 \neq 4$$

EXAMPLE 5   Verifying One Case for the Associative Property

Use Table 13.3, the table for the three-way lamp switch, to verify the associative property if $a = 3$, $b = 2$, and $c = 1$.

Solution   We must show that $(3 \oplus 2) \oplus 1 = 3 \oplus (2 \oplus 1)$.

Table 13.3

⊕	0	1	2	3
0	0	1	2	3
1	1	2	3	0
2	2	3	0	1
3	3	0	1	2

Locate 3 on the left and 2 on the top of Table 13.3. Intersecting lines show 3 ⊕ 2 = 1.

$$(3 \oplus 2) \oplus 1 = 3 \oplus (2 \oplus 1)$$
$$1 \oplus 1 = 3 \oplus 3$$
$$2 = 2$$

Locate 2 on the left and 1 across the top of Table 13.3. Intersecting lines show 2 ⊕ 1 = 3.

Changing the location of the parentheses does not change the answer, 2.

If every choice of three elements from the set $\{0, 1, 2, 3\}$ is checked, it can be shown that the mathematical system in Table 13.3 is associative under the operation ⊕.

The Identity Property

I see your hand on my three-way lamp switch. Please do not turn it because I like the light intensity just the way that it is. If it's off, leave it off: $0 \oplus 0 = 0$. If it's in the low position, leave it there: $1 \oplus 0 = 1$. If it's in the medium position, don't change anything: $2 \oplus 0 = 2$. Finally, if the light intensity is high, on high it will remain: $3 \oplus 0 = 3$.

Does not changing anything remind you of the role that the number 0 plays in addition and the number 1 plays in multiplication? If a represents any real number,

$$a + 0 = a \quad \text{and} \quad 0 + a = a$$
$$a \cdot 1 = a \quad \text{and} \quad 1 \cdot a = a.$$

In each equation, we end with the identical number with which we started, namely a. We call 0 the **identity element of addition** and 1 the **identity element of multiplication**.

In a mathematical system, the **identity element** (if there is one) is an element from the set such that when a binary operation is performed on any element in the set and the identity element, the result is the given element. If a represents any element in the set and the binary operation is represented by $\circ$:

$$a \circ \text{identity element} = a \quad \text{and} \quad \text{identity element} \circ a = a$$

> An element does not change when we perform an operation with an identity element.

EXAMPLE 6   Identifying the Identity Element

Table 13.4

$\circ$	a	b	c
a	c	a	b
b	a	b	c
c	b	c	a

Consider the set $\{a, b, c\}$. A binary operation on this set is given in Table 13.4. What is the identity element for this mathematical system?

Solution   Look for the element in $\{a, b, c\}$ that changes nothing when used in the binary operation $\circ$. Notice that the column under b is the same as the column on the left.

$$a \circ b = a \quad b \circ b = b \quad c \circ b = c$$

Notice, too, that the row to the right of b is the same as the top row.

$$b \circ a = a \quad b \circ b = b \quad b \circ c = c$$

The element b does not change anything. Thus, b is the identity element for the mathematical system.

The Inverse Property

It's time to get this lamp with the three-way switch out of my life. Hope I don't get charged with design pollution while driving it to the dump. I'll start by turning it off. (See Figure 13.6.) If it's already off, I'll leave it there: $0 \oplus 0 = 0$. If it's on low, 1, I'll move it to the off position by 3 clockwise turns: $1 \oplus 3 = 0$. If it's on medium, 2, two turns to the right will quiet the beast: $2 \oplus 2 = 0$. Finally, if it's on high, 3, one right turn will slay the dragon: $3 \oplus 1 = 0$.

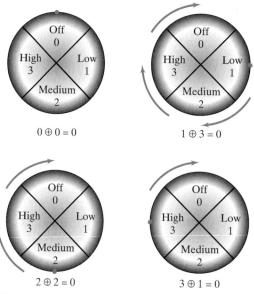

$$0 \oplus 0 = 0 \qquad 1 \oplus 3 = 0$$

$$2 \oplus 2 = 0 \qquad 3 \oplus 1 = 0$$

Figure 13.6 Slaying the dragon

Buried in this lamp rant is a property that applies to many, but not all, mathematical systems. Do you see that the answer to each of the four binary operations in Figure 13.6 is the identity element 0? For example,

$$1 \oplus 3 = 0. \quad \text{identity element}$$

In a situation like this, we say that 1 is the *inverse* of 3 and 3 is the *inverse* of 1. In general, suppose that a binary operation is performed on two elements in a set and the result is the identity element for the binary operation. Under these conditions, each element is called the **inverse** of the other. Inverses restore the identity.

	Element	$\oplus$	Inverse	=	Identity	
0 is its own inverse.	0	$\oplus$	0	=	0	
2 is its own inverse.	1	$\oplus$	3	=	0	*1 and 3 are inverses*
	2	$\oplus$	2	=	0	*of each other.*
	3	$\oplus$	1	=	0	

EXAMPLE 7   Identifying an Inverse

Consider the set of integers

$$\{\ldots, -3, -2, -1, 0, 1, 2, 3, \ldots\}.$$

What is the inverse of 17 under the operation of addition?

Solution   When an element operates on its inverse, the result is the identity element. Because the operation is addition, the identity element is 0. To find the inverse of 17, we answer the question: What integer must be added to 17 to obtain a sum of 0?

$$17 + ? = 0$$

The required integer is -17: $17 + (-17) = 0$. Thus, the inverse of 17 under the operation of addition is -17.

We can generalize from Example 7. If a is an integer, the inverse for the operation of addition is $-a$.

$$a + (-a) = 0$$

$-a$ is often called the **additive inverse** of a.

In Chapter 5, we defined the set of *rational numbers* as the set of all numbers in the form $\frac{a}{b}$, where a and b are integers and $b \neq 0$. Our next example involves a mathematical system with rational numbers.

EXAMPLE 8   Identifying an Inverse

Consider the set of rational numbers. What is the inverse of 17 under the operation of multiplication?

Solution   When an element operates on its inverse, the result is the identity element. Because the operation is multiplication, the identity element is 1. To find the inverse of 17, we answer the question: 17 times what rational number gives 1?

$$17 \cdot ? = 1$$

The required rational number is $\frac{1}{17}$: $17 \cdot \frac{1}{17} = 1$. Thus, the inverse of 17 under the operation of multiplication is $\frac{1}{17}$.

We can generalize from Example 8. If a is any rational number *other than zero*, the inverse for the operation of multiplication is $\frac{1}{a}$.

$$a \cdot \frac{1}{a} = 1$$

$\frac{1}{a}$ is often called the **multiplicative inverse** of a. Zero has no multiplicative inverse because no rational number can be multiplied by 0 to give 1.

Table 13.5

∘	S	L	A	R
S	S	L	A	R
L	L	A	R	S
A	A	R	S	L
R	R	S	L	A

EXAMPLE 9   Identity Element and Inverse Elements

For the mathematical system defined by Table 13.5,

   a. What is the identity element?

   b. Find the inverse for each element in $\{S, L, A, R\}$.

Solution

   a. The identity element is the element in $\{S, L, A, R\}$ that does not change any element to which it is combined in the binary operation ∘. Figure 13.7 shows that the column under S is the same as the column on the left and the row next to S is the same as the row on the top. The element S does not change anything. Thus, S is the identity element.

∘	S	L	A	R
S	S	L	A	R
L	L	A	R	S
A	A	R	S	L
R	R	S	L	A

Figure 13.7 S does not change any element to which it is combined

   b. When an element operates on its inverse, the result is the identity element. Because the identity element is S, we can find the inverse of each element in $\{S, L, A, R\}$ by answering the question: What must each element be operated by to obtain S?

$$\text{element} \circ \text{?} = S$$

Figure 13.8 illustrates how we answer the question. Look at the entries on the left, find S in the body of the table in each row, and then locate the entry across the top that gives S. We see that

∘	S	L	A	R
S→	S	L	A	R
L→	L — A — R — S
A→	A — R — S	L
R→	R — S	L	A

Figure 13.8 Locating inverses

$S \circ S = S$, meaning that S is its own inverse.

$L \circ R = S$, so R is the inverse of L, and vice versa.

$A \circ A = S$, so the inverse of A is A.

$R \circ L = S$, showing again that R and L are inverses of each other.

Exercise Set 13.1

 Practice Exercises

Use the mathematical system given by the table shown to solve Exercises 1–14.

∘	e	a	b	c
e	e	a	b	c
a	a	e	c	b
b	b	c	e	a
c	c	b	a	e

1. What is the set of elements of this mathematical system?

2. What is the binary operation of this mathematical system?

Find

3. $a \circ b$.

4. $c \circ a$.

5. $b \circ c$.

6. $c \circ b$.

7. $e \circ e$.

8. $e \circ a$.

9. $b \circ e$.

10. $c \circ e$.

11. $a \circ a$.

12. $b \circ b$.

13. $c \circ c$.

14. Is the mathematical system closed under the binary operation? Explain your answer.

15. Is the set $\{0, 1, 2, 3, 4\}$ closed under the operation of addition? Explain your answer.

16. Is the set $\{0, 1, 2, 3, 4, 5\}$ closed under the operation of addition? Explain your answer.

17. Is the set of natural numbers $\{1, 2, 3, 4, 5, \ldots\}$ closed under the operation of addition? Explain your answer.

18. Is the set of natural numbers {1, 2, 3, 4, 5, …} closed under the operation of multiplication? Explain your answer.

19. Is the set of natural numbers closed under the operation of subtraction? Explain your answer.

20. Is the set of natural numbers closed under the operation of division? Explain your answer.

*In Exercises 21–22, use the table shown to explain whether or not the mathematical system is closed under the binary operation *.*

21.

*	a	b
a	a	b
b	c	a

22.

*	d	e	f
d	d	e	g
e	e	d	f
f	f	e	d

Use the mathematical system given by the table shown to solve Exercises 23–32.

⊕	0	1	2	3	4
0	0	1	2	3	4
1	1	2	3	4	0
2	2	3	4	0	1
3	3	4	0	1	2
4	4	0	1	2	3

Show that

23. $2 \oplus 4 = 4 \oplus 2$.

24. $3 \oplus 4 = 4 \oplus 3$.

25. $4 \oplus 1 = 1 \oplus 4$.

26. $2 \oplus 3 = 3 \oplus 2$.

27. What property is illustrated in Exercises 23–26? Use the table to explain how to verify this property for all possible cases without having to consider one case at a time.

Find

28. $(3 \oplus 2) \oplus 4$ and $3 \oplus (2 \oplus 4)$. What do you observe?

29. $(4 \oplus 3) \oplus 2$ and $4 \oplus (3 \oplus 2)$. What do you observe?

30. $(2 \oplus 2) \oplus 3$ and $2 \oplus (2 \oplus 3)$.

31. $(4 \oplus 4) \oplus 2$ and $4 \oplus (4 \oplus 2)$.

32. What property is illustrated in Exercises 28–31?

33. Use the table shown at the top of the next column to find

a. $(b \circ c) \circ b$.   b. $b \circ (c \circ b)$.

c. Is the mathematical system associative under the operation ∘? Explain your answer.

∘	a	b	c
a	a	b	c
b	b	a	c
c	c	b	a

34. Use the table shown below to find

a. $(b \circ b) \circ c$.   b. $b \circ (b \circ c)$.

c. Is the mathematical system associative under the operation ∘? Explain your answer.

∘	a	b	c
a	a	b	c
b	b	b	a
c	c	a	c

35. Provide an original example to show that the integers are not associative under subtraction.

36. Provide an original example to show that the integers are not associative under division.

In Exercises 37–40, consider the set of rational numbers.

37. What is the inverse of 29 under the operation of addition?

38. What is the inverse of 43 under the operation of addition?

39. What is the inverse of 29 under the operation of multiplication?

40. What is the inverse of 43 under the operation of multiplication?

Use the mathematical system given by the table shown to solve Exercises 41–56.

∘	a	b	c	d	e
a	a	b	c	d	e
b	b	c	d	e	a
c	c	d	e	a	b
d	d	e	a	b	c
e	e	a	b	c	d

Find

41. $a \circ a$.   42. $a \circ b$.   43. $a \circ c$.

44. $a \circ d$.   45. $a \circ e$.   46. $b \circ a$.

47. $c \circ a$.   48. $d \circ a$.   49. $e \circ a$.

50. What can you conclude about the element a in this mathematical system?

Find the element represented by a question mark.

51. $a \circ ? = a$ 52. $b \circ ? = a$

53. $c \circ ? = a$ 54. $d \circ ? = a$

55. $e \circ ? = a$

56. What is true about the relationship between the elements on the left sides of the equations in Exercises 51–55?

Use the mathematical system given by the table shown to solve Exercises 57–62.

⊕	0	1	2	3	4
0	0	1	2	3	4
1	1	2	3	4	0
2	2	3	4	0	1
3	3	4	0	1	2
4	4	0	1	2	3

57. What is the identity element?

Find the inverse for

58. 0.   59. 1.   60. 2.   61. 3.   62. 4.

63. a. Use the table shown below to find the identity element for this mathematical system.
    b. Find, if possible, the inverse for each element of the set. Do some elements not have inverses? Which ones?

∘	a	b	c	d
a	a	a	a	a
b	a	b	b	b
c	a	b	c	c
d	a	b	c	d

64. a. Use the table shown below to find the identity element for this mathematical system.
    b. Find, if possible, the inverse for each element of the set. Do some elements not have inverses? Which ones?

∘	a	b	c	d	e
a	d	e	a	b	b
b	e	a	b	a	d
c	a	b	c	d	e
d	b	a	d	e	c
e	b	d	e	c	a

 Application Exercises

65. Suppose that a lamp has a four-way switch. The positions of the switch are 0 : off, 1 : dim, 2 : low, 3 : medium, and 4 : high. Describe the relationship between this switch and the mathematical system given by the table shown for Exercises 57–62.

66. An army drill instructor gives you four different commands. They are S: stand still, L: left face (turn 90° to your

left), A: about face (turn 180° to your right), and R: right face (turn 90° to your right). The operation ∘ represents two commands in succession. Describe the relationship between this situation and the mathematical system given by Table 13.5 on page 670.

Let E represent any even number, and let O represent any odd number, as in Example 1 on page 665. However, instead of adding numbers, as we did in Example 1, we will be multiplying them. In order to solve Exercises 67–72, begin by filling in the four missing entries in the table shown.

×	E	O
E	—	—
O	—	—

67. Is the set $\{E, O\}$ closed under the operation of multiplication? Explain your answer.

68. Verify one case of the commutative property.

69. Verify one case of the associative property.

70. What is the identity element?

71. Find the inverse of E.

72. Find the inverse of O.

 Writing in Mathematics

73. Describe what is meant by a mathematical system.

74. What is the closure property? Give an example.

75. What is the commutative property? Give an example.

76. What is the associative property? Give an example

77. What is the identity property? Give an example.

78. What is the inverse property? Give an example.

79. Describe the difference between a nonzero number's additive inverse and multiplicative inverse. Provide an example.

 Critical Thinking Exercises

80. Give an example of a mathematical system that is different than any seen in this section.

81. If $\begin{bmatrix} a & b \\ c & d \end{bmatrix} \times \begin{bmatrix} e & f \\ g & h \end{bmatrix} = \begin{bmatrix} ae + bg & af + bh \\ ce + dg & cf + dh \end{bmatrix}$, find

   a. $\begin{bmatrix} 2 & 3 \\ 4 & 7 \end{bmatrix} \times \begin{bmatrix} 0 & 1 \\ 5 & 6 \end{bmatrix}$.

   b. $\begin{bmatrix} 0 & 1 \\ 5 & 6 \end{bmatrix} \times \begin{bmatrix} 2 & 3 \\ 4 & 7 \end{bmatrix}$.

   c. Draw a conclusion about one of the properties discussed in this section in terms of these arrays of numbers under multiplication.

SECTION 13.2   Rotational Symmetry, Groups, and Clock Arithmetic

Objectives

1. Recognize rotational symmetry.
2. Determine if a mathematical system is a group.
3. Understand clock systems as groups.
4. Understand congruence in a modulo *m* system.
5. Perform additions in a modulo *m* system.

Figure 13.9

1 Recognize rotational symmetry.

Mathematics is about the patterns that arise in the world about us. Mathematicians look at a snowflake in terms of its underlying structure. Notice that if the snowflake in Figure 13.9 is rotated by any multiple of 60° ($\frac{1}{6}$ of a rotation), it will always look about the same. A **symmetry** of an object is a motion that moves the object back onto itself. In a symmetry, you cannot tell, at the end of the motion, that the object has been moved.

The snowflake in Figure 13.9 has **sixfold rotational symmetry**. After six 60° turns, the snowflake is back to its original position. If it takes *m* equal turns to restore an object to its original position, the object has ***m*-fold rotational symmetry**. Consider, for example, a pinwheel. Figure 13.10 shows that as the pinwheel rotates, at each quarter turn it is in a new position, yet it looks exactly the same as it did at the start. If all its petals are the same color, we cannot distinguish the original position from the new position after one quarter turn, two quarter turns, or three quarter turns. After four quarters (that is, after a full rotation), we are back to the starting position. The pinwheel has **fourfold rotational symmetry**. If the blades are colored or numbered, it is possible to keep track of the pinwheel's rotation.

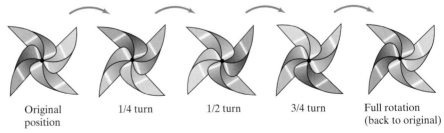

| Original position | 1/4 turn | 1/2 turn | 3/4 turn | Full rotation (back to original) |

Figure 13.10

A two-blade propeller with twofold rotational symmetry

Does the pinwheel remind you of anything? Its symmetry is exactly the same as that of the infamous light switch with its off, low, medium, and high positions. Special kinds of mathematical systems, called *groups*, are used to study the symmetries and hidden structure of our world. Objects that appear to be totally different, such as a pinwheel and a lamp switch, can be unified by the definition of a group. We begin with this definition.

The logo from a Korean bank with fivefold rotational symmetry

The seedpot of the autograph tree (*Clusia Rosea*) with eightfold rotational symmetry

Groups

I went to the movies with a *group* of friends. I bought an interesting *group* of paintings for my living room wall. We use the word *group* in everyday speech when referring to any collection of persons or things. However, in mathematics *group* means something entirely different. A group is a mathematical system meeting four requirements.

Definition of a Group

A mathematical system that meets the following four requirements is called a **group**.

1. The set of elements in the mathematical system is *closed* under the given binary operation, represented in this box by ∘.
2. The set of elements is *associative* under the given binary operation. If a, b, and c are any three elements of the set,

$$(a \circ b) \circ c = a \circ (b \circ c).$$

3. The set of elements contains an *identity* element. When the binary operation ∘ is performed on the identity element and each element in the set, the result is the given element.
4. Each element of the set has an *inverse* that lies within the set. When an element operates on its inverse, the result is the identity element.

Do you notice anything missing from these four requirements? The commutative property does not need to hold for a mathematical system to be a group. If a group does satisfy the commutative property (that is, if $a \circ b = b \circ a$ for any two elements of the set), it is called a **commutative group**.

2 Determine if a mathematical system is a group.

Table 13.6

·	−1	1
−1	1	−1
1	−1	1

EXAMPLE 1   Showing That a Mathematical System Is a Group

Table 13.6 is a mathematical system for the set $\{-1, 1\}$ under the binary operation of multiplication.

a. Show that the mathematical system is a group.

b. Show that the group is commutative.

Solution

a. We begin by checking the four requirements—closure, the associative property, the identity property, and the inverse property—for a mathematical system to qualify as group.

1. **The Closure Property.** The set $\{-1, 1\}$ is closed under the binary operation of multiplication because the entries in the body of Table 13.6 are all elements of the set.

2. **The Associative Property.** Is $(a \cdot b) \cdot c = a \cdot (b \cdot c)$ for all elements a, b, and c of the set? Let us select some values for a, b, and c. Let $a = 1, b = -1$ and $c = -1$. Then

$$\left[1 \cdot (-1)\right] \cdot (-1) = -1 \cdot (-1) = 1$$

and

$$1 \cdot \left[(-1) \cdot (-1)\right] = 1 \cdot 1 = 1.$$

Fivefold rotational symmetry

Sixfold rotational symmetry
Flowers with rotational symmetries

Figure 13.11 Using Table 13.6 to locate inverses

The associative property holds when $a = 1, b = -1,$ and $c = -1.$ This does not prove that the mathematical system is associative. However, we could check every possible choice of three elements from the set. Such a check would verify that the system does satisfy the associative property.

3. **The Identity Property.** Look for the element in $\{-1, 1\}$ that does not change anything when used in multiplication. The element 1 does not change anything:

$$-1 \cdot 1 = -1 \qquad 1 \cdot (-1) = -1 \qquad 1 \cdot 1 = 1$$

An element does not change when we multiply with 1.

Thus, 1 is the identity element. The identity property is satisfied because 1 is contained in the set $\{-1, 1\}$.

4. **The Inverse Property.** When an element operates on its inverse, the result is the identity element. Because the identity element is 1, we can find the inverse of each element in $\{-1, 1\}$ by answering the question: What must each element be multiplied by to obtain 1?

$$\text{element} \cdot ? = 1$$

Figure 13.11 illustrates how we answer the question. If each element in $\{-1, 1\}$ has an inverse that restores the identity element 1, then a 1 will appear in every row and column of the table. This is, indeed, the case. Using 1 in each row, we see that:
$-1 \cdot -1 = 1,$ so the inverse of -1 is $-1.$
$1 \cdot 1 = 1,$ so the inverse of 1 is 1.
Because each element in $\{-1, 1\}$ has an inverse within the set, the inverse property is satisfied.

In summary, the set $\{-1, 1\}$ satisfies the closure property, the associative property, the identity property, and the inverse property under the operation of multiplication. Thus, the mathematical system is a group.

b. To show that the group is commutative, we must show that the commutative property is satisfied. Is $a \cdot b = b \cdot a$ for all elements a and b of $\{-1, 1\}$? We need to examine only one case, the case where a and b have different values.

$$1 \cdot (-1) = -1 \qquad \text{and} \qquad -1 \cdot 1 = -1$$

The order of the factors in the multiplication does not matter. Thus, $\{-1, 1\}$ is a commutative group under multiplication.

If a mathematical system fails to meet even one of the four requirements for a group, that system is not a group. For example, consider the set of integers $\{\ldots, -3, -2, -1, 0, 1, 2, 3, \ldots\}$ under the operation of multiplication. Although the closure property, the associative property, and the identity property are satisfied, the inverses of the integers are not contained within the set. For example, the multiplicative inverse of 3 is $\frac{1}{3}(3 \cdot \frac{1}{3} = 1).$ However, $\frac{1}{3}$ is not an integer. Because there is at least one element, 3, in the set of integers that fails to have an inverse that lies within the set, the integers do not satisfy the inverse property under multiplication. The failure to meet one of a group's four requirements means that the integers are not a group under multiplication.

3 Understand clock systems as groups.

Figure 13.12 A 12-hour clock.

Clock Arithmetic and Groups

Figure 13.12 looks like the ordinary face of a clock, with two differences. The minute hand is left off, and 12 is replaced by 0. If we replace each number by a small tick-mark, we can observe 12-fold rotational symmetry. If the clock is rotated $\frac{1}{12}$ of a rotation, the tick-marks will fall in the same positions and you cannot tell that the clock's face has been moved. Because Figure 13.12 has numbers instead of tick-marks, it takes 12 turns to restore 0 to its original position.

Consider the mathematical system formed by the set of numbers on the 12-hour clock:

$$\{0, 1, 2, 3, 4, 5, 6, 7, 8, 9, 10, 11\}$$

and a binary operation called *clock addition*. **Clock addition** is defined as follows: Add by moving the hour hand in a clockwise direction. The symbol $+$ is used to designate clock addition. Using the definition of clock addition, Figure 13.13 illustrates that $5 + 2 = 7$, $8 + 9 = 5$, and $11 + 4 = 3$.

Figure 13.13

Addition in a 12-Hour Clock System

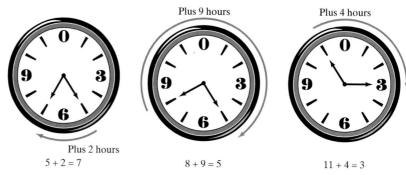

Plus 2 hours
$5 + 2 = 7$

Plus 9 hours
$8 + 9 = 5$

Plus 4 hours
$11 + 4 = 3$

Table 13.7 is the addition table for clock addition in a 12-hour clock system.

Table 13.7   Table for 12-Hour Clock Addition

+	0	1	2	3	4	5	6	7	8	9	10	11
0	0	1	2	3	4	5	6	7	8	9	10	11
1	1	2	3	4	5	6	7	8	9	10	11	0
2	2	3	4	5	6	7	8	9	10	11	0	1
3	3	4	5	6	7	8	9	10	11	0	1	2
4	4	5	6	7	8	9	10	11	0	1	2	3
5	5	6	7	8	9	10	11	0	1	2	3	4
6	6	7	8	9	10	11	0	1	2	3	4	5
7	7	8	9	10	11	0	1	2	3	4	5	6
8	8	9	10	11	0	1	2	3	4	5	6	7
9	9	10	11	0	1	2	3	4	5	6	7	8
10	10	11	0	1	2	3	4	5	6	7	8	9
11	11	0	1	2	3	4	5	6	7	8	9	10

This U.S. stamp celebrating our friendship with Morocco shows a geometric form with 12-fold rotational symmetry. The form, and all objects with such symmetry, can be analyzed by the properties and patterns of the 12-hour clock system.

EXAMPLE 2   The 12-Hour Clock System as a Group

Show that the mathematical system given by Table 13.7 is a commutative group.

Solution   We must check the five requirements—the closure property, the associative property, the identity property, the inverse property, and the commutative property—for a commutative group.

1. **The Closure Property.** The set $\{0, 1, 2, 3, 4, 5, 6, 7, 8, 9, 10, 11\}$ is closed under the operation of clock addition because the entries in the body of Table 13.7 are all elements of the set.

2. **The Associative Property.** Is $(a + b) + c = a + (b + c)$ for all elements a, b, and c of the set? Let us select some values for a, b, and c. Let $a = 4$, $b = 7$, and $c = 9$.

Locate 4 on the left and 7 on the top of Table 13.7. Intersecting lines show 4 + 7 = 11.	$(4 + 7) + 9 = 4 + (7 + 9)$ $11 + 9 = 4 + 4$ $8 = 8$	Locate 7 on the left and 9 across the top of Table 13.7. Intersecting lines show 7 + 9 = 4.

The associative property holds when $a = 4$, $b = 7$, and $c = 9$. As always, this does not prove that the mathematical system is associative under clock addition. However, we could check every possible choice of three elements from the set. Such a check would verify that the system does satisfy the associative property.

3. **The Identity Property.** Look for the element in Table 13.7 that does not change anything when used in clock addition. Table 13.7 shows that the column under 0 is the same as the column on the left. Thus, $0 + 0 = 0, 1 + 0 = 1, 2 + 0 = 2$, $3 + 0 = 3$, and so on, up through $11 + 0 = 11$. The table also shows that the row next to 0 is the same as the row on top. Thus, $0 + 0 = 0, 0 + 1 = 1$, $0 + 2 = 2$, up through $0 + 11 = 11$. Each element of the set does not change when we perform clock addition with 0. Thus, 0 is the identity element. The identity property is satisfied because 0 is contained in the given set.

4. **The Inverse Property.** When an element operates on its inverse, the result is the identity element. Because the identity element is 0, we can find the inverse of each element in $\{0, 1, 2, 3, 4, 5, 6, 7, 8, 9, 10, 11\}$ by answering the question: What must be added to each element to obtain 0?

$$\text{element} + ? = 0$$

Figure 13.14 illustrates how we answer the question. If each element in the set has an inverse that restores the identity element 0, then a 0 will appear in every row and column of the table. This is, indeed, the case. Use the 0 in each row. Because each element in $\{0, 1, 2, 3, 4, 5, 6, 7, 8, 9, 10, 11\}$ has an inverse within the set, the inverse property is satisfied.

The Longest Proof in Mathematics

The *Guinness Book of World Records* mentions the "enormous theorem" that deals with classifying groups into "families." Sounds simple? Not so. Completed in the 1980s, the proof is spread over more than 14,000 pages in nearly 500 articles in mathematical journals, contributed by more than 100 mathematicians over a period of more than 35 years.

+	0	1	2	3	4	5	6	7	8	9	10	11
0	0	1	2	3	4	5	6	7	8	9	10	11
1	1	2	3	4	5	6	7	8	9	10	11	0
2	2	3	4	5	6	7	8	9	10	11	0	1
3	3	4	5	6	7	8	9	10	11	0	1	2
4	4	5	6	7	8	9	10	11	0	1	2	3
5	5	6	7	8	9	10	11	0	1	2	3	4
6	6	7	8	9	10	11	0	1	2	3	4	5
7	7	8	9	10	11	0	1	2	3	4	5	6
8	8	9	10	11	0	1	2	3	4	5	6	7
9	9	10	11	0	1	2	3	4	5	6	7	8
10	10	11	0	1	2	3	4	5	6	7	8	9
11	11	0	1	2	3	4	5	6	7	8	9	10

$0 + 0 = 0$: The inverse of 0 is 0.
$1 + 11 = 0$: The inverse of 1 is 11.
$2 + 10 = 0$: The inverse of 2 is 10.
$3 + 9 = 0$: The inverse of 3 is 9.
$4 + 8 = 0$: The inverse of 4 is 8.
$5 + 7 = 0$: The inverse of 5 is 7.
$6 + 6 = 0$: The inverse of 6 is 6.
$7 + 5 = 0$: The inverse of 7 is 5.
$8 + 4 = 0$: The inverse of 8 is 4.
$9 + 3 = 0$: The inverse of 9 is 3.
$10 + 2 = 0$: The inverse of 10 is 2.
$11 + 1 = 0$: The inverse of 11 is 1.

Figure 13.14 Locating inverses. The arrows illustrate that $1 + 11 = 0$ and $8 + 4 = 0$.

5. **The Commutative Property.** Is $a + b = b + a$ for all elements a and b of $\{0, 1, 2, 3, 4, 5, 6, 7, 8, 9, 10, 11\}$? Let us check a few cases. $6 + 9$ and $9 + 6$ both yield 3. Also, $5 + 8$ and $8 + 5$ both yield 1. Order of clock addition does not matter for these cases.

We can use the method discussed in the previous section to avoid checking the commutative property one case at a time. Draw a diagonal line from upper left to lower right, as in Figure 13.15. The part of the table above the diagonal is a mirror image of the part below the diagonal. For each number in the table, the same number is repeated the same number of times on each side of the diagonal. Thus, the system satisfies the commutative property.

+	0	1	2	3	4	5	6	7	8	9	10	11
0	0	1	2	3	4	5	6	7	8	9	10	11
1	1	2	3	4	5	6	7	8	9	10	11	0
2	2	3	4	5	6	7	8	9	10	11	0	1
3	3	4	5	6	7	8	9	10	11	0	1	2
4	4	5	6	7	8	9	10	11	0	1	2	3
5	5	6	7	8	9	10	11	0	1	2	3	4
6	6	7	8	9	10	11	0	1	2	3	4	5
7	7	8	9	10	11	0	1	2	3	4	5	6
8	8	9	10	11	0	1	2	3	4	5	6	7
9	9	10	11	0	1	2	3	4	5	6	7	8
10	10	11	0	1	2	3	4	5	6	7	8	9
11	11	0	1	2	3	4	5	6	7	8	9	10

Figure 13.15 Showing that a system is commutative by observing numbers above and below the diagonal.

Because the five properties listed above are satisfied, the 12-hour clock system is a commutative group.

4 Understand congruence in a modulo m system.

Figure 13.16 Symmetry in Native American design

Figure 13.17 Mod 7 $\{0, 1, 2, 3, 4, 5, 6\}$

Modular Systems

The 12-hour clock system and the operation of clock addition form what is called a **modulo 12** system, or a **mod 12** system. Although this system is ideal for illuminating the structure of 12-fold symmetry, it would not be a system used to describe the structure of the design in Figure 13.16. Native American pottery has decorations with a wide variety of different kinds of rotational symmetry. This design, similar to those found on Pueblo pottery, has sevenfold rotational symmetry. Its pattern can be studied with a modulo 7 system consisting of seven elements, 0 through 6, and the binary operation of clock addition. The seven-hour clock for the mod 7 system is shown in Figure 13.17.

We perform clock addition in the mod 7 system exactly as we did in the 12-hour clock system. For example, the figure on the right shows how we can find $6 + 3$. We start at 6 and advance the hour hand three hours. This puts the hour hand at 2. Thus, in mod 7, $6 + 3 = 2$. We express this by writing

$$6 + 3 \equiv 2 \ (\text{mod } 7).$$

The symbol $\equiv$ is read "is congruent to." Thus, $6 + 3$ is congruent to 2 in a modulo 7 system.

In the modulo 7 system, regardless of where we start, if we advance the hour hand 7 units, we wind up at the same number. This is also true if we advance the hour hand 14 units, 21 units, or any multiple of 7 units. What counts in terms of where the hour hand stops is given by the remainder after each multiple of 7. This observation should help you to understand each of the following congruences. For simplicity, suppose that we start at 0.

Plus 3 hours

$6 + 3 = 2$
in mod 7

Advance 9 units:	Advance 16 units:	Advance 23 units:
$9 \equiv 2 \pmod 7$	$16 \equiv 2 \pmod 7$	$23 \equiv 2 \pmod 7$
$9 \div 7 = 1$, remainder 2	$16 \div 7 = 2$, remainder 2	$23 \div 7 = 3$, remainder 2

By starting at 0 on the 7-hour clock in Figure 13.17 and advancing 9 units, 16 units, or 23 units, we wind up at 2 in each case.

Generalizing from this situation, we describe *m*-fold rotational symmetry with a **modulo *m*** system. Such a system consists of *m* integers, starting with 0 and ending with $m - 1$. For example, a modulo 5 system (Figure 13.18) consists of five integers, starting with 0 and ending with $5 - 1$, or 4. The integers *a* and *b* are **congruent modulo *m***, denoted by

$$a \equiv b \pmod m,$$

means that if *a* is divided by *m*, the remainder is *b*.

Figure 13.18 Mod 5
$\{0, 1, 2, 3, 4\}$

EXAMPLE 3 Understanding Congruence

Label each statement as true or false.
  a. $22 \equiv 4 \pmod 6$ b. $12 \equiv 4 \pmod 3$ c. $49 \equiv 5 \pmod{11}$

Solution
  a. Is $22 \equiv 4 \pmod 6$? If 22 is divided by 6, is the remainder 4? $22 \div 6 = 3$, remainder 4. Because the remainder is 4, the statement is true.
  b. Is $12 \equiv 4 \pmod 3$? If 12 is divided by 3, is the remainder 4? $12 \div 3 = 4$, remainder 0. Because the remainder is not 4, the statement is false. A true statement is $12 \equiv 0 \pmod 3$.
  c. Is $49 \equiv 5 \pmod{11}$? If 49 is divided by 11, is the remainder 5? $49 \div 11 = 4$, remainder 5. Because the remainder is 5, the statement is true.

5 Perform additions in a modulo *m* system.

Understanding congruence gives us a procedure for performing addition in any modulo system without having to draw a clock.

> **How to Add in a Modulo *m* System**
>
> 1. Add the numbers using ordinary arithmetic.
> 2. If the sum is less than *m*, the answer is the sum obtained.
> 3. If the sum is greater than or equal to *m*, the answer is the remainder obtained upon dividing the sum in step 1 by *m*.

EXAMPLE 4 Modular Additions

Find each of the following sums.

  a. $(2 + 4) \pmod 7$ b. $(4 + 4) \pmod 5$ c. $(9 + 10) \pmod{12}$

Solution
  a. To find $(2 + 4) \pmod 7$, first add $2 + 4$ to get 6. Because this sum is less than 7,

$$2 + 4 \equiv 6 \pmod 7.$$

Symmetry and Physical Attractiveness

Symmetry in the human face is one key to physical attractiveness. An attractive face is almost completely symmetrical, although the symmetry is not rotational. By drawing lines between paired features and marking the midpoints, we can see how the features line up almost perfectly. To most people, an attractive face is one in which each half is an almost perfect mirror image of the other half.

b. To find $(4 + 4)$ (mod 5), first add $4 + 4$ to get 8. Because 8 is greater than 5, divide 8 by 5.

$$8 \div 5 = 1, \text{remainder } 3$$

The remainder, 3, is the desired sum.

$$4 + 4 \equiv 3 \text{ (mod 5)}$$

c. To find $(9 + 10)$ (mod 12), first add $9 + 10$ to get 19. Because this sum is greater than 12, divide 19 by 12.

$$19 \div 12 = 1, \text{remainder } 7$$

The remainder, 7, is the desired sum.

$$9 + 10 \equiv 7 \text{ (mod 12)}$$

Being able to add in a modular system without having to draw a clock means that we can construct an addition table for the system fairly quickly. All such tables represent mathematical systems that are commutative groups. We can show that any modular system is a commutative group under addition by verifying each of the five properties (closure, associative, identity, inverse, commutative) as we did for the modulo 12 system in Example 2.

Modulo systems are also used to solve problems involving cyclical changes, such as calendar problems. Because there are 7 days in a week, we can consider this as a modulo 7 system, in which Sunday is 0, Monday is 1, Tuesday 2, Wednesday 3, Thursday 4, Friday 5, and Saturday 6.

EXAMPLE 5   Solving a Calendar Problem

Suppose today is Thursday, July 2. Which day of the week will it be 47 days from now?

Solution   Dates that differ by a multiple of 7 fall on the same day of the week. This means that we can divide 47 by 7 and keep the remainder: $47 \div 7 = 6$, remainder 5. Equivalently,

$$47 \equiv 5 \text{ (mod 7)}.$$

Thus, the desired day of the week is 5 days past Thursday, or Tuesday.

Exercise Set 13.2

 Practice Exercises

Name the kind of rotational symmetry shown in Exercises 1–4.

1.

2.

3.

4.

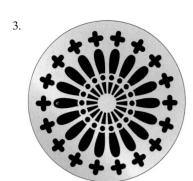

In Exercises 5–19, use the mathematical system given by the table shown.

∘	e	p	q	r	s	t
e	e	p	q	r	s	t
p	p	q	e	s	t	r
q	q	e	p	t	r	s
r	r	t	s	e	q	p
s	s	r	t	p	e	q
t	t	s	r	q	p	e

5. Explain why the closure property is satisfied for the given binary operation.
6. Show that $(p \circ s) \circ t = p \circ (s \circ t)$.
7. Show that $(r \circ t) \circ q = r \circ (t \circ q)$.
8. As in Exercises 6–7, if every choice of three elements is checked, changing the location of the parentheses will not change the answer. What property is satisfied by the mathematical system?
9. What is the identity element?

Find the inverse of

10. *e.*   11. *p.*   12. *q.*   13. *r.*   14. *s.*   15. *t.*

16. Based on Exercises 5–15, what can you conclude about this mathematical system?

17. Find $r \circ p$.   18. Find $p \circ r$.

19. Based on Exercises 17–18, what can you conclude about this mathematical system?

In Exercises 20–22, give one reason why

20. the natural numbers $\{1, 2, 3, 4, 5, \dots\}$ are not a group under addition.
21. the natural numbers $\{1, 2, 3, 4, 5, \dots\}$ are not a group under multiplication.
22. the integers $\{\dots, -3, -2, -1, 0, 1, 2, 3, \dots\}$ are not a group under subtraction.
23. Consider the 6-hour, modulo 6, clock system under the operation of clock addition.
    a. Complete the clock addition table.

+	0	1	2	3	4	5
0						
1						
2						
3						
4						
5						

   b. Show that this mathematical system is a commutative group. Just verify two examples for the associative property.
24. Consider the 7-hour, modulo 7, clock system under the operation of clock addition.
    a. Complete the clock addition table.

+	0	1	2	3	4	5	6
0							
1							
2							
3							
4							
5							
6							

   b. Show that this mathematical system is a commutative group. Just verify two examples for the associative property.

In Exercises 25–34, determine if each statement is true or false. If the statement is false, change the first number on the right to make it true.

25. $7 \equiv 2 \pmod 5$ 26. $8 \equiv 3 \pmod 5$
27. $41 \equiv 6 \pmod 7$ 28. $77 \equiv 5 \pmod{12}$
29. $84 \equiv 1 \pmod 7$ 30. $21 \equiv 5 \pmod 7$
31. $23 \equiv 2 \pmod 4$ 32. $29 \equiv 3 \pmod 4$
33. $55 \equiv 0 \pmod{11}$ 34. $75 \equiv 0 \pmod{25}$

In Exercise 35–42, find each sum.

35. $(3 + 2)$ (mod 6)

36. $(3 + 4)$ (mod 8)

37. $(4 + 5)$ (mod 6)

38. $(5 + 6)$ (mod 8)

39. $(6 + 5)$ (mod 7)

40. $(8 + 7)$ (mod 9)

41. $(49 + 49)$ (mod 50)

42. $(75 + 75)$ (mod 100)

 Application Exercises

To avoid A.M. and P.M. designations, the military uses a 24-hour clock. For example, 11 A.M. is designated 1100 hours, and 11 P.M. (12 noon + 11 hours) is designated 2300 hours. In this system, the first two digits represent hours and the last two digits represent minutes. In Exercises 43–46, find each sum in the 24-hour clock system.

43. $1200 + 0600$

44. $1300 + 1900$

45. $0830 + 1550$

46. $1315 + 0945$

47. Suppose today is Wednesday, July 8. Which day of the week will it be 67 days from now?

48. Suppose today is Tuesday, October 12. Which day of the week will it be 147 days from now?

 Writing in Mathematics

49. Describe the three kinds of rotational symmetry shown by the passionflower in the introduction to this chapter (page 662).

50. Look around and find an object that exhibits rotational symmetry. Describe the object and the kind of rotational symmetry shown.

51. Under what conditions is a mathematical system a group?

52. Describe two ways of finding $8 + 7$ in a modulo 12, 12-hour clock system.

53. Describe two ways of finding $4 + 4$ in a modulo 5 system.

54. Describe the meaning of $a \equiv b$ (mod m) and give an example.

55. The days of the week can be considered a modulo 7 system. Describe another phenomenon that occurs in a cycle. What modulo system is appropriate for this phenomenon?

 Critical Thinking Exercises

56. Consider the following operations on a conditional statement:
    E: leaves the conditional unchanged
    C: changes the conditional into its converse
    I: changes the conditional into its inverse
    CP: changes the conditional into its contrapositive

    The operation ∘ means "followed by."
    a. Show that $C \circ CP = I$ and $C \circ I = CP$.
    b. Fill in the following table.

∘	E	C	I	CP
E				
C				
I				
CP				

    c. Show that this mathematical system is a commutative group. Just verify two examples for the associative property.

57. A mathemanical system consists of the set of integers and the operation ∘ defined by $a \circ b = a - b + ab$. Use an example involving the associative property and explain why the mathematical system is not a group.

58. Give an example of a mathematical system with just one element which is a group.

59. If it is now 5:00 P.M., what time will it be 99,999,999 hours from now?

60. A fascinating collection of readings in mathematics can be found in the four-volume set *The World of Mathematics*, published by Simon and Schuster. Read pages 1552–1557 in volume 3, beginning with the header "A Question for Psychologists." In this part of the selection, the author presents a model in which the "mind" might be viewed within the framework of the group definition. After reading the article, describe an example of nonclosure within your own learning experiences.

 Group Exercise

61. Group members should read the essay on page 680. Then, members should find two pictures of human faces, one which they find attractive and one which they find unattractive. Do an analysis of the facial symmetry, much like that shown in the essay, for each face. Summarize the observations. Are there other characteristics of an attractive face that have nothing to do with symmetry? What are some of these characteristics?

CHAPTER SUMMARY, REVIEW, AND TEST

SUMMARY

13.1 Mathematical Systems

a. A mathematical system consists of a set of elements and at least one binary operation.

b. Certain mathematical systems satisfy the closure, associative, identity, inverse, and commutative properties. These properties are described in the box on page 674. The commutative property is described directly under the box.

13.2 Rotational Symmetry

a. If it takes m equal turns to restore an object to its original position, the object has m-fold rotational symmetry.

Groups

a. A group is a mathematical system meeting the requirements for the closure, associative, identity, and inverse properties.

b. A group that meets the requirements for the commutative property is called a commutative group.

Clock Arithmetic

a. Clock addition is defined by moving a clock's hour hand in a clockwise direction.

b. Our usual 12-hour clock system is a modulo 12 system. It is a commutative group under clock addition.

c. A modulo m system consists of m integers, starting with 0 and ending with $m - 1$.

d. The integers a and b are congruent modulo m, denoted $a \equiv b \pmod{m}$, means that if a is divided by m, the remainder is b.

e. Addition in a modulo m system can be performed using a clock or the rule given in the box on page 679.

f. A modulo m system describes the properties of objects having m-fold rotational symmetry. All such systems are commutative groups under clock addition.

REVIEW EXERCISES

13.1

Use the mathematical system given by the table shown to solve Exercises 1–18.

∘	e	c	f	r
e	e	c	f	r
c	c	f	r	e
f	f	r	e	c
r	r	e	c	f

1. What is the set of elements of this mathematical system?

2. Is the mathematical system closed under the binary operation? Explain your answer.

Find

3. $c \circ f$.   4. $r \circ r$.   5. $e \circ c$.

Find

6. $c \circ r$ and $r \circ c$.   7. $f \circ r$ and $r \circ f$.

8. $f \circ e$ and $e \circ f$.

9. What property is illustrated in Exercises 6–8?

10. Use the table and explain how the property you named in Exercise 9 can be verified for all possible cases without having to consider one case at a time.

Find

11. $(c \circ r) \circ f$ and $c \circ (r \circ f)$.

12. $(r \circ e) \circ c$ and $r \circ (e \circ c)$.

13. What property is illustrated in Exercises 11–12?

14. What is the identity element for the mathematical system?

Find the inverse for

15. e.   16. c.   17. f.   18. r.

19. Is the set $\{0, 1\}$ closed under the operation of ordinary addition? Explain your answer.

20. Is the set $\{0, 1\}$ closed under the operation of multiplication? Explain your answer.

21. Is the set $\{1, 2, 4\}$ closed under division? Explain your answer.

In Exercises 22–23, consider the set of rational numbers.

22. What is the additive inverse of 123?

23. What is the multiplicative inverse of 123?

24. Suppose that $a \circ b$ means to select the larger of the two numbers a and b, or if the numbers are the same, select either number.
    a. Complete the following table.

$\circ$	0	1	2	3	4
0					
1					
2					
3					
4					

    b. What is the identity element?
    c. Does 2 have an inverse? Explain your answer.

13.2

Name the kind of rotational symmetry shown in Exercises 25–26.

25.

Mercedes Benz symbol

26.

Based on the form of a sea urchin

27. Consider the 5-hour, modulo 5, clock system under the operation of clock addition.
    a. Complete the clock addition table.

+	0	1	2	3	4
0					
1					
2					
3					
4					

    b. Show that this mathematical system is a commutative group. Just verify one example for the associative property.

In Exercises 28–30, determine if each statement is true or false. If the statement is false, change the first number on the right to make it true.

28. $17 \equiv 2 \pmod{8}$
29. $37 \equiv 3 \pmod{5}$
30. $60 \equiv 0 \pmod{10}$

In Exercises 31–34, find each sum.

31. $(4 + 3) \pmod 6$
32. $(7 + 7) \pmod 8$
33. $(4 + 3) \pmod 9$
34. $(3 + 18) \pmod{20}$

 Group Exercise

35. One of the reasons that a passionflower is so visually appealing is that it has three different kinds of rotational symmetry: three-, five-, and tenfold. The flower has three stigmas, five stamens, and ten petals. For this activity, each member of the group should find an object or picture of an object that exhibits rotational symmetry. Once each member has shared the object with the group, the group should
    a. Construct a clock addition table for the object's symmetry.
    b. Describe how each of the properties for a commutative group applies to or describes something about the object.

CHAPTER 13 TEST

Use the mathematical system given by the table shown to solve Exercises 1–5.

∘	x	y	z
x	x	y	z
y	y	z	x
z	z	x	y

1. Is the mathematical system closed under the binary operation? Explain your answer.

2. Find $z \circ y$ and $y \circ z$. What property is illustrated?

3. Find $(x \circ z) \circ z$ and $x \circ (z \circ z)$. What property is illustrated?

4. What is the identity element for the mathematical system?

5. Give the inverse for each element in the mathematical system.

6. Is the set $\{-1, 0, 1\}$ closed under the operation of ordinary addition? Explain your answer.

7. In the set of rational numbers, what is the multiplicative inverse of 5? Explain your answer.

8. Name the kind of rotational symmetry shown in the design at the top of the next column. Describe why the design has this particular kind of rotational symmetry.

In Exercises 9–10, consider the 4-hour, modulo 4, clock system under the operation of clock addition.

9. Complete the clock addition table.

+	0	1	2	3
0				
1				
2				
3				

10. Show that this mathematical system is a commutative group. Present your work clearly, naming and explaining one property at a time.

In Exercises 11–12, determine if each statement is true or false. If the statement is false, change the first number on the right to make it true.

11. $39 \equiv 3 \pmod 6$ 12. $14 \equiv 2 \pmod 7$

In Exercises 13–14, find each sum.

13. $(9 + 1) \pmod{11}$ 14. $(9 + 6) \pmod{10}$

Answers to Selected Exercises

CHAPTER 1

Exercise Set 1.1

1. Inductive   **3.** Andrew Johnson   **5.** Answers may vary.   **7.** Answers may vary.   **9.** Answers may vary.   **11.** 28   **13.** 12
15. 729   **17.** 32   **19.** 32
21. **23.**

d	d	d
d	d	

25. a. The original number is doubled.   **27. a.** The result is always 3.
29. a. 14, 17, 20   **b.** 16 in.
37. Deductive—the conclusion comes from the general statement that all people leaving the college administration building every day at 5:00 P.M. are college administrators.
39. 75   **41.** $165 \times 3367 = 555,555$

43. a. The squares all end in 625. The numbers preceding the 625 are 5, 30, 75, 140, 225 or $5(0 + 1)(2 \times 0 + 1), 5(1 + 1)(2 \times 1 + 1),$ $5(2 + 1)(2 \times 2 + 1), 5(3 + 1)(2 \times 3 + 1), 5(4 + 1)(2 \times 4 + 1).$ **b.** $575^2 = 330,625; 675^2 = 455,625$ **c.** Inductive

Exercise Set 1.2

1. $\approx \$2.40$ **3.** ≈ 350 mi   **5.** $\approx \$43$ **7.** $\approx \$100$ **9.** $\approx \$40,000$ per year   **11.** ≈ 68 **13.** $\approx 640,000$ hrs
15. $\approx 140,000$ students   **17.** ≈ 150 people per sq mi   **19. a.** ≈ 240 mi   **b.** ≈ 6 hrs   **21.** $\approx 180,000,000$ people
23. About 17%   **25.** Sony and Levi's   **27.** About $150   **29.** About $30   **31.** About 5%   **33.** 1982; about 9.5%
47. ≈ 2500 years

Trick Questions

1. 12   **2.** The match   **3.** Sister and brother

Exercise Set 1.3

1. Price of the computer   **3.** Number of words per page   **5.** Weekly salary is unnecessary.; $180
7. How much the attendant was given is unnecessary.; $4.50   **9.** $3000 more per year   **11.** $50   **13.** $90   **15.** $4525   **17.** $565
19. 4 mi   **21.** $104.00   **23.** 5 ways   **25.** Answers may vary.   **27.** Answers may vary.   **33.** 20
35. Use one plank across one corner of the square. Use the other plank to go from the stone to the first plank.
37.

Chapter 1 Review

1. Vermont, Virginia, Washington, West Virginia, Wisconsin, or Wyoming   **2.** Any consecutive odd numbers such as 5 and 7 will work.
3. 24   **4.** 112   **5.** 21
6.   **7. a.** The result is the original number.   **8.** $18.00   **9.** $\approx \$640$ **10.** $\approx 90,000$ sec per day   **11.** ≈ 4
12. $\approx \$60$ **13.** ≈ 17 million   **14.** Answers will vary.   **15.** Approximately 46   **16.** Approximately 84
17. 13 years   **18.** Only for men and women born in 1900.   **19.** 1980, approximately 54 million
20. Weight of the child   **21.** The customer giving the driver a $20 bill is unnecessary.; $8.00   **22.** 8 lb   **23.** $885
24. Healthy Bodies by $40   **25.** 5.75 hrs   **26.** $15,500   **27.** 6

Chapter 1 Test

1. $50 \times 2 = 100$ **2.** 20   **3.** $\dfrac{1}{96}$ **4.** 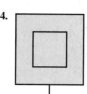   **5. a.** The original number is doubled.   **6.** About $70
7. About $25,000 per person   **8.** ≈ 60 **9.** ≈ 6.8 million acres
10. Outdoor recreation and historical places and museums
11. 1994; about $1.4 billion   **12.** Estes by $12.00   **13.** $14,080
14. 26 weeks

CHAPTER 2

Exercise Set 2.1

1. The known planets in the Solar System.   **3.** The characters of *I Love Lucy*   **5.** Odd natural numbers less than 100.
7. {Winter, Spring, Summer, Autumn}   **9.** {1, 2, 3}   **11.** {January, June, July}   **13.** {*Titanic*}   **15.** True   **17.** True
19. False   **21.** True   **23.** False   **25.** $\notin$ **27.** $\in$ **29.** $\notin$ **31.** {1, 3, 5, 7, 9, 11}   **33.** {101, 102, 103, ..., n}
35. {11, 12, 13, 14, 15}   **37.** 5   **39.** 25   **41.** 0   **43.** True   **45.** False   **47.** True   **49. a.** Not equal   **b.** Not equivalent
51. a. Not equal   **b.** Equivalent   **53. a.** Equal   **b.** Equivalent   **55.** {Gainesville, Los Angeles-Long Beach, Pine Bluff, Miami}
57. {Lawton, New Orleans, Baltimore}   **59.** {Jackson, Miami, New Orleans, Mobile}   **61.** { }   **63.** {1993, 1996}   **65.** $\varnothing$
77. a   **79.** Yes   **81.** No

Exercise Set 2.2

1. Answers may vary.   **3.** Answers may vary.   **5.** {c, d, e}   **7.** {b, c, d, e, f}   **9.** {6, 7, ..., 20}   **11.** {2, 4, 6, 8, ..., 20}
13. $A' = \{21, 22, 23, 24, ...\}$ **15.** $C' = \{1, 3, 5, 7, ...\}$
17. {3, 4, 6, 7}   **19.** {c, d, e}

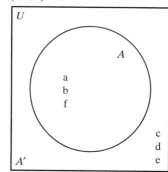

21. {February, March, April, May, August, September, October, November, December}; A' is all the months not beginning with the letter J.

A' is all the months not beginning with the letter J.

23. $\subseteq$ **25.** $\not\subseteq$ **27.** $\not\subset$ **29.** $\not\subseteq$ **31.** $\subseteq$ **33.** $\not\subseteq$ **35.** $\subseteq, \subset$ **37.** $\subseteq$
39. Neither symbol will make the statement true. The second set is smaller than the first.   **41.** True
43. False; {Ralph} is a subset, not Ralph.   **45.** True   **47.** False; The symbol "$\varnothing$" is not a member of the set.
49. $\varnothing$, {Border Collie}, {Poodle}, {Border Collie, Poodle}   **51.** $\varnothing$, {t}, {a}, {b}, {t, a}, {t, b}, {a, b}, {t, a, b}   **53.** $\varnothing$, {0}
55. 16 subsets, 15 proper subsets   **57.** 64 subsets, 63 proper subsets   **59.** 128 subsets, 127 proper subsets
61. 8 subsets, 7 proper subsets   **63.** 32   **65.** 64   **67.** 256   **81.** 0, 5¢, 10¢, 25¢, 40¢, 15¢, 30¢, 35¢

Exercise Set 2.3

1. {1, 3}   **3.** {1, 2, 3, 5, 7}   **5.** {2, 4, 6}   **7.** {4, 6}   **9.** {1, 3, 5, 7}   **11.** {1, 2, 4, 6, 7}   **13.** {1, 2, 4, 6, 7}   **15.** {4, 6}
17. {1, 3, 5, 7}   **19.** $\varnothing$ **21.** {1, 2, 3, 4, 5, 6, 7}   **23.** {1, 3, 5, 7}   **25.** {g, h}   **27.** {a, b, g, h}   **29.** {b, c, d, e, f}
31. {c, d, e, f}   **33.** {a, g, h}   **35.** {a, b, c, d, e, f, g, h}   **37.** {a, b, c, d, e, f, g, h}   **39.** {c, d, e, f}   **41.** {a, g, h}   **43.** $\varnothing$
45. {a, b, c, d, e, f, g, h}   **47.** {a, g, h}   **49.** {1, 3, 4, 7}   **51.** {1, 2, 3, 4, 5, 6, 7, 8, 9}   **53.** {3, 7}   **55.** {1, 4, 8, 9}   **57.** {8, 9}
59. A' is the set of all U.S. cities in which average homes cost less than $200,000.
61. $A \cup B$ is the set of all U.S. cities in which average homes cost more than $200,000 or in which there are more than one million
convention attendees each year.   **63.** $A \cup A'$ is the set of U.S. cities in which average homes cost more than $200,000 or in which average
homes cost less than $200,000.   **71.** b   **73.** Answers may vary.

Exercise Set 2.4

1. $\{1, 2, 3, 5, 7\}$ **3.** $\{1, 2, 3, 5, 7\}$ **5.** $\{2\}$ **7.** $\{2\}$ **9.** $\varnothing$ **11.** $\{4, 6\}$ **13.** $\{b\}$ **15.** $\{a, b, g, h\}$ **17.** $\{b, c, d, e, f\}$
19. $\{b\}$ **21.** $\varnothing$ **23.** $\{c, d, e, f\}$ **25.** II, III, V, VI **27.** I, II, IV, V, VI, VII **29.** II, V **31.** I, IV, VII, VIII
33. a. IV **b.** IV **c.** $(A \cup B)' = A' \cap B'$ **35. a.** I, III, IV **b.** IV **c.** No **37. a.** II, III, IV **b.** I **c.** No
39. The regions represented by $(A' \cap B)'$ are I, II, IV. The regions represented by $A \cup B'$ are I, II, IV. Thus, $(A' \cap B)' = A \cup B'$.
41. a. II, IV, V **b.** II, IV, V **c.** $A \cap (B \cup C) = (A \cap B) \cup (A \cap C)$ **43. a.** II, IV, V **b.** I, II, IV, V, VI **c.** No
45. Answers may vary in form. **47.** V **49.** IV **53.** AB^+ **55.** Yes **57.** Answers may vary.

Exercise Set 2.5

1. 26 **3.** 17 **5.** 37 **7.** 7 **9.** 31 **11.** 27
13. a.

b.

c.

d.

15. a.

b.

c.

d.

e. Answers may vary.

17. a.

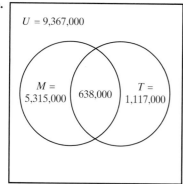

$U = 9,367,000$

$M = 5,315,000$ | $638,000$ | $T = 1,117,000$

b. 479,000
c. 3,573,000

21. a. 0 **b.** 30 **c.** 60
23. Answers may vary.

Chapter 2 Review

1. Natural numbers less than 11. **2.** {Tuesday, Thursday} **3.** ∈ **4.** ∉ **5.** 12 **6.** 15 **7.** ≠ **8.** ≠ **9.** Equivalent
10. Equal **11.**

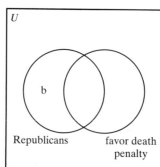

U

3
4
5
6
7

A

1
2
8
9

12. {January, February, March, May, July, August, October, December}
13. ⊆ **14.** ⊄ **15.** ⊆ **16.** ⊆ **17.** ⊂ **18.** False **19.** False
20. True **21.** False **22.** ∅ {1} {5} {1, 5}; {1, 5} is not a proper subset.
23. 32 subsets, 31 proper subsets **24.** 8 subsets, 7 proper subsets
25. {1, 2, 4} **26.** {1, 2, 3, 4, 6, 7, 8} **27.** {5} **28.** {6, 7, 8}
29. {6, 7, 8} **30.** {4, 5, 6} **31.** {2, 3, 6, 7} **32.** {1, 4, 5, 6, 8, 9}
33. {4, 5} **34.** {1, 2, 3, 6, 7, 8, 9} **35.** {2, 3, 7} **36.** {6}
37. {1, 2, 3, 4, 5, 6, 7, 8, 9} **38.** {1, 2, 3, 4, 5} **39.** {1, 2, 3, 4, 5, 6, 7, 8}

40.

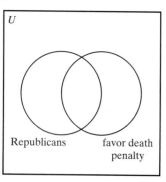

U

A B

True

41.

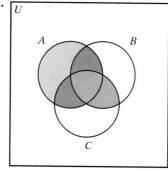

U

A B

C

False

42. 33 **43. a.**

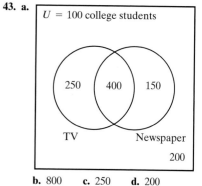

$U = 100$ college students

250 | 400 | 150

TV Newspaper

200

b. 800 **c.** 250 **d.** 200

44. a.

U

Republicans favor death penalty

b.

U

b

Republicans favor death penalty

c.

U

c

Republicans favor death penalty

Chapter 2 Test

1. {18, 19, 20, 21, 22, 23, 24, 25}   **2.** 12   **3.** False   **4.** True   **5.** True   **6.** False   **7.** True   **8.** False   **9.** False
10. False   **11.** $\emptyset$, {6}, {9}, {6, 9}; {6, 9} is not a proper subset.   **12.** {a, b, c, d, e, f}   **13.** {a, b, c, d, f, g}   **14.** {b, c, d}
15. {a, e}   **16.** V   **17. a.**

b. 30   **c.** 57   **d.** 36   **e.** 120

CHAPTER 3

Exercise Set 3.1

1. Yes   **3.** Yes   **5.** No   **7.** No   **9.** Yes   **11.** Yes   **13.** It is not raining.   **15.** Macbeth is a comedy show on television.
17. ~p **19.** ~r **21.** *I Love Lucy* is not a Broadway musical.   **23.** Benjamin Franklin invented the rocking chair.
25. The United States is not the country with the most Internet users.   **27.** Michael is the most common of boys' names.
29. a. There are no whales that are not mammals.   **b.** Some whales are not mammals.
31. a. There exists at least one student that is a business major.   **b.** No students are business majors.
33. a. There exists at least one thief that is not a criminal.   **b.** All thieves are criminals.
35. a. All Democratic presidents have not been impeached.   **b.** Some Democratic presidents have been impeached.
37. b   **47.** Answers may vary.
49. Either his muscularity isn't the reason she's dating him, or his muscularity is the reason she's not dating him.

Exercise Set 3.2

1. $p \wedge q$ **3.** $p \wedge \sim q$ **5.** $p \vee q$ **7.** $p \vee q$ **9.** $p \rightarrow q$ **11.** $\sim p \rightarrow \sim q$ **13.** $p \leftrightarrow q$ **15.** $\sim q \leftrightarrow \sim p$
17. The heater is not working and the house is cold.   **19.** The heater is working or the house is not cold.
21. If the heater is working then the house is not cold.   **23.** The heater is working if and only if the house is not cold.
25. It is July 4th and we are not having a barbeque.   **27.** It is not July 4th or we are having a barbeque.
29. If we are having a barbeque, then it is not July 4th.   **31.** It is not July 4th if and only if we are having a barbeque.
33. It is not true that Romeo loves Juliet and Juliet loves Romeo.   **35.** Romeo does not love Juliet and Juliet loves Romeo.
37. It is not true that Juliet loves Romeo or Romeo loves Juliet.   **39.** Juliet does not love Romeo or Romeo loves Juliet.
41. Romeo does not love Juliet and Juliet does not love Romeo.   **43.** $(p \wedge q) \vee r$ **45.** $(p \vee \sim q) \rightarrow r$ **47.** $r \leftrightarrow (p \wedge q)$
49. If the temperature is above 85° and we finished studying, then we go to the beach.
51. The temperature is above 85°, and if we finished studying then we go to the beach.
53. If we do not go to the beach, then the temperature is not above 85° or we did not finish studying.
55. If we don't go to the beach then we didn't finish studying, or the temperature is above 85°.
57. We go to the beach if and only if the temperature is above 85° and we finished studying.
59. The temperature is above 85° if and only if we finished studying, and we go to the beach.
61. If we don't go to the beach, then it is not true that the temperature is above 85° and we finished studying.   **63.** $p \rightarrow q$
65. $(p \wedge q) \rightarrow r$ **75.** $p \leftrightarrow q$ **77.** $p \wedge \sim q$ **79.** $\sim(p \vee q) \rightarrow \sim r$

Exercise Set 3.3

1. $q \wedge q$ is true   **3.** $p \wedge q$ is false   **5.** $p \wedge q$ is false   **7.** $p \vee q$ is true   **9.** $p \vee q$ is true   **11.** $p \vee q$ is false

13.

p	$\sim p$	$p \vee \sim p$
T	F	T
F	T	T

15.

p	q	$\sim p$	$\sim p \wedge q$
T	T	F	F
T	F	F	F
F	T	T	T
F	F	T	F

17.

p	q	$p \vee q$	$\sim(p \vee q)$
T	T	T	F
T	F	T	F
F	T	T	F
F	F	F	T

19.

p	q	~p	~q	~p ∧ ~q
T	T	F	F	F
T	F	F	T	F
F	T	T	F	F
F	F	T	T	T

21.

p	q	~q	p ∧ ~q
T	T	F	F
T	F	T	T
F	T	F	F
F	F	T	F

23.

p	q	~p	~p ∨ q	~(~p ∨ q)
T	T	F	T	F
T	F	F	F	T
F	T	T	T	F
F	F	T	T	F

25.

p	q	~p	p ∨ q	(p ∨ q) ∧ ~p
T	T	F	T	F
T	F	F	T	F
F	T	T	T	T
F	F	T	F	F

27.

p	q	~p	~q	p ∧ ~q	~p ∨ (p ∧ ~q)
T	T	F	F	F	F
T	F	F	T	T	T
F	T	T	F	F	T
F	F	T	T	F	T

29.

p	q	~p	~q	p ∨ q	~p ∨ ~q	(p ∨ q) ∧ (~p ∨ ~q)
T	T	F	F	T	F	F
T	F	F	T	T	T	T
F	T	T	F	T	T	T
F	F	T	T	F	T	F

31.

p	q	~p	~q	p ∧ ~q	p ∧ q	(p ∧ ~q) ∨ (p ∧ q)
T	T	F	F	F	T	T
T	F	F	T	T	F	T
F	T	T	F	F	F	F
F	F	T	T	F	F	F

33. Texas is not a state or Paris is not a state.

35. *Romeo and Juliet* was not written by Shakespeare or *Jurassic Park* was not written by Shakespeare.

37. Both statements are true, so p ∧ q is true. **39.** First statement is false, second is true. p ∨ q is true. **41.** False **43.** False

45. True **47.** False **57.** Answers may vary. **59.**

p	q	~p	~p ∧ q
T	T	F	F
T	F	F	F
F	T	T	T
F	F	T	F

Exercise Set 3.4

1.

p	q	~q	p → ~q
T	T	F	F
T	F	T	T
F	T	F	T
F	F	T	T

3.

p	q	q → p	~(q → p)
T	T	T	F
T	F	T	F
F	T	F	T
F	F	T	F

5.

p	q	p ∧ q	p ∨ q	(p ∧ q) → (p ∨ q)
T	T	T	T	T
T	F	F	T	T
F	T	F	T	T
F	F	F	F	T

7.

p	q	p → q	~q	(p → q) ∧ ~q
T	T	T	F	F
T	F	F	T	F
F	T	T	F	F
F	F	T	T	T

9. If I don't live in Washington, then I don't live in Seattle.
11. If a plant doesn't wilt, then it is being watered.

13.

p	q	$p \rightarrow q$	$(p \rightarrow q) \wedge q$	$[(p \rightarrow q) \wedge q] \rightarrow p$
T	T	T	T	T
T	F	F	F	T
F	T	T	T	F
F	F	T	F	T

Not a tautology

15.

p	q	$\sim p$	$\sim q$	$p \rightarrow q$	$(p \rightarrow q) \wedge \sim q$	$[(p \rightarrow q) \wedge \sim q] \rightarrow \sim p$
T	T	F	F	T	F	T
T	F	F	T	F	F	T
F	T	T	F	T	F	T
F	F	T	T	T	T	T

This is a tautology.

17.

p	q	$\sim p$	$\sim q$	$p \vee q$	$(p \vee q) \wedge p$	$[(p \vee q) \wedge p] \rightarrow \sim q$
T	T	F	F	T	T	F
T	F	F	T	T	T	T
F	T	T	F	T	F	T
F	F	T	T	F	F	T

Not a tautology

19.

p	q	$\sim p$	$p \rightarrow q$	$\sim p \vee q$	$(p \rightarrow q) \rightarrow (\sim p \vee q)$
T	T	F	T	T	T
T	F	F	F	F	T
F	T	T	T	T	T
F	F	T	T	T	T

This is a tautology.

21.

p	q	$\sim p$	$\sim q$	$p \wedge q$	$\sim p \vee \sim q$	$(p \wedge q) \wedge (\sim p \vee \sim q)$
T	T	F	F	T	F	F
T	F	F	T	F	T	F
F	T	T	F	F	T	F
F	F	T	T	F	T	F

Not a tautology

23.

p	q	$\sim q$	$p \leftrightarrow \sim q$
T	T	F	F
T	F	T	T
F	T	F	T
F	F	T	F

25.

p	q	$p \leftrightarrow q$	$\sim(p \leftrightarrow q)$
T	T	T	F
T	F	F	T
F	T	F	T
F	F	T	F

27.

p	q	$p \leftrightarrow q$	$(p \leftrightarrow q) \rightarrow p$
T	T	T	T
T	F	F	T
F	T	F	T
F	F	T	F

29.

p	q	$\sim p$	$\sim p \leftrightarrow q$	$\sim p \rightarrow q$	$(\sim p \leftrightarrow q) \rightarrow (\sim p \rightarrow q)$
T	T	F	F	T	T
T	F	F	T	T	T
F	T	T	T	T	T
F	F	T	F	F	T

31.

p	q	$p \wedge q$	$q \rightarrow p$	$(p \wedge q) \wedge (q \rightarrow p)$	$[(p \wedge q) \wedge (q \rightarrow p)] \leftrightarrow (p \wedge q)$
T	T	T	T	T	T
T	F	F	T	F	T
F	T	F	F	F	T
F	F	F	T	F	T

33.

p	q	~p	~q	p ∧ q	~(p ∧ q)	~p ∧ ~q	~(p ∧ q) ↔ (~p ∧ ~q)
T	T	F	F	T	F	F	T
T	F	F	T	F	T	F	F
F	T	T	F	F	T	F	F
F	F	T	T	F	T	T	T

Not a tautology

35.

p	q	p → q	q → p	(p → q) ↔ (q → p)
T	T	T	T	T
T	F	F	T	F
F	T	T	F	F
F	F	T	T	T

Not a tautology

37.

p	q	~p	p → q	~p ∨ q	(p → q) ↔ (~p ∨ q)
T	T	F	T	T	T
T	F	F	F	F	T
F	T	T	T	T	T
F	F	T	T	T	T

This is a tautology.

39.

p	q	p ↔ q	p → q	q → p	(q → p) ∧ (p → q)	(p ↔ q) ↔ [(q → p) ∧ (p → q)]
T	T	T	T	T	T	T
T	F	F	F	T	F	T
F	T	F	T	F	F	T
F	F	T	T	T	T	T

This is a tautology.

41.

p	q	r	~q	p ∧ ~q	(p ∧ ~q) ∨ r
T	T	T	F	F	T
T	T	F	F	F	F
T	F	T	T	T	T
T	F	F	T	T	T
F	T	T	F	F	T
F	T	F	F	F	F
F	F	T	T	F	T
F	F	F	T	F	F

43.

p	q	r	p ∨ q	(p ∨ q) → r
T	T	T	T	T
T	T	F	T	F
T	F	T	T	T
T	F	F	T	F
F	T	T	T	T
F	T	F	T	F
F	F	T	F	T
F	F	F	F	T

Not a tautology

45.

p	q	r	p ∧ q	p ∨ r	(p ∧ q) → (p ∨ r)
T	T	T	T	T	T
T	T	F	T	T	T
T	F	T	F	T	T
T	F	F	F	T	T
F	T	T	F	T	T
F	T	F	F	F	T
F	F	T	F	T	T
F	F	F	F	F	T

This is a tautology.

47.

p	q	r	p ∧ q	r → (p ∧ q)
T	T	T	T	T
T	T	F	T	T
T	F	T	F	F
T	F	F	F	T
F	T	T	F	F
F	T	F	F	T
F	F	T	F	F
F	F	F	F	T

Not a tautology

49.

p	q	r	$p \to q$	$q \to r$	$(p \to q) \land (q \to r)$	$p \to r$	$[(p \to q) \land (q \to r)] \to (p \to r)$
T	T	T	T	T	T	T	T
T	T	F	T	F	F	F	T
T	F	T	F	T	F	T	T
T	F	F	F	T	F	F	T
F	T	T	T	T	T	T	T
F	T	F	T	F	F	T	T
F	F	T	T	T	T	T	T
F	F	F	T	T	T	T	T

This is a tautology.

51. False

53. If *The Lion King* sold 3 million more soundtrack albums than *Purple Rain*, then *Titanic* sold 9 million albums. True.

55. If *Titanic* sold 9 million albums, then *The Lion King* sold 3 million more soundtrack albums than *Purple Rain*. False.

57. If *Dirty Dancing* is not the best-selling soundtrack album, then *Titanic* did not sell 9 million albums. False.

59. a.

p	q	$\sim q$	p unless q
T	T	F	T
T	F	T	T
F	T	F	T
F	F	T	F

b. p: The curfew will not be lifted.
q: The violence ends.
The curfew will not be lifted unless the violence ends.

p unless q
↓
$\sim q \to p$
This is false when the curfew is lifted while the violence continues.

67. No—the person could have decided to take the student out to dinner if they got a B.

69.

p	q	$p \lor q$	$p \land q$	$\sim(p \land q)$	$(p \lor q) \to \sim(p \land q)$
T	T	T	T	F	F
T	F	T	F	T	T
F	T	T	F	T	T
F	F	F	F	T	T

71.

p	q	$\sim p$	$\sim p \to q$
T	T	F	T
T	F	F	T
F	T	T	T
F	F	T	F

Exercise Set 3.5

1. A major dam on the upper Nile River is in place or the lower Nile overflows its banks each year.   **3.** a   **5.** c
7. If I am not in Illinois, I am not in Chicago.   **9.** If I can hear you, then the stereo is not playing.   **11.** If you don't die, you laugh.
13. If some troops were not withdrawn, then the president is not telling the truth.   **15.** If no people suffer, then some institutions are not placing profit above human need.   **17.** Converse: If you get a skin rash, then you have touched poison oak. Inverse: If you have not touched poison oak, then you will not get a skin rash.   **19.** Converse: If Shakespeare is the author, then the play is *Macbeth*. Inverse: If the play is not *Macbeth*, then Shakespeare is not the author.   **21.** Converse: If you are not sleeping, then you are driving the car. Inverse: If you are not driving the car, then you are sleeping.   **23.** Converse: If I am not in the West, then I am in Charleston. Inverse: If I am not in Charleston, then I am in the West.   **25.** Converse: If some people wear green, then it is St. Patrick's Day. Inverse: If it's not St. Patrick's Day, then no people wear green.   **27.** I am in Los Angeles and not in California.
29. It is purple and it is a carrot.   **31.** He doesn't, and I won't.   **33.** There is a blizzard, some schools are not closed.
35. Australia is not an island or China is not an island.   **37.** My high school did not encourage creativity or did not encourage diversity.
39. Babe Ruth was not a writer and was not a lawyer.   **41.** The United States has not eradicated poverty and has not eradicated racism.
43. I'm not going to Seattle and I'm not going to San Francisco.   **45.** I do not study and I pass.   **47.** I am going or he is not going.
49. A bill does not become law or it receives majority approval.   **51. a.** True   **b.** If it is not the case that 96% of the patients are women, then the procedure is not a chemical peel.; True   **c.** If 96% of the patients are women, then the procedure is a chemical peel.; False
d. If the procedure is not a chemical peel, then it is not the case that 96% of the patients are women.; False   **e.** The procedure is a chemical peel and it is not the case that 96% of patients are women.; False   **53. a.** True   **b.** There are not 32,383 face lifts per year and it is not the case that 8% of the face lift patients are men.   **c.** False   **63.** b
65. If I get a ticket, then I did not observe the speed limit.
67. Converse: $(\sim q \lor r) \to p$; Inverse: $\sim p \to (q \land \sim r)$; Contrapositive: $(q \land \sim r) \to \sim p$; Negation: $p \land (q \lor \sim r)$

69.

p	q	r	$p \wedge q$	$q \to r$	$p \to (q \to r)$	$(p \wedge q) \to r$
T	T	T	T	T	T	T
T	T	F	T	F	F	F
T	F	T	F	T	T	T
T	F	F	F	T	T	T
F	T	T	F	T	T	T
F	T	F	F	F	T	T
F	F	T	F	T	T	T
F	F	F	F	T	T	T

Exercise Set 3.6

1. Invalid
3. Valid
5. Valid
7. Invalid

9. p: It is cold.
q: Motorcycle started

$$\frac{\begin{array}{l} p \to {\sim}q \\ q \end{array}}{\therefore {\sim}p}$$

Valid

11. p: There is a dam.
q: There is flooding.

$$\frac{\begin{array}{l} {\sim}p \to q \\ q \end{array}}{\therefore {\sim}p}$$

Invalid

13. p: All people obey the law.
q: No jails are needed.

$$\frac{\begin{array}{l} p \to q \\ {\sim}p \end{array}}{\therefore {\sim}q}$$

Invalid

15. Invalid   **17.** Valid   **19.** Valid   **21.** Valid   **23.** Valid   **25.** Invalid   **27.** Invalid   **29.** Invalid   **31.** Valid   **33.** Valid
35. Invalid   **37.** My best friend is not a chemist.   **39.** TV show was cancelled   **41.** All electricity is not off.
43. If I vacation in Paris I gain weight.
45. p: Poverty causes crime
q: Crime sweeps American cities during the Great Depression

$$\frac{\begin{array}{l} p \to q \\ {\sim}q \end{array}}{\therefore {\sim}p}$$

Valid

53. Answers may vary.
55. Valid

57.

p	q	r	${\sim}r$	$q \to r$	$p \to (q \to r)$	$p \wedge q$	$(p \wedge q) \wedge {\sim}r$	$[p \to (q \to r)] \vee [(p \wedge q) \wedge {\sim}r]$
T	T	T	F	T	T	T	F	T
T	T	F	T	F	F	T	T	T
T	F	T	F	T	T	F	F	T
T	F	F	T	T	T	F	F	T
F	T	T	F	T	T	F	F	T
F	T	F	T	F	T	F	F	T
F	F	T	F	T	T	F	F	T
F	F	F	T	T	T	F	F	T

Exercise Set 3.7

1. Valid   **3.** Invalid   **5.** Valid   **7.** Invalid   **9.** Invalid   **11.** Valid   **13.** Valid   **15.** Invalid   **17.** Invalid   **19.** Valid
21. Valid   **23.** Valid   **27.** Answers may vary.   **29.** All opera singers take voice lessons.

Chapter 3 Review

1. If the temperature is below 32° and we finished studying, then we go to the movies.
2. If we don't go to the movies, then the temperature is not below 32° or we did not finish studying.
3. The temperature is below 32° and if we finished studying we go the the movies.
4. We go to the movies if and only if the temperature is below 32° and we finished studying.
5. It is not true that the temperature is below 32° and we finished studying.
6. We won't go to the movies if and only if the temperature not below 32° or we have not finished studying.   **7.** $(p \wedge q) \vee r$
8. $(p \vee {\sim}q) \to r$ **9.** $q \to (p \leftrightarrow r)$ **10.** $r \leftrightarrow (p \wedge {\sim}q)$ **11.** Some houses are not made of wood.
12. Some students major in business.   **13.** No crimes are motivated by passion.   **14.** All Democrats are registered voters.
15. Some new taxes are not for education.   **16.** False   **17.** True   **18.** True

19.

p	q	~p	~p ∧ q	p ∨ (~p ∧ q)
T	T	F	F	T
T	F	F	F	T
F	T	T	T	T
F	F	T	F	F

20.

p	q	~p	~q	~p ∨ ~q
T	T	F	F	F
T	F	F	T	T
F	T	T	F	T
F	F	T	T	T

21.

p	q	~p	~p ∨ q	p → (~p ∨ q)
T	T	F	T	T
T	F	F	F	F
F	T	T	T	T
F	F	T	T	T

22.

p	q	~q	p ↔ ~q
T	T	F	F
T	F	T	T
F	T	F	T
F	F	T	F

23.

p	q	~p	~q	p ∨ q	~(p ∨ q)	~p ∧ ~q	~(p ∨ q) → (~p ∧ ~q)
T	T	F	F	T	F	F	T
T	F	F	T	T	F	F	T
F	T	T	F	T	F	F	T
F	F	T	T	F	T	T	T

24.

p	q	r	~r	p ∨ q	(p ∨ q) → ~r
T	T	T	F	T	F
T	T	F	T	T	T
T	F	T	F	T	F
T	F	F	T	T	T
F	T	T	T	T	F
F	T	F	T	T	T
F	F	T	F	F	T
F	F	F	T	F	T

25.

p	q	r	p ∧ q	p ∧ r	(p ∧ q) ↔ (p ∧ r)
T	T	T	T	T	T
T	T	F	T	F	F
T	F	T	F	T	F
T	F	F	F	F	T
F	T	T	F	F	T
F	T	F	F	F	T
F	F	T	F	F	T
F	F	F	F	F	T

26. a.

p	q	~q	p ∨ q	~q → p
T	T	F	T	T
T	F	T	T	T
F	T	F	T	T
F	F	T	F	F

b. If I get the part, then I learned the lines.

27. c

28. If I am not in the South, I am not in Atlanta.

29. If today is a holiday, I'm not in class.

30. If I fail some courses, I did not work hard.

31. Converse: If classes are cancelled, then there is a storm. Inverse: If there is not a storm, classes are not cancelled.

32. Converse: If we do not talk, then the television is on. Inverse: If the television is not on, then we talk.

33. I am in Bogota and I am not in Columbia.   **34.** I do not work hard and I succeed.   **35.** Chicago is not a city or Maine is not a city.

36. Earnest Hemingway was not a musician and was not an actor.   **37.** I don't work hard and I succeed.

38. She is using her car or she is not taking the bus.   **39.** Invalid   **40.** Valid   **41.** Valid   **42.** Invalid   **43.** Invalid

44. Valid   **45.** Invalid   **46.** Invalid   **47.** Valid   **48.** Valid   **49.** Invalid   **50.** Invalid

Chapter 3 Test

1. If I'm registered and a citizen, then I vote.   **2.** I'll not vote if and only if I'm not registered or not a citizen.

3. It is not true that I am registered or a citizen.   **4.** $(p \land q) \lor \sim r$ **5:** $(\sim p \lor \sim q) \to \sim r$

6. Some numbers are not divisible by 5.   **7.** Nobody wears glasses.

8.

p	q	~p	~p ∨ q	p ∧ (~p ∨ q)
T	T	F	T	T
T	F	F	F	F
F	T	T	T	F
F	F	T	T	F

9.

p	q	$\sim p$	$\sim q$	$p \wedge q$	$\sim(p \wedge q)$	$(\sim p \vee \sim q)$	$\sim(p \wedge q) \leftrightarrow (\sim p \vee \sim q)$
T	T	F	F	T	F	F	T
T	F	F	T	F	T	T	T
F	T	T	F	F	T	T	T
F	F	T	T	F	T	T	T

10.

p	q	r	$q \vee r$	$p \leftrightarrow (q \vee r)$
T	T	T	T	T
T	T	F	T	T
T	F	T	T	T
T	F	F	F	F
F	T	T	T	F
F	T	F	T	F
F	F	T	T	F
F	F	F	F	T

11. b   **12.** If it snows, then it is not August.
13. Converse: $q \rightarrow p$
If I cannot concentrate, then the radio is on.
Inverse: $\sim p \rightarrow \sim q$
If the radio is not playing, then I can concentrate.

14. It is cold and we use our pool.
15. The test is not today and the party is not tonight.
16. It is not true that the banana is green and not ready to eat.
17. Invalid   **18.** Invalid   **19.** Invalid   **20.** Valid

CHAPTER 4

Exercise Set 4.1

1. 25   **3.** 8   **5.** 81   **7.** 100,000   **9.** $(3 \times 10^1) + (6 \times 1)$ or $(3 \times 10) + (6 \times 1)$ **11.** $(2 \times 10^2) + (4 \times 10^1) + (9 \times 1)$ or
$(2 \times 100) + (4 \times 10) + (9 \times 1)$ **13.** $(7 \times 10^2) + (0 \times 10^1) + (3 \times 1)$ or $(7 \times 100) + (0 \times 10) + (3 \times 1)$
15. $(4 \times 10^3) + (8 \times 10^2) + (5 \times 10^1) + (6 \times 1)$ or $(4 \times 1000) + (8 \times 100) + (5 \times 10) + (6 \times 1)$
17. $(3 \times 10^3) + (0 \times 10^2) + (7 \times 10^1) + (0 \times 1)$ or $(3 \times 1000) + (0 \times 100) + (7 \times 10) + (0 \times 1)$
19. $(3 \times 10^4) + (4 \times 10^3) + (5 \times 10^2) + (6 \times 10^1) + (9 \times 1)$ or $(3 \times 10,000) + (4 \times 1000) + (5 \times 100) + (6 \times 10) + (9 \times 1)$
21. $(2 \times 10^8) + (3 \times 10^7) + (0 \times 10^6) + (0 \times 10^5) + (0 \times 10^4) + (7 \times 10^3) + (0 \times 10^2) + (0 \times 10^1) + (4 \times 1)$ or
$(2 \times 100,000,000) + (3 \times 10,000,000) + (0 \times 1,000,000) + (0 \times 100,000) + (0 \times 10,000) + (7 \times 1000) + (0 \times 100) + (0 \times 10)$
$+ (4 \times 1)$ **23.** 73   **25.** 385   **27.** 528,743   **29.** 7002   **31.** 600,002,007   **33.** 23   **35.** 1262   **37.** 11,523   **39.** 2,416,271
41. 14   **43.** 6846   **45.** 3048   **47.** 14,411   **49.** 75,610   **51.** 1776; Declaration of Independence
61.   **63.** $<\vee\ <<<<\vee\vee\vee\vee\vee\vee\vee;\ <\vee\ <<<<<$ **65.** 625   **67.** 592,704

Exercise Set 4.2

1. 23   **3.** 42   **5.** 30   **7.** 11   **9.** 455   **11.** 28,909   **13.** 8342   **15.** 53   **17.** 44,261   **19.** 12_{five} **21.** 14_{seven}
23. 10_{two} **25.** 31_{four} **27.** 101_{six} **29.** 322_{five} **31.** 1230_{four} **33.** 10011_{two} **35.** 12010_{three} **37.** 1442_{six} **39.** 4443_{seven}
41. 153 days = 21 weeks, 6 days   **43.** 35 quarters + 4 pennies   **47.** 887_{nine}, 1000_{nine} **49.** 11111011_{two}, 673_{eight}, $3A6_{\text{twelve}}$ **51.** 37
53. 1000110111_{two}

Exercise Set 4.3

1. 102_{four} **3.** 110_{two} **5.** 1310_{five} **7.** 1302_{seven} **9.** 15760_{nine} **11.** 23536_{seven} **13.** 13_{four} **15.** 4_{five} **17.** 206_{eight}
19. 366_{seven} **21.** 10_{two} **23.** 111_{three} **25.** 152_{six} **27.** 11_{two} **29.** 4011_{seven} **31.** 3114_{eight} **33.** 312_{four} **35.** 20_{four}
37. 41_{five} remainder of 1   **43.** 1367_{eight} **45.** $12F_{\text{sixteen}}$

Exercise Set 4.4

1. 322   **3.** 300,423   **5.** 132   **7.**   **9.**
11.   **13.** 11   **15.** 16   **17.** 40   **19.** 59   **21.** 146   **23.** 1621   **25.** 2677
27. XLIII   **29.** CXXIX   **31.** MDCCCXCVI   **33.** MMMMMDCCCXCII   **35.** 88   **37.** 527   **39.** 2776
41.   **43.**   **45.**   **47.** 12   **49.** 234   **51.** $\mu\gamma$ **53.** $\upsilon\pi\gamma$ **55.** 1776—Declaration of Independence
63. Preceding:
Following:

Chapter 4 Review

1. 121 **2.** 343 **3.** $(4 \times 10^2) + (7 \times 10^1) + (2 \times 1)$ or $(4 \times 100) + (7 \times 10) + (2 \times 1)$
4. $(8 \times 10^3) + (0 \times 10^2) + (7 \times 10^1) + (6 \times 1)$ or $(8 \times 1000) + (0 \times 100) + (7 \times 10) + (6 \times 1)$
5. $(7 \times 10^4) + (0 \times 10^3) + (3 \times 10^2) + (2 \times 10^1) + (9 \times 1)$ or $(7 \times 10,000) + (0 \times 1000) + (3 \times 100) + (2 \times 10) + (9 \times 1)$
6. 706,953 **7.** 740,000,306 **8.** 673 **9.** 8430 **10.** 2331 **11.** 65,536 **12.** Answers may vary. **13.** 19 **14.** 6
15. 325 **16.** 805 **17.** 4051 **18.** 560 **19.** 324_{five} **20.** 10101_{two} **21.** 122112_{three} **22.** 26452_{seven} **23.** 111140_{six}
24. $3A2_{\text{twelve}}$ **25.** 132_{seven} **26.** 1401_{eight} **27.** 110000_{two} **28.** $AD0_{\text{sixteen}}$ **29.** 5_{six} **30.** 345_{seven} **31.** 11_{two}
32. 2304_{five} **33.** 222_{four} **34.** 354_{seven} **35.** 1102_{five} **36.** 133_{four} **37.** 12_{five} **38.** 1246 **39.** 12,432
40. **41.** **42.** 2314
43. DDDDDCCCCBBBBBBBBBAA **44.** Answers may vary. **45.** 163 **46.** 1034 **47.** 1990 **48.** XLIX
49. MMCMLXV **50.** Answers may vary. **51.** 524 **52.** 8253
53. **54.** **55.** 365 **56.** 4520 **57.** G Y I X C **58.** F Z H Y E X D **59.** Answers may vary. **60.** 653 **61.** 678 **62.** $\nu\nu\gamma$
63. $\pi\beta$ **64.** 357 **65.** 37,894 **66.** 80,618
67. WRG **68.** lfVQC **69.** Answers may vary.

Chapter 4 Test

1. 729 **2.** $(5 \times 10^2) + (6 \times 10^1) + (7 \times 1)$ or $(5 \times 100) + (6 \times 10) + (7 \times 1)$
3. $(6 \times 10^4) + (3 \times 10^3) + (0 \times 10^2) + (2 \times 10^1) + (8 \times 1)$ or $(6 \times 10,000) + (3 \times 1000) + (0 \times 100) + (2 \times 10) + (8 \times 1)$
4. 7493 **5.** 400,206 **6.** Answers may vary. **7.** Answers may vary. **8.** 72,731 **9.** 1560 **10.** 113 **11.** 223 **12.** 53
13. 2212_{three} **14.** 111000_{two} **15.** 24334_{five} **16.** 1212_{five} **17.** 414_{seven} **18.** 250_{six} **19.** 221_{five} **20.** 20,303
21. **22.** 1994 **23.** CDLIX **24.** Answers may vary.

CHAPTER 5

Exercise Set 5.1

1. a. Yes **b.** No **c.** Yes **d.** No **e.** No **f.** Yes **g.** No **h.** No **i.** No
3. a. Yes **b.** Yes **c.** Yes **d.** No **e.** Yes **f.** Yes **g.** No **h.** No **i.** Yes
5. a. Yes **b.** No **c.** Yes **d.** No **e.** No **f.** No **g.** No **h.** No **i.** No
7. a. Yes **b.** Yes **c.** Yes **d.** No **e.** Yes **f.** Yes **g.** Yes **h.** No **i.** Yes
9. a. Yes **b.** Yes **c.** Yes **d.** Yes **e.** Yes **f.** Yes **g.** Yes **h.** Yes **i.** Yes
11. True **13.** True **15.** False **17.** True **19.** True **21.** False **23.** True **25.** $3 \cdot 5^2$ **27.** $2^3 \cdot 7$ **29.** $3 \cdot 5 \cdot 7$
31. $2^2 \cdot 5^3$ **33.** $3 \cdot 13 \cdot 17$ **35.** $3 \cdot 5 \cdot 59$ **37.** $2^5 \cdot 3^2 \cdot 5$ **39.** $2^2 \cdot 499$ **41.** $3 \cdot 5^2 \cdot 7^2$ **43.** $2^3 \cdot 3 \cdot 5^2 \cdot 11 \cdot 13$ **45.** 14
47. 2 **49.** 12 **51.** 24 **53.** 38 **55.** 15 **57.** 168 **59.** 336 **61.** 540 **63.** 360 **65.** 3420 **67.** 4560 **69.** 12
71. 10 **73.** July 1 **75.** 90 min **89. a.** $2^{14} \cdot 3^{25} \cdot 5^{30}$ **b.** $2^{17} \cdot 3^{37} \cdot 5^{31}$ **91.** Morning of the third day, at 2:20 A.M. **93.** No

Exercise Set 5.2

1. **3.** **5.** $<$ **7.** $<$ **9.** $>$ **11.** $<$ **13.** 14
15. 14 **17.** 300,000 **19.** -12 **21.** 4 **23.** -3 **25.** 13 **27.** -18 **29.** 0 **31.** 5 **33.** -7 **35.** 14 **37.** 11
39. -9 **41.** -28 **43.** -54 **45.** 21 **47.** -12 **49.** 13 **51.** 0 **53.** 25 **55.** 25 **57.** 64 **59.** -125 **61.** 625
63. -81 **65.** 81 **67.** -3 **69.** -7 **71.** 30 **73.** 0 **75.** Undefined **77.** -20 **79.** -31 **81.** 25 **83.** 13
85. 13 **87.** 33 **89.** 32 **91.** -24 **93.** 0 **95.** -32 **97.** 45 **99.** 44°F **101.** 19,757 ft **103.** $-\$58,300$ million; deficit
105. $-\$7000$ million; deficit **117.** $8 - 2 \cdot (3 - 4) = 10$ **119.** -7 **121.** 150

Exercise Set 5.3

1. $\dfrac{2}{3}$ **3.** $\dfrac{5}{6}$ **5.** $\dfrac{4}{7}$ **7.** $\dfrac{5}{9}$ **9.** $\dfrac{9}{10}$ **11.** $\dfrac{14}{19}$ **13.** 0.75 **15.** 0.35 **17.** 0.875 **19.** $0.\overline{81}$ **21.** $3.\overline{142857}$ **23.** $0.\overline{285714}$

25. $\dfrac{3}{10}$ **27.** $\dfrac{2}{5}$ **29.** $\dfrac{39}{100}$ **31.** $\dfrac{41}{50}$ **33.** $\dfrac{29}{40}$ **35.** $\dfrac{5399}{10,000}$ **37.** $\dfrac{7}{9}$ **39.** 1 **41.** $\dfrac{4}{11}$ **43.** $\dfrac{257}{999}$ **45.** $\dfrac{21}{88}$ **47.** $-\dfrac{7}{120}$

49. $\dfrac{3}{2}$ **51.** $\dfrac{10}{3}$ **53.** $-\dfrac{14}{15}$ **55.** $\dfrac{5}{11}$ **57.** $\dfrac{2}{3}$ **59.** $\dfrac{2}{3}$ **61.** $\dfrac{7}{10}$ **63.** $\dfrac{9}{10}$ **65.** $\dfrac{53}{120}$ **67.** $\dfrac{1}{2}$ **69.** $\dfrac{7}{12}$ **71.** $-\dfrac{71}{150}$

73. $\dfrac{4}{15}$ **75.** $\dfrac{7}{24}$ **77.** $\dfrac{7}{12}$ **79.** $-\dfrac{3}{4}$ **81.** $\dfrac{169}{36}$ **83.** $\$30$ **85.** $\dfrac{16}{25}$ **87.** $\dfrac{31}{50}$ **89.** 285 **91.** $\dfrac{3}{8}$ **93.** $\$588$ **95.** $\dfrac{1}{6}$

109.

say does that   Star-span-gled   Ban-ner   yet   wave   O'er the

Exercise Set 5.4

1. 3 **3.** 5 **5.** 8 **7.** 11 **9.** 13 **11. a.** 13.2 **b.** 13.15 **c.** 13.153 **13. a.** 133.3 **b.** 133.27 **c.** 133.270
15. a. 1.8 **b.** 1.77 **c.** 1.772 **17.** $2\sqrt{5}$ **19.** $4\sqrt{5}$ **21.** $5\sqrt{10}$ **23.** $14\sqrt{7}$ **25.** $\sqrt{42}$ **27.** 6 **29.** $3\sqrt{2}$ **31.** $2\sqrt{13}$
33. 3 **35.** $3\sqrt{5}$ **37.** $-4\sqrt{3}$ **39.** $13\sqrt{3}$ **41.** $-2\sqrt{13}$ **43.** $2\sqrt{5}$ **45.** $7\sqrt{2}$ **47.** $3\sqrt{5}$ **49.** $2\sqrt{2}$ **51.** $34\sqrt{2}$
53. $-\dfrac{3}{2}\sqrt{3}$ **55.** $11\sqrt{3}$ **57.** $\dfrac{5\sqrt{3}}{3}$ **59.** $3\sqrt{7}$ **61.** $\dfrac{2\sqrt{30}}{5}$ **63.** $\dfrac{5\sqrt{3}}{2}$ **65.** $\dfrac{\sqrt{10}}{5}$ **67.** $\dfrac{7\cdot\sqrt{4}\cdot\sqrt{3}}{6}=\dfrac{7\cdot2\cdot\sqrt{3}}{6}=\dfrac{14\cdot\sqrt{3}}{6}$

69. $2\sqrt{5}$ sec   **77.** c   **79.** $>$ **81.** The square root is multiplied by $\sqrt{2}$.   **83.** $\dfrac{3\sqrt{2}}{2}$

Exercise Set 5.5

1. a. $\sqrt{100}$ **b.** $0, \sqrt{100}$ **c.** $-9, 0, \sqrt{100}$ **d.** $-9, -\dfrac{4}{5}, 0, 0.25, 9.2, \sqrt{100}$ **e.** $\sqrt{3}$

3. a. $\sqrt{64}$ **b.** 0 and $\sqrt{64}$ **c.** $-11, 0, \sqrt{64}$ **d.** $-11, -\dfrac{5}{6}, 0, 0.75, \sqrt{64}$ **e.** $\sqrt{5}, \pi$

5. 0 **7.** Answers may vary.   **9.** Answers may vary.   **11.** Answers may vary.   **13.** 4 **15.** 6 **17.** $4; 3$ **19.** 7
21. $30 + 5\sqrt{2}$ **23.** $3\sqrt{7} + \sqrt{14}$ **25.** $5\sqrt{3} + 3$ **27.** $2\sqrt{3} + 6$ **29.** Commutative property of addition
31. Associative property of addition   **33.** Commutative property of addition   **35.** Distributive property of multiplication over addition
37. Associative property of multiplication   **39.** Answers may vary. Example: $1 - 2 = -1$ **41.** Answers may vary. Example: $\dfrac{-2}{8} = -\dfrac{1}{4}$
43. Answers may vary. Example: $(2\sqrt{3})(3\sqrt{3}) = 18$ **45.** No   **47.** Answers may vary.   **57.** c

Exercise Set 5.6

1. $2^5 = 32$ **3.** $4^3 = 64$ **5.** $2^6 = 64$ **7.** $1^{20} = 1$ **9.** $4^2 = 16$ **11.** $2^4 = 16$ **13.** 1 **15.** 1 **17.** $\dfrac{1}{4}$ **19.** $\dfrac{1}{64}$

21. $\dfrac{1}{32}$ **23.** $\dfrac{1}{4}$ **25.** $3^2 = 9$ **27.** $3^{-2} = \dfrac{1}{9}$ **29.** $2^{-4} = \dfrac{1}{16}$ **31.** 270 **33.** $912,000$ **35.** $80,000,000$ **37.** $100,000$
39. 0.79 **41.** 0.0215 **43.** 0.000786 **45.** 0.00000318 **47.** 3.7×10^2 **49.** 3.6×10^3 **51.** 3.2×10^4 **53.** 2.2×10^8
55. 2.7×10^{-2} **57.** 3.7×10^{-3} **59.** 2.93×10^{-6} **61.** $600,000$ **63.** $60,000$ **65.** 0.123 **67.** $30,000$ **69.** $3,000,000$
71. 0.03 **73.** 0.0021 **75.** 2.46×10^{17} **77.** 3×10^3 **79.** 1.9×10^4 **81.** 4×10^{-7} **83.** 4×10^{15} **85.** 9.2×10^3
87. 2.5×10^{-16} **89.** $\$1.6943 \times 10^{12}$ **91.** $\$6 \times 10^{10}$ **93. a.** 6.68×10^7 **b.** 1.67×10^7 **95.** 5.2×10^5 miles

107. d   **109.** $\dfrac{1}{4}$ **111.** 4.1583×10^{58}

Exercise Set 5.7

1. $8, 10, 12, 14, 16, 18$ **3.** $200, 220, 240, 260, 280, 300$ **5.** $-7, -3, 1, 5, 9, 13$ **7.** $-400, -100, 200, 500, 800, 1100$ **9.** $7, 4, 1, -2, -5, -8$
11. $200, 140, 80, 20, -40, -100$ **13.** $\dfrac{5}{2}, 3, \dfrac{7}{2}, 4, \dfrac{9}{2}, 5$ **15.** $\dfrac{3}{2}, \dfrac{7}{4}, 2, \dfrac{9}{4}, \dfrac{5}{2}, \dfrac{11}{4}$ **17.** $4.25, 4.55, 4.85, 5.15, 5.45, 5.75$
19. $4.5, 3.75, 3, 2.25, 1.5, 0.75$ **21.** 33 **23.** 252 **25.** 67 **27.** 955 **29.** 82 **31.** -142 **33.** -43 **35.** -248
37. $\dfrac{23}{2}$ **39.** 1.75 **41.** $4, 8, 16, 32, 64, 128$ **43.** $1000, 1000, 1000, 1000, 1000, 1000$ **45.** $3, -6, 12, -24, 48, -96$

47. $10, -40, 160, -640, 2560, -10, 240$ **49.** $2000, -2000, 2000, -2000, 2000, -2000$ **51.** $-2, 6, -18, 54, -162, 486$
53. $-6, 30, -150, 750, -3750, 18,750$ **55.** $\frac{1}{4}, \frac{1}{2}, 1, 2, 4, 8$ **57.** $\frac{1}{4}, \frac{1}{8}, \frac{1}{16}, \frac{1}{32}, \frac{1}{64}, \frac{1}{128}$ **59.** $-\frac{1}{16}, \frac{1}{4}, -1, 4, -16, 64$
61. $2, 0.2, 0.02, 0.002, 0.0002, 0.00002$ **63.** 256 **65.** 2.32×10^9 **67.** 50 **69.** 320 **71.** -2 **73.** 486 **75.** $\frac{3}{64}$ **77.** $-\frac{2}{27}$
79. -1.82×10^{-9} **81.** 0.1 **83.** Arithmetic; $18, 22$ **85.** Geometric; $405, 1215$ **87.** Arithmetic; $13, 18$ **89.** Geometric; $\frac{3}{16}, \frac{3}{32}$
91. Arithmetic; $\frac{5}{2}, 3$ **93.** Geometric; $7, -7$ **95.** Arithmetic; $-49, -63$ **97.** Geometric; $25\sqrt{5}, 125$ **99.** 139,074 employees
101. \$65,930 **103. a.** \$16,384 **b.** \$536,870,912 **113.** d **115.** $-287,309$ **117.** $\approx 3.595 \times 10^{25}$

Chapter 5 Review

1. $2, 3, 4, 6, 8, 12$ **2.** $2, 3, 5, 6, 9, 10$ **3.** $3 \cdot 5 \cdot 47$ **4.** $2^6 \cdot 3 \cdot 5$ **5.** $3 \cdot 5^2 \cdot 7 \cdot 13$ **6.** $6; 240$ **7.** $6; 900$ **8.** $2; 27,432$
9. 12 people **10.** 11:48 A.M. **11.** $<$ **12.** $>$ **13.** 860 **14.** 53 **15.** 0 **16.** -3 **17.** -11 **18.** -15 **19.** 1
20. 99 **21.** -15 **22.** 9 **23.** -4 **24.** -16 **25.** -16 **26.** 10 **27.** -2 **28.** 17 **29.** $\frac{8}{15}$ **30.** $\frac{6}{25}$ **31.** $\frac{11}{12}$
32. 0.8 **33.** $0.\overline{428571}$ **34.** 0.625 **35.** 0.5625 **36.** $\frac{3}{5}$ **37.** $\frac{17}{25}$ **38.** $\frac{147}{250}$ **39.** $\frac{21}{2500}$ **40.** $\frac{5}{9}$ **41.** $\frac{34}{99}$ **42.** $\frac{113}{999}$
43. $\frac{21}{50}$ **44.** $\frac{8}{3}$ **45.** $\frac{2}{3}$ **46.** $\frac{43}{36}$ **47.** $\frac{37}{60}$ **48.** $\frac{11}{15}$ **49.** $\frac{5}{16}$ **50.** $\frac{15}{112}$ **51.** $\frac{27}{40}$ **52.** $\frac{5}{12}$ **53.** $2\sqrt{7}$ **54.** $6\sqrt{2}$
55. $5\sqrt{6}$ **56.** $10\sqrt{3}$ **57.** $4\sqrt{3}$ **58.** $15\sqrt{2}$ **59.** $2\sqrt{3}$ **60.** 3 **61.** $5\sqrt{5}$ **62.** $-6\sqrt{11}$ **63.** $7\sqrt{2}$ **64.** $-17\sqrt{3}$
65. $12\sqrt{2}$ **66.** $6\sqrt{5}$ **67.** $\frac{\sqrt{6}}{3}$ **68. a.** $\sqrt{81}$ **b.** $0, \sqrt{81}$ **c.** $-17, 0, \sqrt{81}$ **d.** $-17, -\frac{9}{13}, 0, 0.75, \sqrt{81}$ **e.** $\sqrt{2}, \pi$
69. Answers may vary. **70.** Answers may vary. **71.** Answers may vary. **72.** Commutative property of addition
73. Associative property of multiplication **74.** Distributive property of multiplication over addition
75. Commutative property of multiplication **76.** Commutative property of multiplication **77.** Commutative property of addition
78. Answers may vary. Example: $\frac{1}{2}$ **79.** Answers may vary. Example: $4 - 5 = -1$ **80.** 216 **81.** 64 **82.** 16 **83.** 729
84. 25 **85.** 1 **86.** 1 **87.** $\frac{1}{216}$ **88.** $\frac{1}{16}$ **89.** $\frac{1}{49}$ **90.** 27 **91.** 460 **92.** $37,400$ **93.** 0.00255 **94.** 0.0000745
95. 7.52×10^3 **96.** 3.59×10^6 **97.** 7.25×10^{-3} **98.** 4.09×10^{-7} **99.** 390 **100.** $1,150,000$ **101.** 0.023 **102.** 40
103. 3.24×10^{10} **104.** 3.64×10^1 **105.** 2.1×10^3 **106.** 5×10^1 **107.** 1000 yrs **108.** $\$4.05 \times 10^{10}$
109. $7, 11, 15, 19, 23, 27$ **110.** $-4, -9, -14, -19, -24, -29$ **111.** $\frac{3}{2}, 1, \frac{1}{2}, 0, -\frac{1}{2}, -1$ **112.** 20 **113.** -30 **114.** -38
115. $3, 6, 12, 24, 48, 96$ **116.** $\frac{1}{2}, \frac{1}{4}, \frac{1}{8}, \frac{1}{16}, \frac{1}{32}, \frac{1}{64}$ **117.** $16, -8, 4, -2, 1, -\frac{1}{2}$ **118.** 54 **119.** $\frac{1}{2}$ **120.** -48 **121.** Arithmetic; $24, 29$
122. Geometric; $162, 486$ **123.** Geometric; $\frac{1}{256}, \frac{1}{1024}$ **124.** Arithmetic; $-28, -35$ **125.** \$36,261 **126.** \$129,471.03

Chapter 5 Test

1. $2, 3, 4, 6, 8, 9, 12$ **2.** $2^2 \cdot 3^2 \cdot 7$ **3.** $24; 144$ **4.** 1 **5.** -4 **6.** -32 **7.** $0.58\overline{3}$ **8.** $\frac{64}{99}$ **9.** $\frac{1}{5}$ **10.** $\frac{37}{60}$ **11.** $-\frac{19}{2}$
12. $\frac{7}{12}$ **13.** $5\sqrt{2}$ **14.** $9\sqrt{2}$ **15.** $3\sqrt{2}$ **16.** $-7, -\frac{4}{5}, 0, 0.25, \sqrt{4}, \frac{22}{7}$ **17.** Commutative property of addition
18. Distributive property of multiplication over addition **19.** 243 **20.** 64 **21.** $\frac{1}{64}$ **22.** 7500 **23.** 7×10^6
24. $1, -4, -9, -14, -19, -24$ **25.** 22 **26.** $16, 8, 4, 2, 1, \frac{1}{2}$ **27.** 320

CHAPTER 6

Exercise Set 6.1

1. 27 **3.** 23 **5.** 29 **7.** -2 **9.** 140 **11.** 217 **13.** 176 **15.** 30 **17.** 27 **19.** -12 **21.** 12 **23.** -2 **25.** 69
27. 3 **29.** -142 **31.** $3x + 15$ **33.** $16x + 24$ **35.** $4 + 2r$ **37.** $5x + 5y$ **39.** $3x - 6$ **41.** $8x - 10$ **43.** $-8x + 12$
45. $6x - 12$ **47.** $17x$ **49.** $8x$ **51.** $10x$ **53.** $-2y$ **55.** $-4y$ **57.** $7x^2$ **59.** $-3x^2$ **61.** $11x - 3$ **63.** $8y + 10$
65. $10x + 8y - 2$ **67.** $15x + 16$ **69.** $27x - 10$ **71.** $29y - 29$ **73.** $300;$ One can tan for 300 minutes without burning with a number 15 lotion. **75.** $46,560;$ The average yearly earnings for elementary and secondary teachers in the U.S. 10 years after 1990, or in

2000, is $46,560.   **77. a.** 34 mpg; 29 mpg; 24 mpg   **b.** Decreases by 5   **79.** $4.67 million, $8 million, $18 million, $38 million, $198 million; cost increases to an infinitely large number.   **87.** d   **89. a.** $50.5; $5.5; $1   **b.** No

91.

x	y
3	7
4	9
5	11
6	13

Exercise Set 6.2

1. $\{10\}$ **3.** $\{-17\}$ **5.** $\{12\}$ **7.** $\{9\}$ **9.** $\{-3\}$ **11.** $\left\{-\dfrac{1}{4}\right\}$ **13.** $\{3\}$ **15.** $\{11\}$ **17.** $\{-17\}$ **19.** $\{11\}$

21. $\left\{\dfrac{7}{5}\right\}$ **23.** $\left\{\dfrac{25}{3}\right\}$ **25.** $\{8\}$ **27.** $\{-3\}$ **29.** $\{2\}$ **31.** $\{-4\}$ **33.** $\left\{-\dfrac{1}{5}\right\}$ **35.** $\{-4\}$ **37.** $\{5\}$ **39.** $\{6\}$

41. $\left\{-\dfrac{7}{2}\right\}$ **43.** $\{1\}$ **45.** $\{24\}$ **47.** $\{20\}$ **49.** $\{5\}$ **51.** $y = -3x + 6$ **53.** $y = -\dfrac{1}{2}x + 3$ **55.** $y = -\dfrac{1}{3}x + 2$

57. $y = \dfrac{1}{2}x$ **59.** $y = \dfrac{2}{3}x - \dfrac{5}{3}$ **61.** $L = \dfrac{A}{W}$ **63.** $b = \dfrac{2A}{h}$ **65.** $P = \dfrac{I}{rt}$ **67.** $m = \dfrac{E}{c^2}$ **69.** $m = \dfrac{y - b}{x}$

71. $a = 2A - b$ **73.** $r = \dfrac{S - P}{Pt}$ **75.** All real numbers   **77.** $\varnothing$ **79.** All real numbers

81. a. 205 mg per dl   **b.** 375,000; 125,000   **83.** 30 years after 1950 or in 1980   **95.** Answers may vary.   **97.** Yes

Exercise Set 6.3

1. $x + 9$ **3.** $20 - x$ **5.** $5x - 8$ **7.** $\dfrac{15}{x}$ **9.** $2x + 20$ **11.** $7x - 30$ **13.** $4(x + 12)$ **15.** 410   **17.** 136   **19.** 13

21. 108   **23.** 16   **25.** 26   **27.** 5   **29.** 14   **31.** 5   **33.** 50   **35.** 800 mi   **37.** 6 mo
39. Sosa hit 66 runs; McGuire hit 70 runs   **41.** Teacher earns $34,200; surgeon earns $223,800   **43.** 11 hr   **45.** 314 and 315
47. a. Without coupon book: $1.25x$; with coupon book: $21.00 + 0.50x$ **b.** 28 times   **49.** Blacks earn $34,340; whites earn $43,690
55. 17 min   **57.** Woman is 20 yrs; "uncle" is 60 yrs   **59.** Answers may vary.

Exercise Set 6.4

1. $\dfrac{1}{2}$ **3.** $\dfrac{12}{5}$ **5.** $\dfrac{3}{4}$ **7.** $\dfrac{2}{1}$ or $2 : 1$ **9.** $\dfrac{1}{3}$ or $1 : 3$ **11.** $\{14\}$ **13.** $\{27\}$ **15.** $\left\{-\dfrac{9}{4}\right\}$ **17.** $\{-15\}$ **19.** $\left\{\dfrac{7}{2}\right\}$
21. $\{10\}$ **23.** $1115.38   **25.** 20,489   **27.** $950   **29.** 154.1 in.   **31.** 2442 mph   **33.** 607 lbs   **35.** 6.4 lbs
45. 0–8: $\dfrac{11,000}{17,500}$, 0.63; 9–11: $\dfrac{14,000}{21,000}$, 0.67; 12: $\dfrac{17,500}{27,500}$, 0.65; 13–15: $\dfrac{20,500}{31,000}$, 0.66; 16: $\dfrac{27,000}{38,000}$, 0.71; 16+: $\dfrac{32,000}{47,000}$, 0.68.
Woman's income to man's income averages 67%, or $2 : 3$ ratio   **47.** 32

Exercise Set 6.5

1.

3.

5.

7.

9.

11.

13. $\{x | x > 5\}$

15. $\{x | x \le 5\}$

17. $\{x | x < 3\}$

19. $\{x | x < 5\}$

21. $\{x | x \ge -5\}$

23. $\{x | x > 5\}$

25. $\{x | x < 5\}$

27. $\{x | x < 8\}$

29. $\{x | x > -6\}$

31. $\{x | x > -5\}$

33. $\{x | x \le 5\}$

35. $\{x | x \le 3\}$

37. $\{x|x < 16\}$

39. $\{x|x > -3\}$

41. $\{x|x \geq -2\}$

43. $\{x|x > -4\}$

45. $\{x|x \geq 4\}$

47. $\left\{ x \,\middle|\, x > \dfrac{11}{3} \right\}$

49. $\{x|x > 2\}$

51. $\{x|x < 3\}$

53. $\left\{ x \,\middle|\, x > \dfrac{5}{3} \right\}$

55. Raleigh, NC; Seattle; San Francisco; Austin, TX   **57.** San Diego
59. Washington, DC; Lexington-Fayette, KY; Minneapolis; Boston; Arlington, TX   **61.** $x \leq 40.6\%$ **63.** $x > 29\%$
65. a. The average is 88. An A is not possible.   **b.** At least 68 points   **67.** At most 1280 mi   **73.** Exceeds 720 mi

Exercise Set 6.6

1. $x^2 + 8x + 15$ **3.** $x^2 - 2x - 15$ **5.** $2x^2 + 3x - 2$ **7.** $12x^2 - 43x + 35$ **9.** $(x + 2)(x + 3)$ **11.** $(x - 5)(x + 3)$
13. $(x - 3)(x - 5)$ **15.** $(x - 12)(x + 3)$ **17.** Prime   **19.** $(x + 16)(x + 1)$ **21.** $(2x + 1)(x + 3)$ **23.** $(2x - 5)(x - 6)$
25. $(3x + 2)(x - 1)$ **27.** $(3x - 28)(x + 1)$ **29.** $(2x - 1)(3x - 4)$ **31.** $(2x + 5)(2x + 3)$ **33.** $\{-3, 8\}$ **35.** $\left\{ -\dfrac{5}{4}, 2 \right\}$
37. $\{-5, -3\}$ **39.** $\{-3, 5\}$ **41.** $\{-3, 7\}$ **43.** $\{-8, -1\}$ **45.** $\{6\}$ **47.** $\left\{ -\dfrac{1}{2}, 4 \right\}$ **49.** $\left\{ -2, \dfrac{9}{5} \right\}$ **51.** $\left\{ -\dfrac{7}{2}, -\dfrac{1}{3} \right\}$
53. $\{-5, -3\}$ **55.** $\left\{ \dfrac{-5 - \sqrt{13}}{2}, \dfrac{-5 + \sqrt{13}}{2} \right\}$ **57.** $\{-2 - \sqrt{10}, -2 + \sqrt{10}\}$ **59.** $\{-2 - \sqrt{11}, -2 + \sqrt{11}\}$ **61.** $\{-3, 6\}$
63. $\left\{ -\dfrac{2}{3}, \dfrac{3}{2} \right\}$ **65.** $\{1 - \sqrt{11}, 1 + \sqrt{11}\}$ **67.** $\left\{ \dfrac{1 - \sqrt{57}}{2}, \dfrac{1 + \sqrt{57}}{2} \right\}$ **69.** $\left\{ \dfrac{-3 - \sqrt{3}}{6}, \dfrac{-3 + \sqrt{3}}{6} \right\}$ **71.** $\left\{ \dfrac{3}{2} \right\}$
73. a. $10x^2 - 475x + 3750 = 0$ **b.** $\{10, 37.5\}$ **c.** 10 yrs   **79.** Yes; If $b^2 - 4ac$ is negative, there are no real solutions because the square root of a negative number is not real. If $b^2 - 4ac = 0$, then there is one rational solution. If $b^2 - 4ac$ is a positive perfect square, then there are two rational solutions. If $b^2 - 4ac$ is positive, but not a perfect square, then there are two irrational solutions.
81. 3, 4   **83.** 5 sec

Chapter 6 Review

1. 33   **2.** 87   **3.** 15   **4.** $6x - 3$ **5.** $30x - 2$ **6.** $39x - 4$ **7.** 135; You can stay in the sun 135 minutes without burning.
8. 1800; The computer's discount price is $1800.   **9.** 16; It takes 16 seconds.   **10.** $\{6\}$ **11.** $\{2\}$ **12.** $\{12\}$
13. $\left\{ -\dfrac{13}{3} \right\}$ **14.** $\{2\}$ **15.** $y = -3x + 9$ **16.** $y = -2x + 8$ **17.** $T = \dfrac{D}{R}$ **18.** $w = \dfrac{P - 2l}{2}$ **19.** $h = \dfrac{2A}{b}$
20. $B = 2A - C$ **21.** 8 yrs; 1997   **22.** $17 - 9x$ **23.** $3x - 7$ **24.** $5x + 8$ **25.** $\dfrac{6}{x} + 3x$ **26.** 3   **27.** 5   **28.** 5
29. 12   **30.** 23 yrs; 2016   **31.** Green Bay's score was 24; Denver's score was 31   **32.** 17.5 yrs; $24,250
33. a. $\dfrac{15}{11}$ or $15:11$ **b.** $\dfrac{13}{9}$ or $13:9$ **34.** $\{5\}$ **35.** $\{-65\}$ **36.** $\left\{ \dfrac{2}{5} \right\}$ **37.** $\{3\}$ **38.** 324   **39.** 287   **40.** 19,200
41. 784 ft   **42.** 40 lbs
43. $\{x|x < 4\}$

44. $\{x|x \geq -8\}$

45. $\{x|x \geq -3\}$

46. $\{x|x > 6\}$

47. $\{x|x \geq 4\}$

48. $\{x|x \leq 2\}$

49. At least 91   **50.** $x^2 + 4x - 45$ **51.** $12x^2 - 13x - 14$ **52.** $(x - 4)(x + 3)$ **53.** $(x - 5)(x - 3)$ **54.** Prime
55. $(3x - 2)(x - 5)$ **56.** $(3x + 2)(2x - 5)$ **57.** Prime   **58.** $\{-7, 2\}$ **59.** $\{-4, 8\}$ **60.** $\left\{ -8, \dfrac{1}{2} \right\}$ **61.** $\{-5, -2\}$
62. $\{1, 3\}$ **63.** $\left\{ \dfrac{5 - \sqrt{41}}{2}, \dfrac{5 + \sqrt{41}}{2} \right\}$ **64.** $\left\{ -3, \dfrac{1}{2} \right\}$ **65.** $\left\{ \dfrac{3 - 2\sqrt{6}}{3}, \dfrac{3 + 2\sqrt{6}}{3} \right\}$

Chapter 6 Test

1. 64   **2.** $22x - 10$ **3.** \$1,074,000   **4.** $\{8\}$ **5.** $\{2\}$ **6.** 2002; The salary will reach \$48,196 in 2002.   **7.** $y = -\dfrac{1}{2}x + 2$

8. $P = 2L + 2W$ **9.** 63.8   **10.** 11 yrs   **11.** $\dfrac{2}{5}$ or $2 : 5$ **12.** $\{7.5\}$ **13.** $\{3\}$ **14.** 6000 elk   **15.** 137.5 lbs per square inch.

16. $\dfrac{1}{2}$ hr   **17.** $\{x \mid x \le -3\}$ **18.** $\{x \mid x > 7\}$ **19.** At least 92   **20.** $6x^2 - 7x - 20$

$$\xleftarrow{\hspace{2cm}} \overset{}{\underset{-5\;-4\;-3\;-2\;-1}{\bullet}} \xrightarrow{\hspace{2cm}}$$

$$\xleftarrow{\hspace{2cm}} \overset{}{\underset{4\;\;5\;\;6\;\;7\;\;8}{\circ}} \xrightarrow{\hspace{2cm}}$$

21. $(2x - 5)(x - 2)$ **22.** $\{-9, 4\}$ **23.** $\left\{\dfrac{-2 - \sqrt{2}}{2}, \dfrac{-2 + \sqrt{2}}{2}\right\}$

CHAPTER 7

Exercise Set 7.1

1.

(1, 4)

3.

(−2, 3)

5.

(−3, −5)

7.

(4, −1)

9.

(−4, 0)

11.

(0, −3)

13.

(0, 0)

15.

$\left(-2, -3\dfrac{1}{2}\right)$

17.

(3.5, 4.5)

19.

(1.25, −3.25)

21.

23.

25.

27.

29.

31. a. 4   **b.** −3
33. a. 19   **b.** −2
35. a. 5   **b.** 5
37. a. 53   **b.** 8
39. a. 26   **b.** 19

41.

43.

45.

47.

49. Function   **51.** Function   **53.** Not a function   **55.** Function   **57. a.** $A(1989, 295); B(1991, 262); C(1998, 255)$

b. A represents the defense spending for 1989. It is the highest defense spending ever. B represents the defense spending for 1991. It is the lowest defense spending before 1995. C represents the defense spending for 1998.

59. a. The x-coordinate of the intersection point of the graph is 40. This x-coordinate means that if one is to drive 40 miles, he/she will be charged the same amount by both companies.   **b.** 56   **c.** $y = 54$; This value represents the amount of money both companies will charge for a 40 mile drive. The difference is $2.

61. a.

x	$f(x) = 0.1x^2 - 0.4x + 0.6$
0	0.6
1	0.3
2	0.2
3	0.3
4	0.6
5	1.1

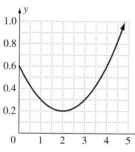

b. 10 A.M. and 12 P.M.

69. a. $f(x) = -\dfrac{x}{2}$ **b.** $f(x) = \dfrac{x + 1}{2}$ **c.** 3

Exercise Set 7.2

1.

3.

5.

7.

9. -1; line falls   **11.** $\dfrac{1}{4}$; line rises   **13.** -5; line falls   **15.** Slope undefined; line is vertical   **17.** -4; line falls   **19.** 0; line is horizontal

21.

23.

25.

27.

29.

31.

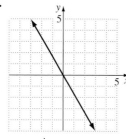

33. a. $y = -3x + 0$

b. Slope $= -3$

  y-intercept $= 0$

c.

35. a. $y = \dfrac{4}{3}x + 0$

b. Slope $= \dfrac{4}{3}$

  y-intercept $= 0$

c.

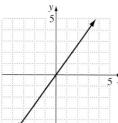

37. a. $y = -2x + 3$

b. Slope $= -2$

  y-intercept $= 3$

c.

39. a. $y = -\dfrac{7}{2}x + 7$

b. Slope $= -\dfrac{7}{2}$

  y-intercept $= 7$

c.

41.

43.

45.

47.

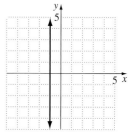

49. a. 179.5 million; 181.85 million; 184.2 million; 186.55 million; 188.90 million
  b. 2.35; It represents the population increase per year (in millions).
  c. 179.5; It represents the U.S. population in 1960 (in millions).
  d. 273.50; It represents the estimated U.S. population in year 2000 (in millions).
  61. 0.2; The slope represents the increase in life expectancy in years per one year increase in year of birth.

Exercise Set 7.3

1. $36,954; It represents the average income in the Unites States for a 30 year old person. **3.** Upward **5.** Downward **7.** 3 and 1
9. 6 and 2 **11.** Approximately -32 and 1.2 **13.** 3 **15.** -12 **17.** -4 **19.** 0 **21.** $(2, -1)$ **23.** $(-1, -8)$ **25.** $(-3, -9)$
27.

29.

31.

33.

35.

37.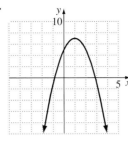

39. (25, 13.50); In practical terms, this indicates that an annual rainfall of 13.5 inches produces the highest level of growth for the redwood tree.
41. 2 seconds; 144 feet   **51.** Answers may vary.
53. 2 x-intercepts

Exercise Set 7.4

1.

3.

5.

7.

9.

11. a. 67.38 million   **b.** 134.74 million   **c.** 269.46 million   **d.** 538.85 million   **e.** Doubles
13. a. 241,786   **b.** 16,123,834
19. c and d have the form of $y = b^x$ where $b > 1$; a and b have the form of $y = b^x$ where $b < 1$ for every positive value of x. $\left(\frac{1}{5}\right)^x < \left(\frac{1}{3}\right)^x < 3^x < 5^x$

Exercise Set 7.5

1. Solution   **3.** Not a solution   **5.** $\{(4, 2)\}$ **7.** $\{(3, 0)\}$ **9.** $\{(-1, 4)\}$ **11.** $\{(3, -4)\}$ **13.** $\{(1, 3)\}$ **15.** $\{(5, 1)\}$
17. $\{(2, 1)\}$ **19.** $\{(-1, 3)\}$ **21.** $\{(4, 5)\}$ **23.** $\left\{\left(-4, \frac{5}{4}\right)\right\}$ **25.** $\{(2, -1)\}$ **27.** $\{(3, 0)\}$ **29.** $\{(-4, 3)\}$ **31.** $\{3, 1)\}$
33. $\{(1, -2)\}$ **35.** $\{(-5, -2)\}$ **37.** $\varnothing$ **39.** $\{(x, y) \mid y = 3x - 5\}$ **41.** $\{(1, 4)\}$ **43.** $\{(x, y) \mid x + 3y = 2\}$ **45.** 4, 7
47. 2, 5   **49.** Maximum length of royal pythons = 35 feet; maximum length of anacondas = 28 feet.
51. In 1995, the number of deaths from gunfire in the United States will be equal to the number of deaths from car accidents. That number is 12.5 per hundred thousand Americans.   **63.** Answers may vary.

Exercise Set 7.6

1.

3.

5.

7.

9.

11.

13.

15.

17.

19.

21.

23.

25. a. Answers may vary.
b. Answers may vary.

27.

Answers may vary.

35.

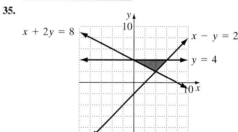

Exercise Set 7.7

1. Maximum value $= 70$, minimum value $= 17$ **3.** Maximum value $= 610$, minimum value $= 0$

5. a.

b. At $(0, 1)$ $z = 0 + 1 = 1$; at $(6, 13)$ $z = 6 + 13 = 19$;
at $(6, 1)$ $z = 6 + 1 = 7$

c. Maximum $= 19$ occurs at $x = 6$ and $y = 13$;
minimum $= 1$ occurs at $x = 0$ and $y = 1$

7. a.

b. At $(0, 10)$ $z = 6(0) + 10(10) = 100$;
at $(4, 8)$ $z = 6(4) + 10(8) = 104$; at $(12, 0)$ $z = 6(12) + 10(0) = 72$;
at $(0, 0)$ $z = 6(0) + 10(0) = 0$

c. Maximum $= 104$ occurs at $x = 4$ $y = 8$;
minimum $= 0$ occurs at $x = 0$ and $y = 0$

9. a. $z = 10x + 7y$ **b.** Constraints; $x + y \leq 20, x \geq 3, x \leq 8$

c.

d. At $(3, 0)$ $z = 10(3) + 7(0) = 30$; at $(8, 0)$ $z = 10(8) + 7(0) = 80$;
at $(3, 17)$ $z = 10(3) + 7(17) = 149$;
at $(8, 12)$ $z = 10(8) + 7(12) = 164$

e. The student can earn the maximum amount per week by tutoring for
8 hours per week and working as teacher's aid for 12 hours per week.
The maximum amount that the student can earn each week is $164.

11. 40 bicycles of Model A and no bicycles of Model B

Chapter 7 Review

1.

2.

3.

4.

5.

6.

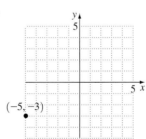

7.

8. 3
9. 26
10. 30
11. −64

12.

x	$f(x) = \frac{1}{2}x$
−6	−3
−4	−2
−2	−1
0	0
2	1
4	2
6	3

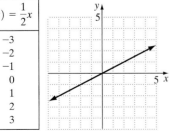

13.

x	$f(x) = x^2 - 2$
−2	2
−1	−1
0	−2
1	−1
2	2

14. y is not a function of x **15.** y is a function of x **16.** y is not a function of x

17.

18.

19.

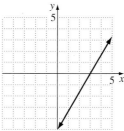

20. $-\dfrac{1}{2}$; line falls

21. 3; line rises

22. 0; line horizontal

23. Undefined; line vertical

24.

25.

26.

27.

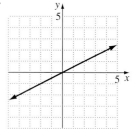

28. a. $y = -2x$

  b. Slope $= -2$

    y-intercept $= 0$

  c.

29. a. $y = \dfrac{5}{3}x$

  b. Slope $= \dfrac{5}{3}$

    y-intercept $= 0$

  c.

30. a. $y = -\dfrac{3}{2}x + 2$

  b. Slope $= -\dfrac{3}{2}$

    y-intercept $= 2$

  c.

31.

32.

33.

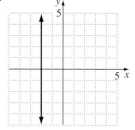

34. a. Upward
b. $(3, -2)$
c. 1.6 and 4.4
d. 7
e.

35. a. Downward
b. $(-1, 4)$
c. -3 and 1
d. 3
e.

36. a. Downward
b. $(1, 4)$
c. -0.15 and 2.15
d. 1
e.

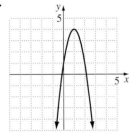

37. Vertex at $(4, 4.27)$

38.

39.

40.

41. 260   **42.** 92.4   **43.** $\{(2, 3)\}$ **44.** $\{(-2, -3)\}$ **45.** $\{(3, 2)\}$ **46.** $\{(4, -2)\}$ **47.** $\{(1, 5)\}$ **48.** $\{(2, 3)\}$
49. $\{(-9, 3)\}$ **50.** $\{(3, 4)\}$ **51.** $\{(2, -3)\}$ **52.** $\varnothing$ **53.** $\{(3, -1)\}$ **54.** $\{(x, y)\mid 3x - 2y = 6\}$
55. The numbers are -3 and 1.
56. The cholesterol intake of an ounce of shrimp is 42 mg. The cholesterol intake of an ounce of scallops is 15 mg.

57.

58.

59.

60.

61.

62.

63.

64.

65. Maximum value is 10; minimum value is 2

66. a.

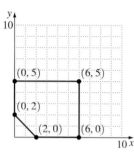

b. At $(0, 2)$ $z = 2(0) + 3(2) = 6$; at $(0, 5)$ $z = 2(0) + 3(5) = 15$; at $(6, 5)$ $z = 2(6) + 3(5) = 27$; at $(6, 0)$ $z = 2(6) + 3(0) = 12$; at $(2, 0)$ $z = 2(2) + 3(0) = 4$

c. The maximum value of the objective function is 27. It occurs at $x = 6$ and $y = 5$. The minimum value of the objective function is 4. It occurs at $x = 2$ and $y = 0$.

Chapter 7 Test

1.

2. 21

3.

4. 3

5.

6.

7. a. Upward   **b.** $(1, -9)$
   c. -2 and 4   **d.** -8
   e.

8.

9. \$7,094,942.74   **10.** $\{(2, 4)\}$ **11.** $\{(1, -3)\}$ **12.** $\{(6, -5)\}$

13.

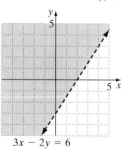

$3x - 2y = 6$

14.

$2x - y = 4$

$2x - y = -1$

15. The maximum value is 24. The minimum value is 6.

CHAPTER 8

Exercise Set 8.1

1. 40%   **3.** 25%   **5.** 37.5%   **7.** 2.5%   **9.** 11.25%   **11.** 59%   **13.** 38.44%   **15.** 287%   **17.** 1487%   **19.** 10,000%
21. 0.72   **23.** 0.436   **25.** 1.3   **27.** 0.02   **29.** 0.005   **31.** 0.00625   **33.** 0.625   **35.** 12.5%   **37.** 30%   **39.** 33,000,000
41. $9   **43. a.** $1008   **b.** $17,808   **45. a.** $103.20   **b.** $756.80   **47.** 10%   **49.** 15%   **51.** 50.4%   **53.** 2% decrease
61. c   **63.** $960 increase   **65.** $18.71   **67. a.** 54%   **b.** 33%   **c.** 9%   **d.** 4%

Exercise Set 8.2

1. a. $240   **b.** $4240   **3. a.** $10.80   **b.** $190.80   **5. a.** $27   **b.** $927   **7. a.** $897   **b.** $10,097
9. a. $262.50   **b.** $20,262.50   **11. a.** $426.25   **b.** $15,926.25   **13. a.** $10,816   **b.** $816   **15. a.** $3655.21   **b.** $655.21
17. a. $12,795.12   **b.** $3295.12   **19. a.** $5149.12   **b.** $649.12   **21. a.** $1855.10   **b.** $355.10
23. a. $49,189.30   **b.** $29,189.30   **25.** 5.5% rate compounded semiannually   **27.** 7% compounded monthly   **29.** $8374.84
31. $7528.59   **33. a.** $247.50   **b.** $4247.50   **35. a.** ≈ $3,052,400,000   **b.** ≈ $3,169,700,000   **37.** $65,728.51   **39.** $21,679.39
47. $8544.49   **49.** $9087.97   **51.** 13.94%

Exercise Set 8.3

1. a. $22,000   **b.** $29,600   **c.** $2600   **3. a.** $1000   **b.** $1420   **c.** $320   **5.** 12.5%   **7.** 14.5%   **9.** 13.0%
11. a. $17,000   **b.** $22,133   **c.** $4633   **d.** 10.0%   **13. a.** $2779.56   **b.** $10,560.79   **c.** $1686.11   **d.** $11,654.24
15. a. $11.05   **b.** $1013.05   **c.** $28   **17. a.** $4.96   **b.** $618.61   **c.** $61.86   **19. a.** $7.50   **b.** $45   **c.** $15
31. b   **33.** Answers may vary.   **35. a.** 30 days; $373.27 average daily balance   **b.** $4.85 finance charge   **c.** $471 balance due

Exercise Set 8.4

1. a. $25,000   **b.** $100,000   **c.** $3000   **d.** $665   **e.** $139,400   **3.** $24,168   **5.** 20-year mortgage at 7.5%
7.

Amortization Schedule			
Annual % rate: 8		Monthly payment: $734	
Amount of mortgage: $100,000		Term: Years 30, Months 0	
Number of monthly payments: 360			
Payment Number	Interest Payment	Principal Payment	Balance of Loan
1	$666.67	$67.33	$99,932.67
2	$666.22	$67.78	$99,864.89
3	$665.77	$68.23	$99,796.66

9. $172,300   **11.** At least $30,000
13. $151,446,400   **23.** Answers may vary.

Exercise Set 8.5

1. a. $73.25; $45.44   **b.** $840   **c.** 2.2%   **d.** 591,500 shares   **e.** $56.38; $54.38   **f.** $55.50   **g.** Up $1.25   **h.** $3.26
3. a. $6485   **b.** $406.25   **5. a.** $15,000   **b.** $300   **7. a.** $4260   **b.** $111.50

Chapter 8 Review

1. 80%   **2.** 12.5%   **3.** 75%   **4.** 72%   **5.** 0.35%   **6.** 475.6%   **7.** 0.65   **8.** 0.997   **9.** 1.50   **10.** 0.03   **11.** 0.0065
12. 0.0025   **13.** 70%   **14.** $11.70   **15. a.** $1.44   **b.** $25.44   **16. a.** $297.50   **b.** $552.50   **17.** 12.5%   **18.** 35%
19. $180   **20.** $2520   **21.** $1200   **22.** $900   **23. a.** $122.50   **b.** $3622.50   **24. a.** $8114.92   **b.** $1114.92
25. a. $38,490.80   **b.** $8490.80   **26. a.** $5556.46   **b.** $3056.46   **27.** 6.25% rate compounded 12 times a year   **28.** $16,653.64
29. $13,175.19   **30. a.** $16,000   **b.** $21,500   **c.** $5500   **d.** Approximately 12.5%   **31. a.** $1074.53   **b.** $3475.47
32. a. $2344.43   **b.** $2205.57   **33.** Answers may vary.   **34. a.** $16.50   **b.** $1756.50   **c.** $49
35. a. $28.80   **b.** $64.80   **c.** $35.77   **36. a.** $29,000   **b.** $116,000   **c.** $2320   **d.** $771.40   **e.** $161,704
37. 20-year mortgage at 8%

38.

Amortization Schedule			
Annual % rate:	7.5	Monthly payment:	$559.20
Amount of mortgage:	$80,000	Term: Years 30, Months 0	
Number of monthly payments:	360		

Payment Number	Interest Payment	Principal Payment	Balance of Loan
1	$500	$59.20	$79,940.80
2	$499.63	$59.57	$79,881.23

39. $769; $699 **40.** $64.06; $26.13
41. $144 **42.** 0.3% **43.** 545,800 shares
44. $61.25; $59.25 **45.** $61
46. $1.75 increase **47.** $1.49
48. a. $9750 **b.** $656.25
49. Answers may vary.
50. Answers may vary.

Chapter 8 Test

1. a. $18 **b.** $102 **2.** 20% **3.** $72 **4.** $2472 **5.** $2797.70 **6.** $697.70 **7.** $14,204.57 **8.** $13,000 **9.** $21,000 **10.** $5000 **11.** Approximately 13.5% **12.** $819.67 **13.** $6680.33 **14.** $15.60 **15.** $1335.60 **16.** $37 **17.** $17.60 **18.** $12,000 **19.** $108,000 **20.** $2160 **21.** $830.52 **22.** $190,987.20 **23.** $61,820 **24.** $25.75; $25.50 **25.** $2030 **26.** $386.25

CHAPTER 9

Exercise Set 9.1

1. 2.5 ft **3.** 360 in. **5.** 0.17 yd **7.** 216 in. **9.** 18 ft **11.** 2 yd **13.** 3.25 mi **15.** 3960 ft **17.** 500 cm **19.** 1630 m **21.** 0.03178 hm **23.** 0.000023 m **25.** 21.96 dm **27.** 35.56 cm **29.** 5.51 in. **31.** 424 cm **33.** 165.625 mi **35.** 13.33 yd **37.** 55.12 in. **39.** 0.4064 dam **41.** 1.5 m **43.** 16.67 ft **45.** 60 mi per hr **47.** 72 km per hr **49.** Meter **51.** Millimeter **53.** Meter **55.** Millimeter **57.** Millimeter **59.** b **61.** a **63.** c **65.** a **67.** 0.216 km **69.** 148.8 million km **79.** 9 km **81.** 11 m **83.** 457.2 cm

Exercise Set 9.2

1. 16 square units **3.** 24 square units **5.** 8 square units **7.** 2.15 in^2 **9.** 37.5 yd^2 **11.** 25.5 acres **13.** 91 cm^2 **15.** 24 cubic units **17.** 74,800 gal **19.** 1600 gal **21.** 9 gal **23.** 13.5 yd^3 **25.** 45 L **27.** 17 mL **29.** 1500 cm^3 **31.** 150 cm^3 **33.** 5.5 people per square mile **35. a.** 20 acres **b.** $12,500 per acre **37.** Square centimeters or square meters **39.** Square kilometers **41.** b **43.** b **45.** 336,600 gal **47.** 4 L **55.** 11,952.64 people per square mile **57.** Answers may vary. **59.** Milliliter; liter; kiloliter **61.** Liters

Exercise Set 9.3

1. 740 mg **3.** 0.87 g **5.** 800 cg **7.** 18,600 g **9.** 0.000018 g **11.** 2.25 lb **13.** 1008 g **15.** 243 kg **17.** 35,840 g **19.** 1200 lb **21.** 222.22 T **23.** 50° F **25.** 95° F **27.** 134.6° F **29.** 23° F **31.** 20° C **33.** 5° C **35.** 22.2° C **37.** −5° C **39.** 176.7° C **41.** −30° C **43.** Gram **45.** Gram **47.** Kilogram **49.** Kilogram **51.** b **53.** a **55.** c **57.** 13.28 kg **59.** 99 cents **61.** Regular size **63.** a **65.** c **67.** 19.4° F **75.** b

Chapter 9 Review

1. 5.75 ft **2.** 0.25 yd **3.** 7 yd **4.** 2.5 mi **5.** 2280 cm **6.** 70 m **7.** 1920 m **8.** 0.0144 hm **9.** 0.0005 m **10.** 180 mm **11.** 58.42 cm **12.** 7.48 in. **13.** 528 km **14.** 375 mi **15.** 15.56 yd **16.** 40 ft **17.** 28.13 mi per hr **18.** 96 km per hr **19.** 0.024 km; 24,000 cm; 2400 m **20.** 4.8 km **21.** 24 square units **22.** 190.8 people per square mile **23.** 18 acres **24.** 333.33 ft^2 **25.** 31.2 km^2 **26.** a **27.** 24 cubic units **28.** 251,328 gal **29.** 76 L **30.** c **31.** Answers may vary. **32.** Answers may vary. **33.** 1240 mg **34.** 1200 cg **35.** 0.000012 g **36.** 0.00045 kg **37.** 94.5 kg **38.** 14 oz **39.** Kilograms **40.** 2.25 lb **41.** a **42.** c **43.** 59° F **44.** 212° F **45.** 41° F **46.** 32° F **47.** −13° F **48.** 15° C **49.** 5° C **50.** 100° C **51.** 37° C **52.** −17.8° C **53.** −10° C **54.** More

Chapter 9 Test

1. 0.00807 hm **2.** 250 in. **3.** 4.8 km **4.** mm **5.** cm **6.** km **7.** 128 km per hr **8.** 9 times **9.** 200.3 people per square mile **10.** 45 acres **11.** b **12.** 1000 times **13.** 74,800 gal **14.** b **15.** 0.137 kg **16.** 40.5 kg **17.** kg **18.** mg **19.** 86° F **20.** 80° C **21.** d

CHAPTER 10

Exercise Set 10.1

1. a. C **b.** Ray CD and ray CB **c.** $\angle C, \angle DCB, \angle BCD$ **3.** 30°   **5.** 90°   **7.** 65°; acute   **9.** Obtuse   **11.** Straight
13. 65°   **15.** 146°   **17.** 42°   **19.** 1°   **21.** 52.6°   **23.** 69°   **25.** 164°   **27.** 90°   **29.** $86\frac{3}{4}°$ **31.** 108°; 72°; 108°
33. 50°; 90°; 50°   **35.** 68°; 68°; 112°; 112°; 68°; 68°; 112°   **37.** Answers may vary.   **39.** Answers may vary.   **41.** Answers may vary.
53. 45°   **55.** 90°

Exercise Set 10.2

1. 67°   **3.** 32°   **5.** 50°; 130°; 50°; 130°; 50°   **7.** Angles A and D, angles B and E, angles C and F; $\overline{AB}$ and $\overline{DE}$, $\overline{AC}$ and $\overline{DF}$, $\overline{BC}$ and $\overline{EF}$
9. Angles N and R, angles P and S, angles M and T; $\overline{NM}$ and $\overline{RT}$, $\overline{NP}$ and $\overline{RS}$, $\overline{MP}$ and $\overline{TS}$ **11.** 5 in.   **13.** 6 m   **15.** 16 in.
17. 17 m   **19.** 39 m   **21.** 12 cm   **23.** 13.2 m   **25.** No; 0.3°   **27.** 32 yd   **29.** 600 yd   **31.** 34 ft   **43.** 21 ft

Exercise Set 10.3

1. Quadrilateral   **3.** Pentagon   **5.** a (square), b (rhombus), d (rectangle), e (parallelogram)   **7.** a (square), d (rectangle)
9. c (trapezoid)   **11.** 30 cm   **13.** 28 yd   **15.** 1000 in.   **17.** 27 ft   **19.** 18 yd   **21.** 84 yd   **23.** 32 ft   **25.** 540°
27. 360°   **29.** 108°   **31.** 540; 140°   **33.** No entry   **35.** Stop, yield, deer crossing   **37.** Equilateral triangle   **39.** Yield
41. $5600   **43.** $9.50   **51.** $6a$

Exercise Set 10.4

1. 18 m²   **3.** 16 in.²   **5.** 2100 cm²   **7.** 56 in.²   **9.** 20.58 yd²   **11.** 91 m²   **13.** 25 cm; 50 cm²   **15.** 38 yd²; 113 yd²
17. 72 m²   **19.** 300 m²   **21.** $556.50   **23.** 148 ft²   **25.** $910   **27. a.** 18 bags   **b.** $215.55   **29.** 126 m   **31.** 376 plants

33. Large pizza   **35.** $34,741.50 (using π) or $34,732 (using 3.14)   **41.** By a factor of $\frac{9}{4}$ **43.** $13,033.60   **45.** 15.3 cm²

Exercise Set 10.5

1. 36 in.³   **3.** 64 cm³   **5.** 175 yd³   **7.** 56 in.³   **9.** 471 cm³   **11.** 9500 in.³ (using π) or 9495 in.³ (using 3.14)   **13.** 151 m³
15. 47 yd³   **17.** 905 m³ (using π) or 904 m³ (using 3.14)   **19.** 3054 cm³ (using π) or 3052 cm³ (using 3.14)   **21.** 62 m²   **23.** 96 ft²
25. 1018 cm³ (using π) or 1017 cm³ (using 3.14)   **27.** $40   **29.** No   **31. a.** 3,386,880 yd³   **b.** 2,257,920 blocks   **33.** Yes
35. 260,120,252,600 mi³ (using π) or 259,988,382,700 mi³ (using 3.14)   **39.** Multiplied by 8   **41.** 168 cm³   **43.** 84 cm²

Exercise Set 10.6

1. $\frac{3}{5}, \frac{4}{5}, \frac{3}{4}$ **3.** $\frac{20}{29}, \frac{21}{29}, \frac{20}{21}$ **5.** $\frac{5}{13}, \frac{12}{13}, \frac{5}{12}$ **7.** $\frac{4}{5}, \frac{3}{5}, \frac{4}{3}$ **9.** 188 cm   **11.** 182 in.   **13.** 7 m   **15.** 22 yd   **17.** 40 m
19. $m\angle B = 50°$; $a = 18$ yd, $c = 28$ yd   **21.** $m\angle B = 38°$; $a = 43$ cm, $b = 33$ cm   **23.** 37°   **25.** 28°   **27.** 529 yd   **29.** 2880 ft
31. 86 ft   **33.** 50°   **35.** 150 ft   **37.** 410 ft   **47.** tan gets very large; tan 90° is undefined

Exercise Set 10.7

1. a. Yes   **b.** Sample path: $DABDCB$ **3. a.** Yes   **b.** Sample path: $ADCBDEAB$ **5. a.** No   **7.** 4   **9.** 2
11. Pitcher and wrench, pretzel and button   **13.** The sum of the angles is greater than 180°.   **15.** Yes   **17.** No
19. Carbon: even; hydrogen: odd
21. a.
b. Yes
c. Answers may vary.

23. a.
b. No

25. a.
b. No

27. Answers may vary.

Chapter 10 Review

1. Acute **2.** Obtuse **3.** Right **4.** 65° **5.** 49° **6.** 17° **7.** 134° **8.** 110°; 70°; 110° **9.** 138°; 42°; 138°; 138°; 42°; 42°; 138°
10. 72° **11.** 51° **12.** 90°; 90°; 140°; 40°; 140° **13.** 5 ft **14.** 3.75 ft **15.** 10 ft **16.** 7.2 in. **17.** 10.2 cm **18.** 12.5 ft
19. 15 ft **20.** 12 yd **21.** Rectangle, square **22.** Rhombus, square **23.** Trapezoid **24.** 30 cm **25.** 4480 yd **26.** 44 m
27. 1800° **28.** 1080° **29.** 135° **30.** $132 **31.** 32.5 ft^2 **32.** 20 m^2 **33.** 50 cm^2 **34.** 135 yd^2 **35.** 63 m; 314 m^2
36. 192 in.^{2} **37.** 28 m^2 **38.** $787.50 **39.** $650 **40.** 31 yd **41.** 60 cm^3 **42.** 1053 m^3 **43.** 402 yd^3
44. 46,919 in.^{3} (using π) or 46,891 in.^{3} (using 3.14) **45.** 905 m^3 (using π) or 904 m^3 (using 3.14) **46.** 126 m^2 **47.** 4800 m^3
48. 651,775 m^3 **49.** $80 **50.** $\dfrac{3}{5}, \dfrac{4}{5}, \dfrac{3}{4}$ **51.** 42 mm **52.** 23 cm **53.** 37 in. **54.** 58° **55.** 807 ft **56.** 31 m **57.** 56°
58. Not traversable **59.** Traversable **60.** 0 **61.** 2 **62.** 1 **63.** 2 **64.** Answers may vary. **65.** Answers may vary.

Chapter 10 Test

1. 126° **2.** 133° **3.** 70° **4.** 35° **5.** 3.2 in. **6.** 10 ft **7.** 1440° **8.** 40 cm **9.** d **10.** 517 m^2 **11.** 525 in.^{2}
12. 126 m **13.** 108 tiles **14.** 18 ft^3 **15.** 16 m^3 **16.** 550 cm^3 **17.** 85 cm **18.** 70 ft **19.** Traversable
20. Answers may vary.

CHAPTER 11

Exercise Set 11.1

1. 80 **3.** 12 **5.** 6 **7.** 40 **9.** 144 **11.** 8 **13.** 96 **15.** 729 **17.** 144 **19.** 676,000 **21.** 2187 **27.** 720 hrs

Exercise Set 11.2

1. 720 **3.** 120 **5.** 120 **7.** 362,880 **9.** 6 **11.** 4 **13.** 504 **15.** 570,024 **17.** 3,047,466,240 **19.** 600 **21.** 10,712
23. 5034 **25.** 24 **27.** 6 **29.** 42 **31.** 1716 **33.** 3024 **35.** 6720 **37.** 720 **39.** 1 **41.** 720 **43.** 8,648,640
45. 120 **47.** 15,120 **55.** 239,500,800 **57.** 2.0923×10^{12} **59.** 144

Exercise Set 11.3

1. Permutations **3.** Combinations **5.** Combinations **7.** Permutations **9.** Permutations **11.** 6 **13.** 126 **15.** 330
17. 8 **19.** 1 **21.** 4060 **23.** 1 **25.** 7 **27.** 20 **29.** 495 **31.** 24,310 **33.** 4495 **35.** 13,983,816 **37.** 735
39. 4,839,570,450 **45.** 5/36 lottery **47.** 9.5 min; 39 min

Exercise Set 11.4

1. $\dfrac{1}{6}$ **3.** $\dfrac{1}{2}$ **5.** $\dfrac{1}{3}$ **7.** 1 **9.** 0 **11.** $\dfrac{1}{13}$ **13.** $\dfrac{1}{4}$ **15.** $\dfrac{3}{13}$ **17.** $\dfrac{1}{52}$ **19.** 0 **21.** $\dfrac{1}{4}$ **23.** $\dfrac{1}{2}$ **25.** $\dfrac{1}{2}$ **27.** $\dfrac{3}{8}$
29. $\dfrac{3}{8}$ **31.** $\dfrac{7}{8}$ **33.** 0 **35.** $\dfrac{1}{4}$ **37.** $\dfrac{1}{9}$ **39.** 0 **41.** $\dfrac{3}{10}$ **43.** $\dfrac{1}{5}$ **45.** $\dfrac{1}{2}$ **47.** 0 **49.** $\dfrac{1}{4}$ **51.** $\dfrac{1}{4}$ **53.** $\dfrac{1}{2}$
55. 0.424 **57.** 0.208 **59.** 0.030 **61.** 0.128 **63.** 0.567 **65.** 0.135 **73.** 0.375

Exercise Set 11.5

1. a. 120 **b.** 6 **c.** $\dfrac{1}{20}$ **3. a.** $\dfrac{1}{6}$ **b.** $\dfrac{1}{30}$ **c.** $\dfrac{1}{720}$ **d.** $\dfrac{1}{3}$ **5. a.** 84 **b.** 10 **c.** $\dfrac{5}{42}$ **7.** 0.000000056; 0.00000556
9. a. $\dfrac{1}{177,100}$ **b.** $\dfrac{6783}{44,275}$ **11.** $\dfrac{3}{10}$ **13. a.** 2,598,960 **b.** 1287 **c.** 0.0004952 **15.** $\dfrac{11}{1105}$ **17.** $\dfrac{36}{270,725}$ **23.** $9,004,730
25. $\dfrac{1}{10}$

Exercise Set 11.6

1. $\dfrac{12}{13}$ **3.** $\dfrac{3}{4}$ **5.** $\dfrac{10}{13}$ **7.** 0.999986 **9.** 0.998559 **11.** 0.931 **13.** 0.864 **15.** 0.153 **17.** $\dfrac{2}{13}$ **19.** $\dfrac{1}{13}$ **21.** $\dfrac{1}{26}$
23. $\dfrac{1}{12}$ **25.** $\dfrac{1}{2}$ **27.** $\dfrac{9}{22}$ **29.** $\dfrac{5}{6}$ **31.** $\dfrac{15}{52}$ **33.** $\dfrac{11}{26}$ **35.** $\dfrac{3}{4}$ **37.** $\dfrac{5}{8}$ **39.** $\dfrac{33}{40}$ **41.** $\dfrac{4}{5}$ **43.** $\dfrac{7}{10}$ **45.** 2 : 1 **47.** 1 : 2
49. 1 : 3 **51.** 1 : 1 **53.** 12 : 1 **55.** 25 : 1 **57.** 47 : 5 **59.** 49 : 1 **61.** 1 : 19 **63.** $\dfrac{3}{7}$ **65.** $\dfrac{4}{25}$; 84 **73. a.** $\dfrac{12}{25}$ **b.** $\dfrac{3}{10}$
75. 5 : 1

Exercise Set 11.7

1. $\frac{1}{6}$ **3.** $\frac{1}{36}$ **5.** $\frac{1}{4}$ **7.** $\frac{1}{36}$ **9.** $\frac{1}{8}$ **11.** $\frac{1}{36}$ **13.** $\frac{1}{3}$ **15.** $\frac{3}{52}$ **17.** $\frac{1}{169}$ **19.** $\frac{1}{4}$ **21.** $\frac{1}{64}$ **23.** $\frac{1}{6}$

25. a. $\frac{1}{256}$ **b.** $\frac{1}{4096}$ **c.** 0.524   **d.** 0.476   **27.** $\frac{7}{29}$ **29.** $\frac{5}{87}$ **31.** $\frac{2}{21}$ **33.** $\frac{4}{35}$ **35.** $\frac{11}{21}$ **37.** $\frac{1}{57}$ **39.** $\frac{8}{855}$

41. $\frac{11}{57}$ **43.** $\frac{1}{5}$ **45.** $\frac{2}{3}$ **47.** $\frac{3}{4}$ **49.** $\frac{3}{4}$ **51.** 0.568   **53.** 0.025   **63.** 0.590

65. a. Answers may vary.   **b.** 0.992   **c.** 0.008   **d.** 0.411   **e.** 23 people

Exercise Set 11.8

1. 1.75   **3. a.** \$29,000   **b.** \$29,000   **c.** \$29,050   **5.** \$0   **7.** \$.73   **9.** Second mall   **11. a.** \$140,000   **b.** No
13. −\$.17   **15.** −\$.053   **17.** −\$.50   **25. a.** 0   **b.** 0.25   **c.** 0.67   **d.** 1.5   **e.** Answers may vary.

Chapter 11 Review

1. 800   **2.** 20   **3.** 9900   **4.** 125   **5.** 243   **6.** 60   **7.** 720   **8.** 120   **9.** 120   **10.** 240   **11.** 800   **12.** 114
13. 990   **14.** 151,200   **15.** 9900   **16.** 32,760   **17.** 1,860,480   **18.** Combinations   **19.** Permutations   **20.** Combinations
21. 330   **22.** 2002   **23.** 210   **24.** 1287   **25.** 1140   **26.** 55,440   **27.** $\frac{1}{6}$ **28.** $\frac{2}{3}$ **29.** 1   **30.** 0   **31.** $\frac{1}{13}$ **32.** $\frac{3}{13}$

33. $\frac{3}{13}$ **34.** $\frac{1}{52}$ **35.** $\frac{1}{26}$ **36.** $\frac{1}{2}$ **37.** $\frac{1}{3}$ **38.** $\frac{1}{6}$ **39. a.** $\frac{1}{2}$ **b.** 0   **40.** 0.302   **41.** 0.288   **42.** $\frac{1}{24}$ **43.** $\frac{1}{6}$

44. $\frac{1}{30}$ **45.** $\frac{1}{720}$ **46.** $\frac{1}{3}$ **47. a.** 0.0000645   **b.** 0.00645   **48. a.** $\frac{1}{14}$ **b.** $\frac{3}{7}$ **49.** $\frac{3}{26}$ **50.** $\frac{5}{6}$ **51.** $\frac{1}{2}$ **52.** $\frac{1}{3}$ **53.** $\frac{2}{3}$

54. 1   **55.** $\frac{10}{13}$ **56.** $\frac{3}{4}$ **57.** $\frac{2}{13}$ **58.** $\frac{1}{13}$ **59.** $\frac{7}{13}$ **60.** $\frac{11}{26}$ **61.** $\frac{5}{6}$ **62.** $\frac{5}{6}$ **63.** $\frac{1}{2}$ **64.** $\frac{2}{3}$ **65.** 1   **66.** $\frac{5}{6}$

67. 0.807   **68.** 0.574   **69.** $\frac{4}{5}$ **70.** $\frac{3}{4}$ **71.** $1:12; 12:1$ **72.** $99:1$ **73.** $\frac{3}{4}$ **74.** $\frac{2}{9}$ **75.** $\frac{1}{36}$ **76.** $\frac{1}{9}$ **77.** $\frac{1}{36}$

78. $\frac{8}{27}$ **79.** $\frac{1}{32}$ **80. a.** 0.04   **b.** 0.008   **c.** 0.4096   **d.** 0.5904   **81.** $\frac{1}{9}$ **82.** $\frac{1}{12}$ **83.** $\frac{1}{196}$ **84.** $\frac{1}{3}$ **85.** $\frac{3}{10}$

86. a. $\frac{1}{2}$ **b.** $\frac{2}{7}$ **87.** $\frac{92}{291}$ **88.** $\frac{55}{103}$ **89.** 3.125   **90. a.** −\$.50   **b.** \$10.00   **91.** \$4500   **92.** −\$.25

Chapter 11 Test

1. 240   **2.** 24   **3.** 720   **4.** 990   **5.** 210   **6.** $\frac{6}{25}$ **7.** $\frac{17}{25}$ **8.** $\frac{11}{25}$ **9.** $\frac{5}{13}$ **10.** $\frac{1}{210}$ **11.** 0.010   **12.** $\frac{1}{2}$ **13.** $\frac{1}{16}$

14. $\frac{1}{8000}$ **15.** $\frac{11}{26}$ **16.** $\frac{3}{5}$ **17.** $\frac{1}{19}$ **18.** $\frac{1}{256}$ **19.** Answers may vary.   **20.** $3:4$ **21. a.** $4:1$ **b.** $\frac{4}{5}$ **22.** $\frac{9}{19}$
23. \$1000   **24.** −\$12.75

CHAPTER 12

Exercise Set 12.1

1. College professors in the United States   **3.** Residents of the United States   **5.** All high school students in Connecticut

9.

Time Spent on Homework (in hours)	Number of Students
15	4
16	5
17	6
18	5
19	4
20	2
21	2
22	0
23	0
24	2
	30

11.

Age	Number of Runners
10–19	8
20–29	13
30–39	7
40–49	6
50–59	4
60–69	2
	40

13.

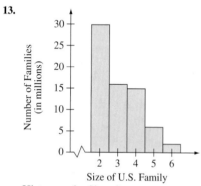

Histogram for Size of
United States Family

Frequency Polygon for Size of
United States Family

15.

Histogram for Time Spent on Homework

Frequency Polygon for Time Spent on Homework

17. c

19.

Stems	Leaves
2	8 8 9 5
3	8 7 0 1 2 7 6 4 0 5
4	8 2 2 1 4 5 4 6 2 0 8 2 7 9
5	9 4 1 9 1 0
6	3 2 3 6 6 3

21. Ages of the actors: 31, 32, 32, 33, 35, 37, 38, 39, 40, 40, 41, 42, 42, 43, 43, 44, 45, 47, 46, 47, 48, 48, 51, 55, 56, 56, 60, 61, 62, 76
Ages of the actresses: 21, 24, 26, 26, 26, 27, 30, 30, 31, 31, 33, 33, 34, 34, 34, 35, 35, 37, 37, 38, 41, 41, 41, 42, 49, 60, 61, 61, 74, 80
23. Answers may vary.   **37.** Answers may vary.

Exercise Set 12.2

1. 4.125   **3.** 95   **5.** 62   **7.** 3.45   **9.** 4.71   **11.** 6.26   **13.** 3.5   **15.** 95   **17.** 60   **19.** 3.6   **21.** 5   **23.** 6   **25.** 3
27. 95   **29.** 40   **31.** No mode   **33.** 5   **35.** 6   **37.** 4.5   **39.** 95   **41.** 70   **43.** 3.3   **45.** 4.5   **47.** 5.5   **49.** $282.33
51. a. 1.79 inches per hour   **b.** No   **c.** 0 in.   **53.** 147.5 lb   **55.** 147.5 lb
57. a. 854.17 words per minute; 850 words per minute; 1000 words per minute; 850 words per minute   **b.** Mode   **c.** Answers may vary.
69. Answers may vary.

Exercise Set 12.3

1. 4   **3.** 8   **5.** 2   **7.** 6   **9.** 4   **11. a.** $-9, -7, -5, 0, 6, 15$ **b.** 0   **13. a.** $-20, -11, -1, 0, 4, 28$ **b.** 0
15. a. 91   **b.** $-6, 4, -1, -6, 9$ **c.** 0   **17. a.** 155   **b.** $-9, -2, 0, 5, 6$ **c.** 0
19. a. 2.70   **b.** $-0.45, 0.80, 0.05, 0.40, -0.80$ **c.** 0   **21.** 1.58   **23.** 3.46   **25.** 0.89   **27.** 3   **29.** 2.14
31. 12, 12, 4.32; 12, 12, 5.07; 12, 12, 6; The samples have the same mean, but different standard deviations.   **33.** 35.3; 18.32
35. 45.2; 13.60   **37.** 529.2; 19.51   **39.** 768.83, 226.56   **49.** Answers may vary.   **51.** a

Exercise Set 12.4

1. 120   **3.** 160   **5.** 150   **7.** 60   **9.** 90   **11.** 68%   **13.** 34%   **15.** 47.5%   **17.** 49.85%   **19.** 16%   **21.** 2.5%
23. 95%   **25.** 47.5%   **27.** 16%   **29.** 2.5%   **31.** 0.15%   **33.** 1   **35.** 3   **37.** 0.5   **39.** 1.75   **41.** 0   **43.** -1
45. -1.5 **47.** -3.25 **49.** 1.5   **51.** 2.25   **53.** -0.5 **55.** -1.5 **57.** Math test   **59.** 500   **61.** 475   **63.** 250
65. 275   **67. a.** 72.57%   **b.** 27.43%   **69. a.** 88.49%   **b.** 11.51%   **71. a.** 24.20%   **b.** 75.8%   **73. a.** 11.51%   **b.** 88.49%
75. 33.99%   **77.** 15.74%   **79.** 86.64%   **81.** 28.57%   **83.** 93.32%   **85.** 27.43%   **87.** 88.49%   **89.** 6.29%   **91.** 45.14%
93. 6.68%   **95.** 24.17%   **97. a.** ±5.0%   **b.** We can be 95% confident that between 21% and 31% of all parents feel that crime is a bad thing about being a kid.   **99. a.** ±1.6%   **b.** We can be 95% confident that between 58.6% and 61.8% of all TV households watched the final episode of *M*A*S*H*.   **101.** 0.2%   **103.** No   **105.** Answers may vary.   **119.** 62 in.

Exercise Set 12.5

1.

There appears to be a strong positive correlation.

3.

There appears to be a strong negative correlation.

5.
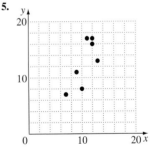
There appears to be a moderate positive correlation.

7.

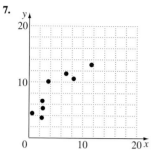

There appears to be a moderate positive correlation.

9. False   **11.** True   **13.** True   **15.** False   **17.** False
19. True   **21.** False   **23.** False   **25.** False   **27.** True   **29.** a
31. d   **33.** 0.855   **35.** −0.954
37. a. 0.75   **b.** $y = 1.52x - 3.38$ **c.** 21 yrs
39. a. 0.885   **b.** $y = 0.85x + 4.05$ **c.** 16 murders per 100,000 people
41. Correlation does exist   **43.** Correlation does not exist
45. Correlation does exist   **47.** Correlation does not exist
61. Answers may vary.

Chapter 12 Review

1. American adults earning $100,000 or more each year   **2.** Rental apartments in San Francisco   **3.** a

4.

Time Spent on Homework (in hours)	Number of Students
6	1
7	3
8	3
9	2
10	$\frac{1}{10}$

5.

6.

7.

Grades	Number of Students
0–39	19
40–49	8
50–59	6
60–69	6
70–79	5
80–89	3
90–100	$\frac{3}{50}$

8.

Stems	Leaves
1	3 4 1 3 7 8
2	4 9 6 9 2 7
3	4 9 6 5 1 1 1
4	4 0 2 7 9 1 2 5
5	7 9 6 4 0 1
6	3 3 7 0 8 9
7	2 3 4 0 5
8	7 1 6
9	5 1 0

9. Answers may vary.
10. 91.2   **11.** 17   **12.** 2.3
13. 11   **14.** 28   **15.** 2
16. 27   **17.** No mode   **18.** 2
19. 91   **20.** 19.5   **21.** 2.5
22. Answers may vary.
23. Answers may vary.

24. a.

Age at first inauguration	Number of Presidents
42	1
43	1
44	0
45	0
46	2
47	1
48	1
49	2
50	1
51	5
52	2
53	0
54	4
55	4
56	3
57	4
58	1
59	0
60	1
61	3
62	1
63	0
64	2
65	1
66	0
67	0
68	1
69	$\frac{1}{42}$

b. 54.86 years; 55 yrs; 51 yrs; 55.5
25. 18 **26.** 564 **27. a.** $-6; -26; -27; -13; 11; 16; 13; 7; 18; 7$ **b.** 0
28. a. 50 **b.** $-14; -24; -26; 40; 24$ **c.** 0 **29.** 4.05 **30.** 5.13 **31.** 49, 76, 24.32
32. 80, 0; 80, 11.55 **33.** Answers may vary. **34.** 86 **35.** 98 **36.** 60 **37.** 68%
38. 95% **39.** 34% **40.** 99.7% **41.** 16% **42.** 84% **43.** 2.5% **44.** 0 **45.** 2
46. 1.6 **47.** -3 **48.** -1.2 **49.** Vocabulary test **50.** 38,000 mi **51.** 41,000 mi
52. 22,000 mi **53.** 91.92% **54.** 96.41% **55.** 88.33% **56.** 10.69% **57.** 75%
58. 14% **59.** 11%
60. a. -1.4%
   b. We can be 95% confident that between 8.4% and 11.2% of all TV households watch *Jeopardy*.

61.

There appears to be a strong positive correlation.

62.

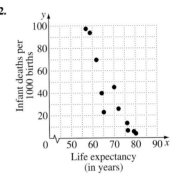

There appears to be a strong negative correlation.

63. False **64.** True **65.** True
66. False **67.** False **68.** False
69. False **70.** c
71. a. 0.972 **b.** $y = 0.509x + 0.537$

72. a.

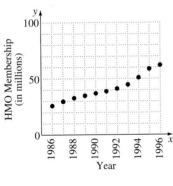

b. 0.973
c. There is a correlation between time and HMO membership.

Chapter 12 Test

1. d **2.**

Score	Frequency
3	1
4	2
5	3
6	2
7	2
8	3
9	2
10	1
	16

3.

4.

5.

Class	Frequency
40–49	3
50–59	6
60–69	6
70–79	7
80–89	6
90–99	2
	30

6.

Stems	Frequency
4	1 8 6
5	9 1 0 5 0 0
6	2 3 7 0 1 1
7	9 3 1 5 8 9 1
8	8 9 9 1 3 0
9	0 3

7. 3.67 **8.** 3 **9.** 4 **10.** 2.34
11. 2.25 **12.** 2 **13.** 2
14. Answers may vary.
15. 34% **16.** 2.5% **17.** Student
18. 8.08% **19.** 41%

20. a. ±10%
b. We can be 95% confident that between 50% and 70% of all students are very satisfied with their professors.

21.

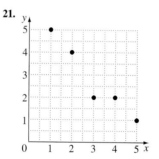

There appears to be a strong negative correlation.

22. True
23. False
24. True
25. Answers may vary.

CHAPTER 13

Exercise Set 13.1

1. $\{e, a, b, c\}$ **3.** c **5.** a **7.** e **9.** b **11.** e **13.** e **15.** No **17.** Yes **19.** No **21.** No
23. $2 \oplus 4 = 1; 4 \oplus 2 = 1;$ So $2 \oplus 4 = 4 \oplus 2$ **25.** $4 \oplus 1 = 0; 1 \oplus 4 = 0;$ So $4 \oplus 1 = 1 \oplus 4$
27. The Commutative Property; since the entries are mirror images about the main diagonal, $\oplus$ is commutative. **29.** $4; 4$ **31.** $0; 0$
33. a. b **b.** a **c.** No **35.** Answers may vary. **37.** -29 **39.** $\dfrac{1}{29}$ **41.** a **43.** c **45.** e **47.** c **49.** e
51. a **53.** d **55.** b **57.** 0 **59.** 4 **61.** 2

63. a. *d*

b.

Element	Inverse
a	None
b	None
c	None
d	*d*

65. Answers may vary.

67. Yes

69. Answers may vary.

71. *E* does not have an inverse.

81. a. $\begin{bmatrix} 15 & 20 \\ 35 & 46 \end{bmatrix}$ **b.** $\begin{bmatrix} 4 & 7 \\ 34 & 57 \end{bmatrix}$ **c.** Not commutative

Exercise Set 13.2

1. 8-fold symmetry **3.** 18-fold symmetry **5.** For any 2 elements in the set, the result is in the set.

7. $(r \circ t) \circ q = p \circ q = e; r \circ (t \circ q) = r \circ r = e;$ so $(r \circ t) \circ q = r \circ (t \circ q)$ **9.** *e* **11.** *q* **13.** *r* **15.** *t* **17.** *t*

19. This mathematical system is not commutative. **21.** Answers may vary.

23. a.

+	0	1	2	3	4	5
0	0	1	2	3	4	5
1	1	2	3	4	5	0
2	2	3	4	5	0	1
3	3	4	5	0	1	2
4	4	5	0	1	2	3
5	5	0	1	2	3	4

25. True **27.** True **29.** False; $84 \equiv 0 \pmod 7$

31. False; $23 \equiv 3 \pmod 4$ **33.** True

35. $3 + 2 \equiv 5 \pmod 6$ **37.** $4 + 5 \equiv 3 \pmod 6$

39. $6 + 5 \equiv 4 \pmod 7$ **41.** $49 + 49 \equiv 48 \pmod{50}$

43. $1200 + 0600 \equiv 1800 \pmod{2400}$

45. $0830 + 1550 \equiv 2380 \pmod{2400}$

47. Sunday **57.** Answers may vary. **59.** 8:00 A.M.

Chapter 13 Review

1. $\{e, c, f, r\}$ **2.** Yes **3.** *r* **4.** *f* **5.** *c* **6.** *e; e* **7.** *c; c* **8.** *f; f* **9.** The Commutative Property

10. Since the table entries are symmetric, the operation is commutative. **11.** *f; f* **12.** *e; e* **13.** The Associative property

14. *e* **15.** *e* **16.** *r* **17.** *f* **18.** *c* **19.** No **20.** Yes **21.** No **22.** -123 **23.** $\dfrac{1}{123}$

24. a.

+	0	1	2	3	4
0	0	1	2	3	4
1	1	1	2	3	4
2	2	2	2	3	4
3	3	3	3	3	4
4	4	4	4	4	4

b. 0

c. No

25. 3-fold symmetry

26. 18-fold symmetry

27. a.

+	0	1	2	3	4
0	0	1	2	3	4
1	1	2	3	4	0
2	2	3	4	0	1
3	3	4	0	1	2
4	4	0	1	2	3

28. False; $17 \equiv 1 \pmod 8$ **29.** False; $37 \equiv 2 \pmod 5$ **30.** True **31.** $4 + 3 \equiv 1 \pmod 6$

32. $7 + 7 \equiv 6 \pmod 8$ **33.** $4 + 3 = 7 \pmod 9$ **34.** $3 + 18 \equiv 1 \pmod{20}$

Chapter 13 Test

1. Yes **2.** *x; x;* Commutative Property **3.** *y; y;* Associative Property **4.** *x*

5.

Element	Inverse
x	*x*
y	*z*
z	*y*

6. No **7.** $\dfrac{1}{5}$ **8.** 6-fold symmetry **9.**

+	0	1	2	3
0	0	1	2	3
1	1	2	3	0
2	2	3	0	1
3	3	0	1	2

11. True **12.** False; $14 \equiv 0 \pmod 7$ **13.** $9 + 1 \equiv 10 \pmod{11}$ **14.** $9 + 6 \equiv 5 \pmod{10}$

Subject Index

Photo Credits

CHAPTER 1 **CO** Leland Bobbe/The Stock Rep, Inc. **p. 6** Rod Planck/Tony Stone Images **p. 7** LSHTM/Tony Stone Images **p. 12** Ken Fisher/Tony Stone Images **p. 17** Suzanne & Nick Geary/Tony Stone Images **p. 19** Harry Harris/AP/Wide World Photos **p. 21** Gregg Adams/New England Stock Photo **p. 23** Jim Cummins/FPG International LLC

CHAPTER 2 **CO** D. Berry/PhotoDisc, Inc. **p. 34** Illustration by John Tenniel, colored by Fritz Kredel. Discoveries Æ. Harry N. Abrams, Inc., Publishers. **p. 35** Globe Photos, Inc. **p. 39** O. Abolafia/Liaison Agency, Inc. Paramount Pictures Corporation, Inc. **p. 49** (Border collie) Bob London/The Stock Market **p. 49** (Poodle) Adolf Schmidecker/FPG International LLC **p. 49** (German shepherd) Labat J. M. Jacana/Scientific Control/Photo Researchers, Inc. **p. 50** (Golden retriever) Donna Svennevik/Liaison Agency, Inc. **p. 50** (Afghan) Mero/Labat J. M. Jacana/Scientific Control/Photo Researchers, Inc.

CHAPTER 3 **CO** SuperStock, Inc. **p. 77** Columbia/TriStar/AP/Wide World Photos **p. 79** Warner Bros./Shooting Star International Photo Agency **p. 80** Paramount Pictures/Kobal Collection **p. 87** Chris Trotman/Duomo Photography Incorporated **p. 91** (top) SuperStock, Inc. **p. 91** (bottom) Carole Elies/Tony Stone Images **p. 95** Alfred Eisenstaedt/*Life* magazine (c) 1962 Time Inc. **p. 96** (top) 20th Century Fox/Archive Photos **p. 96** (bottom) The Disney Publishing Group (c) Disney Enterprises Inc. **p. 119** (top) Ari Ojala/Lehtikuva/SABA Press Photos, Inc. **p. 119** (bottom) Maull & Polyblank/Mary Evans Picture Library **p. 125** Illustration by John Tenniel, colored by Fritz Kredel. Discoveries Æ. Harry N. Abrams, Inc., Publishers. **p. 126** Scott Schulman/Shooting Star International Photo Agency **p. 133** Mary Evans Picture Library **p. 139** Scala/Art Resource, N.Y.

CHAPTER 4 **CO** Chris Noble/Tony Stone Images **p. 152** William Munoz **p. 156** Jasper Johns, *The Number Zero*. (c) Jasper Johns/Licensed by VAGA, New York, NY. **p. 157** Julian Calder/Tony Stone Images **p. 158** M. Beck-Coppola/Reunion des Musees Nationaux RMN **p. 161** Mary Evans Picture Library **p. 162** Phil Degginger/Tony Stone Images **p. 165** Courtesy of International Business Machines Corporation. Unauthorized use not permitted. **p. 168** Lee Snider/The Image Works

CHAPTER 5 **CO** PhotoDisc, Inc. **p. 190** Hulton Getty/Liaison Agency, Inc. **p. 207** The Granger Collection **p. 208** Telegraph Colour Library/FPG International LLC **p. 210** Jim Brandenburg/Minden Pictures **p. 215** Robert F. Blitzer **p. 223** David Weintraub/Photo Researchers, Inc. **p. 224** Charles Rex Arbogast/AP/Wide World Photos **p. 229** Dick Morton **p. 234** Richard Lord/The Image Works

CHAPTER 6 **CO** Nita Winter Photography **p. 244** Jake Rajs/Tony Stone Images **p. 247** Brian S. Wilcox/Adventure Photo & Film **p. 249** U.S. Air Force/AP/Wide World Photos **p. 253** A. Ramu/Stock Boston **p. 267** Kobal Collection **p. 272** Doc White/TCL/Masterfile Corporation **p. 273** AP/Wide World Photos **p. 277** Frans Lanting/Minden Pictures **p. 278** (top) David Woodfall/Tony Stone Images **p. 278** (bottom) Aerial Focus/Adventure Photo & Film **p. 280** Kobal Collection **p. 282** UPI/Corbis **p. 290** Stephen G. Maka/Index Stock Imagery, Inc. **p. 299** Corbis